Encyclopedia of
ACTIVISM and
SOCIAL JUSTICE

Encyclopedia of ACTIVISM *and* SOCIAL JUSTICE

1

Editors

Gary L. Anderson *&* Kathryn G. Herr

New York University   *Montclair State University*

A SAGE Reference Publication

SAGE Publications
Thousand Oaks ▪ London ▪ New Delhi

For information:

SAGE Publications, Inc.
2455 Teller Road
Thousand Oaks, California 91320
E-mail: order@sagepub.com

SAGE Publications Ltd.
1 Oliver's Yard
55 City Road
London EC1Y 1SP
United Kingdom

SAGE Publications India Pvt. Ltd.
B 1/I 1 Mohan Cooperative Industrial Area
Mathura Road, New Delhi 110 044
India

SAGE Publications Asia-Pacific Pte. Ltd.
33 Pekin Street #02-01
Far East Square
Singapore 048763

Printed in the United States of America.

Library of Congress Cataloging-in-Publication Data

Encyclopedia of activism and social justice / [edited by] Gary L. Anderson, Kathryn G. Herr.
    p. cm. — (A Sage reference publication)
Includes bibliographical references and index.
ISBN 978-1-4129-1812-1 (cloth)
    1. Social justice—Encyclopedias. 2. Social action—Encyclopedias. 3. Social movements—Encyclopedias.
4. Social reformers—Biography—Encyclopedias. I. Anderson, Gary L., 1948- II. Herr, Kathryn.

HM671.E53 2007
303.48'403—dc22   2006034804

This book is printed on acid-free paper.

07 08 09 10 11 10 9 8 7 6 5 4 3 2 1

Publisher:	Rolf Janke
Acquisitions Editor:	Todd R. Armstrong
Developmental Editor:	Yvette Pollastrini
Project Editor:	Tracy Alpern
Reference Systems Coordinator:	Leticia Gutierrez
Proofreaders:	Colleen Brennan
	Sally Jaskold
	Anne Rogers
Typesetter:	C&M Digitals (P) Ltd.
Indexer:	Naomi Linzer
Cover Designer:	Candice Harman
Marketing Manager:	Carmel Withers

Contents

Editorial Board, *vi*

List of Entries, *vii*

Reader's Guide, *xix*

About the Editors, *xxxiii*

Contributors, *xxxv*

Introduction, *xlix*

Entries

Volume I: A–D

1–492

Volume II: E–M

493–1000

Volume III: N–Z

1001–1520

Index, *1521–1712*

List of Entries

Abernathy, Ralph
Abolitionist Movements
Abortion
Abraham Lincoln Brigade
Abuelas de Plaza de Mayo
Abu-Jamal, Mumia
Achebe, Chinua
ACORN
Action for Children's Television
Action Medic Groups
Action Research. *See* Participatory
   Action Research
Activism, Social and Political
Activism in Australia and New Zealand
Activism in Postconflict and Reconstruction
ACT UP
Adbusters
Addams, Jane
Adorno, Theodor. *See* Frankfurt School of Critical
   Theory
Advocacy
Affinity Groups. *See* Strategies and Tactics in Social
   Movements
Affirmative Action
Afghan Resistance to Soviet Occupation
African National Congress
African Women and Social Justice
Afrocentricity
Agrarian Socialist Movement
AIDS Memorial Quilt
Air America Radio
al-Banna, Hasan
Albizu Campos, Pedro
Algebra Project
Ali, Muhammad

Alinsky, Saul
Allende, Salvador
Alternative Bookstores
Alternative Health
Alternative Movements
Alternative Press
Amaru, Túpac, II
American Civil Liberties Union (ACLU)
American Federation of Labor (AFL-CIO)
American Federation of Teachers.
   See Teacher Unions
American Gold Star Mothers
American Indian Movement
American Revolution
Amnesty International
Anarchism
Anarcho-Syndicalism
Animal Rights
Anthony, Susan B.
Anti-Apartheid Movement
Anti–Ballistic Missile Treaty
Anti-Busing Movement
Anti-Colonial Movements, Asia
Anti-Colonial Movements, Latin America
Anti-Colonial Movements, Middle East and
   North Africa
Anti-Colonial Movements, South Pacific
Anti-Colonial Movements, Sub-Saharan Africa
Anti-Consumerism
Anti–Death Penalty Movement
Anti-Globalization Movement
Antigonish Movement
Anti-Immigrant Politics
Anti-Imperialism
Anti-Lynching Movement

Anti-Monopoly Movement
Anti-Nuclear Movement
Anti-Pornography Activism
Anti-Prison Movement
Anti-Racist Teaching
Anti-Slavery Movement. *See* Abolitionist
    Movements
Anti-Smoking Campaigns. *See* Koop, C. Everett
Anti-Sweatshop Movement
Anti–Vietnam War Movement. *See* Conscientious
    Objectors to War; Draft Resistance; Johnson,
    Lyndon; War Resisters' International
Anti-Wal-Mart Movement
Anzaldúa, Gloria
Apartheid. *See* Anti-Apartheid Movement
Appropriate Technology Movement
Aquino, Corazon
Arab American Activism
Arafat, Yasser
Arbenz, Jacobo
Arenas, Reinaldo
Arendt, Hannah
Arias, Oscar
Aristide, Jean-Bertrand
Armenian Genocide
Arts-in-Medicine Movement
Ashrawi, Hanan
Asian American and Pacific Islander Activism
Atheism
Attica Uprising
Aung San
Awad, Mubarak

Bachelet, Michelle
Baez, Joan
Bahá'í Faith and Social Action
Baker, Ella
Baldwin, James
Ballot Initiatives
Baraka, Amiri
Basque Separatist Movement. *See* ETA
Basquiat, Jean-Michel
Basta Ya! *See* Ya Basta!
Battle of Seattle
Bauhaus Photographers
Beat Poets
Belafonte, Harry

Bell, Derrick
Benefit Concerts
Benjamin, Medea
Benn, Tony
Berlin Wall Destruction
Berrigan Brothers
Berry, Wendell
Bhabha, Homi. *See* Postcolonial Theory
Bicycle Movement. *See* Critical Mass Bicycle
    Movement
Biko, Stephen
Bilingual Education
Billionaires for Bush
Bill of Rights
Blacklists. *See* Hollywood Blacklists
Black Lung Movement
Black Panther Party
Black Power
Blogging
Boal, Augusto
Boff, Leonardo
Bolívar, Simón. *See* Anti-Colonial Movements,
    Latin America
Bolsheviks
Bonafini, Hebe. *See* Madres de Plaza de Mayo
Bonhoeffer, Dietrich
Bonner, Elena. *See* Soviet Dissidents
Bono
Bourdieu, Pierre
Bové, José
Boxer Rebellion. *See* Anti-Colonial Movements,
    Asia
Boycotts and Divestment
Boyle, Father
Braden, Anne and Carl
Brazilian Workers Party. *See* Partido dos
    Trabalhadores
Bread and Puppet Theater
Breastfeeding Movement
Brecht, Bertolt
Brown, H. Rap
Brown, John
Brown v. Board of Education
Bruce, Lenny
Brutus, Dennis
Burmese Resistance Movement
Busing. *See* Anti-Busing Movement

Butler, Judith
Buy Nothing Day

Caldicott, Helen
Campaign to End the Death Penalty
Campus Antiwar Network
Camus, Albert
Cárdenas, Lázaro
Carmichael, Stokely
Carson, Rachel
Carter, James Earl
Castro, Fidel
Catholic Worker Movement
Centre for Contemporary Cultural Studies
Chautauqua
Chávez, César
Chávez, Hugo
Chicago, Judy. *See* Performance Art, Political
Chicago Democratic Convention
    Demonstrations, 1968
Chicago Seven
Chicano Movement
Child Advocacy
Child Labor Laws
Children's Defense Fund
Chisolm, Shirley
Chomsky, Noam
Christian Base Communities
Christian Right
CIA Repression of Social Movements
Citizen School, The
Citizenship and Patriotism
Civil Disobedience
Civil Rights Acts
Civil Rights Movement
Civil Society
Clamshell Alliance
Clark, Ramsey
Climate Change and Global Justice
Cloward, Richard A., and Piven, Frances Fox
Coalition Building
Code Pink
Coffin, William Sloane
COINTELPRO. *See* Government Suppression of
    Social Activism
Committee for Cleaners' Rights
Commodification

Communism
Communist Manifesto
Communist Party USA
Communitarianism
Community Action Program
Community-Based Ecological Resistance
    Movements
Community Currencies
Community Gardens
Community Organizing
Community Radio and Television
Cone, James H.
Confucius
Congress of Racial Equality
Conscientious Objectors to War
Conyers, John, Jr.
Cooperatives
Corrie, Rachel
Cotton, Samuel
Council to Aid the Jews. *See* Holocaust,
    Resistance
Counter-Recruitment
Counts, George
Coxey, Jacob S.
Craftivism
Crazy Horse
Critical Literacy
Critical Mass Bicycle Movement
Critical Pedagogy
Critical Race Theory
Critical Theory. *See* Frankfurt School of
    Critical Theory
Cuban Literacy Campaign
Cuban Revolution. *See* Castro, Fidel
Culture Jammers
Cyber Rights

Dalai Lama
Dalton, Roque
Dance and Activism
Darrow, Clarence
Darwin, Charles
Davis, Angela
Davis, Ossie
Day, Dorothy
Death Penalty. *See* Anti–Death Penalty Movement
de Beauvoir, Simone

Debs, Eugene V.
Debt Relief Movement
de Certeau, Michel
Deconstruction
Deep Ecology Movement
Dees, Morris
de la Cruz, Sor Juana Inés
Dellinger, David
Dellums, Ronald
Deloria, Vine, Jr.
Democracy
Democratic Socialism
Demonstrations. *See* Strategies and Tactics in
    Social Movements
Derrida, Jacques
Dewey, John
Dickens, Charles
Difference
Digital Activism
Digital Equity
Direct Action
Disability Rights Movement
Disability Studies
Dissent
Dissent Magazine
Divestment. *See* Boycotts and Divestment
Djilas, Milovan
Doctors Without Borders
Dorfman, Ariel
Douglas, Marjory Stoneman
Douglass, Frederick
Dow, Unity
Draft Resistance
Drug Laws, Resistance to
Dubček, Alexander
Du Bois, W. E. B.
Dunayevskaya, Raya
Dussel, Enrique
Dworkin, Andrea
Dylan, Bob

Earth Charter
Earth Day
Earth First!
Earth Summit
East Timor, Resistance to Indonesian Occupation
East Timor Action Network

Ebadi, Shirin
Ecofeminism
Ecopaganism
Edelman, Marion Wright
Ehrenreich, Barbara
Eight-Hour-Day Movement
Ejército Zapatista de Liberación Nacional
Electronic Democracy
Electronic Privacy Movement
Elizabethan Poor Law
Ellacuría, Ignacio
Ellsberg, Daniel
El Saadawi, Nawal. *See* Saadawi, Nawal El
Emancipation Proclamation
Engels, Friedrich
Environmental Movement
Environmental Racism
Equal Rights Amendment
ETA
Ethical Culture Movement
Eugenics Movement
Eurocommunism
Evers, Medgar

Fabian Socialism
Fairness & Accuracy In Reporting (FAIR)
Fair Trade
False Consciousness
Falwell, Jerry. *See* Christian Right
Fanon, Frantz. *See* Postcolonial Theory
Farmworkers' Movement
Farrakhan, Louis
Fascism
Federal Bureau of Investigation (FBI).
    See Government Suppression of Social Activism
Federal Housing Administration (FHA)
Feminism
Feminist Majority Foundation
Feminist Research
Filipino American Activism
Film
First, Ruth
First Amendment to the Constitution.
    See Free Speech Activism
First Nations Peoples. *See* Indigenous People and
    Social Justice
Fisk, Robert

Flores Magón, Ricardo
Flynn, Elizabeth Gurley
FMLN
Fonda, Jane
Foucault, Michel
Frankfurt School of Critical Theory
Franklin, Benjamin
Freedom Rides, 1961
Free Movement Activism
Free Software Movement
Free Speech Activism
Freire, Paulo
French Revolution
Friedan, Betty

Gage, Matilda Joslyn
Gandhi, Mohandas K.
Gangs and Activism
García Márquez, Gabriel
Garvey, Marcus
Gay Liberation Front
Gay-Straight Alliance Network
Gender Equity Movement in Schools
Genital Integrity Activists
Genocide Studies
Genocide Watch
George, Henry
Geronimo
GI Bill
Gideon v. Wainright
GI Movement
Ginsberg, Allen
Gitlin, Todd
Global Exchange
Globalization. See Anti-Globalization Movement;
   Living Wage Movement
Glocalization
Golan Heights Druze Resistance
Goldman, Emma
Gold Star Mothers. See American
   Gold Star Mothers
Gómez-Peña, Guillermo
Gompers, Samuel
Gonzales, Rodolfo "Corky."
   See Chicano Movement
Goodman, Amy
Gorbachev, Mikhail

Gore, Al. See Climate Change and Global Justice
Government Suppression of Social Activism
Graffiti Art
Gramsci, Antonio
Grandmothers of the Plaza de Mayo.
   See Abuelas de Plaza de Mayo
Grange Movement
Grape Boycotts
Gray Panthers
Great Society
Greenback Movement
Green Party
Greenpeace
Gregory, Dick
Guerrilla Girls
Guerrilla Movements. See Urban Guerrilla Movements
Guerrilla Television
Guerrilla Theater
Guevara, Che
Gunder Frank, Andre
Gun Politics
Guthrie, Woody
Gutiérrez, Gustavo

Habermas, Jürgen
Habitat for Humanity
Hamer, Fannie Lou
Hampton, Fred
Hansberry, Lorraine
Harrington, Michael
Harris, Mary. See Jones, Mother (Mary)
Havel, Václav
Hawai'ian Sovereignty Movement
Hayden, Tom
Hezbollah
Hidalgo, Miguel. See Anti-Colonial Movements,
   Latin America
Highlander Center
HIJOS, Children of the Disappeared
Hikmet, Nazim
Hill, Joe
Hill, Julia Butterfly
Hip-Hop
Ho Chi Minh
Hoffman, Abbie
Hollywood Blacklists
Holocaust, Resistance

Homeless Activism
Homeopathy Movement
Home Schooling
Homestead Riot
hooks, bell
Hormel Strikes
Horton, Myles
Hospice Movement
Housing Movements
Huerta, Dolores. *See* Chicano Movement
Hughes, Langston
Hull-House
Human Rights Watch

Identity Politics
Ideology
Immigrant Activism in France
Immigration. *See* Anti-Immigrant Politics;
    Free Movement Activism
Imperialism. *See* Anti-Imperialism
Income Inequality
Indian Mascot Protests
Indigenous People and Environmentalism
Indigenous People and Social Justice
Industrial Areas Foundation (IAF)
Industrial Workers of the World (IWW)
Indymedia
Intelligent Design Movement
International Campaign to Ban
    Landmines
International Criminal Court
Intifada (1987–1992, 2000–2003)
Iranian Revolution (1963–1979)
Iraq Women's Movement
Irish Republican Army (IRA)
Islamic Feminism
Israeli Peace Movement

Jackson, George
Jackson, Jesse
Japanese Internment Camps
Jara, Víctor
Jefferson, Thomas
Jesus Christ
Jihad
Joan of Arc
Johnson, Lyndon B.

Jones, Mother (Mary)
Jordan, Barbara
Judicial Activism
Justice for Janitors
Just War Theory

Kahlo, Frida
Keller, Helen
Kennedy, John F.
Kennedy, Robert F.
Keynes, John Maynard
Khmer Rouge
Killing Fields. *See* Khmer Rouge
King, Coretta Scott
King, Martin Luther, Jr.
King, Rodney. *See* Urban Uprisings,
    United States
Klein, Naomi
Kollwitz, Käthe
Koop, C. Everett
Kozol, Jonathan
Kunstler, William
Kurdish Human Rights
Kuti, Fela
Kwangju Uprising
Kwanzaa
Kyoto Accords

Labor Culture
Labor Law
Laclau, Ernesto
LaFollette, Robert
Landless Movement
La Nueva Canción
La Raza Unida Party. *See* Chicano Movement
Lau Decision
Law and Social Movements
Law of Restitution. *See* Indigenous People and the
    Environment
Leadership, Participatory Democratic
League of Nations
League of United Latin American
    Citizens (LULAC)
Lebrón, Lolita
Lee, Barbara
Lee, Spike
Lenin, V. I.

Lennon, John
Lesbian, Gay, Bisexual, and Transgender (LGBT)
  Movement
Letelier, Orlando
Lewis, Avi. *See* Klein, Naomi
Lewis, John L.
Lewis, Sinclair
Liberalism
Liberation Theology
Libertarians
Lincoln, Abraham
Lippmann, Walter
Literature and Activism
Living Wage Movement
Lobbying
Locke, Alain
Locke, John
Long, Huey P.
López Obrador, Andrés Manuel
L'Ouverture, Toussaint.
  See Toussaint L'Ouverture
Low-Income Housing
Ludlow Massacre
Lukács, Georg
Lula da Silva, Luiz Inácio
Luther, Martin
Luxemburg, Rosa

Maathai, Wangari
Machel, Graca
Machiavelli, Niccolò
Madres de Plaza de Mayo
Malcolm X
Mandela, Nelson
Mandela, Winnie
Mao Tse-tung
Marcos, Subcomandante
Marcuse, Herbert
Marley, Bob
Marshall, Thurgood
Martí, José
Martín-Baró, Ignacio
Martínez, Betita
Marx, Karl
Marxist Theory
Mau Mau Movement
May Day

May Revolution, France
McCarthyism. *See* Government Suppression of
  Social Activism
McGovern, George
McLuhan, Marshall
M.E.C.H.A. *See* Chicano Movement
Media Activism
Media Literacy
Media Reform Movement
Meer, Fatima
Meier, Deborah
Menchú Tum, Rigoberta
Mencken, H. L.
Mendes, Chico
Men's Movement
Merton, Thomas
Mexican American Legal Defense and Education
  Fund (MALDEF)
Mexican Muralists
Mexican Revolution
Mexican Student Movement
Military-Industrial Complex
Militia Movements
Milk, Harvey
Mill, John Stuart
Millennial and Apocalyptic Movements
Miller, Arthur
Million Man March
Mills, C. Wright
Minutemen Project
MIR (Movement of the
Revolutionary Left)
Miranda v. Arizona
Mississippi Freedom Schools
Mohammed, Bibi Titi
Mondragón Cooperatives
Mongela, Gertrude
Montgomery Bus Boycott
Moore, Michael
Moral Majority. *See* Christian Right
Morales, Evo
Moral Panic
Morrison, Toni
Moses, Robert
Mothers of the Plaza de Mayo. *See* Madres de Plaza
  de Mayo
Mother Teresa

Mouffe, Chantal
Movement of the Revolutionary Left. *See* MIR
   (Movement of the Revolutionary Left)
MoveOn.org
Mtintso, Thenjiwe
Muhammad
Muhammad, Elijah
Multicultural Education
Multiculturalism
Multitude
Mumia Abu-Jamal. *See* Abu-Jamal, Mumia
Mural Art
Muslim Brotherhood
Muste, A. J.
Myrdal, Gunnar

Nader, Ralph
Names Project, The. *See* AIDS Memorial Quilt
Nasrallah, Hassan
National Association for the Advancement of
   Colored People (NAACP)
National Consumers' League
National Gay and Lesbian Task Force
National Organization for Women (NOW)
National Rifle Association (NRA)
National Urban League
Nation of Islam
Natural Childbirth Movement
Nazism and Civilian Resistance
Nehru, Jawaharlal
Neoconservatism
Neoliberalism
Neruda, Pablo
New Deal
New Profile
New Social Movements. *See* Social Movements,
   Sociology of
Newton, Huey P.
Ngugi wa Thiong'o
Nguzo Saba. *See* Kwanzaa
Nhat Hanh, Thich
Nietzsche, Friedrich
Nkrumah, Kwame
Nobel Peace Prize
Noncitizen Rights
Non-Governmental Organizations (NGOs)
Non-Partisan League

Nonviolence and Activism
Northern Ireland
Northern Ireland Peace Process
Nuclear Power. *See* Anti-Nuclear Movement

Ocean Hill–Brownsville Teachers' Strike
Ochoa, Digna
Oglala, Incident at
Old Left
Ono, Yoko. *See* Lennon, John; Performance Art,
   Political
Operation Rescue
Operation Solidarity
Option for the Poor
Organic Farming and Agribusiness
Organization of the Petroleum Exporting Countries
   (OPEC)
Organizing. *See* Community Organizing
Orwell, George
Other, The
Outsider Art
Ovington, Mary White
Owen, Robert
Owen, Wilfred
Oxfam

Pacifism
Paine, Thomas
Palestine Liberation Organization (PLO)
Palestine National Council
Palmer Raids
Pan-Africanism
Parents, Families and Friends of
   Lesbians and Gays (PFLAG)
Parks, Rosa
Parra, Violeta
Participatory Action Research
Participatory Democratic Leadership.
   See Leadership, Participatory Democratic
Participatory Economics
Partido dos Trabalhadores
PATCO Strike
Patkar, Medha. *See* Save Narmada Movement
Peace Corps
Peace Education
Peace People, The. *See* Northern Ireland
Peltier, Leonard

People for the Ethical Treatment of Animals (PETA). *See* Animal Rights

People Power Revolution. *See* Philippine People Power Revolution

Performance Art, Political

Performativity

Philanthropy for Social Action

Philippine People Power Revolution

Physicians for Social Responsibility

Picasso, Pablo

Piercy, Marge

Piqueteros

Pittsburgh Rail Strike of 1877

Piven, Frances Fox. *See* Cloward, Richard A., and Piven, Frances Fox

Plato

Play, Creativity, and Social Movements

Plessy v. Ferguson. *See* Civil Rights Acts

Police Brutality

Political Humor

Political Opportunity Structure. *See* Strategies and Tactics in Social Movements

Political Satire

Political Spectacle

Polling

Poor People's Campaign

Popular Front

Popular Unity Government

Populism

Pornography. *See* Anti-Pornography Activism

Postcolonial Theory

Poster Art

Postman, Neil

Postmodernism

Power, Theories of

Prague Spring

Praxis

Prejean, Sister Helen

Prison Abolition Movement. *See* Anti-Prison Movement

Prison-Industrial Complex

Private Property

Professional Activist Organizations

Progressive Movement, Education

Protestantism

Protest Music

Public Access. *See* Community Radio and Television

Public Citizen

Public Theology

Pueblo Revolt

Punk

Quakers

Queer Theory

Rabin, Yitzhak

Racism. *See* Anti-Racist Teaching

Radical Cheerleaders

Rage Against the Machine

Raging Grannies

Rainforest Action Network

Rand, Ayn

Randolph, A. Philip

Ransome-Kuti, Funmilayo

Rastafarians

Rawls, John

Reagon, Bernice Johnson

Recuperated Factories in Argentina

Red Cross

Reed, John

Reed, Ralph. *See* Christian Right

Refugee Resettlement

Reich, Wilhelm

Religious Activism

Religious Society of Friends. *See* Quakers

Reparations Movement

Resistance

Reverend Billy

Rich, Adrienne

Rifkin, Jeremy

Riots. *See* Urban Uprisings, United States

Rivera, Diego

Robertson, Pat. *See* Christian Right

Robeson, Paul

Robinson, Jackie

Robinson, Mary

Rock Bands and Activism

Rock 'n' Roll

Roe v. Wade

Romero, Oscar

Roosevelt, Eleanor
Roosevelt, Franklin D.
Rosenberg, Julius and Ethel
Rousseau, Jean-Jacques
Roy, Arundhati
Rushdie, Salman
Russian Revolution
Rustin, Bayard

Saadawi, Nawal El
Sacco and Vanzetti
Sadker, Myra and David
Said, Edward
Sakharov, Andrei
Salt of the Earth
Sánchez, George I.
Sanctuary Movement
Sandinismo
Sands, Bobby
Sanger, Margaret
Sankara, Thomas
Sarandon, Susan
Saro-Wiwa, Ken
Sartre, Jean-Paul
Save Narmada Movement
Save the Children
Savio, Mario
Schlafly, Phyllis
School of the Americas
School of the Americas Watch
Seale, Bobby
Seaman, Barbara
Seeger, Pete
Semiotic Warfare
Serbian Civil Unrest
Sex Workers' Rights
Sharpton, Al
Shays' Rebellion
Shcharansky, Anatoly. *See* Soviet Dissidents
Sheehan, Cindy
Shepard, Matthew
Shining Path Movement
Sierra Club
Silkwood, Karen
Sinclair, Upton
Sitting Bull

Situationist International
Slam Poetry
Slow Food Movement
Smith, Adam
Smith, Anne Deavere
Smith, Samantha
Sobrino, Jon
Social Constructionism. *See* Identity Politics
Social Democracy
Social Gospel Movement
Socialism
Socialist Feminism
Socially Responsible Investing
Social Movements, Sociology of
Social Movement Unionism. *See* Janitors
    for Justice
Social Reproduction. *See* Willis, Paul
Social Science Fiction
Socrates
Sojourners Movement
Solar Energy Movement
Solidarity, Poland
Solzhenitsyn, Alexander. *See* Soviet Dissidents
Sontag, Susan
Sosa, Mercedes
Southern Christian Leadership Conference
Southern Poverty Law Center
Southern Student Organizing Committee
Soviet Dissidents
Spirituality and Peacemaking
Spivak, Gayatri
Spock, Benjamin
Stanton, Elizabeth Cady. *See* Anthony, Susan B.
Steinem, Gloria
Stiglitz, Joseph
Stonewall Rebellion
Straight Edge Youth
Strategies and Tactics in Social Movements
Street Medics. *See* Action Medic Groups
Student Activism, K–12
Student Activism, Latin American
Student Nonviolent Coordinating Committee
    (SNCC)
Students for a Democratic Society
Subaltern
Sun Yat-sen

Suppression of Social Activism. *See* Government Suppression of Social Activism
Sustainable Living
Suu Kyi, Aung San
Sweatshops. *See* Anti-Sweatshop Movement
Sweet Honey in the Rock

Take Back the Night
Talk Radio. *See* Air America Radio
Taxation and Activism
Teacher Unions
Teamsters for a Democratic Union
Tenant Organizations. *See* Housing Movements
Tennessee Valley Authority
Terkel, Studs
Testimonio
Theatre of the Oppressed
Theodorakis, Mikis
Thich Nhat Hanh. *See* Nhat Hanh, Thich
Think Tanks
Third-Party Politics
Third World Cinema
Thomas, Norman
Thompson, E. P.
Thoreau, Henry David
Tiananmen Square
Tijerina, Reies López
Timerman, Jacobo
Torres Restrepo, Camilo
Touraine, Alain
Toussaint L'Ouverture
Transgender Movement
Treaty of Guadalupe Hidalgo
Treaty Rights Struggle
Trocmé, André
Trotsky, Leon
Trotskyism
Truth, Sojourner
Tubman, Harriet
Tupamaros. *See* Urban Guerrilla Movements
Turner, Nat
Tutu, Desmond
Twain, Mark
Underground Railroad
Unemployed Workers Movement. *See* Piqueteros
Union Movements

Union Songs
United for a Fair Economy
United for Peace and Justice
United Nations Children's Fund (UNICEF)
United Nations Educational, Scientific and Cultural Organization (UNESCO)
Universal Declaration of Human Rights
UPS Strike
Urban Guerrilla Movements
Urban Space, Politics of
Urban Uprisings, United States
Utopian Communities

Vegetarianism
Veterans for Peace
Vidal, Gore
Vietnam War. *See* Johnson, Lyndon B.
Villa, Pancho
Violence, Theories of
Virtual Sit-Ins
Voices in the Wilderness
Voluntary Simplicity
Volunteers in Service to America (VISTA)
Voting Rights. *See* Civil Rights Acts

Wald, Lillian
Wałęsa, Lech
Walker, Alice
Wallis, Jim
Wal-Mart. *See* Anti-Wal-Mart Movement
Warren, Earl
War Resisters' International
Warsaw Ghetto Uprising
War Tax Resistance
Weather Underground
Weavers. *See* Seeger, Pete
Webb, Gary
Welfare Rights Movement
Wellman, Saul
Wells-Barnett, Ida B.
Wellstone, Paul
West, Cornel
Whiskey Rebellion
Whistleblowers
White Privilege

Whitman, Walt
Wildcat Strikes
Wilderness Preservation Act
Wilkins, Roy
Williams, Jody
Willis, Paul
Witness for Peace
Woman's Christian
    Temperance Union
Women in Black
Women's Collective Acts of Resistance
Women's Health Activism
Women's International League for Peace and
    Freedom
Women's Suffrage Movement
Woodson, Carter
Woolf, Virginia
Workers Party, PT. *See* Partido dos
    Trabalhadores
Working-Class Cinema
World Court

World Social Forum
Wounded Knee

Ya Basta!
Yippies. *See* Play, Creativity, and Social
    Movements
Yomango
Young Americans for Freedom
Young Patriots Organization
Youth Organizing and Activism

Zapata, Emiliano
Zapatista Movement. *See* Ejército Zapatista de
    Liberación Nacional
Zenger, Peter. *See* Free Speech
    Activism
Zines
Zinn, Howard
Zionism
ZNet
Zola, Émile

Reader's Guide

The Reader's Guide provides a way to locate related entries in the encyclopedia. For example, if you look under Education, you will find a list of the main entries on that topic, including Critical Pedagogy, Paulo Freire, Peace Education, and Student Activism, K–12. Alternatively, if you are interested in the Catholic Worker movement, you will find the entry under the heading Religious/Spiritual Movements, where you also will find other related entries, Christian Base Communities, Thomas Merton, and Muslim Brotherhood. The Reader's Guide also provides an overview of all the entries in the encyclopedia. You can look through all the headings, including Education or Religious/Spiritual Movements, pick one of particular interest to you, and then choose entries you might want to read.

Activism and Social Justice

Activism, Social and Political
Advocacy
Alternative Movements
Boycotts and Divestment
Civil Disobedience
Coalition Building
Community Organizing
Cooperatives
Direct Action
Dissent
Lobbying
Nonviolence and Activism
Philanthropy for Social Action
Play, Creativity, and Social Movements
Social Movements, Sociology of
Strategies and Tactics in Social Movements
Third-Party Politics
Urban Uprisings, United States
Utopian Communities

The Arts

Literature

Achebe, Chinua
Arenas, Reinaldo
Baldwin, James
Baraka, Amiri
Beat Poets
Brutus, Dennis
Camus, Albert
Dalton, Roque
de la Cruz, Sor Juana Inés
Dickens, Charles
Dorfman, Ariel
García Márquez, Gabriel
Ginsberg, Allen
Hansberry, Lorraine
Hikmet, Nazım
Hughes, Langston
Lewis, Sinclair
Literature and Activism
Miller, Arthur
Morrison, Toni
Neruda, Pablo
Orwell, George
Owen, Wilfred
Piercy, Marge
Political Humor
Political Satire
Rand, Ayn
Rich, Adrienne
Rushdie, Salman

Sinclair, Upton
Slam Poetry
Social Science Fiction
Testimonio
Thoreau, Henry David
Twain, Mark
Vidal, Gore
Walker, Alice
Whitman, Walt
Zola, Émile

Music

Baez, Joan
Belafonte, Harry
Benefit Concerts
Bono
Dylan, Bob
Guthrie, Woody
Hip-Hop
Jara, Víctor
Kuti, Fela
La Nueva Canción
Lennon, John
Marley, Bob
Parra, Violeta
Protest Music
Punk
Rage Against the Machine
Reagon, Bernice Johnson
Robeson, Paul
Rock Bands and Activism
Rock 'n' Roll
Seeger, Pete
Sosa, Mercedes
Sweet Honey in the Rock
Theodorakis, Mikis
Union Songs

Performing Arts

Boal, Augusto
Bread and Puppet Theater
Brecht, Bertolt
Dance and Activism
Davis, Ossie

Film
Fonda, Jane
Gómez-Peña, Guillermo
Guerrilla Theater
Hollywood Blacklists
Lee, Spike
Moore, Michael
Performance Art, Political
Performativity
Play, Creativity, and Social Movements
Political Humor
Political Satire
Radical Cheerleaders
Raging Grannies
Reverend Billy
Robeson, Paul
Salt of the Earth
Sarandon, Susan
Smith, Anne Deavere
Theatre of the Oppressed
Third World Cinema
Working-Class Cinema

Plastic Arts

AIDS Memorial Quilt
Basquiat, Jean-Michel
Bauhaus Photographers
Graffiti Art
Guerrilla Girls
Kahlo, Frida
Kollwitz, Käthe
Mexican Muralists
Mural Art
Outsider Art
Picasso, Pablo
Poster Art
Rivera, Diego

Criticism/Critical Theory

Deconstruction
Derrida, Jacques
Difference
Lukács, Georg
Postcolonial Theory

Said, Edward
Semiotic Warfare
Situationist International
Sontag, Susan
Spivak, Gayatri

Cultural Studies, Popular Culture

Bruce, Lenny
Centre for Contemporary Cultural Studies
Craftivism
Culture Jammers
de Certeau, Michel
Difference
Dunayevskaya, Raya
Dussel, Enrique
Ellacuría, Ignacio
Foucault, Michel
Frankfurt School of Critical Theory
Hip-Hop
Identity Politics
Moral Panic
Multiculturalism
Other, The
Performativity
Postcolonial Theory
Postmodernism
Power, Theories of
Punk
Radical Cheerleaders
Raging Grannies
Resistance
Reverend Billy
Semiotic Warfare
Situationist International
Straight Edge Youth
Subaltern
White Privilege
Willis, Paul
Zines

Consumer Movements

Anti-Consumerism
Anti-Monopoly Movement
Anti-Wal-Mart Movement

Boycotts and Divestment
Buy Nothing Day
Community Currencies
Fair Trade
Nader, Ralph
National Consumers' League
Socially Responsible Investing
Yomango

Education

Algebra Project
Anti-Racist Teaching
Bilingual Education
Brown v. Board of Education
Citizen School, The
Counter-Recruitment
Counts, George
Critical Literacy
Critical Pedagogy
Cuban Literacy Campaign
Dewey, John
Disability Rights Movement
Disability Studies
Freire, Paulo
Gender Equity Movement in Schools
Genocide Studies
Highlander Center
Home Schooling
Kozol, Jonathan
Lau Decision
Media Literacy
Meier, Deborah
Mississippi Freedom Schools
Moses, Robert
Multicultural Education
Multiculturalism
Ocean Hill–Brownsville Teachers' Strike
Participatory Action Research
Peace Education
Postman, Neil
Progressive Movement, Education
Rousseau, Jean-Jacques
Sadker, Myra and David
Student Activism, K–12
Student Activism, Latin American

Student Nonviolent Coordinating
  Committee (SNCC)
Teacher Unions
Think Tanks
Woodson, Carter
Youth Organizing and Activism

Environmentalism

Alternative Health
Animal Rights
Berry, Wendell
Caldicott, Helen
Carson, Rachel
Clamshell Alliance
Climate Change and Global Justice
Community-Based Ecological Resistance
  Movements
Community Gardens
Critical Mass Bicycle Movement
Deep Ecology Movement
Douglas, Marjory Stoneman
Earth Charter
Earth Day
Earth First!
Earth Summit
Ecofeminism
Ecopaganism
Environmental Movement
Environmental Racism
Green Party
Greenpeace
Hill, Julia Butterfly
Homeopathy Movement
Indigenous People and Environmentalism
Maathai, Wangari
Mendes, Chico
Organic Farming and Agribusiness
Rainforest Action Network
Rifkin, Jeremy
Sierra Club
Silkwood, Karen
Slow Food Movement
Solar Energy Movement
Sustainable Living
Thoreau, Henry David
Urban Space, Politics of

Vegetarianism
Voluntary Simplicity
Wilderness Preservation Act

Globalization/Anti-Globalization

Amnesty International
Anti-Globalization Movement
Anti-Immigrant Politics
Anti-Imperialism
Anti-Nuclear Movement
Anti-Sweatshop Movement
Battle of Seattle
Benjamin, Medea
Bové, José
Child Advocacy
Citizenship and Patriotism
Civil Society
Corrie, Rachel
Debt Relief Movement
Doctors Without Borders
Fair Trade
Free Movement Activism
Genocide Studies
Genocide Watch
Global Exchange
Glocalization
Klein, Naomi
Multiculturalism
Multitude
Non-Governmental Organizations (NGOs)
Organization of the Petroleum Exporting
  Countries (OPEC)
Pan-Africanism
Rifkin, Jeremy
Roy, Arundhati
Stiglitz, Joseph
War Tax Resistance
Witness for Peace
Women in Black
World Social Forum

Labor/Socialism/Communism/
Social Class

Agrarian Socialist Movement
American Federation of Labor (AFL-CIO)

Anarchism
Anarcho-Syndicalism
Berlin Wall Destruction
Bolsheviks
Castro, Fidel
Committee for Cleaners' Rights
Communism
Communist Manifesto
Cooperatives
Davis, Angela
Day, Dorothy
Debs, Eugene V.
Democratic Socialism
Eight-Hour-Day Movement
Engels, Friedrich
Eurocommunism
Fabian Socialism
False Consciousness
Farmworkers' Movement
Flynn, Elizabeth Gurley
Goldman, Emma
Gompers, Samuel
Gramsci, Antonio
Guevara, Che
Harrington, Michael
Hayden, Tom
Hill, Joe
Hormel Strikes
Income Inequality
Industrial Workers of the World (IWW)
Jones, Mother (Mary)
Justice for Janitors
Keller, Helen
Labor Culture
Labor Law
Lenin, V. I.
Lewis, John L.
Ludlow Massacre
Lukács, Georg
Luxemburg, Rosa
Marx, Karl
Marxist Theory
May Day
Muste, A. J.
Non-Partisan League
Ocean Hill–Brownsville Teachers' Strike
Old Left

Owen, Robert
Palmer Raids
PATCO Strike
Pittsburgh Rail Strike of 1877
Private Property
Recuperated Factories in Argentina
Reed, John
Robeson, Paul
Rosenberg, Julius and Ethel
Sacco and Vanzetti
Socialist Feminism
Taxation and Activism
Teacher Unions
Teamsters for a Democratic Union
Thomas, Norman
Thompson, E. P.
Trotsky, Leon
Union Movements
Union Songs
UPS Strike
Wellman, Saul
West, Cornel
Wildcat Strikes
Working-Class Cinema

Legal and Judicial System/ Human Rights/Civil Rights

Activism in Postconflict and Reconstruction
Affirmative Action
American Civil Liberties Union (ACLU)
Amnesty International
Anti–Ballistic Missile Treaty
Anti–Death Penalty Movement
Bill of Rights
Brown v. Board of Education
Campaign to End the Death Penalty
Child Labor Laws
Civil Disobedience
Civil Rights Acts
Clark, Ramsey
Conscientious Objectors to War
Cyber Rights
Darrow, Clarence
Dees, Morris
Disability Rights Movement
Doctors Without Borders

Draft Resistance
Drug Laws, Resistance to
Ethical Culture Movement
Free Speech Activism
Gideon v. Wainright
Homeless Activism
Human Rights Watch
International Campaign to Ban Landmines
International Criminal Court
Judicial Activism
Kunstler, William
Kurdish Human Rights
Kyoto Accords
Lau Decision
Law and Social Movements
League of Nations
Miranda v. Arizona
Myrdal, Gunnar
Nhat Hanh, Thich
Nobel Peace Prize
Noncitizen Rights
Ochoa, Digna
Oxfam
Physicians for Social Responsibility
Red Cross
Refugee Resettlement
Roe v. Wade
Save the Children
Sex Workers' Rights
Southern Poverty Law Center
Taxation and Activism
Treaty Rights Struggle
United Nations Children's Fund (UNICEF)
United Nations Educational, Scientific
   and Cultural Organization (UNESCO)
Universal Declaration of Human Rights
Voices in the Wilderness
War Resisters' International
War Tax Resistance
Warren, Earl
Welfare Rights Movement
Whistleblowers
Williams, Jody
Witness for Peace
Women in Black
World Court

Media and Communications

Action for Children's Television
Adbusters
Air America Radio
Alternative Press
Appropriate Technology Movement
Blogging
Community Radio and Television
Culture Jammers
Cyber Rights
Digital Activism
Digital Equity
Dissent Magazine
Electronic Democracy
Electronic Privacy Movement
Fairness & Accuracy In Reporting (FAIR)
Fisk, Robert
Free Software Movement
Goodman, Amy
Guerrilla Television
Indymedia
McLuhan, Marshall
Media Activism
Media Literacy
Media Reform Movement
MoveOn.org
Political Humor
Political Satire
Political Spectacle
Polling
Postman, Neil
Reed, John
Situationist International
Terkel, Studs
Think Tanks
Timerman, Jacobo
Virtual Sit-Ins
Webb, Gary
Zines
ZNet

Political and Social Movements (Africa)

Achebe, Chinua
African National Congress

African Women and Social Justice
Anti-Apartheid Movement
Anti-Colonial Movements, Middle East and
    North Africa
Anti-Colonial Movements, Sub-Saharan
    Africa
Biko, Stephen
Brutus, Dennis
Dow, Unity
First, Ruth
Islamic Feminism
Maathai, Wangari
Machel, Graca
Mandela, Nelson
Mandela, Winnie
Mau Mau Movement
Meer, Fatima
Mohammed, Bibi Titi
Mongela, Gertrude
Mtintso, Thenjiwe
Ngugi wa Thiong'o
Nkrumah, Kwame
Pan-Africanism
Ransome-Kuti, Funmilayo
Sankara, Thomas
Saro-Wiwa, Ken
Tutu, Desmond

Political and Social Movements (Asia/South Asia/Australia/ New Zealand)

Activism in Australia and New Zealand
Anti-Colonial Movements, Asia
Anti-Colonial Movements, South Pacific
Aquino, Corazon
Aung San
Burmese Resistance Movement
Confucius
Dalai Lama
East Timor, Resistance to Indonesian Occupation
East Timor Action Network
Gandhi, Mohandas K.
Ho Chi Minh
Khmer Rouge
Kwangju Uprising

Mao Tse-tung
Mother Teresa
Nehru, Jawaharlal
Nhat Hanh, Thich
Philippine People Power Revolution
Roy, Arundhati
Rushdie, Salman
Save Narmada Movement
Sun Yat-sen
Suu Kyi, Aung San
Tiananmen Square

Political and Social Movements (Europe)

Anarchism
Benn, Tony
Bové, José
Darwin, Charles
Djilas, Milovan
Dubček, Alexander
Elizabethan Poor Law
ETA
Eurocommunism
Fabian Socialism
French Revolution
Havel, Václav
Holocaust, Resistance
Immigrant Activism in France
Irish Republican Army (IRA)
Joan of Arc
May Revolution, France
Mondragón Cooperatives
Nazism and Civilian Resistance
Nobel Peace Prize
Northern Ireland
Northern Ireland Peace Process
Popular Front
Prague Spring
Resistance
Robinson, Mary
Sands, Bobby
Serbian Civil Unrest
Solidarity, Poland
Theodorakis, Mikis
Trocmé, André

Wałęsa, Lech
Warsaw Ghetto Uprising

Political and Social Movements
(Former Soviet Union)

Afghan Resistance to Soviet Occupation
Bolsheviks
Djilas, Milovan
Dubček, Alexander
Dunayevskaya, Raya
Gorbachev, Mikhail
Havel, Václav
Lenin, V. I.
Prague Spring
Russian Revolution
Sakharov, Andrei
Serbian Civil Unrest
Solidarity, Poland
Soviet Dissidents
Trotsky, Leon
Trotskyism

Political and Social Movements
(Latin America and Caribbean)

Abuelas de Plaza de Mayo
Albizu Campos, Pedro
Allende, Salvador
Amaru, Túpac, II
Anti-Colonial Movements,
    Latin America
Arbenz, Jacobo
Arenas, Reinaldo
Arias, Oscar
Aristide, Jean-Bertrand
Bachelet, Michelle
Cárdenas, Lázaro
Castro, Fidel
Chávez, Hugo
Cuban Literacy Campaign
Dalton, Roque
de la Cruz, Sor Juana Inés
Dorfman, Ariel
Dussel, Enrique
Ejército Zapatista de Liberación Nacional
Flores Magón, Ricardo

FMLN
Freire, Paulo
García Márquez, Gabriel
Guevara, Che
Gunder Frank, Andre
Gutiérrez, Gustavo
HIJOS, Children of the Disappeared
La Nueva Canción
Laclau, Ernesto
Landless Movement
Lebrón, Lolita
Letelier, Orlando
López Obrador, Andrés Manuel
Lula da Silva, Luiz Inácio
Madres de Plaza de Mayo
Marcos, Subcomandante
Marley, Bob
Martí, José
Martín-Baró, Ignacio
Menchú Tum, Rigoberta
Mendes, Chico
Mexican Muralists
Mexican Revolution
Mexican Student Movement
MIR (Movement of the Revolutionary Left)
Morales, Evo
Neruda, Pablo
Ochoa, Digna
Parra, Violeta
Partido dos Trabalhadores
Piqueteros
Popular Unity Government
Rastifarians
Recuperated Factories in Argentina
Romero, Oscar
Sandinismo
School of the Americas
School of the Americas Watch
Shining Path Movement
Sosa, Mercedes
Student Activism, Latin American
Testimonio
Timerman, Jacobo
Torres Restrepo, Camilo
Toussaint L'Ouverture
Urban Guerrilla Movements
Villa, Pancho

Ya Basta!
Zapata, Emiliano

Political and Social Movements (Middle East)

al-Banna, Hasan
Anti-Colonial Movements, Middle East and
    North Africa
Arafat, Yasser
Armenian Genocide
Ashrawi, Hanan
Awad, Mubarak
Corrie, Rachel
Ebadi, Shirin
Golan Heights Druze Resistance
Hezbollah
Hikmet, Nazim
Intifada (1987–1992, 2000–2003)
Iranian Revolution (1963–1979)
Iraq Women's Movement
Islamic Feminism
Israeli Peace Movement
Jihad
Muslim Brotherhood
Nasrallah, Hassan
New Profile
Organization of the Petroleum Exporting
    Countries (OPEC)
Palestine Liberation Organization (PLO)
Palestine National Council
Rabin, Yitzhak
Saadawi, Nawal El
Said, Edward
Women in Black
Zionism

Political and Social Movements (North America)

Abolitionist Movements
Abraham Lincoln Brigade
ACORN
Agrarian Socialist Movement
Alinsky, Saul
Alternative Bookstores
American Gold Star Mothers

American Revolution
Anti-Busing Movement
Anti–Death Penalty Movement
Antigonish Movement
Anti-Immigrant Politics
Anti-Nuclear Movement
Anti-Prison Movement
Arab American Activism
Attica Uprising
Ballot Initiatives
Benjamin, Medea
Bill of Rights
Billionaires for Bush
Black Lung Movement
Braden, Anne and Carl
Brown, John
Campus Antiwar Network
Carter, James Earl
Chautauqua
Chicago Democratic Convention
    Demonstrations, 1968
Chicago Seven
Children's Defense Fund
CIA Repression of Social
    Movements
Clamshell Alliance
Clark, Ramsey
Code Pink
Communist Party USA
Communitarianism
Community Action Program
Community Organizing
Cotton, Samuel
Counter-Recruitment
Coxey, Jacob S.
Darrow, Clarence
Dees, Morris
Dellinger, David
Douglas, Marjory Stoneman
Draft Resistance
Drug Laws, Resistance to
Ellsberg, Daniel
Eugenics Movement
Federal Housing Administration (FHA)
Fonda, Jane
Franklin, Benjamin
Gangs and Activism

George, Henry
GI Bill
GI Movement
Government Suppression of
    Social Activism
Grange Movement
Gray Panthers
Great Society
Greenback Movement
Gun Politics
Habitat for Humanity
Hayden, Tom
Highlander Center
Hoffman, Abbie
Hollywood Blacklists
Homestead Riot
Horton, Myles
Hull-House
Industrial Areas Foundation (IAF)
Jefferson, Thomas
Johnson, Lyndon B.
Jones, Mother (Mary)
Kennedy, John F.
Kennedy, Robert F.
LaFollette, Robert
Lincoln, Abraham
Lippmann, Walter
Living Wage Movement
Long, Huey P.
McGovern, George
Mencken, H. L.
Military-Industrial Complex
Militia Movements
Minutemen Project
Moore, Michael
MoveOn.org
Multiculturalism
National Rifle Association (NRA)
New Deal
Non-Partisan League
Operation Rescue
Operation Solidarity
Paine, Thomas
Peace Corps
Philanthropy for Social Action
Police Brutality
Poor People's Campaign

Prison-Industrial Complex
Professional Activist Organizations
Public Citizen
Roosevelt, Eleanor
Roosevelt, Franklin D.
Rosenberg, Julius and Ethel
Sacco and Vanzetti
Sanctuary Movement
Savio, Mario
School of the Americas
School of the Americas Watch
Shays' Rebellion
Sheehan, Cindy
Smith, Samantha
Southern Student Organizing Committee
Spock, Benjamin
Student Nonviolent Coordinating Committee
    (SNCC)
Students for a Democratic Society
Tennessee Valley Authority
Third-Party Politics
Thomas, Norman
Thoreau, Henry David
United for a Fair Economy
United for Peace and Justice
Urban Uprisings, United States
Veterans for Peace
Voices in the Wilderness
Volunteers in Service to America (VISTA)
Weather Underground
Welfare Rights Movement
Wellstone, Paul
Whiskey Rebellion
Young Americans for Freedom
Young Patriots Organization
Zinn, Howard

African American

Abernathy, Ralph
Abolitionist Movements
Abu-Jamal, Mumia
Afrocentricity
Ali, Muhammad
Anti-Lynching Movement
Baker, Ella
Baldwin, James

Baraka, Amiri
Basquait, Jean-Michel
Belafonte, Harry
Bell, Derrick
Black Panther Party
Black Power
Brown v. Board of Education
Brown, H. Rap
Brown, John
Carmichael, Stokely
Chisolm, Shirley
Civil Rights Movement
Congress of Racial Equality
Conyers, John, Jr.
Critical Race Theory
Davis, Angela
Davis, Ossie
Dellums, Ronald
Douglass, Frederick
Du Bois, W. E. B.
Edelman, Marion Wright
Emancipation Proclamation
Evers, Medgar
Farrakhan, Louis
Freedom Rides, 1961
Garvey, Marcus
Gregory, Dick
Hamer, Fannie Lou
Hampton, Fred
Hansberry, Lorraine
hooks, bell
Hughes, Langston
Jackson, George
Jackson, Jesse
Jordan, Barbara
King, Coretta Scott
King, Martin Luther, Jr.
Kwanzaa
Lee, Barbara
Locke, Alain
Malcolm X
Marshall, Thurgood
Million Man March
Mississippi Freedom Schools
Montgomery Bus Boycott
Morrison, Toni
Moses, Robert

Muhammad, Elijah
Nation of Islam
National Association for the
    Advancement of Colored People (NAACP)
National Urban League
Newton, Huey P.
Pan-Africanism
Parks, Rosa
Poor People's Campaign
Randolph, A. Philip
Rastifarians
Reparations Movement
Robeson, Paul
Robinson, Jackie
Rustin, Bayard
Seale, Bobby
Sharpton, Al
Southern Christian Leadership Conference
Student Nonviolent Coordinating
    Committee (SNCC)
Truth, Sojourner
Tubman, Harriet
Turner, Nat
Underground Railroad
Walker, Alice
West, Cornel
White Privilege
Wilkins, Roy
Woodson, Carter

American Indian/First Nation/ Indigenous

American Indian Movement
Crazy Horse
Deloria, Vine, Jr.
Geronimo
Hawai'ian Sovereignty Movement
Indian Mascot Protests
Indigenous People and
Environmentalism
Indigenous People and Social Justice
Menchú Tum, Rigoberta
Oglala, Incident at
Peltier, Leonard
Pueblo Revolt
Reparations Movement

Sitting Bull
Wounded Knee

Asian American

Asian American and Pacific Islander
    Activism
Filipino American Activism
Japanese Internment Camps
Reparations Movement

Feminism/Gender

Abortion
Anthony, Susan B.
Anti-Pornography Activism
Butler, Judith
de Beauvoir, Simone
Dworkin, Andrea
Ecofeminism
Ehrenreich, Barbara
Equal Rights Amendment
Feminism
Feminist Majority Foundation
Feminist Research
Flynn, Elizabeth Gurley
Friedan, Betty
Gage, Matilda Joslyn
Gender Equity Movement in Schools
Genital Integrity Activists
Goldman, Emma
Islamic Feminism
Men's Movement
National Organization for Women (NOW)
Ovington, Mary White
Roe v. Wade
Roy, Arundhati
Sadker, Myra and David
Sanger, Margaret
Schlafly, Phyllis
Seaman, Barbara
Sex Workers' Rights
Socialist Feminism
Steinem, Gloria
Take Back the Night
Wells-Barnett, Ida B.

Woman's Christian Temperance Union
Women's Collective Acts of Resistance
Women's Health Activism
Women's International League for
    Peace and Freedom
Women's Suffrage Movement
Woolf, Virginia

Latino/a

Albizu Campos, Pedro
Anzaldúa, Gloria
Baez, Joan
Bilingual Education
Chávez, César
Chicano Movement
Farmworkers' Movement
Grape Boycotts
League of United Latin American
    Citizens (LULAC)
Lebrón, Lolita
Martínez, Betita
Mexican American Legal Defense and Education
    Fund (MALDEF)
Sánchez, George I.
Tijerina, Reies López
Treaty of Guadalupe Hidalgo

Lesbian, Gay, Bisexual, and Transgendered

ACT UP
AIDS Memorial Quilt
Butler, Judith
Gay Liberation Front
Gay-Straight Alliance Network
Lesbian, Gay, Bisexual, and Transgender (LGBT)
    Movement
Milk, Harvey
National Gay and Lesbian Task Force
Parents, Families and Friends of Lesbians and
    Gays (PFLAG)
Queer Theory
Shepard, Matthew
Stonewall Rebellion
Transgender Movement

Political Philosophy/Ethics

Arendt, Hannah
Atheism
Bourdieu, Pierre
Butler, Judith
Camus, Albert
Chomsky, Noam
Citizenship and Patriotism
Civil Disobedience
Civil Society
Commodification
Communitarianism
Confucius
Critical Race Theory
Darwin, Charles
de Certeau, Michel
Democracy
Democratic Socialism
Engels, Friedrich
False Consciousness
Fascism
Foucault, Michel
Frankfurt School of Critical Theory
Gitlin, Todd
Gramsci, Antonio
Habermas, Jürgen
Ideology
Income Inequality
Jesus Christ
Just War Theory
Keynes, John Maynard
Laclau, Ernesto
Leadership, Participatory Democratic
Liberalism
Libertarians
Locke, Alain
Locke, John
Lukács, Georg
Machiavelli, Niccolò
Marcuse, Herbert
Marx, Karl
Marxist Theory
Mill, John Stuart
Mills, C. Wright
Mouffe, Chantal

Multitude
Neoconservatism
Neoliberalism
Nietzsche, Friedrich
Nonviolence and Activism
Old Left
Participatory Economics
Plato
Populism
Power, Theories of
Praxis
Private Property
Rand, Ayn
Rawls, John
Reich, Wilhelm
Rousseau, Jean-Jacques
Said, Edward
Sartre, Jean-Paul
Smith, Adam
Social Democracy
Socialism
Social Movements, Sociology of
Socrates
Thompson, E. P.
Thoreau, Henry David
Touraine, Alain
Utopian Communities
Violence, Theories of

Religious/Spiritual Movements

Bahá'í Faith and Social Action
Berrigan Brothers
Boff, Leonardo
Bonhoeffer, Dietrich
Boyle, Father
Catholic Worker Movement
Christian Base Communities
Christian Right
Coffin, William Sloane
Cone, James H.
Conscientious Objectors to War
Dalai Lama
Day, Dorothy
Ecopaganism
Gutiérrez, Gustavo

Intelligent Design Movement
Islamic Feminism
Jesus Christ
Just War Theory
Liberation Theology
Luther, Martin
Martín-Baró, Ignacio
Merton, Thomas
Millennial and Apocalyptic Movements
Muhammad
Muhammad, Elijah
Muslim Brotherhood
Option for the Poor
Pacifism
Prejean, Sister Helen
Protestantism
Public Theology
Quakers
Rastafarians
Religious Activism
Reverend Billy
Romero, Oscar
Sanctuary Movement
Sobrino, Jon
Social Gospel Movement
Sojourners Movement
Southern Christian Leadership Conference
Spirituality and Peacemaking
Torres Restrepo, Camilo
Tutu, Desmond
Wallis, Jim
West, Cornel
Woman's Christian Temperance Union
Zionism

Social, Health, and Welfare Rights

Action Medic Groups
Addams, Jane
Advocacy
Alternative Health
Arts-in-Medicine Movement
Black Lung Movement
Breastfeeding Movement
Child Advocacy
Children's Defense Fund
Cloward, Richard A., and Piven,
    Frances Fox
Community Action Programs
Doctors Without Boarders
Edelman, Marion Wright
Ehrenreich, Barbara
Federal Housing
Administration (FHA)
Homeless Activism
Homeopathy Movement
Hospice Movement
Housing Movements
Hull-House
Koop, C. Everett
Low-Income Housing
Natural Childbirth Movement
Physicians for Social Responsibility
Poor People's Campaign
Professional Activist Organizations
Save the Children
Slow Food Movement
Spock, Benjamin
Wald, Lillian

About the Editors

Gary L. Anderson is a professor in the Department of Administration, Leadership and Technology in the Steinhardt School of Education at New York University. His research focuses on critical theory and education, critical ethnography, participatory action research, and issues of youth and violence. He has researched, taught, and presented extensively in Latin America and was the recipient of two Fulbright awards, one in Mexico and the other in Argentina. With Kathryn Herr, he has coauthored two books on action research: *The Action Research Dissertation: A Guide for Students and Faculty* (Sage, 2005) and *Studying Your Own School: An Educator's Guide to Practitioner Action Research* (Corwin Press, 1994; 2nd ed., 2007). His coedited book *Performance Theories and Education: Power, Pedagogy, and the Politics of Identity* was published in 2005 by Lawrence Erlbaum. For nearly 20 years, he has taught politics and policy issues in programs that certify school principals and superintendents.

Kathryn G. Herr is a professor in the College of Education and Human Services at Montclair State University in Montclair, New Jersey. She has published many articles on issues of youth and is coauthor, with Gary Anderson, of the books *Studying Your Own School: An Educator's Guide to Practitioner Action Research* (Corwin Press, 1994; 2nd ed., 2007) and *The Action Research Dissertation: A Guide for Students and Faculty* (Sage, 2005). She is also editor of the interdisciplinary Sage journal *Youth and Society.* Her professional background is in social work and education.

Contributors

Joseph Adamczyk
Attorney

Luis L. M. Aguiar
University of British Columbia–Okanagan

Mario I. Aguilar
University of St. Andrews

Wallace Alcorn
Wallace Alcorn Associates

Özlem Altiok
University of Wisconsin

Julie R. Andrzejewski
St. Cloud State University

Edlyne Anugwom
University of Nigeria, Nsukka

Keith Appleby
University of Oregon

Joyce Apsel
New York University

Alice Arnold
Hunter College, City University of New York

Ronald Aronson
Wayne State University

Josh Ashenmiller
Fullerton College

Elida Babollah
*Urban Scholar in Residence Program at Central
   Magnet High, Bridgeport, Connecticut*

Amanda Bahr-Evola
Southern Illinois University Edwardsville

Robert Edwin Bahruth
Boise State University

Sandeep Bakshi
University of Rouen, France

Meliza Bañales
San Francisco State University

Patricia A. Bauch
University of Alabama

Rosalyn Baxandall
State University of New York College at Old Westbury

Marc Becker
Truman State University

Scott M. Behen
California State University, Fullerton

Dan Berger
University of Pennsylvania

Beth Berila
St. Cloud State University

Andrea Bertotti Metoyer
Gonzaga University

Michael T. Bertrand
Tennessee State University

Pamela Jean Bettis
Washington State University

Douglas Bevington
University of California, Santa Cruz

Markus Paul Bidell
San Francisco State University

Jnan Ananda Blau
Southern Illinois University

Susan G. Blickstein
Clark University

Avital H. Bloch
University of Colima

Robert O. Bothwell
Visions Realized

Betsy Bowman
Grassroots Economic Organizing Newsletter

Jules Boykoff
Pacific University

Maxwell Boykoff
Oxford University Centre for the Environment

Mary (M. J.) Jean Braun
University of West Florida

Kathleen M. Brown
University of North Carolina at Chapel Hill

Sheri Bartlett Browne
Tennessee State University

Christopher G. Buck
Michigan State University (formerly)

Brian Burch
Ganesh Community Development Co-operative

Guy Burton
*London School of Economics and
    Political Science*

Brian Burtt
Syracuse University

Jay Byron
Radio Active Radio

Marco Cabrera Geserick
Arizona State University

Karen Cadiero-Kaplan
San Diego State University

George Caffentzis
University of Southern Maine, Portland

Cenap Çakmak
Rutgers University

Jane E. Calvert
St. Mary's College of Maryland

Ramona Anne Caponegro
University of Florida

Eduardo R. C. Capulong
New York University

Rosemary P. Carbine
College of the Holy Cross

David Lee Carlson
Hunter College, City University of New York

Joseph Carroll-Miranda
New Mexico State University

Valerie J. Carter
University of Maine

Katherine Casey-Sawicki
University of Florida

Graham Cassano
University of Connecticut

Sinan Kadir Çelik
*Middle East Technical University, Ankara,
    Turkey*

Graeme Cheadle

Frank M. Chiteji
Gettysburg College

Dana E. Christman
New Mexico State University

Monica Ciobanu
State University of New York, Plattsburgh

Lisa Hoffman Clark
Florida State University

Charles A. Clements
Burlington College

Aykut Coban
Ankara University

Ronald D. Cohen
Indiana University Northwest

Charlotte Collett
Medgar Evers College Preparatory School

Ed Collom
University of Southern Maine

Harris Cooper
Duke University

Rosa Elena Cornejo
New York University

Mark Douglas Cunningham
University of Texas at Austin

Nunzio N. D'Alessio
University of Texas at Austin

Amy Dahlberg Chu
Brandeis University

Sunny Daly
National Council for Research on Women

Leilah Danielson
Northern Arizona University

Michael E. Dantley
Miami University

Antonia Darder
University of Illinois at Urbana-Champaign

Samuel Marc Davidson
University of New Mexico

Stephanie Daza
Michigan University

Barbara DeAguiar
*Urban Scholar in Residence Program at Central
    Magnet High, Bridgeport, Connecticut*

Jean-Philippe Dedieu
École des Hautes Études en Sciences Sociales

Gregory Dehler
Front Range Community College

Abraham P. DeLeon
University of Connecticut

Jason Del Gandio
Kean University

Nadia Delicata
University of Toronto

Maria Delis
University of Central Florida

Noah De Lissovoy
University of Texas at San Antonio

Ana de Miguel
Universidad Rey Juan Carlos

Audrey M. Dentith
University of Wisconsin–Milwaukee

LaRay Denzer
Northwestern University

Victor G. Devinatz
Illinois State University

Graciela Di Marco
Universidad Nacional de San Martín, Buenos Aires, Argentina

Kit Dobson
University of Toronto

Peter Dolack

Ramon Dominguez
New Mexico State University

Jamel K. Donnor
Washington University in St. Louis

Mary Erina Driscoll
New York University Steinhardt School of Education

Garrett Albert Duncan
Washington University in St. Louis

Maylan Dunn
Northern Illinois University

Suzanne E. Eckes
Indiana University

Mark Engler
Freelance Journalist; Foreign Policy Analyst

Fenwick W. English
University of North Carolina at Chapel Hill

Leona M. English
St. Francis Xavier University

Craig L. Esposito
University of Connecticut

Cory Fairley
University of British Columbia

Robert Todd Felton
Freelance Writer

Kathy E. Ferguson
University of Hawai'i

Jordan Flaherty
Editor, Left Turn *Magazine*

Roger J. Flynn
Clemson University

Catherine Fosl
University of Louisville

Jason Friedman
Michigan State University

Joshua B. Friedman
University of Michigan

Samuel R. Friedman
National Development and Research Institutes, New York

Marie Justine Fritz
University of Maryland, College Park

Angela K. Frusciante
Jackson State University

Marcela A. Fuentes
New York University

Delia Tamara Fuster
Arizona State University

Darlene Galarza
*Urban Scholar in Residence Program at Central
Magnet High, Bridgeport, Connecticut*

Gregor Gall
University of Hertfordshire

Francesca Gamber
Southern Illinois University at Carbondale

Ross Gandy
Universidad Nacional Autónoma México, Aragón

César Cuauhtémoc García Hernández
Boston College

Thomas N. Gardner
Westfield State College

Barbara Garii
State University of New York, Oswego

Philip Gasper
Notre Dame de Namur University

Gregory Geddes
State University of New York, Binghamton

Doğan Göçmen
University of London

Michelle A. Gonzalez
University of Miami

Susan Myers Gordon
Ben Gurion University of the Negev

Paul C. Gorski
Hamline University

Camille Grant
*Urban Scholar in Residence Program at Central
Magnet High, Bridgeport, Connecticut*

Ivan Greenberg
Independent Historian

Betsy Greer
Independent Scholar

Jana Grekul
University of Alberta

David A. Gruenewald
Washington State University

Jeannine Guenette
York University

Rudy P. Guevarra, Jr.
University of California, Santa Barbara

Kristen E. Gwinn
George Washington University

Eric M. Haas
University of Connecticut

Martine Hackett
City University of New York Graduate Center

Jon N. Hale
University of Illinois at Urbana-Champaign

Lee Hall
Rutgers University

Nicole Hallett
Yale University

Bonita Hampton
State University of New York, Oswego

Chong-suk Han
Temple University

Jinghe Han
University of Western Sydney

Shak Hanish
National University

Joy Hardy
University of New England

Matthew L. Harris
Colorado State University–Pueblo

Joy L. Hart
University of Louisville

Andrew Hartman
Illinois State University

Menachem Hecht
New York University

Meeri Hellsten
Macquarie University

Paula-Andrea Hevia-Pacheco
York University

Helen M. Hintjens
Institute of Social Studies

K. Kim Holder
Rowan University

Julie Hollar
FAIR

Arthur Matthew Holst
Widener University

Dwight N. Hopkins
University of Chicago

Matthew S. Hopper
University of California, Los Angeles

Julie Horton
Appalachian State University

Marilyn K. Howard
Columbus State Community College

Michael W. Howard
University of Maine

Richard Hudelson
University of Wisconsin–Superior

Mark Hudson
University of Oregon

Luis Huerta-Charles
New Mexico State University

Emilia Ilieva
Egerton University, Kenya

Stephen Inrig
Duke University

Andrew B. Irvine
Long Island University

Adam Jacobs
University of Wisconsin

David H. Jensen
Austin Presbyterian Theological Seminary

Jørgen Johansen
Coventry University

Eric L. Johnson
Drake University

Richard A. Jones
Howard University

Jeffrey Joseph
*Urban Scholar in Residence Program at Central
    Magnet High, Bridgeport, Connecticut*

Davis D. Joyce
East Central University, Ada, Oklahoma

Craig A. Kaplowitz
Judson College

Vanessa E. Kass
University of Connecticut

Carole Keller
Wayne State University

Anne Keala Kelly
Native Hawaiian Journalist/Filmmaker

Walter J. Kendall, III
John Marshall Law School, Chicago

Jessica Ketcham Weber
Louisiana State University

Kathy P. Kilpatrick
Rowan University

Karla V. Kingsley
University of New Mexico

Teresa Knudsen
Independent Scholar

Carly A. Kocurek
University of Texas

Louis Kontos
John Jay College

Marc Krupanski
Center for Constitutional Rights

Deepa Kumar
Rutgers University

Donald D. Kummings
University of Wisconsin–Parkside

Andrew Kurtz
Bowling Green State University Firelands

Scott Laderman
University of Minnesota, Duluth

Pierre Lamarche
Utah Valley State College

Dorothy A. Lander
St. Francis Xavier University

Thomas J. Lappas
Nazareth College of Rochester

Matthew Lasar
University of California, Santa Cruz

Pat Lauderdale
Arizona State University

John LeBlanc
University of British Columbia–Okanagan

Chris Leslie
City University of New York Graduate Center

Dustin A. Lewis
Harvard University

Mona Lilja
Göteborg University

Renzo Llorente
Saint Louis University, Madrid Campus

William Low
University of Auckland

David E. Lowes

Catherine A. Lugg
Rutgers University

Theresa Catherine Lynch
Massachusetts College of Art

Paul J. Magnarella
Warren Wilson College

Jonathan Makuwira
Central Queensland University

Curry Malott
Brooklyn College

Beatrice Manning
Fitchburg State College

Joanne M. Marshall
Iowa State University

Brian Martin
University of Wollongong, Australia

Marlene Martin
Campaign to End the Death Penalty

Maryann Martin
Independent Scholar

John J. Martino
Victoria University

Paula J. Mathieu
Boston College

Todd May
Clemson University

Rela Mazali
Writer and Independent Researcher

Sara J. McAlister
*New York University Institute for Education and
    Social Policy*

Johonna R. McCants
University of Maryland

Martha M. McCarthy
Indiana University

Tristan McCowan
University of London, Institute of Education

Kathlene McDonald
*City University of New York, City College Center for
    Worker Education*

Conor McGrath
University of Ulster

Carole McKenna
Arizona State University

Ailíse McMahon
Boston College

Dan Taulapapa McMullin
Independent Writer and Artist

Brenda Melendy
Texas A&M University–Kingsville

Derek Merrill
Georgia Institute of Technology

Matt Meyer
Peace and Justice Studies Association

Sharon Michael-Chadwell
University of Phoenix

Alessandro Michelucci
*The Peoples' Library, Associazione per i Popoli
    Minacciati, Florence, Italy*

Natalija Micunovic
University of Belgrade

Kathryn Miles
Unity College

Cynthia J. Miller
Emerson College

Jason E. Miller
Western Washington University

Robert Earnest Miller
University of Cincinnati

Steven P. Miller
Vanderbilt University

Dylan A. T. Miner
University of New Mexico

William A. Mirola
Marian College

Thomas Mogan
Temple University

Carla R. Monroe
University of Georgia

Danelle Moon
San Jose State University

Alberto Morales

Douglas L. Morgan
University of South Australia

Melissa R. Mosley
Washington University

Susan Muaddi Darraj
Harford Community College

Lucy W. Mule
Smith College

Diego I. Murguía
University of Buenos Aires

Da'ad Naserdeen
University of Toledo

Angelene Naw
Judson College

Caryn E. Neumann
Ohio State University

Mitchell Newton-Matza
University of Phoenix

Louie Nikolaidis
National Development and Research Institutes

Elizabeth Noll
University of New Mexico

Yusuf Nuruddin
University of Toledo

Colleen C. O'Brien
Wake Forest University

Mike O'Connor
University of Texas at Austin

Lennox Odiemo-Munara
Egerton University, Kenya

Manal Omar
Women for Women International

Michelle Orihel
Syracuse University

Azadeh Farrah Osanloo
Arizona State University

Raquel Osborne
Universidad Nacional de Educación a Distancia, Madrid

Christian Papilloud
Lüneburg University

Thomas Peri
Montclair State University

James Perkinson
Ecumenical Theological Seminary

Allison Kristian Perlman
University of Texas at Austin

Naomi Jeffery Petersen
Central Washington University

Jesse Phillips-Fein
Brooklyn Friends School

Stephen Pimpare
Yeshiva College/Wurzweiler School of Social Work

Sherrow O. Pinder
Hobart and William Smith Colleges

Alex Plows
Cardiff University

Eric Poinsot
Université Robert Schuman de Strasbourg

Brad Porfilio
D'Youville College

Sarah Potvin
Harvard Business School

Keith C. Pounds
Hofstra University

Janet M. Powers
Gettysburg College

Jeanne M. Powers
Arizona State University

Michael A. Principe
Middle Tennessee State University

Carol Quirke
*State University of New York College,
    Old Westbury*

Tony Rafalowski
University of Missouri

Tania Ramalho
State University of New York, Oswego

Stacey Ingrum Randall
Northern Illinois University

Kamau Rashid
University of Illinois at Urbana-Champaign

Carina Ray
Cornell University

Beth Rempe
Lancaster University

Yolanda Retter Vargas
University of California, Los Angeles

Jesse H. Rhodes
University of Virginia

Nancy E. Rice
University of Wisconsin–Milwaukee

Joerg Rieger
Southern Methodist University

Malila N. Robinson
Rutgers University

Dalia Rodriguez
Syracuse University

Jon Roland
Constitution Society

Eric B. Ross
Institute of Social Studies

Susan L. Rothwell
Syracuse University

Carole Roy
Trent University

Joshua Rubenstein
Amnesty International USA

Markku Ruotsila
University of Tampere

Mara D. Rutten
Northern Virginia Community College

Rebecca M. Sánchez
University of New Mexico

Milagros Sandoval
*National Development and Research
    Institutes–Bushwick Youth Project*

Joseph C. Santora
Thomas Edison State College

Jeff Sapp
California State University, Dominguez Hills

Diego Saravia
Universidad Nacional de Salta

Paul Khalil Saucier
Northeastern University

Scott Schaffer
Millersville University of Pennsylvania

H. E. Schmiesser
University of Florida

David Schweickart
Loyola University Chicago

Helen C. Scott
University of Vermont

Katherine A. Scott
Temple University

Adrian Oscar Scribano
*Universidad Nacional de Villa Maria CEA UN
    Cordoba*

James L. Secor
*Sun Yat-Sem University, Guangzhou City,
    China*

Eden H. Segal
University of Maryland

Maha Shami
United Palestinian Appeal

Muna J. Shami
American University

Benjamin Shepard
California State University, Long Beach

Frederick Shepherd
Samford University

David Sherman
University of Montana

Horacio Sierra
University of Florida

John Sillito
Weber State University

Shawnece Simmons
*Urban Scholar in Residence Program
    at Central Magnet High, Bridgeport,
    Connecticut*

Anneliese A. Singh
Georgia State University

Michael Singh
University of Western Sydney

Daniel A. Smith
University of Florida

David Norman Smith
University of Kansas

Yushau Sodiq
Texas Christian University

Soner Soysal
Middle East Technical University

Andre Spicer
University of Warwick

Stephanie Urso Spina
State University of New York, Cortland

Mark Stern
Syracuse University

Heidi Stevenson
Northern Michigan University

Karsten J. Struhl
City University of New York, John Jay College

Harry Targ
Purdue University

Robert T. Teranishi
New York University

Martha May Tevis
University of Texas–Pan American

Linda C. Tillman
University of North Carolina at Chapel Hill

Myriam N. Torres
New Mexico State University

James Richard Tracy
San Francisco Community Land Trust

Eli Tucker-Raymond
University of Illinois at Chicago

Maureen H. Turnbull
University of California, Santa Cruz

Ruth H. Turner
Hanover College

Concepción M. Valadez
University of California, Los Angeles

Judith Imel Van Allen
Cornell University

Leandro Vergara-Camus
York University

Jenice L. View
Teaching for Change

Javier Villa-Flores
University of Illinois at Chicago

Stellan Vinthagen
Göteborg University

Fabian Virchow
Philipps-University of Marburg

Lori A. Walters-Kramer
State University of New York, Plattsburgh

Nessim Watson
Westfield State College

Jillian Todd Weiss
Ramapo College

Seth G. Weiss
Author

Michael Welch
Rutgers University

Ryan Wells
University of Iowa

Carol Westcamp
University of Arkansas–Fort Smith

Tom Wetzel
San Francisco Community Land Trust

Robert Whealey
Ohio University

Kelly L. Whitaker
New York University

Robert F. Whiteley
University of British Columbia–Okanagan

Joy L. Wiggins
University of Texas at Arlington

Brook Willensky-Lanford
W. W. Norton & Company

Dean Williams
University of Edinburgh

Glen Yahola Wilson
University of Connecticut

Barbara Winslow
*Brooklyn College, City
   University of New York*

C. Sheldon Woods
Northern Illinois University

Sabrina Worsham
Southern Illinois University at Carbondale

Amy Nathan Wright
University of Texas at Austin

Elizabeth Wrigley-Field
Campus Antiwar Network

Tracy Wyman-Marchand
University of British Columbia

Susan R. Wynn
Duke University

Michael A. Yacci
RIT Information Technology

Mehmet Yetis
Ankara University

William Youmans
*Columnist, Arab-American News; Board Director,
   Jerusalem Fund for Education and Community
   Development*

Eric Zassenhaus
City Lights Bookstore and Publishers

Ger J. Z. Zielinski
McGill University

Lynn W. Zimmerman
Purdue University Calumet

Magdalena Zolkos
University of Alberta

Alexander M. Zukas
National University

Lorna Lueker Zukas
National University

Stephen Zunes
University of San Francisco

Gilda Zwerman
State University of New York, Old Westbury

Introduction

Like many scholars whose formative years were in the activist 1960s and early 1970s, we lived for many years with an uncomfortable relationship between our activism and our scholarship. These were supposed to remain separate domains: By day, we produced positivist knowledge to feed the information society; by night, we engaged in political activism to change it. Some scholars chose fields more amenable to making activism and social justice a central and legitimate focus of their research. For most, however, the curriculum of our fields had no place for these issues. As Foucault pointed out, we were well "disciplined" by our respective disciplines—even more so in professional fields like education, in which both of us labor. A shift has occurred among many scholars in a number of different fields as the tensions between our professional and personal goals have become more apparent. Increasingly, scholars see themselves as "public intellectuals" who no longer apologize for advocating for the powerless in society. The brazen advance of neoliberalism, the resurgence of nativist and racist policies, and the arrogance and aggression of a post-9/11 American empire has given scholars a greater sense of urgency. The once-tight boundaries between academia and activism have been breached, to the consternation of some and the approval of others.

So when Todd Armstrong approached us with the idea for an encyclopedia of activism and social justice, we felt that not only was it a way to meld our scholarship and our activism, but that it would bring together a much-needed synthesis of diverse scholarship on both traditional and emerging forms of social, cultural, and aesthetic activism. Because no one could possibly be an expert on activism and social justice worldwide from the beginning of recorded history to the present, we put together a group of associate editors, consisting of a diverse group of scholars representing expertise in numerous fields. With their input, we produced an extensive list of entries to include, and we solicited authors known in these areas. In order to touch base with the greater scholarly community, we put these entries out on a couple of international activist listserves. The response was overwhelming and transformed the encyclopedia into a collective enterprise. Activists and scholars suggested entries on new and emerging areas of scholarship that we never would have thought of including. For instance, we were taken to task by female Africanist scholars for failing to include a single female African activist in our initial list. So we took a new look at the entries with an eye to gender, as well as representative balance among different parts of the world. We also heard from many activists in technology and communication that opened up a world of cyber activism of which we were largely unaware. Unlike most academic writing projects that tend to be fairly matter of fact, contributors to this project produced a sense of excitement and urgency that energized us.

Other decisions had to be made. The Ku Klux Klan or neo-Nazi groups clearly view themselves as activists. And yet, their link to social justice, regardless of how it is defined, is just as clearly absent. Eliminating entries such as those was easy, but some entries fell into a grayer area. As we all know, some view freedom fighters as terrorists and vice versa. One Arab scholar objected to including Zionism. Meanwhile, a Jewish friend was scandalized that I was planning to include Hamas. Should we only include groups that reject violence as a strategy? After struggling with this issue, we felt that a group should be included if social justice was an espoused goal, even if there was a historical consensus that those goals were largely unrealized. So, for instance, V. I. Lenin is included, but not Stalin. Militia movements appear, but not neo-Nazi movements. The entry on abortion includes both pro- and anti-legalization groups. Because social justice has tended to be an espoused goal primarily of the political left, there are fewer movements and activists of the political right represented in the encyclopedia.

One of our associate editors, Brian Martin, helped us with a framework for prioritizing our inclusion of entries. His entry, titled "Activism, Social and Political," serves as a good conceptual introduction to the encyclopedia. In that entry, Martin writes,

> Activism is action that goes beyond conventional politics, typically being more energetic, passionate, innovative, and committed. In systems of representative government, conventional politics includes election campaigning, voting, passing laws, and lobbying politicians. Action outside of these arenas includes neighborhood organizing, protest marches, and sit-ins. The boundary between activism and conventional politics is fuzzy and depends on the circumstances.

Because of the fuzzy boundary between conventional politics and activism, we have included some entries that would be viewed as the former. We prefer to think of activism as occurring both within the conventional political arenas and outside them, as well as perhaps crossing back and forth between the increasingly fuzzy boundaries. As Martin points out, the labor movement and labor parties in various countries worked for change. Both the environmental movement and the Green Party worked for environmental justice.

We also added another kind of activism to Brian Martin's definition: aesthetic activism. Breaking aesthetic paradigms also can be a form of activism, such as the importance of mural art or Walt Whitman's populist poetic structures. We also wanted to privilege collectivist struggle over individual accomplishment. History

is not a story of heroes and villains, but rather movements made up of the collective, everyday acts of courageous people. However, we had hundreds of e-mails from individuals arguing the case for one or another individual activist, and we realized to what extent we have all internalized this view of history. So, while we consciously attempted throughout to favor movements and struggles over individuals, we are not sure to what extent we have been successful. This is also, in part, because we wanted to include social theorists who helped to provide conceptual guidance for activists. Political theorists, liberation theologians, philosophers, and social and literary critics have helped to lay the groundwork for much activism.

From a practical perspective, Brian Martin warned us that once we got to the level of individual activists, the possible entries would number in the thousands. Thus, some readers will not find their favorite activist included. In some cases, this was because a particular contributor to the encyclopedia simply did not come through with a promised entry. In other cases, we had to painfully triage people due to space limitations. The index should provide guidance for individuals or movements that do not have their own entries, but instead are discussed as part of a larger entry.

We would like to acknowledge the assistance of our associate editors. Several made contributions that went above and beyond the call of duty. As already noted, Brian Martin was instrumental in helping us conceptualize the encyclopedia. Jeffrey Paris was largely responsible for the entries in political philosophy and social theory. Joerg Rieger provided copious suggestions for authors and entries on religion and spirituality. Fenwick English, general editor of *Encyclopedia of Educational Leadership and Administration* (Sage, 2006), provided invaluable tips from his experience as an encyclopedia editor. Paul Buhle, coeditor of the classic *Encyclopedia of the American Left,* now in its second edition, also provided useful feedback based on his extensive experience.

It has been a pleasure to work with the team of editors at Sage. As acquisitions editor, Todd Armstrong first brought the idea to us. Leticia Gutierrez was always there to provide logistical support with entries.

Yvette Pollastrini was a constant troubleshooter throughout the development process, and Tracy Alpern deftly handled all production issues. Laura Torres, Elaine Herr, and Thomas Peri helped with editing and fact checking.

Further Readings

Buhle, M., Buhle, P., & Georgakas, D. (1998). *Encyclopedia of the American left* (2nd ed.). London: Oxford University Press.

—Gary L. Anderson and Kathryn G. Herr

ABERNATHY, RALPH (1926–1990)

Born in Linden, Alabama, on March 11, 1926, Ralph David Abernathy was the 10th child of W. L. Abernathy, a farmer, and his wife Louivery. Abernathy became a close friend and partner of civil rights leader Martin Luther King, Jr. and worked to carry on King's legacy as head of the Southern Christian Leadership Conference.

Abernathy received a religious upbringing within the Baptist church. After serving in the army during World War II, he entered Alabama State University in Montgomery in 1945 and there decided to become a minister. He was named pastor of Montgomery's First Baptist Church in 1952, and Martin Luther King, Jr., then pastor of the Dexter Avenue Baptist Church, soon became a good friend. With King, Abernathy was instrumental in the foundation of the Montgomery Improvement Association and in the yearlong boycott of the city's buses after Rosa Parks was arrested in 1955 for refusing to comply with segregation laws.

Abernathy and his family relocated to Atlanta in 1961, and he became pastor of West Hunter Baptist Church. King had also moved to Atlanta, and both men were prominent within the Southern Christian Leadership Conference (SCLC), a civil rights organization founded in 1957. As the civil rights movement escalated, Abernathy was by King's side during its most important battles, including Albany, Georgia, in 1962; Birmingham, Alabama, in 1963; Selma, Alabama, in 1965; and Chicago, Illinois, in 1966. Abernathy was intimately familiar with nearly every tactic that has since made the civil rights movement exemplary. He raised money to release jailed activists, participated in voter registration, helped craft desegregation agreements, and was the southern coordinator for the 1963 March on Washington.

When King was murdered in April 1968, Abernathy—who was with him at the time and identified his body—became president of the SCLC. That summer, Abernathy set up Resurrection City near the Lincoln Memorial in Washington, D.C., to continue the Poor People's Campaign King had started before his death by publicizing the condition of the poor. Abernathy also sustained SCLC involvement in direct action protests, marching with striking hospital workers in Charleston in 1969, supporting César Chávez's United Farm Workers Union, and helping the FBI and Native American activists reach an agreement at Wounded Knee in 1973.

Abernathy left the SCLC in 1977 and ran unsuccessfully for Congress. Disillusioned with the Democratic Party, he campaigned for Ronald Reagan in 1980 and became vice president of the conservative American Freedom Coalition in 1987. He published an autobiography, *And the Walls Came Tumbling Down*, in 1989. Abernathy died on April 17, 1990. His life encompassed both the successes of the civil rights movement and the challenges of sustaining its influence after the 1960s.

—Francesca Gamber

See also Civil Rights Movement; King, Martin Luther, Jr.; Montgomery Bus Boycott; Southern Christian Leadership Conference

Further Readings

Abernathy, D. (2003). *Partners to history: Martin Luther King Jr., Ralph David Abernathy, and the civil rights movement.* New York: Crown.

Abernathy, R. (1989). *And the walls came tumbling down.* New York: Harper & Row.

Garrow, D. (1986). *Bearing the cross: Martin Luther King, Jr., and the Southern Christian Leadership Conference.* New York: Morrow.

ABOLITIONIST MOVEMENTS

Dismantling slavery took hundreds of years of resistance and public outcry and cannot be attributed to one group, nation, or movement. Although Great Britain outlawed British involvement in the slave trade in 1807 (barring the sale and transport of slaves but not outlawing slavery outright), it took 26 more years for emancipation to reach the colonies of the vast British Empire. Member of Parliament William Wilberforce gained a place in history and became an abolitionist role model for the United States as he campaigned for these political reforms, joined by his colleague Thomas Clarkson. The influence of evangelical and cultural beliefs contributed to the political changes as well.

The narratives and letters of former slaves like Olaudah Equiano (Gustavus Vassa) and Ignatius Sancho, for example, helped raise awareness about the horrors of the middle passage and the desire for freedom among enslaved Africans. Jonathan Edwards, Jr., lesser-known anti-slavery activist and son of the famed Congregationalist minister of the First Great Awakening, composed a sermon that denounced 10 common pro-slavery positions. The 1791 document, *Injustices and Impolicy of the Slave Trade and of the Slavery of Africans,* exemplifies some of the religious concerns that would eventually effect political change.

Later that year, the Haitian Revolution, led by Toussaint L'Ouverture in August 1791, led to the abolition of slavery in Haiti and, after more than a decade of struggle, independence from French colonial rule. L'Ouverture, a slave himself, orchestrated major military maneuvers to overthrow French planters and defeat French and Spanish troops on the island of Santo Domingo. As a revolutionary moment in the wake of the American and French Revolutions, Haitian independence put a black face on freedom and self-determination. In Haiti, men of all colors were to become equal citizens. Slaveholders, including Thomas Jefferson, rejected this new brand of independence. Slaveholding colonies and nations alike feared that the revolution in Haiti would spread throughout the New World; thus, governments in the other Caribbean islands and United States constructed a "cordon sanitaire" around the island to prevent news of the insurrection from spreading throughout the Americas, particularly to other rebellious slaves. Although France first abolished slavery in response to the Haitian Revolution, Napoleon Bonaparte reinstated it in 1802.

The age of revolution contributed to anti-slavery activism in the United States as well. On January 1, 1794, representatives from the abolition societies of Connecticut, New York, New Jersey, Pennsylvania, Delaware, and Maryland met in Philadelphia, which became an anti-slavery hotbed due to the presence of middle-class free blacks as well as a large population of anti-slavery Quakers. The petition strategy, which would entreat Congress to prohibit the slave trade and encourage state legislatures to abolish slavery, became the modus operandi of this and many ensuing anti-slavery groups. The rhetoric of these petitions stressed the contradictions of a country that had revolted in 1776 against kings and despots yet permitted men to own and deprive other human beings of their freedom. The Philadelphia delegates of 1794 also published *Minutes of Proceedings of a Convention of Delegates From the Abolition Societies.*

Quaker abolitionist Benjamin Lundy founded anti-slavery newspapers including the *Genius of*

Universal Emancipation, which acquired William Lloyd Garrison as its editor in 1829. Lundy was generally considered a gradualist and endorsed repatriation of freed slaves to a safe haven in Africa or the Caribbean rather than integration into American society. Garrison's views collided with Lundy's, particularly as the former began to see abolition as an immediate and widespread, rather than gradual, solution to the problem of slavery. After a conflict with Lundy and time in jail for libel, Garrison returned to New England to found *The Liberator* in 1831 and the New England Anti-Slavery Society in 1832.

The American Anti-Slavery Society, founded in 1833, was one of the first U.S. national organizations to oppose slavery and take steps to abolish the institution. As a supporter of women's full participation in anti-slavery activities, Garrison welcomed women in leadership roles in the Society and accepted the influence of Susan B. Anthony, Lucretia Mott, Elizabeth Cady Stanton, and other future leaders in the women's suffrage movement.

Denied the right to vote, women used petitions to Congress and state legislatures as a key strategy in making their names and beliefs known to lawmakers. The role of women as abolitionists ushered them into a public arena where traditional gender barriers (such as the idea that women should not speak in public, much less to "mixed" audiences of men and women) shattered. Black and white women established independent anti-slavery societies. Maria Stewart, a black Bostonian, became the first African American woman to deliver a lecture to the New England Anti-Slavery Society in 1832. The Boston and Philadelphia

The large, bold woodcut image of a supplicant male slave in chains appears on the 1837 broadside publication of John Greenleaf Whittier's anti-slavery poem, "Our Countrymen in Chains." The design was originally adopted as the seal of the Society for the Abolition of Slavery in England in the 1780s, and appeared on several medallions for the society made by Josiah Wedgwood as early as 1787. Here, in addition to Whittier's poem, the appeal to conscience against slavery continues with two further quotes. The first is the scriptural warning, "He that stealeth a man and selleth him, or if he be found in his hand, he shall surely be put to death." Exod[us] XXI, 16. Next the claim, "England has 800,000 Slaves, and she has made them free. America has 2,250,000! and she holds them fast!!!!" The broadside is advertised at "Price Two Cents Single; or $1.00 per hundred."

Source: Courtesy of the Library of Congress.

Female Anti-Slavery Societies emerged in 1833; the former, led by author Lydia Maria Child, organized an anti-slavery fair in 1834. In addition to the innovation of featuring female speakers who addressed "promiscuous" audiences, women established the practice of holding fairs at which they offered abolitionist literature and souvenir household items (such as pin cushions) bearing anti-slavery emblems. South Carolina sisters Angelina and Sarah Grimké became the first female agents of the American Anti-Slavery Society in 1836.

As the abolitionist movement grew, the role of women in leadership positions and the constitutional issue led to the formation of new societies. In 1835, the Ladies' New York Anti-Slavery Society formed; they participated in petitioning but believed in a God-given hierarchical structure of society in which the definition of rights established by their more radical sisters did not apply. The "Ladies" did not become suffragists and did not endorse women's presence in the public sphere. When the American and Foreign Anti-Slavery Society broke from the American Anti-Slavery Society in 1840 because Abby Kelley sat on its business committee, the New York Ladies walked out with them.

Women, nonetheless, continued to play an unconventional and nontraditional role in the abolitionist movement. Lydia Maria Child became editor of a major publication, *The National Anti-Slavery Standard*, in 1841. By 1848, most of the leading women in the abolitionist movement would convene at Seneca Falls to demand their own rights. Sojourner Truth, born into slavery in New York in the early 1800s, became one of the best-known spokeswomen for African American and women's rights. The fact that many abolitionist meetings were integrated in race and gender, however, contributed to the reactionary public opinion that abolitionists were indecent and obscene, particularly because opponents characterized abolitionists as "amalgamationists," or persons in favor of the mixing of the races and intermarriage, a topic that severely threatened the social order in the 19th- and even 20th-century United States.

The spirit of reform, which included issues such as temperance, peace, and opposition to Cherokee removal on what came to be known as the Trail of Tears,

likewise fostered the growth of abolitionist activity. The interception of a boatload of anti-slavery tracts by a Charleston, South Carolina, postmaster resulted in the burning of the documents by an angry mob. In the pattern of President Andrew Jackson's recommendation to prevent the circulation of these incendiary materials through the mail, the House of Representatives passed a "gag rule" that automatically tabled any anti-slavery petition without discussion. An angry mob murdered abolitionist publisher Elijah Lovejoy in 1837 in Acton, Illinois; extensive newspaper coverage of this event made Lovejoy a martyr for the movement.

Evangelism also drove the reform spirit of the 1830s. Religious groups such as the Quakers and Unitarians found slavery inconsistent with the teachings of Jesus Christ, and some political leaders agonized over the contradictions inherent in the Constitution of a slaveholding United States. When, in 1846, Lysander Spooner published *The Unconstitutionality of Slavery*, the beginnings of a schism in the abolitionist movement surfaced. Garrison, when challenged by an audience member who claimed that the Constitution protected slavery, stated that the Constitution should then be burned. He and Wendell Phillips opposed Frederick Douglass, Spooner, and Gerrit Smith because the latter three maintained that the Constitution was a pro-freedom document. In 1855, Douglass, Smith, James McCune Smith, and John Brown founded the Radical Political Abolitionist Party, which promoted radical equality and was generally considered extreme and scandalous by more liberal and conservative abolitionists. Informed by Emersonian ideals of personal morality, their militant political agenda accompanied a belief in racial equality and the sacredness of the U.S. Constitution unparalleled by any of their contemporaries.

Douglass, an escaped slave who published his influential *Narrative of the Life of Frederick Douglass* in 1845 and his second autobiography, *My Bondage and My Freedom*, 10 years later, traveled the anti-slavery lecture circuit and began publishing his own newspaper, the *North Star*, with Martin Delany as coeditor in 1847. When the two editors split, the name of the publication was changed to *The Frederick Douglass Paper*. Whereas Douglass's name is fairly familiar in

U.S. history, the similar work of his contemporary Frances Watkins Harper is not. Both worked as writers and lecturers; both joined the women's suffrage movement in the 1850s, and although Harper was born free in Baltimore in 1824, both were in jeopardy of kidnapping under the fugitive slave law after the Compromise of 1850 because they traveled extensively in their lecturing circuits. Douglass and Harper were friends of John Brown, who orchestrated an unsuccessful raid on a military arsenal in Harper's Ferry, West Virginia, in 1859. Brown's plan was to capture the arsenal and lead a massive slave insurrection that would abolish the evil institution permanently. He was captured, tried, and eventually hanged for treason.

The relationship of slave insurrections to the abolitionist movement deserves further inquiry. The alleged Denmark Vesey conspiracy in Charleston, South Carolina, fueled the objectives of the American Colonization Society, a group of South Carolina planters that endeavored to send free blacks (like Vesey) to Africa and thereby erase the visible presence of freedom among African Americans. Although Southerners blamed Nat Turner's Insurrection in 1831 on Garrisonians, no direct evidence suggests that Turner was aware of the Garrisonian movement. Other insurrectionary plots, led by Africans and African Americans, fueled the abolitionist sentiment. The *Amistad* mutiny in 1839 pitted abolitionists against President Martin Van Buren and his administration. The subsequent trial of mutiny leader Joseph Cinquez and his accomplices in New Haven, Connecticut, resulted in a decision, upheld by the Supreme Court in March 1841, to return Cinquez and his surviving friends to Africa. John Quincy Adams represented the Africans before the Supreme Court, making pleas for freedom and justice that applied to enslaved Africans.

In 1852, the publication of Harriet Beecher Stowe's immensely popular novel *Uncle Tom's Cabin,* which sold one and a half million copies in its first year, promoted the abolitionist cause. While the publicity and attention Stowe drew to slavery increased abolitionist sentiment, it is interesting to note that she (unlike the radical abolitionists) did not support racial equality. Stowe endorsed repatriation, the removal of people of African descent to their "fatherland" after a period of seasoning in the North when they could adopt what she explicitly refers to as the Christian and civilized ways of white Americans. After the Civil War, she apologized to the "white ladies" of the South for having precipitated their predicament, stating that she never endorsed social equality between the races.

The 1850s saw the expression of "higher law" in U.S. politics. The evangelical abolitionist beliefs of many abolitionists translated into an interpretation of the Constitution as a document reflecting the equality of all in the eyes of God. At the same time, Northern representatives engaged in a power struggle with the South over the entry of new states into the Union. Slavery had not been economically expedient in the North, hence its abolition in most of New England by 1800. Debates over U.S. expansion in the Caribbean and the question of whether new territories (such as Kansas, where John Brown and his recruits fought pro-slavery Missouri Rangers, and Nebraska) would permit slavery divided Congress, and the issue of slavery became representative of a number of political disagreements between North and South. The Free-Soil Party formed, consolidating the Whigs and the former Liberal Party, to oppose the spread of slavery in territories acquired through the Mexican War. Free-Soiler Charles Sumner of Massachusetts gained a seat in Congress in 1851 and, like many members of his party, became a Republican in the mid-1850s. His vitriolic anti-slavery filibusters almost led to his demise when, in 1856, the nephew of a South Carolina senator whom Sumner had lambasted in a speech nearly caned Sumner to death.

A month after Abraham Lincoln was elected without a single Southern electoral vote, South Carolina, followed by 10 other states, dissolved its ties to the Union. Massachusetts abolitionists in particular celebrated secession, yet conservatives in Boston blamed abolitionists for destroying the Union, and attacks on abolitionist meetings became so common that Wendell Phillips began carrying a revolver. Whereas Garrison was pleased by secession, the likes of Frederick Douglass, Gerrit Smith, and James McCune Smith held on to John Brown's militant vision that the entire nation could repent from its sins through bloodshed.

Although "Abraham Lincoln freed the slaves" is a common historical understanding, the truth is that

Lincoln had no stated intention to abolish slavery in territories where it already existed; instead, he had a vague idea that it would die gradually, and he supported the repatriation of former slaves to Africa rather than the development of social and political equality in the United States. Lincoln hesitated to declare emancipation after the outbreak of the Civil War, in part not to agitate the border states (Maryland, Delaware, Kentucky, and Missouri) who held slaves but had not seceded from the Union. It was only after the battle of Antietam in the fall of 1862 that he declared a Preliminary Emancipation Proclamation.

—Colleen C. O'Brien

See also Brown, John; Douglass, Frederick; Lincoln, Abraham; Toussaint L'Ouverture; Turner, Nat; Women's Suffrage Movement

Further Readings

Cain, W. E. (Ed.). (1995). *William Lloyd Garrison and the fight against slavery: Selections from "The Liberator."* Boston: Bedford.

Douglass, F. (2001). *Narrative of the life of Frederick Douglass, an American slave: Written by himself.* New Haven, CT: Yale University Press. (Original work published 1845)

Jacobs, H. (1987). *Incidents in the life of a slave girl; written by herself* (J. F. Yellin, Ed.). Cambridge, MA: Harvard University Press. (Original work published 1861)

Knight, F. W. (2000). The Haitian Revolution. *American Historical Review.* Retrieved March 8, 2006, from http://www.historycooperative.org/journals/ahr/105.1/ah000103.html

Richards, L. L. (1970). *"Gentlemen of property and standing": Anti-abolition mobs in Jacksonian America.* New York: Oxford University Press.

Ryan, M. P. (1990). *Women in public: Between banners and ballots, 1825–1880.* Baltimore: Johns Hopkins University Press.

Stauffer, J. (2002). *The black hearts of men.* Cambridge, MA: Harvard University Press.

Stowe, H. B. (1994). *Uncle Tom's cabin.* New York: W. W. Norton. (Original work published 1852)

Walters, R. G. (1978). *The antislavery appeal: American abolitionism after 1830.* Baltimore: Johns Hopkins University Press.

Yellin, J. F., & Van Horne, J. (Eds.). (1994). *The abolitionist sisterhood: Women's political culture in antebellum America.* Ithaca, NY: Cornell University Press.

ABORTION

The issue of abortion has polarized the human race as few other issues have done in our recorded history. Perhaps it is because religion, a cornerstone of culture, is central in this debate and cannot be separated from it. It was John Stuart Mills who believed that the only way to acquire wisdom was to hear all aspects and perspectives. This entry attempts to present both sides of this contentious issue.

Definition

An abortion can be defined as the removal or expulsion from the uterus of an embryo or fetus, resulting in or caused by its death. When abortion is discussed by the media or in the political arena, many refer to one that was chosen or induced. According to the medical profession, there are many types of and reasons for an abortion, including (a) spontaneous (miscarriage) and (b) induced (therapeutic and induced). A spontaneous abortion or miscarriage may occur due to an accident or natural causes at any time during pregnancy. Up to 50% of all pregnancies, depending on the age and prenatal care the mother receives, end in a miscarriage. A therapeutic abortion may be used to either save the life of the mother or, in the case of multiple births, end one fetus to save two others. Another case of therapeutic abortion may be to kill a fetus that has been determined to have a fatal disorder that would die if brought to full term. For the remainder of this piece when the word *abortion* is used, it will refer to the general understanding of a chosen termination of pregnancy.

Historical Context of Abortion

The termination of pregnancy has been practiced virtually by most civilizations and by many cultures since ancient times even though many religious doctrines have been interpreted as denouncing the use of abortion as immortal and sinful. Pregnancies have been terminated through a number of methods, including the administration of herbs, the application of abdominal pressure, and the use of sharpened implements. The ancient Greeks relied on herbs and also suggested that women wanting to abort their pregnancies should engage in vigorous exercises. By 1869, the Catholic Church declared abortion a sin punishable by excommunication. Around the same time, women's choices had expanded to pills, powders, and mechanical devices with varying degrees of effectiveness and safety. During this time, the mortality rate from abortion was high, whereas the mortality rate from childbirth was less than 3%.

Only during the past 100 years or so has legislation been passed regulating the practice of abortion. There are no records on the number of abortions performed during this time. The laws in the United States varied until 1800. Assisted by the American Medical Association, bans regarding the practice of abortion were enacted by states, beginning in 1821 and continuing throughout the 19th century. In the United States, legislation regarding abortion has varied with the times. Thus began a steady business in illegal abortions, some of which were done by incompetent doctors in unsafe conditions. Eventually, the development of surgical abortion using standard antiseptic methods made abortion more effective and safer for the mother. The introduction of penicillin in the 20th century reduced the incidence of maternal death enormously.

By the mid-20th century, decisions about abortion often went to hospital review boards. There were also several groups arguing that abortion laws should be changed. During the 1950s, the practice of medicine came under increasing scrutiny, and guidelines were set to define the indications for therapeutic abortion. In 1959, the American Law Institute proposed revisions that were used by a number of states. In the 1960s, an outbreak of German measles (which often causes serious birth defects) led to more abortions. Some doctors, fearing prosecution, argued for more liberal laws. In 1969, Planned Parenthood supported the repeal of anti-abortion laws. In 1973, the U.S. Supreme Court ruled in *Roe v. Wade* that a Texas anti-abortion statute was unconstitutional; this decision led to the legalization of abortion.

Fundamental Concerns of Abortion

In order to fully grasp this complicated issue, one must come to terms with the most deep-seated issue surrounding the topic of abortion: the exact time a human life begins. Thus, the question for mothers, fathers, sisters, and brothers must be "When can life be terminated?" What is the justification morally and legally? Under what circumstances can one or should one choose to terminate a pregnancy? At what time during the pregnancy should an abortion be stopped? Is it ever too late to terminate pregnancy, and if so, is late termination of a pregnancy considered murder? What are the legal ramifications of these choices in the United States and in the global community?

One of the questions central to this issue appears to be philosophical and religious in nature. When does life begin? Does life begin at the time of conception, during the time that cells are dividing, or at birth? There is a lack of consensus on the exact timing to the beginning of personhood. This leads people to polarize into camps of what have been called the "prolifers" and "pro-choicers." Although it is difficult to lump all people into just two belief systems, the basic idea of the two groups are that pro-lifers believe that abortion should be avoided and pro-choicers believe abortion should be a choice. Although both groups believe that once life's existence has been established, this person has rights and should not be killed unless there are dire circumstances, it appears the division still exists on when life actually does begin. This is essential to uncovering the layers beneath; whose rights are more important, the mother or the fetus, and when does that fetus become a child?

The majority of the pro-life camp believes that life occurs at the time of conception because that is when a unique DNA strand first appears. Some pro-lifers would go further to say that abortion is the killing of a baby in the mother's womb. Conversely, most pro-choicers say that personhood occurs much later in pregnancy when movement begins. To add to this argument is that up to 50% of fertilized eggs do not implant and of those that do, between 20% and 50% miscarry; only 10% are successful pregnancies. To add a global perspective, some Aboriginal people worldwide believe that the newborn only becomes a human person when he or she is named.

It has been established that abortions have been used throughout history for unwanted pregnancies.

Can abortion be justified, or is it an immoral act? The use of abortion to preserve the life of the mother has been widely accepted. Early Jewish scholars' interpretation of the Talmud required that the fetus be destroyed if it posed a threat to the mother during delivery. The ancient Greeks allowed abortion under certain circumstances. Ancient Romans did not consider a fetus a person until after birth, and abortion was practiced widely. In modern day, both pro-life and pro-choice supporters tend to agree that an abortion should not be allowed after human personhood is present, except under very unusual circumstances. What those circumstances can be are not as easily determined.

Many pro-life supporters refer to abortion as the murder of an unborn child. The Roman Catholic Church, for example, teaches that an abortion at any stage of pregnancy can never be a valid moral choice but allows an abortion if it is an unintended side effect of a required medical procedure. A small minority believes that an abortion is never a moral choice, even to save the life of the woman, and an even smaller number equate abortion to the Nazi Holocaust, equating abortion clinics with Nazi death camps. In the middle is the belief that abortion should be allowed to save the life of the woman, avoid serious long-term injury or permanent disability to the woman, and perhaps if the pregnancy had been initiated by rape or incest. There is a discrepancy between pro-lifers regarding a forced pregnancy under the above circumstances, but pro-choicers believe a woman should have a choice regarding her future. Most pro-choicers might agree that the alternative to abortion access is enforced childbirth for every pregnant woman. Forcing her to continue an unwanted pregnancy to childbirth is an unwarranted intrusion into the private life of a woman, particularly for those who believe that they are carrying only a potential human life and not an actual human life.

It appears impossible for religious leaders, philosophers, medical professionals, and the rest of the public to reach a consensus about when personhood begins. What limitations, if any, should the State place on a woman's choice to terminate a pregnancy? If a woman, after consultation with her physician and perhaps with her spiritual adviser, decides to have an abortion, then when should the State intrude and deny her that option?

The Supreme Court of the United States decided on January 22, 1973, that women have a right to control their own reproductive destinies, striking down the state laws that had made early abortions illegal. *Roe v. Wade* 1973 upheld the fundamental right of a woman to determine whether to continue her pregnancy. Support for *Roe* comes from those who view the decision as necessary to preserve women's equality and personal freedom.

Complex issues exist in the debate over abortion and are not likely to change over the upcoming decades. Since 1969, the Centers for Disease Control and Prevention have documented the number of abortions in the United States. The number was on the rise until 1999 when that number began to decrease. The highest percentages of abortions were reported for white and unmarried women under the age of 25 years. From 1990 through 1997, the number of legally induced abortions gradually declined. In 1998 and in 1999, the number of abortions continued to decrease, and as in previous years, deaths related to legally induced abortions occurred rarely. The abortion rate worldwide in 1995 was approximately 26 million legal and 20 million illegal abortions, resulting in a worldwide abortion rate of 35 per 1,000 women aged 15 to 44. Among the subregions of the world, Eastern Europe had the highest abortion rate (90 per 1,000) and Western Europe the lowest rate (11 per 1,000). Out of the countries where abortion is legal, the higher rate was reported in Vietnam, 83 per 1,000, and the Netherlands and Belgium reported the lowest, with 7 per 1,000.

Conclusion

The conflict continues, and at least for the time being, abortion is legal in the United States and in most if not all of the developed countries around the world (see Dailard, 1999, for complete breakdown by country and reasons for legal abortion). As travel costs drop and more countries in the world allow women to have at least early abortions if they wish, a local law forbidding elective abortions can be overcome. Many people believe that keeping abortions legal would put an end to the dangerous and/or self-induced back alley abortions. At the same time, who will be the voice for those who cannot be heard? That is the question pro-lifers continue to ask.

According to the Pew Forum on Religion and Public Life, only 29% of Americans would like to see the *Roe* decision repealed. At the same time, the majority of the public believes that there should be more restrictions on abortion, such as parental consent.

—*Julie Horton*

See also *Roe v. Wade*

Further Readings

Beckwith, F. (1998). *Is the unborn human less than human?* Christian Answers Network. Retrieved March 8, 2006, from http://www.christiananswers.net/

Cozic, C. P., & Tipp, S. L. (Eds.). (1991). *Abortion: Opposing viewpoints.* San Diego, CA: Greenhaven.

Dailard, C. (1999, May). Abortion in context: United States and worldwide. Guttmacher Institute *Issues in Brief.* Retrieved March 14, 2006, from http://www.guttmacher.org/pubs/ib_0599.html

Elam-Evans, L. D., Strauss, L. T., Herndon, J., Parker, W. Y., Whitehead, S., & Berg, C. (2002, November 29). Abortion surveillance—United States 1999. *Morbidity and Mortality Weekly Report, 51*(SS09), 1–28. Retrieved February 24, 2006, from http://www.cdc.gov/mmwr/preview/mmwrhtml/ss5109a1.htm

Histories of Abortion. (n.d.). Retrieved January 11, 2006, from http://users.telerama.com/%7Ejdehullu/abortion/abhist.htm

James, D., & Roche, N. (2004). *Therapeutic abortion.* Retrieved March 8, 2006, from http://www.emedicine.com/med/topic3311.htm

Mcfarlane, D. R. (1993). Induced abortion: An historical overview. *American Journal of Gynecological Health, 7*(3), 77–82.

Pew Forum on Religion & Public Life. (2005). *Abortion seen as most important issue for Supreme Court.* Retrieved January 11, 2006, from http://pewforum.org/docs/index.php?DocID=127

Robinson, B. A. (2005). *When does human personhood begin and how do we proceed when we cannot agree?* Ontario Consultants on Religious Tolerance. Retrieved February 10, 2006, http://www.religioustolerance.org/abo_when1.htm

ABRAHAM LINCOLN BRIGADE

Approximately 2,800 Americans joined the International Brigade to fight alongside the Spanish Republican forces against General Francisco Franco's fascist regime during the Spanish Civil War (1936–1939). The Abraham Lincoln Brigade refers to the American component of the international volunteer force that assisted the Spanish Republicans. "Brigade" is a misnomer, as multiple American units existed, such as the George Washington Battalion and the John Brown Anti-Aircraft Battery.

Following Franco's coup against the democratically elected government of Spain in July 1936, the Western democracies opted not to interfere in Spain. The nations of Western Europe signed a nonintervention agreement. The Axis powers of Germany and Italy consistently violated the accord and assisted Franco. The United States passed a neutrality act and enacted an embargo, prohibiting the sale of arms to either side in the Spanish conflict.

The Soviet Union was the only nation to officially support the Republicans. The Soviets sold war materials to the Republican forces. The Comintern, which was the international Communist organization, was responsible for creating the International Brigades, encouraging foreign nationals to aid in the fight against fascism. The Abraham Lincoln Brigade consisted mainly, though not entirely, of American communists and socialists. Those who joined the Lincolns and supported them on the home front felt that backing the Spanish Republican forces was necessary in order to prevent the spread of fascism through Europe.

The Communist Party in the United States organized the Lincoln Battalion of American volunteers, but not all members were communists. The volunteers represented a diverse segment of American society. Approximately 40% of the Lincolns were Jewish. About 100 black Americans volunteered. Women participated in the Brigade as nurses, technicians, ambulance drivers, and truck drivers. An estimated 1,800 returned from Spain, and most remained politically active throughout their lives. Many participated in World War II, opposed McCarthyism, and fought for civil rights in the United States.

The first group of Lincolns went to Spain in 1936, and they continued to arrive until February 1937, when the League of Nations prohibited foreign nationals from participating in the war. American volunteers were particularly prominent in the battles at

Valencia, Madrid, and the Jarama Valley in 1937. Americans also participated in battles at Teruel, Belchite, Zaragoza, and Brunete. Of the almost 3,000 Americans who enlisted in the International Brigades, nearly half lost their lives in Spain. The international forces were sent home in the spring of 1938. On March 31, 1939, the Republic fell and Franco's government became the official power in Spain.

—*Kristen E. Gwinn*

See also Communist Party USA; Old Left; Popular Front

Further Readings

Carroll, P. (1994). *The odyssey of the Abraham Lincoln Brigade: Americans in the Spanish Civil War.* Palo Alto, CA: Stanford University Press.

Eby, C. (1969). *Between the bullet and the lie: American volunteers in the Spanish Civil War.* New York: Holt, Rinehart & Winston.

Rosenstone, R. (1980). *Crusade of the left: The Lincoln Battalion in the Spanish Civil War.* Lanham, MD: University Press of America.

ABUELAS DE PLAZA DE MAYO

Argentina's military regime developed a policy of terror in which the "disappearance" of persons played an important role. Abuelas de Plaza de Mayo (Grandmothers of the Plaza de Mayo), a movement established in 1977, is aimed at searching for sons and daughters of the disappeared taken by the military to be sold or dumped at welfare institutions as unidentified people (Jane/John Doe). Abuelas also seeks to restore these people's true identities and to establish the necessary conditions for these events never to happen again, while they demand that the guilty be punished for these crimes.

The association created under the name Abuelas de Plaza de Mayo works at four different levels: reports and claims submitted to governmental, national, and international authorities; recourse to the Judiciary; requests for the society as a whole to support their goals; and the enforcement of the provisos of a Genetic Data Bank under National Bill No. 23511, which contains genetic maps of all families with missing children under the military regime.

Abuelas has made an impressive contribution to the cause of human rights: By developing the tools for determining the probabilities that children raised in other families might be someone else's grandchildren, their search has contributed to the field of individual identification through genetic tools worldwide. The association has also promoted the Right to Identity as a basic right at the International Convention on the Rights of the Child, approved by the United Nations and included in Argentina's National Constitution.

Through long years of struggle, the members of Abuelas de Plaza de Mayo have never ceased to fight for and demand truth and justice; they have insisted on the investigation of all crimes against humanity committed under the military dictatorship and have demanded that those who were responsible for the regime be incarcerated. Between 1997 and 2000, and as a result of their efforts, Jorge Rafael Videla, Eduardo Emilio Massera, Antonio Vañek, Rubén Franco, and Jorge Acosta were convicted for having taken minors from their original families.

Retired Lieutenant Colonel Ceferino Landa's conviction in 2001 nullified the Full Stop and Due Obedience Laws and declared that crimes such as the taking of minors, changing of their identities, and disappearance of individuals did not enjoy the benefits of immunity and were to be treated as crimes against humanity.

Over the past few years, Abuelas has begun calling on the young to help the association search for missing grandchildren. This gave rise to an intergenerational encounter that enabled both parties to go deeper into the practices of Abuelas and that, together with other organizations such as Madres (mothers) de Plaza de Mayo, Hijos (sons and daughters), and the recent creation Hermanos (brothers and sisters), has endowed family bonds with a new meaning based on identity, memory, and the pursuit of justice.

Out of the approximate figure of 500 young people who are so far ignorant of their family roots, 82 grandparents have been identified.

—*Graciela Di Marco*

See also Amnesty International; HIJOS, Children of the Disappeared; Human Rights Watch; Madres de Plaza de Mayo

Further Readings

Asociación Abuelas de Plaza de Mayo. (2001). *Niños desaparecidos, jóvenes localizados 1976–2001* [Disappeared children, located youth 1976–2001]. Libro Digital [Electronic book].

Arditti, R. (1999). *Searching for life: The grandmothers of the Plaza de Mayo and the disappeared children of Argentina.* Berkeley: University of California Press.

ABU-JAMAL, MUMIA (1954–)

At the date of this writing, 2006, Mumia Abu-Jamal has been in police custody for the alleged murder of Philadelphia police officer Daniel Faulkner for more than 24 years. Most of this time, besides a brief stay in the hospital after the original December 9, 1981, incident in which Mumia was shot and brutally beaten by Philadelphia police, he has been the most notorious inmate on Pennsylvania's death row. But, whereas most inmates in this position have been silenced, censored, and defeated, Mumia Abu-Jamal has been and continues to resist the injustices practiced against him by using his position on death row as a pedestal to critique overarching hegemonic power and, at the same time, to organize and educate those fighting against oppression.

Born Wesley Cook on April 24, 1954, in Philadelphia, Mumia was involved with journalism and radical politics from a very early age. As an activist growing up in an era filled with racial tension, Mumia's first contact with the police happened when he was 14. Protesting at a 1968 rally for the openly racist and pro-segregationist George Wallace, who was at that time running for president of the United States, Mumia was beaten by police and then arrested. In the summer of 1969, Mumia, along with others in Philadelphia, a city known at that point for its police brutality and racial profiling, founded a branch of the Black Panther Party (BPP). Mumia was named Lieutenant Minister of Information and began a journalism career that continues to the present day. He was all of 15 years old. It was at this point in Mumia's life that the Federal Bureau of Investigation (FBI) began a file on the young revolutionary.

In 1970, a fresh-faced Mumia was asked to go to Berkeley to the BPP headquarters. It was across the bay in Oakland, where the BPP came into being when two young students at Merritt College, Huey Newton and Bobby Seale, met and began searching, both vocally and organizationally, for ways to represent a collective voice questioning status quo politics, class inequalities, racial discrimination, and the importance of international solidarity in the pursuit of freedom and emancipation. Mumia was in the Bay Area helping to hawk the party's newspaper, the *Black Panther*, and to work at BPP community-wide free breakfast programs. After another brief stint in prison for jaywalking, Mumia, now more confident and better educated on revolutionary literature such as works by Marx, Lenin, Mao, Fanon, and Kim Il-Sung, was transferred back to Philadelphia and then to the Bronx as Minister of Information. Due to an illegal FBI program known as the Counter Intelligence Program (COINTELPRO), which violated constitutional rights in order to neutralize political dissidents, the BPP was split and ultimately disseminated. Mumia settled in Philadelphia to continue his style of guerrilla journalism.

He was an award-winning journalist for his critical and in-depth pieces on police brutality and other acts of racism. Nicknamed "the voice of the voiceless," he was heard on such broadcasts such as National Public Radio, National Black Network, Mutual Black Network, WHYY Philadelphia, and other national outlets as well as being news director of the Philadelphia station WHAT. At the time of his arrest, he was serving as the president of the Association of Black Journalists. In the 1970s, Mumia became very critical of the Philadelphia police department and the mayor at that time, Frank Rizzo. Mumia, who was an eloquent writer and a testimonial reporter, was labeled by Rizzo as a new breed of journalist who was getting people to believe that his administration and the police department, of which Rizzo was formerly the commissioner, were involved in racial discrimination and other clandestine forms of illegal surveillance and militaristic operations. At a press conference in 1978, Rizzo threatened this "new breed" and publicly claimed that it would be his business and duty to make sure that journalists like Mumia, who at that point was someone both the police and politicians were watching, be held accountable and responsible for reporting what in fact was the truth.

Much of Mumia's reporting during the late 1970s and early 1980s called attention to the police brutality and injustices that happened on a regular basis to MOVE. MOVE was a radical collective of black revolutionaries and naturalists from Philadelphia who were against and resisted all that the dominant system represented. MOVE's work was to stop the pollution of the environment and the enslavement of all life. They helped homeless find places to live, assisted elderly persons, and mediated between local gangs. As their platform became bigger and expanded to greater parts of the city, both police and city officials began to take notice. Rizzo, who had made a political career out of being tough on blacks, began to make the destruction of MOVE, whose membership and appeal was gaining ground, a top priority. In 1977, MOVE staged a major demonstration demanding the release of their political prisoners. Like the BPP, MOVE armed themselves for the purpose of self-defense. When they appeared at this demonstration armed to keep police activity at bay, the city found its catalyst for intervention. In August 1978, hundreds of Philadelphia police officers illegally surrounded the MOVE house and flooded their basement in hopes of forcing them out. A shot was fired from across the street from the house, killing one officer. The police opened fire on the house and family. Nine members of MOVE were brought up on murder charges despite evidence from ballistic experts and witnesses who testified otherwise. The journalist who brought this story to the public and questioned police actions and the relation between these actions and ideologies from city hall was Mumia Abu-Jamal. In 1985, well after Mumia's trial, the city of Philadelphia would drop a bomb on the MOVE house killing 11 (6 children) and causing a fire to burn more than 60 houses in the neighborhood.

As a result of his forthright advocacy for MOVE and for his unwillingness to remain silent on police and State misconduct, Mumia was fired or let go by his broadcast affiliates and began working as a cab driver to supplement his income. On the night of December 9, 1981, Mumia was shot and beaten unconscious by Philadelphia police officers after Officer Daniel Faulkner was shot and killed in the vicinity of where Mumia's cab was parked when he heard gunshots and saw his brother, William Cook, staggering in the street. The case was rushed to trial and began in June, and Mumia was sentenced to death on July 3, 1982, for the murder of the police officer. Mumia has claimed innocence since the beginning. Presiding over the case was Judge Sabo, who not only was a lifelong member of the Fraternal Order of Police but, at the time of the sentencing, had sent more people to death row than any other sitting judge in America (31 at the time, only 2 of them being white).

Sabo would not allow Mumia to represent himself during his trial because he claimed that his dreadlocks would make the jurors nervous. Mumia, who insisted on the assistance of John Africa (spiritual leader of MOVE) as well as his right to self-representation, was removed from the courtroom for the bulk of the prosecution's argument and placed in a holding cell in the courthouse without communication to or from the courtroom. The court appointed an inexperienced attorney who was both unqualified and unwilling to represent him. This was especially damaging because it was Mumia, not the attorney, who had prepared his case. He ended up reading most of what happened in the courtroom from the newspapers.

The inconsistencies and flaws of the trail are overt and numerous. In a court where one is supposed to be tried by one's peers, out of the 11 black possible jury members, only one remained in the end. The prosecution claimed that the shot that killed Faulkner came from Mumia's registered .38 caliber weapon, contradicting the medical report which stated that the bullet removed from the officer was .44 calibers. This information was never told to the jury. Mumia's BPP history and anti-police reporting was consistently something that was brought back into focus even though it had nothing to do with the trial. The prosecution's star witness, a prostitute named Cynthia White, had a long history of arrests, and there was no one who could place her at the scene of the crime that night. A different prostitute testified that she was offered the same deal as the prosecution witness: immunity from arrest in return for her testimony against Mumia. She was working in the same vicinity as Cynthia White on the night in question. In 1987, when Ms. White was in court again, this time on armed robbery charges, a homicide detective intervened in the case and asked that Ms. White be released without posting money because she was a commonwealth witness in a high-profile case. Since the time of the original 1982 trial, a gentleman by the name of Arnold Beverly, backed by two lie detector tests, has confessed to the killing of Officer Faulkner. Beverly was hired to kill Faulkner, who was apparently interfering with Philadelphia mob activity. Numerous others have come out to say that they were forced to confess or testify against their will.

Mumia is a writer, journalist, columnist, and professional revolutionary. He is on death row and continues to write from death row, from a prison cell that he is relegated to 23 hours a day, because he refused and refuses to be silenced against the blatant racism and injustices practiced on a local, domestic, and international scale by those in power. His work has been censored because people like Frank Rizzo and other high-ranking officials are afraid of the consequences if people begin to hear the truths about the ways the system manipulates and cultivates oppression and systemic violence. His imprisonment and pending execution are literal examples of a man who seeks fairness and justice by using his voice and who is being censored by a corrupt system in the business of profiteering and tainted in the legacy of slavery. It is not a coincidence that one of the fastest-growing industries in the United States is the prison system. The use of prison/slave labor is a manner in which corporate America can get cheap labor outside of sight to the general public. Mumia, a political prisoner, a reporter who sought to uncover the corrupt practices of a system responsible of the proliferation of prisoners, naming black prisoners, is on death row for

exposing these ideological, historical, and factual injustices.

Mumia's imprisonment has brought a lot of attention to the problems and questions surrounding the prison system, democracy, racism, economics, and hegemony. As an heir to a long list of revolutionaries writing while incarcerated, Mumia's plight has brought about an array of both national and international support and solidarity. People such as Nelson Mandela, Archbishop Desmond Tutu, Reverend Jesse Jackson, Ossie Davis, Danny Glover, the European Parliament, Amnesty International, Jacques Derrida, Jean Genet, Daniel Mitterand, Stephen Jay Gould, Susan Sarandon, Whoopi Goldberg, the National Lawyers Guild, Fidel Castro, and a long list of others have made public their support for Mumia and their demand for a fair trial.

Mumia's writings continue to inspire people from all over the world to voice their animosity and frustration with the status quo. Through Mumia, many have begun to engage in rereadings of historical periods, the black radical tradition, the prison movement, and also become active and determined members of various forms of local and international political and revolutionary movements. Mumia is a powerful writer and activist whose moral message is to resist today's mightiest of empires for to not would be to assist in one's own oppression.

—*Mark Stern*

See also Anti–Death Penalty Movement; Anti-Prison Movement; Black Panther Party; Police Brutality; Prison-Industrial Complex

Further Readings

Abu-Jamal, M. (1996). *Live from death row.* New York: Avon Books.

Abu-Jamal, M. (2001). *All things censored* (N. Hanrahan, Ed.). New York: Seven Stories Press.

Abu-Jamal, M. (2003). *Death blossoms: Reflections from a prisoner of conscience.* Cambridge, MA: South End Press.

Abu-Jamal, M. (2003). *Faith in our fathers: An examination of the spiritual life of African and African-American People.* Trenton, NJ: Africa World Press.

Abu-Jamal, M. (2004). *We want freedom.* Cambridge, MA: South End Press.

ACHEBE, CHINUA (1930–)

One of the foremost African writers of the late 20th and early 21st centuries, Achebe gives voice to African perspectives on precolonial, colonial, and postcolonial social and cultural developments.

Chinua Achebe was born on November 15, 1930, in Ogidi, Nigeria. His parents named him Albert Chinualumogo Achebe after Great Britain's Prince Albert, husband to Queen Victoria. As a university student, Achebe began writing and publishing short stories, he changed his name to Chinua Achebe, discarding the colonial legacy, and soon earned an international reputation as a writer. His writings eloquently demonstrate African agency, articulating European and African encounters, and scrutinizing the consequences for Africans linguistically, religiously, politically, and economically.

Achebe was 28 years old in 1958 when his first novel, *Things Fall Apart,* was published; he was working for the Nigerian Broadcasting Corporation at that time. After Nigeria's second coup d'état and shortly after publication of *Man of the People* in 1966, Achebe went to work for the Biafran Ministry of Information. He supported the Biafran secessionist movement. He was appointed Senior Research Fellow at the University of Nigeria, Nsukka. The university was destroyed during Nigeria's civil war, as government forces attempted cultural genocide to quell alternative ways of thinking.

Known as a modest man, Achebe has long been an activist and an advocate for social justice. He helped to rebuild the University of Nsukka, with few resources, after the war. He worked with the National Guidance Committee to produce the *Ahiara Declaration,* a document championing the sanctity and dignity of human life, peaceful coexistence, egalitarianism, social justice, and government service as public good rather than a platform for self-aggrandizement. His personal philosophy is to create communal endeavors rather than to promote individuals or commercial ventures; he has worked tirelessly to establish literary journals and other opportunities that have introduced numerous African writers to a wide audience. He convinced a major publishing house to highlight African authors and became the founding editor of the Heinemann African Writer's Series in 1962. He cofounded a publishing company with Nigerian poet Christopher Okigbo in 1966. He founded the journal *Okike—An African Journal of New Writing* in 1971, became the founding editor of the Association of Nigerian Authors in 1981, and founded *Iwa ndi Ibo* in 1984; this bilingual publication was dedicated to Igbo cultural life. He has mentored numerous students and young artists; authors such as Ngugi wa Thiong'o and Flora Nwapa both developed under his tutelage.

He does not shy away from political issues in his novels or in his daily life. In 2004, Achebe criticized the Nigerian government for its failure to utilize national oil resources to support its people. In refusing to accept Nigeria's second highest honor, "Commander of the Federal Republic," Achebe supported labor strikes and called for social and political change in Nigeria. He is the recipient of several international literary awards, has received more than 30 honorary doctorates from universities around the world, and is a member of the American Academy and Institute of Arts and Letters. He holds Nigeria's highest honor for intellectual achievement, the Nigerian National Merit Award. Achebe eventually left Nigeria to lecture and teach in the United States. While he remains Professor Emeritus of English at University of Nigeria, Nsukka, he is currently the Charles P. Stevenson Jr. Professor of Languages and Literature at Bard College in Annandale-on-Hudson, New York.

—*Lorna Lueker Zukas*

See also Literature and Activism

Further Readings

Emenyonu, E. N. (Ed.). (2004). *Emerging perspectives on Chinua Achebe.* Trenton, NJ: Africa World Press.

Ezenwa-Ohaeto. (1997). *Chinua Achebe: A biography.* Oxford, UK: James Currey.

Innes, C. L. (1990). *Chinua Achebe.* Cambridge, UK: Cambridge University Press.

ACORN

The Association of Community Organizations for Reform Now (ACORN) is a multi-issue, direct-membership organization of low- and moderate-income families fighting for social and economic justice. Founded in Little Rock, Arkansas, in 1970 by Wade Rathke, ACORN now counts more than 200,000 members organized into neighborhood chapters in more than 100 cities in 37 states, Canada, Mexico, and Perú. ACORN members conduct local, multistate and national campaigns; elect representatives to city, state, and national boards; and provide the bulk of the organization's budget through membership dues and grassroots fund-raising. ACORN chapters organize on a range of issues, including environmental justice, neighborhood safety, housing, health care, schools, predatory lending, and community reinvestment. In addition to the direct-membership 501(c)(3) organization, ACORN includes a 501(c)(4) that conducts extensive electoral organizing through get-out-the-vote drives, endorsing candidates, and developing campaigns on voting rights and voter participation issues and the ACORN Housing Corporation, which provides free tax preparation, homeownership counseling, and low-cost mortgages to members.

ACORN traces its roots to the work of Fred Ross, an organizer trained by Saul Alinsky. Ross departed from Alinsky's practice of relying on the existing leadership of churches and other institutions and instead organized individual community members house by house into direct-membership chapters. George Wiley used this model in organizing welfare recipients into the National Welfare Rights Organization (NWRO). By the mid-1960s, the NWRO had a strong presence in more than 50 cities, but Wiley believed that welfare recipients would never command real power until they could build alliances with other low-income and working constituencies. Wiley sent one of his young organizers, Wade Rathke, to Little Rock in 1970 to attempt to build such an organization.

In Little Rock, Rathke found quick success organizing to demand welfare recipients' access to clothing and furniture in six neighborhoods, and the nascent neighborhood organizations began developing campaigns on public housing conditions, free school lunches, and other issues of concern to working-class families. In 1972, these neighborhood organizations came together in the successful "Save the City" campaign on a range of quality-of-life issues, including traffic problems facing blue-collar homeowners, racist real estate practices, and insufficient parks in African American neighborhoods. The newly formed Arkansas Community Organizations for Reform Now established offices around the state and organized farmers to stop the construction of a sulfur-emitting plant by the state utility. By 1975, ACORN had chapters in 3 states and an elected executive board to direct policy; by 1980, the organization had grown to 30,000 families in 20 states.

ACORN's structure consists of neighborhood chapters whose members elect representatives to city, state, and national boards. Members are primarily recruited through door knocking by organizers and leaders, although recruitment also occurs through house meetings and through services including loan counseling, tax preparation, and lead paint screening. Members pay annual dues, attend meetings, plan and carry out local campaigns, and work on state, regional, and national campaigns. Local resident-led member boards, and larger state and national boards elected by local chapters, set policy for the organization and direct larger-scale campaigns. The weeklong Leadership School, conducted three times a year, trains emerging leaders in organizing skills. ACORN maintains a legislative office in Washington, D.C., and the annual Legislative and Political Conference brings together 150 leaders from across the country for training on the organization's political work.

ACORN's immersion in electoral politics sets it apart from many community organizing groups. ACORN employs the range of direct-action tactics typical to community organizing groups, but combines these with extensive political work at all levels of government through its 501(c)(4) organization. ACORN members run for office, hold candidate forums and endorse candidates, back ballot initiatives and legislation, and conduct voter-registration and voter-mobilization drives. ACORN maintains a national legislative office in Washington, D.C.

ACORN's approach combined electoral and direct-action tactics from its earliest days. In 1972, ACORN's Political Action Committee endorsed two candidates for the Little Rock school board, and 2 years later, 250 ACORN and International Ladies' Garment Workers union members ran for seats on the Pulaski County (Arkansas) Quorum Court, the county legislative body, and 195 won seats. The first ACORN national assembly in Tennessee, timed to coincide with the 1978 Democratic Party platform-drafting conference, brought together 1,000 members from 10 states and produced a "People's Platform" of demands for economic justice and representation of low-income families. Over the next 2 years, ACORN members presented the People's Platform to state delegations and pushed the Democratic Party to increase participation by low-income and minority communities.

During the 1980s and 1990s, ACORN continued expanding and developing new strategies. Chapters set up tent cities called "Reagan Ranches" to protest the homelessness and poverty created by paltry spending on social programs. Another important tactic was the well-publicized seizure of abandoned buildings, in which ACORN leaders, with the cooperation of local officials and homeowners, would recruit volunteers to rehabilitate and squat in abandoned housing. These squatting campaigns brought national attention to affordable housing issues and resulted in the creation of urban homesteading programs in several cities to turn abandoned buildings over to low-income families. ACORN organized home care workers, hotel workers, and other low-wage service industry employees into what would eventually become two large Service Employees International Union locals. In 1988, ACORN endorsed the Rev. Jesse Jackson and his Rainbow Coalition and contributed substantial energy to his campaign. ACORN won representation on the Resolution Trust Commission, the body overseeing the distribution of funds seized during the federal savings-and-loan bailout, and negotiated agreements with lending institutions under the Community Reinvestment Act. During the 1990s, ACORN won campaign finance reforms and worked

to organize workfare recipients after the 1996 welfare reform. The ACORN Housing Corporation, established in 1987, rehabilitates and maintains affordable housing and provides homeownership counseling and low-cost mortgages to first-time homebuyers.

ACORN has helped win passage of statewide minimum-wage increases in Florida, Illinois, and New Jersey and has sponsored similar initiatives in a number of other states. ACORN has also led coalitions of labor and other groups mobilizing for living wage ordinances in cities across the country, including successful campaigns in Baltimore, Santa Fe, and Philadelphia. The ACORN Living Wage Resource Center in Boston provides technical assistance to living wage campaigns across the country. ACORN has recently focused on forcing states to comply with the National Voting Rights Act and on local and national get-out-the-vote drives, registering 1.1 million voters in 2004. Local chapters have succeeded in changing a number of city and county governing bodies to district-based, rather than at-large, elections, enabling more equitable representation of minorities and low-income families.

ACORN conducts inclusionary zoning and affordable housing campaigns across the country, as well as campaigns to end predatory lending practices and to force compliance with the Community Reinvestment Act, which requires banks to make loans and other investments in the communities where they do business. Chapters work on school quality issues, including teacher turnover and funding, and have opened ACORN-run charter schools and alternative schools in several cities. Efforts are under way in several states to win union representation for home child care workers. Other local campaigns address a range of environmental justice, neighborhood safety, and health care access concerns. In the wake of Hurricane Katrina, ACORN has been involved in relief and rebuilding efforts and has organized the Katrina Survivors Association to ensure community participation in planning for the redevelopment of New Orleans.

—*Sara J. McAlister*

See also Activism, Social and Political; Community Organizing

Further Readings

Delgado, G. (1986). *Organizing the movement: The roots and growth of ACORN.* Philadelphia: Temple University Press.

Fisher, R. (1994). *Let the people decide: Neighborhood organizing in America.* New York: Twayne.

ACTION FOR CHILDREN'S TELEVISION

For close to 25 years, Action for Children's Television (ACT) was among the most prominent media reformers in the United States. Formed by a group of concerned Massachusetts mothers in 1968, ACT sought to protect children from the commercialism of television programming, especially within shows aimed at young viewers. ACT's emphasis on children, and its acceptance of the structure and economics of the television industry, contributed to its success in gaining the ear of broadcasters and their federal regulators.

The first activist group to concentrate on children's television, ACT had two overarching, intertwined goals: (1) to impress on broadcasters and the Federal Communications Commission (FCC) that children constituted a unique audience, more naïve and impressionable than adult viewers, who required special administrative protections; and (2) to eliminate advertising and promotion from children's television. To realize these aims, ACT tried to reform broadcasting practices, researched and published reports on television's impact on children, and staged public events to draw attention to its cause.

In the early 1970s, ACT members met with the FCC and successfully encouraged the Commission to examine rules regarding children's television and to develop a permanent children's unit as part of the agency's infrastructure. In addition, ACT filed a petition with the Federal Trade Commission (FTC) to ban commercials for sugar-based foods (cereals, candy) and toys on television. The FTC agreed to investigate ACT's petition, putting aside its policy of working on a case-by-case basis. Responding to complaints of the sugar lobby, Congress passed a law in 1980 prohibiting the FTC from creating industry-wide rules regarding unfair advertising; this law, in other words, rendered the ACT petition futile. However, despite its logistical defeat, the ACT campaign garnered substantial public interest, drawing attention to ACT's concerns over the health hazards of manipulative television advertising and prompting the transformation of the conventions of cereal commercials to be more sensitive to their impact on young audiences. ACT's concern over advertising and promotion on children's television extended to the content of programming as well. For example, in 1992, ACT filed a petition with the FCC protesting *Yo! It's the Chester Cheetah Show*, a program designed by Frito Lay whose central character was an established animated spokesperson for Frito Lay products.

In addition to its formal petitions, ACT created resources for itself and for like-minded individuals and organizations. In its first 15 years, ACT commissioned 15 studies on children's programming and commercials. Another source of publicity for the concerns of the group were events organized by ACT. For example, ACT staged a rally in which it gave away balloons to children and pens and envelopes to their parents with advice on how to write to the FCC to protest inappropriate commercials or programs for children.

ACT's impact began to diminish in the 1980s, when advocates of deregulation began to control federal administrative agencies, fostering a climate hostile to the interventions that ACT sought to make. Its legacy, however, can be found in current media reformers who see dangers in television's commercialism and in broadcasters' and the viewers' cautious attitudes toward young viewers.

—Allison Perlman

See also Child Advocacy; Media Activism; Media Reform Movement

Further Readings

Cole, B. G., & Oettinger, M. (1978). *Reluctant regulators: The FCC and the broadcast audience.* Reading, MA: Addison-Wesley.

Guimary, D. L. (1975). *Citizens' groups and broadcasting.* New York: Praeger.

Hendershot, H. (1998). *Saturday morning censors: Television regulation before the V-chip.* Durham, NC: Duke University Press.

ACTION MEDIC GROUPS

The enduring scenes from the 1999 Seattle protests against the World Trade Organization include photo after photo of police using clubs, rubber bullets, pepper spray, and tear gas against anyone who was on the street. Protesters, shoppers, businesspeople, students, children, all were targets. In the middle of this chaos, many victims found a measure of relief from the action medics, or street medics, who set up improvised treatment centers to help wash tear gas and pepper spray from people's eyes and to see that seriously injured people were moved on to hospital emergency rooms.

According to Action-Medical.Net, action medics are the all-volunteer "street first aiders" who provide preventative education, emergency first aid, and aftercare to demonstrators working to resist oppression. Alternatively referred to as action medics or street medics, these groups have traditionally maintained an active interest in the safety, health, and well-being of people who are participating in protests. Action medics are politically oriented and anti-authoritarian.

Numerous action medic groups in the United States grew during the 1960s civil rights movement. The Medical Committee for Human Rights started volunteering medical care in Mississippi during the 1964 Freedom Summer. These medics tended to wounded protesters, set up emergency clinics, wrote orientation manuals, and also suffered from police and Ku Klux Klan attacks. Action medic groups continued their activities into the late 1960s protests against the U.S. war in Vietnam, as well as during the American Indian Movement's 1973 action at Wounded Knee.

It was action medics from these groups, including the Colorado StreetMedics, who were called on to help protesters prepare for the 1999 action against the World Trade Organization Ministerial in Seattle, Washington. Many action medic groups subsequently evolved from the 1999 World Trade Organization protests in Seattle, Washington. Among the groups are the Black Cross Health Collective in Portland, Oregon, Medical Activists of New York, Boston Area Liberation Medics, Bay Area Radical Health Collective, Star of Resistance Medics New York City, Cascadia Health Educators, the D.C. Action Medical Network, and On the Ground.

Most action medic groups maintain their own websites with information and training about upcoming protests, preparing for protests, and caring for people during and after protests. The Black Cross Health Collective, formed by health care workers who participated in the Seattle protests, have been among the first to conduct trials to find effective treatments for pepper spray and tear gas. With a policy of being forewarned equals being forearmed, the Black Cross Health Collective writes that they are making the material available so that people might be as safe as possible during street action.

Action medics are often independent people, and making generalizations about them is risky. Nevertheless, many of the action medic groups have grown from radical roots, combining direct action with anarchist organizing principles. Infoshop.org is one anarchist website that lists the Black Cross Health Collective and the D.C. Action Medical Network as favorite links.

Action medic trainings incorporate the principles of anarchist organizing, including a lack of hierarchy, with decision making by consensus. The trainers often introduce themselves by their first names only and make a conscious decision to avoid mentioning any titles or education they have. Although the trainers include medical doctors, nurses, and aides, they also include people without medical training who have shown they can maintain calm in difficult protest circumstances.

Trainings from action medics are designed to be informative and intense. There is generally a section on the ABCs (i.e., checking airways, breathing, and circulation) and overall first aid in emergency situations. Then follows training specific to protests. Trainees learn how to assess a situation and focus on those most severely hurt, how to deal with interfering bystanders and police, how to wash tear gas and pepper spray from people's eyes and skin, how to improvise when medical equipment and personnel are not available, and how to deal with after-protest care of victims.

Action medics often seek additional training as wilderness first responders. By definition, a wilderness area is one hour away from definitive care. In an unpredictable protest situation, a patient might be technically in an urban area, but getting the patient to care might take an hour or more.

Groups planning a protest often contact the action medics to request their services in case there is violence. Yet, despite any violence, medics often report that the most common treatment they administer is for falls from people running.

While action medics have most often been used in protests, the summer of 2005 brought new challenges with the flooding of the Gulf Coast during Hurricane Katrina. As documented, the response of the Bush administration and FEMA (Federal Emergency Management Agency) left many victims to fend for themselves, without medical attention. In the Algiers neighborhood of New Orleans, there was a request for action medics, and in a few days, action medics were riding bikes from house to house, asking if anyone needed medical attention. The action medics set up an impromptu medical clinic named the Common Ground, which is presently turning into a permanent clinic. The name is aptly titled, as on one day when supplies arrived, they were unloaded by the unlikely mixture of National Guard troops and anarchists protesting the war.

With the establishment of the Common Ground, the mission of the action medics has grown to include creating a system of clinics across the country and remaking the health care system. The Common Ground has received a mention in the *New England Journal of Medicine,* taking yet another step in mainstreaming a radical medical group. Besides protests, recent action medical topics of interest include the affects of taser guns, as well as possible preventions, including polyester fabric.

—Teresa Knudsen

See also Activism, Social and Political

Further Readings

Action-Medical.Net. Retrieved April 26, 2006, from http:// zena.secureforum.com/ontheground/action-medical/ index.htm

Berggren, R. E. (2006, April 13). Adaptations. *New England Journal of Medicine, 354*(15), 1550–1551. Retrieved April 21, 2006, from http://content.nejm.org/cgi/ content/full/354/15/1550

Black Cross Health Collective. (2006, January 16). *First aid for radicals and activists.* Retrieved March 16, 2006, from http://blackcrosscollective.org/about

Common Ground Collective. Retrieved July 4, 2006, from http://www.commongroundrelief.org/

DC Action Medical Net. Retrieved July 4, 2006, from http:// damn.mahost.org/

Infoshop. Retrieved April 25, 2006, from http://www .infoshop.org/

Medical Committee for Human Rights. (2004). *Manual for volunteers.* Retrieved July 4, 2006, from http://www .crmvet.org/docs/mchr.htm

O'Carroll, E. (2004, August 11). Meet the BALM squad. Election 2004. AlterNet. Retrieved April 25, 2006, from http://www.alternet.org/election04/19505/

Shorrock, T. (2006, March/April). The street samaritans. *Mother Jones,* pp. 64–67. Retrieved April 25, 2006, from http://www.motherjones.com/news/feature/2006/03/ common_ground_long.html

ACTION RESEARCH

See PARTICIPATORY ACTION RESEARCH

ACTIVISM, SOCIAL AND POLITICAL

Activism is action on behalf of a cause, action that goes beyond what is conventional or routine. The action might be door-to-door canvassing, alternative radio, public meetings, rallies, or fasting. The cause might be women's rights, opposition to a factory, or world peace. Activism has played a major role in ending slavery, challenging dictatorships, protecting workers from exploitation, protecting the environment, promoting equality for women, opposing racism, and many other important issues. Activism can also be used for aims such as attacking minorities or promoting war.

Activism has been present throughout history, in every sort of political system. Yet it has never received the same sort of attention from historians as conventional politics, with its attention to rulers, wars, elections, and empires. Activists are typically challengers to policies and practices, trying to achieve a social goal, not to obtain power themselves. Much activism operates behind the scenes.

There are many varieties of activism, from the face-to-face conversations to massive protests, from principled behavior to the unscrupulous, from polite requests to objectionable interference, and from peaceful protests to violent attacks. Activism is not well defined, so different people often have somewhat different ideas of what constitutes activism.

Activism is not necessarily a good thing or a bad thing. It all depends on the cause and the actions, and a person's judgment of what is worthwhile. One person might say that a protest is a valuable defense of freedom, and another person might say that it is a dangerous attack on human rights.

Activism and Conventional Politics

Activism is action that goes beyond conventional politics, typically being more energetic, passionate, innovative, and committed. In systems of representative government, conventional politics includes election campaigning, voting, passing laws, and lobbying politicians. Action outside of these arenas includes neighborhood organizing, protest marches, and sit-ins. The boundary between activism and conventional politics is fuzzy and depends on the circumstances.

Action on behalf of special causes such as animal rights or anti-abortion goes beyond conventional politics. Sometimes, though, political parties are set up to promote special causes, such as labor parties in many countries in the 1800s and early 1900s or green parties since the 1960s. In this way, activism becomes conventional politics. Often activism and conventional politics operate side by side, such as the labor movement—including unions and rank-and-file activities—alongside a labor party or the environmental and peace movements alongside a green party.

It is also possible to speak of activism inside an organization, such as a corporation, government department, political party, or labor union. Organizations have their usual ways of doing things, such as senior executives making decisions in corporations. If employees organize to challenge a decision or try to alter the usual decision-making process, this can be called activism, though it is much less visible than activism in public places.

What counts as activism depends on what is conventional. In societies in which free speech is respected and protected, making a posting on an e-mail list complaining about the government is a routine occurrence. But in a dictatorship, such a posting might be seen as subversive, and both the sender and the list manager might be punished. Similarly, when strikes are banned, going on strike is a more daring form of activism than when they are legal and routine.

Activism is typically undertaken by those with less power, because those with positions of power and influence can usually accomplish their aims using conventional means. But sometimes those in positions of power might be called activists, when they go beyond normal expectations, such as an "activist president" who pushes through an ambitious agenda or an "activist court" that interprets the law in new ways. Most of the entries in this encyclopedia, though, are about activism from below, often called grassroots activism.

Methods of Activism

The most common image of activism is a public protest, such as a rally, a march, or a public meeting. This is a useful starting place in looking at methods of activism. Researcher Gene Sharp divides the methods of nonviolent action into three main types. First are methods of protest and persuasion, such as speeches, slogans, banners, picketing, protest disrobings, vigils, singing, marches, and teach-ins. To count as nonviolent action—and activism—these need to go beyond conventional behavior. Singing in a choir is not activism, but singing as a protest, for example in a prison or in a church, certainly can be.

The second type of nonviolent action is noncooperation, such as religious excommunication, disobeying social customs, protest emigration, rent strike, producers' boycott, withdrawal of bank deposits, international trade embargo, and a wide variety of strikes. The third type is intervention, including sit-ins, nonviolent occupations, guerrilla theater, fasting, and setting up alternative economic and political institutions. All of these, and more, can be methods of activism—of the nonviolent variety.

Another option is violent action, such as beatings, imprisonment, torture, killing, and bombing. Conventional violent action is carried out by police and military forces. Violent activism would be carried out by those not authorized to do so, who might be called freedom fighters or terrorists. However, this is usually called armed struggle rather than activism.

In between nonviolent action and armed struggle is violence against physical objects, of which sabotage is one variety. This can include damaging a pipeline, destroying genetically engineered crops, or defacing a website. These are activism if done on behalf of a cause. Like other forms of activism, sabotage can be praised or condemned. The Boston Tea Party, a signal event during the American Revolution, involved economic sabotage.

The methods of activism will continue to evolve along with political opportunity and developments in culture and technology. To challenge consumer culture, for example, a new practice has developed called culture jamming, involving a transformation of conventional symbols, such as those used in advertisements, to create a new, confronting message. Cell phone messaging systems are now used to organize rallies. Online activism, called cyberactivism, involves using the Internet to communicate and organize traditional actions and as a direct form of activism itself, such as bombarding a website or sending large files to slow down a system.

Groups and Movements

Many activists are members of groups, which can be small or large, local or global. By operating in groups, activists gain several advantages. They can undertake larger tasks, such as organizing a citywide campaign. They can benefit from specialization, such as when one person responds to queries, another sets up a website, another handles memberships, and yet another talks to the media.

Another vital function of groups is to provide mutual support. Many activists lose heart or burn out through constant struggle and slow progress. Working with others can give a feeling of solidarity and often leads to lasting friendships. Most people who join activist groups do so because they are invited by someone already involved. Groups serve personal and social purposes as well as getting tasks done.

A century ago, nearly all activist groups operated face to face, with coordination between groups via visits, the postal system, and public notices. The telephone allowed rapid coordination across greater distances, and the Internet has made it much easier to coordinate globally.

Activist groups, like groups of any kind, from families to corporations, can have problems, including miscommunication, personal animosities, and power struggles. Getting group members to work well together is vital. Skills like listening, summarizing, and conflict resolution are called maintenance functions, whereas skills for undertaking action outside the group are called task functions.

Many small activist groups are made up entirely of volunteers. Large groups often have some paid staff plus many volunteers. International activist organizations like Amnesty International or Friends of the Earth are made up of numerous local groups, with some paid staff in national or international offices.

Paid activists seldom receive a large salary, though there are exceptions. Because they are committed to a cause, activists are often willing to work at much lower wages than if they took a conventional job. The term *professional activist* can apply to a paid staff member but also—sometime pejoratively—to volunteers who spend so much time doing activism that they are as experienced as a full-time worker.

The easiest way to learn how to be an activist is to join a group and become involved. There are few courses in educational institutions about activism, and even fewer teaching practical skills. Some activist groups run training sessions for their members and others, but most learning occurs on a person-to-person basis, through direct instruction, learning by imitation, and learning by doing. This is supplemented by manuals on community organizing, campaigning, nonviolent action, and other skills, with an ever-growing amount of material available online.

Groups are the main way that activists are organized to get tasks done. In many cases, groups are part of what is called a social movement. A social movement typically includes many groups and individuals acting toward a common goal to change society in a particular way. A movement is broader than any single organization and it has a broader, less precise vision than most groups.

The peace movement, for example, includes a wide variety of groups, including local groups campaigning on a single issue such as against a particular war, national groups with an agenda such as nuclear disarmament, professional networks such as Physicians for Social Responsibility, and international organizations such as War Resisters' International. The peace movement also contains a diversity of general themes, such as opposition to wars and inhumane weapons.

Within any movement, there can be many different beliefs and emphases. Some people and groups in the peace movement oppose any involvement in war or war making, whereas others are primarily concerned about nuclear weapons, land mines, or a particular war.

Other social movements include the labor, feminist, environmental, gay and lesbian, animal rights, and disability movements. Movements provide an important context for activism in several ways. They constitute a network of individuals and groups that is a source of communication, advice, and inspiration. They provide a learning environment, with activists drawing on the experience of other groups to find out what works. And they provide a framework or perspective for understanding society, its problems, possible futures, and ways of bringing about change. This framework, or belief system, develops out of the experience of activists, combined with the ideas of writers and leaders, some who are part of the movement and some who are largely independent of it. For example, the feminist movement has supported activism through the network of individuals and groups, has fostered learning about tactics, and has offered an understanding of the problem of patriarchy through women sharing their experience and through feminist writers presenting ideas that illuminate and inspire their readers.

Most movements have activist and nonactivist aspects. The feminist movement, for example, has included plenty of activism, including confrontation and noncooperation with sexist practices. There are also many important parts of the movement that are less activist or nonactivist. Women's consciousness-raising

groups—in which women share their experiences—were a key part of the second wave of the Western feminist movement, starting in the 1960s, but most of these groups did not engage in action. Similarly, liberal feminists who operated through the system by pushing for equal opportunity laws and procedures were at the less activist end of the spectrum, as were those who put all their energy into feminist scholarship.

This again raises the issue of the boundaries of what is called activism. Someone working on a campaign might spend time listening to the news, reading and sending e-mails, phoning others, participating in a meeting, and writing a grant proposal. None of this is out in public, such as joining a rally or blockade, but it is all an essential part of what makes such public events possible. It is useful to distinguish between "direct action" or "frontline action," in which people are putting their bodies on the line, and support work, which is usually behind the scenes. Without the support work, the frontline action could hardly occur. This is analogous to military forces: Only a few troops are engaged in fighting, with vastly more personnel involved in accounts, cooking, maintenance, and a host of other support activities.

Those involved in behind-the-scenes work, in support of a cause, can either be called activists or supporters or members of an activist group or movement. This is a matter of definition but has a wider significance. For many people who are concerned about the world's problems, and especially in social movement groups, there is status in being called an activist. This can lead to a valuing of dramatic and visible direct action and a corresponding devaluation of routine, less visible activity such as answering correspondence or handling accounts. On the other hand, some people who take action do not think of themselves as activists: In their minds, they are simply doing what is necessary to address a pressing problem.

It is useful to think of an ecology of activism, in which a flower or fruit can only exist with the support of nutrients, roots, stems, pollinators, and sunlight. Analogously, effective direct action depends on prior learning, supportive group members, resources (including funds), and communication. Many people can contribute to making activism effective without necessarily being activists themselves: financial contributors, resource people, teachers, supportive friends

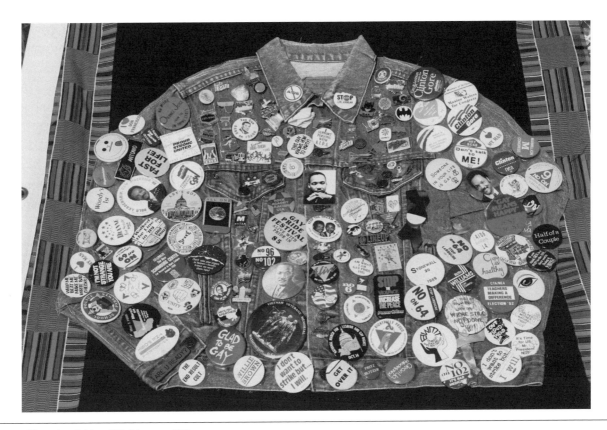

Source: Photo by dbking, Washington, DC.

and family members, and journalists, among others.

There are some activists who operate on their own, largely or entirely independent of groups. They might produce their own leaflets and hold a single-person vigil outside an office. Such individuals, if campaigning on a relevant issue, could be considered part of a social movement. A few such individual activists take up issues that no one else is concerned about. Most activists find it much easier to be part of a group, but this is not an obligation.

Areas of Activism

Activism can be on behalf of a great many causes, such as labor, religious, or environmental goals. Some people associate activism with "progressive" causes that promote equality and the rights of those with less power, but activism can just as well be used to attack the weak. Tim Jordan usefully proposes three types of activism, oriented to the past, present, and future.

Past-oriented or reactionary activism seeks to protect the interests of those with more power, often at the expense of those who are weaker. Examples are

men who assault gays, vigilantes against illegal immigration, and campaigners for aggressive wars.

Present-oriented activism is aimed at changing policies. This is also called *reformism*. Examples are campaigns for laws and regulations, such as on election financing, gun control, or whistleblower protection.

Future-oriented activism—called by Jordan "activism!" with an exclamation point—is about changing social relations, not just policies. Examples are greater equality in the family, worker participation in decision making, and treating animals as valuable. Most of the entries in this encyclopedia are about future-oriented activism.

The idea of the political left and right is often used to classify activism. It is most appropriately applied to labor (left) versus capital (right), but does not work so well as a way of classifying positions on other issues. The so-called new social movements—student, feminist, environmental, and others—that developed in the 1960s and thereafter do not comfortably fit within the left-right classification system.

Those on the left are often called progressives or radicals and those on the right conservatives or reactionaries.

But if conservative means maintaining the status quo and reactionary means harking back to an earlier age, then movements do not always line up in a predictable way. For example, environmentalists campaigning against a waste dump or chemical factory are seeking to maintain the status quo in the face of industries trying to change it. Environmentalists seeking to return a region to earlier vegetation patterns, before human settlement, could be called radicals, because they are challenging the logic of industrial development, or reactionaries, because they want to re-create an earlier time.

It is possible to see activism as a spectrum from the local to the global, both geographically and in relation to the person. Local activism is often about protecting the quality of life of a family or small community, such as when local citizens campaign for better schools or hospitals or against a factory or freeway. This is sometimes disparagingly called NIMBY (Not In My Back Yard) activism.

A broader focus brings concern for groups subject to disadvantage or discrimination, including women, ethnic minorities, the poor, and people with disabilities. Much activism is carried out by people in these groups, supported by some from more privileged groups. For example, some men are pro-feminist activists and some able-bodied people advocate on behalf of those with disabilities.

Traditionally, most activism within a country focused on issues affecting that country. But there is an increasing orientation to issues transcending national borders. Sometimes this is because the issues are global, such as climate change. But in many cases, it is simply because the scope of concern has widened. Torture, a problem in numerous countries, is challenged by human rights groups, often from outside the country where torture takes place.

Local and global forms of activism sometimes pull in opposite directions but can be mutually supportive. For example, NIMBY opposition to a nuclear waste repository assists, and is assisted by, the global anti-nuclear movement.

Traditionally, most activism focused on humans. The animal rights and environmental movements have broadened the area of concern beyond humans to other forms of life and even to inorganic nature. In the future, the boundaries of activism will continue to expand to domains that are now hardly recognized, including human technological creations.

The domain of activism has also expanded inward, from the public sphere into personal and private realms. Examples include sexual harassment, bullying, and domestic violence. These often take place between individuals, out of the public eye. Activism has been central to the response, in two ways. First, activists have identified these as social problems and have campaigned to raise awareness about them. These efforts sometimes have led to laws and procedures being introduced. Second, individuals and small groups have developed techniques to deter and challenge sexual harassers, bullies, and batterers.

Leaders

Leaders play an important role in activist groups and movements. They can play a variety of roles; for example, as figureheads, spokespeople, role models, strategists, and theorists. A few activist leaders become famous. Probably the two most famous activists in the 20th century who did not become heads of state are Mohandas Gandhi, leader of the Indian independence movement from 1915 until independence in 1947, and Martin Luther King, Jr., leader of the U.S. civil rights movement from the late 1950s until his death in 1968. But few activist leaders are as well known as presidents, prime ministers, or dictators.

Activist leaders are important both externally and internally. To the wider public, they are symbols of social concern. Due to their formal position in an organization or to their personal visibility, they receive disproportionate media attention. Inside movements, charismatic leaders can attract and retain members and hold a group together. Wise leaders can give guidance on strategies and internal dynamics. Leaders often come under attack by opposition forces: Discrediting a leader is a way of discrediting an entire movement.

Leaders can also be a source of tension within movements. Some leaders develop their own agendas that clash with the desires of members. Leaders can be co-opted by their opponents, for example, by being given a position in government or industry. The importance of activist leaders is reflected in this encyclopedia, with entries for individuals such as Aung San Suu Kyi and Rosa Parks. Learning about a leader is a useful entry point for learning about an entire movement.

Nevertheless, focusing on leaders can be somewhat misleading, because most activism is a collective activity. Leaders would not exist except for the quiet, unheralded efforts of hundreds of ordinary activists. Furthermore, in some groups and movements, there is a commitment to sharing power and an opposition to formal hierarchy. Such groups might adopt consensus decision making and encourage everyone to develop a range of skills and play a variety of roles. Leadership still exists in such groups, but it is leadership based on contributions and respect, not formal roles.

Much of the feminist movement operates this way. There are certainly quite a number of prominent feminists, but they are more commonly writers and commentators than leaders of activist groups. This can be contrasted with political groups with official leaders. For example, Nelson Mandela was the leader of the African National Congress in South Africa, an activist political movement, and later became head of state, entering the formal political system, where he achieved vastly greater visibility.

Most activist movements contain a combination of formal structure and egalitarian dynamics. In writings about activist movements, it is worth remembering that there is usually much more attention to formal structures and leaders than to ordinary activists and everyday activities.

Theory

Activism, despite its importance historically and in struggles every day, has received relatively little attention from scholars. Most history is written about powerful and prominent people and about official systems and activities, such as governments, elections, militaries, and wars. Even when the focus is on a social problem, such as slavery, there is consideration attention to official actions, such as President Lincoln's Emancipation Proclamation. The vast amount of individual and small-group activism may be given only a brief discussion or be entirely ignored.

News reports give a distorted picture of activism, with vastly more coverage of violence than peaceful activities. In reporting on Israel and Palestine, there is extensive coverage of suicide bombings but hardly any mention of the great amount of nonviolent activism that occurs all the time by both Israelis and Palestinians.

The research most relevant to activism is about social movements. As well as telling the stories of movements, researchers have looked at social structures that influence their origins and survival, resources that movements can use, political opportunities that they can take up, and systems of meaning that enable them to get their message across. However, little of the research on social movements tells much about what activists do and how they can do it better. Few activists pay much attention to research on social movements, because so little is oriented to their practical concerns. In addition, most scholarly research is written in a style that is not attractive to activists.

Far more relevant to activists are manuals that give advice on community organizing, analyzing power structures, group dynamics, decision making, fundraising, and conflict resolution. An example is Coover, Deacon, Esser, and Moore's *Resource Manual for a Living Revolution,* widely used in nonviolent action training in several countries.

Many activists learn about issues—corporate globalization, genetic engineering, or whatever—in a manner analogous to grassroots educator Paulo Freire's method of teaching reading and writing through politically charged words. Activists learn what they can about issues so they can be effective in their actions, and they take action because of what they have learned about issues.

Activists tend to draw on whatever information is useful for their immediate practical purposes. If the problem is homelessness, then they want information about the local situation and what is effective for dealing with it. At the same time, many activists are inspired by eloquent writers.

One of the major interactions between academia and activism is via individuals who are involved in both, including students and academics. These individuals provide a bridge for taking ideas from activism into theory and vice versa.

Activist Trajectories

In parallel with activism are debates about activism. If a particular form of action alienates too many people, then it is hardly worth doing. Therefore, convincing people that forms of action are acceptable is a key part of making activism viable. Debates about activism take place in the media, in everyday conversations, and not least among activists themselves.

Individuals can enter and exit activist roles in a variety of ways. Some begin with a small involvement, such as helping with a street stall or attending a public meeting, and gradually become more engaged over the years, perhaps becoming regular participants or even full-time activists. Others become heavily involved very quickly but drop out of activism due to burnout or other commitments.

It is difficult to maintain a high level of activism in addition to other major commitments, especially a conventional job and a family. Some sorts of activism—crewing on a peace voyage or attending a vigil lasting weeks—are virtually impossible for those with heavy family or job commitments, so it is easier for students or retired people to participate. One of the challenging tasks for social movements is to develop campaigns that allow many people to participate, not just those able to drop all other commitments.

Just like individuals, social movements go through cycles, though there is no fixed pattern. Movements sometimes start with a surge of innovative action, as many people join, attracted by the exciting feeling of change and making a difference. After the first several years, though, the initial enthusiasm can decline, media attention fades, and the movement appears to lose momentum. Activism can become routine, like ritual May Day marches organized by the labor movement.

Some movements fade away entirely. Others are institutionalized; that is, their purposes are incorporated in formal systems, such as welfare services or equal opportunity offices. In these cases, some former activists may become leading officials in the system.

There are also movements that maintain their levels of activism over many years or decades, continuing to innovate and attract new members.

The peace movement has followed a pattern of rapid expansion and decline. For example, the movement against nuclear weapons surged in the late 1950s and faded away in the early 1960s; then in the 1980s, it surged and declined again. There are some antinuclear activists who continue even when the movement is at a low level, but the pattern is one of boom and bust. There is little institutionalization of peace movement agendas; for example, there are few government disarmament departments.

In contrast, the environmental movement has maintained a more consistent level of activism, with a variety of groups that attract members and support. The mix of urgent environmental issues can change—from pesticides to nuclear power to climate change—but the level of involvement has not varied dramatically. Environmental agendas have been institutionalized, with government environment departments and industries adopting environmental programs.

The Future of Activism

It is safe to predict that activism will continue, both with current activist campaigns and branching out into new issues and using new tactics. Activism may decline when institutionalization is seen to address social problems, but new problems keep being brought to attention. Furthermore, some old issues reappear. For example, slavery was thought to have been abolished in the 1800s, but today it occurs in new forms—and there is a contemporary anti-slavery movement.

There are two important reasons why activism is likely to expand and become more sophisticated. First, activists learn from and are inspired by each other; the amount of information available about activism is dramatically increasing, thus laying the groundwork for further activism. Second, people are becoming better educated and less acquiescent to authority, and therefore better able to judge when systems are not working and willing to take action themselves.

Today's political systems of representative government are themselves the outcome of previous activism. If these systems were fully responsive to everyone's needs, there would be no need for activism, but this possibility seems remote. For political systems to co-opt activism, activism would need to become part of the system, with techniques such as strikes, boycotts, and sit-ins becoming part of the normal political process—a prospect as radical today as voting was in the 1700s. When that happens, new forms of activism will arise, challenging the injustices of whatever system is in place.

—Brian Martin

See also Nonviolence and Activism; Social Movements, Sociology of; Strategies and Tactics in Social Movements

Further Readings

Alinsky, S. D. (1971). *Rules for radicals.* New York: Random House.

Coover, V., Deacon, E., Esser, C., & Moore, C. (1981). *Resource manual for a living revolution.* Philadelphia: New Society.

Daloz, L. A. P., Keen, C. H., Keen, J. P., & Parks, S. D. (1996). *Common fire: Leading lives of commitment in a complex world.* Boston: Beacon Press.

Fisher, R. (1984). *Let the people decide: Neighborhood organizing in America.* Boston: Twayne.

Freire, P. (1972). *Pedagogy of the oppressed.* Harmondsworth, UK: Penguin.

George, S. (2004). *Another world is possible if . . .* London: Verso.

Halpin, M. (2004). *It's your world—if you don't like it, change it: Activism for teenagers.* New York: Simon Pulse.

Hedemann, E. (Ed.). (1986). *War Resisters League organizer's manual* (Rev. ed.). New York: War Resisters League.

Jordan, T. (2002). *Activism! Direct action, hactivism and the future of society.* London: Reaktion Books.

Keck, M. E., & Sikkink, K. (1998). *Activists beyond borders: Advocacy networks in international politics.* Ithaca, NY: Cornell University Press.

Loeb, P. R. (1999). *Soul of a citizen: Living with conviction in a cynical time.* New York: St. Martin's Griffin.

McCaughey, M., & Ayers, M. D. (Eds.). (2003). *Cyberactivism: Online activism in theory and practice.* New York: Routledge.

Moyer, B. (with McAllister, J., Finley, M. L., & Soifer, S.). (2001). *Doing democracy: The MAP model for organizing social movements.* Gabriola Island, BC: New Society.

Sharp, G. (2005). *Waging nonviolent struggle.* Boston: Porter Sargent.

Shaw, R. (2001). *The activist's handbook: A primer.* Berkeley: University of California Press.

Shields, K. (1991). *In the tiger's mouth: An empowerment guide for social action.* Sydney: Millennium Books.

van de Donk, W., Loader, B. D., Nixon, P. G., & Rucht, D. (Eds.). (2004). *Cyberprotest: New media, citizens and social movements.* London: Routledge.

Welton, N., & Wolf, L. (2001). *Global uprising: Confronting the tyrannies of the 21st century. Stories from a new generation of activists.* Gabriola Island, BC: New Society.

ACTIVISM IN AUSTRALIA AND NEW ZEALAND

First Nations peoples' activism in Australia and New Zealand developed through three phases: resistance, equal rights, and self-determination. These often overlapped, and the resulting movements may be engaged in one, two, or all three of these phases simultaneously. The experiences of indigenous/First Nations peoples of New Zealand and Australia differ and will be treated separately.

Whereas the sovereignty of the Maori is recognized under the Treaty of Waitangi of 1840, which offers them some legal recourse, for the First Nations peoples of Australia, the primary motivation for activism is unjust treatment. It results from claims to rights and social justice exercised either through traditional law or the legal framework of the dominant (British) culture. Activists seek redress either through active resistance using violent means or through passive resistance—noncompliance with the mechanisms of alien institutions that have replaced their own. In Australia and New Zealand, activism manifests differently depending on the context but involves claims to land and physical, intellectual, and spiritual resources denied by unfair rule of law. Access to legal recourse or the rule of law is mostly exercised in favor of the dominant alien culture.

The First Nations peoples of Australia were invaded and colonized by the British from 1788 through to the late 1800s by force of arms. While the first peoples were guaranteed the rights of British subjects, this was largely ignored by those administering the laws. The loss of lands, resources, and culture were resisted by the First Nations inhabitants at the frontiers. Devastated by introduced diseases and technically superior weapons, they have been reduced to remnant pockets on the fringes of the settlements of invading culture.

Indigenous Australians resisted their displacement and loss of their lands and resources from the beginning. Early place names bear testament to indigenous/First Nations peoples' struggle to maintain their birthrights. Places such as Battle Hill and Murdering Flat dot the landscape, and figures such as Pemulwye and Jimmy Blacksmith in New South Wales and Pigeon in Western Australia led fierce, though short, armed resistance. Pemulwye, a Dharuk man and a skilled strategist, organized armed resistance to European settlement at Parramatta ending with his death in 1802. Armed resistance largely ended with the forced removal of indigenous/First Nations peoples of Australia to church-run missions and government-controlled reserves in the mid- to late 1800s.

Indigenous/First Nations Australians passively resisted occupation through noncompliance with the imposed laws and regulations, from earliest contact to the present, resulting in high rates of incarceration. Many refused to contribute their labor for less remuneration than their European counterparts. In the 1940s, communist agitator Don McLeod led a pastoral strike of indigenous/First Nations Australians in Western Australia and indigenous dock workers went on strike in Darwin. In the 1960s, the Gurindji people walked off the Vesty-owned Wave Hill cattle station in a dispute over unequal pay and conditions. This action evolved into agitation for rights to their traditional lands (Wattie Creek) that was eventually successful in the 1970s. In Sydney, the first Aboriginal Legal Service was established in 1970 to defend the rights of indigenous/First Nations Australians. As a protest over the McMahon government's denial of land rights, activists Kevin Gilbert, Chika Dixon, Gary Foley, and others, with support from around the country, established the Aboriginal Tent Embassy in Canberra to bring national and international attention

to the poor treatment and conditions experienced by First Nations Australians. Although it has been periodically removed (with, on occasion, violent confrontation and arrests for obstruction), it has been continually reestablished as a focal point for activism by indigenous/First Nations Australians.

New Zealand was occupied by the British over a period from the late 1700s through the late 1800s. This was violently resisted in some cases, but many Maori leaders welcomed the protection offered by European weapons and sold their land for settlement while maintaining sovereignty. In 1835, a declaration of independence, presented to the British by the Chiefs of North Island tribes was ignored by the Colonial Office. However a treaty (the Treaty of Waitangi) was negotiated in 1840. Although the intent of the Treaty has been debated, with discrepancies between the Maori and English versions, the Crown has asserted "sovereignty" under the doctrine of "cession." Despite this, the Treaty of Waitangi has served as a basis for Maori rights and offers legal recourse.

In 1860, Land Purchase Commissioner Robert Parris purchased 600 acres from Teira, who was not the legal owner. Te Rangitake, the rightful owner of the land, resisted its survey, and the subsequential Land Wars of 1860–1865 resulted in the confiscation of 3 million acres of Taranaki, Waikato, and Bay of Plenty land and the dispossession of its peoples. When active resistance failed to stem the loss of lands and resources, many First Nations groups began to operate within the colonial systems to secure some of their land and resources.

In 1879, the Maori prophet Te Whiti, along with renowned leader Tohu, led followers in passive resistance to the further confiscation of their lands. In May 1879, Maori ploughmen at Te Whiti's behest ploughed the confiscated lands, and 200 of the Taranaki protestors were arrested and imprisoned for interfering with the survey of the land for European settlement. When Maori fences were constructed across newly made roads, an army of 10,000 was sent to arrest Te Whiti and Tohu and disperse their followers. They passively resisted the troops at Parihaka for 18 days, but Te Whiti and Tohu were arrested and imprisoned on the South Island for 3 years. Although unable to prevent the loss of their lands, Te Whiti and Tohu steadfastly refused to concede rightful ownership of their lands or acknowledge the government's decisions in relation to them, refusing all payment for their "rental." Agitation for lost land never subsided and during the 1970s, the movement grew in strength culminating in the 1975 30,000-strong Land March led by Whina Cooper from Te Hāpua in the north to Wellington's parliament buildings to petition for the preservation of Maori lands in Maori hands. Bastion Point in Auckland was occupied for 506 days by the Maori owners, led by Joe Hawke and the Orakei Maori Action Committee, until May 25, 1978, when the police and army evicted them, arresting 222 protestors and demolishing their meeting house, buildings, and garden.

Despite early calls for better treatment of indigenous/First Nations Australians, most notable from indigenous intellectual David Unaipon (recognized for his invention of the mechanical shears on the Australian $50 note), it was not until the 1920s and 1930s that Pan-Aboriginal movements were established. Fred Maynard founded the Australian Aboriginal Progressive Association, and with the Aborigines Progressive Association led by Bill Ferguson, agitated for civil rights culminating in the 1938 Day of Mourning protests. In the 1950s, organized national action for equal rights began in earnest. In February 1958, Dr. Charles Duguid, a nonindigenous campaigner for indigenous equality, Pearl Gibbs, and Faith Bandler established FCAATSI (Federal Council for the Advancement of Aborigines and Torres Strait Islanders) at a meeting in Adelaide of various state organizations to petition the government for equal rights. This organization was largely responsible for the 1967 referendum by which indigenous/First Nations Australians gained equal citizenship (having been specifically denied this in the Australian Constitution). Supported by many groups and organizations, action by Sydney University's Student Action for Aborigines and Ted Noff of the Wayside Chapel created positive media attention through the Moree/Walgett Freedom Ride. Led by Charlie Perkins, a group of activists traveled to Moree and Walgett in New South Wales in February 1965 to protest discrimination against Aboriginal peoples. Based on the

American civil rights movement, the Freedom Rides generated press coverage of racism and discrimination through protest outside the Walgett Returned Services League and the Moree Memorial swimming pool, where access was segregated.

In addition to acts of civil disobedience such as the Tent Embassy and the Freedom Rides, major protests at the 1988 Bicentennial and action at the 2000 Olympics and 2006 Commonwealth Games highlighted indigenous/First Nations Australians' legal challenges. The most important of these was action taken by Eddie (Koki) Mabo for rights to his traditional land. This resulted in the Mabo decision, which overturned the legal fiction of *terra nullius* (that First Nations Australians had no property rights over the land). The High Court decision established native title for indigenous/First Nations Australians; however, this has been narrowly defined by the Wik Amendment, which affirmed that the rights of pastoral lessees were to prevail over the rights of native titleholders. Legal action on the grounds of racial discrimination and through the international courts has been unsuccessful in overturning this ruling. Despite the watering down of the Mabo decision, it has served as a basis for continuing legal activity.

Although Maori had equal rights guaranteed under the law and designated parliamentary representation (four Maori seats were created in 1867), their interests received secondary consideration to Anglo-European interests, with legislation concerning Maori lands being uninterpreted and rushed through Parliament. In 1911, Pomare (later knighted) was elected to Parliament and agitated for land rights resulting in the 1926 Royal Commission that established that much of the confiscation of lands resulting from the Land Wars and the passive resistance offered by Te Whiti and Tohu was illegal. The situation was remedied with "fair" compensation of two cents per acre per year for 462,000 acres of the 3 million Waitara acres confiscated. Restitution also was made for the actions of Bryce's troops. Three hundred pounds in total was awarded for the destroyed houses, theft of crops and livestock, false imprisonment, and the countless rapes of Maori women.

Despite the fact that the United Nations has determined First Nations peoples' right to self-determination, this has not been ratified by the Australian government. The South Australian governments returned the Pitjantjatjara lands in 1981 and the Maralinga Tjarutja to its peoples, recognizing tribal laws and customs and restricting entry, but it was the Hawke and Keating Labor governments (1983–1996) that implemented significant steps toward First Nations peoples' self-determination. In 1985, the government handed Uluru (Ayers Rock) back to its traditional owners under joint management of National Parks, and in 1989, the Aboriginal and Torres Strait Islander Commission (ATSIC) was established, with representatives elected by First Nations Australians to oversee expenditure of the Commonwealth's Aboriginal and Torres Strait Islander budget. (The ATSIC was disbanded in 2004 by the Howard government.) In 1991, the government established the Aboriginal Reconciliation Council to work for reconciliation by the year 2001; this effort focused national attention on the injustice experienced by First Nations Australians.

Despite calls for a Makarrata (treaty) by First Nations Australians, this was rejected in 1989 when the Constitutional Commission recommended against a treaty, thereby limiting legal recourse. However, the Australian High Court's Mabo decision in 1992 found that indigenous Australians are entitled to compensation for, and access to, lost lands where title is not deemed to be extinguished. The Wik decision of 1996, which granted that native title coexists with leases but that the rights of pastoral lessees prevail over the rights of native title holders, has further eroded this small victory.

The Treaty of Waitangi has served as a basis for Maori rights to self-determination though the Crown asserts sovereignty. Maori peoples have continued to agitate through the courts for just compensation for their illegally confiscated lands and resources. This resulted in the 1992 Sealords and 1995 Waikato-Tainui Deeds of Settlement in recognition of sea and land rights; in addition, the Ngai Tahu iwi won compensation for lost land and the return of land and access to South Island sites. Other gains also have been made, with the Crown accepting an obligation to interpret legislation consistent with principles of the Waitangi Treaty, as well as recognizing bicultural education, Maori language, and cultural law.

The fight for social justice and equal rights continues despite a steadfast adherence to the principles of "liberal neutrality" by the State. The resulting policies are unacceptable to most indigenous/First Nations peoples, as they deny distinctive group rights in favor of assimilationist, undifferentiated rights to citizenship where the government extends individualist and noninterventionist rights and protections to individuals, not groups or distinct cultures.

A limited rights based approach has been pursued by many First Nations Australian activists. Based on a remolded democratic norms and institutions approach, it received limited support from the Labor governments (1983–1996), which established ATSIC to provide limited self-governance. The approach recognizes cultural difference and argues that cultural identity is a social good that may nevertheless disadvantage minority cultures. It argues for a pluralistic State where rights to cultural practices are protected from other groups through groups' specific rights to self-governance and special group representation rights. This approach underpins the most recent activism in Australia, as it recognizes that existing liberal arguments do not comprehend the distinctiveness of indigenous claims to lands and self-determination.

For the Maori of New Zealand, the issues of sovereignty and exercising the rights accorded under the Treaty of Waitangi continue to be a source of current activism. Recent activity is underpinned by the theory of cultural differences, which holds that liberal political thought be applied within the limits of liberal conceptions of equality and autonomy where rights to self-government are based on preeminent sovereignty within an existing state. Activists argue that individual rights should be based on group identity, which preserves the conditions of individual autonomy and freedom, with Maori culture being a primary good deserving of recognition. Although the approach has had some success, it is resisted by the government as endorsing cultural relativism (one law for Maori and another for European New Zealanders).

—*Douglas L. Morgan*

See also Anti-Colonial Movements, South Pacific; Indigenous People and Social Justice

Further Readings

Bandler, F. (1989). *Turning the tide*. Canberra, Australia: Aboriginal Studies Press.

Havemann, P. (Ed.). (1999). *Indigenous peoples' rights: In Australia, Canada & New Zealand*. Oxford, UK: Oxford University Press.

Howe, K. R. (1977). *Race relations: Australia and New Zealand*. Auckland, New Zealand: Longman Paul.

Ivison, D., Patton, P., & Sanders, W. (2000). *Political theory and the rights of indigenous peoples*. Cambridge, UK: Cambridge University Press.

McGinnes, J. (1991). *Son of Alyandabu*. Brisbane, Australia: Queensland University Press.

Owens, J. (1993). *The new wave in* Other boundaries: Inner-city Aboriginal stories. Sydney, Australia: University of Technology, Printing Services.

Scott, D. (1975). *Ask that mountain: The story of Parihaka*. Auckland, New Zealand: Reed/Southern Cross.

ACTIVISM IN POSTCONFLICT AND RECONSTRUCTION

Although conflict has been around throughout history, the nature of conflict in the world has changed. Conflict no longer is limited to a single nation or geographical region. The past 2 decades have seen an emergence of conflicts within nations that have had a global impact. The advancements in media, communications, and technology are among the factors that have influenced this change. Not only has the nature of conflict changed, but how it affects communities has also dramatically changed.

The conflicts that have emerged have been the result of a breakdown of dictatorships or outbreak of civil war. Within these conflicts, military and civilian are not distinguished. The International Rescue Committee, an organization founded in 1933, which works in postconflict countries, helps illustrate this point by comparing the death rate ratio of soldiers to civilians in the wars of the 1950s. In the 1950s, the death ratio of soldiers to civilians was 9 to 1, whereas today for every 1 soldier killed, 9 civilians die. The World Bank estimates that during the 1990s, civilian war-related deaths accounted for 90% of all war-related deaths, and violence created approximately 13 million refugees and 38 million internally displaced persons worldwide. Political forces openly use ethnic, national, and religious differences as a mobilizing force for war and conflict. As a result, it is not nations or countries that are destroyed, but an entire way of life. Human capital, economic infrastructure, and the social contract are ripped apart during times of conflict. The World Bank claims that over the past 15 years, 80% of countries defined as the world's poorest have been through a civil war. It is believed that on average 40% of countries coming out of war may fall back into conflict in the first five years of peace.

The changing nature of conflict has called for a changing approach to postconflict reconstruction. Long gone are the formalized peace treaties signifying the end of war and the beginning of the road of reconstruction. The Treaty of Versailles, the peace settlement reluctantly signed by the defeated countries after World War I, has been acknowledged as an ineffective mechanism to moving forward. Many historians attribute the harsh stipulations from the allied forces on the defeated countries as one of the causes for the conflict that led to World War II. It has become accepted by international actors and by most governments that the concept of punishing a nation for erupting conflict is ineffective for reconstruction and establishing global security. In addition, rarely are there formalized internationally binding peace treaties ending conflicts today. Today's peace negotiations are ongoing; treaties are signed and constantly violated, and postconflict relapses into violent conflict overnight.

These changing forces have led to a new form of activism in postconflict and reconstruction. In the past, assistance to postconflict areas was mainly in the form of emergency aid and humanitarian assistance. Today, non-governmental organizations (NGOs) and international activists work on creating a balanced approach to helping a nation emerging out of conflict. There is a strong belief that, in addition to providing short-term needs and restoring the physical infrastructure, there need to be programs focused on creating a new social contract between the people and their institutions. Conflict resolution mechanisms and new social structures are often introduced to safeguard against a reversion into conflict. Development and aid agencies strongly emphasize that postconflict reconstruction cannot be addressed through one avenue but needs a holistic approach in order to be successful.

Due to the increase of conflicts, particularly after the fall of the Soviet Union, much attention has been dedicated to postconflict reconstruction. In 1998, a World Bank study showed that the World Bank lending to postconflict countries increased by 800% since 1980. More recent estimates set the amount of postconflict assistance at between 20% and 25%.

Attention has also been committed to developing a reconstruction framework to assist practitioners in the field. The objective of these frameworks is to help international and local actors take lessons learned from other postconflict environments and apply them to a new context. The frameworks assist in giving an overall structure for developing programs and projects to assist the postconflict country to stabilize. It is important to note that, although frameworks have been developed and can be useful, there is no one formula for providing assistance in postconflict. Each country has its unique environment, and the local context is among the most crucial factors to determine the success of any program.

In most cases, reconstruction is supported through bilateral aid (aid from government entities, such as the U.S. Agency for International Development or the U.K. Department for International Development) and multilateral organizations (such as the United Nations and World Bank). The World Bank has defined three stages a country must go through to move from conflict to normalization. The first stage is a watching brief, where information is gathered through already existing research of secondary resources. The information allows practitioners to determine future engagement when a country begins to stabilize. The second stage is a needs assessment. The needs assessment is often done with several counterparts, possibly including the new government if it has been put in place. The final stage is the

transitional support strategy that includes a document on the national recovery program. An important part of the document will outline potential risks, including a clear strategy for entry and exit, and potential donors to fund the program.

The Association of the United States Army, in collaboration with the Center for Strategic and International Studies (CSIS), also developed a postconflict reconstruction framework. The framework defines the three stages for a country to transform from violent conflict to normalization as the initial response phase, transformation phase, and fostering sustainability phase. The initial response is a different step to that of the World Bank's watching brief. The initial response argues that, as soon as violence emerges, a quick response on behalf of the humanitarian community is vital to maintaining stability in that country. The second phase, transformation, involves identifying local human capacity, beginning physical reconstruction, stimulating the local economy, and weaving the social fabric back together. The third and final stage, fostering sustainability, is to plant roots in programs and institutions to ensure continuance and to prevent a relapse into conflict. Although most activists and international NGOs find a strong contradiction in the use of international military force for stabilization in the initial response phase, the CSIS framework closely resembles an activist's initial reaction.

All the large international players—World Bank, United Nations, and NATO—recognize that part of intervention to stabilize nations and regions emerging from conflict includes military intervention. In most of the frameworks introduced for postconflict reconstruction, a military component is involved. In most cases, this is in the form of the United Nations peacekeeping troops—such as in Bosnia Herzegovina or the Democratic Republic of Congo. In more recent history, a coalition of countries have formed their own entity and intervened, such as in the cases of Afghanistan and Iraq. This has caused a significant conundrum for international NGOs and activists who are adamantly against military intervention.

As a result, one of the leading questions facing agencies is how to support populations in countries emerging from conflict without serving the specific agenda or interest of another country. This debate was particularly intense with the U.S.-led coalition in Iraq. Many anti-war activists, including powerful donors, wanted to boycott any reconstruction efforts as a form of protesting U.S. aggression. Other organizations, such as Women for Women International and the Campaign for Innocent Victims in Conflict, searched for innovative ways to support the Iraqi people without being tied to a political agenda.

Activism in postconflict environments and during the reconstruction phases continues to take on a challenging approach. Development and reconstruction work can be completely erased and destroyed by any relapse into conflict. This can cause donors millions if not billions of dollars. Understanding the barriers is an important element for activists interested in working on reconstruction in a postconflict area. The International Federation of Red Cross/Red Crescent Societies (IFRCS) outlined barriers to working in postconflict reconstruction. They divide potential barriers into three categories: conceptual, programming, and structural. Defining postconflict and rehabilitation is one of the challenges within the category of conceptual barriers. The timing of the end of a conflict is extremely essential for long-term stability, and many donor countries wait for an official peace accord to be signed before acting. Other countries may be labeled as postconflict but still have an overwhelming amount of daily violence, such as the case of Iraq. Developing much-needed programs is difficult in volatile and unpredictable environments, such as found in countries that continually slip in and out of conflict. Without a certain level of security, development and reconstruction projects may be futile.

In terms of programming barriers, IFRCS lists relief culture, competence, knowledge, attitude, political will, and security as the primary barriers. Relief culture is defined as a top-down approach to emergency aid and can create a dependency that will weaken development programs in the future. It is important for reconstruction efforts that the seeds of long-term development and local ownership are planted in order to see long-term positive change.

Many activists working on reconstruction in postconflict provide strong lip service to involved local communities, but the actual implementation is almost always lacking. Security is another essential barrier to explore before working in postconflict. Many foreign nationals may be targeted by those wishing to see the country alienated from international contact.

The third category of barriers is structural. This includes a weak state or lack of a central government. There is often a problem of human capacity due to a brain drain during conflict, whereas small elite have a strong control over the economic institutions. The elite's control is most often one of the fuels for past and potential future conflicts. IFRCS also lists changed postwar reality and inequitable growth as important challenges. Millions of foreign aid is poured into the country and can potentially upset the balance of wealth within the country. A new society of local NGO and U.N. workers is created, real estate prices soar, and although local economy is stimulated, many nationals can no longer afford to buy things they need. With a weak government structure and institutions, there is plenty of room for corruption, and monitoring and evaluation of aid money become vital. Yet perhaps the most difficult problem to address is a rise in expectations from local communities. The arrival of international aid workers and large multilateral organizations creates the illusion that all problems will be solved. When the reality settles in that the road to recovery is a long and difficult path, many become disillusioned with the process.

Structural barriers are one of the strongest realities in postconflict and one of the most difficult to bypass. In most cases, time is needed to ensure the structure of a nation is rebuilt. One of the biggest challenges many groups working in a postconflict environment and supporting reconstruction projects have identified is a lack of local capacity and institutional infrastructure. Despite the fact that studies have shown that postconflict countries lack absorptive capacity in the first three years following violence, most donor funding is poured in at this time. The World Bank recommends a phased approach to donor funding to be staggered in for a decade. Yet, in most cases, there is a surge of aid from the international communities that tapers off within the first few years. As a result, just as the local communities develop their capacity to implement projects and have established institutional and government frameworks to benefit from programs, donor fatigue begins to settle in and funding significantly decreases.

As challenging as working in a postconflict environment can be, it is clear that a window of opportunity has also been created. During the reconstruction process, a new social contract is being formed between the communities, individual citizens, and the government. Whether it is in the form of developing a new constitution or redefining traditional gender roles, the window of opportunity presents a chance to leap forward in making changes related to women's rights, government participation, free elections, media laws, and many other aspects. Through proper understanding of the larger postconflict and reconstruction experience, coupled with the unique local context surrounding each conflict, activists can develop programs and activities for reconstruction that will either seize or miss this window of opportunity.

—*Manal Omar*

See also Bill of Rights; Coalition Building; Electronic Democracy; Identity Politics; Mandela, Nelson; Power, Theories of; Violence, Theories of

Further Readings

Anderlini, S., & El-Bushra, J. (2005). *Post-conflict reconstruction.* Retrieved December 21, 2005, from http://www.huntalternatives.org/pages/87_inclusive_security_toolkit.cfm

Association of United States Army & Center for Strategic and International Studies. (2002). *Post-conflict reconstruction: Task framework.* Retrieved December 20, 2005, from http://www.csis.org/images/stories/pcr/framework.pdf

Fitzduff, M. (2004). *NGOs at the table: Strategies for influencing policy in areas of conflict.* Blue Ridge Summit, PA: Rowman & Littlefield.

Kreimer, A. (1998). *The World Bank's experience with post-conflict reconstruction.* Washington, DC: World Bank Group.

Orr, R. (Ed.). (2004). *Winning the peace: An American strategy for post-conflict reconstruction.* Washington, DC: Center for Strategic and International Studies Press.

Richardson, D. (2004). *Modeling and analysis of post-conflict reconstruction.* Washington, DC: Storming Media.

Simpson, G. (1997). Reconstruction and reconciliation: Emerging from transition. *Development in Practice, 7*(4), 475–478. Retrieved December 20, 2005, from http://www.csvr.org.za/papers/paprrgs.htm

Zuckerman, E., & Greenberg, M. (2004). *The gender dimension of post-conflict reconstruction.* Washington, DC: Gender Action.

ACT UP

ACT UP was the first organized effort to bring attention to the AIDS epidemic in the United States. The organization has dozens of chapters in the United States and around the world whose purpose is to find a cure to AIDS, while at the same time providing accurate information, help, and awareness about the disease by means of education and radical, nonviolent protest.

The organization's birth was in March 1987 at the Lesbian and Gay Community Services Center in Manhattan. ACT UP, or the AIDS Coalition To Unleash Power, carried out acts of civil disobedience in response to the inaction of the U.S. government to act quickly and effectively in responding to the growing number of HIV infection and AIDS deaths in the United States. By 1987, AIDS had killed almost 60,000 people and more than 40,000 were HIV-positive in the United States alone. In 1984, 41 gay men had died of what was called a "gay cancer." By 1987, the numbers of AIDS deaths in the United States was considered staggering and the gay community was at the center of the statistics. Under the Reagan administration, funding for AIDS-infected patients, research for a cure, and research for drugs to slow down the disease were slow. Due to the homophobic sentiments of many Americans and of the Reagan administration, the gay community felt it

NO MORE BUSINESS AS USUAL!

Come to Wall Street in front of
Trinity Church at 7AM Tuesday March 24 for a

MASSIVE AIDS DEMONSTRATION

To demand the following

1. Immediate release by the Federal Food & Drug Administration of drugs that might help save our lives.

    These drugs include: Ribavirin (ICN Pharmaceuticals); Ampligen (HMR Research Co.); Glucan (Tulane University School of Medicine); DTC (Merieux); DDC (Hoffman-LaRoche); AS 101 (National Patent Development Corp.); MTP-PE (Ciba-Geigy); AL 721 (Praxis Pharmaceuticals).

2. Immediate abolishment of cruel double-blind studies wherein some get the new drugs and some don't.

3. Immediate release of these drugs to everyone with AIDS or ARC.

4. Immediate availability of these drugs at affordable prices. Curb your greed!

5. Immediate massive public education to stop the spread of AIDS.

6. Immediate policy to prohibit discrimination in AIDS treatment, insurance, employment, housing.

7. Immediate establishment of a coordinated, comprehensive, and compassionate national policy on AIDS.

President Reagan, nobody is in charge!

AIDS IS THE BIGGEST KILLER IN
NEW YORK CITY OF YOUNG MEN AND WOMEN.

Tell your friends. Spread the word. Come protest together.

7 AM . . . March 24 . . . You must be on time!

AIDS IS EVERYBODY'S BUSINESS NOW.

The AIDS Network is an ad hoc and broad-based community of
AIDS-related organizations and individuals.

Flyer of the first ACT UP action on March 24, 1987, Wall Street, New York City.

Source: http://www.actupny.org/documents/1stFlyer.html

their responsibility to exert pressure regarding these issues.

The mission of ACT UP was to carry out daily acts of nonviolent protest, using vocal and visual demonstrations, focusing on critical issues regarding the AIDS crisis. One of their first victories was in June 1987, when activists protested Northwest Orient Airlines for not allowing people with AIDS on their flights. The group brought two suits against the airline, and the policy was reversed. By 1988, the group had gained credibility with regard to "AIDS activism." They led protests of misguided news articles, films, and news stations reporting on AIDS, some claiming that women could not get AIDS from straight men and that AIDS could be passed through public bathrooms, pools, and drinking fountains. Through constant public protests, open forums, and information sharing, ACT UP was able to reverse these misconceptions and stereotypes and bring attention to the inadequacies of the U.S. government's treatment of people with AIDS.

In 1991, the group led the largest protest in the world against the discrimination of people with AIDS. Declaring a "Day of Desperation," protesters led mass marches in New York City and delivered coffins to city, state, and federal offices responsible for perpetuating the AIDS epidemic. Many protesters were arrested and throughout the years were subjected to police brutality, as well as anti-gay verbal and physical harassment.

Today, ACT UP has over 70 chapters around the world and has expanded its vision to include a worldwide end to the AIDS crisis. They remain at the forefront of ending the epidemic, and it is argued that their efforts have radically changed the way the world sees the AIDS crisis and the power of the gay rights movement.

—*Meliza Bañales*

See also AIDS Memorial Quilt; Lesbian, Gay, Bisexual, and Transgender (LGBT) Movement

Further Readings

Shilts, R. (1988). *And the band played on.* New York: St. Martin's Press.

ADBUSTERS

Adbusters is the nonprofit, bimonthly publication of Adbusters Media Foundation. In conjunction with the foundation's website (www.adbusters.org), Powershift Advocacy Advertising Agency, Blackspot Anticorporation, and various anti-consumerist campaigns and events, *Adbusters* functions as the self-proclaimed "journal of the mental environment" and urtext of the culture jamming movement.

Currently boasting a staff of 15 people, a magazine circulation of 120,000, and a culture jammers' listserve with more than 91,000 members, the Adbusters Media Foundation was originally founded by filmmakers and activists Kalle Lasn and Bill Schmalz in response to a public relations campaign titled "Forests Forever," sponsored by the British Columbian logging industry. When Lasn and Schmalz attempted to purchase television ad time to counter the logging industry's claims, they were refused by the Canadian Broadcasting Corporation (CBC). This experience led to the creation of the Media Foundation in 1989 and the first issue of *Adbusters* in 1991. Imagined as existing within the continuum of revolutionary projects such as Dadaism, Situationism, punk rock, and culture jamming, *Adbusters* is best known for its use of subvertisements and inversion of corporate and commercial rhetoric through what the Situationists called *détournement.* Lasn describes the artistic-politico work of *Adbusters* as meme warfare or a kind of jujitsu battle over the symbols and signs in our lives and the toxic mental environment created by advertising and the fakery of postmodernism. The publication's stated goal is "to topple existing power structures and forge a major shift in the way we will live in the 21st century." To that end, in addition to the regular publication of culture jamming images and articles, *Adbusters* and the Media Foundation have engaged in several campaigns that directly target commercial culture, globalization, and neoliberal policies. The magazine sponsors an annual Creative Resistance Contest to reward the year's best new subvertisements and is associated with the for-profit Blackspot Anticorporation—an "anti-brand" socially and environmentally conscious shoe company that allows consumers to become voting shareholders.

Most notably, *Adbusters,* with Lasn as a leading voice, has doggedly promoted the concept of "media carta"—the right for the public to reclaim the commons of the airwaves, to have guaranteed media access in the communications age, and to protect net neutrality. The organization has attempted to air commercials for "Buy Nothing Day" and "TV Turnoff Week" and subvertisements for "Autosaurus" and "Obsession Fetish," among others; only the Cable News Network (CNN) has thus far agreed to broadcast the "Buy Nothing Day" spot. This inability to buy televisual time has led Adbusters Media Foundation to file a Canadian Charter legal action against the CBC in 1995, which was dismissed by the Canadian Supreme Court in 1998, and lawsuits against several Canadian broadcasters in 2004. Although *Adbusters* claims to promote an anti-consumerist ethos and the rights of "media carta," it has also been critiqued by some activists and culture jammers for its very commercialization of anti-consumerism in the form of its "culture shop," a naïve vision of revolution, obvious spoofs that are easily subsumed back into commercial culture, and a patronizing attitude toward the masses.

—Katherine Casey-Sawicki

See also Alternative Press; Anti-Consumerism; Buy Nothing Day; Culture Jammers; Media Activism; Situationist International

Further Readings

Adbusters: The Media Foundation. (n.d.). About Adbusters. Retrieved June 20, 2006, from http://www.adbusters .org/network/about_us.php

Bordwell, M. (2002). Jamming culture: *Adbusters'* hip media campaign against consumerism. In T. Princen, M. Maniates, & K. Conca (Eds.), *Confronting consumption* (pp. 237–253). Cambridge: MIT Press.

Graaf, J. de (Writer), & Graaf, J. de, & Boe, V. (Producers). (1998, July 2). Canadian group practices the art of "subvertising." *Bugbuster Profiles. Affluenza* [Television special]. Retrieved June 20, 2006, from http://www.pbs.org/kcts/affluenza/show/adbusters.html

Jordan, T. (2002). *Activism! Direct action, hacktivism and the future of society.* London: Reaktion Books.

Klein, N. (1999). *No logo: Taking aim at the brand bullies.* New York: Picador.

Lasn, K. (1999). *Culture jam: The uncooling of America.* New York: Eagle Brook.

Strangelove, M. (2005). *The empire of the mind: Digital piracy and the anti-capitalist movement.* Toronto: University of Toronto Press.

ADDAMS, JANE (1860–1935)

Jane Addams stands as a giant of democratic social reform and international cooperation. She was a pioneer social change advocate, theorist, philosopher, and sociologist; she cofounded Hull-House and became world renowned as a feminist and peace activist. She was a prolific writer and public speaker on matters of industrial capitalism, social conscience, democracy, and pacifism. Many demands were placed on her time and ill health; her elite social class and her career did not shield her from tragedy and family responsibilities. Until her death, she remained as the administrator of Hull-House. Her latter years were devoted to the realization of world peace and social justice. In 1931, she was awarded the Nobel Peace Prize.

Born in Cedarville, Illinois, her mother Sarah died in childbirth when Addams was 2 years old. After her father's remarriage to a wealthy widow, Anna Haldeman, who had two children, Jane became the youngest of seven siblings. Her special playmate was

Jane Addams' headstone in her family plot in the Cedarville, Illinois, cemetery.

Source: Photo by Patricia A. Bauch.

a stepbrother her own age, George. Addams carried fond memories of their games and play in the woods and streams of the vast Addams estate. As a child she was not vigorous, as she suffered from a congenital spinal defect that was later corrected by surgery, but from which she suffered all her life. Her father John was a prosperous miller and businessman, who served as a senator in the Illinois State Legislature for 16 years. He fought in the Civil War, his home was a stop on the Underground Railroad, and he was an early friend of Abraham Lincoln. Addams attributes to her father the early influences on her life and beliefs. He grounded her in literature, history, social commentary, and moral rectitude. Addams matured as an attractive, intelligent, persuasive, and graceful woman.

In 1881, she graduated from nearby Rockford Female Seminary as the class valedictorian. She was disappointed that her father would not allow her to attend the newly opened Smith College. He died the year of her graduation. In the following year, she was awarded a bachelor's degree when the school received accreditation as Rockford College for Women, now Rockford College. Addams enrolled in medical school but dropped out due to poor health. About the same time, in the midst of difficult postgraduate studies at Johns Hopkins University, George asked for her hand in marriage. Realizing that her refusal was definite, he lived the rest of his life suffering from depression, addiction to opium, and as a recluse in the family home. Addams did not see her future as a life of domesticity.

Not sure of her path in life, for 21 months Addams studied art history and modern languages in Europe. She later came to realize that such studies were useless unless they could be shared with others. On her return, she intermittently cared for family members during illness and childbirth, studied and wrote, and pondered what her life's work should be. As the only unmarried sibling, this "family claim" followed Addams throughout her life including the guardianship and care of two nephews and a niece on the death of a sister. Juggling parental responsibilities and a career was not part of her life's plan. She later came to understand that events were not dependent on her own desires and efforts. On her second visit to Europe with her friend, Ellen Gates Starr, she visited Toynbee Hall, a settlement house in London's East End. This visit influenced her decision to open a similar house with Starr in an immigrant district in Chicago where she would live among and care for the poor. In 1888, with money inherited from her father, she and Starr leased a large home previously owned by Charles Hull located at the intersection of Halsted and Polk Streets. As expressed later, their purpose was to provide a center for civic and social life, to institute and maintain educational and philanthropic enterprises, and to investigate and improve the conditions in the industrial districts of Chicago. Starr and Addams enjoyed setting up housekeeping in the upper-class style and beauty to which they were accustomed.

Addams's social activities included speeches to support the expanding work of Hull-House. The settlement house eventually grew to encompass a square block. She responded to her neighbors' needs for an outdoor playground, child care, and club meetings. Hull-House eventually also included a night school with literacy classes for adults, a circulating library, and a kindergarten; a public kitchen, a coffee house, a swimming pool, and a gymnasium; a book bindery, an art studio and gallery, a music school, and a drama group; a cooperative boarding club for working girls; and an employment bureau and labor museum. She inspired other educated women of her social class to join her, such as Florence Kelley, Julia Lathrop, and Alice Hamilton. These women became accomplished in their own right. Wealthy women such as Louise deKoven Bowen and Mary Rozet Smith contributed financially and personally enabled Addams to form a close group of woman friends. Smith purchased the property that enabled the expansion of Hull-House. Addams visited her neighbors to determine their needs, cared for the sick, and listened to troubled people. She believed it was important to live with and get to know the poor and to share her financial wealth and ability to raise money, as well as her education and experiences with them. She was the consummate fund-raiser and democratic community builder as more staff and residents were added to Hull-House.

Addams took on larger civic responsibilities, including running for garbage inspector for her ward, as a result of her investigations into sanitary conditions. Other studies led to the publication of *Hull-House Maps and Papers* in 1895, widely considered the first sociological investigations into the environmental conditions of immigrants in a large city. This was primarily the work of Julia Lathrop, a trained investigator. With this information, Addams and the women of Hull-House lobbied for factory inspections and labor reform. These investigations helped establish Hull-House as a center of social science work and Addams as one of the main thinkers in the emerging field of sociology. She wrote incessantly in efforts to convince citizens of the need for social reform. Her first book, *Democracy and Social Ethics,* explained how the customs and values of the working-class poor were not the same as those of the middle class. She insisted on seeing the poor in their own context, which was not implicitly inferior to the middle class. This book and her other writings brought paid speaking requests from across the country, which helped her finance Hull-House. Ultimately, Addams wrote more than 500 published articles, many appearing in important scientific journals, and 15 books. She was well established as a respected thinker and much in demand as a lecturer at both the University of Wisconsin and Chicago University.

Addams's first biographer, a nephew James Weber Linn, argues that her love of children permeated her writings and works from those of family members to the child factory workers, to the schoolchildren, to the orphans of war. She organized the forces of society for 14 years before the passage of the Illinois Child Labor Act in 1903. In 1905, Addams was appointed to Chicago's Board of Education and subsequently became chair of the School Management Committee, which she used as a vehicle for investigating the deplorable conditions of the public schools and advocating for reform. In 1908, she participated in the founding of the Chicago School of Civics and Social Philanthropy. It soon was taken over by the new University of Chicago and became the Graduate School of Social Services Administration, with Edith Abbot a longtime Hull-House resident, as Dean. Among her many scholarly friends were George

Herbert Mead and John Dewey, who were influenced by her sociological theories, her application of those theories to her work among the disadvantaged, and her writings. Twice she was invited to teach sociology at the University of Chicago, but she declined so she could continue her social reform work. In 1906, however, she gave a course of lectures at the University of Wisconsin summer session, which she published the following year as a book, *Newer Ideals of Peace.* In 1910, she was the first woman to receive an honorary doctorate from Yale University.

Addams was an ardent feminist in the days before women's suffrage and believed that women should aspire to all levels of leadership and government. Her work at Hull-House and her own philosophy argued against women's duties as being solely maternalistic. She paved the way for women to think of themselves as legitimate citizen activists whose assessments of society should be heard and with the expectation that their ideas would be acceptable because of their roles as citizens. Her writings increasingly emphasized democracy and women's rights. She longed to rid the world of war and spoke against the entry of the United States into World War I. She once said that men, by their nature, are more given to war than women. Due to her opposition to the war, she was maligned in the press and vilified by those who had previously supported her. She was expelled from the Daughters of the American Revolution. She found an outlet for her humanitarian desires as an assistant to Herbert Hoover in providing relief supplies for women and children in enemy nations, which she related in her book *Peace and Bread in Time of War* in 1922. In 1915, she formed and became the first president of the Women's Peace Party, a national organization, and 3 months later president of the International Women's Congress for Peace and Freedom, which convened at The Hague. This group later founded the Women's International League for Peace and Freedom for which Addams served as president until 1929 and as honorary president for the rest of her life. She was a founder of the American Civil Liberties Union, an early member of the National Association for the Advancement of Colored People, and a member of the Progressive Party.

Before the war, Addams spoke and wrote on many topics, including women's rights in a democracy. She also worked with George Herbert Mead on social reform issues, including unfair labor practices, factory working conditions, and strikes, including the famous Pullman Strike. Her offer as a mediator between the company and labor was refused. During the war, however, Addams became a leader. The war brought about a subtle shift in her ideals and activities. She increasingly saw mediation and reconciliation as the means of settling disagreements. Building on organizations she had helped found earlier and as a woman in her 60s and experiencing ill health, Addams devoted the rest of her life to the work of peace and social justice internationally. She still took time to administer Hull-House, but increasingly she traveled the world as a political activist speaking on peace and justice issues.

Addams experienced many personal disappointments and deep sadness during her life. Besides her ill health, near the end of her life, she remarked that she felt that her stepmother had never forgiven her for not marrying George. Addams and her stepmother had a cool relationship, but she fulfilled the family claim by returning home for all funerals if she was not traveling abroad or in the hospital, and she remained a concerned daughter through her visits to Cedarville as her stepmother aged. From her considerable wealth, her stepmother never contributed to any of Addams's projects nor visited Addams at Hull-House. Half her family was supportive of her work and half was not; yet she was expected to be there whenever her large, extended family needed her. She was the last of her family to die. Her decade of personal disappointments, ill health, and family members' deaths weighed heavily on her, but she kept herself immersed in the business of running Hull-House and was never bitter or outraged. In fact, she was known as the humblest of persons. Whenever she was praised for her work, she always said that she did not know that what she was doing was right, that others were often right, and that she did what she could working with others. Her chosen life course was not an easy path, but her ideals, theories, and words are treasured as much today as when she uttered or wrote them.

Addams sustained a heart attack in 1926 from which she never fully recovered. Due to her heart condition, she was admitted to Johns Hopkins hospital in Baltimore on December 10, 1931, the very day she was awarded the Nobel Peace Prize in Oslo. She died in Chicago in 1935, the most famous woman in the world, 3 days after an operation revealed unsuspected cancer. Her funeral service was held in the courtyard at Hull-House. She was buried in the family plot at Cedarville.

In 2006, the State of Illinois declared December 10 as Jane Addams Day.

—Patricia A. Bauch

See also Feminism; Nobel Peace Prize; Progressive Movement, Education; Women's International League for Peace and Freedom

Further Readings

Berson, R. K. (2004). *Jane Addams: A biography*. Westport, CT: Greenwood Press.

Bryan, M. L. M., Bair, B., & deAngury, M. (2003). *The selected papers of Jane Addams: Vol. 1. Preparing to lead, 1860–81*. Urbana: University of Illinois Press.

Davis, A. F. (1973). *American heroine: The life and legend of Jane Addams*. Chicago: Dee.

Deegan, M. J. (1988). *Jane Addams and the men of the Chicago School, 1892–1918*. New Brunswick, NJ: Transaction.

Elshtain, J. B. (2002). *Jane Addams and the dream of American democracy: A life*. New York: Basic Books.

Knight, L. W. (2005). *Citizen: Jane Addams and the struggle for democracy*. Chicago: University of Chicago Press.

Linn, J. W. (1935). *Jane Addams: A biography*. New York: Appleton-Century.

Polikoff, B. G. (1999). *With one bold act: The story of Jane Addams*. Chicago: Boswell Books.

Stebner, E. J. (1997). *The women of Hull-House: A study in spirituality, vocation, and friendship*. Albany: SUNY Press.

ADORNO, THEODOR

See FRANKFURT SCHOOL OF CRITICAL THEORY

ADVOCACY

Advocacy refers to the totality of an organization's efforts to argue its position and influence the outcome of public policy decisions, through both direct and indirect techniques. A number of the principal ways in which advocacy is undertaken are described in this entry.

Increasingly, organizations employ a variety of new technologies in order to pursue their advocacy efforts. Clearly, most significant groups by now have a presence on the Internet, and most use e-mail to communicate. They are able to research and monitor socioeconomic and political developments online. They can place video or audio files on the Internet, which can then be downloaded by interested individuals (known as "podcasting"). Protest movements and charities have perhaps been more effective than corporations at electronic advocacy to date and have used e-media to compensate for their relative lack of resources; for instance, they have been highly innovative in setting up "copycat websites." These are sites that are used by critics of an organization to disseminate their particular perspective, and often they have addresses that are very similar to the organization's, which has the effect of ensuring that they are inadvertently accessed by people wanting to open the official site.

Lobbying

The direct contact between a politician or official and a representative of an organized interest, known as lobbying, is a well-developed feature of all democratic political systems. Criticized by some on the grounds that it affords undue influence over public policy to powerful and resourced interests at the expense of those groups that are already less favored, lobbying is nonetheless a large industry. Its defenders assert that lobbying is merely the manifestation by a group of its constitutionally protected freedom of expression and moreover that it is a mechanism by which voters are able to communicate directly with elected representatives more regularly than by simply voting in general elections.

It is certainly true that policy makers often find it useful to be provided with information by lobbyists about the possible impact of a policy decision. Much lobbying involves a relatively straightforward supply of information—although the information may be slanted to favor the interests of the group providing it, if a policy maker hears from the range of groups lobbying on an issue, he or she generally will be better informed about the issue and thus better able to reach a position on it. Most lobbying is directed at those policy makers who already favor a group's interests (and in this case is intended to provide that person with the information to support his or her position) or at those who have not yet arrived at a firm view on an issue, rather than being aimed at persuading a policy maker to change his or her mind.

Grassroots Campaigns

Organizations often seek to persuade their members and supporters at large to contact policy makers to urge them to support or oppose a particular policy proposal. This grassroots lobbying is based on the idea that "all politics is local"—in other words, that the more constituents who write or call about an issue, the more likely their elected representatives are to pay attention to it. Grassroots advocacy therefore involves organizations using their supporters around the country to influence policy decisions. Grassroots campaigns tend to relate to large, national issues that could have an impact on many people, whereas the resolution of more technical and detailed issues may be better suited to direct and private lobbying. Therefore, those groups that have a large, committed and geographically spread membership or supporter base will tend to be better able to mount an effective grassroots effort.

Grassroots advocacy is particularly common in the United States because it connects to the electoral imperative that drives politicians in America's institutional framework. The relative weakness of U.S. political parties and relative independence of individual members of Congress, as well as the fact that they face election every 2 years, all mean that American politicians tend to be particularly attentive to the views of their constituents. Grassroots campaigns—in which potentially substantial numbers of voters contact their elected officials—can thus give politicians a signal as to how significant a policy decision may be. Although money plays an important role in U.S. electoral politics, astute interest groups recognize that politicians will appreciate votes (or the implicit promise of votes) more than campaign contributions. Most politicians value a check for $1,000 much less than the gratitude of 1,000 voters. In other words, those grassroots lobbying campaigns in which politicians are contacted by large numbers of voters, expressing a strong desire for the politician to support or oppose a policy proposal, will likely be highly influential.

Crucial to the effectiveness of a grassroots lobbying effort, though, is not so much the number of constituent communications generated, but rather that all communications demonstrate the individual voter's genuine views and, as much as possible, relate those views to the constituent's experiences or situation. Politicians are skilled at recognizing communications in which a voter has not invested much effort (such as merely signing a preprinted postcard) and often discount those. However, an individually written letter that makes a well-argued case will be taken seriously.

Grassroots campaigns often start when an interest group sends an alert to its members or supporters urging them to write, phone, fax, or e-mail their elected officials to express a view about a given forthcoming policy decision such as a congressional vote. Another popular technique, known as a "Lobby Day," involves a group's members converging on Washington, D.C., to actually meet their members of Congress and senators in an organized way to deliver their message. This clearly signals a strong commitment to the issue on the part of the group's members and for that reason can be very effective.

A variant of grassroots campaigns is referred to as "grasstops" efforts, in which instead of trying to mobilize large numbers of constituents to contact a politician, an interest group attempts to identify and activate a smaller number of particularly influential individuals. These may be the friends, former colleagues, neighbors of the politician, or key local opinion formers such as business figures or religious leaders. Much less respected are "Astroturf" campaigns, in which those people apparently concerned enough to contact decision makers spontaneously about an issue, have actually been induced artificially to do so, or are unaware that their name had been used on a letter or petition. When discovered, such campaigns are wholly counterproductive.

Advocacy coalitions form when organized interests sharing the same desired outcome of a policy decision coordinate their efforts and pool their resources to maximum effect. Often temporary arrangements, coalitions signal to policy makers that the position being advocated is supported by a number of groups. From the policy maker's perspective, coalitions also help to reduce conflict in the sense that a coalition's members will have already resolved any differences of nuance and interpretation before they approach the politician.

Coalitions provide interest groups with the opportunity to demonstrate that their policy position is not held alone, but shared with others. In this way, groups hope to suggest that their position is not merely a private interest, but rather that it represents the wider public interest and hence makes good public policy. It also enables them to pool their resources. One member of the coalition, for instance, may have money; another may have a large membership base to use in grassroots support; and a third may have good access to a particular set of legislators being targeted.

Interest groups frequently seek to have an effect on public opinion in the hope that this will indirectly influence policy makers. An efficient—and potentially very effective—means to this end is for the group to cultivate good relationships with news journalists and editors. Media coverage can increase a group's visibility and profile, and can magnify the importance of an issue. The extent and tone of media coverage of an issue clearly has an impact on how the issue is framed and perceived by policy makers. Congress passes relatively few pieces of legislation each year, and sustained media reporting can certainly help to elevate an issue to a higher priority among legislators.

Media relations involve a range of activities. At the most basic level, an organization will issue a regular stream of press releases when it has something newsworthy to communicate, such as the publication of a new report or a response to political events. It may choose to hold a press conference at which journalists will have the opportunity to question the group and probe its views in some detail. The organization should make someone available to speak to journalists when they are seeking background information or a quote to use in their story. More proactively, an organization can attempt to persuade journalists that a certain issue is worth covering.

A key element of the public debate on policy issues is made up of television and radio programs that cover public policy, and so interest groups will often seek to have their representative invited as a guest on those political talk shows. Although such programs do not generally have a particular audience, they are watched by legislators, regulators, lobbyists, and others involved in politics and administration; therefore, they are influential in terms of helping to set the priorities and boundaries of the public policy process. The same is true of the print media—there are only a handful of newspapers and current affairs magazines that tend to be read by most senior political figures, and hence receiving positive coverage in those outlets is important to any organization's advocacy efforts.

Astute lobbyists know that media relations can be tied in to other aspects of a wider campaign. For instance, celebrity endorsements of a group's position, or even arranging for a celebrity to testify on an issue before a congressional committee, can result in substantial media coverage. Similarly, every politician's staff will ensure that he or she sees every article that mentions the politician in their local constituency newspaper. Therefore, they will ask their grassroots supporters to write letters to the editors of those papers, in which the politician is urged to adopt a particular policy position.

Interest groups will, from time to time, seek to influence public policy through judicial advocacy. This takes three forms: (1) Groups can bring a legal case in the hope that the court will interpret the law in a way that favors the group's interest, for instance, by declaring a law or policy unconstitutional, as when the National Association for the Advancement of Colored People brought a case (*Brown v. Board of*

Education), which led the Supreme Court to determine that the policy of separate-but-equal provision of school places was unlawful. (2) Groups can file *amicus curiae* (or "friends of the court") briefs in cases in which the group is not a direct participant, but where it wants to add weight to the arguments made by one of the parties; for example, when the Supreme Court is considering abortion legislation, both pro-choice and pro-life groups will file such briefs. (3) Groups can try to influence how the courts interpret the law by seeking to influence the appointment of judges, as when groups lobby legislators who must vote on executive branch nominations to federal and state courts.

Issue Advertising

Whereas the direct lobbying of legislators is often conducted in private, a wider advocacy campaign may be aimed at also affecting public opinion as a means of indirectly influencing policy makers. One form this can take is that groups advertise in the print and broadcast media. The classic example here is Mobil Oil, which has for decades regularly placed issue advertisements (originally in the *New York Times* and now in other major publications also). These ads are not intended to encourage people to buy Mobil gasoline but rather explain, at some length, the company's views about some policy issue it has an interest in. Specific policy issues will generate significant amounts of issue advertising from groups on all sides of the debate, as was seen during the debate over the North American Free Trade Agreement in 1993, which was promoted by business interests and opposed by environmentalists and labor unions.

Television advertisements are also used by advocacy groups as a way of generating mass public opinion. Perhaps the best-remembered example here was when the Health Insurance Association of America ran a series of ads in 1993 and 1994, in which a fictitious married couple ("Harry and Louise") discussed how President Bill Clinton's proposals for health care reform would make their own care plan more expensive and less effective.

—Conor McGrath

See also Activism, Social and Political; Coalition Building; Community Organizing; Digital Activism; Lobbying; Strategies and Tactics in Social Movements

Further Readings

Baumgartner, F. R., & Leech, B. L. (1998). *Basic interests: The importance of groups in politics and in political science.* Princeton, NJ: Princeton University Press.

Goldstein, K. M. (1999). *Interest groups, lobbying and participation in America.* Cambridge, UK: Cambridge University Press.

Milbraith, L. W. (1963). *The Washington lobbyists.* Chicago: Rand McNally.

Nownes, A. J. (2001). *Pressure and power: Organized interests in American politics.* Boston: Houghton Mifflin.

Schlozman, K. L., & Tierney, J. T. (1986). *Organized interests and American democracy.* New York: Harper & Row.

Thomas, C.S. (Ed.). (2004). *Research guide to U.S. and international interest groups.* Westport, CT: Praeger.

Zeigler, H., & Baer, M. (1969). *Lobbying: Interaction and influence in American state legislatures.* Belmont, CA: Wadsworth.

Zorack, J. L. (1990). *The lobbying handbook: A comprehensive lobbying guide.* Washington, DC: Professional Lobbying and Consulting Center.

AFFINITY GROUPS

See STRATEGIES AND TACTICS IN SOCIAL MOVEMENTS

AFFIRMATIVE ACTION

Affirmative action is defined as specific actions in recruitment, hiring, and other areas designed either to eliminate the present effects of past discrimination or to prevent discrimination. In its most general usage, affirmative action refers not only to hiring practices but also to recruitment and admissions in higher education. Typically, this policy involves granting some sort of preference in hiring or admissions to members of a minority group based on sex or race. This is not to be confused with "quotas"—specific numbers or percentages of a whole group who must have a minority status—which are illegal in the United States.

As a policy, affirmative action has been extremely controversial. Some observers believe that affirmative action is reverse discrimination: By giving hiring and admissions preference to members of the minority group, corporations and universities are in fact discriminating against Caucasian males. Others argue that, at its core, affirmative action is meant to prevent new discrimination or to eliminate the negative effects of past or ongoing discrimination.

One of the most common arguments against affirmative action or race-conscious admissions programs is that these programs violate Title VI of the Civil Rights Act of 1964 and the Equal Protection Clause of the Fourteenth Amendment. Title VI promises that citizens should not be subject to discrimination in any program receiving federal financial assistance on the grounds of race, color, or national origin. The Equal Protection Clause ensures that the government provides the equal protection of the laws to its citizens. The Equal Protection Clause has been interpreted to mean that similar individuals should be treated in a similar manner by the government. Affirmative action admissions programs have typically been challenged by white plaintiffs who claim that such admissions programs violate the Equal Protection Clause because minority applicants (similar individuals) are given a preference based on race (dissimilar treatment).

When a court considers the constitutionality of a government action, it will apply one of three standards. The easiest standard to satisfy is the rational basis standard. When the court applies this standard, it will uphold the governmental action if the government is pursuing a legitimate governmental objective and if there is a rational relation between the means chosen by the government and the stated objective. The next highest standard of review is known as mid-level review. Under this standard, the governmental objective has to be important, and the means chosen by the government needs to be substantially related to the important government objective. Strict scrutiny is the highest standard of review used by the courts. Courts have reviewed affirmative action cases, including race-conscious admissions programs and employment issues, under strict scrutiny analysis.

Under strict scrutiny, the state must first show that its decision to treat people differently is justified by a compelling state interest. For example, in affirmative action admissions cases, the court first examines whether promoting diversity in higher education is a compelling governmental interest. Second, the court explores if the means chosen to obtain a diverse student body, through a race-conscious admissions program, are narrowly tailored. In other words, a race-conscious admissions plan may not utilize a quota, but it may use race as a plus-factor. In so doing, the admissions program must be flexible in considering several elements of diversity for each applicant. To be constitutional, a racial classification must satisfy both parts of strict scrutiny. This encyclopedia entry will primarily discuss affirmative action within the context of higher education admissions programs.

Higher Education Admissions

Before 2003, the only U.S. Supreme Court case to address affirmative action in higher education admissions was the *Regents of the University of California v. Bakke* in 1978. In addition to *Bakke,* there were four federal appellate court cases that addressed similar issues within the context of higher education. These cases set the stage for the landmark 2003 *Gratz v. Bollinger* and *Grutter v. Bollinger* decisions ("the Michigan decisions"), which gave further guidance on the constitutionality of race-conscious admissions programs.

The U.S. Supreme Court's 1978 *Bakke* decision addressed a university's consideration of race as part of its admissions program. The plaintiff, Allan Bakke, was a white male who had been rejected twice by the University of California Davis Medical School. Bakke alleged that the medical school's admissions program had violated the Equal Protection Clause because the school had accepted less-qualified minority applicants by reserving 16 out of 100 places for disadvantaged minority students. Bakke claimed that the students who filled these 16 spots had lower grade point averages (GPAs) and test scores than rejected white students. Bakke alleged that the medical school's

program treated him differently than the successful minority applicants, thus violating his rights under the Equal Protection Clause of the Fourteenth Amendment (and under Article I of the California Constitution) by excluding him because of his race.

The U.S. Supreme Court held that the University's program was unconstitutional. The highly divided Court found the medical school's particular policy of setting aside 16 seats to be filled only by minorities was unconstitutional. Thus, the unconstitutionality of using quotas was established. The Court, however, reversed a lower court's ruling that race could never be considered a factor in education. Due to the many rationales apparent in the *Bakke* decision, universities were left to wonder whether or to what extent race could be used in admissions.

After the *Bakke* decision, there was a lack of a clear standard of whether race could be considered in admissions. Also after the *Bakke* decision, appellate courts from the Fifth, Eleventh, Ninth and Sixth Circuits decided affirmative action education cases. The Fifth and Eleventh Circuits did not find *Bakke* binding, whereas the Ninth and Sixth Circuits did. Circuit splits like this often lead to intervention by the Supreme Court.

In a case within the Fifth Circuit, *Hopwood v. Texas* in 1996, Cheryl Hopwood and three other white students were denied admission to the University of Texas Law School in 1992. Hopwood filed suit claiming that the admissions policy violated the Equal Protection Clause of the Fourteenth Amendment and Title VI of the Civil Rights Act, arguing that less-qualified minority applicants were admitted. Within her argument, she contended that the law school had different admissions criteria for white students and minority students. The Fifth Circuit Court of Appeals found in favor of Hopwood, holding that it was unconstitutional to consider race or ethnicity to achieve a diverse student body at the law school.

The Ninth Circuit Court of Appeals was the first circuit court to address the issue after *Hopwood.* In *Smith v. University of Washington Law School* in 2000, the Ninth Circuit Court of Appeals found that diversity was a constitutionally permissible goal. In this case, several white students were denied admission to the University of Washington Law School.

The plaintiffs alleged that the law school was practicing racially discriminatory admissions policies. The court disagreed and found that student body diversity was a compelling state interest and therefore constitutional.

In 2001, the Eleventh Circuit Court of Appeals joined the Fifth Circuit when it intimated that diversity in an academic setting was not a compelling interest. In *Johnson v. Board of Regents,* three white female students were denied admission to the University of Georgia. The plaintiffs claimed that minority applicants were unfairly given extra "points" during the admissions process because of their race. The University implemented an admissions policy that first considered the SAT exam and the student's GPA. In a second round of applicant evaluation, a point system was used that included many factors, including race. Agreeing with the white plaintiffs, the Eleventh Circuit held that the University's affirmative action program was unconstitutional because it mechanically gave diversity bonuses to its nonwhite applicants. The court did not definitively conclude whether diversity was a compelling state interest; instead, it held that the University's policy was unconstitutional because it was not narrowly tailored.

In addition to the Fifth, Ninth, and Eleventh Circuits, the Sixth Circuit saw the issue arise in *Gratz v. Bollinger* and *Grutter v. Bollinger,* wherein the same federal district court found one program constitutional and the other, similar program unconstitutional. Subsequently, the Sixth Circuit Court of Appeals found diversity to be a compelling state interest and upheld the constitutionality of race-conscious admissions programs if the program is narrowly tailored. As noted, when circuits are split on an issue, the Supreme Court may intervene. As such, in 2003, the Supreme Court decided whether race could be considered in university admissions.

In the case involving undergraduate admissions policies, *Gratz v. Bollinger,* the plaintiffs, Jennifer Gratz and Patrick Hamacher, applied to the College of Literature, Science, and the Arts (LS&A) at the University of Michigan, were wait-listed, and later rejected. Gratz had a 3.8 GPA, an ACT score of 25, and an impressive list of high school extracurricular activities. Hamacher had equally impressive credentials.

In October 1997, the plaintiffs filed a class action lawsuit against the Board of Regents of the University of Michigan and various school administrators in the U.S. Eastern District Court of the Sixth Circuit, alleging that the University's admissions program was discriminatory because in making its calculations, the University awarded extra points to minority candidates on the sole basis of their race. Specifically, the undergraduate admissions policy awarded a maximum of 150 points to any given application. Race was considered, along with several other factors such as test scores, alumni relationships, and leadership skills, when determining each applicant's point total. Members of underrepresented minority groups and applicants from socioeconomically disadvantaged backgrounds received an automatic 20 points under the system. The plaintiffs argued that the University's consideration of race in admissions from 1995 to 2003 violated Title VI of the 1964 Civil Rights Act as well as the Equal Protection Clause of the Fourteenth Amendment. The University, on the other hand, alleged that the admissions program was constitutional. Ultimately, the U.S. Supreme Court struck down the University of Michigan's undergraduate admissions program. Although it found student body diversity to be a compelling state interest, the Court did not find the undergraduate program to be narrowly tailored.

In *Grutter v. Bollinger,* regarding law school admissions, plaintiff Barbara Grutter had a 3.8 undergraduate GPA and a law school admissions test (LSAT) score in the 86th percentile. Like the plaintiffs in *Gratz,* she was wait-listed and later denied admission. Grutter and other rejected applicants filed suit in December 1997, challenging the law school's use of race in its admissions program. In her class action suit, Grutter complained that the law school's affirmative action policy favored certain minority applicants and that the policy amounted to racial or ethnic discrimination under the Equal Protection Clause of the Fourteenth Amendment and Title VI of the Civil Rights Act of 1964.

Unlike the undergraduate program's use of points, the law school used race as one of many unquantified factors that could enhance an applicant's chances of admission. In order to demonstrate a commitment to diversity, the law school sought to enroll a critical mass of minority applicants. The term *critical mass* refers to the minimum number of minority students necessary to withstand compartmentalization. The University of Michigan Law School stressed that the presence of more than a few minority students in a classroom encourages all students to think less stereotypically, while allowing the minority students to feel less isolated. In the *Grutter v. Bollinger* U.S. Supreme Court decision, the Court found that student body diversity is a compelling interest.

After the Court reasoned that diversity was compelling, it next addressed whether the law school's program was narrowly tailored. The Court found that the law school's policy was narrowly tailored because, unlike the undergraduate admissions program in *Gratz v. Bollinger*, the law school's affirmative action program adequately ensured that all factors that may contribute to student body diversity were meaningfully considered alongside race in admissions decisions.

Like the University of Michigan Law School did, universities should make clear that there are many possible bases for diversity admissions. The Supreme Court in *Grutter* noted that the law school's policy required admissions officers to consider "soft variables," or other criteria beyond grades and test scores. The bottom line is that the law school gave substantial weight to diversity factors besides race. In other words, universities should take into account a wide variety of characteristics besides race and ethnicity that contribute to a diverse student body.

Also noteworthy in this decision is that the Court acknowledged the amici briefs and studies that highlighted the benefits of diversity. Specifically, the Court noted that major American businesses need a diverse workforce and that the U.S. military needs a racially diverse officer corps for the purposes of national security.

The *Gratz* and *Grutter* decisions will certainly have implications for university admissions teams. The *Grutter* decision is not a license for admissions teams to implement any type of race-conscious plan they choose. Instead, universities may use race only when the admissions policy is narrowly tailored. Indeed, a careful analysis of the Court's reasoning in

Gratz and *Grutter* provides guidance for universities that choose to implement a race-conscious admissions program.

Other Arenas of Affirmative Action Influence

The Michigan decisions discussed in the previous section may also have implications for K–12 admissions programs as well as for employment decisions. Specifically, *Grutter v. Bollinger* offers strong language in support of the consideration of race in other contexts. As a result of the Michigan decisions, it is arguable that student body diversity may also be considered a compelling state interest at the K–12 level. To illustrate, some of the lower courts have permitted the consideration of race in admissions and transfer policies within the K–12 context; however, other courts have not.

Courts are also divided over the use of the diversity argument in hiring practices. Affirmative action proponents have argued that more minorities in the police department or in the faculty of universities would be beneficial. Opponents would argue that any consideration of race in hiring would violate federal law. In addition to Title VI and the Equal Protection Clause, employment cases also involve Title VII, which prohibits employment practices that discriminate on the basis of race, gender, religion, or national origin. Title VII makes it more difficult to consider race in hiring, but some scholars argue that this practice should not be precluded. Indeed, the affirmative action debate is likely to continue within the context of education and employment.

—*Suzanne E. Eckes*

See also *Brown v. Board of Education;* Civil Rights Acts; Civil Rights Movement; Law and Social Movements

Further Readings

Ancheta, A. (2003). *Revisiting Bakke and diversity-based admission: Constitutional law, social science research, and the University of Michigan affirmative action cases.* Cambridge, MA: Harvard University, Civil Rights Project.

Eckes, S. (2004). Race-conscious admissions programs: Where do universities go from *Grutter* and *Gratz? Journal of Law and Education, 33*(1), 21–62.

Glossary of affirmative action terms. (n.d.). University of Rhode Island, Office of Affirmative Action, Equal Opportunity and Diversity. Retrieved December 14, 2005, from http://www.uri.edu/affirmative_action/definitions.html

Gratz v. Bollinger, 539 U.S. 244 (2003).

Grutter v. Bollinger, 539 U.S. 306 (2003).

Hopwood v. Texas, 78 F.3d 932 (5th Cir. 1996).

Joint statement of constitutional law scholars, reaffirming diversity: A legal analysis of the University of Michigan affirmative action cases. (2003). Cambridge, MA: Harvard University, Civil Rights Project.

Regents of the University of California v. Bakke, 438 U.S. 265 (1978).

Smith v. University of Washington Law School, 233 F.3d 1188 (9th Cir. 2000).

AFGHAN RESISTANCE TO SOVIET OCCUPATION

Afghanistan is a southwest Asian state populated by tribal clans with multiple ethnicities and languages. Historically, Afghans have identified with their religion, tribe, and kinship to a much greater degree than with any central government.

In April 1978, a small group of leftist Afghan officers with Soviet ties seized control of the government and established the Democratic Republic of Afghanistan (DRA). President Nur Taraki, the Soviet-backed Marxist leader, quickly announced a program of land reform, liberalized status for women, and changed other policies that ran counter to the centuries-old social order of Afghanistan.

Because many of Taraki's programs were in direct opposition to the social structure based on tribe, kinship, village, and religious identity, the government drew very little support in the countryside. Resistance to Taraki's government grew, and a civil war broke out among tribal clans. Afghan Islamic religious leaders proclaimed *jihad* (holy war) against the Communist régime and bands of *mujahideen* (holy warriors) formed to defend the faith.

On March 15, 1979, the city of Herat was in full rebellion against the DRA government, and most of the Afghan 17th Infantry Division mutinied and joined the anti-government rebellion. The DRA air force bombed the city, and the DRA retook the city by March 21, 1979. An estimated 5,000 Afghans and up to 200 Soviets were estimated to have died in the fighting. Desertions were so rampant in the Afghan army that, by the end of 1979, the actual strength of the DRA's army was estimated to be less than half of its authorized strength of 90,000 men.

In September 1979, Taraki's prime minister, Hafizullah Amin, seized power and had President Taraki killed. Under Amin's rule, the political situation in Afghanistan continued to deteriorate. The Soviet leadership under Soviet Secretary General Leonid Brezhnev determined that military intervention was necessary to restore political and social stability to Afghanistan. The Soviets' prior experiences in quelling large-scale insurrections were Hungary in 1956 and Czechoslovakia in 1968.

Following some advance elements, the Soviet 40th Army invaded Afghanistan in force on Christmas Eve 1979. During the first several days of the invasion, the Soviets seized the government, killed President Amin, and installed Barbak Karmal as president. The Soviet plan was to stabilize the government, reconstitute and strengthen the DRA military, and withdraw the majority of Soviet forces within 3 years. The Soviets originally intended to leave responsibility for combat to the military of the DRA. However, with Afghan mujahideen in full rebellion against the government, the DRA army was ineffective and unreliable, and the possibility of its defeat worried the Soviet leadership. The Soviet 40th Army found itself drawn into direct combat with hundreds of guerrilla groups throughout the country. The 40th Army was a motorized rifle division, whose training predisposed them to conduct conventional large unit combat sweeps supported by artillery fire support and tactical close air support.

The Soviet invasion prompted an Islamic jihad against the Marxist régime in which many foreign nationals arrived, believing it their Moslem duty to defend their faith. For the most part, foreign mujahideen were funneled into one of seven major groups or alliances. Afghan and foreign mujahideen received significant support from numerous outside sources. Foreign countries such as Pakistan, Iran, the United States, China, and some European and Arab states began to supply money and arms to the mujahideen. In the case of the United States, the government did not believe that the mujahideen would be able to defeat the Soviets; the U.S. objective was to make this invasion costly to the Soviets and perhaps cause some reticence on the Soviets' part to embark on other foreign adventures.

Pakistan required, as a condition for their cooperation, that all foreign assistance pass through them. Pakistan's Inter-Service Intelligence (ISI) became heavily involved as an intermediary for financial aid, supplies, weapons, and training. The ISI generally provided assistance and sanctuary to about seven major mujahideen groups, four considered Islamic fundamentalist and three considered religiously moderate. Pakistan's political leaders and the ISI favored the fundamentalist groups, which gave Islamic religious leaders greater influence and likewise tended to undermine the balance of traditional Afghan social structure based on religion, tribe, kinship, and village. Al-Qaeda's involvement was primarily during the latter years of the conflict and was generally one of recruiting, training, and financing foreign jihadists.

Much like the Viet Minh and Viet Cong before them, the mujahideen were facing a modern, technologically advanced enemy with superior firepower. To neutralize the enemy's advantages, the mujahideen avoided large-scale attacks and used highly mobile small-unit guerrilla tactics, choosing when and where to strike, emphasizing the use of rugged terrain, and coordinated ambushes and quick withdrawal to inflict casualties and material losses on the enemy while minimizing their own losses in men and materials. The Soviets and their Afghan allies maintained a tenuous hold on the major cities and highways. The mujahideen targeted enemy lines of communication and supply and government infrastructure, such as the electrical grid, as a means of demonstrating the impotence of the Afghan central government and as a way of demoralizing the DRA, its Afghan supporters, and the Soviet Union.

By late 1985, the U.S. Central Intelligence Agency (CIA) supplied FIM-92 "Stinger" missiles to mujahideen groups. Stinger missiles are portable infrared seeking missiles that can be shoulder-fired by a single operator and are highly effective as anti-aircraft weapons. Stingers reportedly seriously reduced the effectiveness of Soviet helicopter and fixed-wing close air support with approximately 300 Soviet aircraft shot down. The Soviets were forced to change their use of air power in ways that greatly reduced its effectiveness. It is estimated that the CIA provided some 2,000 to 2,500 missiles to the various mujahideen groups. This conflict differed from prior communist-assisted guerrilla movements in that the mujahideen were opposing a communist form of government and believed themselves to be defending their Islamic faith against an atheistic central government that promoted a hostile, anti-religious value system.

In early 1985, Mikhail Gorbachev ascended to the position of Soviet Secretary General. Soviet military casualties in 1985 ended up among the highest of any year of the war for the Soviets. Finally, the Soviet leadership decided that the war was not to be won at any reasonable cost. In early 1986, Gorbachev announced a program to turn over fighting to the military forces of the DRA and began to withdraw Soviet military elements. The 40th Army began to withdraw in 1988 and completed its withdrawal on February 15, 1989.

The lasting effect of the Soviet invasion of Afghanistan was to weaken traditional Afghan tribal kinship ties and strengthen radical Islamic fundamentalists in Afghanistan, a major goal of Pakistan. This occurred to such a degree that the Taliban, considered a particularly harsh form of fundamentalist Islam, became the ruling government of Afghanistan in 1994. The Taliban were noted for providing asylum and protection to Osama bin Laden on his arrival in Afghanistan in May 1996.

—Glen Yahola Wilson

See also Iranian Revolution (1963–1979); Resistance

Further Readings

Coll, S. (2004). *Ghost wars: The secret history of the CIA, Afghanistan, and bin Laden, from the Soviet invasion to September 10, 2001.* New York: Penguin Books.

Jalali, A. A., & Grau, L. S. (2001). *Afghan guerrilla warfare: In the words of the mujahideen.* St. Paul, MN: MBI.

Kakar, M. H. (1995). *Afghanistan: The Soviet invasion and the Afghan response.* Berkeley: University of California Press.

Poole, J. H. (2004). *Tactics of the crescent moon: Militant Muslim combat methods.* Emerald Isle, NC: Posterity Press.

Russian General Staff. (2002). *The Soviet-Afghan war: How a superpower fought and lost* (L. W. Grau & M. A. Gress, Trans.). Lawrence: University Press of Kansas.

AFRICAN NATIONAL CONGRESS

January 8, 2006, marked the 94th anniversary of the founding of the African National Congress of South Africa (ANC). The ANC (the first nonethnic organization in South Africa) was formed on January 8, 1912, in Bloemfontein. This took place against the background of the 1910 formation of the Union of South Africa, which expressly excluded the African people from the political system. For a number of years after its formation, the ANC adopted nonviolence strategies in an attempt to persuade the government to accommodate African political aspirations. In later years, however, economic development—and rapid industrialization in particular—led to the emergence of nascent forms of militant resistance to white rule.

From the outset, the ANC proclaimed its commitment to nonracialism; that is, it viewed the peoples of Africa as one, regardless of skin color. Throughout the early years, the ANC had clung to this commitment. It always advocated a multinational union, insisted on a nonracial principle as being the only solid foundation for sound government of the society, and never sought black domination of the state. The African workers' strikes influenced a change in class composition of the ANC leadership, with the scale being tilted in favor of the workers. The repression of African workers during strikes and the rise in political consciousness accounted for the formation of the African National Congress Youth League (ANCYL) in the 1940s and led to the ANC's adoption of a militant program of action in the beginning of the 1950s.

In political terms, the 1950s were characterized by mass defiance campaigns, the drafting of the Freedom Charter at Kliptown in 1955, the anti-pass laws demonstration, and the treason trial of anti-apartheid activists. This position can clearly be seen in the ANC's 1956 endorsement of the Freedom Charter, drafted by the Congress of the People the previous year in Kliptown. The Charter served as a beacon for ANC future activities and declared that South Africa belonged to all who lived in it, black and white.

The ideological stance as stipulated in the Charter further allowed the ANC to work and cooperate with other nonblacks; this can clearly be seen in the alliance in which the ANC linked up with Coloreds and Indians. Moreover, the fact that the ANC never believed in black exclusivity in the fight for black emancipation allowed the ANC to cooperate with white-dominated groups, such as the communists, and certain white liberals who were sympathetic to their cause.

From its establishment in 1912 until the Sharpeville shootings and its subsequent banning in 1960, the ANC advocated nonviolent tactics in its struggle. However, two differing strategies can be identified even within this period. Until World War II, the ANC was pledged to constitutional protest, such as negotiation, petitions, and deputations. The policy during this period was characterized by cooperation and compromise with the government, as the party believed it could bring about change through the education and enlightenment of the whites in power.

The Sharpeville shootings of 1960 and the banning of the ANC demonstrated the failure of peaceful tactics. The ANC, in exile and at home, adopted a policy of armed struggle under the banner of Umkhonto we Sizwe (MK), which was set up in 1961 to carry out the sabotage campaign. However, by 1963 the MK was smashed by government security forces followed by the arrests and imprisonments of most of its leadership. The ANC was convinced of the need for armed guerrilla warfare, a strategy it remained faithful to until the negotiations and eventual overthrow of the apartheid regime in the 1990s.

The banning of the ANC in March 1960 posed what amounted to insurmountable problems for the organization. Besides the difficult task of readjustment to meet the rigors of underground activity, the discipline involved problems of communication and recruitment, and there was the question of a need for the ANC to meet and review the situation. The ANC could not easily meet inside the country. The problem was further exacerbated by the fact that South Africa was surrounded by white-controlled regimes of Mozambique and Rhodesia (now Zimbabwe), which were hostile to the anti-colonial movements in the region.

What the apartheid regime was unaware of when it banned the ANC and other anti-apartheid movements were that it also inadvertently frustrated the nonviolent strategies that the ANC had used for over 4 decades. Consequently, at the Rivonia trial, Nelson Mandela defended an armed struggle.

The creation of Umkhonto we Sizwe meant the emergence of a new factor in the politics of liberation in South Africa. The politics of Umkhonto we Sizwe was formulated in the December 1961 Manifesto. Those who formed Umkhonto we Sizwe were all members of the ANC, with some support from the South African Communist Party and had behind them the tradition of nonviolence and negotiation as a means of solving problems.

By the end of 1964, the campaign of armed struggle to overthrow the South African government had been broken. It is clear that the ANC and other movements were overoptimistic, perhaps naïve, in their hopes that the South African government would be ended in the rising of the masses. Unlike, for instance, Mozambique and Angola, South Africa did not have the ideal terrain for the establishment of viable guerrilla bases.

The exiled ANC established links with a number of countries for the training of MK members as well as for the launching of diplomatic initiatives. Training camps were established in Tanzania and later in Angola, Mozambique, and Zambia for the instruction of the military of the ANC. Specialized training was undertaken in a number of sympathetic countries, notably the Soviet Union, Libya, and Uganda. The headquarters of the ANC were established in Dar es Salaam, but moved to Lusaka, Zambia, after the Morogoro Conference in 1969, in order to be closer to South Africa. At the Morogoro Conference, it was reiterated that that the armed struggle was the only way to achieve the aims of the ANC.

The pace was set for the 1970s by the historic Morogoro Conference of 1969, where the strategy and tactics that would guide the ANC in the pursuit of its cherished goal—total liberation—were adopted. Thus, by the early 1970s, the strength of the people was manifested in the extensive strike waves, the militancy of the youth and students, and the oppressed people's clear identification with the armed struggles being waged, and won, in neighboring Angola and Mozambique. The whole world reverberated to the barbarity of Boer aggression in the 1976 nationwide uprisings centered in Soweto, which left more than 1,000 youths dead and marked a new stage in the struggle, raising mass resistance on all fronts to unprecedented heights.

As the struggle intensified inside South Africa, the number of people going into exile increased, and the ANC was faced with the task of sustaining a substantial number of refugees from South Africa. The number of exiles increased from possibly 1,000 in 1975 to 9,000 in 1980. In order to accommodate this increase, a new center was established at Mazimbu, near Dar es Salaam, in 1979. Many school-age youngsters were admitted to the ANC's Solomon Mahlangu Freedom College. The period after 1975 was one of reorganization of the ANC, as bases were established closer to South Africa in an attempt to intensify armed struggle against apartheid. Angola became the main ANC military center.

In 1974–1975, Southern Africa was transformed by the intensification of the liberation struggles that led to the collapse of the Portuguese empire, the independence of Mozambique and Angola, and the South African invasion of Angola. The independence of Mozambique and Angola (which attained their freedom through armed struggle) offered hope and inspiration to black South Africans. Within South Africa, the revolutionary fervor in the two Portuguese colonies exploded in the Soweto uprising of 1976. There were, in June 1976, countrywide demonstrations against the imposition of Afrikaans in African schools. The demonstrations spread from Soweto to other South African cities. The heroic struggle of Soweto had a profound impact on the ANC.

For the Africans, the significance of the Soweto uprising and the challenge to white authority that it sparked throughout the country lay in the emergence of a new generation of youthful activists who proved themselves ready to confront armed white power, even with little immediate prospect of success. The demonstration showed that a powerful wellspring of direct defiance could be tapped among Africans from all population groups. There is little evidence that the ANC was initially directly involved, although its leadership and supporters, both on Robben Island as well as in exile, identified with the uprising.

Whereas many African liberation movements attained power through a peaceful decolonization process in which colonizers handed power to the colonized, the ANC's road to power was relatively unique. After nearly 3 decades in exile from where it led both a nonviolent and an armed struggle, the ANC ascended to power. Although organizational mobilization was important in the liberation of South Africa, it was the ANC position in the negotiated transition to a multiracial democracy that was even more crucial. It was a significant breakthrough when multiparty negotiations, bolstered by the bilateral agreement between the ANC and the government, produced tangible products, such as draft legislation on transitional mechanisms to prepare for election and a fairly detailed interim constitution.

Efforts by the ANC facilitated the reacceptance of South Africa into the international community and returned the ANC to the center of the political stage, occupying again the position that it held in the 1950s as the most prominent of the African opposition to the National Party government. With the banning of the ANC on February 2, 1990, and the release of Nelson Mandela on February 11, the anti-apartheid struggle of more than 4 decades entered a new stage.

The ANC and the National Party entered into negotiations to create a nonracial democratic South Africa that resulted in the formation of the ANC government in 1994. In 1990, the government lifted its ban on the ANC, and its leaders were allowed to return to South Africa and conduct peaceful political activities. In return, the ANC suspended its guerrilla struggle against the government. The most important ANC leader in the 1990s was Mandela, who succeeded Tambo as president in 1991. Mandela led the ANC in negotiations (1992–1993) with the government through the transition to an elected government based on universal suffrage. The ANC's opposition to apartheid had won it the allegiance of most black South Africans, and in April 1994, the party swept the country's first all-race elections, winning more than 60% of the vote for seats in the new National Assembly. Mandela was inaugurated as South Africa's first black president on May 10, 1994, heading a government of national unity.

—*Frank M. Chiteji*

See also Anti-Apartheid Movement; Biko, Stephen; Mandela, Nelson; Mandela, Winnie

Further Readings

Benson, M. (1994). *Nelson Mandela: The man and the movement.* New York: W. W. Norton.

Mandela, N. (1994). *Long walk to freedom: The autobiography of Nelson Mandela.* Boston: Little, Brown.

Meli, F. (1988). *South African belongs to us: A history of the ANC.* Harare: Zimbabwe Publishing House.

AFRICAN WOMEN AND SOCIAL JUSTICE

Women across sub-Saharan Africa have a long history of social and political protest. Using precolonial forms of collective action, women protested colonial abuses against them and African men. They became activists as well as supporters for nationalist movements in the 1940s and 1950s. They joined national liberation movements and armed struggles in the Portuguese colonies and in white minority-ruled countries in southern Africa from the 1960s until the last one, South Africa, fell in 1990. In recent decades, women have engaged in pro-democracy and anti-corruption protests in many countries, and as democratization increased political possibilities in the 1990s, women's advocacy groups proliferated, leading to a rich culture of women's activism.

In many African societies, women used shaming practices against men, and sometimes against women, to correct what they saw as violations of appropriate gender behavior. Shaming practices included dancing, ululating, singing derisive songs (usually aimed at men's alleged lack of virility), distinctive forms of dress and body decoration, and sometimes the display, or threat of display, of women's nakedness, as a statement of women's symbolic power of fertility and as a way of taunting men for their perceived cowardice.

Women used shaming practices in anti-colonial and nationalist protests against European men, who in their ignorance of customary meanings often responded with violence. Anti-colonial protests often involved multiple concerns but were often triggered by perceived plans to tax women, a direct threat to their livelihoods as farmers and traders. Because women contributed the bulk of farming labor, and in many areas, particularly West Africa, were active market traders, they reacted strongly to threats to their control over crops or markets and to what they saw as threats to the linked fertility of women and the land. Using market and kinship networks, women could mobilize demonstrations over large areas. Both the 1929 Women's War in southeastern Nigeria and the Anlu rebellion in British Cameroon from 1958 to 1961 mobilized thousands of women over thousands of miles using market and kinship networks. Urban women in French Togo used market women's networks to organize a successful tax revolt in 1933. There are many reports of anti-colonial and nationalist protests in which women attempted to shame African men into action by demanding that the men "Give us your trousers!" or, in earlier times, "your loincloths," as the queen mother Yaa Asantewaa demanded of the Asante chiefs in 1900 to rally them (successfully) to resist the British.

As nationalist parties and movements gained strength and militancy in the post–World War II period, women throughout colonized Africa entered strongly into party and movement campaigns, carrying with them their traditional forms of song, dance, and sexual shaming. In Pare district, Tanzania, in the 1940s, women marched to the colonial headquarters and demanded that the district officer meet their protesting husbands' demands and send them home, or else impregnate all the women himself. In 1949 in Cote d'Ivoire, 500 women marched to the prison, singing, dancing, and using shaming taunts, to demand the release of imprisoned male nationalists, a turning point toward French acceptance of African independence.

Most sub-Saharan nations without white settler colonies attained independence in the 1950s and 1960s without armed struggles, but nationalist leaders were often jailed, protests suppressed, and parties banned. Both educated and uneducated women in cities and villages actively took part in these movements. In West Africa, market women's organizations mobilized protests in support of nationalist parties. Funmilayo Ransome-Kuti of western Nigeria was a well-known women's leader, as were Margaret Ekpo from the east and Garubo Sawaba from the north. Bibi Titi Mohammed in Tanzania used contacts in women's dancing groups to mobilize uneducated women to support Julius Nyerere and the Tanganyikan African National Union (TANU). Aoua Keita, a leader in the Malian socialist party, joined with Aissata Sow in organizing the Malian Union of Women Workers. In French Cameroon, a nonsettler colony where armed struggle did occur, women were active in the militant socialist party and joined in the armed struggle.

Independence was won in settler colonies only after political campaigns coupled with armed struggle. In Kenya, women supported the 1950s rebellion of the Land and Freedom Army (called "Mau Mau" by the British). Wambui Waiyaki Otieno was a principal organizer of women as scouts and food providers. The British eventually confined 13,000 women in guarded camps to try to suppress the rebellion.

In the Portuguese colonies, Mozambique, Angola, and Guinea Bissau, national liberation movements moved to armed struggle in the mid-1960s, and women's detachments were organized. Women villagers provided support for the movements, and women combatants were part of party leadership: Josina Machel in Mozambique, Carmen Pereira in Guinea-Bissau, and Deolinda Rodrigues in Angola. Rodrigues was one of five women combatants assassinated in 1967. In Zimbabwe (then Rhodesia), women joined the armed struggle as couriers and combatants. Joyce Nhongo Mujuru, known as Teurai Ropa—"Spill Blood"—became a leader in the Zimbabwe African National Union and moved into government after independence, as did Margaret Dongo, also a combatant. In Namibia, Pendukeni Iivula-Ithana headed the Southwest Africa People's Organization women's council and became the first woman attorney general.

In South Africa, Winnie Mandela became a symbol of resistance to apartheid, but hundreds of thousands of women historically have engaged in the struggle. Because South Africans had been dispossessed of their land, women's protests grew more out of apartheid restrictions on family life and on women as wage-workers than the linked issues of land and fertility. Many women organizers and much support came from the trade union movement (the Congress of South African Trade Unions [COSATU] after 1985). Organizers from the South African Communist Party (SACP) also played a significant part. Women launched a successful campaign against carrying passes in 1913, shortly after the formation of the African National Congress (ANC), and later formed the ANC Women's League. Women activists joined the Defiance of Unjust Laws Campaign, begun in 1952. In 1954, the multiracial Federation of South African Women (FEDSAW) was organized, made up of women's groups from the Congress Alliance. In 1956, FEDSAW organizers and leaders, including Lillian Ngoyi, Helen Joseph, Frances Baard, Fatima Meer, Dorothy Nyembe, Dora Tamana, Albertina Sisulu, Ray Alexander, and Hilda Bernstein, organized a women's Defiance Campaign demonstration against the proposed imposition of passes for women, bringing more than 20,000 women to Pretoria. Ngoyi, Nyembe, and Joseph, as well as Ruth First, ANC and SACP activist, were among those tried and acquitted in the 1956 treason trial. In the 1970s, many women, notably Mamphela Ramphele, were active in the South African Students Union and the black consciousness movement. Many women were active in parents' groups in Soweto in 1976, and many women and women's groups were active in the United Democratic Front

(UDF) in the 1980s. Women activists were repeatedly banned, put under house arrest, banished, detained, and imprisoned. Many were subjected to solitary confinement and torture. Some were murdered. Many were forced into exile, including Frene Ginwala (ANC activist who returned after 20 years to become National Assembly Speaker in 1994), the singer-activist Miriam Makeba, and Ruth First, who was assassinated in Mozambique in 1982. Young people fleeing the country after the Soweto uprising as well as ANC veterans went into exile or underground and joined the military wing of the ANC, Umkhonto we Sizwe, including Dorothy Nyembe and Thenjiwe Mtintso. Victoria Mxenge, a member of the UDF executive committee, was assassinated in Durban in 1985. Women have continued to be active in the ANC and in its organizational partners, SACP and COSATU, in the new South African government.

Contemporary women's activism has flourished with greater democratization in African countries, stronger recognition of women's rights as human rights, and the growth of regional and Africa-wide women's organizations and coalitions. Women demonstrated for democratization and against corruption, helping to bring about the conditions in which they could act for women's interests. African women's contemporary activism was energized by the third United Decade for Women meeting in Nairobi, Kenya, in 1985, presided over by Margaret Kenyatta (interned during "Mau Mau") and attended by many women from the continent. Activism was further spurred by the Fourth World Conference on Women in Beijing in 1995, chaired by Gertrude Mongella of Tanzania, and by the preconference organization of discussion groups in both urban and rural areas in many African countries. Since 1985, thousands of women's nongovernmental organizations have been organized. Women's groups combine international perspectives and organizational links with their own experiences of local women's needs and concerns. They focus on a wide range of issues, including legal rights and legal reform, representation in political parties and government, economic opportunities, HIV/AIDS and other health issues, environmental protection, war crimes against women, and peacemaking. In many countries, women's resource centers and institutes provide research and coordination for advocacy groups. Many advocacy groups are spearheaded by women lawyers or other professionals and use electoral and jural strategies for change. Others draw their leaders and members from rural women farmers or market women, who put forms of collective action passed down through generations of women to new uses against corporate and government abuses.

In South Africa, women across the political spectrum organized to write the Women's Charter, which was incorporated into the new Constitution. Cheryl Carolus, Frene Ginwala, and Thenjiwe Mtintso have led in bringing a feminist perspective into ANC politics. In Botswana, the regional group Women in Law in Southern Africa joined with the local women's group Emang Basadi! (Stand Up, Women!) and others to support lawyer Unity Dow's successful 1990 lawsuit against a discriminatory citizenship law. Dow was appointed to the Botswana High Court in 1998, as was legal scholar-activist Athaliah Molokomme, a cofounder and first head of Emang Basadi! in 2003. Molokomme, in 2005, was appointed as the first female attorney general in Botswana. In Nigeria, Baobab for Women's Human Rights challenges Shari'a provisions, including physical chastisement of wives, stoning for "adultery" and the requirement of four male witnesses to prove rape. The organization Women in Nigeria pursues issues of reproductive rights, violence toward women, child marriage, education, and housing. In Zimbabwe, the Women's Action Group, organized in response to indiscriminate arrests of "unaccompanied women" in Harare in the 1980s, advocates for women's rights, and the Musasa Project work to reduce domestic violence.

African women have advocated for gender parity in peace negotiations and conflict resolution, including working for the passage of the 1993 Kampala Action Plan on Women and Peace and the formation of the 1998 African Women's Anti-War Coalition. Women's peace groups have been formed in areas of conflict, including Congo, Rwanda, Sudan, Sierra Leone, and Liberia, where Ellen Johnson-Sirleaf, elected president in 2005, was a peace activist. Graca Machel has worked to aid war orphans and children's education. Women have organized to combat HIV/AIDS in many local and national groups and in the Society for Women and AIDS in Africa. Women's groups in areas where female genital cutting is practiced advocate health education and alternative rituals as ways to eliminate the practice.

Since the 1970s, women have formed groups focused on their relationship to the land as farmers and gatherers of fuel and water. The Green Belt movement of Kenya, led by Wangari Maathai, known for planting trees, also uses traditional shaming practices. In the oil-drilling areas of southern Nigeria, women's groups such as Niger Delta Women for Justice use nonviolent protest and shaming practices against oil companies to protest environmental degradation and deepening poverty. Throughout the continent, African women continue long traditions of female protest as they respond to new democratic openings as well as to continued violence and to new burdens imposed by globalizing capitalism.

—Judith Imel Van Allen

See also African National Congress; Anti-Apartheid Movement; Anti-Colonial Movements, Sub-Saharan Africa; Boycotts and Divestment; Communism; Feminism; Non-Governmental Organizations (NGOs); Nonviolence and Activism; Pan-Africanism; Socialist Feminism

Further Readings

Berger, I. (1992). *Threads of solidarity: Women in South African industry 1900–1980.* Bloomington: Indiana University Press.

Geiger, S. (1997). *TANU women.* Portsmouth, NH: Heinemann.

Goetz, A. M., & Hassim, S. (Eds.). (2003). *No shortcuts to power.* New York: Zed Books.

Sheldon, K. (2005). *A historical dictionary of women in sub-Saharan Africa.* Lanham, MD: Scarecrow Press.

Tripp, A. M. (Ed.). (2003). *Women's issues worldwide: Sub-Saharan Africa.* Westport, CT: Greenwood.

Urdang, S. (1989). *And still they dance: Women, war and the struggle for change in Mozambique.* New York: Monthly Review Press.

Van Allen, J. (1976). "Aba Riots" or Igbo "Women's War"? Ideology, stratification and the invisibility of women. In N. J. Hafkin & E. G. Bay (Eds.), *Women in Africa* (pp. 59–85). Palo Alto, CA: Stanford University Press.

AFROCENTRICITY

The African-centered paradigm, also known as Afrocentricity and Africentricity, is both an epistemological framework as well as a mode of social engagement that is centrally concerned with the liberation and empowerment of the global African community. Growing directly out of the scholarship and activism of numerous continental and diasporic Africans from the mid-20th century to the present, the Afrocentric paradigm has also been informed by the historical struggles of African people for self-determination in the wake of European enslavement and colonialism.

As an epistemological framework, Afrocentricity can be defined as a mode of social, historical, and cultural analysis that is centrally concerned with the issues, interest, and destiny of African people in the world. As such, Afrocentricity argues that any substantive discussion of African people must reconcile itself with the historical continuum of African civilization, culture, and humanity. What this means is that African people must be seen as historical beings, growing out of, existing within, and contributing to a particular historical reality. Second, it must endeavor to understand the social practices, traditions, understandings, and behaviors of African people within an African cultural and interpretive framework. This means that one must understand African thought and action within African terms, or within the conceptual logic of the culture in question. Finally, Afrocentricity insists on the necessity of Sankofa, a concept from the Akan culture of Ghana that literally means "to go back and fetch it." For advocates of the African-centered approach, this has meant returning to the source, or facilitating the reconstruction of African culture, history, and civilization. The necessity of Sankofa as a restorative process is understood relative to the Maafa, the historical and ongoing assault on African civilization, culture, and humanity evidenced by the ancient and modern invasions and colonization of the African continent, the enslavement and oppression of African people, and the ongoing exploitation, plunder, and destabilization of African societies (both continental and diasporic).

As a paradigm of social engagement, Afrocentricity has been applied, to varying degrees, to the task of reality transformation or community empowerment for African-descended people. It has found prominent expression within various academic disciplines as well as certain sectors of the African community. Specific disciplines that have been of import to African-centered scholars have been history (and by extension, historiography), psychology, education, and sociology (or social theory). Each of these areas has been quite instrumental in terms of community-based Afrocentric initiatives.

In the field of history, Afrocentric scholars have noted the ways in which African civilization and history have been either distorted or utterly denied in the dominant (Eurocentric) historical narrative. As such, African-centered scholars have paid special attention to historiography, the prevailing theories, methods, and objectives of historical knowledge construction. The maligning of Africa in world history and the reconstructive mandate of the Afrocentric paradigm places the process of historical research, research that accurately represents the achievements and contributions of Africa and African people, as a fundamental objective. Particular emphasis has been placed on Kmt (Ancient Egypt), which has been portrayed in contemporary Eurocentric scholarship as a non-African civilization. Other Afrocentric scholars have studied the history of the various African empires, kingdoms, and societies, as well as their diasporic counterparts.

Noting the psychosocial trauma of the Maafa, Afrocentric psychologists argue that the reordering of African patterns of life relative to the interest of European enslavers and invaders via political, economic, military, religious, and other social and cultural impositions has achieved the conceptual incarceration of the African community. This conceptual incarceration has impaired the psychological and social functioning of Africans by virtue of its estrangement of African people from their own history and culture, as well as separating them from their own indigenous institutions and life patterns. This mode of psychosocial fragmentation is necessary in order to subvert the agency that naturally comes from operation within one's own indigenous cultural, conceptual, and social framework. Moreover, conceptual incarceration has attempted to compel Africans to accept powerlessness and dependency as the legitimate and natural order of African life. Africans are therefore compelled to operate within an ahistorical consciousness by not connecting these realities with European oppression and to avoid, at all cost, the formulation of approaches to end this debilitating malaise. As such, African-centered psychologists have formulated and advocated various approaches to restore the social and cultural integrity of the African community.

In education, Afrocentric scholars and educators have demonstrated the linkages between education (and the formal processes of socialization) and agency. Drawing on Carter G. Woodson's concept of miseducation, African-centered educators and scholars have looked at the ways in which Eurocentric education has achieved the enfeeblement of African consciousness and social engagement. Conversely, African-centered scholars and educators have demonstrated the utility of education in the process of cultural recovery and community empowerment.

Within the context of sociology or social theory, Afrocentric scholars have sought to understand the oppression of Africans and to formulate solutions to this reality. This has been approached from a variety of perspectives. African-centered scholars like Maulana Karenga have been among the most vocal in noting the cultural crisis and its resolution as being imperative in the process of African empowerment. He is joined by Molefi Kete Asante, who has advocated for the utility of Afrocentricity as a paradigm of social engagement and a framework for academic research. Other African-centered social theorists, such as Marimba Ani and Jacob H. Carruthers, have sought to understand the structure and nature of European thought and culture and its proclivity toward war and conflict, oppression and inequality, conquest and control, racism and ethnocentrism, and so on. Ani also has been noted for her efforts to document the enduring vestiges of African spirituality in the Western hemisphere. She is joined by scholars like Rkhty Wimby Amen whose study of Kemetic (ancient Egyptian)

spirituality demonstrates its parallels and relevance to contemporary African practices. In addition to these theorists, scholars such as Nah Dove and Clenora Hudson-Weems have sought to understand the dynamics of gender in African communities, the centrality of women in every facet of African life, and the inadequacy of European-derived paradigms to understand their agency. Lastly, psychologist Amos Wilson has offered a plethora of frameworks for community development in the arenas of economics and politics.

In conclusion, Afrocentric scholars note that the historical process of European enslavement and conquest, in addition to its political and economic components, has been a conceptual, ideological, and cultural assault on African and other non-European people. Calling this paradigm Eurocentrism, advocates of the Afrocentric approach have argued that Afrocentricity is not Eurocentrism in reverse; that is, it is not (nor does it attempt to impose) an alternative hegemony. Instead, it represents an attempt on the parts of African people to restore the damage done by the Maafa, facilitate African empowerment, and restore African civilization.

African-centered scholars contend that the historic disruptions of the Maafa have served to weaken the integrity of African social structures and institutions. In most instances, these impositions have sought to annihilate these structures and institutions entirely. This process is clearly expressed in the deculturalization inherent in the enslavement of Africans in North America and the varying assaults on African culture and humanity throughout the Western hemisphere. It is within that vein that Afrocentric scholars insist on the centrality of culture in shaping social reality, maintaining that culture provides rules for living, frameworks for thinking, and models of human and social development. As such, African-centered scholars have made substantive contributions to a variety of domains related to historical and cultural recovery and community transformation.

Finally, the Afrocentric paradigm has been a collaborative project owing to the efforts of activists, scholars, political leaders, religious and spiritual leaders, and educators in the African world community from the 18th century to the present. It has been devised as a means to facilitate the process of Sankofa; that is, returning to the source—reconnecting with African cultures, traditions, institutions, and ideas for the sake of achieving Weheme Mesu, the rebirth, restoration, and transformation of the African world.

—Kamau Rashid

See also Black Power; Du Bois, W. E. B.; Garvey, Marcus; Kwanzaa; Malcolm X; Toussaint L'Ouverture; Wells-Barnett, Ida B.

Further Readings

Ani, M. (1994). *Yurugu: An African-centered critique of European cultural thought and behavior.* Trenton, NJ: Africa World Press.

Asante, M. K. (1980). *Afrocentricity: The theory of social change.* Chicago: African American Images.

Carruthers, J. H., & Harris, L. C. (Eds.). (1997). *The preliminary challenge.* Los Angeles: Association for the Study of Classical African Civilizations.

Dove, N. (1995). African womanism: An Afrocentric theory. *Journal of Black Studies, 28*(5), 515–539.

Hudson-Weems, C. (1994). *Africana womanism: Reclaiming ourselves.* Troy, MI: Bedford.

Kambon, K. K. K. (1998). *African/black psychology in the American context: An African-centered approach.* Tallahassee, FL: Nubian Nation.

Kershaw, T. (1992). Afrocentrism and the Afrocentric method. *Western Journal of Black Studies, 16*(3), 160–168.

Shujaa, M. J. (Ed.). (1994). *Too much schooling, too little education: A paradox of Black life in White societies.* Trenton, NJ: Africa World Press.

Wilson, A. N. (1998). *Blueprint for black power: A moral, political, and economic imperative for the twenty-first century.* New York: Afrikan World InfoSystems.

AGRARIAN SOCIALIST MOVEMENT

The agrarian socialist movement took root in the rural parts of the United States at the turn of the 20th century. Economic conditions of this time help explain why farmers, an unlikely bunch to adopt Karl Marx's brand of socialism, were drawn to it. Agrarian radicalism after the Civil War developed with the extension of the railroads west of the Mississippi. The new settlers, who expected freedom and security, encountered instead a fluctuating world price for their crops, railroads, and middlemen to market their crops. Growing cash crops that are primarily cotton, wheat, and corn, farmers were suffering under high interest rates and low crop prices.

Under a system called *crop lien,* farmers were brutally exploited by their creditors, who loaned farmers money in return for their crops as collateral. Thus, farmers mortgaged their harvest while it was still on the ground. The merchant who bought the crop during harvest time (at a price determined by him) was, in many cases, the same person as the creditor. Often, farmers would be short of paying back their debt despite a year's hard toil. Increasingly indebted, farmers worked 16 hours a day and overworked the soil to stay afloat. Despite these efforts, many farmers lost their land. Tenancy among white and black farmers was thus increasing as the 1910 census revealed. Many thought monopoly capitalism was the culprit.

Responding to the economic conditions, many farmers organized rural protests. These protests took the form of educational organizations, cooperative organizations to eliminate the profits of middlemen, direct action, and political parties. The Farmers' Alliance, for example, emerged in Texas in the late 1870s as an organization of white farmers, big and small, against industrial and monied interests. The leadership of the Alliance focused on educating the individual farmer and shied away from cooperative action such as crop withholding.

The more militant members of the Alliance who were dissatisfied with the Alliance later moved on to comprise the core of the Populist movement (or the People's Party), which emphasized cooperation. The People's Party posed the strongest challenge to the two-party system in U.S. history. The Populists were successful during 1890s, primarily in the countryside in Kansas and Colorado, where Populist governors were elected. After much debate, Populists chose fusion with the Democrats instead of running their own candidate for the presidential election in 1896. The Democratic candidate William Jennings Bryan lost, and the demise of the Populists began.

Texas Populists continued even in 1898 to garner significant electoral support against Democrats at a time when the People's Party was practically dismantling in all the other southern states. Moreover, Texas Populists were also recruiting black farmers and calling for the need to create unity between industrial workers and farmers. There was a socialist party in the United States at that time, the Socialist Labor Party. However, its contempt for the small farmer had kept even the radical ex-Alliance members and Populists at bay. Politically homeless, many of these militant Populists joined the Socialist Party of America when it was founded in 1901.

Agrarian socialists were extremely sophisticated in their understanding of the agricultural system. This led them to redefine the Socialist Party's position on agricultural issues. Agrarian socialists had also come to be very skeptical of attempts at centralization through their previous organizing experience. Thus, they were committed to conducting Socialist Party's organizational affairs in a democratic and decentralized fashion.

Published by Julius A. Wayland, the socialists' national weekly *Appeal to Reason* was the main link between rural and urban socialists. *Appeal to Reason*'s vision of a cooperative commonwealth appealed to small farmers. Under a cooperative commonwealth, all monopolies, in fact all means of production except for small farms, would be owned and operated by the people. Yeoman farmers would enjoy "fee simple title" to land as long as they did not use it for speculation or the exploitation of hired labor.

What has come to be known as *agrarian socialism* has been the subject of debate among socialists. Many socialists thought that some of the objectives of agrarian socialists clashed with the theoretical underpinnings of Marxism, most importantly when it pertains to land ownership. Many urban socialists envisioned collective farms with increased efficiency and the industrial worker as the backbone of a revolution. As crop prices were falling, farmers were being charged exorbitant interest rates, and more farmers lost their land to big landlords, agrarian socialists were skeptical of any proposal that mimicked what they perceived to be the source of their problems; that is, the concentration of land in fewer and fewer hands.

Agrarian socialism diverged in other important ways from the socialism as understood in prevalent urban centers, such as Chicago and New York City. Agrarian socialists created a synthesis of Marx, Jefferson, and Jesus. Marx offered a relevant analysis of the plight of the oppressed farmer under monopoly capitalism. In many ways, agrarian socialists were Marxists. As they tried to make sense of their place and future in a rapidly industrializing society, many farmers also turned to republican ideals. Specifically, Thomas Jefferson's vision of small yeoman farmers as the backbone of democracy appealed more to the farmer than did collective farms. If Marx and Jefferson provided the economic and political analysis and prescription for a better order, Jesus Christ provided the moral justification for working to achieve that order.

Eugene Debs, Mother Jones, Kate Richards O'Hare, and other inspirational socialist orators toured the country during the height of socialist organizing. These speakers of national fame also attended "socialist encampments" throughout the Plains and the Southwest. Socialist encampments resembled festival-like religious revivals and drew thousands of farmers at a time. Many local agrarian socialists not only used the language of Christianity to deliver the socialist message but also took it seriously. Referring to Jesus as "the carpenter," they evoked his working-class status and attacked usury and greed as non-Christian. Thus, the gospel of socialism was spread in the countryside.

Between 1900 and 1920, socialists were elected to local offices in dozens of cities from Milwaukee, Wisconsin, to Collinsville, Oklahoma. Socialists gained significant support, especially in Texas, Kansas, Louisiana, and Oklahoma. From the standpoint of electoral success, the Socialist Party in Oklahoma was the strongest of all. Oklahoma socialists elected candidates to a variety of state and local-level offices between 1904 and 1920.

By 1916, Oklahoma socialists were strong enough to collect over 64,000 signatures, enough to put the Fair Election Law to a referendum. If enacted, the Fair Election Law would alter the state's political structure. Democratic officials resorted to extreme measures to reverse this extraordinary victory, using their control over the State Election Board and the legislature. In fact, that same year Democrats passed legislation designed to effectively disenfranchise African

Americans and tenant farmers. Importantly, the official stance of the Socialist Party on the so-called Negro question was clear. Whereas the Party rejected economic and political disenfranchisement of African Americans, it did not embrace social equality per se. Integration, even among socialists, was not a universally accepted objective.

As hysteria surrounding World War I encircled the country, the U.S. Congress passed the Espionage and Sedition Acts in 1917 and 1918. The Espionage Act made it a crime to "cause or attempt to cause insubordination, disloyalty, mutiny, or refusal of duty" in the armed forces and was used to prosecute those who opposed the country's involvement in the war. Soon after, the national executive committee of the Socialist Party of America and prominent socialist leaders were on trial for conspiracy. Because of their open opposition to the war, Socialists throughout the country became instant targets of harassment and prosecution by local councils of defense. A surge in the socialist vote came in the 1920 presidential election with Eugene Debs running from his prison cell. Despite this small surge, the destruction of socialist parties in the United States was virtually complete by 1922. Two decades later, agrarian socialism was revived in rural Saskatchewan, Ontario, British Columbia, and Manitoba in Canada by an avowedly socialist party, the Co-operative Commonwealth Federation.

—*Özlem Altıok*

See also Debs, Eugene V.; Populism

Further Readings

Bissett, J. (1999). *Agrarian socialism in America: Marx, Jefferson and Jesus in the Oklahoma countryside 1904–1920.* Norman: University of Oklahoma Press.

Burbank, G. (1976). *When farmers voted red: The gospel of socialism in the Oklahoma countryside, 1910–1924.* Westport, CT: Greenwood Press.

Green, J. (1986). *Grass-roots socialism: Radical movements in the Southwest, 1895–1943.* Baton Rouge: Louisiana State University.

Lipset, S. M. (1968). *Agrarian socialism: The Cooperative Commonwealth Federation in Saskatchewan.* Garden City, NY: Anchor Books.

AIDS Memorial Quilt

The concept of the AIDS memorial quilt was created by gay rights activist Cleve Jones in November 1985. While helping plan the annual candlelight march to honor assassinated gay San Francisco Supervisor Harvey Milk and Mayor George Mascone, Jones decided to recognize San Francisco residents lost to AIDS. He asked each marcher to write on placards names of friends and loved ones who had died of AIDS. After the march, the placards were taped to the walls of the

Nominated for a Nobel Peace Prize in 1989, the quilt is the largest community art project worldwide, representing the ultimate example of art as a tool for activism and social change. As of May 2006, the AIDS Memorial Quilt is composed of more than 5,748 blocks (which are the 12-foot square building blocks seen at displays).

Source: Photo by dbking, Washington, DC.

San Francisco federal building. This wall of names resembled a patchwork quilt.

Motivated by this display, Jones worked with others to plan a larger memorial. The idea was a quilt: a fabric patchwork bearing the names of people lost to AIDS; men, women, and children, remembered by their families and loved ones with a personalized cloth panel. Jones created the first AIDS Memorial Quilt panel in memory of his friend Marvin Feldmen. Jones collaborated with his friend Mike Smith and others in June 1987 to formally organize the Names Project Foundation, which is currently headquartered in Atlanta, Georgia.

The quilt symbol was chosen in a deliberate effort to evoke and recapture the traditional American values that were affected by the AIDS epidemic but that had yet to be applied to it. Public response was immediate as people from other cities most affected by AIDS, such as New York and Los Angeles, sent panels to San Francisco. The inaugural quilt display took place on October 11, 1987, on the National Mall in Washington, D.C., during the National March on Washington for Lesbian and Gay Rights. At that time, the quilt consisted of 1,920 panels and was larger than a football field. After the initial display of the quilt, requests to have the quilt displayed in other locations around the country flooded the organization's office. This was the beginning of the traveling quilt display. The quilt grew as it traveled, for in every city it visited, scores of new panels were added to the collection.

The entire quilt was last displayed in October 1996, when it covered the entire National Mall in Washington, D.C. Each quilt block measures 12 square feet and typically consists of eight separate panels. More than 40,000 colorful panels comprise 5,712 blocks. Currently, 20-plus Names Project chapters exist in the United States with 40 independent AIDS Memorial Quilt affiliates worldwide. Nominated for a Nobel Peace Prize in 1989, the AIDS Memorial Quilt is the largest community art project worldwide, representing the ultimate example of art as a tool for activism and social change.

The Names Project is not a political organization in that the organization takes no position on the various legislative and policy issues surrounding the AIDS epidemic. From its inception, however, the Names Project has sought to have an impact on the political process by helping keep the memory of those lost to the epidemic visible.

—*C. Sheldon Woods*

See also Activism, Social and Political

Further Readings

Brown, J. (Ed.). (1988). *The Names Project: Book of letters.* New York: Avon Books.
Stull, G. (2001). The AIDS Memorial Quilt: Performing memory, piecing action. *American Art, 15*(2), 84–89.

AIR AMERICA RADIO

Although talk radio began in the early part of the 20th century with programs like President Franklin D. Roosevelt's Fireside Chats, it is considered a form of "new media"—media that are not regulated by the traditional media guideline of objectivity but, instead, function to entertain, inform, and persuade listeners to one side versus another. Gallup polls reveal that talk radio grew increasingly more popular with the public during the late part of the 20th century; more radio stations were airing talk radio programming and more listeners were tuning in and contributing to, by and large, extremely conservative discourse. Debuting on March 31, 2004, on five stations, Air America Radio (AAR)—a subsidiary of Progress Media—aimed to offer an alternative to the conservative political talk radio that dominated the airwaves by being the first commercial network to be openly liberal in its outlook.

One of the goals of some of the AAR architects was to offer "formatic purity," which involved producing an entire lineup of shows, not just a program or two, that resonated with nonconservative audiences; audiences that desired programs with the political flavor, but not the staleness, of National Public Radio (NPR); audiences who wanted the entertainment value, but not the right-wing discourse, of popular conservative talk shows like those hosted by Rush

Limbaugh and Bill O'Reilly. Former *Saturday Night Live* writer and regular Al Franken, hired to host a daily 3-hour show, was AAR's biggest name in their lineup. Another former *Saturday Night Live* comedienne and actress, Janeane Garofalo, hosted another show, as did the co-creator of *The Daily Show*, Lizz Winstead, who shared the microphone with rapper Chuck D. Along with these new radio personalities, AAR hired veteran radio personalities Katherine Lanpher of NPR and Randi Rhodes, perhaps the most caustic of all AAR hosts.

Not long after AAR's debut, stories about the network described it as struggling. After only 5 weeks on the air, five of its executives had left. Robert McChesney, known for his critiques of mainstream media, had written—even before the introduction of AAR—that capitalists would not be willing to invest in liberal talk radio programming. In fact, some commentators contended that the network was in disarray because the business of politics, rather than the business of radio, undergirded all of AAR's decisions. To be sure, AAR creators did believe radio could be a vehicle for change in the political landscape and were vocal about their hope that AAR could reinforce Democratic Party efforts to unseat President George W. Bush in the 2004 election.

Of course, AAR did not disrupt George W. Bush's return to the presidency. Some researchers who study the consequences of talk radio would not be surprised, as the effects of talk radio are ambiguous, making it difficult to successfully undermine a campaign via the medium of radio. What talk radio can do, however, is ensure that those who want to talk, laugh, or rant about the political sphere have the outlet to do so.

—*Lori A. Walters-Kramer*

See also Alternative Press

Further Readings

Bachman, K. (2004, May 24). Local media: Still breathing. *Mediaweek*. Retrieved January 24, 2006, from LexisNexis Academic database.

Barker, D. C. (2002). *Rushed to judgment: Talk radio, persuasion, and American political behavior*. New York: Columbia University Press.

McChesney, R. W. (2004). *The problem of the media: U.S. communication politics in the 21st century*. New York: Monthly Review Press.

Moy, P., & Pfau, M. (2000). *With malice toward all? The media and public confidence in democratic institutions*. Westport, CT: Praeger.

Starr, P. (2004, March). Reclaiming the air. *The American Prospect*, p. 57. Retrieved January 24, 2006, from LexisNexis Academic database.

Steinberg, J. (2004, April 2). Liberal voices get a new outlet: Air America aims to counter right's talk-radio dominance. *New York Times*, p. 5. Retrieved January 24, 2006, from LexisNexis Academic database.

AL-BANNA, HASAN (1906–1949)

Hasan al-Banna was the founder of the most influential Islamic revival movement of the 20th century, the Association of Muslim Brothers (*al-Ikhwan al-Muslimun*). Al-Banna was born in Egypt in 1906. He received basic Islamic education in Isma'liyyah and memorized the Qur'an at an early age. His fervor for Islamic spirituality led him to join Hasafiyyah, a Sufi order. After high school, he received training as a teacher at Dar al-Ulum. There he sharpened his organizational skills and became a teacher. As he grew up, he was disturbed by how Muslims were treated by the foreign occupiers of Egypt and decided to change the situation. He encouraged Muslims to regain their lost glory. He preached vigorously and affirmed to his listeners that they could free their country from all foreign occupation by adhering to Islam and practicing it in their daily life. Eventually, he won enough followers to form the movement of the Muslim Brothers in 1928, whose goal was to establish an Islamic State.

Al-Banna was very clear about his objectives and how to achieve them. His goals were to produce a Muslim individual, a Muslim family, a Muslim community, and an Islamic state where Islam would govern the society in all aspects of life. He then designed programs and sets goals to attain these objectives. His treatise, the 20 principles (*al-usul al-'ishrun*), demonstrates how to develop an individual practicing

Muslim. To al-Banna, Muslims should emulate the prophet Muhammad in their daily live.

To create both a Muslim family and society, al-Banna pleaded for Muslim unity and support for one another socially, by creating a healthy environment for all Muslims. Through their networking, the Muslim Brothers established schools, created businesses and jobs, and encouraged education to eliminate poverty. By 1935, the movement spread across Arabia and into other Muslim countries.

Al-Banna wrote books on jihad, Qur'anic interpretation, and instructional pamphlets to illustrate his views and opinions about his new understanding of Islam. He borrowed from Jamal Din al-Afghani, Muhammad Abduh, and Rashid Rida's ideas of reformation and expanded on them. He was able to win many members, including many women, to his movement. Al-Banna was an eloquent speaker, an ardent preacher, a kind and caring teacher, a visionary leader, and a focused reformer. He never deviated from his plans, yet he was wise enough to adjust his programs, accept criticism, and make necessary modifications as the situation dictated.

Toward the end of his life, al-Banna clashed with the Egyptian government, especially after the assassination of the Egyptian prime minister, al-Nukrashi, in 1948. Al-Banna was assassinated by the Egyptian government in 1949. Whereas many movements die with the death of their founders, the Muslim Brothers have had more success since al-Banna's death. His ideas remain extremely influential throughout the Muslim world, as many Muslims wholeheartedly embrace his ideology.

—*Yushau Sodiq*

See also Anti-Colonial Movements, Middle East and North Africa; Religious Activism; Spirituality and Peacemaking

Further Readings

al-Banna, H. (1978). *Five tracts of Hasan al-Banna* (C. Wendell, Trans.). Berkeley: University of California Press.

Kepel, G. (2002). *Jihad: The trail of political Islam* (A. F. Roberts, Trans). Cambridge, MA: Harvard University Press. (Original work published 2000)

Mitchell, R. (1969). *The society of the Muslim Brothers.* London: Oxford University Press.

Shalabi, R. S. (1978). *Hasan al-Banna Wa Madrasatuhu al-Ikhwan al-Muslimun* [Hasan al-Banna and his school: The Muslim Brotherhood.]. Cairo: Al-Ansar Press.

ALBIZU CAMPOS, PEDRO (1891–1965)

Dr. Pedro Albizu Campos is considered the most renowned Puerto Rican patriot of the 20th century. He was a fierce advocate for the reclamation of Puerto Rico's culture, language, identity, and flag from colonial rule. The son of an ex-slave and a Spanish landowner, he was born in Ponce on September 12, 1891. During his lifetime, Albizu Campos experienced colonialism under the rule of both Spain and the United States. This lived history of colonized impoverishment and brutality profoundly influenced his uncompromising position in the struggle for Puerto Rican independence and anti-colonial struggle in the Caribbean Antilles.

A highly intelligent man, Albizu Campos was awarded several scholarships to study in the United States and became the first Puerto Rican to graduate from Harvard, with degrees in chemical engineering, military sciences, and law. A deeply sensitive and committed man, Albizu Campos matured in his understanding of U.S. racism and its damaging impact during his military service in an African American unit during World War I. Fluent in a variety of languages, Albizu Campos was offered several lucrative official posts with the U.S. government. He rejected these offers, choosing instead to return to Puerto Rico and unite with his compatriots in the fight against U.S. colonialism.

On his return in 1921, Albizu Campos became active in the burgeoning independence movement. With his impassioned oratory style, he quickly became a leading force within the Puerto Rican Nationalist Party. In 1927, as vice president of the party, he conducted diplomatic visits to the Dominican Republic, Haiti, Cuba, Mexico, Panama, Peru, and Venezuela, in an effort to raise consciousness regarding the colonial atrocities in Puerto Rico and garner support for a unified anti-colonial struggle. Elected party president in 1930, Albizu Campos initiated a massive political organizing and education campaign for Puerto Rican self-determination.

By 1932, the nationalist campaign for a free Puerto Rico, unable to make headway into the formal political system of the island or contend with increasing police repression, advocated violent revolution. This led to a series of dramatic confrontations with island authorities during the next 6 years, resulting in the death of insular police chief E. Francis Riggs in 1936 and the bloody Ponce Massacre of March 21, 1937. In response, the leadership of the Nationalist Party was arrested and charged for seditious conspiracy to overthrow the government. Despite court appeals, Albizu Campos and his compatriots were sent to the federal penitentiary in Atlanta, Georgia, until 1947, beginning a 25-year period spent mostly in prison.

On their return, the battle for Puerto Rican independence was reignited in the hopes of disrupting the proposed plan to grant Puerto Rico commonwealth status. Albizu Campos, along with 3,000 independence supporters, were arrested after the revolt of 1950, in which Puerto Rican nationalists staged the Jayuya Uprising, as well as attacks on the Puerto Rican governor's mansion and the Blair House, where U.S. president Truman was staying during renovations of the White House. In 1951, Albizu Campos was arrested and sentenced to an 80-year term in prison. He received a pardon in 1953 from Governor Luis Muñoz Marin. However, the pardon was rebuked a year later following the 1954 attack on the U.S. House of Representatives by Lolita Lebrón, Irving Flores Andrés Figueroa Cordero, and Rafael Cancel Miranda, an action staged to attract the world's attention to U.S. military occupation of Puerto Rico.

While in prison, Albizu Campos's health began to deteriorate, and he suffered a stroke in 1956. He alleged that he was poisoned with radiation, a practice confirmed in 1994 by the U.S. Department of Energy, which disclosed that human radiation experimentation was, in fact, conducted on prisoners without their consent. Pardoned, once more, by Governor Luis Muñoz Marin in 1964, Albizu Campos died on April 21, 1965, never to see his dream of a free Puerto Rico realized. Nevertheless, for many, Dr. Pedro Albizu Campos, *el maestro,* is considered the first great theorist of the anti-colonial struggle in the Caribbean.

—*Antonia Darder*

See also Anti-Imperialism; Lebrón, Lolita

Further Readings

Corretjer, J. A. (1991). *Albizu Campos* (2nd ed.). Chicago: Editorial El Coqui.

Rodríguez Cruz, J. (1994). *Pedro Albizu Campos: Un asomo a su vida y su época* [Pedro Albizu Campos: A portrayal of his life and times]. San Juan, Puerto Rico: Centro de Estudios Graduados de Puerto Rico y el Caribe.

Vasallo, R., & Torres Martinó, J. A. (1990). *Pedro Albizu Campos: Reflexiones sobre su vida y su obra* [Pedro Albizu Campos: Reflections on his life and his work]. San Juan, Puerto Rico: Editorial Marién.

ALGEBRA PROJECT

This is the name of a curriculum for mathematics education born out of indignation for the apathy commonly found in schools of the inner city and rural areas. Robert P. Moses, a veteran of the civil rights struggles of the late 1960s, is the originator of this program. For this work, he drew on experiences helping the black community of Mississippi seek political power through the vote. In the South, he had discovered that gaining political power was not a simple matter of urging people to vote. There was a series of interrelated questions that had to be addressed: What is the vote for? Why do we want it in the first place? What must we do to ensure that it will work for us and will benefit our community? Answers to these questions resulted in important political consciousness building and to the formation of the Mississippi Freedom Democratic Party.

In 1982, Moses found that a similar set of questions needed to be answered with respect to mathematics and students failing this subject. Moses, by then a celebrated mathematics educator and a

MacArthur Fellow at the time, volunteered to help at a school in Massachusetts where large numbers of students were failing algebra. Moses, now a parent-organizer, approached the challenge of improving mathematics learning by posing, to the school staff and the parents, an initial set of questions (What is algebra for? Why do we want children to study it?), followed by the broad political questions, What does success in mathematics gain for you and your children? What does failure in mathematics deny you and your children? Once the relationship between success in mathematics and access to college was made, establishment of the content followed, along with the instructional approach of the mathematics program. Parent involvement and self-determination on the part of the students are important factors in the curriculum. The initial goal was that middle school students be engaged personally in the process of learning mathematics that would provide access to college preparatory courses in high school. The Algebra Project has since evolved to include courses in high school.

The political consciousness of individual parents, students, and teachers plays a key role in the Algebra Project. There are still many schools where inner-city and rural students are not expected to succeed. Moses accuses these schools of offering a sharecroppers' curriculum, where students are being prepared only to work for others and at minimum wage. The Algebra Project demands that mathematical literacy be accessible to all students, joining the traditional skills of reading and writing commonly associated with the term *literacy*. The struggle for citizenship and equality includes mathematical literacy, the Algebra Project asserts.

The Algebra Project's curriculum is interactive, calling for students to use their physical surroundings as references to mathematical ideas. The process can be summed up as having five steps: (1) Students experience an event, such as a field trip, followed by (2) creating a model or a picture of the event and then (3) writing about that event in an informal and creative manner. The language used to (4) describe the event is then formalized to accurately depict the activity. The last step is (5) the development of a symbolic representation of the event using mathematical

concepts. The Algebra Project is being implemented in several urban and rural school districts in the United States, with high levels of success.

—*Concepción M. Valadez*

See also Moses, Robert

Further Readings

Moses, R. P. (1994). Remarks on the struggle for citizenship and math/science literacy. *Journal of Mathematical Behavior, 13,* 107–111.

North Central Regional Education Laboratory. (1991). *Schools that work: The research advantage* [Video series]. *Videoconference 2: Children as problem solvers.* Naperville, IL: Author.

ALI, MUHAMMAD (1942–)

A well-known athlete, Muhammad Ali (Cassius Clay) has enjoyed fame for the past 45 years. He himself recognizes that and calls himself "the greatest." Ali was born on January 17, 1942, in Louisville, Kentucky. He began his training as a boxer at age 12. By age 18, he had won many local titles. He won a gold medal in lightweight championship in the Rome Olympics in 1960. On his return, he vowed to reach the top, the world heavyweight championship.

Ali engaged in 61 national and international bouts (fights), winning 56 of them. He challenged all of the heavyweight champions of his time and won all of those fights. He was a self-disciplined boxer who took charge of his own affairs and invented his own styles of boxing. He became a heavyweight champion three times: in the years 1964–1967, 1974–1978, and 1978–1979. At the height of his glory, he converted to Islam and joined the Nation of Islam, led by Elijah Muhammad. His conversion caused him many problems. In the late 1960s, when he refused to be inducted into the U.S. Army because he opposed the Vietnam War, he was sentenced to 5 years imprisonment, and all his boxing licenses were suspended. He appealed the court order, won his freedom back after 3 years, and resumed his boxing career. Ali remains a loyal follower of Elijah Muhammad and a devout Muslim even today.

Ali retired from boxing in 1981 after 2 decades of boxing. Even though he was diagnosed with Parkinson's disease in 1984, he did not withdraw into the disease. Rather, he became an activist and a promoter of peace. He spends his time and wealth assisting others in achieving their goals and reaching their potential. He established several charitable organizations, which have provided more than 232 million meals to the hungry in Africa and Asia. Ali has won many local, national, and international awards, including the Presidential Medal of Freedom Award, given to him by President George W. Bush in 2005; the Greatest Athlete of the 20th century, awarded by the BBC in London and *USA Today;* and the United Nations Messenger of Peace.

Ali is well known throughout the world. After his retirement, he engaged in civil activities and established a civic center in 2005: the Muhammad Ali Center in Louisville, Kentucky. The center serves as an international educational and cultural institute, which promotes respect, hope, and understanding. Ali continues to inspire adults and children to be as great as they can be. His contributions to the world peace and relief efforts are enormous. He lit the Olympic Cauldron during the Olympic Games opening ceremonies in Atlanta, Georgia, in 1996.

Muhammad Ali is married and has a number of children. Although Parkinson's disease prevents him from public speaking, he attends many functions and continues to serve humanity through his generosity, thoughts, and encouragement.

—Yushau Sodiq

See also Conscientious Objectors to War; Nation of Islam

Further Readings

Burchard, M. (1975). *Muhammad Ali.* New York: Putnam.

Garrett, L. (2002). *The story of Muhammad Ali.* New York: DK.

Myers, W. D. (2001). *The greatest: Muhammad Ali.* New York: Scholastic Press.

ALINSKY, SAUL (1909–1972)

Saul Alinsky was known as a great social activist, organizer, and iconoclast. He perfected the practice of grassroots organizing. On his death, he was referred to by one newspaper columnist as someone who had antagonized more people than anyone else in America. But his influence remains strong, and his legacy of activism remains as the gritty road toward confrontation, conflict, compromise, and change that characterized his life and his work.

Saul Alinsky was born to Russian, orthodox Jewish parents on Chicago's Maxwell Street, an area of high density of Jewish immigrants, where his father, Benjamin, was a tailor. The family later moved to a more middle-class section where young Saul grew up. Despite the youth of his mother (she was 17 when he was born), Sarah Alinsky was the driving force behind her son. She had the reputation among those who knew her as a troublemaker. Her son would learn her style well.

Alinsky did reasonably well in school, despite having sustained a hip injury playing football with friends; the injury left him immobilized for a year. During his recuperation, he began to read extensively, a habit he carried throughout his life. In the fall of 1926, Saul Alinsky entered the University of Chicago. He did not fare well academically, ending up on probation at the end of his first year. Also, he had a reputation of being a loner. His biographer, Sanford Horwitt, indicates that Alinsky did not lack social skills; he was just not an organization person.

Saul Alinsky did not take a liking to academic life until he enrolled in the University of Chicago's sociology department, considered by many to be one of the finest in the nation. The Chicago sociological faculty had developed the perspective that crime, disease, and urban blight were caused by social disorganization and not heredity. The slum itself was the cause of a breakdown in the social order. Alinsky began to do fieldwork in the city's life, first studying dance halls where he learned the role of participant-observer. Later, in graduate work, he would begin a study of crime and juvenile delinquency. He tried law school, but lasted only two quarters. He pursued a Ph.D. but lacked some of the core courses. Alinsky preferred to learn his lessons on the street. He developed friendships with some of Chicago's more notorious crime figures, such as Frank Nitti. He also began working on Chicago's West Side with street gangs through the Institute for Juvenile Research. Alinsky worked with the Sholto Street gang for more than 10 years. He won their friendship and respect, and he convinced them to write accounts of their gang's exploits. Alinsky also did research and work at Illinois' famous Joliet Prison for 3 years.

Alinsky was assigned through the Chicago sociology department's research to work in the infamous Back of the Yards, the huge urban slum that included the stockyards and the sights and smells of animal death and decay that dominated this area of the city. It was also during this time that the Congress of Industrial Organizations (CIO) was involved in organizing the meatpacking industry under the leadership of the charismatic John L. Lewis. Lewis's main man in the Back of the Yards was Herb March. March and Alinsky formed a friendship. Alinsky impressed March with his nondoctrinaire approach to organizing. Alinsky avoided labels and overtly political extremes because, pragmatically, he believed it hampered good organizing work and the art of compromise.

Alinsky began to work to bring unity to the Back of the Yards, a task made difficult because the area was balkanized by nationalities, and even within these nationalities there were divisions. The intellectual idea behind Alinsky's work was to identify the indigenous leaders within the Back of the Yards and work with them to create a community-wide action group. Although this technique had worked in homogeneous areas in past work, it had never been tried before with widely disparate, ethnic and religious groups. This was the great challenge to organizing community action in the Back of the Yards. The key to grassroots organizing within this environment was the churches, most of which were Catholic and served various nationalities. In his organizing efforts, Alinsky made contact with Chicago's auxiliary Catholic bishop, Bernard Sheil. Subsequently, he brought Sheil and

John L. Lewis together on the same platform, an event that had national implications for unionism and the Back of the Yards Neighborhood Council (BYNC).

Alinsky worked the community with other key players to develop a budget. He worked every angle to empower the BYNC financially and politically. In the organizing efforts, Alinsky's connection to the sociology department at the University of Chicago finally ended. Alternative support was made possible through Bishop Sheil and a connection to magnate Marshall Field. Field established a foundation to support the fledging BYNC. It was called the Industrial Areas Foundation.

Alinsky evolved a kind of credo for his work. First, to be a "citizen" meant that one had to participate in the community. It meant activism. It meant that people had to question decisions made elsewhere by "authorities," and it meant being involved in larger events outside the community. It also involved learning the processes of functional democracy, such as engaging in debate, constructing bylaws and regulations, electing representatives, and working to focus their actions on important targets for concerned action to change things.

The success of the BYNC threatened the professional social work establishment and the existing Chicago political machine. The latter barrier was the more formidable one. Alinsky and his backers wanted independence in the Back of the Yards. The political machine feared such independence. And it feared bringing together the disparate ethnic neighborhoods over a common agenda. The political machine ran on continued ethnic suspicions and hatreds. The loss of these divisions was a political threat. What ensued was a political battle for control fought out in the city's newspapers, the Chicago machine using the *Chicago Tribune* and the BYNC the *Chicago Sun.* After a period of jousting and muscle flexing, both sides agreed to compromise. What was important was that the BYNC had been able to battle the city's infamous political machine to a draw.

As Saul Alinsky's fame grew and his work with the BYNC expanded, he wrote *Reveille for Radicals*, published in 1946. This work endures to this day and is still read by radicals the world over. In the book,

Alinsky spurned liberals as talkers but not activists. It was only through becoming an activist that social justice would actually happen, and that required the use of power. In the chapter in this book about defining a radical, Alinsky said that a radical believed completely in *real* equality of opportunity for all peoples, regardless of race, color, or creed. Alinsky also asserted that radicals should and would fight privilege and power, no matter what their source. A radical would fight any clustering of power, which is hostile to a broad, popular democracy. *Reveille for Radicals* astounded the experts by making the *New York Times* bestseller list, an anomaly for a book published by a university press. On the personal side, the second edition of the book, published in 1969, bore the inscription, "To the memory of Helene," a remembrance of the loss of his wife to a tragic drowning incident in Lake Michigan in 1947.

In 1948, Alinsky began a biography of his hero, John L. Lewis. Although Alinsky professed independence from his subject, the work was largely very sympathetic to the labor leader, and critics charged he left out of the book some of the more unflattering moments in Lewis's career.

Alinsky worked on community organizing in California with Fred Ross, and in 1952, he remarried a New York divorcée named Jean Graham. Alinsky also was able to secure funding for his work from the Schwarzhaupt Foundation, a very large grant that enabled him to continue working in California with Fred Ross and a newly emerging community organizer named César Chávez.

Perhaps Saul Alinsky's most stellar work was his utilization of techniques that attacked racial segregation in Chicago, a city called the most segregated city in the North.

Alinsky's strategy was to organize an African American community organization that would be considered powerful. To this end, he turned his attention to Woodlawn and its various problems. Alinsky believed that economic or social justice was not possible without power, and power came from two sources: organized people and money. Alinsky had no sympathy for the "do-gooders" who thought progress could be obtained through Christian love, and he abhorred professional social workers because they were not activists.

Alinsky taught that change occurred when one agitated to the point of conflict. Conflict produced the crucible in which organized power could be applied to provide the leverage for social change. Alinsky believed that people had to experience coming into their own sense of authority and apply power in social situations. He wrote in his book *Rules for Radicals* that change meant movement and that movement invariably created friction. To this end, Alinsky worked in creating a black community organization that would push for the integration of Chicago. The result was the Temporary Woodlawn Organization, later renamed the Woodlawn Organization (TWO).

After much organizing, based on tried and true Alinsky organizational techniques, the TWO began a caravan of 46 buses with more than 2,500 African Americans on their way to city hall to register to vote. This was only the beginning. One of the overriding issues in Woodlawn was the overcrowded, segregated schools. Chicago maintained a segregated school system. With Alinsky's proven grassroots strategies, his penchant for creating tension, and a flair for the dramatic, the TWO began social activism to force the issue of overcrowding based on race into the public arena.

The campaign began with 300 TWO supporters appearing at a board meeting. One hundred fifty crowded into the boardroom while the rest marched outside. When the school board president refused to accommodate requests for some to testify, the supporters marched out. A week later they were back, only this time they wanted the resignation of the city's school superintendent, Benjamin Willis. Willis had consistently denied that there was any evidence that the schools were deliberately segregated.

One of Saul Alinsky's rules for change was that an enemy had to be created by which political power would become polarized. It was polarization that created the lynchpin for action. In his 13th rule in *Rules for Radicals,* Alinsky had urged that in social action one had to pick a target, focus on it (or freeze it), personalize it, and polarize it. This tactic is necessary because in a complex society, it is hard to attach blame to any one person because many are part of the problem. But for an opposition group, such complexities can reduce or dilute the consequences of their collective actions. In the case of the segregation of Chicago's schools, TWO picked on the school superintendent, Benjamin Willis.

TWO held its own inquiry about school conditions in a local hotel. It brought in several teachers to testify about the conditions in the schools, but they put sheets over themselves to protect their identities. TWO supporters dressed in black capes to symbolize a "death watch" over the fate of African American children. African American mothers barged into all-white schools with cameras to take pictures of the empty classrooms in the buildings. These "truth squad mothers" were arrested for trespassing, but they caused moral terror for school administrators. In polarizing the school desegregation fight, Alinsky resorted to his fourth rule in *Rules for Radicals;* that is, use ridicule. Calling it man's most potent weapon because it was nearly impossible to counterattack and it infuriated the enemy who had to concede your advantage in conflict, Alinsky called the school system's use of portable classrooms on wheels at overcrowded schools, "Willis Wagons." TWO also organized a school boycott of a targeted elementary school. On May 18, 1962, at Carnegie Elementary School, nearly 1,200 out of 1,350 students stayed out of school. The successful 1-day boycott was widely publicized in Chicago's press.

Alinsky's work in Chicago brought him fame. He was called on to help other communities around the nation in their community activism. He responded to an invitation to assist the organization of the African American community in Rochester, New York, in which he penned one of his most famous barbs of ridicule: that the only thing Eastman Kodak ever did to improve race relations in Rochester was to invent color film. In describing his work for a popular magazine of the day, Alinsky described his tactics as a kind of mass jujitsu in which the tactics of the politically powerful were turned against them by provoking a response from those in power. Although Rochester was judged a success in community organizing for Saul Alinsky's group, rising black nationalism began to distrust all white leaders who were out to help them. black power required black leadership. Rochester was the last

African American community assisted by Saul Alinsky to organize for political purposes.

In the late 1960s, Saul Alinsky became a national icon. But he found himself at odds with leaders of the New Left. In his mind, they failed to understand that the acquisition of power was about social change and that one had to work inside the system, not engage in efforts to blow it up. The voices of the New Left eschewed authority and hierarchy and wanted to identify with the poor. Alinsky's approach was structured, centralized, and required strong leadership. When some of the New Left groups turned violent, Alinsky was unsparingly scathing in his remarks about them, saying that they should be getting paid by the extreme right for their actions. Alinsky's last book, *Rules for Radicals,* was criticized by New Left writers as devoid of any vision of the good society. It was a question of ends and means to which Alinsky had long answered. Such criticism hinged on the notion that Saul Alinsky had no ideology to his methods. In *Rules for Radicals,* he unequivocally rejected any ideology when he asserted that he hated and feared dogma in any form. To the criticisms of the New Left writers who accused him of not stating his vision for the future, Alinsky responded that such moralists were committed to a kind of mystical objectivity where human passion was suspect. Then, in his patented style of ridicule that was part and parcel of his approach to politics and power, Alinsky indicated that such means-and-ends moralists were non-doers and always wound up on their ends without any means.

Saul Alinsky died of a heart attack on June 12, 1972, while standing on a street corner in Carmel, California. One of his eulogists portrayed him as a cactus pear, prickly on the outside but sweet on the inside. However he is characterized, his life's work and writings continue to serve as inspiration for those interested in social change.

—Fenwick W. English

See also Civil Disobedience; Civil Rights Movement; Coalition Building; Community Action Program; Community Organizing; Direct Action; Dissent; Labor Culture; Political Humor; Political Satire; Professional Activist Organizations; Religious Activism

Further Readings

Alinsky, S. (1969). *Reveille for radicals* (2nd ed.). New York: Vintage Books. (Original work published 1946)

Alinsky, S. (1971). *Rules for radicals.* New York: Vintage Books.

Horwitt, S. (1989). *Let them call me rebel: Saul Alinsky, his life and legacy.* New York: Knopf.

ALLENDE, SALVADOR (1908–1973)

Salvador Allende Gossens was president of Chile from November 4, 1970, until September 11, 1973. On that day, a military coup d'état led by General Augusto Pinochet stormed the La Moneda presidential palace. The coup resulted in the dissolution of the Socialist government and in Allende's death. Augusto Pinochet's subsequent 17-year rule as leader of the military junta was responsible for a climate of political oppression that saw the death or "disappearance" of opposition members and revolutionary activists. Allende now stands as one of Chile's most notable historical figures and has become a controversial sociopolitical icon, both in Chile and throughout Latin America, with a legacy variously hailed and reviled.

Though he would spend most of his early formative years in the port city of Valparaíso, he was born June 26, 1908, in the Chilean capital of Santiago, son to Salvador Allende Castro, a lawyer and notary, and Laura Gossens Uribe, an accountant. He married Hortensia Bussi in 1940, with whom he had three daughters, Laura, María Isabel, and Beatriz. His grandfather, Ramón Allende Padín, founded Chile's first secular school in 1871, was a congressional representative for the *Partido Radical* (Radical Party), and was Grand Master of Chile's Masonic Order. Allende attended primary school in the desert north of Chile, in Tacna, where he witnessed the plight of copper mine laborers as they struggled against conditions of indentured servitude. Allende's formative years, spent as a member of a radical political family,

thus played an important role in fostering the concerns for social justice and economic equality that would shape his life and undergird his political career.

Allende became a medical student in 1926, eventually earning his degree as a surgeon. His doctoral thesis was titled *Higiene Mental y Delincuencia* (Mental Hygiene and Delinquency). During the course of his university years, he became president of the Students' Center of the School of Medicine at the Universidad de Chile. Allende was arrested several times as a result of his vocal opposition to the dictatorship of General Carlos Ibañez. In 1933, he cofounded the Chilean Socialist Party, which adhered to Marxist thought but wanted to distance itself from the Soviet-influenced Communist Party. In 1937, he was elected to be a deputy in Chile's National Legislature as member and leader of the *Frente Popular* (Popular Front). In 1939, then President Pedro Aguirre Cerda appointed him to be Minister of Health. He became a senator in 1945 and eventually became its president, a post he would maintain until he was successfully elected, after a few failed attempts, to become president of Chile.

He was elected president of Chile in 1970, on a Socialist platform that touted "*La vía chilena al socialismo*" ("the Chilean way to socialism"). He is known to have been a somewhat charismatic speaker who was well liked and revered by a significant portion of Chile's population, especially those who resonated strongly with his vision of social and economic reform. His program of reform included nationalizing large-scale industries (notably copper mining and banking), reorganizing the health care system, retooling the educational system, and furthering his predecessor Eduardo Frei Montalva's agrarian reform (wherein land was seized from wealthy owners and subsequently redistributed), among others.

Allende is the first Marxist ever to have gained power in a free election. However, although he was democratically elected by Chile's population, his presidency rather quickly met with strong opposition both within and outside of the country. His ties to socialism and communism and, especially, his cultivated relationship with Fidel Castro and Cuba (he also renewed diplomatic relations with the U.S.S.R., China, and East Germany) were met with unease by both the U.S. government and U.S. corporate and economic interests, who were concerned that Allende's program of social reform and industry nationalization might spread to other countries. Throughout Latin America, conditions of great social, political, and economic disparity made Socialist programs such as Allende's attractive to large masses of marginalized and disenfranchised people.

Though he would later deny that the plans were ever implemented, Henry Kissinger, then secretary of state under U.S. president Richard Nixon, has admitted that he was instructed to organize a coup against Allende and his Socialist government. Declassified Central Intelligence Agency (CIA) documents have subsequently documented, however, that the U.S. government and other interested parties, through both official and unofficial operations, played a role in undermining the success of Allende's programs of reform in Chile and, eventually, in supporting Allende's ousting at the hands of Pinochet's military coup.

Salvador Allende's legacy several decades after his death is one characterized by controversy and conflicting versions of history. His time as president of Chile saw both the cultivation of hope for long-needed social and economic reform and the sometimes harsh realities of their failure to come to their fullest fruition. Allende's lack of success as a president and social reformer is mitigated, however, by the uneasy and complicated truths of U.S. involvement in and efforts at undermining his government's efficacy as an agent of social justice. Nevertheless, Allende enjoyed (and continues to enjoy) a significant amount of support and affection from a substantial portion of Chile's population. His figure, in the years since General Augusto Pinochet stepped down from power in 1990, has steadily gained visibility as a cultural and political icon, not unlike the figure of his personal friend, Ernesto "Che" Guevara.

—Jnan Ananda Blau

See also CIA Repression of Social Movements; Communism; Guevara, Che; Marxist Theory; Socialism

Further Readings

Alegria, F. (1993). *Allende: A novel* (F. Janney, Trans.). Palo Alto, CA: Stanford University Press.

Allende, S. (2000). *Salvador Allende reader: Chile's voice of democracy* (J. D. Cockroft, Ed.). New York: Ocean.

Garretón, M. A. (2003). *Incomplete democracy: Political democratization in Chile and Latin America* (R. K. Washbourne & G. Horvath, Trans.). Chapel Hill: University of North Carolina Press.

Haslam, J. (2005). *The Nixon administration and the death of Allende's Chile: A case of assisted suicide.* New York: Verso.

Kaufman, E. (1988). *Crisis in Allende's Chile: New perspectives.* Westport, CT: Greenwood Press.

Salvador Allende Gossens. Retrieved February 13, 2006, from *Archivos Internet Salvador Allende:* http://www .salvador-allende.cl

ALTERNATIVE BOOKSTORES

Serving communities that are not always represented by the larger book industry, alternative bookstores have been key to disseminating information not found in more traditional media outlets. Though specialty bookstores have always existed to cater to specific communities of readers, and political publishers of every stripe have long had their own bookselling outlets, it was the postwar burgeoning of political activity combined with the mores of the modern book industry that provided an opening for the massive proliferation of "alternative" bookshops around the world.

Before World War II, publishers printed mostly hardcover editions; only a small number of paperbacks were printed, and these were commonly thought of as disposable, subpar books. The shortages of World War II and the high cost of paper made it both expedient and patriotic for publishers to print and consumers to purchase more paperback titles. This confluence meant that cheaper editions of scholarly and literary titles became available to a larger number of people, revolutionizing an industry that had previously preferred to publish in hardcover only, and reducing the stigma of the paperback book, though most stores were still somewhat reluctant to carry them. In addition, a new breed of literature began to take shape, rebelling against the mores of conventional society in the 1950s. New bookstores began to spring up, aided in part by the rise in new means of distribution and production and a public hungry for these and other authors not regularly carried in most bookstores. Lawrence Ferlinghetti's City Lights in San Francisco began, in part, to cater to this new audience. In 1953, it became the first paperback-only bookstore and would continue on as a nexus of cultural and political activity for decades afterward.

In the 1960s and 1970s, as social justice movements and these fledgling literary movements began to intrigue a larger reading audience, there were still few outlets available to carry their most basic tracts. Many bookstores evolved to fill this gap. Most were fly-by-night shops that lasted only a few years, offering literature and a space for progressive and radical communities to share ideas and organize. Conceived more as contributions to culture or a cause rather than strictly commercial enterprises, many of these shops functioned as salons where customers were encouraged to linger and read. The Hungry Mind Bookstore in St. Paul, Minnesota, and Left Bank Books in St. Louis, Missouri, both steeped in the anti-war movement, were among the longest lasting. Coming out of the civil rights struggle of the 1960s, Oakland, California's Marcus Books was among the first African American bookstores in the United States and became a meeting place for the Black Power struggles of the late 1960s and 1970s. A Different Light Bookstore in San Francisco and Amazon Bookstore Cooperative in Minneapolis were crucial in informing the growing gay liberation movement. A Room of One's Own in Madison, Wisconsin, and Women and Children First Bookstore in Chicago helped galvanize the feminist movement of the 1970s and inspired kindred booksellers across the world. The creation of these and many other stores, in turn, stimulated publishers to release more books on progressive issues and provided new authors with sympathetic readers.

By the 1990s, a new model of the bookstore began to take shape: the corporate chain store. Drawing on many of the innovations of independent bookstores—the in-store café, the reading room, newsletter, and

so forth—many of these chain bookstores began aggressive campaigns, using their muscle and momentum to shut down competition from alternative and independent bookstores alike. As chain stores began to proliferate, they demanded deeper discounts for their purchases from publishers and were then able to sell the books at heavily discounted prices. Many opened stores in close proximity to long-standing independent booksellers in direct competition. Their larger reserves of cash allowed them to continue offering books at ridiculously discounted prices long enough to put nearby competitors out of business. The advent of online book vendors made it all the more difficult for independent bookstores to operate. By the end of the decade, nearly two thirds of independent bookstores had closed. Membership in the American Booksellers Association—the trade organization representing booksellers—had declined by half of what it had been a decade before.

Despite the odds, alternative bookstores continue to provide a curatorial role for their readers, offering literature that would otherwise go unstocked and unnoticed at the larger corporate bookstores. Most provide their communities throughout the world with a quiet space to read and a place to meet.

—Eric Zassenhaus

See also Alternative Press; Literature and Activism

Further Readings

Buzbee, L. (2006). *The yellow-lighted bookshop.* St. Paul, MN: Graywolf Press.
Laties, A. (2005). *Rebel bookseller.* New York: Vox Pop.
Schiffrin, A. (2000). *The business of books.* New York: Verso.

ALTERNATIVE HEALTH

The term *alternative health* is a general phrase used to describe any preventative, diagnostic, or healing medical practices, procedures, systems of thinking, or lifestyle choices that do not fit into the traditional idea of allopathic, or traditional, medicine and have often not been proven effective through traditional scientific medical studies. Although the movement is considered new and even misguided or dangerous by some individuals, conventional health practitioners, health insurance companies, and pharmaceutical companies, many of the ideas that fall under this umbrella term are influenced by, or directly descended from, ancient medical practices from all over the globe.

The latest wave of alternative health interest came in the 1970s, possibly as a result of growing dissatisfaction with conventional medical care. Currently, health care professionals hold a variety of opinions and condone alternative health practices to varying degrees. These opinions can affect the cost and availability of treatment. Due to this and other factors, sometimes alternative health practices are implemented as complementary medicine. *Complementary medicine* is a term that refers to any alternative health practice used in conjunction with conventional medical practices, as opposed to in place of them.

Some give alternative health no credence based on the fact that it is not often tested in the same scientifically rigorous manner as more conventional practices. Even in the cases where data have been collected, it is all too often evidence that demonstrates a correlation between treatment and recovery or prevention, not a clear cause-and-effect relationship. Because of the stigma attached to some of these practices, people may even participate without admitting so to their conventional health care professionals. Because some alternative health practices are linked to spirituality, people may also make the decision to participate in them secretly, or choose not to participate at all, based on their existing spiritual beliefs.

Still others have completely abandoned traditional medicine in favor of these practices and report positive results treating everything from anxiety to cancer. It is up for argument how much the placebo effect may be in play, and also how much that matters, if the end result is an end to symptoms and good health. In other words, whether it is the practice itself or the belief that the practice will work, if a health condition is prevented or successfully treated, then the alternative health practice is likely to receive further attention.

One major area of concern is self-prescribing of alternative health practices without the supervision of a health care professional, which, like the casual or misinformed utilization of any medical treatment or practice, can result in injury or even death. People may, for instance, utilize herbal remedies without informing their primary physicians, because they are not aware of possible interactions with other prescription drugs.

Alternative health practices often focus on the connection between the body and the mind and take a holistic approach to treatment, with the aim of achieving a balance of some sort. The terminology in this field is used loosely, and often there is more than one term that refers to the same practices or similar practices. A term coined by the National Center for Complementary and Alternative Medicine (NCCAM) is *complementary and alternative medicine.* The NCCAM divides complementary and alternative health practices into five main categories: alternative medical systems, mind-body interventions, biologically based therapies, manipulative and body-based methods, and energy therapies.

Alternative medical systems are all-inclusive systems that have evolved separately from conventional, allopathic medicine. One of these is Oriental medicine, of which traditional Chinese medicine (TCM); Tibetan, Korean, and Japanese medicine; and many other practices originating in Asia are all a part. TCM is the most prevalent and familiar to those in Western culture; it is in itself a general term that includes acupuncture, Chinese herbalism, meditation, and exercise, often in particular qigong or T'ai Chi. All of these practices originated thousands of years ago and are based on the Taoist belief in the relationship between mind and body and that the body's *qi* (vital energy) must be balanced.

Acupuncture does this through the insertion of fine needles into specific places on the body, sometimes with the addition of heat or electrical stimulus to the needles. Acupuncture often is used in conjunction with herbal remedies, also administered with the goal of balancing *qi.* Closely related to acupuncture is acupressure, in which manual pressure takes the place of the needle insertion. Meditation is likewise used with this goal in mind. T'ai Chi, which combines slow body movements with breathing exercises and meditation, is one of the most popular components of TCM worldwide. Qigong is another form of physical exercise, similar to T'ai Chi but even more focused on the manipulation of *qi* and the flow of *qi* through channels in the body, or meridians.

Ayurvedic medicine is also ancient in origins; it is believed to be more than 4,000 years old. This alternative health system originated in India. Like TCM, it is based on a belief that the relationship between mind and body is central to promoting balance, and therefore health. The Hindu term *prana* is used to describe a very similar concept to the Taoist concept of *qi*. Ayurvedic medicine provides guidelines for more detailed diagnosis, however, based on body types, or "energetic constitutions." An imbalance in the *doshas*—combinations that make up these energetic constitutions, not just of human beings, but of everything in the universe—can cause illness. Most Ayurvedic practices revolve around dietary issues, meditation, and exercise, in particular yoga.

Ayurvedic dietary practices are meant to not only heal the body but also prevent disease. Depending on a person's constitution, different kinds of foods (e.g., sweet, salty, moist, dry) should either be added to the diet or avoided. Transcendental meditation, introduced to the Western world by Maharishi Mahesh Yogi, is the Ayurvedic version of meditation, and the meditator utilizes *mantras;* that is, verbal sounds that have no meaning and therefore cannot lead the mind away from the stillness the meditator is trying to achieve. Meditation is not only practiced by itself in Ayurveda; it is also an important component of yoga, as is physical movement. Patanjali, credited with creating yoga nearly 5,000 years ago, designed a series of postures and breathing exercises to purify the mind and body and reconnect them to *prana,* the universal life force.

Alternative health systems have also evolved within Western culture, even alongside traditional medicine. German doctor Samuel Hahnemann is credited with coining the term *homeopathy* in the late 18th century. Despite resistance from the conventional medical community, Hahnemann's practices of stimulating the immune systems of sick patients with plant, mineral, or even animal substances that cause the same symptoms those patients are having gained a following. For instance, a smallpox patient may be given a small dose of cowpox. This practice is based on the Law of Similars, which traditional medicine also utilizes in the way of vaccinations. The Law of Similars, in homeopathy, operates on the concept that the body cannot defend itself against all kinds of attacks and that, by administering minute doses of a substance that mimics the symptoms of the current ailment, the homeopathic specialist is helping the body learn to fight off that particular kind of attack.

Naturopathy began employing similar practices to homeopathy in the early 1900s, starting with the philosophy that the entire body needs to be healthy and balanced to cure ailments and prevent future health problems. Naturopaths make it their primary goal to help create the ideal environment for the body to heal itself and stay balanced. The actual methods used to achieve this status are often borrowed from other realms of alternative health; for example, acupuncture, supplements, and meditation may all be prescribed by naturopaths.

Mind-body interventions refer to a more generalized set of ideas and practices. The meditation practiced in TCM and Ayurveda could be considered a mind-body intervention, as could prayer, one of the most widespread practices that can be categorized as an alternative health practice; art or music therapy; or any other practice that hopes to implement changes in the body through changes in the mind. Increasingly, mind-body interventions are being accepted and practiced in traditional medical communities. They have gained the most acceptance in mainstream medicine out of all alternative health practices, possibly because they have been largely successful in treating a variety of conditions. For instance, hypnosis has been used to help people quit smoking, and guided imagery has been successful in promoting stress reduction and relaxation.

Biologically based therapies, again, share some overlap with alternative health systems; for example, the substances administered in homeopathy and naturopathy, and also the herbal remedies of TCM could be considered biologically based therapies. Anything that is administered to directly affect the biological aspect of the body, but has not been accepted by mainstream medicine, falls into this category, including herbs, dietary choices, vitamins, and dietary supplements.

Orthomolecular medicine, which utilizes substances already familiar to the human body in larger doses, is an example of a biologically based therapy. The use of glucosamine, chondroitin, or both to treat osteoarthritis is one example of orthomolecular medicine that has gained popularity in the allopathic medical community as of late. Diet-based therapies, such as macrobiotic diets and raw food diets, are also increasingly popular methods of fostering overall wellness.

Both osteopathy and chiropractic medicine are considered by the NCCAM to be manipulative and body-based methods of alternative health, as is massage, even though it is also a part of several alternative health systems. Reflexology is closely related to massage and is considered another kind of manipulative and body-based method. Both massage and reflexology utilize practices that can be very similar to acupuncture and acupressure.

Osteopathy is a relatively new facet of alternative health and medicine. Like homeopathy, it is structured around the belief that it is more productive to treat the underlying condition causing a symptom or set of symptoms than to treat the symptoms alone. In the case of osteopathy, the underlying cause is traced to the relationship between the structure of the body and the way all of those parts function, separately and in conjunction. The founder of osteopathy is Andrew Taylor Still. He first articulated and promoted his theories in the 1800s. Osteopathy seeks to treat illness primarily through manipulation of the body's structure (i.e., the musculoskeletal system) and its relationship to the circulatory system. Through Still's work, osteopathy gained acceptance in the United States, but is has yet to be fully accepted in other areas of the world.

Chiropractic medicine also got its start in the United States in the 19th century, but it is seen as evolving out of much older traditions. Daniel David Palmer is credited with formally introducing it in 1890; at that time, it was based on the belief that many diseases originate from skeletal problems, in particular, misalignment of the spine. Earlier chiropractors claimed to be able to heal a variety of problems wider than is currently accepted, but the practice is still used to treat a spectrum of conditions. Modern chiropractic medicine bases its practices on a model that takes into account the complexity of the relationships not just between the spine and spinal nerves, but also other bones and nerves, as well as blood vessels, ligaments, and muscles. This newer theory gained acceptance in the 1980s. Today, the field of chiropractic medicine has recovered from the onslaught of criticism by the traditional medical community to gain not only acceptance but popularity worldwide.

In the 1960s, chiropractor George J. Goodheart introduced applied kinesiology, which uses the testing of muscle reactions through manual stimulation to assess medical conditions and proper treatment. This led to the subfield of diagnostic kinesiology, which uses these methods specifically to diagnose muscular problems. Applied kinesiology is still taught in some chiropractic schools; however, it has not gained the popularity that other chiropractic methods have.

The term *massage* can refer to any sort of manipulation of the body's tissues, whether through light touching, kneading, or applying manual pressure to certain points of the body. It is used with increasing commonness to treat not only musculoskeletal pain but also stress and anxiety. It is one of the few alternative health practices to receive credit from the traditional medical community, as it has been shown to improve immune system function. It is used in many different ways by many different cultures. Over centuries, many different styles of massage have evolved—Swedish, Thai, Shiatsu, and neuromuscular are just a few.

Reflexology focuses specifically on applying pressure to, stretching, or moving certain places on the hands and feet that are thought to correspond with various systems of the body, or even specific organs. It is thought to engage the peripheral nervous system and is used to decrease physical as well as mental stress by helping the body achieve a balanced state.

The last NCCAM category is energy therapies. These are divided into two main categories: biofield therapies and bioelectromagnetic-based therapies. *Biofield therapies* is a term used to define the elements of alternative health systems that are meant to affect energy fields, like *qi* or *prana,* which in turn affect the body and mind. Reikki is an example of a biofield therapy, in which light touch is used to affect the body's energy fields. *Bioelectromagnetic-based therapies* refer to practices that attempt to manipulate electromagnetic fields, such as the use of magnets, in the form of anything from magnetic jewelry to magnetic mattresses, to alleviate pain and treat certain existing medical conditions; for example, asthma or carpal tunnel.

All of these practices, and the many others that can be defined as facets of alternative health, share a tendency toward treating well-being holistically and acknowledging interconnectedness, whether that be between the mind and the body, different systems of the body, or the body and its surrounding environment. They are accepted to varying degrees, depending on the specific practice, surrounding culture, and the emerging research that will either support each practice or refute its effectiveness.

—*Heidi Stevenson*

See also Homeopathy Movement

Further Readings

Gerson, S. (2006). *Basic principles of Ayurveda*. Retrieved May 12, 2006, from the National Institute of Ayurvedic Medicine website: http://niam.com/corp-web/basicstoc .html

Health World Online. (2006). Alternative Medicine Center. Retrieved May 12, 2006, from http://www.healthy.net/ scr/center.asp?centerid=1

National Center for Alternative and Complementary Medicine. Retrieved May 12, 2006, from http://nccam .nih.gov/

Wessel, C. B. (2006). The alternative medicine homepage. Retrieved May 12, 2006, from http://www.pitt.edu/~cbw/ about.html

ALTERNATIVE MOVEMENTS

Social movements are organized, collective efforts to promote or resist change to some aspect of society. Alternative movements are one type in which participants create their own social space and live differently, in defiance of mainstream social institutions.

Community currencies and home schooling are two notable examples. The struggle for social justice takes many forms, and some choose to exit the system and build their own alternative communities. Despite their prevalence, alternative social movements have received very little scientific attention from researchers.

In their attempt to understand the dynamics of social movements, scholars have defined and categorized movements in a variety of ways. Those with more stringent conceptions often cite five different elements: (1) collective challenge, (2) common claims and interests, (3) collective identity, (4) disruptive tactics, and (5) sustained interaction with opponents. In accord with the first three criteria, alternative social movements are collective efforts waged by people with common claims and a collective identity. Yet, alternative movements are not based on, nor do they usually involve, the use of disruptive tactics or interaction with opponents. As these are "do-it-yourself" efforts, alternative social movements do not necessarily directly protest against other groups or social institutions.

The lack of attention to alternative movements in the larger social movement literature is at least partially attributable to the fact that those adhering to strict conceptions do not consider these efforts to be social movements. Many other definitions of social movements are looser and do not stress the use of disruptive tactics, seeing these forms of collective behavior as movement activity.

Popular typologies of social movements tend to exclude alternative movements. One oft-cited scheme contains four movement types by differentiating between the amount of change sought (partial vs. total) and the locus of change (individual vs. social structure). *Alternative* movements seek partial change in individuals' behaviors or habits. Self-help movements such as Alcoholics Anonymous and Drug Abuse Resistance Education are representative of alterative movements. *Redemptive* movements seek total personal transformation and are typically religious in nature. *Reformative* movements, the most common form of social movements, attempt to change parts of existing society in some fashion. *Transformative* movements seek revolutionary change and replacement of the existing social order.

Alternative social movements are not easily placed within this typology. In the criterion concerning the amount of change sought, some alternatives seem to fit squarely in the "partial" side. The home schooling and community currency movements, for example, do not seek total change in either individuals or society. On the other hand, communes and utopian socialist communities may represent "total change" examples of these types of movements. Problems emerge when the other criterion of the typology—locus of change—is considered. These alternative efforts are more difficult to pigeonhole, as they do not really attempt to reform the existing social structure; rather, they create an alternative to it. Yet, the change is greater than at just the individual level, as whole new communities are created. Alternative social movements fall somewhere in between micro-level (individual) and macro-level (social structural) change. They are most appropriately considered as meso-level change because they build new communities.

Some have referred to alternative collective efforts to live everyday life differently as *communal* or *communitarian* social movements. These movements seek to create small-scale social systems to remedy the ills of the larger society. Participants choose to live (at least some portion of their lives) according to their own values, outside of mainstream social institutions. Unlike reformative and transformative movements, alternative social movements are not oppositional. They create their own social space to defy mainstream institutions (rather than engaging in sustained, disruptive interaction with them). The alternative versus oppositional dichotomy is an important one when considering social movements. Indeed, alternative movements may have greater impact on their participants than oppositional movements do. The alternative arrangements that are constructed make these efforts everyday social movements in which actions are history making insofar as participants are influencing the conditions and terms of their everyday lives.

Alternative social movements may also be considered as examples of new social movements because they break the boundary between politics and personal life. Major movements of the 1970s (such as the peace, environmental, feminist, gay rights, and animal rights movements) are argued to represent a new postindustrial era in which class conflict is no longer fundamental. New social movements tend to emphasize quality of life and identity issues and result in participants living their everyday lives differently. Thus, alternative social movements are one form of new social movements.

In the United States, the growing home schooling and community currency efforts exemplify alternative social movements. Parents who have chosen to home educate their children do not tend to act in isolation. They work together through networks and organizations. By sharing teaching materials and ideas, taking their children on group field trips, and engaging in other social activities, home schooling parents build a community. Such interaction is likely to reinforce their decision to home educate and to contribute to the formation of a collective, "us" feeling.

Community currency systems are created by local activists seeking to empower the economically marginalized and build social capital. These local trading networks create an alternative currency as a medium for the exchange of services and goods. Unlike conventional bartering (where two actors trade directly with one another), local currencies expand commerce by connecting a network of people (and often businesses). Participants in these alternative local economies are intentionally building community and providing opportunities for the disadvantaged outside of the mainstream economy.

Alternative social movements span the political spectrum; they are not only waged by liberals and progressives. Parents critical of governmental control over their children's education may seek to create their own alternatives just as those who are critical of the decline of the welfare state and the failure of the market economy to meet social needs may build local alternative solutions. The rising discontent and widespread activism witnessed in the past decade suggest that alternative social movements are likely to grow and continue to be an important avenue for the pursuit of social justice.

—*Ed Collom*

See also Community Currencies; Home Schooling

Further Readings

Aberle, D. (1966). *The peyote religion among the Navaho.* Chicago: Aldine.

Collom, E. (2005, September). Community currency in the United States: The social environments in which it emerges and survives. *Environment and Planning A, 37*(9), 1565–1587.

Collom, E., & Mitchell, D. E. (2005). Home schooling as a social movement: Identifying the determinants of homeschoolers' perceptions. *Sociological Spectrum, 25*(3), 273–305.

Croteau, D. (1995). *Politics and the class divide: Working people and the middle-class left.* Philadelphia: Temple University Press.

Kanter, R. M. (1972). *Commitment and community: Communes and utopias in sociological perspective.* Cambridge, MA: Harvard University Press.

McAdam, D., & Snow, D. A. (1997). Social movements: Conceptual and theoretical issues. In D. McAdam & D. A. Snow (Eds.), *Social movements: Readings on their emergence, mobilization, and dynamics* (pp. xviii–xxvi). Los Angeles: Roxbury.

Rothschild-Whitt, J. (1979, August). The collectivist organization: An alternative to rational-bureaucratic models. *American Sociological Review, 44,* 509–527.

Tarrow, S. (1998). *Power in movement: Social movements and contentious politics* (2nd ed.). Cambridge, UK: Cambridge University Press.

ALTERNATIVE PRESS

Alternative press, at its best, is a source of accurate, well-documented, counterhegemonic, investigative reporting and analysis that can advance social movements and serve as the basis for effective social and environmental justice activism. The term *alternative press* is most often used to refer to noncorporate social and environmental justice print and, more recently, Internet media. Other times, it refers to all sources of alternative media, including books, radio, video, film, and television. Although blogs may also serve as a source of independent information, this discussion will focus on alternative newspapers, magazines, journals, newsletters, and website media, primarily in the United States.

Accurate information and analysis are essential for ordinary people who care about and want to work toward creating a better world. Democratic decision making can be based on nothing less. Self-serving elites, governments, and business interests have long been aware that the easiest way to control people is to restrict access to information and to shape public perspectives of reality in ways that increase power and profits for the rich and powerful. Thus, various methods of censorship and propaganda have been used separately and in combination to misinform and/or disinform (lie to) people. Yet, despite such manipulation, ordinary people have often sought or created alternative ways of investigating, analyzing, and sharing information crucial for the well-being of themselves, others, and the earth. Thus, it is not surprising that the first alternative press in the United States emerged from black, Native American, women's, and working-class movements.

To understand why independent media sources are viewed as a powerful alternative, it is necessary to examine significant characteristics of mainstream corporate-owned media. Media analysts Herbert Schiller, Benjamin Bagdikian, and Carl Jensen (founder of Project Censored) led scholars of journalism in critiquing and documenting the methods and consequences of corporate media ownership and concentration. They exposed the inherent conflict of interest between maximizing profits and informing the public. Early in the 20th century, media corporations discovered they could make more money by selling advertisements (actually selling affluent audiences to advertisers) than selling the most papers (circulation). With this change, Bagdikian documented how media businesses became uninterested in groups that had little or no disposable income.

As media companies grew larger, they found it beneficial to interlock their boards of directors with other large manufacturing corporations, thus consolidating the interests of wealthy elites. Through purchases and mergers, the mass media became concentrated in the hands of fewer and fewer corporations, whose primary interest was—and still is—in maximizing profits, not informing the public. These corporations, who also dominate industries like weapons and fossil fuels, understand that if the public were fully informed about corporate and government activities, more than a few of which are unethical and even criminal, it would be difficult or impossible to continue them. Contrary to the myths of objectivity and fairness in reporting, this financial conflict of interest creates conditions for censorship, manipulation, propaganda, and disinformation to dominate mainstream media outlets. Corporate media and public relations firms have developed methods of creatively packaging selective information designed to gain public support for policies and practices beneficial to corporations and government collaborators and detrimental to the public interest. Herman and Chomsky aptly labeled this shaping of public opinion "manufacturing consent."

Thus, *alternative press* is one of the contemporary terms describing communication media that provide information and analysis not normally available through mainstream corporate-owned media. Also known as *independent media,* meaning independent *from* corporate ownership and control of elites, no consensus has emerged on a set of criteria for alternative press, although new media organizers are seeking to transform thinking, methods, and effectiveness of the alternative press.

While noncorporate media may span the political spectrum from left to right, the term *alternative press* usually applies to those outlets that might variously be described as critical, progressive, leftist, underground, dissident, environmental, activist, oppositional, radical, counterhegemonic, or socially responsible. If "alternative press" is typed into a search engine, a majority of sites that emerge reveal these types of perspectives. Some corporate or right-wing media sources may try to present themselves as alternative to mainstream, but if they are closely examined, important aspects of alternative press will be missing.

Some characteristics most likely to be associated with alternative press are (1) committing to a mission that fosters peace, social justice, and/or ecological sustainability in some way; (2) giving voice to marginalized populations; (3) being a nonprofit organization or profitability not being a priority; (4) critiquing and challenging misinformation and disinformation; (5) investigating, documenting, and gathering information from many sources; (6) printing socially responsible

advertisements or no advertisements; (7) encouraging action; (8) being indexed in alternative reference lists; and (9) aspiring to become democratic, nonhierarchical organizations. Although a particular medium may not have all of these characteristics or criteria, this list might help activists, or people aspiring to become more active, distinguish the social justice alternative press from other sources of information. There are, however, exceptions to some of these characteristics among alternative media sources.

Although they may share some values and characteristics, the alternative press is not monolithic. It offers great variation in information, evidence, analysis, opinion, and proposed solutions. Each publication, e-newsletter, or website has its own interests, approach, theoretical foundation, and activism. There may be vehement disagreement on many facets of an issue among, and even within, alternative press publications. Because of the great diversity available, readers of alternative press can cross-check evidence and sources, and compare analytical frameworks.

Characteristics of Alternative Press

• *Alternative press has a mission of social justice, peace, and/or ecological sustainability.* Alternative media usually do not claim to be objective. They may even point out that objectivity is not possible, as there are values in every aspect of selecting and presenting information. Thus, each alternative media organization has a mission that expresses both its values and focus. Some alternative press organizations have a broad mission and others a more specific focus. More often than not, alternative press publications make their value positions directly available to their readers. If the mission is not printed in their publication, it is likely to be available on their website.

• *Alternative press gives voice to populations not heard and views not seen in corporate media.* The voices and perspectives of indigenous peoples (*Cultural Survival Quarterly: World Report on the Rights, Voices and Visions of Indigenous Peoples*), poor and nonrich people (*Dollars and Sense*), communities of color (*Colorlines*), women (*Off Our Backs*), people with disabilities (*Ragged Edge*), queer people (*The Gay and Lesbian Review*), colonized peoples in other countries (*NACLA*), animals (*Animal Issues*), grassroots and activist organizations (*Earth First! Journal*) all find expression in alternative press. People marginalized within government (such as the Black Caucus and the few elected officials committed to peace, earth, and justice within the Congress) are provided a forum (*In These Times*), as are whistle-blowers who expose government or corporate wrongdoing (*Bridging the GAP* by the Government Accountability Project). The voices of these groups critique the self-serving policies, practices, and propaganda of dominant and privileged groups, reveal the consequences, and propose creative actions and solutions to social, environmental, and global problems.

- *Alternative press organizations are either nonprofit organizations, or their mission far exceeds profits as their primary objective.* Most alternative media organizations have nonprofit status. With a few exceptions, most do not seek, nor do they receive, large amounts of funding from advertisers. Their funding, which is often limited, is usually derived from subscriptions; donations; social or environmental justice organizations, foundations, or institutes that support a particular cause; or some combination of these sources.

Some alternative media sources are an outgrowth of a particular organization that already has nonprofit status (*Amnesty International, Public Citizen, Sierra*). For others, readers can usually locate the mission and nonprofit status of a publication by looking at the masthead page that provides information about the publication or the webpage of the media organization.

If there is no statement about nonprofit status, then it is likely that the publication has a for-profit status. This legal status, however, does not necessarily mean they are actually making a profit. Some important exceptions to the nonprofit status characteristic are *The Nation* and *Utne Reader,* which are profit based. *The Nation,* one of the longest continuous alternative press publications in the United States beginning in 1865, is technically a for-profit publication. However, they have actually lost money in all but 4 or 5 years, where they broke even or made a small profit.

Utne Reader, started in 1883 and with a current circulation of 225,000, is another for-profit publication careful not to compromise its values for money. For-profit alternative press publications are challenged to cover all their costs through subscriptions and advertising because they receive little to no financial support from other sources. The strong value-based missions of these publications, their employees, and their constituencies maintain their advocacy for peace, social justice, environmental concerns, and oppressed or persecuted groups.

It is important to differentiate these strong value-based independent publications from city entertainment weeklies that may call themselves alternative press and have some content that challenges corporate and government elites but which are profit-based publications that survive on nonrestricted advertising.

- *Alternative press is counterhegemonic, critiquing and challenging corporate, government, and/or dominant group misinformation and disinformation.* Another role of alternative press is to check the accuracy and credibility of evidence, and rebut false claims and fake news made through corporate, public relations, and dominant group media outlets. Although all alternative presses perform this role on their particular topics of interest, some alternative media focus their critique on the corporate media directly. Some examples are *Fairness & Accuracy In Reporting (FAIR), Project Censored, Center for Media and Democracy,* and *Media Matters in America.*

One organization, Project Censored, demonstrates the significance of this role by exposing the top 25 stories censored by the mainstream media every year (www.projectcensored.org). Almost all of these stories are revealed by alternative press publications. Because they do not have to ingratiate themselves to the powerful or the corporations to get copy or be published, alternative presses are free to pursue stories that corporate editors eschew for fear of offending their parent companies or advertisers.

- *Alternative presses provide evidence and documentation from many places, not just official sources from government and corporations.* Because alternative press challenges the myths, misinformation, and false realities generated by the corporate media, many alternative press publications go to special lengths to provide evidence, documentation, and sources in their articles. In contrast to corporate media, which continue to reduce the size of the news staff while passing on the views and claims of elites, politicians, or corporate public relations releases as news, alternative presses seek out and publish investigative reports, independent journalists, and research conducted by human rights, peace, animal rights, or environmental advocacy organizations. Alternative publications often cite their sources so readers can investigate the accuracy of the information for themselves.

Commondreams.org is a good example of an alternative press website that posts breaking news and analysis daily from independent journalists and alternative newswires, highlights key reports from activist organizations, draws the best reporting and analytical pieces from corporate sources, and links to international articles of import. In some cases, investigative journalists are hired or sponsored by alternative media. At times, they provide reports at great personal risk in war zones or in places contaminated with hazardous substances, venturing into life-threatening situations to bring eyewitness accounts, pictures, and critical news. This material may then be located in a variety of places: in the sponsoring journal, on the reporter's website, picked up by other alternative Internet sites, or published in alternative print publications.

• *Alternative press either has no advertisements or accepts only socially responsible advertisements.* Although some publications take no advertisements (*Worldwatch, Yes!*), and others use their publications to disseminate a catalogue of their own products (People for the Ethical Treatment of Animals), many alternative press publications do accept some advertisements. Most commonly, they publish advertisements for other alternative press or books, for socially responsible investment funds, for activist organizations, and for educational programs. When products are advertised, they usually have some claim for

health, environmental, or social responsibility, such as organic or fair trade products (beverages, food, clothing, furniture, personal care, homecare); recycled products; vegetarian or vegan products or restaurants; socially conscious Internet, phone, or automobile companies; or art, music, and festivals. Because alternative presses, for-profit or nonprofit, do not have to worry about offending advertisers, which can result in the withholding of millions of dollars in revenue, alternative press organizations have the freedom to investigate and critique dominant corporations, office-holders, and their policies and practices.

• *Alternative press organizations encourage readers to engage with social movements and may provide suggestions and resources for activism.* In contrast to corporate media, carefully documented alternative press publications tend to energize readers, encouraging them to take action for themselves, for others, and the environment. Alternative press organizations often try to publish specific actions, campaigns, conferences, or organizational websites where readers can influence policies or practices of governments or corporations. Actions may range from boycotts, to buying fair trade products, to screening documentaries, to writing letters to officials or editors, to marching in rallies or protests, to initiating creative new methods.

Alternative press websites facilitate grassroots organizing further by providing quick links to sign petitions or letters to Congress or others about a particular issue, even writing out key points readers can use if they wish. Some political web organizations like MoveOn.org and InternationalANSWER.org (Act Now to Stop War and End Racism) emerged out of specific activist agendas. While not claiming to be alternative presses, they still serve the purpose of disseminating critical information using extensive e-mail lists to stimulate mass actions.

Similarly, state and local activist organizations may disseminate information to their members or communities through newsletters or newspapers. Although these publications may not have large circulations, they serve a powerful role by announcing local events, encouraging local actions, and making connections between local and state events with national and international movements.

● *Alternative press publications are often found in alternative indexes or through media analysis sources.* Many alternative presses and their publications can be found in alternative reference sources. Bibliographic and Web Tools for Alternative Publications lists such references as the Alternative Press Index, Alt-Press Watch, Alternative Internet Directory, Ethnic News Watch, Environmental Periodicals Bibliography, INK, the International Directory of Little Magazines and Small Presses, the Left Index, MediaChannel, NewPages, and Street Librarian: Independent & Non-corporate Media.

The Alternative Press Center (www.altpress.org) has the most comprehensive list of U.S. alternative media on the Internet. It still only accesses a portion of the publications available. Some alternative presses with larger circulations or longevity of publication also may be listed in the mainstream indexes (e.g., Readers' Guide to Periodical Literature), but most are not. Alternative press organizations increasingly are collaborating (rather than competing) to support their collective goals and needs through groups like the Independent Press Association (United States), Independent Media Center, or the Independent News Collective (United Kingdom).

● *Alternative presses try to live the values they espouse, organizing themselves in more democratic, nonhierarchical ways.* This criterion may have the most variation in practice. In theory, however, because the alternative press is challenging injustice and seeking to give voice to underrepresented groups, decision making, work assignments, and salaries should be socially just and established through democratic, cooperative processes and policies. As Michael Albert, one of the founders of *Z Magazine,* contends, strong efforts should be made to reject and reduce hierarchies based on race, class, gender, or any other oppressive category. Still, if the mastheads, websites, the authors or editors of articles of alternative press publications are perused, it may reveal that some are not be as inclusive as they might wish or claim to be.

Electronic Alternative Information Dissemination

Activist Organizations: National, State, and Local

Some organizations with limited staff and/or budgets, or who focus their energies on particular areas of activism, not information dissemination per se, may not publish extensive monthly or quarterly publications. Instead, they may communicate primarily through newsletters, e-newsletters, and their own websites (MoveOn.org, *Rachel's Environment and Health Weekly* magazine, Organic Consumers Association's online *Progressive Grocer Magazine*). These sources of alternative information and organized actions have quickly motivated millions of people to donate money, contact senators and representatives, and participate in local and national actions.

Alternative Press Websites

Alternative press websites like commondreams, truthout, alternet, indymedia, tompaine, and zmag are the most significant development in the history of alternative press, reaching millions of readers per month as opposed to tens of thousands. They have dramatically increased access to alternative press, bringing censored information to the public and exposing propaganda as it happens. The immediacy and flexibility of the Internet allows these sites to draw news, opinions, announcements, studies, and reports quickly from sources that ordinary people would previously be unlikely to encounter. In some cases, print circulation has actually decreased with the advent of an extensive website, but the immediacy increases the knowledge and power of busy readers who can take action quickly on issues of concern instead of having to wait to get their publication in the mail.

To support participatory democracy, alternative Internet media organizations provide links to the websites of key grassroots, nonprofit, and advocacy organizations, which often encourage readers toward a variety of actions or provide action links on their sites. Further, many provide opportunities to directly contact state and federal senators and representatives. Because these information outlets are making it much more difficult for elites to control the opinions and actions of the populace, plans and policies to severely curtail or inhibit access are being promulgated. Given the increased consciousness of the public through these websites, it remains to be seen if they will be successful.

The Importance of Open and Fair Internet to the Alternative Press

Maintaining an Internet environment that is free from corporate, government, or military domination of content and access will be an ongoing struggle. Despite initial and continued campaigns to maintain diversity and democracy in print, radio, and television media, they all were eventually severely compromised by corporate ownership, censorship, and propaganda with alternative press relegated to nonthreatening roles on the fringe. Accessed only by readers, listeners, and viewers who knew mainstream media outlets disseminated corporate biases, they had to go to some trouble to locate and use alternative, accurate, well-documented information for the public interest.

The Internet dramatically changed this scenario by making alternative information and viewpoints quickly and easily available to anyone who had access to a computer. Because computers are expensive and differentially available in public schools, libraries, and the like, this still leaves a substantial component of the United States and global population without access. Even with this restriction, the popularity of independent information from alternative media, nonprofit organizations, and blogs has spread through other channels to produce a public sea change on many key policies. However, this open and fair exchange of information on the Internet is threatened by two sources: corporations and the Pentagon.

Corporate Domination or Internet Neutrality

Internet neutrality, according to Freepress.net means that all online activity must be treated equally; companies like AT&T, for example, must allow access to small blogs as well as the large corporate websites. In

what is likely to be just one of many attempts to control and profit from the Internet, giant telecommunications corporations who own the telephone and cable lines (Verizon, Bell South, Comcast, AT&T, Time Warner) are lobbying for legislation to operate the Internet as their own private service free from government oversight. To confuse the public, they have set up phony front groups like Hands Off the Internet to disseminate propaganda touting the benefits of privatization. They want to be able to decide for the public, like they do for cable TV, what sites will be available for what prices, the speed of the sites, and even be able to block sites altogether. Examples of blocking content for purposes of censorship have already occurred. Content providers and individuals would have to pay for most or all online activities, with preference given to the telecom's own services and to content providers who can pay the most for high visibility and speedy access—primarily other corporations. Under these conditions, Chester suggests that civic and noncommercial online programming may become less and less accessible to the Internet user.

Further, phone and cable companies have new technologies that can create a detailed profile of each individual Internet user for purposes of tracking, marketing, metering, and billing. In addition to further corporate targeting, such technologies may inhibit Internet users from accessing alternative press Internet sites because the Patriot Act allows surveillance of private citizens without one's knowledge. Revelations of illegal government surveillance and harassment continue to emerge. Public accessibility, already limited to people who can gain access to computers, could be further curtailed.

Information Democracy or Propaganda Warfare

In an equally disturbing development, the British Broadcasting Corporation has revealed a Pentagon plan, obtained through the Freedom of Information Act, to use the Internet for military propaganda, psychological operations, and electronic warfare. Using expressions like "fight the net," the Information Operations Roadmap, a Pentagon document written in 2003, lays out strategies to control, plant, or disrupt information, even to destroy communications systems.

Among the many questions are, who would be defined as the "enemy," and what are their plans for the U.S. and global publics.

In conclusion, there is no single requirement for social movements more important than accurate well-documented information on which people can take action. Alternative press, now available to millions of people 24 hours a day through the Internet, must be preserved in order to provide the foundation for such democratic citizenship and activism.

—*Julie R. Andrzejewski*

See also Abu-Jamal, Mumia; *Adbusters;* Alternative Bookstores; Blogging; Culture Jammers; Cyber Rights; Digital Activism; Dissent; Electronic Privacy Movement; Fairness & Accuracy In Reporting (FAIR); Free Speech Activism; Indymedia; Media Activism; Media Literacy; Media Reform Movement; Mencken, H. L.; MoveOn.org; Political Satire; Timerman, Jacobo; Virtual Sit-Ins; Webb, Gary; Yomango; Zines; ZNet

Further Readings

Aaron, C., & Fitzgibbon, T. (2006, April 26). *House ignores public, sells out the Internet.* Retrieved April 29, 2006, from www.savethenet.com

The case for AlterNet. (2006). Retrieved March 18, 2006, from http://alternet.org/about/

Chester, J. (2006, February 1). The end of the Internet? *The Nation.* Retrieved February 12, 2006, from www .thenation.com

Herman, E., & Chomsky, N. (1988). *Manufacturing consent: A propaganda model.* New York: Pantheon Press.

Smith, J. (1996). The fifth column of the fourth estate: A brief history of the alternative press in America. In J. Smith (Ed.), *Afflict the comfortable, comfort the afflicted: A guide for campus alternative journalists* (pp. 19–32). Cambridge, MA: Campus Alternative Journalism Project.

Whitney, M. (2006, February 14). The Pentagon's war on the Internet. *Alternative Press Review.* Retrieved March 20, 2006, from www.altpr.org

AMARU, TÚPAC, II (1738–1781)

Túpac Amaru II was the leader of the largest indigenous uprising in the Americas during the period of European colonization. From November 1780 until his death in May 1781, Túpac Amaru II headed a powerful movement that quickly spread through the South American Andes and rocked elite colonial society to its core.

Born José Gabriel Condorcanqui in 1738 outside of Cuzco, the former capital city of the Inca Empire, Túpac Amaru II traced his lineage to Túpac Amaru, the last Inca emperor, who was executed by Spanish Viceroy Francisco de Toledo in 1572. His father was a *curaca* (chief) over the region of Tinta (Cana y Canchis) southeast of Cuzco and operated a successful trade route. The young Condorcanqui enjoyed the benefits of a Jesuit education, was fluent in both the colonial Spanish and indigenous Quechua languages, and could operate quite well in both worlds.

On his father's death in 1750, José Gabriel inherited his mule train as well as his curaca status. He became a successful trader, gaining power and prestige throughout the central Andean highlands. At the same time, he also engaged in repeated legal battles with the Spanish colonial authorities to retain his curaca status. He also witnessed Spanish abuses of the indigenous population and growing discontent with colonial rule. Economic reforms had improved the efficiency of tax collection, which increasingly alienated Creole and mestizo populations.

Finally, on November 4, 1780, Condorcanqui took the name of Túpac Amaru and called for the expulsion of the Spanish and for the establishment of an independent Inca empire. He arrested the local Spanish official (*Corregidor*) Antonio de Arriaga and, after a summary trial, executed him. Túpac Amaru II pledged to destroy the hated colonial labor systems (*mita* and *obrajes*), roll back the new taxes, and free Indians to live in peace and harmony with mestizos and Creoles.

As news of the uprising spread, people flooded to join Túpac Amaru's forces with his ranks quickly swelling to 60,000 troops. He attacked Spanish estates (haciendas), freed Indians from prison, and removed colonial authorities from power. Although seen as an indigenous uprising, much of the leadership came from the Creole and mestizo colonial middle class. The bulk of the fighting force, however, remained overwhelmingly indigenous and included both men and women. They were motivated primarily by local issues, and their interest waned as the army moved further away from their homes.

Micaela Bastidas, the wife of Túpac Amaru II, played a particularly important role in the movement, serving as chief strategist and propagandist. She had advocated the death of Arriaga and urged her husband to move more quickly in his attacks. A delay until the end of December to attack Cuzco allowed royalist forces to go on the counteroffensive, and the revolt began to fall apart. On April 6, 1781, the Spanish captured the leadership and took them to Cuzco. On May 18, Túpac Amaru II watched the torture and execution of Bastidas and other family members before he was drawn and quartered and his limbs distributed throughout the area as a lesson to discourage other indigenous revolts.

After the uprising, the Spanish engaged in a severe campaign of repression designed to destroy cultural elements of neo-Inca nationalism. The revolt, however, continued in a more radical phase under Túpac Katari's leadership in the southern Andes. Historians sometimes interpret Túpac Amaru II's uprising as a failed precursor to independence 40 years later. Ongoing debates disagree as to whether the uprising should be seen as a messianic movement or a class-based struggle. In either case, the name Túpac Amaru remains today as a potent symbol of resistance.

Reference to Túpac Amaru can also be found in contemporary guerrilla movements, such as the Túpac Amaru Revolutionary Movement (MRTA) in Peru and Tupamaros in Uruguay, even though most of them have no actual link with indigenous struggles but with left-wing tendencies. Several operas and compositions were inspired by the story of Túpac Amaru. Examples include *Túpac Amaru, la deconquista, il Pachacuti* by Luigi Ceccarelli and *Suite Túpac Amaru* by Marcela Pavia, both composers of contemporary music.

—*Marc Becker and Alessandro Michelucci*

See also Indigenous People and Social Justice; Reparations Movement

Further Readings

Campbell, L. G. (1987). Ideology and factionalism during the great rebellion: 1780–1782. In S. J. Stern (Ed.), *Resistance, rebellion, and consciousness in the Andean world, 18th to 20th centuries* (pp. 110–139). Madison: University of Wisconsin Press.

Glave, L. M. (1999). The "Republic of Indians" in revolt (c. 1680–1790). In F. Saloman & S. B. Schwartz (Eds.), *The Cambridge history of the native peoples of the Americas* (pp. 502–557). Cambridge, UK: Cambridge University Press.

Stavig, W. (1999). *The world of Túpac Amaru: Conflict, community, and identity in colonial Peru.* Lincoln: University of Nebraska Press.

Thomson, S. (2002). *We alone will rule: Native Andean politics in the age of insurgency.* Madison: University of Wisconsin Press.

Walker, C. (1999). *Smoldering ashes: Cuzco and the creation of republican Peru, 1780–1840.* Durham, NC: Duke University Press.

AMERICAN CIVIL LIBERTIES UNION (ACLU)

The American Civil Liberties Union (ACLU) is a private, nonprofit organization charged with protecting and promoting select rights and liberties codified in the U.S. Constitution and Bill of Rights. Despite pressure to expand its reach internationally, the organization operates exclusively within the United States. Its national board, which is composed of state-affiliate and at-large representatives, formulates the organization's policy and oversees its operations. The ACLU's national headquarters is in New York City; a legislative office is located in Washington, D.C., and a regional office is in Atlanta, Georgia. Although bound to the policy decisions of the national board, state affiliate branches retain significant autonomy over local resource allocation, including deciding which cases to take. The ACLU reports to have more than 500,000 current (in 2006) members and to handle over 6,000 cases annually. Volunteer and permanent attorneys, administrators, and interns staff the ACLU, while membership dues, donations, grants, and attorneys' fees fund the organization. Profoundly controversial since its founding in 1920, the ACLU quickly attained, and continues to retain, a uniquely influential position in the United States' legal landscape.

The ACLU originally deployed a civil liberties agenda, which was animated by the principle of freedom from unnecessary governmental intrusion, and later adopted a hybrid civil liberties and civil rights agenda, which called on government to ensure equality and other constitutionally protected rights. Derived from the text of the Bill of Rights of 1791 and the process by which the Bill of Rights' protections became applicable to every state, the primary liberties the ACLU seeks to secure include freedom of speech, freedom to practice religion, freedom from government endorsement of religion, the right to privacy, the right to due process, and the right to equal treatment under the law. From the beginning, the ACLU has employed various legal mechanisms, including litigating cases; providing (often free) legal counsel; and filing numerous *amicus curiae,* or "friend of the court," briefs in cases it does not litigate. Public-education campaigns, lobbying lawmakers, and advising law-enforcement actors directly have also figured prominently in the ACLU's work.

The ACLU has instituted a policy of political neutrality: It purportedly defends all Americans' liberties regardless of political orientation or ideology. This policy has been critiqued in theory and in practice, especially during wartime. In 1940, for instance, the ACLU formally barred Communist Party members from its leadership positions. Elizabeth Gurley Flynn, a founding ACLU board member as well as a Communist Party member, was expelled from the ACLU's board. (Flynn was reinstated posthumously in 1976.) Critics maintain, moreover, that the ACLU has disproportionately defended, and attempted to advance, liberal or leftist causes. Pointing to the ACLU's call for the impeachment of Richard Nixon and its opposition to the Supreme Court nominations of Robert Bork and Samuel Alito Jr., some contend the organization is merely a liberal wing of the Democratic Party. The ACLU's *amicus* support of Lieutenant Colonel Oliver North's Fifth Amendment rights during the Iran-Contra affair has been similarly impugned as a political ruse deployed during a highly contentious presidential election. Conversely, the ACLU has come under attack by various liberals, both for its stance against the constitutionality of hate-speech legislation and for its support of Nazi and Ku Klux Klan members' freedom-to-assemble and free-speech rights. Despite such protestations from liberals, however, many critics continue to tie the ACLU to a leftist political agenda.

The ACLU initially emerged out of the tumultuous period surrounding America's entry into World War I. The American Union Against Militarism (1916) and the National Civil Liberties Bureau (1917) were the ACLU's direct antecedents. Both the AUAM and the NCLB defended conscientious objectors in the WWI draft and, later, political dissidents prosecuted under the Espionage Act of 1917 and the Sedition Act of 1918. Boston native Roger Nash Baldwin transformed the NCLB into the ACLU in 1920, endowing the new organization with a more broadly conceived mission than its predecessors. The ACLU's first board members included political activists Helen Keller and Crystal Eastman, as well as future Supreme Court justice Felix Frankfurter, then a Harvard Law School professor. Among its first efforts, the newly formed ACLU denounced the sweeping countrywide police raids against alleged subversives authorized by Attorney General Mitchell Palmer. The ACLU's publicity campaign helped to end the raids, bolstering the fledging organization.

In 1925, the so-called Scopes Monkey Trial served as the first high-exposure case in which the ACLU helped provide counsel. The ACLU joined in the defense of a Tennessee high school instructor accused of teaching the theory of evolution despite a state law forbidding it. Although the teacher lost the trial, his conviction was later overturned on a technicality. The ACLU's involvement in the case was the first of what would become numerous attempts to foster both the right to academic freedom and a separation between church and state. That same year, the ACLU's earliest Supreme Court victory came in *Gitlow v. New York.* Clarence Darrow, who also served as co-counsel in the *Scopes* case, represented a man accused under New York criminal syndicalism laws of advocating in a flyer the overthrow of the U.S. government. Although it upheld Gitlow's lower-court conviction, the Supreme Court's decision nonetheless established that the Fourteenth Amendment's due process clause extended the First Amendment's freedom-of-speech guarantee to every state in the union.

Since *Gitlow,* the ACLU has participated in numerous foundational Supreme Court decisions. Within the sphere of religion, the organization has maintained an especially influential role. Its involvement in *West Virginia v. Barnette,* in which a compulsory school flag salute statute was held to be unconstitutional, helped secure legally sanctioned freedom of conscience for Jehovah's Witnesses. In *Engel v. Vitale,* the ACLU supported the Supreme Court's decision ruling that voluntary, nondenominational school prayer violates the Constitution's establishment clause. In 1989, the ACLU successfully persuaded the nation's high court, in *County of Allegheny v. ACLU,* that public-sponsored holiday displays could, under certain circumstances, constitute government endorsement of religion. In 2005, the ACLU served as co-counsel in *Kitzmiller v. Dover Area School Board,* a federal district–level case in which a Pennsylvania judge struck down an attempt by a local school board to incorporate intelligent design into the biology curriculum.

Among the ACLU's core concerns, free speech has been granted prioritized status. In 1934, after a decade-long battle fought in part by the ACLU, the Supreme Court allowed James Joyce's novel *Ulysses* to enter the United States. In 1938, the ACLU obtained an injunction against the mayor of Jersey City, Frank Hague, ordering him to cease his harassing anti-union activities. Conversely, the ACLU later successfully argued on behalf of Henry Ford's right to express anti-union views so long as he did not directly threaten individuals. The Supreme Court articulated a new free-speech standard in *Brandenburg v. Ohio* in 1969—declaring expression is unconstitutional if it attempts to incite imminent lawless action and is likely to do so—a case in which the ACLU defended the Ku Klux Klan against charges of unlawful advocacy. The ACLU's legal defense of the right for Nazis to march in the largely Jewish Skokie suburb of Chicago in 1977 drew the ire of numerous ACLU members, many of whom left the organization and withdrew funds.

In the realm of national security, the ACLU has elicited some of its sharpest criticism, most often from those who contend the organization prioritizes civil liberties over physical security. In 1944, the ACLU unsuccessfully argued against the detention of Japanese Americans in *Korematsu v. United States.* The organization spoke out against government loyalty oaths during the McCarthy era, prompting the FBI to

track its activities and members. The ACLU also supported the constitutionality of the 1973 publication of the *Pentagon Papers.* In the wake of September 11, 2001, the ACLU was one of the most vocal opponents of the USA Patriot Act's provision that simultaneously expanded FBI and police surveillance power while it lowered the threshold of evidence required to commence a search. Utilizing the Freedom of Information Act, the ACLU has also acquired countless national security–related government documents.

The ACLU's attempt to foster and protect a right to privacy has come under fire as well. The organization lent its support both to *Griswold v. Connecticut,* in which the Supreme Court first articulated a right to privacy derived from the Bill of Rights and Constitution, and to *Roe v. Wade* in 1973, in which the court recognized women's constitutional right to an abortion. Under the direction of future Supreme Court Justice Ruth Bader Ginsburg, during the 1970s the ACLU's Women's Rights Project coordinated a public-education, legislative, and litigation campaign directed at preserving a woman's right to an abortion. Ginsburg argued six gender-equality cases in front of the Supreme Court, winning five.

Utilizing the Fourth Amendment's search-and-seizure and the Fifth Amendment's self-incrimination clauses, the ACLU defended and expanded the rights of those accused and convicted of crime. For instance, in 1961 in *Mapp v. Ohio,* the Supreme Court limited the power of prosecutors and the police to use illegally obtained evidence, and in 1966 in *Miranda v. Arizona,* the Court required police to advise suspects of their rights prior to interrogation. Through enforcement of the Fourteenth Amendment's equal protection clause, the ACLU has engaged in various racial-justice issues. As with *Mapp* and *Miranda,* the ACLU supported the Supreme Court's decisions both in *Brown v. Board of Education* in 1954, which struck down segregation in public schools as unconstitutional, and in *Loving v. Virginia* in 1967, which invalidated various states' laws criminalizing interracial marriage.

Under the leadership of Executive Director Ira Glasser (1978–2001) and President Nadine M. Strossen (1991–present), who is the first woman to hold the position, the ACLU has increasingly emphasized a civil rights–based agenda. The ACLU has expanded the scope of its programs to establish and protect the rights of legally disenfranchised constituencies, including gays and lesbians, people with disabilities, and immigrants. The organization conducts projects on children's rights, prisoners' rights, capital punishment, and women's rights. And the ACLU backs affirmative action in college and university applications, despite some members' protestations that affirmative action is inherently discriminatory.

The ACLU continues to protect the right to untrammeled expression, even so-called hate speech and pornography, with at least one exception. The Northern California branch supported a prior restraint on speech in a workplace racial harassment case called *Aguilar v. Avis*. The affiliate's stance contravened the ACLU's support of the Supreme Court decision in *Near v. Minnesota* in 1931, which declared prior restraints on speech unconstitutional. Nonetheless, the ACLU has defended government whistleblowers, and, in the age of the Internet, the ACLU has attempted to extend legal protection to cyber communications. It argued, successfully, against the constitutionality of the Communications Decency Act and the Child Online Protection Act. The ACLU's opposition to provisions of both Acts derived from what it considered to be the unnecessary and unwarranted limitations the Acts placed on protected speech.

The ACLU recently became mired in controversy after Executive Director Anthony Romero (2001–present) acknowledged that he advised the Ford Foundation to mimic the Patriot Act in its grant agreements. The ACLU also initially agreed to sign an agreement with the Ford Foundation that included restrictions on speech and advocacy. After considerable internal debate, the agreement was revoked. Yet, in order to gain access to a charitable giving program for federal employees, the national organization signed a contract with the federal government in which the ACLU certified its compliance with federal laws prohibiting it from hiring anyone targeted by government watch lists.

—*Dustin A. Lewis*

See also Abortion; Affirmative Action; Bill of Rights; Civil Rights Movement; Communist Party USA; Darrow, Clarence; Democracy; Dissent; Free Speech Activism; Government Suppression of Social Activism; Liberalism; Libertarians; Palmer Raids

Further Readings

Cottrell, R. (2001). *Roger Nash Baldwin and the American Civil Liberties Union*. New York: Columbia University.

Donohue, W. A. (1985). *The politics of the American Civil Liberties Union*. New Brunswick, NJ: Transaction.

Donohue, W. A. (1994). *Twilight of liberty: The legacy of the ACLU*. New Brunswick, NJ: Transaction.

Gibson, J. L., & Bingham, R. D. (1985). *Civil liberties and Nazis: The Skokie free-speech controversy*. New York: Praeger.

Lamson, P. (1976). *Roger Baldwin, founder of the American Civil Liberties Union: A portrait*. Boston: Houghton Mifflin.

Strossen, N. (2000). *Defending pornography: Free speech, sex, and the fight for women's rights*. New York: New York University.

Walker, S. (1999). *In defense of American liberties: A history of the ACLU* (2nd ed.). Carbondale: Southern Illinois University.

AMERICAN FEDERATION OF LABOR (AFL-CIO)

The largest labor federation representing American workers, founded in 1886 and led for many years by Samuel Gompers, the American Federation of Labor (AFL) was a craft union championing the slogan, "a fair day's wage for a fair day's work." With this slogan, the AFL differentiated its craft unionism from the more radical efforts first of the Knights of Labor and then, after 1905, of the Industrial Workers of the World. Unlike the Wobblies, the AFL sought to protect the privileges of a small segment of the industrial working class, skilled craft workers.

In the early 20th century, even the moderate craft unions affiliated with the AFL fought a difficult battle against capital. Nonetheless, the years between 1909 and 1919 represented an important period of union growth. As historian David Montgomery has argued, union strength waxed and waned with fluctuations in the economy. During boom years, when skilled workers were in high demand, unions gained membership, whereas recessions reduced workers' bargaining power, and union strength declined. But with the onset of World War I, in return for a "no-strike" pledge from the AFL leadership, the U.S. government began to actively support union efforts. Through this new capital/labor accord, union leaders found themselves, for the first time, in the corridors of Washington power. In 1913, President Wilson established the Labor Department and appointed former United Mine Workers leader, William Wilson, to a cabinet-level position overseeing its operations. Furthermore, to ensure steady wartime production and to quiet labor unrest, President Wilson put in place the National War Labor Board, with representatives from labor and management. This new board gave official sanction to the right of workers to organize and bargain collectively through their own chosen representatives. Between 1915 and 1920, union membership in the United States doubled. At the same time, the new capital/labor accord and the union movement's increasing reliance on governmental support reinforced the "business unionism" that already characterized much of the AFL's program. This situation led one contemporary observer, the radical political economist, Thorstein Veblen, to view the AFL as yet another vested interest. He wrote, in 1921, that its purpose and ordinary business is to gain a little something for its own members at a more-than-proportionate cost to the community.

Although Veblen's words rather accurately described the organizational attitudes of the AFL's leadership, craft workers were not all so parochial. In fact, within locals, craft unionists were often more radical than their moderate leadership. This radical craft unionism, with roots in the European syndicalist tradition, led to a series of wildcat "control strikes" that took place even while the AFL's official no-strike pledge remained in force. Radical craft workers were striking not for wages but for control over the means of production. This quest for industrial democracy only grew stronger with the war's end. After the armistice, organized labor expressed its new sense of confidence during the unprecedented Red Summer of

1919. Strikes, both sanctioned and unsanctioned, disrupted production on a national scale. Coming just 2 years after the Bolshevik Revolution in Russia, and led, at least in part, by radical syndicalists, this postwar strike wave inspired the fear and ire of America's ruling class. Rather than securing the labor movement's foothold in American political economy, the Red Summer resulted in a red scare, the Palmer raids, and new legal and extralegal forms of political repression. Labor's defeat in 1919 led to a 30% drop in union membership. The gains made during the early part of the century seemed to vanish into dust.

Once the Great Depression hit, workers became increasingly restive, searching for a voice that would represent their interests. A series of general strikes (in San Francisco, Toledo, and Minneapolis), a national textile strike, militant street actions, rent strikes, and general protests led the Roosevelt administration to enact the National Labor Relations Act (also called the Wagner Act) in 1935. This law gave legal support to labor's right to organize and bargain collectively. Buoyed by new legislative openings, John L. Lewis, Philip Murray, Sidney Hillman, and other labor leaders, already dissatisfied with the limits of the AFL's craft unionism, founded the Congress of Industrial Organizations (CIO). The CIO set out to organize workers along industrial lines and had early success unionizing the steel and rubber industries. In addition, the CIO made use of a radical cadre of activists, many affiliated with the Communist Party and other radical political organizations. Promoting a brand of egalitarian unionism that was often as much about workers' power in the community as on the job site, the CIO fostered multiple "cultures of solidarity" that helped create a moment of radical social democratic possibility for American workers. Although these cultures of solidarity could not have been built without significant support from the state apparatus, they also relied on militant worker action. This was evident during the 1936–1937 wave of sit-down strikes. After workers at General Motors were able to secure union recognition through the militant technique of sitting down at their machines and occupying the plant, workers all over the nation followed suit, and the CIO became a new symbol of hope for an otherwise desperate working class.

After 1937, some CIO leaders (most notably, Sidney Hillman) became increasingly close to the Roosevelt administration, whereas others, including Lewis, thought such close union-state cooperation was a danger to the movement. Hillman and his faction won. When the United States entered World War II, the CIO once again offered a no-strike pledge in return for continued support from the state apparatus. Although this no-strike pledge could not stop the many wartime wildcat work actions, it did have the effect of alienating the more militant and energetic local workers and leaders from the national CIO. After the war, workers and returning soldiers had confidence in their union strength and a sense of entitlement derived from having sacrificed so much for the national cause. This led to a massive postwar wave of strikes. Once again, this postwar strike wave was followed by a new red scare, political repression, and, most importantly for labor, the passage of the 1947 Taft-Hartley Act. Written in part by the National Association of Manufactures, some of the Taft-Hartley Act's more important provisions included the outlawing of union-only "closed shops"; the outlawing of all secondary boycotts to support unionizing drives and union struggles; and the requirement of all union leaders to sign an oath that they were not communists. This last provision was particularly devastating for the CIO's organizational structure, forcing the federation to expel many militant and radical organizers and to disaffiliate unrepentant radical unions. Finally, the Taft-Hartley Act completed the process of bureaucratizing union grievance procedures and thus made militant action, if not impossible, at least extremely difficult.

By the 1950s, between 33% and 35% of all nonagricultural workers were members of a trade union. But the new CIO's moderate business unionism no longer differed from the practices promoted by the AFL and the two unions affiliated, producing the AFL-CIO. In the early years of the AFL-CIO, union workers gained ground, securing pensions, health care, and relatively high wages. This new workers' prosperity made possible a blue-collar middle class, as union members purchased homes, automobiles, and college educations for their children. To some extent, union prosperity and sheer union density benefited all American workers, even those left out of direct unionization campaigns. Whereas this moderate, Cold War unionism benefited American workers, abroad the AFL-CIO often served as a functionary for the U.S. State Department, or, worse still, for the Central Intelligence Agency. Under the banner of anti-communism, the AFL-CIO used its considerable resources to support right-wing labor and political leaders. In one of the most notable incidents during this period, between 1971 and 1973, the AFL-CIO's American Institute for Free Labor Development worked closely with the CIA to channel millions of dollars to right-wing unions and political parties opposed to the rule of Chile's Salvador Allende.

But the era of labor's close cooperation with the state was coming to an end. With the period of deindustrialization that began in the 1970s, labor lost membership, strength, and influence. When President Ronald Reagan broke the air traffic controllers' strike in 1981, it was clear that a new pattern of union busting and state-sanctioned union hostility had emerged. In 1995, with union membership at a postwar low, John Sweeney was elected president of the AFL-CIO on a reform platform. Sweeney promised renewed emphasis on organizing and reached out to new constituencies, including activists usually associated with the new social movements that came out of the 1960s. In 1999, when Sweeny gave labor's official sanction to the Seattle protests against the World Trade Organization, it did seem that a new day for labor had dawned. In the years that followed Sweeney's election, however, labor continued to lose ground and now comprises approximately 8% of the nongovernmental, nonfarm workforce. At the same time, despite his reformist credentials, Sweeney continued the AFL-CIO's questionable foreign policies, providing material support for the right-wing oil unions during the failed U.S.-sponsored coup against President Chávez in Venezuela.

As traditional, industrial unions affiliated with the AFL-CIO lost strength, however, nontraditional, service sector unions, like Service Employees International Union (SEIU), actually grew in size and influence. Frustrated by the AFL-CIO's failure to deliver on its post-1995 promises, SEIU disaffiliated with the AFL-CIO in 2005. Since then, several other unions, including the Teamsters and HERE-UNITE, have joined with SEIU to form the Change To Win coalition (CTW), a labor federation in competition with the AFL-CIO. As John Sweeney did in 1995, CTW promises a new emphasis on organizing and militant action. With organizers culled from the ranks of the new social movements, and with a constituency consisting of the least privileged and most exploited of American workers, CTW hopes to reenergize the labor movement and, in particular, promises to organize Wal-Mart. Sympathetic observers, workers, and activists remain uncertain whether this new division within the labor movement will lead to concrete improvement or whether it will be just another factor preventing organized labor from completing the social democratic project of workplace and community justice initiated by the founding of the CIO in 1935.

—Graham Cassano

See also Gompers, Samuel; Industrial Workers of the World (IWW); Labor Culture; Lewis, John L.; Palmer Raids; PATCO Strike

Further Readings

Babson, S. (1999). *The unfinished struggle: Turning points in American labor, 1877–present.* New York: Rowman & Littlefield.

Fantasia, R. (1988). *Cultures of solidarity: Consciousness, action, and contemporary American workers.* Berkeley: University of California Press.

Lichtenstein, N. (2002). *State of the union: A century of American labor.* Princeton, NJ: Princeton University Press.

Montgomery, D. (1979). *Workers' control in America.* New York: Cambridge University Press.

Shorrock, T. (2003, May 19). Labor's cold war. *The Nation.* Retrieved October 6, 2006, from http://www.thenation.com/doc/20030519/shorrock

Veblen, T. (1921). *Engineers and the price system.* New Brunswick, NJ: Transaction.

AMERICAN FEDERATION OF TEACHERS

See TEACHER UNIONS

AMERICAN GOLD STAR MOTHERS

American Gold Star Mothers is a remembrance and service organization for mothers of military personnel who have died in the line of duty. Members of the organization offer emotional support to each other as well as services to care for veterans who are receiving treatment in government hospitals. The organization was founded in 1928 by Grace Darling Siebold, whose son died in 1918 during World War I. The organization was named for the memorial flag that families hung in the front window of their homes to commemorate the deceased veteran. Membership is open to all mothers whose children served and died in the line of duty. Mothers who join must support the goals of the organization, which include allegiance to the United States, service to the State and the Nation, and the promotion of peace and goodwill nationally and internationally.

The Gold Star Mothers original charter was written to support mothers who hold American citizenship whose sons died during World War I. The charter was revised during World War II and again during the Korean War to allow mothers whose sons died in those wars to join the organization. More recently, Gold Star Mothers again revised their charter to include mothers whose sons or daughters died in the line of duty in any U.S. military operation. Noncitizen mothers, however, were still denied membership. In 2005, Carmen Palmer and Ligaya Lagman, both permanent residents of the United States, became the first noncitizen mothers allowed to join Gold Star Mothers. Earlier in the year, both women applied to join the organization and were refused membership. In early 2005, the organization reviewed the matter and voted to maintain the citizenship requirement. This refusal led to a national outcry and Gold Star Mothers revised their charter in June 2005 to allow mothers who are legal residents of the United States to join the organization.

Although the organization is nominally apolitical, its focus has been supportive of most military endeavors. The organization often works with military service organizations to ensure that active duty military personnel and veterans are recognized for their service and sacrifices. In addition, Gold Star Mothers chapters operate on military bases to support grieving families. Its 2000 individual members volunteer in communities nationwide to assist veterans and their dependents with claims made to the Veterans Administration, and individuals and chapters work with various organizations to inspire patriotism. Traditionally, Gold Star Mothers have distanced themselves from anti-war activities, but in 1971, Gold Star Mothers led a 5-day anti-war protest in Washington, D.C., sponsored by Vietnam Veterans Against the War. Because Gold Star Mothers is traditionally apolitical, in response, Gold Star Families for Peace was chartered in 2005 to represent families of deceased service members who oppose U.S. military involvement overseas.

—Barbara Garii

Further Readings

American Gold Star Mothers, Inc. (2005). *American Gold Star Mothers.* Retrieved March 1, 2006, from http://www .goldstarmoms.com/agsm/Home/index.htm

Erlbaum, M. (2002). What legacy from the radical internationalism of 1968? *Radical History Review, 82,* 37–64.

Piehler, G. K. (1995). *Remembering the war the American way.* Washington, DC: Smithsonian Institution Press.

AMERICAN INDIAN MOVEMENT

The American Indian Movement (AIM) was started in 1968 by George Mitchell, Dennis Banks, and Clyde Bellecourt and initially was focused on getting fair treatment for American Indians by police and the legal system in Minneapolis, Minnesota. Although there were other American Indian groups addressing American Indian rights at this time, the goals of the organization quickly expanded to protecting the rights of all American Indians. What was unique to this organization, however, was that it was urban based when most American Indian organizations were started on reservations located in remote areas. In the first meeting in July 1968, 250 people showed up to voice their concerns about the status of American Indians with regard to racism, school dropout rates, and the number of arrests in the area.

During the first year of AIM's existence, the organization focused on increasing employment opportunities and better housing, improving education, and monitoring police activities in Minneapolis. Such activity received national attention as well as resulted in fewer police arrests and more humane treatment of American Indians. In addition to these issues, the AIM organization also focused on the need to protect treaty rights and the sovereignty of Native American Nations, and to preserve Native spirituality and culture. Prior to this time, the U.S. government had mandated boarding schools for American Indian children, which had taken them away, often far away, from their families and communities. There had been forced relocation programs for American Indian young adults and other government-backed methods of assimilation.

In November of 1969, 14 Native Americans "repossessed" Alcatraz Island off the coast of San Francisco, California. Banks and others wanted to bring national attention to the poverty, poor housing, and lack of education most American Indians experienced in their daily lives. The activists saw the occupation of the deserted prison and island of Alcatraz much like they viewed American Indian reservations, and they cited treaty rights that had guaranteed the return of unoccupied federal lands to American Indians. Shortly after the initial occupation, about 100 American Indians joined Banks and others, claiming Alcatraz as "Indian Country." The occupation lasted 19 months, until June 1971. All negotiations and meetings between the activists and U.S. government were unproductive, but the media attention brought national attention to American Indian problems.

During the occupation, takeover of government land started to take place all over the United States. Of particular note was the encampment by American Indians on Mount Rushmore to protest the desecration of the Black Hills. As well, there was an attempt to seize Ellis Island near Jersey City, New Jersey, as a way of uniting the Red Power movement from both coasts.

Besides the moves on Mount Rushmore and Ellis Island, there was a sit-in at the Bureau of Indian

Affairs (BIA) office in Littleton, Colorado, which stemmed from a formal complaint of job discrimination that had been filed against the BIA and a local industry. The National Indian Youth Council filed the initial complaint, and Banks and AIM of Minneapolis supported the sit-in. Three days later, police emptied the building and arrested 12 of the activists, who became known as the Littleton 12. The media reported that a wave of demonstrations was being set off around the country, all in support of the Littleton 12. Those activists arrested in Littleton were charged with trespassing but pled innocent and received a jury trial. However, BIA officials dropped the charges the next year before the trial could begin.

Due to the attention of the national media, membership grew rapidly and the dress and accessories of the AIM activists became widespread among activists and others across the country. To continue to draw attention to the broken treaties and treatment of American Indians, AIM members and others began to fly the American flag upside down as a distress signal.

In 1972, AIM held a series of national meetings. At the September AIM National Council, members developed a list of 20 major problems in Native American communities in the United States. The organization stressed self-governance of tribes and exchanged letters with the White House. They planned an event known as the Trail of Broken Treaties, which also included such organizations as the Native American Rights Fund, the National Indian Brotherhood of Canada, the National Indian Lutheran Board, the United Native Americans, and others. This event was actually a march on Washington, D.C., which ended in the occupation of the BIA headquarters and the presentation of a 20-point solution paper to then president Nixon.

Beyond the significance of the 20-point solution paper were the events in 1973. By this time, AIM had members from many different tribes and nations. One event of importance surrounded the death of a local American Indian man, Wesley Bad Heart Bull, who was stabbed to death in a town just outside the Pine Ridge Reservation. The white man accused of his death was charged with second-degree manslaughter. AIM members protested, claiming that the charge was

evidence of how little Indian life was valued by the white power structure. In February, as part of the protest against the charges filed for the death of Bad Heart Bull, AIM and other American Indian demonstrators took over the courthouse in Custer, South Dakota, and later burned the courthouse and an unoccupied Chamber of Commerce. The situation came under control following federal marshals' use of tear gas. Numerous arrests were made.

Other events leading up to the occupation of Wounded Knee centered on tribal politics. In the years prior to the protest, American Indians on the Pine Ridge Reservation had used every means available to them to persuade the U.S. government to address more than 150 civil rights violations by the tribal government headed by Richard Wilson. After all efforts had failed, Oglala and Brule Sioux elders asked the AIM membership to help them stage a protest. The elders and the AIM leadership decided that Wounded Knee would be the place to stage the protest, as it was an historical and sacred site. The occupation of the community of Wounded Knee began on February 27 when approximately 200 members and supporters of AIM met outside of the community of Pine Ridge and made their way to Wounded Knee, South Dakota, the site of the 1890 massacre of several hundred Oglala Sioux men, women, and children by the Seventh Cavalry.

The government, under President Richard Nixon, responded to the protest and occupation with an impressive show of force. Over the 71 days, the National Guard, Federal Bureau of Investigation (FBI), federal marshals, and local police were present. Law enforcement agency staff were well armed and even brought armored personnel carriers to the community. Government officials from the Attorney General's Office, the BIA, the Department of the Interior, U.S. senators from South Dakota, media personnel, members of the clergy, and supporters for the protesters were also present.

Throughout the occupation, negotiations were held between the protesters and government officials. On May 5, a dispossession agreement was signed by government officials, including Solicitor for the Department of the Interior Kent Frizzell; Director of the U.S. Marshal Service Wayne Colburn; Deputy

Assistant Attorney General Richard Hellstern; and by Leonard Crow Dog, Franklin Fools Crow, and others on behalf of AIM, the traditional Oglala leaders, and the occupants of Wounded Knee. On the morning of May 8, 71 days after the occupation had started, the occupation ended. Of the 129 people who left Wounded Knee, 85% were American Indians and 33 were residents of Wounded Knee. Fifteen arrests were made following the evacuation, which brought the total number of people arrested for the protest to 237.

The Wounded Knee trial in Minnesota for AIM leaders Dennis Banks and Russell Means lasted 8 months. The prosecution spent 6 of those months in presenting its case on 11 counts against the two activists. The judge, Fred Nichol, dismissed 5 of the 11 charges. The other counts were scheduled to go to a jury. At the conclusion of the trial, the two men were acquitted and all charges dropped. Other Wounded Knee trials were going on in three states. The Custer County Courthouse trials were also taking place in Rapid City, South Dakota.

Following the occupation of Wounded Knee, there was heavy government monitoring of AIM activities, and public interest in AIM declined dramatically as attention became concentrated on other events, namely the Watergate scandal. Distrust became strong among the AIM leadership, as they felt that there were informants for the federal authorities among them. They felt that the FBI's COINTELPRO (Counter Intelligence Program) was being used against the organization. Indeed, AIM leaders eventually discovered that Douglass Durham, a supposed AIM member who had joined the protest at Wounded Knee and was acting as Dennis Banks's assistant and coordinator of the Wounded Knee Legal Defense/Offense Committee, was actually a government informant. Public anti-AIM sentiment was also on the rise, especially in South Dakota.

In 1975, AIM member Leonard Peltier, Darrell "Dino" Butler, and Robert Robideau were accused of shooting and killing two FBI agents, Jack Coler and Ronald Williams, on the Pine Ridge Reservation. The legal defense fund of AIM provided money for the defense of the three men. Butler and Robideau were acquitted because the court believed they acted in self-defense, but in 1977, Leonard Peltier was found guilty and received two life sentences for the killings of the FBI agents.

In 1978, AIM organized a nationwide demonstration called the Longest Walk. The purpose of the walk was to educate the American and world communities about the struggle of American Indians and to bring public attention to 11 anti-Indian bills before Congress. In the opinion of AIM, the bills would take away the self-determination of American Indian people. Beginning in March in California, the walk was supported by church organizations, social groups, and even heavyweight boxer, Ken Norton. Thousands of American Indians arrived in Washington, D.C., in mid-July and camped in a nearby park in Virginia. The protest was deemed a success as the bills were defeated.

In the years following Wounded Knee, many of the leaders of AIM had to undergo trials, and AIM shifted direction back to regional social concerns. One issue that the organization investigated was the destruction of Native American graves and human remains. Members lectured and held public awareness meetings about the problem. The states of Indiana and Kentucky passed laws to protect gravesites as a result of AIM's activities. Eventually, a federal law was passed called the Native American Graves Protection and Repatriation Act (NAGPRA) [25 U.S.C. 3001 et seq. Nov. 16, 1990], which provides for the repatriation of the objects and remains of Native ancestors that were appropriated, collected, manipulated, sold, or displayed by Europeans and Americans. Over this time, AIM also supported the activities of other activist groups, such as the United Farm Workers, led by activist César Chávez, as well as Mexican American groups and black nationalists.

Twenty years following the second Wounded Knee, AIM members and many others returned to Wounded Knee, meeting at the gravesite of the 1890 Wounded Knee massacre. Whereas in 1973, the times had been acrimonious and violent, in 1993 times were much more harmonious. The memorial ceremony was solemn and peaceful.

In 1994, AIM organized the Walk for Justice, another event that began in California and ended in Washington, D.C. The walk was intended to bring about national awareness to the grievances of Native Americans as well as a means to collect signatures of people who were urging the release of Leonard Peltier. Later, in 1997, Banks led the *Bring Peltier Home* campaign that included teach-ins, concerts, and petition drives. AIM chapters and Peltier support groups from all over the world came together to talk about how to get Peltier released. A *Run for Freedom* from Cincinnati, Ohio, to Tulsa, Oklahoma, was also held in 1997. Since then, AIM has also taken legal action against the names of sports organizations, such as the Washington Redskins and Cleveland Indians.

AIM was organized as a civil rights organization, but the membership also became known for founding culturally relevant schools for American Indian children, an emphasis on traditional spirituality, and a focus on treaty rights. AIM became an interstate organization with largely autonomous chapters in many states. Throughout its nearly 40-year history, the organization has endured, waxing and waning in strength and popularity among both American Indians and the U.S. public.

—*Dana E. Christman*

See also Civil Rights Movement; Oglala, Incident at; Treaty Rights Struggle; Wounded Knee

Further Readings

Cheatham, K. (1997). *Dennis Banks: Native American activist.* Springfield, NJ: Enslow.

Dewing, R. (Ed.). (1973). *The FBI files on the American Indian Movement and Wounded Knee* [Microfilm]. Frederick, MD: University Publications of America.

Sanchez, J., Stuckey, M. E., & Morris, R. (1999). Rhetorical exclusion: The government's case against American Indian activists, AIM, and Leonard Peltier. *American Indian Culture and Research Journal, 23*(2), 27–52.

Wittstock, L. W., & Salinas, E. J. (n.d.). *A brief history of the American Indian Movement.* Retrieved February 4, 2006, from http://www.aimovement.org/ggc/history.html

AMERICAN REVOLUTION

American Revolution is the term given to the war for independence fought by the British North American colonies from 1775 to 1783. For a century and a half following the first English settlements along the coast of North America, the British government mostly ignored them. All of the colonies had written charters, issued either by the King or by the corporate structure that had originally funded them. By the 1750s, most of the colonies had a royal governor, appointed by the King. The colonies were expected to levy their own taxes to pay for the upkeep of the governor, the other executive offices, and their court systems. Beyond that, little was expected of the colonists beyond trade with the mother country. In fact, the colonial legislatures usually used their responsibility to support the governor as a weapon against him. Governors demanding too much power or being otherwise unpopular with the elites who controlled the local legislatures often found themselves unpaid.

The French and Indian War between Great Britain and France (1754–1763; known in Europe as the Seven Years' War) saw North America become a major theater of operations. Several armies from the mother country were dispatched to the colonies, which were expected to support them. Depending on the tact and persuasive powers of the English commanders, many of the colonists began to view the "protection" offered by the armies as a mixed blessing. To this uneasiness was added the personal arrogance of many of the British officer corps, and their widespread contempt for the colonials. The upper-class Americans took this disdain particularly badly, having considered themselves "country squires" every bit as well off as their English counterparts. In fact, many of the American officers who would later lead the Revolution began their military careers during this war and remembered, with disgust, being looked down on by their English counterparts.

After the Seven Years' War ended in 1763 with a crushing English victory, the British government found itself with a massive war debt and a much enlarged empire to police. The government decided that the colonists should pay a portion of the costs that were, from the government's perspective, incurred to protect them. The colonists thought otherwise. Over the next 10 years, Parliament tried repeated schemes to impose some kind of tax on the colonies; each attempt was met with increasing, and increasingly violent, resistance.

Massachusetts in particular found itself in a cycle of increasingly violent response to Parliament's attempts to exercise control. After Bostonians dumped a load of taxed tea in the harbor (the famed Boston Tea Party) on December 16, 1773, London shut down the port and occupied it with British regular army forces. The rest of the colonies rallied to Massachusetts' support, mindful that any of them could be next to feel Parliament's wrath. A Congress of all of the colonies was called for Philadelphia.

War for Independence

The crisis boiled over in May 1775. The British commander in Boston decided to try to extend his power into some of the surrounding towns. He sent a force of 1,800 soldiers marching to Lexington and Concord, inland from Boston, to confiscate some weapons and arrest a couple of the local radicals. Instead, the townspeople resisted, sending the British back to Boston with heavy casualties.

The colonies in general, and New England in particular, were galvanized into action. Within days, New England militia had surrounded and besieged Boston. The Continental Congress sent a Virginia plantation owner and veteran of the French and Indian War, George Washington, to command the rebel forces surrounding the city.

From the beginning, the British were hamstrung by several factors. First and foremost was distance. It could take 6 weeks for messages from the colonies to reach London and even longer for a response to make it back. Within weeks, rebels had overthrown almost every loyalist government in the 13 colonies, giving them the advantage of controlling the governmental structures before the British even knew there was a problem. The second problem was that many of the British in Parliament and especially in the military sympathized with the rebels' complaints.

Despite King George's defiant rhetoric and Parliament's moves to send much stronger forces to suppress the rebels, by the winter of 1776 the British were forced to evacuate Boston. That summer, however,

the British landed in force at New York. The Americans suffered a series of defeats and were chased out of New York City and, by late December, out of New Jersey. Washington rallied his forces, however, and surprised the British with a series of counterattacks starting at Trenton, New Jersey, on the day after Christmas. By late January, Washington's forces had recaptured much of New Jersey.

In the meantime, the King's aggressive rhetoric had two effects in the colonies, neither of them good for the Empire. Most of the colonists had been of the opinion that their quarrel was with Parliament and the King's ministers, not the King himself. The King, they hoped, would mediate the dispute. These moderates were disabused of the notion. The King's stance also narrowed the rebels' perceived options to submission or independence. In July 1776 (July 2, not July 4, which was the date the final version was published), the colonists chose independence.

It would be easy, in retrospect, to view American independence as inevitable, but it did not appear so to the participants. For the next 4 years, the British were able to conquer almost any city they chose, though they were never able to control the rural areas. The rebels were constantly plagued with financial difficulties and political divisions. They were never able to adequately supply their armies, and at times, the soldiers were near starvation. Washington and the other American generals soon understood, however, that maintaining what later analysts would call a force in being was more important than winning battlefield victories.

In 1777, the British suffered a devastating defeat when an army marching south from Canada was cut off from its supplies and forced to surrender. This victory encouraged the French and subsequently the Spanish and Dutch to join the war against Britain. These foreign allies changed the nature of the war. For Britain, North America was now a sideshow in a world war encompassing the wealthy Caribbean islands, India, and the European continent.

The climax of the war came in October 1781. A British army that had marauded across the South without being able to control much more than the land they were standing on was cornered in Yorktown, Virginia. They surrendered to a combined French and

American army after the French navy had beaten the British navy's attempt to reinforce them in the Chesapeake Bay. Everyone now conceded the independence of the Americans, but the British were still fighting the European powers, and final terms were not worked out until the Treaty of Paris was signed on September 3, 1783.

Civil War

Support for the Revolution was far from unanimous in the colonies. John Adams later said that one third of the colonists were for the rebellion, one third of the colonists were loyalist, and one third did not care. Historians believe his analysis was broadly accurate.

In New England, support for the rebellion was probably overwhelming, outside of Boston and the other big cities, which had substantial loyalist minorities. Virginia was probably also largely opposed to the Crown. The King enjoyed broad support in New York City and, at first, in New Jersey, although the repeated depredations of the British army as it marched across the colony, beginning in the winter of 1776, quickly eroded that support.

The pacifist Quakers of Pennsylvania and southern New Jersey opposed the war and ranged from neutrality to passively loyalist in attitude. The French of what is now Quebec and Ontario saw little to choose between the Anglophone protestant Americans and Anglophone protestant English, and ignored the Americans' attempts to recruit them to the cause. Nova Scotia, heavily dependent on the British naval base at Halifax, never seriously considered joining the rebellion. Generally, the loyalists in the North supported the British when they occupied any particular city, such as Boston, New York, or Philadelphia, and, when the soldiers left, evacuated with them.

In the northern colonies, the rebels also benefited from their control of the governments. As long as they provided the necessary public services (primarily access to the courts and land registration), the majority of the populace, especially the apolitical persons, was content to acquiesce.

By far the bloodiest struggle between loyalists and rebels took place in South Carolina and North Carolina. Here, the conflict between loyalists and rebels was complicated by conflict between the tidewater landowners, who had controlled the colonial governments before the war, and new settlers moving into the river valleys of the Appalachian Mountains.

This conflict was, in large part, based on class and ethnicity. The newcomers were poor—and violent— Scots-Irish who were leaving Ulster and Scotland and migrating down the Great Valley from Pennsylvania and Virginia. The conflict also preceded the Revolution; the Scots-Irish immigrants had been fighting both the Cherokee Indians and the state governments (especially of South Carolina) since they started moving in a generation previously.

By 1780, the entire region had deteriorated into a wave of atrocity and counteratrocity as fighting degenerated into neighbor versus neighbor killings. What side any one individual chose was as likely to be predicated on the side his hated neighbor next door took or on what side had killed his brother or looted his farmstead as on ideological concepts.

The loyalist militias were particularly brutal in their treatment of real and presumed rebels, especially after the British regular army conquered Charleston in May 1780, and began to march into the countryside. Indeed, by September of that year, almost all organized resistance by the rebels had collapsed in South Carolina, and it appeared that the colony would be won back for the Crown.

In October, however, a group of frontiersmen from what is now eastern Tennessee, who had been threatened by the loyalist leaders if they did not submit, surrounded, fought, and defeated a loyalist force of some 1,100 loyalists, butchering many of them after the battle. This battle, along with new leadership of the regular rebel army, led to a resurgence of rebel fortunes in the South. By summer 1781, the British army and their few surviving loyalist supporters were holed up in Charleston and Savannah, Georgia.

As the war wound down and the British evacuated the remaining cities, most of the loyalists left with them. Some moved back to Great Britain, but most moved to Canada, settling in the Maritime Provinces and along Lake Ontario and the Niagara River. Their sons stoutly resisted the American attempts to conquer them in the War of 1812, and their descendents have held ambivalent feelings toward the United States ever since then.

Social Revolution

The leaders of the American Revolution did not couch their rhetoric in terms of ethnic nationalism, as the leaders of so many later wars of independence have done. This would have been difficult because they considered themselves the same as their cousins in England. Indeed, they argued they were fighting for the same rights their English brothers possessed. The rebels therefore used—indeed, largely invented, the language of liberty and political rights to justify their actions.

In using such expressions as "all men are created equal" and, later, "freedom of speech," most of the first generation of leaders had a much more limited concept of equality than what it came to mean for later generations. For these prosperous businessmen and lawyers, it would have been "equality of opportunity" and "equality of protection before the law," certainly not social or political equality. The language they used and the forces it unleashed, however, changed the world far more than the mere independence of 13 economically marginal colonies on the far side of a wide ocean.

The colonies had never had hereditary, titled nobility as existed in England and most of Europe. Nevertheless, it was a highly stratified and vertically structured society, based on connections to sponsors and family, however distantly related. Individuals were expected to defer to their "betters." Even the most democratized colonies, such as Rhode Island, were, in fact, run by a few small, interlocking, if competing, clans. Skill and ability could lead to success; especially in the northern colonies. Benjamin Franklin is proof of that. By and large, however, a person's prospects were determined more by his connections than by his competency.

Most of the first generation of founding fathers probably had no conscious thought of making significant changes in the arrangement; they were, after all, its beneficiaries. Most were deeply fearful of democracy, for them a synonym for mob rule. The Constitutional Convention of 1787 was at least as much a response to signs of increasing unrest among

what later generations would call "the workers" as it was a response to the institutional inadequacies of the Articles of Confederation, set up by the Continental Congress during the War for Independence.

The institutionalized evidence of this fear of the masses is visible in the Constitution drafted by the Convention. Only members of the House of Representatives were directly elected by the people. The Senate was chosen by the state governments, the president by the electoral college, and the Supreme Court by the president and Senate. Not as obvious was the implied limitation on the people. Almost every state had a property ownership requirement for voting, some of which were quite large. This was considered entirely appropriate by the conservatives; only people with a stake in the land and the wealth to own such a stake were likely to make wise and considered decisions, instead of being swept up as part of "the mob."

The conservative instincts of the writers of the Constitution were only heightened by the French Revolution. In the 1790s, the French had absorbed the egalitarian rhetoric of the American Revolution and quickly took it to bloody extremes, culminating in the Reign of Terror and subsequent counter-revolution leading to the dictator Napoleon. The American conservatives, now coalesced into a protopolitical party, the Federalists, attempted to stifle the increasingly vitriolic American debate through such measures as the Alien and Sedition Acts, which allowed criminal prosecutions for anti-government speech.

It was too late. The Americans, too, were pursuing the language of liberty and equality to where it led. The 1800 election pitted the increasingly centralizing and authoritarian Federalists against Thomas Jefferson and his Republicans, who argued for more individual rights. Most of the Jeffersonians were by no means "democrats" in the sense of supporting such concepts as universal suffrage, but they did represent a step toward the integration of more people into the political discourse. After losing the election, the Federalists were never again a serious national party, and they and their elitist concept of government faded away within 15 years.

Jeffersonian democracy was still not universal (white, male) suffrage, however. Jefferson and his successors were agrarians with a limited view of the people. They favored less federal government involvement in the lives of the people, and greater personal liberties than did the Federalists, but, by and large, they feared the malignant power of the urban and rural poor almost as much as the Federalists.

State by state, the right to vote spread to more and more white men. Between 1824 and 1828, under the pressure of an enraged politician and frontier war hero, Andrew Jackson (he felt the elites had stolen the 1824 presidential election from him), almost every state allowed almost every white man to vote. The results were astonishing. In 1828, 314% more Americans voted than in 1824, and the populist "man of the people," Jackson, was elected president in a landslide.

The American Revolution was not completed, of course. Blacks were not freed from slavery until the 1860s and were not given a meaningful opportunity to vote until the 1960s and 1970s. Women did not receive the right to vote until 1920. But the America that Alexis de Toqueville saw in the 1830s would have been unimaginable 60 years before then. The structured, hierarchical society of connection and deferment had been replaced by a society that viewed itself as based on opportunity and merit; on what a person could do, not who he knew.

—Joseph Adamczyk

See also Bill of Rights; Jefferson, Thomas

Further Readings

Bowen, C. D. (1966). *Miracle at Philadelphia: The story of the Constitutional Convention May to September 1787.* Boston: Little, Brown.

Ferling, J. (2004). *Adams vs. Jefferson: The tumultuous election of 1800.* New York: Oxford University Press.

Middlekauff, R. (1982). *The glorious cause: The American Revolution, 1762–1789.* New York: Oxford University Press.

Nash, G. B. (2005). *The unknown American Revolution: The unruly birth of democracy and the struggle to create America.* New York: Viking.

Wills, G. (1978). *Inventing America: Jefferson's Declaration of Independence.* New York: Simon & Schuster.

AMNESTY INTERNATIONAL

Amnesty International (AI) is generally considered the most important international human rights nongovernmental organization (NGO) worldwide. A winner of the Nobel Peace Prize in 1977, it holds consultative status with a number of international organizations, including the United Nations and the Council of Europe, and claims a membership of nearly 2 million in 150 countries and territories. The London-based International Secretariat employs roughly 450 staff members, with an annual budget of more than £28 million. Over its 45 years of existence, AI has gone from a movement for the defense of freedom of opinion and religion, in reference to articles 18 and 19 of the U.N.'s Universal Declaration of Human Rights, to a much broader organization, which campaigns for internationally recognized human rights.

AI was originally set up to seek the immediate and unconditional release of "prisoners of conscience," people imprisoned only for having voiced an opinion, without resorting to violence or advocating the use of violence. Today, AI, drawing on the Universal Declaration of Human Rights and other international human rights standards, undertakes actions focused on preventing and ending grave abuses of the rights to physical and mental integrity, freedom of conscience and expression, and freedom from discrimination.

AI started on May 28, 1961, first as a 1-year campaign for the release of prisoners of conscience under the name Appeal for Amnesty 1961, when London barrister Peter Benenson (1921–2005) published an article titled "The Forgotten Prisoners" in the English weekly *The Observer.* Benenson already had some experience in the fields of politics and human rights: He had been a Labour candidate at local elections, had attended political trials in other countries on behalf of the Trade Union Congress, and had taken part in 1956 in the foundation of the organization Justice, which brought together members from the three major political parties' societies of lawyers and subsequently became the U.K. branch of the International Commission of Jurists. After his conversion to Catholicism in 1958, he resigned from the bar in 1959 for health reasons.

Because Benenson played a key role in the creation of AI, he must be considered the actual founder of the movement. He led a group of jurists, academics, and journalists, which included, among others, Eric Baker, a prominent Quaker activist and chair of the British section of AI; Neville Vincent, a lawyer and businessman, who became AI's first treasurer; and Irish lawyer and politician Sean MacBride (1904–1988), secretary general of the International Commission of Jurists, chair of AI's International Executive Committee (1961–1974), and winner of both the Nobel Peace Prize (1974) and the Lenin Prize (1977).

Benenson's idea was to call on international public opinion and to involve ordinary citizens, not just lawyers, in the struggle for human rights. His article met with a favorable response and was reproduced in newspapers worldwide. AI's first members formed "Threes groups" at the local level, which each took the defense of three prisoners of conscience: one from the Western world, one from the communist world, and one from a nonaligned country. After a year, there were 70 active groups in seven countries. A central office was set up in London to provide information and coordinate groups' activities. Still in 1961, Benenson published the book *Persecution '61,* which presented nine cases of prisoners of conscience, and AI adopted its official logo: the flame in barbed wire, designed by group member Diana Redhouse on an idea from Benenson. AI then became a permanent organization after a meeting in Luxembourg in July 1961, and the name Amnesty International was formally adopted the following year.

AI's main objective was to assert the utmost importance of human rights in the context of the Cold War, at a time when all political issues were interpreted within the framework of the fundamental East–West conflict. AI condemned human rights violations as such, without supporting or opposing any political or economic system: AI is neither a capitalist nor a communist organization. That attitude was then a real novelty; it was also not an easy position to maintain. Until the fall of the Berlin Wall, AI was regularly accused of being an agent either of the KGB or of the CIA. AI's

impartiality and independence manifested themselves both in its strategy (groups adopted prisoners from both sides, and AI condemned human rights abuses in both worlds) and in its financial policy (it was decided that AI would take no fund from governments or international organizations). The actual reality was not that clear-cut, however. Throughout the 1960s, AI was constantly under surveillance from the British secret services, if not funded by the British government, which partially explains Benenson's resignation and departure in 1967. AI's position also took into account other preexistent human rights movements, especially the elitist and liberal International Commission of Jurists, and the communist National Council of Civil Liberties. Benenson thought that because of their political orientation, these organizations were unable to defend human rights very effectively, and AI's impartiality and independence were a response to these limitations.

AI is a highly centralized and integrated structure, whose core is the London-based International Secretariat. It accommodates, in particular, the movement's researchers, who conduct field investigations and write reports. The International Secretariat's prominent figure is the Secretary General, appointed by AI's International Executive Committee. The Secretary General is the operational leader of the movement, as well as its spokesperson. It is often considered the most important position within the organization, which has been held since 2001 by Irene Khan from Bangladesh, who took over from Pierre Sané from Senegal (1992–2001). The International Executive Committee is AI's central political authority. It is made of nine members, who are elected to a 2-year term at the biannual International Council Meeting, AI's supreme decision-making body, which brings together representatives from all countries where the movement is active and sets up its general policy.

At the moment, there are 72 AI national sections or structures in the world, which all work under the authority of the International Secretariat and whose policy must be consistent with AI's general strategy. The sections are active at national level: They bring together local groups and individual members, lobby national authorities, and undertake fund-raising actions, AI's first financial resource. Until 2001, AI section members were not allowed to work on human rights abuses in their own respective countries. The biggest sections are in the United States, the United Kingdom, the Netherlands, Germany, and France. AI is a unique body, in the sense that it has both a strong supranational element (the International Secretariat) and an important local presence, with its many members, groups, and networks. Unlike some other, more institutionalized, NGOs, it is considered not only a voluntary organization but also a grassroots movement and a democratic organization, where crucial decisions are made after long internal debates and only when a consensus is reached.

AI's actions are based on international human rights law and humanitarian law, which are used in the struggle for human rights. International law is a central resource for AI, but it can become, in certain circumstances, a limitation, as AI is a legalist organization whose demands do not go further than existing international law. It is also quite a slow organization, which takes action only on the basis of reliable and confirmed information. It intervenes by first calling on public opinion and then asking its numerous members and supporters to send letters, cards, and petitions to put pressure on governments and those responsible for human rights abuses. Thanks to an important network of members and supporters, AI is able to take action quickly and on a large scale. Members also regularly undertake awareness and fund-raising activities. AI is recognized for the quality of its publications and its expertise in the field of human rights. Its reports and press releases are often used and quoted by the press, which serves as another medium for AI. Furthermore, AI lobbies international organizations actively and has permanent representatives in New York to the United Nations and in Brussels to the European Union, in order to encourage the adoption of international treaties.

AI's mandate underwent several crucial reviews. In the 1970s, AI ran its first campaigns against torture and the death penalty; in the 1980s, it took the defense of refugees and asylum seekers; in the 1990s, it intervened in armed conflicts and toward armed political groups; and, more recently, it began addressing grave abuses of economic, social, and cultural rights. From 1961 to 2001, the mandate evolved in an incremental way, one concern paving the way for another, without any substantial change of logic: from prisoners of conscience to conditions of detention, then from torture to the death penalty, and so forth. Evolution was slow, as it had to be accepted by a vast majority of the members and often prompted some heated debates. The mandate also only grew larger and larger: New topics were added, and nothing was ever taken away.

By the end of the 1990s, the mandate had become a list of what AI could or could not do, a list that some considered too restrictive and not flexible enough. At the 2001 International Council Meeting in Dakar, delegates decided that a new vision and mission would take the place of the mandate, in order for AI to address human rights abuses more effectively. AI then adopted its first Integrated Strategic Plan for the period 2004–2010, which defines its midterm policy and priorities. It now also addresses violations of economic, social, and cultural rights (right to education, to food, to health, etc.), as well as civil and political rights (freedom of opinion, freedom of conscience, right to physical and mental integrity, etc.), which were always part of its mandate. These two generations of human rights were most notably recognized in the two 1966 U.N. covenants, the distinction itself being to a large extent a by-product of the East–West conflict.

The end of the Cold War was regarded as a major turn, not only by AI but also by the human rights movement as a whole. Various actors hoped for a reorganization of international relations around multilateral institutions, especially the United Nations. Fundamental rights were put at the forefront of the international stage and received global recognition, which did not necessarily mean drastic changes in actual policies. This recognition at least encouraged NGOs to become more professional, with dramatic increases in budget and staff. It also involved more competition: In the 1990s, Human Rights Watch became AI's first rival. It is sometimes considered that such professionalism and competition tend to pull NGOs away from their original missions of advocacy and criticism of governments.

The 1990s were also a time of great confusion, and, contrary to what was once thought, no "new world order" based on democracy and global respect of human rights came into being. Because of the increasing number of local conflicts, AI had to review its policy regarding the use of armed force, especially after such crises as the genocide in Rwanda, the war in Chechnya, the Great Lakes in Africa, the Darfur conflict in Sudan, and others. The 9/11 terrorist attacks on the World Trade Center in New York and the Pentagon in Washington, D.C., and the subsequent "war on terror" represent another major challenge for AI, as the organization now works in a context where rights regarded as fundamental are undermined in the name of security, where individual freedoms are threatened, and where the universality of human rights is questioned.

—Eric Poinsot

See also Advocacy; Human Rights Watch; Law and Social Movements; Nobel Peace Prize; Non-Governmental Organizations (NGOs); Strategies and Tactics in Social Movements; Universal Declaration of Human Rights

Further Readings

Buchanan, T. (2002). "The truth will set you free": The making of Amnesty International. *Journal of Contemporary History, 37*(4), 575–597.

Buchanan, T. (2004). Amnesty International in crisis, 1966–7. *Twentieth Century British History, 15*(3), 267–289.

Clark, A. M. (2001). *Diplomacy of conscience.* Princeton, NJ: Princeton University Press.

Hopgood, S. (2006). *Keepers of the flame: Understanding Amnesty International.* Ithaca, NY: Cornell University Press.

Mihr, A. (2002). *Amnesty International in der DDR.* Berlin: Ch. Links.

Power, J. (2002). *Like water on stone.* London: Penguin.

ANARCHISM

Anarchism, which was once thought to have passed with the 19th century, has made a resurgence in recent years. Particularly since the fall of the Berlin Wall, progressive activists have turned increasingly toward anarchism for a framework within which to understand and orient their work. From Seattle to Genoa, anarchism has once again found support among organizers. Nineteenth-century anarchists are being read anew, and recently the theoretical tradition of anarchism is being expanded by writers and thinkers who see themselves either as anarchists or inspired by anarchism.

There is good reason to return to anarchism, particularly in the wake of the experience of the 20th century. The main theoretical alternative to anarchism as a framework for progressive thought, Marxism, was derailed during the last century, giving rise to social and political systems that were a betrayal of progressive hopes. Whether or not the totalitarianism associated with Marxist states was or was not in keeping with Karl Marx's writings is a vexing theoretical question. In any case, anarchists of the 19th century, criticizing Marx, predicted with uncanny accuracy the problems that beset Marxist states in the 20th century.

What distinguishes anarchism from Marxism, a distinction that both drives the mutual suspicion between them and that makes anarchism relevant for us today, is anarchism's embrace of radical equality and its consequent rejection of an avant-garde party. For anarchism, all social change must happen on the basis of recognition of the equality of participants in that change. There is no distinction to be drawn between those who lead and those who follow, between those who have knowledge and those who trust them, or between party members and nonmembers. To believe in these distinctions is to fail to grasp the fundamental problem besetting almost all previous existing social orders, that of hierarchy. Whereas for Marx the issue to be overcome in capitalism is exploitation, for anarchists it is domination.

There is more to this difference than the substitution of one term for another. For Marx, exploitation occurs in a specific sector of society; exploitation is an economic phenomenon. Recall Marx's concept of exploitation: It is the extraction of surplus value from the workers. Surplus value, in turn, represents the amount of labor performed by the workers that is not returned to them by the capitalist. Other areas of society may well foster or reinforce exploitation, but it is exploitation itself that is the lynchpin of Marx's analysis of capitalism.

This has two consequences. First, all social change, if it is to be effective, must focus on the economic relations between the capitalist and the worker. Marx was the first thinker to claim, in effect, that "it's the economy, stupid." Second, if the economy is to be the central focus of social change, then it is best for those who know how the economy works and how to change it to lead the struggle, hence the emergence of the avant-garde party in Marxist political tradition.

The anarchist concept of domination is different from that of exploitation, and not because it points elsewhere than the economy. It is, in fact, a different kind of concept. Whereas exploitation points to a specific social sector, domination does not. Domination occurs wherever there is hierarchy, wherever one person or group holds sway over another in a way that forces the latter to do the bidding of the former. There is domination in gender relationships, in racial relationships, around the issue of sexual orientation, in political movements, and elsewhere. Although some hierarchies may be more deleterious or have wider ramifications than others, domination in all its forms is to be resisted. There is no privileged point of focus, as there is with the concept of exploitation.

As a consequence of this, there can be no avant-garde party in anarchism, and it is precisely this point that concerned 19th-century anarchists about the evolution of Marx's thought. An avant-garde party implies hierarchy, and for anarchists, once one starts with a hierarchy, there will always be relationships of domination. Hierarchy in, hierarchy out. It is a claim for which the politics of the 20th century, whether in its Marxist, fascist, or liberal democratic guises, has provided compelling evidence.

If there is to be no avant-garde party, then political change must focus not only on the outcome of political action but on its process as well. It is not enough to say that at the end of the day, there will be equality. Equality is fragile. To maintain it, it must be fostered at all moments and at all levels of the political process. This concern for process can be seen increasingly in recent progressive political movements. It lies in the recognition that all participants in social change must be included and respected and that decisions that are made must reflect the willingness of all, in one way or another, to ratify those decisions. It is a concern that has animated anarchism from its very beginning.

So far, anarchism has appeared to be a seamless whole. In fact, it is not. There are two main streams of anarchist thought: individualist anarchism and collectivist (or communist) anarchism. The former privileges the concept of liberty, whereas the latter places more importance on equality.

Although there are important overlaps between liberty and equality (which is why the distinction between the two types of anarchism is simplistic), for individualist anarchists the important thing is to allow individuals to act as they like. Domination, for them, consists in constraining the individual in ways that the individual would not ratify. Thinkers in this tradition include Max Stirner, Ayn Rand, Robert Nozick, and even economists such as Milton Friedman. Essentially, individualist anarchism is reflected in the political movement known as *libertarianism,* a radical free market version of capitalism.

The other type of anarchism, collectivist or communist anarchism, emphasizes the notion of equality. Peter Kropotkin, in a famous article on anarchism, defined *communist anarchism* as the name given to a principle or theory of life, in which conduct is conceived without government. Harmony in such a society is obtained by free agreements among various groups rather than by submission to law or obedience to any authority. For anarchists, particularly anarchists of the 19th century, if all institutions of hierarchy are suspect, that of the state, alongside capitalism, is perhaps the most suspect because it concentrates power within itself. Kropotkin represents the third of the three great anarchists of the 19th century, after Pierre-Joseph Proudhon and Mikhail Alexandrovich Bakunin. A glance at the history of collectivist or communist anarchism, however, suggests the best figure to start with is the Englishman William Godwin.

Godwin (1756–1836) is perhaps the first systematic thinker to present an anarchist viewpoint. It appears in his major work, *Enquiry Concerning Political Justice,* where he argues that human beings are perfectible and that it is government that stands in the way of their achieving that perfection. Like many thinkers of the 19th century, Godwin relies on a belief in the ability of humans to think and act rationally in order to support his view that humans are capable of conducting their lives without concentrating their power in an overarching authority.

Among the 19th-century anarchists, Proudhon (1809–1865) is the most elusive in his thought. He is famous for the phrase, "Property is theft" from his first major work, *What is Property?* but it is sometimes unclear what he means by property, for in other writings he refers to property as freedom. He criticizes government harshly but spent time as a member of France's Constituent Assembly after 1848. What binds his thought into a whole is his concern and faith in people's activity of self-development and a suspicion of those who would direct from above. His most lasting contribution may be that of *mutualism,* the view that the best economic arrangement is one characterized by mutual cooperation among small enterprises. In fact, while a member of the Assembly, Proudhon tried, unsuccessfully, to start a popular bank that would help finance mutualist projects. The mutualist picture of an anarchist society will remain compelling throughout the history of anarchist thought and provides a model for more recent ecologically oriented anarchists like Murray Bookchin.

If Proudhon is the often considered the father of anarchism, then Bakunin (1814–1876) would be its most fiery messenger. Bakunin's writings are often topical in nature, addressing issues of the day. His most systematic work, *God and the State,* is an excerpt from a larger project that criticizes the role religion and government play in the subjection of human potential. Bakunin's contribution to anarchism has more to do with what he did than with his writings. A tireless speaker and organizer, Bakunin was involved in the first International Workingman's Association, representing the anarchists against Marx and the communists. His idea, in keeping with anarchist thought, was to struggle directly against capitalism without, as Marx wanted, becoming involved in parliamentary activity. It is during this period that Bakunin issued his telling prediction that revolutions that focused on taking over the state would result in a one-party dictatorship.

Kropotkin (1842–1921) is the most systematic of the 19th-century anarchist theorists. Like Bakunin and Proudhon before him, he was active in revolutionary movements and spent time in prison. However, his distinction is to articulate the most sustained view of what anarchism is and how it can come about. His views are often articulated on a Darwinian basis, which is counter to the dominant Spencerist current of the 19th century, which saw in Darwin a justification of remorseless competition. Kropotkin, by contrast, articulates a view of Darwin that is now considered to be more accurate both to Darwin and to evolution in general. He argues, particularly in his book *Mutual Aid,* that it is not only competition but also cooperation that characterize the successful maintenance and reproduction of the species. Moreover, this cooperation is not imposed from above but seems to be as much a natural endowment of creatures as any competitive instinct would be. On this basis, Kropotkin builds a view of anarchism as one that can exploit this natural endowment to create a successfully reproducing society in which the cooperative aspects of humanity are brought to the forefront. He articulates the movement toward anarchism in his book *The Conquest of Bread,* where he argues, in good anarchist fashion, that any revolution to create anarchism must emerge from below rather than from the state and must spread by offering models of cooperative living that can provide both the means of living (i.e., bread) and the possibility of constructing significant lives with one another.

After World War I, the anarchist theoretical tradition went into a long decline. There are a number of reasons for this, but among them is the protracted failure of what came to be called "propaganda of the deed." Arising during the late 19th and early 20th century, the propaganda of the deed promoted the spread of anarchism through the performance of spectacular political acts that were, it was hoped, a spur to others to act. Most of these deeds were violent, and in the end they seemed more successful in smearing the reputation of anarchism than in spreading its development.

This is not to say that there were no significant moments of anarchism in the early to mid-20th century. Indeed there were several. In the United States, the International Workers of the World, or Wobblies, engaged in union activity on the basis of anarchist rather than hierarchical organization. Emma Goldman, both in her writings and in her speeches, helped spread the word of anarchism, and feminism alongside it, particularly in workers' struggles. In Italy, anarcho-syndicalism (an anarchist viewpoint that privileges labor syndicates as centers of decision making) gained a number of adherents. And most striking of all, the anarchist component of the Spanish revolution of the 1930s introduced, at least temporarily, anarchism into entire towns. However, it would not be until the 1960s that the themes of anarchism would make a return to prominence, and the 1990s before anarchism as such was rediscovered as a framework for political thought and action.

What the 1960s brought, particularly in Europe, is the first sustained resistance to Marxism from the left. The key events were the Prague Spring of 1968 and May '68 in France. The former was an uprising against the communist regime in Czechoslovakia, displaying the bankruptcy of the states that labeled themselves workers' states. The latter was a more general uprising, but one that eventually turned against the French Communist Party when it aligned itself against the strikers because they did not cede direction to the party. May '68, in particular, introduced into progressive movements the idea that domination is not simply a matter of exploitation but in fact occurs in many ways and on many levels.

In the wake of the movements of the 1960s, a number of anarchist strains developed. The earliest among them was Colin Ward's anarchism, forcefully discussed in his book *Anarchy in Action,* which details both the complexity of domination and instances of resisting it without appeal to state intervention. Murray Bookchin's ecologically oriented anarchism is perhaps best represented in his book *Post-Scarcity Anarchism,* in which he argues presciently that contemporary capitalism is leading to an ecological disaster and that people need to embrace an anarchism that focuses on human beings' place within nature rather than on any attempt to dominate it.

With the collapse of the Berlin Wall, and with it much of the hope invested in Marxism, anarchism has again become a dominant framework for thinking about progressive political action. Recent thinkers like Bookchin and Ward are being rediscovered, and the subtlety of writers like Kropotkin is beginning to receive recognition. In addition, several theorists have begun to integrate the insights of more recent political theories like those of Michel Foucault and Gilles Deleuze into the anarchist tradition, creating a new dimension for anarchist thought. Moreover, many organizers are finding their way to anarchism after recognizing that many of the practices they were engaged in were already anarchist in orientation and that anarchism gives them a way to conceive and to extend their work more clearly. Anarchism, so long thought the province of disturbed men in trench coats carrying bombs, is beginning to be recognized as a set of powerful theories and practices of organization and resistance.

—Todd May

See also Goldman, Emma; Libertarians

Further Readings

Kropotkin, P. (1995). Anarchism. In M. Shatz (Ed.), *The conquest of bread and other writings.* Cambridge, UK: Cambridge University Press.

ANARCHO-SYNDICALISM

Also known as revolutionary syndicalism (often abbreviated simply as syndicalism), anarcho-syndicalism is a revolutionary strategy for workers' liberation from class oppression that aims to create a socialized economy based on workers' self-management of production. Most anarcho-syndicalists also advocate the application of self-management to decision making in all aspects of society. Syndicalism is Left-libertarian in the sense that it interprets liberty as self-determination or control over one's life, and believes that freedom for the working class requires the elimination of working-class subordination to capitalist or state bosses.

The word *syndicalism* derives from the word for unionism in languages derived from Latin (*syndicalisme* in French, e.g.). At the beginning of the 20th century, the labor movement in countries such as France, Spain, and Italy had been strongly influenced by the libertarian Left, with a strong emphasis on mass direct action by workers, and a revolutionary conception of unionism.

The principles of the first International Workers Association (IWA), formed in 1864, included the slogan "The emancipation of the working class must be the work of the workers themselves." Anarcho-syndicalists take this principle very seriously. The syndicalist political tendency can trace its lineage back to the anti-statist, libertarian socialist tendencies in the first IWA, grouped around Mikhail Aleksandrovich Bakunin.

Syndicalists oppose a strategy for achieving a post-capitalist economy through electoral or parliamentary politics, or through the building up of a political party to gain control of a state, with the aim of implementing its program top-down throughout the state. This is because syndicalists believe that the hierarchical nature of the state, and subordination of workers to such a hierarchical apparatus, would imply continued subordination and exploitation of the working class.

The strategy proposed by syndicalists involves the development of large-scale worker solidarity and mass actions that develop a sense of power and class consciousness; a sense of "us versus them." The massive national general strike in Russia in 1905 encouraged the development of this strategic vision for social change in the European labor movement in the period between 1906 and World War I. Syndicalists believe that a revolution in which the working class would gain control of society presupposes a process of the development of class consciousness, the capacity for self-organization, and self-confidence within the working class.

Syndicalists believe that direct management of industry by workers and the absence of a hierarchical state standing above society are essential for the emancipation of the working class. Most anarcho-syndicalists advocate ownership of the means of production by the entire society, with a system of grassroots social planning, not a system of privately owned collectives competing in a market economy.

Anarcho-syndicalists advocate the development of mass organizations of workers that would be directly controlled by them, without subordination to a hierarchical apparatus of paid officials. Anarcho-syndicalists believe that if the working class is to create a set of new institutions through which the people control their own lives and through which workers run the industries where they work, the process of self-management—collective control by the rank and file—must first emerge in the self-management of struggles in the existing society. In the syndicalist view, the self-managed mass organizations prefigure self-management of social production by workers and the direct self-governance of society by the mass of the people.

In the early 20th century, syndicalism usually was based on organization at the point of production. In more recent times, extensions of the syndicalist idea have been proposed, such as the "student syndicalism" advocated in the United States in the early 1960s or, more recently, extension of the concept to self-organized mass organizations in struggles arising in working-class communities outside the workplace, such as struggles of tenants.

Syndicalism in the United States emerged as a labor tendency in opposition to the "business union" ideology and practice of the American Federation of Labor (AFL). Labor radicals in the United States during the late 19th century began to talk about building classwide solidarity of workers and using large-scale actions, such as general strikes, to effect major changes, eventually replacing capitalism with a "cooperative commonwealth." This radical labor vision was opposed by the organizers of the AFL. Seeing entrenched racism in the United States, and a flood of immigrants from Europe speaking many languages, the organizers of the AFL viewed the radical strategy of classwide solidarity as unrealistic. The AFL focused on organizing groups of workers in particular crafts—especially skilled, white male workers—to simply negotiate a better deal with employers. A layer of paid officials emerged, running AFL unions like businesses, a change not inspired by a vision of workers' liberation. Although the AFL membership quadrupled in the economic boom after 1898, the anti-union "open shop" drive of the employers in 1903 brought this union growth to a halt and exposed the limits of the AFL approach.

Intense class conflict in the United States between the 1890s and World War I led a number of groups of workers to seek a different form of labor organization that could be more effective than the AFL as a challenge to employers in the United States. This new form of labor organization would be based on the idea of solidarity of all workers, irrespective of craft, race, nationality, or gender. This led to the formation of the Industrial Workers of the World (IWW; also called Wobblies) in 1905, the most important expression of syndicalism in the United States in the early 20th century. The IWW had been formed on the initiative of the Western Federation of Miners and developed a significant following among lumber workers in Louisiana and the Pacific Northwest, longshoremen in Philadelphia and maritime workers on the West Coast, and farm workers and miners in the western part of the United States. World War I and the anti-radical hysteria after the war led to severe repression of the IWW, including fascist-style vigilante violence, mass arrests for speech against the war, and the passage of "criminal syndicalism" laws by many state legislatures. A failed attempt by the Communist Party to capture control of the IWW in 1924 further depleted the organization. Nonetheless, the IWW continued to have thousands of members into the early 1930s.

Syndicalism also took other forms in the United States in the period after 1900, including militant, grassroots unions like the first Auto Workers Union, formed by syndicalist-influenced socialists in 1918. There was also the Syndicalist League, formed as a political syndicalist group in 1912, with the aim of organizing activists for efforts at broader solidarity in the AFL unions.

Italy also saw various approaches taken by anarcho-syndicalists in the World War I era. Anarchists had formed rank-and-file direct action committees in the Italian labor movement by the early 1900s. In 1910, this movement formed the Unione Sindacale Italiana (Italian Syndicalist Union) on the basis of the IWW platform. At the same time, there also were some Italian anarcho-syndicalist political groups. The Turin Libertarian Group, working with Marxian-syndicalists in the Turin branch of the Italian Socialist Party, worked to build a shop assembly and stewards' council movement, independent of the union bureaucracy of the CGL, the Socialist Party–controlled union federation. With the Turin councils' emphasis on workers' management of production and direct democracy of workplace assemblies, the council model was embraced by the Unione Sindacale Italiana also. During the mass occupation of the factories by over 600,000 workers in Italy in September, 1920, the anarcho-syndicalists were a major influence trying to extend the occupation into a revolutionary reorganization of Italian society.

The Communist International attempted to rally revolutionary labor groups around the world under the Communist banner after World War I. But the statist central planning, managerialist control of workers in the new Soviet economy, and the repression of Russian syndicalists tended to dampen the enthusiasm of syndicalists for the Soviet regime. Although the French Communist Party eventually gained control of the ex-syndicalist CGT in France, most of the large syndicalist unions—the USI in Italy, CNT in Spain, CGT in Portugal, FORA in Argentina, FORU in Uruguay, and FORB in Brazil—joined in the formation of a second IWA, built on an anarcho-syndicalist platform in 1922.

The high point of anarcho-syndicalism was achieved in the workers' revolution in Spain in 1936. With the defeat of a repressive right-wing government after elections in February 1936 and the freeing of thousands of anarcho-syndicalist and socialist union members held in prison, workers in Spain felt they had an opening to push forward in the development of their movement and pressing for their aims. In the months after February 1936, there were dozens of partial and city-wide general strikes in Spain, many of them initiated by the anarcho-syndicalist Confederación Nacional de Trabajo (CNT). With about 1.7 million members, the CNT was the majority labor organization in Spain. There were also tens of thousands of farm workers, mostly organized by the Socialist Party's UGT union federation, participating in mass takeovers of *latifundia*, large agricultural estates, creating worker cooperatives to run them. The intense class polarization and politicization of Spain culminated in an attempted military takeover on July 18, 1936.

This takeover attempt had been anticipated by the CNT, which had armed many of its members and set up a Workers Defense Committee to coordinate fighting back. Street fighting in Barcelona on July 19–20, the defense groups of the CNT defeated the Spanish army, with the aid of rank-and-file police and air force pilots. The CNT union federation then seized the arms and army bases of the Spanish army in the Barcelona area and built its own union militia. Each of the military divisions within the militia was self-managing, with assemblies and election of the commanding officer (chief delegate) of that division. The CNT set up a militia committee to run its army. The CNT metal workers union seized the Spanish motor vehicle manufacturing industry to convert it to the manufacture of armored vehicles for the union army.

With armed power in the hands of the CNT in Catalonia, the CNT unions began seizing the means of production. In some cases, the union itself took over management of an industry—for example, health care, barbering, and furniture manufacturing—in Catalonia. In most cases, however, a separate industrial federation or collective was created to manage an industry or facility, with assemblies of the workers being the ultimate decision-making body. This was the situation in the motion picture, public transit, public utility, railway, telephone, textile manufacturing, and other industries. Historian Robert Alexander estimates that 80% of the economic assets in Catalonia were seized, perhaps half the economy in all of the nonfascist part of Spain. The assets were seized in the name of the people of Spain; it was not intended that facilities be the collective private property of the workers working there. The CNT's ultimate aim was to create, from below, a democratically planned, socialized economy, based on workers' self-management of production.

With the failure of the CNT to build a union-controlled political power, the armed forces fighting the fascists were reorganized by the Popular Front government into a conventional, hierarchal military.

The Communist Party ultimately gained most of the officer positions in the new army. The increasing power of the Communists led to attacks on agricultural and industrial worker collectives and demoralization of CNT members who made up a majority of the rank and file in the anti-fascist army. Writers such as George Orwell and Jose Peirats saw this as one of the causes in the defeat of the anti-fascist side in the Spanish civil war. The question of whether the CNT unions should have "taken political power" in Spain divided the Spanish anarcho-syndicalists, suggesting that anarcho-syndicalism itself is subject to multiple interpretations.

—*Tom Wetzel*

See also Communism; Industrial Workers of the World (IWW); Libertarians; Orwell, George; Socialism

Further Readings

Alexander, R. J. (1999). *The anarchists in the Spanish Civil War* (2 vols.). London: Janus.

Leval, G. (1975). *Collectives in the Spanish Revolution.* London: Freedom Press.

Orwell, G. (1952). *Homage to Catalonia.* New York: Harcourt, Brace & World.

Peirats, J. (1974). *Anarchists in the Spanish Revolution.* Toronto: Solidarity Books.

Rocker, R. (2004). *Anarcho-syndicalism: Theory and practice.* Edinburgh, UK: AK Press. Retrieved from http://www.multimania.com/anarchives/site/rocker/asindex.htm

Thorpe, W. (1989). *The workers themselves: Revolutionary syndicalism and international labour, 1913–1923.* Dordrecht, Netherlands: Kluwer Academic.

Williams, G. A. (1975). *Proletarian order: Antonio Gramsci, factory councils and the origins of communism in Italy 1911–1921.* London: Pluto Press.

ANIMAL RIGHTS

Animal rights stem from early animal welfare organizations. However, there is a difference between the two movements. Animal rights advocates believe in letting animals live according to their nature and not be used as commodities. These activists believe that animals are similar enough to humans to deserve serious moral consideration and deserve a life lived not according to human goals. Thus, they do not eat meat, dairy products, or eggs; they do not wear leather, fur, or wool products; and they do not patronize corporations that produce these items or participate in animal testing. Animal welfare advocates believe that animals may not be able to reason, but they still feel pain and can suffer. This view differs from the animal rights perspective in that they can be used as commodities but must be treated humanely. Another term often used in animal rights circles is *speciesism*. Speciesism is the unjust discrimination of members of other species.

The theory of animal rights stems from feminism and environmentalism. These theories stem from the critique of instrumentalism. Instrumentalism is said to prevail in contemporary society in which nature, women, and animals are reduced to the status of tools and things to promote technology, markets, and bureaucracies. Theorists argue that animals and humans should not be used for economic gains. Animal rights activists believe that animals should not be used as a means to an ends but allowed to lead their own lives. This idea of "rights" is a non-negotiable moral value in which living, sentient beings have a right to live as they choose.

Charles Darwin's evolutional theory began to question the creation theory by reexamining human origin. This theory sought to show the similarities of humans and nonhumans by exhibiting common ancestry and the remnants of both anatomical and systemic similarities, in addition to common mental powers. Darwin found that animals felt pain, guilt, despair, joy, devotion, ill temper, anxiety, disgust, pride, helplessness, fear, horror, shyness, and modesty. Biological research supports this notion of anthropomorphic sensibilities in nonhumans. People seem to anthropomorphize their pets and wild animals, whether contained or in the wild. This furthers the notion that animals can feel emotions and pain.

By the 1860s, the first societies were formed to prevent animal cruelty. Humans began to see animals more as pets rather than as instruments of labor and production. By 1950, the Humane Society was formed and focused on overpopulation, abandonment,

shelters, and cruelty to animals. Philosopher Peter Singer, from New York University, taught a course on animal liberation, thus beginning to inform most of the early movements around the animal rights belief system. He also wrote the books *Animal Liberation* and *In Defense of Animals*.

By the 1970s, advocates started to target larger systematic activities of institutions. By researching scientific abstracts and grant proposals, Henry Spira, a student of Peter Singer, started to mobilize animal rights sensibilities into the beginning of contemporary animal rights activism. The American Museum of Natural History in Manhattan funded two psychologists in the Department of Animal Behavior. They were studying the neurological bases of sexual behavior through experiments on cats deprived of various sensations and brain functions. Procedures involved removing parts of the brain, severing nerves in the penis, and destroying their sense of smell. Spira and other protestors took to the streets of Manhattan and mobilized a massive protest stating that the experiments were sadistic, greedy, and only a way of getting government grants in exchange for animal blood and agony. Spira and other advocates also started a letter-writing campaign against the museum and found scientists who were willing to say that the experiments had no validity. This would be the beginning of animal rights protests on a large scale.

Rather than target doctors and certain companies for animal testing or circuses for the mistreatment of animals, animal rights advocates believe that animals should not be used at all under any circumstances. Arguments against animal testing and use for human goals stems from the notion that a life is a life whether human or nonhuman. It is rooted deeply in a moral belief system. The difference between humans and nonhumans is clear; however, some people believe that a human life is worth more than a nonhuman life and that an animal can be used for human use. However, animal rights advocates contend that this is a matter of belief and not based on evidence.

In 1980, Henry Spira organized a protest using fake white rabbits to protest Revlon's use of white rabbits to test cosmetics. The cosmetic company then paid Rockefeller University $750,000 to research alternative ways of testing the safety of their products. In 1984, the Animal Liberation Front (ALF) destroyed $20,000 and stole videotapes to later give to the People for the Ethical Treatment of Animals (PETA). The videotapes showed the research of Thomas Gennanilli, who used baboons to test severe head injuries. The baboons were subjected to severe shocks and injuries to the head.

PETA, founded by Ingrid Newkirk and Alex Pacheco, began to shift the focus of animal rights to scientific research. In May 1981, Alex Pacheco found immense cruelty and filthy conditions in a laboratory led by scientist Edward Taub in Silver Spring, Maryland. Taub was conducting neurological research involving severing nerves in the limbs of monkeys. The monkeys gnawed and attacked their numb limbs. Pacheco kept a diary and took photographs of feces, urine, and rust all over the cages. After the police seized the property and monkeys, Taub was found guilty on six counts of cruelty and fined $500. Although not highly successful, this case, along with the ALF's 1984 seizing of 60 hours of videotapes, allowed Pacheco and Newkirk to gain publicity to build animal rights' first successful letter-writing campaign.

By 1990, 300,000 people had become members of PETA. By 1987, many companies ended live animal testing. By 1990, several thousand animal welfare organizations and several hundred new animal rights groups had formed. In June 1990, 30,000 people marched on Washington to promote animal rights. Most of these protests argue against wildlife traffickers, hunters and trappers, laboratories where animal testing is performed, cosmetics and pharmaceutical firms, slaughterhouses, butchers, fur ranchers and retailers, rodeos, circuses, carriage drivers, and zoos. Animals used for entertainment such as racing, trained animal shows, bullfighting, animal fighting, and animal training for these events are deemed unnecessary and cruel. Animal testing for biomedical research is also a heated issue. Protests and education concerning alternatives to this kind of testing have been promoted by the Center for Alternatives to Animal Testing at John Hopkins established in 1982. Many animal rights advocates are also vegetarians and promote the benefits of this lifestyle to the planet and healthy living.

A meat-based diet is a waster of water, grain, and land because it wastes all these resources raising cows for slaughter. Issues like factory farming and fur companies have ranged from a question of cruelty to include a critique of the materialism of a consumer society and political critique of an economic system that encourages profits at the expense of animals. Stopping the use of animals as commodities is a goal shared by all in the animal rights movement.

Three movements, welfarist, pragmatist, and fundamentalist, make up the animal protection groups. Welfarists accept most current uses of animals but believes the pain and suffering should be minimized. The most influential animal welfare organizations are the Society for the Prevention of Cruelty to Animals (SPCA) and the Humane Society of the United States. Their primary strategies are protective legislation, education (on the humane treatment of animals), and shelters. Pragmatists believe that animals can be used when the benefits outweigh the suffering. They seek to reduce animal use through legal actions, political protest, and the pragmatic cooperation, negotiation, and acceptance of short-term compromises. Fundamentalists believe that animals should never be used regardless of the benefits. The ALF is one such fundamentalist organization. Their primary strategies use moralist rhetoric, condemnation, direct action, civil disobedience, and animal sanctuaries. These three movements range in their flexibility. Some believe in the fundamentalist belief system but protest in more pragmatic ways. Pragmatists and welfarists tend to contest what a full life is for an animal and the range of their cognitive awareness, thus creating further tensions within the movement. Fundamentalists believe that cows not only should not be slaughtered painfully but not used at all for human use. Chickens should not only be cage-free but should not be used for their eggs at all. These movements inform many of the goals of current animal welfare and rights organizations today.

Animal rights organizations vary in focus and sometimes on specific animals. More fundamentalist and pragmatist organizations focus on all animals, including PETA, ALF, the Humane Society of the United States, the Animal Legal Defense Fund, the American Anti-Vivisection Society, the International

Society for Animal Rights, and SPCA. These organizations are growing in number and in political and economic power.

—*Joy L. Wiggins*

Further Readings

Jasper, J. M., & Nelkin, D. (1992). *The animal rights crusade: The growth of a moral protest.* New York: Free Press.

LaFollette, H., & Shanks, N. (1996). The origin of speciesism [Electronic version]. *Philosophy, 71,* 41–60. Retrieved October 9, 2006, from http://www.stpt.usf.edu/hhl/papers/species.htm

Regan, T. (2003). *Animal rights, human wrongs: An introduction to moral philosophy.* Lanham, MD: Rowman & Littlefield.

Regan, T. (2004). *Empty cages: Facing the challenge of animal rights.* Lanham, MD: Rowman & Littlefield.

UNESCO. (1978). *Universal Declaration of Animal Rights.* Retrieved October 9, 2006, from http://league-animal-rights.org/en-duda.html

ANTHONY, SUSAN B. (1820–1906)

Susan B. Anthony was an advocate of temperance and abolition before she turned her attention to women's suffrage. Her dedication to the socially and politically marginalized grew out of her faith, which was shaped by the Quaker and then Unitarian faiths of her father as well as the Universalist upbringing of her mother. Her parents supported the temperance movement, a cause to which she was very devoted at a young age. Later, and again inspired by her parents, she focused her energy on the abolitionist movement, and as a result, in 1856 she was selected to be the New York State agent for the American Anti-Slavery Association. Although her work for these causes is not ignored, she is best known for her contribution to what is now known as the first wave of feminism. Her first encounter with Elizabeth Cady Stanton, the woman she would end up associated with in the suffrage movement and in mainstream narratives of women's history, was in 1851, 3 years after her parents and sister attended a women's

rights convention in Rochester, New York, where Stanton spoke. One year after meeting Stanton, Anthony attended a women's rights convention in Syracuse. It would be the first of many such conventions for the teacher-turned-reformer.

In 1868, Anthony and Stanton launched *The Revolution,* a weekly feminist newspaper. The next year, Anthony and Stanton formed the National Woman Suffrage Association (NWSA), an event that was followed in the same year by the creation of the American Woman Suffrage Association (AWSA) by Lucy Stone and Julia Ward Howe. Whereas the NWSA wanted Congress to pass a suffrage amendment, the more conservative AWSA focused its efforts on converting the country state by state. Later, largely due to the collaboration of Anthony and Stone, the two associations merged under the name of the National American Woman Suffrage Association (NAWSA).

After black men received suffrage, Anthony and 14 other suffragists claimed that women were able to vote under the Fourteenth Amendment—the first federal document to define *citizenship.* Anthony claimed that because the definition did not exclude women, women could no longer be prohibited from voting. On November 5, 1872, Anthony cast her ballot in Rochester, New York, only to be served a warrant on November 18 for doing so. Her willingness to violate the law caused the public to think of Anthony as a militant, a label that would be used to describe future advocates of women's rights who loudly and visibly protested the status quo.

Although she was not allowed to speak at her yearlong trial, she addressed many audiences during that year, publicly refuting the indictment that she voted illegally. Anthony was not the first woman to vote before women's suffrage, nor was she the first to argue that women are citizens and, like black men, have a right to vote under the Fourteenth Amendment. Yet, unlike those who came before her, Anthony had the distinct ability to draw substantial numbers of male and female listeners to speaking engagements.

In her frequently delivered speech during the year of her trial, titled "Is It a Crime for a U.S. Citizen to Vote?" Anthony asserted that women are dissatisfied with the current form of government—a government that enforces taxation without representation, forces women to follow laws that were created by men only, and grants men complete power within the institution of marriage. She asks her audiences, Are women persons? If the audience members can only conclude that women, indeed, are persons, then Anthony says women must also be considered citizens and therefore have the right to vote that is provided to all citizens by the Fourteenth Amendment. Anthony maintains that women are also covered under the Fifteenth Amendment, which states that citizens cannot be prevented from voting due to race, color, or previous condition of servitude. Women, asserted Anthony, should be considered people in servitude because women are subjected to the will of others, including their husbands and politicians who create the laws that disempower women.

Indeed, by the time of her trial, Anthony was considered a proficient speaker, known for her extemporaneous style of delivery and her use of statistics and facts to support her claims. During the 1850s and 1860s, Anthony participated in town meetings, met with others to organize associations, and spoke on programs. In the 1870s, she spoke across the nation, delivering speeches for which she earned money and at which her black dress and red silk crepe shawl developed into her trademarks. Yet, in her early days as a reformer, public speaking proved to be a great challenge for her. Stanton came to her rescue several times, helping Anthony write speeches and providing the less-experienced speaker with encouragement and confidence.

After the trial, considered by many to be a farce when the judge demanded a vote of guilty from the jury, Anthony wrote what is now the Nineteenth Amendment, an amendment that was introduced to Congress first as the Sixteenth Amendment, then as the Seventeenth Amendment, and later as the Eighteenth Amendment before being approved as the Nineteenth Amendment 35 years after it was first introduced to Congress. As she had predicted, an amendment would take a long time to be ratified. The long wait was something she tried to avoid by working diligently to persuade the public that women were already covered under the Fourteenth and Fifteenth

Amendments, and therefore, a new amendment to address women's right to vote was not necessary.

Although agreeing on many issues and having great respect for each other, Stanton and Anthony did have disagreements. Whereas Stanton and Matilda Joslyn Gage were willing to take Christianity to task for its role in the subjugation of women, Anthony considered articulation of that sentiment dangerous to the women's suffrage movement. What is more, participants of the Christian women's movement considered Anthony an ally. When speaking to clergy at the dedication of the Young Women's Christian Association in Rochester, Anthony argued that they should support women's suffrage because women were their best allies. Women, she said, would be able to move political power from the "saloon men"—the men responsible for constructing political institutions of the day—to clergymen. One of the conservative suffragists she worked with was Helen Barrett Montgomery, a Baptist and advocate of domestic feminism, a form of feminism embraced by many people who believed that men and women have different (and complementary) emotional and physical abilities. In fact, Anthony was known to use the language of domestic feminism whenever the occasion required it. Although some questioned Anthony's alliances with conservatives, it cannot be denied that these partnerships resulted in advances for women. For example, Montgomery and Anthony developed Rochester's Women's Educational and Industrial Union and worked to make the University of Rochester coeducational.

Stanton also was dismayed at the merger of the NWSA and the AWSA into the NAWSA, a merger that Anthony endorsed. However, after years of speaking to and partnering with conservative Christians, Anthony defended Stanton's criticism of the Church when NAWSA wanted to disassociate itself with Stanton's *Woman's Bible*. Anthony argued that the platform on which suffragists stand must be wide enough for people of all creeds. Yet, perhaps it is because of Anthony's willingness to appease others (and Stanton's refusal to do so), regarding the role of Christianity in women's oppression, that Anthony remains a larger figure in the women's suffrage movement than Stanton. In her biography, Stanton commented on the money and material goods Anthony had received, whereas she received only criticism for her radical ideas.

Scholars have since employed racial and global perspectives to challenge the traditional narrative of the suffrage movement and the first wave of feminism—a narrative that focuses on Anthony, Stanton, and other white suffragists while ignoring the black women who fought for women's rights. For example, many black suffragists who were connected with the AWSA are missing from Stanton, Anthony, and Gage's book, *History of Woman Suffrage.* In addition, some contemporary scholars express dismay that the work of suffragists in other countries is overlooked in the narrative of the first wave of feminism. As a result, the influence of international suffrage movements on the U.S. women's suffrage movement is essentially forgotten.

When she died, Anthony was commended for her work in the temperance, abolition, and women's rights movements. She was also applauded for the doors she opened up for other women who wanted to speak in public. In 1979, the U.S. Mint released the one-dollar Susan B. Anthony coin, the first U.S. coin on which a female was represented. The coin was in production until 1999.

—Lori A. Walters-Kramer

See also Abolitionist Movements; Citizenship and Patriotism; Feminism; Quakers; Women's Suffrage Movement

Further Readings

Campbell, K. K. (1989). *Man cannot speak for her: Vol. 1. A critical study of early feminist rhetoric.* New York: Praeger.

Campbell, K. K. (1989). *Man cannot speak for her: Vol. 2. Key texts of the early feminists.* New York: Praeger.

Ginzberg, L. D. (2002, Summer). Re-viewing the first wave. *Feminist studies, 28*(2), 419–436. Retrieved February 17, 2006, from InfoTrac OneFile Plus database.

Grube, M. (2003, Summer). Belief and unbelief among nineteenth-century feminists: The dark side of Susan B. Anthony. *Free Inquiry, 23*(3), 44–46. Retrieved February 17, 2006, from InfoTrac OneFile Plus database.

Linder, D. (2001). *Susan B. Anthony: A biography.* Retrieved February 17, 2006, from http://www.law.umkc.edu/faculty/projects/ftrials/anthony/sbabiog/html

McDavitt, E. E. (1944). Susan B. Anthony, reformer and speaker. *Quarterly Journal of Speech, 30,* 173–180.

Mobley, K. P. (2005, Summer/Fall). Susan B. Anthony and Helen Barrett Montgomery: An intergenerational feminist partnership. *Baptist history and heritage, 40*(3), 80–90.

Victory for Woman Suffrage. (1920, August 20). *Plattsburgh sentinel.* Retrieved February 20, 2006, from the Northern New York Library Network's Historical Newspapers website: http://news.nnyln.net

ANTI-APARTHEID MOVEMENT

Social movements are rarely born in isolation, and the anti-apartheid movement (AAM) in South Africa is no different. The AAM grew out of ongoing resistance movements and the efforts of many within South Africa and the international community to end racial inequality and the oppressive policies of enforced racial segregation in South Africa known as *apartheid.*

Resistance to long-standing racial inequality in South Africa was evident before the beginning of the 20th century. Organized resistance began with groups such as the Natal Indian Congress, African churches, labor and trade unions, the African National Congress (ANC), and the Communist Party. Subsequent organizations such as the Pan Africanist Congress (PAC), founded in 1959 by Robert Sobukwe, the South African Student's Organization (SASO), founded in 1969 by Stephen Biko, and the United Democratic Front, founded in 1983 proved instrumental in ending apartheid. Early forms of resistance were primarily peaceful, including mass demonstrations, civil disobedience, boycotts, and strikes. These strategies, employed by various groups in an effort to achieve social justice and to bring an end to the oppressive white South African government, never quieted. However, as a result of ongoing racial segregation, subsequent generations of African leaders determined that violent measures were necessary in order to gain freedom.

The 1940s witnessed a number of important events that became crucial for the AAM, both in South Africa and abroad. Within South Africa, Nelson Mandela, Walter Sisulu, and Oliver Tambo formed a youth league within the ANC to develop new strategies of resistance. Around the same time, the ever-growing oppression was forcing growing numbers of South Africans into exile in London. After the 1960 Sharpeville massacre, the banning of ANC and PAC, and the arrests of movement leaders in South Africa, the efforts of exiled leaders proved crucial for the AAM becoming a key means for banned liberation movements to continue their work. During this time, women also began to play a larger role in resistance movements.

Events That Fueled the Movement

In the 1940s, women moved into active resistance from passive support and social welfare activities. In 1943, women were allowed equal membership in the ANC, and a women's branch was formed to facilitate women's involvement in anti-apartheid efforts. The need for labor during World War II ushered many black women into the industrial workforce and the labor movement. Coming mainly from the Communist Party and the trade unions, women began to take active roles in resistance alongside men, and the federation of South African Women (FSAW) was founded in 1954 by Ray Simons, Helen Joseph, Lillian Ngoyi, and Amina Cachalia. The FSAW quickly became an active multiracial anti-apartheid force in alliance with other groups. In conjunction with the ANC, this woman's group directed campaigns against pass laws and quickly fell under government intimidation. However, strong and active women like Ruth First, Albertine Sisulu, and Winnie Mandela were not easily intimidated.

Throughout the late 1940s and early 1950s, the National Party government in South Africa strengthened the racist policies of the white government and enacted new apartheid legislation. The Population Registration Act and the Group Areas Act became cornerstones of apartheid. All individuals were labeled black, white, or colored, and the labeling predetermined their place in society, determining where they lived, worked, and went to school. On the heels of this legislation, two other laws were passed: the Separate Representation of Voters Act, which limited the rights of colored people to vote, and the Bantu Authorities

Act, which abolished the Natives' Representative Council, the one indirect forum of national representation for Africans. The apartheid government also stepped up its attempts to prevent anti-apartheid actions; they arrested leaders, harassed civic groups, and intimidated individuals. In addition, the government passed the Suppression of Communism Act, which was used later to arrest most of the movement's leaders.

In the aftermath of World War II, the ANC adopted new plans to push for black freedom and equality. Walter Sisulu was appointed Secretary General of the ANC, and it adopted a more militant anti-apartheid strategy. This action transformed the ANC from a reactive group organizing protest movements to a proactive mass organization. Sisulu worked tirelessly to foment social, political, and economic change despite growing oppression from the white South African government. The ANC initiated a Defiance Campaign in 1952 to challenge the apartheid laws and overtax the legal system by violating the apartheid laws and forcing the arrest of violators. The plan was to fill the jails and keep the police force working at full force until it became ineffective.

Two additional campaigns during the 1950s helped to solidify the anti-apartheid movement. The ANC, the South African Indian Congress, the South African Colored People's Congress, the South African Congress of Democrats, and the South African Congress of Trade Unions joined forces to establish the Congress Alliance. This group was responsible for the Freedom Charter and convening a Congress of the People. Individuals and groups from all over South Africa submitted ideas to the Congress about the type of society in which they wanted to live. Ideas were adopted by acclamation by the more than 3,000 delegates at the Congress of the people on June 25, 1955 (often referred to as Freedom Day). These two campaigns united the anti-apartheid forces in South Africa.

In 1952, Albert Luthuli became president of the ANC. In 1953, he was banned under the Suppression of Communism Act and unable to participate in public meetings. At least 41 other leaders of the ANC also were banned. In 1956, the white South African government arrested 156 members of the AAM and charged them with high treason. Whereas the majority of those arrested were African (104), 8 colored, 21 Indian, and 23 whites also were arrested. Ultimately, only 30 of the 156 faced charges, and finally in 1961, all charges were dropped. The arrests were attempts to harass and intimidate leaders and put an end to anti-apartheid protests. This repression of movement leaders did not stop people's resistance efforts. On August 9, 1956, nearly 20,000 women took part in an anti-pass law march in Pretoria. In 1957, a bus boycott was organized in Alexandria to protest cost increases. Thousands of residents walked as many as 10 miles to work until prices were reduced. Other boycotts and work stoppages continued in these years.

In December 1959, the ANC called for a series of 1-day actions against the pass laws. PAC suggested an expansion of this campaign and called for a series of demonstrations at police stations. March 21, 1960, was the day chosen by the PAC to hold a protest march in Sharpeville. As demonstrators gathered, the police opened fire on the unarmed crowd, killing 69 protesters and injuring 180. The massacre of people in Sharpeville turned the tide again for the anti-apartheid movement, which initiated strikes and work stoppages. The government declared a state of emergency. International attention was focused on South Africa. A proposal to initiate economic sanctions against South Africa was put forward at the United Nations, but it was vetoed by the United States and Britain. Increasing criticism of the South African Nationalist Party led them to withdraw from the British Commonwealth. The Republic of South Africa was determined to continue its apartheid state.

Protests against apartheid did not stop. In 1961, Umkhonto we Sizwe (translated "Spear of the Nation" and also referred to as MK), a guerrilla army, was launched under the direction of Nelson Mandela and Joe Slovo. It began a program of sabotage and tactical violence against government installations. Armed struggle was deemed necessary, as all peaceful efforts for change had failed and the government was increasingly violent against demonstrators. On June 12, 1964, the ANC and PAC were banned and the leadership jailed. As a result of the Rivonia trial, Nelson

Mandela, Walter Sisulu, Govan Mbeki, Ahmed Kathrada, Taymond Mhlaba, Elias Motsoaledi, and Andrew Mlangeni were sentenced to life in prison on Robben Island. In jail, the men were sentenced to hard labor, and they were allowed only one family visit and one letter every 6 months. However, these men were neither forgotten nor abandoned. They protested their living and working conditions through hunger strikes and go-slow protests. Pressure brought by the international community gradually brought an end to their sentences of hard labor. They were also then given access to newspapers and were allowed to receive letters and visitors twice a week. Perhaps the most important accommodation was the right to study. Nelson Mandela studied Afrikaans, economics, and history. During Mandela's 27 years in prison at Robben Island, Pollsmore Prison, and then Victor Verster Prison, his determination never faltered, and his confidence in the future for majority rule in South Africa continued to grow.

The imprisonment, banning, and exile of movement leadership slowed the struggle against apartheid, but they did not stop it. On June 16, 1979, almost 25 years after the creation of the Freedom charter and the meeting of the People's Congress, 20,000 Soweto schoolchildren took to the streets in protest over a government order that Afrikaans was to be used as the language of instruction at all black secondary schools. The student uprisings are best contextualized within the SASO, founded in 1969 by Steven Biko, and his black consciousness movement (BCM). SASO and the BCM filled a void left by the banning of the ANC and PAC. Considered a danger to the apartheid system, Biko was murdered by the South African police while in custody in September 1977. In 1979, the South African student movement organized a protest against learning in the language of Afrikaans. This protest revealed ingrained resentment toward apartheid and its policies of pass control, forced removals, denial of political rights, police terror, housing shortages, and inferior education for blacks. The BCM asserted black pride in African culture and heritage and challenged black youth to step forward and take their rightful places in South African society. The anti-apartheid movement was revitalized in the children of

South Africa. As they marched, they called for the release from prison of Nelson Mandela, Walter Sisulu, and other ANC leaders. Rather than deny the leadership of the movement, they sang praises to them. The police shot and killed several students.

Winnie Mandela, Nelson Mandela's wife, was blamed for the Soweto uprising by the white South African government. To support the children, she founded the Black Parents Association. This organization helped build necessary bridges between PAC, BCM, and the ANC. In the aftermath of Soweto, Winnie Mandela was arrested with a dozen other women as political detainees.

The youth accepted Winnie Mandela as a leader in the struggle. Neither movement leadership nor arrest and detention were new to her. Her first arrest came in 1958 as a result of her involvement in the anti-pass campaign. She was chair of the ANC Women's League when the ANC was banned; she turned her energies to the FSAW to continue her work. She remained outspoken and active during Nelson Mandela's incarceration, and she was often arrested, detained, and harassed by the government. From 1962 to 1975, she was banned under the Suppression of Communism Act and twice charged with contravening her banning order. In 1970, she was acquitted of wrongdoing but had been held in solitary confinement for 17 months under Section 6 of the Terrorism Act. Throughout the 1970s, Winnie Mandela continued to ignore banning orders and to speak out against apartheid.

Following the Soweto uprising, she was banished to Brandfort in the Orange Free State. Her house was bombed, but she continued to actively oppose apartheid and ignore posted segregation signs and orders. In 1985, she began a media campaign to inform the public about Nelson Mandela's life in prison. She vocally criticized the government and became as much of an icon of the anti-apartheid movement as her husband. Despite her legal difficulties, her sometimes abrasive behavior, and her eventual divorce from Mandela, Winnie Mandela continued to serve the people and the ANC. In 1993, she became president of the ANC Women's League, and in 1994, she became Deputy Minister of Arts, Culture, Science, and Technology in the new Unity government.

She eventually left government service but continued to campaign for the poor and disaffected in South Africa.

The South African Council of Churches, under the leadership of Archbishop Desmond Tutu, helped to facilitate the anti-apartheid struggle within black churches. This council supported civil disobedience as a proper response against racist laws. Churches delivered the message of the BCM. The church was banned in 1977. Tutu attempted to meet with P. W. Botha to discuss deteriorating conditions. When these talks collapsed, Tutu called for international economic sanctions against South Africa and criticized apartheid vociferously. He was an outspoken advocate for African freedom and encouraged boycotts and other forms of resistance. He criticized U.S. president Ronald Reagan and British prime minister Margaret Thatcher for their failure to uphold sanctions against South Africa. He was awarded the Nobel Peace Prize in 1984. Other religious leaders also worked to end apartheid. For example, C. F. Beyers Nande, an Afrikaner clergyman, founded the Christian Institute and began the Study Project on Christianity in Apartheid Society. Nande and his institute were banned in 1977 for providing a multiracial platform for challenging the official view of the Dutch Reformed Church.

In 1983, the United Democratic Front (UDF) was formed to continue the anti-apartheid struggle. The coalition of nearly 600 churches, civic associations, trade unions, women's groups, student organizations, community groups, and sports clubs joined forces to fight oppression. Albertina Sisulu became copresident. With broad appeal and populist support, UDF reenergized the black rejection of apartheid and fueled mass participation in a boycott against the newly proposed tricameral government. At the same time the National Forum emerged from the former Black Consciousness members of the Azanian People's Organization and the Cape Unity Movement. This group based its work on principles of noncooperation with whites and rejected the broad mass appeal of UDF. From 1984 to 1986, there was an increase in widespread rebellion and mass protests. Eventually workers, students, and other groups were able to overcome differences, and despite heavy state oppression, they coalesced into a strong movement. Once again ANC banners appeared, and Nelson Mandela and Oliver Tambo were upheld as leaders of the movement. Despite their strength and numbers, the resistance was still not sufficiently organized to take over.

The International Anti-Apartheid Movement

Nelson Mandela and others active in the AAM in South Africa have credited the pressure put on South Africa by the international community for helping to bring about the end of apartheid. With movement leaders within South Africa imprisoned and others forced to live in exile, an international AAM grew up in Britain and spread elsewhere. During a meeting of South African exiles and their supporters in London in 1959, Chief Albert Luthuli suggested the formation of an AAM in Britain.

The organization organized boycotts, published the newspaper *Boycott News,* organized public meetings in support of the ANC and PAC, and worked diligently to enlist the active involvement of the United Nations, the British Commonwealth, the Non-Aligned Movement, the Organization of African Unity, and many other international organizations in their struggle. AAM began by promoting the establishment of anti-apartheid groups in other West European countries, lobbying the Commonwealth in 1960–1961 and the International Olympic Committee in 1962, launching the World Campaign for the Release of South African Political Prisoners in 1963, and organizing the International Conference on Sanctions against South Africa in 1964. Its campaigns for people's boycotts, government sanctions, and the arms embargo soon spread far beyond the borders of Britain. AAM was responsible for a broad range of actions from public boycotts to U.N. sanctions, from the provision of humanitarian assistance to refugees to military and nonmilitary assistance to the liberation movement.

Oliver Tambo was the ANC president-in-exile from 1967 to 1991, and he was charged with mobilizing international opinion. In exile, Tambo's efforts supported the combined armed struggle and mass political actions in South Africa as he mobilized

international support. He organized and raised funds for an armed struggle, negotiated with other governments to house and train liberation forces, maintained contact with ANC forces within South Africa and developed diplomatic missions with other countries. He eventually established missions in 27 countries. Oliver Tambo returned to South Africa in December 1990, Nelson Mandela was released from prison on February 10, 1990, and South Africa's first democratically held elections, signifying the end of apartheid were held on April 27, 1994. The movement finally succeeded.

—Lorna Lueker Zukas

See also African National Congress; Biko, Stephen; Mandela, Nelson

Further Readings

Biko, S. (1996). *I write what I like: A selection of his writings* (A. Stubbs, Ed.). London: Bowerdean.

Eades, L. M. (1999). *The end of apartheid in South Africa.* Westport, CT: Greenwood Press.

Mandela, N. (1994). *Long walk to freedom: The autobiography of Nelson Mandela.* New York: Holt, Rinehart & Winston.

Mandela, N. (1996). *Mandela: An illustrated autobiography.* New York: Little, Brown.

Mandela, W. (1984). *Part of my soul went with him.* New York: W. W. Norton.

Schuster, L. (2004). *A burning hunger: One family's struggle against apartheid.* Athens: Ohio University Press.

South African History Online. Retrieved July 26, 2006, from http://www.sahistory.org.za/pages/mainframe.htm

Waldmeir, P. (1997). *Anatomy of a miracle: The end of apartheid and the birth of the new South Africa.* New York: W. W. Norton.

ANTI–BALLISTIC MISSILE TREATY

A ballistic missile is so called because it is launched at such high speed and elevation as to require a great trajectory as it seeks its target. They are typically armed with nuclear warheads. By comparison, ground launch cruise missiles are not ballistic; they are launched in response to first strike ballistic missiles and are thus anti–ballistic missiles. Both are the subjects of diplomatic efforts to avoid war.

The Treaty on the Non-Proliferation of Nuclear Weapons, signed in 1968 and in effect by 1970, was followed by rounds of Strategic Arms Limitation Talks (SALT I and II), resulting in the Anti–Ballistic Missile Treaty of 1972, signed by Richard M. Nixon, president of the United States, and Leonid Breshnev, general secretary of the Central Committee of the Communist Party of the Soviet Union. The difference between the two treaties is that the one restricts development of weapons whereas the other monitors technology intended to detect and destroy incoming missiles. The Cold War distrust between the two superpowers prompted the diplomatic efforts to avoid a nuclear war that would be impossible to survive, as suggested by Carl Sagan's famous analogy of standing knee-deep in gasoline, one person with three matches and his competitor with five. The diplomatic strategy was called *détente,* meaning that threat will inhibit aggression, maintaining a stalemate.

The treaty included provisions for amendment and also for review every 5 years (Article XIV). The first two, in 1977 and 1982, resulted in brief statements acknowledging the review activity and the continuation of each side's commitment to the treaty. In 1988, each side issued lengthy statements seething with accusations of noncompliance and righteous indignation. The American statement warned that the United States will not accept Soviet violations or a double standard of treaty compliance and will reserve the right to take appropriate and proportionate responses in the future. The corresponding Soviet statement defended its radar station under construction in the Krasnoyarsk region for the tracking of space objects, dismissed American claims as assumptions and subjective evaluations, and countered with accusations of American subterfuge in Shemya, an Aleutian island relatively close to Soviet shores.

Just 5 years later, in 1993, there were no Soviet representatives at the fourth review because the Soviet Union had dissolved in 1991. Instead, a mildly worded statement acknowledged that representatives from the new sovereign nations of Belarus, the Russian Federation, and Ukraine had joined the American delegation in Geneva. Not only was there no fifth review in 1998, but before the sixth review, the United States withdrew and effectively terminated the treaty.

However, the original nonproliferation treaty remained in effect, with its own 5-year reviews. In addition, the G-8 partnership of countries with nuclear capabilities has added several other issues to the topic of nonproliferation, including chemical weapons, bioterrorism, and nuclear safety—especially following the 1986 Chernobyl disaster. In 1998, Russia became a more fully functioning member of G-8, a collaboration among the nations known in World War II as Axis and Allied powers. Also, on January 1, 2002, a U.N. resolution for voluntary "transparency in armaments" called on all member states to provide annual reports on imports and exports of conventional arms. This was intended to encourage bilateral and regional dialogues on security concerns—one of the goals prompting the original talks leading to the Anti-Ballistic Missile Treaty and mentioned in the 5-year reviews as a rationale for continuing the agreement. On May 24, 2002, President George W. Bush and President Vladimir Putin signed the Moscow Treaty on Strategic Offensive Reductions, agreeing to reduce strategic nuclear warheads nearly two thirds below current levels.

—Naomi Jeffery Petersen

See also Anti-Globalization Movement; Anti-Nuclear Movement; International Campaign to Ban Landmines

Further Readings

Anti-Ballistic Missile Treaty. Retrieved October 12, 2006, from http://www.state.gov/www/global/arms/treaties/abmpage.html

Treaty on the Non-Proliferation of Nuclear Weapons. Retrieved October 12, 2006, from http://www.iaea.org/Publications/Documents/Treaties/npt.html

U.N. Department for Disarmament Affairs. (2002). *United Nations register of conventional arms.* Retrieved October 12, 2006, from http://disarmament.un.org/cab/register.html

The White House. (2002, June 13). *Statement on withdrawal from the ABM Treaty* [Press release]. Retrieved October 12, 2006, from http://www.whitehouse.gov/news/releases/2002/06/20020613-9.html

ANTI-BUSING MOVEMENT

From the late 1960s through the subsequent 2 decades, the policy of busing represented arguably the most controversial proposal for ending public school segregation, whether in a *de jure* (legalized) or, especially, a *de facto* (e.g., residence-driven) capacity. Busing involved the transportation of students across traditional school district lines (which tended to coincide with geographical proximity) for the purpose of achieving racial balance reflective of the larger school system. Concomitantly, opposition to court-ordered "forced busing" became the most salient means by which activists and their mostly white sympathizers resisted school desegregation. While the anti-busing movement cut across the political spectrum (and included a few minorities, as well), it paralleled a resurgence in grassroots conservative activism that began in the 1970s.

As with most policies concerning school desegregation, busing programs developed largely as a consequence of federal court mandates. Court-ordered busing began as a response to segregation in southern schools, which had persisted (especially in the Deep South) into the late 1960s. In *Green v. County School Board of New Kent* (VA) *County* in 1968, the Supreme Court outlawed "freedom of choice" plans and other indirect methods school boards had used to evade desegregation. Instead, the Court called for as much integration as possible. This decision, along with another ruling requiring an immediate end to school segregation (*Alexander v. Holmes County* (MS) *Board of Education,* 1969), indicated a more aggressive interpretation of the Court's existing dictum that desegregation should proceed with "all deliberate speed." The Court began to consider the structural factors—namely, residential patterns—underlying school segregation. In areas with substantial residential segregation, race-conscious student assignment programs (and, with them, busing) emerged as viable options to ensure that school systems did not perpetuate historical patterns of racial separation. In *Swann v. Charlotte-Mecklenburg* (NC) *Board of Education* in 1971, the most important busing decision, Supreme Court upheld a judicially prescribed busing order there, arguing that the need for racial balance outweighed the tradition of neighborhood school districts.

Busing became a national controversy when it moved outside of the South. The policy represented one of the first attempts to grapple with the existence of segregation well above the Mason-Dixon line. In *Keyes v. School District Number One, Denver, Colorado* in 1973, the Court applied the reasoning of *Swann* to a district lacking a legacy of Jim Crow laws. Both *Swann* and *Keyes* addressed city school districts, which in certain metropolitan areas contained only a fraction of the overall population. Most suburbs remained largely white, as did their schools. When district courts consequentially began to apply busing to larger metropolitan regions, the Supreme Court balked. First in a case involving Richmond, Virginia, then more influentially in *Milliken v. Bradley* in 1974, which concerned Detroit, the Court exempted from busing programs suburban areas not linked with city school districts. As a result of these rulings, the most effective busing programs occurred in cities (such as Charlotte) that had previously merged with their adjacent suburbs. Most large American cities lacked such an arrangement, however, meaning that busing programs largely occurred in inner-city, working-class communities. Many white students from wealthier families, meanwhile, attended suburban schools or could afford private education.

As suggested in the preceding discussion, busing programs derived almost exclusively from court decisions. Despite strong support from many African Americans and white liberals, busing never gained substantial popular backing. To the contrary, busing decisions garnered vocal resistance from a host of elected politicians, including state legislators (both northern and southern), congressional leaders, and presidents Nixon and Ford. This predicament left municipalities under busing mandates sandwiched between watchful courts and energized civil rights activists, on the one hand, and upset citizens and unsympathetic politicians, on the other hand. Whereas some communities implemented successful programs (often supported by image-conscious civic leaders not normally associated with civil rights causes), most districts backed into the policy of busing.

Following a 1974 district court ruling, Boston emerged as the poster child for the white backlash against busing. The vocal, emotional anti-busing movement there—especially in such white working-class neighborhoods as South Boston and Charleston—publicized the reality that virulent and sometimes violent opposition to integration was not the exclusive property of Birmingham or Selma. In 1976, millions of Americans saw a shocking, Pulitzer Prize–winning photograph of a young white busing opponent attempting to spear a black man with an American flag pole. Less publicized were other dynamics suggesting that racism was not the only factor behind opposition to busing in Boston. Because suburban Boston vastly exceeded the city proper in both population and wealth, poor whites and blacks bore the bulk of the busing burden. Even though studies showed that busing neither decreased the quality of education for white students nor significantly increased their travel time, many white parents in Boston and elsewhere saw busing as an attempt by outsiders to disrupt their closely knit communities and family lives.

By the late 1970s, busing policies had lost momentum. This happened not only because of grassroots white resistance but also because many African Americans had begun to question whether busing programs justified their own sacrifices. As was the case in Nashville, desegregation programs threatened the existence of cherished, historically black schools. In the 1990s, a more conservative Supreme Court relaxed its integration mandates and returned to a policy of simply banning racial discrimination in school systems. Since then, both Boston and Charlotte have brought their busing policies to a close; desegregation programs persist elsewhere, although often through voluntary school-transfer or school-choice systems.

The significance of the anti-busing movement extends beyond this seeming victory through attrition. Demographically, opposition to busing was one of many factors contributing to the phenomenon of "white flight," by which white families moved to racially uniform suburbs beyond the reach of desegregation policies. Districts under court-ordered integration plans lost an average of around 50% of their white students during the first decade of the programs. In the South, busing and other integration mandates led to a sudden proliferation of all-white private schools (nicknamed "seg. Academies") during the early 1970s.

Many scholars have interpreted the anti-busing movement as part of a larger turn in American political culture toward conservatism and the Republican Party. In certain respects, the grassroots organizations of the anti-busing movement resembled contemporaneous citizens' groups created to fight other school reforms, such as sex education or prohibitions against school prayer. One historian views the Boston movement as a manifestation of "reactionary populism," or the popular defense of the local status quo in the face of presumably elitist judges, liberals, and policy experts. Although reactionary populism was not exclusively conservative in outlook—and although many local Democrats resisted busing programs—it tended to benefit right-leaning Republicans, particularly on a presidential level. In such strongly Democratic cities as Boston, opponents of busing came to view the policy as a sign that the party's liberals had shifted from defending New Deal economic programs to embracing intrusive, unpopular civil rights experiments. Busing was thus one of several issues contributing to the demise of the Democrats' hitherto successful political coalition, which in northern states had united working-class whites, African Americans, and liberals. The unsuccessful anti-busing movement in Charlotte may have been the origins of color-blind conservatism, a viewpoint that subsequently influenced attacks on other race-conscious programs, such as affirmative action. In both Boston and Charlotte, anti-busing activists consciously invoked the language of the civil rights movement to criticize race-based assignment policies and to defend their right to neighborhood schools. Charlotte activists sang "We Shall Overcome," while the most visible anti-busing organization in Boston was named ROAR (Restore Our Alienated Rights).

Among civil rights leaders and within progressive circles in general, busing became one of several issues (including proportional representation and affirmative action) that complicated the legacy of the civil rights movement. As early as the mid-1970s, some black activists grew ambivalent about the benefits of insisting on desegregation programs; instead, they chose to emphasize educational quality. Such sentiments contributed to an overall decline in what had been a deep confidence in racial integration as the best cure for the nation's history of racial injustice. Amid these debates, American schools returned to levels of segregation not seen since before the busing controversy commenced.

—*Steven P. Miller*

See also Affirmative Action; *Brown v. Board of Education*

Further Readings

Bell, D. (2004). *Silent covenants:* Brown v. Board of Education *and the unfulfilled hopes for racial reform.* New York: Oxford University Press.

Formisano, R. P. (1991). *Boston against busing: Race, class, and ethnicity in the 1960s and 1970s.* Chapel Hill: University of North Carolina.

Lassiter, M. D. (2004). The suburban origins of "color-blind" conservatism: Middle-class consciousness in the Charlotte busing crisis. *Journal of Urban History, 30*(4), 549–582.

Pride, R. A., & Woodward J. D. (1985). *The burden of busing: The politics of desegregation in Nashville, Tennessee.* Knoxville: University of Tennessee.

Schulman, B. J. (2001). *The seventies: The great shift in American culture, society, and politics.* New York: Free Press.

Wolters, R. (2004). From *Brown* to *Green* and back: The changing meaning of desegregation. *Journal of Southern History, 70*(2), 317–326.

ANTI-COLONIAL MOVEMENTS, ASIA

The competition among the emerging modern European nations for the control of the spice trade in the 16th century eventually led to the spread of colonialism and imperialism in Asia. The earliest colonization started with the Spanish domination of the Philippines in 1565. By 1900, with a few exceptions, almost all the societies in Asia were under some form of colonial rule: the British colonies of India, Burma (Myanmar), and Malaya; the Dutch colony of the Netherlands East Indies (Indonesia); the French colony of Indochina (Vietnam, Cambodia, and Laos); and the U.S. colony of the Philippines (1898–1946).

China was not a colony, but its sovereignty was controlled by different foreign entities.

Generally, the first stage of resistance to the Western intrusion in Asia came from the traditional ruling class, who were motivated by the desire to defend traditional institutions and economic interests, and also from some traditional religious groups or leaders, who tried to defend native religious beliefs. But these early traditional resistance movements met with little success when the colonial authorities responded with their powerful weapons and well-organized armies. The real challenges to colonial rulers began to take shape in the early 20th century when the subject peoples developed a sense of their own identities and the consciousness of modern nationhood through the education brought by the Western rulers. This growth of nationalism in the early 20th century changed the traditional resistance movements to modern anti-colonial movements. Under the systematic leadership of the modern educated elites, nationalist parties were formed, and political movements dedicated to the overthrow of the colonial rule emerged. These new leaders proclaimed the independence from the foreign rule together with the establishment of a new nation. By the mid-20th century, almost all the colonized nations in Asia were free from Western colonial rule.

British colonization started with the British East India Company's victory over Indian forces in 1757. By 1857, most of India was directly or indirectly controlled. Prior to the annexation, India was in a state of chaos because of the collapse of the Mughal Empire. With no single effective ruler, the Indian princes were not strong enough to respond to the British East India Company's well-equipped troops.

Anti-colonial sentiments first appeared among the upper-class, Western-educated Hindu elites. These elite groups began to stir the Indian society by initiating literary and debating societies. Among them was Ram Mohan Roy (1772–1833), who formed the *Brahmo Samaj* (Society of Brahman) in 1828. Early movements focused primarily on the traditional religious identity while stirring national sentiment, posing little threat to the colonial power.

The first anti-colonial movement that alarmed the British was the Sepoy Rebellion of 1857. Indian soldiers, called *sepoys,* formed the vast majority of the rank and file of the British army in India. The cartridges used by the sepoys' rifles, which were routinely opened by the soldier's mouth, were covered in cow or pig fat. The Hindus and Muslims were insulted by this slight to their culture. Although the British changed the cartridges, the rumor persisted and when the British officers forced the use of these cartridges, the soldiers protested. The military mutiny quickly became a war against the British when traditional rulers, such as the last emperor of the Mughal dynasty and the queen of Jhansi, joined in the fight with the support of the Indian military personnel and civilians. The British managed to reassert its control by July 1858.

The 1857 rebellion failed, but it brought significant changes to India. The British government abolished the British East India Company's rule and took over the power. All the territories of the Company became British India, controlled by the British parliament. India was carved into states and ruled by the princes who signed treaties with Great Britain and agreed to accept British hegemony. The British Crown created more Indian representation within the administration and promised equal treatment under British law.

On the other hand, the Sepoy Rebellion had stimulated Indian nationalist aspirations and enhanced the anti-colonial movement. Resenting the racial discrimination to which they were subjected, the Indian nationalists began to criticize the British colonial regime. Whereas some of these Indian leaders demanded a larger role in the government, some spread the ideas of the needs for Indians to reform their society and build a truly national community. Many political societies and organizations flourished. Among these was the Indian National Congress (INC), founded in 1885 by a group of British educated elites.

Approved by the British, the INC initially served as a debate society. Its prominent members included the moderate nationalists like Gopal Gokhale (1866–1915), who advocated for social reforms, and Rabindranath Tagore, a national poet who led Indian crowd marching with the song he composed in protest of the partition of Bengal in 1905. A radical wing within the INC was initiated by Gangadhar Tilak (1856–1920), who urged the Indian people to take pride in the pre-British Hindu

Indian tradition and culture rather than emulating Western ideas. His call for the ousting of British from India brought many noneducated Hindus into the anti-colonial movement. As Tilak's group prevailed at the 1905 congress session, the INC started to demand for *swaraj,* or self-government absolutely free of British control. The boycotting of British goods by the INC during this period was very successful and led the British to make a series of constitutional reforms in 1909.

Constituting a fifth of the population, Muslims began their own organization, the All-India Muslim League, in 1906 but played little part in the protests against the British. In recognition of the league's support, the British increased the number of elective offices reserved for Muslims in the India Councils Act of 1909. In 1916, the All-India Muslim League joined the INC in demanding for self-rule.

In response to the demands and protests led by the INC, the British passed the 1918 Montagu-Chelmford Reforms, expanding provincial legislatures with higher numbers of Indians legislators. But the Indians felt that the reforms did not give them enough power, and the protest increased. The INC would become the core of independent movements after the addition of British-trained lawyer Mohandas Gandhi. He traveled around India, spreading his message of mass protest against oppression. Drawing on traditional Hindu values, he set up a resistance movement based on nonviolent civil disobedience called *Satyagraha.* When the government promulgated the Rowlatt Act in 1919, enhancing the wartime martial law, Gandhi organized peaceful mass protests calling his followers to refuse to obey the new regulations. A similar mass protest led by the Sikh leaders in Amritsar resulted in the killing of 400 unarmed civilians. The Amritsar massacre increased the Indian people's resolve for freedom.

Becoming the leader of the INC in 1920, Gandhi declared *purna swaraj* (complete self-government) as its goal. He organized boycotts of British imported goods. Through his campaign of making and wearing Indian traditional handwoven cotton, the spinning wheel became a nationalist symbol. With millions of followers, Gandhi had transformed the INC, which was initially an educated elite organization, into the most powerful mass political organization in India.

In December 1929, under the presidency of Jawaharlal Nehru, the INC authorized a civil disobedience movement throughout India and to observe January 26, 1930, as Purna Swaraj Day, which was joined by many other Indian political parties and leaders. Gandhi led his famous Salt March campaign in March and April 1930. In response, the British arrested more than 100,000 people, including Gandhi, Nehru, and other leaders. The economic hardship caused by the civil disobedience movements forced the British government to acknowledge Indian nationalism and release all political prisoners in 1931. After his release, Gandhi was invited to London for negotiations, but when the British declined to give a deadline for withdrawal from India, Gandhi returned and resumed his civil disobedience movements in 1932.

A new constitution for India was announced in 1935, and in the 1937 nationwide elections the INC became the dominant party, winning the majority of the nearly 40 million votes. The All-India Muslim League, that had left the INC in 1920 and was now under the leadership of Mohammad Ali Jinnah, failed to win the majority of seats reserved for the Muslims. Unlike Gandhi and Nehru, who were always against the separation of the Indian subcontinent into Hindu and Muslim, Jinnah's goal was to build a separate Muslim state. This difference in religious positioning would ultimately lead to the formation of Pakistan.

While the negotiation for the independence was on the way, the British made an announcement that India would join Britain in World War II. This enraged the Indian nationalists, culminating in the resignation of all INC provincial ministries. Gandhi's "Quit India" movements led to the arrest of Gandhi, Nehru, and other INC leaders. After a series of negotiations and bloodshed, India gained its independence from the British on August 15, 1945.

Burma became a British colony after three Anglo-Burmese wars: 1825, 1852, and 1885. After dethroning the last king of the Konbaung dynasty, the British made Burma a province of India. The traditional chiefs and the Buddhist monks resisted the new administration, but the British managed to pacify the whole country and the colonial institutions became well established in the early 1900s.

The Western-educated Burmese elites played the leading role in organizing a systematic anti-colonial movement. It began with the forming of cultural societies spreading national consciousness. One of these was the Young Men Buddhist Association, which was formed in 1906, emulating the Young Men Christian Association. In 1916, the name was changed to General Council of Burmese Association, aiming to unify all of the Burmese people under its umbrella to resist foreign domination. From a religious-based organization, it was transformed into a political organization, protesting British rule. These protests led to reforms in the British legislature that allowed some educated Burmese a small role in the government.

The strongest anti-British movement in the 1930s was led by a former Buddhist monk, Saya San, who won the support of thousands of peasants. Only after launching severe repressive measures could the British quell the rebellion. Meanwhile, the young university students, feeling discriminated by the authorities, became agitated. The All-Burma Students' Union was formed to demand self-rule; many of them joined the Dobama Asi-Ayone (We, the Burmese Association), where the members addressed one another *Thakin* (Master), a title that was reserved for the British. Their active participation in the 1936 university strike, 1937 student strikes, and the 1300 Revolution (1938–1939) brought student leaders like Nu and Aung San to the surface as nationalist leaders of Burma. From this point, Aung San played a key role in the Burmese independence movements, collaborating with the Japanese to be free from British colonialism, and then turned to the British for help to save Burma from the yoke of Japanese fascism. The Anti Fascist People's Freedom League (AFPFL), formed in 1943 under the leadership of General Aung San, fought the Japanese forces. When the British came back after World War II and resumed its control of Burma, the AFPFL became the strongest political party to challenge British rule. It organized protests throughout the country, demanding independence. Finally, on January 4, 1948, Burma gained its independence.

In Asia, the people of the Philippines had the longest experience of colonial domination under three different foreign rulers: Spain (1565–1898), the

United States (1898–1946), and Japan (during an interim period, 1942–1944). After a century of Spanish rule, most Filipinos converted to Catholicism. Having both civil administrative and ecclesiastical power in their colony, the Catholic religious establishment became very influential over the native subject, and the Spanish friars resisted the ordination of Filipino priests. This unequal treatment in religious order aroused nationalist sentiment and encouraged the movements for social and political reforms. However, in 1872, three Filipino leaders who challenged the authority were executed in public.

The growth of education and the influence of Western political ideas gave rise to the Western-educated middle class called the *ilustrados,* who began to demand independence from Spain. The most prominent nationalist leader was Jose Rizal, whose 1887 novel stirred public sentiment and enraged the religious authority. He was executed in 1896 by the Spanish for his freedom movement. In 1892, a secret revolutionary organization, Katipunan, with its goal to overthrow the Spanish rule, was founded by Andres Bonifacio. Katipunan became the core of revolutionary movement under the leadership of Imilio Aguinaldo, with whom the government negotiated for political reforms. According to the agreement, Aguinaldo left for Hong Kong but came back in May 1898 and organized his forces after the U.S. fleet defeated the Spanish in Manila. Aguinaldo gained popular support and declared the independence of the Philippines on June 12, 1898. Believing in the American claim against colonialism and assuming that the United States would support their independence move, Aguinaldo and the Filipino nationalists agreed to join U.S. troops in fighting the remaining Spanish forces on the islands. In return, the United States had promised to grant independence in exchange for their cooperation.

After the Spanish transferred the Philippines to the United States following the signing of a peace treaty in December 1898, Aguinaldo again claimed the promise of independence. When it was unattained, he declared the independence of the Philippine Republic on January 23, 1899. Aguinaldo's troops began to fight the United States in February, and the war ended only in March 1901, after the United States' brutal suppression and the capture of Aguinaldo.

Eventually, the United States began to prepare the Philippines for independence and allowed Filipino representation in the government. By 1935, the Philippines became a commonwealth with its own elected government. With these political developments and the growth of the economy, Filipino bitterness over the U.S. betrayal subsided. When the Japanese invaded the islands on December 10, 1941, the people of the Philippines fully cooperated with the United States, fighting the Japanese. The Philippines achieved its complete independence on July 4, 1946.

The Dutch arrived on the Indonesian islands in the 16th century, but actual colonization started in the 18th century when the Dutch East India Company began to control the trade of the region called the Dutch East Indies or the Netherlands Indies. The Dutch government took over the company's rule in 1798. Except for the periods of British (1811–1816) and Japanese occupation (1942–1945), Indonesia was a Dutch colony from 1798 to 1949.

Resistance movements began from the early years of annexation, but the strongest revolt, under the leadership of a Javanese prince named Diponegoro, started in 1825 and lasted 10 years. The modern nationalist movement for independence came in the early 20th century. In 1908, a retired Javanese doctor established a society called Budi Utomo (High Endeavor). Its aims were more cultural than political, but its movements were fully supported by the Western-educated Javanese elite, who demanded reforms. In 1912, another anti-Dutch nationalist organization, called Sarekat Islam (Islamic Association), was formed by Muslim traders. Its initial goal was to protect the batik merchants, but under the leadership of Omar Said Cokroaminoto, it attracted many followers and became one of the largest political organizations of the time to challenge the Dutch rule.

To quiet these nationalists, the Dutch government established the Volksraad (People's Council) in 1916, offering some Indonesian representation on it. In reality, the council had little power or control over the government. Adopting a noncooperation policy as a way of continuing their fight for independence, many nationalist leaders began to refuse the seats in the assembly. Meanwhile, the Indies Social Democratic Association, founded by the Dutchman Hendricus Sneevliet, became the Indonesian Communist Party in 1920 and led a series of revolts in 1926 and 1927.

Many other nationalist organizations were formed after 1926, including the prominent Partai Nasional Indonesia (Indonesian Nationalist Party) led by Sukarno, who called for complete independence. In response, in the 1930s the Dutch government banned the Partai Nasional Indonesia and other noncooperating political organizations, arresting and exiling their leaders, including Sukarno and Mohammad Hatta.

Japanese occupation of Indonesia from 1942 to 1945 interrupted the Dutch rule. By collaborating with the Japanese, Sukarno and Hatta reinforced their leadership roles, while their position in the military administration developed their political, strategic, and military skills. The harsh Japanese military training given to thousands of Indonesian young men also made them prepared for future struggle for independence. After the Japanese surrendered to the Allies, on August 17, 1945, the Indonesian nationalists declared an independent Republic of Indonesia, with Sukarno as president and Hatta as vice president. Soon in November 1946, the Republic had to continue its fight for freedom when the Dutch came back to reassert their control of Indonesia. Fierce fighting and negotiations went on; with a stronger sense of national identity, the Indonesian people were determined to fight for their independence. The Dutch continued to attack the Republic in 1947 despite protest from some members of the United Nations. In December 1948, the Dutch recaptured the Republic's capital and arrested Sukarno and Hatta. However, under pressure from the United Nations and the United States, at a conference in The Hague in November 1949, the Netherlands agreed to grant independence to all of Indonesia except West Irian (Irian Jaya). Consequently, the United States of Indonesia was established on December 27, 1949.

French Indochina was established in 1885 encompassing Vietnam, Cambodia, and Laos. As elsewhere in Asia, the first resistance came from the traditional leaders and the religious groups. In 1905, the Vietnamese nationalists Phan Boi Chau and Phan

Chau Trinh called for the improvement of education in Vietnam. In 1916, 18-year-old Emperor Duy Tan led a revolt, but he was arrested and exiled. Two religious sects played significant roles in the early Vietnamese nationalist movements: Cao Dai, combining aspects of traditional animism, Buddhism, and Christianity, was founded in 1926, and the Hoa Hao sect of Buddhism was founded by Huynh Phu So in 1938.

Nguyen Thai Hoc formed the Vietnamese Nationalist Party in 1927 and attacked the French administration. He was executed after a failed uprising in 1930. Most of the nationalist leaders before World War II were killed, jailed, or exiled.

Anti-colonial struggles in Vietnam began to assume importance under the leadership of Ho Chi Minh (1890–1969). He was a member of the Communist International and in exile from 1911 to 1941. In 1925, Ho Chi Minh formed the Vietnamese Revolutionary Youth League, which became the Indochinese Communist Party (ICP). In 1941, the ICP was reorganized as the League for the Independence of Vietnam (Viet Minh), emphasizing anti-imperialism and land reforms.

During WWII, when Vietnam came under the Japanese control, Ho collaborated with the Chinese to oust the Japanese. After the Japanese surrendered, Ho declared the formation of the Democratic Republic of Vietnam (DRV) on September 2, 1945, giving an augural speech emulating the American Declaration of Independence. But as the French returned to reestablish its control over Vietnam, Ho and his Viet Minh continued their fight for independence. The Viet Minh began to attack the French in Hanoi, on December 19, 1946. In 1949, the French established the State of Vietnam with a nationalist Bao Dai as its head to crush the Viet Minh.

Fighting between the Viet Minh and the French from 1946 to 1954 had been the Vietnamese battle against French colonial rule. Communist Chinese aid to the nationalist communist leader Ho and the Viet Minh from 1950 entangled Vietnam in the Cold War contest. After the French defeat at Dienbienphu in 1954, a peace conference was held in Geneva, where a decision was made to temporarily divide Vietnam at the 17th parallel, with North Vietnam under communist Ho and South Vietnam under noncommunist Bao Dai. In addition, national elections for the reunification of Vietnam were scheduled to be held before July 1956, under the supervision of an international commission.

In October 1956, Ngo Dinh Diem proclaimed South Vietnam the Republic of Vietnam (RVN), assuming the presidency and refused to hold elections. Fearing that the free elections might result in a Communist victory, the United States supported Diem's decision. Ho wanted the reunification of Vietnam and urged the different armed groups to join together for a powerful armed resistance. In December 1960, the National Front for the Liberation of South Vietnam (the Viet Cong) was established to lead the insurrection in South Vietnam. In 1965, the United States increased its support to the RVN, including bombing campaigns. With support from China and the Soviet Union, Viet Cong forces launched guerrilla operations against U.S troops.

In 1973, a cease-fire agreement was signed by DRV, RVN, and the United States. After the withdrawal of U.S. troops, the DRV continued to fight until the capital of South Vietnam fell in April 1975. The Socialist Republic of Vietnam was established after the unification of the DRV and RVN in 1976.

Beginning with the Treaty of Nanjing after the first Opium War in 1842, Western powers gained control of the important Chinese ports. By 1900, China lost 90 ports and had to sign a series of treaties that granted exclusive economic rights and the extraterritoriality to each of the foreign nations.

The carving of China into the sphere of influence by the colonial powers posed an insult to the sense of national pride of the Chinese, who were ruled by the Manchus (the Qing dynasty) from 1644. Several uprisings occurred, but the most dangerous one was the Taiping Rebellion (1850–1864), which split China into two camps: one led by Christian-leaning Hong Xiuquan and the other by the Confucian-oriented Qing court. The Qing government crushed the rebellion with military assistance from the Westerners.

Realizing its weakness, the Qing government attempted reforms for the growth of economy and the military strength. One was the Self-Strengthening movement (1860–1895), led by Li Hongzhang and supported by Manchu Prince Gong, who wanted to preserve Confucian values while adopting Western technology. Another was the Hundred Days reforms of 1898, led by scholars, who instigated radical changes in the imperial system, with the support of the emperor Guangxu, who planned to transform China into a constitutional monarchy.

The reforms failed, and the foreign powers continued to strip China by annexing its tributary states. In 1899, the U.S. imposition of the Open Door Policy allowed all nations equal rights in China. The situation enhanced anti-Western sentiment, creating associations like the Society of Righteous and Harmonious Fists (Boxers), which led the Boxer Rebellion of 1900. The Boxers attacked not only all foreigners but also Chinese who had ties with foreigners in northern China. Supported by the Qing empress dowager Cixi, a bloody retaliation was launched by a joint armed force of British, French, Russian, U.S., German, and Japanese troops. The defeat further strengthened foreign control of China.

The incompetence of the Qing government bred a new generation of reformers who were determined to overthrow the monarchy and who called for national unity. Among these was Sun Yat-sen, a Western-educated physician, who devoted himself to the revolution in 1894. Success came on October 11, 1911, when the revolutionary troops took Wuchang, followed by a series of victories that overthrew the Manchu.

In December 1911, a provisional government was set up in Nanjing. In January 1912, Sun was inaugurated as president of the New Republic, but to avoid civil war, he stepped down and gave the presidency to Yuan Shikai, a former Qing general. Yuan's attempts to reestablish a monarchy with himself as an emperor caused insurgencies in many provinces, leaving China in the hands of the military warlords after his death in 1916. However, the foreign powers continued to recognize the government of China in Beijing. In 1917, Sun, leader of the Guomindang (National People's Party), with the support of the southern warlords set up a rival government in Guangzhou to overthrow the government at Beijing and to reunite the country.

Meanwhile, the young Chinese intellectuals, feeling that China was not given fair treatment, staged a mass demonstration protesting the Versailles peace conference on May 4, 1919, known as the May Fourth movement. It was followed by public strikes and boycotts of foreign goods, leading to the fall of the cabinet.

The May Fourth movement strengthened anti-colonialism and the drive for political revolution, especially among the intellectuals, who began to call for the reorientation of traditional values that some found in communism. Sun's Guomindang was joined by these early communist groups and became the leading organization in the nationalist movement.

Sun's successor, Chiang Kai-shek, launched his famous Northern Expedition military campaign in 1926, defeating the warlords, while trying to eliminate Communist rivals in 1927. After capturing Beijing in 1928, Chiang reestablished the Republic of China with its capital at Nanjing. But the broken relationship between the Guomindang and the Communists led to a civil war while Japan continued to extend its influence in Manchuria in 1931 and northern China in 1936. Preoccupied with the Communists, Chiang ceded to Japanese demands, until his troops forced him to make an alliance with the Communists, forming a united front.

The Japanese occupied Nanjing and most of eastern China by 1938. Chiang's forces had to retreat to southwest China, with its new capital at Chongjing in Sichuan. During World War II, China received aid from the Allies, but the cost of the war weakened the Nationalist government, resulting in a loss of popularity. Inflation and corruption added chaos. The Communists, under the leadership of Mao Tse-tung, who became the leader of the Communist Party during the famous Long March of 1935, gained popular support in northern China where the Japanese army was repelled. Communist land redistribution programs in the countryside attracted the peasants, the core of the population. By 1945, the Communists had 19 base areas with a population of nearly 100 million.

After the Japanese troops withdrew from China, competition for national control began. A U.S. attempt at resolution in 1946 failed, heightening hostilities. The Communists triumphed, and on October 1, 1949,

Mao proclaimed the establishment of the People's Republic of China with its capital in Beijing. Finally, China regained its sovereignty over all of mainland China.

—*Angelene Naw*

See also Aung San; Gandhi, Mohandas K.; Ho Chi Minh; Mao Tse-tung; Sun Yat-sen

Further Readings

Chandra, B. (1989). *India's struggle for independence, 1857–1947.* New York: Penguin Books.
Fairbank J. K. (1986). *The great Chinese revolution: 1800–1985.* New York: Harper & Row.
Hay, S. (Ed.). (1988). *Sources of India tradition* (Vol. 2). New York: Columbia University Press.
Steinberg, D. J. (1987). *In search of Southeast Asia: A modern history.* Honolulu: University of Hawaii Press.

ANTI-COLONIAL MOVEMENTS, LATIN AMERICA

From the early nativist revitalization uprisings to the wars of independence, Latin America has been the stage of numerous, variegated, and complex anti-colonial movements. Reflecting the multiethnic, multicultural, and conflictive nature of their societies, anti-colonial struggles were propelled by an impressive diversity of political views and utopian agendas. Insurgents did not always look for a radical break with colonialism, and demands for equal treatment, better living and working conditions, or religious recognition did not necessarily imply repudiating the monarchs across the Atlantic. Anti-colonial programs were often contradictory, exclusionary, and in need of a great deal of improvisation. They evidenced the complicated nature of relations of resistance and domination under colonialism and the multiple sources of anti-colonial thought and activism in Latin America.

As early as 1564, the Spanish Crown faced a movement, the Taqui Onkoy, which aimed to end European domination and restore the supremacy of the ancient gods. The Taqui Onkoy ("dance of sickness") was a

Pan-Andean movement of revitalization that broke out near Cuzco and soon expanded from La Paz to Chuquisaca, Huamanga, and even to Lima and Arequipa. The taquiongos, for the most part Indians who had become Christians, danced and trembled while being possessed by huacas (Andean gods). Using the taquiongos as mouthpieces, the huacas reprimanded the Indians for abandoning them and threatened to kill all those who did not leave Christianity or stopped cooperating with the Spaniards. At its peak, the movement allegedly gathered 8,000 individuals. Its revivalist message exposed a moral crisis of old patterns of reciprocity that had been undermined by Spanish colonialism. Although the Taqui Onkoy aimed at a solidarity transcending old ethnic divisions, it did not succeed in building a Pan-Andean coalition and was brutally repressed by Spanish authorities.

Like the Taqui Onkoy, many other rebellions had a limited impact because of their incapacity to build a united front against the colonizers. In 1680, however, the Pueblo caciques of Taos, Picuris, San Lorenzo, Santo Domingo, Jémez, and Pecos set aside their differences to rebel under the leadership of a medicine man named Popé. The Puebloans had endured years of drought, famine, pestilence, and death, and Popé blamed the colonizers for their suffering. Only after killing the Spaniards and their God, he claimed, would the katsina (the ancient gods) return, bringing along a new era of prosperity. On August 10, 1680, an army of 8,000 Indian warriors razed churches and pillaged Spanish settlements, killing more than 400 settlers within hours. After several days of resisting in Santa Fe, the Spaniards fled south toward El Paso. They would not come back until 1692, when Diego de Vargas, New Mexico's new governor, succeeded in subduing the rebels.

During the 18th century, a number of popular rebellions and insurrections made evident the social and racial tensions and economic inequalities that riddled the colonies. Many of these movements were protests against the absolutist policies of the Bourbons in Spain and Sebastião José de Carvalho, the Marquis of Pombal, in Portugal. Implemented to rationalize colonial exploitation, strengthen the colonies' links to the metropolis, improve tax collection, and revamp the entire colonial administration, the Bourbon reforms also discouraged popular expressions of piety and collective devotion as unnecessary and extravagant. The combined impact of these socioeconomic, political, and religious reforms brought together different social groups against the government. For instance, between 1749 and 1752, cacao producers of Venezuela rebelled against the imposition of below-market prices by the monopolistic Guipúzcoa Company. A few years later, in 1765, an anti-tax movement rose in Quito in the context of a decline of the textile industry. In 1788 and 1789, a similar anti-tax revolt took place in Ouro Preto, in the mining district of Minas Gerais. Most of these movements looked for reforms and rarely challenged colonialism per se. This was not, however, always the case.

In 1712, a Pan-Mayan coalition known as the Cancuc Rebellion inaugurated a new era of indigenous revolts. Unlike its predecessors, the uprising in Cancuc, Chiapas, did not aim at reviving ancient religious customs but rather at challenging Spanish monopoly of Catholicism. To be sure, a series of Indian movements in highland Chiapas made similar demands between 1708 and 1713, but only Cancuc became an organized armed rebellion. Around May, a 13-year-old Indian, María de la Candelaria, claimed to have seen the Virgin Mary in the outskirts of the town. The priest of Cancuc dismissed the miracle as the devil's invention, but the inhabitants decided to build a chapel on the spot where the miracle occurred. To the dismay of ecclesiastical authorities, the Virgin cult drew the support of people from 32 Tzotzil, Tzeltal, and Chol villages. Rebel leader Sebastián Gómez de la Gloria announced that there was no longer a king, a bishop, or tributes to pay, and he began ordaining Indian priests. As the rebel confederation grew stronger, they moved on to Chilan, wiping out the Spanish army. Some time later, in Ocosingo, they killed all Spanish men and children and carried the women off to Cancuc. In the following months, the confederation started to fall apart because of the appearance of rival cults and the increasing attacks by Spaniards. By November, Spanish forces had retaken Cancuc, but the Indian leaders were never captured.

In Peru and Bolivia, the rebellion of Túpac Amaru II in the 1780s represented the climax of an impressive number of uprisings dating from the late 17th century.

Born José Gabriel Condorcanqui Noguera, Túpac Amaru II was a mestizo *curaca* (hereditary ruler) of Tinta and a moderately successful muleteer. In the 1770s, he assumed the name of the last Inca ruler, Túpac Amaru, and litigated in favor of the Indians in his jurisdiction before Spanish courts. After years of asking the Crown to put an end to the *reparto* (forced sale) of merchandise to Indians and the excesses of *corregidores* (local officers), Túpac Amaru II decided to rise in arms. Using his muleteer network to orchestrate the rebellion, Amaru II led a massive uprising that spread through southern Peru after initiating in Cuzco in November 1780. By December, Amaru II commanded an army of 40,000 soldiers composed not only of Indians but also mestizos, black slaves, and even whites. Many Indians refused to join the movement, and at least 20 curacas decided to fight with the Spanish forces. This notwithstanding, the movement harvested important victories but, inexplicably, Túpac Amaru II hesitated to attack the city of Cuzco, a crucial target. The Spaniards recovered from their surprise and defeated the movement within 6 months. Túpac Amaru II and his family were brutally executed in May 1781, but his relatives continued a second phase of the rebellion for 2 more years in Bolivia. In the wake of Amaru's rebellion, the Crown abolished the reparto of merchandise and replaced the corregidores with intendants, but these actions did not put an end to the abusive behavior of colonial officers.

While colonial authorities in Peru were dealing with the Andean uprisings, a new popular mobilization emerged in New Granada (Colombia). The Comunero revolt in 1781 was a popular movement to protest the recent increase in the alcabala sale taxes and in the price of monopolized products such as tobacco and brandy, as well as other exactions to finance Spain's war against England. News of popular uprisings in Socorro and San Gil reached Bogotá in March, and by May an army of 20,000 protesters, including Creoles, mestizos, Indians, and blacks, marched on the defenseless capital. Colonial authorities then sent Archbishop Antonio Caballero y Góngora to negotiate with the rebels. The result was a compromise settlement signed in Zipaquirá on June 8, 1781. Unfortunately, Spanish authorities refused to

honor the accords once the rebels dispersed. Some former comunero leaders, such as José Antonio Galán, a mulatto rebel, continued the fighting, but they were hunted down and executed between 1782 and 1783.

The most important and radical of the late colonial uprisings took place in the French island colony of Saint-Domingue (modern Haiti) in the 1790s. With a production equivalent to two thirds of the world's sugar and almost half of the world's coffee, Saint-Domingue was the jewel of the French Crown. The colony had a population of over half a million black slaves, 40,000 whites, and nearly 25,000 mulattoes and free blacks. After the outbreak of the French Revolution, the colony witnessed 2 years of vicious fighting between the whites and free people of color who demanded equal rights. Taking advantage of the situation, slaves decided to rebel on their own under the leadership of Boukman, who was replaced after his death in battle by Toussaint L'Ouverture, an ex-slave and ex-slaveowner. Toussaint proved to be a formidable commander. When Great Britain and Spain sent expeditionary forces hoping to seize the island, the rebel fended them off successfully. By 1801, Toussaint's forces controlled the French colony and had even expanded to the Spanish segment of the island. That same year, the leader promulgated a new constitution abolishing slavery and giving equality and citizenship to all inhabitants. Then, to the profound irritation of Napoleon Bonaparte, he made himself governor for life. In 1802, Napoleon sent his brother-in-law and 10,000 of his best soldiers to Saint-Domingue, but they were soundly defeated. Toussaint attempted to negotiate a settlement, but the French commander arrested him and sent to France, where he died of consumption in prison. His former lieutenant, Jean-Jacques Dessalines, took up the leadership and drove out the French. On January 1, 1804, Saint-Domingue, now renamed Haiti, became the second republic of the Americas and the first one to have abolished slavery on the continent.

Napoleon's imperial ambitions contributed not only to the independence of Haiti but also to the liberation of a good part of Latin America. The imperial crisis began in 1807 when, with the permission of Charles IV, Napoleon's troops crossed Spanish territory to invade Portugal as punishment for supporting England. As the French approached Lisbon, the Portuguese royal court left for Rio de Janeiro. As Napoleon occupied part of northern Spain, Charles IV's son Ferdinand orchestrated a riot at Aranjuez that forced the king to abdicate in his favor in March 1808. Offering himself as a mediator, Napoleon lured father and son to Bayonne, where he forced them both to abdicate in favor of his brother Joseph. Meanwhile, in Madrid, a popular insurrection broke out on May 2 and spread throughout the country. To organize the resistance, the rebels created *juntas* (provisional bodies) that were later joined together under a central junta in Seville. Across the Atlantic, Spanish Americans debated whether to recognize the Junta Central or to seize the opportunity to gain independence. In most of the colonies, Creoles (native-born Spaniards) swore allegiance to the king, but argued that, in the absence of the monarch, sovereignty reverted to the people. They thus moved to organize local juntas mainly composed of Creoles to rule in name of Ferdinand VII. In 1810, however, French troops took Seville and the Junta Central moved to Cádiz, where a Regency replaced it. The Regency then called for a meeting of the Cortes, a legislative body, and tried to secure the support of the colonies by inviting them to send representatives. After much discussion, the Cortes drafted a liberal constitution that established a constitutional monarchy but ruled that the American colonies could not be granted autonomy. When Ferdinand returned to the throne in 1814, he dissolved the Cortes, abolished the constitution, and tried to recover control of the colonies by sending a massive number of troops to South America. Unfortunately for him, Colonel Riego led a mutiny within the army that soon turned into an insurrection. The king was forced to restore the constitution, but the return of liberal policies was not enough to quiet down the autonomist impulse in the colonies.

The first country to declare its independence in Spanish America was Venezuela. After the collapse of the Central Junta in Seville, Creole militia officers formed a junta and deposed the captain general in April 1810. One year later, a congress convened to declare independence and drafted a federalist constitution that excluded most of the population from political participation. When Spanish troops from Puerto Rico landed in northwest Venezuela, many free blacks and mulattoes readily joined them. Then on March 26, 1812, an earthquake struck Venezuela, causing massive destruction in the regions controlled by the rebels. The royalist cause received a major boost when royalist clergy interpreted this disaster as divine punishment against the rebels. As the rebel forces crumbled under Spanish attack, commander in chief Francisco de Miranda struck a deal with the royalist general and tried to flee with part of the republic's treasury. Before he could leave the country, however, Creole officer Simón Bolívar captured him and turned him in to the Spaniards as a traitor. In exchange, Bolívar obtained a safe conduct to Colombia, where he led a successful campaign against the royalists in the east. In 1813, Bolívar returned to Venezuela with 500 men, but he suffered a humiliating defeat by an army of black and mulatto cowboys called *llaneros,* who were despised and mistreated by the insurgents. By July 1814, Bolívar was back in Colombia fighting again the Spaniards, but the country was deeply divided. Believing the situation to be hopeless, Bolívar left for Jamaica in May 1815. Later, he traveled to Haiti, where President Alexandre Pétion promised to help him in return for a promise to abolish slavery. On his return to Venezuela in 1816, Bolívar made an alliance with the llaneros and free blacks. With his new forces, Bolívar crossed the Andes and defeated the Spaniards in Colombia in 1819. Two years later, Venezuela was liberated, and Bolívar expanded the campaign to Ecuador with the help of his lieutenant, José de Sucre. By 1822, Colombia, Venezuela, Ecuador, and even Panamá had been liberated.

The independence movement in Buenos Aires started as early as 1806, when a Creole force led by Santiago Liniers repelled a British attack while Viceroy Sobremonte fled the city. In February 1807, the Audiencia (the high court) appointed Liniers as temporary viceroy, to the peninsula's great displeasure. Although the Creoles were in control of the colony, they pledged to be loyal to Spain and accepted the appointment of a new viceroy in 1809. One year later, however, Creole militia officers demanded an open town meeting to discuss the crisis in Spain. On

May 21, 1810, the participants voted to depose the viceroy and establish a junta to govern on behalf of Ferdinand VII. The junta then attempted to consolidate its authority over the interior provinces, but the leaders of Uruguay, Paraguay, and Upper Peru (Bolivia) resisted Buenos Aires' ascendancy. After a triumvirate headed by Bernardino Rivadavia assumed power in 1811, the capital sent military expeditions to subdue the provinces, with terrible results. By the end of that year, Buenos Aires was forced to acknowledge the independence of Paraguay. In 1813, José de San Martín, the son of Spanish officer, led a coup d'état against Rivadavia but this did not change Buenos Aires' policy toward the provinces. In 1814, Paraguay became independent. On July 9, 1816, a constituent congress gathered in Tucumán and declared the independence of the United Provinces of the Río de la Plata. But the union did not last: Uruguay became independent in 1828, and the rest of the territory was only unified under the dictatorship of Juan Manuel de Rosas (1829–1852).

Chile made its first move toward independence on September 18, 1810. On that date, an open meeting of Santiago's town council deposed the Spanish governor and established a junta. The Creoles were divided, however, regarding the direction the movement should take. Whereas the reformists wished to remain within a Spanish framework, the revolutionaries, led by Bernardo O'Higgins, advocated for full independence. Soon, the country was beset by bitter disputes between factions and regions. In 1814, royalist forces defeated the divided patriots in Rancagua forcing O'Higgins and others into exile in Argentina, where they joined San Martín's forces. Three years later, in an amazing feat, San Martín led a force of 5,500 men across the Andes over six mountain passes. The insurgents defeated the Spaniards on the hill of Chacabuco in February 1817, but Chile was not set free until the decisive defeat of Spain at Maipú on April 5, 1818. San Martín then turned his attention to the liberation of Peru. For this new expedition, he gathered a force of 4,500 soldiers and the naval support of mercenary Thomas Cochrane. San Martín arrived in Peru in 1820 and tried to find a way for a negotiated peace, but to no avail. In July 1821, however, Spanish authorities abandoned Lima and San Martín's forces entered unopposed and proclaimed Peru independent. The following year, San Martín met with Bolívar in Guayaquil. It remains a mystery what transpired in the meeting, but San Martín decided to abandon the insurgent cause afterward and leave the liberation of Peru and Upper Peru to Bolívar. Having landed in Callao in September 1823, Bolívar undertook a final offensive in the south of Peru the following year. Liberation was finally accomplished when Antonio José de Sucre defeated the Spaniards at Ayacucho on December 9, 1824. Four months later, on April 1, 1825, Sucre sealed Bolivia's independence by defeating Governor Olañeta in Tumusla.

In Mexico, the collapse of the Spanish prompted Creoles to establish a junta with the support of the opportunistic Viceroy José de Iturrigaray, but the calls for autonomy were suppressed when peninsular leaders staged a military coup on September 15, 1808. Whereas the Creoles in Mexico City hesitated to rebel, those living in the provinces organized several conspiracies. In 1810, colonial authorities learned of a new conspiracy in Querétaro and moved to arrest the plotters, which included Father Miguel Hidalgo y Costilla. Knowing of his impending arrest, Hidalgo issued the "Grito of Dolores" on September 16, 1810, calling on his parishioners of Dolores to rebel against the government. As the rebels marched through the Bajío, a region struck by years of drought, hunger, and unemployment, Hidalgo's forces grew by the thousands in a matter of days. After the uncontrollable mass of Indians and mestizos attacked and burned the granary in Guanajuato, even provincial Creoles repudiated the revolt and joined the Spanish forces. In late October, Hidalgo's mob of 80,000 faced a small royalist force in Monte de las Cruces, outside of Mexico City. Although the rebels won the battle, Hidalgo lost half of his contingent in desertions and decided not to attack the capital. He was captured on his way to Querétaro and executed on July 31, 1811. With Hidalgo dead, leadership passed on to José María Morelos, a mestizo priest of humble background. Preferring a smaller but better trained and armed army, Morelos recovered much of the ground lost to the royalists. By the beginning of 1813, he controlled most of southern Mexico and felt confident enough to convene a constitutional congress in Chilpancingo, which issued a declaration of independence on November 6, 1813. His program called for the abolition of slavery, tributes, and caste distinctions, and the redistribution of property of the wealthy. Like Hidalgo, however, Morelos hesitated to attack Mexico City, and after a series of losses, he was captured and shot on December 22, 1815. By the end of 1817, only rebels Vicente Guerrero and Felix Fernandez (alias Guadalupe Victoria) led isolated efforts of resistance in the east and west of the country. Then a surprising turn of events won Mexico's conservative sectors over to the side of independence. In November 1820, Royalist General Agustín de Iturbide was sent by Viceroy Apodaca to fight against Vicente Guerrero. Instead of carrying out his orders, Iturbide negotiated an alliance with Guerrero and declared Mexico's independence in the Plan de Iguala. Because the plan argued for the adoption of a constitutional monarchy, the protection of the church, and the preservation of the old bureaucracy, the conservatives had no qualms in embracing it. In September 1821, Iturbide returned, in victory, to Mexico City, thus putting an end to 11 years of bloody fighting. Mexico's independence also brought freedom to Guatemala, El Salvador, Honduras, Nicaragua, and Costa Rica. In 1823, however, these countries separated into the United Provinces of Central America.

Brazilian independence was markedly different from the rest of Spanish America: There was no prolonged independence war, little racial upheaval, rapid expansion of slavery instead of its progressive decline, and finally, creation of an independent empire rather than a republic. Brazil's different path to independence started in November 1807, when the royal family and a host of nobles and functionaries left Portugal to escape French troops. The arrival of the Portuguese court in Rio de Janeiro brought about dramatic changes in the colony, such as the introduction of printing presses in Rio and Salvador, the establishment of two medical schools, the creation of a Bank of Brazil, and the active promotion of the colony's manufacturing industry. By 1815, Portugal had been liberated from Napoleonic rule, but King John VI decided to stay in Brazil, raising the colony's status to

a kingdom. Five years later, however, the Portuguese liberals revolted in Lisbon and Oporto, thus forcing the king to return. On July 26, 1821, his 22-year-old son Pedro assumed Brazil's regency in blatant defiance of Portugal's authority. As in Spain, the liberals had convoked a meeting of the Cortes, which now demanded Dom Pedro to return to Portugal. On September 7, 1822, Dom Pedro proclaimed the independence of Brazil and assumed the title of constitutional emperor. In 1831, the monarch abdicated in favor of his son Pedro II, who ruled the country until 1889 when Brazil became a republic.

By the end of the 19th century, Spain had lost most of its American possessions, except for Cuba and Puerto Rico. In Cuba in 1868, nationalists started a 10-year war of liberation, but the rebels failed to gain the support of the elite and were defeated by the Spanish government. That same year, on September 23, Ramón Emeterio Betances, Segundo Ruíz Belvis, and close to 600 men and women revolted in Lares, Puerto Rico, without success. Back in Cuba, a new revolt broke out in 1895, led by a group of revolutionaries that included poet-lawyer José Martí, who would be killed in battle. For the next 3 years, the country was engulfed in a brutal war that received wide coverage in the United States. After the USS Maine inexplicably exploded and sank in Havana Harbor, the U.S. Congress declared war on Spain. The war lasted only a few months, and by December 1898, Spain granted independence to Cuba. The United States also obtained sovereignty over Guam, Puerto Rico, and the Philippines. In 1901, the Cubans drafted a new constitution that included, under U.S. pressure, a proviso (the Platt Amendment) giving the United States the right to intervene in Cuban affairs. Although the amendment was abrogated in 1934, the United States enjoyed total hegemony over the island until the triumph of the Cuban Revolution of 1959. As for Puerto Rico, the island was granted commonwealth status in 1952, thus making it in practice neither a colony nor a state.

—*Javier Villa-Flores*

See also Amaru, Túpac, II; Martí, José; Toussaint L'Ouverture

Further Readings

Barman, R. J. (1998). *Brazil: The forging of a nation, 1798–1852.* Palo Alto, CA: Stanford University Press.

Fink, C. E. (1990). *The making of Haiti: The Saint Domingue Revolution from below.* Knoxville: University of Tennessee Press.

Gosner, K. (1992). *Soldiers of the Virgin: The moral economy of a colonial Maya rebellion.* Tucson: University of Arizona Press.

Gutiérrez, R. (1991). *When Jesus came, the corn mothers went away: Marriage, sexuality, and power in New Mexico, 1500–1846.* Palo Alto, CA: Stanford University Press.

Kinsbruner, J. (1994). *Independence in Spanish America: Civil wars, revolutions, and underdevelopment.* Albuquerque: University of New Mexico Press.

Kraay, H. (2001). *Race, state, and armed forces in independent-era Brazil: Bahia, 1790–1840s.* Palo Alto, CA: Stanford University Press.

Pérez, L. A., Jr. (1995). *Cuba: Between reform and revolution* (2nd ed.). New York: Oxford University Press.

Schroeder, S. (Ed.). *Native resistance and the Pax Colonial in New Spain.* Lincoln: University of Nebraska Press.

Stern, S. (1992). *Peru's Indian peoples and the challenge of Spanish conquest: Huamanga to 1640* (2nd ed.). Madison: University of Wisconsin Press.

Van Young, E. (2001). *The other rebellion: Popular violence, ideology, and the Mexican struggle for independence, 1810–1821.* Palo Alto, CA: Stanford University Press.

ANTI-COLONIAL MOVEMENTS, MIDDLE EAST AND NORTH AFRICA

As with other colonies, a number of anti-colonial resistance movements sprang up in the Middle East and North Africa. The circumstances of colonialism in this region, however, differed quite substantially from those in other areas. In particular, three things set this region's history apart from that of other colonized regions: (1) the relative recency of colonialism as an organized regime in these areas, (2) the placement of a wide number of what are now sovereign nation-states under the protection of the League of Nations and later the United Nations, and (3) the relatively peaceful decolonization of these regions.

Colonialism as an organized system—that is, a system in which one country conquers, settles, rules, and economically exploits a second country—was a recent phenomenon in much of the Middle East and North Africa. Although many have argued that the Ottoman Empire constitutes a colonialist regime, its decline was already noted in the early part of the 19th century. As well, the Berlin Conference of 1884–1885, which divided the continent of Africa into colonial zones governed by France, Britain, Portugal, Germany, Belgium, Spain, and Italy only legitimated the already existing colonial presences in North Africa, whereas in sub-Saharan Africa, new expansion by the colonial powers was made possible by the Berlin Conference. This encyclopedia entry will treat colonialism in this region as commencing with the 1830 invasion of Algeria by France.

After the defeat of the Ottoman Empire in World War I, its territorial holdings were spun off into semi-sovereign states that were, at least nominally, made protectorates or mandates of the new League of Nations. With this new protectorate status—continued after the demise of the League of Nations and the creation of the United Nations at the conclusion of World War II—a variety of countries were able to have influence on the protectorates, which simultaneously complicated the colonial situation and diffused the power that any one colonial power could have over the protectorates.

Finally, unlike much of sub-Saharan Africa, many of the colonized countries in the Middle East and North Africa achieved independence in a relatively amicable manner. This is not to say that the decolonization process was entirely peaceful, rather that most countries in the region did not go through either full-blown revolutions or wars for independence. Algeria (1954–1962) and Israel (1946–1948) are the two notable exceptions; however, there are other instances of rebellions and other types of uprisings in many of these countries.

This entry provides a short overview of the key anti-colonial movements in the Middle East and North Africa. These movements are presented according to their categorization in a four-part schema based on their primary ideology and are generally presented moving eastward from Morocco to Iran. Those countries in which an explicitly colonial regime did not exist—in particular, most of the protectorates known collectively as the Trucial States, Saudi Arabia, and Iran—are not addressed here; however, contemporary movements that claim an anti-colonial program vis-à-vis a current colonizing or colonialist-style occupying force are discussed.

Types of Anti-Colonial Movements in the Middle East and North Africa

For the purposes of this entry, the term *anti-colonial movement* will be defined in two ways: (1) as a political party (legal or otherwise) or clandestine movement that has as its goal the independence of the nation within which it operates and which struggles against a specified colonial power or powers that have control over its nation, or (2) as a larger organization that takes on an anti-colonial discourse and policy vis-à-vis international affairs. As well, while recognizing that this schema developed by Hassan Hanafi is necessarily an artificial one, this entry will characterize anti-colonial movements as belonging to one of four categories, arranged in concentric circles from first to last: pure nationalism, Arab and/or Pan-Arab Marxist nationalism, religious nationalist movements, and Third World movements.

Beyond Hanafi's schema, however, it seems that once anti-colonial movements in one country are successful, they very frequently begin to transition to an orientation further out in these concentric circles, so that pure nationalist movements will begin to become more Pan-Arab or even Arab Marxist in their ideology, Pan-Arab movements take on Islamist overtones, and so on. Particularly in the Middle East and North Africa, with countries in such close proximity to one another, the bleed-over of one anti-colonial movement into another is both likely and, for Pan-Arab movements and further out in this schema, highly desired, and very often successful anti-colonial movements get involved in or mobilize solidarity with movements in other countries. With this internationalist (or at least regionalist) orientation, then, the full picture of anti-colonial movements in this region is necessarily complicated, often sloppy, and frequently unable to be fully depicted in a short representation of the

phenomenon. Nevertheless, where appropriate, this entry will sketch out the ways in which successful anti-colonial movements have sought to continue the collapse of colonialism as a world system.

Pure Nationalist Movements

Pure nationalist movements are those that are dedicated to the independence and self-determination of a particular nation by its national members, without explicit reference to belonging to the Arab world, to Islam as the basis for all laws in the postcolonial society, or to furthering the cause of *tiers-mondisme* (third worldism). These movements rely on a burgeoning concept of national membership, often one that is either received from or imposed by the colonizing country (e.g., "You are all Algerians"), or one that is indigenously developed through the use of conceptual tools gained from the colonizing country, generally through the education of indigenous elites by institutions in the *métropole.*

Throughout North Africa, the earliest of anti-colonial movements generally held to pure nationalist ideologies. The first of Morocco's movements, La Koutla de l'Action Nationale, was an attempt to unify the people of Morocco in response to the French-issued Berber Decree of 1930 (which strove to divide Imazighen and Arabs) and articulated the nationalist goals of "the Moroccan people"; between then and 1937, La Koutla maintained a contentious relationship with the French governor-general, and was closed in 1937. At that time, with the support of Egyptian student movements, new nationalist parties such as L'Alliance pour la Défense de Maroc and Le Parti de la Réforme formed, and contributed in 1944 to the promulgation of the Manifeste de l'Indépendance et Democratie. The year 1944 also saw the establishment of the Hezb al-Istiqlal (Independence Party), which went clandestine in 1953 and relied on Algerian support and a merger with the Reform Party to gain preeminence on the eve of independence in 1956.

Likewise, Algerian parties such as the Front de la Libération Nationale and the Mouvement National Algérien articulated a nationalist response to French colonial rule, utilizing the discourse of the American

Bill of Rights and the French Declaration of the Rights of Man and the Citizen as the basis for their resistance. Three core groups participated in the development of Algerian nationalism: the assimilationists (or Young Algerians), who would accept the permanent incorporation of Algeria into metropolitan France if citizenship came with it; Muslim reformers, who created the Association des Uléma Musulmans Algériens; and the followers of Ahmed Messali Hadj, who eventually formed the Front de Libération Nationale. Even before the organization of the Front de Libération Nationale in 1953, nationalist resistance to French colonialism had been widespread in the 1830s with the Sufi leader 'Abd al-Qadir ibn Muhyi al-Din leading a campaign of nearly 2 decades.

Tunisia's Young Tunisians, Destour Party (1918–1920), and Neo-Destour Party (1933–1938) did the same. The Neo-Destour Party began an armed resistance campaign in 1953, and the more conservative Destourist leader Salah bin Youssef took up arms against the agreement on full Tunisian autonomy.

The Middle East also saw the development of a wide variety of pure nationalist movements, though these often had to take account of the particular demographics of the region. Even before direct British rule through the invasion of 1882, Egypt saw a number of nationalist leaders, including Jamal ad-Din al-Afghani, who wanted to modernize Egypt while distancing itself from the West, and Colonel 'Urabi Pasha, who created the parliament, which Britain invaded to eliminate. Both the Wafd Party, which came from the 1918 move for Egyptian independence, and Colonel Jamal 'Abd al-Naser (Gamal Nasser) wanted to develop an independent form of Egyptian nationalism over and against the involvement of Western countries.

In Syria, the establishment of the People's Party in 1925 yielded the first anti-colonial movement in the country; later, this party joined with members of the Druze religious community to form the National Bloc in 1936, which later ushered in Syria's declaration of independence. Lebanon had its Nationalist Party, led by Bishara al-Khuri, which drew from a cross-section of Lebanese society and pushed for an independent Lebanon rather than unification with Syria or a Pan-Arab state;

as well, the Phalange Party (1936–1982), a right-wing radical Maronite movement (and later a pro-Israel militia), also utilized a pure nationalist ideology.

More recently, the Polisario Front has declared itself to be a movement fighting the colonization of Western Sahara by Morocco. Founded in 1973 out of the remnants of the Harakat Tahrir Sagula Al-Hamra wa Oued Ad-Dahab (Organization for the Liberation of Saguia El Hamra y Rio de Oro), the Polisario Front fought against both Morocco and Mauritania while the latter made territorial claims to Western Sahara; in 1979, Mauritania renounced its claims, leaving the Polisario Front to declare Morocco a colonizing country, evidenced with the Green March, organized by Moroccan king Hassan II to ensure that Moroccans were counted as voters in the U.N.-organized referendum on independence for the region. In 1982, the Organization for African Unity (and its successor, the African Union) accepted the Polisario-declared Saharawi Arab Democratic Republic as a member, while blocking Morocco from accession because of its colonial repression in the Saharawi Arab Democratic Republic.

Arab and Pan-Arab Marxist Movements

The second type of anti-colonial movements, Arab and Pan-Arab Marxist movements, are motivated not only by the direct need for national independence from the colonial powers but also by the fact of having a common language, set of traditions, and history with other Arab nations and therefore a common set of political, economic, and social needs and concerns across the Arab world. These movements draw their inspiration not only from the desire for decolonization from within the nation but also on the fact of other Arab nations throwing off their colonial chains. As well, Pan-Arab movements can also become involved in the anti-colonial movements in another country in a version of the kind of internationalism practiced by such revolutionaries as Che Guevara.

Few of the anti-colonial movements in the Middle East and North Africa started from a Pan-Arab ideology. The two notable exceptions, however, are the

Palestine Liberation Organization (PLO) and the Front for the Liberation of (Occupied) South Yemen. The PLO was a creation of the 1964 Arab League summit, when it was decided (particularly by Egypt) that there should be a centralized organization to unify the various factions resisting what was seen as Israeli colonialism. Most of the factions that fell under the PLO umbrella—including the Democratic Front for the Liberation of Palestine, al-Fatah, the Popular Front for the Liberation of Palestine, and al-Sa'iqah—had one or more national members of the Arab League as their sponsor(s) and relied on some form of a Marxist-Leninist or Arab socialist ideological position; thus, it can be claimed that the PLO itself represented a Pan-Arab approach to Palestinian liberation.

Between 1963 and 1968, the Egyptian-sponsored Front for the Liberation of (Occupied) South Yemen competed with the indigenous Marxist-oriented National Liberation Front for dominance in Aden and a position as the representative of the Yemeni people. The National Liberation Front eventually gained control and took over after Britain granted South Yemen its independence.

The most widely known Pan-Arab movements developed that element of their political ideology and agenda after independence. In addition to the PLO, the Egyptian leader Gamal Nasser, Libya's Mu'ammar al-Qaddafi, and the Ba'ath parties of both Syria and Iraq have all taken on Pan-Arab ideologies and worked to support anti-colonial movements elsewhere in the Arab world, often as an expression of their own national self-interest. Nasser facilitated the 1958 creation of the United Arab Republic out of the merger of Egypt and Syria and hoped to create a larger Pan-Arab state, in particular by attempting to conquer Yemen; however, the United Arab Republic was disbanded in 1961.

Religious Nationalist Movements

Hanafi's framework includes Islamic movements as the third type of nationalist movement. Islamic movements are those that predicate themselves on the tenets of Islam as the basis of anti-colonial activity, either in the sense of relying on the cross against the crescent motif (discussed by Frantz Fanon as an inspiration for anti-colonial political or revolutionary activity) or on the tenets of Shari'a (Islamic law) for the establishment of a postcolonial social and political order.

However, the Middle East and North Africa differ from other colonized regions in one particular way—that is, it is a multireligious region, with Muslims, Christians, Jews, Druze, and Tamazight and Imazight (Berber) adherents, among others, living in close proximity with one another, as well as multiple sects of each of the religions in close quarters (e.g., Sunni and Shi'a Muslims, as well as Coptic and Maronite Christians). Therefore, it makes more sense, given the histories of countries in this region, to speak more broadly of religious nationalist movements, those whose societal organizing principles, either as a basis for resistance to the colonial order or in the core tenets of the postcolonial order, are predicated on any of the religions at work in the area.

The obvious examples in this region are the Irgun Zvai Leumi (1931–1948) and the Haganah (1920–1948), both Jewish nationalist movements in the British Mandate of Palestine. Each of these movements and their associated political parties (the Herut and Revisionist Parties in the case of the Irgun and the Histadrut [General Federation of Labor] for the Haganah) had opposing political ideologies and targets. The Irgun, a right-wing clandestine organization that left the Zionist movement's congress in 1935, took their struggle first against Arab Palestinians and then against the British. The Haganah, on the other hand, remained a more left-leaning Zionist organization, resisting the British mandate and the White Paper on the two-state solution before and after World War II, while at the same time forming the Jewish Brigades of the Royal Armed Forces during the war. Nevertheless, both the Irgun and the Haganah, which were eventually folded together in the creation of the Israeli Defense Forces with independence in 1948, were motivated by the notion of creating a "Jewish state" with all that phrase entailed.

At the same time within British-mandated Palestine, the Arab Revolt (1936–1939) represented another religiously motivated anti-colonial movement. Sparked by ardent followers of the religious leader Sheikh 'Izz ad-Din al-Qassam after his murder by British forces in 1935, the spontaneous violence of the sheikh's followers was channeled into a coherent rebellion by the Arab High Committee, which was eventually dissolved by the British after a declaration of martial law in 1937. Still, after the release of the Peel Report and its statements that Britain's obligations to both Jews and Arabs were mutually irreconcilable, the violence of the Arab Revolt was accelerated through the 1939 release of the White Paper, which addressed the Arab rebels' demands for control over Jewish immigration and land transfers.

However, there were other religiously based anti-colonial movements, rebellions, and uprisings in the region. In what was the Spanish Sahara (now Western Sahara), Abd al-Krim led an uprising (1921–1926) against Spanish colonial forces, declaring the establishment of the Republic of the Rif, based on Tamazight and Imazight (Berber) traditional institutions and cultural practices; eventually, the rebellion was quashed by a joint French-Spanish expeditionary force.

In Libya, both the Bedouin resistance to Italian colonialism and the Sanusi Muslim movement that sparked two Italo-Sanusi wars (1914–1917 and 1923–1931) were religiously motivated; the Bedouins wanted nothing more than to preserve their ability to practice Islam without Western interference, while 'Umar al-Mukhtar, the Sanusi leader, looked to establish an Islamic republic in Libya. Eventually, Idris I, the Sanusi sultan, was accepted by both Tripolitania (the coastal region) and Cyrenaica as the leader, and he was instrumental in deciding that the best way to defeat Italian colonialism was to support Great Britain during World War II. After independence and the military coup against the monarchy organized by the Free Officers, Mu'ammar al-Qaddafi transitioned from Pan-Arabism to an Islamic socialism, detailed in his *Green Book*.

Finally, in post–World War I Iraq, ruled by Great Britain, three anti-colonial secret societies developed in primary urban areas across the country. Jamiyat an-Nahda al-Islamiya (The League of Islamic Awakening), Al-Jamiya al-Wataniya al-Islamiya (Muslim National League), and Haras al-Istiqlal (The Guardians of Independence)—all composed of both Sunni and Shi'a members from across class strata and the rural/urban divide, joined together in the 1920 Great Iraqi Revolution (Ath-Thawara al-Iraqiyya al-Kubra), which was quashed by British colonial forces. Finally, the Zaydi imam Yahya Mahmud al-Mutawwakil of North Yemen led that region toward an Islamist resistance to Ottoman, and later British, influence on the Saudi peninsula.

More recently, after former Israeli prime minister Ariel Sharon's declaration that the site of the Al-Aqsa Mosque would always remain an Israeli possession, more Islamist-oriented resistance groups such as Hamas, Islamic Jihad, and Hezbollah have come to the fore in what has been called the "Al-Aqsa Intifada." Some scholars might argue that these movements represent Islamic anti-colonial movements, claiming that Israel is the colonial force in these areas. This entry takes no stand on these claims, given that the Israeli occupation of the West Bank and Gaza does not meet all of the criteria of the definition of colonialism presented earlier. As well, because there was no clear colonial dominator in Iran, the claims of the Islamic Revolution of 1979 to be an anti-colonial movement are not treated herein. Finally, the Al-Qaeda network, the Iraqi insurgents during the Second Gulf War, and other jihadist organizations utilize a Pan-Arab, Islamist discourse in their edicts against the imperialism of the United States; however, because U.S. interventions in the affairs of the Middle East do not meet the criteria of colonialism, the treatment of this discourse will be left aside.

Third World Movements

The final type of anti-colonial movement Hanafi outlines is the Third World movement. Unlike the common usage of this term, the true connotation is with the Non-Aligned Movement (NAM), or what has also been known as the "positive neutrality" movement. NAM was a response both to the history of Western colonialism and to the bipolar nature of the Cold War international order, and many countries that gained their independence through decolonization struggles chose to remain unattached to either the United States–dominated Western bloc or the Soviet Union. Egypt's Gamal Abdel Nasser was one of the five founding members (along with the leaders of India, Yugoslavia, Ghana, and Indonesia).

One of the core tenets of NAM is the resistance to colonialism or infringements on its members' sovereignty of any kind and to promote equity and economic and cultural cooperation among its member states. Although the original 29 member states that met at Bandung, Indonesia, in 1955 showed considerable solidarity and support for the principles expressed in the Bandung Declaration, the tacit alignment of many of the member countries with the Soviet Union began to weaken the organization. Nevertheless, NAM maintained its opposition to colonialism or imperialism of any kind into the 21st century and has been integral in the struggle against neocolonial measures that economically developed countries have attempted to impose through the World Trade Organization and other multilateral economic institutions.

Nearly all of the former colonies in the Middle East and North Africa, save for Israel, are members of NAM, as is the Palestinian Authority. The organization currently serves as a parallel institutional structure for the countries now generally referred to as the "global South."

Conclusion

Leaving aside the current issues of the Western Sahara and the Israeli occupation of the West Bank and Gaza Strip, the era of classical colonialism is over. Many movements operating in the early 21st century in the Middle East and North Africa claim that colonial domination continues to exist on the part of the United States and Israel and utilizes one of the four types of anti-colonial ideology and discourse discussed herein. As time has gone on, however, anti-colonial movements in this region have moved from particular national struggles for independence, whether based on a burgeoning indigenous conception of nationhood or a religiously based membership ideal, to a larger political stance of countering colonialist and imperialist forms of domination. As this transition has taken place, movements have shifted their particular stance toward more regionalist or internationalist approaches to countering

interference in their sovereign affairs by other nations. So long as this kind of interference continues to occur—and in an era of increasing globalization, one would expect that it will continue—anti-colonial movements in the Middle East and North Africa will continue to struggle against domination.

—*Scott Schaffer*

See also Anti-Globalization Movement; Anti-Imperialism; Guevara, Che; Hezbollah; Intifada (1987–1992, 2000–2003); Palestine Liberation Organization (PLO); Postcolonial Theory; Social Movements, Sociology of; Strategies and Tactics in Social Movements

Further Readings

Betts, R. (2005). *Assimilation and association in French colonial theory, 1890–1914.* Lincoln: University of Nebraska Press.

Chouieri, Y. M. (2001). *Arab nationalism: A history.* London: Blackwell.

Cleveland, W. L. (1999). *A history of the modern Middle East.* Boulder, CO: Westview Press.

Dawisha, A. (2002). *Arab nationalism in the twentieth century: From triumph to despair.* Princeton, NJ: Princeton University Press.

Eldan Shahin, E. (1998). *Political ascent: Contemporary Islamic movements in North Africa.* Boulder, CO: Westview Press.

Fanon, F. (2005). *The wretched of the earth.* New York: Grove Press.

Hanafi, H. (2004). Qu'est-ce que le colonialisme? [What is colonialism?]. *Rencontres d'Averroès, 10,* 15–25.

Milton-Edwards, B. (2000). *Contemporary politics in the Middle East.* Cambridge, UK: Polity Press.

Peters, R. (1996). *Jihad in classical and modern Islam: A reader.* Princeton, NJ: Markus Wiener.

Tibi, B. (1997). *Arab nationalism: Between Islam and the nation-state.* London: Palgrave Macmillan.

Anti-Colonial Movements, South Pacific

From the beginning of Western contact with islands of the South Pacific, there have been anti-colonial actions that were characterized by Westerners as acts of simple savagery or cannibalism. On first contact with Westerners, the people of the South Pacific suffered great losses in numbers due to epidemics of Western diseases, and the superior firepower of Western guns and cannons overcame native forces. A famous early conflict led to the killing of Captain Cook by Hawaiians in 1779. Other incidents included the deaths of a group of Frenchmen led by the Count de la Perouse to Samoa in 1787 and the death of the London Missionary Society's South Pacific leader John Williams in Vanuatu in 1839.

The original representation of the South Pacific as a natural paradise, as mythologized by Western writers in the 18th century, changed to one of a paradise lost by the 19th century. The London Missionary Society sent its very first mission to the island of Tahiti in 1796 but did not establish itself there until the conversion of King Pomare. Meanwhile throughout the South Pacific, Western influence centered on paramount chiefs weakening the much-decentralized systems of governance traditionally in place.

A search for Pacific routes to Asia and Australia set the United States of America onto great natural harbors at Pearl River in the Kingdom of Hawai'i and Pagopago Bay in Samoa. U.S. naval strategists were incited by 19th-century admiral Alfred Mahan's theory that there were three keys to sea power: production with its exchange, shipping, and colonies to facilitate and enlarge the operations while multiplying points of safety. Today, the U.S. Seventh Fleet, headquartered in Hawai'i, is the largest fleet in the U.S. Navy with about two thirds of its combat capability, where most of the transpacific sea-lanes pass through the Hawaiian Islands.

With missionaries and militarism, tourism also has played a large role in South Pacific colonialism. In French Polynesia, after World War II, Tahitian soldiers returning from fighting for France questioned the oppression of Tahitians by the French. The independence movement they started, however, was suppressed and their leaders imprisoned when the 1962 Hollywood film production of *Mutiny on the Bounty* with Marlon Brando came to Tahiti, resulting in a sharp rise in tourism. With the 1980s anti-nuclear movement, the Tahitian or Maohi pro-independence parties returned, and eventually its most prominent

leader, Oscar Temaru, was elected president of French Polynesia in 2004. A similar anti-nuclear movement was organized in the Marshall Islands where nuclear testing that began in 1946 on the island of Bikini led to entire island relocations and the contamination of these islands. The United States has yet to decontaminate and reinstate any of the Marshall Islands that were used for nuclear testing sites.

The socioeconomic concept of a "Pacific Rim," often used to describe Pacific interests, exploits Pacific Island sea-lanes and sea resources, including fishing rights. Twenty-one Pacific Rim nations, including the United States and Canada, are members of the Asia-Pacific Economic Cooperation (APEC), which was established in 1989 to provide a forum for discussion on a broad range of Pacific economic issues. Except for the larger countries of Papua New Guinea, Australia, and New Zealand, APEC does not include any Pacific island nation. The Pacific island nations are members of the Pacific Islands Forum, which includes the independent nations of Cook Islands, Federated States of Micronesia, Fiji, Kiribati, Nauru, Niue, Palau, Papua New Guinea, Republic of the Marshall Islands, Samoa, Solomon Islands, Tonga, Tuvalu, Vanuatu, Aotearoa-New Zealand, and Australia. Nonmember colonial states, which are gaining some autonomy, such as Tahiti (French Polynesia) and New Caledonia, have been allowed to send observers to Pacific Islands Forum meetings.

U.S. unincorporated organized territories include Guam and the Commonwealth of Northern Mariana Islands. The unincorporated unorganized territories include American Samoa (technically unorganized but self-governing under a 1967 constitution) and several islands and atolls uninhabited by indigenous peoples. The Samoa Islands today are divided into the independent nation of Samoa and the U.S. territory of American Samoa. The U.N. Committee on Decolonization includes Guam and American Samoa on the U.N. list of non-self-governing territories, along with the Pacific island nations of Pitcairn (New Zealand), Tokelau (New Zealand), and New Caledonia (France). Other island nations like Rapanui (or Easter Island, Chile) are seeking to be (re)instated on the U.N. list of non-self-governing territories with the goal of independence.

In the 1950s in Nouvelle Calédonie (New Caledonia), France granted greater autonomy, but with the rise in nickel mining in the 1960s, France reinstated its former colonial position. The immigration of mostly French and some Polynesian settlers who came to outnumber the native Kanaks, led to race conflicts that began in the 1980s and continue today where the population is about 43% Kanaky, 37% French, and 9% Polynesian from Wallis and Futuna. There is now a Kanak Customary Senate representing the Kanaky interest toward independence.

The great island of Papua is divided between the independent nation of Papua New Guinea and the Indonesian province of Irian Jaya, also called West Papua. In the 1950s, West Papua was moving toward independence from the Netherlands when a naval war broke out with Indonesia over West Papua. Seeking to ally itself with Indonesia, the United States held secret meetings with the Dutch and Indonesians, leading to the New York Agreement of 1962 creating the Indonesian province of Irian Jaya. Free Papua Movement (Organisasi Papua Merdeka) was established in 1965, but an estimated 100,000 Papuans have been killed by Indonesian military forces since 1963. In 1988, Dr. Tom Wanggai organized a peaceful West Papuan flag-raising demonstration; the Indonesian military arrested him, and he was sentenced to 20 years in prison where he died in 1996. In 1998, the military opened fire on flag-raising civilians in the island of Biak, killing dozens of people. Despite killing, imprisonment, and torture, flag raisings still occur throughout West Papua. In 2000, an estimated 20,000 West Papuans gathered in the capital Jayapura, and the Papua Presidium Council (Presidium Dewan Papua) was formed, a nonviolent body charged to achieve dialogue with the Indonesian authorities and promote the West Papuan case abroad. In November 2001, its chairperson, Theys Eluay, was strangled to death by the Indonesian military. Countries that have supplied arms to the Indonesian military include the United States, the United Kingdom, Canada, the Netherlands, Australia, New Zealand, Russia, France, Germany, Belgium, Sweden, Thailand, South Korea, Japan, South Africa, and China. Freeport/Rio Tinto operates the largest copper and gold mining enterprise

in the world in the subdistrict of Timika. The company signed its contract to operate with the Indonesian government in 1967, two years before the discredited "Act of 'Free' Choice." Former U.S. secretary of state Henry Kissinger has sat on its board of directors for decades, and he remains a director emeritus and consultant to the company. Freeport/Rio Tinto have been regularly accused of complicity in human rights abuses and environmental destruction in the area in which they operate. British Petroleum has begun to operate in the Bintuni Bay area of West Papua, where it plans to extract and export gas. Human rights abuses in Wasior subdistrict have led to fears that the Indonesian military will continue to abuse West Papuans and increase its presence in the area.

Other sovereignty movements have grown among indigenous peoples in Aotearoa-New Zealand, Guam, Hawai'i, and Australia. The Maori Party was established in 2004 in Aotearoa-New Zealand, in response to the Labour Government's Foreshore and Seabed Bill, which took away many traditional Maori sea rights. The U.N. Committee on the Elimination of Racial Discrimination cited the bill for discrimination against the Maori.

The anti-colonialist movements of the South Pacific are often manifested in the return to traditional polytheism, native language education, and the contemporary arts, where indigenous peoples of Aotearoa-New Zealand have often taken a lead in the South Pacific, and where an strong indigenous arts movement is gathering world attention through the visual arts and films, such as Maori writers Alan Duff's *Once Were Warriors* and Witi Ihimaera's *Whalerider.*

—*Dan Taulapapa McMullin*

See also Anti-Nuclear Movement; Hawaiian Sovereignty Movement; Indigenous People and Social Justice

Further Readings

Allard K. Lowenstein International Human Rights Clinic, Brundige, E., King, W., Vahali, P., Vladeck, S., & Yuan, X. (2004, April). *Indonesian human rights abuses in West Papua: Application of the law of genocide to the history of Indonesian control.* New Haven, CT: Yale Law School, Allard K. Lowenstein International Human Rights Clinic. Retrieved October 12, 2006, from http://www.westpapua .net/docs/papers/paper12/yale-wphr.pdf

Barker, J. (Ed.). (2005). *Sovereignty matters: Locations of contestation and possibility in indigenous struggles for self-determination.* Lincoln: University of Nebraska Press.

Hau'ofa, E. (Ed.). (1993). A *new Oceania: Rediscovering our sea of islands.* Suva, Fiji: University of the South Pacific Press.

Leibowitz, A. (1996). *Embattled island: Palau's struggle for independence.* Westport, CT: Praeger.

Maclellan, N., & Chesneaux, J. (1998). *After Moruroa.* Melbourne, Australia: Ocean Press.

Trask, H.-K. (1993). *From a native daughter: Colonialism and sovereignty in Hawai'i.* Monroe, ME: Common Courage Press.

Vaai, S. (1999). *Samoa Faamatai and the rule of law.* Apia: National University of Samoa Press.

ANTI-COLONIAL MOVEMENTS, SUB-SAHARAN AFRICA

Anti-colonial movements rose in opposition to colonial rule throughout sub-Saharan Africa from the onset of colonialism. They varied considerably over time, reflecting specific constellations of indigenous institutions, colonial policy, local leadership, social change, and opportunity. Variables included the character of colonial imposition, the indigenous perception of the effectiveness of such imposition, the structure of the society being defended, the political abilities of the leaders, and access to modern arms and organizational strategy. Initially, resistance took the form of armed rebellion, but as colonial administrations became entrenched, it also took the form of strikes, tax evasion, black market activity, boycotts, and migration to a colony with less-oppressive laws. Equally important was mental resistance expressed through song, dance, religion, art, and everyday insubordination. All forms of rebellion sought to reclaim lost freedom and self-assertion, to reform government policy, to air grievances, or sometimes to expel the Europeans.

Between 1884 and 1914, Great Britain, France, Belgium, Portugal, Italy, and Spain conquered African states and polities and incorporated them into national empires. Only the empire of Ethiopia in northeast Africa and the Republic of Liberia in West Africa escaped takeover. Their existence as independent states became a symbol of hope and possibility for African anti-colonialists until Africans regained their autonomy in the independence and revolutionary movements that dominated the continent's history after the 1950s.

Widespread resistance rose against the imposition of European colonial rule throughout the continent. African states mobilized armies that waged scores of wars of resistance during the 1880s and 1890s. The most successful were organized by professional military leaders. The Malinke general Samori Toure fought the French from 1888 to 1898 over a vast terrain from what is now Guinea and southern Mali to Ivory Coast (now Côte d'Ivoire) and Ghana. In East Africa, Khalifa, the Sufi head of the Mahdist state in Sudan, campaigned against the British from 1885 to 1898. Ultimately, these armies were defeated by the superior weaponry of the European armies, and their leaders died in battle or were exiled. Resistance was not always led by professional soldiers. In 1896–1897, spirit mediums linked to ancestral cults in Southern Rhodesia (now Zimbabwe) led the Shona in a fierce rebellion against the British that became known as the First Chimurenga. Across the continent in the Gold Coast (now Ghana) in 1900, a woman chief, Yaa Asantewaa, led the Asante against the British in an effort to restore political autonomy and bring back the king from exile.

Although military resisters failed, these resistance wars revealed the strength of African sociopolitical organization, the scope of religious ideas and leadership, and the power of women as last-ditch defenders of their communities. These elements shaped future anti-colonial movements, as Africans continuously reinterpreted traditional ideas and institutions in the changing colonial situation. The resistance leaders became the heroes of the nationalist movements, regarded today as founders of their nations.

Prior to the imperial conquest, some of these nations had established small coastal commercial outposts. Early interaction between Europeans and Africans in these enclaves resulted in the rise of educated Eurafrican elites, who became influential mediators between the small European settlements and the larger African populace. In West Africa, Eurafricans held high positions as colonial government servants, Christian clergy, merchants, journalists, educators, and lawyers and regarded themselves as the intelligentsia. Often educated in Europe, they had the requisite skills and knowledge to deal with the new colonial administrations at their own level. Indeed, they had initially aspired to be part of the new colonial setup. Whereas the policy of assimilation resulted in the *evolués* of French West Africa and Afro-Portuguese being included in the new administrations, the educated elite in British West Africa quickly realized that the rise of racism and institutional inequality excluded them from participation in the colonial government. Resentment about exclusion from the new order compelled them to organize the first modern colonial pressure groups to preserve indigenous rights, to reform colonial policy, and to agitate for greater participation in colonial public bodies. They also took up their pens from which emanated a stream of books and pamphlets, petitions and memoranda, and newspaper articles voicing opposition to colonial rule, including methods of conquest, new legal codes, and land and labor laws—laying the intellectual groundwork for future anti-colonial and nationalism movements.

In 1898, the Gold Coast elite joined with traditional rulers to establish the Aborigines Rights Protection Society to oppose a land alienation scheme proposed by the British government. They drew up a lengthy petition and sent a delegation to London, which succeeded in getting the proposed legislation repealed. Similar legislation was also prevented by opposition from southern Nigerian groups. Likewise, in Bechuanaland (now Botswana), united action among Batswana chiefs stopped the British from handing over their territory to the white settlers of Rhodesia. In South Africa, the educated elite founded the South African Native National Congress in 1912, which changed its name to the African National Congress in 1923. While these movements pursued a moderate form of anti-colonialism, their tactics of petitions, delegations, making alliances with like-minded European pressure groups, and campaigning

in both local colonial capitals and the imperial metropole became standard procedure in anti-colonial protest until independence.

Each colonial power evolved distinct philosophies of colonial administration. In West Africa and Uganda, the British pursued a policy of indirect rule based on empiricism, but in the white settler colonies of East, Central, and South Africa, a dual system provided for indirect rule for Africans and representative government for white minorities. The French applied two main administrative policies. Assimilation operated in the four Senegalese communes and with Africans who demonstrated fluency in French culture and language, while association formed the basis for governing for the much larger Muslim and non-Christian populations in French West and Equatorial Africa. Since 1871, citizens of the communes could vote and send representatives to the National Assembly in Paris. The Belgians adopted the policy of paternalism that sought to instill European middle-class values on its colonial subjects. The Portuguese, Spanish, and Italian administrations employed variants of assimilation and association.

No matter what type of policy was asserted, economic motives dominated the goals of colonial administrations. The main goal was to extract maximum material resources—cash crops (palm products, cocoa, tea, coffee, cotton, sisal, rubber, and peanuts) and minerals (gold, diamonds, bauxite, iron, and coal)—for use in European manufacture overseas. To accomplish this, early colonial governments focused on building roads and railroads and expanding mining enterprises and cash crop agriculture. When Africans showed little enthusiasm to work in the mines and on plantations, they were encouraged to do so through alienation of their best land for use of white settlers, laws prohibiting Africans from growing specific cash crops, taxation rates designed to force Africans into wage labor, and outright forced labor. Another policy objective was to impose "good government" on indigenous peoples through new legal systems and new regulations for chieftaincy and social relations. Taxes, land alienation, imposing chiefs where none existed before, and labor laws became the flash points for anti-colonial resistance for the entire colonial period.

Before World War I, colonial governments confronted outbreaks of armed rebellion in many areas. Although most centralized states had been defeated, a few states still rebelled against European rule, but the colonial authorities easily restored control. In 1903, Attahiru, the Caliph of Sokoto, the largest Hausa state in northern Nigeria, attempted to evade certain British conquest by conducting a hijira, withdrawing eastward toward Sudan. In South Africa in 1906, the Zulu rose against the collection of taxes. It proved more difficult to quell rebellions in noncentralized polities who organized resistance through social and religious organizations based on generational principles, ancestor cults, and the leadership of spirit mediums. In Ivory Coast, proclaimed a colony in 1893, it took the French 20 years to impose control on the Baule. In southeastern Nigeria, Igbo resistance, often organized by youth organizations and in some places called the Ekumeku, continued to 1910. In southwestern Africa, the Herero and Nama revolted against their German overlords from 1904 to 1907. In southern Tanzania, the Maji Maji Rebellion broke out in 1905 among farmers resisting being forced to grow cotton for export. The resisters, armed only with spears and protected by sprinkling a magic water called maji-maji, held out against the Germans for 2 years. Religious institutions were especially resilient vehicles for the organization of widespread resistance that often cut across ethnic groups and colonial boundaries. Between 1908 and 1928, the Nyabingi cult coordinated recurrent rebellions in British Uganda and German (later Belgian) Rwanda. Similar cults were found throughout the intralacustrine area as well as in East and Central Africa.

Organized armed resistance rapidly collapsed under the harsh measures and sheer brutality of the colonial armed forces. Villages were burned, crops destroyed, and resistance leaders executed or exiled. Many died. Twenty-six thousand Maji Maji resisters were killed in action, and an estimated 50,000 villagers died in the famine that followed. Causalities inflicted on the Herero amounted to genocide: Only 16,000 of the previous population of 80,000 remained in their homeland at the end of 1905. Such wholesale devastation did not end the will to resist, but leaders realized the futility of open resistance.

World War I widened African global experience and expectations. In a few places, some local leaders saw the war as a second opportunity to oust the Europeans or defy their authority. Perhaps the most remarkable of these movements was the uprising led by John Chilembwe, an American-trained Baptist pastor in Nyasaland (now Malawi), who led a small band of followers from his Providence Industrial Mission against local white plantation owners. Influenced by the example of John Brown, he deplored the conscription of local men to fight in the British army against the Germans in Tanzania without any immediate benefit to themselves, oppressive treatment of plantation workers, and racism. Profoundly depressed, he called for the execution of white plantation owners and the destruction of their property, but presented no plan of action to ameliorate grievances. Three white men and a few Africans were killed, some property was destroyed, and Chilembwe himself was killed while fleeing toward Mozambique.

Several hundreds of thousands of Africans served as carriers and soldiers on the battlefronts of Africa, Europe, and the Middle East. They gained greater knowledge of different colonial situations, white interethnic rivalry, and modern organization. Returning from the war, their expectations of rewards for their service dwindled as war bonuses were slow to materialize.

Meanwhile, the educated elite was influenced by wartime discussion of the importance of democracy and self-determination of nations. In addition, there was growing interest in Pan-African movements in the United States, especially the Universal Negro Improvement Association led by Marcus Garvey and the Pan African Congress led by W.E.B. Du Bois. These movements differed significantly in objectives and style, but both sought to influence African policy. While the West African educated elite agreed with the basic tenets of cultural unity, they rejected the notion that yet another group of foreigners should voice their demands and grievances. In 1920, the National Congress of British West Africa met in Accra (Gold Coast) and drew up a lengthy memorandum, which demanded a limited franchise, greater involvement in the colonial legislatures, and administrative reforms.

Following the model set by earlier groups, it sent a delegation to England to submit its demands to the Colonial Office. Although the imperial government rejected the demands, by 1927, it had instituted significant constitutional reforms in all four colonies, granting a small number of electoral seats in the legislatures. This marked the beginning of formal political parties and election campaigns. Meanwhile, London and Paris became important centers of Pan-African movements organized by resident colonials with more direct experience in anti-colonial politics at home and in the metropole.

Throughout the colonial era, African anti-colonialists and political activists had found ready support for their causes from European anti-imperialist pressure groups that opposed the growth of imperialism, the brutality of the wars of conquest, and the abuse of human rights in the colonies. These included the venerable Anti-Slavery Society (founded in 1787) and the Aborigines' Protection Society (founded in 1837). The most important source of anti-imperial theories and movements was the European Left, which not only maintained constant pressure on metropolitan governments but also recruited candidates for leadership training from among colonial students and workers residing in the imperial capitals. During the interwar period, the Soviet Union played an active role in promoting anti-colonial movements in Africa through the Comintern (founded in 1919), which sought to create communist parties across the world, and the League Against Imperialism (founded in 1927), a pressure group to publicize colonial grievances. In sub-Saharan Africa, their efforts concentrated on those areas with a substantial emergent working class: South Africa, Nigeria, Kenya, and Sudan. Communist parties were set up in South Africa and Sudan but did not succeed elsewhere. Efforts to encourage trade unionism and other grassroots movements were somewhat more successful. In 1927, it set up the International Trade Union of Negro Workers whose journal, *The Negro Worker,* was widely distributed by African seamen despite a ban by the colonial authorities. Articles carried information about how to organize trade unions and peasant movements and spread news related to grievances and organizational

activities throughout the black world. Although many Africans like Jomo Kenyatta rejected communist approaches, others like the Sierra Leonean I.T.A. Wallace-Johnson wrote for *The Negro Worker* and underwent a brief training course in Moscow in the early 1930s. After his return to West Africa, he was involved in organizing workers and founded the mass-based West African Youth League in the Gold Coast and Sierra Leone. Youth movements proliferated after the 1930s, but many of them adopted moderate methods of protest.

The years between the two world wars represented the high point of colonial socioeconomic and institutional development. Many Africans found ways of realizing their ambitions within the system, yet this period was punctuated by the growth of Christian prophetism, the rise of Sufism, tax riots, strikes, boycotts, market women's protests, large-scale migrations seeking better opportunities in another colony, and political agitation. These movements were expressions of self-assertion, seeking to wrest reform and better conditions from the authorities. Occasionally, a large-scale movement surprised the authorities as did the women's war in southeastern Nigeria in 1929 that involved women from five ethnic groups. Organized on the basis of indigenous women's associations, they demanded the removal of oppressive chiefs, reforms in the legal system, and the departure of the white rulers. Armed force was used to restore control, but the war was followed by two official commissions and sweeping changes in the system of indirect rule.

World War II involved Africans on a larger scale than the previous war. Although racial arrogance convinced the colonial authorities that business would resume as usual after the war, African leaders at home and abroad were equally convinced that colonialism could not survive the war. In 1945, the Manchester Pan-African Congress brought together colonial trade unionists, politicians, and other activists to plot a strategy to regain independence. One of them was Kwame Nkrumah, who obtained his education in the United States. Two years later, he returned to the Gold Coast where he launched a militant nationalist movement that achieved national independence in 1957, only 10 years after his return. Nationalism dominated colonial politics throughout the continent, and by the mid-1960s, most colonies had become independent states with the exception of those governed by recalcitrant white minorities in Rhodesia, Angola, Mozambique, Guinea-Bissau, and South Africa. In these countries, African nationalists were forced to conduct revolutions to drive the colonialists out.

—LaRay Denzer

See also Du Bois, W. E. B.; Garvey, Marcus; Nkrumah, Kwame

Further Readings

Cooper, F. (2002). *African since 1940: The past of the present.* Cambridge, UK: Cambridge University Press.

Crowder, M. (1978). *West African resistance* (2nd ed.). London: Hutchinson.

Hodgkin, T. (1956). *Nationalism in colonial Africa.* New York: New York University Press.

Padmore, G. (1971). *Pan-Africanism or communism.* Garden City, NY: Doubleday.

Rotberg, R. I., & Mazrui, A. A. (1970). *Protest and power in black Africa.* New York: Oxford University Press.

ANTI-CONSUMERISM

Historically, consumerism and its antithesis, anti-consumerism, have fallen under a variety of descriptions in different times, regions, and as part of various cultures. Defining anti-consumerism can be a somewhat thorny task because it can be difficult to establish just what consumerism is. In some contexts, consumerism, like that often referred to in the phrase "consumer society," is a pejorative. However, in other contexts, "trickle-down economics" for instance, consumerism is considered a positive and integral part of modern, capitalist economies.

Consumerism generally refers to the creation, purchase, and use of goods and commodities over and above the material needs of those purchasing and utilizing the goods. This phenomenon is certainly not new, and many have argued it is as old as human civilization itself, but it has reached unprecedented levels in recent decades. In addition, consumerism is also closely associated not only with excess goods but with acquiring new and novel goods, as well as the status associated with such possessions. One result is a plethora of, strictly speaking, unnecessary consumer goods and a seemingly insatiable demand for a continual supply of new and novel products. The role of the commodity and its consumption is thus elevated beyond both its use value and exchange value. This feature, in particular, links modern consumerism closely with what Karl Marx called the fetishism of commodities and what Thorstein Veblen described as conspicuous consumption.

The primary criticisms of consumerism have most often come from three sources: religious groups, secular conservatives, and a somewhat loose collection of social and political activist perspectives that often coalesce around certain issues. Of course, criticisms have originated from other sources as well, but these three seem to capture those that dominate most anti-consumerism discourse. The first two have played important historical roles in the development of consumerism, but it is the last of the three that is most commonly referenced by the term *anti-consumerism* in contemporary discourse. However, it remains useful to look briefly at anti-consumerism based both on religious concerns and on conservative secular values, even if only to demonstrate the penetration of consumerism into various aspects of human social, political, and economic life.

Religious anti-consumerism generally turns on the view that human beings ought to focus their energies on spiritual matters rather than on the acquisition of worldly goods. Those holding this perspective have often argued that the focus on material goods produced by and within consumer culture detracts from the ability of individuals to focus on their spiritual existence. This view is not necessarily limited to any one religion, culture, or region. Buddhism, Hinduism, Islam, and Christianity, among others, all contain within their belief systems prohibitions against focusing on the corporeal world and the acquisition of material goods.

However, it is worth noting that even in areas where these faiths are dominant, consumerism often has taken root and exercised great influence. In some instances, forms of consumerism have become absorbed into religious practice itself in the form of elaborate churches, mosques, and temples or in the creation and accumulation of ornate religious artifacts. In a way similar to that of individual consumer goods and purchases, rhe acquisition of such religious goods or the construction of such structures has often been viewed as a means of establishing status or even proving the favor of deities.

Nonreligious, secular conservative ideologies also have manifested brands of anti-consumerism. Issues of social status have produced anti-consumerism criticisms on a variety of fronts. The oft-heard contemporary critique of consumerism expressed in the colloquialism "keeping up with the Joneses" takes aim at the desire to attain the appearance of a certain level of material wealth. Such criticism generally takes aim at the desire to "keep up." Yet anti-consumerism critiques have also come from quite a different perspective too—that of the proverbial "Joneses" themselves. While some have criticized "keeping up with the Joneses" on the grounds that it encourages people to buy things they don't need, others have criticized it on the grounds that it encourages people to buy things they should simply refrain from desiring and pursuing.

Although it is true that such a critique is sometimes based on religion, it more often emanates from groups defined primarily on secular grounds (such as the aristocracy) and which are concerned with maintaining the perception of privilege in their social position. Such secular movements have argued that consumerism and the status seeking it both expresses and encourages threatens traditionally established social and economic hierarchies. It has been argued that consumerism, by encouraging those of lower social stations to desire and attempt to acquire goods traditionally reserved for the upper classes, threatens established boundaries between classes. For this reason, among others, growing consumerism also received criticism not only from those concerned about increased inequality but also from those advocating certain kinds of inequality viewed as appropriate and natural.

Although religious and secular conservative perspectives have played a role in anti-consumerism, the bulk of contemporary criticism of consumerism derives from individuals and groups concerned with contemporary social issues and problems they see as inextricably linked to the growth and expansion of consumerism.

Anti-consumerism (and consumerism itself) often focuses largely on the reasons goods are acquired; on why and how certain commodities are bought and consumed by individual members of societies. One of the primary criticisms of consumerism concerns the purchase of consumer goods on the basis of novelty or because of artificially manufactured perceived needs.

The central criticism involved here is that people purchase things they really have no need or even use for simply because they are the latest and most novel products on the market (or latest version of some older product). On such a view, consumerism produces or contributes to several objectionable outcomes including, but not limited to, resource depletion and environmental degradation, the creation of artificial needs, consumer debt, competitive or conspicuous consumption, unequal distribution of wealth, and global poverty.

Rampant consumerism leads to the depletion of resources because the demand for more products, as well as the new and novel, outpaces the ability to produce such goods in a sustainable manner. Increasing demand for a variety of products produced from nonrenewable or relatively hard to reproduce resources, such as oil or certain varieties of wood, can and does lead to a depletion of such resources. In addition, procuring or locating many such resources (drilling for oil or harvesting timber) often causes environmental damage. The specifically anti-consumerism feature of this objection is that many of the consumer activities associated with these harms are not strictly necessary but rather meet demands for novelty or status, such as fuel for sport utility vehicles or furniture fashioned of relatively rare and expensive wood.

Another of the charges often leveled against consumerism includes that, through advertising, those attempting to sell consumer goods generate artificial desires or perceived needs for novel but unnecessary products. The idea is that corporations, for example, depend on continually increasing market share, sales, and profits. They do this, in part, by continually creating, marketing, and selling new products. However, this depends on the ability of the companies in question to convince individuals—consumers—to purchase these products. Those critical of consumerism often argue that this is accomplished largely via manipulative advertising and the subsequent creation of artificial needs in consumers. Essentially, the public is convinced that in order to live a full life, or to appear respectable to their friends and neighbors, they need to purchase certain products; they need the latest style of automobile, cellular phone, laptop computer, or brand of designer jeans. What drives such consumption, it is argued, is not a need or use for a given product, but rather a desire, born largely of manipulation, to achieve or maintain a certain level of social status.

This phenomenon leads to the third objection listed earlier. Such a desire among the working class and the poor to emulate the higher social and economic strata of society has led to criticisms of consumerism on the basis that it encourages, or perhaps necessitates, high levels of unsustainable consumer debt. The argument is that those with limited financial resources are encouraged to increase their social status through the purchase of consumer goods, many of which they have no intrinsic need for. In order to do this, however, those in the lower economic strata must go into debt purchasing such consumer goods. The consumer good is purchased not for its use value or even for its exchange value, but rather for its social value in terms of the prestige bestowed on its owner. However, as large groups begin to partake of this type of consumption, the relative necessity to purchase and own certain goods rises while the relative level of prestige associated with their ownership falls. The result, then, is a cycle of consumption leading to ever-increasing consumer debt loads with the added feature that such debt works to effectively prohibit those in the lowest economic strata from actual and lasting economic progress.

Anti-consumerism advocates argue, then, that rather than bringing about some sort of economic and social equality, as those purchasing goods might hope, consumerism actually exacerbates existing inequality while also creating additional and more severe inequalities. In the effort to attain and maintain certain levels of social status, the race to own the latest and trendiest consumer products seems endless. This trend depletes the income of those in the lowest economic strata while increasing debt. As the trendiest products become ubiquitous, they become less desirable and the next "must have" product is introduced. However, only the affluent can afford to stay atop the latest trends, and so purchases made in the seeking of status bestowed by ownership of consumer goods leads to a decrease in relative status, resulting in greater inequality rather than an increase in equality.

In addition, anti-consumerism advocates charge that consumerism not only breeds poverty, inequality, and wastefulness domestically, but that it also is deeply connected to the plight of the global needy. Many consumer products are manufactured overseas in foreign countries with lax labor laws, corrupt government officials, and by vulnerable working populations ripe for exploitation. The same consumer goods that signal high social rank and affluence in the developed world often are produced by workers who live in abject poverty and are unable to afford the products they produce. Anti-consumerists claim that consumerism in developed countries is worsening this situation by encouraging firms to provide a steady and abundant supply of new, novel, and relatively inexpensive consumer goods. Yet, in order for this demand for abundant and cheap products to be met while high profit levels persist, the cost of production must be kept low, and it is foreign workers that bear the brunt of this trend.

As the previous discussion demonstrates, the issues with which anti-consumerism advocates are concerned are often closely linked to or even the same as those addressed in anti-globalization, anti-corporate, or, among others, environmentalist movements and organizations. In fact, many see these issues as inextricably linked to one another. The result is that identifying activities, actions, and causes that are specifically demonstrative of anti-consumerism per se is not always easy. Perhaps the most clearly identifiable manifestation of collective anti-consumerism action is International Buy Nothing Day. This event, which occurs in Canada and the United States on the Thursday after the U.S. Thanksgiving (and the following Saturday elsewhere) is designed to encourage consumers to refrain from consuming by not making any purchases. The primary point of Buy Nothing Day, activists maintain, is to make consumers aware of the constant and demanding role consumption plays in their lives.

Although Buy Nothing Day may be one of the most recognizable and visible manifestations of it, anti-consumerism also finds expression as part of a variety of other movements, such as *Adbusters* magazine, culture jamming, anti-globalization activities, or smaller, organic movements to reduce consumption through co-ops or the resale and reuse of goods. Neither consumerism nor anti-consumerism appears to be a recent invention, but the exponential growth of consumerism in recent decades has thrown into sharper relief the issues and potential problems surrounding it and, as a result, as consumerism increases and intensifies, anti-consumerism continues to grow along with it.

—Cory Fairley

See also *Adbusters;* Anti-Globalization Movement; Anti-Sweatshop Movement; Buy Nothing Day; Environmental Movement

Further Readings

Heath, J., & Potter, A. (2004). *The rebel sell: Why the culture can't be jammed.* Toronto: HarperCollins.

Klein, N. (2000). *No logo: Taking aim at the brand bullies.* Toronto: Random House.

Marx, K. (1992). *Capital: Vol.1. A critical analysis of capitalist production* (F. Engels, Ed.; S. Moore & E. Aveling, Trans.). New York: International Publishers.

Stearns, P. N. (2001). *Consumerism in world history: The global transformation of desire.* New York: Routledge.

Veblen, T. (1963). *The theory of the leisure class: An economic study of institutions.* New York: New American Library.

ANTI–DEATH PENALTY MOVEMENT

The anti–death penalty movement, also called the abolitionist movement or the new abolitionist movement, seeks to end capital punishment. The movement's members view capital punishment as a human rights violation, which is frequently associated with other social justice issues, like racism, classism, and inadequate judicial processes. While the anti–death penalty movement itself works toward the abolition of capital punishment, its members approach and argue the issue from a wide variety of viewpoints. Various arguments made against the death penalty include its religious and humanistic immorality, its detrimental effect on victims' family members, its likelihood of executing an innocent person, its arbitrary and often racist or classist application, its ineffectiveness as a deterrent, and its high financial cost. Even though the anti–death penalty movement as a whole aims to abolish the use of the death penalty throughout the world, most of the recent efforts against capital punishment have been centered on the United States, one of the last democratic countries to still execute its citizens.

The anti–death penalty movement in America has its roots in English opposition to the death penalty, which was documented as early as the 1640s, but the movement has existed on American soil, in one form or another, since the 1700s. Initially, many individuals only opposed capital punishment as a sentence for property crimes like theft, but by the 1780s, abolitionists began to protest the use of the death penalty as a response to any crime, including murder. From this point on, Herbert H. Haines describes organized resistance to the death penalty in America as cyclical, with four significant periods of protest and condemnation: the 1830s and 1840s, the 1890s to the beginning of World War I, the mid-1950s and 1960s, and the late 1970s to the present day. While the early era of the 1830s and 1840s—frequently called the anti-gallows movement—accomplished the goal of having executions take place behind prison walls rather than in town squares or courtyards, the anti–death penalty movements of later eras have worked toward the complete abolition of capital punishment.

In fact, the U.S. Supreme Court's 1972 ruling in *Furman v. Georgia,* which struck down all existing capital statutes in America as violations of the Eighth and Fourteenth Amendments to the Constitution, was initially hailed as just such a victory for the anti–death penalty movement, but the Supreme Court's ruling only applied to the capital statutes in effect at that time. Thus, in response to the justices' concerns, voiced in their *Furman v. Georgia* decision, about the random and, therefore, unconstitutional application of the death penalty, many states adopted new capital sentencing statutes designed to make the sentencing phases of capital trials less arbitrary and discriminatory. In 1976 in the *Gregg v. Georgia* decision, the U.S. Supreme Court upheld the constitutionality of the new death penalty statutes, and executions became legal again in the United States.

Since the return of American capital punishment in 1976, the anti–death penalty movement has included a diverse array of members, both from the United States and from other countries. Abolitionist leaders have included activists, attorneys, law enforcement personnel, religious leaders, family members of death row inmates, family members of murder victims, and exonerated death row inmates. Some of these abolitionists work in organizations—such as the National Coalition to Abolish the Death Penalty, Citizens United for Alternatives to the Death Penalty, and Journey of Hope: From Violence to Healing—that consider the abolishment of the death penalty as their primary goal. Other active anti–death penalty organizations, such as Amnesty International, the American Civil Liberties Union, and the NAACP's Legal Defense and Education Fund, Inc., oppose the death penalty as one of many human rights violations that they are trying to end. Moreover, members of both types of organizations employ different strategies in their attempts to end capital punishment, including lobbying legislators, filing petitions in the court systems, educating the public about the issue, and engaging in acts of protest and civil disobedience.

Even as different abolitionists choose different strategies by which to accomplish their goal, they also emphasize different arguments against the death penalty. These arguments typically fall into three broad categories based on moral and religious beliefs, on personal experiences, and on statistical data about the application and administration of capital punishment. Of course, many abolitionists use arguments from more than one of these three general categories when they are making a case against the death penalty.

In arguing against the death penalty on moral grounds, a common argument is that, because both society and prison security have evolved and executions are no longer necessary to keep society safe, capital punishment has become nothing more than murder, the same crime for which people are being executed. Other abolitionists claim that the Mosaic Law, an eye for an eye, was designed to limit the measures that individuals and governments could take in exacting revenge for a wrongdoing; it was not mandating that offenders be dealt exactly the same treatment that they may have inflicted on others. Additionally, continuing the biblical argument, some death penalty opponents contend that capital punishment violates the philosophy of love and forgiveness that is advocated for in the New Testament.

Other abolitionists draw on personal experiences with the death penalty, either their own or those of other individuals, in order to make their arguments against its practice. For example, supporters and members of groups like Murder Victims' Families for Reconciliation, Murder Victims' Families for Human Rights, and Journey of Hope: From Violence to Healing, point out that the death penalty makes celebrities out of the executed and the condemned but not out of the victims. These abolitionists also denounce the idea that executions bring peace and closure to the victims' families, arguing instead for the healing power of forgiveness and for the importance of not creating another set of victims among the death row inmates' family members. Similarly, exonerated death row inmates and their supporters relate personal stories, stressing the likelihood of the criminal justice system executing individuals for crimes that they did not commit, since the National Coalition to Abolish the Death Penalty reports that more than 118 innocent people have been released from death row since 1972.

In addition to anti–death penalty arguments based on personal experiences and on moral and religious objections, arguments are also made about the application and administration of capital punishment, with many abolitionists stating their belief that, because the death penalty cannot be fairly administered, it should not be administered at all. Stephen B. Bright cites two studies done in Georgia that demonstrate that, when a murder victim is Caucasian, prosecutors are more inclined to seek a capital sentence and jurors are more likely to vote for one. Like race, class is also considered by numerous anti–death penalty activists to be a central determinant in an individual's receiving a death sentence because defendants who can afford private, high-quality legal representation are more likely to avoid the death penalty. Additionally, as the National Coalition to Abolish the Death Penalty states, the death penalty is not a deterrent to other violent criminals: Two studies conducted in Oklahoma and California failed to find a relationship between the use of capital punishment and the rate of violent crime. Moreover, abolitionists contend that the cost of a capital trial, appeals, and execution is greater than the cost of incarcerating an inmate for life.

While the anti–death penalty movement has made arguments like these against capital punishment for more than 300 years, there were more than 1,000 executions in America alone between 1976 and 2005. Yet, the tide may be turning for the movement since two U.S. Supreme Court decisions, *Atkins v. Virginia* in 2002 and *Roper v. Simmons* in 2005, limited the scope of the death penalty by ruling it unconstitutional to execute either the mentally retarded or those who committed their crimes as juveniles. The anti–death penalty movement will have to convince many more people of the validity of their arguments, however, before their ultimate goal of worldwide abolition of the death penalty is realized.

—*Ramona Anne Caponegro*

See also Amnesty International; Campaign to End the Death Penalty; Prejean, Sister Helen; Sarandon, Susan

Further Readings

Banner, S. (2002). *The death penalty: An American history.* Cambridge, MA: Harvard University Press.

Bright, S. B. (2002). Discrimination, death, and denial: Race and the death penalty. In D. R. Dow & M. Dow (Eds.), *Machinery of death: The reality of America's death penalty regime* (pp. 45–78). New York: Routledge.

Haines, H. H. (1996). *Against capital punishment: The anti–death penalty movement in America, 1972–1994.* New York: Oxford University Press.

National Coalition to Abolish the Death Penalty. Retrieved October 10, 2006, from http://www.ncadp.org

Stassen, G. H. (Ed.). (1998). *Capital punishment: A reader.* Cleveland, OH: Pilgrim Press.

Anti-Globalization Movement

Anti-globalization movement is a disputed term referring to the international social movement network that gained widespread media attention after protests against the World Trade Organization (WTO) in Seattle, Washington, in late November and early December 1999. Activists and scholars debate whether it constitutes a single social movement or represents a collection of allied groups, a "movement of movements." Including diverse constituencies with a range of ideological orientations, the global movement is broadly critical of the policies of economic neoliberalism, or "corporate globalization," that has guided international trade and development since the closing decades of the 20th century. Varied communities organizing against the local and national consequences of neoliberal policies, especially in the global South, connect their actions with this wider effort. Movement constituents include trade unionists, environmentalists, anarchists, land rights and indigenous rights activists, organizations promoting human rights and sustainable development, opponents of privatization, and anti-sweatshop campaigners. These groups charge that the policies of corporate globalization have exacerbated global poverty and increased inequality.

Internationally, the movement has held protests outside meetings of institutions such as the WTO, the International Monetary Fund (IMF), the World Bank, the World Economic Forum, and the Group of Eight (G8) heavily industrialized nations. Its own annual gathering, the World Social Forum, serves as a site for activist networking and transnational strategizing. Movement participants have also launched campaigns targeting multinational corporations, such as Nike and Monsanto, and have mobilized resistance to U.S.-led military intervention in Iraq and Afghanistan.

While opposing neoliberalism, the anti-globalization movement advocates participatory democracy, seeking to increase popular control of political and economic life in the face of increasingly powerful corporations, unaccountable global financial institutions, and U.S. hegemony. A focus on democracy is reflected in many of the movement's organizational structures. These tend to emphasize grassroots participation, cooperative decision making, and "horizontalism" over hierarchy. Rather than promoting a single model for social reorganization, anti-globalization activists defend diversity and, adopting a slogan of the Mexican Zapatistas, envision a world in which many worlds fit.

Terminology

The term *anti-globalization movement* has more often been imposed by movement critics and by the media than used for self-identification. Many activists reject the label, arguing that the term falsely implies a stance of isolationism. A hallmark of the movement is its use of advanced communications and Internet technology to unite activists across borders. In some cases, such as the No Borders campaign prominent in Europe, participants rally under the slogan "No one is illegal" and advocate the elimination of national boundaries altogether. Leading voices in the movement express the ambition to create a global network that is as transnational as capital itself. Countering the spread of multinational corporations, they aspire instead to globalize hope, globalize resistance, or globalize liberation.

To reflect this internationalism, activists commonly use terms such as the *global justice movement, globalization from below,* and *alter-globalization* as alternatives to *anti-globalization*. Some refer to the international network simply as the *globalization movement*.

Many globalization activists explicitly state their opposition to neoliberalism, a variant of market-driven capitalism promoted in the developing world through the 1970s, 1980s, and 1990s by the World Bank, the IMF, and the U.S. Treasury. Neoliberal policies include privatizing public industries, opening markets to foreign investment and competition, creating fiscal austerity programs to curtail government spending, removing controls on capital flows, reducing tariffs and other trade barriers, and ending government protections for local industry. Movement participants argue that these policies have created sweatshop working conditions in the developing world, threatened unionized jobs and environmental protections in the global North, benefited the wealthy at the expense of the poor, and endangered indigenous cultures.

Because the term *neoliberalism* is not widely used in the United States, advocates refer to this system as "corporate globalization" or "the Washington Consensus." In opposing neoliberal policies, activists contend that the international debate does not concern whether or not globalization will take place in some form; rather, it concerns what shape globalization will take and whom it will benefit.

Movement Origins

"It didn't start in Seattle" serves as the widely accepted slogan among globalization activists, refuting the belief common in the mainstream media that the movement first arose in protests against the WTO's Third Ministerial Meeting in 1999. Many participants and theorists instead trace the lineage of the movement through a 500-year history of resistance against European colonialism and U.S. imperialism. Other commentators see the anti-globalization movement as continuous with the anti–Vietnam War mobilizations of the 1960s and 1970s, with worldwide uprisings in 1968, and with protests against structural adjustment in Africa, Asia, and Latin America in the 1980s and 1990s.

Perhaps the most symbolically significant moment of origin for the movement was the uprising of the Zapatista Army of National Liberation (EZLN) in Chiapas, Mexico, on January 1, 1994. On the same day that the North American Free Trade Agreement went into effect, the Zapatistas launched a 2-week campaign of armed clashes with the Mexican military. Their effort subsequently became a nonviolent movement for land reform and indigenous rights. The EZLN eschewed traditional models of hierarchical leadership. It used the Internet to spread poetic critiques of capitalist injustice throughout a network of international supporters. As a rebel army seeking not to claim state power but to create spaces of autonomy and direct democracy, the EZLN both paid homage to earlier models of national liberation struggle and transformed them. Their example became an influential one for the nascent globalization movement.

In 1996, the EZLN hosted an International Encounter for Humanity Against Neoliberalism in the jungles of Chiapas. Some 5,000 activists from over 40 countries attended. A follow-up meeting in Geneva in 1998 resulted in the formation of Peoples' Global Action, a network of autonomous organizations united in their rejection of capitalism, imperialism, and cultural domination. Participating organizations include groups as diverse as the indigenous Maori of New Zealand; the Gandhian State Farmers' Association of Karnataka, India; and the Canadian Postal Workers' Union. The Peoples' Global Action has helped organize many of the international direct action mobilizations associated with the globalization movement.

The 1999 "Battle of Seattle," while not the first appearance of the global movement, dramatically altered the debate about trade and development taking place within international institutions. It served as a prototype for many future protests and also marked the moment when *anti-globalization* as a term gained widespread usage. In Seattle, an estimated 75,000 activists organized an unusually colorful and confrontational demonstration against the meetings of the WTO. Groups like Art and Revolution created giant puppets to carry in the demonstrations, activists inspired by British Reclaim the Streets actions held parties in intersections blocked by protesters, and musicians formed activist marching bands. While the labor movement led a mass march on the organization's ministerial meetings, student, anarchist, and militant environmentalist "affinity groups" formed a nonviolent human blockade around the convention center, preventing trade ministers from holding the opening session of the meetings. Police responded to the blockades with tear gas and rubber bullets. Shortly thereafter, a black bloc of anarchists vandalized downtown storefronts of major banks and corporations like Nike. Authorities temporarily enacted martial law, and more than 600 protesters were arrested for acts of civil disobedience during the week of action.

Ultimately, the Seattle round of trade negotiations deadlocked when developing nations, bolstered by grassroots resistance, rejected U.S. and European demands. The week delivered a lasting setback to the WTO and represented a turning point for neoliberal advocates, who adopted a defensive posture in subsequent negotiations and in their public justifications of the free trade agenda.

National and International Protests

Continued protests outside of international financial institutions serve as only the most highly publicized manifestations of a much broader body of action taking place at the local and national levels. More localized embodiments of the globalization movement include strikes by unions in South Korea, fights against water privatization in Bolivia and South Africa, the mass mobilization of civil society in Argentina following the country's 2001 economic collapse, the struggle against development of hydroelectric dams in rural India, Indonesian protests in the wake of the 1997 Asian financial crisis, actions of the landless farmers movement (MST) in Brazil, African efforts to secure access to low-cost generic AIDS drugs, and demonstrations in Central America against the adoption of trade agreements with the United States.

Nevertheless, the financial institutions promoting corporate globalization have provided critical rallying points for the movement. By bringing together groups with diverse complaints about the international deliberations, these organizations have helped disparate movements make common cause and have strengthened transnational coalitions of activists. For example, resistance to the WTO has united labor unionists who argue that the organization is depressing wages and lowering protections for workers, farmers in the global South who protest agribusiness dominance in international markets, food safety advocates concerned about the spread of genetically modified foods, environmentalists who contend that current free trade agreements weaken local protections for the natural world, indigenous rights activists defending cultural diversity, and anti-capitalists who see the institution as a mechanism of corporate expansion. On college campuses, groups such as the United Students Against Sweatshops, an organization that has waged transnational campaigns to improve the labor conditions of garment workers who make university apparel, have energetically supported mobilizations against the international financial institutions.

While often not as large as mobilizations taking place at the local level in the global South, actions surrounding international summits have received the most attention from the media in the United States and Europe, and they have most consistently been identified as part of the anti-globalization movement.

Like the WTO, the World Bank and IMF have drawn significant protests for their role in promoting neoliberalism. Tens of thousands demonstrated against the institutions' meetings in Washington, D.C., in April 2000 and in Prague, Czech Republic, in September 2000. In response to movement criticism, the World Bank has worked to refashion its image as an anti-poverty institution. It officially ended its support of structural adjustment, although critics contend that its lending practices remain problematic.

The globalization movement has staged several mass protests against the creation of the Free Trade Area of the Americas (FTAA). In April 2001, tens of thousands rallied outside the Summit of the Americas in Quebec City, Canada. The tightly guarded summit served as occasion for what was then the largest security operation in Canadian history. In an act of civil disobedience, protesters dismantled sections of a large chain-link fence that blocked the public from entering the summit grounds. Police clashed with activists and, as in Seattle, filled the city with tear gas. Subsequent FTAA demonstrations in Miami, Florida, in 2003 and in Mar del Plata, Argentina, in 2005 also faced a heavily militarized police response and contributed to the collapse of the trade agreement.

In July 2001, some 300,000 demonstrators gathered outside G8 meetings in Genoa, Italy. One protester, 23-year-old Carlo Giuliani, was shot dead during a clash with Italian security forces. Giuliani became the first Northern protester killed at a major summit action, although many activists in the developing world had died previously in police and military repression of anti-neoliberal demonstrations.

Owing to large-scale civil uprisings and concerns about security, trade officials have opted to hold some meetings in remote and publicly inaccessible locations. Such meetings include the WTO's 2001 Ministerial in Doha, Qatar, and the 2002 G8 summit in Kananaskis, Alberta, Canada.

World Social Forum and Anti-War Activism

The World Economic Forum, an annual convention of influential politicians and business elites held in a Swiss resort near the town of Davos, has attracted regular protest from globalization activists. More significantly, the meeting inspired the French-based Association for the Taxation of Financial Transactions for the Aid of Citizens (ATTAC) and the Brazilian Workers' Party to organize a grassroots countersummit. First held in January 2001, the World Social Forum (WSF) convened for several years in Porto Alegre, Brazil. The forum provides a space for local and national social movements to network, strategize for future action, and assert an identity as a unified international movement. The WSF has been institutionalized as a regular event and is organized by a committee of representatives from prominent civil society groups throughout the world. Additional social forums have also been organized at the regional level on virtually every continent. While the first WSF hosted some 12,000 participants, subsequent forums have drawn crowds of over 100,000.

After September 11, 2001, critics charged that the anti-globalization movement would fade into obscurity. While summit demonstrations in U.S. and European cities indeed grew less frequent, challenges to neoliberalism continued throughout the global South. Meanwhile, many activists turned to highlight connections between corporate globalization and U.S. power, and led organizing against the George W. Bush administration's "war on terror." The November 2002 European Social Forum issued the first call for a February 15, 2003, day of action against the impending U.S.-led invasion of Iraq. The resulting demonstrations involved tens of millions of people in over 500 cities and constituted the largest coordinated global day of action in history.

Protests against international financial institutions also continued. Demonstrations outside the WTO's

Fifth Ministerial Meeting in Cancún, Mexico, in September 2003 turned sober after the suicide of South Korean Lee Kyang Hae, who stabbed himself while wearing a sign reading, "WTO Kills Farmers." Like at the Seattle talks, outside pressure helped to feed resistance from developing countries, organized in Cancún as the G20+, and resulted in the collapse of trade talks. The December 2005 WTO Ministerial in Hong Kong, at which the beleaguered organization was able to produce a compromise agreement, faced opposition from at least 10,000 protesters.

For over a decade, globalization movement groups like the Jubilee Coalition have vigorously campaigned for debt relief for poor countries. Protests and cultural events in July 2005 pressured G8 leaders meeting in Gleneagles, Scotland, to act on this demand. Ultimately, the G8 agreed to an accord canceling debts owed by 18 of the world's poorest countries to the IMF, the World Bank, and the African Development Bank.

Ideological and Strategic Debates

Although some constituent groups, especially within labor and non-governmental organizations, maintain more traditional leadership structures, the globalization movement as a whole claims no formal leaders. In the absence of official spokespeople, well-known writers or intellectuals are often called on to represent the movement in public forums. Prominent figures include Canadian journalist Naomi Klein, Indian ecofeminist Vandana Shiva, U.S. intellectual Noam Chomsky, Filipino analyst Walden Bello, ATTAC cofounders Bernard Cassen and Ignacio Ramonet, Brazilian MST leader João Pedro Stédile, Indian writer Arundhati Roy, South African community leader Trevor Ngwane, theorists Michael Hardt and Antonio Negri, British journalist George Monbiot, French farmer and anti-McDonald's activist José Bové, Subcomandante Marcos of the EZLN, and Susan George of the Transnational Institute in Amsterdam.

A lack of official spokespeople, agreed-upon manifestos, or overarching organizational structures means that many ideological and strategic issues within the movement remain unresolved. Diverse constituencies disagree about whether existing international financial institutions should be reformed or abolished, whether tactics such as property destruction should be deployed in international protests, and whether capitalism itself is responsible for global problems. In general, globalization movement organizations represent groups based in civil society, rather than traditional communist, socialist, or social democratic parties. Activists have long debated how the movement should interact with state power, and this discussion has intensified with the rise of progressive governments in Latin America.

Conclusion

Because institutions such as the WTO, World Bank, and the IMF remain intact, countries continue to broker free trade pacts, and multinational corporations extend their reach, critics charge that the globalization movement has proven ineffective. Advocates, however, point to debt relief, expanding fair trade and anti-sweatshop agreements, the scuttling of the FTAA, a curtailed WTO agenda, local victories against privatization, and the rise of anti-neoliberal governments in Latin America as evidence of the movement's impact. Pressure from civil society, in addition to a series of regional financial crises, has gone far in discrediting the long-dominant Washington Consensus in trade and development policy, and the future of neoliberalism is now in question. Whatever its final legacy, the globalization movement will remain historically noteworthy for its contribution to revitalizing the international left in the post–Cold War era.

—*Mark Engler*

See also Anarchism; Anti-Imperialism; Anti-Sweatshop Movement; Battle of Seattle; Bové, José; Chomsky, Noam; Civil Disobedience; Culture Jammers; Debt Relief Movement; Direct Action; Fair Trade; Global Exchange; Klein, Naomi; Landless Movement; Living Wage Movement; Marcos, Subcomandante; Neoliberalism; Roy, Arundhati; World Social Forum; Ya Basta!

Further Readings

Brecher, J., Costello, T., & Smith, B. (2000). *Globalization from below*. Cambridge, MA: South End Press.

Klein, N. (2002). *Fences and windows: Dispatches from the front lines of the globalization debate.* New York: Picador.

Mertes, T. (Ed.). (2004). *A movement of movements.* London: Verso.

Notes from Nowhere Collective. (Ed.). (2003). *We are everywhere: The irresistible rise of global capitalism.* London: Verso.

ANTIGONISH MOVEMENT

The Antigonish movement is a cooperative movement that began in the 1920s in the impoverished rural area around the university town of Antigonish, Nova Scotia, to address the decline of the fisheries, agriculture, and coal mining industry. The reform-minded priests who have become synonymous with this movement are Father Jimmy Tompkins and his cousin, Father Moses Coady. Under their leadership, the Extension Department of St. Francis Xavier University in Antigonish was created in 1928 with Coady as its first director. Both Tompkins and Coady were committed to the university going to the people, and not the other way around.

Although the Antigonish movement has much in common with the social gospel movement, its program of social justice was influenced most heavily by the church teachings in the papal encyclicals Rerum Novarum of 1891 and later Quadragesimo Anno of 1931. The visionary leaders of the movement were diocesan priests and the Sisters of St. Martha, the service-focused religious order established in Antigonish in 1900.

The Antigonish movement is well known for linking emancipatory adult education practices to the local context of "social Catholicism." The adult education initiatives for organizing people for cooperative action in the early days of the movement included mass meetings, study clubs, kitchen meetings, lending libraries, leadership courses, radio broadcasts, pamphlets, and conferences. In the late 1920s, Moses Coady held a first meeting with 600 people and then proceeded to travel 13,000 kilometers in 10 months, organizing up to four meetings a day in fishing villages. By the summer of 1930, Coady had brought together 200 delegates from fishing communities to Halifax for the inaugural meeting of the United Maritime Fishermen, a marketing cooperative. Through study clubs, the members gained skills in fish conservation, marketing, refrigeration, and so forth; as the cooperative grew, housing and banking were added to their repertoire. Before Coady assumed leadership of the Extension Department, Jimmy Tompkins had been working for several years in the remote coastal towns of Canso and Dover. In 1933, Father Tompkins and the Sisters of St. Martha established the Canso Library and this was the departure point for promoting local libraries, which led to the regional library system.

Although the recognized leaders of the Antigonish movement are male, women were active leaders in many of the programs that endure to the present day. The life-long friendship between Father Tompkins and the Sisters of St. Martha opened up opportunities for women to lead adult education programs in household management. Sisters Monica Doyle, Denis Marie, Augustine, and Jean Doyle created an educational environment for the women of Canso, with a focus on learning to provide necessities for their families. They held workshops and meetings, and taught the women to sew, mend, and dye clothing. The main publication of the movement, the *Maritime Co-operator,* was managed entirely by local women during the first decades, with leadership from Coady's secretary, Kay Thompson DesJardins. Sister Irene Doyle organized a handicraft conference in 1942 that led to the Nova Scotia government setting up a program that included the marketing of handicrafts. Lilian Burke of Cheticamp, Northern Nova Scotia, created the floral designs that were the trademark in the rug hooking industry that she developed in the 1920s and 1930s as part of the movement, an industry now estimated to generate more than $3 million yearly.

In 1937, Mary Ellicott Arnold (1876–1968) and her life companion Mabel Reed visited Nova Scotia as members of the Cooperative League of the United States of America to study the Antigonish movement. They stayed on as fieldworkers of the Extension Department to organize a cooperative housing project in a mining community, which was named Tompkinsville after Jimmy Tompkins. Mary Arnold was the operational and educational force behind the cooperative housing project—11 single-dwelling houses were built in the year 1937. Mary and Mabel opened up their home, which was the first model home in the project, as the center of education for the men working on the technical and business details of the housing project and also for women meeting to focus on the house plans and furnishings.

The Antigonish movement continues today through the St. Francis Xavier University Extension Department, working with wood lot owners, inshore fishers, and Mi'Kmaq communities on such community development issues as labor education and affordable housing. In 1959, St. Francis Xavier University inaugurated the Coady International Institute as a way of extending the Antigonish movement to the less-developed regions of the world. To date, community leaders from 120 countries have taken part in the institute's campus-based programs to learn the community development and adult education approaches of the Antigonish movement. The movement's focus on social justice has implications for local community development as well as for global economic reform, political restructuring, technological change, and the HIV/AIDS pandemic.

—Dorothy A. Lander

See also Community Organizing; Cooperatives; Housing Movements; Social Gospel Movement

Further Readings

Alexander, A. (1997). *The Antigonish movement: Moses Coady and adult education today.* Toronto: Thompson Educational Publishing.

Neal, R. (1998). *Brotherhood economics: Women and co-operatives in Nova Scotia.* Sydney, Nova Scotia: UCCB Press.

Welton, M. R. (2001). *Little Mosie from the Margaree: A biography of Moses Michael Coady.* Toronto: Thompson Educational Publishing.

ANTI-IMMIGRANT POLITICS

From early on in U.S. history through present times, a nativist reaction to immigration has fostered hostile politics. Still, while the debate over immigration remains politically charged, it is difficult to accurately surmise an individual's position on the issue based on party affiliation. Many liberals support greater restrictions for immigration while many conservatives do not. As the arguments over immigration heated up again, political observers acknowledged that the issue had indeed created strange bedfellows. Among those opposing freer immigration are Patrick J. Buchanan, the conservative commentator and former Republican presidential candidate; Dianne Feinstein, the liberal California Democrat; and her fellow liberal counterpart Barbara Jordan of Texas. Proponents of freer immigration include conservatives William Bennett, Jack Kemp, and Rudolph Giuliani; Robert Dornan, a gay-bashing California Republican; and Representative Barney Frank, the Massachusetts Democrat who is openly homosexual.

Rather than trying to force-fit the dialogue on immigration into traditional categories of political party alliance, the topic ought to be understood in terms of the various immigration ideologies found among liberals and conservatives alike. For instance, *free marketeers* support immigration arguing that the free flow of people across national borders, like that of goods and capital, contributes to prosperity while on the other side of the issue, *nativists* oppose immigration policies that allow nonwhites to enter the United States because they dilute the whiteness of American culture. Conversely, *civil rights* and *ethnic advocates* oppose immigration policies that discriminate against people of color, insisting that such an approach to immigration is racist and a violation of human rights. Some *environmentalists* and *population control advocates* recommend strict limits on immigration to the United States because they contend that overpopulation places undue strain on natural resources; similarly, *job protectionists* believe that immigration contributes to income stagnation and takes work from unskilled Americans. Rounding out the field, *anti-government libertarians* oppose the call for a national identification card verifying citizenship status while *antitax advocates* reject proposals requiring employers to pay a tax on every foreign worker they sponsor. Overall, it is important to note that the political debate on immigration has been shaped by overt economic considerations. Whereas some commentators oppose immigration, arguing that U.S. citizens are adversely affected by job displacement as well as having their tax dollars spent on social services for so-called illegal aliens, others argue that the economy benefits from immigration.

In a democratic society, debate over public policy ought to engage competing points of view along with systematic appraisals of legislation. However, the most recent immigration law, the Illegal Immigration Reform and Immigrant Responsibility Act, passed by Congress in 1996, was influenced less by sound policy making and more by exaggerated political rhetoric that issued warnings that foreigners pose a threat to the American social and economic order.

Adverse societal reaction to immigrants is nothing new. Throughout U.S. history, many citizens have shunned immigrants, viewing them with contempt and suspicion, thus reinforcing social inequality, hostility, and discrimination. A clear example of anti-immigrant politics can be traced to the 1840s when manifest destiny inspired white Anglo-Saxon Protestants (WASPs) to uphold a racist ideology professing that they were an elite people chosen by God to cultivate and civilize the country. That pernicious version of nativism condemned immigrants as cultural, political, and economic threats to a WASP-dominated society. Such militant nativism reached a flash point in Philadelphia, where in 1844, members of the Native American Party unleashed their fury on Irish Catholics, sparking 3 days of violence known as the Kensington Riots in which the homes, schools, and churches of Irish immigrants were burned and razed.

During the 1880s, discrimination against Asians peaked when Congress passed the Chinese Exclusion Act of 1882, a law halting immigration from China and even stripping Chinese Americans of their U.S. citizenship. Eventually, similar hostility was directed at Southern and Eastern Europeans during the immigration wave of the 1910s. In years leading up to World War I, mistrust of foreigners, especially those suspected of being political dissidents, influenced the passage of the Immigration Act of 1917. During the "Red Scare" of that period, thousands of foreign-born people suspected of political radicalism were arrested and brutalized by federal law enforcement officers;

hundreds were deported without a hearing. The 1917 law also established various classes of undesirable immigrants who would be denied admission to the United States, including illiterates, vagrants, alcoholics, the mentally ill, and those perceived as being immoral. Additionally, the statute along with the Immigration Act of 1924 (also known as the National Origins Act) contained restrictions against Asians and Africans.

Again, in the early 1990s, the perception that immigrants endangered American society gained considerable acceptance among political commentators and eventually the public. In 1992, conservative journalist Peter Brimelow published a controversial article in the *National Review* titled "Time to Rethink Immigration" in which he delivered scathing attacks on current immigration policy, arguing that it was already destroying American society. The essay drew enormous attention, placing the issue of immigration back on the political table; later, the debate over immigration would degenerate into a crusade against immigrants. Brimelow and other nativists, including Patrick J. Buchanan, realized that they had hit a public nerve with the immigration issue. While Buchanan campaigned for president spreading his brand of nativist rhetoric, Brimelow expanded his magazine article into a widely publicized book, *Alien Nation: Common Sense About America's Immigration Disaster.* Casting apocalyptic images of a doomed American society, *Alien Nation* was not viewed merely as nativist ranting; rather, it inflamed fears of immigrants and heightened anxiety among huge segments of the public. Brimelow's book, along with growing anti-immigrant sentiment, sounded the alarm that America was under siege, galvanizing a nativist crusade that would succeed in revising federal immigration laws in 1996 along with a host of state-sponsored initiatives.

Particularly in California, Texas, and Florida—as well as in the nation's capital—politicians took notice of growing public concern over immigration. However, instead of offering their constituents enlightened interpretations of the issue, many political leaders reinforced fears of immigrants. Politicizing immigration is significant because political rhetoric not only inflames public anxiety but also shapes the content of legislation. In the early 1990s, California Governor Pete Wilson stirred public anxiety over immigrants by introducing several proposals, including the abolition of birthright citizenship, a measure considered extreme even by nativist standards. During that period, California drew national attention for its Proposition 187, an initiative designed to crack down on undocumented immigrants, prohibiting them from receiving publicly funded education, medical care, and social services. Critics observed that the campaign was tuned to a range of Anglo anxieties and fears: a declining standard of living and quality of life; a faltering and changing economy; a sense of being overwhelmed by a range of cultures and peoples of color; and concern for dilution of American values, institutions, and ways of life. Demonstrating widespread public anxiety over immigrants, Proposition 187 won in an astounding landslide vote among California voters in 1994. A California federal judge, however, ruled that Proposition 187 was unconstitutional, a decision based on a 1982 Supreme Court case preventing Texas from denying illegal immigrant children an education.

Despite harsh criticism from advocates for immigrants, the nativist campaign reached critical mass in 1996 when Congress passed a deeply politicized form of legislation, namely the Illegal Immigration Reform and Immigrant Responsibility Act. The law granted the immigration service new and expansive powers. Proponents of tough law-and-order strategies praised the immigration service for its commitment to rid the nation of criminal aliens; by contrast, immigration advocates argued that the law unfairly targets immigrants who have had minor brushes with the law. Under the new immigration act, numerous crimes were reclassified as aggravated felonies requiring detention and possibly deportation, including minor misdemeanors such as shoplifting and low-level drug violations. Typically, persons convicted of those crimes rarely served jail terms and were placed on probation. Compounding the harshness of the revised statutes, enforcement was retroactive, meaning that persons who had been convicted before 1996 also were subject to detention and deportation; furthermore, judges have little or no discretion in determining under which conditions the law applies. Whereas

the Illegal Immigration Reform and Immigrant Responsibility Act produced several ongoing hardships for immigrants, those controversies have moved to the forefront of the American conversation on immigration since September 11, 2001. The terrorist attacks on the World Trade Center and the Pentagon have given the political debate over immigration control a new resonance, especially given that at least 15 of the 19 terrorists involved in the hijackings had entered the country legally on some form of temporary visa (i.e., tourist, business, or student visa). Consequently, significant changes in policy were inevitable, thus altering the course of the debate over immigration. Public opinion polls after 9/11 consistently showed virtually all segments of American society overwhelmingly felt the government was not doing enough to screen those entering the nation. Since then, the Department of Homeland Security has expanded the federal screening system at all ports of entry, a measure that is intended to serve dual functions: national security and immigration control.

Prevailing anti-immigrant political messages echo themes of criminal justice and public safety; for example, adding more armed border police, imposing mandatory detention, and building a 700-mile fence to keep out those who pose a threat to American society. In New Hampshire, a sheriff tried to charge illegal immigrants with trespassing on U.S. territory, a claim that had no legal merit but earned him support from an angry, anti-immigrant constituency. Similarly, in Connecticut, a community banned volleyball because it is considered a sport of choice for South American workers. In the realm of economics, the proposal for a guest worker program that was shelved after 9/11 has reentered the discussion over immigration. While some elected leaders in the United States push for a greater clampdown on "illegal aliens," politicians in Mexico and Central America complain that the rhetoric is shamefully xenophobic and anti-Latino. Astute political analysts recognize the danger of injecting too much ethnicity into immigration discourse since both major political parties seek votes from Hispanic Americans.

From a sociological point of view, anti-immigrant politics contribute to the prejudice and discrimination of immigrants, making them vulnerable to being criminalized, marginalized, and scapegoated. Stoking anti-immigrant hostility, nativists and restrictionists commonly resort to criminalizing immigrants by casting them as predatory villains, drug dealers, and even terrorists. Compounding matters, stereotypes have a potent effect on the general public since at times it is willing to uncritically accept inaccurate versions of tragic events. In 1995, the bombing of a federal building in Oklahoma City contributed to growing fears about terrorists and fueled suspicion of Arab immigrants, even after investigators determined that the bombing was not the handiwork of Muslim terrorists but that of Timothy McVey, a white, Christian, U.S. citizen and former serviceman. Anti-immigrant rhetoric also marginalizes economically poor immigrants, casting them as being part of America's underclass. Nativists contribute to the stigma of being immigrant by insinuating that they drain tax dollars in the form of public assistance, adding that immigrants are drawn to the United States for its so-called magnet of the American welfare state.

Scapegoating involves the placing of blame for one's troubles onto an individual or group incapable of offering resistance. Due to anti-immigrant politics, immigrants are commonly scapegoated, becoming convenient targets for public anger over social and economic unrest. Scapegoating further creates unique paradoxes—or catch-22s—for immigrants. On the one hand, some immigrants are portrayed as lazy and unskilled, thus draining social and welfare services; on the other hand, they are blamed for stealing jobs from hardworking U.S. citizens. In sum, anti-immigrant politics are potent albeit divisive tactics that polarize opinions over immigration. It is ironic that such nativist campaigns are capable of generating such widespread support in the United States, a country that also takes enormous pride in being a nation of immigrants. It ought to be noted that anti-immigrant politics are not confined to the United States. Likewise, in Europe, such politicization continues to gain momentum in regions where migrants—especially from Africa and the Middle East—are met with public alarm.

—*Michael Welch*

See also Free Movement Activism; Immigrant Activism in France

Further Readings

Calavita, K. (1996). The new politics of immigration: "Balanced-budget conservatism" and the symbolism of Proposition 187. *Social Problems, 43*(3), 285–305.

Johnson, K. (2004). *The "huddled masses" myth: Immigration and civil rights.* Philadelphia: Temple University Press.

Miller, T. A. (2005). Blurring the boundaries between immigration and crime control after September 11th. *Boston College Third World Law Journal, 25*(1), 81–123.

Reimers, D. M. (1998). *Unwelcome strangers: American identity and the turn against immigration.* New York: Columbia University Press.

Welch, M. (2002). *Detained: Immigration laws and the expanding I.N.S. jail complex.* Philadelphia: Temple University Press.

Welch, M. (2003). Ironies of social control and the criminalization of immigrants. *Crime, Law and Social Change: An International Journal, 39*(44), 319–337.

ANTI-IMPERIALISM

Anti-imperialism has transformed throughout several phases, each with distinct social, economic, and political motivations and objectives. Attempts to annex countries like Santo Domingo and Cuba failed in the U.S. Congress from the 1850s through the 1870s, largely due to very conservative politics. It was not until the aftermath of the Spanish-American War, when the Anti-Imperialist League became part of the progressive movement, that anti-imperialism became a social cause. Finally, later in the 20th century, anti-imperialists objected to U.S. expansion and military involvement in places such as Vietnam, Central America, and the Middle East.

In its first phase, which is ideologically and tactically very different from the second and third, anti-imperialist sentiment in the United States consisted mainly of congressional representatives who opposed the annexation of territories in the Caribbean, South Pacific, and Mexico. In large part, the slavery debate influenced the congressional refusal to annex overseas territories; annexation would not only alter the balance of free and slave states but also usher thousands to millions of new citizens into the body politic. The racial background of these potential citizens, who were overwhelmingly non-European, proved a deterrent against the annexation of their homelands because racist ideology and political rhetoric claimed they were not capable of self-government and not civilized. Ulysses S. Grant's 1870 plan to annex Santo Domingo and make it a refuge for former slaves illustrates some of the complicated racial politics of imperialism. While, prior to 1900, many political anti-imperialists believed that islands like Santo Domingo, Cuba, and Hawai'i were inhabited by "primitive" cultures and thus unappealing and possibly a contaminant to the Anglo-American polity, an equally racist mix of missionary impulses and the desire to remove former slaves from the U.S. mainland informed imperial ventures.

By 1900, anti-imperialism was associated with the progressive movement and informed by an anti-racist agenda. This second phase of anti-imperialism, that turned anti-imperialism into a social movement, began after the Spanish-American War. When Cuba, Puerto Rico, and the Philippines came under U.S. control, numerous factions continued to debate the status of these new territories, and their subjects, within the body politic. President William McKinley engaged the United States in a war with Philippine nationalists after the United States defeated Spanish forces in the Philippines. In November 1898, a group of prominent Boston citizens organized the Anti-Imperialist League. Within a year, their ranks had soared to more than 30,000 members. The highly controversial war with the Philippines, which McKinley insisted was the only alternative to even more bloodshed among Philippine nationals, the Spanish, and Japanese, brought McKinley much criticism and centered the Philippines on the Anti-Imperialist League's agenda.

The Anti-Imperialist League's leaders included Chicago reformer Jane Addams, the steel magnate Andrew Carnegie, Samuel Gompers of the American Federation of Labor, and Moorfield Storey, a prominent Boston lawyer who later became the first president of the National Association for the Advancement of Colored People (NAACP). Other members included W. E. B. Du Bois and James Weldon Johnson, who would become prominent figures in the NAACP. The ranks of the Anti-Imperialist League

also included suffragists and former abolitionists such as Mary Livermore and Oswald Garrison Villard.

Some of the Anti-Imperialist League's most pertinent political philosophies yielded from democratic principles evidenced in founding documents such as the Declaration of Independence. The history of the United States as a British colony, they argued, indicated that the nation's very founding was based on anti-colonial principles. Anti-imperialists likewise objected to the acquisition or control over territories whose subjects could not become citizens of the United States, vote, or create independent republics.

Some African American leaders attacked McKinley for trying to establish a Republican government in the Philippines when the government failed to take action to curb the widespread lynching and political disenfranchisement of African Americans in the United States. While journalists like Ida B. Wells-Barnett openly opposed McKinley, the experience of black soldiers in the Spanish-American War and the possibility that, through military service and patriotism, blacks in the United States could gain full citizenship rights curbed the anti-imperialist sentiment in many black communities.

The rather illustrious and prestigious list of founding members suggests that financial resources and established social power distinguished the Anti-Imperialist League from anti-imperialist social movements later in the 20th century that mobilized through support of the masses. Nonetheless, the league soon gained a mass following; the Anti-Imperialist League's first action, a petition to the Senate protesting American sovereignty in the Philippines without the consent of the people of the archipelago, succeeded in collecting 50,000 signatures. Partisan politics, however, would hinder the organization almost immediately. Theodore Roosevelt's election isolated the Anti-Imperialist League, and by 1904, the national organization had collapsed. The Philippine Independence Committee's position on an agenda for liberation was more compromising, and in an attempt to curry favor with Republicans, some anti-imperialists supported the organization. A combination of changes in Filipino leadership, international events, and the increasing strength of domestic imperialist interests forestalled Philippine independence. Organizations such as the American-Philippine Company, founded in 1912 to safeguard U.S. financial interests in the archipelago, represented imperialist interests.

According to Jim Zwick, the Anti-Imperialist League, which disbanded in 1921, preceded other social movements that opposed U.S. intervention throughout the globe. In the 1920s, several of the league's leaders served as officers of new anti-imperial organizations, such as the Haiti-Santo Domingo Independence Committee of 1921, a coalition among NAACP and former Anti-Imperialist League officers who opposed the U.S. occupation of Haiti (1915–1934) and Santo Domingo (1916–1924); the American Fund for Public Service Committee on American Imperialism of 1924, which provided funding for liberal and leftist causes and opposed economic imperialism; the All-America Anti-Imperialist League of 1925, affiliated with the Workers' Party (Communist Party) and dedicated to organizing workers throughout the Caribbean; and the Women's International League for Peace and Freedom (WILPF), which dispatched an investigatory panel to Haiti in 1926 to document the U.S. Marine occupation there. Jane Addams, the international president of WILPF, won the Nobel Peace Prize in 1931 for her work with the organization.

Some scholars view anti-imperialism in the United States and Europe as a precursor to independence movements in Asia and Africa in the 1950s and later. Cuban and Filipino nationals José Martí and José Rizal opposed Spanish rule over their respective islands in the late 19th century. The independence movements inspired by these two men anticipated the U.S. intervention in 1898 that led to U.S. expansion. Native American tribes that fought against settlers likewise modeled a militant anti-imperialism. In that sense, they might be considered some of the Western hemisphere's first anti-imperialists.

—*Colleen C. O'Brien*

See also Addams, Jane; Gompers, Samuel; National Association for the Advancement of Colored People (NAACP); Wells-Barnett, Ida B.

Further Readings

Love, E. (2004). *Race over empire: Racialism and U.S. imperialism 1865–1900*. Chapel Hill: University of North Carolina Press.

Women's International League for Peace and Freedom. (1998). *History of WILPF*. Retrieved March 13, 2006, from http://www.wilpf.int.ch/history/hindex.htm

ANTI-LYNCHING MOVEMENT

During the late 19th century and the first half of the 20th century, lynching or mob violence was a powerful tool that was used by commonplace citizens to enforce the social aspects of Jim Crow and to terrorize African American communities. In this sense, the victims of lynching were mostly black men. Although participants in the lynching rarely hid their identities, many of them were never arrested for their crimes. As a result, lynching of blacks continued to triumph. In the 1890s, African Americans and their white allies formed an anti-lynching movement. In an effort to publicize the mob violence, various strategies were used, including petitions, marches, demonstrations, and rallies. Also, plays, songs, visual art, films, and cartoons were used to emphasize the humanity of the victims and to educate the American public about the scope of the lynching. The main aim of the movement was to reprove lynching and to pressure the government to pass a federal anti-lynching law. Nonetheless, even though the movement never did achieve its legislative goal, the shameful history of the lynching of black Americans was given voice, and it brought enormous attention to lynching in the United States, especially in the South.

Many black women played a significant role in the anti-lynching movement on a number of fronts. For example, with the financial support of the Black Women's Club movement, journalist Ada B. Wells-Barnett was able to travel throughout the United States and went to Britain twice to speak out against lynching. Wells-Barnett published two anti-lynching pamphlets, *Southern Horrors: Lynch Law in All Its Phases* (1892) and *The Red Record* (1895). In 1896, the National Association of Colored Women was founded. Its main focus was to denounce lynching and to develop anti-lynching strategies. Also, the National Association for the Advancement of Colored People (NAACP) was formed as a result of efforts to combat lynching.

Eventually in 1918, Representative Leonidas Dyer (R-Missouri) introduced in Congress his anti-lynching bill, which was known as the Dyer Bill. Initially, the NAACP did not support the passage of this bill because of the recommendations of Moorfield Storey, a lawyer and the first president of the NAACP. Storey eventually altered his position, and in 1919, the NAACP launched a campaign against lynching. The Dyer Bill was passed by the House of Representatives on January 26, 1922. Nonetheless, the very idea of protecting blacks from mob violence prompted a considerable number of white supremacist senators to use filibuster, which succeeded in preventing the bill from ever reaching a vote in the Senate.

Many efforts to pass similar legislation were not taken up again until the 1930s with the Costigan-Wagner Bill, which was proposed by Senators Edward P. Costigan (D-Colorado) and Robert Wagner (D-New York). Its aim was to make sure that sheriffs who failed to protect their prisoners from lynching mobs were punished. However, President Franklin D. Roosevelt refused to support this bill because he was afraid of losing the support of the white voters in the South and, as such, of losing the 1936 presidential election. Another anti-lynching bill, the Gavagan Bill, was passed in the House of Representatives in 1937 and again in 1940, but both times it died in the Senate because of Southern filibusters. Although a federal law making lynching a crime failed to pass, lynching had almost disappeared in the 1950s. Between 1950 and 1959, about six African Americans were lynched.

—*Sherrow O. Pinder*

See also National Association for the Advancement of Colored People (NAACP); Wells-Barnett, Ida B.

Further Readings

Brundage, W. F. (1993). *Lynching in the New South, Georgia and Virginia, 1880–1930.* Chicago: University of Illinois Press.

Holden-Smith, B. (1996). Lynching, federalism, and the intersection of race and gender in the Progressive Era. *Yale Journal of Law and Feminism, 8*(1), 31–78.

Kellogg, C. F. (1967). *NAACP: A history of the National Association for the Advancement of Colored People, 1909–1920* (Vol. 1). Baltimore: Johns Hopkins Press.

ANTI-MONOPOLY MOVEMENT

The anti-monopoly movement in the United States roughly parallels the rise of the modern corporation. It has drawn to its ranks many different kinds of activists, from farm populists to working-class advocates, and from middle-class reformers to corporate leaders who sought to make the capitalist system more predictable and rational.

Anti-monopolist sentiment in the United States has often been galvanized by specific legal instances. One of the earliest and most celebrated anti-monopoly causes centered on the controversial Charles River Bridge case. In 1837, after a long, protracted legal battle, the U.S. Supreme Court ruled that the state of Massachusetts could build a free bridge over the Charles River, even though it had earlier chartered a toll bridge close by. The proprietors of the first bridge protested that the new project represented a breach of contract. Advocates of the new corporate charter and much of the public regarded this objection as little more than an attempt by the privileged to impede progress.

Such sentiments had been percolating since the American Revolution. Property did not help society, wrote Revolutionary War veteran and Massachusetts Senator Theodore Sedgwick when gotten by unfair dealings, fraud, oppression, or monopoly. Anti-monopoly activists in the second half of the 19th century often regarded the absence of any legal protections for farmers and workers as de facto privileges for the wealthy, especially the wealthy who controlled the nation's railroads, coal, and oil refining industries. Farmer and labor advocates and small business owners all clamored for federal laws that would protect them from price fixing and economic coercion. In response, Congress gave them two very weak laws in the last 2 decades of the 19th century: the Interstate

Commerce Act of 1887 and the Sherman Antitrust Act of 1890.

The Interstate Commerce Commission did not seriously inhibit the shipping practices of the railroads, wrote historian Nell Irvin Painter, and the Sherman Act was at first ineffective, but the statute came to life under the leadership of Theodore Roosevelt, made president by the assassination of William McKinley in 1901. Angered by the personal arrogance of men like financier J. P. Morgan and fearful that popular discontent would move the country to the left, Roosevelt authorized the selective prosecution of prominent monopolies like the vast Northern Securities railroad company.

Roosevelt's "trust-busting" battles captured the public's imagination during the Progressive Era. A generation of writers and journalists further nourished the anti-monopoly impulse by exposing the underside of corporate power in their articles and books. Their most famous contributions included Upton Sinclair's *The Jungle,* a fictional but compelling account of the Chicago meatpacking industry, and Ida Tarbel's *History of the Standard Oil Company.*

But modest regulatory reform also received the support of much of the corporate sector, whose principals saw in greater government oversight a more predictable business environment and the ability to maintain an advantage over smaller competitors. This influence weakened more radical efforts to reign in monopoly power. In addition, anti-monopoly activists during this period often remained divided on how to confront corporate dominance. Some advocated a vigorous regimen of antitrust activity; others counseled the acceptance of large corporations within the context of a strong regulatory environment.

The anti-monopoly movement remained scattered and divided throughout the 1930s and largely paralyzed the attempts of President Franklin D. Roosevelt to come up with a coherent philosophy for the management of corporations. As historian Ellis W. Hawley notes, the Great Depression intensified conflicting demands among reformers both for more government planning and rationalization and for the punishment of big business and the restoration of competitive ideals. In addition, beginning in the early 20th century, many

corporations, especially AT&T, launched lengthy and vigorous public relations (PR) campaigns. AT&T's PR campaign, which emphasized the corporation's commitment to public service and the welfare of widow stockholders, helped it survive a late 1930s investigation of anti-competitive behavior launched by the Federal Communications Commission. When the U.S. government finally bore down on the monopoly in the early 1980s, it was in large part at the behest of rival telecommunications firms that had also launched sophisticated PR offensives.

In 1976, consumer advocates Ralph Nader, Mark Green, and Joel Seligman, disappointed by the weakness of state corporate charters, proposed the federal chartering of corporations. Their proposed Federal Chartering Act would have covered all corporations that sold more than $250 million in goods or services or employed more than 10,000 workers. It would have included requirements for more corporate openness and accountability to consumers and shareholders and a bill of rights for corporate employees. Twenty years later, computer users and software developers empowered by the Internet cheered when the U.S. Department of Justice launched an investigation against Microsoft, responding to charges that the corporation engaged in anti-competitive behaviors against Netscape, a web browser competing with Microsoft's own Internet Explorer. These outbursts of vision and activism indicate that Theodore Sedgwick's concerns may be difficult to implement, but they are anything but dormant in our time.

—Matthew Lasar

Further Readings

Hawley, E. W. (1966). *The New Deal and the problem of monopoly: A study in economic ambivalence.* New York: Fordham University Press.

Lloyd, H. D. (1898). *Wealth and commonwealth.* New York: Harper & Row.

Marchand, R. (2001). *Creating the corporate soul: The rise of public relations and corporate imagery in American big business.* Berkeley: University of California Press.

McGerr, M. (2003). *A fierce discontent: The rise and fall of the Progressive movement in America, 1870–1920.* New York: Free Press.

Nader, R., Green, M., & Seligman, J. (1976). *Taming the giant corporation: How the largest corporations control our lives.* New York: W. W. Norton.

Painter, N. I. (1987). *Standing at Armageddon: The United States, 1877–1919.* New York: W. W. Norton.

Reid R. H. (1997). *Architects of the Web: 1,000 days that built the future of business.* New York: Wiley.

Stone, A. (1989). *Wrong number: The breakup of AT&T.* New York: Basic Books.

ANTI-NUCLEAR MOVEMENT

The anti-nuclear movement is a social movement opposed to production of nuclear weapons and generation of electricity by nuclear power plants. It is often assumed that this perspective on the anti-nuclear movement has dominated since the early days of atomic power; however, the anti-nuclear movement has almost as long and contested a history as nuclear power itself. Today, the anti-nuclear movement is truly global in nature, exhibiting a range of social goals and ideology. The movement is rooted in early atomic energy research in Germany and the United States.

During the late 1930s and early 1940s, when the Nazi regime was attempting to build an atomic weapon, a liberal and internationalist attitude toward atomic power was prevalent. Atomic research was expensive and generally funded by the government and military. Early atomic scientists were focused primarily on scientific potential and advancement, largely unaware of either the potential dangers of radiation and atomic reactions or of the full potential for negative application of atomic power for military purposes. By the time the negative aspects of non-peaceful uses of atomic power were realized, the government and military controlled atomic energy. In 1945, when Los Alamos Laboratory scientists exploded the first plutonium bomb, scientists were becoming increasingly concerned about the destructive potential of atomic power.

Even at this early stage of atomic research, it was apparent that the technology was advancing faster than the understanding of the scientific phenomena involved. The explosive power of the first plutonium bomb was substantially higher than what had been predicted. A movement of scientists developed to try and prevent military control of atomic energy, resulting in the foundation of the Federation of American Scientists. This was led by physicist J. Robert Oppenheimer, one of the fathers of atomic power research, director of the Manhattan Project, and a symbol of the ethical dilemma that scientists can face when their research interests and national interests conflict. The U.S. attack on Japan in 1945 was the beginning of a strong public anti-nuclear movement.

In late 1945, the Federation of American Scientists attempted to mandate civilian control of atomic power through the McMahon Act, but this effort was not successful. As the Cold War escalated, gaining increasing international and national attention, military power and national security became paramount. National security doctrines established during this time deemed that all nuclear power policy decisions in the United States would be controlled by the government and military. The rise of the United States to an atomic superpower and the anti-communism of the McCarthy era changed the perspective on nuclear energy from liberal scientific research to one where dissension against nuclear power was the equivalent of an act of treason. Scientists who were actively against military use of nuclear power were discredited, and Julius and Ethel Rosenberg were tried and executed for espionage after communicating atomic energy secrets to the Soviet Union. This environment was the beginning of an era of government and nuclear secrecy that continues today, now enhanced by the need for protection against terrorists.

In the 1950s, increasing efforts were made to support international cooperation and sharing of nuclear materials through President Eisenhower's Atoms for Peace proposal to the United Nations. While this provided a level of control over nuclear research, it also led to nuclear weapons development in other countries. During this time, both government and private industry were developing the first commercial nuclear power plants, government research into applications of nuclear power research was continuing, and the environmental effects of radiation were being investigated. Critics of nuclear power were becoming increasingly vocal, expressing concerns about the testing of nuclear weapons in the atmosphere, radioactive fallout, and the potential for radiation to cause genetic mutations. The First World Conference Against Atomic and Hydrogen Bombs was held in Hiroshima in 1955.

Politically, the change of the 1950s resulted in President Kennedy's Test Ban Treaty in 1962. Socially, the anti-nuclear movement grew throughout the 1960s, in part via beatnik philosophies of world destruction through nuclear war. The Cold War resulted in elevated fear of nuclear attack, construction of backyard nuclear bomb shelters, and regular duck-and-cover drills in grade schools. The "ban the bomb" movement began in Britain, construction of missile bases were protested, and increasing controversy developed over construction of commercial nuclear power plants. In 1968 the Nuclear Non-Proliferation Treaty was signed, placing commercial nuclear materials under the control of the Atomic Energy Commission.

Although the anti-nuclear movement continued in the United States during the late 1960s and into the 1970s, some momentum was lost as many other social issues came to the forefront, such as the Vietnam War, women's rights, black rights, and many other environmental issues. One environmental issue that strongly affected the anti-nuclear movement was concerns about thermal pollution due to hot water discharge from nuclear power facility cooling systems. Although the effects of thermal pollution were minimal and have been corrected through regulation and improved technology, concerns about thermal pollution in the early 1970s led the way to environmental impact challenges of nuclear power facilities by citizen groups.

A resurgence of interest in the anti-nuclear movement began in the mid-1980s after higher than normal numbers of deaths from children's leukemia were reported for residents near several types of nuclear facilities. This began a lengthy controversy, which continues today, into the effects of exposure to low-level radiation.

The anti-nuclear movement became a major social movement after the energy crisis of the early 1970s. The energy crisis and associated efforts to both expand nuclear power and provide improved nuclear safety brought many nuclear issues and concerns to the forefront. During this time, commercial nuclear power continued to develop across the globe, as did both public concerns about nuclear power and awareness of the benefits of nuclear power. The anti-nuclear movement as it is today was born when Ralph Nader, the Sierra Club, and Friends of the Earth called for a moratorium on nuclear power development. Safety of commercial nuclear power plants became a public issue, escalated by issuance of a government report, the Rasmussen report, on reactor safety (a report that was challenged by the Sierra Club and the Union of Concerned Scientists); national concerns about earthquake damage to nuclear power plants; and a fire at the Browns Ferry reactor. Anti-nuclear activities were brought to worldwide attention in 1979 when the Three Mile Island nuclear power plant accident occurred in Pennsylvania. The late 1970s also saw expansion of anti-nuclear activities in Western Europe, as protests against NATO deployment of nuclear weapons, the NATO stance that conventional deterrence is not nearly as effective as nuclear deterrence, and opposition to American military interests in Europe increased.

During the 1980s, the focus of the anti-nuclear movement in the United States shifted to adjust to a large number of political and social changes, including large cuts in funding for development of alternative energy sources, new Department of Energy policies, production of plutonium for nuclear weapons, streamlining of the commercial nuclear power plant licensing process, expansion of nuclear research and military deployment in Western Europe, and increased European and Japanese pressure for nuclear disarmament. Anti-nuclear activism was now largely directed at issues of a Soviet-American treaty to halt testing, deployment, and development of nuclear weapons, renewed fears of a Cold War resurgence, radioactive waste disposal, and emergency evacuation plans in the event of an accident at a nuclear power plant. The anti-nuclear movement influenced arms control agreements between Mikhail Gorbachev and Ronald Reagan and positively contributed to nuclear disarmament and avoidance of nuclear war.

In 1986, the anti-nuclear movement again received a boost from a nuclear power plant accident, this time at the Chernobyl plant in Ukraine. This was by far the most serious nuclear accident in history, with widespread physical effects and global political effects. While this accident substantially added strength to the anti-nuclear movement, particularly at the grassroots level where it became a global symbol for anti-nuclear activism, it also helped spread technical knowledge about nuclear power. Public and media discussion of the extensive lack of safety systems and appropriate operator training at Chernobyl, and resulting comparisons with nuclear power plant technology in the United States and worldwide, have expanded public knowledge of the safety, technology, and culture associated with properly operated and maintained power plants. Proponents of nuclear power argue that since Three Mile Island, regulatory and cultural improvements within the commercial nuclear power industry in the United States have resulted in a strong, safety-oriented, high-performing culture with a focus on communications and social responsibility that is being studied by other industries.

Since Chernobyl, concerns about terrorist activities have once again changed the politics, technology, and culture of nuclear power and have provided a new focus for the anti-nuclear movement. Trends in increasing violence and disobedience at some anti-nuclear protest activities have also raised some concerns about the potential for anti-nuclear protests to result in possible terrorist violence.

From a standpoint of social goals and ideology, the anti-nuclear movement exhibits several subjective orientations. On a global scale, both national and regional differences are likely to be significant. Subjective orientations include emphasis on peace/ecology and environmentalism, intellectual social activism based on knowledge of nuclear technology, and political/moral activism based on conflicts between nuclear power applications and policies and personal values. These same subjective orientations can be applied to pro-nuclear activists who support nuclear energy as a more environmentally safe and feasible power source than fossil fuels, support education on nuclear power technology, and morally support peaceful uses of advanced nuclear power designs.

Goals of anti-nuclear movement organizations include a moratorium on nuclear development and research, emphasis on alternative energy sources,

dangers of proliferation of nuclear weapons, environmental hazards, and safety of nuclear industry workers. The emphasis on goals and ideology varies across organizations. Supporting beliefs tend to include assumptions that nuclear weapons that are produced will eventually be used, nuclear-related terrorist attacks and nuclear accidents are probable, radioactive wastes cannot be adequately disposed of, and that alternative energy technologies can meet the needs of the human race prior to depletion of fossil fuels. When contrasted with the beliefs of pro-nuclear organizations—which include assumptions that nuclear weapons can be controlled and hopefully eliminated, terrorist attacks and nuclear accidents are largely preventable, radioactive wastes can be safely disposed of, and that alternative energy sources cannot possibly meet the energy needs of the human race and thus new nuclear power designs are required—it is very apparent that nuclear power is a social concern that will not only continue to be prominent in our society but is likely to become even more so.

Currently, with oil prices rising rapidly, concerns growing about global warming, and technological advances in alternative energy sources well behind prior predictions, many are again arguing that nuclear energy is a necessary and economically important source of electrical power. They argue that advances in technology, training, and safety culture can prevent another Three Mile Island or Chernobyl and that new power plant designs can provide more efficient and safer sources of power than ever before. Commercial nuclear power is likely to once again come to the forefront of energy and environmental policy decisions. A variety of efforts to impose, monitor, and enforce nuclear weapons development and testing policies are continuing, at international and national levels, with various degrees of success. Nuclear proliferation and terrorist threats are critical political and social issues worldwide. The anti-nuclear movement is likely to continue to be a global social force for the foreseeable future.

—*Susan L. Rothwell*

See also Community-Based Ecological Resistance Movements; Environmental Movement; Nader, Ralph; Sierra Club; Solar Energy Movement; Tennessee Valley Authority

Further Readings

Domenici, P. (2004). *A brighter tomorrow.* Lanham, MD: Rowman & Littlefield.

Dougherty, J., & Pfaltzgraff, R. (Eds.). (1985). *Shattering Europe's defense consensus: The anti-nuclear protest movement and the future of NATO.* Elmsford, NY: Pergamon-Brassey's International Defense Publishers.

Heaberlin, S. (2003). *A case for nuclear-generated electricity.* Columbus, OH: Battelle Press.

Price, J. (1990). *The antinuclear movement.* Boston: Twayne.

Rees, J. (1994). *Hostages of each other.* Chicago: University of Chicago Press.

Smith, J. (Ed.). (2002). *The antinuclear movement.* Greenhaven Press.

Wittner, L. (2003). *Toward nuclear abolition.* Palo Alto, CA: Stanford University Press.

ANTI-PORNOGRAPHY ACTIVISM

Anti-pornography activism is the term used to describe the actions of those who argue, from a variety of legal, feminist, and religious perspectives, that pornography has a large number of harmful effects, including violence toward women and minors, increased crime in areas with sex shops and strip clubs, links to organized crime, and harm to the family unit. Pornography, in general, is an issue that gets many people, including its adamant censors and perceived advocates, agitated. Yet, for all of the commotion that it causes, pornography has no accepted, static legal definition. Definitions of pornography often differ due to things such as one's upbringing, religious views, sexual preference, viewing context, position on pornography, or life situation. Under current federal obscenity laws, the majority of pornographic images are not illegal; only material that is considered to be obscene is legally unacceptable. The Supreme Court created the Miller Test, in *Miller v. California,* 423 U.S. 15, 40 (1972), which stated that in order for material to be considered obscene it must first be determined

(a) whether "the average person, applying contemporary community standards" would find that the work, taken as a whole, appeals to the prurient interest, . . . (b) whether the work depicts or describes, in a patently offensive way, sexual conduct specifically defined by the applicable state law and (c) whether the work, taken as a whole, lacks serious literary, artistic, political, or scientific value.

Generally, the U.S. government may not regulate speech because of its message, its ideas, its subject matter, or its content (*Erznoznik v. City of Jacksonville,* 422 U.S. 205 [1975]). In *Hustler Magazine, Inc. v. Falwell,* 485 U.S. 747, 781 (1982), the Court rejected the theory that there can be permissible content regulation within a category of protected speech. However, in *Chaplinsky v. New Hampshire,* 315 U.S. 568,571–72 (1942), the Court stated "certain well-defined and narrowly limited classes of speech . . . are no essential part of any exposition of ideas, and are of such slight social value as a step to truth" that the government can regulate them without raising First Amendment concerns. In cases like *Young v. American Mini Theaters,* 427 U.S. 50 (1976), *FCC v. Pacifica Foundation,* 438 U.S. 726 (1978), and *N.Y. v. Ferber,* 458 U.S. 747, 781 (1982), courts have ruled that offensive but nonobscene words and portrayals dealing with sex may be regulated when the expression plays no role or even a minimal role in the exposition of ideas. For example, in *Barnes v. Glen Theatre, Inc.,* 501 U.S. 560 (1991), commercial speech is protected by the First Amendment, but it is less protected than other speech and is subject to content-based regulation.

Many activists and politicians have expressed concern over the ease and availability of Internet pornography. Currently in the United States, the crux of the legal debate surrounding pornography deals with the regulation of cyberpornography and is focused on how to protect children from the wide range of sexually explicit images that are available, without encroaching on the First Amendment rights of adults. Computer technology continues to advance rapidly and children now often have unrestricted access to explicit pornographic electronic images at home, in school, and in libraries. The Child Online Protection Act (COPA) is a U.S. law passed in 1998 that purported to protect children from harmful sexual material on the Internet but actually focused on limiting commercial speech originating in the United States. COPA required individuals who fall within the scope of the statute to undertake specified steps to restrict children's access to materials that are considered to be "harmful to minors." COPA defined material that is "harmful to minors" as "any communication, picture, image, graphic image file, article, recording, writing, or other matter of any kind that is obscene" under the aforementioned Miller Test.

The law was effectively blocked by the courts and has never taken effect. For example, in *ACLU et al. v. Janet Reno,* 31 F. Supp. 2d 473 (E.D. Pa. 1999), the court enjoined enforcement of COPA because it constituted an unconstitutional regulation of speech in violation of the First Amendment. The court decided that COPA was unconstitutional because the government did not sufficiently prove that the regulation was the least restrictive means available to achieve the compelling state interest of protecting children. The court also pointed out that the statute might result in the unwanted self-censorship of Internet providers who felt coerced into removing questionable content to avoid prosecution. It was decided that commercially available blocking software that could be installed in the home by concerned parents was a less restrictive way to achieve the government's goal of protecting children. The court also noted that COPA would not prevent minors from accessing harmful materials from foreign sources or even sites that were not commercial in nature.

COPA was just one part of the struggle of anti-pornography lawmakers against the proliferation of Internet pornography. Prior to COPA, the Communications Decency Act had been struck down as unconstitutionally vague by the Supreme Court; COPA was a direct response to that decision and an attempt to narrow the range of material covered.

The feminist position on pornography is divided. Some, like Andrea Dworkin, Catharine MacKinnon, and Susan Brownmiller, believe that all pornography should be completely banned. These feminists assert that pornography is degrading to women and promotes violence against women. This violence is seen not only in its production, where the abuse is often caught on tape, but also in its consumption. This feminist camp believes that because pornography

eroticizes the humiliation and domination of women in sexual situations, it works to reinforce the harmful sexual and cultural attitudes that surround crimes like rape, sexual harassment, and abuse. In the 1970s, anti-pornography radical feminists formed organizations such as Women's International Terrorist Conspiracy from Hell (W.I.T.C.H.), New York Radical Women, and Women Against Pornography, which attempted to raise awareness of what they saw as the harmful content of pornography and the toxic sexual subculture in pornography shops and live sex shows.

On the other side, some feminists believe that some types of pornography are fairly harmless; therefore, they do not support a complete ban on it. Many, like Laura Kipnis and Susie Bright, believe that although the pornography industry is often exploitative and abusive, pornography could be and sometimes is feminist, as seen through the power of the sexual revolution. These feminists believe that viewing some types of pornography allows people to safely experience sexual alternatives that could help to satisfy their sexual curiosities. In this day and age when AIDS and many other sexually transmitted diseases threaten the lives of the sexually inquisitive, these feminists believe that it is much safer for someone curious about things like having a ménage à trois to view it on the Internet rather than to seek out numerous sexual partners. Thus, they seek to drastically reform the harmful side of the pornography industry rather than totally oppose pornography in general.

Finally, some religious conservatives or fundamentalists, such as Jerry Falwell, Charles Humphrey Keating, Jr., Jonathan Christian Webster III, and Patricia Bartlett, along with organizations like the American Family Association and the Christian Legion Against Media Pornography, criticize pornography on moral and ethical religious grounds. They say sex is reserved for heterosexual married couples and assert that use of pornography leads to an increase in behavior that is considered by the Church to be sexually immoral. This unwanted behavior includes crimes such as rape, assault, battery, and abuse and activities such as homosexuality, polygamy, sex with minors, and adultery.

—Malila N. Robinson

See also American Civil Liberties Union (ACLU); Bill of Rights; Christian Right; Dworkin, Andrea; Feminism; Free Speech Activism; Media Activism; Media Reform Movement; National Organization for Women; Religious Activism; Sex Workers' Rights

Further Readings

Dines, G., Jensen, R., & Russo, A. (1998). *Pornography: The production and consumption of inequity.* New York: Routledge.

Dworkin, A. (1997). *Life and death: Unapologetic writings of the continuing war against women.* New York: Simon & Schuster.

Lederer, L., & Delgado, R. (Eds.). (1995). The price we pay: The case against racist speech, hate propaganda, and pornography. New York: Hill & Wang.

Leidholdt, D., & Raymond, J. (Eds.). (1990). *The sexual liberals and the attack on feminism.* Elmsford, NY: Pergamon Press.

MacKinnon, C. A. (1993). *Only words.* Cambridge, MA: Harvard University Press.

MacKinnon, C. A., & Dworkin, A. (Eds.). (1997). *In harm's way: The pornography civil rights hearings.* Cambridge, MA: Harvard University Press.

Russell, D. (1994). *Against pornography: The evidence of harm.* Berkeley, CA: Russell.

ANTI-PRISON MOVEMENT

The individuals and organizations that comprise the contemporary anti-prison movement are working to create a world without prisons. This national and international force is also known as the prison abolition movement. Prison abolitionists believe that imprisoning people does not prevent crime, make society safer, or address the root causes of crime and violence. Instead, anti-prison activists locate the root causes of crime in pervasive inequality, structural oppression, and a dominant culture of violence. They also question the definitions of *crime* and *criminal* and seek to dismantle state violence and capitalism, which play key roles in the criminalization of entire communities. The foundations of existing efforts to abolish prisons lie in the earlier prison abolitionist movement of the 1960s and 1970s. The existence of a prison-industrial complex provides the political and economic context of the contemporary movement and serves as the target of anti-prison activists.

To achieve the anti-prison movement's long-term goal of solving social problems and generating public safety without warehousing millions of people, organizers work to educate the public about the problems with prisons, prevent the construction of new prisons, promote alternatives to incarceration, and implement community-based solutions to violence. A diversity of people and organizations are involved in working toward a world without prisons, including grassroots organizations, prisoners and former prisoners, activist-scholars, policy advocacy groups, youth organizers, and artists. Many anti-prison activists also participate in movements to end violence against women, stop police brutality, protect the rights of prisoners, increase funding for education and social services, free political prisoners, and stop environmental injustice, among other progressive goals.

Arguments for Prison Abolition

Prisons do not make society safer. Prisons are used to punish offenders after a violent crime has been committed; they do not prevent violence from occurring. Incarceration also fails to protect people from state violence such as police brutality. Instead, imprisonment increases violence by subjecting nonviolent offenders to violent conditions in prison, such as rape and assault by other prisoners and prison guards. Some of these previously nonviolent offenders go on to commit acts of violence once they are released, after having lived in such a violent environment.

Prisons do not address the root causes of crime. Most crime and violence are caused by economic inequality, structural oppression, and a pervasive culture of violence, not moral failures or individual pathologies. Many people commit crime because they have limited legal means to gain resources needed for their own survival. Forms of oppression engrained within social structures exclude entire groups from opportunities for legal employment and adequate income. Society also promotes a culture of violence through mass media, government policies, and dominant values that celebrate violence, especially violence against women. Rather than addressing these economic and cultural causes of crime, prisons exacerbate the social conditions that fuel it.

Prisons do not address the needs of crime victims or offenders. Incarceration does not help to repair the harm done to individuals who have suffered losses as the result of crime. Similarly, instead of allowing communities to meet existing needs, through drug treatment or quality mental health care, for instance, incarceration simply isolates those in need. Most prisoners have been victims of crime before their own involvement in committing crime. By only considering the most recent act of victimization and fostering an artificial binary between "victims" and "perpetrators," the criminal punishment system fails to holistically address the needs of everyone affected by crime and violence.

Prisons are used to suppress marginalized people. Those with political and economic power create laws against activities that threaten their own views and interests. For instance, to maintain a white supremacist, patriarchal, and heterosexist social order, women's suffrage, same-gender sex, and interracial marriage were previously defined as crimes. Contemporary crimes such as prostitution and undocumented immigration may be viewed similarly in hindsight. White, upper-class, heterosexual men remain the majority of lawmakers. Though people of all races and classes break the law, poor whites and people of color are far more often arrested, convicted, and incarcerated. Prison helps to keep these disenfranchised members of the population from rebelling against an oppressive social order.

Prisons are used to generate profit. Many individuals and institutions profit from imprisoning people. There are companies that own prisons, build prisons, supply prisons with goods, and use prisoners' labor for manufacturing and service work. Altogether, corporations that profit from incarceration comprise the fastest-growing industry in the United States. Many of these corporations successfully lobby for laws that lengthen prison sentences and otherwise drive the binge for more prisons. This underlying profit motive guarantees the growth of the prison system despite a decrease in crime.

Imprisonment perpetuates oppression. The criminal punishment system has proven to be racist, classist, sexist, and homophobic. Policies and stigmas that prevent prisoners and former prisoners from voting, receiving federal assistance for higher education, and procuring meaningful employment further exclude already marginalized groups from meaningful participation in society. Prisons also exacerbate oppression by fomenting racism, classism, sexism, homophobia, and other forms of domination behind bars.

Imprisonment is a form of slavery. The Thirteenth Amendment to the U.S. Constitution states that slavery and involuntary servitude cannot exist in the United States, except as a punishment for crime. This amendment was passed after the Civil War, when the system of chattel slavery was forced out of existence. Coinciding with the Thirteenth Amendment, southern states passed Black Codes, laws that made acts like unemployment and insubordination illegal for African Americans only. States also instituted or expanded convict leasing, which permitted people convicted of crimes to be rented out to companies and plantation owners for labor. The collective impact of these policies allowed states to exchange one form of slavery for another. Though most prisoners in the 21st century do not work, the total ownership and control of incarcerated persons by governments and private corporations constitute a condition of slavery.

Prison reform will not alleviate the problems with prison. Rather than solve incarceration's enduring abuses, prison reforms often widen the net of the criminal punishment system or make it more efficient. Many of the reforms successfully fought for by activists in the 1970s, such as fixed sentences and increased parole and probation, prevent judges from considering extenuating circumstances and bring more people under the authority of the criminal punishment system.

Movement History

After being sentenced to 1-year-to-life at the age of 18 for allegedly stealing $70 from a gas station in 1958,

George Jackson became one of the leading theorists of the anti-prison struggle during the black power movement. In his 12th year of prison, Jackson and two other black men were accused of murdering a white prison guard. The same year, Angela Y. Davis, an activist and former philosophy professor at the University of California–Los Angeles, was arrested and imprisoned on charges associated with trying to free Jackson and the other men from Soledad Prison. The Soledad Brothers, as they came to be known, were acquitted of all charges, but Jackson was killed by prison guards before the court case. Incited by Jackson's murder and inhumane prison conditions, prisoners staged a mass riot at Attica Correctional Facility in New York in 1971 and several smaller revolts around the nation. In 1972, Davis was acquitted of all charges stemming from the Soledad Brothers' case and continued her career as a leading activist and scholar in the women's liberation, black power, and anti-prison movements.

As the U.S. prison population doubled in the late 1980s and tripled in the mid-1990s, organizers and communities began a widespread outcry against mass incarceration. Activists and writers began using the term *prison-industrial complex* to explain the proliferation of prisons after sociologist Mike Davis (no relation to Angela Davis) promulgated the term in a 1995 magazine article. In 1997, Angela Davis and other activists, academics, and former prisoners began to organize a national conference designed to build a mass movement against the prison-industrial complex. The conference, which occurred in Berkeley, California, in 1998, drew 3,500 participants and resulted in the formation of Critical Resistance, a national organization dedicated to prison abolition. Many local and regional anti-prison groups, including a strong coalition of youth organizers, also grew from the 1998 conference. Two years later, a subsequent conference called the Color of Violence brought together women of color involved in the anti-violence and anti-prison movements. A new organization, Incite: Women of Color Against Violence, emerged from this conference. Working with other anti-racist feminist organizations, Incite has centered concerns for safety from violence within the anti-prison movement while challenging anti-violence advocates to consider approaches for public safety that do not rely on law enforcement. Women of color, as well as young people, former prisoners, community organizers, and scholars, continue to work at the forefront of the contemporary anti-prison movement.

The Context of the Contemporary Anti-Prison Movement

The United States incarcerates more people than any other nation in the world. In the year 2000, the U.S. prison population reached 2 million. During the 1990s, more people were added to the nation's prison population than during any other decade in U.S. history. Currently, 2.1 million people are held in U.S. prisons, over 70% for nonviolent offenses. Most of these convictions stem from drug-related arrests fueled by the War on Drugs. Though people of color do not commit more crime than whites in any category of crime, half of all prisoners are African American and over 70% are people of color. The prison-industrial complex (i.e., the confluence of private and public institutions within the criminal punishment system) ties imprisonment to political and economic interests that feed off of such racist practices. Many politicians have found promises to get "tough on crime" are successful at generating votes. Companies that own prisons (e.g., the Corrections Corporation of America) sell their stocks on the U.S. stock exchange, allowing members of the general public to literally invest in incarceration. In addition to eradicating prisons, the anti-prison movement seeks to sever public and private investments in an industry of punishment.

Prominent Campaigns Within the Anti-Prison Movement

Educating Communities About the Prison-Industrial Complex. Anti-prison activists foster public education and awareness of the problems about the prison-industrial complex through a variety of methods, including teach-ins, conferences, publications, and workshops. The Blackout Arts Collective, a national organization of artists of color, works to further this campaign through art. Blackout artists travel around the United States to share visual art, poetry, music, and theater about the prison industry as part of an annual summer tour called Lyrics on Lockdown.

Preventing the Construction of New Prisons. Grassroots organizers work to prevent the construction of new prisons by generating mass opposition to new prison development and organizing for state moratoriums on new prison construction, among other strategies. In 2000, Critical Resistance and the California Prison Moratorium Project filed a lawsuit against the California Department of Corrections to prevent construction of a new prison. The two anti-prison groups worked closely with environmental justice organizations. In 2001, a California judge halted construction of the prison, ordering studies of its environmental impacts.

Promoting Alternatives to Incarceration and Community-Based Solutions to Violence. Organizations that emphasize alternatives to incarceration and community-based solutions to violence help to answer the question most asked of prison abolitionists, "What will you do about the murderers and the rapists?" These groups promote a wide range of alternatives to incarceration and community-based solutions to violence, including conflict mediation, violence-free zones within communities, and group confrontations that hold offenders accountable. Radical feminist organizations such as Incite specifically focus on developing solutions that keep women of color safe because women of color are often left unprotected by law enforcement, have experienced violent abuse by police, and are distrustful of the criminal punishment system. Another organization, Generation Five, aims to stop child sexual abuse in five generations, by developing and implementing community responses to violence against children without reliance on the state. Most anti-prison organizations advocate restorative and transformative justice models that rely on principles of engagement, accountability, and reparations instead of isolation, punishment, and retribution.

—*Johonna R. McCants*

See also Davis, Angela; Drug Laws, Resistance to; Jackson, George; Prison-Industrial Complex

Further Readings

Braz, R., Brown, B., DiBenedetto, L., Gilmore, R., Gilmore, C., Hunter, D., et al. (2000). The history of Critical Resistance. *Social Justice, 27*(3), 6–10.

Davis, A. Y. (2003). *Are prisons obsolete?* New York: Seven Stories Press.

Davis, M. (1995, February 20). Hell factories in the field: A prison-industrial complex. *The Nation, 260*(7), 229–234.

Herzing, R., & Paglen, T. (2005). Abolishing the prison-industrial complex. *Recording Carceral Landscapes.* Retrieved July 27, 2006, from http://paglen.com/carceral/interview_rachel_herzing.htm

Knopp, F. H. (1976). *Instead of prisons: A handbook for abolitionists.* Syracuse, NY: Prison Education Action Research Project.

Sudbury, J. (2003). Toward a holistic anti-violence agenda: Women of color as radical bridge builders. *Social Justice, 30*(3), 134–141.

ANTI-RACIST TEACHING

For social justice–minded educators, teaching is indeed a political act, and teachers and students are constantly negotiating power relations both within and outside of the classroom walls. These negotiations have the potential to be both deconstructive and reconstructive. Anti-racist teaching stems from a position that racism is endemic to the global society. Through the unveiling of how racism functions through education, racism's deleterious effects in schools and classrooms can be analyzed and deconstructed. Reconstruction occurs when people ask, anti-racism for what ends? The answer differs for stakeholders in the educational system and results in a diverse set of approaches to anti-racist education.

Anti-racist education is also a response to disproportionately lower levels of success for students of color and higher racial violence in schools. In the field of education, the United States, Canada, and Australia have appropriated theories from British anti-racist education to theorize reform and social change through education. An increasing number of scholars have focused their research on the preparation of teachers for anti-racist teaching. Teachers have also published accounts of anti-racist teaching. This work shows that education may be employed as an instrument to bring awareness of unjust educational practices to students, teachers, families, and policymakers.

A Multicultural Movement in Education

Anti-racist education emerged out of a progressive social movement in education that included an emphasis on both culturally responsive teaching and multicultural education. Culturally responsive instruction centers on the idea that students have different histories of participation with literacy, schools, and social relationships, and schools are responsible for valuing these events and experiences. Multicultural education includes the cultural traditions, languages, and perspectives into the school curriculum and expands the artistic and literary curriculum to include works authored by racial and ethnic groups outside of the traditional Western canon.

In some educational debates, anti-racist education has been posited in opposition to multicultural education, although there are significant overlaps in the impetus for these pedagogies and how they are implemented. Anti-racist education emerged because multicultural education has often focused on culture without considering how cultural differences are accorded different value. Teaching from multicultural perspectives does not always include noticing and naming educational inequalities, equipping students and their families to understand how cultural differences are assigned value, and examining equity in terms of material and economic outcomes. Further, multicultural educators have failed to emphasize race in an attempt to eradicate racism from the classroom. In addition, anti-racist teaching has added a focus on institutional and individual racism, as well as a focus on class, which are absent in the multicultural movement. Finally, anti-racist teaching has an added

emphasis on critical dialogue to explicate injustices, a feature that is often absent in multicultural education.

Perspectives in Anti-Racist Teaching

Educators with diverse perspectives and methods conduct anti-racist teaching and research. Anti-racist teaching had its major impetus in the social movements of Canadian and British educators. Practices related to anti-racist teaching can bring awareness to inequities based on the negative valuation of ethnic, racial, or cultural characteristics. An anti-racist education provides opportunities for teachers and students to question racist or stereotyped thinking and how racial differences lead to inequalities in employment, breeches in human and civil rights, and violence against subjugated groups. Anti-racist educators hold a great number of theories about how anti-racism develops within individuals and social groups as well as in institutions.

Some progressive educators hold that anti-racist teaching is fundamentally social. Informed by critical theories of race that posit that conflict between races is a threat to society, anti-racist educators view race as a fundamental principle of social organization. Therefore, anti-racist education relies on what Paulo Freire called critical dialogue, in which many perspectives come into conversation with one another. Together, people draw on cultural knowledge to engage in a comparative or contrastive dialogue to build theories that hold the power to reshape society.

Anti-racist teaching also attends to individual growth and identity development. Identities often acquire their meaning from the other, and the structures in society provide privilege for some and injustice for others. Understanding the individual's identity within a group's experience is a central goal of anti-racist pedagogy. Often, movements for social change have excluded the multiple subject positions of identity groups. Therefore, anti-racist pedagogy includes an emphasis on the subjectivities of individuals; for example, young African Americans experience racism in different ways based on gender, class, and sexual orientation.

In addition, anti-racist educators posit that racism acts as a screen door between youth and opportunity. Therefore, anti-racist education holds to the idea that outcomes are as important as intentions. Outcomes that would signal anti-racist education's success include equitable job opportunity and the revision of who holds cultural capital and power in society.

Anti-Racist Education Approaches

There are various ways to teach in anti-racist ways. Often, anti-racist teaching occurs through the careful selection of materials. Teaching materials are often chosen because they represent a variety of cultures in an authentic and sensitive manner. Teachers often choose materials that reflect a multitude of perspectives and bring these perspectives into dialogue. Anti-racist educators often employ critical dialogue, problem posing, and critical literacy pedagogy to the examination of carefully selected materials.

Often, anti-racist educators will use students' language and experience as the basis for an anti-racist lesson. For example, a teacher may ask students to investigate language practices or cultural practices in their families and communities that are misunderstood by other cultural groups. However, one caution from anti-racist educators is that teachers must explore their own culture and language from a critical perspective before attempting this pedagogy with students.

Many scholars have drawn on the burgeoning field of whiteness studies with white teachers who are learning to teach in university programs or in professional development settings. Whiteness studies connect the construction of white racial identity to the reproduction of racism. The idea behind whiteness studies is to take a close look at what our hegemonic culture holds as values, goals, and assumptions and to question the normalization of such an ideology.

Likely, institutions become anti-racist, culturally responsive, and multicultural in stages, as people begin to think about how racism exists within the institution and work to change the conditions. Often, this might begin with a group investigation of current practices, followed by experimentation with anti-racist initiatives. However, much anti-racist teaching occurs in everyday interactions between teachers, students, and families, so it is essential that members of a school participate in individual and collective efforts to understand how race and racism function at various levels.

Challenges to Anti-Racist Teaching

There have been a number of challenges to anti-racist teaching. On one hand, anti-racist teaching has been posed as reductionist: assigning inequality in education to inadequate binaries, therefore increasing racial tensions or reifying the construction of race. On the other hand, anti-racist teaching focuses on the political dimensions of society and may function to remove emphasis from academic achievement. Finally, anti-racist educators have been critiqued for not clearly defining racism and how it functions in society.

Relating to the first point, educators and administrators are fearful that explorations of race and racism may lead to increased tension in a school. Over time, public schools have been thought of as politically neutral spaces. Whereas multicultural education purports to be neutral and unbiased, anti-racist teaching is often named as political.

Further, anti-racist practices often focus on the black–white binary that is assigned meaning in Marxist theories of social class. This position is problematic for whites and ethnic groups that have a minority status. For whites, such an approach makes it difficult to name and notice racist practices; for other ethnic groups, there are increasing stakes for nonwhite groups that may be invisible within the binary construction of race.

In an age of standards and accountability in Western schooling, the question of equity in education has been complicated. The idea that education should awaken and reform current inequalities is often subverted by an emphasis on raising achievement on standardized, high-stakes tests. The consequences of a political education are that if the necessary attention is not paid to test preparation, a school can literally be put out of business.

Many anti-racist educators have been critiqued for not working from a clear understanding of racism. Moreover, many educators are not aware of the emotions and understandings about race that have been learned over time and therefore do not successfully implement anti-racist instruction. Indeed, anti-racist teaching cannot be learned in a short-term course for teachers. Educators usually have found the most success when participating in long-term racial awareness training with a cohort or support group as the process of teaching about race and racism begins.

—Melissa R. Mosley

See also Critical Literacy; Freire, Paulo; Multicultural Education

Further Readings

Dei, G. J. S. (1996). *Anti-racism education theory and practice.* Halifax, Nova Scotia: Fernwood.

Figueroa, P. (1991). *Education and the social construction of "race."* London: Routledge.

Gillborn, D. (1995). *Racism and antiracism in real schools: Theory, policy, practice.* Buckingham, UK: Open University Press.

Giovanni, N. (1994). *Racism 101.* New York: William Morrow.

Howard, G. (1999). *We can't teach what we don't know: White teachers, multiracial schools.* New York: Teachers College Press.

Mansfield, E., & Kehoe, J. (1994). A critical examination of anti-racist education. *Canadian Journal of Education, 19,* 418–430.

McIntyre, A. (1997). *Making meaning of whiteness: Exploring racial identity with white teachers.* Albany: SUNY Press.

Tatum, B. D. (1997). Teaching white students about racism: The search for white allies and the restoration of hope. *Teachers College Record, 95,* 462–476.

ANTI-SLAVERY MOVEMENT

See ABOLITIONIST MOVEMENTS

ANTI-SMOKING CAMPAIGNS

See KOOP, C. EVERETT

ANTI-SWEATSHOP MOVEMENT

Sweatshop practices have existed in labor history since the Industrial Revolution in the late 18th and early 19th century. Since that time, collective protests and welfare reforms have succeeded in enacting and enforcing progressive labor laws. From the end of the 20th century on, the globalization of capitalism and the development of transnational corporations have brought back this social issue on an unprecedented scale in North America, Western Europe, and more predominantly, in the Third World countries. Through structural adjustment programs, the International Monetary Fund and the World Bank have exerted considerable pressure on low-income states to embrace neoliberal reforms, create export-oriented industries, and promote free-trade zones. To manufacture their products, Europe- and U.S.-based clothing and apparel manufacturers have taken advantage of these policy shifts and have been increasingly subcontracting companies whose assembly-line plants are set up in Africa and Asia as well as in the Caribbean Basin and Central America.

Since the early 1990s, anti-sweatshop movement activists have denounced the abuse of workers in factories overseas by the subcontractors of manufacturers and retailers such as Liz Claiborne, Nike, Phillips–Van Heusen, Sears, Gap Inc., and Wal-Mart, among others. Workers, mainly young women, are not only exposed to excessive compulsory overtime, lack of insurance coverage, and low pay (which is far below subsistence wage), but they are also submitted to forced birth control, unhealthy food, and verbal harassment. Furthermore, their unionization efforts have been continuously repressed by governments that rely heavily on foreign investors to meet the multilateral agencies economic requirements. These social struggles often involve physical intimidation, death threats, and mass firings of union supporters by company management, which may ultimately decide to close down and relocate the factory. The resulting lockout leaves workers unemployed and, very often, without any other viable livelihood.

To contest these working conditions and labor law violations, multilayered strategies have been elaborated by local activists, international labor unions, and non-governmental organizations such as the Campaign for Labor Rights, the National Labor Committee, the Union of Needletrades, Industrial and Textile Employees, and the United Students Against Sweatshops. Their difficult implementation reveals the tangled complexities of the globalization process. The strength and the durability of these transnational networks are in fact conditioned by their ability to cross gender, geographical, linguistic, and social boundaries in order to develop an effective local activism in the Third World countries and to warn the consuming audience in the Western postindustrial centers against these illegal manufacturing processes.

For the most part, garment workers are facing a domestic historical and political context that makes problematical even the possibility of establishing trade unions and calling for collective bargaining. For instance, the authoritarian nature of Latin American states has long been supported by the United States and, to a lesser extent, by the American Federation of Labor–Congress of Industrial Organizations in order to contain communist movements and popular protests. Deprived of a solid union tradition and submitted to desperate socioeconomic conditions, workers are frequently reduced to coordinating their activities on a clandestine basis before being able to create their own independent organization and initiate negotiations. Their legal recognition is contested not only by subcontractors but also by local governmental authorities, which may receive the implicit support of U.S. embassies.

Supported by a wide range of collective actors, cross-border tactics are designed to convey these domestic protests at an international level and to put pressure on both companies and states. A multiplicity of strategies is brought into play, such as boycott, leafleting, petitions, picketing, or sits-in on university campuses. Along with media campaigns, these strategies attempt to give emphasis to contradictions between the ethical brand image carefully marketed by companies among Western consumers and the oppressive sweatshop labor surreptitiously experienced by their factory workers in the developing countries. Corporations are thus compelled to curtail the exploitation system set up by their subcontractors. These strategies may also lead the U.S. government to place under review the low-income states that are entitled to the benefits of the Generalized System of Preferences. Instituted in 1976, this program provides countries with preferential duty-free treatment for their products under restrictive conditions, such as workers' rights to organize and bargain collectively as well as receive minimum wages.

The combination of domestic and cross-border activism turned out to be valuable in the short run. Transnational corporations and local ministries of labor have often been obliged to rehire fired workers, recognize the independent unions, and negotiate an agreement. However, as several scholars and social justice activists have pointed out, these victories are limited in the long run. For instance, unionized factories can be relocated by subcontractors.

Institutional responses have also had limited results. In October 1996, the Clinton administration set up the Apparel Industry Partnership, a task force designed to develop regulatory codes of conduct and principles of monitoring the workplace. However, representatives of the manufacturing industry, labor unions, grassroots organizations, and the task force never succeeded in agreeing on independent monitoring, freedom of association, and minimum wages. Formally founded in 1999, its successor, the Fair Labor Association, succeeded in imposing external and internal audits; the effectiveness of these audits has yet to be properly evaluated. If the anti-sweatshop movement has not yet been able to counter the social injustice generated by global capitalism, this activism reveals the existence of a real and hopeful cross-border labor solidarity whose conceptualization and implementation remains to be deepened.

—*Jean-Philippe Dedieu*

See also Anti-Globalization Movement; Government Suppression of Social Activism; Social Movements, Sociology of

Further Readings

Armbruster-Sandoval, R. (2005). *Globalization and cross-border labor solidarity in the Americas: The anti-sweatshop movement and the struggle for social justice.* New York: Routledge.

Keck, M., & Sikkink, K. (1998). *Activists beyond borders: Advocacy networks in international politics.* Ithaca, NY: Cornell University Press.

Louie, M. (2001). *Sweatshop warriors: Immigrant women workers take on the global factory.* Cambridge, MA: South End Press.

Rosen, E. (2002). *Making sweatshops: The globalization of the U.S. apparel industry.* Berkeley: University of California Press.

Starr, A. (2000). *Naming the enemy: Anti-corporate movements confront globalization.* London: Zed Books.

ANTI–VIETNAM WAR MOVEMENT

See CONSCIENTIOUS OBJECTORS TO WAR; DRAFT RESISTANCE; JOHNSON, LYNDON; WAR RESISTERS' INTERNATIONAL

ANTI-WAL-MART MOVEMENT

Founded in 1962 by Sam Walton, Wal-Mart has grown to become one of the largest corporations in the world. By 2006, Wal-Mart operated nearly 5,000 outlets in 15 countries with 1.3 million–plus direct employees. In the fiscal year ending January 31, 2006, Wal-Mart reported earnings of more than 312 billion U.S. dollars and a profit of more than $11 billion. In many ways, Wal-Mart seems a corporate success story, but in recent years, harsh criticism of Wal-Mart's practices has arisen on a variety of fronts.

Wal-Mart has been accused of a wide range of unethical, unfair, and even illegal business and employment practices. The company has been the subject of a class action suit over gender discrimination (the largest ever certified against a private employer) and has been accused of systemic racial discrimination; predatory pricing aimed at eliminating local competition in order to create effective monopolies;

destroying local businesses and economies; encouraging exploitation and massive human rights violations in its dealings with foreign manufacturers (particularly in China); substantially lowering overall retail wage rates; failing to provide adequate and affordable health care benefits to employees; subsidizing its low wage and benefit rates through publicly funded programs like Medicaid and food stamps programs; actively and aggressively working to prevent unionization of its workforce, including intimidation and store closures; failing to pay employees for overtime hours worked; causing environmental damage in the construction and operation of its stores; contributing substantially to urban sprawl; failing to contribute to the communities in which it operates. This is not a complete list, but it does capture many of the primary issues around which the anti-Wal-Mart movement is generally focused.

Wal-Mart denies most of these accusations, citing their operations as engines of economic growth providing jobs both in North America and abroad. The company also argues that it contributes to communities not only by providing jobs but also by providing competitive pricing and access to relatively inexpensive goods that are a benefit to low-income and working families. Those involved in the anti-Wal-Mart movement generally acknowledge that Wal-Mart undoubtedly employs many people and provides access to cheap consumer products, but that these benefits are limited and do not outweigh the harms caused by Wal-Mart in the previously listed ways. Moreover, they argue that Wal-Mart reaps enormous profits via the causing of these harms and by exploiting the poorest segments of the population both domestically and in overseas manufacturing plants.

In contrast to many other movements, such as anti-globalization or environmentalism, for example, the anti-Wal-Mart movement is not necessarily focused on one specific set of issues but rather consists of a range of issue-oriented campaigns and groups coalescing around a single target. As a result, the anti-Wal-Mart movement has, in recent years, brought together perhaps unlikely partnerships. Anti-globalization activists, trade unionists, and environmentalists often work together with small business owners and free enterprise supporters to fight the expansion of Wal-Mart in various communities.

Pittsfield Community First is a grassroots citizens group of more than 350 Pittsfield Township, Saline, and Ann Arbor area residents joining forces to stop the building of a proposed Wal-Mart. The group has organized phone-call and letter-writing campaigns to government officials and has appeared at township and county meetings. Such community-based collective grassroots anti-Wal-Mart campaigns are increasing throughout North America and elsewhere and meeting with some success.

Source: Photo © Brave New Films.

Although the issues of concern to trade unionists or anti-globalization activists may be quite different from those of free enterprise supporters concerned with Wal-Mart's attempts to monopolize markets, or small business owners combating predatory pricing practices, these parties find common ground in opposition to Wal-Mart.

In uniting diverse groups around a common cause, the anti-Wal-Mart movement perhaps exemplifies a shift in social activism practices. Whereas activist groups have often focused on specific issues and causes, such as environmentalist groups concerned primarily with pollution or anti-globalization activists focused on international trade, the anti-Wal-Mart movement brings a diverse range of groups together around a central objective. In many areas in the United States, for example, whole communities, featuring diverse sets of interests and concerns, have come together in a common movement to successfully halt Wal-Mart expansion into their communities. Such community-based, collective, grassroots anti-Wal-Mart campaigns are increasing throughout North America and elsewhere and meeting with some success. In addition, the public focus that the anti-Wal-Mart movement has focused and continues to focus on such a diverse group of activists and such a wide range of issues helps connect global concerns, such as human rights violations, exploitive labor practices, and global environmental degradation, with local issues, such as domestic job loss, falling wage rates, and the destruction of local communities.

The enormous growth of Wal-Mart and its domination of the retail market have forced many of its competitors to adopt new strategies in order to survive. Similarly, it seems that Wal-Mart's power, influence, and the litany of allegations directed against it have encouraged the diverse groups of activists and organizations making up the anti-Wal-Mart movement to employ new strategies in combating what they see as a common and powerful enemy.

—*Cory Fairley*

See also Anti-Consumerism; Anti-Globalization Movement; Anti-Sweatshop Movement; Environmental Movement; Union Movements

Further Readings

Fishman, C. (2005). *The Wal-Mart effect: How the world's most powerful company really works—and how it's transforming the American economy.* New York: Penguin Press.

Greenwald, R. (Director). (2005). *Wal-Mart: The high cost of low price* [Video recording]. Culver City, CA: Brave New Films.

Ortega, B. (1998). *In Sam we trust: The untold story of Sam Walton and how Wal-Mart is devouring America.* New York: Times Business.

Quinn, B. (2005). *How Wal-Mart is destroying America and the World: And what you can do about it* (3rd ed.). Berkeley, CA: Ten Speed Press.

ANZALDÚA, GLORIA (1942–2004)

Gloria Evangelina Anzaldúa was an influential Chicana feminist scholar and activist. Born in the Rio Grande Valley of Texas in 1942, Gloria Anzaldúa worked as a migrant worker in her youth and fell in love with reading at age 9. She went on to earn a B.A. degree from Pan American University and her M.A. from the University of Texas at Austin. At the time of her death, Anzaldúa worked as a lecturer at University of California at Santa Cruz where she was weeks away from defending her doctoral dissertation. Anzaldúa was 61 when she passed away on May 16, 2004, from complications related to diabetes.

Gloria Anzaldúa's ideas and writings have influenced and shaped discussions about feminism, cultural theory, queer theory, communication theory, spirituality, and Chicano/a studies. Her writings and edited anthologies are widely used in colleges and universities globally. In addition to her academic contributions, Anzaldúa serves as an activist role model for many communities. Through her efforts to raise consciousness about various forms of oppression, Anzaldúa helped to build an inclusive feminist movement.

Anzaldúa's writing career was over 23 years long and includes essays, poetry, children's books, scholarly research, folk tales, autobiography, and political commentary. Her works mix genres and go beyond a monolingual approach. Anzaldúa wrote in a flowing combination of English and Spanish. She was among the first Chicana writers to claim and write about her lesbian identity. Anzaldúa also wrote about her own spirituality as influenced by her grandmother.

She is best known for her book *Borderlands/ La Frontera* (1987), which was named one of the 100 Best Books of the century by the *Utne Reader* and *Hungry Mind Review*. *Borderlands/La Frontera* examines the conflict inherent to the border between the United States and Mexico and tells the history of the twice-conquered people. Anzaldúa addresses causes of oppression and linguistic terrorism and discusses the necessarily fluid mestiza consciousness.

Other published works by Anzaldúa include, but are not limited to, a collection coedited with Cherríe Moraga titled *This Bridge Called My Back: Writings by Radical Women of Color* (1981) and *Making Face, Making Soul /Haciendas Cara: Creative and Critical Perspectives by Feminists-of-Color* (1990). Anzaldúa authored two children's books, *Friends from the Other Side/Amigos del otro lado* (1993) and *Prietita and the Ghost Woman/Prietita y la Llorona* (1995). Another collection of feminist writings, coedited with AnaLouise Keating, is titled *This Bridge We Call Home: Radical Visions for Transformation* (2002).

Anzaldúa received numerous awards for her writings and activism. Some of the awards are the Before Columbus Foundation American Book Award, the Lambda Lesbian Small Book Press Award, NEA (National Endowments for the Arts) Fiction Award, the Lesbian Rights Award, the Sappho Award of Distinction, and the American Studies Association Lifetime Achievement Award.

—*Sabrina Worsham*

See also Chicano Movement; Feminist Research; Queer Theory

Further Readings

Benavides, Y. (2004, May 30). Gloria Anzaldúa—poet, critic, feminist, seeker of dignity: South Texas scholar died this month. *San Antonio Express News*, p. 7J.

de la Tierra, T. (2004, July 1). Gloria E. Anzaldúa, author of *Borderlands*, dies. *Criticas*, p. 8.

Martinez, T. (2005, September/October). Making oppositional culture, making standpoint: A journey into Gloria Anzaldúa's *Borderlands*. *Sociological Spectrum, 25*(5), 539–570.

Tavitas-Williams, J. (2004, May 18). Anzaldúa wrote books for kids and adults; Scholar's *Borderlands/La Frontera* collection made two top 100 lists. *San Antonio Express-News*, p. 4B.

Woo, E. (2004, May 28). Radical feminist author: Acclaimed writings merged genres. *Montreal Gazette*, p. E7.

APARTHEID

See ANTI-APARTHEID MOVEMENT

APPROPRIATE TECHNOLOGY MOVEMENT

The underlying philosophy of the appropriate technology (AT) movement continues to be a provocative approach to directing development and studying technology. At the heart of the movement is the idea of technology choice: Alternative technologists assert that there are many possibilities for adopting technologies, each having a social consequence, and these possibilities must be evaluated in light of the long-range needs of the community where the technology will be used. One of the most provocative legacies of AT is the idea that any given technology is a manifestation of a particular cultural, social, and economic arrangement and a certain environment. These variables make the technology of one region unsuitable for direct implementation in another.

The movement was established in the early years of the Cold War, when the difficulty of industrialization was of critical importance. The struggle between the capitalist First World and the communist Second World for control over the developing Third World led to the effort to modernize economies through the transplantation of "inappropriate" technologies. Appropriate technologists deplored the fact that industrial development benefited only a few industrialists. Furthermore, the imported industrial processes ignored the local knowledge of the host country; because there was no corresponding research and development effort in the host country, the burgeoning industry would be dependent on the knowledge and support of the industrial exporters. What is more, these exported industries used raw materials available only in the exporting country, and even though the host country might have an available substitute, the resources of the host country were ignored because the country did not have technical experts who were able to adapt the industrial processes. These conditions meant that the developing countries lacked the capital, industrial infrastructure, and technical knowledge to become truly developed nations and instead became increasingly dependent despite their newly won independence from colonialism.

Although AT acknowledges its debt to Gandhi's program of satyagraha, most say the movement was born in 1965 as the Intermediate Technology Development Group Limited in London, founded by Ernst Friedrich Schumacher, George McRobie, and Julia Porter. Schumacher first promoted the idea of "intermediate technology" with his colleagues at an Oxford University conference in 1968 and brought the idea to a wider audience in his book *Small Is Beautiful* in 1973. The idea of an intermediate technology is one that is somewhere between the un- or underdeveloped state of the Third World and the highly advanced state of the First or Second World. Instead of deploying advanced technology as part of a program of international aid, Schumacher suggested a middle, intermediate step that would be more beneficial to the host country.

Schumacher was distressed by the large-scale institutionalized poverty in developing countries. Schumacher focused on villages or small regions for development, promoting labor-intensive methods with low capitalization in the hope that these would provide greater employment and benefit the overall population. Sharma and Quereshi discuss an example of this type of AT program; that is, the idea of modernizing India's paper production industry. A factory that creates paper completely by hand can produce 100 kg of paper per day, while factories in industrialized countries can make 500 metric tons per day. The decision of what to do for India can be discussed through the lens of AT by considering the availability of raw materials, finances, local knowledge, and time required to set up a factory.

One proposition for India is to build factories that can make 200 metric tons of paper a day. For such a large enterprise, capital expenditures are significant: Raw materials have to travel 300 km; a water supply, a power plant, and means to treat the effluent must be developed, as they are not part of the local infrastructure; and chemicals must be imported. Employment at such mills is not large; a mill that produces

100 metric tons per day at a cost of 400 million rupees employs 3,000 people; thus, 130,000 rupees are spent to create one job.

On the other hand, smaller mills—ones that create 5 to 20 metric tons per day, which would be impractical in industrial countries—can use local agricultural material like cotton waste, rice straw, and wild grass. The capital cost per ton is 1.5 million rupees, and each such mill employs 150 people. A small mill requires only 50,000 rupees to create one job as opposed to 130,000 rupees; thus, the small mill creates more employment for the same investment. Furthermore, a small mill is not a strain on water resources, and the effluent is not noxious. Because this type of mill cannot be imported, in order to build these mills, India would have to standardize its own equipment, thus spurring local knowledge development. Thus, the AT analysis shows that the best option for India is to set up a large number of smaller paper mills.

In the popular ethos of the 1970s, AT became more about alternative technologies that would lead to self-sufficiency. In his critique of this attitude, *Paper Heroes*, Rybczynski finds failure with many appropriate technologists because they fail to consult the population where a technology is going to be implemented before deploying their plan; appropriate technology, he asserts, only works when it is accompanied the understanding of an affected people. Rybczynski concludes that most technologies that are offered as alternatives simply benefit the wealthier and landed classes. In his analysis of bio-gas plants, for instance, he points out that only large-scale farmers have the ability to benefit from the alternative; smaller farmers—the ones for whom AT is supposed to be a benefit—have neither sufficient agricultural waste nor a place to process it.

A collection of Schumacher's essays, *This I Believe*, covers AT-related issues. McRobie builds on the ideas in Schumacher's *Small Is Beautiful* by suggesting practical implementations. In addition, Willoughby provides a thoroughly researched academic treatment of the movement.

—*Chris Leslie*

See also Gandhi, Mohandas K.

Further Readings

McRobie, G. (1981). *Small is possible.* New York: Harper & Row.

Rybczynski, W. (1980). *Paper heroes: A review of appropriate technology.* Garden City, NY: Anchor Press.

Schumacher, E. F. (1973). *Small is beautiful: Economics as if people mattered.* New York: Harper & Row.

Schumacher, E. F. (1997). *This I believe and other essays* (S. Kumar, Ed.). Totnes, Devon, UK: Green Books.

Sharma, K. D., & Qureshi, M. A. (1979). *Alternative technology: Proceedings of the seminar held in September 1975 under the joint auspices of the IIAS, Simla and CSIR, New Delhi.* Simla, India: Indian Institute of Advanced Study.

Willoughby, K. W. (1990). *Technology choice: A critique of the appropriate technology movement.* Boulder, CO: Westview Press.

AQUINO, CORAZON (1933–)

Corazon "Cory" Aquino was president of the Philippines from 1986 to 1992. The country's—and Asia's—first female head of state, she personified the 1986 "People Power" uprising that overthrew the dictator Ferdinand Marcos and restored elite democracy in the Philippines.

Aquino was born into one of the Philippines' richest landowning families, the Cojuangcos of Tarlac Province. She was formally educated in the Philippines and the United States. In 1955, Aquino married Benigno "Ninoy" Aquino, Jr., a rising star in Philippine politics. Ninoy later became provincial governor, senator, and then Marcos's chief rival. When Marcos declared martial law in 1972, he jailed Ninoy, as well as other political opponents. In 1980, with Cory and the rest of his family, Ninoy was granted permission to travel to the United States for heart surgery. He returned in 1983 and was assassinated in the airport.

Aquino remained in her husband's shadow—a self-described housewife—until his assassination. Thereafter, she came to symbolize Filipino suffering under the dictatorship, which committed countless human rights atrocities. She considered herself to be the best-known victim of the atrocities. Under pressure economically and politically—investors deserted the Philippines and mass grassroots opposition developed after the assassination—Marcos called for a "snap" presidential election for February 7, 1986. On December 3, 1985, after the acquittal of military officers accused of killing her husband, Aquino announced that she would run against Marcos, vowing to be his complete opposite. With vice-presidential bet Salvador "Doy" Laurel, Aquino's candidacy galvanized the left-liberal opposition. She is widely acknowledged to have handily won the election, though Marcos cheated her out of her victory. The vote fraud created an electoral crisis that then led to the defection of key Marcos allies and military factions to Aquino's camp. On February 22, 1986, millions of Filipinos rose in mass revolt in what was to become the People Power uprising. People Power disintegrated the Marcos dictatorship and swept Aquino into power. She was sworn into the presidency on February 25, 1986.

Despite her sweeping mandate, Aquino squandered the opportunity to fundamentally transform Philippine society. As president, Aquino restored a multiparty system, released political prisoners, pursued peace talks with the Maoist and Muslim insurgencies, and convened a constitutional commission, which finished a new constitution the following year. Filipinos relished the "democratic space" that she helped usher in. At the same time, however, she retained key Marcos personnel and economic policies during her administration. And, like Marcos, she allied herself with the United States, the political godfather behind the dictatorship. Aquino developed a reputation for being apolitical and standing above the fray between left and right. Yet, her decisions progressively catered to the right. In the face of repeated coup attempts, Aquino relied increasingly on the military—and in particular, former Marcos crony and turncoat General Fidel Ramos—for political survival. In 1992, she anointed Ramos her successor. Though she symbolized a high point in Philippine grassroots activism, in the end, Aquino succeeded in restoring traditional politics in the Philippines.

—*Eduardo R. C. Capulong*

See also Philippine People Power Revolution

Further Readings

Reid, R. (1995). *Corazon Aquino and the Brushfire Revolution.* Baton Rouge: Louisiana State University Press.

ARAB AMERICAN ACTIVISM

Arab Americans are U.S. citizens and permanent residents of Arab descent. Arabs speak Arabic and trace their roots to Algeria, Bahrain, Djibouti, Egypt, Iraq, Jordan, Kuwait, Lebanon, Libya, Mauritania, Morocco, Oman, Palestine, Qatar, Saudi Arabia, Somalia, Sudan, Syria, Tunisia, United Arab Emirates, and Yemen.

With no officially ethnic demographic category, estimates of the Arab American population vary from 1.2 to 3.5 million in 2000 and 25% are under the age of 18. While the majority of Arabs in the world are Muslim, the majority of Arab Americans are Christian (63%) and 24% are Muslim. The Arab American population is growing with an estimated 40% increase in the 1990s. More than 80% are U.S. citizens. An estimated 46% were born in the United States. Forty-eight percent of Arab Americans live in California, Florida, Michigan, New Jersey, and New York.

There were three major waves of Arab immigration to America. The initial wave of immigration occurred before World War II. The majority were Christians from Greater Syria who sought economic betterment. Consistent with the experiences of other immigrant groups, the first wave of Arab Americans largely assimilated into the dominant culture. This included Americanizing their family names and adopting English.

The second wave took place through the 1960s. Later waves of immigration brought a more nationally and religiously diverse as well as educated Arab population. Many were forced out of their countries of origin due to postcolonial social and political turmoil. The sociopolitical currents of the time, combined with a societal shift toward pluralism in America, gave rise to an Arab American identity in the late 1960s.

Early Arab American Activism

The challenges of economic betterment, assimilation, and the lack of a strong Pan-Arab identity limited early Arab American activism in the public sphere. However, literary and intellectual circles formed, and civic life increased. The nascent community increasingly focused on domestic and international issues.

One of its earliest causes was over racial classification and citizenship. Initially categorized as Turks and Syrians, legal battles ensued over whether Arabs were to be classified as "white" or not. Given the privileges associated with the "white" category, early organizations protested their classification as "Asiatic." After a ruling in a Georgia court case affirmed their nonwhite status, the Association for Syrian Unity was organized and sent a delegation to lobby in Washington, D.C. Despite Arab Americans obtaining legal "white" status in 1923, this did not protect Arab immigrants from disenfranchisement and segregation in the American South, nor did it prevent immigration limits from non-European countries.

Ameen Rihani, one of the renowned members of Khalil Gibran's Pen League, lectured on Arab independence, wrote extensively against the Ottoman empire, and promoted Arab thinkers. Arabic newspapers sprung up in New York and several other cities across America, with 102 Arabic periodicals and newspapers in 1929. Articles written by expatriate Arabs, such as Rihani and Gibran, had a profound effect in the Arab world. The Pen League revolutionized Arabic prose and advocated for national independence from the postwar colonial domination of the Arab world.

The 1917 British declaration of support for a Jewish homeland in Palestine sparked an international debate. Arab American organizations advocated against the establishment of a Jewish homeland in historic Palestine, whose indigenous population is largely Arab and of multiple faiths. They wrote articles and letters to the secretary of state, spoke before Congress, and organized a protest in Brooklyn. The Palestinian Antizionism Society and the Ramallah Young Men's Society attracted 500 demonstrators to the protest.

One of the longest-running Arab American organizations was founded in 1917. The Syrian Ladies' Aid Society was formed to help new immigrants. Local and national Arab American women's clubs have continued to flourish since then. They were social, charitable, or political. Some were transnational, such as the General Union of Palestinian Women. The Arab Movement of Women Arising for Justice draws parallels with communities of color.

Arab Americans have been prominently involved in other domestic and international movements since World War II. For example, Arab American civil rights activist and NAACP member, Ralph Johns challenged segregation by encouraging the 1960 sit-in at a Woolworth's lunch counter in Greensboro, North Carolina. Among other Arab Americans who made an impact are Ralph Nader, the leading force behind the consumer protection movement. Nagi Daifullah, a labor organizer and farmworker, was the first casualty in the struggle to unionize farmworkers in the grape fields of California's central valley. Candy Lightner founded Mothers Against Drunk Driving (MADD). In later years, Arab American activists worked in coalition with other movements, such as the anti-apartheid movement for South Africa.

Growth of Arab American Activism

The 1960s began a new phase of communal political involvement. In the Six-Day War of 1967, Israel destroyed the militaries of the surrounding Arab countries. This awakened Arab Americans to the critical need for activism. The war exposed the impotence of the Arab states. A just response to the Palestinian experience of loss and displacement appeared further away. The war also heightened popular anti-Arab bias, which resulted in general disdain for the Palestinians and their Arab allies. It also increased support for Israel.

In the context of the active student movement of the 1960s, Arab American student activism took root. The growth of the Arab American student movement was supported by the second wave of immigration and the arrival of foreign students after the passage of the Immigration and Nationality Services Act of 1965. One of the first major national student groups was the Organization of Arab Students, which grew to more than 50 chapters by the 1980s. Another national group, the General Union of Palestinian Students, emerged. It was in this post-1967 fallout that a young academic named Edward Said became politicized. He would go on to become a preeminent intellectual.

Though some groups existed during the 1967 war, such as the American Federation of Ramallah, Palestine, and the Southern Federation of Syrian Lebanese American Clubs, many more emerged in the immediate years after the war, including the Arab American Medical Association, the Association of Arab-American University Graduates, the National Association of Arab Americans, and the Palestine Congress of North America. Charity groups proliferated as well, such as the Beit Hanina Charity groups, the Jerusalem Fund, American Near East Refugee Aid, and United Palestinian Appeal.

In 1972, community activists in Detroit mobilized to prevent the demolition of an Arab American neighborhood. The city wanted to convert it into an industrial park. The success of the campaign led the activists to form the Arab Community Center for Economic and Social Services (ACCESS). It grew into a model for ethnic groups around the country. ACCESS established the Arab American National Museum in Dearborn, Michigan, in 2005.

In the late 1970s, agents working on the FBI ABSCAM sting operation dressed up as oil sheiks to bribe members of Congress. Their reliance on a stereotype inspired U.S. Senator James Abourezk to cofound the American-Arab Anti-Discrimination Committee (ADC) in 1980. The group's mission was to counter anti-Arab portrayals in the media. ADC's mission has since expanded to include civil rights and advocacy for balanced U.S. policy in the Middle East.

In 1985, James Zogby founded the Arab American Institute to increase Arab American involvement in political and civic life, such as its voter mobilization campaign called "Y'allah (Go) Vote!" The Census Bureau has designated the Arab American Institute as the Census Information Center for data on the Arab American community.

As Arab American activists organized, they faced increased governmental hostility and organized opposition. Several officials running for office refused to accept campaign contributions from Arab American organizations. With the Lebanese civil war, the Iran-Iraq war, and the bombing of Pan Am flight 103, Arabs were increasingly viewed as irrational and violent. Arab American activists, such as the "LA 8," faced deportation for their activism.

Other organizations targeted Arab American activists. One settled a 1993 class-action lawsuit with Arab American and progressive groups that accused the organization of espionage. This foreshadowed the plethora of post-9/11 groups committed to monitoring Arab American and Muslim institutions.

Though rare, some individuals attacked the offices of Arab American organizations, community spaces, businesses, and mosques. Alex Odeh, ADC's Southern California Regional Director, was killed in 1985 by a bomb attached to the door of the ADC office in Santa Ana, California. The FBI identified members of the Jewish Defense League as suspects. In 2005, Jewish Defense League leader Earl Krugel was convicted for a 2001 plan to blow up a Los Angeles–area mosque, the office of an Arab American congressman, and the office of the Muslim Public Affairs Council.

Arab American activism endured a roller coaster ride of events starting in the late 1980s. The Palestinian *intifada* (uprising) expanded American public sympathy for the Palestinians. While some activists supported American efforts in the Gulf War in the early 1990s, others opposed it. After the war, U.S.-led sanctions on Iraq caused a humanitarian disaster. Arab American activists adopted this issue. As for Palestine, Arab Americans largely supported the Oslo Accords and peace process.

As the Cold War receded, the traditionally secular left in the Arab world increasingly gave way to religionists. Asserting religious identity, some Arab American activists began to organize via local mosques and churches.

The 1996 Anti-Terrorism and Death Penalty Act allowed the use of secret evidence to deport suspected terrorists. Under this Act, the government began detaining prominent Muslim activists on the basis of evidence they could neither see nor contest. This foreshadowed the civil liberties issues that would arise out of the government's war on terrorism in 2001.

In 2000, a new Palestinian uprising began after the demise of the peace process. This inspired a new generation of Arab American and solidarity activists from diverse backgrounds. Student groups began organizing the Palestine Solidarity Movement. After the formation of Students for Justice in Palestine at the University of California, Berkeley, chapters spread across the country. Students and churches launched campaigns for divestment from companies profiting from Israel's occupation of Palestinian land. Since 2002, the Palestine Solidarity Movement has held annual conferences calling for divestment. Organizing alongside Palestinians, solidarity activists in the United States helped form the International Solidarity Movement in 2001; this organization facilitates nonviolent activism in the occupied territories.

Critical Arab American Issues and 9/11

In September 1999, the Michigan Advisory Committee to the U.S. Commission on Civil Rights held a community forum in Dearborn, Michigan, which has one of the largest concentrations of Arab Americans in the nation. The three primary issues that emerged at the forum as areas of concern regarding the civil rights of Arab Americans were racial profiling and detainment at airports and other ports of entry, denial of due process in deportation hearings, and discrimination. While the issues facing Arab Americans did not begin on September 11, 2001 (9/11), they have since then grown more significant.

According to ADC, over 700 violent incidents were reported in the first 9 weeks after 9/11, including several murders. With the launch of the war on Iraq in March 2003, an Afghan man was set on fire by two men in Indianapolis, Indiana. Someone bombed a Palestinian family's van in Burbank, Illinois. Others faced threats, harassment, vandalism, and attacks on religious institutions, all of which contributed to fear and anxiety.

The State Advisory Committees of the U.S. Commission on Civil Rights addressed civil rights concerns of Arab Americans after 9/11. In addition, community forums helped it document and respond to civil rights issues. Some of the critical issues facing Arab Americans include stereotyping and lack of understanding about Arabs and Islam; media bias; harassment, threats, and hate crimes; threats to civil liberties; racial profiling; changes in immigration policies; lack of government representation; preservation and continuity of Arab culture; and educational, employment, housing, and transportation discrimination. Further, educators were concerned by increasing threats to academic freedom at schools and universities across the country.

Federal, state, and local government officials and law enforcement actively intervened to address the violent backlash against the Arab, Muslim, and South Asian communities. In the week after 9/11, President George W. Bush addressed the nation from the Islamic Cultural Center in Washington, D.C. Congress passed a resolution asserting protection of civil rights and civil liberties. It condemned discrimination and attacks.

At the same time, the affected communities felt subject to government suspicion. U.S. authorities secretly detained hundreds of men of Middle Eastern descent in the days and weeks following 9/11. At the height of the detentions, there were over 1,100 individuals held indefinitely without charge, many of whom were later deported.

The USA PATRIOT Act broadened government powers regarding investigation, detention, and deportation. The three primary areas of concern regarding the Patriot Act are the legalization of indefinite detentions with little or no due process, expanded powers for surveillance and search and seize, and guilt by association. The FBI questioned thousands of Arabs and Muslims at home and work based on their country of origin. They scrutinized Arab and Muslim small business owners to search for financial ties to terrorist groups.

Arab American Activism After 9/11

The 9/11 attacks on the United States shifted Arab American activists away from Palestinian rights to the backlash and then the subsequent wars. Despite the climate of fear and silencing, Arab American activists worked to defend the civil rights of community members. They launched campaigns to educate Arabs and Muslims about their rights. In addition, legal activists confronted increasing discrimination faced by the community.

While Arab American activists focused much of their work on the protection of civil liberties in America, they did not lose sight of international issues. The struggle for justice in Palestine continued with the call for boycott, divestment, and sanctions. The Palestine movement linked with the mass mobilization in opposition to the 2003 war on Iraq and energized many activists. Though a vocal minority of Arab Americans supported the war on Iraq, Arab American organizations largely called for a nonviolent solution.

Activists responded to the increased interest in the Arab American community in several ways. Arab American media has proliferated in the age of the Internet with the establishment of online resources such as *Electronic Intifada, Arab-American News*, and *Palestine Chronicle.* Arab America began asserting itself culturally through artists, activists, writers, musicians, rappers, and comedians. Arts and culture publications, such as *Al-Jadid* and *Mizna,* progressed. Similarly, increased access to Arab media outlets provided Arab American activists information they could not find in the American media. Since 9/11, Arab Americans and their young institutions are better positioned for self-representation and agency with the government.

—*William Youmans and Muna Shami*

See also Nader, Ralph; Said, Edward

Further Readings

American-Arab Anti-Discrimination Committee. (2003). *Report on hate crimes and discrimination against Arab Americans: The post–September 11 backlash—September 11, 2001–October 11, 2002.* Washington, DC: ADCRI.

Arab American Institute. (2006). *Arab American cemographics.* Retrieved June 1, 2006, from http://www.aaiusa.org/arab-americans/22/demographics

Brittingham, A., & de la Cruz, G. P. (2005). *Census 2000 Special Reports: We the people of Arab ancestry in the United States.* Washington, DC: U.S. Census Bureau.

Hagopian, E. (Ed.). (2004). *Civil rights in peril: The targeting of Arabs and Muslims.* London: Pluto Press.

Kayyali, R. A. (2005). *The Arab Americans (The new Americans).* Westport, CT: Greenwood Press.

Naber, N. (2000). Ambiguous insiders: An investigation of Arab American invisibility. *Ethnic and Racial Studies, 23*(1), 37–61.

Suleiman, M. (Ed.). (2000). *Arabs in America: Building a new future.* Philadelphia: Temple University Press.

ARAFAT, YASSER (1929–2004)

Yasser Arafat, a controversial and polarizing leader for the Palestinians, became a key figure in the decades-long struggle between Israel and Palestine. Renowned for his red and white keffiyah headdress, Palestinians hailed Arafat as a martyr while Israelis ostracized him as an instigator and terrorist. Arafat began his political activism in the late 1940s during the Arab-Israeli War by smuggling in arms to Palestine and founding the militia group Al-Fatah. Arafat gained international status when he became chairman of the Palestine Liberation Organization (PLO). A milestone in Arafat's legacy was his declaration that the PLO would renounce violence and officially recognize Israel's statehood, paving the way for the 1993 Oslo Peace Accords, for which Arafat shared the 1994 Nobel Peace Prize.

Mohammed Abdel-Raouf Arafat As Qudwa al-Hussaeini was born on August 24, 1929, in Cairo, although it is believed that his birthplace may well be Jerusalem or Gaza. Yasser, his childhood name, lost his mother when he was 5 years old and moved in with his maternal uncle in Jerusalem, the capital of the British Mandate of Palestine. Four years later, Arafat's father had him return to Cairo. During the Arab-Israel War in 1947, Arafat returned to Jerusalem to fight in the Gaza area. In defeat, he returned to Cairo and studied engineering at the University of Cairo.

After graduating in 1956, Arafat briefly worked in Egypt and then moved to Kuwait and successfully ran his own contracting firm. He donated most of his profits to his political activities and his recently created Al-Fatah organization. In 1964, Arafat left Kuwait to become a revolutionist. That same year, the PLO was created by the Arab League.

Arafat became chairman of the PLO in 1969 and formed a military headquartered in Jordan, which then moved to Lebanon, and eventually reestablished in Tunisia. In 1988 Arafat changed policies; while addressing the United Nations, he announced that the PLO condemned terrorism, supported an independent Palestine, and acknowledged Israel as a state. With new prospects for peace, Arafat, Israeli prime minister Rabin, and Israeli foreign minister Peres negotiated the Oslo Peace Accords of 1993.

The 1996 Palestine elections made Arafat president of the Palestine Authority, governing the West Bank and Gaza Strip. In September 2000, the Second Intifada began. By 2003, Israeli prime minister Sharon had banned Arafat from peace talks to end the intifada and trapped him at home through constant bombing raids. A frail Arafat left his home to seek medical attention in Paris. Although Arafat's dream of an independent Palestinian state never materialized, the people for whom he had fought for more than 60 years remained faithful until his death on November 11, 2004, in Paris. A bachelor until 1990, Arafat is survived by his wife Suha and daughter Zahwa, named after his mother.

—Da'ad Naserdeen

See also Intifada (1987–1992, 2000–2003); Palestine
    Liberation Organization (PLO)

Further Readings

Gowers, A. (1994). *Arafat: The biography.* London: Virgin
    Books.
Wallach, J., & Wallach, J. (1997). *Arafat: In the eyes of the
    beholder.* New York: Lyle Stuart.

Arbenz, Jacobo (1913–1971)

Jacobo Arbenz Guzmán, who was elected president of Guatemala in 1951 and overthrown by a U.S.-organized coup in 1954, was born in Quetzaltenango, Guatemala, on September 14, 1913. He attended the national military academy, where he also taught for a number of years, during which time he married Maria Cristina Vilanova, daughter of a Salvadorean landowner, whose socialist ideas and associations deeply influenced his own views and subsequent policies.

Arbenz became a secret opponent of the Guatemalan dictator, Jorge Ubico, who, during the 1930s, had supported the ambitions of the powerful U.S.-based United Fruit Company, Guatemala's largest landowner and state within a state. In 1944, Arbenz helped lead a coup against Ubico's successor, General Francisco Ponce, bringing to power a provisional junta that wrote a new, progressive constitution, ending censorship, outlawing racism, and legalizing unions. Democratic elections led to the presidency of Juan Jose Arevalo, a former university professor who returned to the country after years in exile, and a period of widespread reforms. In 1951, the popular Arbenz, who had served as Defense Minister in the Arevalo government, was elected president, with 65% of the vote.

On June 17, 1952, Arbenz announced a new agrarian reform program, to redress the country's terrible problem of land inequality. In the process, 200,000 acres of uncultivated land owned by the United Fruit Company were appropriated, triggering the company's aggressive propaganda campaign in Washington, D.C., to induce the Eisenhower administration to overthrow the Arbenz government on the grounds that it was under Soviet influence. Although Arbenz had close relations with leading members of the small Guatemalan Communist Party, he was not a member (he joined only in 1957, long after the coup), nor was there any evidence of Russian influence on his policies. However, the argument was appealing to many prominent political figures, who often had long-standing relations with the United Fruit Company. These included Secretary of State John Foster Dulles, who characterized Guatemala as the scene of a communist type of terrorism.

The Central Intelligence Agency had actually started planning to bring down the Arbenz government through psychological warfare, political intervention, and, if need be, assassination, before the land reform program. That plan (named PBSuccess), which backed an ambitious army officer, Carlos Castillo Armas, culminated in a successful coup in mid-June 1954, which forced Arbenz into exile. In the subsequent months, political parties and peasant organizations were banned, and the land reform program was reversed. Under Armas, who was assassinated in 1957, and a succession of military dictators, Guatemala degenerated into one of the region's most repressive countries, where, for more than 30 years, an ongoing civil war claimed an estimated 100,000 lives, chiefly among Guatemala's indigenous (Mayan) communities. Arbenz eventually settled with his family in Cuba in 1960. Ten years later, he and his wife moved to Mexico City where, worn-out and depressed, not least by the suicide of his daughter several years earlier, he was found drowned in his bathtub on January 27, 1971. His remains were returned to Guatemala in 1995.

—Eric B. Ross

See also CIA Repression of Social Movements; Indigenous People and Social Justice

Further Readings

Cullather, N. (1999). *Secret history: The CIA's classified account of its operations in Guatemala, 1952–1954.* Palo Alto: Stanford University Press.

Doyle, K., & Kornbluh, P. (1997). *CIA and assassinations: The Guatemala (1954) documents.* Washington, DC. (National Security Archive Electronic Briefing Book No. 4)

Gleijeses, P. (1991). *Shattered hope: The Guatemalan Revolution and the United States, 1944–1954.* Princeton, NJ: Princeton University Press.

Harbury, J. (2000). *Searching for Everardo: A story of love, war and the CIA in Guatemala.* New York: Warner Books.

ARENAS, REINALDO (1943–1990)

Reinaldo Arenas was born in Cuba on July 16, 1943. His literary career began in 1963 when he won a contest hosted by the Biblioteca Nacional José Martí (José Martí National Library). He gained a post in the prestigious library and national acclaim. He then embarked on a prolific writing career dedicated to Cuban independence from what he perceived to be the despotic rule of Fidel Castro. Still, to this day, he is considered among the leading figures of Cuban literature to emerge since the revolution of 1959. He committed suicide on December 7, 1990, preferring to free himself from, rather than succumb to, AIDS complications. As is suggested by his autobiography's title, *Before Night Falls,* Arenas championed every human being's right to freedom and happiness, even in his dying days. He preferred death to a life full of suffering, just as he preferred political activism to a life of oppression. In all things, he espoused self-autonomy, no matter the fight or its outcome.

Cantando en el pozo (Singing From the Well) was the first in a series of five novels collectively called the Pentagonia. Though fiction, the Pentagonia, his most famous work, is framed as the secret history of Cuba under Fidel Castro. It is told from the perspective of an ever-changing protagonist who appears in each novel at a different stage of his life. *Cantando* is told from a child's perspective. *El palacio de las blanquisimas mofetas* (The Palace of the Pure White Skunks) is the second in the series and is told from the perspective of an adolescent. The next novel, *Otra vez el mar* (Farewell to the Sea), took three attempts to write, each time anew, because Castro confiscated it twice. The fourth is *El color de verano* (The Color of Summer). The fifth, *El asalto* (The Assault), protrays the protagonist later in his life.

Arenas was able to publish only one novel in Cuba, *Cantando.* The Cuban revolutionary government did not allow artists to write counterrevolutionary art, nor were they allowed to publish overseas. Given this climate, Arenas was forced to secretly publish in other countries and was subsequently arrested in 1970. He continued to write while in prison, secretly smuggling out his work. He remained in prison until 1976, after which he was forbidden to write. In 1980, during the Mariel Boatlift, he escaped Cuba amid the confusion of the 10,000 people who stormed the Peruvian embassy in the hope that they would be able to leave. He then lived out his life in the United States. At first he admired the United States for its ostensible ideals, but later he became disenchanted with the racist and hierarchical nature of the society and the division between classes, facts he parodied in his *El Portero* (The Doorman).

Apart from his novels, Arenas wrote several collections of short stories, began a monthly publication called *Mariel* and published on matters dealing with national and international cultural politics in several publications. He received numerous awards, including best foreign novelist in France 1969 and a Guggenheim fellowship in 1982. He was a professor for a brief time and spoke at several universities.

Much like his patron saint, Friar Servando Teresa de Mier, whose biography Arenas rewrote under the title *El mundo alucinante,* published in English as *The Ill-Fated Preregrinations of Fray Servando,* Arenas spent his life speaking truth to power, confronting the lethal blade of oppression. He lived his life as a gay dissident intellectual in the hopes of enjoying life, throughout its briefness, if not as a free human, then as one who fought for freedom until the very end.

—Alberto Morales

See also Castro, Fidel; Literature and Activism

Further Readings

Arenas, R. (1993). *Before night falls.* New York: Viking.

Solé, C. A., & Abreu, M. I. (Eds.). (1989). *Latin American writers.* New York: Scribner.

Soto, F. (1994). *Reinaldo Arenas: The Pentagonia.* Gainesville: University Press of Florida.

Soto, F. (1998). *Reinaldo Arenas.* New York: Twayne.

ARENDT, HANNAH (1906–1975)

Hannah Arendt was a German American political theorist, philosopher, and political commentator. Considered to be one of the most original and influential philosophers of the 20th century, Arendt became known for her application of phenomenological methods to her study of politics and for her analyses of totalitarianism, the public sphere, political action, freedom, and revolution.

Arendt was born in Hanover, Germany, and reared in Köningsberg. She studied theology and classics, as well as philosophy with Martin Heidegger at Marburg University. In 1929, she completed her doctoral dissertation on Saint Augustine's concept of love under the supervision of Karl Jaspers at Heidelberg University. In 1933, she was arrested for her work for the Zionist movement (a project on the Nazi anti-Semitic propaganda). On her release, she moved to France where she worked with Youth Aliyah, a Jewish children's refugee organization. In 1941, Arendt managed to emigrate to America, where she taught at the University of California, Berkeley, in 1955, the University of Chicago, 1963–1967, Wesleyan University and the New School for Social Research in New York, 1967–1975; cooperated with the journals *Jewish Social Studies, Jewish Frontier, Aufbau* and *Partisan Review;* and worked as an editor for the publishing house Schocken Books. During the years 1949–1951, she worked as an executive director of the Commission on European Jewish Cultural Reconstruction. She was a recipient of numerous academic distinctions and awards, such as the Lessing Prize in 1959, the Sigmund Freud Prize of the German Akademie für Sprache und Dichtung in 1967, and the Sonning Prize for Contributions to European Civilization in 1975.

In 1951, Arendt published *The Origins of Totalitarianism,* in which she analyzed the emergence of totalitarianism and investigated its relationship to the modern forms of anti-Semitism and 19th-century imperialism. In *The Origins of Totalitarianism,* she was one of the first political analysts to emphasize the analogy between Nazism and Soviet communism in (a) their annulment of the distinction between the private and the public arenas; (b) their bureaucratic socialization of citizens into loyal, powerless, and thoughtless dependents; (c) their ideological justifications; and (d) the accompanying terror and collapse of moral standards. Arendt suggested that modern totalitarianism proved the traditional understandings of evil inadequate. She therefore introduced the concept of "radical evil," understood as a systematic eradication of the conditions of humanity, such as plurality, autonomy, and individuality. For Arendt, the radical evil entailed the effect of making humanity superfluous. In *The Origins of Totalitarianism*, Arendt also discussed the issue of human rights and statelessness. She claimed that if human rights were derived solely from the concept of humanity and natural equality of people, they would be ineffective and unenforceable. She stated famously that people as rights-recipients were not born equal but became equal through their political agency. She also argued that human rights needed to be linked to the institution of citizenship in a sovereign state.

In 1958, Arendt published what is considered her major work in political theory, *The Human Condition*. In it, she dealt with the concerns of political life and the distinction between the public and private. She proposed that human activities could be categorized as labor (the biological necessities of human existence), work (the construction and fabrication of the non-natural world), or action (the liberating political engagement of people). She argued that characteristic of modern times was the expansion of the realms of labor and work at the expense of action. She also claimed that the conceptual distinction between the private and the public realms was inadequate, and argued instead for the recognition of the social realm, which she understood as an encroachment of the economic matters into public activities, and the subsequent commodification of political and moral values.

In 1958, Arendt published the biography of Rahel Varnhagen, which she wrote during her stay in Germany in the 1930s, titled *Rahel Varnhagen: The Life of a Jewish Woman*. In that book, Arendt was concerned with the problems of Jewish identity and assimilation. In the book, she employed her well-known notion of a "pariah," an observer and outsider who speaks from a position of difference. A year later, Arendt published her controversial essay on the African American civil rights movement, *Reflections on Little Rock*, in which she criticized the state practices of desegregation.

In her book *On Revolution* (1961), Arendt undertook a historical-philosophical analysis of revolutionary human action. She endorsed the paradigm of the American Revolution as an expression of free human action and as an impulse toward popular sovereignty and political responsibility for one's own community. In this way, Arendt challenged the liberal (French) model of the revolution, which seemed preoccupied with the principle of state noninvolvement rather than the establishment of popular government, as well as criticized the Marxist (Russian) revolutionary moment.

In 1961, Arendt traveled to Jerusalem where she worked as a correspondent for *The New Yorker*, covering the trial of Adolf Eichmann. Eichmann was an S.S. officer responsible for the realization of the "final solution to the Jewish question" during World War II. Her correspondence led to the publication of one of the most controversial of Arendt's books, *Eichmann in Jerusalem: A Report on the Banality of Evil* (1963). In this book, Arendt famously declared that Eichmann's evilness was "banal." While the meaning of that contention has remained contested, Arendt's argumentation linked the banality of Eichmann's evil to his inability to reflect critically on his own actions; that is, to think and articulate judgment. Arendt's students suggested later that the notion of the banality of evil was either inspired by her correspondence with Jaspers or suggested to her by her second husband, Heinrich Blücher. In *Eichmann in Jerusalem*, Arendt also claimed that the Jewish councils complied with the Nazi politics of the "final solution" in that they provided lists of German citizens of Jewish background. For those reasons, *Eichmann in Jerusalem* caused great controversy among the Jewish communities and resulted in the famous correspondence between Arendt and Gershom Scholem, founder of the scholarly study of Kabbalah, who accused Arendt of a lack of love for the Jewish people.

In the final years of her life, Arendt embarked on a project to write three volumes titled *The Life of the Mind*, which dealt with three human faculties and conditions for moral responsibility: *Thinking*, *Willing* (both published posthumously in 1978), and *Judging* (never completed). In the first volume, *Thinking*, Arendt presented her understanding of thinking not as a cognitive activity but as a purgative moral dialogue with oneself. This work was greatly influenced by

Arendt's reading of Kant, which also surfaced in her famous lectures "Some Questions of Moral Philosophy" at the New School for Social Research in New York in 1965 and in the Gifford Lectures in Aberdeen, Scotland, 1972–1974. Arendt died in New York on December 4, 1975.

While Arendt drew inspiration from various schools of philosophical thought, what is characteristic of her scholarship is the difficulty to identify it with one particular tradition. Different students of Arendt pointed at her affinities with St. Augustine in her conflict between the love of the world and the feelings of nonbelonging and estrangement; with Aristotle in her conceptualization of citizenship and civicness; with Machiavelli in her understanding of public action and her republican sympathies; with Kant in her ideas on reflective judgment; as well as with Nietzsche, Heidegger, and Jaspers, and others. Controversies were also raised by Arendt's alleged unorthodox and unsystematic reading of philosophy.

Another debate emerged around Arendt's classification as either a conservative or progressive thinker. During a famous interview with Hans Morgenthau, Arendt refused to submit to any of those labels. Her commentators emphasize her unique ability to connect the radical views on the possibility of political liberation with the conservative preoccupation with the (institutional and communal) limitations of political change.

An important issue concerning Arendt's scholarship is its various interpretations by feminist theorists and Arendt's puzzling approach to the category of gender. While some feminists have discussed Arendt's private/public dichotomy in explicitly negative terms, others have contextualized that dichotomy as a bulwark against totalitarianism rather than against patriarchy. Some feminists tried to incorporate in contemporary feminism Arendt's reflections on her Jewish identity and her concept of "natality," which she linked to the political importance of the categories of birth, vitality, and human life.

Another important debate concerning Arendt's influences is her designation as a precursor of postmodern political theory. Many researchers have emphasized the tension in Arendt's writings between the modern and the postmodern. This has been exemplified by her dissociation of political judgment from any universal concept of ethics, or by her rejection of an essentialist understanding of identity and its linkage to difference rather than sameness.

—*Magdalena Zolkos*

See also Democracy; Feminism; Feminist Research; Identity Politics; Noncitizen Rights; Postmodernism; Zionism

Further Readings

Benhabib, S. (1996). *The reluctant modernism of Hannah Arendt.* London: Sage.

Hansen, P. (1993). *Hannah Arendt: Politics, philosophy and citizenship.* Palo Alto: Stanford University Press.

Moruzzi, N. (2000). *Speaking through the mask: Hannah Arendt and the politics of social identity.* Ithaca, NY: Cornell University Press.

Ville, D. R. (1999) *Politics, philosophy, terror: Essays on the thought of Hannah Arendt.* Princeton, NJ: Princeton University Press.

Young-Bruehl, E. (2004). *Hannah Arendt: For love of the world* (2nd ed.). New Haven, CT: Yale University Press.

ARIAS, OSCAR (1940–)

Oscar Arias was president of Costa Rica from 1986 to 1990 and reelected for the presidency for the 2006–2010 period. Oscar Arias was also the winner of the Nobel Peace Prize in 1987 and has written books about political groups in Costa Rica.

Arias was born in 1940 in Heredia, Costa Rica. Member of an affluent family dedicated to the production of coffee, he studied economics and law at the University of Costa Rica. As a college student, Arias became involved in politics as a member of the *Partido Liberación Nacional* (PLN), a social democratic party. In 1967, he moved to England to pursue graduate studies. He obtained his Ph.D. in 1974 from Essex with a dissertation titled *¿Quién gobierna en Costa Rica?* (Who governs in Costa Rica?).

On his return to Costa Rica, Arias resumed his political involvement with the PLN. As a member of the PLN, he became minister of national planning and political economy from 1972 to 1976, international secretary of the party in 1975, general secretary of the party in 1979, and member of the legislature from 1978 to 1981.

In 1986, Oscar Arias was elected president of Costa Rica. His presidency was marked by the armed conflicts in Nicaragua, Guatemala, and El Salvador. Contrary to the previous administration official position of "neutrality," Arias promoted a more active role and sought diplomatic solutions to the conflicts in the region. With these efforts, he challenged the U.S. policy in Central America. In 1987, he proposed a peace plan and convinced the presidents of Guatemala, El Salvador, Honduras, and Nicaragua to sign the Esquipulas II Accords. The same year, Arias was awarded the Nobel Peace Prize. The funds awarded were used to create the Arias Foundation for Peace and Human Progress, which focused on the promotion of women rights, demilitarization, and conflict resolution.

In 2006, after the approval of a controversial constitutional amendment allowing presidential reelection, Arias became president for a second term. The 2006 election was one of the most contested elections in modern Costa Rican history, with Arias obtaining 40.9% of the votes against 39.8% for the opposition. The decisive issue in the 2006 election was Arias's support for the ratification of the CAFTA (Central America Free Trade Agreement) with the United States.

Oscar Arias's intellectual work has as a main focus the role of pressure groups. This focus includes not only the interference in governmental decisions on the part of special interest groups but also social movements and organizations that could exert any degree of nonformal influence over governments and political parties. In his publications, Arias defines social movements as formed mainly by activists, whom he considers as a minority that could become a majority in the future.

—*Delia Tamara Fuster and Marco Cabrera Geserick*

See also FMLN; Nobel Peace Prize; Sandinismo; Student Activism, Latin American

Further Readings

Anglade, C. (1988). President Arias of Costa Rica. *Political Science and Politics, 21*(2), 357–359.

Arias Sánchez, O. (1983). *Grupos de presión en Costa Rica* [Pressure groups in Costa Rica]. San José, Costa Rica: Editorial Costa Rica.

Arias Sánchez, O. (1984). *¿Quién gobierna en Costa Rica?* [Who governs in Costa Rica?]. San José, Costa Rica: EDUCA.

ARISTIDE, JEAN-BERTRAND (1953–)

Jean-Bertrand Aristide has twice been president of Haiti. The nature of his rise to power and his removal from power (twice, in 1991 and in 2004) has made him an international figure of great significance. Throughout his career as a radical Catholic priest and a politician, he has sided firmly with the poorest inhabitants of a poor country. His radicalism has led to both great hope and great instability in Haiti, especially as the United States has intervened in Haitian politics.

Aristide was ordained as a Salesian priest in 1983. Most of his work as a priest took place in the slums of Port-au-Prince. His exposure to the extraordinary poverty in these areas affirmed his more radical religious beliefs, expressed in his book *In the Parish of the Poor.* He first came to national prominence in the mid-1980s when he broadcast his sermons on national Catholic radio. This exposure quickly drew the wrath of both the Duvalier dictatorship and the Catholic authorities. In 1988 (2 years after Duvalier's ouster), Aristide was expelled from the Salesian order for incitement to hate and violence and exaltation of class struggle. Aristide ran for president in 1990, at the head of a movement he labeled Lavalas (meaning "the flood"). The election was a stunning victory for Aristide and for poor and marginalized Haitians: He won over two thirds of the national vote and took office in February 1991. Despite the democratic opening and Duvalier's departure, an entrenched elite remained very much in place. The military, with support from the elite, moved quickly to oust Aristide. He was forced into exile in September 1991. The bulk of Aristide's exile was spent in the United

States, where he worked tirelessly to secure his return to the presidency of Haiti. Growing international pressure, combined with a relatively sympathetic Clinton administration, created the political conditions for Aristide's return. He was reinstalled in October 1994, in the wake of a massive deployment of U.S. troops.

Aristide's chosen successor, Rene Preval, won 88% of the vote in the 1995 presidential election, and Aristide (constitutionally permitted to run again) prevailed with over 90% of the vote in 2000. This election came under heavy criticism from the international community and from opposition groups in Haiti, many of whom refused to participate. Conditions polarized over the next 3 years. Aristide and his opponents repeatedly refused to compromise, Aristide's supporters formed gangs to intimidate opposition figures, and the opposition responded in kind. As the violence worsened in 2004, many of the gangs linked to Aristide defected and directed their violence at his supporters. Anti-Aristide insurgents eventually succeeded in controlling two larger Haitian cities, and by late February, they were advancing on Port-au-Prince. In this increasingly anarchic atmosphere, the United States took the unilateral step of removing Aristide from power, transporting him on a U.S. aircraft to Africa on February 29, 2004. Aristide maintains that he was taken against his will by U.S. troops. Numerous high-level U.S. officials claim that he went willingly. Aristide has continued to argue his case while in exile in South Africa. Rene Preval, Aristide's former close associate, won the presidential election in February 2006 and has begun to consider the issue of Aristide's return.

Jean-Bertrand Aristide has always reflected the tremendous inequity in Haitian society. His commitment to impoverished Haitians and his effective use of democratic political tactics were fundamentally destabilizing in a society where the poor accounted for an overwhelming majority. He has been a polarizing figure in a polarized society.

—*Frederick Shepherd*

Further Readings

Aristide, J.-B. (1990). *In the parish of the poor: Writings from Haiti* (A. Wilentz, Trans.). Maryknoll, NY: Orbis.

Farmer, P. (2005). *The uses of Haiti* (3rd ed.). Monroe, ME: Common Courage Press.

Wilentz, A. (1990). *The rainy season: Haiti since Duvalier.* New York: Touchstone.

Armenian Genocide

The genocide visited on the Armenian population between 1915 and 1917 living within the boundaries of the Ottoman Empire is also known as the "forgotten genocide." The Ittahad's ruling party of the secular Young Turks perpetrated it. While its survivors commemorated it 50 years later, the international community and the West in general took even longer to admit that what happened in 1915 was a planned, well-organized, and systematic attempt at exterminating the Armenian population. The United Nations and the European Parliament officially acknowledged the genocide in 1985 and 1987; the French Senate passed a resolution into law in 2000, and the United States, although it issued a formal statement in 1990, stopped short of passing a bill that explicitly refers to the 1915 tragedy as genocide.

Most of the Armenian territories located between the Black, Caspian, and Mediterranean seas were incorporated into the Ottoman Empire in the 16th century. As a Christian minority in a Muslim-dominated empire, the status of Armenians was second-class citizens or "tolerated infidels." The genocide was preceded by centuries of political and economic persecution as well as by two massacres, in 1894–1896 and 1909, resulting in the loss of 200,000 lives. Acts passed in 1839 and 1856, a result of the politics of "humanitarian intervention" practiced by Russia vis-à-vis Christian minorities in the Ottoman Empire that granted religious minorities equal rights, were never put into practice. Equally powerless in protecting the Armenians was article 62 of the 1878 Treaty of Berlin that placed the Armenians under the protection of the Great Powers.

Turkey's entry into World War I gave the nationalistic regime of the Young Turks an opportunity to solve the Armenian question. The genocide, which was preceded by confiscation and the expropriation of the Armenian properties, was carried out during the

1915 deportation with the help of mobilized groups of criminals. It resulted in the death of one million people caused by killings, torture, starvation, and rape. At the time, this tragedy was very well documented in the United States by the media. In 1915 the *New York Times,* for example, published almost 150 articles on the subject.

Despite Turkey's military defeat in World War I, the Great Powers—England, France, and Russia—did not entirely occupy Turkey. Moreover, they allowed the new government of Mustafa Kemal to prosecute the organizers of the genocide in local Turkish courts. These decisions destroyed the most important provision of the 1920 Treaty of Sèvres: international adjudication regarding crimes perpetrated against the Armenians. In consequence, the trials were not successful in punishing any of the war criminals. Many of them fled the country, as was the case with the most important participants—Talat, Enver, Celat, and Nazim—who were either sentenced to death in absentia by court-martial or set free. Vakhan Dadrian explains the failure of these trials as resulting from three factors: the persisting influence of partisans of the Young Turks in the police, the limited powers the courts were provided, and the allies' pursuit of political interest at the expense of justice. Ultimately, the courts-martial were abolished, and the 1923 Treaty of Lausanne, in avoiding the subject of war crimes, made no provisions for the survivors of the genocide. Although the United States did not sign the treaty initially, diplomatic relations with Turkey were established 4 years later. Eventually, in the 1950s, as a member of the North Atlantic Treaty Organization, Turkey became an important strategic and military partner of the West during the Cold War.

After the Treaty of Lausanne, successive Turkish governments were quite successful in erasing Armenia from Turkish history. Historians explain this as the result of Mustafa Kemal's attempt, in founding the Turkish Republic, at creating the myth of a homogenous Turkish nation. But after half a century of silence, the second and third generations of Armenian survivors in the diasporas of France and the United States reintroduced the genocide in the court of international public opinion through commemorations, academic publications, artistic endeavors, and political lobbying. At the same time, radical Armenians did not shy away from engaging in terrorist acts against Turkish targets. The memory of the genocide was also revived by the 1998 violent conflict between the former Soviet republics of Armenia and Azerbaijan.

However, despite recent pressures put on Turkey by the European Union as a precondition for accession, the Turkish government continues to deny the past. The official version is that only 300,000 Armenians died and that the deportations were a necessary action since Armenians were willing to support Turkey's enemy Russia during the Great War. Under article 301 of the penal code, any person who publicly denigrates the memory of Kemal or "Turkishness" can be prosecuted and punished. As a result, a number of intellectuals were tried under this law, and an academic conference on the Armenian genocide in 2005 was almost blocked. The most notable recent case is that of the novelist Orhan Pamuk who, in an interview in 2005, was indicted for criticizing the Turkish government's denial of the genocide. His trial was terminated through the intervention of the European Union.

—*Monica Ciobanu*

See also Genocide Watch

Further Readings

Akcam, T. (2004). *From empire to republic: Turkish nationalism and the Armenian genocide.* London: Zed Books.

Balakian, P. (2003). *The burning Tigris: The Armenian genocide and America's response.* New York: HarperCollins.

Dadrian, N. V. (1989). Genocide as a problem of national and international law: World War I and the Armenian case and its contemporary legal ramification. *Yale Journal of National and International Law, 14*(2), 221–355.

Hovannisan, G. R. (1994). Etiology and sequelae of the Armenian genocide. In G. Andreopoulous (Ed.), *Genocide: Conceptual and historical dimensions* (pp. 111–140). Philadelphia: University of Pennsylvania Press.

Peuch, J.-C. (2005, April 24). *Armenia: Tragedy remains on Europe's political map.* Retrieved from http://www.rferl .org/features

ARTS-IN-MEDICINE MOVEMENT

Although the healing power of the arts has a long history, the arts-in-medicine movement as a modern grassroots movement evolved from therapeutic art in psychiatry in the 1940s and art therapy as an acknowledged profession by 1960. The expanded focus of the movement in the late 20th century was the nonclinical concept of art and artists. The arts-in-medicine movement distinguishes between passive enjoyment of art created by others and art that participants—patients, their families, and caregivers—create. The involvement of a patient in the creative process (and increasingly self-help for caregivers) serves to enhance self-esteem, autonomy, and ability to take charge of a critical situation.

The healing power of the arts featured in the temple rituals and dream work of the Greek god of healing, Asklepios. In modern times, there are three main areas of art activity within health care. First, art in health care settings assumes that enhancing the physical environment of health care facilities promotes patient care; examples include architectural design and signage, art installations, sculptures, and live performances in public and private spaces. Second, community art refers to the practice of using art to deliver health promotion messages to wider communities in order to have an impact on the health and well-being of the population. Examples include anti-smoking billboards and popular theater performances in shopping centers and public squares. Third, medical humanities, as part of higher education and continuing professional education for doctors and nurses, is designed to change the way in which health care practitioners interact with patients. As a daily practice of the arts-in-medicine movement, medical staff and volunteers alike are encouraged to find the artist within and add creative expression to their healing approaches. Nurses are often in the best position to make the link between patients and artist, identifying both artist and art form (visual, music, dance, puppets, magic, clowning, etc.) that meet the patient's needs and creative energies. The so-called artists-in-residence—both paid and volunteer—are increasingly part of the health care team in hospitals and hospices in North America and Europe. The incorporation of the arts as an integral component of health care was formalized with the founding of the Society for the Arts in Healthcare in 1991. The society's website and annual conference are primary resources for identifying the programs, research, and professional opportunities that are available internationally.

Patch Adams, M.D., portrayed by Robin Williams in the 1998 film *Patch Adams,* is perhaps the most visible social revolutionary of the arts-in-medicine movement. He is the inspiration for healer-clowns in many health care settings. With a few colleagues, Patch Adams founded the Gesundheit Institute in Virginia in 1972—a home-based family medical practice that advocates for humor, clowning, and healing art to accompany traditional medical treatment. Gesundheit Institute charges nothing for its services and raises funds in order to welcome anyone from anywhere. Gesundheit Institute grew out of a recognition of the health care crisis in the United States and as a provocative stimulus to a peaceful revolution, opposing the "for-profit-not-people" health care system in America. The mission statement on Patch Adams's website underscores that the arts-in-medicine movement aspires to a snowball effect of activism that supports sustainability of individual and community health.

John Graham-Pole, a physician and poet, with visual artist Mary Rockwood Lane, cofounded Arts in Medicine at Shands Hospital at the University of Florida in Gainesville in 1991. This program has helped de-professionalize art in health care venues, taking the approach that all people are artists. The mission of the University of Florida Center for the Arts in Healthcare, Research, and Education is to identify the many connections between the creative and the healing arts in an academic medical setting. Key to this approach has been to involve not only artists from the community and the university but also those emerging from patients, family members, staff, and volunteers. The effective healing potential within the relationship established between the sufferer and the carer through art and creativity is connected to an unexpressed acknowledgment that both are fully and equally human. Healing art is not a domain restricted to established artists and art therapists. The executive director of Hospice King-Aurora in Ontario, Canada, tells of hospice volunteers responding to a dying woman's dream of a trip to Paris with her husband: The volunteers created a "café" in the couple's living room. They set up tables with red-checkered cloths, played Edith Piaf, served French food, and gave the couple their evening in Paris.

Arts in medicine is committed to using the arts to transform the health care environment from a barren, depersonalized setting to an interactive healing ambience, complete with color, texture, sound, movement, and conversation. The Healing Wall in the atrium of Shands Hospital at the University of Florida is a 30-foot structure, consisting of more than 800 ceramic tiles painted by cancer patients, their families, and the Shands Cancer Center staff. The messages and images on the tiles start up conversations between strangers. A grand piano is a permanent feature of the atrium, and a musical performance takes place every Friday during the noon hour. In the United Kingdom, Paintings in Hospitals is a registered charity that loans 400 pictures to more than 250 hospitals, hospices, and other health care facilities. A study of the effects of live music performed in the waiting room of the clinic in the Chelsea and Westminster Hospital in London revealed the lowering of blood pressure and a shorter duration of labor (2.1 hours shorter). The University of Michigan Hospital's Art That Heals program, initiated in 1987, provides performing and visual arts activities, including an art cart, which is a traveling library of framed poster prints from which patients select and exchange art work for their rooms. *Lilian,* a rock musical written by Michael Bishop and community members in Tasmania in 1989, about the visible/invisible presence of people with mental health problems, has been performed several times over the past 15 years throughout Australia. The production moved out of hospital settings into the wider community and increasingly has combined with discussion groups and workshops to engage audiences in critical reflection and action plans to reduce the stigma of mental health problems.

Graham-Pole frames the arts-in-medicine movement as a renaissance that celebrates the marriage of art and science in health care. Although the movement is testimony that the biomedical model is giving way, Graham-Pole emphasizes the importance of creating a balance. The emergence of the arts-in-medicine movement coexists with the global exploration of body-mind-spirit connections and alternative health care options as adjuncts to mainstream or modern medicine. More recently, art-based research in health care is making the case that art experiments like random controlled trials are evidence based. This balance of art and science, often associated with the emerging field of psychoneuroimmunology, is supported by evidence- and narrative-based studies on the effects of art on clinical outcomes (e.g., pain relief, reduced anxiety, raised pain thresholds, increased life span, lowered blood pressure, and lowered stress hormone levels). For example, studies show that patients exposed to nature scenes through a window or as an artistic representation reported less anxiety, requested less pain medication, and had a quicker postoperative recovery time than those without such views. Physicians at the Sloan Kettering Hospital in New York reported that many of their patients with cancer, who visited the Museum of Modern Art to view Monet's *Water Lilies,* described their emotional state afterward as a letting go of their concerns.

Art in medicine as a modern social movement is in its early stages. Healing art as self-care for the caregiver is a fairly new innovation. The University of Florida Center for the Arts in Healthcare, Research, and Education program, *Days of Renewal,* offers a whole-day experiential, art-based workshop for nurses and other caregivers. In 2002, the Society for the Arts in Healthcare in the United States initiated a research program with their counterpart in Japan to assess the field of caregiver support using the arts. The effect of healing art in recruiting and retaining staff and volunteers requires further study. Also worthy of research and education are the issues around integrating art forms into health care culture so as to honor cultural differences (social inclusion) related to class, gender, religion, race, ethnicity, age, and generation. The importance of healing art as a response to collective trauma experiences, such as the AIDS pandemic in Africa, 9/11 terrorist attacks in New York and Washington, D.C., earthquakes in Pakistan, and

Hurricane Katrina in New Orleans, Louisiana, have only recently captured the attention of this movement.

—*Dorothy A. Lander*

See also Play, Creativity, and Social Movements

Further Readings

Adams, P., & Mylander, M. (1998). *Gesundheit*. Rochester, VT: Healing Arts Press.

Graham-Pole, J. (2000). *Illness and the art of creative self-expression*. Oakland, CA: New Harbinger.

Lander, D. A., Napier, S. D., Fry, B. F., Brander, H., & Acton, J. (2006). Memoirs of loss as popular education: Five palliative caregivers remember through the healing art of hope and love. *Convergence, 38*(3), 44–56.

McNiff, S. (1998). *Art-based research*. London: Jessica Kingsley.

Society for the Arts in Healthcare. (2003). *Caring for caregivers: A grassroots USA-Japan initiative*. Washington, DC: Author.

Staricoff, R. L. (2004). *Arts in health: A review of the medical literature*. London: Arts Council. Retrieved from http://www.artscouncil.org.uk/documents/publications/phpcOeMaS.pdf

Ashrawi, Hanan (1946–)

Hanan Daoud Khalil Ashrawi emerged as a political activist and voice for Palestinians when she returned to her homeland of Palestine in 1973. On her return, Ashrawi developed the Department of English at Birzeit University in the West Bank. As a voice for human rights, she has distinguished herself both politically and academically as she has earned herself a seat in the theater of Palestinian politics. She has utilized her scholarly insight by writing numerous articles, poems, and short stories regarding Palestinian culture, literature, and political plight. In 1998, Ashrawi created MIFTAH, an organization committed to human rights, democracy, and peace in Palestine. In 2003, she was awarded the Sydney Peace Prize.

Hanan Ashrawi was born in Ramallah in 1946, then a part of the British Mandate of Palestine. Her father, Daoud Mikhail, was a founder of the Palestine Liberation Organization (PLO). Ashrawi received her bachelor's and master's degrees in English literature from the American University of Beirut and her Ph.D. in medieval and comparative literature from the University of Virginia. She began her activism in 1974 when she created the Birzeit University Legal Aid Committee/Human Rights Action Project as a response to the sporadic closures of Birzeit University by the Israeli military. She served as chair of the Department of English at Birzeit University from 1973 to 1978 and again from 1981 to 1984. From 1986 to 1990, she served as dean of the Faculty of Arts. Ashrawi remained a faculty member at Birzeit until 1995.

Her political involvement took center stage in 1988 during the First Intifada. She joined the Intifada Political Committee and served on the Diplomatic Committee until 1993. From 1991 to 1993, she served as the official spokesperson of the Palestinian delegation to the Middle East peace process. When the peace accords were signed by Arafat and Rabin in 1993, Dr. Ashrawi founded and headed the Preparatory Committee of the Palestinian Independent Commission for Citizens' Rights in Jerusalem. In 1996, she served as Minister of Higher Education and Research until 1998 when she resigned in protest against political corruption, especially Arafat's handling of the peace talks. In August 1998, she founded the Palestinian Initiative for the Promotion of Global Dialogue and Democracy, otherwise known as MIFTAH.

Dr. Ashrawi serves on numerous international advisory boards, including the Council on Foreign Relations, the United Nations Research Institute for Social Development, and the World Bank Middle East and North Africa. In 1995, she published her autobiographical book, *This Side of Peace: A Personal Account*. Through her scholarly work and political involvement, Dr. Ashrawi has become known as an advocate for peace with justice for the Palestinians and Israelis. Ashrawi's wish is to end the Israeli occupation based on humanitarian rather than historical or ideological foundation.

—*Da'ad Naserdeen*

See also Intifada (1987–1992, 2000–2003); Palestine Liberation Organization (PLO); Palestine National Council

Further Readings

Ashrawi, H. (1995). *This side of peace: A personal account.* New York: Simon & Schuster.

Victor, B. (1994). *A voice of reason: Hanan Ashrawi and peace in the Middle East.* San Diego, CA: Harcourt Brace.

ASIAN AMERICAN AND PACIFIC ISLANDER ACTIVISM

There are many assumptions about the Asian American and Pacific Islander (AAPI) population that often mask their actual participation in, and contributions to, American society. Some scholars have identified AAPIs as the "invisible Americans" because of the lack of visibility they are afforded in scholarly research, public policy, the media, and the political arena. At the same time, there is a common perception of AAPIs as a successful or model minority. Because of the perceived success of AAPIs, they have often been excluded altogether from racial discourse on social issues because it is believed that there is no need to address their needs.

While the disregard of Asian American and Pacific Islanders continues, the population has grown to become the third largest racial minority group in the United States after Latino/as and African Americans. The U.S. Census Bureau found that in 2003, there was an estimated 13.3 million AAPIs in the United States, representing 4.5% of the total population. The number of AAPIs increased nearly 50% since 1990 and doubled from 1980. Furthermore, the growth of the AAPI population is expected to continue, maintaining AAPIs as the fastest-growing racial group in the nation. The U.S. AAPI population is also extremely diverse. Through classification by the U.S. Census Bureau, the AAPI racial designation is inclusive of more than 50 different ethnic groups who speak more than 300 languages.

Despite their lack of recognition by American society, the AAPI population has a long history of political, social, and legal activism. In fact, like most minority populations in U.S. society, the gains in civil liberties would not be enjoyed today if it were not for the initiative that was put forth by the AAPI population. The AAPI population has fought to gain rights as U.S. citizens, attain equal opportunity in education and employment, and end discrimination and racial profiling. There has also been a rise in AAPI political representation that has helped to bring more attention to the needs and challenges faced by the population. Key movements in the history of AAPIs have made significant gains in the fight against basic social problems such as inequality, poverty, and discrimination.

Probably the most visible social movement among the AAPI population is when the Japanese American community succeeded in pushing for the passage of the Civil Liberties Act of 1988. The act provided redress for Japanese American internees, evacuees, and persons of Japanese ancestry who lost liberty or property because of discriminatory action by the federal government during World War II. As a result of the war with Japan, many people in the United States did not trust people of Japanese ancestry, and even Japanese Americans who were born in this country were mistakenly thought to be loyal to Japan. As a result, President Franklin D. Roosevelt in 1942 issued Executive Order 9066, which began this prohibition. In 1978, the national convention of the Japanese American Citizens League adopted a resolution calling for redress and reparations for the internment of Japanese Americans. In 1980, the Commission on Wartime Relocation and Internment of Civilians was established by Congress, which reviewed the impact of Executive Order 9066 on Japanese Americans and determined that they were the victims of discrimination by the federal government.

Long before the struggle Japanese Americans faced in this country during World War II, many generations of Asian immigrants had struggled for their right to gain American citizenship. For example, provisions such as the Chinese Exclusion Law suspended immigration of laborers for many years. Prior to 1965, immigrants from Asia were prohibited by law from becoming U.S. citizens, and children of immigrants were barred from attending "white" schools. As a result of their status in the United States, and other targeted efforts to hurt the population, Asian Americans were stripped of many civil liberties, such as voting, testifying in court, or owning property. For example, in California, a law was passed that the alien land law that prohibited "Asians ineligible to citizenship" from buying or leasing land. Not only did Asian immigrants face the challenge of gaining access to the United States, there was an added burden over naturalized citizenship, which made it difficult if not impossible for the children of Asian immigrants to gain citizenship. Asians fought these exclusions in a series of legal and political battles.

Along with challenges to their citizenship, many AAPIs faced many labor disputes. For example, Chinese immigrants that worked in railroads and mining in the late 1800s fought for equal wages to those earned by their coworkers of European ancestry. Japanese and Filipino plantation workers staged strikes to gain equality in employment throughout Hawai'i and the West Coast. Their struggles were met by white workers, who formed unions to oppose the companies that sought to employ the Asian Americans. There were a number of initiatives set forth to prevent municipalities and corporations from employing Chinese workers.

In the 1960s and 1970s, Asian Americans were active in fighting for equal opportunity to education, effective language policy, affirmative action, and ethnic studies in colleges and universities. One of the most important Supreme Court decisions related to education involving Asian Americans was *Lau v. Nichols*, 414 U.S. 563 (1974), which ruled that school districts must provide children who speak little English with bilingual education. Another important movement throughout the country that began in the late 1960s and continues today is the creation of Asian American and ethnic studies programs in colleges and universities. The first protest was in 1968, when students went on strike at San Francisco State University to demand the establishment of ethnic studies programs. These programs have been vital to bringing attention to the Asian American community through scholarship and mentorship of future AAPI leaders.

Other contemporary challenges the AAPI community faces include racism, violent assaults, and other forms of discrimination. In the post-9/11 environment, Arabs, South Asians, and Muslims are at risk for racial profiling, discrimination, and violent acts.

Another struggle faced by the AAPI population has been political representation. It was not until the 1960s that AAPIs gained access to Congress. In that decade, Daniel K. Inouye became a U.S. senator; Spark Matsunaga, a U.S. Congressman; and Patsy Takemoto Mink, the first Asian American woman to serve in Congress.

Just as diverse as the AAPI population is, so are the issues that different ethnic populations have faced throughout their history in the United States. AAPIs have often struggled to find common ground in social movements. For example, while the Pacific Islander population is included in the AAPI racial designation, they face their own struggle to be recognized and treated with sovereignty status. Prior to 1996, Filipinos in California were long considered eligible for affirmative action while other AAPI groups were excluded. Despite the individual groups' challenges, the similarities in their struggles outweigh their differences. As a whole, Asian Americans and Pacific Islanders have actively protected and promoted their civil rights, as well as the rights of minorities as whole, through litigation, advocacy, education, and organization.

—*Robert T. Teranishi*

See also Anti-Immigrant Politics; Filipino American Activism; Japanese Internment Camps

Further Readings

Aguilar-San Juan, K. (1994). *The state of Asian America: Activism and resistance in the 1990s*. Boston: South End Press.

Louie, S., & Omatsu, G. (2001). *Asian Americans: The movement and the moment*. Los Angeles: UCLA Asian American Studies Center Press.

Zia, H. (2000). *Asian American dreams: The emergence of an American people*. New York: Farrar, Straus & Giroux.

ATHEISM

Atheism is the denial of the existence of God and of any supernatural being or force. Atheism mainly rejects the Judaist, Christian, and Islamic notion of a god who is divine and the creator of the universe. Atheists reject God by refuting theists' arguments for the existence of God, such as argument of the first cause, argument for design, and argument of religious experience. Atheists argue that there is a lack of evidence to prove the existence of God. Some atheists go beyond a mere absence of belief in gods: They actively believe that particular gods, or all gods, do not exist. Just lacking belief in gods is often referred to as the "weak atheist" position, whereas believing that gods do not (or cannot) exist is known as "strong atheism."

Atheism should not be identified with deism, pantheism, or religious freethinking. Broadly defined, atheists are those who do not believe in any deities, such as nontheists, agnostics, and even Buddhists. Buddhism affirms that nonbeing, or Nirvana, is the goal of all temporal effort. Taoism has no affirmation of an existing god. Denial of God should be distinguished from agnosticism, which holds that the existence of God cannot be proved.

In ancient Greece, people who rejected the gods of popular religions were called atheists. Atheism comes from Greek prefix *a-* (meaning without) and *theos* (meaning deity). Democritus and Epicurus were among atheist intellectuals of Greek time. Several leading thinkers of the Enlightenment and beyond were atheists, including Holbach, Diderot, Shelley, Byron, Hardy, Voltaire, Sartre, Turgenev, Twain, Sinclair, Feuerbach, Marx, Schopenhauer, Nietzsche, Russell, and Freud.

Atheists are strong advocates of the legal separation of religion and state. Some atheists educate the public to install a scientific and materialistic world outlook and to help overcome religious prejudice. The dominant Soviet ideology of Marxism-Leninism was to undermine religion. For Marx, religion was a reflection of socioeconomic order and was to him an alienation of humans from their products and true nature. Mass atheist movements used mass media and the Internet to spread their message and to draw believers and weak believers into active social, cultural, and political activities, to free them from religious influence and create a new culture based on science.

There is often a misperception of atheism as of being immoral and evil and that morality and purpose in life cannot exist without a belief in God. Atheists' ethical goals are determined by secular aims and concerns. Atheists believe that human beings must take responsibility for their destiny. Therefore, atheists are no less moral than theists.

Among the leading American atheist organizations are the American Atheists, the Internet Infidels, America First, Atheists United, the American Humanist Association, American Rationalist Federation, American Association for the Advancement of Atheism, and Freedom From Religion Foundation.

Most of atheists' reasoning is based on philosophical ground, a lack of evidence supporting theist claims, the belief that science is sufficient to conclude that there is no evidence to support religious doctrines, or the belief that religion is self-contradictory. To atheists, scientific explanation is more rational than faith.

Atheists are largely protected in the developed world but condemned in the developing world where religion is strong and associated with the state. Nonreligious and anti-religious groups constitute about 14% of the world's population.

—*Shak Hanish*

Further Readings

Edis, T. (2002). *The ghost in the universe: God in light of modern science.* Amherst, NY: Prometheus Books.

The Secular Web. Retrieved October 12, 2006, from www.infidels.org

Smith, G. H. (1980). *Atheism: The case against God.* Amherst, NY: Prometheus Books.

ATTICA UPRISING

Perhaps no other prison riot has received as much notoriety as the uprising at Attica (New York). The penitentiary became a metaphor for numerous social problems, including racism, oppression, and injustice. As a result of the riot, between September 9 and 13, 1971, a total of 43 persons died; most significantly, 39 were killed, and more than 80 others were wounded by gunfire during the 15 minutes it took the state police to retake the institution.

Attica was not unlike most maximum-security prisons in the nation in the early 1970s. At the time of the uprising, the prison was vastly overcrowded with more than 2,200 inmates. Compounding overcrowding, the prisoners were simply "warehoused" since few meaningful programs of education and rehabilitation were offered. Like many large prisons in the nation, the inmate population was becoming increasingly urban and minority (54% black, 37% white, and 8.7% Spanish-speaking, almost 80% from downstate urban ghettos). By contrast, prison officials and staff members were predominately white and from rural communities. Racism between the officers and the inmates was mutual. Rural white officers were suspicious of prisoners from the ghettos, and minority inmates did not trust the staff, who were viewed as "hicks," "cowboys," or "Good ol'boys."

The chronology of events began the day before the riot when a misunderstanding between guards and prisoners led to an officer being assaulted by an inmate. That night, two prisoners were removed from their cells and placed in administrative detention. Other inmates vowed revenge, and the next morning the officer, who was at the center of the controversy, was attacked. Violence spread as prisoners attacked officers, took hostages, and destroyed property. Following a few days of negotiations, prisoners rejected Commissioner Oswald's revised set of demands; as a result, state police were ordered to storm the prison.

Regaining control of the prison, however, did not end the violence. Hundreds of prisoners were subsequently stripped naked and beaten by correction officers, troopers, and sheriffs' deputies. The ordeal was prolonged further because prison officials withheld immediate medical care for those suffering from gunshot wounds and injuries stemming from the widespread reprisals. When the shooting stopped, there were only 10 medical personnel available to treat more than 120 seriously wounded prisoners and hostages, and only 2 of them were physicians. Doctors at local hospitals who could have attended to the wounded were not dispatched by prison officials until 4 hours later.

After years of legal wrangling, a class action suit moved forward in the courts. Eventually, a jury found Deputy Warden Pfeil liable for violent reprisals following the riot for permitting police and guards to beat and torture inmates. But in 1999, a federal appeals court overturned that ruling saying that the 1992 liability finding against Pfeil was invalid. Then in 2000, a federal judge announced that the inmates who were beaten and tortured during the riot would receive an $8 million settlement from New York State.

—*Michael Welch*

Further Readings

Attica: The official report of the New York State commission. (1972). New York: Bantam Books.

Welch, M. (2004). *Corrections: A critical approach* (2nd ed.). New York: McGraw-Hill.

Welch, M. (2005). *Ironies of imprisonment.* Thousand Oaks, CA: Sage.

Wicker, T. (1972). *A time to die.* New York: Quadrangle.

AUNG SAN (1915–1947)

Aung San, the father of Aung San Suu Kyi, leader of the movement for democracy against the present Burma's military junta, was a Burmese revolutionary fighting British capitalism and Japanese fascism. Born to a family descendent of a Burmese patriot beheaded by the British, as a child, Aung San's dream was to rebel against the British. He grew up a committed nationalist leader obsessed with a single goal: independence for Burma. His dedication to the cause earned him the title, "the architect of Burma's freedom."

Attending the national high school established by the Burmese nationalists strengthened Aung San's deep-rooted nationalist sentiment. During this period, the teenager Aung San joined the student union and urged his fellow students to take an interest in the country's affairs and work toward freedom from British bondage.

Aung San started his political apprenticeship during his university years from 1932 to 1938. Choosing political science and history as his specialization, Aung San read a variety of political ideologies (including that of Karl Marx) and constantly sought for opportunities to share his knowledge and thoughts. Soon he found his political platform at the debates and seminars organized by the Rangoon University Student Union (RUSU). The debates were held in English, the language that Aung San was still struggling to master at the time. However, whenever time was given to the audience, Aung San always rose from his seat to talk. For his clumsy English, the audience booed and yelled him to stop, but Aung San would continue his speech until he finished. Such uncommon courage in these debates earned him the title "crazy Aung San." In 1936, Aung San was assigned the editorship of *Oway,* the RUSU magazine, while he was also writing articles for other magazines and newspapers. His initial success came with the change of his reputation from "crazy" Aung San to "editor" Aung San.

The university strike of 1936 was the major turning point in Aung San's political life. A series of students' dissatisfactions led to the strike, but what ignited the fire was the expulsion of the editor Aung San from school due to his refusal to reveal the identity of the author of an article, "A Hell Hound at Large," that appeared in *Oway* attacking a university official.

With the name "Aung San" repeatedly appearing in the daily newspaper during the strike, he came to be regarded as the future leader of the country. Aung San helped maneuver the student movements into the forefront of national politics. He became the vice president of the RUSU in 1936 and president of both RUSU and the All Burma Student Union in 1938. In October 1938, Aung San joined the Dobama Asi Ayon (DAA), or *Thakin* organization, a political organization led by the older nationalist leaders who encouraged the 1936 student strike. Although the common goal was to obtain the independence of Burma, these leaders were divided into factions. When Aung San became the general secretary of DAA, he called for unity under DAA. With the formation of a mass base of workers, peasants, students, and even monks, DAA played a crucial role during the Revolution of 1300.

Aung San's role in the nationalist movement became more substantial when he persuaded other Burmese political parties to join him in forming the Freedom Bloc Party in 1939. He was elected the party's general secretary and promptly claimed that "Britain's war (in Europe) was Burma's opportunity" and that the time had come to fight British imperialism. His anti-British speeches were not confined to the Burmese people. In 1940, when he attended the India National Congress in India as the DAA delegation leader, he delivered public speeches in various places expressing his desire to cooperate with the Indian people in fighting against the British imperialism.

Aung San shifted from political to military leader through his contact with the Japanese. While the Burmese nationalists were searching for help, the Japanese, who wanted to push the British out of Asia, offered their aid. After his meeting with the Japanese in China, military training was given to Aung San and 29 other young Burmese nationalists, "thirty comrades," on Hainan Island in 1941. The Japanese appointed Aung San the military leader of the Japanese-trained Burma Independence Army, which eventually became the Burmese National Army.

Soon after the Japanese occupied Burma in 1942, Aung San was made the defense minister and became increasingly popular among the Burmese people by the title "Bogyoke," (Supreme General). When Japanese fascism turned out to be more oppressive than British imperialism, Aung San initiated a clandestine anti-Japanese campaign and formed the Anti-Fascist Organization, which later became the Anti-Fascist People's Freedom League. He tried also to unite the underground groups to work against the Japanese. Crucial to his plan was allying with the Karen people who never severed their ties with the British. When contact was resumed with the British, Aung San won the support of Lord Louis Mountbatten, who was then the commander in chief of the Allied army in Southeast Asia.

In 1945, the British returned to Burma with the White Paper Policy, claiming that Burma would remain under British rule for 3 more years followed by an election. Because the terms were unacceptable, Aung San and his Anti-Fascist People's Freedom

League orchestrated political uprisings throughout the country, which led to the final negotiation. The British government invited Aung San to London as the representative for final negotiation, and Burmese independence within 1 year was promised by the signing of Aung San-Atlee Agreement in January 1947.

Aung San's dream to build a new sovereign state with all of Burma's minority ethnic groups became a reality when the Panglong Agreement was signed with the various minority representatives in February 1947. The tragic assassination of Aung San on July 4, 1947, left the people of Burma to celebrate their official independence on January 4, 1948, without Aung San, "the architect of Burma's freedom."

—Angelene Naw

See also Suu Kyi , Aung San

Further Readings

Aung San Suu Kyi. (1991). *Aung San of Burma: A biographical portrait by his daughter.* Edinburgh, UK: Kiscadale.

Naw, A. (2001). *Aung San and the struggle for Burmese independence.* Chiang Mai, Thailand: Silkworm Books.

AWAD, MUBARAK (1951–)

Mubarak Awad is a Palestinian American nonviolent activist, youth advocate, and educator. A Christian pacifist, he has emerged as one of the leading Arab voices in support of nonviolent action. Born in 1951 in Jerusalem, then under Jordanian control, he immigrated to the United States in 1968, receiving his bachelor's degree from Bluffton University, a master's degree in education from St. Francis University, and a Ph.D. in psychology from the International Graduate School in St. Louis, Missouri.

In 1978, he became the founding president of the National Youth Advocate Program, a private nonprofit international organization that serves troubled youth and families, focusing on the development and

administration of programs that provide alternatives to restrictive or institutional placement for youth in need of substitute care. Emphasizing an advocate model that aims to support and surround troubled youth with positive role models in one-to-one relationships, it has served as a model for private, nonprofit youth advocate organizations worldwide and has played a role in reforming state policy in Ohio, West Virginia, and Indiana.

In 1985, Awad returned to Palestine, where he founded the Palestinian Center for the Study of Nonviolence in Israeli-occupied East Jerusalem, providing educational materials on nonviolent resistance and supporting nonviolent direct action by Palestinians living under occupation. The center also established a family reunification project and the publication and translation of writings on the theory and practice of nonviolence into Arabic. The utilization of nonviolent action on a massive scale during the first Palestinian initifada drew the attention of Israeli occupation authorities, who arrested and deported Awad in 1988.

Back in exile in the United States, in 1989 Awad became the founding president of Nonviolence International, a nonprofit organization dedicated to educating people worldwide about nonviolent resistance and supporting the training of activists in methods of nonviolent action for social justice. In addition to its headquarters in Washington, D.C., Nonviolence International has since established regional offices in Jerusalem, Bangkok, Belfast, Kamenshikov (Russia), and Aceh (Indonesia).

In 1994, following the Oslo Accords, Awad returned to Palestine, where he became the founding director of the Palestinian Center for Democracy and Elections. An educational project funded by the National Endowment for Democracy, the center has provided educational materials and training to Palestinians in the West Bank and Gaza Strip experiencing their first opportunity to participate in open municipal and general elections and to encourage incorporating democratic concepts into the governance structure of the Palestine Authority.

Awad has lectured before audiences worldwide on nonviolent solutions to the Palestinian and Israeli conflict and support for human rights, children's rights, and the implementation of governmental policies that will improve the lives of young people. He has also served annually as adjunct faculty at the American University's School for International Service, teaching courses on the theory and methods of nonviolent action.

—Stephen Zunes

See also Nonviolence and Activism; Intifada (1987–1992, 2000–2003); Youth Organizing and Activism

Further Readings

Awad, M. (1984). Nonviolent resistance: A strategy for the Occupied Territories. *Journal of Palestine Studies, 13*(4), 22–36.

Awad, M., & Hubers, P. (1993). Nonviolence in the intifada: Long-term costs and values. *Peace Research, 25*(3), 61–68.

Ingram, C. (1990). *In the footsteps of Gandhi: Conversations with spiritual social activists.* Berkeley, CA: Parallax Press.

B

BACHELET, MICHELLE
(1951–)

Michelle Bachelet is the current (2006–2010) president of Chile and the first woman to fill this position. Prior to this, she was Chile's first female defense minister, in which position she personally embodied the democratic transition of the country where she had been a victim of its military regime.

A Socialist member of the center-left Concertación alliance, Bachelet was elected with 53.49% of the vote in a second-round runoff against José Piñera's center-right candidacy in January 2006; she took office in March 2006. Her first cabinet was notable for its equal division of posts by gender.

Bachelet's first 100 days as president were marked by large street protests by secondary school students demanding education reforms. In June 2006, the demonstrations ended after Bachelet made concessions; these included a presidential advisory panel and a review of the education system. During that first 100 days, she also began work on 36 measures, including legislation introducing automatic voter registration, reforming the electoral system, making the army a volunteer-based force, increasing educational spending, and ensuring pension entitlement for all people aged over 65.

Bachelet served as health minister (2000–2002) and defense minister (2002–2004) in the Concertación government under Ricardo Lagos. As health minister, she oversaw a national health care reform program and sought to improve health care quality and coverage. Her appointment as Chile's first female defense minister heralded efforts to enhance civil power over the military, make changes to the military service system, introduce equal opportunities for women, and comply with the Ottawa Convention by destroying land mine stockpiles.

Born in 1951, Bachelet studied medicine at the University of Chile and became a left-wing student leader. Her father, a general, was arrested for his involvement with the left-wing Allende government after the 1973 coup and tortured, which contributed to his death. Nevertheless, Bachelet continued to help those sought by the regime until her own arrest and imprisonment in the secret police center at Villa Grimaldi in January 1975. Released a month later, Bachelet went into exile, first to Australia and then to East Germany.

Bachelet returned to Chile in 1979 and worked as a pediatrician and for various pro-democracy groups. With the return of democracy in 1990, she worked for various national and international health organizations and for the Health Ministry. She became increasingly concerned about civil-military relations and undertook a course of study at the National Academy of Political and Strategic Studies, finishing first in her class. This granted her a presidential scholarship to complete her studies at the Inter-American Defense College in Washington, D.C., in 1997. In 1998, she returned to Chile, where she was employed by the Defense Ministry.

Active in the Socialist Party, on its Central Committee, and as a key manager of Lagos's presidential campaign in 1999, Bachelet resigned as defense minister in October 2004. Bachelet initially faced a challenge from the Christian Democratic Party's Soledad Alvear for the Concertación nomination, but the latter dropped out of the race in May 2005.

—Guy Burton

See also Popular Unity Government; Social Democracy; Socialist Feminism

Further Readings

Neira Fernández, E. (2006). Socialismo a la Bachelet. [Socialism à la Bachelet]. *Observatorio de Política Internacional II. AMERICAS.* Retrieved June 26, 2006, from http://www.saber.ula.ve/observatorio/
Presidency of the Republic of Chile. (2006). Biography. Retrieved June 26, 2006, from http://www.presidency ofchile.cl/view/viewBiografia.asp?seccion=Biografia

Baez, Joan
(1941–)

Folk singer and activist Joan Baez was born January 9, 1941, on Staten Island, New York, to Dr. Albert Baez, a Mexican-born physicist, and Joan Bridge Baez, of Scottish and English descent. She was the second of three daughters. Joan Baez's older sister was Pauline Baez. Her younger sister, born Margarita Mimi Baez, was a singer, guitarist, and activist in her own right as Mimi Fariña (Fariña died of neuroendocrine cancer in 2001).

Dr. Baez and his wife were practicing Quakers, and Dr. Baez had turned down lucrative defense industry jobs during the Cold War. The family moved frequently due to Dr. Baez's work, living in towns across the United States as well as in France, Switzerland, Italy, and Iraq. Baez was only 10 when her family moved to Baghdad, but the poverty and inhumane treatment of the people there deeply affected her. The family ultimately settled in the

Boston area in the late 1950s after Dr. Baez took a position at MIT.

As a teenager, Baez learned to play the ukulele first, then the guitar. She also sang in her school choir. She began her political involvement early. While still in high school, Baez attended a conference with the Quakers' social-action wing, the American Friends Service Committee; it was at this conference that she met 27-year-old Martin Luther King, Jr. Baez also involved herself in issues in her hometown. When she boycotted a high-school air-raid drill, saying that the drills were false and misleading, she made front-page news in her hometown.

After graduating from high school, Baez attended Boston University but dropped out after one semester to spend her time performing as a singer-songwriter at the clubs and coffeehouses that lined Harvard Square. Baez's most significant venue at that time was Club 47 on Mount Auburn Street in Cambridge, where she was paid $20 a night to perform twice a week. Baez gained substantial exposure when she made her debut at the Newport Folk Festival in 1959. She signed with Vanguard Records, which was a small folk label at the time, and released her first album, *Joan Baez,* in 1960; *Joan Baez, Volume 2,* followed in 1961. Early in her career, Baez worked within the historical folk

Peace activist and singer Joan Baez performs on stage during a free performance on the National Mall near the Ellipse in conjunction with an anti-war demonstration on Saturday, September 24, 2005, in Washington.

Source: AP Photo/Pablo Martinez Monsivais.

repertoire, adding more political content in the 1960s. Her first albums earned her a position in the American roots revival; she worked with other artists, including Bob Dylan, with whom she toured in the 1960s.

Baez has a long history of engagement with civil rights issues. She was involved with the struggle for migrant workers' rights as well as with the black rights movement. In 1963, she sang "We Shall Overcome" at Dr. Martin Luther King, Jr.'s March on Washington, a performance that linked her permanently to the song in the public consciousness. In 1966, she participated in the migrant farmworker strikes led by César Chávez.

As the Vietnam War escalated, the folksinger turned her attention toward war and draft protests. In 1964, Baez announced that she was refusing to pay 60% of her income taxes, as that percentage would go to fund U.S. military operations, and she encouraged draft resistance at her concerts. She also participated in the Free Speech Movement at the University of California at Berkeley and traveled to Hanoi with the U.S.-based Liaison Committee. With Ira Sandperl, Baez founded the Institute for the Study of Nonviolence in 1965 in Carmel Valley, California, and helped establish the presence of Amnesty International on the U.S. West Coast. Baez's work, both musically and politically, was often controversial. In 1967, the Daughters of the American Revolution denied her permission to perform at Constitution Hall. That same year, Baez was arrested twice (and once jailed) for blocking the entrance of the Armed Forces Induction Center in Oakland, California, as an act of civil disobedience. In 1968, she married David Harris, a Vietnam draft protestor and anti-war organizer who was ultimately imprisoned for draft resistance. Harris spent most of the couple's marriage in jail, but his interest in country music steered Baez toward country rock influences, which emerged in her work beginning with the appropriately titled *David's Album.* The couple had one child, Gabriel Earl, before divorcing in 1973.

Baez was among the performers at the original historic Woodstock music festival in 1969. In the 1970s, she began writing her own material, including the well-known song "Diamonds and Rust" (which was later covered by Judas Priest). In 1972, Baez traveled to North Vietnam as a member of a peace delegation to address human rights issues and deliver mail to American POWs. The delegation was caught in the United States' Christmas bombing of Hanoi.

Baez was appalled by the Vietnamese communists' human rights record, and she eventually arranged for the publication of a full-page newspaper advertisement describing its failures and offenses. The advertisement, which ran in four major newspapers in the United States, isolated Baez politically, as many American leftists were hesitant to criticize what purported to be a left-wing regime. The incident made Baez aware of the problems of partisanship within the human rights movement. This new awareness led her to found the Humanitas International Human Rights Committee, an organization focused on criticizing all oppressive regimes, regardless of where they fall within the political spectrum. She headed that organization for 13 years.

As the war in Southeast Asia drew to a close, Baez turned her attentions to problems in South America. She dedicated her first album sung entirely in Spanish to the Chilean people, who were then enduring the oppressive rule of Augusto Pinochet. Included on that record was a Spanish-language version of "We Shall Not Be Moved" ("No Nos Moveran"), which had been banned from public performance in Spain for more than four decades under Generalissimo Franco's regime. Baez was the first to perform the song publicly in 1977, 3 years after Franco's death. In 1981, Baez mounted a tour of Chile, Brazil, and Argentina but was not allowed to perform, as none of the three countries wished to give her a public forum in which to air her criticisms of their human rights practices.

Baez has also dedicated time and energy to the struggle for gay and lesbian rights in the United States. In an interview in the mid-1970s, she said that she considers herself bisexual, making her one of the first celebrities to publicly "out" herself. She performed at benefit concerts held to help defeat the 1978 Briggs Initiative (California's Proposition 6), which would have banned homosexuals from teaching in public schools, and participated in memorial marches for Harvey Milk, San Francisco's assassinated, openly gay city supervisor.

Even while taking a long hiatus from recording in the late 1980s, Baez continued her political activities. She participated in rallies for the nuclear freeze movement and played a significant role in 1985's Live Aid concert. Baez has also participated in a number of other human rights tours, including Amnesty International's A Conspiracy of Hope Tour in 1986. In 1991, Baez performed for crowds protesting the Persian Gulf War, and in 2003, she performed at two rallies in San Francisco protesting America's invasion of Iraq. In 2004, she participated in the filmmaker Michael Moore's Slacker Uprising Tour, advocating for young adults to vote for peace candidates in the national election. In 2005, she appeared at the anti-war protest started by Cindy Sheehan near President George W. Bush's ranch in Crawford, Texas, participated in a tribute to the survivors of Hurricane Katrina held at the Temple in Black Rock City during the annual Burning Man festival, and participated in protests held in Washington, D.C., against the Iraq War.

She has spoken out against the death penalty. In 1992, she appeared at a vigil protesting the execution of Robert Alton Harris, who was the first man executed after the reinstatement of the death penalty in California, and in 2005, she participated in the protest against the execution of Tookie Williams at San Quentin prison in California. Baez still contributes a stipend from the royalties of her album *Come From the Shadows* to the Resource Center for Nonviolence in Santa Cruz, California.

Baez has earned many awards, including the American Civil Liberties Union's Earl Warren Civil Liberties Award in 1976, the Jefferson Award from the Institute of Public Service in 1980, the Lennon Peace Tribute Award in 1982, and the Chevalier from the Légion d'Honneur, France, in 1983. Eight of Baez's records have reached gold status for sales, and she has been nominated for six Grammys. In 1980, Baez was awarded two honorary doctorates: one from Antioch University and the other from Rutgers University.

—*Carly A. Kocurek*

See also Amnesty International; Civil Disobedience; Civil Rights Movement; Conscientious Objectors to War; Dylan, Bob; Nonviolence and Activism

Further Readings

Baez, J. (1988). *And a voice to sing with: A memoir.* New York: Signet Books.

Fuss, C. J. (1996). *Joan Baez: A bio-bibliography.* Westport, CT: Greenwood Press.

Hajdu, D. (2002). *Positively 4th street: The lives and times of Joan Baez, Bob Dylan, Mimi Baez Fariña and Richard Fariña.* New York: North Point Press.

Jaeger, M. (2006). *Joan Baez and the issues of Vietnam: Art and activism versus conventionality.* Stuttgart, Germany: Ibidem-Verlag.

BAHÁ'Í FAITH AND SOCIAL ACTION

The Bahá'í is an independent world religion that promotes social justice through social action by advancing processes leading to world peace. In the Bahá'í value-hierarchy, social justice is the cardinal principle of human society. On the theory that all human actions flow from consciousness, Bahá'ís believe that world peace can only be established on a foundation of human solidarity—the harmony of races, religions, and nations. The purpose of justice, according to Bahá'u'lláh (1817–1892), prophet-founder of the Bahá'í Faith, is the achievement of unity in human society. International peace and security are unattainable, Bahá'u'lláh counsels, unless and until world unity is firmly established. Acting globally through interfaith alliances and national and international agencies, including the United Nations, Bahá'ís actively promote race unity, human rights, social and economic development, moral development, and the advancement of women. They draw international attention, in particular, to human rights violations against the Bahá'ís in Iran while advocating universal human rights for all. Bahá'ís aim to achieve these humanitarian goals through practical applications of Bahá'í principles of unity. Bahá'í philosopher Alain Locke (1885–1954), whose work is cited here to illustrate Bahá'í teachings, wrote that world peace depends on discovering necessary common values involved in the application of democracy on a world scale. World democracy thus entails building infrastructures that can best canalize efforts to achieve social justice, to which Bahá'í institutions and programs of social action contribute.

Bahá'ís at the United Nations

Ethics-based and religious non-governmental organizations (RNGOs) are playing increasingly significant roles in their consultative collaborations with the United Nations. As a RNGO, the Bahá'í International Community (BIC) represents a network of 182 democratically elected National Spiritual Assemblies that act on behalf of over 5.5 million Bahá'ís worldwide. Accordingly, the BIC is the voice of the worldwide Bahá'í community in international affairs. On the 60th anniversary of the United Nations in October 2005, the Bahá'í International Community issued a statement, "The Search for Values in an Age of Transition," presenting its recommendations for human rights, development, democracy, and collective security. Commending the international community's commitment to democracy, the BIC stressed that democracy is good governance—an essentially moral exercise (what Alain Locke calls a "moral democracy"). Democracy will succeed only if it is coefficient with personal integrity (gaining respect of the governed), moral principles, transparency, objective need assessments, and ethical applications of scientific resources. Democracy, according to the BIC, must be rooted in moral values that promote social welfare both within and beyond the nation-state. Without this principled anchor, democracy falls prey to the excesses of individualism and nationalism, which tear at the fabric of the community, both nationally and globally. As sociomoral forces, Bahá'í principles of unity serve as a moral bedrock for building a world democracy.

Principles of Unity

In his epistle to Queen Victoria (c. 1869), Bahá'u'lláh endorsed parliamentary democracy as an ideal form of governance. Referring to his own mission as that of a "World Reformer," Bahá'u'lláh promulgated social principles that are wider in scope than the process of electing governments. The Bahá'í community, in a measured participation in political democracy, eschews

partisan politics as polarizing and divisive. While exercising their civic obligation in voting, individual Bahá'ís distance themselves from the political theater of party politics. Embracing democracy, they shun campaigning. Instead, Bahá'ís work with the body politic, applying Bahá'í principles to better society. These principles include the following:

1. Human unity
2. Social justice
3. Racial harmony
4. Interfaith cooperation
5. Gender equality
6. Wealth equity (economic justice)
7. Social and economic development
8. International law
9. Human rights
10. Freedom of conscience
11. Individual responsibility
12. Harmony of science and religion
13. International scientific cooperation
14. International standards/world intercommunication
15. International language
16. Universal education
17. Environmentalism
18. World commonwealth
19. World tribunal
20. World peace
21. Search after truth
22. Freedom of conscience
23. Love of God
24. Nobility of character (acquiring virtues)
25. Advancing civilization (individual purpose)
26. Work as worship
27. Ideal marriage
28. Family values
29. Model communities

30. Religious teleology (Progressive Revelation)

31. Bahá'í doctrinal integrity

32. Bahá'í institutional support (the "Covenant")

33. Promoting Bahá'í values

In 1925, Alain Locke stated that Bahá'í principles—and the leavening of America's national life with its power—are to be regarded as the salvation of democracy. Only in this way can the fine professions of American ideals best be realized.

Bahá'ís in Iran

The Bahá'í Faith originated in Persia, now Iran, where the Bahá'í community has experienced a century and a half of persecution. In the years immediately following the 1979 Islamic revolution in Iran, clerics, with state sanction, ordered the arbitrary arrest of Bahá'ís, the use of torture, and the execution of more than 200 members (particularly elected members of Bahá'í administrative councils)—sometimes demanding that families pay for the bullets used to kill their loved ones. Other actions taken against Bahá'ís include confiscation of property; seizure of bank assets; expulsion from schools and universities; denial of employment; cancellation of pensions and demands that the government be reimbursed for past pension payments; desecration and destruction of Bahá'í cemeteries and holy places; criminalization of Bahá'í activities, thereby forcing the dissolution of Bahá'í institutions; and pronouncement that Bahá'í marriages were illegal acts of prostitution. State-instigated incitements to violence took the form of relentless propaganda campaigns aimed at inflaming anti-Bahá'í passions to instigate mob violence and crimes against Bahá'ís.

A new and insidious anti-Bahá'í strategy was formalized in a secret 1991 memorandum from the Iranian Supreme Revolutionary Cultural Council on "the Bahá'í question." Personally endorsed by Ayatollah Ali Khamenei on February 25, 1991, this document advises government officials to expel Bahá'ís from universities once Bahá'í identity becomes known. The directive—still in force—instructs officials to refuse Bahá'ís employment if they identify themselves as Bahá'ís, to bar their promotion to any position of influence, and to deny to all Bahá'ís the right to a higher education. No Bahá'í can, in practice, attend university in Iran. Iranian columnist Iqbal Latif calls Iran's denial of Bahá'ís' access to a university education "intellectual cleansing" of their ethnic brothers by the clergy-dominated regime. This phase of the anti-Bahá'í campaign has aptly been described as civil death—a cultural expurgation that collectively affects a community estimated to include more than 300,000 Iranians.

On March 20, 2006, the U.N. Special Reporter on Freedom of Religion or Belief, Asma Jahangir, issued a press release regarding a confidential letter sent October 29, 2005, by the Chairman of the Command Headquarters of the Armed Forces in Iran. The press release informed government officials that the Supreme Leader, Ayatollah Khamenei, had instructed Command Headquarters to identify all Bahá'ís and closely monitor their activities. In the wake of mounting media attacks on the Bahá'ís, such surveillance aggravates an already dangerous situation. Anti-Bahá'í propaganda campaigns have typically preceded government-led assaults on the Bahá'ís in Iran. In 2006, another U.N. special reporter reported that the regime is now confiscating family homes, thereby worsening the economic strangulation.

A New Model of Local Democracy

In marked contrast to Iran's efforts to extirpate the Bahá'í community, the Bahá'í Faith, as a global, supranational community, represents a new social experiment. In its joint RNGO statement, "Family and Social Development" (1994), the BIC stresses that the values of democracy and social justice must first be taught at home. The family, says the BIC, is the first environment to teach the values of local democracy, human rights, social responsibility, tolerance, and peace, thus enabling individual members to become advocates for social justice. These values, seen as the spirit of democracy, extend to each local Bahá'í community. The Universal House of Justice (the world Bahá'í governing body) speaks of the Nineteen-Day Feast (a Bahá'í worship service and consultative meeting held roughly every 3 weeks throughout the year) as an arena of democracy at the very root of society. This is where the Local Spiritual Assembly (the Bahá'í council annually elected by plurality vote with no campaigning allowed) and the members of the community meet on common ground, where individuals are free to offer their gifts of thought, whether new ideas or constructive criticism, to the building processes of an advancing civilization. Based on these and similar practices, the Universal House of Justice speaks of Bahá'u'lláh having prescribed a system that combines democratic practices with the application of knowledge through consultative processes.

Interfaith Cooperation

In accordance with Bahá'u'lláh's call to peace and fellowship among religions, Bahá'ís have taken part in the Parliament of the World's Religions, the World Bank's World Faiths Development Dialogue, and the Committee of RNGOs at the United Nations. In 1950, the annually elected governing body of the American Bahá'í community, the National Spiritual Assembly of the Bahá'ís of the United States (NSA) inaugurated World Religion Day to promote interfaith ecumenism. In April 2002, the Universal House of Justice issued a public letter addressed "To the World's Religious Leaders." This letter called on religious leaders worldwide to achieve common cause through a greater appreciation of their common ground and to unequivocally renounce all claims to exclusivity or finality, as such claims have precluded religious unity and have been the single greatest factor in justifying religious hatred and violence.

America's World Role

On December 23, 2001, shortly after the infamous 9/11 terrorist attacks, the NSA of the Bahá'ís of the United States published a statement, "The Destiny of America and the Promise of World Peace," as a full-page advertisement in the *New York Times*. It closes with an excerpt from a Bahá'í prayer: "May this American Democracy be the first nation to establish the foundation of international agreement. May it be the first nation to proclaim the unity of mankind. May it be the first to unfurl the standard of the Most Great Peace." This prayer envisions America's role in building a world democracy—not by force, but by example, in accordance with universal, moral principles.

Strengthening Human Rights

The BIC notes that the rise of democracy worldwide is a positive trend wherever nations have adopted free elections, representational governance, and strong human rights standards. In promoting social democracy, American Bahá'ís have taken leadership roles in advocating U.S. ratification of U.N. human rights treaties, including the U.N. Convention to Eliminate Racial Discrimination; the International Covenant on Civil and Political Rights; the International Convention on the Prevention and Punishment of the Crime of Genocide; and the International Convention against Torture and Other Cruel, Inhuman, or Degrading Treatment or Punishment. Current ratification efforts center on the Convention on the Elimination of All Forms of Discrimination Against Women and the Convention of the Rights of the Child.

Promoting Race Unity

In 1921, the NSA of the United States and Canada inaugurated a series of race amity conferences in Washington, D.C., and throughout the United States, in a historic contribution to what Alain Locke (who joined the Bahá'í Faith in 1918) called a "racial democracy" or, more broadly, a "social democracy." The spirit of efforts (which Locke personally helped organize) to promote interracial harmony lives on today. In 1957, the NSA inaugurated Race Unity Day (second Sunday in June)—an event now recognized by the United Nations—to promote interracial harmony. In 1991, the NSA issued "The Vision of Race Unity," a statement addressed to all Americans. Since racism is really a global issue, the NSA had urged the United States to become a party to the International Convention on the Elimination of All Forms of Racial Discrimination, which was finally ratified in 1994. In 1997, sponsored by the

National Spiritual Assembly, a video, called "The Power of Race Unity," was broadcast on the Black Entertainment Network and on other networks across America. The video characterizes the Bahá'í Faith as a "spiritual democracy."

Social and Economic Development

Economic solutions to global poverty require that economic values be predicated on spiritual values. In promoting economic justice and prosperity (what Alain Locke calls "economic democracy"), Bahá'í communities have launched more than 1,500 development projects worldwide, including more than 600 schools and seven radio stations broadcasting educational, health, and agricultural programs. Projects are tracked by the Bahá'í Office of Social and Economic Development, an agency of the Bahá'í World Center in Haifa, Israel. Published in December 2004, *In Service to the Common Good: The American Bahá'í Community's Commitment to Social Change* profiled, from among more than 400 Bahá'í-sponsored initiatives, a handful of projects in the fields of education, health care, race unity, community development, and women's rights. These projects include, among others: Health for Humanity, Tahirih Justice Center, Women for International Peace and Arbitration, Bahá'í Institute for Race Unity, Native American Bahá'í Institute, Children's Theater Company, and Parent University. In what Locke calls "cultural democracy," one must not forget the various Bahá'í artists, American Indian dancers, Bahá'í-sponsored musical groups, ballets, and youth dance workshops that reinforce progressive social values.

Advancement of Women

In "The Search for Values in an Age of Transition: A Statement of the Bahá'í International Community on the Occasion of the 60th Anniversary of the United Nations" (October 2005), the BIC states that a healthy democracy must be founded on the principle of the equality of men and women. Member states of the United Nations, in their efforts to promote democracy, must vigilantly work for the inclusion of women

in all facets of governance as a practical necessity. These Bahá'í-sponsored initiatives represent, but do not exhaust, efforts by the worldwide Bahá'í community and its democratically elected institutions to promote social justice through social action.

—*Christopher G. Buck*

See also Democracy; Human Rights Watch; Religious Activism

Further Readings

Bahá'í International Community. (2005, April 30). *Bahá'í International Community response to the Secretary General's Report, "In Larger Freedom: Towards Development, Security and Human Rights for All."* http://www.bahai.ch/pdf/LargerFreedom.pdf

Bahá'í International Community. (2005, October). *The search for values in an age of transition: A statement of the Bahá'í International Community on the occasion of the 60th anniversary of the United Nations* (BIC Document No. 05-1002). http://www.bic-un.bahai.org/pdf/05-1002.pdf

Bahá'í International Community. (2006, January). *A new framework for global prosperity: Bahá'í International Community's submission to the 2006 Commission on Social Development on the review of the First United Nations Decade for the Eradication of Poverty* (BIC Document No. 06-0101). http://www.bic-un.bahai.org/pdf/06-0101.pdf

Berger, J. (2003, March). Religious nongovernmental organizations: An exploratory analysis. *Voluntas: International Journal of Voluntary and Nonprofit Organizations, 14*(1), 15–39.

Buck, C. (2003). Islam and minorities: The case of the Bahá'ís [Special issue]. *Studies in Contemporary Islam, 5*(1–2). English: http://www.iranian.com/Opinion/2005/June/Bahai/Images/BuckBahais2005Eng.pdf; Farsi: http://www.iranian.com/Opinion/2005/June/Bahai/Images/BuckBahais2005.pdf

Buck, C. (2005). *Alain Locke: Faith and philosophy.* Los Angeles: Kalimát Press.

Gervais, M. (2004). The Baha'i curriculum for peace education. *Journal of Peace Education, 1*(2), 205–224.

Ghanea, N. (2003). *Human rights, the UN and the Bahá'ís in Iran.* Leiden, Netherlands: Martinus Nijhoff.

Hassall, G. (2000). Rights to human and social development: A survey of the activities of the Bahá'í International Community. In T. Tahririha-Danesh (Ed.), *Bahá'í-inspired perspectives on human rights* (pp. 102–122). Hong Kong: Juxta. http://www.juxta.com/main.cfm?SID=22

National Spiritual Assembly of the Bahá'ís of the United States. (2004). *In service to the common good: The American Bahá'í Community's commitment to social change.* http://www.bahai.us/in-service-to-the-common-good

BAKER, ELLA (1903–1986)

Ella Josephine Baker, an African American civil rights and political activist, was influential in a broad range of 20th-century social justice movements for almost half a century. Baker is one of a group of significant, but not widely known, African American women who made crucial contributions to the civil rights movement. Her radical vision of social change emphasized grassroots organizing, commitment to listening to people, and then working together to address their problems and needs.

Baker, born in Norfolk, Virginia, was influenced by growing up in Norfolk and rural North Carolina as the granddaughter of former slaves. Family members, such as her grandfather, Mitchell Ross, a farmer and Baptist minister, and her mother, Georgianna Ross Baker, whose religious beliefs and sense of moral obligation spurred her to help the sick and others in need in the community, set examples that would influence Baker's activism for the eradication of poverty, racism, and other inequities. Baker was sent to the Shaw Academy and University in Raleigh, North Carolina, and graduated as class valedictorian in 1927.

Within a year, she moved to Harlem, where she encountered what she described as radical thinking and saw firsthand the terrible impact of the Great Depression on ordinary people's lives. She held jobs ranging from waitressing and factory labor to editorial and management work for the *American West Indian News* and the *Negro National News.* Through working at the Harlem Branch Library, helping organize speakers for the Adult Education committee, attending Brookwood Labor College (established to train labor organizers) in Katonah, New York, for a semester in 1931, Ella Baker became immersed in the radical political debates of the time.

Ella Baker worked on tenant and consumer rights with the Dunbar Housewives' League, as well as on a variety of community cooperative projects. Along with George Schuyler, in 1930 she helped organize and became executive director of the Young Negroes' Cooperative League, a black consumer cooperative formed to combat the economic effects of the Depression and to promote mutual aid, communalism, and community-based action. In the 1930s, Ella also taught consumer education through the Works Progress Administration. She was married to Thomas J. Roberts for several decades but kept her maiden name, and she raised her niece Jacqueline Brockington.

Ella Baker's organizing abilities and capacity to be an effective grassroots trainer were central to her work with the National Association for the Advancement of Colored People (NAACP). In the 1940s, she traveled in the South and throughout the country as a field secretary and helped recruit members, organized campaigns locally, and raised money as director of branches. She worked closely with people on everything from job training for African Americans to anti-lynching campaigns and thus created a network of individuals committed to social and economic change. This network would become an important source for the civil rights activities of the 1950s and 1960s. By 1952, Baker resigned from the NAACP in part to raise her niece but also because of her disaffection with the bureaucracy and the lack of a group-centered leadership. Baker returned to Harlem and was elected president of the New York City NAACP branch. By building coalitions, she organized campaigns on issues such as desegregation, school reform, and police brutality. Her involvement in coalition politics resulted in her unsuccessful run for elective office for the New York City Council on the Liberal Party ticket.

In 1956, Baker, along with Stanley Levison and Bayard Rustin (both men would become advisors to Martin Luther King, Jr.), founded In Friendship, an organization that raised funds to aid the growing civil rights struggle in the South, including the Montgomery Improvement Association, the coordinator of the Montgomery bus boycott. In 1957, Baker and Rustin went south to help organize the founding meeting of the Southern Christian Leadership Conference

(SCLC). As in her earlier work in the NAACP, Baker played an important if largely unacknowledged role in the SCLC. Her criticism of its reliance on charismatic male leaders and hierarchical organizational structures would cause tension with the SCLC leadership, including Martin Luther King, Jr. She was instrumental in organizing the successful May 17, 1957, Prayer Pilgrimage for Freedom held at the Lincoln Memorial in Washington, D.C. Attended by 25,000 to 30,000 people, it provided a national political stage for the SCLC. In 1958, Baker moved to Atlanta and worked for the SCLC directing the voter rights campaign, Crusade for Citizenship. Baker continued to urge SCLC leaders to promote mass action programs, to target women's involvement, and to develop youth and action work.

In April 1960, following a series of student desegregation sit-ins, Baker invited students and other leaders to a conference at Shaw University, her alma mater. Later that year, she helped them form the Student Nonviolent Coordinating Committee.

Baker encouraged and mentored the founding of an independent youth organization that provided a more egalitarian, grassroots-based model than that of the SCLC. Four years later, the Mississipi Freedom Democratic Party was created as a grassroots political party challenging the all-white, segregated Mississippi Democratic Party. Baker established the Mississippi Freedom Democratic Party's Washington, D.C, office. She delivered the keynote speech at its state convention in Jackson, Missisippi, and eulogized the three recently murdered white civil rights workers.

Baker continued to work on a series of projects, including the Southern Conference Education Fund, which was organized to promote cooperation between black and white people. From serving on the Puerto Rican Solidarity Committee to ties with the Third World Women's Alliance to the Angela Davis Defense Committee, Ella Jo Baker lent her support and name to a range of activities that promoted her vision for radical change and elimination of racial, economic, and political injustice.

—Joyce Apsel

See also Civil Rights Movement; King, Martin Luther, Jr.; National Association for the Advancement of Colored People (NAACP); Southern Christian Leadership Conference; Student Nonviolent Coordinating Committee (SNCC)

Further Readings

Grant, J. (Producer/Director). (1981). *Fundi: The story of Ella Baker* [Video film]. (Available from First Run Icarus Films, 32 Court Street, 21st Floor, Brooklyn, NY 11201)

Grant, J. (1998). *Ella Baker: Freedom bound.* New York: Wiley.

Ransby, B. (2003). *Ella Baker and the black freedom movement: A radical democratic vision.* Chapel Hill: University of North Carolina Press.

BALDWIN, JAMES (1924–1987)

James Arthur Baldwin was born in Harlem, New York City, on August 2, 1924. He was the eldest of nine children. His stepfather, a hard and cruel man, was a storefront preacher. A voracious reader as a child, Baldwin published his first story at the age of 12 in a church newspaper. At the early age of 14, he became a preacher in a Pentecostal church in Harlem, but in his late teens, he converted from the love of religion back to his first love, literature. Baldwin's literary genius would take him all over the world, but he was always rooted in the influences of his childhood. The influences on his writing style included the rhythms and rhetoric of the King James Bible and the storefront church. Family, race, and sexuality would become his topics of choice. His writings were influential in informing a large white audience about growing up black in America.

The year that Baldwin was born was also the year of the Detroit race riots of 1924, one of the bloodiest race riots of the century. The day of his stepfather's funeral, on Baldwin's 19th birthday, a race riot broke out in Harlem as well. Indeed, as they drove to the graveyard, Baldwin later wrote, injustice, anarchy, discontent, and hatred were all around them. As a black man in America, Baldwin seemed destined to confront race, and he approached it with the evangelical fervor of his youth. He had been a child preacher, and he still believed in the possibility of mass conversion regarding race in America.

Baldwin's rage toward racism was fueled by a job he had in a defense plant in New Jersey during the war. It was there that he felt the sting of segregation at the bars, diners, and bowling alleys that were closed to him. He insisted on going to these places even though he knew he would be refused service. He felt compelled to suffer the rejection and force whites to tell him they would not serve him.

Baldwin began writing full-time in 1943 and, although publishers rejected his work, his book reviews and essays helped garner him the prestigious Rosenwald Fellowship in 1948. Baldwin's difficult relationship with his stepfather, his confusion with his sexual orientation, the suicide of a friend, and the ever-present strain of racism in America drove him to move to Paris in 1948. It was in Europe that Baldwin finished *Go Tell It on the Mountain*; this novel garnered him fame when it was published in 1953. In this and subsequent works, Baldwin fused autobiographical material with a keen analysis of prejudice and social injustice. In his book *Love in a Dark Time: And Other Explorations of Gay Lives and Literature,* Colm Tóibín says that Baldwin was both freed and cornered by his heritage. He was freed from being a dandy and freed into finding a subject. Then he was cornered into being a spokesman or an exile.

Baldwin was always conscious of his otherness and wrote about it often. In an essay, "Stranger in the Village" (1953), he describes traveling to a small Swiss village. The children call him a nigger in Swedish, and he realizes that American beliefs originated right there in Europe. He had not escaped racism at all by going to Europe; he had only found its roots.

Baldwin's play *The Amen Corner,* published in 1955, was also written during his time in Europe; it speaks to another of Baldwin's major topics, that of family. He was the oldest child in his family and once commented that his family had saved him because they kept him so busy caring for them. Many of his writings had a theme of brotherhood and, often, of one brother helplessly watching the other spiral down into death and despair. The title essay in *Notes of a Native Son* (1955) was autobiographical.

In 1956, Baldwin published his second novel, *Giovanni's Room,* the story of a white American expatriate who must come to terms with his sexual orientation. This beautifully written story about gay love has come to symbolize the confining space occupied by gays in the past. It is considered by many to be the finest example of gay prose ever created. Baldwin's inclusion of gay themes resulted in a brutal criticism from some in the black community. Eldridge Cleaver, of the Black Panthers, said that Baldwin's writings displayed a total hatred of blacks. Editors in New York felt that publishing a black writer was fascinating, but they also felt that publishing a black homosexual writer was totally impossible. Publishers told him point-blank not to write about his homosexuality. When he did, they refused to publish it.

Baldwin returned to America from Europe in 1957 to participate in the struggle for school desegregation in the South. He offered a vital literary voice during the era of the civil rights movement and activism during the 1950s and 1960s. Many other famous black literary figures would have nothing to do with the civil rights movement; Langston Hughes took no part, nor did Ralph Ellison. Baldwin's writing and passion was always connected to the world of his family and his country. It was inevitable that he would become passionately involved in the movement. The movement, though, offered him no safe haven.

The civil rights movement was hostile to homosexuals. There were only two known gay men in the movement, Baldwin and Bayard Rustin. Rustin was a veteran activist by the time the movement came to national prominence. He had been imprisoned as a conscientious objector, beaten by police as early as 1942 for his refusal to obey segregation laws, and served on a chain gang in 1947 for his participation in the first Freedom Ride organized by the Congress of Racial Equality. Rustin and King were very close, as Rustin received credit for the success of the March on Washington. Whereas King was not bothered by Rustin's homosexuality, many of his colleagues were. Eventually homophobic pressure resulted in King distancing himself from Rustin. This may also be why Baldwin was conspicuously uninvited to speak at the end of the March on Washington. During his involvement in the movement, Baldwin made speeches, went on television, traveled, and organized boycotts. He wrote very little during this time; many believe it was because his work was directly political.

Published in 1962, the novel *Another Country* was about racial and gay sexual tensions among New York intellectuals. It was criticized for having weak characters. Also published in 1962, *Nobody Knows My Name* was a collection of essays that explored, among other issues, black-white relations in America, Faulkner's views on segregation, and the work of Richard Wright. It became a bestseller in 1963 under the title *The Fire Next Time*; in it, Baldwin warned readers that violence would result if white America did not change its attitudes toward black America. Like King and others during the civil rights movement, Baldwin attracted the attention of the Federal Bureau of Investigation, which had a 1,750-page file on him.

When Martin Luther King, Jr. was assassinated in 1968, Baldwin began to acknowledge that violence was the way to racial justice. Optimism and peaceful solutions crept back into his work later. His novel *Tell Me How Long the Train's Been Gone* (1968) was also criticized as simpleminded and one-dimensional. *If Beale Street Could Talk* (1974) showed an artistic renewal as Baldwin penned a moving and poetic love story that emphasized the importance of family bonds and the simple power of love as a means of survival. *The Evidence of Things Not Seen* (1985) was an account of the brutal, unsolved murders of 28 black children in Atlanta in 1980 and 1981. It also disappointed critics. Baldwin became Five College Professor in the Afro-American Studies Department of the University of Massachusetts at Amherst in 1983. He spent his last years, however, in St. Paul de Vence on the Riviera, in France, where he died of stomach cancer on November 30, 1987.

Baldwin was compelling because he embodied so many contradictions. He was artist and agitator. He was political and engaged. He was Harlem and Greenwich Village and Paris. He was social and a loner. In his writings he explored the parts of the self that most people conceal and attempt to hide even from themselves. He wanted it all illuminated; he wanted to bare it all. Always the child preacher, Baldwin demonstrated the

necessity of recognizing our sins, and not just those of racism and homophobia, but our refusal to really know each other, to accept differences, and to love. He believed not in guilt, but in responsibility.

—Jeff Sapp

See also Civil Rights Movement; Congress of Racial Equality; Freedom Rides, 1961; King, Martin Luther, Jr.; Literature and Activism; Nonviolence and Activism; Other, The

Further Readings

Baldwin, J. (1953, October). Stranger in the village. *Harper's, 207,* 42–48.

Baldwin, J. (1953). *Go tell it on the mountain.* New York: Knopf.

Baldwin, J. (1954, July). The amen corner. *Zero, 2,* 4–8, 11–13.

Baldwin, J. (1955). *Notes of a native son.* Boston: Beacon Press.

Baldwin, J. (1956). *Giovanni's room.* New York: Dial.

Baldwin, J. (1962). *Another country.* New York: Dial.

Baldwin, J. (1963). *The fire next time.* New York: Dial.

Baldwin, J. (1968). *Tell me how long the train's been gone.* New York: Dial.

Baldwin, J. (1974). *If Beale Street could talk.* New York: Dial.

Baldwin, J. (1985). *The evidence of things not seen.* New York: Holt, Rinehart & Winston.

Tóibín, C. (2001). *Love in a dark time: And other explorations of gay lives and literature.* New York: Scribner.

BALLOT INITIATIVES

Perhaps more than anywhere else in the world, activists clamoring for social justice have used ballot initiatives in the American states to advance their progressive causes. The initiative is one of the three mechanisms of direct democracy (along with the popular referendum and the recall).

Originating in Switzerland, direct democracy was imported to the United States during the 1890s, the heyday of the populist movement. Of the three mechanisms, the initiative is by far the most widely used. It allows citizens to participate directly in the making of public policy by casting their votes on ballot measures. In order to place either a statutory or a constitutional amendment measure on the ballot for fellow citizens to adopt or reject, a specified number of valid signatures must be collected by petition. Activists for social justice, of course, do not hold a monopoly on the initiative process; corporate interests along with social conservatives also place initiatives on the ballot and have done so with considerable success.

Most of the two dozen states that allow the initiative process today adopted the mechanism during the early 20th century. The practice of direct democracy grew out of the doctrines put forth by the Populist (People's) Party, the single-taxers led by Henry George, and the Farmers' Alliance during the late 19th century. In 1898, the citizens of South Dakota became the first in the Union to adopt the initiative, and in 1904, citizens in Oregon were the first to collect signatures to successfully qualify initiatives for the ballot. The number of statewide initiatives on the ballot increased rapidly during the 1910s but tapered off after World War I. Use of the process regained popularity in the 1970s.

Along with Henry George, social reformers James W. Sullivan of New Jersey, John Randolph Haynes of California, Benjamin B. Lindsey of Colorado, and William S. U'Ren of Oregon, were all early proponents of the mechanisms of direct democracy. Many progressive politicians also aligned themselves with the effort in the states to adopt direct democracy. Republican U.S. Senator Jonathan Bourne, Jr. from Oregon and several Progressive governors (both Republicans and Democrats, including California's Hiram Johnson) were outspoken advocates of the "People's Rule," as the initiative was often called. Perhaps most prominently, former president Teddy Roosevelt stumped in 1912 for the adoption of direct democracy, maintaining that the initiative could serve as an institutional check on unresponsive state legislatures. If legislators failed to recognize or respond to the wishes of the public, citizens could resort to direct action by passing initiatives that either amended the state constitution or enacted a statute. Woodrow Wilson, an erstwhile critic of the process, eventually jumped on the direct democracy bandwagon during the 1912 presidential campaign, calling the initiative a gun behind the door that could persuade legislators to act in accordance to the wishes of the people.

Once states adopted the initiative, progressive activists used ballot initiatives to call for numerous issues promoting social justice, after being rebuffed by political party bosses who were in cahoots with corporate interests and controlled the agendas of the state legislatures. Self-styled Progressive Era reformers in numerous states placed initiatives on the ballot calling for women's suffrage, the direct primary, the direct election of U.S. senators, the abolition of the poll tax, home rule for cities and towns, 8-hour work days for women and minors, and the regulation of public utility and railroad monopolies. Voters adopted many of these measures on election day. In circumventing their co-opted state legislatures, these reformers used the initiative to advance public policy that promoted transparency in public life, equal economic opportunity, and broader social welfare.

Not surprisingly, the popular expression of the *vox populi* has not always been synonymous with a progressive agenda advancing the causes of social justice. Even during the Progressive Era, many economic interests—from railroads to public utilities to mining operators to fishermen to ranchers to newspaper owners to morticians—turned to the initiative process to advance their narrow agendas. Big money, too, has always been part of the process. In 1922, for example, over $1 million was spent in California on seven measures on the ballot. In one of the ballot measure campaigns that year—the Pacific Gas and Electric Company's effort to defeat the Water and Power Act—over $660,000 was spent. As is the case today, vested interests were not always successful in their endeavors; economic interests traditionally have had an easier time defeating initiatives than passing them. But the historical record from the Progressive Era suggests that the initiative process was just as dangerous to progressive forces as it was empowering to them.

Today, ballot initiatives in the United States continue to reflect a mix of both progressive and conservative issues. Voters have passed progressive ballot initiatives boosting the minimum wage, requiring utilities to invest in renewable energy, allocating public dollars for embryonic stem cell research, requiring environmental cleanup, proposing public financing of candidate campaigns, recommending nonpartisan electoral redistricting and fusion voting, providing for dedicated revenue streams for public education and class-size requirements, demanding increased land-use conservation, guaranteeing animal protection, legalizing medical marijuana, and taxing tobacco for health education programs. Many of these same voters, however, have also passed an array of conservative ballot measures, including same-sex marriage bans, tax cuts and limits on governmental spending, caps on medical malpractice lawsuits, prohibitions on affirmative action and welfare benefits for illegal immigrants and their children, abortion restrictions, and English Only requirements. Direct democracy knows no ideological bounds; rather, it is a populist reflection of the sentiments of those who turn out to vote.

One of the strongest and most enduring criticisms of the initiative made by advocates of social justice is that the majoritarian process inherently leads to policy outcomes that threaten the rights of minorities and the representation of minority interests. There is considerable anecdotal evidence that some initiatives do have harmful consequences for racial, ethnic, sexual, and language minorities, and more indirectly, that the process of voting on divisive issues may contribute to the suppression of minority rights by negatively affecting public attitudes toward already marginalized groups. Yet, the classic argument against the initiative—that when contrasted with state legislatures, the process systematically disadvantages racial and ethnic minorities—has found limited empirical support.

Supporters of the initiative argue that ballot measures have an educative quality that can help promote democratic deliberation and engagement. Though cognizant that economic interests could use the initiative too, many Progressive Era reformers long ago realized that the merit of the citizen initiative was not limited to its substantive policy outcomes. Pointing to its educative value, reformers highlighted the beneficial procedural byproducts of having citizens serve as lawmakers. They argued that ballot initiatives not only provide additional political information to citizens, they give them more reason to participate in the electoral process. Pedagogically, the act of voting on ballot measures can help educate citizens, stimulating them to become more politically engaged and involved in civic affairs.

There is considerable scholarly evidence that the initiative process does have these so-called educative effects. Across a slate of democratic participatory dimensions, citizens living in initiative states are generally more civically involved than those living in noninitiative states. Being exposed to ballot measures encourages voters to turn out to vote, become more civically engaged in the political process, and have more trust in their government. Survey data show that citizens living in states with frequent exposure to ballot initiatives vote with more frequency, are better informed about politics and discuss politics more often, and express more confidence in government responsiveness than citizens living in noninitiative states. These findings are particularly robust in low-information contexts, such as midterm elections when ballot issue campaigns are less likely to compete with media coverage of candidate races.

Ballot campaigns also can alter the dynamics of candidate elections, alternatively hurting or helping progressive candidates. Following the lead of conservatives, activists for social justice have tried to harness the power of ballot measures for electoral purposes. Some ballot measures can be used to underscore campaign themes and set the agenda in candidate elections. Since there are no limitations on how much can be raised or spent on ballot measure campaigns, other measures can be used to circumvent contribution limitations in candidate races. Finally, ballot measures can help increase voter turnout as well as drive wedges into the opposing party's base. While conservatives appear to have discovered some sure-fire issues to mobilize supporters to the polls, including tax cuts and socially divisive measures, such as anti-gay marriage and affirmative action, progressives are still searching for issues, such as increases to the minimum wage, the protection of civil liberties, and environmental protection, that may help them to activate their base.

In order to more strategically push ballot measures, several progressive organizations, along with organized labor, came together in the late 1990s to create the Ballot Initiative Strategy Center (BISC). BISC was established to counteract conservative ballot initiatives and proactively craft progressive ones. Today, BISC acts as a catalyst, bringing together national, state, and local organizations to coordinate efforts to challenge conservative ballot measures and support progressive initiatives. One of BISC's principal goals is to help educate the progressive political and donor community about the value and power of ballot initiatives. In addition to its national tracking and response center, which improves the capacity for handling defensive priorities so that more progressive issues get more attention, BISC works with progressive groups in initiative states to develop campaign strategies and dispatch strategic intervention staff to set up grassroots campaign operations. To this end, BISC has led training courses to educate hundreds of individuals to work on ballot initiative campaigns and has identified professional consultants who are able to lend their services. As the key facilitator of progressive ballot initiatives, BISC plays a central role in using the process of direct democracy to advance issues of social justice.

—*Daniel A. Smith*

See also ACORN; Affirmative Action; Coalition Building; Progressive Movement, Education; Strategies and Tactics in Social Movements; Union Movements; Women's Suffrage Movement

Further Readings

Allswang, J. (2000). *The initiative and referendum in California, 1898–1998.* Palo Alto, CA: Stanford University Press.

Bowler, S., & Donovan, T. (1998). *Demanding choices: Opinion, voting, and direct democracy.* Ann Arbor: University of Michigan Press.

Bowler, S., Donovan, T., & Tolbert, C. (Eds.). (1998). *Citizens as legislators: Direct democracy in the United States.* Columbus: Ohio State University Press.

Cronin, T. (1989). *Direct democracy: The politics of initiative, referendum, and recall.* Cambridge, MA: Harvard University Press.

Ellis, R. (2002). *Democratic delusions: The initiative process in America.* Lawrence: University Press of Kansas.

Gerber, E. (1999). *The populist paradox: Interest group influence and the promise of direct legislation.* Princeton, NJ: Princeton University Press.

Goebel, T. (2002). *A government by the people: Direct democracy in America, 1890–1940.* Chapel Hill: University of North Carolina Press.

Magleby, D. (1984). *Direct legislation: Voting on ballot propositions in the United States.* Baltimore: Johns Hopkins University Press.

Matsusaka, J. (2004). *For the many or the few? The initiative, public policy, and American democracy.* Chicago: University of Chicago Press.

Schrag, P. (1998). *Paradise lost: California's experience, America's future.* New York: New Press.

Smith, D. A. (1998). *Tax crusaders and the politics of direct democracy.* New York: Routledge.

Smith, D. A., & Tolbert, C. J. (2004). *Educated by initiative: The effects of direct democracy on citizens and political organizations in the American states.* Ann Arbor: University of Michigan Press.

Waters, M. D. (Ed.). (2001). *The battle over citizen lawmaking.* Durham, NC: Carolina Academic Press.

Waters, M. D. (Ed.). (2003). *The initiative and referendum almanac.* Durham, NC: Carolina Academic Press.

Baraka, Amiri (1934–)

Writer, intellectual, and activist Amiri Baraka, alternately associated with the Beat movement, black nationalism, and socialism, was born Everett LeRoi Jones in 1934 in Newark, New Jersey. The son of a postal worker, Baraka attended Rutgers University and Howard University before joining the air force.

Upon discharge in 1957, Baraka, then known as LeRoi Jones, took up residence in Greenwich Village, soon after marrying Hettie Cohen. Together, they edited a literary magazine, *Yugen,* and became associated with the bohemian scene, in particular with the up-and-coming writers of the Beat movement. He soon founded Totem Press, which would be the first to publish Allen Ginsberg and Jack Kerouac. Baraka's own first published work appeared in 1958, a play titled *A Good Girl Is Hard to Find.*

In 1961, Baraka's first volume of poetry, *Preface to a Twenty-Volume Suicide Note,* was published. From 1961 to 1963, he coedited *The Floating Bear* with Beat writer Diane Di Prima. During this time, he was also teaching at the New School for Social Research in New

York. In 1963, he published his first book of music criticism, *Blues People: Negro Music in White America*.

Baraka became more widely known in 1964 with the production of another play, *Dutchman*, which won an Obie. It was later made into a film. Soon after the assassination of Malcolm X in 1965, Baraka aligned himself with the black nationalists. He left his wife, moved to Harlem, and founded the Black Arts Repertory Theatre/School, which influenced black theaters nationally but was short-lived.

In 1967, Baraka moved back to Newark, married poet Sylvia Robinson, and founded another company of actors, the Spirit House Players. A black nationalist volume of poetry, *Black Magic*, was published.

He adopted the Muslim name Imamu Amiri Baraka in 1968 (later dropping Imamu), and his wife adopted the name Amina Baraka. He became involved in Kawaida, a Black Muslim organization; he was also chairman of the Congress of African People, and led the organization of the National Black Political Convention.

By 1974, Baraka had rejected the black nationalist viewpoint and instead declared himself a socialist. From that point on, he produced several socialist works, including essays, plays, and poetry collections. He guest lectured at several universities before working in the Africana Studies Department at SUNY-Stonybrook. He became a full professor in 1984 and remained at SUNY until his retirement in 1999.

Baraka has since remained active in his artistic and political pursuits. He has continued to publish and, in 2002, became poet laureate of the state of New Jersey. A year later, after controversy surrounding his poem about the events of 9/11, "Somebody Blew Up America," state lawmakers voted to eliminate the poet laureate post. Baraka insisted that the poem had been misinterpreted.

—*Heidi Stevenson*

See also Beat Poets; Black Power; Literature and Activism

Further Readings

Baraka, A. (1995). *The autobiography of LeRoi Jones*. Southwest Harbor, ME: A Cappella.

Baraka, A. (1999). *The LeRoi Jones/Amiri Baraka reader* (W. J. Harris, Ed.). Emeryville, CA: Thunder's Mouth Press.

BASQUE SEPARATIST MOVEMENT

See ETA

BASQUIAT, JEAN-MICHEL (1960–1988)

Neo-Expressionist painter Jean-Michel Basquiat, a controversial member of the New York art scene, was known for his accessible works that rejected material culture. Originally a graffiti artist who painted New York City subway trains, he integrated a bicultural stance into his art. His "tag" or signature, SAMO, which stood for "same old shit," was included in nearly all his work through the early 1980s. His often nonpictorial paintings incorporated provocative words and phrases, questioning racism, discrimination, and prevailing middle-class values. His style was a response to the inaccessibility of mid-century minimalist and conceptual art movements, and it built on elements of 1920s surrealism.

Although raised in the middle class, Basquiat identified himself as a street artist whose ideas came from poverty and outsider status. He embraced his Puerto Rican and Haitian backgrounds, although as a man of color, he was a marginal member of the mainstream art community. However, due to his background and education, he was not fully accepted in the African American art community. Thus, his work reflected his search for identity, bringing a multiethnic perspective to his artistic endeavors.

Basquiat entered the art scene during "Reaganomics": The economy was booming and newly rich technocrats invested in art as tax write-offs. These new investors sought works that reflected their political questions and idealism. Basquiat's popularity was a reflection of his outsider status; his neo-Expressionist style made his work accessible and understandable to naïve collectors.

Although he had no formal art training, the scope of his work was broad and he acknowledged influences from Twombley, Debuffet, Pollack, and Picasso.

Basquiat's oeuvre is divided into three eras. Between 1980 and 1982, he painted crude skulls, masks, and body parts in a spiky, repetitive style. In 1982, he destroyed all unsold pieces. He is best known for collages he created between 1982 and 1985, integrating images from African art and culture and major figures in American black history and jazz with his signature word art, thereby creating heroic portraits of black males, crowned and haloed. Between 1985 and 1988, he painted huge canvases, filled with letters.

In the early 1980s, Basquiat became close friends with Andy Warhol. Together they created a series of paintings and exhibited them at a collaborative show in New York City. One critic referred to Basquiat as Warhol's mascot, which led to Basquiat's breaking away from the friendship to ensure his own identity.

Basquiat died in New York City in 1988 of a heroin overdose, leaving a mixed legacy. He is often lauded as an innovative artist whose exploitation of his own bicultural background gave his work a political edge, transforming art from background to foreground. Others suggest that his work was naïve and crude and that his popularity was tied to the economic excesses of the time.

—Barbara Garii

See also Literature and Activism

Further Readings

Marshall, C. (1999). Jean-Michel Basquiat, outsider superstar. *International Review of African American Art, 16*(4), 32–36.

Basta Ya!

See Ya Basta!

Battle of Seattle

The Battle of Seattle consisted of a series of marches, direct actions, protests, and "black bloc" tactics carried out from November 28 through December 3, 1999, in a successful effort to disrupt the World Trade Organization (WTO) Ministerial Conference. Comprising a broad and diffuse coalition of the American Federation of Labor (AFL-CIO) and other labor unions, student groups, non-governmental organizations (NGOs) such as Global Exchange and Oxfam, Earth First!ers, Jubilee 2000, media activists, international farmers and industrial workers, the Ruckus Society, groups allied with the Direct Action Network (DAN), anarchists, and others, the Battle of Seattle is often referred to as "the coming-out party" of the anti-neoliberal-globalization movement.

The Battle of Seattle was one of the first major international mobilizations to be coordinated via the Internet. It was reported online with streaming audio and video clips by the Seattle Independent Media Center. While 400,000 people took part in a virtual sit-in of the WTO website organized by the Electrohippies, the ground war was a loose populist assemblage of more than 40,000 protestors (some estimates are as high as 60,000) opposing everything from specific WTO policies to free trade and neoliberal paternalism to the human rights failures of globalization. Replete with NGO-sponsored debates, lectures, and various teach-ins throughout the week, the battle is most notable for the events of N30 (code for November 30, 1999)—the AFL-CIO People's Rally and March and the "Shut down the WTO-Mass Nonviolent Direct Action" blockade—and the resulting escalation of police force.

By the morning of N30, an estimated 10,000 protestors, including DAN-organized affinity groups, surrounded the Paramount Theatre and Convention Center—the location of many WTO functions. Through a variety of solidarity tactics, such as street theater, sit-ins, chaining affinity groups together, and activists locking themselves to metal pipes in strategic locations, the protestors prevented the opening ceremony from taking place. In response to this civil disobedience, the police utilized close-range pepper sprays, tear gas grenades, and rubber bullets in their efforts to disperse the crowd; some protestors responded in kind by throwing sticks and water bottles. At the same time, the permitted AFL-CIO

People's Rally and March of over 25,000 Teamsters, Longshoremen, and environmental activists began at Memorial Stadium. As the march gradually moved downtown toward the Convention Center, a few hundred anarchists used targeted black bloc property destruction tactics against Starbucks, Nike, Nordstrom, and other stores, and a few protestors burned trash-cans and broke store windows. By midday, Seattle's central business district was clogged with marchers from the People's Rally, DAN blockaders, and other dissenters; consequently, several WTO events were cancelled. The mayor of Seattle, looking to quell the massive protests in anticipation of President Clinton's arrival the following day and finally running out of riot control chemicals, declared a 7 P.M. to 7 A.M. cur-few in the area.

The following day, December 1, 1999, saw the illegalization of gas masks and the creation of a 50-block "no protest zone" in the central business district; moreover, the Seattle police were joined that morning by members of the Washington National Guard and the U.S. military. More mass dissentions and acts of civil disobedience, some vandalism, and curfew violations resulted in reprisals by the police forces and the eventual arrest of more than 500 people on December 1 alone. On December 2 and 3, thousands of demonstrators staged sit-ins outside the Seattle Police Department to protest what was seen by many as the department's brutal tactics against peaceful protestors. Finally, December 3 ended with U.S. Trade Representative Charlene Barshefsky and WTO Director-General Michael Moore announcing the suspension of the WTO Ministerial Conference in response to both the street actions and disagreements between the various delegations.

Seattle was left with millions of dollars in property damage and lawsuits by protestors arguing civil rights violations. While many of the affiliations formed by divergent political groups dissolved within the next few years, the Battle of Seattle did jumpstart a series of international anti-corporate-globalization protests and helped progressive movements realize the power of the Internet for mobilization and coalition building. Also, the Battle of Seattle allowed media activists to grasp the potential of the Indymedia model, which quickly spread and propagated throughout the country and abroad.

—*Katherine Casey-Sawicki*

See also American Federation of Labor (AFL-CIO); Anarchism; Anti-Globalization Movement; Direct Action; Earth First!; Global Exchange; Indymedia; Non-Governmental Organizations (NGOs); Nonviolence and Activism; Oxfam; Police Brutality; Strategies and Tactics in Social Movements; Virtual Sit-Ins

Further Readings

Big Noise Productions, Changing America, Headwaters Action Video Collective, Paper Tiger TV, Video Active, Whispered Media, and IMC (Producers/Directors). (1999). *Showdown in Seattle: Five days that shook the WTO* [Documentary film].

Cockburn, A., St. Clair, J., & Sekula, A. (2000). *5 Days that shook the world: Seattle and beyond.* London: Verso.

Independent Media Center. (2006, April 6). Indymedia documentation project. http://docs.indymedia.org/view/Global/FrequentlyAskedQuestionEn

Infoshop.org. (1999, August 31). NO2WTO. http://www.infoshop.org/no2wto.html

Klein, N. (2002). Seattle: The coming-out party of a movement. In *Fences and windows: Dispatches from the front lines of the globalization debate.* New York: Picador.

Meikle, G. (2002). Backing into the future. In *Future active: Media activism and the Internet.* New York: Routledge.

Starhawk. (2002). *Webs of power: Notes from the global uprising.* Gabriola Island, BC, Canada: New Society.

The WTO History Project. (2001, August). http://depts.washington.edu/wtohist/index.htm

BAUHAUS PHOTOGRAPHERS

The Bauhaus photographers (1919–1933) have been described by scholars as one of the most influential and experimental groups of artists in the 20th century. They were a part of the larger Bauhaus School, which thrived in Germany during the famous Weimar Republic, the liberal government that was set up after World War I. Bauhaus was established in 1919 in Weimar, moved to Dessau in 1925, then to Berlin in 1932. One of the most progressive groups of artists and designers in 1920s Germany, the Bauhaus School believed in furthering Modernism and freethinking. Their talents spanned across a number of disciplines, particularly architecture, art, design, and photography. Unlike others in these areas, the Bauhaus believed that all art and design should exist to promote a more harmonious society and foster human connections. They accomplished this by highlighting a more human effect to their work, experimenting with bright colors, using newer and lighter materials, and emphasizing the relationships society would have with their work rather than just its functionality.

The Bauhaus photographers Andreas Feininger, Florence Henri, László and Lucia Moholy-Nagy, and Grete Stern carried these beliefs along with their passion for experimentation in their photographs. Although photos had existed for quite some time, it was not until the turn of the 20th century that the act of taking pictures was brought to attention. Most early photos (pre–20th century) were portraits that emphasized great events in history or were records of family lineage. Bauhaus photographers were interested in capturing real life. They were some of the first photographers to take self-portraits and action shots, pictures of everyday activities that were unstaged and unexpected. Often they were the subjects of their photos, since they lived and worked together.

Bauhaus photographers were fascinated with experimentation and pushing the limits of a picture, playing with lighting, different developing effects, and shooting at unusual angles. They were interested in the body and took some of the first critical photos of nudes, using natural light and shadows to create an almost fantastical quality to the human body.

They also kept the idea of fostering human connections as the basis for their work. They viewed their photos not only as historical documents but also as celebrations of human relationships, citing a responsibility to contribute to society in this way.

In 1933, Germany was met with the rise of the Nazi Party. Movements like the Bauhaus were pushed out of Berlin and seen as a threat by the new regime. Much of their work was hidden and taken out of Germany by the artists and are thankfully available for viewing today. The rest was seized and destroyed by the Nazis.

The Bauhaus influence thrives today, with scholars finding the photographs and their makers to be prime examples of the beauty of Modernism and the Weimar Republic. Today's artists continue to be influenced by the Bauhaus's experimentations with light, shadow, and angle as well as how a subject in a photo can foster greater human connection.

—*Meliza Bañales*

See also Activism, Social and Political

Further Readings

Fiedler, J. (Ed.). (1990). *Photography at the Bauhaus.* Cambridge: MIT Press.

Girard, X. (2003). *Bauhaus.* New York: Assouline.

Smock, W. (2004). *The Bauhaus ideal, then and now: An illustrated guide to modernist design and its legacy.* Chicago: Academy Chicago.

Beat Poets

Beat Poets refers to a literary cluster of poets and writers who achieved notoriety during the years after World War II through the early 1960s. The literary movement, which also included novelists and essayists, was located primarily in New York City and San Francisco. Writers now accepted as central parts of the American canon were then thought of both by the mainstream literary establishment and themselves as fringe writers. The loose affiliation of writers included Alan Ginsberg, Jack Kerouac, Gregory Corso, and William Burroughs in New York City, who merged with the San Francisco Renaissance poets Kenneth Rexroth, Lawrence Ferlinghetti, Michael McClure, Gary Snyder, and Philip Whalen. Although the group is now known primarily for its writers, others were not primarily writers: Neil Cassady, the ultimate Beat figure and the model for Kerouac's protagonist in *On the Road;* Herbert Huncke, the New York City street hustler; Carolyn Cassady, one of Neil's wives, who offered her perspective on the Beats.

The term *beat* was originally used by jazz musicians and New York City street hustlers to describe something that was worn down, tired, or poor. An old, threadbare jacket with holes was beat. By the time this word reached the group of men gathering around Alan Ginsberg and William Burroughs, it suggested to Jack Kerouac a special spirituality. For Kerouac, the son of a strong Catholic mother, beat alluded to the beatitudes and being beatific. Shortly after this, Kerouac used the phrase to define his generation in a late-night conversation with another writer friend, John Clellon Holmes.

The term was then officially launched by Holmes in November 1952. Based on his conversations with Kerouac and his observations of Ginsberg, Neil Cassady, and Kerouac, Holmes had written a novel titled *Go* (one of Cassady's catchphrases). That November, he also wrote an article, "This Is the Beat Generation," for the Sunday *Times*. His novel and article began to raise public interest about the Beats and their mission.

The group of East Coast writers and thinkers were trying to articulate what they called a new vision of art that was more organic and less rule-bound. At the heart of their search was the belief that an alternative consciousness laid behind or beyond our everyday consciousness and that it could be reached through literature. This quest inspired them to push the boundaries in both social and literary realms.

On the social side, many of the early group considered themselves outcasts and, as such, had greater freedom to move beyond society's rules. They experimented with drugs, in particular heroin; occasionally stole money for drugs or forged prescriptions; and did not keep steady jobs. In addition, the homosexuality and sexual freedom of many of the Beats further shocked conservative America.

On the literary side, the East Coast Beats experimented with the forms and rules of literature, freeing both prose and poetry from conventions in favor of more personal and spontaneous methods of creating. They consciously styled their writing on jazz artists, including Dizzy Gillespie and Charlie Parker. These influences, in turn, gave birth to wildly experimental poems and novels, such as Ginsberg's "Howl," Kerouac's *On the Road*, and Burroughs's *Naked Lunch*.

"Howl" is one of Ginsberg's best-known works, and its publication in May 1957 clearly marked him as a central figure in what had come to be known as the Beat Generation. With its frequent references to drugs, sex, and genitalia, along with profanities, "Howl" landed its publisher, Lawrence Ferlinghetti, and its author in court battling obscenity charges. The well-publicized trial in San Francisco did much to solidify Ginsberg's reputation as a major poet, and after his acquittal, sales of the book rose dramatically.

Appearing just after Ginsberg's trial, Jack Kerouac's novel *On the Road* put Kerouac at the center of the Beat movement. A loosely autobiographical novel condensing 10 years of traveling into four distinct trips, *On the Road* put Kerouac on the map for both his energetic, improvisational prose style and for his portrayal of Neil Cassady as the character Dean Moriarty. Moriarty burns with a frenetic nonconformist energy that made the book into the archetype of American 1950s counterculture.

The third work of major importance from the East Coast Beat scene was William Burroughs's *Naked Lunch*. Burroughs, a Harvard graduate living in New York City during the early 1950s, mentored the younger members of the group, including Ginsberg and Kerouac, in fiction and poetry. However, it was not until he wrote his memoirs as a drug addict in New York City (published as *Junk* in 1953) that he really thought of himself as a writer. His next book, *Naked Lunch*, was published in 1959 and firmly established Burroughs as an important voice in describing the subculture of heroin addicts.

The close-knit group that made up the East Coast Beats in New York City had little overall impact in American culture before the mid-1950s, when Ginsberg and Kerouac went to California and combined their talents with those of the San Francisco Renaissance Poets. While Ginsberg and Kerouac were dropping out of Columbia University and attempting to articulate their new vision of American art, San Francisco was hosting its own developing counter-literature scene. Poets Kenneth Rexroth, Robert Duncan, Weldon Kees, Ruth Witt-Diamant, and others had helped renew interest in poetry in the Bay Area. Rexroth held weekly meetings in his apartment to discuss poetry, politics, and social issues. These gatherings frequently overflowed into the hall and into a downstairs meeting hall. Duncan had also gathered a group around him across the bay in Berkeley. Kees organized the Poet's Follies, and Witt-Diamant founded the San Francisco State College Poetry Center. In addition, numerous underground and small print-run publications, such as *Circle, Ark,* and *The Illiterati*, appeared. These presses were active in publishing the poetry of the lesser-known poets and translations of poetry from other countries.

Ginsberg arrived in the middle of this energy in 1954. By the summer of 1955, he had enrolled in the University of California at Berkeley graduate school program in English. However, that summer and fall, Ginsberg would be involved in two other ventures which did much more to bring the new vision before the American public: the writing of "Howl" and the October 7 poetry reading at the Six Gallery.

The reading at the Six Gallery has now become legendary for introducing five Beat writers to the world. In addition to Ginsberg, the readers were Michael McClure, Gary Snyder, Philip Whalen, and Philip Lamantia. Kenneth Rexroth served as the master of ceremonies. Ginsberg read his newly written poem, "Howl," to the loud acclaim of the audience.

With the publication of *Howl and Other Poems* and *On the Road*, the obscenity trial around "Howl," and the Gallery Six reading, the Beats were firmly established as a literary group with followers and imitators across the country. There was soon a canon of work by Ginsberg, Kerouac, Corso, Burroughs, Snyder, Ferlinghetti, McClure, Whalen, and Kaufman. These men produced a variety of works that appeared in a slew of anthologies with the word *Beat* in the title.

However, as the movement swelled and gained national notoriety during the mid-1960s, it dissipated somewhat, morphing into the hippie culture of the 1960s and 1970s. Now, the Beat Generation is being studied on campuses nationwide not just for the timeliness of their work but also for their relationship to and impact on mainstream society.

—*Robert Todd Felton*

See also Dissent; Ginsberg, Allen; Literature and Activism

Further Readings

Charters, A. (Ed.). (1992). *The portable Beat reader.* New York: Penguin.

BELAFONTE, HARRY (1927–)

Known as the "King of Calypso," Harold George Belafonte, Jr. has achieved fame as a recording artist, actor, composer, producer, and author, as well as for serving as an outspoken advocate and activist for global human rights issues. Born in Harlem, New York, Belafonte was the son of Caribbean-born immigrants. When he was 8 years old, his mother sent him to her native home in Jamaica, where he lived until 1939. Living there fostered a deep love of Caribbean music that would later catapult him to stardom. After serving in the navy during World War II, Belafonte resettled in New York to follow a career of musical performance and acting that would span more than five decades.

A prolific recording artist, Belafonte has released more than 40 original albums, and his third album with RCA Victor, *Calypso* (1955), made him the first recording artist with album sales of over a million copies. Belafonte has also made numerous significant contributions to theater, film, and television, often using his art to foster cultural and racial awareness and understanding. In 1960, President John F. Kennedy appointed Belafonte as the entertainment industry's first cultural advisor to the Peace Corps, an experience that heightened his awareness of global human rights issues, particularly in Africa. Since that time, his art has often given voice to the struggles and gifts in the lives of people of color—such as in his 1969 production of the off-Broadway "To Be Young, Gifted, and Black" and, in 1987, his coproduction of the drama "Asinamali," about life in prison in South Africa.

Belafonte's ongoing humanitarian and activist efforts have often mixed controversy with his celebrity, as he has maintained close alignment among his personal, professional, and political lives. Throughout the 1950s and 1960s, he was a prominent figure in the U.S. civil rights movement, and a close friend and advisor of Dr. Martin Luther King, Jr. According to the William Morris Agency, King cited Belafonte's global popularity as a key ingredient in the global struggle for freedom. After King's assassination, Belafonte chaired the New York State Martin Luther King, Jr. Commission and spearheaded the Martin Luther King, Jr. Institute for Nonviolence. He was a vigorous anti-apartheid activist and a close associate of Nelson Mandela. Most recently he has publicly criticized the Bush administration for its policies in Cuba and Venezuela and for its failure to support the struggle of blacks globally.

Belafonte has received honors from a wide range of artistic and humanitarian organizations, including Grammy, Tony, and Emmy awards; the Nelson Mandela Courage Award; the American National Medal of the Arts in 1994; and the Recording Academy Lifetime Achievement Award in 2000. He was appointed Goodwill Ambassador for the United Nations Children's Fund in 1987 and has been repeatedly honored for his ongoing work with children and youth. He has also been recognized by the National Association for the Advancement of Colored People, the Urban League, the National Council of Black Mayors, the American Civil Liberties Union, and the American Jewish Congress.

—*Cynthia J. Miller*

See also Anti-Apartheid Movement; Civil Rights Movement; King, Martin Luther, Jr.; Mandela, Nelson

Further Readings

Fogelson, G. (1996). *Harry Belafonte: Singer and actor.* Belmont, CA: Wadsworth.
Williams, J., & Bond, J. (1988). *Eyes on the prize: America's civil rights years, 1954–1965.* New York: Penguin.

BELL, DERRICK (1930–)

Derrick Bell is widely regarded as providing the conceptual basis for critical race theory, a legal theoretical perspective grounded in the historical and social experiences of racial groups in the United States. Bell's contribution to the genesis of critical race theory is derived from using race as an intellectual and methodological approach to explain racism and social inequity.

Bell, a former attorney with the National Association for the Advancement of Colored People Legal Defense Fund during the civil rights movement, viewed traditional strategies—such as filing amicus briefs and conducting protests, marches, and boycotts—as producing minimal and temporary results for oppressed racial groups, particularly African Americans. In addition, Bell argued that laws and policies designed to eradicate racial discrimination or provide remedies for racial injustice on the basis of color-blindness and merit generally secured and advanced the political and economic interests of middle- and upper-class whites.

According to Bell, racism is not indiscriminate but is instead a permanent component of American society. Developing an analytical construct he termed the interest-convergence principle, Bell explained how race and racism are perpetuated and maintained by society's dominant group. In contrast to de jure methods of exclusion and oppression to maintain its power, the dominant class, according to the interest-convergence principle, maintains its position through an elaborate process of marginalization using society's governing institutions. This process includes the use of law and public policy to construct and situate the political and economic interests of the dominant group around social resource management, distribution, and production. Paradoxically, the rights of subordinate groups are only recognized and legitimated when they further the interests of the dominant class and society's governing institutions.

An example of a convergence of interests is the decision in *Brown v. Board of Education* (1954). For Bell, the U.S. Supreme Court's decision to overturn segregation in *Brown* was more a matter of advancing America's national interests than of reconciling a fundamental discrepancy within its democratic tenets. Using the legal history of African Americans as a precedent, Bell explained that, prior to *Brown,* claims that segregated schools were inferior had been met with unsympathetic responses from the courts or addressed with court orders requiring equal facilities. Bell asserts that the Supreme Court's decision to abolish de jure segregation on the basis of race was necessary for the United States to secure its position as an international superpower. The image of America legally subordinating its nonwhite citizens undermined its effort to combat the spread of communism to Third World countries. Under the interest-convergence principle, the passage of *Brown* is viewed as "progress" requiring the coincidence of a pressing social issue rather than a commitment to justice.

Derrick Bell's intellectual and social significance stems from his departure from traditional legal theory. Through a social-constructionist perspective of race, he introduced a new line of critical thought to explain the continuance of racism and social injustice. Bell's critical race scholarship, which used unconventional, nonanalytic methods—such as narrative, storytelling, and racial allegory—articulated how judicial and civil rights strategies designed to promote equality simultaneously worked to preserve America's social hierarchy.

—*Jamel K. Donnor*

See also Critical Race Theory

Further Readings

Bell, D. (1987). *And we are not saved: The elusive quest for racial justice.* New York: Basic Books.

Bell, D. (1992). *Face at the bottom of the well: The permanence of racism.* New York: Basic Books.

Bell, D. (1992). *Race, racism and American law* (3rd ed.). Boston: Little, Brown.

Dudziak, M. L. (1988). Desegregation as a cold war imperative. *Stanford Law Review, 41*(1), 61–120.

BENEFIT CONCERTS

The mixing of popular music and political causes since approximately 1970 has inspired a number of labels conveying a primarily positive sensibility. Organized events such as Band Aid, Live Aid, Concerts for Bangladesh, Farm Aid, Hearing Aid, We Are the World (USA for Africa), Hands Across America, Rock Against Racism, Freedomfest, Sun City, Tibetan Freedom Concert, the Concert for Monserrat, the Paris Concert for Amnesty International, America: A Tribute to Heroes, and Live 8 have variously been identified as charity rock, philanthropic pop, political pop, conscience rock, and benefit concerts. Large-scale benefits draw from differing cultural and political moments: the early 1970s, the early and later 1980s, and the early 21st century. The roots of the modern benefit, however, began much earlier.

Music and social protest have a long historical connection. Music has been important in the formation and remembrance of a wide range of social movements from civil rights (e.g., the March on Washington) to anti-war protests. Songs of protest and the revival of folk music in the 1960s can be credited to such earlier acts as the Wobblies in Washington, Woodie Guthrie during his travels through the American Southwest, Pete Seeger, and the Kingston Trio (widely considered the starters of the folk revival of the 1960s). The commercial folk of the Limeliters and the New Christy Minstrels helped generate renewed interest in traditional folk music, and by the early 1960s, folk music was back in the limelight. With its songs of protest, cries for equality, and, at times, acts of violence, the civil rights movement influenced the folk revival and brought forward new protest folk stars, including Bob Dylan.

As political culture over the past half century continues to shift, culture and politics are becoming

Fans wave flags, the U.S. Stars and Stripes, and Britain's Union Jack, at Wembley Stadium, London, July 13, 1985, at the end of the Live Aid famine relief concert for Africa.

Source: AP Photo/Joe Schaber.

increasingly interconnected. Artists have lent their celebrity to many different causes, ranging from charity concerts for Amnesty International, environmental issues, race relations, aid-relief for famines and war-torn countries, and support for various political parties. The Concert for Bangladesh is widely considered the first modern benefit concert. George Harrison organized it in 1971 after his friend, Ravi Shankar, told him about the plight of the refugees in Bangladesh. Proceeds provided assistance to refugees threatened by starvation, lack of sanitation, and illness. The No Nukes concert series of 1979 supported the anti-nuclear power movement and also deserves mention as an early example of the modern benefit. However, Bob Geldof is credited with making charity rock a widely known phenomenon. In 1986, after watching a documentary about the Ethiopian famine, Geldof and Midge Ure wrote the song "Do They Know It's Christmas?" and organized fellow artists for Band Aid; proceeds were donated to famine relief.

If the 1960s and 1970s were marked by change and social and political upheaval, the 1980s brought forward a resurgence and increase in the number of benefit concerts, leading some to acknowledge a revival of conscience in popular music and of the dormant notion that rock and roll could indeed change the world. In the summer of 1985, Live Aid became the most-watched program in television history with between 1.5 and 2 billion viewers. The 1980s also witnessed We Are the World, Farm Aid, Freedomfest, and Sun City; most of these events turned attention to Africa.

Just as large-scale benefit concerts are tied to particular social and political movements, they are also responses to historical and technological developments and are dependent upon social conditions and contexts. Benefits often continue to raise awareness and money long after the concerts are over through television specials, books, videos/DVDs, and CDs.

Benefit concerts have also sparked criticism and controversy. Extensive media undertakings such as Live Aid and Freedomfest, for example, are remembered as much for their organizational successes as for controversies over which networks would or would not air the shows, accusations of network censorship by participants, and questions about what versions of the concerts would be shown to viewers in different countries. Critics claim that the potential of benefits to effect lasting change is minimal, explaining that the average commitment to important issues and causes is fleeting. Mixed feelings also permeate the relationship between benefits and big-business advertising. Some critics have suggested lesser-known artists participate in megabenefits to boost their careers and gain free exposure.

In 2001, the United States became an unlikely site in need of awareness and aid. A number of benefit concerts, compilation music CDs, and individual recordings were organized in the days and weeks following 9/11 to provide financial aid for individuals and families affected by the terrorist acts: God Bless America (CD), What's Going On: To Benefit the United Way's September 11th Fund and Artists Against Aids Worldwide (CD), The Spirit of America (recording by Daniel Rodriguez), The Concert for New York City (concert and CD), and America: A Tribute To Heroes (concert and CD), among others. In Canada, the SARS (severe acute respiratory syndrome) Benefit Concert in 2003, featuring the Rolling Stones, helped show the world that Toronto was again a safe place to visit.

In July 2005, aid turned outward once again through Geldof's organization of Live 8, a series of benefit concerts that preceded the G8 Summit in Scotland and took place in the G8 nations and South Africa. Although the concerts coincided with the 20th anniversary of Live Aid, Geldof insisted that Live 8 was not Live Aid 2. The focus of Live 8 was not to raise money but to raise awareness and to pressure world leaders to drop the debt of, increase aid to, and negotiate more fair trade rules for the world's poorest nations.

Benefit concerts surface during times of dire emotional and physical disasters. In July 2005, Tsunami Relief: A Concert of Hope brought actors and singers together to help raise money for relief efforts in Southeast Asia. That same year, a number of benefit concerts were organized to help provide relief for victims of flooding in New Orleans.

—*Maryann Martin*

See also Guthrie, Woody; Protest Music; Rock Bands and
    Activism; Seeger, Pete

Further Readings

Crosby, D., & Bender, D. (2000). *Stand and be counted: Making music, making history: The dramatic story of the artists and events that changed America.* San Francisco: HarperSanFrancisco.

Eyerman, R., & Jamison, A. (1998). *Music and social movements: Mobilizing traditions in the twentieth century.* Cambridge, UK: Cambridge University Press.

Garofalo, R. (Ed.). (1992). *Rockin' the boat: Mass music and mass movements.* Boston: South End Press.

Szatmary, D. P. (2000). *Rockin' in time: A social history of rock-and-roll* (4th ed.). Englewood Cliffs, NJ: Prentice Hall.

BENJAMIN, MEDEA (1952–)

Medea Benjamin has emerged as one of the leading American activists and progressive political leaders, particularly in the areas of global economic justice and opposition to the war in Iraq. Raised on Long Island in New York in a middle-class Jewish family, she received a master's degree in public health from Columbia University and a master's degree in economics from the New School for Social Research. She spent the subsequent decade working as an economist and nutritionist in Latin America and Africa for the United Nations Food and Agriculture Organization, the World Health Organization, the Swedish International Development Agency, and the Institute for Food and Development Policy.

In 1988, Benjamin became founding director of Global Exchange, a membership-based international human rights organization, with offices in San Francisco, dedicated to promoting global social, economic, and environmental justice. Through her work with Global Exchange, Benjamin helped build support in the United States for the pro-democracy movement to oust the U.S.-backed General Suharto in Indonesia and for the right of self-determination for Indonesian-occupied East Timor. She also supported the peace process between the Zapatista rebels and the Mexican government, fought to lift the embargoes against Cuba and Iraq, and was active in the movement to stop U.S. military aid to repressive regimes in Central America. She has served as an election observer and led fact-finding delegations to dozens of countries.

Benjamin became a major figure in the anti-sweatshop movement, spearheading campaigns against Nike, The GAP, and other U.S. apparel manufacturers. In 1999, Medea helped expose the problem of indentured servitude among garment workers in Saipan, part of the U.S. Commonwealth territory of the Northern Marianas Islands, which led to a billion-dollar lawsuit against 17 U.S. retailers.

After several fact-finding visits to China, Medea cosponsored with the International Labor Rights Fund an initiative to improve the labor and environmental practices of U.S. multinationals in China. The ensuing Human Rights Principles for U.S. Businesses in China have been endorsed by major companies such as Cisco, Intel, Reebok, Levi Strauss, and Mattel.

During the World Trade Organization meeting in Seattle in December 1999, Benjamin played a major role in the nonviolent protests, helping to draw world attention to the need to place labor and environmental concerns over corporate profits. In September 2003, Medea was in Cancun, Mexico, challenging the policies of the World Trade Organization and, in November, she was in Miami protesting the proposed Free Trade Area of the Americas and highlighting the coalescing of the global peace and economic justice movements.

Benjamin has also promoted fair trade alternatives to benefit to both producers and consumers, helping form a national network of retailers and wholesalers in support of fair trade. She was instrumental in pressuring coffee retailers such as Starbucks to start carrying fair trade coffee. In 2000, Benjamin became the Green Party nominee for the U.S. Senate in California, challenging incumbent Democratic Senator Dianne Feinstein on such issues as raising the minimum wage, increased support for education, criminal justice reform, and universal healthcare. During the 2001 energy crisis in California, Benjamin led a broad coalition of consumer, environmental, union, and business leaders fighting market manipulation by the big energy companies and the rate hikes that cause hardship for low-income ratepayers and small businesses. The coalition also worked for clean and affordable power under public control.

The U.S. wars in Afghanistan and Iraq brought Benjamin into greater prominence in the peace movement, where she helped bring together the diverse groups forming United for Peace and Justice. She accompanied four Americans who lost loved ones in the 9/11 terrorist attacks on a trip to Afghanistan to meet people there who lost relatives during the U.S. bombing of that country. This trip received such media attention as to pressure the U.S. government to address the issue of civilian casualties and to create a compensation fund for Afghan victims.

She was also the cofounder of CODEPINK: Women for Peace, a women's group known for its creative nonviolent actions protesting the Iraq War and occupation. She traveled several times to Iraq and helped establish the Occupation Watch International Center in Baghdad, which monitors the military occupation forces and foreign corporations, hosts international delegations, and keeps the international community updated about the occupation forces' activities. She has led a number of delegations of U.S. military families to Iraq and assisted in the distribution of humanitarian aid.

—*Stephen Zunes*

See also Anti-Sweatshop Movement; East Timor, Resistance to Indonesian Occupation; Global Exchange; Nonviolence and Activism; Women's Collective Acts of Resistance

Further Readings

Benjamin, M. (1989). *Don't be afraid, gringo: A Honduran woman speaks from the heart: The story of Elvia Alvarado.* New York: HarperCollins.

Benjamin, M., & Evans, J. (Eds.). (2005). *Stop the next war now! Effective responses to violence and terrorism.* San Francisco: Global Exchange.

Benjamin, M., & Freeman, A. (1989). *Bridging the global gap: A handbook to linking citizens on the first and third worlds.* Santa Ana, CA: Seven Locks Press.

Benjamin, M., & Rodolfo-Sioson, M. (2003). *The Peace Corps and more: 220 Ways to work, study, and travel at home and abroad.* San Francisco: Global Exchange.

Rosset, P., & Benjamin, P. (Eds.). (1996). *The greening of the revolution: Cuba's experiment with organic farming.* New York: Ocean Press.

BENN, TONY (1925–)

Born in 1925, Antony Wedgewood Benn entered the House of Commons of the British Parliament in 1950. Initially, he was a protégé of right-wing Labour leader High Gaitskell and was shortly brought into the shadow cabinet by him. However, following the death of his father, Viscount Stansgate, Benn was elevated to the House of Lords, thus disbarring him from the Commons. He spent the next 3 years fighting to change the law so that he could renounce his hereditary peerage and contest an election for a seat in the Commons. This was the first act that, in hindsight, marked Benn out as a radical and rebel, albeit one that was an English, Christian socialist.

Prior to 1970, Benn was on the right wing of the Labour Party, but the disillusioning experience of the 1964–1970 Labour governments, in which he was a Minister, saw him move to the left. Benn opposed British support for the United States in Vietnam and Labour's attempt to regulate the unions. These, and the industrial struggles in the early 1970s, saw Benn establish his links with the Institute of Workers' Control and campaign against the precursor to the European Union—the European Economic Community.

The trajectory of moving further left was aided by the disastrous Labour government of 1974–1979, in which Labour attacked the unions and began implementing monetarist policies, ultimately paving the way for Thatcherism in 1979. Benn became the rallying point for a renewed left movement within Labour and the unions, whereby he just lost the election to become Labour deputy-leader to a right-winger (by 0.5%) in 1981 but succeeded in democratizing the internal processes and structures of the party.

In the early 1980s, many on the left who had previously been outside Labour joined Labour, encouraged by Bennism, and as a result, Benn became the single most important defender of the peace, anti-nuclear, pro-women, pro-gay, union, and anti-racist movements. Although he lost his Bristol seat in Labour's disastrous showing in the general election of 1983,

Benn reentered the House of Commons the next year as a member of Parliament for Chesterfield.

Benn stood out against Labour's move to accommodate to Thatcherism and neoliberalism under successive Labour leaders, thus becoming the unassailable elder statesman of the British left. When he left Parliament in 2001, he did so, in his own words, to spend more time in politics.

Politically, Benn is an intriguing character. A lifelong and committed Christian, his political compass comes from moral indignation against injustice. He has always been on weaker ground on his alternative to capitalism, and to the extent that he is a socialist, he is best characterized as a radical social democrat. One of his particular campaigns has been to democratize the British state, in the historical tradition of the Levellers and Chartists. Despite being a dogged critic of Labour, he remains committed to Labour as the vehicle for social change, believing that pressure from outside Parliament and the unions will lead to Labour being reclaimed for his brand of socialism. In tune with this, Benn has taken a nonsectarian approach to working with the different parts of the left.

—Gregor Gall

See also Social Democracy; Union Movements

Further Readings

Benn, T. (1980). *Arguments for socialism.* London: Penguin.
Benn, T. (1996). *The Benn diaries* (Abridged version).
    London: Arrow.

BERLIN WALL DESTRUCTION

The Berlin Wall, erected in August 1961 to stop the hemorrhage of Germans seeking to leave East Germany (the German Democratic Republic, or GDR), achieved symbolic proportions that almost outstripped its physical function. For 28 years, it served as the concrete realization of the metaphorical Iron Curtain dividing Eastern and Western Europe. Although this most recognizable symbol of the Cold

War fell 2 years before the dissolution of the Soviet Union ended that conflict in 1991, once the Berlin Wall stopped dividing East and West, the Cold War was for all intents and purposes over.

The destruction of the Berlin Wall rests on the convergence of two historical phenomena. One of these was the series of top-down reforms triggered by Mikhail Gorbachev in the U.S.S.R. Gorbachev's openness to change, as evinced by his policies of glasnost and perestroika, laid the essential groundwork by permitting the east bloc countries more freedom in determining their own policies; among these were emigration issues and relations with neighboring nations in Western Europe. Gorbachev's reforms also signaled the end of the threat

Berliners celebrate on top of the wall as East Germans (backs to camera) flood through the dismantled Berlin Wall into West Berlin at Potsdamer Platz, November 12, 1989.

Source: AP Photo/Lionel Cironneau.

of Soviet military force to regulate satellite states' internal affairs. The opening of the Austrian-Hungarian border in May 1989 demonstrated the significance of this change. Not only did the act carry symbolic importance as the first breach in the Iron Curtain, but it also heralded the destruction of the Berlin Wall in a very practical way when thousands of East Germans took advantage of summer vacations in Hungary to escape to the West. By September, more than 10,000 East Germans had crossed from Hungary into Austria, forcing the GDR to restrict travel of its citizens to Hungary. Thousands of East Germans besieged the West German embassies in Warsaw and Prague, claiming West German citizenship and a passport to travel to the West. Humanitarian crises threatened in these overcrowded conditions, in full view of the Western media.

This summer exit crisis revealed the pressing need for political change in a society lacking a public forum for open discussion. Embracing the spirit of glasnost, a number of political reform groups formed; the largest and most important was the New Forum. Its founding manifesto, with more than 200,000 signatures, urged democratic dialogue about reform.

The second, opposing trend was the ground-up popular movement. This movement was rooted in the East German peace movement that had begun in the early 1980s in response to NATO's plan to deploy Pershing II missiles in Western Europe. Beginning in 1982, peace prayers were held almost every Monday night at Leipzig's St. Nikolai Church. At first no more than 30 participants gathered, but beginning in 1988 the meetings began to attract more than 1,000, and as participation grew, the Monday night peace prayers began concluding with public marches and became increasingly political.

The Leipzig peace prayers recommenced on September 4, 1989, and provided a focus and meeting point for the emerging mass citizen movement. That night, 1,000 marchers carried banners reading "Freedom of Assembly" and "Freedom to Travel." The movement had evolved from prayers opposing missile deployment to a full-fledged call for political reform within the GDR. With each passing week, the number of protesters multiplied exponentially, as did the potential for conflict with the security forces.

The October 9 march portended a likely showdown between protesters and the police. General Secretary Erich Honecker had issued orders to shoot to kill, Leipzig hospitals were told to prepare, and arrest lists were drawn up. The prospect of another Tiananmen Square, where the Chinese Army had brutally suppressed demonstrators just 4 months earlier, loomed.

Following the peace prayers that night, 70,000 to 100,000 marchers paraded peacefully around the Ring, the wide boulevard enclosing Leipzig's historic downtown, watched by a heavy police presence. When demonstrators passed the headquarters of the secret police without incident, the atmosphere of the GDR irrevocably changed. Citizens took up the chant, "We are the People" and experienced, for the first time in the GDR, the rights of peaceable assembly and free speech.

The regime sustained rapid and fundamental change over the next month. On October 17, party leaders forced Honecker to step down; they subsequently dismissed other top party functionaries. On October 30, about 300,000 protesters marched in Leipzig; the demonstration was covered live by East German television, another first. When the border with Czechoslovakia reopened, nearly 23,000 East Germans fled, prompting the new government to address the emigration issue.

A tentative policy to issue passports and permit limited tourism and limited emigration was developed the morning of November 9, 1989. The committee reasoned the bureaucratic process of obtaining passports would slow the rush to emigrate. But when the new policy was announced at a televised press conference, astonished reporters asked when the new policy would go into effect, and an unrehearsed party official said that it would take effect immediately.

As the news spread over the airwaves, East Berliners rushed en masse to the nearest checkpoint. Although police tried to restore order by announcing no visas would be issued that night, and reinforcements were ordered to the borders, it was clear to the border guards that they could not, even with their machine guns, hold off the crowds pressing to the checkpoints. Finally, they simply stepped aside. All checkpoints had opened by midnight, and 20,000 East Germans crossed to West Berlin just to visit.

Unforgettable images of joyous Berliners dancing atop the wall at the Brandenburg Gate, or swinging pickaxes and sledgehammers at the wall, were broadcast to an astonished world audience.

Ultimately, the Berlin Wall collapsed under its own weight. Forty years of suppressed dissident sentiment, combined with the removal of the threat of Soviet intervention, encouraged a mass movement that brought down the Wall. The people of East Germany converted the most enduring symbol of Cold War oppression into a symbol of determination and unity.

—*Brenda Melendy*

See also Anti-Nuclear Movement; Dissent; Free Movement Activism

Further Readings

Joppke, C. (1995). *East German dissidents and the Revolution of 1989.* New York: New York University Press.

Maier, C. S. (1997). *Dissolution.* Princeton, NJ: Princeton University Press.

Snodgrass, W. (2000). *Swords to plowshares.* Huntington, NY: Nova.

BERRIGAN BROTHERS

Two Catholic priests, Philip Berrigan (1923–2002) and Daniel Berrigan (1921–), were known as anti-war protestors. They are especially remembered as organizers and participants of the anti-Vietnam demonstration called the Catonsville Nine. On May 17, 1968, the brothers led seven others into a Catonsville, Maryland, draft board office, removed nearly 400 Selective Service records, and burned them in the parking lot with homemade Napalm. Encircling the blaze, these seven men and two women offered prayers and hymns as television and print journalists recorded images, although most pictures show only the Berrigans. All were arrested, tried, and found guilty the following October, and each sentenced to varying terms of federal imprisonment. Philip was given 3½ years to run concurrently with a 6-year

sentence he was already serving for involvement in the earlier Baltimore Four raid. After appeal, Daniel served 3 years. Acts of civil disobedience and protest continued as the brothers turned their attention to the possession of nuclear weapons, racism, abortion, and the AIDS epidemic.

Philip was a World War II artillery officer and a 1949 graduate of the College of the Holy Cross in Massachusetts. He was ordained a Josephite priest in 1955. Much of his priestly ministry was spent with inner-city black communities in New Orleans, Louisiana (1956–1963), and Baltimore, Maryland (1966). Between 1962 and 1963, he became the first Catholic priest to participate in a civil rights movement freedom ride. The Baltimore Four refers to events on October 27, 1967, when he and three others entered the Baltimore Customs House and poured blood on draft files. In 1970, he left the priesthood and married an activist nun, Elizabeth McAlister. Together they had three children: Frida in 1967, Jerry in 1975, and Kate in 1981. The family settled in Baltimore, and Philip, when not protesting or in prison, was a housepainter. Although never convicted, in 1971 J. Edgar Hoover named him a coconspirator in the Harrisburg Seven's plan to kidnap Henry Kissinger and bomb utility tunnels under U.S. capitol buildings. Between 1980 and 1999, he participated in five more actions that resulted in 7 years' imprisonment, including pouring blood on Mark 12A warheads. He cofounded Jonah Community in 1973, where he died in 2002 from kidney and liver cancer. The author of six books, his autobiography appeared in 1996.

Daniel was ordained a Jesuit priest in 1952. He studied at Woodstock College, Massachusetts; the Gregorian University, Rome; and did some postgraduate work in France. An intermittent teacher of Latin, English literature, and theology, in 1967 he took a campus ministry position at Cornell University, by then a northeastern hub of student anti-war sentiment. Daniel had a long correspondence with Thomas Merton, a Trappist monk who exerted a profound influence on the Jesuit. However, after many acts of civil disobedience, a prophetic turn and a renewed concentration on writing mark Daniel's later years. A prolific poet and essayist, he is the author of more than 40 volumes, including his 1987 autobiography. His prose and poetry register what he sees as the dissonant, purgatorial, and at times absurd reality of violence in the Americas.

The brothers' papers were deposited as the Daniel and Philip Berrigan Collection at Cornell University Library. At various points, both have lived as underground fugitives and have appeared on the FBI's most wanted list. Collectively their activities are considered to concretize the Catholic Left or Catholic Resistance Movement, whose roots are in the Catholic peace movement's pacifism of resistance. Throughout their long and active lives, the Berrigan brothers have remained self-professed gadflies and holy outlaws.

—*Nunzio N. D'Alessio*

See also Anti-Nuclear Movement; Catholic Worker movement; Civil Disobedience; Draft Resistance; Merton, Thomas; Pacifism

Further Readings

Allitt, P. (1985). *Catholic intellectuals and conservative politics in America, 1950–1985.* Ithaca, NY: Cornell University Press.

Au, W. A. (1985). *The cross, the flag, and the bomb: American Catholics debate war and peace.* Westport, CT: Greenwood Press.

Berrigan, D. (1970). *The trial of the Catonsville Nine.* Boston: Beacon Press.

Berrigan, D. (1972). *America is hard to find.* Garden City, NY: Doubleday.

Berrigan, D. (1973). *Prison poems.* Greensboro, NC: Unicorn Press.

Berrigan, D. (1987). *To dwell in peace: An autobiography.* New York: Harper & Row.

Berrigan, D. (1997). *Ezekiel: Vision in the dust.* Maryknoll, NY: Orbis.

Berrigan, D. (2002). *Lamentations: From New York to Kabul and beyond.* New York: Sheed & Ward.

Berrigan, D. (2006). *Genesis: Fair beginnings, then foul.* Lanham, MD: Rowman & Littlefield.

Berrigan, P. (1969). *A punishment for peace.* New York: Macmillan.

Berrigan, P. (1970). *Prison journals of a priest revolutionary* (V. McGee, Ed.). New York: Holt, Rinehart & Winston.

Berrigan, P. (1973). *Widen the prison gates: Writing from jails April 1970–December 1972.* New York: Seabury.

Berrigan, P. (with Wilcox, F. A.). (1996). *Fighting the lamb's war: Skirmishes with American empire. The autobiography of Philip Berrigan.* Monroe, ME: Common Courage Press.

BERRY, WENDELL (1934–)

Wendell Erdman Berry was born in 1934 in Kentucky to a family that had farmed for generations along the Kentucky River. After establishing himself as an author and an academic, in 1964 he returned to Kentucky to farm and to write.

He is the author of novels, books of essays, short stories, and poetry. His major theme eulogizes the destroyed communal life of family farmers. His fiction details how generations of farmers dealt with the impact of changes in U.S. agriculture over the past century in the fictional town of Port William. He affirms the values of hardworking men and women, their struggles, and their lives of caring for each other and the land.

Berry's belief that humans must acknowledge that there are limits to how we can live informs his argument against bigness of all sorts, especially that of agribusiness. Factory farming has removed 98% of the population from the land and from a fundamental appreciation of nature that comes from the proper, loving care of the land.

Berry admires the Amish for their choice in farming practices, particularly their use of draft animals. His argument that we should not automatically assume that what is new is an improvement over the inherited ways has earned him the label of a Luddite. Berry is a spokesman in the anti-globalization movement and has cataloged the damage that multinational corporations have inflicted on the inhabitants of small towns. Other threats that he has opposed include nuclear power and suburban sprawl.

The most systematic presentation of his agrarian philosophy is *The Unsettling of America: Culture and Agriculture* (1986), wherein he argues against the beliefs that work is to be avoided, that uniformity provides freedom, and that humans can be whole apart from healthy communities.

Humans aware of limits understand the fertility cycle, in which all is related; for example, life is intimately connected to death, both in nature and in the human community. Such an awareness comes from being at home in the world, being a good husband of the natural resources, and acknowledging that what has been inherited must be treasured. Because much of modernity rejects these deep commitments, Berry writes out of a deep anger at the practices of coal companies in eastern Kentucky and the unlimited sprawl of urban areas.

His concern with natural history, geography, and the place of humans in the larger natural world are present throughout his poetry and his other writings. Some of his poems address contemporary politics, such as his anti-war poem "Upon Seeing a Siberian Woodsman." Much of it ponders the mysterious connections of generations living and dead, as well as the emotional geography of being deeply rooted in a place.

—*Ruth H. Turner*

See also Anti-Globalization Movement; Deep Ecology Movement; Environmental Movement

Further Readings

Angyal, A. (1995). *Wendell Berry.* New York: Twayne.

Berry, W. (1986). *The unsettling of America: Culture and agriculture.* San Francisco: Sierra Club Books.

Berry, W. (2004). *That distant land: The collected stories.* Washington, DC: Shoemaker & Hoard.

Bhabha, Homi

See Postcolonial Theory

Bicycle Movement

See Critical Mass Bicycle Movement

Biko, Stephen (1940–1977)

Stephen Biko was the most prominent leader of the black consciousness movement, which flourished among African students from the late 1960s through the 1970s. His life reflected the lot of frustrated young African intellectuals. In his death, he became a symbol of the martyrdom of African nationalists whose struggle focused critical world attention on South Africa more strongly than at any time since the Sharpeville shooting in 1960.

His early schooling started at Lovedale, in the Eastern Cape. He later moved to Natal to attend a Roman Catholic boarding school and later enrolled at the University of Natal Medical School (Black Section) in 1966. Biko gave up what could have been a comfortable life as a medical doctor; instead, he devoted his life to selflessly work for the total liberation of South Africa. He and his colleagues founded the South African Students' Organization in 1968, and Biko was elected its first president. The organization was born out of the frustrations African students encountered within the multiracial National Union of South African Students and geared itself toward addressing those frustrations and problems. But the black students, under his leadership, went on to further argue that they were black before they were students and argued for a black political organization in the country. Opinions were canvassed; finally, the Black People's Convention was founded in July 1972 and inaugurated in December of the same year.

Through his inspiration, the youth of the country at high-school level were mobilized, and this resulted in the formation of the South African Students' Movement. This is the movement that played a pivotal role in the 1976 Soweto uprisings, which accelerated the course of the liberation struggle in South Africa. In 1973, a flurry of political restrictions were gradually imposed on African youth in black institutions. They culminated in banning orders, and in June 1976, high-school students and police clashed violently and fatally, and continuing widespread urban unrest threatened law and order.

In the wake of the Soweto revolt of 1976 and with the prospects of national revolution becoming increasingly real, security police detained Biko. He was taken to Port Elizabeth and on September 11, 1977, he was moved to Pretoria, Transvaal, where he mysteriously died. The apartheid authorities made every effort to conceal how he died, claiming, among other explanations, that Biko died of a hunger strike. This story was dropped after it was revealed by Donald Woods, the editor of the *East London Daily Dispatch*, that Biko died of brain damage caused by beatings by the South African police.

This disclosure was very damaging to South African authorities, and Biko's death made him a martyr. When, in 1997, his killers appeared before the Truth and Reconciliation Commission to request amnesty for the death of Biko, they only claimed responsibility for assaulting him and maintained that his death was accidental. His death caused a worldwide outcry, and he became a martyr and symbol of black resistance to the oppressive apartheid regime. As a result, the South African government banned a number of individuals, including Donald Woods and those black consciousness groups closely associated with Biko. The U.N. Security Council imposed an arms embargo against South Africa. Stephen Biko's contribution to the liberation struggle was finally commemorated with the unveiling of a memorial statue of him in his birthplace at King Williamstown.

—*Frank M. Chiteji*

See also Anti-Apartheid Movement

Further Readings

Biko, S. (2002). *I write what I like: Selected writings.* Chicago: University of Chicago Press.
Woods, D. (1987). *Asking for trouble: the autobiography of a banned journalist.* New York: Atheneum Press.
Woods, D. (1990). *Biko.* New York: Henry Holt.

BILINGUAL EDUCATION

Bilingual education is a model of educating students in public schools in their native language and in English.

The goal of bilingual programs is the attainment of biliteracy. Biliteracy includes communicative and academic literacy skills of listening, speaking, reading, and writing in one's native language and in English. Within this model, a student's native language and culture are valued and recognized as assets to learning and society. Bilingualism is achieved in most programs in which a student's native language/literacy is the foundation for transitioning to English only or mainstream classroom instruction. This approach, considered subtractive bilingualism, systematically replaces the native language with English. James Tollefson reports that the loss of language is accompanied by a loss of culture. In subtractive programs, students are forced to assimilate into the dominant group, oftentimes leaving their native language and culture behind.

A biliteracy model is based on the ideology of cultural pluralism, which ensures that students maintain both their language and their culture while acquiring the language of the dominant culture. This is additive bilingualism, in which a student's native language and culture are seen as an asset to learning.

As linguistic and cultural diversity increase in the United States, many students in classrooms will speak with parents and grandparents in languages other than English. David Berliner and Bruce Biddle report that by 2020, at least 50% of school-age children will be of non-Euro-American background, and by 2030, language minority students will make up 40% of the school population.

One common ideal held by most Americans is that English is not only the most viable but also pedagogically the most suitable language in which to learn. Critical pedagogists have put forth credible debates concerning the need to include cultural democracy and social justice as alternative ways of viewing bilingual education. Even when social justice is considered in educational conversations, the question of language of instruction is rarely raised and most often is relegated to the margins. In considering social justice in the context of bilingual education, it is acknowledged that language and literacy are more than parts of speech (e.g., nouns, verbs, adjectives) and sound systems (e.g., phonemes, morphemes). Language use and teaching methods also reflect an ideology that has the potential to empower or marginalize learners. Jim Cummins reports that language is inherently tied to one's culture and community and that language cannot be separated into discrete skills apart from the person, culture, or community. Kenji Hakuta and Catherine Snow state that language is not a unitary skill, but a complex configuration of abilities.

English language development occurs on two planes; first is English for social communication skills, referred to as playground English, or what Cummins names basic interpersonal communication skills. The second plane is academic English, or cognitive academic proficiency skills (CALPS). CALPS, according to Cummins, is the cognitively demanding language that children need to succeed in school. Basic interpersonal communication skills tend to be acquired rapidly by most children in and out of school, whereas CALPS is acquired in school, over a period of 5 to 7 years. The result of biliteracy is proficiency in social and academic literacy in two languages.

Historically in the United States, bilingual education programs have been at the heart of political debates derived from two dominant program policies, defined by Maria Brisk as compensatory or quality. A compensatory education policy focuses on the choice of language, where the policy makers determine which language of instruction is utilized. Within this policy model, the overriding goal of education is to teach students English as quickly as possible. English is considered the only language appropriate to acquire content knowledge (i.e., math and science can only be understood and assessed in English). A compensatory policy views students' fluency in English as the only condition necessary to receiving education.

A quality education policy, according to Brisk, focuses on a student's right to a good education with the goal of educating students to their highest potential, and English is an element of the educational goal. In a quality approach, ethnolinguistically diverse learners have the opportunity to access knowledge and be assessed in English and in their native language. A quality policy recognizes and values students' varied cultural experiences and knowledge.

Colin Baker outlines common models for bilingual education that can be contextualized within compensatory or quality policies. Each program model values different outcomes for non-native English speakers. The most common bilingual programs throughout the 1980s were transitional bilingual programs. Transitional bilingual education supports students in developing their native language while learning English, with the goal to transition to English mainstream classroom instruction in 2 or 3 years (early transition) or 4 to 6 years (late transition). Transitional programs provide academic instruction in students' native language with a gradual transition to academic instruction in English. Typically, if children begin a transition program in kindergarten or Grade 1, they will receive instruction to build literacy in their native language for the first two years, with English gradually introduced; by fourth or sixth grade, the majority of instruction is in English. Transition programs can fall into either compensatory or quality approaches depending on the amount of native language support and instruction available. Early transition could be considered compensatory since the ultimate goal is to achieve English literacy as quickly as possible.

The process of transition from a native language to a second language is an important factor in acquiring a new language. Krashen contends that students learn to read by reading, that is, by making sense of what appears on the page. This skill is acquired more readily when the text is in a language the readers already understand. Cummins refers to this as underlying language proficiency and contends that the ability to read and write in the native language transfers to learning these skills in a new language. This transfer is most successful when students develop literacy in their native language first.

Dual-language or two-way immersion is considered a quality bilingual education model; it is designed to educate both non-native speakers of English and monolingual English speakers in developing biliteracy. Dual-language programs group approximately equal numbers of native English-speaking students and native speaking language minority students together. Program models include 90/10 and 50/50. In the 90/10 model, 90% of the school time is in the minority language, and 10% is in the majority language. These percentages gradually shift through the grade levels until 50% of schooling is divided between languages. In the 50/50 model, 50% of schooling is in each language.

The language division can be established through alternating subjects, parts of day, days of week, weeks, or half semester.

The goal of a dual-language immersion program is to create bilingual and biliterate students in both the language minority and majority groups. Baker suggests additional goals of this additive program include positive cross-cultural attitudes and behaviors. Students educated through quality dual-language immersion programs are bilingual and biliterate and display high levels of personal and social competence.

Children reared bilingually from birth and those who enter school speaking a language other than English benefit from grade-level academic work in two languages. Dual-language models are beneficial academically to English-speaking children whose parents choose to enroll them in two-way bilingual classes. Overall, children in well-implemented, one-way and two-way bilingual classes show greater academic achievement on standardized measures over their counterparts in well-implemented monolingual classes.

The following characteristics should be present for a dual-language program to be successful:

- A pedagogically sound model of instruction that fits the demographic realities and resources of the school community
- Fidelity to the model of instruction in all aspects of implementation
- A means of assessing and addressing appropriately, and in a timely manner, any incongruity between the model of dual-language instruction, the needs of the school community, and the systems created to faithfully implement the model

Baker reports five elements to ensure quality and equity of language and culture for bilingual education:

1. The two languages of the school have equal status and are taught as a medium of instruction.

2. The school ethos is bilingual. Displays, newsletters, curriculum resources, and school functions are bilingual.

3. Biliteracy and bilingualism are the goals of the program. Reading and writing are a part of the curriculum in both languages.

4. Staff, including teachers, paraprofessionals, secretaries, custodial staff, and parent help, are often bilingual. Where there is difficulty staffing bilingual teachers, teachers may be paired to work as a team. Minority parents are encouraged to participate in the classroom.

5. To work toward success in dual-language education, sufficient time (minimum 4 years) must be allocated for program implementation and assessment.

According to Sonia Nieto, a myth of meritocracy exists in the United States, which places education as a key factor in an individual's success in this country. This myth has been consciously and purposefully engrained in marginalized communities, fostering the belief that all people, regardless of race, culture, class, gender, age, or sexual preference, have equal access to a quality education as long as they are willing to work for it. Therefore, if a person does not obtain a quality education, it is not due to lack of access, resources, or mediocre schooling; rather, it is because that person did not take full advantage of opportunities presented.

To address this notion of access, Michael Apple asserts that current neoconservative agendas promote policies in education that have resulted in mandatory curriculum and high-stakes standardized testing. This agenda fuels a fear of others who are different. In the case of bilingual education, the "other" is made up of marginalized communities, such as urban immigrants, who are subjected to societal and educational policies that limit their access to equity.

It is this conservative agenda toward bilingual education that promotes the hegemony of English as a way to maintain positions of power. Thus, education has become one entity, among many, used to enforce this hegemony of language through a particular instructional delivery system. This perpetuates what Macedo calls "linguistic racism" by imposing the idea that the learning of English, in and of itself, is education; this type of imposition is a form of neocolonialism that strips children of various ethnicities of their own identity, language, and culture.

Research indicates that public policy for bilingual education has direct correlations to political agendas within specific historical-cultural-political moments. In this context, any real meaning of a language should be considered in relation to assumptions that govern the language along with the social, political, and ideological relations to which it points. Often the issue of accountability, in terms of effectiveness of programming, hides the true role of language; the dominant language is not just a subject matter to be taught or a skill to be acquired, but it promotes and maintains the values and interests of the dominant class.

Therefore, the issues of effectiveness and validity for bilingual education become the tool or measure that masks the underlying social, political, and ideological order within which a group's native language exists.

Critical social researchers contend that in order for bilingual education to succeed in the United States within public schools, an ideology of cultural pluralism and social justice must be considered. Any program approach for bilingual education requires an interrogation of the sociopolitics and culture that inform program choices, models, and, ultimately, implementation in schools.

—Karen Cadiero-Kaplan

See also Multicultural Education

Further Readings

Baker C. (2001). *Foundations of bilingual education and bilingualism.* New York: Multilingual Matters.

Cadiero-Kaplan, K. (2004). *The literacy curriculum and bilingual education: A critical examination.* New York: Peter Lang.

Crawford, J. (1999). *Bilingual education: History, politics, theory, and practice* (4th ed.). Los Angeles: Bilingual Educational Services.

Cummins, J. (1996). *Negotiating identities: Education for empowerment in a diverse society.* Los Angeles: California Association for Bilingual Education.

Nieto, S. (1999). *The light in their eyes: Creating multicultural learning communities.* New York: Teachers College Press.

Thomas, W., & Collier, V. (1997). *School effectiveness for language minority students.* Washington, DC: National Clearinghouse for Bilingual Education.

BILLIONAIRES FOR BUSH

Billionaires for Bush is a nonpartisan campaign to expose politicians and systems of power that are supported by, and aligned with, corporate interests at the expense of the majority of Americans. It is a unique, grassroots approach that uses irony, humor, street theater, and blatantly outrageous slogans and statements to convey its positions. Because the Billionaires for Bush are able to attract public attention through comical antics and signature ball gowns, tuxedos, and political songs, the organization has been effective in spreading its views through major media venues, including television, newspapers, magazines, the Internet, and other popular outlets. Billionaires for Bush is an outcrop of United for a Fair Economy's Billionaires for Steve Forbes 1996 campaign. In 2000, the campaign Billionaires for Bush (or Gore) began as people trained in street theater and media activism and well versed in political humor arranged demonstrations at key political events.

The group literally dress like billionaires, complete with top hats, decadent jewels, and sometimes ready for a game of croquet. They wield banners and signs and sing poignant, outlandish songs in support of the most unpopular policies and positions of well-known politicians. Slogans include "Make Social Security Neither," "Widen the Income Gap," "Leave No Billionaire Behind," and many slogans that target Bush's policies in particular, such as, "We Paid for Eight Years," "Privatize Everything," and "Four More Wars!" With the vision statement of a world where no industry lobbyist has to ask twice, the Billionaires' goals include allowing corporations to run for office, one dollar for one vote, paying appointed officials and public servants in stock options, eliminating corporate liability, and scrapping social programs. A strong point of this particular grassroots organizing is that the campaign is not tied to any single issue so it can react to current events and abominations.

Billionaires for Bush consists of a board of directors, each with a pseudonym, such as Phil T. Rich and Dee Forestation; a board of advisors, such as Hal E. Burton and Paul Tax; and national cochairs and affiliates, such as Countessa Frie de Marquette and Felonius Ax. As of January 2006, Billionaires for Bush was a network of 90 chapters nationally, with an online community of more than 10,000. The Billionaires for Bush website (billionairesforbush .com) keeps members and aspiring billionaire activists informed by administering a B4B Listserv that posts upcoming events, pictures, videos, and descriptions of recent events. Billionaires for Bush is run entirely by volunteers; money is raised for events, supplies, and administrative costs through key contributors, online donations, and event revenue.

The largest events are the Re-Coronation Inaugural Ball, last held in January 2005 to "celebrate" George W. Bush's victory, and the "Get on the Limo Tour." It has been said that political leaders are more afraid of satirists than of their political opponents, as it is easier to silence criticism than laughter. Using language, slogans, and songs designed to elucidate and highlight horrific trends and disturbing top-level policies, Billionaires for Bush is a campaign designed to

Using language, slogans, and songs designed to elucidate and highlight horrific trends and disturbing top-level policies, Billionaires for Bush is a campaign designed to emphasize the structural, class-based injustice of the American political system, and its effect in just a few short years has been impressive.

Source: Photo by Matt Luce, www.mattluce.com.

emphasize the structural, class-based injustice of the American political system, and its effect in just a few short years has been impressive.

Some of B4B's main actions are as follows:

• *Tax Day:* On April 15, 2004, Billionaires for Bush celebrated National Tax Day by showing up at 15 local post offices to acknowledge the contribution of ordinary taxpayers to corporate America. Holding placards that read "Thank YOU for paying OUR taxes," the activists educate people on facts about tax cuts and how they benefit the rich.

• *Billionaire Croquet Party:* As part of the Republican National Convention Extravaganza, a series of actions in which the Billionaires joined thousands of activists to show Republicans that they were not welcome in New York, on August 29, 2004, B4B organized a croquet party on the Great Lawn in Central Park. They called groups of fewer than 20 people to gather there dressed in billionaire regalia to play croquet. The action was supposedly part of a campaign to privatize Central Park, but in reality it was a response to Mayor Michael Bloomberg's measure banning activists from holding an anti-war rally in that area, alleging that they would ruin the lawn.

• *Social Security Auction:* On March 21, 2005, on the popular e-commerce site eBay, B4B launched an auction offering the Social Security system to private bidders. The announcement addressed President Bush's plan for Social Security reform and listed facts exposing how the president's reform would be profitable for brokerage houses and detrimental to those in need of social welfare.

By putting on the Billionaires' disguise, B4B unmasks the discreet lobbying practices that undermine a fair democratic system. Some critics express doubts about the efficacy of B4B's actions on the grounds that their heavy use of irony can obscure their message and lead to confusion. Responding to this criticism, the Billionaires point out that their theatrical, parodic style conveys pressing issues amid a polluted media landscape. The existence of 90 chapters across the United States suggests that other activists consider the Billionaires' voice a useful tool to end the rule of governing for private interest.

—*Marcela A. Fuentes and Sunny Daly*

See also Culture Jammers; Guerrilla Theater; Performance Art, Political

Further Readings

Billionaires for Bush. (2004, Fall). Multimedia presentation. Retrieved March 14, 2006, from http://hemi.nyu.edu/journal/1_1/b4b.html

Haugerud, A. (n.d.). Leave no billionaire behind: Political dissent as performance parody. *P-rok: Princeton Report on Knowledge, 1*(1). Retrieved from http://prok.princeton.edu/1-1/inventions

BILL OF RIGHTS

The Bill of Rights enumerates the basic rights of citizens of the United States of America. The first 10 amendments to the U.S. Constitution, the Bill of Rights, entitles citizens to fundamental rights such as freedom of speech, press, and religion; peaceable assembly; the keeping and bearing of arms; and protection from unreasonable search and seizure. The first Continental Congress of the United States of America passed the Bill of Rights on September 25, 1789, and then submitted it to the states for ratification. The Bill of Rights was not made into law until all the former colonies ratified the document, which occurred on December 15, 1971. The inclusion of the Bill of Rights as amendments into the constitution was controversial. The issue split the Continental Congress into two groups: federalists and anti-federalists. The federalists wanted the Bill of Rights included in the Constitution in order to form a stronger centralized

federal government. The anti-federalists were proponents of states' rights and believed that the Bill of Rights would diminish the states' rights. The Ninth Amendment was included to appease the anti-federalists; it returned power to the states for anything that was not outlined in the Constitution or in the Bill of Rights.

The interpretation of the rights outlined in the Bill of Rights has been disputed since the day they were written. Even as recently as the 1960s, some states required daily Bible readings in public schools, and the U.S. African American population was systematically denied the rights guaranteed by the Constitution and the Bill of Rights. The U.S. judicial system, from the local district courts to the U.S. Supreme Court, is constantly reviewing and re-reviewing decisions in order to maintain the best possible adherence to the Constitution, the Bill of Rights, and prior decisions (precedents) of the courts.

The First Amendment limits congressional power in regard to freedom of religion, speech, press, assembly of the people, and the ability to petition the government with concerns:

> Congress shall make no law respecting an establishment of religion, or prohibiting the free exercise thereof; or abridging the freedom of speech, or of the press; or the right of the people peaceably to assemble, and to petition the Government for a redress of grievances.

The freedom of religion is distinctly itemized as both the freedom to establish religion and the freedom to exercise religion. These itemizations are known as the establishment clause and the free exercise clause, respectively. The establishment clause has been interpreted to mean that there exists an impassable wall between the government and the people in respect to religion, so much so that religious iconography of any kind is forbidden in government facilities, for example. The free exercise clause protects the people's right to choose to practice or not to practice religion of any kind without government interference. Freedom of speech and press are also protected under the First Amendment. Essentially, freedom of speech and freedom of press are treated in the same manner, in that they are both ways to express one's views. In 1931, in the case of *Near v. Minnesota,* the U.S. Supreme Court ruled that except in the most extraordinary of circumstances, the government cannot influence or force a media publication to publish or not publish their material. An example of extraordinary circumstances where the government did intervene is in the case against Manuel Noriega in 1990. Taped conversations implicating Noriega were obtained by the Cable News Network (CNN) before Noriega had the chance for a fair trial. The Supreme Court ruled that CNN could not broadcast the tapes because the broadcast of the tapes could impair Noriega's right to a fair trial.

The Second Amendment protects the people's right to keep and bear weapons. Although there is no doubt that this amendment clearly states that the individual citizen is granted the right to keep and bear arms, there is much controversy about the exact circumstances to which this amendment is meant to apply. In 1939, the Supreme Court made it clear that states were prohibited from keeping militias without express consent of Congress. They stated that the writers of the Bill of Rights felt that, during their time, "The sentiment of the time strongly disfavored standing armies; the common view was that adequate defense of country and laws could be secured through the Militia . . ." Even with this judgment, Congress still cannot infringe on the individual's ability to keep and bear arms, but it does have the power to limit the extent to which a citizen can bear arms. The 1993 Brady Handgun Violence Prevention Act is an example of this power.

The Third Amendment protects citizens against unwillingly quartering troops:

> No Soldier shall, in time of peace be quartered in any house, without the consent of the Owner, nor in time of war, but in a manner to be prescribed by law.

The writers of the Constitution knew firsthand of the victimization of troops forcing themselves on houses in the former colonies. British soldiers would demand food and shelter from the people before and during the Revolutionary War. This amendment's relevance has waned since then and has had almost no legal challenges since its inception.

The Fourth through Eighth Amendments deal specifically with the protection of rights of the criminally accused. The Fourth Amendment protects the criminally accused against illegal search and seizures, and proper warrants are issued on probable cause.

> The right of the people to be secure in their persons, houses, papers, and effects, against unreasonable searches and seizures, shall not be violated, and no Warrants shall issue, but upon probable cause, supported by Oath or affirmation, and particularly describing the place to be searched, and the persons or things to be seized.

The case law surrounding this amendment is vast, and constant updates address specific circumstances. An important aspect of this amendment that has come out of case law is the so-called exclusionary rule, whereby evidence seized illegally cannot be presented as evidence in the court. Also notable is that citizens are granted a "reasonable expectation of privacy" in their homes and persons; however, if something found to be illegal is in plain sight of an officer, it is acceptable cause for a more rigorous search.

The Fifth Amendment assures both U.S. citizens and noncitizens the right to due process of law, the protection against seizure of private property without compensation, protection from double jeopardy, and protection against having to be a witness in one's own trial:

> No person shall be held to answer for a capital, or otherwise infamous crime, unless on a presentment or indictment of a Grand Jury, except in cases arising in the land or naval forces, or in the Militia, when in actual service in time of War or public danger; nor shall any person be subject for the same offence to be twice put in jeopardy of life or limb; nor shall be compelled in any criminal case to be a witness against himself, nor be deprived of life, liberty, or property, without due process of law; nor shall private property be taken for public use, without just compensation.

These protections and rights are essential guarantees for a fair and balanced legal system. Without these rights, a government would be free to seize property, imprison citizens and noncitizens without trial, and hold the criminally accused for indefinite periods of time. The criminally accused could be forced to testify against themselves in trial and could be tried more than once for the same offense. These rights and provisions are vitally important to the existence of life, liberty, and the pursuit of happiness.

The Sixth Amendment guarantees trial by jury and other rights of the criminally accused:

> In all criminal prosecutions, the accused shall enjoy the right to a speedy and public trial, by an impartial jury of the State and district wherein the crime shall have been committed, which district shall have been previously ascertained by law, and to be informed of the nature and cause of the accusation; to be confronted with the witnesses against him; to have compulsory process for obtaining witnesses in his favor, and to have the Assistance of Counsel for his defense.

The right to a speedy and public trial is ensured and by an impartial jury in the same state where the crime allegedly occurred. It also guarantees that the defendant must be presented with the charges against him. Confrontation, or cross-examination, of witnesses is also assured. Finally, in the Sixth Amendment, the defendant is given the right to have counsel to assist in the defense in the trial. Only in *Powell v. Alabama* (1932) did the Supreme Court rule that if defendants are unable to pay for their own counsel for defense, the court must provide them with the necessary counsel.

The Seventh Amendment draws the distinction between criminal and civil trials:

> In suits at common law, where the value in controversy shall exceed twenty dollars, the right of trial by jury shall be preserved, and no fact tried by a jury, shall be otherwise reexamined in any Court of the United States, than according to the rules of the common law.

The outcomes of civil trials are determined in monetary amounts. In the English system, there were two courts, one of common law and one of equity. The Seventh Amendment maintains that tradition of having the outcome of criminal trials determined in one court and the outcome of monetary settlements determined in a different court.

The Eight Amendment grants citizens the right to not have excessive bail required in order to maintain freedom while a trial is pending, that excessive fines are not imposed, and that cruel and unusual punishments are not implemented:

> Excessive bail shall not be required, nor excessive fines imposed, nor cruel and unusual punishments inflicted.

Regarding excessive bail, the U.S. Supreme Court ruled in *United States v. Salerno* (1987) that "the government's proposed conditions of release or detention not be 'excessive' in light of the perceived evil." This decision basically states that if the criminally accused remains a threat to others upon release, that extraordinary monetary amount for bail is not excessive and does not violate the Fifth Amendment or any of the Eighth Amendment.

The Ninth Amendment states that the rights outlined in the Constitution and in the Bill of Rights should not be construed so as to limit the rights of the people:

> The enumeration in the Constitution, of certain rights, shall not be construed to deny or disparage others retained by the people.

This amendment appeased the anti-federalist faction of the original Constitutional Congress, who feared that future lawmakers could interpret the Bill of Rights and the Constitution to be the people's only and all rights, instead of maintaining the presumption of the liberty of the people.

Finally, the Tenth Amendment states that the federal government does not have any more power than is given to it by the Constitution and that the states have whatever power is not enumerated in the Constitution:

> The powers not delegated to the United States by the Constitution, nor prohibited by it to the states, are reserved to the states respectively, or to the people.

For many, this may seem an obvious truism; however, the Tenth Amendment was important again in the political debate between the federalists and the anti-federalists during the writing of the Constitution. The anti-federalists wanted to make sure that the federal government was not granted extraordinary powers not foreseen by the writers at that time and that any powers overlooked by them then would be given to the states and then to the people.

—Arthur Matthew Holst

See also American Civil Liberties Union (ACLU); Free Speech Activism

Further Readings

Burns, J. (2003). *Government by the people.* Upper Saddle River, NJ: Prentice Hall.
Ginsberg, B. (2001). *We the people.* New York: W. W. Norton.
Levy, L. (2001). *Origins of the Bill of Rights.* New Haven, CT: Yale University Press.
Wikipedia. (2006). *United States Bill of Rights.* Retrieved February 19, 2006, from http://en.wikipedia.org/wiki/United_States_Bill_of_Rights

BLACKLISTS

See HOLLYWOOD BLACKLISTS

BLACK LUNG MOVEMENT

In approximately 18 months, miners executed one of the most important movements in the coal industry. This grassroots effort, called the black lung movement, shut down mining in West Virginia, the nation's largest coal producer. Its goals were compensation for disabled miners and prevention programs. The movement ultimately secured federal action.

Several terms refer to black lung disease (e.g., *pneumoconiosis, miners' asthma*), and because it involves a spectrum of problems, there is not a confirmatory medical test. Despite some compensation for silicosis, when workers could prove damage from "hard" particles confirmed via X-rays, bituminous miners faced a difficult situation, because soft coal dust harms the lungs differently.

Black lung disease results from coal dust particles clogging the lungs. Over time, the body's ability to intake oxygen lessens, leading to heart enlargement, which, in turn, often leads to heart failure. Victims experience shortness of breath and inability to perform basic tasks.

"Miners' asthma" appeared in medical reports by the mid-1800s. In the early 1940s, the United Kingdom began compensating workers. At most United Mine Workers of America (UMWA) conventions from the early 1940s to the late 1960s, miners demanded actions to prevent black lung disease and compensate those affected. However, the U.S. medical establishment, company owners, and the union resisted acknowledging black lung.

Early in 1968, miners requested UMWA priorities on black lung prevention and compensation, but the union took little action. Later, in November, an explosion at Consol Number 9, near Farmington, West Virginia, claimed 78 lives and highlighted mine safety as a national issue.

In late January 1969, displeased with union response and concerned about safety, more than 3,000 miners attended a Charleston meeting, with talks by miners, physicians, and politicians. From this meeting and similar ones across the state, the West Virginia Black Lung Association was formed.

During West Virginia's legislative session, several bills on black lung issues were introduced. Many miners attended; they were joined by members of the Association of Disabled Miners and Widows. Group members sometimes staged funerals for fallen coworkers or wore armbands listing mine deaths. When a promised bill was not delivered, disgruntlement increased.

On February 18, miners at the Winding Gulf Coal Company's East Gulf Mine in Raleigh County refused to work. By the next day, miners at nine sites were on strike. Within the week, the wildcat strike included more than 7,000 workers and garnered media attention, reinforcing worker concerns nationally.

Absences of more than 30,000 workers shut down production in West Virginia's southern mines and more than half of the northern mines by late February. Union attempts to compel miners to work and legal action by company owners failed. By March, with over 40,000 striking, West Virginia's mines were closed. On March 11, West Virginia Governor Moore signed the black lung bill. Then, on December 30, President Nixon signed the Federal Coal Mine Health and Safety Act of 1969, which included the Black Lung Benefit Program.

The movement, fueled by West Virginia, Kentucky, Ohio, and Pennsylvania miners, focused attention on occupational disease. The federal act was significant; however, costs were borne by taxpayers rather than by mining companies. In the 1970s, focus centered on alleviating compensation problems. In mid-1972, the Black Lung Benefits Act, more broadly defining the illness, was passed.

More than half a million miners or their widows have received compensation, totaling greater than $30 billion, since the federal program's approval. However, it is unknown how many miners suffered or are suffering from the disease.

—Joy L. Hart

See also Labor Culture; Labor Law; Union Movements; Wildcat Strikes

Further Readings

Derickson, A. (1998). *Black lung: Anatomy of a public health disaster.* Ithaca, NY: Cornell University Press.

Lockard, D. (1998). *Coal: A memoir and critique.* Charlottesville: University Press of Virginia.

Smith, B. E. (1987). *Digging our own graves: Coal miners and the struggle over black lung disease.* Philadelphia: Temple University Press.

Black Panther Party

The Black Panther Party was a black human rights and self-defense organization active in the United States during the 1960s and 1970s. The passage of 1960s civil rights legislation following the landmark 1954 U.S. Supreme Court ruling in *Brown v. the Topeka Board of Education* brought minimal economic and social relief to the masses of black people living in cities throughout North America. Chronic poverty and reduced public services characterized these urban centers, where city residents were subject to poor living conditions, joblessness, chronic health problems, violence, and limited means to change their circumstances. Such conditions contributed to the urban uprisings of the 1960s and to the increased use of police violence as a measure to impose order on cities throughout North America.

It was in this context, and in the wake of the assassination of Malcolm X, that Merritt Junior College students Huey P. Newton and Bobby Seale founded the Black Panther Party for Self-Defense on October 15, 1966, in West Oakland, California. Shortening its name to the Black Panther Party (BPP), the organization immediately sought to set itself apart from the black cultural nationalist organizations, such as the Universal Negro Improvement Association and the Nation of Islam, to which it is commonly compared. Although the groups do share certain philosophical positions and tactical features, the BPP and cultural nationalists differ on a number of basic points. For instance, whereas black cultural nationalists generally regard all white people as oppressors, the BPP distinguishes between racist and nonracist whites and ally themselves with progressive members of the latter group. Also, whereas cultural nationalists generally view all black people as oppressed, the BPP believes that black capitalists and elites can and typically do exploit and oppress others, particularly the black working class. Perhaps most importantly, whereas cultural nationalists place considerable emphasis on symbolic systems, such as language and imagery, as the means to liberate black people, the BPP believes that such systems, though important, are ineffective in bringing about liberation. In its view, symbols are woefully inadequate to ameliorate the unjust material conditions, such as joblessness, created by capitalism.

From the outset, the BPP outlined a Ten Point Program, not unlike those of the Universal Negro Improvement Association and Nation of Islam, to initiate national black community survival projects and to forge alliances with progressive white radicals and organizations of people of color. A number of positions outlined in the Ten Point Program address a principle BPP stance: Economic exploitation is at the root of all oppression in the United States and abroad, and the abolition of capitalism is a precondition of social justice. This socialist economic outlook, informed by a Marxist political philosophy, resonated with other social movements in the United States and in other parts of the world. Therefore, even as the BPP found allies both within and beyond the borders of North America, the organization also found itself squarely within the crosshairs of the Federal Bureau of Investigation (FBI) and its counterintelligence program, COINTELPRO. In fact, in 1968 FBI Director J. Edgar Hoover considered the BPP the greatest threat to national internal security.

The Impact of the Black Panther Party

The BPP came into the national spotlight in May 1967 when a small group of its members, led by its chair Seale, marched fully armed into the California legislature. Emboldened by the view that black people had a Constitutional right to bear arms, the BPP marched on the body as a protest against the pending Mulford Act. The BPP viewed the legislation, a gun control bill, as a political maneuver to thwart the organization's effort to combat police brutality in the Oakland community. Newton's arrest later that year, after a shoot-out with police in which an officer was killed, perhaps did more than the iconic gun-toting images of BPP members ascending the steps of the council building to ignite the growth of the group from an Oakland-based organization into an international one with chapters in 48 states in North America and support groups in Japan, China, France, England, Germany, Sweden, Mozambique, South Africa, Zimbabwe, Uruguay, and elsewhere.

In addition to challenging police brutality, the BPP launched more than 35 Survival Programs and provided community help, such as education, tuberculosis testing, legal aid, transportation assistance, ambulance service, and the manufacture and distribution of free shoes to poor people. Of particular note

was the Free Breakfast for Children Program that spread to every major U.S. city with a BPP chapter; to the chagrin of Hoover, the government adopted it as a federal program. The program survives today in the free breakfast and lunch programs found in schools throughout North America.

Notwithstanding the vital social services the BPP provided to neglected communities across the country, the FBI declared the group a communist organization and an enemy of the U.S. government. Director Hoover had pledged that 1969 would be the last year of the BPP and devoted the resources of the FBI, through COINTELPRO, toward that end. In a protracted program of aggression against the BPP, COINTELPRO used agent provocateurs, sabotage, misinformation, mayhem, and lethal force to eviscerate the national organization. The measures employed by the FBI were so extreme that, years later when they were revealed, the agency issued a public apology, printed on the front page of the *New York Times,* for the tactics COINTELPRO used to destroy the BPP. COINTELPRO documents also revealed the complicity of a cultural nationalist organization, whose central leadership was on the agency's payroll.

FBI-led assaults on nearly every BPP chapter and program punctuated 1969, including those that destroyed breakfast programs, free clinics, and batches of *Black Panther,* the BPP newspaper. The 1969 assaults culminated in December in a 5-hour police shoot-out with the Los Angeles office and an Illinois state police ambush in which Chicago BPP leader Fred Hampton was killed. From the mid-1970s throughout the 1980s, the activities of the BPP had all but completely ceased. Although COINTELPRO contributed to the demise of the BPP, the dissolution of the party's leadership also contributed to the downfall of the organization. Assata Shakur went into exile in Cuba. Kathleen Cleaver earned a law degree and took an appointment as a professor. Having returned from exile in Cuba, Huey P. Newton was killed in a drug dispute in August 1989, perishing in an alley in West Oakland, not far from where he and Seale founded the first BPP chapter. Eldridge Cleaver designed clothes in the 1970s and 1980s before joining the anti-Communist Unification Church en route to becoming a born-again Christian and a registered member of the Republican Party; he succumbed to prostate cancer at the age of 62 in 1998.

Legacies of the Black Panther Party

Since it was founded in 1966, the influence of the Black Panther Party has assumed a transnational character that goes beyond the creation of support groups for the organization. Activists in Australian urban centers, for example, incorporated the works of BPP members into their social movements. In addition, the oppressed Dalits in India emulated the rhetoric of the BPP, and the representatives of the Vietnamese National Liberation Front, who called themselves Yellow Panthers, also used the organization as a model. Closer to the United States, the Vanguard Party of the Bahamas closely studied the BPP, drew on its political philosophy, adopted its use of uniforms and its Ten Point Program, and published the newspaper *Vanguard,* whose scope and format mirrored *Black Panther,* to shape its program of activism.

Forty years after the founding of the organization, the BPP survives in the public imagination in the United States as a result of the publication of a number of memoirs by its members and the use of its rhetoric in rap music. Some of the more notable memoirs include *Soul on Ice* by Eldridge Cleaver, *Blood in My Eye* by George Jackson, *Assata: An Autobiography* by Assata Shakur, and *A Taste of Power: A Black Woman's Story* by Elaine Brown. Similarly, rap group Public Enemy highlights the BPP on two of its compact discs, *It Takes a Nation of Millions to Hold Us Back* and *Fear of a Black Planet.* Rap artist Tupac Shakur's music video "Dear Mama," a tribute to his mother Afeni Shakur, a BPP member, includes images of *New York Times* headlines announcing her arrest. And, the self-styled Black Panther of Rap, Paris, includes short biographies of BPP members in the liner notes of his compact discs and regularly employs their rhetoric in his recording tracks.

Finally, in 1990 Milwaukee Alderman Michael McGee, a former BPP member, resurrected the organization when he formed the Blank Panther Militia in response to the neglect of his community by local politicians and business leaders. The militia inspired other chapters and eventually became the New Black Panther Party (NBPP). By 1998, Khallid Abdul Muhammad, the former national spokesperson for the Chicago-based Nation of Islam, had assumed the de facto leadership of the group when he led 50 shotgun- and rifle-toting NBPP members to Jasper, Texas, in the wake of the murder of James Byrd, Jr., the 49-year-old black man who had been dragged behind a pickup truck by three members of the Ku Klux Klan. The NBPP once again came into the public spotlight in 2000 when it led a Million Youth March in Harlem, New York.

Many NBPP activities clearly replicate those of the original BPP. At the same time, however, the NBPP embraces a staunchly cultural nationalist orientation, leading some former BPP leaders to denounce the NBPP for using the Black Panther Party name and for appropriating its legacy. Members of the NBPP, however, are unapologetic and summarily reject such condemnation, contending that they have only taken up the struggle for social justice and freedom that the original BPP failed to sustain.

—Garrett Albert Duncan

See also Government Suppression of Social Activism; Hampton, Fred; Jackson, George; Newton, Huey P.; Seale, Bobby

Further Readings

Brown, E. (1992). *A taste of power: A black woman's story.* New York: Anchor Books.

Cleaver, E. (1991). *Soul on ice.* New York: Rampart. (Originally published 1968)

Cleaver, K., & Katsiagicas, G. (Eds.). (2001). *Liberation, imagination, and the Black Panther Party: A new look at the Panthers and their legacy.* New York: Routledge.

Foner, P. S. (Ed.). (1995). *The Black Panthers speak.* New York: Da Capo Press.

Jackson, G. (1970). *Soledad brother: The prison letters of George Jackson.* Chicago: Lawrence Hill Books.

Jackson, G. (1990). *Blood in my eye.* Baltimore: Black Classic Press.

Jones, C. E. (Ed.). (1998). *The Black Panther Party (reconsidered).* Baltimore: Black Classic Press.

Morrison, T. (Ed.). (1995). *To die for the people: The writings of Huey P. Newton.* New York: Writers & Readers.

Olsen, J. (2000). *Last man standing: The tragedy and triumph of Geronimo Pratt.* New York: Doubleday.

Seale, B. (1991). *Seize the time: The story of the Black Panther Party and Huey P. Newton.* Baltimore: Black Classic Press.

Shakur, A. (1987). *Assata: An autobiography.* Chicago: Lawrence Hill Books.

BLACK POWER

The intense period of African American activism for social justice, commencing with the National Association for the Advancement of Colored People Legal Defense Fund's victory in *Brown v. Board of Education* and continuing until 1975, is often referred to as the civil rights movement. Yet, that period was actually composed of two distinct phases and characterized by two successive movements: the civil rights movement (1954–1965) and the Black Power movement (1965–1975). Mainstream histories of the 1960s freedom struggle tend to valorize the civil rights movement as heroic and inspirational but downplay and even demonize the Black Power movement (BPM) as an explosive expression of rage, reverse racism, and retaliatory violence—the menacing, threatening evil twin of the civil rights movement, which was responsible for its demise. Such assessments are largely the manufactured consensus of corporate media. Radical histories tend to give a more objective and balanced account, although there are some leftist analyses, which are nonetheless marred by the Eurocentric biases—for example, blaming the BPM for a betrayal of the radical Enlightenment tradition of Marxist class solidarity, the destruction of black-white coalitions, the death of the New Left movement, and the onset of divisive identity politics.

From an anti-imperialist perspective, however, many aspects of the BPM were comparable to the national liberation movements in Africa and Asia during the same historical period. However, the movement, which stressed unity without uniformity, was not monolithic but a broad tent encompassing many tendencies: bourgeois and socialist, reformist and revolutionary, pluralist and separatist, culturalist and

materialist, spirited and analytical. The common ideological threads running through all of these tendencies that defined Black Power were group solidarity, self-definition, self-determination, and self-defense. Ethnic or racial *group solidarity* included an emphasis on collective advancement rather than individual achievement and assimilation. *Self-definition* involved the rejection of imposed definitions; the redefining of group interests, goals, and objectives, as well as the means for advancing those interests and attaining those goals and objectives; and re-identification as Black or Afro-American rather than Negro, and as a people of color who constituted a global majority rather than an American minority. *Self-determination* ranged widely—from black people taking the lead in their own movement for liberation rather than letting others lead them, to community empowerment via building alternative institutions and taking control of existing ones, to plans for sovereignty and nation-building. Self-determination efforts included initiatives to acquire political power, economic power, and educational and cultural autonomy and to end institutional racism and white domination in these spheres. *Self-defense* measures ranged from community patrols to spontaneous insurrections as responses to police brutality to more organized forms of armed struggle against white supremacist repression and aggression.

Black Power as a Political Slogan

The term *Black Power* entered the arena of public discourse in June of 1966 and caused a storm of controversy and contention among civil rights activists and the general American public. Student Nonviolent Coordinating Committee (SNCC) activists Willie "Mukasa" Ricks and Stokely Carmichael (Kwame Ture) are credited with launching the term into the public sphere, though they did not coin it. The term had been used previously (as early as 1954) by the author Richard Wright, the militant activist Robert F. Williams, and Harlem congressman Adam Clayton Powell. Ricks introduced the slogan as a political chant on June 16, 1966, during a defiant civil rights march from Memphis to Jackson in support of James

Meredith, who had been shot when he attempted a solo march along the same route 11 days earlier. Indignant marchers responded enthusiastically to the "Black Power" chant, and the charismatic Carmichael, who immediately understood its political currency, popularized it. Dr. Martin Luther King, Jr. called the term an unfortunate choice of words. Other moderate civil rights leaders denounced it more vociferously, while militant leaders jumped to its defense and network news sensationalized it, making the terms *Black Power* and *Black Power advocate* household words. SNCC soon released a position paper titled "The Basis of Black Power," and Carmichael coauthored, with political scientist Charles Hamilton, *Black Power: The Politics of Liberation* (1967).

The Onset of the Black Power Movement

The phase of the 1960s freedom struggle, which became known as the Black Power movement, actually began in 1965 (prior to the sloganeering of Ricks and Carmichael), when there was a major shift in the mood and direction of the freedom struggle. Three key events in 1965 signaled and precipitated this shift. The first event was the assassination of Malcolm X on February 21. Controversial in life, Malcolm, in death, was elevated to the status of a heroic martyr. The second event involved Dr. Martin Luther King, Jr.'s loss of stature and credibility during the planned Selma to Montgomery marches of March 7 and 9. King was inexplicably absent during the first march, which ended in rampant police brutality and became known as Bloody Sunday. He led the second attempted march but, based on a secret deal cut with the Johnson administration, soon ordered the determined marchers to retreat when faced with police barricades to avoid a second confrontation; this fiasco was derided as Turn-Around Tuesday. Though King led a third successful march 2 weeks later, for many dauntless activists, anxious to make their unflinching resolve and presence felt, it was too late. The first two marches revealed King's compromised politics and the bankruptcy of the philosophy and tactics of nonviolence. King's reputation was severely damaged; he was accused of being manipulated by the white power structure. The unrestrained rebelliousness of the black masses finally came to the fore in Los Angeles in the third historical event of 1965—the Watts Rebellion of August 11–16, which left 34 dead, more than 1,000 wounded, more than 3,400 arrested, and estimated damages of $40 million. While seven cities, including New York, Chicago, and Philadelphia, had experienced civil insurrections in 1964, none had been of this magnitude. Watts was the first of the seismic urban quakes that would send shockwaves across the nation, and the several years of long hot summers that were to follow included major eruptions in Detroit and Newark. Until Watts, the freedom struggle had been exclusively focused on the problems of de jure segregation in the South. Watts brought attention to the intractable problems of racism, poverty, police brutality, and de facto segregation beyond the South. The shift from the civil rights movement to the BPM was also marked by changes in ideology, political consciousness, psychological attitudes, and cultural aesthetics.

King and Malcolm represented the two ideological extremes of the freedom struggle. Though Malcolm, toward the end of his life, secretly strategized to assist King in obtaining his moderate but just demands by assuming the posture of the feared alternative to King, their differences were real rather than feigned or theatrical. King's advocacy of nonviolence and integration, his southern-based constituency and strategy, middle-class background, emphasis on constitutional rights, and beliefs in the basic goodness of humanity, the power of moral suasion, and the American Dream contrasted sharply with Malcolm's advocacy of militant self-defense, his northern urban constituency and savvy, grassroots background, emphasis on human rights, understanding of white supremacy, grasp of realpolitik, and vision of an American nightmare. Malcolm's posthumous ascendancy to greatness and King's temporary loss of stature were indicative of the direction of the ideological shift in the black community.

There was a maturation of the political consciousness of the African American masses around domestic and international events. Black people were simultaneously buoyed by the successes of collective struggle, yet disillusioned by the vicious backlash of white supremacy, the cautious stalling of the federal government, and the intractable problems of de facto segregation in the North. They were inspired by a rediscovery of Garveyism and Pan-Africanism, and by anti-colonialist and national liberation movements in Africa and other parts of the Third World. In fact, the colonial analogy—the concept that the African American Black Belt South and northern inner cities constituted a ghetto-colony, internal colony, domestic colony, or colonized nation within the United States—though much debated and disputed, fueled much of the efforts for political self-determination. Rejecting the term *minority*, blacks redefined themselves as part of a global majority who constituted the rising tide of history. Black Power conferences were held, and the one that took place in Newark shortly after the 1967 rebellion received national attention. There was a profusion of revolutionary and nationalist literature, including the monumental treatise of the movement, Harold Cruse's *The Crisis of the Negro Intellectual.* Mental decolonization was as important as political anti-colonialism. Frantz Fanon and other radical mental health professionals provided models for liberating oneself from internalized racism. The nigrescence models or negro-to-black conversion experience models described the mass shift in identity and analyzed the stages of the process. The phrases "Black Pride" and "Black Is Beautiful" summarized a new cultural aesthetic characterized by natural Afro hairstyles and African fashions. This embracing and celebration of African heritage, kinky hair, black skin, thick lips, broad hips, Ebonics, and soul food was a bold step, because the Negro integration-assimilationist thrust of the 1950s and early 1960s had de-emphasized racial and cultural differences. Assimilationists had accepted, for example, white norms as a standard of beauty and suppressed all black so-called deviation from these norms—the use of hair-straightening techniques and skin-lightening creams had been pervasive. The Black Arts movement—a renaissance in literature, visual arts, and performing arts—was the aesthetic wing of the BPM; the movement to establish Black Studies in the university was the academic and intellectual wing. Warrior poets and guerrilla scholars advanced to the front line of battle, alongside militant activists, in the war for black liberation, as the literary canon and the academy itself became sites of confrontation. The so-called culture wars being waged today in the public sphere and the university had their origin in the BPM.

Major Tendencies of the Black Power Movement

Analysts have noted that the BPM had several tendencies. Many analytical schemas exist. The essential tendencies that appear in most schemas are pluralism, nationalism, and Pan-Africanism. *Pluralists*, who included community development advocates and black capitalists, concentrated their efforts within the system, on the goal of community empowerment or community control—black ownership and/or control of the educational, economic, and political institutions in the community—as a base or springboard for empowerment at the state and national levels. Although community development advocates often attempted to obtain empowerment through the creation of nonprofit entities, such as alternative schools or community development corporations, black capitalists sought empowerment through entrepreneurship, retail stores, manufacturing plants, development banks, and enterprise zones.

Nationalists, in contrast to pluralists, were fatalistic about the prospects of reforming the system or gaining power within it. They rejected mainstream values, avoided entering into entangling alliances with the establishment, and were advocates of social, cultural, and political autonomy. The nationalist camp was further subdivided into four tendencies: (1) *sovereign nationalists* or *territorial separatists,* advocates of a separate territory for a black-governed, sovereign nation-state (e.g., the organization the Republic of New Africa); (2) *revolutionary nationalists*, nationalists who embraced scientific socialism and advocated worldwide socialist revolution (e.g., the Black Panther Party); (3) *cultural nationalists,* advocates of an African-centered cultural renaissance as a key component of the struggle (e.g., Karenga's organization US); and (4) *religious nationalists,* faith-based communities of nationalists (e.g., the Nation of Islam,

Black Hebrew Israelites, and Black Christian Nationalists).

Pan-Africanists included (a) *global Pan-Africanists,* who advocated solidarity, mutual aid in political struggles and economic development, and cultural exchange between blacks in all regions of the African diaspora (including the United States and the Caribbean Basin) and the continent of Africa; and (b) *continental Pan-Africanists,* who advocated repatriation to and development and political unification of the motherland, envisioning an eventual United States of Africa. There were no rigid lines of demarcation between these various tendencies, and there was often much overlap between pluralists, nationalists, and Pan-Africanists in both vision and practice. However, organizational allegiances were strong, as were interorganizational rivalries.

Demise of the Black Power Movement

The inter-organizational rivalries were exploited by infiltrators and agent provocateurs from local police agencies and the Federal Bureau of Investigation's counterintelligence program, COINTELPRO. Some deadly internecine conflicts erupted, for example, between the Black Panthers and the cultural nationalist organization US. The demise of the Black Power movement is attributed to many factors. Some, such as the factionalism of intergroup and intragroup rivalries and ideological conflict over the question "Which way forward?" (i.e., nationalism or socialism) were internal. Others were external: police and government repression and illegal surveillance, co-optation of local and national leaders by private foundations (such as buying out leaders by offering them high salaried positions or lucrative grants), and co-optation of the movement by the film, TV, and other popular media that made a concerted effort to distort, deride, destroy, and satirize the image of the Black Power movement as an outdated fad (e.g., clownish, rainbow-colored Afro wigs) and to market new fads and fashions (e.g., jherri curl hairdos and a cocaine culture as portrayed in the 1970s Hollywood blockbuster *Superfly*). Equally important was a change in the economic climate, the onset of a recession—actually a depression in the inner city, which helped foster an individualist/survivalist mentality (the "Me Generation") that eroded group solidarity. The legacy of the movement, however, still persists. For example, the gangsta rap of hip-hop culture, expresses resistance to countervailing forces.

—Yusuf Nuruddin

See also Black Panther Party; Carmichael, Stokely; Civil Rights Movement; King, Martin Luther, Jr.; Malcolm X; Pan-Africanism; Student Nonviolent Coordinating Committee (SNCC)

Further Readings

Carmichael, S., & Hamilton, C. (1967). *Black Power: The politics of liberation.* New York: Vintage.

Joseph, P. E. (Ed.). (2001, Fall–Winter). Black Power studies: A new scholarship [Special issue]. *Black Scholar, 31*(3–4).

Joseph, P. E. (2006). *Waiting 'til the midnight hour: A narrative history of black power in America.* New York: Henry Holt.

McCartney, J. T. (1993). *Black Power ideologies: An essay in African American political thought.* Philadelphia: Temple University Press.

Marable, M. (1991). *Race, reform and rebellion: The second renaissance in Black America, 1945–1990* (2nd ed.). Jackson: University Press of Mississippi.

Student Nonviolent Coordinating Committee. (1966). *The basis of Black Power* (Position paper). Retrieved August 13, 2006, from http://www.hartford-hwp.com/archives/45a/index-bi.html

Van Deburg, W. F. (1992). *New day in Babylon: The Black Power movement and American culture, 1965–1975.* Chicago: University of Chicago Press.

BLOGGING

Blogging is a term that refers to the act of posting entries on a blog. Blogs are personal or organizational websites that allow their authors to publish texts and multimedia materials online without the intervention of an editor or a webmaster. Blogging entails an active or activist use of the Internet, in which a passive mass of users becomes an active and responsive public.

Through a structure marked by personal opinion rhetoric, and many times a firsthand reporting style, blogging represents a community of Internet users who produce their own coverage of current events in order to contest the monopoly of information distribution by mainstream media corporations.

By securing a versatile technology, apt for users' continual posting, web developers opened up the possibility for cyberspace to turn into a blogosphere, a networked environment of blogs that functions as an open forum for public debate. The architecture that facilitates this virtual blogging community is basically made out of hyperlinks. They connect diverse perspectives on a certain topic by highlighting the threads within a given conversation of posts in response to previous posts.

Specialists agree that in the United States after 9/11, blogs became increasingly influential in generating public opinion and collective response. In the context of George W. Bush's war on terror campaign, people turned to the web as a channel to support or to oppose the government's policies regarding issues such as homeland security and terrorism. Blogging also became a privileged ground for firsthand reporting from the areas of conflict in order to point to the horrors of the actually "lived" state of war.

Blogs played an influential part in the 2004 U.S. presidential elections. Democratic candidate Howard Dean was one of the main political figures to use this medium to install his image in the public scene. By that time, blogs had become a self-sustained space for electoral campaigning and political scrutiny.

In countries subjected to a heightened state of surveillance and censorship, blogs help citizens to get their reports out for fellow bloggers to spread the word about human rights abuses. Unfortunately, this approach to blogging as a tool that bypasses the regulations imposed by hegemonic authority has its limits. Reports indicate that in compliance with authoritarian governments, or perhaps obliged by them, Internet providers police these websites and shut them down when they find information denouncing the government's performance.

As specialists in the field note, effective blogging means not only a seizing of the means of production by writers but also the possibility of reaching a massive audience. More and more, this is ensured by the networked community, who digs in the corners of the blogosphere to reach out to those who need to be heard.

—*Marcela A. Fuentes*

See also Digital Activism; Electronic Democracy; Indymedia

Further Readings

Kline, D., & Burstein, D. (2005). *Blog! How the newest media revolution is changing politics, business, and culture.* New York: CDS Books.

Rebecca's Pocket. Retrieved March 12, 2006, from http://www.rebeccablood.net/

Riverbend. (2005). *Baghdad burning: Girl blog from Iraq.* New York: Feminist Press.

BOAL, AUGUSTO (1931–)

As a theater director, literacy advocate, politician, and theorist, Augusto Boal is responsible for creating the Theatre of the Oppressed, a theatrical practice designed to raise literacy, critical thinking, and expression skills for disenfranchised populations. His body of work, from writing to community and activist theater practice, is aimed at countering the passivity-inducing effects of political and artistic practice. Born and raised in Brazil, his works stirred controversy in his homeland, and in 1971 he was exiled to Argentina, and later fled to Paris. Among his goals is helping to foster the capacity to be one's own political and community advocate. Boal's perspective resonates with Paulo Freire's Marxist reworking of educational philosophy, where even the most illiterate and impoverished person possesses a sophisticated ability to think and reason critically. Augusto Boal views all artistic expression, including theatrical practice, as intrinsically political. In the Theatre of the Oppressed, Boal critiques the Aristotelian tragedy as a form of theatrical practice that coercively encourages passivity in its audience. A key element in Boal's approach is the development of audience-actors, or spect-actors, who become empowered not merely to reflect on change, but to take action for themselves.

A significant part of a theater of the oppressed is an ability to work with symbols that are meaningful to the communities in which it is practiced. In the early 1970s, Boal worked in South America with indigenous rural populations to teach literacy. Believing that there are multiple ways to be literate, Boal developed such practices as newspaper theater, invisible theater, photo-romance theater, masks and rituals, to name just a few, to engage peasants and workers, many of whom had never heard of the theater. Boal's method consists of four stages: knowing the body, making the body expressive, theater as language, and theater as discourse, all of which lead to a rehearsal theater as opposed to the closed loop of Aristotelian bourgeois theater. For instance, in forum theater, part of developing the language of theater, participants may stage a situation in which a worker is being exploited by a boss who cruelly expects long hours of hard labor. Members of the community offer potential solutions for the situation that may range from destroying equipment to creating breaks for workers to organizing a union. Each suggestion is then acted out so that community members can see what works and what does not. The director is transformed into a facilitator who helps guide participants through the activity. Another technique, invisible theater, places performers in actual settings of oppression where they then enact a preplanned event to bring different injustices to light. Invisible theater is designed as a direct action against society about a specific problem where the aim is to foster public debate. Boal has taught these practices at numerous festivals and conferences around the world. He returned to Brazil after the military junta lost power and served as an elected vereador in Rio de Janeiro, formed numerous performance companies, and founded the Centre for the Theatre of the Oppressed in Rio.

—*Keith Pounds*

See also Critical Literacy; Freire, Paulo; Theatre of the Oppressed

Further Readings

Boal, A. (1985). *Theatre of the oppressed* (C. A. McBride & M.-O. L. McBride, Trans.). New York: Theatre Communications. (Original work published 1974)

Boal, A. (1998). *Legislative theatre: Using performance to make politics* (A. Jackson, Trans.). New York: Routledge.

BOFF, LEONARDO (1938–)

A former Franciscan priest, Leonardo Boff was a preeminent force in the development of liberation theology in its expression in Latin America. Like that of Dietrich Bonhoeffer, his work had two foci: taking seriously theological concerns such as eschatology and Christology while meeting the pastoral concerns of the communities in which he lived. His work was woven around the concept of "a preferential option for the poor"—that the role of the church is to take seriously the needs of the oppressed, learn from their struggles, and participate fully in dialogue and practical solidarity with forces of radical social transformation.

Liberation theology, for Boff, was not a discipline but a process—one did liberation theology, not study it. Its most visible expression was in the Base Ecclesial Community movement, which involved grassroots activists in the study of scripture and church documents through the lens of challenging the oppressive structures in which they lived and worked. The role of theologians was to give shape to this experience, as a mirror of a transforming social force.

Boff's approach to theology is closer to a social science approach than a religious one, and more dialectical than descriptive. It is analytical in approach, being informed by the struggles for justice and, directly or indirectly, applying this knowledge in ways that work toward a radical reconstruction of society in harmony with the strands within Christian tradition and Christian scripture that call for justice.

His early work was a direct response to the changes of Vatican II, and particularly the call to renew the church in true partnership with all the voices within the church. In Brazil, with the support of the institutional church, he studied doctrines such as grace and the nature of the incarnation of Jesus in a spirit of radical openness to previously unheard voices within the church and worked to ensure that the church itself found ways to be in active solidarity with the poor and oppressed.

In mid-career, his work took on a directly political note. He more clearly and openly called for open support of movements for social transformations outside of those initiated or controlled by church bodies. Moreover, he clearly challenged the institutional church, which led to his temporary silencing by the Vatican in 1985. The silencing was primarily in response to his book *Church: Charisma and Power,* which looked at the institutional church through the same lens with which transnational corporations and oppressive institutions of the nation state were examined.

In more recent times, his work has often taken on a more mystical bend, responding to the ecological crisis of modern times with a blending of liberation theology and gaia spirituality. His perspective is still that of a preferential option for the poor; the lens is still that of the experience of the oppressed. However, there is greater emphasis on the spiritual and creative and somewhat less on analysis and dialectics. The preservation and healing of creation is linked to ensuring the dignity and autonomy of individuals and local communities bound together through shared experiences.

—*Brian Burch*

See also Bonhoeffer, Dietrich; Liberation Theology

Further Readings

Boff, L. (1979). *Jesus Christ liberator: A critical Christology for our time* (P. Hughes, Trans.). Maryknoll, NY: Orbis. (Original work published 1972)

Boff, L. (1979). *Liberating grace* (J. Drury, Trans.). Maryknoll, NY: Orbis. (Original work published 1976)

Boff, L. (1985). *Church: Charisma and power* (J. W. Diercksmeier, Trans.). New York: Crossroad. (Original work published 1981)

Boff, L. (1988). *When theology listens to the poor* (R. R. Barr, Trans.). San Francisco: Harper & Row. (Original work published 1984)

Boff, L. (1995). *Ecology and liberation: A new paradigm* (J. Cumming, Trans.). Maryknoll, NY: Orbis. (Original work published 1993)

Boff, L. (2006). *The Lord is my shepherd: Divine consolation in times of abandonment.* Maryknoll, NY: Orbis.

Boff, L. (n.d.). *Leonardoboff.* Retrieved August 1, 2006, from http://www.leonardoboff.com/

Smith, C. (1991). *The emergence of liberation theology: Radical religion and social movement theory.* Chicago: University of Chicago Press.

BOLÍVAR, SIMÓN

See ANTI-COLONIAL MOVEMENTS, LATIN AMERICA

BOLSHEVIKS

Bolsheviks (Russian for "members of the majority") developed as a significant faction within the revolutionary socialist Russian Social Democratic Labor Party (RSDLP) as a result of ideological and organizational splits in the party's ranks at its 1903 Congress. The other important faction that emerged was called Mensheviks ("members of the minority"), and while nominally part of the same socialist party, the two factions often worked independently of each other until the Bolsheviks formed a separate party in 1912. The Bolsheviks are historically significant because, led by N. Lenin (1870–1924), they overthrew the Russian government in October 1917 and set the former Russian Empire on its way to becoming the Soviet Union, the first avowedly communist and anti-imperialist nation in the world that also became a major superpower in the 20th century.

The RSDLP, a political party formed illegally by Russian socialists at a congress at Minsk in 1898 to unite various Russian revolutionary associations into one political force, was based on the Marxist doctrines of class struggle, the historical necessity of proletarian revolution to end all human exploitation, and the desirability of a future non-alienated, communist society of socially equal citizens. Activism and social justice were at the top of their agenda. The delegates were arrested by the Tsarist regime, which outlawed all independent political activity in the autocratic Russian Empire. The year before the Second RSDLP Congress in 1903, a young revolutionary by the name of Vladimir Ilyich Ulyanov, better known by his revolutionary alias N. Lenin, published *What Is to Be Done?* In the conditions of Tsarist autocracy, which tolerated no political parties and no parliamentary government, the pamphlet outlined Lenin's strategic vision for the RSDLP's activism and fight for social justice: Composed of disciplined activists and agitators organized along democratic centralist lines, the party was to be the vanguard of proletarian revolution. Party members would be full-time revolutionaries while sympathizers would remain outside the party organized into auxiliary institutions like trade unions and other "mass" organizations. Lenin called his model a party of a new type, one that was not interested in electoral success but in inculcating revolutionary consciousness and activism in the mass of workers and peasants and in organizing the revolutionary overthrow of the government in order to clear the way for a just society based on socialist principles. He proposed a theory of democratic centralism to govern all internal party processes and debates. The democratic aspect referred to the freedom of party members to discuss and debate matters of policy and direction freely and openly within the party and to vote for leaders democratically; however, once the members came to a decision by majority vote, all members, even the dissenters and/or losers, were expected to support and follow that decision in public. This latter aspect denoted the doctrine's centralism. As Lenin characterized it, democratic centralism consisted of freedom of discussion and criticism tied to unity of action and purpose.

Following a robust tendency within Marxism, Bolsheviks held that socialism could only be achieved by revolutionary means, which meant overthrowing the existing state and then using the state's coercive power to consolidate socialism and defeat its enemies, the old ruling classes. Lenin held that the revolution would be followed by a dictatorship (i.e., emergency rule) of the proletariat, which he characterized as a class-based democracy in which workers and peasants would hold political power through elected councils known as *soviets.* Lenin and his followers steadfastly contended that any attempt to achieve socialism by reforming capitalism was doomed to failure because the ruling classes would turn the class-based power (i.e., "dictatorship") of the present state against workers and peasants seeking reform as it had done in the past.

At the Second Congress, Lenin's faction, centered on the editorial board of the party's newspaper *Iskra* (Spark), lost the vote that the core of the party should consist of professional revolutionaries only: The RSDLP majority voted that the party should be a mass organization open to radical trade unionists, revolutionary workers, and sympathizers. Lenin's faction won a less-important vote on the composition of *Iskra's* editorial board. It was this victory that earned the faction the label *Bolshevik.* Unwilling to compromise on democratic centralism and the vanguard nature of a revolutionary party, in the aftermath of the congress, the Bolsheviks left the RSDLP. The split between the Bolsheviks and the Mensheviks became formalized in early 1905 when the Bolsheviks held a Bolsheviks-only meeting in London in April 1905, which they called the Third Party Congress, and the Mensheviks organized a rival conference.

At the Fourth (Unification) Conference in Stockholm in April 1906, the Bolsheviks and Mensheviks attempted a reconciliation and worked together again within the RSDLP. At the Fifth Conference in London in May 1907, the Bolsheviks regained majority support but the two factions once again began to operate independently of each other. After defeating the urban revolutionary uprisings of 1905–1906, in which the Bolsheviks played a relatively small role, the government of Tsar Nicolas II (1868–1918) instituted minor political reforms, including the legalization of parliamentary political parties, a restricted franchise, and an elected *Duma* (parliament) with very limited authority. Divisions appeared within Bolshevik ranks, as Lenin and his followers Grigory Zinoviev (1883–1936) and Lev Kamenev (1883–1936) argued for Bolshevik participation in the new Duma while Alexander Bogdanov (1873–1928) argued for a boycott of the Duma by the RSDLP representatives. After Lenin's attack on Bogdanov's views in *Materialism and Empiriocriticism,* Lenin regained majority support at a Bolshevik mini-conference in Paris the same year. Lenin opposed reunification with the Mensheviks, and contacts between the two groups in 1910 came to naught.

In January 1912, a Bolshevik-only party conference in Prague formally expelled Mensheviks as well as Bogdanov and his supporters from the RSDLP. At the Prague conference, the Bolsheviks ceased to regard themselves as a faction within the RSDLP and declared themselves to be an independent party, the RSDLP (Bolshevik). During World War I (1914–1918), the Bolsheviks took a principled stance based on Marxist internationalism and refused to support the Russian war effort. They saw nationalism, Russian or otherwise, as an ideology that divided the workers of the world and deflected proletarian revolutionary energies into a patriotic fever that bolstered an oppressive status quo that the Bolsheviks were determined to change. As far as the Bolsheviks were concerned, the war as a whole pitted conscript worker-soldiers from one nation against conscript worker-soldiers from another, and the Bolsheviks, following Marx and Engels, firmly believed that the proletariat had no country but needed to direct its energies into overthrowing ruling classes and capitalist and semi-capitalist regimes around the world in order to establish regimes based on social justice. Adopting an internationalist stance, Bolsheviks emphasized solidarity and comradeship between the workers and soldiers of the belligerent nations and left the socialist Second International when its leading parties, German Social Democrat and French Socialist, voted to support their ruling classes and national governments in the conflict.

The Russian Army and economy collapsed under the war effort. Egged on by Bolshevik agitators, peasants and workers deserted the army while casualties, officer incompetence, and complete routs on the battlefield mounted in 1916. With starvation and physical deprivation growing steadily by early 1917, Russia was ripe for revolution amid strikes and food riots in every major city inspired and led by local Bolsheviks. To preserve freedom of action and the clandestine nature of their seditious activities, most of the Bolshevik leaders (including Lenin and Zinoviev) lived abroad. In early 1917, German authorities helped numerous Bolshevik leaders travel to Russia

and provided them with financial support on the premise that strengthening the anti-war Bolshevik movement would hasten Russia's withdrawal from hostilities directed at Germany's eastern front. Increasingly unpopular with his people as a result of his disastrous handling of the Russian war effort and the economic breakdown at home, Nicholas II abdicated in February 1917 and a provisional government was formed. This February Revolution was nearly bloodless and the Bolshevik leadership living in exile was not involved although local Bolshevik organizers were instrumental in initiating the daily strikes and street demonstrations.

In this chaotic and unsettled revolutionary situation, major policy differences between Bolsheviks and Mensheviks reemerged. Mensheviks and other moderate socialists held that an industrially backward country like Russia was nowhere near the stage of achieving socialism on the basis of a mature capitalist economy and class-conscious proletariat required in classic Marxist theory. They supported the Provisional Government and argued that Russia needed a liberal-capitalist revolution so that the country could transition to socialism at a later date. In his *April Theses,* Lenin opposed cooperating with the Provisional Government, which continued Russia's ruinous participation in World War I, and the Bolsheviks rallied mass support for their position with the slogans of "All Power to Soviets" and "Land, Bread, and Peace." These slogans appealed to Russia's urban working class, soldiers, and huge peasant population tired of the misery of economic injustice, starvation, and war. Remaining within mainstream Marxist analysis but adding a new interpretive twist based on their internationalism, Bolsheviks believed that a socialist revolution in Russia would be the beginning of a wave of classic proletarian socialist revolutions in the more capitalistically and industrially developed countries of Western Europe, who would then assist their Bolshevik comrades in achieving a socialist transformation of Russian society. Lenin regarded Russia as weakest of the great imperialist powers. When that weak link broke, there would be no stopping the collapse of the old order throughout Europe.

The Russian link broke when the Bolsheviks launched an insurrection on October 24, 1917, and seized state power quickly with very little loss of life. The head of the Petrograd soviet, Leon Trotsky (1879–1940), helped stage the uprising after formally joining the Bolsheviks in mid-1917. The Second All-Russian Congress of Soviets met during this seizure of power and established a new government, the Council of People's Commissars. The soviet elected Lenin to lead the new government, Trotsky became People's Commissar for Foreign Affairs, and other Bolshevik leaders directed major government ministries. Bolsheviks had achieved the first Marxist-socialist revolution in world history by riding a wave of radical popular discontent among the peasantry and proletariat of Russia. Announcing a radical break with the past, in March 1918, the Seventh Party Congress of the RSDLP (Bolsheviks) met and changed the name of the party to the All-Russian Communist Party (Bolsheviks). The word *Bolsheviks* was retained when the party changed its name to the All-Union Communist Party (Bolsheviks) in December 1925 after the formation of the Soviet Union. *Bolsheviks* was dropped from the party's formal name in October 1952. Well before that date, the term *Bolshevik* came to designate the Communist Party's pre-revolutionary days of exile and underground struggle.

—*Alexander M. Zukas*

See also Communism; Lenin, V. I.; Russian Revolution; Trotsky, Leon

Further Readings

Carr, E. H. (1985). *The Bolshevik Revolution, 1917–1923* (Vol. 1). New York: W. W. Norton.

Cohen, S. F. (1980). *Bukharin and the Bolshevik Revolution: A political biography.* New York: Oxford University Press.

Haimson, L. H. (1985). *Russian Marxists and the origins of Bolshevism.* Boston: Beacon Press.

Ulam, A. B. (2005). *The Bolsheviks: The intellectual and political history of the triumph of communism in Russia.* Cambridge, MA: Harvard University Press. (Original work published 1965)

BONAFINI, HEBE

See MADRES DE PLAZA DE MAYO

BONHOEFFER, DIETRICH (1906–1945)

Born on February 4, 1906, in Breslau, Germany, to a prominent family, Dietrich Bonhoeffer resolved to become a pastor early in life. Studies at Union Theological Seminary, New York, in 1930–1931 proved pivotal, as he observed the racism of white America, encountered the vibrancy of black church life, and became a devoted pacifist. Two days after Hitler became German chancellor in January 1933, Bonhoeffer delivered a radio broadcast denouncing the *Führer* that was interrupted by government censors. In an essay composed later that year, Bonhoeffer outlined three responses to a state that abuses its authority: (1) verbal criticism of the state, (2) the unconditional obligation to aid victims of state action, and (3) a call to political subversion as a last resort.

As Nazi sympathizers mounted their takeover of the Protestant church, Bonhoeffer helped form the dissident Confessing Church. In the midst of these struggles, Bonhoeffer wrote *Discipleship,* an exposition of the Sermon on the Mount that outlined the costs of Christian commitment and pacifism. Bonhoeffer directed the Confessing Church's seminary at Finkenwalde during 1936–1937 until it was shut down by the Gestapo. Subsequent reflection on the seminarians' common life led to the publication of *Life Together,* a highly regarded devotional work.

When German pastors were instructed to take an oath of loyalty to Hitler in 1938, Bonhoeffer and many of his students refused. In that year, Bonhoeffer began to question some of his earlier pacifism and became more directly involved with the Resistance movement. Through contact with his brother-in-law, a member of German *Abwehr* (counterintelligence), Bonhoeffer was informed of military plots to overthrow the Nazi regime. An invitation to teach at Union Seminary in the summer of 1939 lasted only briefly, as Bonhoeffer resolved to return home at the dawn of war, vowing to share in the trials of his homeland. In 1940, Bonhoeffer became an agent of the Abwehr, ostensibly to advance the war but actually serving the Resistance, traveling abroad and using his church contacts to keep allies abreast of conspiracy efforts.

Bonhoeffer used these contacts in helping plan Operation 7, a clandestine effort that smuggled 14 Jews to Switzerland. Most notable of his resistance activities was his involvement in a plot to place a bomb aboard Hitler's airplane in March 1943. In April, Bonhoeffer was arrested for his involvement in the foiled assassination attempt and spent the remainder of his life in prison, writing several letters now regarded as classics of theological and resistance literature. He was executed on April 9, 1945, at Flössenburg concentration camp, during the waning weeks of World War II. Bonhoeffer's writings and biography have been enormously influential, having a broad impact on theologians, ethicists, and political activists who have emerged in his wake.

—*David H. Jensen*

See also Nazism and Civilian Resistance; Pacifism; Religious Activism

Further Readings

Bethge, E. (2000). *Dietrich Bonhoeffer: A biography.* Minneapolis, MN: Fortress Press.

Bonhoeffer, D. (1996). *Life together: Prayerbook of the Bible* (G. B. Kelly, Ed.; D. W. Bloesch & J. H. Burtness, Trans.). Minneapolis, MN: Fortress Press.

Bonhoeffer, D. (1997). *Letters and papers from prison.* New York: Touchstone.

Bonhoeffer, D. (2003). *Discipleship.* Minneapolis, MN: Augsburg Fortress. (Original work published 1937)

BONNER, ELENA

See SOVIET DISSIDENTS

BONO
(1962–)

Bono, who was born Paul David Hewson on May 10, 1962, in Dublin, Ireland, is the lead singer of the rock band U2 and one of the world's leading advocates for debt relief and aid to poorer countries. As a result of his many efforts in this area, Bono has been nominated for the Nobel Peace Prize several times and, in December 2005, was named *Time* Person of the Year along with Bill and Melinda Gates.

Bono's storied career in social activism began in 1984, when he appeared on Band Aid's charity recording "Do They Know It's Christmas?" After witnessing images of terrible poverty in Ethiopia on British Broadcasting Company television, Bono was inspired to travel to Ethiopia with his wife Ali shortly after U2's historic Live Aid performance of 1985. There they spent several weeks helping with an education and famine relief project. In 1986, U2 headlined Amnesty International's Conspiracy of Hope tour. In addition, Bono traveled to Central America during the fall of 1986, where he spent time in Nicaragua and El Salvador. His experiences there inspired the writing of several songs on the band's 1987 breakthrough album, *The Joshua Tree.*

The 1990s saw a period of personal and professional introspection for Bono, yet his experiences in Africa stayed with him through 1999, when he joined the Jubilee 2000 campaign. Jubilee 2000 was a church-based international movement designed to persuade the World Bank, the International Monetary Fund, and the G8 (Group of 8 industrialized nations) to cancel third world debts. During the Jubilee 2000 campaign, Bono spoke before the United Nations and the U.S. Congress and met with key figures such as Pope John Paul II and Bill Clinton.

In March 2002, Bono founded DATA (Debt, AIDS, Trade, Africa) with Bobby Shiver and activists from the Jubilee 2000 campaign. DATA calls on the world's wealthy nations to put more resources toward Africa and to adopt policies that help, rather than hinder, African nations in achieving long-term prosperity. Bono gained a great deal of publicity for DATA when he embarked on a 2-week tour of Africa with U.S. Treasury Secretary Paul O'Neill in May 2002.

Bono's work for Africa drew well-deserved admiration from politicians and the media in 2005. On February 25, 2005, the *Los Angeles Times* suggested in an editorial that Bono should be named president of

Irish pop star Bono, left, buys palm nuts at a local market in Accra, Ghana, on Wednesday, May 24, 2006. Bono was visiting Ghana during the last leg of a 10-day tour that took him across Africa in an effort to bring attention to the need for more help to Africans from rich countries.

Source: AP Photo/Olivier Asselin.

the World Bank. Bono met with many of the leaders of the G8—including U.S. President George W. Bush and British Prime Minister Tony Blair—leading up to their July 2005 summit. Bono was also instrumental in organizing the Live 8 concerts, which were designed to put pressure on the leaders of the G8 to increase assistance to Africa. The G8 agreed to cancel $40 billion of African debt and pledged another $25 billion to combat poverty and disease on the African continent.

—*Thomas Mogan*

See also Amnesty International; Debt Relief Movement; Rock Bands and Activism

Further Readings

Assayas, M. (2005). *Bono: In conversation with Michka Assayas.* New York: Riverhead.

Jackson, L. (2003). *Bono: His life, music, and passions.* Secaucus, NJ: Citadel Press.

BOURDIEU, PIERRE (1930–2002)

Pierre Bourdieu analyzed and denounced social inequalities and demanded social justice. Bourdieu was born in Denguin, France. He studied philosophy and literature in Paris, Alger, and Lille (1951–1964) before working as a sociologist. His main focus was describing differences in human action through empirical observation of distinctive practices. According to Bourdieu, distinctive practices typify themselves in the expression of personnel preferences and value judgments. In other words, making differentiations locates, positions, determines, and particularizes individuals. It is the difference itself that legitimates the right to have an identity recognized and defended by others. Social reality is defined by difference, which can be summarized as follows: Real life is practical and social because it is relational.

The Relational (Habitus, Capitals, and Fields)

In this context, the word *relational* expresses the interdependence of social determinations. This interdependence is present everywhere. It can be located in individual behavior, the life of social groups, and the evolution of societies. Bourdieu describes the level of individuality with the concept of habitus or sometimes with habitus of class. *Habitus* is a structured and structuring ensemble of ways of being and living. Individuals inherit them from the social environment into which they were born, that is, their own class. Bodily and intellectual dispositions (*hexis*) give individuals their social and cultural identities (*ethos*), which are markers that direct them in life. Individuals are never born isolated from their social context. They develop conscience through the mediation of a social background that supports their growth. Thus, individuals are not social actors, Bourdieu believed, but rather agents of society.

Heritage relies on four principal resources that Bourdieu called *capitals*. He distinguished the symbolic (indications of prestige like high-school diplomas), the economic (material richness and means of obtaining it), the social (the network of relatives and friends), and the cultural capital (know-how and savoir-vivre). Each heritage implies a precise volume and structure of capital. The way they take shape depends on their position inside the class system and its corresponding habitus in society. Heritages determine the trajectory of individuals and groups within a society. They reflect the social career of habitus and classes in the various domains of everyday life. Bourdieu defined them as *fields*.

There are many social fields (e.g., the fields of economics, politics, cultures, religions), each of which is likely to be divided into specialized subfields (e.g., finance within economy, haute couture within fashion). All social fields and their subfields have a relative autonomy, and they are all more or less interdependent. The sum of the social fields is the *social space*. This space reflects the social allocation of resources in a society according to the various habitus and their classes. It draws a picture of the interdependency between social determinations within a society and of the shapes interdependencies can take according to the point of view of each social class.

The Reproduction of Society

Everyday life is composed of the meeting of different habitus equipped with their capitals in the various fields and subfields of the social space. Bourdieu gives the following formula of practical life in his famous work *Distinction: A Social Critique of the Judgment of Taste* (1984): [H(abitus) x C(apitals)] + F(ields) = P(ractice). This equation indicates that the interdependency of social determinations takes place on all levels of society. It also implies that individuals and society are not opposites. Society builds the individuals, who build society on the basis of their heritages. This points to the three cardinal characteristics to Bourdieu's sociology. First of all, it is a structuralist and a genetic sociology. It highlights the correspondences between the structures of habitus, capitals, and social fields. Second, it is constructivist sociology because it assumes that the facts of society—habitus, capitals, fields, and the social

space—are collective constructions. Last but not least, it is a sociology of social change, focusing more on what is preserved by changes than on the changes themselves. Consequently, Bourdieu's prior interest was to describe, explain, and possibly even to predict the reproduction of practical life, as well as to understand its conditions of possibility and its guidelines.

The aim of all social existence is its own reproduction, that is, the reproduction of its structures. This assumes the reproduction of conditions as the foundation of each social position. Each habitus, each social group, each society, and each culture evolves or moves with a task to maintain, even to reinforce their own structures for their time being. This conservatism, however, has more than just a functional significance: Social reproduction tries to maintain not only social differences, for an optimal flow of resources in the social space, but also inequality between social differences, thus reproducing social inequalities.

The dynamic of this reproduction is a dynamic of conflict, which takes place in all fields of society. Habitus are fighting against each other to obtain or preserve a dominant position in a field. A position is dominant when a class of habitus imposes the structure of their field, their sense of the conflict, and their definition of the stakes for which all habitus have to fight. When all habitus believe in it, that is, when they develop an interest for a fight in a particular field and a sense for the social game (illusion), the dominant positions occupied by the dominant habitus have been legitimated, that is, acknowledged as dominant by the dominated habitus. In a social space of such, the practice of violence is legitimated as well as legitimating.

Legitimate Violence and Political Fight

In the modern societies, legitimate violence is no longer physical. The law of the strongest is no longer always the only and best one. Instead, violence is now symbolic. Employers no longer beat employees to force them to work. Instead, employers exert a financial, moral, or psychological pressure on employees. The sociological investigations directed by Bourdieu indicate that victims of this type of oppression are very often forced to accept it. Indeed, very often these individuals do not have sufficient knowledge of the criteria that legitimate the dominating position, either because they do not know them or because they are hidden. Consequently, it is difficult, even impossible, for these individuals to threaten the dominant position. The dominating habitus understands this as the acknowledgment of its power of domination. This dialectic of misjudging or acknowledging regulates the reproduction of societies. It also indicates that all social games are asymmetrical. They are made of legitimated and legitimating injustices, of conscious compromises based on rules kept hidden by the dominant classes. The fields of education, art and literature, religion, economy, and politics point out the same social operating mode: Equal habitus recognize and support each other mutually not only within the framework of their practical competences but also in everyday life.

For Bourdieu, his work was more than just a descriptive scientific report; it was a weapon to denunciate social injustices and to stimulate political activism. Sociology is a "fighting sport," according to Bourdieu. It has to report the state of the fight in social space as cold and disillusioned, that is, as true as possible. This gives a better understanding of how to make sociological determinations lie. From this perspective, sociology is a tool that can be used to mobilize the masses for political fight. In the mid-1990s, Bourdieu gradually set himself free from academic sociology. Leaving his position as a seismograph of society behind, he committed himself to debates on television, demonstrations in the streets, and confrontations in the French *banlieues*. He spoke against the technocratic measurements imposed by democratic institutions and pleaded for the right for self-determination of the precarious populations. In *Weight of the World: Social Suffering in Contemporary Society* (1999), Bourdieu gave a megaphone to people "at the bottom" of society, whose speech disturbs the legitimate order and who have been denied any social importance or any public relevance, noblesse oblige. Caricatured by his detractors as a powerful populist orator, a chief of clan without a heart, or even an intellectual terrorist and adored by others as the saver of desperate causes, Bourdieu disturbs by being different;

after all, both rigor and commitment fashion his rebellious humanity.

—*Christian Papilloud*

See also Difference; Power, Theories of; Violence, Theories of

Further Readings

Bourdieu, P. (1984). *Distinction: A social critique of the judgment of taste.* Cambridge, MA: Harvard University Press.

Bourdieu, P. (1998). *Practical reason: On the theory of action.* Cambridge, MA: Polity Press.

Bourdieu, P. (1999). *Weight of the world.* Cambridge, MA: Polity Press.

Schwartz, D. (1998). *Culture and power. The sociology of Pierre Bourdieu.* Chicago: University of Chicago Press.

BOVÉ, JOSÉ (1953–)

José Bové is a farmer, activist, cofounder of the Confédération Paysanne farmers union, and spokesperson for the international peasant movement Via Campesina. His advocacy of an alternative form of globalization based on popular democratic participation reflects a primary concern for human and environmental welfare over corporate interest and is typified by support for traditional agriculture over genetic modification and industrialized food production. Bové comes from the Bordeaux region of France, where he spent his infancy and teen years, and attributes many of his motivations to regional influence: anarcho-syndicalism, nonviolent direct action, and the combination of symbolic action with mass struggle.

In an interview given to the *New Left Review* in 2001, he describes the relevance of these factors to his involvement in struggles against military service and for the rights of conscientious objectors and deserters during the early 1970s. Around the same time, Bové and others involved in that campaign joined farmers in the Larzac region of France in resisting the expansion of a military base. They symbolized their opposition through the building of a stone sheep barn on military land between 1973 and 1975 and establishing squats in vacant farms owned by the military in 1976. This and much of Bové's subsequent activity and tactics are clearly informed by the principles of nonviolent direct action and the use of bold gestures to publicize and make connections between causes.

As part of Confédération Paysanne, for example, he helped organize the 1988 "Plowing the Champs Élysées" demonstration in Paris, which involved farmers in tractors protesting against European agricultural policy. Opposition to genetic modification of food has involved the destruction of modified maize in a Novartis facility at Nerac, genetically engineered rice at a CIRAD crop agency research center in Montpellier in 1999, and Brazilian corn and soybeans grown by Monsanto in 2001. Again in 1999, Bové helped other activists to dismantle a half-built McDonald's restaurant in Millau, Aveyron, in protest of 100% duties placed on imports of Roquefort cheese into the United States. Typically, the target was chosen because it was considered to represent a symbol of fast food, industrialized agriculture, and the use of hormone-treated beef.

On the international stage, Bové has sought to demonstrate the connectivity of different causes. Examples include joining Greenpeace action against renewed French nuclear weapons testing in the Pacific Ocean in 1995, demonstrating against the World Trade Organization in Seattle in 1999, and attending protests against Israeli occupation of the West Bank and Gaza in 2001 in Al-Khader, Bethlehem, and in Ramallah during 2002. In 2006, however, he was refused entry to the United States, where he had been invited to address a conference on Global Companies organized by the Cornell University Labor Center.

—*David E. Lowes*

See also Anarcho-Syndicalism; Anti-Globalization Movement; Direct Action

Further Readings

Bové, J. (2001, November/December). A Farmers' International? *New Left Review, 12.* Retrieved August 12, 2006, from http://newleftreview.org/?view=2358

Bové, J. (2002). *The world is not for sale: Farmers against junk food.* London: Verso.

Boxer Rebellion

See Anti-Colonial Movements, Asia

Boycotts and Divestment

Not cooperating with those that oppress oneself or others is the basis behind boycott and divestment campaigns. At their heart, such efforts state that one will no longer be complicit with actions that are wrong. The targets can be directly involved with a problem—an example of which was the boycott of General Electric for its involvement in nuclear weapons production. Alternatively, the campaign can be to put pressure on a third party, such as the campaign to get Queen's University to divest its holdings in Noranda because of its operations during the Pinochet regime. They can be local, such as the Montgomery Bus Boycott, or global, such as the ongoing call to boycott goods from China because of its occupation of Tibet. Along with the stated goal of not buying something or ending one's investment in a corporation until the demands are met is the implied promise that if the demands are met, one will return as a customer or one will once again become an investor.

While the tactic has been around for a long time, the term *boycott* was coined during an Irish Land League struggle. By 1879, there had been seven consecutive poor harvests. A campaign began for the redistribution of land that included such tactics as refusing to pay rent, work on the fields of English landlords, or cooperate with evictions; those who did not refuse were ostracized. One particularly brutal land agent was Captain Charles Boycott, who gave his name to this particular form of economic noncooperation.

The tactic certainly predates the Irish land struggle. One of the better-known examples was the refusal to purchase goods produced under slavery, a campaign that began in 1781 and continued for several decades. A specific focus was refusing to purchase slave-produced sugar while buying sugar produced elsewhere.

Consumer boycotts often have been called in support of labor struggles. J. P. Stevens was boycotted from 1976 through 1980 in a successful effort to support the right of the Amalgamated Clothing and Textile Workers Union to organize textile plants in the southern United States. The California-based United Farm Workers have had several boycott campaigns, of various degrees of success, to push for the rights to organize and improve specific working conditions, such as elimination of the use of certain pesticides on food crops.

Corporate Accountability International, formerly called INFACT, coordinated three major consumer boycott campaigns of which two achieved substantial success. Its boycott of Nestlé in the late 1970s and early 1980s led to the company agreeing to follow World Health Organization guidelines for the sale and distribution of infant formula. In the 1990s, when Nestlé backed away from their commitments, other organizations emerged to resurrect the Nestlé boycott. In the late 1980s, INFACT took on General Electric on the issue of manufacturing components for nuclear weapons systems. By the end of the decade, General Electric had divested itself of nuclear weapons manufacturing. They have been less successful, to date, in their campaign against the tobacco giant Philip Morris, which includes a boycott of its subsidiary Kraft Foods.

Boycotts have been an important part of national liberation struggles. Perhaps the best known of these campaigns was the boycott of English-manufactured textile goods in India in the 1930s. The famous salt march, which encouraged Indians to manufacture their own salt, involved both an economic boycott of British-manufactured salt and a civil disobedience campaign to break the laws prohibiting Indians from making their own salt.

Global solidarity has also been expressed in both targeted and general boycott campaigns. Coca-Cola has been the subject of several international boycott campaigns due to poor labor practices. Pepsi-Cola was a subject of a successful boycott campaign to pressure it to withdraw from Burma. More general boycotts of all goods from South Africa during the later part of the anti-apartheid struggles and the current call to boycott all goods from China are more diffuse, and the impact is harder to measure. However, such calls for solidarity serve a number of purposes

beyond the potential economic impact. Like the ostracizing of Captain Boycott and his supporters, such campaigns indicate a wider rejection of oppressive practices while indicating that there is an alternative that will be supported. Raising public awareness, encouraging a simple action that individuals can take, and having definable goals are essential parts of all successful boycott campaigns.

Perhaps the highest profile sustained consumer boycott in the United States was the Montgomery Bus Boycott of 1955–1956. This effort successfully changed discriminatory state laws. Unlike many other boycotts, there was no easy alternative for those refusing to ride public transit in Montgomery, Alabama, although supporters worked hard to organize alternative transportation—which included a defiance of state court injunction on car-pooling.

A variant on boycotting is *divestment*—ceasing to invest in corporations or purchasing government bonds until a particular goal is achieved. Divestment campaigns are most often a part of other initiatives related to corporate responsibility.

During the later part of the struggle against apartheid, a number of organized campaigns focused on getting corporations to withdraw from South Africa until apartheid ended. Universities, labor union pension funds, and religious orders holding shares and bonds in such companies were encouraged to speak out against apartheid and demand that the companies they invested in cease to be active in South Africa or they would withdraw their investments. While the effectiveness of such campaigns was hard to measure, it helped to further international solidarity with the anti-apartheid struggle, indeed to grow in areas and among sectors that would not necessarily have been expected to engage in struggles for social change.

Despite limited definable successes, divestment campaigns have played a role in a number of solidarity campaigns. Student and church groups opposed to the Pinochet regime conducted a divestment campaign directed at Noranda that wanted to prevent Noranda from expanding its holdings and activities in Chile while Pinochet was in power.

More recently, Talisman Energy was a target of a divestment campaign to pressure it to withdraw from

Sudan. Talisman and other Western oil companies have been the target of a campaign to end their involvement in oil exploration and extraction in the Sudan until the oppressive conditions in the country, most notably in the southern regions, end. There has been some success in convincing companies to end their activities, but other companies, particularly those based in China, have moved in to replace them.

—Brian Burch

See also Anti-Consumerism; Strategies and Tactics in Social Movements

Further Readings

Baby Milk Action. Retrieved August 20, 2006, from http://www.babymilkaction.org/

Boycott Made in China Campaign. (2006). *Boycott made in China: Free Tibet.* Retrieved August 20, 2006, from http://www.boycottmadeinchina.org/

Boycotts in history. (2005). Retrieved 20 August, 2006, from http://www.pbs.org/now/society/boycott.html

Bringing GE to light. (1990). Philadelphia: New Society Press.

Canadian Friends of Burma. (1997). *Pepsi withdraws completely from Burma.* Retrieved August 20, 2006, from http://www.perc.ca/PEN/1997–02/s-byrma.html

Co-op America. (2005). *Boycotts: Economic action to stop corporate irresponsibility.* Retrieved August 20, 2006, from http://www.coopamerica.org/programs/boycotts/

Corporate Accountability International. Retrieved August 20, 2006, from http://www.stopcorporateabuse.org/

Corporate Campaign, Inc. (n.d.) *ACTWU vs. J.P. Stevens: 1976–1980.* Retrieved August 20, 2006, from http://www.corporatecampaign.org/stevens.htm

Cox, S. (1983, July 27). UBS reinvests in Noranda. *The Ubyssey,* p. 1. Retrieved August 20, 2006, from www.library.ubc.ca/archives/pdfs/ubyssey/SUBYSSEY_1983_07_27.pdf

Divestment. (2006). Retrieved August 20, 2006, from http://en.wikipedia.org/wiki/Divestment

Ethical Consumer. (2006). *Boycotts list.* Retrieved August 20, 2006, from http://www.ethicalconsumer.org/boycotts/boycotts_list.htm

Matthiessen, P. (1969). *Sal si puedes: César Chávez and the new American revolution.* New York: Random House.

Powers, R. S., & Vogele, W. B. (Eds.). (2006). *Protest, power, and change: An encyclopedia of nonviolent action.* New York: Garland.

Williams, D., & Greenhaw, W. (2006). *The thunder of angels.* Chicago: Lawrence Hill.

BOYLE, FATHER (1954–)

Father Boyle, or Greg Boyle, is a Jesuit priest who has spent the past 20 years working with former gang members in East Los Angeles. He is founder of Homeboy Industries, a gang rehabilitation program that provides employment opportunities for young men and women, primarily Latino/a, who want to leave the dangerous and violent life of street gangs. Former pastor of Delores Mission, Fr. Boyle, or "G" as his homies (ex–gang members) affectionately call him, has dedicated his life to ministering to the modern-day outcasts of contemporary U.S. culture: young, poor, brown men and women who are caught in a seemingly endless cycle of violence and crime.

A native of Los Angeles, Fr. Boyle attended Loyola High School and was influenced by the liberation theology of the Jesuit community. He was ordained in 1984 and was immediately posted in a small rural Bolivian parish. The challenge of this experience radicalized him, and he describes this as the turning point in his life. After his time in Latin America, he realized

Father Greg Boyle, left, talks with Edgar Augilar, 22, at the Homeboy Industries headquarters in East Los Angeles on Thursday, November, 23, 2004. Boyle, a Jesuit priest, began working in 1984 with eight neighborhood gangs. Today, his group works with more than 360 gangs across Los Angeles County.

Source: AP Photo/Kevork Djansezian.

that he wanted to work with the poor. In 1986, he was transferred to Dolores Mission, where the 32-year-old priest was confronted with new challenges, for Delores Mission is situated in one of the most dangerous and gang-infested areas of East Los Angeles. Parishioners in the area were at first resistant to this young Anglo priest. In order to gain their favor, Fr. Greg spent countless hours in the community, walking the streets and meeting individuals. Under his leadership, the parish opened a homeless shelter and a day care center.

Fr. Greg began to notice that the gang problem was the center of most of the community's problems. In 1988, he opened a junior high and high school for gang members called "Dolores Mission Alternative." He also began hiring gang members to work around the church. Fr. Greg grounds his ministry in the gospel message of Jesus' inclusive vision of community that embraces the marginalized and oppressed. He came to understand that poverty is at the root of street gangs' power. Individuals stay in gangs out of necessity, confronted with rejection whenever they attempt to seek employment outside of illegal gang life. Providing jobs for ex–gang members was the starting point of his ministry. His initial outreach to ex–gang members has evolved into a substantial center that includes a job referral program, free tattoo removal, a silk-screening company, a bakery, a graffiti removal service, and a café. In addition to the concrete economic opportunities Fr. Greg facilitates, he also empowers these young men and women by recognizing their full humanity, a subversive act within a society that devalues gang members as hopeless criminals unworthy of opportunities. Through the respect and trust he instills upon thousands of men and women and the economic opportunities he provides them, Fr. Greg is combating the gang problem in Los Angeles one soul at a time.

—Michelle A. Gonzalez

See also Liberation Theology

Further Readings

Fremon, C. (1995). *Father Greg and the homeboys.* New York: Hyperion.

BRADEN, ANNE AND CARL (1924–2006 AND 1914–1975)

Carl Braden and Anne McCarty Braden were long-time southern organizers and journalists who were among the civil rights movement's strongest white allies in the post–World War II South. Despite numerous attempts in the Cold War years to discredit them as revolutionaries and "reds," the pair applied their journalistic skills and left-wing vision to the causes of civil rights and civil liberties for almost three decades. After Carl's death, Anne Braden remained among the nation's most outspoken white anti-racist activists. Over her nearly six decades of activism, her life touched almost every modern U.S. social movement, and her message to them all was the centrality of racism and the responsibility of whites to combat it.

Both Bradens were natives of Louisville, Kentucky, where they met in 1947 as reporters on the daily newspapers. Anne McCarty—younger than Carl Braden by a decade—had grown up in rigidly segregated Anniston, Alabama, and was the child of a middle-class family that accepted southern racial mores wholeheartedly. A devout Episcopalian, Anne had questioned the southern social order as a youth. Yet she was never a reformer herself until she returned to Louisville and teamed up with Carl, a labor journalist who had grown up poor, the child of socialists and committed trade unionists.

In 1948, the two married and immersed themselves in Henry Wallace's idealistic Progressive Party run for the presidency. Soon after Wallace's defeat, they left mainstream journalism to apply their writing talents to the interracial left wing of the Congress of Industrial Organizations (CIO).

Even as the postwar labor movement splintered and grew less militant, civil rights causes heated up. In 1950, Anne Braden spearheaded a hospital desegregation drive in Kentucky. With southern white supporters of racial equality few and far between, she endured her first arrest in 1951 when she led a delegation of southern white women organized by the Civil Rights Congress to Mississippi to protest the execution of Willie McGee, an African American man convicted of the rape of a white woman.

Still, the Bradens might have remained rank-and-file local activists had they not found notoriety when they helped to desegregate an all-white suburb of their border-South city—an action that got them charged with sedition and vilified nationally as Communists. Days before the U.S. Supreme Court condemned school segregation in its historic *Brown v. Board of Education* ruling in May 1954, the Bradens acted as the "fronts" for African Americans Andrew and Charlotte Wade, who, because of Jim Crow housing practices, had been unsuccessful in their quest to purchase a new suburban home on their own. Upon discovering that blacks had moved in, white neighbors burned a cross in front of the new home, shot out windows, and condemned the Bradens for buying it on the Wades' behalf. Six weeks later, amid constant community tensions, the Wades' new house was dynamited one evening while they were out.

What began as an act of housing desegregation turned into a local variation of the anti-communist hysteria known nationwide as "McCarthyism," when the chief investigator began proclaiming that the purchase and subsequent dynamiting had all been a Communist plot to destabilize local race relations. The investigation turned from segregationist violence to the alleged Communist Party affiliations of those who had supported the Wades in their housing quest. In October 1954, Anne and Carl Braden and five other whites were charged with sedition, a vaguely defined charge that had rested inert in Kentucky law since its adoption in 1919 during an earlier Red Scare. The Bradens became local pariahs, and their children had to be sent to live temporarily with grandparents.

That December, after a sensationalized trial, Carl Braden—the perceived ringleader—was convicted of sedition and sentenced to 15 years' imprisonment. A paid FBI informant had connected him to the Communist Party, though not to the violence or any plot. As Anne and the other defendants awaited a similar fate, Carl served 8 months and was out on a $40,000 bond when a Supreme Court decision invalidated state sedition laws because of their capricious use. All charges were dropped.

Rarely had an anti-communist prosecution rested so firmly on racist underpinnings, and the Wades were never again able to live in their house or seek prosecution for its destruction. The Bradens traveled the nation raising consciousness as well as money for their defense by linking their civil liberties violations with the emerging civil rights movement and the repression of dissent in the South. Blacklisted from local employment, they took jobs as field organizers for the Southern Conference Educational Fund (SCEF), a small, New Orleans–based civil rights organization that had also been charged as a "Communist front" by the un-American investigating committees of the U.S. Congress. The couple's work to recruit sympathetic white Southerners to the movement was steadily hampered by their being smeared as seditionists. These attacks made them controversial figures even within the movement, but they used every attack as a platform for the right to dissent.

In the years before southern civil rights violations made national news, the Bradens developed their own media, both through SCEF's monthly newspaper, *The Southern Patriot,* and through numerous pamphlets and press releases publicizing major civil rights campaigns. In 1958, Anne wrote *The Wall Between,* a memoir of their sedition case. One of the few books of its time to unpack the psychology of white southern racism from within, it was praised by human rights leaders such as Martin Luther King, Jr. and became a runner-up for the National Book Award. That same year, Carl insisted on his First Amendment rights of free beliefs and association and refused to answer questions at a House Un-American Activities Committee (HUAC) hearing investigating the southern civil rights movement. Carl and his codefendant, anti-HUAC organizer Frank Wilkinson, lost a resulting First Amendment test case and served almost a year in prison in 1961.

Anne remained free and wrote a booklet titled *HUAC: Bulwark of Segregation,* which she circulated widely to social movement allies. The Bradens helped to launch the National Committee to Abolish HUAC, and they continued to highlight connections between civil rights and civil liberties to a younger generation now igniting a new southern student sit-in movement. In the 1960s, they became respected elders, and younger activists knew them as a "movement family" whose

Louisville home was always open. Later in the 1960s, the couple became directors of SCEF and moved its headquarters to Louisville. When young blacks suggested that whites organize among themselves, Anne Braden defended the Black Power movement, and many young white New Left activists gravitated to SCEF. The Bradens faced a second sedition charge in 1967 in eastern Kentucky as a result of a SCEF community-organizing project against strip-mining. The challenge they mounted finally got the state sedition law declared unconstitutional.

Ideological conflicts within the New Left and disillusionment with the pace of change brought about SCEF's decline in 1973, but the Bradens continued writing and organizing on behalf of African American activists under government attack, such as Angela Davis in California and the Wilmington Ten in North Carolina. With Davis, Carl Braden became a coinitiator of the National Alliance Against Racist and Political Repression. Yet Carl's life ended abruptly with a heart attack in 1975.

Anne's activism continued unabated, and she soon formed a new regional multiracial organization, the Southern Organizing Committee for Economic and Social Justice, which initiated battles against environmental racism. She became an instrumental voice in the Rainbow Coalition of the 1980s and in the two Jesse Jackson presidential campaigns, as well as organizing across racial divides in the new environmental, women's, and anti-nuclear movements that sprang up in that decade.

No longer a pariah, Anne received the ACLU's first Roger Baldwin Medal of Liberty in 1990 for her contributions to civil liberties. As she aged, her activism focused more on Louisville, where she remained a leader in anti-racist drives and taught social justice history classes at local universities.

For many activists of the 1960s and beyond, both Bradens, but Anne in particular, became a rare symbol of white southern resistance to segregation and racism. Despite the repression directed upon them in the Cold War era, the couple never dissociated from Marxism, the Communist Party, or the left generally. Yet neither would they ever affirm, deny, or detail their relationship to the Communist Party, believing firmly that there should be no attacks on the left and that First Amendment principles should protect all such beliefs. Until the ends of their lives, they were unyielding in keeping the struggle against racism at the center of their activism, while connecting it to war, poverty, and other social ills.

—Catherine Fosl

See also Civil Rights Movement; Communist Party USA; Davis, Angela; Government Suppression of Social Activism

Further Readings

Braden, A. (1999). *The wall between* (Rev. ed.). Knoxville: University Press of Tennessee. (Original work published 1958)

Fosl, C. (2006). *Subversive Southerner: Anne Braden and the struggle for racial justice in the Cold War South* (Rev. ed.). Lexington: University Press of Kentucky. (Original work published 2002)

Woods, J. (2003). *Black struggle, Red Scare: Segregation and anti-communism in the South, 1948–1968.* Baton Rouge: Louisiana State University Press.

BRAZILIAN WORKERS PARTY

See PARTIDO DOS TRABALHADORES

BREAD AND PUPPET THEATER

Theatrical historians call the Bread and Puppet Theater of Peter Schumann the East Coast counterpart of the San Francisco Mime Troupe, but this is somewhat incorrect. This designation came about because of Bread and Puppet's involvement in the Vietnam War protests, for which it paraded down the streets of New York with huge puppets. Schumann's involvement was not that of a protester but rather a statement of humanitarian principles, because he does not protest, he says. A protester is someone who is upset about something and gets up and shouts about it. The Bread and Puppet Theater is not interested in ideology. The Bread and

*Peter and Elka Schumann stand at their Bread and Puppet Theater Museum in Glover, VT, on Wednesday, June 4, 2003.
The Schumanns marked 40 years of Bread and Puppet's creativity and activism, which began in New York City's Lower
East Side in the 1960s. Performers gave a variety of short puppet and picture shows on Sunday, June 8, 2003, including a
revival of one of theater's oldest works, an allegory on the abuse of power.*

Source: AP Photo.

Puppet Theater is interested in exposing the problem
of inhumanity and saying what needs to be said; what
the audience does after the performance is out of the
theater's hands.

Rebelling against the comfort and conditioned
reactions of traditional theater, which Schumann
found superfluous in American society, the Bread and
Puppet Theater was established to feed the audience.
The theater should be as basic as bread. Before performances, the actors bake bread and hand it out to their
audience. Thus the name Bread and Puppet Theater. In
accordance with Schumann's belief about conventional theater, Bread and Puppet performs outdoors, in
the streets, and in the parks. Why? Because sometimes his point is made just by being there, for sud-
denly there is this thing right in front of people,
confronting them, and they cannot escape it.

Another reason for outdoor performances is that
Schumann believes that theater is a community occurrence. With this in mind, Bread and Puppet began giving back to the community by going into the schools

and working with children, often using shows developed by these children. Many of the shows are based
on biblical themes, which perhaps fuel his moral challenge to action. For this reason, often depicted are the
victims of injustice, war, hunger, or other forms of
oppression.

Outside in the streets and parks, what is needed
in this simple theater—with puppets that range in size
from 6 inches to 18 feet—is intensity. Puppets, more
than live actors, have intrinsic power. They can say
things that humans cannot say—just by their size.
Movement and music are more important than dialogue, and for this reason, Bread and Puppet's scripts
are minimally written, the performances more or less
improvised. Movement and pacing is of necessity simple and slow because the puppets are so large.

The Bread and Puppet Theater has gained international fame, with performances throughout Europe.

—James L. Secor

See also Performance Art, Political

Further Readings

Brecht, S. (1968, Winter). Peter Schumann's Bread and Puppet Theatre. *TDR: The Drama Review, 12*(2), 44–95.

Brecht, S. (1988). *The Bread and Puppet Theatre: The original theatre of the City of New York from the mid-sixties to the mid-seventies* (2 vols.). London: Methuen.

Hamilton, R. C. (1978). *The Bread and Puppet Theatre of Peter Schumann: History and analysis* (Doctoral dissertation, Indiana University, 1978). (UMI No. 7821732)

BREASTFEEDING MOVEMENT

The movement to promote breastfeeding emerged in the 1930s in response to the growing popularity of bottle-feeding. Around the turn of the 20th century, companies had begun marketing bovine milk products as infant food. By the 1950s, bottle-feeding was more fashionable and considered scientifically superior to breastfeeding. In the developing world, early breastfeeding advocates argued that formula was expensive for poor families and had extremely negative health consequences for babies. Meanwhile, in the United States and other industrialized countries, white, middle-class women argued that breastfeeding was an important aspect of mothering. Since then, an internationally organized breastfeeding movement has formed to challenge multinational corporations, influence international policy, educate citizens, and support breastfeeding women throughout the world.

The breastfeeding movement in the United States largely grew out of the first La Leche League meeting in 1956. That day, seven women in the suburbs of Chicago met to support each other's efforts to breastfeed. Critical of modern, "scientific" methods of mothering (including bottle-feeding, infant schedules, and anaesthetized childbirth), these women saw breastfeeding as the path to good mothering. They asserted that breastfeeding unified mother and baby, as well as the family and society. La Leche League soon became a source of information and encouragement for mothers throughout the United States. The first edition of a popular manual, *The Womanly Art of Breastfeeding,* was published in 1958 and has sold over 2 million copies. With new groups in Canada, Mexico, and New Zealand, the organization changed its name in 1964 to La Leche League International (LLLI). By the mid-1980s, there were over 4,000 LLLI support groups in 48 countries.

In the developing world, health care professionals connected bottle-feeding to infant death and disease in the 1930s. In 1939, a British pediatrician practicing in Singapore made the first public statement addressing the problem in a speech titled *Milk and Murder.* In the 1960s, the formula industry embarked on an aggressive marketing campaign in the developing world. The breastfeeding movement gained momentum in the early 1970s when an exposé in the *New Internationalist* magazine and a book titled *The Baby Killer* sparked international outcry against formula companies. In 1976, Roman Catholic Sisters of the Precious Blood filed a lawsuit against Bristol Myers with support of other shareholders, resulting in an international investigation. In 1977, the Minneapolis group INFACT (Infant Formula Action Coalition) organized a citywide boycott of Nestlé products. Within months, the boycott spread throughout the United States and was soon initiated in Europe, Canada, New Zealand, and Australia. Activists wrote thousands of letters to Nestlé and implored politicians to act.

In 1978, Senator Edward Kennedy held a Senate hearing to examine the marketing practices of the formula industry. At his request and the urging of a growing movement, the World Health Organization convened a meeting in October 1979. After various drafts, the World Health Assembly adopted the International Code of Marketing Infant Formula in May 1981, the first international code for transnational corporations. Among other things, the code stated that companies should accurately label their products, minimize advertising, avoid distributing free samples to mothers, and maintain high quality standards. Due to corporate lobbying, the code was passed as a recommendation rather than a regulation, which is more difficult to enforce. In response, various grassroots organizations soon formed the International Baby Food Action Network (IBFAN) to promote the code and monitor the formula industry's compliance with it. In 1984, the Nestlé boycott was suspended after the company agreed to abide by the code. After numerous warnings, the boycott was resumed in 1988 and was extended to other formula companies due to grievous code violations. The boycott has spread to numerous countries and remains in place to this day.

In 1990, the Innocenti Declaration for the Protection, Promotion and Support of Breastfeeding was adopted by 32 countries and 10 international agencies. It emphasized exclusive breastfeeding for young babies and called all governments to pass legislation that supports and protects breastfeeding. In 1991, World Alliance for Breastfeeding Action was founded in Penang, Malaysia, to act on the Innocenti Declaration. This umbrella organization of researchers, support groups, health care professionals, and community developers facilitates international breastfeeding advocacy and initiates worldwide events, including World Breastfeeding Week.

Breastfeeding organizations continue to grow in strength and number and provide more services than ever before. By 2003, LLLI had accredited nearly 41,000 leaders and published informational materials in 24 languages. IBFAN consists of over 148 organizations in 74 countries and trains high-ranking government health officials and lawyers. The Community Human Milk Bank held at the National Capital Lactation Center in Washington, D.C., provides donated breast milk to women by prescription.

In recent years, advocates in the United States have sought to increase public respect for breastfeeding. In 2004, over two dozen "lactivists" held a nurse-in at a Starbucks in Maryland after a mother was asked to nurse in the bathroom. Starbucks later issued a statement welcoming nursing mothers, and Burger King adopted nursing-friendly policies after a similar protest in Utah. In 2005, over 200 lactivists, organized by LLLI and other groups, peacefully gathered outside the ABC TV studio in response to anti-breastfeeding comments made on *The View*. Meanwhile, many U.S. activists remain in solidarity with mothers in developing countries by continuing to boycott formula companies and expressing new concerns about international aid

groups providing infant formula to victims of the Iraq war.

—*Andrea Bertotti Metoyer*

See also Alternative Movements; Feminism; Natural Childbirth Movement; Women's Collective Acts of Resistance; Women's Health Activism

Further Readings

DuPuis, E. M. (2002). *Nature's perfect food: How milk became America's drink.* New York: New York University Press.

La Leche League International. (2004). *The womanly art of breastfeeding.* New York: Plume.

La Leche League International. Retrieved October 23, 2006, from http://llli.org

Menon, L. (2003). *The breastfeeding movement: A sourcebook.* Penang, Malaysia: World Alliance for Breastfeeding Action.

Palmer, G. (1993). *The politics of breastfeeding.* London: Pandora Press.

Van Esterik, P. (1989). *Beyond the breast-bottle controversy.* Piscataway, NJ: Rutgers University Press.

Weiner, L. (1994). Reconstructing motherhood: The La Leche League in postwar America. *Journal of American History, 8*(4), 1357–1381.

World Alliance for Breastfeeding Action. Retrieved October 23, 2006, from http://www.waba.org.my/

Brecht, Bertolt (1898–1956)

Bertolt Brecht was arguably one of the foremost playwrights, composers, dramaturges, and political activists of the 20th century. Born in Augsburg, Bavaria, he grew up to study medicine and worked in a hospital in Munich during World War I. After the war he moved to Berlin, where he found his passion and talent for the theater. He was inspired by the influential critic Herbert Ihering, who told him how the public was hungry for modern theater. He also befriended Erich Engel, a man who directed most of Brecht's plays throughout Brecht's life. Brecht managed to put up his first two plays in Munich right after the war, *Baal* and *Drums in the Night*. But his first success came from his third play, *In the Jungle of the Cities,* which Engel directed in Berlin.

Brecht lived in Berlin during the 1920s, a time when the world looked to Berlin for the finest art, culture, and fashion. It was also the era of the Weimar Republic, a liberal government set up after World War I. Brecht and his work thrived during this time, taking advantage of the public's positive attitudes toward a more democratic government. By the early 1920s, Brecht had formed his infamous writing collective, whch included such great German artists as Elisabeth Hauptmann, Margarete Steffin, Emil Burri, Ruth Berlau, and Helene Weigel (his second wife). The collective focused its attention on furthering Brecht's work and ambitions to use theater as a means of social change and was one of the most influential literary and theatrical movements during the Weimar Republic. The collective put on a number of Brecht's plays, works they called *Lehrstücke* (teaching plays), for the large worker arts organization in Germany and Austria. These works were written to transform passive audiences into active audiences whose attention was drawn to participation and social change.

Along with Brecht's original works, the collective also adapted John Gray's *The Beggars Opera,* renaming it *Die Dreigroschenoper* (*The Three Penny Opera*). For this work, Brecht composed his own songs and music; it became the most successful play in Berlin in the 1920s. The play focused on the hardships of the working class and the unemployed in Germany, showing the hypocritical views of the Church toward these people. The play also centered around the workers as people rather than numbers. It remains one of Brecht's most well-known plays.

The collective was also where Brecht developed a new, radical approach to the theater. Brecht believed in socialist values and the power of art to move people to better society. He wanted to design an entire method of theater where the audience experienced a sense of alienation, something he called *Verfremdungseffekt* (distancing effect or estrangement effect). Brecht called this new theory epic theater, the theory that a play should not simply cause the audience to emotionally identify with the scenes onstage, but rather it should invoke personal self-reflection and analysis, wherein a critical view of the stage would be developed and would move the person to enact change. Brecht wanted audiences to realize that the play was not reality but merely a representation of reality.

Brecht's epic theater utilized a number of new techniques to heighten the audience's sense of estrangement, such as direct addresses to the audience by actors, songs rather than long monologues, strange and unnatural stage lighting, few props, and signs with explanatory messages aimed toward the audience. Brecht was also fascinated with Asian theater, especially its use of masks. He took the literal use of masks in Asian plays and re-created them metaphorically in his epic theater, often pointing out the hypocritical attitudes of labor bosses and the Church toward the working poor. The masks of Asian theater were also the key influence for Brecht to use alienation and estrangement in his work. In fact, some scholars argue that the explanatory signs were inspired by the masks of Asian theater.

Brecht's epic theater has become the staple way to perform his plays today. Although Brecht's theory has been used so often and mirrored by other artists that it is now considered "theatrical canon," some scholars and audiences feel that the effect of epic theater is lost after seeing a few similar plays that employ it. Yet, it is still considered the first form of political theater, where the audience was encouraged to understand its meaning and invoke critical thought. Brecht was also the first to use multimedia in the semiotics of the theater with the use of his trademark explanatory signs.

Throughout the 1920s to the early 1930s, Brecht and his collective flourished creatively, and he was seen as a success by German and Austrian audiences. Along with being a successful playwright, Brecht also published several books of both poetry and essays. He was also involved in early moviemaking. He wrote the screenplay to the semi-documentary film *Kuhle Wampe* (made in 1932), directed by Slatan Dudow. The film, dealing with the more human side of mass unemployment, was praised for its use of sarcasm, subversive humor, sharp cinematography by Günther Krampf, and musical score by Hanns Eisler. Along with his successful plays, Brecht also wrote operas and collaborated with such musical talents as

Kurt Weill (who composed the musical score for the *Three Penny Opera*). Brecht and Weill wrote the opera *Aufstieg und Fall der Stadt Mahoganny* (*The Rise and Fall of the City of Mahoganny*), which premiered amid Nazi protests in Leipzig in 1930. The opera ran again in Berlin in 1931 and was hailed a success.

By 1933, Brecht's beloved home of Berlin had changed dramatically. The Nazi Party had risen to power with Adolph Hitler winning the German election in 1933. Fascism was quickly taking over the country. Brecht knew that his socialist beliefs could put him and anyone associated with him in danger. Fearing for his life, he immediately went into exile with only his wife, Helene. In exile, he consistently changed locations to evade Nazi persecution, living in Austria, Switzerland, Denmark, Finland, Sweden, England, Russia, and the United States. He did not return to his home of Berlin until about 1947, after the Nazi occupation.

Though Brecht lived as an "enemy alien" of the Nazi regime from 1933 to 1945, his time in exile was spent continuing his groundbreaking work. He and his wife continued to write and stage his plays, showing his work to anyone who desired it. His most famous plays and operas were written during his exile; these included *Galileo, Mother Courage and Her Children, Mr. Puntila and His Man Matti, The Resistable Rise of Arturo Ui, Caucasian Chalk Circle, The Good Person of Sezuan,* as well as many others. These productions were politically and socially charged works, highlighting the oppression of the Third Reich, the hardships and trials of the working poor, the hypocrisy of the Church, and the need for freethinking. In the spirit of his former collective, Brecht also adapted such Greek tragedies as *Antigone,* giving the classic play a new, modern life.

In April 1941, he used his influence and connections to secure a visa to the United States. Traveling through Russia as a known enemy alien, he managed to make the boat to America and arrived in New York in July 1941. In a surprise twist, Brecht chose to live in Hollywood, California. Many believed he would stay in New York City, where his plays were sure to be welcomed. Yet, he chose to move to Hollywood and work in the budding movie industry as a scriptwriter. During the early 1940s, he worked on a few scripts but had no viable success at it. In fact, Brecht hated the movie business. He published a number of essays including *On Film,* in which he described movies to be the downfall of public theater. He also believed that unless film was used to challenge audiences and promote social consciousness, it had the power to destroy theater and society at large.

Remaining in Hollywood for a couple of years after the war, Brecht and his art were thrown into another political situation: the Cold War. Many countries began to test and harbor nuclear weapons, including countries with communist governments. The United States, in particular, viewed communism as a major threat to the American way of life and to the safety of the nation. The U.S. government felt communist governments like Russia would use nuclear weapons against them. U.S. officials also felt that the ideals of communism promoted the use of nuclear weapons. The country fell into a panic known as the Red Scare, the fear that anyone could fall "victim" to the "disease" of communism. To combat the communist "threat," the U.S. established the House Un-American Activities Committttee (HUAC) headed by Senator Joseph McCarthy. The HUAC and McCarthy were known to target people on the social fringes of society as well as the artistic elite.

In 1947, the HUAC set its sights on Brecht, harassing him about his communist allegiances. He was blacklisted by the bosses of every major motion picture studio in Hollywood, never to be allowed to work for them again. In November 1947, Brecht and 30 other movie industry workers were subpoenaed to testify before the HUAC regarding communist activities and ties. At this time, Brecht had already left the United States and returned to East Berlin where he ran the Berliner Ensemble Theater, a postwar, German touring theater that primarily performed Brecht's plays. Though he swore he would ignore the subpoena, he did testify stating that he was not, nor was he ever, a member of the Communist Party either in the United States or abroad. He and 10 others were not cited for contempt, and he returned to Europe the next day.

The last years of Brecht's life were spent doing what he loved most: writing. He stayed relatively out of public and political controversy and wrote mostly poetry, including the well-known "Buckower Elegies." He wrote a few more plays, but none of them were as famous as his earlier works. He lived comfortably until a sudden heart attack in the summer of 1956 took his life; he was 58 years old. He was buried in the Dorotheenfriedhof in Berlin.

Brecht's influence is still alive today. Helene Weigel, his wife and close friend, continued to stage his works until her death in 1971, and he also left her the Berliner Theater. In his wake, Brecht left three children, Hanne Hiob, Stefan Brecht, and Barbara Brecht, all of whom went on to become well-known German actors, critics, and poets (Barbara also holds the current copyrights to all of her father's work). Today, Brecht's epic theater is considered a basic principle of Postmodernism. In fact, though some scholars find Brecht's epic theater to be in the tradition of Modernism (the mood of the 1920s), other scholars argue that Brecht may have been one of the first Postmodernists, paving the way for Postmodernism by dispelling the ideas of theater in his time and creating an entirely new theater, a political theater.

His poetry has also found a large following in today's readership. Though during his life he was best known for his plays and operas, his essays and poems have come into recent attention and acclaim since the 1980s, highlighting similar techniques used in epic theater, such as direct address and feelings of estrangement, offering readers the opportunity to look at his poems as invitations to self-analysis and independent thought. In his lifetime, Brecht wrote and staged almost 30 plays. Even in political exile, he continued his work, emphasizing the hardships and triumphs of the working class. He valued theater, writing, art, culture, and politics that carried more than a message, but also a chance to think freely and independently. His theories, plays, and writings are still performed to sold-out audiences around the world, in dozens of languages, and he is hailed as one of the finest theatrical thinkers and writers of the 20th century.

—Meliza Bañales

See also Film; Hollywood Blacklists; Literature and Activism; Performance Art, Political; Postmodernism

Further Readings

Brecht, B. (2003). *Brecht on art and politics* (L. Bradley, S. Giles, & T. Kuhn, Trans.). London: Methuen.

Brecht, B. (2003). *Poetry and prose* (R. Grimm & C. Molina y Vedia, Eds.). New York: Continuum.

Esslin, M. (1971). *Brecht: The man and his work.* New York: Anchor Books.

Rennert, H. (2004). *Essays on twentieth-century German drama and theater: An American reception 1977–1999.* New York: Peter Lang.

Thompson, P., & Sacks, G. (1994). *The Cambridge companion to Brecht.* London: Cambridge University Press.

BROWN, H. RAP (1943–)

H. Rap Brown's firebrand anti-American rhetoric and militant stances made him synonymous with the 1960s Black Power movement. Coming to political consciousness during the turbulent 1964 Mississippi Summer Project in Lowndes County, Brown became the chairman of the Non-Violent Action Group at Howard University in 1965. That same year, Brown achieved national notoriety by confronting President Lyndon B. Johnson. According to Ekwueme Thelwell, who knew Brown at the time and wrote the foreword to the 2002 reissuing of Brown's *Die Nigger Die!* he rebuffed President Johnson's comments that black demonstrations over the vicious riot on the Pettus Bridge in Selma, Alabama, had prevented his daughters from getting a good night's sleep. In 1967, Brown succeeded Stokely Carmichael as chairman of the Student Nonviolent Coordinating Committee. With the movement divided among U.S. Supreme Court Justice Thurgood Marshall's conciliatory legalistic approach, Martin Luther King, Jr.'s nonviolent mass movement demonstrations, and the Black Panther Party's increasingly militant revolutionary vanguard call for "Black Power," Brown's endorsement of Black Power further fragmented the civil rights movement.

H. Rap Brown's work as a community organizer and black revolutionary was exemplified in the speech he gave in 1967 in Cambridge, Maryland. He urged blacks to arm themselves and be ready to die. This inflammatory speech led to a riot in which gunshots between protesters and the police were exchanged. He was subsequently charged by the State of Maryland with "incitement to riot," and this began his ongoing confrontations with state law enforcement agencies and the Federal Bureau of Investigation (FBI). In 1970, Brown was a fugitive on the FBI's Ten Most Wanted list. In 1972, he was shot in an alleged attempted robbery for which he subsequently served 5 years in prison. In Attica prison, H. Rap Brown converted to Orthodox Islam (Sunni Muslim) and changed his name to Jamil Abdulla Al-Amin. However, despite this conversion, the militant revolutionary polemic of his 1969 book *Die Nigger Die!* remains a unique and powerful statement of black revolutionary struggle. In this powerful political tract, Brown argues that all activities are political, America is a neocolonizing power, black men should not fight in the wars of a colonizing power, and it is legitimate to arm oneself to achieve freedom. In Brown's analyses, there is only freedom or slavery, no middle ground. Brown lambastes blacks who are used by whites in maintaining the false consciousness of "White Power Politics" as "Toms."

After almost two decades of silence in the media, Jamil Abdulla Al-Amin reemerged as imam of a mosque in Atlanta, Georgia. Imam Al-Amin is deeply respected in the Muslim communities he served. Yet, always haunted by his militant revolutionary past and harassed by federal law enforcement agents, when the World Trade Center was first bombed in 1993, Al-Amin was interrogated as a suspected conspirator. In 2000, Al-Amin was arrested and charged with four counts of felony murder for the shooting of two sheriff's deputies. In 2002, he was convicted and sentenced to life in prison without parole.

—*Richard A. Jones*

See also Black Panther Party; Black Power; Kunstler, William; Student Nonviolent Coordinating Committee (SNCC)

Further Readings

Brown, H. (1969). *Die nigger die!* Chicago: Lawrence Hill Books.
Brown, H. (1993). *Revolution by the book: The rap is live.* Beltsville, MD: Writers' Inc. International.
Thelwell, E. M. (2002, March 18). H. Rap Brown/Jamil Al-Amin: A profoundly American story. *The Nation.* http://www.thenation.com/doc/20020318/thelwell

BROWN, JOHN (1800–1859)

John Brown was born May 9, 1800, in Torrington, Connecticut, to white parents who were fiercely Calvinist and opposed to slavery. He carried their legacy, developing a spiritual hatred for racism and raising his family to abhor oppression.

It was in North Elba, Ohio, around 1849, that Brown, after years of largely unsuccessful vocational ventures, began to turn the entirety of his attention toward the abolition of slavery. His house was a stop on the Underground Railroad. He corresponded regularly with ardent abolitionists, including Frederick Douglass. It was during this time that Brown began drafting plans for a mass slave rebellion—the plan that would eventuate in his attack on the U.S. military armory at Harpers Ferry, Virginia.

In 1854, shortly after the passing of the Kansas-Nebraska Act, several of Brown's sons traveled to the area to support the free-state cause. Brown soon joined them. It was there that he would assert his abolitionary leadership on a larger scale. Angered by the violent actions of the pro-slavery contingent in the territory and Preston Brooks's near-deadly caning of Senator Charles Sumner, Brown and his sons retaliated by killing five men. Later, he led a defense of free-state settlement Prarie City. But it was his short-handed defense of Osawatomie, Kansas—a failed defense—that gave Brown his initial celebrity among abolitionists.

Brown returned east in 1856, determined to acquire money and weapons for his war on slavery. Within 2 years, he had rededicated himself to the Harpers Ferry plan. For the next few years, he traveled, led raids freeing dozens of slaves, and continued seeking support, particularly from wealthy New England abolitionists.

By fall of 1859, Brown had gathered 21 men, including five African Americans, and begun preparations for the Harpers Ferry raid. Late at night on

October 16, 18 of the men descended upon the town. They secured the armory without incident, but a lack of response from local slaves (Brown assumed they would quickly join his cause) and the fast-spreading word of their attack doomed the maneuver. On October 18, Marines stormed the engine house in which Brown and his men had taken refuge. Seven of the original raiders, including Brown, were captured.

Brown was tried and convicted of murder and treason and sentenced to hang. Despite attempts by supporters to organize a rescue, Brown insisted that he was worth more hanging than alive. He was executed on December 2, 1859. On his way to the gallows, he handed a guard a note stating that he was certain that the crimes of the guilty land would never be purged without bloodshed. Brown's prophecy proved true. He was eulogized in essays and speeches by Ralph Waldo Emerson, Henry David Thoreau, and other prominent voices of the time. Union Civil War soldiers marched into battle singing "John Brown's Body."

—Paul C. Gorski

See also Abolitionist Movements; Douglass, Frederick; Underground Railroad

Further Readings

Du Bois, W. E. B. (2001). *John Brown.* New York: Modern Library.

Peterson, M. D. (2002). *John Brown: The legend revisited.* Charlottesville: University Press of Virginia.

Renehan, E. J. (1997). *The Secret Six: The true tale of the men who conspired with John Brown.* Columbia: University of South Carolina Press.

Reynolds, D. S. (2005). *John Brown, abolitionist: The man who killed slavery, sparked the Civil War, and seeded civil rights.* New York: Knopf.

BROWN V. BOARD OF EDUCATION

Brown v. Board of Education of Topeka et al. was argued December 9, 1952, and reargued December 8, 1953, in the U.S. District Court for the District of Kansas. Considered by many to be the most important legal decision of the 20th century, the case commonly known as *Brown v. Board of Education* was decided on May 17, 1954, by the U.S. Supreme Court. In a 9–0 unanimous decision, Chief Justice Earl Warren and the Court ruled,

> We come then to the question presented: Does segregation of children in public schools solely on the basis of race, even though the physical facilities and other "tangible" factors may be equal, deprive the children of the minority group of equal educational opportunities? We believe that it does . . . We conclude that in the field of public education the doctrine of "separate but equal" has no place. Separate educational facilities are inherently unequal. Therefore, we hold that the plaintiffs and others similarly situated for whom the actions have been brought are, by reason of the segregation complained of, deprived of the equal protection of the laws guaranteed by the Fourteenth Amendment.

The *Brown v. Board of Education* Case

Oliver L. Brown of Topeka, Kansas, attempted to enroll his 7-year-old daughter Linda in a white elementary school. However, the school principal refused to allow Brown's daughter to attend the school. This incident became the impetus for a class action suit filed by the National Association for the Advancement of Colored People (NAACP) on behalf of Oliver L. Brown, Mrs. Richard Lawton, Mrs. Sadie Emanuel, and other parents in the states of Kansas, South Carolina, Virginia, and Delaware, and the District of Columbia whose children were being discriminated against in their school districts. The U.S. Supreme Court consolidated the Kansas, South Carolina, Virginia, and Delaware cases in 1952 when it agreed to hear appeals in each of them, as well as in a fifth case against segregation in the District of Columbia. More than 200 plaintiffs were included in the *Brown v. Board of Education* case. The states of Delaware, South Carolina, and Virginia had state constitutions or statutes that required segregation. Segregation was permitted but not legally required in the state of Kansas and in Washington, D.C. The landmark case bears the name of Linda C. Brown, the plaintiff. The attorneys who argued the case were Thurgood Marshall (Chief

Counsel), Robert Carter, and Jack Greenberg, from the National Association for the Advancement of Colored People Legal Defense Fund; and Charles Bledsoe, Charles Scott, and John Scott, from the Kansas NAACP. The common thread in the cases was that the 1896 separate but equal ruling in *Plessy v. Ferguson* violated the Fourteenth Amendment of the U.S. Constitution, which reads,

> No State shall make or enforce any law which shall abridge the privileges or immunities of citizens of the United States; nor shall any State deprive any person of life, liberty, or property, without due process of law; nor deny to any person within its jurisdiction the equal protection of the laws.

In the South Carolina case, *Briggs v. Elliott,* 20 African American plaintiffs filed suit to integrate the public schools of Summerton in Clarendon County in 1947. In the Virginia case, *Davis v. County School Board of Prince Edward County,* the lawsuit stemmed from a 1951 protest by African American students who were denied bus transportation and had to walk 3 miles to attend the all-black school. In the Delaware case, two separate cases—*Belton v. Gebhart* and *Bulah v. Gebhart*—were brought by African American parents in the Wilmington suburb of Claymont and in rural Hockessin; the parents challenged the inferior conditions of two schools designated for black children and argued for the right to send their children to the local white high school. The Washington, D.C., case, *Bolling v. Sharpe,* originated in the fall of 1950 when African American students were denied admission to the new John Philip Sousa Junior High School. The Kansas case is the most famous of the five cases. *Oliver Brown et al. v. The Board of Education of Topeka* was filed in 1951 by 13 African American parents who wanted to integrate the city's public elementary schools. State law permitted but did not require cities of 15,000 residents or more to maintain separate school facilities for black and white children. The public junior high and high schools in the community were already integrated. A three-judge federal panel in the Kansas case concluded that segregation did have a detrimental effect on black children. However, the

court denied relief to the plaintiffs—including Oliver Brown who had sued on behalf of his daughter Linda.

The legal question in the *Brown v. Board of Education* case was the following: Did segregation of children in public schools solely on the basis of race, even when physical facilities and other tangible factors were equal, deprive black children of equal opportunities? The Supreme Court held that segregating children in public schools exclusively on the basis of race, even when physical facilities and other tangible factors were equal, did deprive black children equal educational opportunities. The Court concluded that segregation could also have detrimental psychological effects on black children that could lead to an inferiority complex. The Court ruling essentially overturned the *Plessy* ruling that separate educational facilities are inherently unequal and in violation of the equal protection as guaranteed by the Fourteenth Amendment.

On May 17, 1954, the U.S. Supreme Court struck down the applicability of the separate but equal doctrine with respect to education in its unanimous decision, *Brown v. Board of Education of Topeka Kansas.* The court held that de jure segregation (segregation that is imposed by law) deprived black students equal protection of the laws guaranteed by the Fourteenth Amendment of the Constitution. However, the court did not give states specific instructions for implementing desegregation in their schools. In the 1955 case known as *Brown II,* the Supreme Court reviewed the 1954 decision and the lack of progress toward implementing desegregation. The Court reiterated that segregation was unconstitutional and held school authorities responsible for implementing desegregation and addressing any problems associated with implementation. The court also ruled that the lower courts were responsible for determining whether actions taken by school authorities constituted good faith implementation of the constitutional principles that required the dismantling of de jure segregation in schools. The Supreme Court acknowledged that school districts would need time to create plans to eradicate discrimination, but in *Brown II,* the Court ordered public schools to admit students on a racially nondiscriminatory basis with all deliberate speed.

Key Individuals in the *Brown v. Board of Education* Case

The legal strategy that led to the *Brown* victory was designed to dismantle all vestiges of segregation in the United States—segregation in education, public transportation, and access to public accommodations such as restaurants and restrooms. The NAACP legal team, led by Howard University Law School Dean Charles Hamilton Houston and his protégé Thurgood Marshall, planned a series of lawsuits demanding that black students be given the same type of education (books, facilities, transportation) as that available to white students. As a precursor to the *Brown* case, the NAACP filed several lawsuits from 1930 to 1950 that challenged the *Plessy* decision and focused on the right to an equal education in K–12 and higher education. In 1950, Thurgood Marshall, the director-counsel of the NAACP Legal Defense Fund, won two cases that would complete the legal foundation for *Brown*— *Sweatt v. Painter* and *McLaurin v. Oklahoma*. After consecutive legal victories, NAACP strategists began to look for a case that would overturn the *Plessy* decision and its "separate but equal" doctrine. Another African American lawyer, Robert Carter, is considered to be the major strategist behind the *Brown* case. Carter argued three of the five cases that together constituted the *Brown* case—*Briggs v. Elliott, Davis v. Prince Edward County,* and *Brown v. Board of Education of Topeka, Kansas*. Carter used the work of Dr. Kenneth Clark as part of his legal argument to attack the separate but equal doctrine. Dr. Clark, an African American psychologist, became an expert witness for the NAACP in the *Brown* case. His work with black and white students in the South and his doll theory showed how segregation adversely affected the educational achievement of black children. The NAACP legal staff, known as the *Brown Team,* also included Constance Baker Motley, Spotswood Robinson III, James M. Nabrit, Jr., and Jack Greenberg.

The social and political activism of other prominent figures was directly related to the *Brown* case. In 1950, Judge Collins Jacques Seitz ruled that the education in white and black colleges in the state of Delaware was inequitable. As a result of Judge Seitz's ruling, the University of Delaware became the first state-financed institution in the United States to be desegregated at the undergraduate level by court order. In 1952, Seitz became the first U.S. judge to order segregated white schools in the state of Delaware to admit black children immediately rather than allowing state and school authorities to engage in lengthy deliberations about the implementation of desegregation. The NAACP cited Judge Seitz's ruling in the *Brown* case. Rev. J. A. DeLaine, an African American Episcopal minister, was also a key figure before and during the *Brown* case. For over a decade, DeLaine helped organize a series of lawsuits to obtain school bus transportation, better school facilities, and higher teacher pay. In 1951, he led 20 petitioners seeking to desegregate schools in the Clarendon, South Carolina, case, *Briggs v. Elliott*. More than others, Rev. DeLaine suffered severe reprisals for his courage. He was fired from his teaching job, was removed from his church, his house was burned down, and angry whites fired shots at him and his family. A warrant was issued for his arrest after he returned fire, and he fled South Carolina and lived in exile in New York until his death in 1974.

Court Cases Preceding *Brown v. Board of Education*

The separate but equal doctrine originated in the 1896 *Plessy v. Ferguson* case. Homer Plessy, an African American, challenged segregation laws in Louisiana by riding in a whites-only train car. In the *Plessy* case, the U.S. Supreme Court upheld the doctrine of separate but equal, and the Court's decision paved the way for continued segregation throughout the country. The law held that segregation was legal as long as the facilities for blacks were equal to those established for whites. While the *Plessy* case was about public transportation, the case would have broader implications for society, particularly with respect to education.

Several court cases set the stage for the Supreme Court decision in *Brown v. Board of Education*. The first lawsuit challenging school segregation, *Roberts v. City of Boston,* was filed in Boston, Massachusetts, in 1849. The black plaintiffs in that case had been denied the right to enroll their children in the all-white public schools in Boston. The Massachusetts court concluded that commonwealth law entitled colored persons to equal constitutional, political, civil, and social rights. Nevertheless, the court found that the laws that provided separate schools for colored children did not violate any of these rights. The court concluded that the school committees did have the power to separate white and black students, particularly if the education was equal. In many ways, *Roberts v. City of Boston* is the origin of the separate but equal doctrine in education.

The Supreme Court ruled in two important higher education cases that would also have implications for the *Brown* case. In the 1950 *Sweatt v. Painter* case, Herman Sweatt was denied admission to the University of Texas Law School in 1946 because he was black. The Supreme Court found that although the school had established a separate but equal facility, the Equal Protection Clause of the Fourteenth Amendment required that Sweatt be admitted to the law school. As a result of the ruling, *Sweatt v. Painter* became one of the cases that provided the NAACP with a legal strategy for school desegregation cases.

In another 1950 case, *McLaurin v. Oklahoma State Regents for Higher Education,* McLaurin was a black student with a master's degree who applied to the doctoral program in education at the University of Oklahoma. McLaurin was denied admission based on a state law that made it a misdemeanor to maintain or operate, teach or attend a school at which both whites and blacks were enrolled. McLaurin filed a complaint alleging that the action of the school authorities and the statutes upon which their action was based were unconstitutional and deprived him of equal protection as guaranteed by the Fourteenth Amendment. McLaurin won his case at the district court level, and the legislature amended the statute to permit the admission of blacks to postsecondary institutions attended by whites. However, the Court's ruling only made it possible for McLaurin to be admitted in situations where institutions offered courses that were not available in the schools for blacks, and in such cases, the program of instruction was to be given only under segregated conditions. Consequently, university officials enforced the law that allowed segregation and

subjected McLaurin to unfair treatment. He could not sit in the same classroom with white students; rather, he was required to sit at a designated desk in a room adjoining the regular classroom. He was also required to sit at a designated table and to eat at a different time than white students in the school cafeteria. The Supreme Court concluded that the conditions to which McLaurin was subjected in order to receive an education deprived him of his right to the equal protection laws as guaranteed by the Fourteenth Amendment.

Resistance to the *Brown v. Board of Education* Decision

Black students, parents, and educators bore the burden of attempting to desegregate schools while school boards reluctantly created plans that, in theory, were in compliance with the 1954 *Brown I* ruling. Efforts to desegregate Little Rock (Arkansas) Central High School in 1957 is one of the most famous and most compelling stories in the struggle to desegregate schools in the South. Thelma Mothershed, Elizabeth Eckford, Melba Pattillo, Jefferson Thomas, Ernest Green, Minniejean Brown, Carlotta Walls, Terrence Roberts, and Gloria Ray, known as the Little Rock Nine, were the students chosen to integrate the school. The Little Rock Nine experienced emotional distress as they resisted Governor Orval Faubus, the Arkansas legislature, and angry mobs of white citizens who met them each morning as they attempted to enter the school building. White citizens, who were determined to maintain segregation as a way of life in the South, shouted at the students and threatened to harm them. As a result, the Little Rock Nine had to be escorted to classes by law enforcement officials. Attempts to desegregate Little Rock Central High School would result in six legal cases being tried in the federal courts to allow the nine black students to attend school with 2,000 white students. The events at Little Rock Central High School were illustrative of the turbulent times in school systems across America, and particularly in the South.

Numerous lawsuits were filed in efforts to enforce the mandates of *Brown*. Cases such as *Goss v. Board of Education of the City of Knoxville* in 1963, *Rogers v.*

Paul in 1965, *Griffin v. County School Board of Prince Edward County* in 1964, and *Green v. County School of New Kent County* in 1968 were heard in the courts in the decade following *Brown*. The *Green* case was the first school desegregation case following the appointment of Thurgood Marshall to the Supreme Court and articulated the distinction between de jure and de facto segregation. The ruling in this case marked the end of school choice programs that were segregated based on race. The *Green* case is considered the first case that moved schools toward a unitary status—the elimination of dual school systems. Under unitary status, black schools for black students and white schools for white students would no longer be permitted. Another prominent case, the 1971 *Swann v. Charlotte-Mecklenburg Board of Education* case marked the beginning of the use of busing to desegregate schools and to support unitary status. In the *Swann* case, white suburbs surrounded mostly black urban areas such as Charlotte-Mecklenburg, North Carolina. A plan to achieve racial balance was approved by the North Carolina District Court and by the Fourth Circuit Court. The Court noted that in the *Swann* case, while numerical ratios and quotas were not constitutionally required, they could provide a starting point for implementing school desegregation.

In 1974, 20 years after the *Brown v. Board of Education* decision, *Milliken v. Bradley* (known as *Milliken I*) would impede desegregation efforts, particularly in urban school districts. The ruling in the case marked a major shift in the Supreme Court's views on school desegregation. In *Milliken I*, the Supreme Court held that it was improper to impose a multidistrict remedy for Detroit, Michigan's single-district de jure segregation in the absence of findings that the surrounding suburban districts had failed to operate unitary schools or had contributed to segregation in Detroit schools. The Court restricted school desegregation to a single, predominantly black and racially isolated district (Detroit) rather than allowing a multidistrict remedy that would include the surrounding suburban school districts. In his dissent, Justice Thurgood Marshall believed the majority opinion of the Supreme Court in *Milliken I* was based on perceptions that enough had been done to enforce constitutional guarantees for black students at the expense of the enforcement of neutral constitutional principles.

In 1990, almost 30 years after the *Brown v. Board of Education* decision, one of the most significant desegregation cases to reach the Supreme Court was *Missouri v. Jenkins*. In this case, the primary issue was whether the federal judiciary could impose a tax increase to fund school desegregation. The Supreme Court affirmed the authority of federal judges to increase taxes beyond those set by state statute to pay for the cost of desegregating schools.

The *Brown* decision adversely affected many African Americans for many years after it was rendered. For example, Linda C. Tillman wrote in 2004 that while black educators in general were affected, it was black teachers who were most often the victims of segregated policies and practices that cost them their jobs. In 1954, the year of the *Brown* decision, approximately 82,000 African American teachers were responsible for the education of the nation's 2 million African American public school students. A decade later, over 38,000 African American teachers had lost their positions in 17 southern and border states. Another 21,515 African American teachers lost their jobs between 1984 and 1989. African American principals also lost their jobs as a result of resistance to the *Brown* decision. When the states of Oklahoma, Missouri, Kentucky, West Virginia, Maryland, and Delaware closed most of their all black schools between 1954 and 1965, more than 50% of the African American principals in these states were dismissed.

White Southerners and some white Northerners who wished to maintain a segregated educational system refused to comply with the Supreme Court's decision. In many southern states, local officials shut down entire school systems to avoid desegregation. Some politicians also refused to accept the Court's decision. One hundred members of Congress adopted the Southern Manifesto and vowed to oppose the decision and maintain segregation. Supreme Court Justice Earl Warren was also a target of southern hostilities, and "Impeach Warren" signs were visible on highways all across the South. In some states, governors stood at the doors of schools to prevent African American students from attending classes with whites.

The Supreme Court's mandate to desegregate schools with all deliberate speed has taken many years to become a reality. In the first decade after *Brown I,* only 2.14% of African American children in 7 of 11 southern states attended desegregated schools. In 2001, approximately 40% of the nation's 7.9 million African American students still attended schools that were at least 90% minority. In the 2003–2004 school year, of the five states in the *Brown* case, the school district in Clarendon County, South Carolina, was 96% African American; the New Castle school district in Delaware was 35% African American; the Prince Edward school district in Virginia was 59% African American; the District of Columbia school district in Washington, D.C., was 84% African American; and the Topeka school district in Topeka, Kansas, was 22% African American. De facto segregation (segregation, especially in schools, that happens in fact but is not required by law) continues to exist to a significant extent in U.S. schools.

The 50th Anniversary of the *Brown v. Board of Education* Decision

The year 2004 marked the 50th anniversary of the *Brown v. Board of Education* decision, and numerous celebrations and commemorations were held across the country. Educational organizations such as the American Educational Research Association and the National Education Association; postsecondary institutions including the University of Michigan, New York University, Wayne State University, and Harvard University; legal organizations, including the American Bar Association; and school systems across the country held conferences, panel discussions, and other commemorative events. Participants included educational scholars, teachers, students, and lawyers. Members of the Brown family—Linda Brown-Thompson, Cheryl Brown Henderson, and their mother, Mrs. Leola Brown Montgomery—also participated in many of these events. The federal government established a commemorative site for the landmark U.S. Supreme Court's decision, the Monroe School located in Topeka, Kansas. Congress posthumously honored four individuals—Rev. Joseph A. DeLaine, a minister; Levi Pearson, a farmer; and

Harry Briggs, a gas station attendant and his wife, Eliza, a hotel maid—all of whom were instrumental in the *Briggs v. Elliott* school desegregation lawsuit in South Carolina, the first of the five *Brown* cases.

Since the *Brown* decision, key figures in the case have lamented the unfulfilled mandates of *Brown.* In 1974, Thurgood Marshall, the lead attorney for the case, lamented that 20 years after the Court's decision, there had been no substantial progress toward desegregation.

During the year-long 50th anniversary celebration, scholars as well as teachers, students, and parents also debated the negative and positive impacts the *Brown* decision has had on the education of African Americans and society as a whole. Some scholars have noted that the *Brown* case was not only about school desegregation but was, in part, based on the convergence of the interests of African Americans and whites who wanted to improve the U.S. national image, remove the possibility of racial riots, stimulate the economy, improve the condition of education for African American children, and promote social mobility. Other scholars have noted that while the *Brown* decision eventually helped to desegregate schools and led to other court decisions that desegregated public transportation, restaurants, and housing, African American students continue to attend segregated schools and lag behind their white peers with respect to standardized test scores, high school graduation rates, and entry into postsecondary education.

Linda Brown-Thompson, the plaintiff for whom the case is named, did not directly benefit from the decision. By 1954, she was enrolled in an integrated junior high school in Topeka. She reflected on the legacy of *Brown* and commented that, given the hatred, hostility, and violence that many African Americans endured, she wondered if the decision to take the case to the Supreme Court benefited children or the nation as a whole. She observed that 50 years after the decision, the Court's ruling was still unfulfilled.

Brown v. Board of Education Timeline

Selected legal cases and social activism preceding and following the *Brown v. Board of Education* decision are presented here in chronological order.

1896—*Plessy v. Ferguson* is decided by the U.S. Supreme Court, finding that separate but equal public facilities were permissible under the U.S. Constitution.

1909—National Association for the Advancement of Colored People is founded.

1947—Freedom Riders and sit-ins first challenge segregation on buses and in public places.

1954—*Brown v. Board of Education, Topeka, Kansas,* is decided by U.S. Supreme Court; separate but equal education and de jure segregation are overruled.

1955—*Brown II* is decided by the U.S. Supreme Court, ordering schools to desegregate with all deliberate speed.

1957—The Little Rock Nine are the first African American students to integrate the all-white Central High School in Little Rock, Arkansas.

1960—Ruby Bridges is the first African American to integrate the all-white William Franz Elementary School in New Orleans, Louisiana.

1964—Congress passes the Civil Rights Act of 1964.

1968—*Green v. County School Board of New Kent County* (Virginia) is decided by the U.S. Supreme Court, making the first distinction between de jure and de facto segregation.

1974—In *Lau v. Nichols,* the U.S. Supreme Court decides that public schools must teach English to students whose native language is not English.

1976—On April 30, the original liability order was filed in U.S. District Court for the Buffalo Public Schools, mandating that the schools be desegregated.

1978—*Regents of University of California v. Bakke* is decided by the U.S. Supreme Court, ruling against the use of affirmative action in medical school admissions.

1996—On October 10, the Buffalo School District was released from 20 years of court-ordered supervised desegregation into unitary status.

1999—*Eisenberg v. Montgomery County Public Schools,* the Fourth Circuit decided that a school district may not deny a student's request to transfer to a magnet school because of his or her race as a part of voluntary nonremedial desegregation program.

2001—*San Francisco NAACP v. San Francisco Unified School District.* The San Francisco Unified School District settled a desegregation claim regarding discrimination in the assignment decisions of students to specific schools and discrimination in the assignment of qualified teachers within the school district.

2003—*Grutter v. Bollinger* and *Gratz v. Bollinger,* two cases involving the University of Michigan, are decided by the Supreme Court, affirming the use of affirmative action in university admissions.

—Linda C. Tillman

See also Affirmative Action; Anti-Busing Movement; Civil Rights Movement; *Lau* Decision; Mississippi Freedom Schools

Further Readings

Bell, D. (2004). *Silent covenants:* Brown v. Board of Education *and the unfilled hopes for racial reform.* New York: Oxford University Press.

Brown Foundation. Retrieved October 12, 2006, from Brownvboard.org

Brown v. Board of Education, Topeka, 347 U.S. 483 (1954).

Cose, E. (2004). *Beyond* Brown v. Board: *The final battle for excellence in American education.* A report of the Rockefeller Foundation.

Gooden, M. (2004). A history of black achievement as impacted by federal court decisions in the last century. *Journal of Negro Education, 73*(3), 230–238.

Irons, P. (2002). *Jim Crow's children: The broken promise of the Brown decision.* New York: Penguin.

Kluger, R. (2004). *Simple justice: The history of* Brown v. Board of Education *and black America's struggle for equality.* New York: Vintage.

Ladson-Billings, G. (2004). Landing on the wrong note: The price we paid for *Brown. Educational Researcher, 33*(7), 3–13.

Ogletree, C. J., Jr. (2004). *All deliberate speed: Reflections on the first half century of Brown v. Board of Education.* New York: W. W. Norton.

Orfield, G., & Lee, C. (2004). Brown *at 50: King's dream or* Plessy's *nightmare?* Cambridge, MA: Harvard University, Civil Rights Project. www.civilrightsproject.harvard.edu

Tillman, L. C. (2004). African American principals and the legacy of *Brown. Review of Research in Education, 28,* 101–146.

Tillman, L. C. (2004). (Un)intended consequences? The impact of the *Brown v. Board of Education* decision on the employment status of black educators. *Education and Urban Society, (36)*3, 280–303.

The verdict on equal education [Special issue]. (2004, May/ June). *The Crisis.*

BRUCE, LENNY (1925–1966)

Lenny Bruce—born Leonard Alfred Schneider, in Mineola, Long Island (New York), the son of an Anglo-Jewish shoe clerk and a dancer, who divorced when he was 5 years old—was a U.S. nightclub entertainer and social satirist during the 1950s and early 1960s. While public authorities increasingly denounced his performances as dirty and sick and courts across the United States tried him for obscenity, Bruce was widely esteemed by artists and intellectuals and, after his death, emerged as a cultural icon among advocates of free speech and political humor.

Bruce gave his first professional performances shortly after the end of World War II. After changing his name to Bruce (because Schneider sounded too Hollywood) and following an obligatory stint in New York's Borscht Belt, he married a stripper named Harriet Harlowe (née Jolliff) in 1951 (the marriage ended in 1957). They moved to California, where he experimented with his material and technique in the strip clubs and burlesque houses in and around Los Angeles. In April 1959, Bruce appeared on the nationally televised Steve Allen Show, where he was introduced as the most shocking comedian of our time, just a few months before *Time* magazine described him as a sick comic. He himself said that it was impossible to label him.

A turning point was Bruce's performance in 1961 to a packed house at New York City's Carnegie Hall. If, as one of Bruce's prosecutors would later observe, he said things that the establishment did not want said, such newly found prominence inevitably brought more intense police and judicial persecution. Later that year, he was charged with violating California's obscenity law at San Francisco's Jazz Workshop. The jury acquitted him, but more arrests followed. Twice, the trials resulted in a hung jury, but in Illinois, he was sentenced to a year in jail. While that conviction was being appealed, he was deported from England, and in March 1964, he was arrested again on obscenity charges in southern California. The cumulative stress of continued police harassment and prosecution was taking its toll,

physically, emotionally, and financially. (He was officially declared a pauper by the U.S. District Court in San Francisco in 1962.) What Albert Goldman called his nihilistic rage was fading, when in April 1964, Bruce was arrested in New York for his performances at the Café Au Go Go in Greenwich Village.

This arrest evoked tremendous support, including a petition signed by a formidable array of U.S. artists and intellectuals, including Reinhold Neibuhr, Woody Allen, Bob Dylan, James Baldwin, Saul Bellow, Joseph Heller, Lillian Hellman, Norman Mailer, Arthur Miller, Susan Sontag, William Styron, John Updike, Gore Vidal, and Allen Ginsberg. A host of prominent personalities and academics testified on Bruce's behalf, one of whom, Daniel Dodson, professor of comparative literature at Columbia University, compared Bruce's moral outrage to that of Swift and Rabelais.

Nonetheless, on November 4, the Criminal Trial Court of New York City found Bruce guilty of obscenity. At a time when most U.S. nightclubs had blacklisted him, the personal consequences were profound. His health and state of mind rapidly deteriorated. His last performance was on June 26, 1966, at San Francisco's Fillmore Auditorium. Five weeks later, on August 3, 1966, he died of a morphine overdose in his home in Hollywood Hills, California. Almost 40 years after Bruce's death, the governor of New York, George Pataki, would issue him an unprecedented posthumous pardon.

Bruce's performances raised issues that tested the legal system's capacity to deal with social change. While New York's Chief Justice Murtagh had no doubt that the three performances were obscene within the meaning of Section 1140-a of the Penal Law, in a dissenting opinion, Justice Creel noted that decisions in U.S. obscenity cases had amply demonstrated the limitations of the judicial process and of judges in solving this type of social policy problem. The performances—and the trials—of Lenny Bruce had pushed the question of what obscenity was and who should define it beyond the courts into the hands of the people themselves. They had reinstated the role of satire and social criticism in U.S. comic art. Above all, both Bruce's challenge to establishment values—at a time of growing social and political protest in matters of race, gender, and foreign policy—and the official response to him revealed fundamental and pervasive contradictions in the nature of American democracy. In the end, he was not persecuted just because he used obscene language but because his performances went so far beyond the comfortable norms of conventional comedy.

—*Eric B. Ross*

See also Free Speech Activism; Political Humor; Political Satire

Further Readings

Bruce, L. (with Krasner, P.). (1965). *How to talk dirty and influence people: An autobiography.* Chicago: Playboy Press.

Collins, R., & Skover, D. (2002). *The trials of Lenny Bruce: The fall and rise of an American icon.* Naperville, IL: Sourcebooks.

Greenhut, R. (Producer), Fosse, B. (Director), & Barry, J. (Writer). (1974). *Lenny* [Motion picture]. United States: United Artists.

BRUTUS, DENNIS (1924–)

With more than a dozen books to his name, Dennis Brutus is considered one of Africa's greatest poets, his work widely anthologized and reprinted. Born of South African parents in Rhodesia under white minority rule, Brutus graduated from his native University of Witwatersrand to begin a career as a high school English teacher. Active in the anti-apartheid movements of the early 1960s, he played a central role in the international sports boycott which ultimately led to South Africa's suspension from the Olympic Games in 1964. Arrested in 1963, Brutus was sentenced to 18 months of hard labor for breaking a travel ban by attempting to leave the country. He was sent to South Africa's infamous prison camp on Robben Island, housed in the same cell in which Mohandas Gandhi had done time years earlier. During his stay in jail, he worked on his writing and poetry, befriending fellow inmate Nelson Mandela.

Brutus's first book of poetry, *Sirens, Knuckles, and Boots,* was published in Nigeria while Brutus was still in prison. Awarded the Mbari Poetry Prize for distinction among black authors, Brutus, who was considered "Colored" by the apartheid regime, refused the honor on the grounds that it was racially based. After his release from Robben Island, Brutus fled South Africa, eventually winning the right to reside in the United States as a political refugee, after a much-publicized legal struggle. From his positions as professor at Northwestern University, Swarthmore College, the University of Denver, and the University of Texas at Austin, he continued to fight against apartheid, serving as honorary president of the South African Non-Racial Olympic Committee. As Distinguished Visiting Humanist at the University of Colorado, Brutus was the first non–African American to receive the Langston Hughes Award for literature; he also was granted the first Paul Robeson Award, in 1989, for his artistic excellence, political consciousness, and integrity.

After the fall of apartheid and the democratic election of Nelson Mandela to South Africa's presidency, Dennis Brutus's political work shifted, in his words, from national liberation to global justice. Working against what he has popularly termed *global apartheid*— that is, the economic policies of neoliberalism, the International Monetary Fund, and the World Bank— Brutus has been a founding patron of the Jubilee 2000 Africa campaign, working for total cancellation of Africa's external debt. He has campaigned for independence and for freedom of political prisoners across the globe, and has served as judge on special panels relating to the death penalty and to the case of African American death row journalist Mumia Abu-Jamal, also participating in nonviolent civil disobedience actions for those causes. Brutus served as chief judge for the Special Tribunal on Colonialism, held in Vieques, Puerto Rico, in 2000. Now Professor Emeritus of Africana Studies at the University of Pittsburgh, Brutus has intensified his international travel for the causes of social justice since his retirement from academic life.

—*Matt Meyer*

See also Abu-Jamal, Mumia; Literature and Activism; Mandela, Nelson

Further Readings

Brutus, D. (1963). *Sirens, knuckles, and boots.* Nairobi: Mbari.

Brutus, D. (1973). *A simple lust.* Oxford, UK: Heinemann.

Sustar, L., & Karim, A. (Eds.). (2006). *Poetry and protest: A Dennis Brutus reader.* Chicago: Haymarket Books.

BURMESE RESISTANCE MOVEMENT

The Burmese resistance movement, otherwise known as the Burmese pro-democracy movement, has worked for democratic reforms inside and outside Burma since a military junta took control of the country in 1988. Facing severe repression in Burma, many pro-democracy activists have taken refuge in neighboring Thailand and the United States, where they have set up a government-in-exile in Rockville, Maryland. The most famous pro-democracy activist, Nobel Peace Prize winner Aung San Suu Kyi, remains under house arrest in Rangoon, while many of her fellow activists have been imprisoned and often killed at the hands of the oppressive State Peace and Development Council.

The Burmese resistance movement first mobilized in 1988, when mass demonstrations and riots threatened to bring down the government of General Ne Win, who had controlled the country since a military coup in 1962. After the resignation of Ne Win, another military junta, named the State Law and Order Restoration Council (SLORC; renamed as the State Peace and Development Council in 1997) took control of the country. Pro-democracy activists, including Suu Kyi, called for democratic elections. A mass uprising spread throughout the country, which the SLORC violently suppressed, killing thousands. In response, Suu Kyi and other pro-democracy activists formed the National League of Democracy (NLD) and continued to push for democratic reforms.

The embattled military junta agreed to hold democratic elections in 1990, assuming that it could manipulate the results to stay in power. When the NLD won 82% of the seats in Parliament, the SLORC declared the results void and refused to let the new government assume office, placing Aung San Suu Kyi under house arrest and imprisoning NLD Chairman U Tin Oo. The military junta has continued to violently suppress the pro-democracy movement, and scores of activists have been imprisoned or killed. In 2003, a convoy carrying Aung San Suu Kyi was attacked by the military, and many NLD supporters were killed. Suu Kyi herself barely escaped but was later caught and imprisoned. In all, she has spent 12 of the past 17 years under house arrest. The State Peace and Development Council routinely prohibits international observers from meeting with NLD members, and all pro-democracy activities are illegal and punishable by imprisonment or death.

Because continued resistance within Burma has remained so difficult, many members of the NLD and its coalition partners formed the National Coalition Government of the Union of Burma on December 18, 1990, and elected Sein Win, the first cousin of Aung San Suu Kyi, as its prime minister. The exiled government, headquartered in Rockville, Maryland, has as one of its founding principles that it will dissolve as soon as new elections can be held. The Burmese resistance movement has garnered extensive international support from foreign governments, the United Nations, and many non-governmental organizations whose sole purpose is to support democratic reform in Burma. In May 2006, the U.N. Undersecretary-General for Political Affairs, Ibrahim Gambari, met with Aung San Suu Kyi in Rangoon, the first foreign dignitary to meet with her since 2004.

—*Nicole Hallett*

See also Democracy; Nobel Peace Prize; Resistance; Suu Kyi, Aung San

Further Readings

Carey, P. (Ed.). (1997). *Burma: The challenge of change in a divided society.* London: Macmillan Press.

Carey, P. (1997). *From Burma to Myanmar: Military rule and the struggle for democracy.* London: Research Institute for the Study of Conflict and Terrorism.

Clements, A., & Kean, L. (1994). *Burma's Revolution of the spirit: The struggle for democratic freedom and dignity.* New York: Aperture.

Lintner, B. (1995). *Outrage: Burma's struggle for democracy* (2nd ed.). Edinburgh, UK: Kiscadale.

Mawdsley, J. (2001). *The heart must break: The fight for democracy and truth in Burma.* London: Century.

BUSING

See ANTI-BUSING MOVEMENT

BUTLER, JUDITH
(1956–)

Judith Butler is an illustrious poststructuralist philosopher who has made contributions to ethics, feminism, social and political philosophy, and queer theory. Born on February 24, 1956, Butler grew up in Cleveland, Ohio. She received her Ph.D. in philosophy from Yale University in 1984. In the mid-1980s Butler was introduced to the works of Michel Foucault. His ideas soon became a major influence on her philosophical thoughts and writing. She is currently Maxine Elliot Professor in the Department of Rhetoric and Comparative Literature at the University of California, Berkeley.

Butler strongly believes that philosophy does not mean inaction. She asserts that actions are performed because of principles and that principles come from the desire for philosophy. Thus, she believes it is important politically for people to ask what is possible and then to believe in that possibility. She feels that without this belief, people will be unable to advance. Philosophy makes people think about possible roles (gender or otherwise), and it gives people the chance to think about the world in different ways.

In the late 1980s, Butler was involved in poststructuralist efforts within Western feminist theory questioning the assumptions of feminism. Butler believes that feminism incorrectly asserts that women are a group with common characteristics, goals, and interests. Butler asserts that gender is a relation among socially constituted subjects in specifiable contexts. This means that rather than being a static attribute in a person, gender should be viewed as a fluid variable that shifts and changes in different contexts, situations, and times.

Butler further asserts that gender is a performance rather than an identity; thus, gender is what people do at particular times rather than who they are. Butler argues that because we all put on a gender performance, it is not a question of whether to do a gender performance but rather what form (traditional or nontraditional) that performance will take. That identity is a performance is one of the key ideas in queer theory. Specifically, it is not our identity that causes our performance; rather, our identity is the effect of our performance.

Butler hopes that by choosing to think differently, people will be able to change gender norms and the basic understanding of masculinity and femininity. Her writings guide the reader to the idea that people live their gender and their sexuality in different ways and that there is room for people to live happy and content lives in non-normative ways.

—*Malila N. Robinson*

See also Activism, Social and Political; Feminism; Feminist Research; Foucault, Michel; Queer Theory

Further Readings

Butler, J. (1987). *Subjects of desire: Hegelian reflections in twentieth-century France.* New York: Columbia University Press.

Butler, J. (1990). *Gender trouble: Feminism and the subversion of identity.* New York: Routledge.

Butler, J. (1993). *Bodies that matter: On the discursive limits of "sex."* New York: Routledge.

Butler, J. (1997). *Excitable speech: A politics of the performative.* New York: Routledge.

Butler, J. (2001). Doing justice to someone: Sex reassignment and allegories of transsexuality. *GLQ: A Journal of Lesbian and Gay Studies, 7*(4), 621–636.

Butler, J. (2004). *Undoing gender.* New York: Routledge.

Butler, J. (2005). *Giving an account of oneself.* New York: Fordham University Press.

Gauntlett, D. (n.d.). *Judith Butler.* Retrieved October 25, 2006, from http://www.theory.org.uk/ctr-butl.htm

BUY NOTHING DAY

Conceived of by Canadian artist Ted Dave, Buy Nothing Day has become a worldwide day of protest against rampant consumerism and mindless materialism. Typically observed the Friday after Thanksgiving, one of the busiest shopping days of the year in the United States, participants of Buy Nothing Day pledge to buy absolutely nothing for 24 hours. The Buy Nothing Day movement has evolved into an expansive day of action, with major celebrations happening in Asia, Europe, North America, South America, and Australia. Though the particular actions differ from community to community, the same concerns about the political, psychological, ecological, and physical consequences of consumer culture are expressed.

The protest also purports to send a signal to corporations, to let them know that citizens do have economic power. While participants are not necessarily anti-corporate activists, many use Buy Nothing Day to raise awareness about Do-it-yourself culture and the unhealthy propaganda that corporations feed to consumers. Buy Nothing Day activists claim that citizens used to buy just what they needed, but now citizens just buy. Many argue that corporations and their intimate relationship with government have eroded a sense of democracy and citizenship and replaced active citizens with passive consumers.

The political magazine *Adbusters* and its founder, Kalle Lasn, are largely responsible for bringing Buy Nothing Day to its current international success. For more than a decade, *Adbusters* magazine and its website have provided free downloads of T-shirt designs, stickers, flyers, pamphlets, and more. Community-specific organizing takes place not only on the *Adbusters* website but also on other websites, such as International Buy Nothing Day. Particular actions are shared in *Adbusters* magazine and on the website as well.

Every year, Lasn makes an attempt to air an "uncommerical," advertising Buy Nothing Day. For years, Lasn was rejected by broadcast television networks and radio stations and told that they were not legally bound to broadcast anything that they didn't want to broadcast. Finally, Cable News Network agreed to show the spot on *Headline News,* but only after being publicly challenged to articulate a reason to reject the television spot.

—Jessica Ketcham Weber

See also *Adbusters*; Anti-Consumerism; Culture Jammers; Reverend Billy

Further Readings

Berner, R. (1997). A holiday greeting networks won't air: Shoppers are "pigs." *Wall Street Journal—Eastern Edition, 230*(100), A1.

Billy, R. (2006). We are the magic. . . . *Ecologist, 36*(1), 66.

Klein, N. (2000). *No space, no choice, no jobs, no logo.* New York: Picador.

Lasn, K. (1999). *Culture jam: The uncooling of America.* New York: Eagle Brook.

C

CALDICOTT, HELEN (1938–)

Helen Caldicott is a pediatrician and social activist born August 7, 1938, in Melbourne, Australia. She has developed an international career by arguing persuasively against the use of nuclear energy, the buildup of nuclear waste, and the proliferation of nuclear weapons. She first became involved in social activism when she wrote a letter to a newspaper exposing radioactivity in Adelaide's water supply. In the early 1970s, she headed the Australian citizen revolt against France's detonation of nuclear weapons in the South Pacific, and she successfully lobbied against the exportation of uranium from Australia.

In 1978, after a year teaching at Harvard Medical School, Caldicott became president of Physicians for Social Responsibility. During her 5 years as president, she built the international membership to more than 30,000, and she contributed to a worldwide anti-nuclear movement that helped end the nuclear arms race. Because many members of Physicians for Social Responsibility saw her as a "radical," she left this post. She cofounded the International Physicians for the Prevention of Nuclear War, an organization that received the 1985 Nobel Peace Prize. Caldicott herself was nominated for the Nobel Peace Prize. In 2003, she received the Lannan Cultural Freedom Prize.

Caldicott was a founding president of the Nuclear Policy Research Institute, established to educate the public on the medical, environmental, political, and moral consequences of the use of nuclear weapons, power, and waste. Other public advocacy groups she cofounded or led include Women's Action for Nuclear Disarmament; Nuclear Freeze Voter Initiative Campaign; Standing for Truth About Radiation; Green Labor, an interest group in the Australian Labor Party; and Parents Protecting Our Children Against Radiation. In 2000, she established a new political party in Australia called Our Common Future Party.

Politically, Caldicott was very influential. She met privately with Canadian prime minister Pierre Elliot Trudeau, Soviet ambassador Anatoly Dobrynin, and U.S. president Ronald Reagan. In order to appeal directly to their emotions, she insisted on meeting these leaders without their advisors present. She often speaks to unions and working people to counter what she views as misinformation emanating from nuclear proponents and the media. One of her current campaigns is exposing how the nuclear industry contributes to global warming.

During lectures and presentations, Caldicott graphically describes the effects of radioactivity on people and then offers renewable energy alternatives. From 1995 to 1998, she hosted a weekly one-hour radio program—"Fair Dinkum" in New York—on which she clearly articulated her moral, political, and humanist beliefs. She has been awarded a total of 19 honorary degrees from European, Canadian, Australian, and American universities, and she is prominently featured in the 1982 Academy Award–Winning documentary *If*

You Love This Planet. She has written six books focusing on the perils of nuclear energy and weaponry and an autobiography. The Smithsonian Institute has named Caldicott one of the most influential women of the 20th century.

Caldicott's personal convictions have driven her life work and enabled her to speak with passion to people throughout the world. She demonstrates that it is possible to prompt those held in high esteem in our society to adopt socially and morally responsible positions.

—*Robert F. Whiteley*

See also Activism, Social and Political; Advocacy; Anti-Nuclear Movement

Further Readings

Caldicott, Helen (1985). *Missile envy.* New York: Bantam Books.

Caldicott, H. (1992). *If you love this planet: A plan to heal the earth.* New York: W. W. Norton.

Caldicott, H. (1996). *A desperate passion: An autobiography.* Sydney, NSW: Random House.

Caldicott, H. (2006). *Nuclear power is not the answer.* New York: New Press.

CAMPAIGN TO END THE DEATH PENALTY

The Campaign to End the Death Penalty (CEDP) is a national grassroots organization, founded in 1995, that has approximately 20 chapters in various cities across the United States, including in California, Illinois, Indiana, Maryland, New York, Ohio, Texas, and Washington, D.C. Its mission is to build public awareness of and public opposition to the death penalty.

The campaign places an emphasis on organizing a network of grassroots activists, prisoner family members, and former and current death row prisoners. The CEDP's stated goal is to put a human face on the death penalty, by giving voice to those who are directly affected by the death penalty: family members of those on death row and death row prisoners themselves. Family members and exonerated death row prisoners speak at various CEDP local and national CEDP events, and writings of death row prisoners are featured in the organization's bimonthly newsletter, the *New Abolitionist.* This connection—a relationship between activists on the outside and prisoners on the inside of prison walls—is a signature feature of the CEDP.

The CEDP has been involved in local and national struggles against the death penalty. Some examples are the fight for justice for the Death Row 10, prisoners sent to death row based on confessions tortured from them by Chicago police; the fight to save Maryland death row prisoner Vernon Evans from execution; the fight for California death row prisoner Kevin Cooper, who came within 4 hours of execution; and the national and international effort for Stan Tookie Williams, who was put to death in California in December 2005. In 2004, the organization won a grant from the Ford Foundation, under its Leadership for a Changing World program.

Each fall, the CEDP hosts an annual convention in Chicago, bringing together chapter members with other anti–death penalty activists. During these conventions, the work of the CEDP is critically assessed, and plans are forged for the coming years' work. The organization says that it models itself on the grassroots organizing of the 1960s. CEDP chapters organize public forums; "Live From Death Row" events, during which death row prisoners call in via speaker phone to address live audiences; press conferences, protests, and visits to death row. The organization also maintains a national listserve and a website: www.nodeathpenalty.org.

—*Marlene Martin*

See also Anti–Death Penalty Movement

Further Readings

New Abolitionist [Newsletter of the Campaign to End the Death Penalty]. Available at www.nodeathpenalty.org or CEDP, P.O. Box 27730, Chicago, IL 60625

CAMPUS ANTIWAR NETWORK

The Campus Antiwar Network (CAN) is the largest campus-based anti-war organization in the United

States, with chapters at more than 50 colleges and high schools. Describing itself as independent, democratic, and grassroots, CAN strives to connect anti-war activism across campuses and thereby foster a stronger student movement.

CAN was founded during the movement to prevent the war in Iraq. Students organized a series of national meetings and conferences, culminating in a 300-person conference in Chicago in February 2003, representing 100 schools. This conference established a structure for the group, based on elected delegates from school-based anti-war coalitions. Shortly after the war began, CAN adopted, through a series of regional student conferences, a position opposing the occupation of Iraq.

One of CAN's most significant activities has been counter-recruitment: opposing military recruitment in schools. CAN's counter-recruitment activities range from organizing speaking events with anti-war veterans to producing educational materials about the U.S. military, but the tactic that has received the most attention has been CAN's tendency to directly protest military recruiters in schools. More than a dozen CAN chapters have organized protests sufficiently lively to induce military recruiters to leave the premises.

This phenomenon first received national attention after January 20, 2005, when—during George W. Bush's second inauguration—300 Seattle Central Community College students walked out of classes and marched to the military recruitment table on campus. There, students made confetti from the recruiter's literature until he left, then followed him down the hallway, chanting, "Don't come back!" A photograph of this scene was widely circulated on the Internet and inspired similar actions around the country.

In addition to counter-recruitment, CAN's most significant activity has been defending student free speech. Since the Iraq war began, nine colleges have threatened students with expulsion for their involvement in peaceful anti-war protests. In each case, CAN organized a defense campaign, protesting at the school and mobilizing support around the country, charges being dropped.

CAN also has been the target of governmental surveillance. Nearly 20% of the actions listed in the Pentagon surveillance database leaked in December 2005 were organized by CAN. One, a protest at the University of California at Santa Cruz, is the only protest in the database labeled both "credible" and a "threat." In April 2006, additional Pentagon documents were released, showing that the government had sent an undercover agent to a protest organized by the CAN chapter at Southern Connecticut State University. In response to these revelations, CAN has announced that it will investigate whether university administrations are cooperating with government surveillance on campus, and it will not be deterred from continuing to organize anti-war and counter-recruitment activities.

—Elizabeth Wrigley-Field

See also Counter-Recruitment; Free Speech Activism

Further Readings

Campus Antiwar Network. Retrieved July 20, 2006, from http://www.campusantiwar.net

Grim, R. (2005, October 12). Protest and pushback on campus. *The Nation.* Retrieved July 20, 2006, from http://www.thenation.com/doc/20051031/protest_and_pushback_on_campus

Traprock Peace Center. (n.d.). Campus Antiwar Network history. Retrieved July 20, 2006, from http://www.traprockpeace.org/campus_antiwar.html

Camus, Albert (1913–1960)

Albert Camus was born in French colonial Algeria, spending his career as a philosopher, writer, and activist. During World War II, Camus was active in the French resistance newspaper/cell *Combat*. In 1957, he became the second-youngest recipient of the Nobel Prize in Literature. Camus spent the early years of his life in North Africa studying philosophy at the University of Algiers. Camus contracted tuberculosis in 1930, henceforth affecting his lifestyle and writing.

In 1934, Camus joined the Algerian Communist Party (PCA) to aid in combating domestic and foreign fascism. In 1937, Camus was expelled from the PCA for pursuing peaceful alternatives to the violence brought by the colonization of Algeria's indigenous Muslim population.

Camus founded Théatre du Travail (Workers Theater, 1935–1939), renamed Théatre de l'équipe (The Team's Theater), which produced plays by Dostoyevsky, Faulkner, Malraux, and others. Camus remained active in the theater his entire life.

Before World War II, Camus acted as an editor and journalist for the socialist *Alger-Republicain* newspaper, covering topics such as the plight of Algerian Muslims in Kabylie. Camus's first literary works comprise his series known as "the Absurds": *The Stranger, The Myth of Sisyphus,* and *Caligula. The Stranger,* published during the austerity of World War II, brought him fame as an author. *The Myth of Sisyphus* explores whether or not life has any inherent meaning, therefore inferring that it is legitimate to explore the question of suicide.

During World War II, Camus joined *Combat,* the clandestine resistance cell and newspaper, serving as editor under the pseudonym Beauchard. These experiences served as an impetus for Camus's novel *The Plague,* written as an allegory in regard to occupied Paris. Under occupation, Camus became acquainted with existentialist philosopher Jean Paul Sartre. Camus's most significant and self-described contribution to philosophy is his idea of absurdism (in which man's historical pursuit to find meaning in the universe will be in vain, since no such meaning exists). The publication of Camus's philosophical essay *The Rebel* in 1951 consummated the end of his failing relationship with Sartre. *The Rebel* explores rebellion and revolution, illustrating how ideals can be corrupted into tyranny.

In the 1950s, Camus's public efforts were directed toward human rights: confronting totalitarianism and capital punishment. During the Algerian War for Independence in 1954, Camus favored a Swiss-style federated nation creating a Franco-Muslim community to resolve the conflict. Faced with war, he continued his denouncement of not only French colonial oppression but also Algerian rebel terrorism, while affirming his allegiance with all Algerians. He proposed a civil truce between the opposing parties to protect and respect the civilian population—a movement that gained momentum but to no avail.

Camus's resistance to capital punishment was elucidated in his essay "Reflections on the Guillotine" for which he received the Nobel Prize in 1957. Camus died as a passenger in a car accident near Sens, France, on January 4, 1960.

—*Jay Byron*

See also Anti-Colonial Movements, Middle East and North Africa

Further Readings

Camus, A. (1991). *The rebel.* New York: Vintage.
Lottman, H. R. (1979). *Albert Camus.* Garden City, NY: Doubleday.

CÁRDENAS, LÁZARO (1895–1970)

Lázaro Cárdenas was one of the most respected presidents of Mexico. His rigid honesty, integrity, and radicalism shaped his politics. He joined the Mexican revolutionary forces in 1913 and made general in 1920. As the result of his military service, he became governor of Michoacan in 1928. The concerns Cárdenas had for the poor and common people shaped his actions. Thus, he built schools and roads and organized agricultural projects for the peasants. After being a state governor, Cárdenas served as Mexico's secretary of state, and in 1934 he was elected president of Mexico.

Cárdenas's openness and avant-garde leadership marked his actions as president. He attempted to make real the social justice ideals of the Mexican Revolution expressed in the Constitution of 1917. Cárdenas focused directly on the articles that addressed Mexico's propriety of the land and its natural resources as well as the commitment to achieve improved living conditions and respect for the workers' and peasants' rights.

The first action Cárdenas took as president was to cut his salary by 50%. He made a stance for the presidency to be a position for serving people and not a space for becoming rich and powerful, as it had been used previously. For that reason, he also dedicated one day of the week for holding public meetings, especially for the poor in order to give them an opportunity to be heard. Cárdenas organized an agrarian reform effort that included the distribution of land to *campesinos* (farmers). The amount of land he distributed was about 18 million hectares (or 49 million acres). Cárdenas helped the campesinos create *ejidos* (communal or collective farmlands) for establishing small agrarian production units for their economic independence and food self-sufficiency.

In 1938, Cárdenas expropriated and nationalized the oil industry. The oil companies had been owned by foreign interests and had exploited Mexico's natural resources. A dispute among owners and workers sparked the conflict with Cárdenas. Cárdenas attempted mediation, but the owners' unwillingness to yield led them to challenge and resist his resolution. Because of those differences, Cárdenas made the decision to nationalize the oil and expropriate all foreign oil companies. Mexican people from all social classes supported the action. The U.K. and the U.S. governments tried to economically boycott Mexico. However, the outbreak of World War II made oil a sought-after resource that compelled the boycotters to negotiate with Mexico for its oil supply.

Cárdenas considered education as a necessity for supporting Mexico's progress. As an example, he created technological higher education institutions with the purpose of preparing highly qualified technical personnel for oil extraction and production. Cárdenas also was recognized for supporting political refugees from all over the world, allowing them to live in Mexico, including the likes of Trotsky from Russia and 40,000 Spaniards during Spain's civil war. Those actions won him national acclaim; however, by the end of his life, he was criticized for supporting Fidel Castro and the Cuban Revolution against U.S. interests. He also advocated for the liberation of students that were incarcerated during the Mexican student movement of 1968. Although some people saw these actions as a signal of his age, it could be said that Cárdenas was just being coherent with the social justice principles he advocated for

through his participation in the Mexican Revolution. He is still an icon of the Mexican left.

—*Luis Huerta-Charles*

See also Mexican Revolution

Further Readings

Mares, R. (2004). *Lázaro Cárdenas.* Mexico City: Grupo Editorial Tomo.

Townsend, W. (1979). *Lázaro Cárdenas: A Mexican democrat.* New York: International Friendship.

CARMICHAEL, STOKELY (1941–1998)

One of the most passionate and radical leaders of the civil rights era, Stokely Carmichael endorsed militant direct action protest and the formation of independent black political parties. He entered the national spotlight in 1966 when he publicly challenged Martin Luther King, Jr. and the philosophy of nonviolence, openly opposed white participation in the movement, and popularized the controversial "Black Power" slogan. In his 1967 *Black Power,* coauthored by Charles V. Hamilton, he explained his philosophy of political self-determination and black pride. As chairman of the Student Nonviolent Coordinating Committee (SNCC) in 1966–1967, Carmichael pushed the organization toward an increasingly radical and nationalist perspective. After moving to Guinea in the early 1970s, he devoted his life to promoting Pan-Africanism.

Born June 29, 1941, in Port-of-Spain, Trinidad, Carmichael immigrated to the United States at the age of 11. He attended the Bronx High School of Science and Howard University, where he joined the Nonviolent Action Group and participated in demonstrations in the Washington, D.C., area. In 1961, he joined the Freedom Rides, was arrested in Jackson, Mississippi, and served 49 days in Mississippi's Parchman Prison. After his release, he joined SNCC and participated in both direct action and voter registration campaigns. During the 1964 Freedom Summer, he effectively organized voters in Mississippi's 2nd Congressional district. The following March, he moved into Lowndes County, Alabama, and launched SNCC's voter registration project. By 1966, Carmichael had registered hundreds of voters and aided local activists in the creation of an independent black political party, the Lowndes County Freedom Organization. Huey P. Newton and Bobby Seale adopted their symbol—a black panther—when they formed the Black Panther Party in Oakland, California, in October 1966.

In May 1966, Carmichael narrowly defeated John Lewis and became the national chairman of SNCC. He encouraged the group to abandon their earlier commitment to nonviolent, inter-racial activism. In June 1966, Carmichael helped lead James Meredith's March Against Fear, alongside Martin Luther King, Jr. and the Congress of Racial Equality's Floyd McKissick, after Meredith was shot on the second day of the march. Carmichael used the march as an opportunity to introduce the slogan "Black Power" and publicly challenge King's nonviolent philosophy.

After H. Rap Brown replaced Carmichael as SNCC's national chairman in 1967, Carmichael traveled abroad to Cuba, China, North Vietnam, and finally Guinea, where he met with Pan-Africanist leader Kwame Nkrumah. Carmichael returned to the United States, and in February 1968, he became the Black Panther Party's prime minister. In 1971, Carmichael moved with his wife, South African singer Miriam Makeba, to Guinea, West Africa, and wrote *Stokely Speaks: Black Power Back to Pan-Africanism.* The following year, he helped form the All-African People's Revolutionary Party and worked as an aid for Guinea's prime minister, Sékou Touré. In 1978, he changed his name to Kwame Ture to honor the two African socialist leaders who had befriended him. He died in Guinea on November 15, 1998, at the age of 57.

—*Amy Nathan Wright*

See also Black Panther Party; Black Power; Brown, H. Rap; Civil Rights Movement; Freedom Rides, 1961; King, Martin Luther, Jr.; Lewis, John L.; Newton, Huey P.; Pan-Africanism; Seale, Bobby; Student Nonviolent Coordinating Committee (SNCC)

Further Readings

Carmichael, S. (1971). *Stokely speaks: Black Power back to pan-Africanism.* New York: Random House.

Carmichael, S., & Hamilton, C. V. (1967). *Black Power: The politics of liberation in America.* New York: Vintage.

Carmichael, S., & Thelwell, E. M. (2003). *Ready for revolution: The life and struggles of Stokely Carmichael (Kwame Ture).* New York: Scribner.

Carson, C. (1981). *In struggle: SNCC and the Black awakening of the 1960s.* Cambridge, MA: Harvard University Press.

CARSON, RACHEL (1907–1964)

Rachel Carson, considered to be the founder of the modern environmental movement, shattered attitudes toward the natural environment by proving the negative consequences of long-term use of chemical pesticides such as DDT among many kinds of living things, including humans. Carson is regarded as one of the most influential writers of the 20th century.

Rachel Carson was born in Springdale, Pennsylvania, on May 27, 1907, to Robert and Maria Carson. Her father, who was 43 years old when she was born, was often away from the family for long periods of time while he traveled and sold insurance. She was raised almost entirely by her mother, and as a small child,

Rachel Carson (1907–1964) is considered to be the founder of the modern environmental movement.

Source: Courtesy of the Library of Congress.

Carson spent her childhood engulfed in books and exploring the wooded areas around her home. Her love of nature as a child developed her interests in writing. She was often found writing and illustrating short stories about animals. Her first published work was a short story titled "A Battle in the Clouds"; it appeared in a St. Nicholas League magazine when she was only 11 years old. After graduating first in her class from Parnassus High School in New Kensington, Pennsylvania, Rachel was given an academic scholarship to an elite, private Christian college in Pittsburgh in 1925. At the Pennsylvania College for Women (later known as Chatham College), she studied English and changed her major to biology at a time when women were not typically thought of as being intellectually fit to study or physically capable to practice scientific procedures.

Carson continued on to Johns Hopkins University, where she received her master's degree in zoology in 1932. While teaching zoology at the University of Maryland shortly thereafter, she continued her education during the summer months by studying at the Marine Biological Laboratory in Woods Hole, Massachusetts. While studying over the summers, Rachel developed an intense love for the sea and its natural wildlife. Even though her first passion was research in the field, she first began her professional career in the Bureau of Fisheries (later known as the Fish and Wildlife Services) in Washington, D.C., by writing science radio scripts. She later became chief of publications. This eventually led to a full-time job as an aquatic biologist. Carson was only the second woman hired by the Bureau of Fisheries for a nonsecretarial position. In addition to her work as a biologist, she wrote articles for newspapers on marine zoology; her writing served as an additional means of income.

With support from an editor, Carson submitted an article titled "Undersea" to the *Atlantic Monthly,* which was published in 1937. This article led to her first published book, *Under the Sea Wind,* in 1941. This work was critically acclaimed, but went publicly unnoticed in the wake of the uproar of the Pearl Harbor tragedy. Rachel's love for the oceans spawned her next literary venture, titled *The Sea Around Us,* in 1951. This book stayed on the bestseller list for 86 weeks, was noted in numerous books and magazines, and was translated into 33 different languages. In 1952, *The Sea Around Us* won the John Burroughs Medal and the National Book Award for nonfiction. Within its first year of publication, *The Sea Around Us* sold more than 200,000 copies in hardcover.

After her newly acclaimed success by the public and scientific community, Carson left her job at the Bureau of Fisheries to fully concentrate on writing topics of interest. She purchased 1.5 acres of the Southport Island at the tip of Boothbay Peninsula in Maine facing the sea. This motivated her next work, *The Edge of the Sea* (1955), which was praised for its accessibility, beauty of language, and scientific accuracy. She republished *Under the Sea Wind* and became famous as a naturalist and science writer for the uninformed public. She published two other articles—"Help Your Child to Wonder" and "Our Ever-Changing Shore"—and planned another book based on the ecology of life. Basically all of Carson's writings were based on ideology of human beings as a part of nature distinguished with the notions defining humanity—the one part of nature with the ability to alter it, and unfortunately enough, the ability to alter it irreversibly for the worse.

In the midst of the World War II era, the concept of chemical warfare was becoming more of a reality to people all over the country. This especially interested Rachel Carson, and she studied the possible effects of such an attack on the oceans and surrounding wildlife. Her view on writing shifted dramatically, from concern for the natural environment to the effects of the use of synthetic chemical pesticides. She spent much of the rest of her life attempting to warn the public about the use of these pesticides and their negative effects. As early as 1945, Carson and a fellow colleague, Clarence Cottam, became distressed by increasing government abuse of newly produced chemical pesticides, DDT in particular; the government was using poisons to kill both predator and pest problems with little regard for its effects on other aspects of nature. During that year, she wrote an article specifically for *Reader's Digest* on the topic of insecticide experiments conducted near Patuxent, Maryland, which sought to determine the effects of DDT on all aspects of life. *Reader's Digest* was not interested in the article and did not publish it.

Carson then refocused her attention on her trilogy of books about the seas and only returned to the issue of insecticides and pesticides when her books had been completed.

Meanwhile, the federal government was threatening to release a number of pesticides—including DDT, dieldrin, parathion, malathion, and others—to the Department of Agriculture for commercial and public sale and manufacture. In 1962, Carson published *Silent Spring,* in which she challenged the practices of agricultural scientists and their government counterparts in insect prevention among plants. Carson fought against the use of pesticides like DDT that could potentially harm humans through absorption in plants. The publishing of *Silent Spring* led to nationwide attention for people in all walks of life, including farmers, the chemical industry, members of Congress, newspaper editors, and even President Kennedy, who set up special sessions of his Science Committee to discuss the issue of pesticides. In 1972, legislation was passed to ban DDT from commercial and private use. Congressional sessions also led to increased public concern and interest over the general use of pesticides and other chemicals. Carson made it known that the use of pesticides was connected to the entire environment: The elimination of one organism and attempts to poison an insect will result in the poisoning of animals and humans.

Once *Silent Spring* was published, Carson was immediately bombarded with criticism on her data, her interpretation of the data, and even her scientific credentials. Many chemical companies went as far as to call her unprofessional and even a Communist. Another criticism leveled against her was the misconception that she was calling for the elimination of the use of all pesticides, though she was actually encouraging responsible, careful use of the pesticides, marked by a definite awareness of their impact on the environment. Her publisher, Houghton Mifflin, was also pressured to suppress further publishing and advertising of the book, but the publisher refused.

In April 1963, Carson appeared on a CBS TV special in a debate with a chemical company spokesman. Later that year, she was elected to the American Academy of Arts and Sciences and awarded the Cullen Medal of the American Geographical Society.

Rachel Carson died of breast cancer on April 14, 1964, at the age of 56. In 1980, she was awarded the Presidential Medal of Freedom, the highest civilian honor that can be awarded in the United States.

After 7 full months of testimony and Carson's death, the Environmental Protection Agency determined that DDT is not harmful to humans. In addition, DDT was shown to be helpful in the prevention of malaria through the destruction of malaria-carrying insects in many selective environments. Great scrutiny was placed on Rachel Carson after she died—even though she had advocated putting a stop to the use of pesticides in agriculture, not in medicine.

—*Arthur Matthew Holst*

See also Environmental Movement

Further Readings

Graham, F., Jr. (1978, December). Rachel Carson. *EPA Journal.* www.epa.gov.history/topics/perspect/carson.htm

Lear, L. (1997). *Rachel Carson: Witness for nature.* New York: Henry Holt.

Payton, B. (n.d.). *Rachel Carson.* http://earthobservatory.nasa.gov/Library/Giants/Carson

CARTER, JAMES EARL (1924–)

When Georgia governor James Earl "Jimmy" Carter announced that he would run for president, he was virtually unknown outside his home state. But after a 2-year campaign during which he cultivated a reputation as a Washington outsider, Carter won the 1976 presidential election with 50.1% of the popular vote, edging out the Republican incumbent Gerald Ford. During his tumultuous one term in office, Carter's outsider credentials evaporated. Democrats were disappointed by his compromises and his moralistic tone. Republicans found Carter to be a convenient scapegoat for the economic and foreign policy setbacks of the late 1970s.

During his campaign, Carter took advantage of his political strengths. As a Southerner, he portrayed himself as a simple peanut farmer and born-again Baptist. In 1976, he won the electoral votes of every southern state except Virginia. To sway voters outside the South, Carter emphasized his governorship, which reversed the segregationist tradition of former Georgia governor Lester Maddox. Trained at the U.S. Naval Academy as a nuclear power engineer, Carter described himself as a pragmatic problem-solver. He impressed journalists, even jaded reporters such as *Rolling Stone*'s Hunter S. Thompson, with his ability to speak eloquently about the theology of Reinhold Neibuhr and the lyrics of Bob Dylan. Most effectively, Carter convinced voters of his plainspoken honesty, a trait very much in demand following the resignation of President Nixon in 1974 and his subsequent pardon from Gerald Ford.

Carter won with the backing of a coalition of social groups that had supported Democrats since the era of Franklin D. Roosevelt: southern Democrats, African Americans and ethnic minorities, urban voters in cities run by Democratic machines, and working-class voters who distrusted the anti-union Republican Party. After two terms of Republican presidents, many of these groups expected Carter to reanimate the Great Society reforms of the Johnson-Kennedy years. But Jimmy Carter's term proved to be a disappointment.

Carter envisioned the presidency as an office of moral leadership that should rise above the horse-trading of interest-group politics. He also strove to make the federal government more efficient and cost-conscious. So when a crisis erupted during his first months in the White House—a shortage of home heating oil during a bitterly cold winter—Carter responded with a plan that aggravated Americans of all political persuasions. One part of the plan called for removing price controls on fuel in order to encourage conservation. Critics on the left assailed price deregulation as a regressive policy that harmed poor families the most. Thinking like an engineer focused on comprehensive solutions, Carter created a cabinet-level Energy Department, which critics on the right detested as a wasteful expansion of government. The energy crisis also created one of the enduring images of Jimmy Carter in the public mind: wearing a cardigan sweater in the Oval Office and urging national television viewers to turn down their thermostats.

The energy crisis persisted throughout Carter's term, and it was part of a larger economic malaise that Carter could not remedy. Unemployment and inflation began their upward spiral in the early 1970s and by 1980 added up to over 20%, a benchmark economists began calling the Misery Index. Simultaneously high rates of unemployment and inflation defied Keynesian economic theory, which held that the two rates should always move in opposite directions. As a result, Carter began slowly to embrace monetary theory as a way to cure the ailing economy. Many of the policies later championed by Ronald Reagan, such as deregulation of industries and raising interest rates to bring down prices, were Carter initiatives. As such, Carter's policies disillusioned many core Democrat voters who felt he had abandoned the party's traditional method of stimulating the economy through government spending.

Many of these same citizens felt abandoned when Carter seemed to break away from the social movements of the 1950s and 1960s. Although he appointed more African Americans and other non–Anglo Americans to high government positions and judgeships than had any previous president, Carter did not take a strong civil rights stand on symbolic issues, such as school busing and affirmative action. He succeeded in defending fair housing regulations and government contracting set-asides for minority-owned contractors, but Carter frequently expressed his preference that the nation's social problems be solved by private institutions, both for-profit and nonprofit. Similarly, Carter began his term by elevating dozens of women to positions of authority, but by the end of his term, he was receiving criticism from women's rights activists because he did not throw his full weight behind the stalled Equal Rights Amendment. Perhaps the only movement Carter satisfied was the anti-war movement. He carried out a campaign promise to offer amnesty to any Vietnam-era draft resisters who had refused to register or had left the country. Carter received little benefit from granting amnesty because the war was over. But he earned the wrath of veterans groups and conservative politicians.

Carter went through with the amnesty because he felt it was morally correct, and in foreign policy decisions, he often paid a high price for adhering to moral principle. For example, he negotiated a treaty that promised to return Canal Zone control to Panama in the year 2000; Republicans criticized the move as a sacrifice of national autonomy. Carter also responded to the Soviet invasion of Afghanistan by cutting off grain exports to the USSR and boycotting the 1980 summer Olympics in Moscow, decisions that did not endear him to American farmers and sports fans. He won praise for facilitating the peace treaty between Israel and Egypt and for negotiating a reduction in nuclear weapons at the SALT II talks. But these accomplishments were overshadowed by the Iranian Revolution of 1979. Carter initially supported the ousted Shah of Iran, a U.S.-installed autocrat hated by his people. Then when student revolutionaries in Tehran took some 100 Americans hostage for over a year, Carter was powerless to secure their release.

For all the disappointment and criticism Jimmy Carter inspired as president, his post-presidency efforts to eradicate treatable diseases in poor countries, promote human rights worldwide, and build affordable housing in the United States have received almost undiluted praise. Beginning in Panama in 1989, he served as an unofficial U.S. ambassador to war-torn nations struggling to hold democratic elections and prosecute war criminals. He also played a key role in trying to normalize relations between the United States and North Korea and Cuba. In 2002, at the age of 78, Carter won the Nobel Peace Prize.

—*Josh Ashenmiller*

See also Draft Resistance; Equal Rights Amendment; Great Society; Habitat for Humanity; Iranian Revolution (1963–1979); Liberalism

Further Readings

Fink, G. M., & Graham, H. D. (Eds.). (1998). *The Carter presidency: Policy choices in the post–New Deal era.* Lawrence: University Press of Kansas.

Haas, G. (1992). *Jimmy Carter and the politics of frustration.* Jefferson, NC: McFarland.

Hargrove, E. C. (1988). *Jimmy Carter as president: Leadership and the politics of the public good.* Baton Rouge: Louisiana State University Press.

Horowitz, D. (2005). *Jimmy Carter and the energy crisis of the 1970s: The "Crisis of Confidence speech" of July 15, 1979: A brief history with documents.* Boston: Bedford/St. Martin's.

Kaufman, B. I. (1993). *The presidency of James Earl Carter, Jr.* Lawrence: University Press of Kansas.

Castro, Fidel (1926–)

Fidel Castro Ruz has indelibly marked the political history of Cuba, Latin America, and the Third World in the second half of the 20th century. The leader of the Cuban revolutionary process and founder of the first socialist state in the Americas, Castro has distinguished himself in defending the rights of his people and opposing the imperialistic policies of the U.S. government. A leader of the Non-Aligned Movement and at the forefront of the Cuban Revolution, he has contributed substantially to the development of national liberation in Latin America, solidarity with the people of Vietnam and Indochina, the struggle for the decolonization of Africa, the defense of progressive political processes in the Americas, and the end of apartheid in South Africa.

He was born on August 13, 1926, on a farm called Birán, part of the township of Mayarí (in the old province of Oriente, today known as Holguín). He is the third of seven children from the second marriage of Angel Castro Argiz, an emigrant from the peninsula, who was a well-established sugarcane farmer.

Known as a brilliant student, an enthusiastic athlete, and a gifted and original orator who loved to debate in the lecture halls and who radiated leadership potential, Fidel was, by the late 1940s, the guiding force of the Federation of University Students. Later, as a young politician in the vanguard of the nationalist group Pueblo Cubano, he fought Cuban administrative government corruption.

During this time, Fidel was an avid reader of the work of José Martí where he found the political elements necessary to inspire him to fight for the unfinished goal that the Cuban national hero had sought: a democratic and revolutionary republic. Also at this time, he began reading socialist literature and was exposed to Marxist writings. As a proponent of Martí's philosophy, he was a nationalist and ardent anti-imperialist who viewed the neocolonial domination of the United States in Cuba and Latin America as an insult. As a result, he actively participated in solidarity work, the Puerto Rican independence movement, and a group he served as president for, Pro Independencia Dominicana. Between July and September 1947, Fidel was part of a failed expedition to the Dominican Republic to destroy the dictatorship of Rafael Ieónida Trujillo. Later he helped organize an anti-imperialist continental student congress. In 1950, Fidel Castro received a law degree and opened a law office, but his professional activities were aimed at defending laborers and the poor.

During the disturbances of May 10, Castro was able to recruit a contingent of young patriots to capture the Moncada Barracks, the second most important military installation in the country. The spectacular attack on the Moncada Barracks on July 26, 1953, failed for unforeseeable reasons, but in spite of this military failure, the movement led by Castro achieved a huge following among the masses and demonstrated the very real possibility of organizing a struggle to reestablish the constitutional mandate. The dictatorship, for its part, tortured and killed many of the captured combatants. Castro was sentenced to 15 years in prison; his argument in self-defense was "History will absolve me." This was to become the rallying cry, an anti-Batista political force that resulted in amnesty for Castro in 1955 and his exile to Mexico. In Mexico, he organized an armed expedition with which he returned to Cuba on December 2, 1956.

After an unfortunate journey and the loss of the majority of the expeditionary force, on December 18, Castro reorganized a small detachment with only 16 survivors. With this scanty guerrilla group, the No. 1 José Martí Column was founded to penetrate the inhospitable Sierra Maestra and begin the struggle against the 40,000 soldiers of the professional army of the Batista dictatorship.

Castro was effective in his work with farmers, and soon the guerrilla movement he commanded won the confidence and support of the agricultural community.

These folks flocked to the fight and swelled the ranks of the rebels. Organized by Movimiento 26 de Julio, contingent groups of workers and students from the cities arrived in the Sierra Maestra and other rebel zones.

A methodical advance ensued across the length of the island along with other revolutionary organizations such as Directorio Revolutionario 13 de Marzo and Partido Socialista Popular. After 2 years of revolutionary war, the dictatorship fell, and the tyrant Fulgencio Batista fled La Habana on December 31, 1958.

Due to the proclamation of revolutionary laws such as agricultural reform, the political attacks of the U.S. government increased in strength. Following January 1, 1959, the United States gave shelter and protection to the torturers and abusers of the public trust of the dictatorship and soon after began to train and support terrorist groups. On April 16, 1961, on the eve of the invasion that the U.S. government organized to stamp out the revolution, Castro declared the socialist character of the revolution. Forces that he commanded defeated the mercenary brigade in 72 hours at the Bay of Pigs. Along with political and military tasks, Castro led a profound educational and cultural revolution whose first great victory was the declaration, on December 22, 1961, that Cuba is a territory free of illiteracy.

Castro's embrace of Marxism/Leninism created a climate of conflict with the counterrevolutionary policy of the U.S. government and brought about an alignment of the Cuban leader with the USSR and the so-called socialist camp. The USSR developed a policy of solidarity and financial support resulting in the survival of the Cuban Revolution. This happened despite criticism of Castro because of the lack of intelligence by the USSR that determined the end of the October Crisis and the removal of nuclear missiles from the island in 1962.

On October 3, 1965, the process of unity and creation of a political vanguard of the Cuban Revolution were reinforced with the founding of the Cuban Communist Party, an organization that elected Castro as its first secretary. Castro's relationship with the European socialist bloc did not interrupt his relationship with either the liberation movements in Latin America or those progressives in Africa and Asia who were at the front of those revolutionary processes. This became a point of contention with the USSR and, at the same time. a reaffirmation of the political independence of Castro and the Cuban revolutionaries.

Cuba played an important part in supporting the government of Salvador Allende in Chile in 1971, and thousands of civilian Cuban collaborators helped in literacy campaigns after the triumph of the Sandinistas in Nicaragua in 1979. Outside Latin America, Castro occupied an important role within the Non-Aligned Movement. In 1973, he was the first head of state to travel to Vietnam with the war in progress and visit the liberated territories of the South. In 1975, Castro directed Operation Carlota, which developed in Angola, 10,000 kilometers from Cuba. In Angola, the Cuban internationalists were able to stop, almost at the doors of Luanda, a powerful offensive of South African invaders, fighting against the recently established republic.

When the counterrevolutionary reformism of perestroika began in the USSR, Castro distanced himself, and in his speech of July 26, 1988, he rejected it completely. Due to the crisis of socialism in Europe and the dissolution of the Soviet Union, Cuba lost the principal bases of its economy and trading partners. At the same time, the United States increased the strictures against Cuba and approved new laws (e.g., the Torricelli Act in 1992 and the Helms-Burton Act in 1996) that further strengthened the embargo.

The kidnapping of Elian Gonzales by American Cubans in Miami on December 5, 1999, was the beginning of a new stage in the struggle of the Cuban people, a stage in which once again the historic personality of Fidel Castro played a role. The event served as a review of the principal problems and insufficiencies that plague the Cuban socialist society. In this new stage, Castro's leadership appears to have had an impact on the youngest generations of Cuban revolutionaries. In July 2006, due to a serious illness, Castro transferred power to his brother Raúl for an indeterminate length of time.

—*Robert Edwin Bahruth*

See also Anti-Imperialism; Cuban Literacy Campaign

Further Readings

Volker, S. (2004). *Fidel Castro: A biography.* New York: Polity Press.

CATHOLIC WORKER MOVEMENT

The Catholic Worker, a movement of Catholic lay people founded during the Great Depression, has since served as one of the most significant forces on the Christian left in the United States. Largely identified with Dorothy Day (1897–1980), its cofounder and leading voice until her death, the movement combines religious piety, a broadly anarchistic attitude toward the state, voluntary poverty, and a firm commitment to nonviolence. The Catholic Worker movement is known for its Houses of Hospitality, present in cities across the country, which provide food, shelter, and other material needs to the poor. Also well known is its newspaper, the *Catholic Worker,* published by the founding community in New York City. Catholic Workers have been influential in reviving the pacifist tradition in American Catholicism and have been leaders in the use of civil disobedience to advance struggles for peace, nuclear nonproliferation, labor rights, and social justice.

Early History

The Catholic Worker movement was born in December 1932, when cofounders Day and Peter Maurin (1877–1949) met in New York City. Day, a recent convert to Catholicism, was a left-wing journalist and veteran of Greenwich Village bohemian and socialist circles. Maurin, French by birth, was an itinerant laborer and public intellectual, who was well read in Catholic theology. Having assumed a Franciscan embrace of poverty, he developed a program for the communitarian transformation of society through the implementation of Gospel teachings and Catholic social doctrine. He emphasized hospitality for the poor, regular study and prayer, and the development of agrarian communes. Day, seeking a more concrete way to integrate her radical convictions with the principles of her new faith, ultimately took responsibility for putting Maurin's ideas into practice and administering the Catholic Worker movement.

The Catholic Worker newspaper served as the main vehicle for the early spread of movement ideas. The first issue was distributed at a 1933 May Day rally in

New York's Union Square Park. Publishing nearly monthly, with Day as editor, the circulation of the *Catholic Worker* grew from 2,500 copies of the first issue to 110,000 copies by May 1935, to almost 200,000 by 1939. The paper outlined the movement's fundamental ideas in essays by Maurin and Day, as well as quotations from Church leaders. These appeared alongside articles on local labor campaigns and other current events. Over time, notable contributors would include Jacques Maritain, Michael Harrington, and Thomas Merton.

The movement was forced to relocate several times in its early years before settling in the Bowery neighborhood of Manhattan, where it established long-standing Houses of Hospitality. By 1936, Catholic Workers also founded their first satellite farm community. The movement grew rapidly, with communities formed in cities across the United States and Canada. By 1939, the Catholic Worker movement boasted 23 Houses of Hospitality, 2 farms, and 13 affiliate study groups in cities such as Boston, St. Louis, Los Angeles, and Portland.

Philosophy and Principles

Although contemporary activists debate which beliefs represent the fundamental tenets of the Catholic Worker movement, commonly noted principles include personalism, hospitality, voluntary poverty, intentional community, prayer, and pacifism.

Personalism entered the movement through Maurin's study of French philosophy, particularly the works of Emmanuel Mounier. Although often invoked in a philosophically imprecise manner, the concept emphasizes the dignity of every human person, especially those most marginalized by society. Implicit in personalism is a critique of statist communism and the treatment of workers as an undifferentiated social class. In accord with personalist philosophy, Catholic Workers focus on taking personal responsibility for social problems and evince an anarchist distrust of state welfare structures. Many Houses of Hospitality refuse to seek tax-exempt status from the government, arguing that the works of charity and compassion should not be regulated by the state.

Hospitality, voluntary poverty, and intentional community combine in the ethos of the Catholic Worker houses, where volunteers live in solidarity with the poor. There they perform what are known as the corporal works of mercy, which include feeding the hungry, clothing the naked, and harboring the homeless. Christian hospitality draws inspiration from the monasticism of St. Benedict, who instructed monks to view those seeking help as Christ himself. Catholic Workers subsist without salaries, living communally on donations and shunning material acquisition. This has helped to create small, tight-knit communities of individuals unusually committed to their work; many adherents are willing to make extraordinarily personal sacrifices, including spending time in jail for civil disobedience, to advance social justice aims.

Amid the prevailing secularism of the American left, the Catholic Worker movement's distinctive marriage of political radicalism and orthodox religiosity stands out. Dorothy Day attended Catholic services daily and confessed her sins weekly. A controversial figure for decades, Day became almost universally revered by the end of her life, and supporters within the Church have since pushed to have her canonized as a saint.

Day's devout Catholicism, which has carried on as a hallmark of the movement, frequently helped to dispel tensions between Catholic Worker houses and the Church hierarchy. Many Houses of Hospitality operate with open support of local bishops. While stressing Church doctrine on peace and justice issues, many movement activists also take positions on abortion and sexuality that stand in line with traditional Catholic teachings.

Resuscitating a tradition of Catholic pacifism, which previously was virtually unknown among American Catholics, has been one of the movement's foremost contributions and likely its most controversial. In 1936, the *Catholic Worker* advanced an editorial stance of pacifist neutrality regarding the Spanish Civil War. The position cost the newspaper many subscribers, angering both leftists who supported the anti-fascist Spanish Republicans and American Catholics who saw Franco as a defender of the Church.

Later Development

Resolute Christian pacifism proved even less popular during World War II, when Day led the movement in taking an unyielding stance of conscientious objection. Many supporters and subscribers grew increasingly alienated by Day's anti-war position, and the circulation of the *Catholic Worker* dropped during the war years to 50,500. By 1942, over a dozen Catholic Worker houses had closed, and by the war's end, only 10 remained.

The movement began a gradual rebound in the 1950s, receiving renewed public attention after the 1952 publication of Day's autobiography, *The Long Loneliness.* Through the era of McCarthyism, however, some attention was based on critical suspicion. The Federal Bureau of Investigation (FBI) closely monitored the group's activities, and FBI Director J. Edgar Hoover suggested that Day be placed in custodial detention in cases of national emergency.

From 1955 to 1961, in order to dramatize resistance to the nuclear arms race, Catholic Workers in New York began organizing civil disobedience against the annual air raid drills mandated by the Civil Defense Act. Day was arrested in several consecutive years for her refusal to take shelter during a simulated attack and served jail sentences as long as 30 days.

Another leader in the civil defense protests was Ammon Hennacy (1893–1970), a longtime radical who had been imprisoned for draft resistance during World War I. During his tenure with the Catholic Worker, Hennacy also became known for his penitential fasts and pickets in front of tax offices and U.S. military installations to protest Cold War militarism. His example helped to inspire more militant acts of nonviolent direct action in the movement.

In the 1960s, the movement experienced a resurgence fueled by opposition to the Vietnam War. Catholic Workers were among the first young people to publicly burn their draft cards. A new cohort of volunteers helped organize the Catholic Peace Fellowship to promote religious conscientious objection; Catholic Workers also helped to found Pax Christi, USA. The brothers Daniel and Philip Berrigan, two priests renowned for raiding draft boards in Catonsville, Maryland, and burning the draft cards as acts of civil disobedience, maintained close ties with the Catholic Worker, and movement activists were responsible for similar raids.

Renewed youthful interest in the Catholic Worker movement continued throughout the 1970s, even as Day, advancing in age, became more reclusive, limiting her writing and travel before her death in 1980. The circulation of the *Catholic Worker* grew from 65,000 at the start of the 1960s to near 100,000 by 1980, where it has remained. In the 1970s and 1980s, Catholic Workers were active in the Central American solidarity and nuclear disarmament movements, maintaining a particularly strong presence in the Plowshares civil disobedience actions inspired by the Berrigan brothers.

Today there exist over 150 self-identified Catholic Worker communities in the United States, as well as a smaller number abroad, facilitating works of mercy and acts of resistance. Many of the communities produce their own publications in the tradition of the original *Catholic Worker.* Because the movement has had no formal organizational structure and no clear leader since Day's death, the Houses of Hospitality exhibit considerable autonomy and variety, especially in their relationships with the clerical hierarchy and their levels of emphasis on overt religiosity. In the decades since Maurin's death, agrarianism has faded in importance for the movement. Many communities devote the bulk of their energies to providing hospitality for homeless populations that include individuals with serious mental illness and chemical addictions. Political action supported by the movement tends to be individual acts of moral witness, often resulting in jail time, rather than the organization of mass campaigns.

—*Mark Engler*

See also Anarchism; Anti-Nuclear Movement; Berrigan Brothers; Civil Disobedience; Day, Dorothy; Draft Resistance; Jesus Christ; Nonviolence and Activism; Option for the Poor; Pacifism; Religious Activism; Spirituality and Peacemaking; War Tax Resistance

Further Readings

Coy, P. (Ed.). (1988). *A revolution of the heart: Essays on the Catholic Worker*. Philadelphia: Temple University Press.

Miller, W. D. (1973). *A harsh and dreadful love: Dorothy Day and the Catholic Worker movement*. New York: Liveright.

Roberts, N. L. (1984). *Dorothy Day and the Catholic Worker*. Albany: SUNY Press.

Zwick, M., & Zwick, L. (2005). *The Catholic Worker movement: Intellectual and spiritual origins*. New York: Paulist Press.

CENTRE FOR CONTEMPORARY CULTURAL STUDIES

In 1963, Richard Hoggart helped found the Centre for Contemporary Cultural Studies (CCCS) at the University of Birmingham. The CCCS (which became known as the Birmingham School) was a research center, which had as its central focus the newly emergent field of study known as cultural studies. The impact of the pioneering work of members of the Birmingham School extends to established disciplines such as sociology, media, politics, history, and education. The work of the Birmingham School led to the creation of cultural studies as a specific focus for academic study.

The key idea underpinning the work of the Birmingham School was to move away from traditional elite cultural thinking, which emphasized the importance of "high culture," toward a focus on contemporary "lived experience" and popular culture. The founders of the Birmingham School set themselves the task of developing a sociology of literature or of culture and posed a number of specific questions for further exploration. These questions concerned

- the role of writers and artists,
- the significance of audiences,
- how and through whom opinions are formed and transmitted,
- how written and spoken words are produced and distributed,
- and the complex nature of interrelations.

The Birmingham School has its intellectual roots in the following publications: Richard Hoggart's *The Uses of Literacy* (1957), Raymond Williams's *Culture and Society* (1958) and *The Long Revolution* (1961), and E. P Thompson's *The Making of the English Working Class* (1964). This body of work set the frame for the evolution of a distinct approach to the study of literature and society, an approach that focused on the conditions of the working class and embodied the rejection of elitist notions of culture in favor of a common culture. The Birmingham School's notion of a common culture was open enough to encompass what had hitherto been shunned by academic discourse, that is, popular or mass culture.

The Birmingham School provided the space for the blending of literary studies with the sociological study of society. The establishment of the Birmingham School marked a complete break from both the elitist traditions within English literary discourse and, in the case of sociology, the positivism and conservative nature of American structural-functionalism. The work of the Birmingham School has been characterized by a reliance on qualitative research methods, in particular, the use of ethnography as a research tool. The use of qualitative methodology can be seen as an attempt to distance the Birmingham School from what they regarded as the conservative and overly positivistic state of English academic tradition.

One of the significant theoretical contributions made by the Birmingham School, in particular through the work of Stuart Hall, was the development of a unique blend of structuralism that drew on Lacan and Althusser and the Marxist notion of hegemony first articulated by Italian Marxist Antonio Gramsci. This blending provided later writers, such as Willis, Hebdige, McRobbie, and Chambers, with an analytical toolbox with which to identify and subsequently examine subcultural practices within British society. These subcultures were marked out as pivotal in the process of social identity construction and as zones of ideological conflict.

During the second half of the 20th century, the Birmingham School provided the intellectual basis for the establishment of a global academic phenomenon, the emergence of cultural studies as a specific discipline study. In many countries, cultural studies has supplanted more traditional humanities and social science disciplines, such as sociology, politics, English, and literary studies. Much of the recent criticism of the work of the Birmingham School has focused on its shift away from positivistic academic traditions in sociology and literary theory toward Marxism and, more recently, Postmodernism.

—*John Martino*

See also Critical Literacy; Gramsci, Antonio; Marxist Theory

Further Readings

Lipsitz, G. (1990). Listening to learn and learning to listen: Popular culture, cultural theory, and American studies. *American Quarterly, 42*(4), 615–636.

Rojek, C., & Turner, B. (2000). Decorative sociology: Towards a critique of the cultural turn. *Sociological Review, 48*(4), 629–648.

Schulman, N. (1993). Conditions of their own making: An intellectual history of the Centre for Contemporary Cultural Studies at the University of Birmingham. *Canadian Journal of Communication, 18*(1), 51–73.

CHAUTAUQUA

Chautauqua refers most often to the Chautauqua Institution, a village of learning begun on Lake Chautauqua, in western New York State, in 1874. The institution was founded by John Heyl Vincent, a Methodist minister, and Lewis Miller, an industrialist, as a 2-week retreat and summer school for Sunday School teachers in the Methodist church. This summer school was intended to parallel the normal school experience for teachers. The term *Chautauqua* can also be used in reference to the independent Chautauquas, affiliated with the Chautauqua Institution, which offered similar academic and entertainment programs for those who could not attend the institution. In addition, there were the circuit, or tent, Chautauquas that traveled to provide programming to rural America. Finally, the name Chautauqua can be used to refer to a magazine, *The Chautauquan* (1880–1914), which provided a means of continuing communication throughout the year when the summer school was done.

In its first session, Chautauqua attracted some 4,000 participants, who each paid a meager fee. Notables who attended the Chautauqua Institution when it was in its heyday were the inimitable Jane Addams, founder of Hull-House, a settlement house in Chicago for the poor; William James, distinguished psychologist and writer; Rudyard Kipling, writer and poet; as well as noted suffragettes Susan B. Anthony and Julia Ward Howe. Even into the 21st century, Chautauqua continues as a meeting place and speaking venue for authors on topics such as religion and public life.

In the early 20th century, Chautauqua became a meeting place and shorthand for the social gospel movement that united those with religious and social justice leanings. The social gospel movement, strong in public life during this time, was a belief that to be a Christian meant to be involved with improving the social order through speaking, acting, and preaching. Religion and justice went hand in hand for social gospel advocates, who were undoubtedly influenced by Marxist ideas and who embraced the social gospel as a way of combining their religious heritage with a renewed world order.

Begun as a Sunday School initiative, Chautauqua drew numerous people to give speeches, worship, and enjoy the pleasures of Lake Chautauqua and gentrified country living. The idealized perspective of American life drew its share of critics, who saw in Chautauqua an appeal to the middle class and a perpetuation of idealized and romantic notions of summers on the lake. Chautauqua's library, speaking venues, groomed gardens, and rows of neat, wooden houses with verandas contributed to this caricature and critique. Its strict laws against smoking and drinking helped reinforce its image as a euphoric retreat from real America. Critics of Chautauqua point out that for all its promotion of social movements, it managed to evade the larger questions of race and class, and it remained isolated in many ways from people it could well have helped. It would be difficult, for instance, to ignore the homogenous groupings and the largely Christian emphasis of the institution, which continue, by and large, to the 21st century. As well, Chautauqua, for all its social gospel connections, was largely concerned with promoting liberalism, the cultivation of class, education, and the arts.

Yet, Chautauqua had another side. The combined halcyon quality and religious affiliation at Victorian Chautauqua helped it to provide a respectable refuge and opportunity for women to engage in activism and social causes in a way not then allowable in the public sphere. Its largest activist achievement was hosting one of the largest temperance meetings in the United States, which was well attended by women activists who saw in the temperance movement a significant means of eradicating family violence. This temperance meeting sparked the creation of the Woman's Christian Temperance Union, one of the most successful movements in women's activism of the late 19th and early 20th centuries. Canadian Letitia Youmans, who was in attendance at the inaugural meeting, was to become the leader of the movement for the entire Dominion (Canada). As a seemingly innocuous women's social cause, the Woman's Christian Temperance Union was to upset conventional notions of women's behavior and to do so with the sanction of a religious sponsor, Chautauqua. The women who became involved with this movement, including the American and international temperance leader Frances Willard, found in Chautauqua a place where they could actually be the ones doing the speaking to audiences of men and women, or a mixed audience as it was then called, and in which they could link their immediate cause—temperance and family violence—to other women's rights, including suffrage. Chautauqua also spawned the national Congress of Mothers, now known as the PTA (Parent Teacher Association). Chautauqua offered access to the middle class for working-class aspirants and a consolidation of class identity for women already of the middle-class social sphere.

Susan B. Anthony debated women's rights at voting at Chautauqua in 1892. Other topics that were addressed at Chautauqua were peace and the war and factory systems. In no small measure, Chautauqua made possible not only women's gathering but women's organizing. Though hidden or cloaked in themes of home protection and family, women's interests that were cultivated at Chautauqua became forerunners of modern social movements such as Mothers Against Drunk Drivers and the National Action Committee on the Status of women.

Chautauqua also provided access at a minimal cost, to a college education, which by and large was inaccessible to most women at the time. The cultivation of leisure and the concomitant release from regular household duties at the institution facilitated and legitimated women's entry into education and learning. The Chautauqua Literary and Scientific Circle, a 4-year home study course for women, started by Vincent in 1878, was an offshoot of Chautauqua that advanced reform for women and legitimated the formation of reading groups in which to begin or complete their studies at locations far removed from the idyllic town of Chautauqua. In many ways, this home study course became the forerunner of correspondence and other distance education initiatives that continue to address the needs of women who have work, child care, and other responsibilities and who need the flexibility, affordability, and access that distance education provides. The imprimatur of the church, so to speak, on this educational endeavor made it acceptable and accessible for women of this time.

The Chautauqua Institution survives into the 21st century as a 9-week summer school that offers classes and lectures in literature and the arts, as well as dance and music performances. It is an exemplar of the popularization and democratization of education to the masses, with some attributing to it the birth of adult education and lifelong learning, especially through its influential yet short-lived Chautauqua University (1883–1892), which offered diplomas and degrees. Among those who attended or had leadership roles there was William Rainey Harper, a prominent teacher and principal of Chautauqua University, who carried some of the ideas (including extension, summer schools, and the university press) from Chautauqua to his presidency of the University of Chicago in 1892. These initiatives helped develop a model of higher education in the United States, which promoted education of the masses and access for all. As well,

University of Wisconsin's extension program, formed under the presidency of Charles R. Van Hise, can be said to have its genesis in Chautauquan practices. In no small measure, Chautauqua prospered and waned because of its own success; the higher education ideas and practices of Chautauqua were carried on to other organizations and times and made huge reforms and initiatives in American higher education possible.

Chautauqua was as much an idea as it was a place. Its singular greatest achievement was its provision of learning for women who might never have participated in higher education. Chautauqua also provided a place for women to speak to mixed groups, a situation unheard of at that time. In giving women such as Susan B. Anthony a podium and a meeting place, it provided them with the impetus and the venue to organize for action around issues most directly affecting women's lives. It allowed them to stir up unrest and to advance causes such as temperance and an end to family violence.

—Leona M. English

See also Addams, Jane; Anthony, Susan B.; Social Gospel Movement; Woman's Christian Temperance Union; Women's Suffrage Movement

Further Readings

English, L. M. (2005). Historical and contemporary explorations of the social change and spiritual directions of adult education. *Teachers College Record, 107*(6), 1169–1192.

Forsythe, A., & Lander, D. A. (2003). A reflexive inquiry of two non-smokers: A trans-generational tale of social gospel and social norms marketing. *Reflective Practice, 4*(2), 139–162.

Kilde, J. H. (1999). The "predominance of the feminine" at Chautauqua: Rethinking the gender-space relationship in Victorian America. *Signs, 24*(2), 449–486.

Morrison, T. (1974). *Chautauqua: A center for education, religion and the arts in America.* Chicago: University of Chicago Press.

Reiser, A. C. (2003). *The Chautauqua moment: Protestants, progressives and the culture of modern liberalism 1874–1920.* New York: Columbia University Press.

Schultz, J. R. (2002). *The romance of small-town Chautauquas.* Columbia: University of Missouri Press.

Scott, J. C. (1999). The Chautauqua movement: Revolution in popular higher education. *Journal of Higher Education, 70*(4), 389–412.

CHÁVEZ, CÉSAR (1927–1993)

Cesário Estrada Chávez, cofounder of the United Farmworkers Union, is one of the most successful 20th-century labor organizers the Western hemisphere has known. Chávez was born March 31, 1927, on his family farm near Yuma, Arizona. For the first decade of his life, Chávez grew up in an adobe structure on the farm that his grandfather had homesteaded in the late 19th century. In 1937, as the result of depression-era economics, as well as drought and Anglo-American swindling, the Chávez family was forced from the farm and entered the "migrant stream." As a result of his new migratory lived experiences, Chávez quit school in 1942 following the eighth grade. He subsequently labored full-time in the field to supplement his family income. Although Chávez's narrative is not significantly unique, as many ethnic Mexicans endured similar racist and classist incidents, his resiliency and subsequent labor organizing mark him as one of the most significant figures of the organized labor movement.

Following their eviction from their familial lands, Chávez established permanent roots in the San José barrio Sal Si Puedes (translating as "Get Out If You Can") and traveled the San Joaquin migrant cycle. At age 17, looking for an alternative to his laborious circumstances, Chávez enlisted in the U.S. Navy. Although instilling a sense of "discipline" in Chávez, the events that transpired in the armed forces simply replicated those he experienced in civilian life. In fact, within both military and civil society, Chávez was expelled from restaurants and movie theaters for attempting to integrate into whites-only sections. In response to his horrific, albeit common, experiences as a racialized Mexican in the United States, Chávez undertook a life of radical civil service and union organizing.

Upon an honorable discharge from the navy, Chávez married Helen Fabela in 1948. Although only 21, the couple had already known each other for 5 years, meeting at a Mexicano/a maltshop, La Baratita, in Delano, California. Much like Chávez, Fabela also traveled the migrant circuit with her family and was required to renounce formal education to economically assist her family. Together, Chávez and Fabela would have eight children.

One of the most significant events in Chávez's life occurred in 1952, when he met Fred Ross, an organizer with the Community Service Organization (CSO). The CSO was an association formed in Los Angeles to give Mexican Americans a political voice through voting. As a CSO organizer, Ross worked throughout southern California organizing Chicanos/as in their struggle for environmental and economic justice. Attempting to organize Chicanos/as in the San José area, Ross was directed to Chávez by a local priest. Following an apprehensive first meeting, Chávez volunteered for a CSO voter registration drive in East San José; Ross quickly became Chávez's friend and chief mentor. Working closely with Ross, Chávez organized more than 20 CSO chapters across California. Under the direction of Chávez, CSO enabled ethnic Mexicans access to their full rights as U.S. citizens, by way of voter registration drives, fighting police brutality, and improving public services in the barrio. Although initially Chávez worked as a volunteer for the CSO, he was hired full-time when Ross received money from Chicago-based radical organizer Saul Alinsky.

Not surprisingly, Chávez experienced an immense deal of red-baiting, even from within the Chicano/a community. On many occasions, particularly early on, Chávez was accused of being a Communist. Although Chávez embraced an unorthodox ideology, he always operated within a framework of reformation, whereas others within the Chicano/a movement espoused revolution. In the late 1960s, however, Chávez would be criticized by Chicano/a activists for not being radical enough. Either way, Chávez was a fervent believer in, and supporter of, the Roman Catholic Church, as well as popular Catholic praxis, which was often at odds with Marxist (particularly Leninist) doctrine. In fact, before entering into alliance with a Filipino/a farmworker strike, Chávez was so spiritually motivated that he put his faith in God to give him guidance.

In 1962, Chávez met resistance from CSO leadership about the prospects of working more closely with unions. In turn, Chávez resigned from his CSO appointment, closed the Los Angeles office where he had been working, and relocated to Delano, California. Along with Gil Padilla and Dolores Huerta (collectively known as *los tres*), Chávez convened the first conference of the National Farm Workers Association (NFWA) in Fresno, California. The first project of the NWFA was to organize the *campos* between Arvin and Stockton—86 farmworker communities in all. Initially structured similar to other *mutualistas* (mutual-aid societies), with dues helping fund life insurance for members, the NFWA chose to avoid using the term *union* in its official moniker. While this aversion to identifying the NFWA as a union could be connected with his previous experiences of being red-baited, it was more likely a response to the social vision of Chávez. Unlike many mainstream unions, Chávez did not envision the NFWA simply as a working-class bureaucracy; rather, he believed that this organization formed the moral fiber for what he called *la causa* (cause) or *el movimiento* (movement): a self-determining movement where farmworkers would take control of their own lives. In this regard, Chávez was insistent on building a union from the bottom up. In other words, Chávez was committed to organizing at the site of struggle: in the fields, at workers' homes, and during "leisure" activities. These NFWA organizing strategies contrasted with the AFL-CIO affiliate Agricultural Workers Organizing Committee (AWOC), a top-heavy union, where white union-bureaucrats used ethnic Mexicans and Filipinos/as as "middle-men."

The first NFWA-supported *huelga* (strike) occurred in 1965 when workers on a McFarland, California, rose farm aligned with the union to ensure higher wages and rectify on-the-job problems. Through union pressure, the workers received their demands, and the NFWA was catapulted into larger and more difficult struggles. On September 16, 1965, the predominately Chicano/a NFWA joined the picket line with Filipino organizer Larry Itlong and AWOC grape workers in the Delano Grape Strike. This strike, lasting 5 years, put tremendous economic pressure on the union but projected "the fight in the field" into the national consciousness. Through direct action, the support of activist solidarity, the production of community-based art-making, and international media coverage, the farmworker struggle was on the lips of workers and politicians alike. Among the most significant supporters of Chávez and the huelga was ex–Attorney General and U.S. Senator Robert Kennedy. On the night of his assassination, Kennedy had been with NFWA cofounder Dolores Huerta.

In 1966, following a 300-mile march from Delano to the state capitol in Sacramento, the NFWA negotiated a union contract with Schenley Vineyards. This contract was the historic first in the United States between a grower and agricultural workers. As this long-term strike persisted, AWOC and NFWA merged to form the AFL-CIO affiliated United Farm Workers (UFW). Shortly thereafter, DiGiorgio, another large grape grower, conceded to UFW stipulations and signed a union contract. However, even with individual union victories, Chávez remained firm, and beginning in 1967, the UFW called for a boycott of all California-grown table grapes. Supporters across North America rose in solidarity, boycotting non-union grapes. Artists, musicians, poets, and actors came to the aid of the union. El Teatro Campesino (The Farmworker Theater), organized in 1965 by Luis Valdéz, used Brechtian guerrilla theater as the medium to highlight the plight of the farmworker. Chávez knew the power of the arts in organizing workers and constructing support. As such, Chávez and the NWFA began publishing *El Malcriado,* the union newspaper, in 1965. The newspaper, initially published solely in Spanish, included English and Spanish editions and incorporated artworks by many of the most active Chicano/a artists and muralists of the period. Muralist Antonio Bernal painted a mural on the exterior of a union hall in 1968, and Carlos Almaraz painted a 16- by 24-foot mural for the 1972 UFW convention.

Following in the vein of Gandhi and Martin Luther King, Jr., Chávez advocated nonviolence and engaged in fasting as a way to cleanse his soul. As a very spiritual individual, Chávez combined Catholicism with direct action to produce a more just society. Still actively involved in UFW struggles, Chávez died in his sleep on April 29, 1993, at the home of an Arizona farmworker. Posthumously, Chávez was awarded the Medal of Freedom by President Clinton. Much like the spirit of union organizer Joe Hill, César Chávez can be found wherever there are farmworkers struggling to create a more just world.

—*Dylan A. T. Miner*

See also American Federation of Labor (AFL-CIO); Chicano Movement; Community Organizing; Farmworkers' Movement; Grape Boycotts; Guerrilla Theater; Pacifism

Further Readings

Ferriss, S., & Sandoval, R. (1997). *The fight in the fields: César Chávez and the farmworkers movement.* New York: Harcourt Brace.

Mariscal, J. (2004). Negotiating César: César Chávez in the Chicano movement. *Aztlán, 29*(1), 21–56.

Rosales, F. (1997). *Chicano! The history of the Mexican American civil rights movement.* Houston, TX: Arte Público.

Ross, F. (1989). *Conquering Goliath: César Chávez at the beginning.* Keene, CA: El Taller Gráfico.

CHÁVEZ, HUGO (1954–)

Since having been elected president of Venezuela in 1998, Hugo Rafael Chávez Frías has become an extremely contentious and polarizing figure both domestically and internationally. He was a charismatic and personalistic leader who appealed to those who felt as if they never before had had anyone in power who understood them, but he alienated the white power elite of which he was an outsider. To his opponents, his nationalistic and populist rhetoric was seen as authoritarian demagoguery that harmed Venezuela's economic growth and threatened political stability. For the poor, indigenous, and Afro-Venezuelan underclass who formed his base of support, Chávez represented their best hope for re-making a world that responded to their needs.

Chávez was born on July 28, 1954, the child of provincial school teachers. He became a career military officer, one of the few avenues for social advancement available to common people in Latin America, eventually rising to the rank of lieutenant colonel. In the military barracks, Chávez gained a political consciousness as he observed economic exploitation and racial discrimination. In 1983, with both military and civilian co-conspirators, Chávez formed the MBR-200 (Movimiento Bolivariano Revolucionaro 200

[Bolivarian Revolutionary Movement 200]), so named for the birth of Venezuelan independence hero Simón Bolívar, to challenge the existing political system and open the way for social change.

1992 Coup

Chávez first burst on the political scene in Venezuela after a failed February 4, 1992, military-civilian coup d'état against the elected government of Carlos Andrés Pérez. As president in the 1970s and belonging to the left-leaning social-democratic Acción Democrática (AD [Democratic Action]) Party, Pérez nationalized the country's large petroleum industry. In 1989, Pérez returned to power, but this time he implemented draconian International Monetary Fund structural adjustment measures that curtailed social spending and removed price controls on consumer goods. These neoliberal policies disproportionately hurt poor people and on February 27, 1989, triggered massive street riots. Security forces killed hundreds of protesters in the capital city of Caracas in what became known as the *caracazo.*

Although Chávez did not play a role in these protests, it set the stage for his eventual rise to power. It convinced him that Venezuela's political system was fundamentally corrupt. He blamed a 1958 power sharing agreement known as the Pact of Punto Fijo between Pérez's AD and the conservative Social Christian Party COPEI for excluding the vast majority of Venezuelans from participating in the political system. The 1992 coup quickly fell apart, and Chávez made a brief appearance on national television to call for other rebels to give themselves up to prevent further bloodshed. His statement that they had failed for the moment indicated that he would continue the struggle. Taking a stand against corruption and elite rule made him a hero for Venezuela's impoverished masses who had not benefitted from the country's economic growth.

After spending 2 years in prison, Chávez received a presidential pardon. He continued his struggle, this time in the electoral arena rather than through military means. In 1997, he founded the Movimiento Quinta República (Fifth Republic Movement), which he rode to power in presidential elections the following year.

President Chávez

Once in office, Chávez began to remake Venezuela's political landscape. He implemented policies that expanded social spending and halted privatization plans, although he never took steps away from the country's extreme dependency on petroleum exports. This led some early observers to comment that Chávez's bark was worse than his bite, that is, that his strident anti-neoliberal rhetoric was not reflected in his economic policies. Building on his support among the poor, however, Chávez did proceed to redraw the country's political structures. This included drafting a new constitution to replace the one in force since 1961. The new constitution increased presidential power while at the same time implementing socioeconomic changes, including expanding access to education and health care. It increased civil rights for women, indigenous peoples, and others marginalized under the old system. It also changed the name of the country from the Republic of Venezuela to the Bolivarian Republic of Venezuela, pointing to an internationalist vision that built on Bolívar's Pan–Latin Americanism.

The new constitution so fundamentally rewrote Venezuela's political structures that it required new elections for the National Assembly and presidency. Chávez handily won reelection in 2000 with about 60% of the vote, a margin of support he consistently enjoyed. Despite earlier involvement in a military coup, Chávez was content to remake the face of Venezuela through the political process and relished the challenges of electoral campaigns.

Missions

With consolidation of his power, Chávez proceeded to implement a series of social programs called "missions," designed to attack endemic poverty that plagued about a third of the population. Often these were named after national heroes. One of the most successful was Plan Robinson, a literacy program named after Bolívar's tutor Samuel Robinson. Similarly, an agrarian reform program carried the name of Ezequiel Zamora, a radical 19th-century peasant leader who advocated a far-reaching land reform program. Barrio

Adentro (To the Neighborhood) brought Cuban doctors to poor neighborhoods that never before had received sufficient medical attention. Other programs provided for subsidized food and education.

Opposition

Everything from Chávez's mannerisms and colloquial speech patterns to his social policies and economic priorities alienated him from Venezuela's small minority that had traditionally held political power. During his first term in office (2000–2006), Chávez faced three significant challenges and overcame each one. The first and most dramatic was an April 11, 2002, coup that removed Chávez from office for 2 days, but a wellspring of popular support from poor neighborhoods brought him back to power. A December 2002 manager and employee strike in the state oil company Petróleos de Venezuela (Venezuela Petroleum) significantly damaged the economy but failed to undermine Chávez's popular support. Finally, after failing in these extra-constitutional efforts to remove Chávez, the elite turned to a provision in Chávez's own constitution that allowed for the recall of elected officials midway through their terms. Chávez handily won the August 15, 2004, vote, further strengthening his hold on power. These defeats for the opposition further discredited the traditional political parties AD and COPEI. Facing a complete rout in the 2005 congressional elections, they withdrew, handing Chávez and his allies complete control over the National Assembly.

In the United States, the Bush administration continued to denounce and undermine Chávez through a variety of avenues including the National Endowment for Democracy. Chávez accused the United States of plotting his assassination and condemned U.S. imperialism and neoliberal economic policies. Chávez sought to break dependency on oil exports to the United States by signing agreements with China, India, and other new markets. Chávez presented the Alternativa Bolivariana para la América (Bolivarian Alternative for Latin America) as a substitute to the U.S.-sponsored Free Trade Area of the Americas. His demands to put people before capital gained him a good deal of support as it challenged U.S. hegemonic control over the region.

Socialism

Chávez initially denied that he intended to implement a socialist agenda in Venezuela, instead emphasizing a nationalistic Bolivarian Revolution that followed in Bolívar's footsteps. As Chávez consolidated power, however, he increasingly embraced a socialist discourse. He pointed to the failures of savage capitalism and argued that capitalism can only be transcended with socialism through democracy. In 2006, the World Social Forum moved to Caracas where Chávez presented an even stronger statement that the world faces two choices: socialism or death, because capitalism was destroying life on earth. He also consistently utilized religious language.

Since Chávez first won the presidency in 1998, Latin America has taken a significant shift leftward with the election of labor leader Luiz Inácio Lula da Silva in Brazil, Néstor Kirchner in Argentina, Tabaré Vázquez in Uruguay, Michelle Bachelet in Chile, and most significantly the socialist indigenous leader Evo Morales in Bolivia. Critics began to speak of two lefts: (1) a more moderate trend, represented by Argentina, Brazil, and Chile, which was willing to work within the confines of existing market economies; and (2) a "crazy" left, led by Fidel Castro in Cuba and joined by Venezuela and Bolivia. Opponents condemned these radicals for returning to allegedly discredited nationalist, clientelist, and statist models of governance.

Populism

Chávez will leave a historical legacy for Venezuela, but as of the time of this writing, it is not clear exactly what that might be. He is often called a populist, and in a Latin American context, *populist* has negative connotations of following the authoritarian and corporatist legacy of Getúlio Vargas in Brazil and Juan Perón in Argentina. Populists often opportunistically appeal to the impoverished masses for support but implement policies designed to secure their hold on power rather than remaking state structures with the goal of realizing social justice for the dispossessed. Detractors complained that Chávez used skyrocketing petroleum prices to fund social programs to shore up his base, while supporters noted that these were the same policies he had always embraced. Chávez is sometimes called a left-populist, indicating that he uses rhetoric to appeal to the poor but also implements concrete policies to shift wealth and power away from the elite. It is his potential for success that gives so much hope to his supporters and apprehension to his opponents.

—Marc Becker

See also Anti-Colonial Movements, Latin America; Castro, Fidel; Morales, Evo

Further Readings

Chávez, H., & Guevara, A. (2004). *Chávez: Venezuela and the New Latin America.* Melbourne, Australia: Ocean Press.

Chávez, H., & Harnecker, M. (2005). *Understanding the Venezuelan Revolution: Hugo Chávez talks to Marta Harnecker.* New York: Monthly Review Press.

Ellner, S., & Hellinger, D. (Eds.). (2003). *Venezuelan politics in the Chávez era: Class, polarization, and conflict.* Boulder, CO: Lynne Rienner.

Golinger, E. (2005). *The Chávez code: Cracking U.S. intervention in Venezuela.* Havana, Cuba: Editorial José Martí.

Gott, R. (2005). *Hugo Chávez and the Bolivarian Revolution.* London: Verso.

Wilpert, G. (Ed.). (2003). *Coup against Chávez in Venezuela: The best international reports of what really happened in April 2002.* Caracas, Venezuela: Fundación Venezolana para la Justicia Global & Fundación por un Mundo Multipolar.

CHICAGO, JUDY

See PERFORMANCE ART, POLITICAL

CHICAGO DEMOCRATIC CONVENTION DEMONSTRATIONS, 1968

Originally numbering eight, the Chicago Seven were a group of radical protest leaders arrested at the Democratic National Convention (DNC) in Chicago, Illinois, in 1968. Members of the group were charged with conspiracy, crossing state lines with the intent to incite a riot, obstructing justice, and promoting the use of incendiary devices (stink bombs) during an act of civil disobedience that drew thousands of protestors to the city.

The demonstration, initially conceived as a nonviolent disruption of the DNC, was intended to express opposition to the war in Vietnam and to mock the electoral process represented by the convention. Protestors spoofed the convention by staging a carnivalesque "Festival of Life"—music, poetry, and a guerrilla theater performance in which demonstrators announced the candidacy of a pig, Pigasus the Immortal, for president. As the demonstrators resisted police intervention, the protest escalated to a significant component of one of the most controversial riots in American history.

Tensions around the convention were high, as Chicago became a focal point for radical activist groups and their supporters planning massive demonstrations. In response, the city's mayor, Richard Daley, issued severe statements about maintaining order and summoned more than 5,000 National Guardsmen to support Chicago's police force. Clashes between demonstrators and police grew increasingly violent in response to curfew and other restrictions and antagonism from both sides. The climax was reached when protestors marching on the convention hall were met with sanctioned, excessive force by the police, and several hundred were injured and arrested. Key among these were the Chicago Eight.

The original Chicago Eight were Abbott (Abbie) Hoffman and Jerry Rubin, founders of the Youth International Party (Yippies); peace activist and chairman of the National Mobilization Against War, David Dellinger; Rennie Davis, national director of the community organizing program of the Students for a Democratic Society (SDS); SDS founding member, Tom Hayden; SDS member and founder of the Radical Science Information Service, John Froines; Lee Weiner, local organizer and activist; and Bobby Seale, founding member of the Black Panther Party. The Eight became the Chicago Seven when Seale's case was severed from the rest, after receiving 16 citations for contempt for repeated inflammatory outbursts. Seale was ordered bound and gagged in the courtroom and was subsequently sentenced to 4 years on the contempt charge.

The trial of the Chicago Seven ran from September 24, 1969, until February 18, 1970, and its proceedings were marked by mockery and farce delivered by the defendants, while their attorneys, William Kunstler and Leonard Weinglass, of the Center for Constitutional Rights, delivered a steady stream of celebrity witnesses, including Phil Ochs, Timothy Leary, Dick Gregory, Arlo Guthrie, Norman Mailer, Allen Ginsberg, Jesse Jackson, and Judy Collins. Ultimately, Froines and Weiner were acquitted of all charges, and the remaining five defendants were convicted of crossing state lines with the intent to start a riot, sentenced to 5 years each, and fined $5,000. These convictions were overturned on November 21, 1972, by the U.S. Court of Appeals for the Seventh Circuit, due to judicial bias and the inability of defense attorneys to question prospective jurors on their cultural biases.

—Cynthia J. Miller

See also Chicago Seven; Dellinger, David; Guerrilla Theater; Hayden, Tom; Hoffman, Abbie; Kunstler, William; Seale, Bobby; Students for a Democratic Society

Further Readings

Babcox, P., & Babcox, D. (Eds.). (1969). *The conspiracy: The Chicago 8 speak out*. New York: Dell.

Dellinger, D. (1993). *From Yale to jail: The life story of a moral dissenter*. New York: Pantheon.

Hoffman, A., & Wasserman, H. (2005). *Revolution for the hell of it: The book that earned Abbie Hoffman a five-year prison term at the Chicago conspiracy trial*. New York: Thunder Mouth Press.

Rubin, J. (1970). *Do it! Scenarios of the revolution*. New York: Touchstone.

CHICAGO SEVEN

Associated with the trial some historians portray as uniquely symbolic of the conflict of values characteristic of U.S. society in the late 1960s, the Chicago Seven were seven men indicted during the spring of 1969 for conspiracy to incite a riot. Originally made up of eight defendants, including Black Panther Party cofounder Bobby Seale, the charge made reference to the widespread unrest that occurred at the time of the Chicago-based August 1968 Democratic National Convention. The group—including Youth International Party (YIPPIE) founders Abbie Hoffman and Jerry Rubin, pacifists Dave Dellinger and Rennie Davis, Students for a Democratic Society leader Tom Hayden, and locally active academics Lee Weiner and John Froines—had a diverse and sometimes conflicting sense of appropriate courtroom strategy and tactics. With all convictions overturned late in 1972 by a Circuit Court of Appeals, the ultimate judicial decision affirmed a comment made by Abbie Hoffman about eight men who had never (before the trial) met as a single group: They could hardly agree to a conspiracy when they couldn't even agree on lunch! The legacy of the trial suggests that courtroom dramatics can play a powerful role in challenging legal and political authority.

Most observers, including an independent commission and Lyndon Johnson's Attorney General Ramsey Clark, concluded that the violence at the 1968 Democratic National Convention was caused by an out-of-control police force, under the direction of militaristic Chicago Mayor Richard Daley. Daley's insistence on getting a federal judge to convene a grand jury on the matter resulted in the eight indictments. Defense attorneys William Kuntsler and Leonard Weinglass submitted questions intended to reveal cultural bias among potential jurors to trial judge Julius Hoffman (including whether they knew who Jimi Hendrix was or whether they let their daughters dress without bras), who refused to allow that line of inquiry. There is little doubt that Judge Hoffman's strict and narrow interpretation of the law, combined with his open distaste for the defense, helped set up a dynamic that encouraged outrageous defense theatrics.

After one month of struggling to get a postponement so that Black Panther lawyer Charles Garry could be added to the defense team, Bobby Seale, angered at being forced to represent himself, intensified his challenges to the judge. Hoffman, in turn, ordered Seale bound and gagged, an incident not missed by the national media. Seale's case was quickly severed from the remaining seven. Later in the trial, during defense testimony, witnesses appeared to vouch for the defendant's peaceful intentions. These witnesses included folk singers Judy Collins, Pete Seeger, Arlo Guthrie, and Phil Ochs; beat poet Allen Ginsberg, who led the courtroom in chanting OM; and LSD guru Timothy Leary. Abbie Hoffman and Jerry Rubin entered the courtroom on occasion wearing mock judicial robes. Dellinger, the oldest of the group and a World War II conscientious objector, admonished the judge for wanting people to behave like "good Germans" and go along with the Vietnam War, then like "good Jews," going along quietly during a prosecution made up largely of testimony by police officers and paid informants.

Despite more than contempt citations, and a sentence of five years' imprisonment and steep fines for most of the seven as well as their lawyers, the trial could hardly be seen as a success for the state. Even before the reversal on appeal, all eight initial defendants became radical celebrities, leading to significant speaking tours throughout the 1970s. News of the statements and actions of the Chicago Seven bolstered the anti-war movement as a whole.

—Matt Meyer

See also Chicago Democratic Convention Demonstrations, 1968; Dellinger, David; Hayden, Tom; Hoffman, Abbie; Kunstler, William; Seale, Bobby; Students for a Democratic Society

Further Readings

Clavir, J., & Spitzer, J. (Eds.). (1970). *The conspiracy trial.* New York: Bobbs-Merrill.
Linder, D. O. (1999). The Chicago Seven conspiracy trial. www.law.umkc.edu/faculty/projects/ftrials/Chicago7/ Account.html

CHICANO MOVEMENT

The Chicano movement, or *el movimiento,* grew out of the turbulent civil rights movement of the 1950s and 1960s. Similar to their African American counterparts, Chicanos/as struggled for social, political, and economic parity and to subvert discriminatory laws and practices. Within the civil rights movement, Chicanos/as challenged institutionalized systems of oppression that, for decades, had relegated them to second-class citizenship, principally in the U.S. Southwest. Their efforts to achieve complete citizenship were inspired by African American activists struggling for self-determination against the Jim Crow laws in the South. Historian F. Arturo Rosales points out that the African American civil rights struggle was crucial in leading Mexican Americans to forge their own movement. Indeed, the involvement of Mexican Americans in African American organizations, such as the National Student Association and the Student Nonviolent Coordinating Committee, provided them with insightful community-organizing experiences. Undeniably, this second generation of Mexican Americans, or Chicanos, matured politically in an era of social dissent.

As the Chicano movement evolved during the late 1960s, Chicanos/as called for a cultural renewal and search for identity. Their political self-identification distinguished them from their parents' generation, which they thought was more accommodating. Chicanos/as contended that the term *Mexican American* reflected assimilationist tendencies. Like their African American peers, Chicanos/as challenged European American definitions of Mexican Americans. Instead, they espoused phrases that were self-empowering, such as "Brown is beautiful," and called themselves *Chicanos/Chicanas,* a term their parents despised.

As a community, Chicanos/as demanded an educational curriculum that reflected their historical presence in, and contributions to, the United States; their cultural achievements; and their desire for control over their own communities. They also adopted an indigenous identity, or *indigenismo,* that celebrated their native ancestry, especially that of the Aztec civilization. This cultural affiliation tied the Aztec's mythical origins to the Southwest, or *Aztlán.* Thus, it became easier for Chicanos/as to situate themselves between two nations that rejected them for being culturally distinct. In turn, these claims concretized their identity and induced an activist philosophy largely based on racial pride and cultural nationalism, *Chicanismo.* This newfound ideology mobilized the Chicano movement differently throughout the Southwest. In addition, what distinguished the Chicano movement from the previous Mexican American generations was its broad activist base. Chicano/a activists came from different walks of life. Many were high school and college students, community and grassroots activists, and working-class citizens. In contrast, the Mexican American generation was composed of middle-class citizens and leaders, who addressed their concerns through the judicial and legislative systems.

The relationship between Chicano/a activists and the Mexican American generation was one of discord. Chicanos/as were critical of the Mexican American generation for their patience and belief in a system that prolonged social, political, and economic inequality. Instead, Chicano activists appealed for a militant form of activism. The absence of a national leader and disagreements over an ideological platform and long-term strategy, according to Rosales, complicated the Chicano movement. For instance, Reies López Tijerina founded the *Alianza Federal de las Mercedes* (Federal Alliance of Land Grants). Tijerina's main goal was to garnish support to reclaim land grants that were lost in New Mexico. In the late 1960s, Tijerina occupied various locations on behalf of the people, such as the Echo Amphitheatre, the Carson National Forest, and Tierra Amarilla, where he intended to make a citizen's arrest of District Attorney Alfonso Sánchez. As a result of his activities, Tijerina was sent to prison, where he became a symbolic political prisoner. He was released in 1971.

In 1966 in Denver, Colorado, Rodolfo "Corky" Gonzales formed the Crusade for Justice, a community-based organization. A former featherweight contender and the first Chicano district captain of the Democratic Party, Gonzales later became the director of Denver's war on poverty youth programs. Cognizant of the politically charged times, Corky Gonzales organized the historical National Chicano Liberation Youth Conference in March 1969 in Denver, to discuss issues affecting the Chicano/a community. During this conference, Corky Gonzales issued *El Plan del Barrio* (The Barrio Plan). This proclamation focused on self-determination, by calling for separate public housing for Chicanos/as, bilingual education, barrio economic development, and restitution of land. It was also at this conference that Corky Gonzales wrote and performed his epic poem, "I Am Joaquin." This moving poem quickly became the anthem of the Chicano movement. Out of the conference, *El Plan Espiritual de Aztlán* (The Spiritual Plan of Aztlán) was also born. This second manifesto called for separatism, community self-determination, and cultural pride. In Santa Barbara, California, Chicano/a university students incorporated the plan and sought to unify all student groups under one unified organization, known as El Movimiento Estudiantil de Aztlán. It was there that the *Plan de Santa Barbara* (Santa Barbara Plan) was created, which called for the creation and implementation of Chicano Studies programs in every school campus. The Santa Barbara Plan also called for a curriculum that would train the next generation of Chicano/a leaders and activists.

José Angel Gutiérrez came to prominence in his native town of Crystal City, Texas. He was one of the founders of the Mexican American Youth Organization and a leader among students in the movement. Distraught over the blatant racism in Crystal City, he participated in a citizens' organizing committee and vowed to take control of the school board at the 1970 election. Out of this group's action came the La Raza Unida Party (LRUP), an alternative political party for Chicanos/as. At the local level, LRUP garnered 15 city officials, including 2 mayors, 2 school board majorities, and 2 city council majorities; this was the first of its kind in the Winter Garden area of Texas. However, the party was short-lived. Splits between the leadership, insufficient funds, the absence of an attractive platform, and limited membership denied the party of any significant growth.

Most prominent of all other leaders, César Chávez arguably led the fight in a two-prong offensive. Chávez played the roles of civil rights leader and labor leader. In 1965, Filipino farm workers, under the leadership of Larry Itliong, Pete Velasco, Philip Vera Cruz, and others, struck in the grape fields of Delano, California, demanding union recognition, as well as better wages and working conditions in an industry that exploited its workers. In a strategic move, Filipinos in the Agricultural Workers Organizing Committee (AWOC) joined with the National Farm Workers Association and their leader, César Chávez.

Once they joined forces, the farmworkers movement took off full force, propelling César Chávez into worldwide recognition. The Agricultural Workers Organizing Committee and National Farm Workers Association merged to become the United Farm Workers Organizing Committee, which later became the United Farm Workers. Under the *huelga* (strike) banner, César Chávez, Dolores Huerta, Larry Itliong, Philip Vera Cruz, and thousands of other farmworkers moved on the offensive against California's grape growers, including Di Giorgio, Guimarra, and other growers in the San Joaquin and Coachella Valleys. Soon, the national boycott reached international proportions, and the 5-year strike and boycott finally brought growers and workers together at the table for a fair contract. The United Farm Workers became a major symbol of hope for the Chicano movement.

The fight for land took on other fronts outside those headed by Tijerina in New Mexico. In San Diego, the Chicano community of Barrio Logan fought the city to reclaim a piece of land under the Coronado Bridge that was set aside for a community park. The land dispute emerged when the city decided to build a police station instead. The response from the community was swift. Activists, students, and other members of the community got together and stopped the construction of the highway patrol substation by forming human chains and occupying the land. Through a concerted effort involving legal channels, media attention, and community support throughout California, the Chicano/a community of Barrio Logan won its battle and secured the land for the park. Symbolically, Barrio Logan had successfully reclaimed a piece of Aztlán on behalf of the *movimiento*.

Cultural productions blossomed during the Chicano movement. Cultural achievements and legacy were expressed through various venues. Chicano/a muralists, such as Salvador "Queso" Torres, Yolanda López, Judith F. Baca, Jose Montoya, Mario Torrero, Victor Ochoa, and mural groups, such as Mujeres Muralistas and Congreso de Artistas Chicanos en Aztlán, created a new Chicano/a image, highlighted the community's history, and educated the public about the Chicano/a plight. Others, such as Alurista, Moctezuma Esparza, and Luis Valdez, made similar contributions in literature and film. Each participated in producing cultural

images and messages that proclaimed their cultural pride and identity.

On the education front, Mexicans and Chicanos/as have been fighting against school segregation and educational parity for decades. What makes the Chicano movement distinct, however, is the fact that for the first time the protest and activism came directly from the students. Such was the case with the East Los Angeles high school walkouts on March 1, 1968, when students took to the streets to protest mistreatment, inadequate education, poor school conditions, and for an overhaul of the curriculum. The event was noted by the *Los Angeles Times* as "The Birth of Brown Power." During the "East L.A. blowouts," 10,000 to 12,000 students walked out of several Los Angeles Unified School District schools to express their grievances against the school system. The events in Los Angeles inspired other walkouts throughout the Southwest and Midwest. In the arena of higher education, Chicanos/as were entering college in increasing numbers than previous generations. They, too, saw the need for a curriculum that spoke to them, and they created campus organizations, such as the Mexican American Youth Organization in Texas, United Mexican American Students and El Movimiento Estudiantil de Aztlán in California, and the Crusade for Justice in Denver. Students and community members also formed their own defense groups in the barrio, such as the Brown Berets. The Brown Berets stemmed from the Young Citizens for Community Action in 1967 in East Los Angeles. They functioned similarly to the Black Panthers and Puerto Rican Young Lords, in that they were paramilitary, and provided defense from police brutality.

One of the most profound events in the Chicano movement was the Chicano Moratorium. On August 29, 1970, the Chicano/a community organized a day of protest against the Vietnam War. At the time, it was the largest Chicano/a protest in the history of Los Angeles. Estimates indicate that 20,000 to 30,000 people came to protest the Vietnam War and bring attention to the fact that over 23% of the casualties from the Southwest were of Mexican origin, even though they only constituted 10% of the total population in the area at the time. The demonstration was peaceful until the police used a small altercation at a liquor store as the excuse to move against the crowd. Without much warning, the police attacked the crowd, swinging their clubs, trampling people, and hitting those that got in their way. Tear gas was fired into the crowd, which caused protesters to defend themselves by throwing objects at the deputies. More than 1,200 Los Angeles police officers and sheriff's deputies were present making mass arrests. In the chaos that ensued, two casualties were reported; one was a 15-year-old boy. The second victim was Rubén Salazar, a news reporter for KMEX-TV, a Spanish-language television station. Reports and witnesses indicate that Salazar was killed when officers shot a tear gas projectile into the bar where he was having a beer with two coworkers from the station. The projectile struck Salazar in the head, killing him instantly. As Rosales noted, Salazar's death made him the most powerful martyr of the Chicano movement.

Although the Chicano movement's goals of instilling cultural pride and advocating for self-determination, while combating institutional racism, police violence, lack of access to private and public facilities, and inadequate education made some headway, it was not without its problems. First, the Chicano movement lacked a coherent national agenda. For example, the term *Chicano* was a point of debate. José Angel Gutiérrez advocated for the use of *La Raza* (the race, or the people) as the best social identification for Mexican Americans, because the term *Chicano* was not known throughout the Southwest and Midwest. Furthermore, the ways in which the movement was led was highly debated. This led to clashes between rising leaders and limited the movement from maturing thoroughly. This was most evident in the LRUP, which rose as a third party to the Democrats and Republicans in the 1970s. With José Angel Gutiérrez as its leader, the LRUP had minor successes at the local level, especially in the state of Texas, but it failed to achieve the vision of Chicano/a activists. Yet, its legacy showed the political participation of Chicanos/as as a force to reckon with. Another internal problem was patriarchal relations within the movement. Chicanas were critical of male leaders. Also, they voiced their discontent and demanded more representation, their own caucuses, and an agenda that included a gender analysis as well. Although they did stand with their male counterparts, it was not without friction or resentment, as Chicanas often took on most of the organizing responsibilities and groundwork. As women of color, Chicanas had to deal with the triple oppression of racism, classism, and sexism. In addition to the absence of gender analysis, the movement was homophobic and dismissed the lesbian/queer community.

Beyond the movement's control was the use of violence by the state, which, historian Rodolfo Acuña notes, clubbed the movement into submission. In addition, the rhetorical concepts of the Chicano movement were too radical and challenged the integrationist tendencies of American politics. As a result, the police, the Federal Bureau of Investigation (FBI), and other government agencies harassed and arrested Chicano leaders and rank-and-file members. The movement's leaders, key organizers, and most influential organizations were under constant surveillance. COINTELPRO, an FBI counterintelligence program, targeted radical political organizations and organizers. These factors led to the decline of the Chicano movement. Although it has been argued that little progress was ever made and goals were not completely achieved, the fight for social and economic justice has not subsided. The struggles of the Chicano/a community endure, and the *movimiento* continues to reinvent itself to deal with contemporary issues. In California, the Chicano/a community rallied around legislation such as Propositions 187, 209, and 227 in the 1990s. Most recently, the current mobilization of millions of protesters to defend the rights of Mexican immigrants, both legal and illegal, has been a point of mobilization and activism for the Chicano/a community across the nation. Indeed, as current activism in the Chicano movement shows, the struggles of the 1960s and 1970s were but one thread in an intricate historical web of Mexican, Mexican American, and Chicano/a activism, which began with the U.S. takeover of Mexico in 1848. What the Chicano movement did, however, was define a generation who mobilized under the banner of social and economic justice for *los de abajo* (those from below).

—*Rudy P. Guevarra, Jr.*

See also Chávez, César; Civil Rights Movement; Critical Race Theory; League of United Latin American Citizens

(LULAC); Martínez, Betita; Mexican American Legal Defense and Education Fund (MALDEF); Mexican Muralists; Tijerina, Reies López

Further Readings

Acuña, R. (2000). *Occupied America: A history of Chicanos* (4th ed.). New York: Longman.

Cockcroft, E. S., & Barnet-Sánchez, H. (Eds.). (1999). *Signs from the heart: California Chicano murals*. Albuquerque: University of New Mexico Press.

García, I. M. (1997). *Chicanismo: The forging of a militant ethos among Mexican Americans*. Tucson: University of Arizona Press.

García, I. M. (1989). *United we win: The rise and fall of La Raza Unida Party*. Tucson: University of Arizona, Mexican American Studies & Research Center.

Gómez-Quiñones, J. (1990). *Chicano politics: Reality and promise, 1940–1990*. Albuquerque: University of New Mexico Press.

Munoz, C., Jr. (1989). *Youth, identity, power: The Chicano movement*. New York: Verso.

Rosales, F. A. (1997). *Chicano! The history of the Mexican American civil rights movement*. Houston, TX: Arte Público Press.

Vigil, E. B. (1999). *The crusade for justice: Chicano militancy and the government's war on dissent*. Madison: University of Wisconsin Press.

CHILD ADVOCACY

Child advocacy, the act of supporting children's rights, encompasses a variety of social and political issues in countries worldwide. They include, but are not limited to, hunger, child labor, disease and other health risks, homelessness, physical and emotional abuse and neglect, sexual exploitation, and education. These issues usually do not exist in isolation, and poverty is often a central element. Economic disenfranchisement, combined with status as "under-age," nonvoting citizens, leaves children politically powerless.

The primary goals of child advocates are to prevent harm to children's physical, mental, and emotional well-being and to change existing conditions that are harmful to children. Child advocacy is undertaken by individuals; grassroots groups and nonprofit organizations; relief agencies; religious groups; corporations; and both non-government and government-sponsored agencies. These entities operate in a variety of ways (e.g., as independent sponsors, through outreach programs, in networks) and for a variety of purposes (e.g., to conduct research, inform the public, impact policy, provide support and resources). Their efforts take place in local communities and at national and international levels.

Child advocates represent a number of different philosophies, one of which is the perspective of social justice based on the conviction that it is an ethical and moral responsibility to act on the behalf of children who are marginalized or have been rendered voiceless. They advocate for individuals as well as to promote the collective good. Following are descriptions of child advocacy efforts that address three of the issues listed above: child labor, abuse and neglect, and child health and health care.

Child Labor

One of the earliest social ills to be addressed by rights advocates on behalf of children was child labor. During the rise of industrialism, an increasing number of children were sent to work in factories, mines, and mills. They worked up to 16 hours a day in unsanitary and dangerous conditions. Publications by Karl Marx and Charles Dickens were instrumental in focusing public criticism on the practice of child labor. In particular, Dickens's novel *Oliver Twist,* published in 1838, was a social critique of London's workhouses and captured the attention of widespread audiences.

In the United States, one of the first child labor advocacy groups was the National Child Labor Committee, a private, nonprofit organization of social workers. Begun in 1904, the National Child Labor Committee continues to this day to advocate on behalf of children to prevent exploitation in the workplace, to improve the health and education of young migrant workers, and to increase public awareness of child labor laws. It also now collaborates with other organizations and corporations nationwide to sponsor a variety of programs.

Other child labor advocacy groups include the Child Labor Coalition, UNICEF, Campaign for Labor Rights, and the United Farm Workers. These and other groups seek to end the exploitation of children working in sweatshops, the child sex market, drug trade, commercial farming, and businesses. It is estimated that as many as 246 million children are currently engaged in child labor.

Abuse and Neglect

Whereas child labor is an issue that primarily affects children from economically poor backgrounds, child abuse and neglect occur across all socioeconomic groups. When one thinks of advocacy and protection for abused and neglected children, government-funded social service agencies or child protective services may come to mind first. These agencies respond to reports of suspected child abuse or neglect, conduct investigations, and provide support services or, in imminently dangerous situations, remove the child from the environment.

Advocates for abused and neglected children also include teachers, counselors, doctors, day care workers, and certain other individuals who come into contact with minors and in whom children often place their trust. These individuals are required by law to report suspected abuse and neglect to child protective or law enforcement agencies.

What constitutes physical abuse is not universally agreed upon. Corporal punishment of children by teachers and parents, for example, once considered an appropriate form of disciplining children in the United States, is now illegal in schools in more than half of the states. Spanking by parents as a form of discipline has become less socially acceptable overall, as organizations such as the American Psychological Association, the American Medical Association, and others have spoken out against it. Yet, there has been a backlash in recent years by far-right religious conservatives who claim that physical discipline is in the best interest of the child. Citing the Bible, they contend that they are advocating not only for what is best for children but also for the future moral health of our country.

Health and Health Care

The United Nations Universal Declaration of Human Rights states that "everyone has the right to a standard of living adequate for the health and well-being of oneself and one's family, including food, clothing, housing, and medical care." Yet, for millions of children worldwide who live in poverty, poor health and insufficient or absent medical care are a part of life. Contaminated water, exposure to lead, poor nutrition, and disease are some of the health-related problems addressed by child advocacy organizations, including UNICEF; Children NOW; AIDS Alliance for Children, Youth, & Families; and Save the Children Alliance. These organizations work for improved children's health worldwide through field service, fund-raising, backing local health care initiatives, providing medical aid and supplies, and policy change.

The widening divide between rich and poor is reflected in the increasing disparity in the accessibility and quality of health care. Soaring costs of health care and health insurance make it impossible for many poor and working-class families to protect their children. Cutbacks in Medicaid, a government-sponsored health care program for the poor, have had a negative impact on medical care for families and children. Advocacy groups, such as Healthcare for the Homeless (which partners with local, state, and national organizations to provide comprehensive medical care to the homeless) and the Children's Defense Fund are two groups that advocate for change in health care policy and systems. Based on the belief that health care is a human right, they and others lobby for a national health care system that would provide equal access and quality for everyone, regardless of the ability to pay for services.

—Elizabeth Noll

See also Advocacy; Child Labor Laws; Children's Defense Fund; Dickens, Charles

Further Readings

Grover, S. (2005). Advocacy by children as a causal factor in promoting resilience. *Childhood, 12*(4), 527–538.

Robinson, A., & Stark, D. R. (2005). *Advocates in action: Making a difference for young children.* Washington, DC: National Association for the Education of Young Children.

Tompkins, J. R., Brooks, B. L., & Tompkins T. J. (1998). *Child advocacy: History, theory, and practice.* Durham, NC: Carolina Academic Press.

Whittier Journal of Child and Family Advocacy. Costa Mesa, CA: Whittier Law School.

CHILD LABOR LAWS

Child labor laws are the legal guidelines in place to prevent or regulate the employment of children. The effort includes banning the employment of very young children and monitoring the employment of older children. While great strides and improvements have been made, the laws have not been totally effective. Children over the world are exploited as low-paid laborers, bonded servants, and slaves. In addition, they are often found as prostitutes, soldiers, and prisoners of war.

The employment of children has undergone many manifestations since the beginning of the human race, with children involved in hunting and gathering, as well as participating in all aspects of their society and culture. This use of children continued with the development of agriculture, with children working in the fields to plant, tend, and harvest crops. Children worked in homes or assisted their parents and caretakers in all tasks and employments considered necessary for the survival of the family.

Generally, the Industrial Revolution is considered as the most significant event to spawn the increased use of children in deplorable working conditions. When Benjamin Franklin toured midland and northern England, he observed children as young as 5 years old working in a silk mill. Besides mills, young children worked in all types of factories, mines, and domestic servitude.

British Child Labor Laws

Early laws relating to children were harsh and unforgiving. In 1723, parishes founded "unions" or workhouses empowered to manacle children to prevent their escape. In 1740, legislation was passed dealing with child theft, allowing a child to be hanged by the neck until dead for the stealing of a handkerchief. Yet, by 1761, a campaign was started to protect child chimney sweeps, and legislation came about in 1788.

Between 1780 and 1840, there was a dramatic increase in the intensity of exploitation. The plight of working children was the topic of writers, most famously poet William Blake in his books *Songs of Innocence* (1789) and *Songs of Experience* (1794). In particular, "The Chimney Sweeper" describes in heartbreaking phrases the lives of small children doomed to enter the dangerous world of chimney-cleaning.

British social reformers worked to enact a series of legislation to regulate child labor. Among these were the 1842 Mines Act, which prohibited women and young children from working in the mines. In 1844, the Society for the Prevention of Cruelty to Children was founded, and members pushed for a series of acts related to child labor. The 1844 Factory Act reduced the number of hours children ages 8 through 13 were allowed to work. This act was amended in 1850, and while it adjusted the daily hours that children worked, it also increased the weekly hours from 58 to 60. The year 1864 saw the Chimney Sweeper's Act, effected in part by Charles Kingsley's poignant tale *The Water Babies* (1863). In 1867, the Factory Extension Act was extended to factories and workplaces not included in the original laws.

In 1870, the Education Act required elementary schooling for children but still allowed them to work. The 1891 Factory Act raised the minimum age of child workers from 10 to 11.

American Child Labor Laws

Laws in America tended to follow the British legislation and originated initially at a state level. During the American Industrial Revolution, children worked for a pittance in a 70-hour work week. They might begin work at age 4 or 5, in terrible conditions that threatened their life and limbs. Children in factories and mines developed a host of medical conditions, including bronchitis, tuberculosis, and paralysis. As in Britain, many of these children died from the harsh conditions. Efforts to stop these tragedies began in 1832 with minimum age laws in Massachusetts, providing the first of many factory safety and health laws, followed by other states that enacted a variety of similar laws.

By 1904, American social reformers wanting to end child labor founded the National Child Labor Committee. They comprised activists from across the political spectrum, including Socialists, Communists, and anarchists. One reformer, Jane Addams, the founder of Chicago's Hull-House, noted that over 2 million children under the age of 16 were employed in America, and linked this number to the 580,000 children between ages 14 and 16 who could not read or write. She and other activists also documented the severe mental and physical illnesses affecting child workers.

In 1907, Congress granted a charter to the National Child Labor Committee, who hired educator Lewis Hine to photograph child workers in an effort to document the problem. Hine took thousands of photographs. In one, he documented the tormented image of a young cotton mill worker who fell into a spinning machine, cutting and mangling the boy's fingers. Another of his photographs documents very young children employed as oyster shuckers, who also kept watch over babies. Other photos depict the exhausted faces of children working in mines. Hine's photographs struck a nerve with the American public and thus began a series of legislative efforts on the part of Congress to control the abuse of children in the workforce.

The 1916 Keating-Owen Act was the first national labor bill. Congress banned the sale of articles produced by children younger than age 14, or made by children between ages 14 and 16 who had worked more than 8 hours a day, or overnight, or more than 6 days a week. The law applied specifically in the areas of factories, canneries, and mines and also regulated the number of hours a child could work. In 1918, the U.S. Supreme Court considered the case of *Hammer v. Dagenhart,* in which Roland Dagenhart, the father of two young sons under the age of 16, argued that Congress had violated his sons' freedom to work. The U.S. Supreme Court ruled that the Keating-Owen Act was unconstitutional, interfering with interstate trade. The Supreme Court also struck down the 1918 Second Child Labor Law, which would have placed a 10% tax on industries that used children under the age of 16.

With the Great Depression of 1929, followed by widespread adult unemployment, President Franklin D. Roosevelt cited the emergency situation to initiate his plan for economic recovery in the New Deal. One of his efforts involved the development of the National Recovery Administration, which would develop codes for fair trade. To this effort, Congress passed the 1933 National Recovery Act, which outlawed all child labor, and the 1933 National Industrial Recovery Act. Both of these were again struck down by the Supreme Court.

The efforts to eliminate child labor finally took hold in June 1938 with the Fair Labor Standards Act. Also known as the Federal Wage and Hour Law, this legislation prohibited child labor on interstate goods. Also, outside of school hours, children had to be 14 or older to work at nonmanufacturing jobs. They could work during school hours when they became 16. Only at age 18 were they allowed to work in hazardous occupations.

At present, the Fair Labor Standards Act generally keeps to the same guidelines as those originally legislated in 1938. States have enacted their own laws, often stricter than the Fair Labor Standards Act, and employers must adhere to both state and federal laws. Some exceptions include yardwork, babysitting, and agricultural labor.

Nevertheless, millions of children in the United States, Britain, and around the world still labor under exploitative and cruel working conditions. In the United States, migrant children toil with their parents on farms, in private homes, and in industry. Worldwide, the situation is also deplorable. Domestic child laborers are often forced into prostitution. In Sierra Leone, diamond mine barons use child slaves, many of whom were kidnapped and forced to serve as child soldiers. They now work on "blood diamonds," the gemstones harvested under conditions of war and cruelty. In India, bonded children cut and polish diamonds. In Pakistan, children are chained to carpet looms, a practice that stunts the children's growth.

A high-profile case is that of Ipqul Masih, who was sold as a bonded servant when he was 4 years old. At age 10, after having been beaten and abused, he managed to escape and become acquainted with labor activists. He visited schoolchildren in the United States, who noted his smallish height and great courage. He became a spokesperson for ending child labor, in 1994 receiving the Reebok Human Rights Youth in Action award. He returned to Pakistan to be educated, with the goal of becoming an attorney, but was shot dead on Easter Sunday, 1995.

In 1999, the International Labor Organization enacted a Convention against the most exploitative types of child labor. Yet, efforts by the International Labor Organization, the United Nations, and a host of other organizations and lawmakers worldwide have not yet succeeded in ending exploitative child labor practices. With the 2003 U.S. invasion of Iraq, a current focus is on child labor in Iraq, with the Ministry of Labor and Social Affairs documenting children as young as 2 years old street-begging, and a 15% increase since the United Nations imposed sanctions against Iraq, before the 2003 U.S. invasion.

—Teresa Knudsen

See also Child Advocacy; Labor Law; Youth Organizing and Activism

Further Readings

Ellenbogen, M. (2004, April 30). Can the Tariff Act combat endemic child labor abuses? The case of Cote d'Ivoire. *Texas Law Review, 82*(5), 1315–1317.

Hine, L. (1912, October 23). *Accident to a young mill worker. Giles Edmund Newsom* [Photograph]. Retrieved July 26, 2006, from http://memory.loc.gov/service/pnp/nclc/02600/02697v.jpg

Kuklin, S. (1998). *Iqbal Masih and the crusaders against child slavery.* New York: Henry Holt.

Lavalette, M. (1999). *A thing of the past? Child labor in Britain in the nineteenth and twentieth centuries.* New York: St. Martin's Press.

National Child Labor Committee. (n.d.). Lewis Hine photographs. Washington, DC: Library of Congress, Prints and Photographs Division. Retrieved July 26, 2006, from http://www.loc.gov/rr/print/res/097_hine.html

Sarbaugh-Thompson, M., & Zaid, M. (1995). Child labor laws: A historical case of public implementation. *Administration and Society, 27*(1), 25–52.

UNICEF. (n.d.). *Convention on the rights of the child.* Retrieved July 26, 2006, from http://www.unicef.org/crc/

U.S. Department of Labor. (n.d.). *Compliance assistance— Fair Labor Standards Act.* Retrieved July 26, 2006, from http://www.dol.gov/esa/whd/flsa/

Watts, P. (2006, January 8). Bush advisor says President has legal power to torture children. *Information Clearing House.* Retrieved July 24, 2006, from http://www.informationclearinghouse.info/article11488.htm

CHILDREN'S DEFENSE FUND

The conceptual motivation for, and later development of, the Children's Defense Fund (CDF) rests with the civil rights movement and social leaders' aim to fulfill the promise of a democratic society by meeting young people's humanistic needs. Two outgrowths of the civil rights movement—the Poor People's Campaign and the Washington Research Project—specifically situated poverty and hunger as national problems that, in part, characterized social inequities throughout the country. Former attorney general Robert Kennedy's visits to the Mississippi Delta to document and understand living conditions among economically disadvantaged groups largely ushered the severity of such problems into the nation's collective consciousness. In 1973, Marion Wright Edelman, a Washington Research Project co-organizer, established the CDF as an independent entity dedicated to improving the lived experiences of under-served children, families, and communities. The institutional mission of the CDF is to eradicate racial, social, and economic disparities via a populist support base focused on children's welfare and needs. Although the alliance aims to enhance the well-being of all children, leaders devote special consideration to efforts that benefit the most vulnerable. Focusing on children and youth, organizational supporters and staff believe, enables the CDF to facilitate broad-based social change, as raising standards among families and communities is a natural consequence of assisting children. Since its inception, the CDF has functioned as a private, non-profit group financed by individual donors, foundations, and corporations. Into the 21st century, Marian Wright Edelman continued to serve as the group's president.

CDF efforts are grounded in education, advocacy, research, and community service initiatives related to public education, national policy, health care, poverty, and juvenile justice, among other areas. Because the CDF staff is composed of educators who hold expertise in different fields (e.g., health care providers, community organizers, and individuals with legal training), the association is able to target a multiplicity of needs from alternative angles and using wide-ranging approaches. Examples include media campaigns, service learning options, and scholarly investigations. The result is an organizational effort that attends to complex, inter-related forces that undergird the challenges at hand. Since 1974, the association has followed a tiered implementation approach by operating local, state, regional, and national branches. The governance structure enables the group to put broad-based plans into practice by targeting a substantial bloc of intended recipients in lieu of individual cases that, while important, are limited in scope and reach. The CDF Board of Directors provides additional oversight and guidance.

Both national and local drives have advanced equity-based goals by reshaping civic institutions, such as schools, to be more conducive to meeting the needs of diverse students than in previous years. The 1973 CDF report *Children out of School,* for instance, shed light on the problem of minors who were not being formally educated, a significant number of whom were youths with disabilities. Subsequent efforts to redress the problem contributed to the passage of the Education of All Handicapped Children Act, now the Individuals With Disabilities Education Act, a landmark piece of legislation designed to protect the rights of individuals with disabilities. In recent years, CDF leaders have pressed for full enactment of the Dodd-Miller Act to Leave No Child Behind, a comprehensive bill reflective of CDF goals for schooling, poverty, health care, hunger, literacy, housing, violence prevention, and quality of life concerns.

The CDF Education and Youth Development Division guides overarching efforts to correct inequities that arise as a function of discrepancies in funding and opportunity structure, especially for students who are poor, come from communities of color, have disabilities, and do not speak English as a first language. Although much of the work completed by the division is research based, the organization sponsors programs such as the Haley Farm and CDF Freedom Schools, which create spaces to transform articulated goals into living ideas. For example, the Haley Farm was acquired, in part, as a training location for CDF workers. Freedom Schools supply structured literacy opportunities. The CDF staff has worked to cultivate a cadre of young people committed to the ideals that foreground the organization's existence. Current projects include the Ella Baker Child Policy Training Institute and the Student Leadership Network for Children. In a closely related vein, health care and legal thrusts are grounded in the intersection of research, education, and advocacy. CDF is well known for efforts to lower teen pregnancy rates, decrease gun violence, and close health care disparities, and correlational indicators generally suggest a positive CDF influence on policy and practice. For example, the 1974 Juvenile Justice and Delinquency Prevention Act was reauthorized in 1998 and included key provisions regarding the protection of minority children; the act's 2002 reauthorization added additional measures stemming from the confinement of minors with adults.

Despite general esteem for the CDF as a vanguard for child advocacy, the organization receives regular criticism from observers who fault the group as a proponent for government expansion. The critique is supported by traditionally conservative arguments that increasing personal responsibility and promoting local governance are the most worthwhile strategies for solving social problems. In recent years, elements of the CDF's traditionally liberal support base have weakened as some analysts have questioned the effectiveness of emotionally based appeals for the common good. Abandoning effective strategies, critics contend, would push the organization away from methods and arguments that many view as impractical and dated, particularly given shifts in coalitions of power and economic vicissitudes as well as unintended and competing interests of a capitalistic society.

—*Carla R. Monroe*

See also Child Advocacy; Edelman, Marion Wright

Further Readings

Children's Defense Fund. (1994). *Wasting America's future: The Children's Defense Fund report on the costs of child poverty.* Boston: Beacon Press.

Edmunds, M. (2000). *All over the map: A progress report on the state of Children's Health Insurance Program (CHIP).* Washington, DC: Children's Defense Fund, Health Division.

Johnson, C. M. (1991). *Child poverty in America.* Washington, DC: Children's Defense Fund.

Mihaly, L. K. (1991). *Homeless families: Failed policies and young victims.* Washington, DC: Children's Defense Fund.

CHISHOLM, SHIRLEY
(1924–2005)

An educator and politician, Shirley Anita St. Hill Chisholm was an outspoken advocate for social and economic change. A woman who billed herself for her integrity, she was a skilled orator and writer, the first black woman elected to Congress, and the first black woman to campaign for the presidency. Opposed to relying exclusively on the votes of the black community or women, Chisholm represented herself as the candidate of the people, attempting to reshape society as more just and free.

Chisholm was a well-known orator and writer. Scholar-activists analyzing black womanhood, including Patricia Hill Collins, cite Shirley Chisholm as an early leader in addressing the multiple forms of oppression that shape black women's experiences. Early in her career, Chisholm wrote and spoke openly about issues still current today: racism and segregation, sexism, urban poverty, and the power dynamics of politics. She was a critic of the House of Representatives' seniority-based committee system and spoke on behalf of other people of color, including Native Americans and Latino/a migrants. Her legacy includes energetic speeches supporting controversial positions, including opposition to the Vietnam War and support for the Equal Rights Amendment. It also includes two books, *Unbought and Unbossed*, an autobiography, and *The Good Fight,* chronicling her bid for the 1972 Democratic presidential nomination.

Chisholm financed her early campaigns with personal savings and small grassroots donations. Since she became the first black woman in Congress in 1968, there have been 13 others, one of whom, Barbara Lee, worked on Chisholm's presidential campaign. During her seven terms in Congress, Chisholm sustained constituent support despite her unwillingness to endure political conventions. She was a founding member of the Congressional Black Caucus, although she routinely voted based on her conscience rather than her colleagues. She was known, but not apologetic, for not playing by the rules; this often left her at odds with political colleagues.

After leaving Congress, Chisholm was named to the Purington Chair at Mount Holyoke College in South Hadley, Massachusetts, where she taught for 4 years. In 1984, she helped found the National Political Congress of Black Women. Because of ill health, she was unable to accept President Clinton's 1993 nomination as Ambassador to Jamaica. Chisholm died January 1, 2005.

—*Eden H. Segal*

See also Civil Rights Movement; Equal Rights Amendment

Further Readings

Amer, M. L. (2005, September 22). *Women in the United States Congress: 1917–2005*. Washington, DC: Library of Congress, Congressional Research Service. Retrieved December 25, 2005, from http://www.senate.gov/reference/resources/pdf/RL30261.pdf

Chisholm, S. (1970). *Unbought and unbossed.* Boston: Houghton Mifflin.

Chisholm, S. (1973). *The good fight.* New York: Harper & Row.

Hill Collins, P. (1998). *Fighting words.* Minneapolis: University of Minnesota Press.

Lynch, S. (Director). (2004). *Chisholm '72: Unbought and unbossed* [Motion picture]. United States: REALside Productions.

CHOMSKY, NOAM
(1928–)

Through his theory of generative grammar, in which he insists that human beings are born with an innate capacity for language, Noam Chomsky has revolutionized the field of linguistics and effectively shaped contemporary philosophy, psychology, and the cognitive sciences. Yet, this influential intellectual—a faculty member at the Massachusetts Institute of Technology since 1955; the most cited living scholar according to the Arts and Humanities Citation Index, between 1980 and 1992; and the eighth most cited thinker of all times—is also a keen political activist, an outspoken critic of Western capitalism and U.S. foreign policy, and a mass media and propaganda analyst.

Born Avram Noam Chomsky in Philadelphia, Pennsylvania, on December 7, 1928, he is the eldest of two sons of a Russian Jewish father and a Philadelphia-born Jewish mother. Both parents taught Hebrew at the religious school of the Mikveh Israel congregation. Dr. William Chomsky, a scholar in medieval Hebrew, later joined the faculty of Gratz College, a teachers training college, and Dropsie College, a graduate school of Jewish and Semitic studies. Elsie Chomsky brought to the family a keen interest in politics and a passion for issues of social justice. All of the Chomskys, including young Noam and David, were actively involved in the retrieval of Jewish culture, the Hebrew language, and Zionism, even though Chomsky's particular form of Zionism, which stresses Arab-Jewish cooperation in a socialist framework through the organization of kibbutzim, is today considered by many to be anti-Zionist. In 1955, Chomsky and his wife Carol Schatz (with whom he grew up as a child and shared the dream of moving to Israel to settle in a kibbutz) lived in a libertarian community for about 6 weeks, where people shared in manual and intellectual labor.

Chomsky was particularly drawn to politics from a very young age. When he was 10 years old, he contributed an article for his school newspaper on the fall of Barcelona during the Spanish Civil War—an event that shaped the rest of his life. Writing of the article reflected the nourishing environment of Chomsky's elementary school, Oak Lane Country Day School, which was an experimental institution inspired by John Dewey, who believed that education must provide an environment for creative and self-fulfilling exploration. Chomsky's later critique that educational institutions indoctrinate their students to conform to the values of the market culture is based on this formative experience and the shift he noticed between the intellectual freedom of his Dewey elementary school and the restraining competitiveness of traditional high school. He believed the traditional educational system in a capitalist culture teaches competition, regimentation, and prestige, while hindering creativity and cooperation.

Chomsky's interest in the Spanish Civil War also awakened his interest in theories of libertarianism, which he embraced with remarkable consistency for the rest of his life. His political option for anarcho-syndicalism, or libertarian socialism, was sharpened in his youth through the works of thinkers like George Orwell and Rudolph Rocker. This anarchism is not anarchy; that is, it is not hedonistic in character but allows people to freely choose to be active and creative participants, according to their own talents, in a communal culture for the flourishing of all. It is a political model grounded in a philosophy of rationalism, where the human person is understood to be a rational being enabled by innate biological structures that promote flexibility, creativity, and mutual concern. Just as human beings have a predisposition for language—Chomsky's revolutionary claim in linguistics—they also have a predisposition for Cartesian common sense that freely chooses mutual collaboration. Accordingly, in Chomsky's view, political discourse falls into this realm of common sense, which all human beings, including children, can understand, actively participate in, and contribute to. Thus, the organization of a society should be free of any hierarchy: political, economic, or otherwise.

If this understanding of humankind sounds too optimistic, it is because people's development is often distorted, and their natural predispositions are trampled upon. A case in point, according to Chomsky, is the private economic power that controls contemporary democratic societies. While governments are elected to represent the people's interests, capital is the real source of power, and it remains in the hands of only a few individuals. Consequently, the economy is not controlled democratically, because private corporations who have access to capital control governments. Yet, citizens unquestioningly submit to this hegemony, because the economic elite, surrounded and protected by servile governments and the intellectual elite, maintains the status quo through thought control. Propaganda machines manufacture consent through the mass media by creating smokescreens to distract the public; entertainment industries deflect attention from real political concerns, while the mainstream media, like the *New York Times,* define and limit the spectrum of public discourse.

In turn, the educational system restricts human creativity and freedom and transforms future citizens—particularly the most educated—into docile servants of the state who are indoctrinated to conform to established societal and capitalist expectations. Intellectuals are thus elevated to the paradoxical status of being not only elite guardians of culture but also blind servants. Together with the media, intellectuals define the public imagination, narrate its stories, and shape its history, all to protect the interest of the economic elite. This biased worldview constricts the people's freedom and disables them from protecting their interests and reclaiming communal wealth. A clear example of intellectual and media bias, for instance, is the public depiction of anarchism itself. Because anarchism challenges all forms of hierarchy, and accordingly is a threat to the interests of the powerful, the guardians of capitalist-democratic culture often present it as anti-establishment and opposed to the common good. Chomsky's answer to this intellectual and media bias, inspired by Bertrand Russell's example as a philosopher and political activist, is to call for the responsibility of intellectuals, who, because of the privilege of their greater leisure time, should direct their energies to exposing the truthful facts masked by political propaganda, in order to open up authentic public discourse and encourage civic responsibility.

These themes of economic privilege, thought control, and the responsibility of the intellectual ground much of Chomsky's activist agenda, in particular his critique of U.S. foreign policy. Chomsky's political activism has developed simultaneously with his outstanding academic achievements. In his undergraduate studies, Chomsky chose as a mentor the linguist Zellig Harris, because he was inspired by Harris's politics and the open debates that occurred in his class. Growing up in a household of Hebrew scholars, Chomsky was immediately intrigued by the field of linguistics. Chomsky was already producing original ideas in his undergraduate dissertation—a trend that continued throughout his graduate studies and later research. By the 1960s, however, when he was already a full professor at MIT and an academic of high stature, Chomsky's energy and commitment were just as dedicated to activism, particularly the anti–Vietnam War movement. In Chomsky's judgment, the Vietnam War was a clear example of how the United States did not fight against communism but rather defended its capitalist agenda by successfully limiting the economic development of a world region.

Chomsky's critique of U.S. foreign policy has gathered even more momentum since the events of September 11, 2001, and the United States' "war on terrorism." Following the definition used by a U.S. army manual, where terrorism is calculated violence or the threat of violence to inculcate fear, through which governments, societies, and even one's own people can be controlled, Chomsky argues that the terrorist actions that take place in the world are often led by the world's major economic powers. Chomsky's most recent and controversial claim is that "terrorism" has become the latest catchphrase for thought control in democratic societies, especially in the United States.

—*Nadia Delicata*

See also Activism, Social and Political; Alternative Press; Anarchism; Anarcho-Syndicalism; Dissent; East Timor, Resistance to Indonesian Occupation; Zionism

Further Readings

Barsky, R. B. (1997). *Noam Chomsky: A life of dissent.* Cambridge: MIT Press.

Chomsky, N. (n.d.). Noam Chomsky Archive. *ZNet.* Retrieved April 20, 2006, from http://www.zmag .org/Chomsky

Chomsky, N. (n.d.). The Noam Chomsky website. Retrieved April 30, 2006, from http://www.chomsky.info

McGilvray, J. (Ed.). (2005). *The Cambridge companion to Chomsky.* Cambridge, UK: Cambridge University Press.

Mitchell, P. R., & Schoeffel, J. (Eds.). (2002). *Understanding power: The indispensable Chomsky.* New York: New Press.

CHRISTIAN BASE COMMUNITIES

Christian base communities are small, grassroots neighborhood groups dedicated to reading the Bible and encouraging participants to mobilize in order to achieve social justice. The Second Vatican Council provided much of the theological and political basis for these groups, and they emerged throughout the Catholic world but became especially significant in the Latin American countryside. They have become closely identified with liberation theology and have participated directly in movements for social justice.

Christian base communities (often known by their Spanish name, *comunidades eclesiales de base*, or CEBs) were a logical extension of the new theology and politics emerging out of Vatican II (1962–1965). Vatican II had a multilayered impact on Catholic theology and practice, but at the most general level, it represented an attempt to increase Catholicism's accessibility and to emphasize its commitment to social justice. Vatican II encouraged a rereading of the Bible, and it encouraged a far greater variety of people to put themselves in a position to read, teach, and lead, based on this rereading. The groups engaged in this rereading took many forms (and by no means supplanted the church and the chapel), but probably the most common was the Christian base community. Christian base communities immediately came to provide a forum in which even the poorest and least educated could take part. Their structure encourages all participants to actively engage Church representatives and to emphasize the progressive and even revolutionary teachings of Christianity. The Church representatives who have led these groups come from all sectors of society.

Christian base communities proliferated rapidly in the late 1960s and 1970s, for several reasons. First, they established a presence in many remote areas, in which they came to represent a fundamental religious and political reality to their participants. For a poor, marginalized peasant to take part in a base community was often a transformative act. Second, the conditions prevailing in and around Christian base communities gave credence to the reformist and revolutionary ideas expressed in liberation theology. The more radical words of Christ applied immediately and directly to these conditions. For both of these reasons, Christian base communities became most numerous and politically significant in Latin America, a region marked by dictatorship and inequality in the 1970s. The cultural dominance of Catholicism in Latin America also was crucial: Catholicism was so deeply entrenched that some of the radicalism of the region was bound to be channeled through the Church.

If CEBs had an original "home," it was Brazil, where Paulo Freire pioneered the practice of "conscientization"

(which, in its Spanish and Portuguese forms, means a mixture of education and politicization). But they spread quickly throughout the region. There was, in fact, a close correspondence between the CEB presence and the amount of poverty and oppression in a particular country. In this context, then, CEBs became a fixture in the Latin American rural areas during the 1970s, and many of the most prominent advocates for social justice and revolution got their starts in these organizations. Variations of Christian base communities have emerged throughout the world and are by no means limited to Catholicism. But they owe a political and theological debt to the rethinking of Christianity that took place during Vatican II.

—Frederick Shepherd

See also Liberation Theology

Further Readings

Flannery, A. (Ed.). (1996). *Vatican Council II: Constitutions, decrees, declarations*. New York: Costello.

Freire, P. (2000). *Pedagogy of the oppressed.* New York: Continuum.

Peterson, A. L., Vásquez, M. A., & Williams, P. J. (Eds.). (2001). *Christianity, social change, and globalization in the Americas*. Piscataway, NJ: Rutgers University Press.

CHRISTIAN RIGHT

The U.S. Christian Right is an umbrella term describing a political and social movement comprised largely of Protestant evangelicals and fundamentalists, who are deeply conservative in their political orientation. Some of the most important social and political issues for the Christian Right are their strong opposition to abortion, sexuality education, and unrestricted access to birth control; women's rights; racial desegregation and the African American civil rights movement; the lesbian, gay, bisexual, and transgendered civil rights movement; evolution in public school science curricula; and any limits on religious expression and practice in public schools. By contrast, Christian Right adherents have been very vocal in their support for unrestricted public monies for private religious schools (both direct aid, such as federal and state grants, and indirect aid, such as tax deductions), unrestricted home schooling, unrestricted religious proselytization through public schools, criminalization of abortion and the doctors who perform the medical procedure, and the maintenance of criminal statutes that bar all forms of non-procreative sexual expression.

While the roots of the U.S. Christian Right can be found in the early decades of the 20th century, it gathered as a political force largely in reaction to several social and political liberation movements, including the African American civil rights movement, the women's movement, and the gay and lesbian rights movement. However, perhaps the most important motivational trigger was the U.S. Supreme Court's 1973 landmark decision in *Roe v. Wade,* which legalized abortion across the United States. Both conservative Protestants and Catholics were horrified by the decision, viewing it as akin to legalized infanticide and emblematic of a permissive sexual cultural ethos that had pervaded the United States. Although each side had long viewed each other with more than a measure of antipathy and loathing, these diverse (and divergent) religious adherents began to subsume generations of religious animosity to work together toward the common goal of overturning *Roe.*

Two major intellectual developments, Christian Recontructionism and dominion theology, spurred the entry of conservative Protestants into the Christian Right, particularly Christian fundamentalists, regardless of individual denomination. Prior to the 1970s, many fundamentalists had shunned involvement with politics out of religious conviction. Adherents were to stay focused on the return of Christ and not involve themselves with worldly affairs, particularly those of government, which was seen as both morally corrupt and corrupting. Consequently, not only were fundamentalists largely apolitical, but many did not vote—out of religious conviction.

However, several activists urged that this apolitical stance be reconsidered. Claiming that Christ would not return until "His kingdom" was established on this earth, Christian Right activists grounded in Christian Reconstructionism stated that the United

States had been founded on "Godly principles" and needed to reflect these. Reconstructionists advocated that activists work to establish an Old Testament–style theocracy, where only avowed Christians (i.e., Reconstructionists) would lead or even have basic citizenship rights. Only when the United States was truly a "Christian Nation" would Jesus Christ return to reign for 1,000 years.

A central political focus for Reconstructionism is its utter hostility toward legalized abortion, which they equate with murder. Reconstructionists have provided both the political and the legal firepower in attacking the right to abortion in the United States. A few Reconstructionists have gone farther, targeting women's clinics with aggressive picketing. And others—whether actual Reconstructionists or not, but inspired by Reconstructionist writings—have targeted for assassination doctors and medical staff who provide abortions. Given their radicalism and appetite for violence (both physical and rhetorical), Reconstructionists tend to operate beneath the political surface.

Dominion theology is a variant of Reconstructionism, less harsh in the policy pronouncements. Dominionists claim the United States has been a Christian nation (in law as well as culture) since its inception. Consequently, they strive to reshape existing political structures of government to adhere to what they believe already exists. Unlike Reconstructionists, Dominionists became part of the mainstream of the Republican Party during the late 1970s, when the larger Christian Right emerged. Both Reconstructionism and Dominionism have played important intellectual roles in justifying the Christian Right's embrace of political action for Christian fundamentalists, who had previously been studiously apolitical.

The Christian Right rose to national political prominence during the presidency of Jimmy Carter. Carter, who as a presidential candidate in 1976 repeatedly trumpeted his evangelical religious roots, ran afoul of Protestant conservatives when he made policy decisions that differed from their political inclinations. By 1979, conservative Protestants, led by Rev. Jerry Falwell, a little-known (at that time) Baptist televangelist, formed the Moral Majority. In organizing the Moral Majority, Falwell received the assistance of other

New Right activists, including Paul Weyrich, Richard Viguerie, Ed McAteer, and Robert Billings. They incorporated the organization as a charitable organization, which meant it was exempt from federal taxes.

By the 1980 presidential campaign, the Moral Majority had grown to be a force within Republican Party politics. In fact, Falwell nearly obliterated his organization's tax-exempt status by encouraging the faithful to vote for the Reagan of their choice, an attempt to skirt federal bans on charities endorsing political candidates. The party's nominee, Ronald Reagan, also reached out to members of the Christian Right, making numerous campaign statements about the evils of the *Roe v. Wade* decision and activist federal judges. Reagan promised to appoint judges whose values would be congruent with those of religious Americans.

Once elected, Reagan faced significant constraints in pursuing the political goals of the Christian Right. While the Republican Party swept to victory during the Senate elections of 1980, the House of Representatives remained firmly in control of the Democratic Party. This political arrangement made any sweeping change in social policy nearly impossible. Additionally, Reagan focused most of his political energies on his two main policy priorities: a massive defense buildup and massive tax cuts, particularly for upper-income Americans. Such expansive spending, combined with two major reductions in budget revenue (the tax cuts and a major recession), limited Reagan's options in pursuing any additional programmatic innovation. Instead, Reagan made repeated rhetorical nods to reestablishing vocal prayer in public schools, and overturning *Roe v. Wade*, but he invested very little capital in realizing these goals of the Christian Right. By the close of Reagan's presidency, some members of the Christian Right were vocal in their disappointment with Reagan, particularly because *Roe v. Wade* still stood. Although Reagan had shifted the federal judiciary considerably to the right of where it had been prior to his presidency (and turned a blind eye to an explosion of abortion clinic violence), activists' hopes of a speedy repeal of *Roe v. Wade* were dashed.

The movement itself was also experiencing internal shifts and conflicts. Falwell, who had been a lightning rod for criticism both from his political critics and

like-minded Christian Right activists, was displaced as the nominal head of the Christian Right by fellow televangelist Marion (Pat) Robertson. Robertson, who ran against then vice president George H. W. Bush in the Republican Party primaries, generally faired poorly against Bush, particularly in the South. Nevertheless, Robertson gained vital national political exposure and experience at a time when Falwell was ensnared in the lurid James Baker (another televangelist) scandal. Consequently, the politically weakened Falwell was displaced by Robertson as the perceived leader of the Christian Right. The Moral Majority, which had been launched with great fanfare in 1979, quietly disbanded in 1989.

Robertson moved from political candidate to political kingmaker, by establishing his political organization, the Christian Coalition, in 1989. He hired Ralph Reed, a longtime Republican and right-wing activist, to serve as the Christian Coalition's director. Although in his late 20s at the time of his hiring, Reed was well versed in grassroots organizing and political strategizing, serving in the College Republicans and Students for America.

By the mid-1990s, the Christian Coalition was a major component of the national Republican Party. Perhaps the Christian Coalition reached its zenith immediately after the 1994 congressional elections, when the Republican Party was swept to electoral victory during the mid-term elections. Yet, throughout most of the 1990s, the White House was retained by Bill Clinton, a Democrat. Consequently, much of Christian Right's agenda remained stalled.

Christian Right activists were heartened when George W. Bush entered the White House after the disputed 2000 presidential election. Bush had run on a platform espousing conservative Christian policy preferences, and he was well known in some Reconstructionist and Dominionist circles. Initially, Bush made numerous overtures to the Christian Right, including establishing the Office of Faith-Based Initiatives, which, despite Constitutional bans on involving the state with the work of the church, sought to fund religious organizations doing charity work. Furthermore, in 2001, Bush tightly curtailed federal funding exploring possible uses of embryonic stem cells. Bush also appointed numerous long-serving Christian Right activists to positions scattered throughout the executive branch, particularly in areas of domestic policy.

Yet, like Reagan's support, much of Bush's support has been far more symbolic than substantive, particularly if the political choices involved selecting policies that would aid major corporations versus aiding the Christian Right. Bush's policy options have also been constrained due to the ballooning federal budget deficit coupled with the ill-defined and extravagantly funded military missions in Afghanistan and Iraq. Consequently, some Christian Right activists have grown increasingly disenchanted with both the Bush administration in particular and the political sphere in general.

As a political movement, the Christian Right has slowed in its momentum, as many of the long-standing leaders are approaching their 70s or 80s (Pat Robertson, Billy Graham, Jerry Falwell) or have moved on to become major players within the larger Republican Party (Ralph Reed). Furthermore, the movement suffered a nasty national rebuke in 2005 regarding their involvement with the Terry Schiavo case. Schiavo was in a persistent vegetative state, and her husband eventually won the legal right to remove her from life support. Her parents vigorously disagreed with her husband and had sued him for custody of Ms. Schiavo. Various Christian Right organizations and like-minded politicians intervened on the side of the parents, who saw it as a major "right to life" case. Most Americans, however, viewed the case through the lens of family privacy and were appalled by the circus-like atmosphere surrounding the litigation as well as Ms. Schiavo's last days in a Florida nursing home.

In the aftermath of the Schiavo political spectacle, the Christian Right continues to be a central component of one of the two major U.S. political parties, but it is clear the movement has entered a period of transition. Since the 1970s, the United States itself has experienced a shift in religious expression, with Americans increasingly shopping for various faiths as they would any other consumer product. As the U.S. population becomes increasingly spiritual instead of religious, the Christian Right may have to seek ways to reinvent

itself to maintain both its saliency and political currency. Yet, this task will be difficult given the influence of Christian Reconstructionism and Dominionism on the movement and movement adherents.

—*Catherine A. Lugg*

See also Religious Activism

Further Readings

Detwiler, F. (1999). *Standing on the premises of God: The Christian Right's fight to redefine America's public schools*. New York: New York University Press.

Diamond, S. (1995). *Roads to Dominion: Right-wing movements and political power in the United States*. New York: Guilford Press.

Diamond, S. (1998). *Not by politics alone: The enduring influence of the Christian Right*. New York: Guilford Press.

Kramnick, I., & Moore, R. L. (1996). *The Godless Constitution: The case against religious correctness*. New York: W. W. Norton.

Lugg, C. A. (1996). *For God and country: Conservatism and American school policy*. New York: Peter Lang.

Martin, W. A. (1996). *With God on our side*. New York: Broadway Books.

Roof, W. C. (2001). *Spiritual marketplace: Babyboomers and the remaking of American religion*. Princeton, NJ: Princeton University Press.

CIA REPRESSION OF SOCIAL MOVEMENTS

Following the experience of the surprise attack on Pearl Harbor, the U.S. Congress established the Central Intelligence Agency (CIA) in 1947. The CIA's role, as originally envisioned, was information gathering, intelligence analysis, and forecasting. The Cold War and the falling of the Iron Curtain over Eastern Europe following World War II soon provided the justification for the development and use of new capabilities by the CIA—covert action, paramilitary operations, and espionage/counterespionage operations—and provided the CIA with a larger, more encompassing mission of protecting the national security of the United

States. Two major functions became the backbone divisions of the CIA: the Directorate of Intelligence (intelligence analysis) and the Directorate of Plans, later and currently called the Directorate of Operations (recruiting of foreign assets or agents, covert actions such as propaganda and political intrigue, and small- to large-scale paramilitary operations). In very short order, the Directorate of Operations eclipsed the Directorate of Intelligence and became the more pre-eminent and prestigious directorate.

Following the creation of the CIA, U.S. administrations were, to varying degrees, enamored of the CIA's covert action and paramilitary capabilities to further American government policy goals with secrecy or at least deniability. In the years after World War II, the currents of nationalism and anti-colonialism surged all across the world, especially in the former colonies. The rise of nationalism and anti-imperialism made it more difficult for the United States to justify the raw use of military force to achieve its policy goals.

During President Eisenhower's administration, the CIA worked covertly in the 1950s to overthrow two democratically elected governments (Iraq in 1953 and Guatemala in 1954) and thwart another election where the anticipated outcome was not acceptable to U.S. interests (Vietnam in 1954). President Kennedy inherited an ill-advised plan from Eisenhower for a secret army and attempted an invasion and coup in Cuba in 1961 at the Bay of Pigs. U.S. frustration with Vietnamese President Diem and his decreasing popularity and support caused Kennedy to support a CIA-assisted military coup against Diem on November 1–2, 1963. In 1970, President Nixon directly instructed the CIA to intervene in Chile to remove the democratically elected president, Salvador Allende.

In Iran, Prime Minister Mohammad Mossadegh, a passionate nationalist and democrat, came to power in 1951 and tried to secure greater government control of Iran's oil resources. Mossadegh was determined to renegotiate, expel, or nationalize the Anglo-Iranian oil company (later called British Petroleum), which paid Iran only 16% of what it earned in selling Iranian oil, and use the money generated to develop Iran. In Iran, nationalism meant taking control of the country's oil resources. Democracy meant vesting political power

in the elected parliament and prime minister rather than in the monarch, Mohammed Reza Shah. In the spring of 1951, both houses of the Iranian parliament voted unanimously to nationalize the oil industry. Iran suggested to the British government that a 50/50 earning split, as American oil companies were negotiating in neighboring countries, would be acceptable. The British rejected this offer out of hand.

British oil interests and the British government began to undermine Mossadegh and finally decided that a coup to return the former monarch, Mohammed Reza Shah, to the Peacock Throne was the best course of action. Mossadegh caught wind of the British plot and, on October 16, 1952, ordered the British Embassy closed and all embassy employees to leave Iran. This action crippled the British intelligence services in Iran and effectively put a halt to British covert operations in Iran. British officials then asked the American government for assistance in overthrowing Mossadegh. The British understood that the easiest way to ensure America's help was to characterize Mossadegh and his government as sympathetic to socialism and communism. In a CIA-orchestrated coup in 1953 (Operation TPAJAX), Mossadegh's government was overthrown and replaced by the restoration of the royal monarchy under Mohammad Reza Shah Pahlavi. American investors then acquired a major slice of Iranian oil production. The Shah ruled Iran in an increasingly authoritarian and repressive manner. The role of the United States and its long association with the Shah's secular and repressive rule led to a wave of anti-Americanism and ultimately to the Islamic Revolution in Iran and to the rise to power of the Ayatollah Khomeini.

In Guatemala, Jacobo Arbenz Guzmán was inaugurated as president in March 1951. It was the first peaceful transfer of power in Guatemala through the electoral process. The Agrarian Land Reform Law unanimously passed in June 1952 by the National Assembly authorized the government to seize and redistribute uncultivated land on estates larger than 673 acres, with compensation set at the land's declared tax value. The Guatemalan government planned to take over some 234,000 uncultivated acres owned by a U.S. corporation, the United Fruit Company. With some prodding and public relations work, United Fruit helped convince the U.S. government that the Arbenz government was part of a global pattern of pro-communist activity. The citizens of Guatemala saw President Arbenz not as a communist but as a progressive reformer. With President Eisenhower's strong backing, the CIA plotted Arbenz's overthrow in 1954 (Operation PBSUCCESS) and helped install a right-wing dictatorship.

In the case of Vietnam, the Viet Minh fought the Japanese during World War II with material assistance provided by the United States. Following the defeat of the Japanese, nationalist leader Ho Chi Minh, in a speech given on September 2, 1945, declared Vietnam's independence. He also declared that all men are created equal and have inalienable rights to life, liberty, and the pursuit of happiness. Ho Chi Minh was said to harbor a great admiration for Americans and attempted to gain the support of the U.S. government several times. Instead, the United States bowed to the desires of its wartime allies France and England to reestablish their colonial empires, and Ho Chi Minh's requests for American recognition and assistance fell upon deaf ears.

The French attempted to reestablish their colonial rule in Vietnam. After having suffered great military losses, the French met with the Viet Minh in Geneva and negotiated their withdrawal from Vietnam. The French departed Vietnam in October 1954. Under the Geneva accords, the country was to be temporarily partitioned into two separate governments: North Vietnam under communist control and South Vietnam under the control of France and its former allies. The agreement was that there would be nationwide free elections in 1956, and North and South Vietnam would be unified. Ho Chi Minh's stature as the nationalist that defeated the French practically guaranteed that he would win a fair election.

The Eisenhower administration, afraid of the Vietnamese electing a communist government, decided to intervene covertly to undermine the Geneva accords and make Vietnam's division permanent. Following a régime change template that was successfully used in other countries, the United States merely had to find a suitable and compliant leader to be installed as president of South Vietnam. The United States settled on Ngo Dinh Diem. Although Diem was not well known to U.S. officials, they decided he had suitable credentials: Diem had studied public administration, had served as interior minister, and was a devout Catholic and a dedicated anti-communist. Several months before the French withdrawal, Diem was sworn in as prime minister of the Republic of South Vietnam on July 7, 1954. Notwithstanding CIA propaganda and psychological techniques in support of Diem, it was apparent that Ho Chi Minh would easily win a fair election. Upon this realization, Diem and U.S. Secretary of State Dulles argued for the decision to cancel the nationwide election scheduled for 1956. Without an election, there could be no reunification of the two Vietnams into one country. By the end of 1955, Diem deposed the Emperor Bao Dai in a referendum and became chief of state. As chief of state, Diem expanded his power through constitutional changes. Poor military results coupled with U.S. frustration with Diem and his decreasing popularity and support caused President Kennedy to support a CIA-assisted military coup against Diem, which resulted in the death of Diem and his brother, Nhu Dinh Diem, on November 1, 1963. Knowing about U.S. complicity in the deaths of Diem and his brother, President Johnson may have felt a responsibility to South Vietnam and a reluctance to withdraw. By the time the Vietnamese War ended on April 30, 1975, 58,168 Americans had lost their lives there.

In Chile, avowed socialist Salvador Allende ran for the Chilean presidency in the September 4, 1970, election. Allende won a plurality of the vote with 36.3%. In such cases, the Chilean Congress has traditionally selected the leading candidate within 50 days after the election. Allende was a nationalist and a socialist who vowed to nationalize the American-owned companies that dominated the Chilean economy. Major American companies such as International Telephone and Telegraph, Pepsi-Cola, Chase Manhattan Bank, Kennecott Copper, and Anaconda Copper all had major investments in Chile and by September 14, 1970, had a representative meet with President Nixon to ask for a last-ditch effort to prevent Allende from taking office. By the next day, Nixon held a 13-minute meeting with Attorney General John Mitchell, CIA Director Richard Helms, and National Security

Advisor Henry Kissinger. In the meeting, Nixon directly instructed the CIA to intervene in Chile to prevent the installation of the democratically elected president, Salvador Allende. Although no minutes or tapes of the meeting have ever surfaced, notes taken by CIA Director Richard Helms stated the following:

l in 10 chance perhaps, but save Chile!

Worth spending

Not concerned risks involved

No involvement of embassy

$10,000,000 available, more if necessary

Full-time job—best men we have

Game plan

Make the economy scream

48 hours for plan of action

The CIA implemented a two-track plan: Track 1, a propaganda and disinformation campaign warning of dire consequences if Allende becomes president; and Track 2, the active encouragement of a military coup. A part of the Track 2 option was Operation FUBELT, a severe and multipronged disruption of the Chilean economy. The CIA's efforts failed, and on November 4, 1970, Allende was inaugurated president of Chile. However, Nixon and American commercial interests continued to be obsessed with bringing down President Allende. The CIA and American companies' continued destabilization campaign brought the economy to a halt, with labor strikes and street disturbances commonplace. With CIA encouragement and assistance, the military overthrew the Allende government on September 11, 1973. Allende was killed, and a right-wing military junta was installed.

PBSUCCESS in Guatemala taught Latin American reformers that the United States would not allow democratic nationalism, especially in Latin America. Seeing the United States consistently favor repressive right-wing dictatorships over progressive democracies caused many reformers to lose faith in the democratic process as a means of change. This pushed reformers to begin embracing more radical alternatives. Fidel Castro's Cuba became the model. Once in power, they should not work through existing democratic institutions but rather destroy existing institutions—such as the legislative bodies, the judiciary, the army, and the

landowning elite—and expel or nationalize foreign corporations.

—Glen Yahola Wilson

See also Allende, Salvador; Arbenz, Jacobo; Castro, Fidel; Ho Chi Minh; Iranian Revolution (1963–1979); Johnson, Lyndon B.; Letelier, Orlando

Further Readings

Anonymous. (2004). *Imperial hubris: Why the West is losing the war on terror*. Washington, DC: Brassey's.

Conboy, K., & Morrison, J. (1999). *Feet to the fire: CIA covert operations in Indonesia, 1957–1958*. Annapolis, MD: Naval Institute Press.

Cullather, N. (1999). *Secret history: The CIA's classified account of its operations in Guatemala 1952–1954*. Palo Alto, CA: Stanford University Press.

Escalante, F. (2004). *CIA covert operations 1959–62: The Cuba project*. Melbourne, Australia: Ocean Press.

Jarecki, E. (Director). (2006). *Why we fight* [DVD]. United States: Sony Pictures Classics.

Karnow, S. (1983). *Vietnam: A history*. New York: Viking.

Kessler, R. (2003). *The CIA at war: Inside the secret campaign against terror*. New York: St. Martin's Press.

Kinzer, S. (2006). *Overthrow: America's system of regime change from Hawaii to Iraq*. New York: Times Books.

Citizen School, The

The Citizen School (*Escola Cidadã*) is an educational framework developed in Brazil in the late 1980s. It was created in opposition to dominant neoliberal approaches to education and in response to the failures of the public system to provide quality schooling for all. Its aims are to democratize schooling, making education policy and curriculum more responsive to the needs of the community, and to empower students for effective political participation. The best-known instance of the initiative is in the city of Porto Alegre, although there are similar experiences in other regions of the country.

The distinctive approach of the Citizen School has its roots in the work of the Brazilian educationist Paulo Freire. He is influential through both his theoretical writings and his experience as secretary of education of the city of São Paulo from 1989 to 1991, when he brought about a number of policy changes aimed at ensuring greater community participation in the running of schools. Inspiration for the initiative also came from the Citizenship Schools established by Myles Horton in the United States. The term *Citizen School* was first used in Brazil in a 1989 journal article by Genuíno Bordignon. The notion was subsequently developed by a number of theorists associated with the Paulo Freire Institute in São Paulo, including Moacir Gadotti, José Eustáquio Romão, and Paulo Roberto Padilha. The institute has published a number of works on the subject, dealing with issues such as participatory planning, evaluation, and school councils.

The theoretical framework of the Citizen School involves a new form of school autonomy, in which funding is provided by the State and entry is free-of-charge to the students, but in which institutions determine their own expenditure and curriculum. Decision making is not the sole responsibility of the teaching or administrative staff, but extends, as far as is possible, to the whole of the school community, including parents and the students themselves. School, thereby, begins to serve the interests of the community rather than those of central government or the business community. The curriculum is constructed using as its base the historical and cultural specificity of the community, about which participatory research is continually conducted. The overarching orientations of the school are defined in what is called a politico-pedagogical plan. Evaluation too must be carried out by the school community and not be imposed by external evaluators.

Community participation in the running of the school is considered important not only in terms of more efficient use of resources but also as an educational experience for those involved, leading to democratic empowerment for marginalized populations. The process is also seen to educate the State, increasing its awareness of, and ability to respond to, the needs of the people. All of this is intended to create a new citizenship, based on radical democracy in the "non-State" public sphere.

The framework of the Citizen School is constructed in opposition to neoliberal ideas of the commodification of knowledge and of decentralization of financial rather than administrative responsibility, to a large extent concretized in the policy recommendations of the World Bank and International Monetary Fund. The term *citizen*, liable to multiple and sometimes contradictory interpretations, in this case is used in opposition to the ideas of client and consumer. At the same time, the Citizen School opposes centralized bureaucratic socialism and aims to allow communities to determine their own political priorities.

These theoretical ideas might not have made the transition to implementation in policy had it not been for the propitious political climate in Brazil. The end of the military dictatorship in 1985, and the period leading to its demise, had seen an unprecedented popular mobilization and the creation of a number of popular organizations and trade unions. An important event in this process of democratization was the foundation of the Workers' Party (*Partido dos Trabalhadores* [PT]) in 1980, whose later successes in municipal elections would facilitate significant changes in education policy at this level.

The Popular Administration, a coalition of left-wing parties headed by the PT, came to power in Porto Alegre in 1989. The city, with approximately 1.5 million inhabitants, is the capital of Brazil's southernmost state, Rio Grande do Sul. The coalition was subsequently reelected three times; in its 16 years in power, it attracted international attention due to its social policy and its hosting of the World Social Forum. One influential policy innovation was the participatory budget (*orçamento participativo*), through which local communities were able to vote on government spending priorities in their area.

From the start of the administration, there were efforts to expand the municipal school system, with new schools being built in the areas least served by the existing network (predominantly run by the state government). The number of enrolled students more than doubled between 1989 and 1999. Significant improvements were also brought about in teachers' conditions and pay. The new municipal schools were mainly in the *favela* (shantytown) areas, many of them won by the communities through the participatory budget, and therefore faced significant social and economic challenges. The Citizen School framework itself was only implemented in 1993, on the first reelection of the coalition. Efforts would now be made not only to improve access but also to bring a radical change in the culture of schooling itself.

The first step was to create the Constituent Congress of Education (*Constituinte Escolar*), a citywide mobilization of communities to establish the priorities and organizing principles of policy. From this process emerged three axes: democratization of access to schooling, democratization of management, and democratization of access to knowledge. At the start of the administration, the municipality suffered from the high rates of repetition and dropout characteristic of all parts of Brazil, through which students from the poorest segments of society were routinely excluded from formal education. In response, a new grade structure—known as cycles (*ciclos de formação*)—was created, through which students would be promoted automatically, progressing through three periods of 3 years: childhood, pre-adolescence, and adolescence. Extra support was provided for those who were progressing more slowly than their peers. As a result of this and other policies, the dropout rate fell from 9% in 1989 to 0.97% in 1998.

Democratization of management involved two important mechanisms. First was the creation of school councils to oversee expenditure and curriculum, two areas that had previously been controlled centrally. These councils had 50% representation of teachers and administrative staff and 50% representation of parents and students. Reversing previous policies of centralized budgeting, the municipal secretariat of education devolved financial decisions to the school councils, making the funds available every 3 months. The second aspect was the election of headteachers by the community. The introduction of these elections, in place of indication from central government, was seen to have brought a greater commitment and responsiveness to the community.

Lastly, the Citizen School framework involved attempts to democratize knowledge in municipal schools. It challenged the distinction between core (academic) and periphery (popular) knowledge using action research in the community to establish key themes on which interdisciplinary work in the schools would be based. Attempts were also made to tackle issues such as race, valuing the African origins of many of the students and developing new forms of African Brazilian culture.

An indication of increases of community ownership of schools is the fact that vandalism rates, still high in state-run schools, dropped to negligible levels in municipal schools during this period. While commentators generally point to the successes of the project, some problematic areas have also been noted. One of these is the failure of the initiative to fully address the factors of gender and race (in spite of initiatives focusing on African Brazilian culture), subordinating them to the factor of class and not attending to their distinctness as forms of oppression. Another problem stems from the potential overload of participation, with working people unable to devote so much of their time to school debates and planning. The role of teachers was also problematic, with only partial success being achieved in incorporating their existing knowledge and practices into the new framework and opposition generally dismissed as conservatism. Lastly, the political nature of the project was potentially its own downfall; being closely identified with the PT and the Popular Administration, the project was unlikely to survive without them. Since the voting out of the Popular Administration in 2002, a number of elements of the Citizen School have been maintained—such as the cycles and the school councils—but the new government has not kept the name Citizen School and there are signs that the radical participatory nature of the initiative is being gradually diluted.

Aside from Porto Alegre, a number of other local governments in Brazil have adopted the Citizen School framework, although not always using the same name. Among these is the Plural School (*Escola Plural*) of the municipal government of Belo Horizonte. The word *plural* here refers to the origins of the policy framework in the multiplicity of experiences in the school network. This initiative, developed in 1993, involves a similar grade structure of cycles and other policies, aiming for a radical transformation of traditional schooling so as to combat social exclusion. Similar initiatives have been implemented in a number of other municipalities, such as Natal in the northeast state of Rio Grande do Norte, Belém in the

Amazonian state of Pará, Uberaba in Minas Gerais, and Gravataí and Pelotas in Rio Grande do Sul.

Most of these experiences have been located in municipalities and have involved the PT. However, there have been some cases of implementation through state governments: Paraná was the site of some of the first experiments in democratic administration, implementing direct elections of headteachers, school councils, and administrative and financial autonomy. In 1999, the state of Rio Grande do Sul also implemented policies aimed at increasing popular participation in education. The experiences of all these diverse contexts were debated at the First National Meeting of Citizen Schools, organized by the Paulo Freire Institute in 2001, and again at the First International Meeting of Citizen Schools the following year.

The Citizen School has attracted international interest due to its ambitious attempts to break with the neoliberal policy consensus and create schools that are democratic in both their functioning and their purpose. There is little to suggest that it will be adopted as a national framework within Brazil, but it continues to inspire localized initiatives within and outside of the country. In attempting to foster participatory citizenship in contexts of extreme social and political marginalization, and translating its theoretical ideas into concrete proposals, the Citizen School represents a highly significant development in education policy and practice.

—Tristan McCowan

See also Freire, Paulo; Partido dos Trabalhadores

Further Readings

Abers, R. (2000). *Inventing local democracy: Grassroots politics in Brazil.* London: Lynne Rienner.

Freire, P. (1993). *Pedagogy of the city.* New York: Continuum.

Gadotti, M., & Romão, J. E. (Eds.). (1997). *Autonomia da escola: princípios e propostas* (2nd ed.). São Paulo, Brazil: Cortez.

Gandin, L. A., & Apple, M. (2002). Challenging neo-liberalism, building democracy: Creating the Citizen School in Porto Alegre, Brazil. *Journal of Education Policy, 17*(2), 259–279.

CITIZENSHIP AND PATRIOTISM

An examination of American responses after the Pearl Harbor attacks and the September 11 attacks leads to the colloquially described "Days of Infamy." The social movements that emerged after each tragic event created formal and informal educational reactions. This discussion of Pearl Harbor helps make clear the philosophical implications of national unity, tragedy, citizenship, and education. In addition, it provides a historical sounding board from which current responses to terror can be documented as well as used to further normative questioning. While some may challenge the analogy (e.g., Pearl Harbor was initiated by a sovereign state and was considered an act of war, whereas 9/11 was a terrorist act), the comparison is important as it elucidates a penetrating thread in U.S. history, that is, the binary of West and the "other."

During both significantly marred historical periods, multilayered sociopolitical responses helped to bind the nation. These movements, or reactions, can be categorized in three ways: (1) a call to national action, (2) school-based responses, and (3) government intervention. The national lore surrounding the histories of both Pearl Harbor and 9/11 aids the understanding that both events are unique American stories and the underpinnings of citizenship. For a country that had been in the privileged position of never witnessing the destructive effects of modern warfare on its own soil, both Pearl Harbor and 9/11 stand out as attacks at "home" that caused sudden, massive casualties and led to protracted war. Each event has been memorialized and institutionalized in American culture and thus plays a significant role in the discourse of citizenship education.

A Call to National Action

The "new" American patriotism that has emerged since 9/11 is reminiscent of the spirit of America that was created after the Pearl Harbor attacks. The sneak attack by the Japanese on Pearl Harbor on December 7, 1941, brought about a spirit of national unity and patriotism among Americans. Nearly 60 years later, that same spirit was revitalized as the nation mourned and joined together in the apocalyptic aftermath of 9/11. The essence of the patriotic unity is predicated upon the fact that both attacks took place on American soil and were aimed at Americans. Thus, the target was not contained to the focal points of the attacks but reached further to encompass America as a whole. This led to an urgency of patriotism and social solidarity that was more nationally based than globally based. The constant discourse about valor, honor, heroism, duty, and American pride was illustrated by the outpouring of tangible and commoditized patriotic items. Everywhere, flags, songs, ribbons, bumper stickers, and T-shirts highlighted the rise of patriotism. This spectacle of patriotism could be viewed as a new focus of national interest aimed at unifying the country. This devout patriotism resulted in a rise of racism.

Pinpointing an "enemy among us" furthered the newly erupted patriotism: the Japanese during Pearl Harbor and Arab Americans since 9/11. Increased nationalism, combined with a "marked" foe, led to new intolerance and racism. How combative Americans acted toward the enemy could now be used to measure patriotism. The large number of civilian casualties exacerbated the hatred aimed at the enemy exotics. The anger, fear, and racial prejudice associated with Pearl Harbor led to more than 100,000 people of Japanese origin being held in internment camps on the West Coast. Executive Order 9066, signed by President Franklin D. Roosevelt on February 19, 1942, allowed for military commanders to designate areas from which any or all persons may be excluded.

These tendencies are xenophobic in nature and have been reiterated post-9/11. The hatred generated by the American public since 9/11 is often supported by, and helps to inform, governmental policies. The intolerance exhibited toward Arab and Middle Eastern Americans is evident in the Patriot Act. The context of 9/11 and the Patriot Act have positioned Middle Easterners in a tenuous space within the current political climate. Arab and Middle Eastern men have experienced undue suspicion post-9/11. That suspicion has been exacerbated since the passing of the Patriot Act. Federal agents have interrogated more than 8,000 Arab and Middle Eastern immigrants, and thousands of Arab and Middle Eastern men have been held in secretive federal custody for weeks and months, sometimes without any formal charges filed against them. The government has refused to publish their names and whereabouts, even when ordered to do so by the courts.

Public distress after 9/11 has produced a new level of racial profiling—the officially improper, but widely used police technique of identifying potential terrorists based solely on race. In a January 2002 public agenda survey, two thirds of respondents stated that greater scrutiny of Middle Eastern people is understandable. More generally, the majority of Americans of all races say that greater scrutiny of Middle Eastern people by law enforcement concerned with terrorism is again understandable.

Both of these periods of overt racism were shrouded under the rhetoric of national security. It is interesting to note that 60 years after Pearl Harbor and subsequent apologies and reparations made to the Japanese, racial intolerance post-9/11 has not only been acted upon, but even has a new fortitude and resilience. Thus, it is imperative to construct a pedagogy that addresses the need for a civic education that counters totalitarian policies embedded in the notions of freedom and safety.

The patriotism after 9/11 may have been subtler due to the humility associated with the recognition of how the rest of the world looks at the United States. In 2001, Americans were more aware of how the rest of the world looked at the United States than in 1941. This juxtaposition between an emerging national meaning of *American* and the need for a global intelligence regarding the meanings of *democracy, freedom*, and *citizenship* calls for discussion. In addition, ending periods of isolationism, both Pearl Harbor and 9/11 demanded a revitalization of civic education.

School-Based Response

During both times, U.S. schools have revisited social studies and civic education curricula. After the attack in 1941, formal lesson planning was amended to incorporate new learning objectives. The goals specified that students be able to explain the sequence of events leading to, during, and following Japan's surprise attack on Pearl Harbor in 1941; recognize the human dimension of events at Pearl Harbor through the personal accounts of people who were there; use a timeline to understand historical events in relationship to one another; analyze the influence of geographic location and geographic features on political events; and become familiar with vocabulary associated with war and military combat. Similar new course lessons have been adopted for guidelines and planning inclusive of a post-9/11 discourse. Both conservative and liberal agendas have embraced the unifying language of 9/11 and adopted educative platforms that challenge the efficacy of previous learning objectives. Former goals do not encompass queries regarding the United States' position in the global world, nor do they highlight different cultural vantages of the same historical periods in time. Additionally, civic education curricula have been shaped to stem from standards, data-driven, and theoretical bases.

It is important to note that while educational lesson plans have changed to include new instruction in terminology and geography, the theoretical dimensions of democracy, citizenship, justice, and freedom have not been addressed. Academic concern, both then and now, has caused scholars to focus greater attention on civic education. As such, specific concerns for accurate and meaningful civic education curricula, inclusive of a liberal democracy, egalitarianism, and social justice, lead to the framing question on what concepts should civic education be based post-9/11. This query is especially important to consider in the wake of American sociopolitical tragedies such as Pearl Harbor and 9/11 because after both events, the American government reacted by engaging in overseas wars, which, in important ways, proves the necessity of educating citizens in multicultural understanding.

Government Intervention

December 7, 1941, propelled the United States into a complex war, and public sentiment was behind President Franklin D. Roosevelt. Unity and eagerness to help were the backdrops of public support for both the president and U.S. involvement in World War II. In

2001, references comparing 9/11 to Pearl Harbor immediately flooded the news media and halls of government. This led to the concomitant escalation of militarism. The scale of destruction and devastation begged for the comparison to be made, and the mass news media obliged. Elected officials furthered the opportunity-laden comparisons. Senator John Warner of Virginia referred to "our second Pearl Harbor"; Senator Hagel of Nebraska called the attacks this generation's Pearl Harbor. Cable News Network reported that the external relations commissioner for the European Union, Chris Patten, compared the attack with that deployed by the Japanese at the U.S. naval base Pearl Harbor in 1941.

By comparing the events of 9/11 to the attacks on Pearl Harbor, social cohesion was created within the public, making it easier to embark on the War on Terror. This parallels the cohesion of Pearl Harbor days, when World War II was known as America's good war. The history of Pearl Harbor has been used to help contextualize and explain the public reaction to the aftermath of 9/11. The incomprehensible attacks served to align the nation in patriotic membership, education goals, and the pursuit of justice through war. The interplay between national history and war helped to create the central duality of evil (the "other"), and innocence (America). This binary was reproduced in the media, in both the 1940s and the 2000s, although through different means.

The way that information was disseminated and received during Pearl Harbor was markedly different from 9/11. In 1941, the radio stood as the main immediate technological source of information. News was gathered and broadcast primarily without immediate backup imagery. This visual void enabled people to evoke their own images of the event, leading to inconsistent subjective imagery. By 2001, the evolution of technology meant that Americans not only saw images of the attacks, but they saw them as they occurred, transmitted in televised accounts that now constitute a densely documented video record of history. The events of 9/11 were amplified by the availability and proliferation of the television media. Memorializing of 9/11 takes place not only in tangible artifacts but also in the "flashbulb memory" of our minds. The flashbulb memory effect describes an event sufficiently important enough to rivet the attention of an entire society, leading people to remember where they were when they first heard the news. Television helped secure similar images of the 9/11 attacks in the flashbulb memory of worldwide viewers.

The advent of the television has served to perpetuate American ideology. The amplification of 9/11 by the visual media contributed to an increase in national unity. The combination of the oversaturation by media and a post-9/11 climate created cohesion, solidarity, and togetherness in a vulnerable, attacked American people. It also led to strong patriotism that has gone beyond pride and honor in country and may be described as jingoism anchored in xenophobia. *Jingoism* is characterized by an intense and excessive patriotism that fosters hostility toward other countries. Jingoistic attitudes are closely linked with monoculturalism, isolationism, and nationalism. This anxiety can be exacerbated after devastating political events. Jingoism and xenophobia have led to further unity among the American people. A patriot can be defined as a person who loves, supports, and defends his or her country. It is important to note that patriotism is distinguishable and different from jingoism. Patriotism can be a useful tool for unity and should be encouraged, whereas jingoism is inherently negative, limiting, and parochial.

—*Azadeh Farrah Osanloo*

See also Anti-Racist Teaching; Multicultural Education; Peace Education

Further Readings

Abowitz, K. (2002). Imagining citizenship: Cosmopolitanism or patriotism. *Teachers College Record,* Vol. 104. Retrieved July 7, 2005, from www.tcrecord.org

American Civil Liberties Union. (2002). *Insatiable appetite: The government's demand for new and unnecessary powers after September 11.* Washington, DC: Author.

Apple, M. W. (2002). Patriotism, pedagogy, and freedom: On the educational meanings of September 11. *Teachers College Record,* Vol. 104. Retrieved October 15, 2005, from www.tcrecord.org

Giroux, H. (2002). Democracy, freedom, and justice after September 11th: Rethinking the role of educators and the politics of schooling. *Teachers College Record, 4*(6).

Giroux, H. (2004). *George Bush's religious crusade against democracy: Fundamentalism as cultural politics.* Retrieved October 25, 2005, from www.dissidentvoice.org

CIVIL DISOBEDIENCE

The definition, not to mention the accepted practice, of *civil disobedience* has been blurry and disputed over the years. It is most generally acknowledged to mean a nonviolent, public, submissive violation of unjust laws with the intent to educate and effect change. It is nonviolent in that it does no harm to the mental or physical well-being of individuals or damage to property or the polity. The modifier *civil* in this case describes the forum in which the disobedience takes place. It is an act that citizens undertake openly in the public sphere. It is also appropriate to interpret *civil* as meaning orderly, decent, or humane. The word *polite*, however, would be incorrect, implying courteous behavior; civil disobedience is intentionally disruptive and usually challenges social norms as well as instituted laws. In addition to being conducted in the civil or public sphere, the act must be for the public good rather than private or sectarian interests. Disobedients must also submit willingly to the penalties of the laws they are breaking. Accepting punishment fulfills two important purposes: First, it demonstrates respect for the rule of law that holds the polity together; and second, it brings publicity to the cause of the disobedient. Finally, the breaking of the law must be an intentional, not inadvertent, attempt to persuade public opinion toward reform.

For civil disobedience to take place, a number of political requisites must exist. First, there must be a democratic element of the system that gives the people a say in the laws. Second, and most importantly, there must be a sense of moral obligation on the part of the disobedient to the constitution and government for the protest to be legitimate. There is, in other words, no basis for dissent in anarchy. Third, there must be a substantial degree of stability in the polity in order that the disruption caused by the disobedience will not lead to the disintegration of the entire government.

Advocates of civil disobedience argue that it is an important part of the democratic process for several reasons. First, it is one of the most direct forms of popular participation in the governing process. It is a way citizens comment directly on the laws, virtually repeal unjust laws, and model just practice in their place. Also, far from being disrespectful of government or law, civil disobedience shows the highest respect for the Constitution by holding subsequently enacted laws to the fundamental principles on which it was founded. In undertaking civil disobedience, individuals highlight the distinction between what is legal and what is constitutional. They use their consciences as a guide and attempt to appeal to and persuade the conscience of the nation.

On the other side, opponents of civil disobedience claim that it is not part of the democratic process at all. Rather, they argue that it is an extralegal act that is fundamentally disrespectful of the system. If a system is democratic, they say, then citizens should all agree to abide by the decisions of the majority, whether or not they agree with the established policy. Advocates of civil disobedience would counter that this position does not take into account the possibility of the tyranny of the majority and the necessity of dissent to improve society. An extreme example of the dangers of majoritarian hegemony is, of course, Germany under the Third Reich. Further, America has never been envisioned as a government by the majority; rather, the framers of the Constitution saw the stability and liberties of the polity being preserved by dissent rather than uniformity of opinion.

Civil disobedience is located on a continuum of resistance to government. At one extreme is pacifistic nonresistance, which holds that the government must not be resisted by force and the individual should have as little to do with the institutions of government or civil society as possible. At the other extreme is the violent overthrow of government and anarchy. Many acts of civil resistance that have been called civil disobedience do not actually meet the criteria outlined above. Among these, at one extreme, are peaceful acts such as the Amish conscientious objection to certain

kinds of taxes and clandestine activities such as the Underground Railroad. On the other extreme are violent acts of resistance. These include mob activities of the sort practiced by the Americans prior to the Revolution, John Brown's raid on Harper's Ferry, rebellions and revolutions in general, and acts of terrorism, such as suicide bombings. Civil disobedience is a *via media*. When conducted properly, it is disruptive but not destructive.

Martin Luther King, Jr. (1929–1968) laid out the basic steps of civil disobedience in his 1963 "Letter from Birmingham Jail." There must first be a collection of facts as proof of the injustices. Individuals must then purify themselves to ensure their actions are based on disinterested motives. The disobedients must negotiate with the authorities. They then break the law without violence, and finally, they accept their punishments lovingly.

Most theory and practice of civil disobedience have been based on Christian theology. It made its first appearance in 17th-century England with the Religious Society of Friends (Quakers). Several important ideas converged at this time and with this particular group to allow the concept of civil disobedience to arise. These ideas were relatively new in that they had not existed simultaneously in any other previous era. First, since the rise of Christianity, most people living in England and Western Europe believed that the civil government was ordained by God. This meant that man had a duty to respect, obey, and preserve it. A second important idea, arising from Lutheranism and reformed Calvinism, was the idea that if the laws of man and the laws of God were not the same, man has a duty to resist ungodly civil laws. Thus, the theory of political revolution was born. A third crucial factor in the formula for civil disobedience was pacifism. This originated in the West with the early Christians, nearly died out in the reign of Constantine, and then was revived with the Anabaptists of the early 16th century.

Quakerism arose in Interregnum England (1649–1660) and was a mixture of the theology of reformed Calvinism and Anabaptism. Quakers thus believed that God created the British government, man had a duty to disobey ungodly human laws, but, according to the teachings of George Fox (1642–1691), they were obliged to do so in a peaceful way that would preserve the British Constitution.

Quakers were dissenters from the Church of England and believed that liberty of conscience should be a civil liberty. They protested publicly to change the laws that restricted the freedom of worship. Their conscious aim, however, was to gain religious toleration not merely for themselves but for all religious dissenters. For their protest, they were punished by the civil authorities. Their punishments included having their property confiscated, imprisonment, branding, whipping, and having their tongues bored through with hot irons and their ears cropped. Four Quakers were also hanged by the Puritan authorities in Massachusetts. Quakers not only accepted these punishments, they actively sought them out so they could obtain publicity for their cause by becoming martyrs. Their actions were the same steps that King would enumerate 300 years later in Birmingham, Alabama. And they were successful as they gained converts to Quakerism and helped to establish the first laws protecting religious dissenters in England and America.

Since the Quakers pioneered this form of civil dissent, groups and individuals around the world have followed this model. The example of the Quakers directly informed the practice of reformers throughout U.S. history. The first national civil disobedience movement was the initial peaceful resistance to the British in the American Revolution. The nominal leader of the movement was Quaker-influenced John Dickinson (1732–1808), who advocated that Americans peacefully disobey the 1765 Stamp Act that dictated every official document must bear the stamp of the British government. The act was repealed the following year.

Although Quakers were the pioneers of civil disobedience, three non-Quaker figures are generally considered to be the foremost originators and proponents of civil disobedience. They are Henry David Thoreau (1817–1862), Mohandas Gandhi (1869–1948), and Martin Luther King, Jr.

Thoreau is widely considered to be the founder of the theory and practice of civil disobedience, and his ideas were a powerful influence on subsequent thinkers and activists. But Thoreau himself was not a disobedient. His actions in disobeying laws do not meet the generally accepted criteria for civil disobedience discussed here and advocated by Gandhi and King. The resistance he practiced was not always public, peaceful, or respectful of government. It was not intended to be educative, and neither did he espouse any philosophy about accepting the punishments for his transgressions, which he did only for lack of any alternative. His position was akin to a typical sectarian conscientious objector position, which seeks to preserve the moral purity of the individual or sect, not claim universal validity or attempt to change society or the law. His writings on civil resistance, however, were intended for a wide audience, and he profoundly influenced many of the greatest proponents of civil disobedience.

Mohandas Gandhi was one of the most prominent advocates and practitioners of civil disobedience. His thought was shaped by several influences: the work of Thoreau and Christian anarchist Leo Tolstoy (1828–1910); and the New Testament, specifically, the Sermon on the Mount. Interwoven with these were attitudes about nonviolence he inherited from Hinduism, Jainism, and Buddhism. Gandhi called his principle of resistance *satyagraha,* which is defined as "firmness in truth." In order to free India from British rule and oppression, he borrowed selectively from all these thinkers and systems, rejecting the aspects that did not comport with the most extreme form of peaceful protest, civil disobedience. Gandhi's civil disobedience ultimately gained Indian independence from Britain without revolution.

The best-known American civil disobedient is Martin Luther King, Jr., leader of the civil rights movement. He was strongly influenced by the thought of Thoreau and Gandhi, as well as Christian theology. He was also a follower of Quakers Richard Gregg (1885–1974) and Bayard Rustin (1912–1987). King's impact on American society was considerable. A Baptist minister, King preached that disobedience to unjust laws was showing the highest respect for the constitution of a state by showing respect for principles on which it was founded. He taught a generation of Americans how to protest peacefully and helped secure the passage of the Civil Rights Act of 1964.

Often unintended consequences attend the widespread advocacy of civil disobedience. Even when advocates and practitioners of civil disobedience do not resort to violence themselves, their teachings and example can lead to greater disruption of the system than they intended. Evidence of this is that the peaceful protest against Britain advocated by Dickinson in the 1760s led to Revolution in 1776; Gandhi's resistance resulted in violence by the British against Indians, and also violent retaliation by Indians; and followers of King's protests against the Vietnam War ultimately turned away from nonviolent techniques.

These developments notwithstanding, the intentions of civil disobedients are to secure civil liberties through peaceful means—and the methods advocated by Quakers, Thoreau, Gandhi, King, and many others have been used successfully around the world against war, colonialism, abridgement of women's and workers' rights, apartheid, and genocide.

—Jane E. Calvert

See also Civil Rights Movement; Direct Action; Gandhi, Mohandas K.; King, Martin Luther, Jr.; Nonviolence and Activism; Pacifism; Quakers; Religious Activism; Resistance; Rustin, Bayard; Thoreau, Henry David

Further Readings

Bedau, H. A. (Ed.). (1969). *Civil disobedience: Theory and practice.* New York: Pegasus.

Childress, J. F. (1971). *Civil disobedience and political obligation: A study in Christian social ethics.* New Haven, CT: Yale University Press.

Rawls, J. (1971). *A theory of justice.* Cambridge, MA: Belknap Press.

Spitz, D. (Ed.). (1967). *Political theory and social change.* New York: Atherton Press.

Walzer, M. (1970). *Obligations: Essays on disobedience, war, and citizenship.* New York: Simon & Schuster.

Zinn, H. (1968). *Disobedience and democracy: Nine fallacies on law and order.* New York: Vintage.

CIVIL RIGHTS ACTS

The Civil Rights Acts of U.S. congressional legislation were passed to enforce constitutional rights for minorities. The Thirteenth, Fourteenth, and Fifteenth Amendments to the Constitution, passed in the late 1860s immediately after the Civil War, provided the constitutional basis for the emancipation of slaves and granted them the full set of rights provided to other citizens. However, these amendments were meaningless in the face of opposition from the states, especially those of the former Confederacy. The white people of the South in particular, and most of the nation in general, were resistant to the idea that blacks should be allowed to freely participate in the wider, white-dominated society. The Civil Rights Acts were passed to enforce the equality of citizenship that the Amendments promised.

The first Civil Rights Act was passed in 1866, in an attempt to preempt southern whites' attempts to reenslave the blacks in all but name. Several of the states had passed Black Codes, which required former slaves to sign up yearly for jobs or leave the state and which denied them voting and legal rights. In response, the Congress passed (over the veto of President Andrew Johnson) the Civil Rights Act of 1866. The act declared that all persons born in the United States were now citizens, without regard to race, color, or previous condition of servitude. As citizens they could make and enforce contracts, sue and be sued, give evidence in court, and inherit, purchase, lease, sell, hold, and convey real and personal property. Persons who denied these rights to other individuals were guilty of a misdemeanor and, upon conviction, faced a fine not exceeding $1,000, or imprisonment not exceeding one year, or both.

This early Civil Rights Act was a part of a larger effort by Congress to integrate the newly freed slaves into the nation, at least politically. This effort, known as Reconstruction, mainly involved ongoing occupation of the South by federal troops, which allowed blacks to exercise political power. Governments elected by blacks and their white allies controlled several states in the region during this period.

This power was destined not to last, however. As the troops were withdrawn, whites rapidly regained power, through legal means and, very often, through intimidation and violence. Once back in power, the whites disenfranchised and marginalized the blacks.

By 1896, the Supreme Court endorsed the complete disenfranchisement of blacks that occurred after the end of Reconstruction. Their ruling in *Plessy v. Ferguson,* that separate but equal facilities for minorities met the requirements of the law, cemented the Jim Crow laws that regulated the lives of blacks.

The 1866 Civil Rights Act was a powerful statement of equality, but the Congress provided no public enforcement mechanism. Only individuals had any right to redress under the legislation. That is, the federal government did not have the power to force compliance on violators of the law. This power was left to the private individual whose rights were violated. This essentially eviscerated the law. First, most of the abuses took place against poor freedmen with little access to the legal system. Even if they were able to get into the courts, they were unlikely to get a sympathetic hearing from the white, southern judges who would hear the case, even in federal court.

Blacks and other minorities were facing two larger obstacles as well. Despite the language of the act, the federal government of the late 19th century was not institutionally prepared to intervene in the relationship between a state and its citizens. Federal enforcement of civil rights against actions of the state and local governments would not become a realistic possibility until Earl Warren led the Supreme Court during the 1950s and 1960s.

An even greater obstacle faced by minorities in the 19th and early 20th centuries was that most whites heartily agreed with the exclusion of blacks and other minorities from the larger society. While some Northerners may have disliked some of the harsher aspects of the way the South treated its blacks, almost everyone agreed with the concept.

Blacks were kept marginalized by a combination of laws, customs forced on them, and the ever-present threat of violence. States, for example, could not ban blacks from voting, but they could impose tests that whites always passed and blacks always failed. Some southern states allowed blacks to vote in general elections but not in primaries, which were privately run by the political parties. Since only Democrats were ever elected in the South, the primaries decided the winners.

Another set of obstacles were the social mores that were imposed, especially in the South. Blacks were expected to show obsequiousness to whites at all times;

if a white man was walking down a sidewalk, blacks were expected to step off into the streets. Even looking at a white woman might earn a black man a beating, or worse. Blacks were refused service in restaurants, were separately seated in (poorly maintained) rail cars, and forced to sit in the backs of buses and stand if the seats reserved for whites were filled and a white person got on. Worse, blacks were unable to find employment in all but a few, limited professions. Essentially, they were limited to working as manual laborers and servants.

This was enforced by the ever-present threat of violence, ranging from anonymous beatings in the middle of the night for acting "uppity" to public lynching, mob-based hangings of blacks accused of crimes against whites. In the 1920s and 1930s, as many as 120 cases of lynching per year occurred in the United States. Most were in the former Confederacy, but many occurred in the North and Midwest, as well.

After World War II, pressure began to build within the black community and among northern members of the Democratic Party to ameliorate at least the most repressive conditions in the South. Spurred by a fiery speech to the 1948 Democratic National Convention by the mayor of Minneapolis, Hubert H. Humphrey, northern Democratic senators (soon joined by Humphrey) began yearly efforts to pass a civil rights bill to at least make lynching a federal crime, taking it out of the hands of the southern state courts and their all-white juries. Even when the northern Democratic senators were able to enlist the support of moderate Republicans, the efforts were inevitably scampered by threats of filibusters by the southern senators (a filibuster is a procedural blocking technique requiring the votes of two thirds of the Senate to stop). In response to the Birmingham bus boycott and other examples of growing unrest among the blacks in the South, and in response to several high-profile cases of lynching in the region, moderate white Southerners in the Senate, most notably Lyndon Johnson, the Senate majority leader from Texas, began to realize that some kind of legislation was necessary for political reasons.

The Civil Rights Bill that passed made it a federal offense to infringe on someone's right to register and vote but allowed trials by jury to determine guilt, effectively putting the power back in the hands of the all-white juries that had been the force oppressing the blacks all along. The bill had no teeth, but it had passed—the first civil rights bill in almost 100 years. The precedent of federal intervention in state voter registration and voting procedures had been established.

The 1960 Civil Rights Act introduced little direct intervention in the states beyond the 1957 act, but represented yet more precedent in support of federal intervention. It also created a Civil Rights Commission, empowered to analyze the condition of blacks in America. In practice, black voting in the South was little changed between the 1956 and 1960 presidential elections.

On the other hand, black leaders were increasingly concluding that the right to vote was the key to gaining the rest of their rights. Once white politicians had to compete for their votes, they hoped, conditions would improve.

The civil rights movement steadily increased in intensity, and in the violence it was met with, in the early 1960s. Pressure increased from the rest of the country on the new administration to intervene more directly and, at minimum, to protect the black protestors from state-sponsored violence. John F. Kennedy, however, never had the political power to push any significant legislation through the Congress on this issue. It was not until after his assassination that the new president, the Texan Lyndon Johnson, was able to force movement.

Johnson was a Southerner with a reputation as a powerful leader in the Senate before he became vice president. He had also been born into poverty, had worked his way through college, and had taught Hispanics in south Texas who were even poorer than he had been. He decided to confront the issue of racism and discrimination directly and publicly. He referred to the martyred President Kennedy's support for civil rights to galvanize the support of the people. He relied on his own legendary knowledge of the senators and Senate proceedings to cajole and browbeat senators into supporting legislation. To everyone who would listen, he invoked the morality of what he was demanding. The Civil Rights Act of 1964, which he signed into law on July 2, was one of the most important pieces of legislation of the 20th century.

The Civil Rights Act of 1964 gave the federal government the right to end segregation in the South. It prohibited segregation in public places, which it defined as anywhere that received any form of federal (tax) funding. An Equal Employment Commission was created. Federal funding would not be given to segregated schools, and companies doing business with the federal government had to have a civil rights plan in place.

The Voting Rights Act of 1965 was the natural follow-up to the 1964 act. Violence in the South against blacks had actually increased after the passage of that act, largely against voter registration efforts. The 1965 Voting Rights Act outlawed literacy tests and poll taxes. It established Justice Department oversight of voting procedures in several southern states.

The Voting Rights Act had a dramatic effect. By the end of 1966, only 4 out of the traditional 13 southern states had less than 50% of African Americans registered to vote. By 1968, even hard-line Mississippi had 59% of African Americans registered. The act was originally designed to operate for 5 years. By 1970, however, its operation had been so self-evidently successful that it was renewed with little controversy. It was renewed again in 1975, and in 1982, it was renewed for 25 years.

The 1968 Civil Rights Act expanded on previous acts and prohibited discrimination— based on race, religion, national origin, and sex—concerning the sale, rental, and financing of housing. It was later amended to include prohibitions against discrimination based on handicap and family status. Many of these provisions had been in the 1866 law but had no enforcement provisions. It also provided protection for civil rights workers. Title VIII of the act is also known as the Fair Housing Act of 1968. The act establishes two paths for relief in court. The federal government can prosecute under the Fair Housing Act, or a private individual may pursue relief under the 1866 act. The private action is called a Section 1982 claim, because the applicable section of the law is located at Section 1982 of Title 42 of the U.S. Code.

The Civil Rights Restoration Act of 1988 clarified sections of the previous acts and specified that the recipients of federal funds must comply with civil rights laws in all areas, not just in a particular program or activity that receives federal funding. This language reversed an earlier Supreme Court case.

The Civil Rights Act of 1991 was also passed to address Supreme Court rulings that limited the rights of employees who had sued their employers for discrimination. It also allowed trial by jury on discrimination claims.

The Civil Rights Acts of the 1960s made the federal government the active protector of the civil rights of individuals against abuses by other individuals for the first time. The acts, and the follow-up enforcement efforts by the Justice Department, went a long way to alleviating the discrimination faced by blacks, as well as other minorities, including Hispanics and Native Americans, in the United States.

—Joseph Adamczyk

See also Civil Rights Movement; Johnson, Lyndon B.; King, Martin Luther, Jr.; White Privilege

Further Readings

Branch, T. (1989). *Parting the waters: America in the King years 1954–63.* New York: Simon & Schuster.

Branch, T. (1999). *Pillar of fire: America in the King years 1963–65.* New York: Simon & Schuster.

Branch, T. (2006). *At Canaan's edge: America in the King years 1965–68.* New York: Simon & Schuster.

Kotz, N. (2005). *Judgment days: Lyndon Baines Johnson, Martin Luther, Jr., and the laws that changed America.* New York: Houghton Mifflin.

CIVIL RIGHTS MOVEMENT

The civil rights movement describes a period in U.S. history when large numbers of ordinary people and organizations mobilized to destroy the legal segregation and second-class citizenship of African Americans, Latinos/as, Asian Americans, and indigenous peoples encoded in federal and state laws and enforced by the proliferation of violence at all levels of society and in every region of the country. The purpose of the civil rights movement was to secure economic and political equality, empowerment, and democracy.

While resistance to discrimination and racism has existed since the very first contact among Europeans, Africans, and indigenous peoples in the 15th century, the modern civil rights movement often is thought of beginning with the 1954 U.S. Supreme Court decision banning school segregation and ending with the passage of the 1965 Voting Rights Act or the 1968 assassination of Martin Luther King, Jr.

The civil rights movement is interconnected with the historical and ongoing human call for justice worldwide. In the 20th century alone, the civil rights movement was connected with the anti-lynching movement, Spanish Civil War resistance, the labor movement, tenant farmer organizing, Roosevelt's New Deal, Mohandas Gandhi and India's independence, the desegregation of U.S. military forces, anti-colonial movements in Africa and Asia, the American Indian Movement, the Chicano movement, the Asian Pacific Islander movement, the farmworkers' movement, the women's movement, the anti-war movement, the anti-apartheid movement, the Solidarity movement, liberation theology, the Sanctuary movement, gay liberation, environmental justice, and, even, some would argue, the tactics used in the anti-abortion and religious fundamentalist movements.

The civil rights movement can best be understood within the larger context of the Reconstruction Era (1865–1877), an attempt to reconstruct the U.S. economy and expand political democracy following the end of the Civil War in 1865. For more than 250 years, Africans were enslaved, and land was stolen from indigenous peoples and Mexico to create the United States. By 1865, more than 4 million formerly enslaved people were expected to transform themselves into free laborers and equal citizens with no land, no money, and no laws to protect their rights. They worked extremely hard and successfully to create their own societies and economies in a hostile environment.

In addition, the Bureau of Refugees, Freedmen and Abandoned Lands (known as the Freedmen's Bureau) was an agency of the U.S. government formed to help freedmen gain a basic education, an opportunity to work for pay, and voting rights. By 1877, 18 African Americans had been elected to state governments, 16 had been elected to the U. S. Congress, and more than 1,000 schools were established for African Americans. Yet, the process of amending the U.S. Constitution and providing federal resources to the freedmen angered many white women suffragists, southern landowners, white-dominated labor unions, and poor whites. Repressive state laws and violence against African Americans often resulted. In the meantime, the federal government continued its campaigns to appropriate Indian land, deny citizenship to Asian immigrants, and oppress Mexicans.

The Reconstruction Era ended when federal troops abruptly left the South in 1877. By 1895, the white citizenry succeeded in enforcing domination over people of color, most notably through a U.S. Supreme Court decision—*Plessy v. Ferguson*—which stated that separate but equal public accommodations did not violate the Fourteenth Amendment of the U.S. Constitution. States flagrantly disregarded the Fifteenth Amendment, which guaranteed voting rights regardless of race and ethnicity. This backlash to Reconstruction (often called the Jim Crow Era) institutionalized racism in schools, banks, churches, the workplace, real estate agencies, law enforcement, the judicial system, and other institutions that governed daily life, with the purpose of exploiting people of color and preserving white privilege. Mob and police violence were used systematically and frequently—against both whites and people of color—to enforce racism.

In the period between Jim Crow and the modern civil rights movement, houses of worship, schools and universities, civic and fraternal organizations, labor unions, cultural institutions, and businesses were established to sustain the people living in segregated communities and to develop their leadership for promoting an equitable society. Some of the leaders and organizations that emerged during this period were Ida B. Wells-Barnett, anti-lynching crusader and journalist; Charles Hamilton Houston, dean of the Howard University Law School; W. E. B. Du Bois, a founder of the National Association for

the Advancement of Colored People (NAACP); Eugene K. Jones, an early leader of the National Urban League; Mary McLeod Bethune (founder) and Dorothy Height of the National Council of Negro Women; A. Philip Randolph, founder of the Brotherhood of Sleeping Car Porters; Carter G. Woodson, founder of the Association for the Study of Negro Life and History; Bayard Rustin, an organizer for the Fellowship of Reconciliation and a planner for the Congress of Racial Equality (CORE); Elijah Muhammed, founder of the Nation of Islam; the Southern Tenant Farmers' Union; the Highlander Center; Thurgood Marshall, a major lawyer with the NAACP (later the first African American Supreme Court justice); and Ella Baker, a field secretary and organizer for the NAACP. Katherine Dunham, Marian Anderson, Paul Robeson, and Jackie Robinson were important cultural activists during this period.

There were many significant events during the civil rights movement, including the murders of 41 known martyrs (including Medgar Evers, Addie Mae Collins, Denise McNair, Carole Robertson, Cynthia Wesley, Herbert Lee, Harry T. Moore, James Chaney, Andrew Goodman, and Michael Schwerner) and private, local, state, and federal government violence against countless unnamed victims.

African Americans carrying signs for equal rights, integrated schools, decent housing, and an end to bias, August 28, 1963.

Source: Courtesy of the Library of Congress.

In 1954, the U.S. Supreme Court decision *Brown v. Board of Education* banned separate-but-equal public schooling and all other public accommodations, overturning *Plessy v. Ferguson*. The national publicity following the 1955 murder of 14-year-old Chicago native Emmett Till while visiting relatives in Mississippi heightened awareness that lynching and mob violence were still realities in the United States. The Montgomery Bus Boycott, aimed at desegregating the public transportation system in Montgomery, Alabama, began in December 1955 when Rosa Parks deliberately broke segregation laws, immediately prompting JoAnn Robinson and the Women's Political Council, E. D. Nixon, and others to organize a long-anticipated boycott that lasted 381 days. President Eisenhower ordered the intervention of federal marshals in 1957 to protect nine African American students who wanted to desegregate Central High School in Little Rock, Arkansas.

African American college students in Greensboro, North Carolina, organized the first sit-ins in 1960 to desegregate public facilities such as lunch counters; the idea spread to other communities throughout the South. That same year, Ella Baker nurtured the formation of the Student Nonviolent Coordinating Committee (SNCC), a youth organizing effort to engage in direct action and voter registration. In 1961, CORE revived an idea first attempted in 1947 to conduct Freedom Rides to enforce the desegregation of interstate public transportation. Children and youth in Birmingham, Alabama, organized and participated in the 1963 Children's March to protest segregation in ways that their parents could not. In August of that same year, over 250,000 people came to Washington, D.C., for the March for Jobs, Freedom and Equality to petition the federal government. By December 1963, Birmingham was again in the spotlight when four little girls were murdered by a Klan bomb in the basement of the 16th Street Baptist Church as they prepared for Sunday school.

The Council of Federated Organizations, consisting of SNCC, the NAACP, CORE, and the Southern Christian Leadership Conference, organized the 1964 Freedom Summer campaigns to register new voters in the state of Mississippi, to teach citizenship rights to a population that had received little formal education, and to challenge the legality of the Mississippi delegation to the Democratic National Convention. Among the challengers were Fannie Lou Hamer, Annie Devine, and Victoria Gray Adams, Mississippi women demanding to be recognized as the authentic representatives of the state's African American majority.

By 1965, African Americans and other people won passage of the Voting Rights Act, largely as a result of the violence that accompanied the march from Selma to Montgomery, where SNCC organizer John Lewis was severely beaten and two whites—Rev. James Reeb and Viola Luizzo—were murdered. Two months later, Malcolm X, black nationalist leader and former

The March on Washington: a crowd of African Americans and whites surrounding the Reflecting Pool and continuing to the Washington Monument, August 28, 1963.

Source: Courtesy of the Library of Congress.

spokesperson for the Nation of Islam, was murdered in New York City. That same year in California, Larry Itliong, César Chávez, and Dolores Huerta organized the first of many grape boycotts and agricultural strikes to secure fair wages, better working conditions, and schooling for Filipino and Latino farmworker families.

The term *Black Power* was expressed by Stokely Carmichael during the 1966 March Against Fear from Memphis, Tennessee, to Jackson, Mississippi, as the first public statement of conflict between younger, more militant activists and older activists. Similarly, in 1996, the militant Young Lords began its evolution from being a gang to being a political organization for Puerto Rican activists. Martin Luther King, Jr. led a march in 1967 in Cicero, Illinois, to bring attention to poverty in the North and poor housing conditions caused by racial discrimination, shocking the nation by highlighting the same kind of white backlash as had been demonstrated throughout the South. In 1967, the Brown Berets (Chicano) and the Black Panther Party (African American) formed both to create community services in neighborhoods that had been ignored or abandoned by government and to resist police brutality. In April 1968, at the urging of Coretta Scott King, African American sanitation workers continued their strike in Memphis to secure fair wages, despite the assassination of her husband Martin Luther King, Jr., who went to lend support. Similarly, the Southern Christian Leadership Conference, led by Ralph Abernathy, continued with its Poor People's Campaign in April 1968 to bring national attention to the economic concerns of all peoples in the United States. Asian American activism became more strident with the 1969 formation of Yellow Seed. Prisoners at Attica State Prison in New York staged a revolt in 1971 to protest human rights abuses. A 1975 shoot-out in Oglala (Pine Ridge), South Dakota, between federal agents and members of the American Indian Movement led to the political imprisonment of Leonard Peltier and was one of the later events of the modern civil rights movement.

The effort of the civil rights movement to eliminate legal segregation was only one part of dismantling the continuing vestiges of institutionalized racism.

Some of the approaches used during the period to secure civil and human rights included legal challenges to the constitutionality of existing laws; the creation of new laws; mass mobilizations, such as marches, demonstrations, and boycotts, to bring widespread attention to injustices; direct action organizing, such as sit-ins and Freedom Rides, and campaigns to fill the jails and refuse bail to challenge the inherent righteousness of state and local laws; voter registration drives to broaden the political involvement of populations that had been systematically denied the right to vote; organized self-defense against police brutality and the terror of groups such as the Ku Klux Klan; nationalism and sovereignty campaigns to create culturally specific alternatives to the political and economic structure of the United States; the creation of new political parties to compete with the dominance of racially exclusive parties; freedom and liberation schools to guide youth to achieve excellence, prepare for public leadership, gain critical analytic skills, and learn to uphold many cultures; school busing to enforce the desegregation of public schools; appeals to the international policy bodies to put political pressure on the U.S. government to enforce human rights abuses; resistance to the military draft; the creation of new government programs to address economic, housing, employment, and health disparities; and affirmative action programs to promote the advancement of populations that had been systematically excluded from employment and educational opportunities.

Contrary to popular understanding, women were the central activists and leaders of the civil rights movement. Through organized religion, conventional wisdom, and the law, women have often been discouraged (if not banned) from participation in public debate and from holding leadership outside of female-only groups. Nevertheless, women have voiced public opinion and exercised leadership from the earliest days of European encounter, slavery and abolition, various wars, women's suffrage, and women's liberation movements. During the civil rights movement, groups such as the National Council of Negro Women and SNCC offered space for women to redefine their own leadership and to work with and against the strategies for change expressed by African American and white men. Women in the civil rights movement were strategists, public speakers, organizers, teachers, and protesters.

In addition, some of the distinctive "women's" ways of shaping social change movements included strong, religious-based lay leadership; intelligence gathering through their encounters with white employers; and facilitating dialogues among people with conflicting ideas. Mississippi's Mae Bertha Carter, like so many other mothers, offered her children as warriors in the fight to desegregate schools.

The 1963 Birmingham Children's March and SNCC are two of the countless examples from the civil rights movement showing young people exercising strategic thinking, challenging the authority of white supremacy and of community elders seeking to protect them, and altering the turn of political events at the local and national levels.

The role of community organizing is an important aspect of the civil rights story. The celebrity media culture became even more pervasive with the widening popularity of television in the 1950s and 1960s. The coincidental timing with the civil rights movement was both a blessing and a curse. On the one hand, people worldwide witnessed the unedited brutality of white supremacy and helped put pressure on policymakers for change. However, mass media also glamorized the product (the marches, the rallies, the arrests, etc.) at the expense of the long, sometimes boring, and always difficult process of organizing people to change their attitudes, behaviors, votes, and spending habits. The focus on charismatic individuals robs power from the collective efforts of the many hard-working people who made social movements happen. This emphasis also downplays the mistakes, the second-guessing, and the conflicts among planners and activists. Culture defines what (and who) is beautiful, funny, worthy of praise, nourishing, comforting, and the source of a group's strength. Enduring movements for social change transform the landscape of people's daily lives, or their culture. The interracial and cross-generational nature of the civil rights movement created new symbols and new uses for culture as a way to attract more participants. Many of these cultural shifts—in music, visual images, language, clothing/hair, religion, and leadership styles—also influenced other social movements. During the civil rights movement, familiar culture (such as songs and call-and-response oratory) was used as an organizing tool, cultural expressions were central rather than peripheral to building a community of activists, and the political and economic choices made by organizers and activists were rooted in from their daily lives, foods, songs, and worship. Some of the cultural workers during the civil rights movement include Harry Belafonte, James Baldwin, Amiri Baraka, Ossie Davis, Ruby Dee, Dick Gregory, Lorraine Hansberry, and Bernice Johnson Reagon.

Through an understanding of the civil rights movement, young people can learn useful strategies to address pressing problems in their lives and community and to see themselves as agents of change. Over the 20th century and into the 21st century, economic and social forces have reduced the public role of youth to little more than consumers. The primary "action" performed by contemporary youth is to shape a separate, media-driven culture, generating billions of dollars for adult companies. Politically, youth are expected to absorb and conform to adult society uncritically. Yet, an understanding of themselves as the makers of history, not passive customers, is an important step for contemporary youth.

Some of the legacies of the civil rights movement include the 600% to 1,000% increase in the number of elected officials of color; the phenomenal growth of the middle class among communities of color; and an improvement in the positive media images of people of color. Contemporary hip-hop culture has direct links with the Black Power and Black Arts movements of the late 1960s. At the same time, there are continuing (and in some cases, increasing) racial disparities in income, wealth, health and education, environmental injustices, racial inequalities in incarceration and sentencing rates, and employment and housing discrimination. The struggle for civil and human rights continues.

—Jenice L. View

See also Abernathy, Ralph; Affirmative Action; American Indian Movement; Anti-Lynching Movement; Baldwin, James; Baker, Ella; Belafonte, Harry; *Brown v. Board of Education;* Chávez, César; Community Organizing; Congress of Racial Equality; Direct Action; Evers, Medgar; Farmworkers' Movement; Grape Boycotts;

Gregory, Dick; Hamer, Fannie Lou; Highlander Center; Jackson, Jesse; King, Coretta Scott; King, Martin Luther, Jr.; Marshall, Thurgood; Mississippi Freedom Schools; Montgomery Bus Boycott; Moses, Robert; National Association for the Advancement of Colored People (NAACP); National Urban League; Parks, Rosa; Poor People's Campaign; Randolph, A. Philip; Robeson, Paul; Robinson, Jackie; Rustin, Bayard; Southern Christian Leadership Conference; Student Nonviolent Coordinating Committee (SNCC)

Further Readings

Acuña, R. (2004). *Occupied America: A history of Chicanos* (5th ed.). New York: Longman.

Carson, C. (1995). *In struggle: SNCC and the black awakening of the 1960s*. Cambridge, MA: Harvard University Press.

Louie, S., & Omatsu, G. (Eds.). (2001). *Asian Americans: The movement and the moment*. Los Angeles: UCLA Press.

Menkart, D., Murray, A. D., & View, J. L. (Eds.). (2004). *Putting the movement back into civil rights teaching*. Washington, DC: Teaching for Change and Poverty & Race Research Action Council.

Takaki, R. (1994). *A different mirror: A history of multicultural America*. New York: Back Bay Books.

Williams, J. (2004). *My soul looks back in wonder: Voices of the civil rights experience*. New York: Sterling.

CIVIL SOCIETY

For the past two decades, the concept of civil society has been embraced and used by a diverse range of actors including academics, activists, representatives of local and national governments, and international organizations whose interests vary from economic development to democratic governance. The possibility of presenting the idea of civil society to broad audiences transcending group and geographical boundaries is given in the normative character of the concept, that is, a set of value orientations that define what constitutes a good social order. In this respect, there is no doubt that values such as civility, tolerance, pluralism, freedom, justice, and individualism are generally seen as conducive to the production and maintenance of stable, harmonious societies. This is precisely why civil society discourse continued after the end of the Cold War, when divisions between totalitarian communist regimes and Western liberal democracies were replaced with divisions created by new forms of repression based on extreme nationalism, enduring authoritarianism, or religious fundamentalism.

But for such norms of civil discourse to become embedded in any social order, institutions are needed. This leads to a second dimension of the concept of civil society, a sociological one. Jean Cohen and Andrew Arato include in their definition of civil society four arenas of social life that are distinct from both economic society and political society: an intimate sphere (primarily the family), associations, social movements, and forms of public communications. The associations of civil society, generally voluntary organizations, are extremely diverse and embrace professional, civic, educational, and cultural activities. In addition, there are issue-oriented associations that represent the interests of specific groups, such as women, youth, and sexual minorities, or embrace a specific agenda, for example, the environment. This diverse spectrum of associations points toward one of the essential features of civil society, its pluralistic nature, since no group claims to represent the interests of the whole. Various forms of public communication also represent an important component of this definition of civil society and facilitate the flow and circulation of ideas and information. Other authors (e.g., Ernest Gellner, Victor Pérez-Díaz) give an even broader definition of civil society by adding economic markets and sociopolitical institutions.

The difficulty in analyzing civil society lies in grasping, conceptually and empirically, the circumstances under which it takes shape. Jeffrey Alexander argues that civil society can be empirically studied as a sphere of solidarity at the level of social motives, social relations, and social institutions. He further states, however, that one paradox of civil society lies in its inability to openly engage its opponents in dialogue. From a sociological point of view, then, the idea of civil society appears either vague or incomplete. A review of the history of civil society and how it has been conceptualized can provide some further clarification of the concept and at the same time reveal its complexity.

The roots of the ideas can be traced to the 17th century and are associated with the Protestant Reformation in England, which released new ideas of individualism and implied that social or civil relations could not simply be taken for granted as some undefined area beneath the level of the state. To a different extent, philosophers such as Adam Smith and George W. Hegel emphasized the role of individualism in shaping social order. But it was only in the 18th century in Europe, under conditions created by modernity—the rise of long-distance trade, changes in the means of communication, and the creation of a mass print culture—that the existence of an active civil society can be acknowledged. Jürgen Habermas, in *The Structural Transformation of the Public Sphere,* captured this historical moment as well as its implications for the capitalist order of the late 20th century. According to Habermas, the public sphere of civil society was conceived in the mid-18th century, especially in Great Britain, by the bourgeoisie on the basis of the emerging bourgeois constitutional state. During this period, major institutions of the public sphere—coffeehouses, salons—brought together members of the bourgeoisie, intellectuals, and the wider strata of the rising middle class. An important characteristic of these institutions was that they gathered people together not as members of certain social groups but as citizens to engage in critical debates about important social issues. However, Habermas's account of civil society, from these hopeful beginnings to the context of late capitalism and the welfare state, is rather pessimistic since as he saw it, the development of a mass culture of consumption leads to a degradation of the public sphere and the erosion of civil society.

The question that arises now is whether civil society as a project could only be undertaken by the liberal bourgeoisie or, in more contemporary terms, within Western liberal democracies. The recent rise of civil society movements in non-Western, noncapitalist, and nonliberal societies challenges this assumption and raises new questions about the characteristics of civil society.

Totalitarian regimes such as fascism or communism attempted to bring society fully under the authority of the state, in the name of a common national or collective interest, and thus to destroy both individualism and autonomous social groups or relations. However, even under such repressive conditions, neither fascism nor communism succeeded in completely annihilating the idea of freedom and public discourse in such homogenized societies. The important role that civil society movements played in the overthrow of the communist regimes in East and Central Europe before 1989 is a good case in point. Here, civil society became an intellectual and moral project oriented toward the reconstruction of human solidarity and freedom. These were the values that energized the various dissident movements in the former socialist countries whether they took the form of a mass-type movement as the workers' Union of Solidarity in Poland, the culture of *samizdat* (unofficial publications) in the Soviet Union, or of small centers of independent thought gathered in universities or in intellectual circles represented by dedicated thinkers like Václav Havel in the former Czechoslovakia, Janos Kiss in Hungary, or Adam Michnik in Poland. What they all had in common was the idea of society as something independent from the party-state.

However, it should be emphasized that the irreconcilable opposition between civil society and the state has to end once democratic institutions and procedures are put into place. As Philippe Schmitter shows, by facilitating the interaction between the individual and the state, civil society influences public policy and contributes to the process of democratic consolidation. Without in any way substituting for political society, civil society becomes a major factor in the democratic process by monitoring and restraining the power of the state. It also stimulates political participation and therefore contributes to the development of democratic citizenship. But when polarized on ethnic, religious, or territorial lines, civil society may have a negative and divisive impact on the democratization process. It inhibits negotiation and compromise and leads to intolerance, human rights violations, or even civil war. Such extreme cases occur in parts of the world where ethnic or religious groups that originally initiated the struggle for rights and liberties continued to define their interests and rights exclusively on sectarian lines.

But civil society and religion by are no means always incompatible. Alexis de Tocqueville, one of the first sociologists to distinguish civil society as an autonomous entity, suggested an important role played by the churches in the formation of civil society in 19th-century America. More recently, Jose Casanova analyzed the potential of modern churches to become an integral part of civil society when religions embrace the Enlightenment conception of the universality of human rights. This was the case of the Roman Catholic Church in the 1960s with the publication of *Dignitatis Humanae*, known as Vatican II. Almost 200 years after de Tocqueville, Robert Putman indicates the important role played by churches in America in preserving and developing social capital.

The realities of these experiences point toward the historical dimension of the concept of civil society. Today, civil society discourse exists under the circumstances of an emerging new world order characterized by a reconfiguration of national borders as a result of the flow of international capital, information, and widespread immigration. For Pérez-Díaz, this transformation of previously homogenous societies toward more pluralistic ones represents a chance and a challenge for civil society. The challenge is to accommodate diversity through a set of values and institutions that would shape a modern transnational world.

Scholars, as well as social and political activists, recognize the importance of this new type of civil society frequently referred to as transnational or global in nature. It can take a variety of forms, such as a single international non-governmental organization with chapters in many countries (e.g., Transparency International), or more informal transnational or international coalitions of organizations devoted to particular goals. These organizations are active in human rights, as well as social, political, and economic rights. They may promote their agendas peacefully (e.g., by working closely with national governments and international organizations) but also more aggressively (e.g., through public protests). However, some social movements cannot be characterized as standing for civil society since they promote intolerance, xenophobia, and hatred against certain groups (e.g., white supremacists, neo-Nazi movements, religious extremists).

Some authors (e.g., Ann Florini) consider transnational civil society as the third major force in global politics alongside states and transnational corporations. Others, without contesting its strong impact and potential for developing a global public sphere through media and the Internet, question its universality. John Keane, for example, makes the point that due to extreme forms of inequalities between the wealthiest regions of the North and the most underdeveloped and poorest regions of the South, large areas in the world have no opportunity to participate in this global civil society. This is both because of the existence of global markets represented by multinational corporations and in spite of a world polity based on international treaties and international institutions of justice. A problematic aspect of global civil society also relates to the question of the extent of moral authority given the fact that there is a wide range of relationships between movements, international non-governmental organizations, and governments from opposition to dependency.

Despite its weaknesses, the potential that global civil society has for mobilizing large audiences in the face of human suffering caused by wars, natural disasters, or oppressive governments cannot be denied. Otherwise, significant international philanthropic activities targeted at the disastrous effects of recent famine in Africa or earthquakes in Asia or the strong mobilization of public opinion in 2004 in support of democracy movements in Ukraine and against ethnic cleansing in Darfur (Sudan) could not be readily explained.

—*Monica Ciobanu*

See also Communism; Democracy; Fascism; Habermas, Jürgen; Ideology; Non-Governmental Organizations (NGOs); Socialism; Social Movements, Sociology of

Further Readings

Alexander, J. C. (Ed.). (1998). *Real civil societies: Dilemmas of institutionalization*. London: Sage.

Casanova, J. (2001). Civil society and religion: Retrospective reflections on Catholicism and prospective reflections on Islam. *Social Research, 68*(4), 1041–1080.

Cohen, J., & Arato, A. (1992). *Civil society and political theory*. Cambridge: MIT Press.

Florini, A. (Ed.). (2000). *The third force: The rise of transnational civil society*. Washington, DC: Carnegie Endowment for International Peace.

Habermas, J. (1962). *The structural transformation of the public sphere*. Cambridge: MIT Press.

Keane, J. (2003). *Global civil society?* Cambridge, UK: Cambridge University Press.

Pérez-Díaz, V. (1995). The possibility of civil society: Traditions, character and challenges. In J. A. Hall (Ed.), *Civil society: Theory, history, comparison*. Cambridge, UK: Blackwell.

Putnam, D. (2000). *Bowling alone: The collapse and revival of American community*. New York: Simon & Schuster.

Schmitter, P. (1997). Civil society East and West. In L. Diamond (Ed.), *Consolidating the third wave democracies: Themes and perspectives*. Baltimore: Johns Hopkins University Press.

Tocqueville, A. de (2004). *Democracy in America* (A. Goldhammer, Trans.). New York: Library of America. (Original work published 1835)

CLAMSHELL ALLIANCE

The Clamshell Alliance is an anti-nuclear alliance in New England which spearheaded a movement against Seabrook nuclear power plant during the 1970s. Its egalitarian organization forms and nonviolent direct action style became a classic model among anti-authoritarian and anti-nuclear movements throughout the United States and Europe. On April 30, 1976, in their third and biggest action, about 2,500 persons organized in autonomous action groups, "affinity groups" of 3 to 15 persons, occupied the site of the planned Seabrook plant. More than 1,400 activists were kept in National Guard Armories for almost 2 weeks, during which activists conducted workshops and nonviolent action trainings (with role-plays and action simulations). The action was a great success in that it fueled a movement against nuclear power.

The term *affinity groups* originates from the Spanish *grupos de afinidad*, intimate political discussion and action groups that shaped anarchism during the Spanish Civil War as well as women's consciousness-raising groups. Clamshell Alliance integrated and developed consensus decision making in mass direct actions with the help of affinity groups and used nonviolence guidelines and trainings to facilitate

action discipline and creativity. Rotating facilitators managed discussions and "vibes-watchers" took care of emotions and group energy. Spokespersons passed on decisions made by groups to the coordinating committee meetings, which in their decisions had to find agreement with the groups. The alliance attempted mutual accommodation of the individual and the collective. Consensus expressed the alliance's freedom fight against an undemocratic society as well as a belief in collective truth.

The alliance is part of a long-standing left libertarian tradition in the United States. It viewed nuclear power as an instrument of dominance and violence which citizens and local communities were entitled to resist with their civil disobedience. The internal organization of the Clamshell Alliance was an alternative to a hierarchical society symbolized by nuclear power. The alliance fought a liberty struggle internally through egalitarian organization and externally through nonviolent resistance.

Although the alliance popularized a decentralized model of direct action, they were not the first to use it. The alliance were inspired and grew from the anti–Vietnam War movement, in addition to other anti-nuclear groups such as the more than 25,000 persons who occupied the site and stopped the plant construction in West German Wyhl in 1975.

Local authorities dealt rather efficiently with the Clamshell Alliance and, after 1977, frustration grew. Organizational changes and physical nonviolence in resistance to removal during occupations did not help. The final factional split of the alliance is often attributed to ideological conflicts of the egalitarian organization form, especially the consensus decision-making form. What made them famous was perhaps also their weakness. The alliance showed the possibility of decentralized mass action and creative skill-sharing through nonviolence training. At the same time, it involuntarily showed the problems and limits of radical egalitarian ideology in movements. Nevertheless, the Seabrook plant was never fully completed, and the model is still inspiring movements.

—*Stellan Vinthagen*

See also Anti-Nuclear Movement; Civil Disobedience; Direct Action; Nonviolence and Activism

Further Readings

Downey, G. L. (1986, June). Realizing the Clamshell identity: Organizational dilemmas in the anti-nuclear power movement. *Social Problems, 33*.

Epstein, B. (1993). *Political protest and cultural revolution: Nonviolent direct action in the 1970s and 1980s.* Berkeley: University of California Press.

CLARK, RAMSEY (1927–)

Ramsey William Clark was born in Texas, the son of Tom C. Clark, attorney general under President Harry Truman and later an associate Supreme Court Justice. Ramsey followed his father into the law, graduating from University of Chicago law school before moving briefly into private practice on his way to the U.S. Justice Department during the early days of the Kennedy administration. Clark would emerge as one of the Justice Department's more radical lawyers, often at odds with prevailing opinions on civil rights law enforcement. During the dark and dangerous days of the early 1960s, when civil rights campaigners literally took their lives in their hands in challenging the Jim Crow laws of the South, Ramsey Clark, as assistant attorney general in the lands division from 1961 to 1965, was one of the few senior department figures to advocate a more active role for the Justice Department in protecting civil rights activists.

With the passing of the Civil Rights Act in 1964 and the Voting Rights Act in 1965, the Justice Department of President Lyndon Johnson became much more active in the field of civil rights. Yet, the Justice Department found itself struggling to understand and deal with the massive waves of civil unrest that convulsed the nation throughout much of the decade, as frustration grew at the perceived slow pace and limited scope of change, and against the Vietnam War. Clark was thrust further into this environment as he became deputy attorney general in 1965, acting attorney general in October 1966, and finally attorney general in March 1967.

Clark won both acclaim and condemnation for his work as attorney general largely as a result of his delicate balancing act in weighing the interests of the State against individual rights to privacy and protest. Indeed, Richard Nixon would make him a central issue during the 1968 presidential campaign, promising that among the first things the nation would get would be a new attorney general. In addressing civil unrest, Clark implemented the Community Relations Service and the Office of Law Enforcement Assistance Administration programs. Through them, Justice began placing increasing emphasis on riot prevention capabilities and the fostering of effective police-community relations. He also sought to defend the right to privacy by denying wiretaps requested under a dubious catchall provision of the 1968 Omnibus Crime and Safe Streets Act. At the same time, though, he prosecuted a huge number of draft evasion cases—more than 1,500 in 1968 alone—including Dr. Benjamin Spock, for conspiracy to encourage draft evasion.

Unfortunately for Clark, his balancing act came crashing down when he created the Interdivisional Information Unit to collate, store, and disseminate data on the composition and motivations of "dissident groups"—with a view to using this information to prevent civil unrest rather than merely reacting to it. Though he did not know it, by using the Federal Bureau of Investigation (FBI) as the chief source of these data without providing a framework within which it should operate in this role, Clark helped to pave the way for information to be used to target groups like the Black Panthers and the Student Nonviolent Coordinating Committee for repressive action, as part of the FBI's COINTELPRO operations, that grossly violated their civil liberties.

Upon leaving office as Nixon became president, Clark, freed from the confinements of government service, embraced his activist tendencies with a passion. In his legal work, he took on clients like Vietnam War protester Father Daniel Berrigan, and he proceeded to lay out his views on criminal justice in his first book, *Crime in America.* Crime, for Clark, emerged from the dehumanizing effects of poverty, racism, ignorance, and violence, and America needed to deal with these problems through education and rehabilitation rather than resorting to more and bigger prisons—mere criminal hothouses devoid of rehabilitative content—which only exacerbated the problem.

In addition to championing a more holistic approach to criminal justice, Clark sought to address specific issues. In 1973, *Search and Destroy: A Report by the Commission of Inquiry Into the Black Panthers and the Police,* for which he and the NAACP's Roy Wilkins served as chairs and wrote the introduction, launched an excoriating attack on the Chicago police department and the State's attorney for their roles in the shooting deaths of Panthers Mark Clark and Fred Hampton in December 1969. In the introduction, Clark identified what he saw as a common thread running through the Clark and Hampton killings, the Attica prison, Jackson State and Kent State killings, and B-52 raids over Vietnam—that we value others less than ourselves and hence see no wrong in seeking to control or destroy them. This charge would be the leitmotif of Clark's subsequent political activism as his emphasis shifted from U.S. government actions at home to actions abroad.

Since the 1970s, Ramsey Clark has opposed U.S. military interventions wherever they have occurred—Vietnam, Grenada, Panama, Nicaragua, Libya, Somalia, Iraq, the Balkans, and Iraq again—largely organized through his International Action Center. It is in his opposition to U.S. actions in Iraq that Clark has attracted the most attention. In 1992, he wrote *The Fire This Time: U.S. War Crimes in the Gulf,* in which, in addition to accusing the United States of war crimes, he condemned the United Nations for its policy of sanctions against Iraq and the American media for failing to inform the American public and world opinion. The previous year, he had been instrumental in establishing an International War Crimes Tribunal, whose report condemning the United States was published in 1998 as *War Crimes.*

It is, though, his choice of legal clients that has made Ramsey Clark notorious and laid him open to the most sustained attacks. Clark has represented such controversial characters as Slobodan Milošević, Radovan Karadžić, Pastor Elizaphan Ntakirutimana—accused of leading Hutu killing squads against Tutsis in Rwanda and ultimately convicted of genocide—and at home, Lyndon LaRouche. In all of these cases, Clark has contended that his clients could not receive justice at the hands of their accusers; however, he has been widely accused of employing some dubious moral and legal logic in making these claims—such as in his condemnation of the International Tribunal for Rwanda for dispensing "colonial" justice unfair to Hutus.

In 2005, Ramsey Clark's legal practice and political activism combined again when he joined Saddam Hussein's defense team in the former Iraqi leader's trial for crimes against humanity. In his most recent crusade, Clark has become a leading figure in a campaign to impeach President George W. Bush over the Iraq war.

—*Dean Williams*

See also Berrigan Brothers; Black Panther Party; Civil Rights Acts; Draft Resistance; Johnson, Lyndon B.; Spock, Benjamin; Student Nonviolent Coordinating Committee (SNCC); Wilkins, Roy

Further Readings

Chomsky, N., Said, E., & Clark, R. (1999). *Acts of aggression: Policing rogue states.* New York: Seven Stories Press.

Clark, R. (1970). *Crime in America: Observations on its nature, causes, prevention, and control.* New York: Simon & Schuster.

Clark, R. (1992). *The fire this time: U.S. war crimes in the Gulf.* New York: Thunder's Mouth Press.

Clark, R. (Ed.). (1998). *NATO in the Balkans: Voices of opposition.* New York: International Action Center.

Clark, R., et al. (1992). *War crimes: A report on United States war crimes against Iraq.* Washington, DC: Maisonneuve Press.

Clark, R., & Wilkins, R. (Chairs). (1973). *Search and destroy: A report by the Commission of Inquiry Into the Black Panthers and the Police.* New York: Metropolitan Applied Research Center.

CLIMATE CHANGE AND GLOBAL JUSTICE

Climate change and the pursuit of global justice are vitally linked: Those who are most responsible for human-induced climate change are typically not those who are the most vulnerable and who experience detrimental impacts of those changes in the climate.

Historically, environmental movements for global justice have sought to contest environmental degradation, as well as collective human disenfranchisement from the factors and institutions that give rise to, and perpetuate, unjust conditions. These movements have contested political, economic, social, cultural, and environmental factors that shape this uneven terrain: from colonial and imperialist legacies, to unequal power and protection, as well as access to resources and decision making. Specific to climate change, climate justice movements have challenged inequities regarding differential consumption of carbon-based energy and adverse impacts from that consumption. Moreover, these movements have raised questions regarding who is responsible, that is, who can and should take action to alleviate the detrimental impacts from human-induced climate change.

The climate on planet Earth is moderated by input from energy of the sun and the loss of this back into space. Incoming solar radiation enters the earth's atmosphere and is partly absorbed or trapped, while being partly reflected back to space. The composition of the atmosphere dictates the balance between these forces; this is called the planetary energy budget. Certain atmospheric gases are critical to this balance and are known as greenhouse gases (GHGs). These GHGs include carbon dioxide (CO_2), methane (CH_4), nitrous oxide (N_2O), tropospheric ozone (O_3), halocarbons (CFCs, HFCs, HCFCs) and water vapor (H_2O_v). Emissions of GHGs into the atmosphere cause climate changes, which include increases in temperature. There is both a natural greenhouse effect and an enhanced greenhouse effect. The natural greenhouse effect makes the world habitable. Without it, the Earth would, on average, be about 60° Fahrenheit (F) cooler, and the planet would be covered with ice. With this natural greenhouse effect, humans have been able to

This unnamed lake is at the snout of the Jacobsen Glacier in British Columbia, at the north end of the Monarch Icefield south of Bella Coola. The whole lake was a glacier circa 1976. The snout has retreated about 2.5 miles (4 kilometers).

Source: Photo by Drew Brayshaw.

enjoy the benefits of a livable climate, as well as forest and food growth.

The terms *climate change* and *global warming* signify slightly different things. Climate change is a broader term, which accounts for changes in many climate characteristics, such as rainfall, ice extent, and sea levels. Global warming refers to a more specific facet of climate change: the increase in temperature over time. Clearly, temperature increases do not occur in isolation from other climate characteristics. Rather, many other sources and feedback processes contribute to changes across time and space. Partly due to these tightly bound connections, these terms have become commonly used synonymously in policy and popular discourse, despite the fact that global warming is a much more specific term. Temperature (particularly temperature increases) is seen as the most clear and distinguishable climate characteristic that indicates more general climate change. Moreover, many consider temperature to be climate change's "fingerprint." Since 1900, the global average temperature has risen about 1.1°F and is projected to increase 2.5–10.4°F by 2100.

Human activities comprise the enhanced greenhouse effect. These are also called anthropogenic: *anthropo-* referring to humans, and *-genic* referring to the generating of GHGs. In the climate science community, there is overwhelming consensus that climate changes in the past two centuries have been largely driven by human activity and are not merely the result of natural fluctuations. For many decades, climate scientists have stated with increasing confidence that humans play a distinct role in changes to the climate. Led by the Intergovernmental Panel on Climate Change (IPCC)—a group of more than 3,000 of the top climate scientists from around the world—this consensus has also been supported by top U.S. science organizations such as the American Geophysical Union, the National Oceanic and Atmospheric Administration, the American Association for the Advancement of Science, and the American Meteorological Society.

Specifically, research shows that three quarters of atmospheric warming since 1850—the beginning of the Industrial Revolution—has been attributed to anthropogenic sources. These anthropogenic sources include fossil fuel burning (primarily coal, gas, and oil) and land use change. In the United States, roughly a quarter of anthropogenic climate changes can be attributed each to transportation, industry, household use/infrastructure, and land use and land-cover changes. Atmospheric carbon dioxide is the greenhouse gas changing most directly because of these human activities. That is one key reason why the focus of GHG emissions is often on CO_2. Another is that the increase in CO_2 has contributed the most to warming compared to other GHGs. Also, CO_2 emitted into the atmosphere can stay there for a long time (50 to 200 years), referred to as "residence time." So effectively, emissions from a 1911 Model T Ford are potentially in the atmosphere today. After time in the atmosphere, GHGs cycle into a sink. For example, carbon is taken up in the biosphere through photosynthesis in forests. The carbon can stay in this reservoir until the forest dies and decomposes, is cut down, or is burned. Measurements of atmospheric CO_2 concentration over time show that atmospheric CO_2 concentrations have now risen to approximately 380 parts per million (ppm). When the experiment began in 1957, the rate of

increase was approximately 1% (or 3 ppm) per year. However, data have shown that in recent years this increase has gone up to approximately 5 ppm per year. There remain many contentious discussions regarding what threshold will constitute "dangerous climate change." While some argue that it has already been crossed, others place this threshold at 450 ppm or 560 ppm (a doubling of pre-industrial levels of CO_2).

These data have been aggregated with other climate proxy data. Proxy data can come from a wide range of human sources, such as vintner and gardening diaries, captain's ship logs, and records from trading posts. Also, climate proxies are obtained from what are considered natural sources, such as ice cores, tree rings, corals, and sediment cores. Together, these proxy data have shown that recent increases in atmospheric CO_2 exceed the bounds of natural variability experienced during the preceding 650,000 years. While there has been discussion of the passing of the peak in economically recoverable global oil that is commercially available for consumption, many in the climate science community consider the atmospheric concentration of GHGs to be of more pressing concern.

Moving from climate science explicitly to climate policy, international negotiations over anthropogenic global climate policy have most prominently taken shape as the Kyoto Protocol. The Kyoto Protocol was the product of the U.N. Framework Convention on Climate Change, drafted at the 1992 U.N. Conference on Environment and Development, or Earth Summit. The Kyoto Protocol has been signed by 140 countries; despite U.S. nonparticipation, the protocol entered into force in February 2005. The treaty calls on a first phase of 34 industrialized countries (or Annex I/B Parties) to reduce emissions on average 5.2% from 1990 levels by 2012. In 2012, a second phase is scheduled to begin that includes other nations, such as those from the global South.

Concurrently, carbon-based industry and society are riddled with inequities. Consumptive habits are differentiated at many scales. Emissions from the global North account for about two thirds of total global emissions each year. However, emissions in the global South are increasing at a faster rate than those in the global North and are on pace to overtake the global

North in emissions by 2035. It is important to distinguish between what has been called luxury emissions (such as driving an SUV [sports utility vehicle] to the corner store for a pint of ice cream) and survival emissions (such as burning wood for cooking). Moreover, many of the carbon-based, energy-intensive—and hence emissions-intensive—activities that take place in the global South are done to service demands in the global North. Approximately 80% of raw materials that are produced in the global South are consumed in the global North. In terms of GHG emissions by country, the United States—consumer of 20 million barrels of oil a day—is the world leader, accounting for 25% of global emissions. China follows second as a large consumer of coal, accounting for about 14% of global GHG emissions. Left unchecked, many predict that Chinese emissions will surpass those of the United States by 2030. Rounding out the top five emitters on planet Earth are Russia (7%), Japan (5%), and India (5%). This can also be considered through per-capita—or individual—emissions. The United States leads the planet in per-capita emissions, with 19.1 metric tons per year. Despite ranking as the second largest emitter of GHGs at the country level, the individual emissions of a typical resident of China are less than 1/8 that of the United States. The individual emissions of a typical Russian or Japanese are both about one-half that of a citizen in the United States, while a resident of India emits less than 1/20 of what someone in the United States does. This per-capita approach provides a much different picture of GHG emissions.

Looking from sources to impacts, there are also critical differences. Those who typically emit more GHGs into the atmosphere have been less vulnerable to the consequences of their behaviors. Conversely, those who emit fewer GHGs have been more vulnerable to shocks associated with climate change impacts. These unequal relations link concerns over climate change and global justice. Research by Piers Blaikie, Terry Cannon, Ian Davis, and Ben Wisner has asserted that impacts are not merely a result of detrimental events associated with climate change but rather are the product of the combination of a trigger event and social, political, and economic factors that differentially structure people's lives and livelihoods. Many of the poor in the global South are highly dependent on natural resources, while also having a limited capacity—and less infrastructural support—to adapt to changes in the climate. Moreover, these challenges are manifested through varied concerns over future impacts of climate change. For example, sea level rise is of great concern to many poorer island nations that are not financially capable of building large dykes and levee systems to guard against gradual rises as well as increasingly threatening storm events. Since 1900, the global average sea level has risen 8 inches, and IPCC climate scientists predict a rise of another 4 to 37 inches by 2100. In ongoing negotiations of the Kyoto Protocol, the Alliance of Small Island States has called for more severe cuts in GHG emissions, in order to limit this sea level rise. Many citizens of member nations such as Kiribati and the Marshall Islands risk becoming the first wave of climate refugees.

In 1991, Anil Agarwal and Sunita Narain wrote a seminal piece that traced differential impacts in the global North and global South, titled *Global Warming in an Unequal World: A Case of Environmental Colonialism*. They discuss concerns of intragenerational equity, or inequality across segments of the contemporary global community. They consider vastly different levels of consumption—and hence GHG emissions—across populations and call for a rights-based approach to determinations regarding what is a fair share of atmospheric space. Many others have examined the economic structures that support carbon-based industry, which, in turn, has grown to fuel, support, and encourage particular forms of consumption with related GHG emissions. Also, others have looked at political economic impacts, critically exploring for whom the economy potentially booms. This leads to further analysis regarding emissions reductions based on historical rates of emissions at a per-capita and country level. For example, Aubrey Meyer first introduced the proposal of contraction and convergence, where overall GHG emissions are reduced (contraction) while emissions reductions from the global South would be less aggressive than those of the global North through per-capita allocation, so as to enable development in the global South as well as flexibility for a transition from carbon-based energy sources to renewable energy sources.

There is also sensitivity to intergenerational equity, or how future generations will be affected by current carbon-based consumption. This leads to two broad forms of action: adaptation and mitigation. First, adaptation is the alteration of an organism or the capacity to make changes to suit conditions different than those normally encountered. Differential vulnerability engenders challenges for some human populations to adapt to climate changes. Second, mitigation is an intervention that reduces the sources of GHGs. This can take shape through efficiency improvements (such as greater automobile fuel efficiency), fuel switching to less carbon-intensive fuels (such as switching from oil to natural gas for power generation), or mode switching to renewable technologies (such as solar or wind power). Mitigation can also include enhancements of sinks, and is often a more technologically centered and controversial approach.

Moreover, there have emerged many capitalist economic ideas that have gained salience in climate policy circles regarding anthropogenic climate change solutions. For example, market-based GHG permits to be bought and sold have been introduced in places such as the European Union so as to create an explicit cost to pollute. Furthermore, investments by companies in renewable energy technologies in countries of the global South can earn credits for GHG emissions reductions and thereby spur technological shifts in energy production in developing countries. These economic initiatives have been incorporated into the Kyoto Protocol as flexible mechanisms in order to create more opportunities to achieve emissions reductions. However, a number of participants have cautioned that this could lead to the overwhelming privatization of the global public good of our shared atmosphere.

Overall, climate change and global justice represent some of the most pressing issues of modern times. Many organizations are working to grapple effectively with these complex interactions, and they seek opportunities for meaningful and democratic decision making in future transitions of energy sources and consumption. These groups include Centre for Science and Environment, Redefining Progress, the Climate Justice Institute, Ecoequity, Climate Action Network, Rising Tide, Global Commons Institute, Friends of the Earth International, Greenpeace, and Union of Concerned Scientists. Also, new movements associated with these pursuits can be seen to reframe and bolster the aims that have traditionally concerned these groups. For instance, in the United States, increasing numbers of city officials, business leaders, religious groups, and leaders in the recreation industry have voiced concern over threats from anthropogenic climate change. In 2005, more than 180 U.S. mayors signed the Climate Protection Agreement to meet the goals of the Kyoto Protocol in each of their cities, in lieu of U.S. federal support for the treaty. In California, a wide range of business interests from insurance groups to the ski industry supported the Pavley Bill—signed into law in 2002—to reduce CO_2 emissions from personal automobiles. In 2006, many Evangelical Christian leaders signed a statement calling for more aggressive U.S. action on anthropogenic climate change.

Prominently, also in 2006, a film titled *An Inconvenient Truth*, featuring Al Gore—and a book authored concurrently by Gore—was released around the world. This has reinvigorated the issue of climate change and justice in international public and policy discourse. Former U.S. vice president Al Gore has long been a proponent of multifaceted action on climate change, and this new endeavor has renewed attention to climate change and has created space and opportunities for greater policy considerations.

Each day, more concerned citizens are determining that it is critical to link issues of climate change and global justice in order to achieve practical and acceptable policy solutions. These human rights–based approaches do not endeavor to enable formerly unequal communities the freedom to pollute like those who have done so in the past. Rather, what these groups seek is a more just approach to accessible, flexible, and equitable opportunities for alternatives to carbon-based industry and society, and to de-carbonize energy demands.

—*Maxwell Boykoff*

See also Deep Ecology Movement; Environmental Movement; Environmental Racism; Social Movements, Sociology of; Solar Energy Movement

Further Readings

Agarwal, A., & Narain, S. (1992). *Global warming in an unequal world: A case of environmental colonialism.* New Delhi, India: Centre for Science and Environment.

Athanasiou, T., & Baer, P. (2002). *Dead heat: Global justice and global warming.* New York: Seven Stories Press.

Blaikie, P., Cannon, T., Davis, I., & Wisner, B. (2005). *At risk: Natural hazards, people's vulnerability, and disasters.* New York: Routledge.

Gupta, J. (2002). *Our simmering planet: What to do about global warming?* New York: Palgrave Macmillan.

Houghton, J. T., Ding, Y., Griggs, D. J., Noguer, M., Linden, P. J., & Xiaosu, D. (2001). *Climate change 2001: The scientific basis* (Contribution of Working Group I to the Third Assessment Report of the Intergovernmental Panel on Climate Change, Summary for Policymakers and Technical Summary). Geneva, Switzerland: IPCC.

Pedace, R., Vaughan, B., & Doherty, A. (2005). *Climate debt: Making historical responsibility part of the solution.* Amsterdam: Friends of the Earth International.

Peet, R., & Watts, M. (Eds.). (2004). *Liberation ecologies: Environment, development, social movements.* London: Routledge.

CLOWARD, RICHARD A., AND PIVEN, FRANCES FOX (1926–2001 AND 1932–)

Richard A. Cloward and Frances Fox Piven occupy an unusual place in American social welfare history, having been influential both as scholars and as activists. Cloward was a student of juvenile delinquency and a founder of Mobilization for Youth in 1962, which served as a model for the Great Society's Community Action Program. Cloward and Piven, a researcher at Mobilization for Youth, were among the founders of the National Welfare Rights Organization (NWRO) in 1966. The NWRO was born, in part, of "A Strategy to End Poverty," a paper Piven and Cloward circulated in late 1965 and published in *The Nation* in 1966. Their research showed that only half of eligible poor women actually received welfare benefits, and they argued that the welfare system was able to function only because it actively excluded so many. They proposed to enroll all those who were

eligible, thereby bankrupting local relief agencies and forcing the federal government to establish a national relief program. NWRO executive director George Wiley was never fully convinced of this strategy and ultimately built the NWRO as a membership organization instead of the network of activists and organizers Piven and Cloward proposed. But their thinking nonetheless informed much of the welfare rights movement's activities. Though largely defunct by the early 1970s, the NWRO helped expand the food stamp program, forced tens of millions of dollars in relief money to be put into the hands of poor women, helped bring landmark welfare rights cases before the U.S. Supreme Court, mobilized opposition to Richard Nixon's Family Assistance Plan, and helped bring poor black women into politics as actors and agents of change.

In 1973, they published *Regulating the Poor,* a book that would become a classic in the academic social sciences but which was also widely read among activists. In it, they argue that welfare programs are not instituted as benevolent efforts to aid poor people (as most scholarship then suggested) but are rather created or expanded only in times of crisis in order to placate the poor. When that disruption subsides, however, they argue that relief programs are then cut back in order to force recipients into the low-wage labor market. Relief has thus historically expanded and contracted to regulate both civil disorder and low-wage employment. The claim continues to be debated among scholars. *Poor People's Movements* followed in 1977. In this work, they examined the history of American social movements, outlining the conditions under which people are most likely to unite in opposition to injustice and describing the conditions that lead governments to quash movements, co-opt them, or grant them their demands. It, too, has become a classic text.

In 1983, they founded Human SERVE (Human Services Employees Registration and Voter Education), whose research and activism ultimately led to the 1993 National Voter Registration Act. The law requires public agencies, including departments of motor vehicles and welfare offices, to offer easy access to voter registration forms (thus, it is often referred to as the "Motor Voter" law). In *Why Americans Still Don't Vote* (an updated version of *Why Americans Don't Vote,* which showed how the poor have been excluded from democratic politics throughout American history), they explain why the National Voter Registration Act succeeded in registering large numbers of new voters but had little impact on actual voting rates. Human SERVE continues its efforts to bring more Americans into electoral politics.

Together and individually, Cloward and Piven and their works have received awards from the Society for the Study of Social Problems, Eugene V. Debs Foundation, Council on Social Work Education, American Public Health Association, National Association of Secretaries of State, the American Sociological Association, and many others.

Richard A. Cloward died in 2001. Frances Fox Piven is Distinguished Professor of Political Science and Sociology at the City University of New York Graduate Center. She is a former vice president of the American Political Science Association and 2006–2007 president of the American Sociological Association.

—Stephen Pimpare

See also Community Action Program; Praxis; Social Movements, Sociology of; Welfare Rights Movement

Further Readings

Cloward, R., & Piven, F. F. (1966, May 2). The weight of the poor: A strategy to end poverty. *The Nation.*

Piven, F. F., & Cloward, R. A. (1977). *Poor people's movements: How they succeed, why they fail.* New York: Pantheon Press.

Piven, F. F., & Cloward, R. A. (1993). *Regulating the poor: The functions of public welfare* (2nd ed.). New York: Vintage. (Original work published 1973)

Piven, F. F., & Cloward, R. A. (2000). *Why Americans still don't vote: And why politicians want it that way.* Boston: Beacon Press.

Schram, S. F. (2002). *Praxis for the poor: Piven and Cloward and the future of social science in social welfare.* New York: New York University Press.

Trattner, W. (Ed.). (1988). *Social welfare or social control: Some historical reflections on regulating the poor.* Knoxville: University of Tennessee Press.

West, G. (1981). *The national welfare rights movement: The social protest of poor women.* New York: Praeger.

COALITION BUILDING

Coalition building occurs when groups with a common interest in a particular policy outcome will cooperate with each other to work for its advancement. A coalition involves organizations electing to work together with the specific intent of influencing a particular public policy decision. It is well established by now that coalitions play an important—often decisive—role in determining the effectiveness of an advocacy strategy. Over the years, several political scientists have conducted large-scale surveys of the activities that U.S. lobbyists report undertaking. These surveys universally suggest that participation in lobbying coalitions appears to be very common—the proportion of lobbyists surveyed who stated that they took part in coalitions is generally well over 90%.

Coalitions tend most often to be ad hoc or temporary arrangements. Typically, a coalition is formed to work around one specific policy issue; once that issue has been resolved by policymakers, the coalition will dissolve. Indeed, some political scientists have described Washington lobbying as an infinite pattern of whirlpools: Groups come together to form one set of whirlpools on all sides of a policy issue, and when it is concluded, the groups break up and then re-form in different configurations to create a new set of whirlpools dealing with a different issue. In large part, this is due to the relatively fractured state of American government, in which no political party can always direct the policy agenda. By contrast, in the United Kingdom, a government with a large majority in Parliament can more or less guarantee to pass its legislation. The fact that U.S. congressional and White House politics ensures that power is more diffuse and constantly shifting makes it inevitable that interest groups have to work in coalitions in order to be successful. The relatively weak party system in Congress, for instance, means that lobbying coalitions can be highly effective at creating voting majorities on any given issue by drawing on cross-party support in the House and Senate.

Groups commonly find that they need to work on one issue with another organization but that they will be opposing that organization on another issue. In

Washington, it is said that groups can have no permanent allies and no permanent adversaries, merely permanent interests which require any group to cooperate with any other group that shares its position on a particular policy goal while acknowledging that they continue to differ on separate policy objectives. To take one practical example of the diverse range of organizations that may form a coalition, we could consider a proposal to increase the regulation of beer. Such a proposal could face opposition from a coalition of all the various interests involved in that single industry: farmers (who grow hops, wheat, and barley), breweries (from global brands to micro-producers), labor unions (representing workers in the industry), bottle and can manufacturers, beer wholesalers and distributors (and their employees), retailers (bars, clubs, hotels, restaurants, liquor stores, and groceries), and consumers (represented by groups such as the 300,000-strong Beer Drinkers of America).

As that example illustrates, the partners in a coalition may well have varying reasons for supporting the same ultimate policy objective. As long as the end goal is shared, however, they can set aside their other differences to work cooperatively on that issue. Coalition partners very often decide to work together on a policy issue precisely because each partner brings to the united effort a very particular resource, for example, information, membership, money, access to an influential legislator, and so on. In a coalition, organizations that may well be competitors on other issues choose to set aside those differences in order to maximize their joint impact on public policy by exchanging their individual resources to mutual benefit.

Coalitions can serve a number of purposes for the groups that form them. As noted earlier, they enable organizations to pool their financial and other resources in order to maximize the impact of their campaign. In addition, they help to make the campaign appear more credible. A coalition of interests can certainly enable its members to argue more persuasively together than separately that the viewpoint being expressed represents the public interest. In other words, policymakers are more likely to listen favorably to the views of a coalition rather than similar views expressed by a number of groups separately. This is

even truer if the coalition represents what political scientists term *nontraditional allies.* Such coalitions substantially benefit from the perception among policymakers that if groups which do not commonly work together nevertheless find it possible to cooperate on a particular issue, that in itself suggests that the policy objective represents "good" policy. Examples of nontraditional coalitions would include liberal media organizations and religious cults working together on issues relating to the First Amendment of the U.S. Constitution; Communists and energy companies uniting to oppose the development of nuclear power stations; and religious congregations and horse-racing interests combining to defeat the proposed introduction of a state lottery. In each case, the coalition partners would have very different reasons for joining the alliance, but in the end they would share a very particular policy goal. In each case, policymakers would certainly pay attention to the fact that such diverse groups had achieved some measure of common ground.

Coalitions can prove useful, not just from the perspective of the groups involved in the alliance but also so far as the targets of their activity are concerned. Decision makers are able to communicate and negotiate efficiently with a coalition, and coalitions reduce risk for decision makers. By reducing the level of conflict within the lobbying community on an issue, coalitions help to provide policymakers with a certain "comfort level." Coalitions minimize the undoubted cacophony that can result from a number of groups each lobbying individually on the same issue, all expressing largely similar views although each asking for something slightly different or emphasizing different factors. A coalition ensures that this level of negotiation and compromise is undertaken internally, before policymakers are approached. As Kevin Hula noted, lobbying coalitions serve the function of requiring interest groups to predigest policy proposals (by mediating and resolving any internal conflicts within the coalition) before lobbying legislators and regulators. When interest groups have privately settled points of detail, it then becomes much easier for policymakers to support the end proposals.

Managing and coordinating the work of a coalition can be problematic in itself. To begin with, it is necessary that a lobbyist dealing with a policy issue is sufficiently entrepreneurial to actually identify and approach other groups which may be likely to share the same, narrow interest on that particular issue. Some potential coalition partners may be relatively obvious in that they face clear and similar threats or opportunities from the issue, whereas others can be identified if the lobbyist is a little more creative in considering all the implications of the policy. A useful approach is suggested by Edward Grefe, who categorizes potential members as "family" (such as employees, shareholders, and spouses), "friends" (those who have some economic relationship with the organization, like customers or suppliers), and "strangers" (other groups that could conceivably have an interest in the policy issue).

Once members have been recruited, it becomes necessary for them to establish explicit guidelines regarding the organization and management of the coalition. Given that most coalitions are temporary arrangements focused solely on the achievement of limited goals, they have the potential to be relatively flexible. However, it remains crucial that a number of issues are fixed at an early stage. All members must know which of them will be undertaking particular functions (such as research, communication, the coordination of intelligence, planning a grassroots effort) within the coalition; the means of funding and resourcing the coalition's activities must be established; some mechanisms for running and coordinating the campaign have to be negotiated; a strategy has to be decided upon; and all members must be able to settle upon the key messages to be delivered to policymakers.

Even (perhaps especially) large coalitions must be managed on a day-to-day basis by a small number of members. Coalitions are useful only for as long as they stay focused on achieving a specific policy outcome. One of the most common dangers of any coalition is that if each partner in the alliance needs to go back to his or her organization for approval of decisions and strategies, that process will inevitably become so time consuming that the coalition collectively will cease to operate flexibly and to respond to events speedily. The policy objective of the coalition should be as focused as possible in order to minimize the chances of some members being pulled away from the coalition as a result of minor or symbolic concessions from policymakers.

Perhaps the defining value of lobbying coalitions is that, by uniting around an issue, they can better enable organizations with particular self-interests to present their case in terms of the broad public interest, rather than of each group's narrow and sectional interest. The basis of coalitional lobbying is that the larger the coalition that can be swung behind any policy goal, the more likely that goal is to be achieved: Coalitions are the aggregate or sum of a number of private interests, and collectively, they can be portrayed as representing the public interest.

—*Conor McGrath*

See also Activism, Social and Political; Lobbying; Strategies and Tactics in Social Movements

Further Readings

Costain, D. W., & Costain, A. N. (1981). Interest groups as policy aggregators in the legislative process. *Polity, 14*(2), 249–272.

Gray, V., & Lowert, D. (1998). To lobby alone or in a flock: Foraging behavior among organized interests. *American Politics Quarterly, 26*(1), 5–34.

Heaney, M. T. (2003). *Coalitions and interest group influence over health care policy.* Paper presented at the annual meeting of the American Political Science Association, Philadelphia, PA.

Hula, K. (1999). *Lobbying together: Interest group coalitions in legislative politics.* Washington, DC: Georgetown University Press.

Loomis, B. A. (1986). Coalitions of interests: Building bridges in the balkanized state. In A. J. Cigler & B. A. Loomis (Eds.), *Interest group politics* (2nd ed., pp. 258–274). Washington, DC: CQ Press.

Mack, C. S. (1997). *Business, politics, and the practice of government relations.* Westport, CT: Quorum Books.

Nownes, A. J. (2001). *Pressure and power: Organized interests in American politics.* Boston: Houghton Mifflin.

CODE PINK

Code Pink is an international organization dedicated to uniting women against domestic and international violence and oppression. The name *Code Pink* was developed as a satirical take on the color-coded terror alert system put in place by the U.S. Department of Homeland Security.

The Code Pink organization is loosely structured and resists hierarchy; yet it is very effective. Code Pink conducts anti-war actions at the national, state, and local levels. The group follows feminist ideals and advocates open and respectful communication. Code Pink does not restrict membership based on sex or gender. Code Pink often works with other groups, including Veterans for Peace, Military Families Speak Out, and the National Organization for Women. Code Pink also has a large presence at Camp Casey, the encampment of anti-war protesters, originating with Cindy Sheehan, outside the George W. Bush ranch in Crawford, Texas.

Code Pink events put a new spin on traditional forms of protest, such as petitions and marches. The creative and unique tactics often provide a parody of what is seen as feminine while honoring the members' strength. One example is the mock firing of government officials where a symbolic Bush and Cheney received a "pink slip" in the form of women's lingerie. Further, the image of women defended by Code Pink is not necessarily a maternal one, marking a change from previous feminist peace campaigns. Code Pink aims to include all women who are against the war.

Using the Internet, media coverage, pop culture, and parody, Code Pink events represent enjoyable activism, including creative protests, die-ins, and teach-ins. During the Christmas shopping season, Code Pink protested against violent toys that perpetuate an idealized version of war, including G.I. Joe. Code Pink members have been able to stage protests inside meetings, such as the Democratic and Republican National Conventions. These creative options are often highly visual and play well in the media.

Code Pink has protested the war in Iraq on both national and international levels. The group holds ongoing vigils in locations like Washington, D.C. Some members have traveled to protest in the West Bank for peace and against the Israeli security wall. Other Code Pink efforts include fund-raising for victims of the Iraq War and coordinating visits between American and Iraqi families that had lost loved ones to the war.

Code Pink has over 100 local chapters in the United States that engage in grassroots actions. The tactics of local chapters include marches, protests, vigils, and work with the anti-recruitment campaigns. Significantly, these chapters also provide the structure for a local support network. Many women find a sense of sisterhood at Code Pink functions. Code Pink has, and will continue to be, a strong, creative, and feminist presence in the forefront of efforts to curtail and prevent the war.

—Sabrina Worsham

See also Feminism; Nonviolence and Activism; Play, Creativity, and Social Movements; Sheehan, Cindy; Strategies and Tactics in Social Movements

Further Readings

Baumeister, R. F. (1993). Exposing the self-knowledge myth [Review of the book *The self-knower: A hero under control*]. *Contemporary Psychology, 38*, 466–467.

Doolittle, A. (2005, December 13). Code Pink fights sales of G.I. Joe. *Washington Times*, p. A02.

Featherstone, L. (2003, March 23). Mighty in pink. *The Nation*, pp. 23–25.

Groves, S. (2005). Interview with code pink co-founder Jodie Evans. *Feminist Studies, 31*(1), 200–203.

Hannity, S., & Colmes, A. (2003, March 10). Interview with Code Pink cofounder Medea Benjamin [Television broadcast]. In *Hannity & Colmes*. New York: Fox News Channel.

Haughley, C. (2003, March 28). Protestors in New York stage "die-ins": Hundreds arrested with spread of civil disobedience. *The Washington Post*, p. A38.

Powell, S. (2003, May). Code Pink for peace. *Washington Report on Middle East Affairs*, p. 80.

COFFIN, WILLIAM SLOANE (1924–2006)

William Sloane Coffin was the chaplain at Yale University from 1958 to 1975 and the senior minister of Riverside Church in New York City from 1977 to 1987, the most visible and activist pulpit in the United

States. Coffin is most popularly known as the inspiration for the Reverend Sloan character in Garry Trudeau's immortal comic strip *Doonesbury*.

Bill Coffin, as he was known to his friends, was born to an affluent family in New York City in 1924. He was the nephew of Henry Sloane Coffin, once president of the activist Presbyterian school, Union Theological Seminary in New York City, and moderator of the Presbyterian Church in the United States. A classmate of George H. W. Bush, Coffin graduated high school from Phillips Academy in Andover, Massachusetts, in 1942, and went on to spend his young adult years variously as a gifted pianist, army member, and Central Intelligence Agency official. He graduated first from Yale University in 1949 and then later from Yale Divinity School and was ordained as a Presbyterian minister in 1956. A product of social gospel thinking, which combined the insights of Marx and Christianity in its quest for justice for all, Coffin was heavily influenced by the justice manifestos of his Yale seminary teacher, H. Richard Niebuhr, as well as the growing national foment for civil rights and integration.

In the years he spent at Yale University as a chaplain, Coffin was well known and contested as a supporter of student uprisings and as an opponent of segregation and the United States' participation in the Vietnam War. He became a vocal and prominent leader in the Freedom Riders, a group of activists who rode interstate buses in an effort to desegregate the South in the 1960s. In his time at Riverside Church, his interests moved, along with current national events, to nuclear disarmament. One of his high-profile activities during these years was his presidency of SANE/FREEZE (now called Peace Action), the United States' largest disarmament organization. This contribution was radical and bold in a time when ministers often were quiet about injustice on a global scale. Most significantly, Coffin used nonviolent means to achieve peace and stood against a bureaucracy that was pro-war.

Among Coffin's many publications is his unerringly honest autobiography, *Once to Every Man*, and his signature *The Heart Is a Little to the Left*, a reference to a speech he once heard from Dom Helder Camara, a Brazilian activist bishop. Coffin's biography, written by Warren Goldstein, titled *William Sloane Coffin Jr.: A Holy Impatience*, was reviewed in every major publication in the United States, including the *New York Times*, adding support to the author's largely undisputable argument that Coffin was, and is, along with Martin Luther King, Jr., the most influential Protestant religious figure in the United States. He will be remembered for the boycotts, his use of his influential positions to effect social change, and as one of the great religious leaders of the 20th century.

He retired to Vermont with his third wife, Virginia Randolph Witson (Randy). He died in April 2006.

—*Leona M. English*

See also Anti-Nuclear Movement; Civil Rights Movement; Conscientious Objectors to War; Freedom Rides, 1961; Protestantism; Public Theology; Social Gospel Movement; Spirituality and Peacemaking

Further Readings

Coffin, W. S. (1977). *Once to every man: A memoir*. New York: Atheneum.

Coffin, W. S. (1999). *The heart is a little to the left: Essays on public morality*. Hanover, NH: University Press of New England.

Coffin, W. S. (2004). *Credo*. Louisville, KY: Westminster John Knox Press.

Goldstein, W. S. (2004). *William Sloane Coffin Jr.: A holy impatience*. New Haven, CT: Yale University Press.

COINTELPRO

See GOVERNMENT SUPPRESSION OF SOCIAL ACTIVISM

COMMITTEE FOR CLEANERS' RIGHTS

In the 1980s, the Committee for Cleaners' Rights mobilized unions, community groups, and activists to pressure the government of Ontario to introduce labor legislation to help secure job security for cleaners and improve their prospects for joining a union. The committee met two ministers of labor in the Liberal Party's government of Ontario to argue for the importance of introducing a clause in the provincial Labor Code that would extend "successor rights" to cleaners. This legislation would have improved cleaners' ability to retain their jobs if, or when, their cleaning contractor was outbid in the tendering of a bid to clean a building. In addition, under successor rights, a contractor was obliged to recognize and abide by— where present—the existing union contract, even if the original "signatory" to that agreement were defeated in the tendering exercise. However, in spite of the committee's campaigns to rectify this gap in labor legislation, cleaners today remain exposed to a deregulating labor market and a postindustrial citizenship that has no sympathy for cleaners' issues and protections.

The Committee for Cleaners' Rights was the creation of a coalition of unions, community groups like the Portuguese Interagency Network, and New Democratic Party (NDP) politicians, including Bob Rae who later became the first NDP premier of the province of Ontario in 1990. The committee organized a meeting with William Wrye, minister of labor, to impress upon him the insecurities cleaners face in the labor market and to consider the option of extending successor rights to them. This first campaign failed in getting Minister Wrye to make a move. A second campaign evolved out of the committee's meetings and focused on organizing a petition in the community for labor law change in support of cleaners' rights. Ten thousand signatures were collected and brought to the office of the NDP's labor critic, Bob Mackenzie. The latter used the petition to introduce a Private Member's Bill to the provincial legislature for the purpose of getting successor rights protection for cleaners. Bill 132 was presented to members of the legislature and voted on. The vote count defeated the bill, 41 to 23. All NDP members of the legislature, as well as three Conservative Party members voted in favor, whereas all Liberal Party members voted against. Shortly after this disappointment, the Committee for Cleaners' Rights made another attempt to get the minister of labor (this time,

Greg Sorbara) to reconsider the case of building cleaners. Minister Sorbara refused to proceed with any legislative change, leaving the committee frustrated and out of steam. After a decade of organizing and politicking for legislative change, the Committee for Cleaners' Rights disbanded in 1989.

The importance of the committee in mobilizing a coalition of groups—some of which are intense rivals in organizing workers in the same sector— cannot be underestimated. Nonetheless, some aspects of their practices need to be questioned. First, the committee focused on Ontario alone, leaving unions with a national orientation—such as the Canadian Union of Postal Workers—with little to mobilize cleaners elsewhere in the country. Second, the proposed legislative change—successor rights— would do little to bridge the employment relation between cleaners and other workers with whom they share work space. Cleaners would remain contract workers employed by contractors rather than in-house employees sharing the same employer as most other workers in property management. This is an important point because it relates to issues of building solidarity toward resolving common workplace issues. Third, the committee seemed focused on successor rights as if it were a panacea, in the process displaying little vision on how to move with a broader approach to cleaners' reality. This lack of vision partly explains the disbanding of the Committee for Cleaners' Rights.

—*Luis L. M. Aguiar*

See also Justice for Janitors

Further Readings

Aguiar, L. L. M. (2000). Restructuring and employment insecurities: The case of building cleaners. *Canadian Journal of Urban Research, 9*(1), 64–93.

Aguiar, L. L. M. (2006). Janitors and sweatshop citizenship in Canada. *Antipode, 38*(3), 441–462.

Conaghan, J. (2003). Labour law and the "New Economy" discourse. *Australian Journal of Labour Law, 16*, 9–31.

White, J. (1993). Unorganized women. Chapter in J. White, *Sisters & Solidarity: Women and unions in Canada* (pp. 159–206). Toronto, ON: Thompson Educational.

COMMODIFICATION

In contemporary dictionaries and encyclopedias, the concept of commodity is hardly referred to—least of all commodification. But it is one of the most central categories of capitalist society. The concept of commodity is as old as class societies. In precapitalist societies, it occupied a minor place as a social category, but it came to occupy a central place in social and political theories in the age of capitalist society. The principal theorists of commodification are Adam Smith (1723–1790) and Karl Marx (1818–1883).

In the *Communist Manifesto* of 1848, Marx and Engels write that everything that is a need will be turned by capitalism into a commodity. They describe the development of capitalism as a process of permanent commodification. What is interesting about this assertion is the close association of the concepts of needs and commodity. *Commodities* are goods that are produced to satisfy certain human needs. This qualitative aspect of commodities refers to what political economists since the publication of Smith's *Wealth of Nations* call use-value. Since they are, however, exchanged as commodities, they are also necessarily quantified and reduced to what Marx called abstract human labor. This quantitative aspect of commodities is called exchange-value. In capitalism, the primary goal of production is the production of exchange-values rather than use-values. In other words, the satisfaction of human needs is the secondary goal of capitalist production. In the *Critique of Political Economy,* Marx refers to capitalism therefore as a society in which wealth appears to be an immense accumulation of commodities.

In terms of human relations, this negative relationship between use-value and exchange-value in a commodity is referred to as a paradox of values. The concept of commodification points to the spread of this paradox to all human relations, leading to what Marx called alienated labor and commodity fetishism. There are two primary prerequisites for commodification: the social and technical division of labor and monopolization of the means of production in the hands of a few. There are three spheres of human life that are subject to commodification: the external natural world, the external social world, and the internal or psychological social and individual world. The debate about ecological crisis refers to the commodification of nature, and the debate about economic and social crises points to the widening and limits of the commodification of human relations.

—*Doğan Göçmen*

See also Marx, Karl; Marxist Theory; Smith, Adam

Further Readings

Marx, K. (1918). *A contribution to the critique of political economy*. Chicago: Progress.

Marx, K. (1977). Economic and philosophical manuscripts. In D. McClellan (Ed.), *Karl Marx: Selected writings.* London: Oxford University Press.

Marx, K. (1978). *Capital* (Vol. 1). Chicago: Progress. (Original work published 1867)

Marx, K., & Engels, F. (1977). The communist manifesto. In D. McLellan (Ed.), *Karl Marx: Selected writings.* London: Oxford University Press.

Smith, A. (1981). *An inquiry into the nature and causes of the wealth of nations* (Vol. 1). New York: Liberty Fund. (Original work published 1776)

COMMUNISM

Communism can be understood as a form of social organization, a set of ideals, and a movement toward those ideals and the kind of social organization that would embody them. As a form of social organization, communism would abolish private property in the means of production, articles of consumption, or both. In so doing, it would try to realize such ideals as a rationally ordered and just society, a society that prioritizes communal and social welfare, a cooperative and caring community that transcends individual competition and egoism, and an egalitarian and classless society. From ancient times to the present, a variety of different kinds of communist experiments have been attempted, and a number of communist utopian ideals have been proposed. Self-conscious communist movements and utopian proposals have taken both religious and secular, ascetic and materially affluent, celibate and sexually promiscuous forms. They have also taken authoritarian, democratic, and libertarian forms. In the 19th and 20th centuries, the dominant political movements were inspired by Marxist or anarchist thinkers who, for the most part, assumed that a general social and political revolution was necessary to bring about communism.

There is good reason to believe that early hunting gathering societies were communist, as such societies could not have a developed division of labor or class structure. Karl Marx and Frederick Engels labeled such social forms "primitive communism." The Greek philosopher and mathematician Pythagoras organized a communist experiment in southern Italy, which was a combined university and monastic order. The Pythagoreans were mystics who believed that the physical universe and moral universe could be reduced to a harmonious system of numbers. Thus, for the Pythagoreans, private property, which destroyed the harmony and equality of the whole, was the origin of social injustice. The example of the Pythagorean community, as well as the philosophy of Pythagoras himself, influenced Plato's conception of justice as described in *The Republic*. Plato's utopian ideal divides society into three classes: (1) artisans, who are allowed to have private property as long as it is kept within supervised limits; (2) auxiliaries, who are a combination of soldiers and police force and who are allowed to have some degree of luxuries but not private property; and (3) Guardians, who rule the society and are allowed neither private property nor material luxury. The basis of the society is the division of labor, each part of which must evidence a certain virtue in harmony with the society as a whole. For Plato, the society is just if each of these classes is fulfilling its appointed task well. As the Guardians have the responsibility for the society as a whole, it is especially important that anything that would promote self-interest or would divert them from being wise and socially responsible must be eliminated. Hence, they must live communally without any private property or material luxury. Plato also insists on the equality of women and the ability of women to be Guardians. However, insofar as family ties would promote private

interests over communal interests, the Guardians are also not allowed to form separate families, and their children must be raised communally. Plato's conception of communism may strike the modern reader as strange, because it emphasizes class distinctions and is communism only for the ruling class. However, it is important to recognize that Plato's allowance of private property for the artisans is based on his assumption that only certain people can have the sort of knowledge required for wisdom. If, however, one makes the modern assumption of the potential equality of all human beings, Plato's reasoning for the necessity of communism could be generalized to everyone.

Another early communist experiment arose in Palestine in the middle of the second century BC and lasted until the end of the first century AD. This was a Jewish sect known as the Essenes. Martin Larson, an American scholar of religions, claims the Essenes were influenced by the Pythagoreans. The Essenes established communities throughout Palestine. They were an apocalyptic sect and were generally monastic, ascetic, vegetarian, and celibate. Their communism was total, as they lived and ate in common and possessed nothing of their own, not even their clothes. It is generally assumed that John the Baptist was an Essene, and some scholars believe that Jesus of Nazareth was considerably influenced by the Essenes, if he were not indeed himself a Nazarene Essene. In any case, the words ascribed to Jesus in the Gospels are very much in accord with the communist ideas of the Essenes (e.g., The Sermon on the Mount). In the second and fourth chapters of Acts, the apostles are described as owning everything in common, selling their possessions, and distributing their money and goods to each person according to their need. However, once Christianity became a state religion, the communism of the early Christians was relegated to monastic communities. Major Christian figures like St. Augustine argued that the sharing of goods was only possible for those who lived within the monastery walls.

The ideal of communism as a wider social ideal emerged during the Reformation. In the mid-14th century, John Wyclif, an Oxford philosopher and theologian, insisted that the Church should follow the model of the early apostolic poverty. While he did not oppose private property outside the Church, he assumed that human beings in a state of grace would hold all things in common. However, his followers, known as Lollards, often went further, attacking not only the Church's property but that of the nobility. Some of the Lollard preachers went from England to Bohemia where they, in the beginning of the 15th century, influenced Jan Hus, who was rector of the University of Prague. Hus's challenge to the power of the Church in Bohemia led ultimately to his execution. Although Hus was a reformer, many of his followers were radicals and, at the news of his execution, organized a general uprising in Prague. These Hussites then arranged a truce and left to form a Christian communist community, which they called Tabor, under the leadership of Jan Zizka. In Tabor, there was a complete sharing of goods. Anyone who joined the community was expected to put their possessions into a huge tub; the goods were then distributed among the entire community. The armies of the Pope and the emperor attempted to invade Tabor. They were at first repulsed, but in 1434, Tabor was defeated. The Taborites were forced underground but reemerged in a variety of radical sects. In 1528, an offshoot of the Anabaptists, known as Hutterites, after their leader Jacob Hutter, formed a community in Austerlitz, Moravia. There, the Hutterites organized communal workshops, communal farms, and communal households, dining rooms, and schools. As a result of persecution, many Hutterites emigrated to Ukraine and later to Canada and the United States.

In 1516, Thomas More published *Utopia,* a work that was clearly influenced by Plato's *Republic.* In Book II of *Utopia,* More offers an account of a well-ordered, fictional community in which neither private property nor money exists. In this utopia, the burdens of agricultural labor are shared, and all goods are stored in general warehouses and distributed to everyone according to their needs. In Book I, More offers a satirical account of the English land Enclosure Acts, which had the effect of impoverishing small farmers and pushing them off the land. In 1649, Gerrard Winstanley organized a group of poor laborers and landless peasants to take over the common land on St. George's Hill in southern England. This group became known as Diggers and under Winstanley's leadership,

they began to cultivate the land in the spirit of religious communism. Winstanley had probably read More's *Utopia* but was primarily inspired by the communist ideas in the Gospels. He argued that God had created the earth for all to possess in common and that the Fall of Adam was the introduction of private property. The Diggers assumed that their example would spread across England and that this would initiate a new age in human development. However, while the Diggers were expelled less than a year later, their example continued to inspire communist movements into the 20th century. The Diggers may be considered the first attempt to initiate communism through what Marx would later call the expropriation of the expropriators.

The late 18th and the whole the 19th century witnessed two kinds of communist movements. The first was a proliferation of communist experiments, especially in North America. Most of these communist experiments were inspired by religious ideals. Perhaps the most famous and one of the most long lived of these was the Shaker community, which, under the leadership of Ann Lee, believed in the complete equality of men and women, total common ownership of possessions, and celibacy. Other major religious communist communities were Zoarites in Ohio, which stressed democratic decision making, and the Oneida society, which had a system of communal marriage. The secular communist societies in North America were shorter lived. They were inspired primarily by three utopian thinkers: (1) Etienne Cabot, whose *Voyage to Icaria* was influenced by More's *Utopia* and which contained the phrase, subsequently used by Marx to describe a communist society, "from each according to his ability, to each according to his need"; (2) Robert Owen, an English mill owner, who believed firmly that human character could be perfected by perfecting social conditions; and (3) the French political philosopher Charles Fourier, who proposed a complicated system of self-organizing communities.

The second kind of communist movement in the late 18th and 19th centuries was the attempt to organize the revolutionary overthrow of the existing order. Among them was that of François Émile Babeuf, who organized a secret society, called the Conspiracy of Equals, and attempted to overthrow the Directory that had taken power after the French Revolution. Babeuf was arrested and executed but became the exemplar of the professional communist revolutionary. In 1847, the Communist League, formerly the League of the Just, asked Karl Marx and Friedrich Engels to write a declaration of principles for their organization. The result was the *Manifesto of the Communist Party,* later retitled *The Communist Manifesto,* which was published in February 1848, at the same time as the first of many 1848 revolutionary insurrections throughout Europe occurred. With this pamphlet, Marx and Engels became the leading theorists of communist revolutionary movements. In 1864, they helped initiate the first communist international organization in London, and in the latter part of the 19th century and the entire 20th century, their theories dominated communist movements.

For Marx and Engels, communism needed to be divested of its utopian ideas and be put on a scientific basis. The way to do this is through a scientific analysis of historical change, which they called the materialist theory of history. This theory begins with the assumption that human beings are essentially social producers who not only produce what they need but also, in the process, produce who they are historically. This historical process, then, may be understood as a continual transformation of human nature. Because economic production is the most basic form of human activity, it provides the foundation for all other forms of production (e.g., social and political institutions, art, and philosophy). From this, it follows that the underlying roots of historical change must be located at the level of the mode of production. Class struggle, then, is the motor force of history. Class struggle, in turn, is generated by the conflict between the forces, or means, of production (land, labor, raw material, and tools) and class relations. Thus, when, in the feudal era, the development of industrial technology reached the point where the feudal organization of production prevented its further development, a class struggle arose between the emerging bourgeoisie (capitalist class) and the feudal lords. Similarly, Marx and Engels argued, the capitalist organization of production, based on the necessary pursuit of private profit, is incompatible with the rational utilization of the enormous productive forces created by capitalism. The result is a new class struggle, now between the bourgeoisie and the proletariat (working class). The abolition of

capitalism is, thus, a historical necessity, and it requires the abolition of classes, commodity production, and private ownership of the means of production. Thus, revolutionary movements for communism need to ground themselves in a historical analysis of capitalism. What is wrong with utopian communities is that they can occupy, at most, a temporary corner of capitalist society. What is wrong with utopian socialist theories, like those of Owen and Fourier, is that they think that moral reasoning can, by itself, create communism.

However, while Marx and Engels eschewed utopian thinking, they had an elaborate vision of communism. This vision can be divided into two stages: what Marx, in the *Critique of the Gotha Program,* called "first phase communism" and "second phase," or "full communism." This is because, for them, communism in its full form cannot exist immediately after the overthrow of capitalism. There are two reasons for this. The first is that the capitalist mentality cannot be changed overnight. The second is that members of the former capitalist class will attempt to regain their power. To satisfy the first problem, first phase communism needs to provide a form of capitalist incentive. Therefore, it may allow some degree of private ownership and market activities. It will distribute the goods according to the output of work and level of skill. To respond to the second problem, first phase communism will need to maintain a state apparatus, controlled no longer by the capitalist class but by the working class, a State which is now the dictatorship of the proletariat. Nonetheless, first phase communism will open the possibility of a more fully developed communism. It will socialize the major industries of production. It will provide essential goods and services so that everyone has access to them (e.g., free education, free medical care, free child services). It will reorganize the State as a workers' democracy in such a way that its repressive apparatus can begin to whither away. Thus, when the forces of production are advanced enough, first phase communism will pave the way for full communism. In full communism, work becomes a source of creative fulfillment; distribution of goods is in accord with needs; classes will no longer exist; individuals will have abundant free time to develop their many potentials; and there is no longer a need for a repressive state apparatus. Many commentators have argued that this final vision is indeed a form of utopianism. Marx and Engels would answer that their approach does not deny vision but insists on grounding it in historical possibility.

The 20th century has not confirmed Marx's vision. The Soviet Union, created by the Bolshevik Revolution in 1917, had very little in common with Marx's first phase communism. The dictatorship of the proletariat became the dictatorship over the proletariat by a party and managerial bureaucracy that were ruled, in turn, by a very small elite within the Central Committee. The State, far from beginning to wither away, became an elaborate instrument of ever-increasing repression. A new class system developed. By the 1970s, after an earlier period of rapid industrial development, the economic system had become stagnant. In 1985, Mikhail Gorbachev tried to reform the system through *glasnost* (political openness) and *perestroika* (economic restructuring). In 1989, the Soviet Empire began to unravel. In December 1991, after an attempted putsch by forces opposed to the reforms, Gorbachev resigned, the Soviet Union was dismantled, and Russia attempted a transition to capitalism. Much the same could be said about Chinese communism: Today, China is attempting to become a capitalist country under the direction of the Communist Party. The First International was split between the followers of Marx and Engels and those who followed the Russian anarchist Mikhail Bakunin. Bakunin differed with Marx on a number of strategic questions, and his main opposition to Marx was focused on first phase communism. For Bakunin, it was important to oppose not only the rule of Capital but the rule of the State. Maintaining a repressive state apparatus would, he insisted, create an authoritarian bureaucracy and undermine the egalitarian goal of communism. In effect, Bakunin, like other anarchist-communists, believed it is possible and necessary to go directly to what Marx called full communism without an intermediary stage. Peter Kropotkin, the Russian naturalist and perhaps historically the most important theorist of anarchist-communism, envisioned a society based on democratic communes, which would be federated with one another rather than having a central authority. In his book, *Mutual Aid,* Kropotkin argues that cooperation rather than competition is what enables

species in general to survive and that human beings are not an exception to this rule.

Different conceptions about human nature often reflect people's political positions. Those who think that human nature is innately competitive and selfish or that there is an aggressive instinct will use these conceptions to support the claim that communism, in any form, is impossible. If Marx is right, human nature is continuously transformed throughout history. If Kropotkin is right, the motive for communism is built into human nature. The 20th century has not confirmed Marx's vision of communism, but neither has it disconfirmed it. At the most, it demonstrates that communism needs to be organized in a different way, and the history of communist thinking and experiments shows that there are many possible communist alternatives.

—Karsten J. Struhl

See also Anarchism; Bolsheviks; *Communist Manifesto;* Engels, Friedrich; Marx, Karl; Marxist Theory; Utopian Communities

Further Readings

Elmen, P. (1954, September). The theological basis of digger communism. *Church History, 23*(3), 207–218.

Holloway, M. (1966). *Heavens on earth: Utopian communities in America 1680–1880.* New York: Dover.

Minar, E. L. (1944). Pythagorean communism. *Transactions and Proceedings of the American Philological Association, 75,* 34–46.

Ollman, B. (1979). Marx's vision of communism. In B. Ollman, *Social and sexual revolution: Essays on Marx and Reich* (pp. 48–98). Boston: South End Press.

Rexroth, K. (1974). *Communalism: From its origins to the twentieth century.* New York: Seabury Press.

Sayers, S. (1999). Communism and the individual. In S. Sayers, *Plato's Republic: An introduction* (pp. 45–55). Edinburgh, UK: Edinburgh University Press.

COMMUNIST MANIFESTO

By Karl Marx (1818–1883) and Friedrich Engels (1820–1895), the *Communist Manifesto* was first published in February 1848 and is reportedly the world's most widely read book after the Bible. Marx and Engels had been involved with the left-wing Young Hegelian movement in Berlin but came to reject its view that human freedom could be won by changing people's ideas (including their acceptance of alienating religious doctrines) rather than addressing the material realities underlying them. In the early 1840s, both concluded that human emancipation required the abolition of private property and its replacement by communal ownership of the means of production, and that the working class was the key to the revolutionary transformation of society. In 1844, they began a political collaboration that was to last until Marx's death.

The 1840s were a period of growing political and economic crises in Europe. In response, Marx and Engels established the Communist Correspondence Committee in 1846, which enabled them to forge ties with communists and other radicals in both Europe and the United States. They developed links with some of the left-wing leaders of the Chartists in Britain (the first mass working-class movement, fighting for a charter of democratic reforms) and with the League of the Just, a radical organization of perhaps 200 German workers, many living in Paris and London. The League of the Just organized secretly and had a romantic and conspiratorial view of revolution, in which a dedicated minority would seize power on behalf of the masses, but in London its leading members were influenced by the growth of trade unions and by the Chartists.

In early 1847, Marx and Engels joined the League of the Just, and in June of that year, Engels attended an international congress convened by the league in London, aimed at unifying communists from several countries. At this conference, the association renamed itself the Communist League; reorganized itself on more open, democratic lines; and abandoned its previous abstract slogans concerning justice and equality in favor of the call "Workers of All Countries, Unite!" The June congress produced a communist "confession of faith," written by Engels as a series of questions and answers, for discussion among the league's members in preparation for a second congress in November. In October, following further debates, Engels wrote an improved version titled "Principles of Communism." Shortly afterward, he told Marx that

because the document needed to bring in a certain amount of history, the catechism (question and answer) form should be abandoned, and it should be retitled the *Communist Manifesto.*

On November 29, the second Congress of the Communist League began in London. After much debate over 10 days, Marx and Engels fully won the organization to their ideas, and Marx was commissioned to write the league's official program. Marx wrote the *Manifesto* over the next several weeks in Brussels, where he was living in exile, but he drew heavily on Engels's earlier drafts; thus, both Marx and Engels are rightly credited as authors. The process evidently took longer than expected, because on January 24, Marx received a letter from the league in London complaining about the delay. In mid-February, the *Manifesto* was finally published in German in London, with the title *Manifest der Kommunistischen Partei* (Manifesto of the Communist Party).

In the preamble to the *Manifesto,* Marx and Engels announce their intention to dispel the myths about communism and to state its actual ideas and goals. Section I begins by emphasizing the historical importance of class and class struggle and then goes on to explain the rise of the bourgeoisie (the owners of the means of production under capitalism). Marx and Engels argue that the bourgeoisie came to power as a result of a growing contradiction between the forces of production (including tools, technology, and the organization of production and exchange) and the relations of production (in particular, class structure) in feudal society. Even though the bourgeoisie has revolutionized society, expanded to all corners of the globe, and played a historically progressive role in developing the productive forces, they argue a similar contradiction is emerging in modern society, giving rise to regular economic crises that will eventually lead to the bourgeoisie's downfall at the hands of the proletariat (the class of wage laborers). Marx and Engels describe the development of the proletariat and explain why its economic and social position—concentrated in large workplaces and urban centers—makes it capable of playing a revolutionary role. They argue that the victory of the proletariat will bring about the end of class exploitation.

Section II starts by describing the relation of organized communists to the rest of the working class. According to Marx and Engels, communists do not set themselves up as rivals to other genuine working-class organizations, but are simply the most politically advanced and militant section of the workers' movement. The central idea of communism is the abolition of bourgeois private property (which is distinguished from the abolition of all property). After responding to various objections, Marx and Engels set out the program that might be implemented by a successful workers' revolution, including the abolition of inheritance, the expansion of public ownership, and free education, all predicated on democratic control of the state. They predict that such a state of affairs will evolve into a communist society in which classes have disappeared, and "the free development of each is the condition for the free development of all."

In Section III, Marx and Engels criticize other tendencies identified as socialist (in the broad sense of addressing the social dislocations of modern society). *Feudal socialism* was an unsuccessful attempt by sections of the old landed aristocracy to promote its own agenda by manipulating working-class grievances. *Petit-bourgeois socialism* was put forward by sections of the middle class that objected to modern industry destroying small businesses. *True socialism* was a German variant of petit-bourgeois socialism, which ignored historical circumstances and substituted moralism for class politics. All of these were reactionary ideologies. *Bourgeois socialism* was an attempt to solve capitalism's social problems without fundamentally changing the economic system. Finally, various forms of *critical-utopian socialism* made valuable criticisms of capitalism, but because they saw workers merely as victims, they had no serious strategy for transforming society.

In the brief final section, Marx and Engels explain the relation of communist to non-working-class opposition parties. Communists support all progressive movements but, at the same time, refuse to hide their political differences. Marx and Engels believed the struggle against feudalism in Germany was of particular importance, because if successful, it would lead almost immediately to a workers' revolution. Communists bring the issue of private property to the

forefront in every struggle and refuse to hide their aims. The *Communist Manifesto* ends with a rousing call for revolution and international solidarity.

As Marx was completing the *Manifesto* in late January 1848, revolution was already breaking out in parts of Italy. Within days of its publication, revolution had spread to Paris and soon to much of the rest of Europe, including Germany. Marx, Engels, and other members of the Communist League took part in the revolutionary movement in Germany, where they hoped the bourgeoisie would overthrow feudalism and create more favorable conditions for a workers' revolution. But in Germany, the bourgeoisie proved more concerned about the threat from the working class than the repressive status quo, and the revolution was defeated in 1849. Elsewhere, too, the forces of counterrevolution were eventually victorious. Marx and Engels went into exile in England and soon left the Communist League, arguing that revolutionary conditions would not reemerge for several decades. The league itself quickly ceased to function.

At the time of its initial publication, the *Communist Manifesto* had little direct impact, in part because there was no time to distribute it before the revolutionary crisis broke. A Swedish translation appeared in late 1848 and an English one (by Helen Macfarlane) in 1850, but it was to be many years before editions in other languages were published. The *Manifesto* only began to reach a wider audience after Marx gained attention in 1871 for his defense of the Paris Commune, in which working people ran the city for 2 months before their experiment was brutally repressed by the French establishment. Both Marx and Engels viewed the Paris Commune as a model of the kind of society they advocated.

As the socialist movement grew in the late 19th and early 20th centuries, the *Communist Manifesto* became the most popular brief introduction to Marx's ideas. Later, it was widely distributed in the Soviet Union and other self-described Communist countries, although little in those regimes bore much resemblance to Marx and Engels's vision of a society democratically run by the working class.

Contemporary commentators across a wide political spectrum have praised the *Communist Manifesto* for its brilliant analysis of the underlying dynamic of capitalist society and its description of what we now call "globalization," but most reject the view that the working class will play a revolutionary role in opposing capitalism. Defenders of Marx argue that the critics are short sighted and ignore both the growth of the working class and class struggle internationally, as well as the continued tendency of capitalism to go into crisis over the long term.

—*Philip Gasper*

See also Communism; Engels, Friedrich; Marx, Karl; Marxist Theory

Further Readings

Draper, H. (1994). *The adventures of the* Communist Manifesto. Berkeley, CA: Center for Socialist History.

Gasper, P. (2005). (Ed.). *The* Communist Manifesto: *A road map to history's most important political document.* Chicago: Haymarket Books.

COMMUNIST PARTY USA

Undoubtedly, from its origins in 1919 until the latter part of the 1950s, the Communist Party USA (CPUSA) was the most important left-wing organization in the United States. Reaching 85,000 members at its peak in 1942, just as America entered World War II, and with party supporters expanding the organization's strength an additional tenfold, the CPUSA enthusiastically rallied for backing the Soviet-American war effort against the Nazis. In addition, through their tireless roles as industrial union organizers during the mid- to late 1930s, Communist Party members had already become a major force in several important Congress of Industrial Organizations (CIO) unions by the early 1940s. In New York City, a stronghold of party support where Communists actively engaged in housing struggles, CPUSA candidates were elected to the city council during its zenith.

Inspired by the Bolshevik Revolution, two U.S. communist parties emerged from the left wing of the Socialist Party of America (SPA) in 1919: (1) the Communist Party of America (CPA), composed of the SPA's foreign-language federations and led by the sizeable and influential Russian Federation, and (2) the Communist Labor Party (CLP), the predominantly English-language group. Although the two parties feuded with each other, and various factions broke away to establish competing communist groups, the Communist International encouraged the unification of these organizations. In 1922, the CPA merged with the United Communist Party (which was established when the CLP joined a schism from the CPA) to create the legal and aboveground Workers Party of America (WPA). When the United Toilers of America, a group that adopted the same tactics as the WPA, combined with the latter organization, the party renamed itself the Workers (Communist) Party, finally settling on the CPUSA in 1929.

During the 1920s, the CPUSA's trade union arm, the Trade Union Educational League, bore from within the craft-union-oriented American Federation of Labor (AFL) to promote industrial unionism. When this strategy proved unsuccessful, upon orders from Moscow, the CPUSA transformed the Trade Union Educational League into the Trade Union Unity League in 1929, which was dedicated to organizing largely unskilled immigrant, African American, and women workers into industrial unions. Although the Trade Union Unity League was not nearly as successful as the AFL, it did provide a training ground for CPUSA organizers when they became active in the CIO unions.

During the early years of the Great Depression, the CPUSA emerged as committed militants within the unemployed movement. Later in the 1930s, with approximately 65,000 members and New Deal liberalism sweeping the country, the CPUSA became influential in many aspects of life in the United States. At this time, CPUSA members became national, regional, and community leaders in liberal, cultural, and student organizations.

With the onset of the Cold War and the rise of anti-Soviet sentiment after World War II, the CPUSA increasingly came under attack. Deprived of significant influence in the labor movement when the CIO expelled 11 CPUSA-led unions in 1949 and 1950, the CPUSA suffered additional loss of power in many left-liberal organizations when it was subjected to McCarthyism in the early 1950s. In 1956, support for the Soviet invasion of Hungary and the revelation of Joseph Stalin's crimes in Nikita Khruschev's "secret speech" at the Twentieth Soviet Party Congress led to mass defections from the CPUSA. Although Communists held leadership positions in several anti–Vietnam War organizations during the 1960s and 1970s, they exerted little sway in the U.S. labor movement. While the party made many significant contributions to the radical movement, especially during the 1930s and 1940s, the CPUSA's unswerving support for Stalin and the Soviet Union harmed the party, not only in the eyes of broad segments of the population but among other liberal and left-wing activists as well.

—*Victor G. Devinatz*

See also Abraham Lincoln Brigade; Bolsheviks; Communism; Davis, Angela; Old Left; Popular Front; Rosenberg, Julius and Ethel; Russian Revolution; Trotskyism

Further Readings

Draper, T. (1957). *Roots of American communism.* New York: Viking Press.

Draper, T. (1960). *American communism and Soviet Russia.* New York: Viking Press.

Isserman, M. (1987). *Which side were you on? The American Communist Party and the Second World War.* New York: Basic Books.

COMMUNITARIANISM

The term *communitarianism* has different meanings, depending on one's philosophical worldview. In its basic form, the term is used to denote collective responsibility, particularly when used in reference to one's position in a community. Communitarianism is an oppositional viewpoint that rejects ideologies that encourage individualism largely based on market economy and that often come with oppressive power structures that subjugate people who are usually at the periphery of society. By rejecting both authoritarian and individualistic practices, proponents of the communitarian perspective espouse the kind of politics that adhere to the ideals of moral citizenship founded on principles of social, political, economic, and cultural inclusiveness.

Communitarian ideas have evolved over the years, informing modern ways of governance in both public and private spheres. Commentators in this field of scholarship identify four main phases.

The first phase, which began around the 4th century BC, was characterized by Aristotle's rejection of the argument by Plato that there are objects of higher power beyond reach. According to Aristotle, such an argument elevated people to superhumans whose claim to knowledge appropriation was without proper justification. In Aristotle's view, this line of argument perpetuated class; hence, he believed that knowledge can be generated from lived experience, cooperative inquiries, or both.

Aristotelian thought was further advanced by Francis Bacon, whose thinking constituted what is regarded as the second phase of the communitarian evolutionary process. Other thinkers resonated with Bacon in acknowledging that knowledge appropriation based on ancient authorities or particular individual claims is worthless. He argued against bias in such claims and proposed that any such knowledge can be regarded valid if positive results are subjected to practical experimentation. Bacon's argument emphasized what he called "organized research," which allows for the participation of other people in cooperative ventures. In other words, Bacon's philosophical viewpoint aimed to guard against systematization of knowledge transfer, often done without proper security even when such knowledge claims come from powerful authorities.

The third phase in the evolution of communitarian thinking gained prominence in the mid-19th century. This time witnessed an amalgamation of two seemingly different but highly interrelated philosophies. The phase was characterized by the argument about how knowledge claims can be evaluated and how participatory decision-making processes are conducted. Proponents of these views, in particular, Robert Owen and John Mills, argued against market economy, which they believed was greed driven and alienating and caused communities to become powerless because the system seemed to advocate for centralized power and governance. As such, the main thrust during this period was a transformation of communities through participatory decision-making processes of issues that affected the communities themselves. Communitarian advocates argued that to achieve this, better provision of education as the main ingredient to awareness raising was necessary. In addition, communitarian thinkers believed that participatory democracy would provide power to both men and women to hire and fire any elected member of the chosen organizations as a means of improving efficiency, effectiveness, transparency, and accountability.

The fourth phase of this process was advanced by four major figures: Thomas Grean, Leonard Hobhouse, John Dewey, and Émile Durkheim. The major concern that emanated from these communitarian thinkers was the issue of individual rights, which they argued had been misinterpreted and used to exploit the relevance of community. They argued that the liberalization of this discourse was a dangerous precedent for the cohesion of communities. According to Dewey and others, liberalism was to be understood as a building block to enhancing the freedom of association through establishment of inclusive communities founded largely on the fundamental belief of common good. It is this aspect of common good that these four communitarian advocates believed to be the cornerstone for creating checks and balances and also as an instrument in safeguarding themselves from oppressive regimes and dictatorial tendencies. Similarly, unlike misconstrued ideas of liberalism, communitarian liberalism (which is emancipatory) has a powerful and catalytic role to enable people to learn, question, and deliberate as a team with minimal intimidation.

Closer scrutiny of the four phases provides a clear standpoint on which the communitarian thesis was launched. These elements include social democracy or good; a rebirth of the idea of community; active partnership between society and state (i.e., every member of the society is considered an active participant in the social good); inter- and intracommunity partnerships (i.e., inclusive communities that are mutually supportive in order to effect or raise awareness to any barriers

to sustainable community, political, and citizenship development); decentering the state as a strategy to increase civic participation (also known as empowerment); and the development of a pluralistic and democratic state. Many of these elements are interconnected. More importantly, these elements emphasize the challenges of liberalism, individualism, and greed. In other words, these communitarian arguments provide a third strand of thought: a renewed political will that is meant to counter authoritarianism by building responsive communities.

Emanating from the concept of "responsive communities" as part of a communitarian thesis are various threads of thought. First and foremost, communitarian theories, no matter how they might differ in their philosophical viewpoints, have one thing in common: participation in society. Therefore, at a community level, participation is critical. Inclusive communities are not to be seen from a narrow lens but rather from a wider perspective where community means families, neighborhoods, schools, business and social organizations, state institutions, professional groups, voluntary associations, and national and international networks. Being inclusive at each level of these structures ensures not only that the voices of ordinary individuals are heard but also that community members are part of the decision-making processes that affect their lives. For example, if there is need for a particular school reform, it would be appropriate and practical to engage not only parents of schoolchildren but also other structures and organizations that constitute the community. This practical aspect of communitarian spirit not only creates a sense of ownership but also helps to build personal relationships where those involved in the activities see each other as rich resources and building blocks to each other's lives.

The communitarian thesis has another dimension that requires closer scrutiny and understanding. Commentators such as Ametai Etzioni, Alasdair MacIntyre, Charles Taylor, Michael Sandel, and Andrew Cohen have alluded to one fundamental tenet of active participation and active society in order to underscore the argument that by participating in the larger life of our society, people become more empowered. It is this argument of fostering the spirit of community that has emerged with the idea that "one person is no person," because to be a person requires interaction with the wider society from which people draw their values, beliefs, and attitudes. As such, a person can claim citizenship by being an active member of that society. Put simply, people's contribution to the social good of individuals is dependent on their participation as subjects rather than objects of a given process.

While the view to active participation has received ascendancy in recent times (in particular, in the areas of development studies, community development, and international development), the praxis is not as deep as the proponents of communitarianism would perhaps acknowledge. Communitarianism goes beyond a simplistic view of participation to encapsulate what Damaine calls "wider movement," which aims to transform and maintain a supracommunity or a community of communities. The purpose, as argued by communitarians, is to develop a responsible community with a custodial stance that is activated by a change of heart and the manner in which individuals in communities see themselves—not only linked to each other but also having a collective responsibility that transcends the boundaries of family, clan, tribe, political, or religious affiliation.

The communitarian claim of building a strong relationship between citizenry and states is also an issue that development discourse highlights as one of the fundamental tenets of social good. However, the nature of state politics and communitarian philosophy seem to be in disagreement. Society-state interaction is highly political and often skewed because citizens are usually passive subjects in "representative" democracies. If, for example, communities demand their governments be inclusive, one of the challenges that arises is usually associated with conflict of interests. In many developing nations today, tribal wars and ethnic conflicts are pervasive and tell a story of disintegration of the idea and originality of the spirit of community. Rebuilding such a supracommunity may seem to contradict the "winner takes all" mentality, which is highly practiced in developing democracies. Thus, it is the failure to engage society in active negotiation in the policy formulation debate or processes that creates exclusion, elitism, and authoritarianism. Those known to represent the communities take it upon themselves to assume the authority and to decide without the proper consultation of their constituencies.

If the goal of the communitarian movement is to transform social and political aspects of community life toward a greater responsible participation as equal citizens on issues that affect citizens, decentering the state may seem a possibility. In essence, this means giving up power from the top to the lower levels of social governance. It also means providing citizens and governance structures with the freedom to operate with minimal or no political interference. The question of legitimacy for individual communities to govern themselves, with the assistance of community-based organizations, may appear to be a problem given the current global critique of the role of civil society organizations in facilitating participation in the decision-making processes. Communitarians often argue that for citizens to operate and flourish as individuals, they must have a common vision of life that ultimately reflects a good community.

Over and above some of the key issues communitarian citizenship advocates for is the nature and process of education. A well-informed citizenry is able to contribute to the function of state structures. This view has gained currency through such programs as education for all, gender education, education for the youth, and adult education. Communitarianism largely rejects the notion of looking at education from a narrow lens of only preparing or equipping citizens for an industry-related job. Rather, communitarian philosophy advocates for education for conscientization, that is, education that empowers individuals to contribute to the decision-making processes that affect their lives.

Related to the nature and process of education, communitarian thinkers offer their own standpoint with regard to the role of parents and schools. Overall, communitarianism sees parent-child relationships as that of power bargaining rather than that of control and dominance. Schools, therefore, have a fundamental role to cooperate with parents and other community-based organizations to foster the spirit of inclusiveness and nurture cooperation between the two entities in order to engender results whose ripple effects will benefit not only immediate society or communities but also statewide governance structures.

In rapidly changing societies, communitarian ideas should be understood with utmost care, as they can easily be misconstrued to mean a return to communism. Undergirding this philosophy is the argument that creating inclusive and responsible communities for all implies that any good person or a member of a good society has a responsibility to contribute to the common good of society. In this respect, there should be reciprocity for respect for all through social inclusion regardless of race, ethnicity, gender, sexuality, religious and political affiliation, disability, nationality, or any form of identity.

—Jonathan Makuwira

See also Civil Society; Community Action Program; Community Organizing; Dewey, John; Liberalism; Neoliberalism; Plato; Power, Theories of; Social Democracy; Utopian Communities

Further Readings

Cohen, A. J. (1999). Communitarianism, "social constitution," and autonomy. *Pacific Philosophical Quarterly, 80*(2), 121–135.

Demaine, J., & Entwistle, H. (Eds.). (1996). *Beyond communitarianism: Citizenship, politics and education.* London: Macmillan.

Etzioni, A. (1993). *The spirit of community: Rights, responsibilities and the communitarian agenda.* New York: Crown.

Etzioni, A. (1995). *New communitarian thinking: Persons, virtues, institutions, and communities.* Charlottesville: University Press of Virginia.

Etzioni, A. (2001). *The road to the good society.* New York: Basic Books.

MacIntyre, A. (1984). *After virtue* (2nd ed.). Notre Dame, IN: University of Notre Dame Press.

Sandel, M. J. (1982). *Liberalism and the limits of justice.* Cambridge, UK: Cambridge University Press.

Tam, H. (1998). *Communitarianism: A new agenda for politics and citizenship.* London: Macmillan.

Walzer, M. (1990). The communitarian critique of liberalism. *Political Theory, 18*(1), 6–23.

Community Action Program

The Community Action Program (CAP) was a U.S. federal initiative created through the Economic Opportunity Act of 1964. An extension of President John F. Kennedy's commitment to anti-poverty, CAP was the initial centerpiece of the Johnson administration's war on poverty within the era's Great Society efforts. CAP was initially housed in the executive office as an element of the Office of Economic Opportunity (OEO). Other early programs housed within OEO included Job Corps, Youth Conservation Corps, work-study programs, VISTA, and Head Start. Alongside these categorical programs, CAP promoted a community-based, bottom-up, comprehensive approach for mobilizing resources and attacking the root causes of poverty by maximizing both investment in areas devastated by poverty and participation of residents of those areas. The base strategy of CAP involved the direct federal funding of local community action agencies (CAAs), both public and private, that were to advocate with low-income residents. In 1966, a year after CAP was initiated, the actual spending for CAP, as documented in the U.S. budget, was $246,495,000 (excluding Head Start funds).

The CAP strategy emerged from decades of effort on the part of activists and reformers concerned with the impact of inequity within industrialized capitalist democracies and concerned with the plight of individuals not represented through the organization of interests, organization that is necessary to access the benefits of democratic representation. Efforts of settlement houses, voluntary social welfare programs, and demonstration projects such as the Ford Foundation's Grey Areas Project impelled the concept of community action into the politics of the presidency. Once community action was introduced as a concept for federal programming, CAP (later referred to in budget documents as "community action operations") became an exemplar of the complexities and tensions in the pragmatic positioning of social change ideals and ultimately the resilience of progressive interests once these are structured into organizations within networks of activity, government funding, and civic support.

CAP's Movement Through Federal Institutions

CAP, as housed within OEO in the executive office, was immediately greeted with critique and resistance. In the executive arena, and with the coordination authority to inquire into the anti-poverty efforts of other federal agencies, CAP enjoyed a vantage envied by agencies and critiqued by congressional leaders wanting to have more influence over CAP's activities. From this vantage, and based in the ideas that federal, state, and local resources could be mobilized to end poverty, supporters of CAP attempted to alter the trickle-down notions of political power and financial resources. Through a federal infusion of resources, local communities that had not had the financial base or skill sets that contribute to effective civic engagement now had the foundation for collective participation in local, state, and national arenas. In a system where groups with the financial resources to organize had maintained control of political processes, the introduction of a new organized voice was scrutinized by legislators, bureaucrats, and elected officials, who expressed their fears that state and local political authority would be hindered by direct federal funding of low-income community advocacy.

Although the CAAs funded through CAP were restricted from partisan lobbying, advocacy was at the heart of their mission. As CAAs increased their advocacy efforts, criticism of CAP also increased. Concern about CAP's impact on state power was first addressed through the granting of programming veto power to state governors. However, by 1967, the pressure from city mayors became so intense that the Green Amendment was passed to alter the authorization processes so as to require CAAs to obtain formal designation from their local officials and thus to operate more solidly within existing political structures. The amendment also formalized the structure of CAA boards by requiring one-third representation of elected public officials or their representatives, at least one-third low-income people or their representatives, and the remaining members from private and nonprofit organizations. Activists criticized this requirement as a dilution of the voice of the poor. Indeed, this requirement internalized a negotiated structure, ensuring that community action, as federally funded, would include the influence of professionals and investors in community action. This structure was essential for community action, as a concept, to move through the ongoing political attacks and accountability challenges.

By 1973, dismantling of the OEO was under way under the Nixon administration, first through efforts to restrict OEO's functions to research and development, then through the devolution of funding and oversight to the states, and ultimately to OEO's closure in 1974. With this closure, the Ford administration removed CAP from its direct link to the presidency and relocated community action funding to the oversight of the newly created Community Services Administration (CSA), an independent agency replacing OEO. The Ford administration further institutionalized CAP, as CSA was changed from an independent agency to a department within Health, Education, and Welfare. Through 1996, increases in CAP funding were minimal, not even keeping pace with inflation.

However, under the Carter administration, community action was quietly revitalized, and by 1977, actual spending jumped to $710 million (excluding Head Start funds that had become disconnected from community action funding). Within government publications, community action was again represented with respect to its creative origins of local, state, and federal interaction and original focus on local leadership. The conceptual and financial resurgence was short-lived. In the shadow of economic and energy crises, funding for community action efforts declined. With Reagan's conservatism and rising inflation came further reductions in spending for domestic social programming, the closing of CSA, and ultimately the shift to consolidation ideas that led to the 1981 Community Service Block Grants (CSBGs) that, once created, Reagan attempted to terminate. CSBGs were administered by the newly created Office of Community Services, operating within the Department of Health and Human Services. Under presidents George H. W. Bush and Clinton, CAAs continued to receive their funding through CSBG funds, but the Office of Community Services was moved further down in the institutional hierarchy, becoming a program under the Department of Health and Human Services' Administration for Children and Families. Although the government was supportive in rhetoric and still providing funds for CAAs, the shift to CSBG funding severely reduced the federal role in acknowledging the causes of poverty.

With community action's increased institutionalization within the federal bureaucracy, grants no longer encouraged nationally supported community innovation and action; rather, they became distribution vehicles to provide service program money to localities through states. CAAs expanded their categorical service activities, providing financial counseling, housing support, training, medical assistance, and food provision. With attention to service delivery and physical and economic development, some CAAs set aside the more assertive advocacy mechanisms of protest, choosing to advocate within a service delivery paradigm rather than in the overtly political arena.

Nevertheless, CAAs were once again targeted when George W. Bush's administration proposed a consolidation plan that both reduced funding for community service programming and relocated a number of community-oriented funding sources out of institutional homes in social services and development and into the Department of Commerce. This move, guised as a centralizing/efficiency effort and titled the Strengthening America's Communities Initiative, accompanied both a reduction in funds and a rhetoric that attempted to solidify poverty as a market phenomenon to be combated with increased individual and private enterprise and tax incentives rather than a sociopolitical one to be addressed with greater association, democratic participation, and voice. Bush's budget requests for fiscal year 2006 thus did not include requests for specific CSBG funds.

The ongoing political challenges faced by community action as a program occurred alongside the challenges of enacting, monitoring, and managing advocacy and comprehensiveness within institutional structures. As CAP moved through the federal government structure, supporters were forced toward pragmatism in negotiating around the appropriate blend of bricks-and-mortar and social development, about formal board structures, about the extent to which advocacy should be publicly funded, and about the types of evaluation and leadership appropriate in comprehensive programming. The transparent collaboration between private and public officials and citizens, which was the very foundation of community action as conceptualized in CAP, also left local CAAs vulnerable to claims of

conflicts of interests. In addition, community action grappled with ways to focus on community assets rather than solidifying the disadvantage of low-income neighborhoods by further institutionalizing poverty categorizations. Despite tensions, community action as a concept and as pragmatically structured has been quite resilient, as shown through the adoption of community action as a concept in categorical programs such as community policing and community schools.

Over the years, community action has vied for identity and support alongside other programs and agency missions such as urban development and education, initiatives grounded in specific cultural groups, and civil rights and national service efforts. However, the community action concept has retained an identity through its resistance of solely categorical solutions to comprehensive problems, through its ongoing commitment to local participation as one form of advocacy, and through its formal board requirements that made tangible one notion of a board structure for private/public partnership. This identity has survived through the coalitional and lobbying activity of the Washington D.C.–based Community Action Partnership (CAP) and the National Community Action Foundation, and in connection with affiliated state associations; operating and fund distribution entities; training, evaluation, policy, and support service intermediaries; and knowledge experts—all forming a network of participation in support of the cadre of similarly structured local organizations. The network's strength, within the federal funding structure, as well as in local practice, depends not only on its ability to face ongoing political and monetary challenges but also on its own interaction with contemporary forces of social change.

CAP's Interaction With Social Change

The social changes now affecting the community action network are reminiscent of earlier issues but are also uniquely current: generational shifts, the depletion of human resources through military demands and the traumatizing of low-income women, and the growing demand for inclusion of contemporary feminized conceptualizations of community, action, and leadership. As the current generation of activists moves out of civic service, community action is relying upon generations of potential citizen supporters and participants who have had little, if any, training in concepts of civic action and social entrepreneurship. These generations are distant enough from the 1960s civil rights history that they do not have experiential or even parental input about the importance of community action; in addition, they have been inundated, through education and media, with individualistic market-based education principles. Their technological exposure and social stresses have made them both restless with the status quo and resistant to organized change. At the same time that community action is pressed for the financial resources to attract these generations and mobilize their energy, community action is also in dire need of the sensibilities, media savvy, and peculiarly hyper spirit of these younger generations.

At the same time, military service is increasingly consuming the community resources of low-income neighborhoods, with women leaving their communities at a higher rate than ever before. Low-income U.S. communities face multiple challenges. Those community residents returning from military duty in Iraq and Afghanistan, for example, are in need of social services, acknowledgement of their sacrifices, and a feeling of social connectedness. Women who return from military service may have concerns related to their children's welfare during their absence. Industrialized women from various cultural backgrounds also may have special needs.

Finally, community action is also facing an exciting challenge as more women internationally attain positions of formal leadership in the political, private, public, and nonprofit arenas. New opportunities center on the inclusion of contemporary feminized concepts of community, action, and leadership. Community action, with its historical roots in the war on poverty, is challenged to attract support from citizens leery of the utilization of violent rhetoric and divisive metaphors and searching for new approaches that unite advocacy around holistic concepts and experiences.

—Angela K. Frusciante

See also Activism, Social and Political; Coalition Building; Community Organizing; Great Society; Income Inequality

Further Readings

Baum, H. S. (1997). *The organization of hope: Communities planning themselves.* Albany: SUNY Press.

Burnham, M. (1989, July 24). Legacy of the 1960s: The Great Society didn't fail. *The Nation, 249,* 122–124.

Clark, R. F. (2000). *Maximum feasible success.* Washington, DC: National Association of Community Action Agencies.

Flanagan, R. (2001, December). Lyndon Johnson, community action, and management of the administrative state. *Presidential Studies Quarterly, 31*(4), 585–608.

Marris, P., & Rein, M. (1967). *Dilemmas of social reform: Poverty and community action in the United States.* New York: Atherton Press.

O'Connor, A. (2001). *Poverty knowledge: Social science, social policy, and the poor in twentieth-century U.S. history.* Princeton, NJ: Princeton University Press.

COMMUNITY-BASED ECOLOGICAL RESISTANCE MOVEMENTS

Community-based ecological resistance movements emerge within struggles against environmental degradation that disturbs the symbiotic relationship between community and environment. These movements are devoted to the prevention of community life from environmentally harmful activities and to the investigation of means to mobilize local capabilities in resisting these activities. The awareness that the community lives with and within the environment is the key factor in the political mobilization of community members. The constitutive elements of these movements—such as the aim, perceived threat, organizational structure, activists, and activists' demands, targets, resistance strategies, and tactics—are articulated into a political project to protect community-environment interactions in a particular locality. With this political project, community-based ecological resistance movements differ from various types of environmental movements, such as single-issue local movements, nature conservationist movements, and mainstream environmental movements.

The characteristic aim of community-based ecological resistance movements is to protect and sustain the symbiotic relationship between community and the constitutive environment. As community members do not see their community and the particular environment they engage with as separate entities, the political demand around which they mobilize is to save both rather than one or the other. Ecological resistance generally communicates through a language of communal self-determination concerned with the socio-natural reproduction of the community. The counterhegemonic discourse articulates a denotative narrative based on legal community rights expressed as an integral part of the community. So, when a small indigenous community in a rural and impoverished region wages its struggle against a multinational logging activity giving rise to environmental conflicts, the discursive aim is readily knitted around ancestral rights and tribal customs. But, in another place, an urban community of middle-class inhabitants living in a highly complex social context and facing the threat of a harmful industrial activity integrates civic rights discourse with the similar aim of defending their way of life.

The environment is not conceived as raw materials and sinks in the service of capital accumulation, as in developmentalist claims manifesting themselves in harmful industrial activities. Instead, activists' claim about the same environment is based on its significance for the spiritual, cultural, social, and economic life of their communities. Thus, a general discursive justification for establishing a resistance strategy lies in the dependence of community existence on various aspects of the environment. It is a strategy for self-defense. In all resistance cases, ecologically unsound activities or projects are regarded as having detrimental effects on the integrity of community life inseparable from the quality of the environment. The perceived threat is a threat to this integrity. It is not merely the actual forms of air, water, and land pollution or that of the destruction of flora and fauna that pave the way for a reflexive and reactive movement of a community; community activism also arises in response to the potential ecological threats of proposed projects. A perceived threat, as such, prompts a spontaneous direct resistance movement aimed at defending and protecting the community's well-being.

Environment-related claims are of paramount importance in mobilizing communities against a threat, but environmental orientation does not thoroughly determine these movements, as is the case where anthropocentric or ecocentric thought shapes the identity of environmental movements. Because human-environment interactions are addressed in a relational/coexistential manner, activists of community-based ecological resistance movements have to reject dualist views emphasizing that nature and humankind are on two different planes. They use and transform the natural world for the necessities of community life, but they do not treat nature in an instrumentalist manner; instead, they show respect and care for nature.

Other significant differences between mainstream environmentalism and community-based ecological resistance movements are found in participant features and organizational structure. Unlike mainstream environmentalism based on a particular kind of institutionalization fostered by expert knowledge, ecological resistance movements rely mainly on community activism, local leaders, and resources. However, exchanges, solidarity bonds, and alliances are forged with similar local movements and national or international environmental organizations in order to make the local conflict a public issue by geographically expanding the position of resistance. Almost all members of the community, including children and elders, are active participants in an ecological resistance movement. Depending on the major economic activity of the community, the class origin of the participants might vary from peasantry to the middle classes. A relatively low level of class differentiation in the community is conducive to wider community participation. While it can be argued that communal relationships have been undermined in the face of modernization and globalization, organic ties among the members of the community still develop, albeit in unconventional resistance patterns. The shared views about the community's predicament, the threat, its causes, and consequences are the cement binding the members of the community together in the movement. There is a broad consensus of opinion among activists that outsiders in collaboration with the State are, for their short-term profits, abusing and destroying that which the community is dependent on, that is, respect and values.

The tactics employed by activists in community-based ecological resistance movements range from usually militant and sometimes illegal forms to nonviolent, peaceful, and legal ones, such as press conferences, petitions, lobbying, civil disobedience, demonstrations, meetings, marches, road blockades, and sit-ins. A massive involvement of community members in all of these actions demonstrates the degree of large-scale resistance and determination. By having recourse to these actions, activists are not calling for an improved environmental policy at the local or national level but rather the withdrawal of outsiders from the locality where the outsiders are acting in opposition to the will of the community. Though it is a long and expensive way, activists also use the tactic of legal actions by filing administrative appeals and lawsuits. Taking legal actions usually helps exert the pressure of the law on administrative authorities or corporations responsible for harmful industrial activities. In some cases, the cessation of these activities appears as a result of activists' judicial struggles as well as their direct actions.

Some examples of such movements in rural and urban settings around the world are the Mǔang fǎǎi farmers' movement against logging in Thailand; the Penan people's movement against logging in Malaysia; the village movements against the construction of infrastructural facilities in Mexico, Costa Rica, and Nicaragua; the U.S. movements against coal mining in eastern Kentucky, against the proposed zinc-copper mine in Crandon, Wisconsin, and against the proposed solid-waste incinerator in south-central Los Angeles; the Chipko, Appiko, and Bastar movements against forest destruction; the movement against the Narmada dam project in India; and the movements against a sewage treatment plant, a toxics storage-treatment facility, and a geothermal power plant in rural Greece.

The Bergama movement in Turkey is an interesting example in this respect. The villagers' resistance was against a noxious gold mining investment by a multi-national corporation in the small town of Bergama. Heavily engaged in agriculture, they saw the mine as a threat to community life, the environment, and future generations. The early mobilizations took the form of meetings, panels, press conferences, and petition campaigns to declare their opposition. The movement was sparked off in the mid-1990s when 5,000 community members blocked the main road connecting two big cities to protest the felling of thousands of olive trees for the open pit operation. As the corporation (backed by the Turkish government) insisted on putting the mine into operation, the community persisted with the demand for the cessation of its activities by employing confrontational tactics not only in their region but also in other cities of the country in the following years. They also took legal actions against the government authorities that issued mining permits and allowed the corporation to commence gold extraction. Despite the court decisions emphasizing the right to healthy living and a healthy environment, the mining activity continued while the villagers' struggle went on in the court and on the streets. Gold mining was politicized at the national level through these direct and legal actions. Alliances and connections with professional organizations, environmentalist groups, trade unions, and human rights activists helped the movement to make the local conflict a national issue, as well as providing movement leaders with expert knowledge and technical assistance. The struggle also politicized the community by opening up a new political participation channel, as almost all community members with no previous experience in any political activism except voting became committed activists to defend the community-environment symbiosis.

—*Aykut Coban and Mehmet Yetis*

See also Civil Disobedience; Community Organizing; Environmental Movement; Environmental Racism; Indigenous People and Environmentalism; Resistance; Save Narmada Movement; Strategies and Tactics in Social Movements

Further Readings

Coban, A. (2004). Community-based ecological resistance: The Bergama movement in Turkey. *Environmental Politics, 13*(2), 438–460.

Gedicks, A. (1993). *The new resource wars: Native and environmental struggles against multinational corporations*. Boston: South End Press.

Martinez-Alier, J. (2002). *The environmentalism of the poor: A study of ecological conflicts and valuation.* Cheltenham, UK: Edward Elgar.

Taylor, B. R. (Ed.). (1995). *Ecological resistance movements: The global emergence of radical and popular environmentalism.* Albany: SUNY Press.

COMMUNITY CURRENCIES

Community currencies have emerged as a means to empower the economically marginalized and to build social capital. This alternative social movement, comprised of autonomous, local systems, has proliferated in the past two decades. While all local currencies differ, each is premised on an alternative currency as a medium for the exchange of services and goods. Unlike conventional bartering (where two actors trade directly with one another), local currencies expand commerce by connecting a network of people (and often businesses). The provider of a service or good receives credit in the form of the community currency that can be used for making purchases from other participants in the system.

There are three notable systems in operation: Local Exchange Trading Systems (LETS), time banks, and hours systems. LETS (originating in British Columbia in 1983) have been the most widespread form of local currencies. Although LETS have never been widely pursued in the United States, there have been an estimated 1,500 LETS groups in 39 countries. Yet, researchers have concluded that LETS activity peaked in the mid-1990s and that a substantial proportion of LETS are no longer operating.

The Time Dollar Network was launched in 1983 in Miami, Florida, as a diverse and flexible program to formalize volunteering among the socially marginalized, that is, the young, the elderly, the poor, and the disabled. Whereas some of these programs are part of existing organizations, others are independent, alternative economies (e.g., LETS). These local currencies, now known as "time banking," continue to expand in the United Kingdom (where there are 80 active banks and more than 25 in development) and the United States (where there are over 40 programs).

In 1991, an activist in Ithaca, New York, started Ithaca Hours, a printed local currency. This paper format makes Ithaca Hours quite different than LETS and time banks. The latter require substantial coordination and organization as every transaction is accounted for. With paper notes, neither computerized accounting system nor accountant is needed. Since Ithaca Hours was founded, 82 communities in the United States have replicated the model. However, only about 20% of these systems are currently active.

Researchers have identified several major areas of difficulty that community currencies face. They include the recruitment of dedicated administrators, the continual recruitment of participants, redundant listings and the lack of useful services available in the systems, and insufficient resources to administer the systems.

Considering the movement as a whole, it is evident that LETS and hours systems have been less successful in surviving than time banks. The success of the latter is at least partially attributable to the fact that they tend to formally employ staff to broker exchanges, and they are often based in existing organizations. Participants in time banks differ to some extent from those in LETS and hours systems too. Whereas LETS and hour systems are favored by educated, alternative, and progressive people, time banks tend to be used more by the elderly and the poor. Although all of these efforts can be considered community currencies, it is clear that there are substantial differences in the actual practices.

—*Ed Collom*

See also Alternative Movements; Community Organizing

Further Readings

Cahn, E. S. (2000). *No more throw-away people: The co-production imperative.* Washington, DC: Essential Books.

Collom, E. (2005, September). Community currency in the United States: The social environments in which it emerges and survives. *Environment and Planning A, 37*(9), 1565–1587.

Meeker-Lowry, S. (1996). Community money: The potential of local currency. In J. Mander & E. Goldsmith (Eds.), *The case against the global economy* (pp. 446–459). San Francisco: Sierra Club Books.

North, P. (2003). Time banks—learning the lessons from LETS? *Local Economy, 18*(3), 267–270.

Seyfang, G., & Smith, K. (2002). *The time of our lives: Using time banking for neighbourhood renewal and community capacity building.* London: New Economics Foundation.

Williams, C. C., Aldridge, T., Lee, R., Leyshon, A., Thrift, N., & Tooke, J. (2001) *Bridges into work? An evaluation of Local Exchange Trading Schemes (LETS).* Bristol, UK: Policy Press.

COMMUNITY GARDENS

Community gardens are tracks of land, jointly tended by local residents for either collective or mutual individual benefit. Participants share resources and engage in cooperative decision making about the use of the land. Although community gardens may be located in rural areas, urban community gardens, established in the United States in the late 1800s, often make news as they have come to be understood in relation to a variety of purposes and processes necessary in industrialized areas. Community gardens are increasingly being embraced for providing the physical and spatial context for educational, social, and individual or environmental health purposes, through which the processes of ritual building and communal experience can also occur. Existentially, community gardens also provide a lingering memory of the physical and social landscape prior to the days of extensive privatized land division. As such, community gardening, through its combined spatial and process dimensions, serves as a symbol of sustainable human connection amid the forces of individualized conceptions of urban life and development.

From an education standpoint, community gardens can become laboratories for learning about nature and ecology. For youth, participation can also facilitate a sense of pride and an awareness of community responsibility. For teens, lessons may become more relational in terms of social skill building, cooperation for a common goal, and leadership development. For adults, community gardening can enhance a sense of belonging, providing an opportunity to collaborate with others and build support groups. Adults can also role-model cooperation and engage in cross-generational learning with younger participants.

Community gardens can provide social opportunities for isolated individuals and for cultural building. When gardened by individuals from similar backgrounds, the gardens offer a space for maintaining traditions centered on nature. When utilized by diverse individuals, community gardening can facilitate cross-cultural and cross-racial exchange, serving to break down barriers through common activity and dialogue. As a cooperative urban agriculture endeavor, community gardens are also slowly becoming appreciated for their role in microeconomics wherein low-income communities provide resources to their residents.

Community gardens can support health, both on an individual level in terms of good nutrition and environmentally in terms of air quality, open space, and city aesthetics, although the extent of their contribution to air quality and overall beautification is debated. When used for rehabilitative purposes, specific healing community gardens can provide a community space for people dealing with mental or physical disorders, for those that need help readjusting to social interactions, or for those that need assistance in the self-esteem building necessary after physical or emotional abuse. Community gardening can also provide opportunities to build communal reliance and a sense of holism, experiences that are not always accessible in industrialized systems of compartmentalized production.

Community gardening is not without challenge. When utilized within institutions such as hospitals, prisons, and schools, community gardening risks becoming co-opted as a placating activity to reduce challenges to the forces of control, rather than being considered as an arena for cooperation and collaborative skill building and democracy. In addition, issues of property ownership, zoning regulations, short leases, public liability insurance, resource needs, and the pressures of capital development threaten the sustainability of community gardens. Community gardens have been threatened in cities across the country, with politicians and government planners tending to support community gardening when property values are low and when funds are available through blight, education, anti-crime, and environmental programs, but abandoning them by giving in to development pressures when values rise.

In 2006, community gardens were challenged in the city of Bridgeport, Connecticut, when a number of the city's community gardens were slated to be sold for private development. Although publicly supporting the sale of inactive gardens, Mayor John Fabrizi led the city council to postpone the sale decision until after the growing season. The postponement presented both resident gardeners and city planners with a challenge: to find ways to demonstrate the value of community gardening and cooperative action, not antagonistically against forces of capital investment and private development but as inherent components of the social fabric necessary to sustain livable communities that can harness development to the best interests of residents.

—Angela K. Frusciante,
Elida Babollah, Camille Grant,
and Shawnece Simmons

See also Community Organizing; Cooperatives; Environmental Movement

Further Readings

Ferris, J., Norman, C., & Sempik, J. (2001). People, land and sustainability: Community gardens and the social dimension of sustainable development. *Social Policy & Administration, 35,* 559–568.

Glover, T. D. (2004). Social capital in the lived experiences of community gardeners. *Leisure Sciences, 26,* 143–162.

Schmelzkopf, K. (1995). Urban community gardens as contested space. *The Geographical Review, 85,* 364–381.

COMMUNITY ORGANIZING

As an idea, community organizing has recently gained ascendancy within community development discourse. With varying meanings, *community organizing* is understood to mean mobilizing people to work together to solve a shared problem. It is essentially a process in which people organize themselves to take charge or control of their situation and, in doing so, develop a sense of ownership of their community.

When people or communities become marginalized and disempowered, community organizing can be a powerful tool in bringing awareness to people to take action against the forces that discriminate against them. As such, organizing essentially involves two major things. First, it rectifies the challenges of power dynamics. Although this is not easy to do, it is through the process of organizing people that there is a shift in power from the dominant forces (corporate and social institutions) to ordinary people as the process itself enhances accountability and transparency for both parties. Second, organizing people is about transforming people's attitudes. Thus, by organizing people, individuals and communities become authors of public good rather than just passive recipients of things, processes, and decisions decided elsewhere without their participation.

Community organizing does not occur in a vacuum; rather, it is carried out under clear guidelines and a set of rules and principles. It is underpinned by philosophies. The central ingredient of effective community organizing that distinguishes it from other social change strategies is the fact that it builds power that is meant to result in social justice. To achieve this power, the following contemporary principles are employed:

- *Participation*—Community organizing organizations view participation as an end in itself, particularly through skills development, knowledge building, and being responsible custodians.
- *Inclusiveness*—It is fundamentally vital for communities to be as inclusive as possible. Often, membership of the group is drawn from a diverse section of communities, in most cases, those that are usually at the periphery of decision-making processes or from minority groupings.
- *Scope of mission and vision*—Community organizing requires clear and precise aims and goals. This principle is about ensuring that the mission and vision cover broader issues that affect community rather than being narrowly focused.
- *Critical perspective*—In trying to change the behavior of social institutions, community organizing groups can be a polarizing force. However, viewed from a broader context, community organizing is about advocating for positive policy and institutional change.

When governed well, community organizing can stimulate active participation, encourage ownership, and institutionalize accountability and transparency in organizations and institutions that marginalize people.

Community organizing, while focusing on solving present-day problems, gains its strengths from history. Those involved in organizing or mobilizing communities build their confidence by reflecting on the success and failures of the past social movements and social change groups. History is rich with stories of patience, persistence, courage, triumph, and victory against all odds. Against this background are also lessons about tactics and strategies that previous activists used in solving their problems and achieving social justice. In brief, the history behind community organizing is about sensitizing the present generation to the problems and possibilities of positive change.

Community organizing takes different forms in different parts of the world. In the United States, for example, neighborhood organizing is a form of community organizing. In the United States, the history of community organizing is divided into seven distinct periods.

During the Progressive Era (1895–1929), progressives attempted to document the common social problems people encountered. The second period, during the Great Depression, resulted in significant social movements. The third period was the period leading up to World War II until the end of the Eisenhower presidency; community organizing during this period was conservative, protecting the status quo rather than alleviating social problems. The fourth era, during the time of the Great Society, saw community organizing geared toward poverty alleviation and challenges to sexism and racism. The fifth period, during the Reagan administration, saw a resurgence of conservatism that fought back the gains of the 1960s. The final period, the Clinton period, was probably a mix of some sophisticated neighborhood social change that highlighted tension between conservatism and modernity. The ushering in of the new millennium has seen community organizing being promoted by transnational civil society organizations in many forms across the globe and engaged in different activities such as policy advocacy, human rights, community development, and gender equity.

While community organizing can be considered a powerful tool in mobilizing people, its success lies in the effectiveness of organizers. Thus, it is vital that those intending to engage in such activities have a broader understanding of leadership or, simply, leading. The leadership in community organizing can be voluntary or paid work. The leaders can be professionals in their own rights or social justice activists who are simply passionate about making a difference in the lives of others. The crux of their role is therefore not necessarily leading but rather facilitating. An effective facilitator must have a thorough understanding of the characteristics and, more importantly, the power dynamics of the communities in which they work. This means that the organizers have to conduct extensive interviews in communities.

Another very important aspect of community organizing leadership is listening. Being open to people's concerns and establishing ways in which pressing issues are dealt with are vital. Being a listener means encouraging people to voice their concerns and, equally so, making them take control of the measures intended to solve the community's problems. In other words, community organizers or leaders can play the role of facilitating the processes that deal with administration, planning, policy development, program development, training of local leadership, and any public relations matters.

A central principle of community organizing is to ensure that people remain motivated. It is through motivation that social change is gradually achieved as people realize that the issues they struggle to solve are theirs and the solutions can come only from them and not from outside the community. To be effective, community organizers must function as catalysts, teachers, facilitators, and liaisons to other communities and networks. With effective organizers and active participants, communities can take charge of their destinies.

—*Jonathan Makuwira*

See also Communitarianism; Power, Theories of; Social Democracy; Utopian Communities

Further Readings

Etzioni, A. (1993). *The spirit of community: Rights, responsibilities and the communitarian agenda.* New York: Crown.

Etzioni, A. (1995). *New communitarian thinking: Persons, virtues, institutions, and communities.* Charlottesville: University Press of Virginia.

Etzioni, A. (2001). *The road to the Good Society.* New York: Basic Books.

Gittell, R., & Vidal, A. (1998). *Community organizing: Building social capital as a development strategy.* London: Sage.

Rubin, H. J., & Rubin, I. (2001). *Community organizing and development* (3rd ed.). Boston: Allyn & Bacon.

COMMUNITY RADIO AND TELEVISION

Community radio and television is a system that provides production equipment, training, and airtime on local channels so that members of the public can produce programming and broadcast to a mass audience. It developed as an alternative to commercial and state-run broadcast media to open mass media to all citizens. Mass media is considered a key component of political communication, a type of public sphere in democratic societies where people participate in the discussion and construction of government policies. However, most traditional broadcast media are ratings driven, market oriented, and privatized, limiting the range of views presented and offering few opportunities for active and equal participation by the public. In response to these restrictions, a grassroots social movement developed that offered communities access to media technologies and broadcasting platforms in order to encourage diversity, creativity, and participation in the public discourse. Based on the concept that the airwaves belong to everyone, community radio and television (also called community access or public access) provide a vital forum for people around the world to organize, participate, and even spark social change.

The social movement for the development of community radio and television was facilitated by technological changes that made the tools of media production easier, cheaper, and more accessible. Innovations such as the development of a consumer portable video recorder, the Sony Porta-Pak (developed in 1968), meant that video production could be mobile and streamlined. The development of the videocassette in the early 1970s replaced film as a recording medium—it did not need to be processed in a lab and was easily transported. Also in the early 1970s, cable television allowed for broadcasting possibilities beyond state-run or commercial networks. By the late 1970s, small silicon chips replaced bulky, fragile, and complicated vacuum tubes to amplify and tune radio signals, and the development of FM transmitters and antennas made it easier to broadcast radio programs without interference. These new technologies served to release the tools of production to nonprofessionals and to level the playing field between the official sources of broadcast media and media produced by interested citizens.

The democratization of media production in North America is considered to have started with the National Film Board of Canada. The Challenge for Change program encouraged community participation in documentary filmmaking about social and environmental issues in the late 1960s. These films and later videos were shown to other members of the community and government officials to promote discussion, debate, and resolution of local issues. In the United States during the late 1960s and early 1970s, community media were more the province of activists and artists who were expressing themselves and communicating to others via emerging video technologies. These groups were considered to be radical, and many were based in New York City. Collectives such as Videofreex, People's Video Theater, Global Village, Top Value Television, and the Downtown Community Television Center used the latest equipment to record and produce their perspectives on local, national, and international current events and news stories. By 1981, the Paper Tiger Television Collective was established, a group that still exists today and that created television studio–based programming that many consider to be revolutionary in its style and scope.

Community television in the United States was assisted on a national level by federal regulations that were mandated as a result of the growth of the cable television industry in the early 1970s. By 1972 the

Federal Communications Commission authorized the creation of at least one channel, and as many as three, on new cable systems in the top 100 television markets that would be available for state and local government, educational, and community public access purposes. Cable companies would be required to provide studio space and equipment that could be used by any member of the community to produce programs that would then be broadcast on these public access channels. The facilities would be offered to anyone who signed up and would allow any noncommercial programming to be aired as long as it adhered to basic libel and obscenity laws. This resulted in programming from voices not normally heard in mainstream television, some of whom were able to build a following and establish a media identity over the years.

The types of programs produced on community radio and television include talk shows, educational programs, cultural shows, religious programs, children's shows, cooking shows, political shows, and a variety of music programs. For some media critics, the contribution of some of these public access programs to democracy is questionable. As a site open to all citizens, community radio and television occasionally feature programs that focus on edgy topics (e.g., sex, race, and fascism) that may be offensive to others in the community. However, community media offer the space for rebuttal and to debate issues of free speech, decency, and politics that is not available in the mainstream mass media.

Historically, community radio has been a significant medium in Latin America, where it has been used to get members of a community to work with each other for social and economic improvement. In many of these countries, where political repression, censorship, violence, and poverty are pervasive, community radio is one of the few outlets for free speech and indigenous voices to be heard. These community radio stations often are not sanctioned by the government; yet, they foster democratic participation by allowing citizens to discuss everything from politics to culture. Community radio is considered to have contributed significantly to ending the Pinochet dictatorship in Chile in 1990. Radio stations that were operated by churches and political organizations in the 1970s and 1980s provided information that the military would not allow through official channels and kept the public informed and ready for action to create a democratic society. Community radio in the Americas also has contributed to democratic expression in Columbia, Venezuela, and Haiti, among others.

Community radio and television provide a rare opportunity in this time of consolidated media ownership for the presentation of alternative outlooks and opportunities to debate and discuss issues of local interest. Though some of the programming may be considered controversial or radical, the freedom to present these perspectives contributes to freedom for all.

—*Martine Hackett*

See also Alternative Press; Free Speech Activism

Further Readings

Fuller, L. K. (1994). *Community television in the United States*. Westport, CT: Greenwood Press.

Kellner, D. (1990). *Television and the crisis of democracy*. Boulder, CO: Westview Press.

Ryan, C. (1991). *Prime-time activism*. Boston: South End Press.

Skidmore, T. (2001). *Television, politics, and the transition to democracy in Latin America*. Baltimore: Johns Hopkins University Press.

CONE, JAMES H. (1938–)

James H. Cone, Charles A. Briggs Distinguished Professor of Systematic Theology, has taught at Union Theological Seminary (New York City) since 1969. Cone published *Black Theology and Black Power* in March of that same year. His first book introduced liberation theology into the academy and in church circles. Prior to the spring of 1969, theological conversations in the United States swung between liberal and conservative discussions about God. With Cone's creation of black theology of liberation, a whole new way of thinking about and doing theology arose. Cone's work crystallized the thought and ministry of black

American pastors who had supported the call for Black Power in June 1966. Significantly, these African American preachers from diverse denominations (i.e., the National Committee of Negro Churchmen) moved their faith reflections and African American constituencies out of the civil rights struggle into the Black Power movement.

Indeed, the friction between these two streams of black people's resistance—civil rights integration versus black power self-determination; black suffering to convert white racists versus black folk's self-defense—demanded a reinterpretation of the North American religious landscape. How do pastors lead a congregation whose communities are occupied by the National Guard or threatened by local sheriffs in Ku Klux Klan groups? What should seminaries and divinity schools teach when urban America is burning literally blocks from their classrooms?

Cone returned to the Bible to hear a new "word from the Lord." There he discovered the foundational mission and criteria of the historical Jesus as liberation of the economically poor, binding the wounds of the brokenhearted, and organizing to set oppressed people free. In the 1960s, the most marginalized communities in the United States were among black people. Jesus Christ, therefore, called on the church to radically do away with the old and forge an entirely new economic and political system of the United States for poor blacks and other downcasts. Thus, the emergence of a new (psychological and cultural) black individual self and revolutionary (political and economic) black communal selves fostered all sharing in collective control of wealth, equal political participation, and affirmation of cultural differences. By resurrecting the radical Jesus Christ in the particularity of black theology, Cone created a universal liberation theology for the least of these throughout the world.

Cone's family of origin had laid the basis for his future elaboration of liberation theology. Born in Arkansas in 1939, he grew up in a black, working-class church that offered black self-love, communal solidarity, and an acute theological understanding that white supremacist Christians contradicted the love and justice of Jesus Christ. How could Jesus embrace white Christians if they monopolized all resources and claimed white phenotype as the normative image of God? Cone's *Black Theology and Black Power* answers by calling white liberals and conservatives, as well as black churches, to conversion. The Bible's purpose is for the oppressed. Christ's presence is among the downtrodden. And God's heaven on earth belongs to the materially poor.

Cone's career has produced dozens of Ph.D. students, three generations of black theologians, including some of the third-generation womanist scholars in North America, and doctoral students from Africa, Asia, the Caribbean, and Latin America. With roughly 10 honorary degrees and books translated into Dutch, German, Japanese, Korean, Italian, Spanish, Portuguese, Malayalam (in India), and French, he is known globally as the father of black theology of liberation.

—*Dwight N. Hopkins*

See also Black Power; Jesus Christ; Liberation Theology; Religious Activism

Further Readings

Cone, J. (1990). *A black theology of liberation* (20th anniversary ed.). Maryknoll, NY: Orbis. (Original work published 1970)
Cone, J. (1997). *God of the oppressed.* Maryknoll, NY: Orbis.

Confucius (c. 551–479 bc)

Confucius, whose real name was Kung fu-tzu, is the best known of all Chinese philosophers. Although the system that bears his name—Confucian society—has been officially discredited in China, the influence he had on Chinese society lasted well into modern times.

Confucius came to prominence during the Later Chou dynasty (c. 1050–256 bc), also known as the Period of the Warring States. China broke apart into 8 to 12 states. It was a period of political disunity and chaos. Although this was a period of disorder, there was at the same time a flourishing of philosophical thought as people sought to understand what was causing the problems and what could be done to correct them.

Confucius came from a family of low aristocratic status. Confucius deduced that the problem with current society was that people, particularly the leaders, lacked virtue and morality. For more than 10 years, Confucius traveled the Chinese provinces seeking an official who would not only employ him but allow him to put his ideas into practice. Failing in his quest, Confucius returned to his home district where he began to teach.

Confucius never wrote down any of his teachings. Rather, these were collected by his students into a volume known as the *Analects*. In this work, Confucius outlines his plans for a civilized, well-functioning society. Confucius is not referred to by his name but by the title of "Master." Much of the *Analects* are questions posed to Confucius, followed by his answers. Confucian philosophy is a humanistic philosophy; Confucius was concerned with current times rather than spirituality. This is not to say that he had no religious beliefs. While he sometimes invoked the nature of Heaven and spirits, his focus was on the present world.

Confucius argued that besides lacking virtue and morality, people needed to know their *li*, that is, the rights and rules of behavior according to one's status in family and society. In short, it was knowing how to behave at the proper moment. Confucius stressed education as a way to learn virtue, morality, and proper behavior. Young men would study history, philosophy, and literature because they presented examples of proper and improper behavior. To foster their inner harmony, they would also study poetry and music. On completing a Confucian education, the "graduates" would then pursue careers in either the government or education.

Followers of Confucius took these ideas and created the five cardinal relationships: (1) father/son, (2) ruler/subject, (3) husband/wife, (4) older brother/younger brother, and (5) friend/friend. This is not an egalitarian society, for the first four relationships are based on a Superior/Inferior relationship. One must defer to the other. The only relationship based on equality is that between friends.

When China was reunified, the Confucian model was adopted for society. Obtaining a government job depended on one of two methods: appointment by the emperor (which usually required family connections), or the civil service exam. To obtain a post and rise within the ranks, a rigorous examination system was used. Knowledge of Confucianism was paramount.

Confucius took ill and died at age 73. He was buried in Lu, which is along the River Sze. His importance carried on for centuries, although Confucian philosophy was discredited from time to time throughout Chinese history. With the Xinhai Revolution in 1911, culminating with the abdication of the emperor in February 1912, Confucianism was officially discredited as a state ideology. However, many of its tenets, such as the emphasis on social deference, still remain.

—*Mitchell Newton-Matza*

Further Readings

Clements, J. (2004). *Confucius: A biography.* Stroud, UK: Sutton.

Dawson, R. S. (1982). *Confucius.* New York: Hill & Wang.

Fingarette, H. (1972). *Confucius: The secular as sacred.* New York: Harper & Row.

Johnson, S. (1979). *The value of honesty: The story of Confucius.* La Jolla, CA: Value Communications.

Kaizuka, S. (2002). *Confucius: His life and thought* (G. Bownas, Trans.). Mineola, NY: Dover.

Liu, W. (1972). *Confucius: His life and times.* Westport, CT: Greenwood Press.

CONGRESS OF RACIAL EQUALITY

A pioneering organization in the civil rights movement, the Congress of Racial Equality (CORE) was established in 1942 by a group of white and African American activists. The founders of CORE had previously been active in the Chicago chapter of the pacifist Fellowship of Reconciliation. CORE was intended to be an interracial organization dedicated to ending racial inequality through protest according to Gandhian principles of nonviolence.

CORE would establish crucial precedents in the techniques used by civil rights activists of the 1960s and beyond. After a 1946 Supreme Court decision forbade segregation on trains and buses used in transportation across state lines, black and white CORE activists launched a freedom ride on April 9, 1947, to test the implementation of that ruling in the upper South. CORE also sponsored summer sessions from 1947 to 1954 to instruct new activists in nonviolence and direct action tactics.

After the 1960 sit-ins in Greensboro, North Carolina, direct action protests became the tactic of choice for civil rights groups. CORE's experience positioned it as mentor to the new student activists entering the civil rights movement, and it soon extended its work from the upper to the lower South. Under the leadership of national director James Farmer, who served from 1961 to 1966, CORE entered its most prominent period in the civil rights struggle. CORE pioneered the jail-in tactic, in which incarcerated civil rights workers would stay in jail rather than pay fines or bail. It launched a freedom ride in May 1961 to test another Supreme Court decision that barred segregation in interstate travel terminals and facilities. It also participated in a number of key civil rights moments, including the 1963 March on Washington and Freedom Summer in 1964.

By 1965, the passage of the Civil Rights and Voting Rights Acts convinced many in CORE that direct action protest might have reached the limits of its effectiveness. Debates arose regarding the search for new techniques, CORE's continued commitment to nonviolence, and the role of whites in the civil rights movement. Northern CORE activists also urged the organization to try to improve the conditions of African American life in urban neighborhoods. CORE began to focus on generating racial solidarity and activism within black communities based on their particular needs. Yet the organization fractured as separatist, black nationalist ideologies gained more influence in the civil rights struggle. Farmer resigned in 1966 and was succeeded as national director by the avowed nationalist Floyd McKissick. The turn away from integration had alienated many of CORE's white supporters and donors and saddled the organization with financial problems. Roy Innis replaced McKissick as national director in 1968, and CORE continues to concentrate on black community organizing and economic empowerment.

—*Francesca Gamber*

See also Black Power; Civil Rights Movement; Direct Action; Freedom Rides, 1961; Nonviolence and Activism

Further Readings

Meier, A., & Rudwick, E. (1975). *CORE: A study in the civil rights movement, 1942–1968.* Urbana: University of Illinois Press.

Niven, D. (2003). *The politics of injustice: The Kennedys, the Freedom Rides, and the electoral consequences of a moral compromise.* Knoxville: University of Tennessee Press.

CONSCIENTIOUS OBJECTORS TO WAR

Conscientious objectors are people who, for religious, moral, or political reasons, oppose war. Conscientious objectors may refuse to contribute labor, resources, or both to war. Conscientious objection can take a variety of forms, such as not serving in the military, not registering for the draft, or not paying war taxes.

Conscription (compulsory military service on behalf of the state) dates back to feudal obligations, but it was formalized as a permanent institution in the Revolutionary France of 1793. Even though it has been recognized institutionally in the 20th century, primarily by the Protestant countries of continental Northern Europe, conscientious objection, too, goes back further in time. It is linked with the major religious movements in Europe.

Unlike in many countries in continental Europe, in Britain conscription was taken for granted after the 19th century. These European traditions are reflected in some of the institutions in the New World. Former Spanish colonies, many Latin American countries of today, followed continental Europe in instituting universal male conscription. Former British colonies, such as the United States, Canada, Australia, and New Zealand, on the other hand, did not adopt conscription.

Despite an absence of universal conscription, military service was expected of the new settlers in North America as Puritans fought Native Americans. Members of the peace churches—Quakers, Brethren, Mennonites, Rogerenes, and Schwekenfelders—refused to fight or aid in the building of forts. They were often persecuted for their refusal to fight. By the mid-17th century, some colonies had exempted Quakers and others from military service. Other citizens were fined or imprisoned for refusing to serve in militias or maintain forts. Colonial governments forced conscientious objectors to pay for substitutes or face property confiscation.

During the American Revolution, anti-British forces raided the property of those who refused to contribute to the war effort. In the face of soldier shortage, pacifists were forced into military service. Peace church members continued to resist military service and to refuse payment of fines or war-related taxes. As a consequence, many pacifists had their property confiscated by local authorities.

In the 1830s, organizations such as the American Peace Society and the New England Non-Resistance Society linked Christian ethics, abolition of slavery, and pacifism. In 1846, both groups led an organized campaign against the Mexican War. In his essay on civil disobedience, Henry David Thoreau, a representative of political pacifism, presented his rationale for refusing to pay war taxes, and his subsequent imprisonment became a classic example of nonviolent resistance as a means of social change.

During the Civil War, U.S. Congress enacted the first federal conscription legislation, requiring all male citizens between the ages of 20 and 45 to serve in the military if called. Passed in 1863, the act provided no exemptions for conscientious objectors, but excused from service anyone who paid 300 dollars. The class bias in this legislation was so transparent that draft riots erupted among poorer citizens in many major cities. Rioters also included white citizens who attacked and killed African Americans who they perceived to be the cause of the Civil War.

Quakers, too, objected to commutation fees and, in 1864, pressured the U.S. Congress into passing the first national legislation allowing members of peace churches to perform noncombatant alternatives to military service. The law also exempted those whose beliefs forbade any form of service or commutation payment. However, in the South as well as the North, overzealous officers, enlistees, and civilians subjected some objectors to forced service and physical abuse.

The second draft in U.S. history came with World War I. During World War I, only members of recognized peace churches were granted exemption from combatant military service. Those who opposed war for political reasons were court-martialed and sentenced to terms in military camps and prisons. Of the 500 U.S. conscientious objectors who were court-martialed, 17 received death sentences and 142 received life terms. Although no death sentences were carried out and other terms were reduced, physical abuse in military camps was common.

The majority of World War I objectors were Quakers, Mennonites, Molokans, Seventh-day Adventists, Jehovah's Witnesses, Brethren, and members of other peace churches and political objectors, including socialists, anarchists, members of the International Workers of the World, and nonaligned radicals. Social worker Jane Addams, anarchist leader Emma Goldman, and Socialist Party founder Eugene Debs were outspoken supporters of conscientious objectors and of the First Amendment rights of all Americans to voice opposition to war. However, with the passage of the Espionage Act of 1917 and Sedition Act of 1918, the U.S. government effectively suspended constitutional rights to freedom of the press, speech, and assembly, deporting or imprisoning leaders like Goldman and Debs.

In Britain, conscription was introduced because recruitment of volunteers could not keep up with the speed with which soldiers were killed during the war. As a result, Britain introduced conscription, despite controversy, and as a compromise, the right to conscientious objection was also recognized. The entire island of Ireland, then part of the British Empire, was exempted for fear of a revolt.

During World War II in the United States, those who objected war for religious beliefs were given the option of doing alternative service. Some conscientious objectors worked in civilian public service camps on conservation projects, staffed mental hospitals, or volunteered to be human guinea pigs in government-sponsored experiments on diet, endurance, and the transmission and control of malaria, hookworm, typhus, and infectious hepatitis. Objectors received no pay or benefits and had to rely upon families and churches for support.

Not all conscientious objectors were willing to perform alternative services that still aided the war effort. Those who refused to register for the draft, opposed compulsory service, or failed the test for religious conviction were sentenced to prison. Most imprisoned objectors were Jehovah's Witnesses and radical pacifists affiliated with the War Resisters League, the Catholic Worker movement, or the Socialist Party.

Approximately 400 African Americans also refused to serve in the military in World War II. Some belonged to the Nation of Islam, which viewed the war as a white man's conflict. Others refused to serve in a Jim Crow army or to fight for a country that denied basic democratic freedoms to its black citizens.

In Canada, too, exemption from military service was limited to Christians who held a conscientious objection to war. Even then, it was not a full exemption; rather, it was a postponement subject to policy that could change.

During the Vietnam War, the number of political objectors in the United States went far beyond those who held deep religious convictions. While the Selective Service denied exemption to conscientious objectors whose views were essentially political, sociological, or philosophical, objectors enjoyed a great deal of public support. Unlike World War II, the Vietnam War was hugely unpopular because it was viewed as unjust.

By the mid-1960s, the peace movement included radical pacifists, civil rights activists, nonpacifist anti-imperialists, liberals, and members of the traditional peace churches. This coalition not only helped objectors file for exemption but encouraged those who were denied objector status to resist induction. An estimated 250,000 never registered, and another 110,000 burned their draft cards. By the end of the war, 50,000 conscientious objectors had fled the country or assumed false identities in the United States. Many

Canadian activists welcomed U.S. draft dodgers at border towns and helped with their immigration paperwork. Massive noncompliance with the draft, wide opposition to the war, and declining military morale forced the U.S. government to finally accept defeat and retreat from Vietnam.

Following the Vietnam War, many Quakers, members of other religious groups, and radical pacifist organizations (e.g., the War Resisters League) advocated nonpayment of taxes allocated for military use and the creation of an alternative Peace Tax Fund. In the 1980s, with the reinstatement of draft registration, these organizations supported a new generation of conscientious objectors who refused to register. Tax resistance and nonregistration—both federal offenses—became the central forms of American conscientious objection.

Conscription is not a prerequisite for conscientious objection. With the U.S.-led coalition's invasion of Iraq in 2003 and the subsequent occupation, the U.S. military saw many conscientious objectors. The Iraq war, perceived by many to be an immoral, unjust, and illegal war, caused an increase in the numbers of conscientious objectors in the United States. Many National Guard members who had joined the military voluntarily, primarily to go to college, found themselves in combat in Iraq in 2003. Sgt. Camilo Mejia of Florida, a permanent resident of the United States, thus became one of the first Iraq war veterans to refuse to go back to Iraq on grounds of his conscientious objection to the war. He was sentenced to one year in a military prison. Mejia had taken the necessary steps to establish his release from the army based on his conscientious objector status and legal right as outlined in his 8-year contract, which had expired. Amnesty International adopted him as a prisoner of conscience. The details of his trial demonstrate the enormous difficulties in the official recognition of conscientious objector status for individuals even when such a right exists.

Despite many legal, political, and social pressures, many Iraq war veterans and some not yet deployed to Iraq applied for conscientious objector status; an overwhelming majority was denied. An unknown number of others, like Jeremy Hinzman, have gone to Canada to seek refugee status there. As the U.S. military is stretched thin amid its biggest quagmire since Vietnam, many have started to register their conscientious objection to war in advance. While many peace churches remain active in the peace movement, many conscientious objectors also cite political and moral reasons for refusing to serve in the military.

While some states and non-governmental organizations like Amnesty International have evolved to recognize the right to conscientious objection to war, this right goes beyond any legal recognition. In Israel, where conscription includes females, many soldiers refuse to serve in the occupied Palestinian territories despite an almost certain punishment of imprisonment.

In fact, the institutionalization of the right to conscientious objection has its roots in challenging the very basis of law. While many seek legal ways to register their objection to war, conscientious objectors do not deem it the prerogative of any official body or state to *grant* them this status. In fact, in countries like Turkey where universal male conscription is the rule, despite an exemption for homosexuals and the physically unfit, one objector, Mehmet Tarhan, has refused to put on a uniform, has cut his hair, and has testified to his "inability" to serve. Tarhan was imprisoned in April 2005. The Central Committee for Conscientious Objection, Amnesty International, National War Tax Resistance Coordinating Committee, Peace Tax Fund, Savas Karsitlari, *Refusniks,* Veterans for Peace, and Iraq War Veterans are some of the organizations that support the right to conscientious objection.

—*Özlem Altıok*

See also Amnesty International; Draft Resistance; Israeli Peace Movement; Pacifism; Veterans for Peace; War Resisters' International; War Tax Resistance

Further Readings

Altıok, Ö. (2004, December). Refusing to fight: An interview with Maritza Castillo. *Zmag, 17*(12). http://zmagsite.zmag.org/Dec2004/altiok1204.html

Cooney, R., & Michalowski, H. (1977). *The power of the people: Active nonviolence in the United States.* Culver City, CA: Peace Press.

Ferber, M., & Lynd, S. (1971). *The resistance.* Boston: Beacon Press.

Keim, A. N., & Stoltzfus, G. (1988). *The politics of conscience: The historic peace churches and America at war, 1917–1955.* Scottdale, PA: Herald Press.

Muste, A. J. (1972). *Non-violence in an aggressive world.* New York: Harper. (Original work published 1940)

Peck, J. (1958). *We who would not kill.* New York: Lyle Stuart.

CONYERS, JOHN, JR. (1929–)

John Conyers, Jr. is the longest-serving African American member of Congress. Born in Detroit and educated in Detroit's public schools, he earned his LL.B. from Detroit's Wayne State Law School in 1957. Cofounder and dean of the U.S. Congressional Black Caucus, Conyers was first elected to the 89th Congress as a Michigan Democrat in 1965. Since then, he has been reelected 20 times and has served on and chaired many important committees in the House of Representatives. In 1968, to the consternation of many conservatives in Congress, Conyers introduced legislation for the Martin Luther King, Jr. Holiday. It took 15 years for the bill to finally pass in 1983.

Conyers is highly identified with his cause—reparations for African Americans. In 1989, Conyers sponsored H.R. 40 ("40" signifying the "forty acres and a mule" promised freed slaves after the U.S. Civil War) and has reintroduced it every year since then, but the bill has never made it out of committee. H.R. 40, or the Commission to Study Reparation Proposals for African Americans Act, seeks to acknowledge the fundamental injustice, cruelty, brutality, and inhumanity of slavery in the United States and the 13 American colonies between 1619 and 1865 and to establish a commission to examine the institution of slavery, subsequent de jure and de facto racial and economic discrimination against African Americans, and the impact of these forces on living African Americans, and to make recommendations to the Congress on appropriate remedies. Key points in Conyers's argument are that the U.N. World Conference Against Racism in Durban, South Africa, in 2001 agreed that the trans-African slave trade was a crime against humanity and that there are precedents for legislative bodies providing redress, including the U.S. Civil Rights Redress Act, which awarded reparations to Japanese Americans interned during World War II; Canada's ceding of 250,000 square miles to Indians and Eskimos in 1988; and Germany's payment of $852 million in 1952 to Jewish Holocaust survivors.

Although the intent of H.R. 40 is not primarily monetary, those who oppose it characterize it as a massive giveaway that will do little to correct the prior harms of slavery. Conyers describes the bill's intent as an exploratory commission to investigate whether formal apologies from the U.S. government are required, compensation warranted, and if so, in what form and under what eligibility criteria. Opponents argue that none of the 4 million slaves is alive today and that most living Americans neither owned slaves nor profited from their labor. The reparations controversy, with Conyers at its center, along with ongoing affirmative action debates, continues to be one of the most divisive civil rights issues today. Many political polls reveal that 90% of white Americans are opposed to reparations in any form, whereas 65% of black Americans favor monetary payments from the government. Calculations of the monetary value of slave labor unpaid during slavery range between $1.5 trillion and $14 trillion. Currently, Conyers's H.R. 40 has more than 40 cosponsors in Congress, and city councils in Detroit, Atlanta, Cleveland, and Chicago have passed bills in its support.

—*Richard A. Jones*

See also Affirmative Action; Reparations Movement

Further Readings

Bowen, M. D. C. (2000). *HR 40: Bill summary & status for the 106th Congress.* Available at http://www.mdcbowen.org/p2/rap/hr40.htm
Conyers, J., & Watson, J. (2003). Reparations: An idea whose time has come. In R. Winbush (Ed.), *Should America pay: Slavery and the raging debate on reparations* (pp. 14–21). New York: Amistad.
Robinson, R. (2000). *The debt: What America owes blacks.* New York: Dutton.

COOPERATIVES

A cooperative (also co-operative and co-op) is an autonomous association voluntarily formed to meet its members' economic, social, and cultural needs through a jointly owned, democratically controlled enterprise. Cooperatives are created by a pooling or mixing of economic interests or labors. Members "throw in their lot" with others who do the same, with a view to realizing certain benefits impossible by action on their own—such as economies of scale or increases in productivity. A cooperative is distinguished from a capitalist enterprise by its goal, structure, and status: Its goal is the mutual benefit of members, with the result that if profit is sought, it is as a means only, not as an end. Equally, cooperatives are autonomous with regard to states, even though they are typically socially owned in undivided shares.

Because of their distinctive property form, neither private nor public, cooperatives are said to be part of a "third sector" or "social economy." Under the latter category are grouped other democratic economic practices such as fair trade, social currencies, and credit unions. Advocates of cooperatives and the social economy differ with respect to viewing cooperatives as either complements to capitalism or replacements for it. At the World Social Forum held in Caracas in January 2006 under the slogan "Another world is possible," over one third of all sessions were devoted to cooperatives and the social economy, mostly as replacements for capitalism.

As for producer cooperatives, most comparative studies show them to be more productive and profitable than similar capitalist firms, especially in networks. Thus, a cooperative *sector,* not just the odd co-op, might outcompete and replace traditional firms. Co-ops' comparative advantage may be due either to the stake each worker-owner has in the co-op's success or to the freedom of co-ops from the burden of costly managers and absentee shareholders. In a cooperativized economy, instead of capital hiring and bringing workers together, workers first voluntarily join together and then hire capital for their ends.

Any business activity can be run on the cooperative model. Cooperatives may be generally classified either as consumer or producer co-ops, or by sector. They exist in the traditional economic sectors of agriculture, banking and credit, consumer, fisheries, housing, insurance, travel, and production (workers' cooperatives). Each of those eight sectors has its own global organization whose members are the corresponding national associations that represent their nation's individual co-ops of these types. Uniting the eight global organizations is the International Cooperative Alliance, headquartered in Geneva and a part of the International Labor Organization, which is, in turn, an agency of the United Nations. But cooperativism currently permeates many other activities, including car-pooling, child and elder care, health and social care, funerals, computer consultants, orchestras, schools, sports, tourism, utilities (electricity, water, gas, etc.), and transport (taxis, buses, etc.).

Cooperatives are major economic actors. Over 800 million people worldwide are members of a cooperative. Cooperatives provide 100 million jobs worldwide, 20% more than multinational enterprises. According to the International Cooperative Alliance, in Europe, the most cooperativized continent, there are 140 million members of cooperatives of all kinds. In France, typical of several other Western European nations, 10% of all employment is in cooperatives. In the United States, the National Co-operative Business Association reports that co-ops of all kinds serve some 120 million members, or 4 in 10 U.S. citizens. These co-ops include 10,000 credit unions, 1,000 rural electric co-ops, 1,000 mutual insurance companies, 6,400 housing co-ops, 3,400 farmer co-ops, 270 telephone co-ops, and about 300 worker co-ops. In Venezuela and Argentina, worker cooperatives are the most frequently encountered type; in Mexico, it is credit unions, and in Cuba and Brazil, it is agricultural co-ops.

History of Cooperatives

Since the beginnings of the cooperative movement, it has presented itself as an alternative to the exploitative economic relationships demanded by capitalism. While the utopian community set up by Robert Owen preceded the Rochdale Society of Equitable Pioneers founded in England in 1844, Rochdale is usually considered the first successful cooperative enterprise. Its principles are certainly the basis for the modern movement. Of the following seven principles of cooperativism, agreed to in 1995 by representatives of the global movement, four were initiated at Rochdale (i.e., numbers 1, 2, 3, and 5): (1) voluntary and open membership; (2) democratic member control; (3) member economic participation; (4) autonomy and independence; (5) education, training, and information; (6) cooperation among cooperatives; and (7) concern for community.

As mechanization was increasingly forcing skilled workers into poverty, a group of 28 weavers and other Rochdale artisans opened their own store in December 1844, selling food items they could not otherwise afford. Over the previous 4 months, they had struggled to pool together 1 pound sterling per person for a total of 28 pounds of capital. The store opened with a meager selection of butter, sugar, flour, oatmeal, and a few candles. Within 3 months, they expanded their selection to include tea and tobacco, and they were soon known for providing affordable, high-quality, unadulterated goods. In a trajectory that was to become all too common, when, to raise more capital, they took on nonworker members, the new members outvoted the pioneers and set up a standard capitalist enterprise.

The subsequent history of co-ops is characterized by sudden upsurges followed by equally sudden collapses. In 1848, cooperativism as an alternative was often behind the first popular protests against capitalism all over Europe. Co-ops of all sorts flourished under the Paris Commune of 1871, and in France in May 1968, the idea of self-management swept through the entire economy, temporarily democratizing not just factories but apartment blocs, corporate offices, and the like, showing the possibility of radical change in a developed nation. Opposed by the de Gaulle government and massively subverted by the Communist Party, 1968 also proved to be a flash in the pan.

A new wave of cooperativism has arisen in Latin America in response to effects of neoliberal globalization. In the southern state of Chiapas, Mexico, starting in 1994, the Zapatistas have developed a network of agricultural cooperatives or "communities in struggle" aimed at a regional economic autonomy that can both survive and replace globalization. Since roughly 2000, the wave of workplace democracy hit Argentina, Uruguay, and Brazil. An even more sudden expansion, resulting in a cooperative sector, has taken place in Venezuela, with government encouragement. Abstaining from expropriation, the government is hoping that the greater productivity of co-ops will outstrip Venezuela's still-dominant capitalist sector, attracting mass defection from it. Whereas enterprises were merely occupied in France in 1968, the factories and lands occupied in the new wave—almost all bankrupt, closed, or unused—have been made co-ops by their workforces who restarted production *and* self-supporting sales. This shows cooperativization to be a powerful tool for social change in the direction of economic democracy.

There are risks facing the project of starting in a market economy and transforming it by a process of nonviolent cooperativization into something better than capitalism. First, co-ops will develop "enterprise consciousness," putting themselves first and losing sight of their solidarity with workers in the same sector, becoming unworthy as models of a new, postcapitalist order. Second, if ownership is by divisible stock shares, the co-op's greater productivity can so increase a share's value that the original cooperators will have strong incentives to sell out, given the pressures of a market economy. But these two risks are mere versions of the overall problem of being re-assimilated into capitalism, which has dogged all experiments in cooperativism from Rochdale to the astonishingly successful Mondragón Cooperative Corporation in Spain's Basque Country.

There are counterstrategies: (1) Begin with disciplined organizers whose goal is economic democracy and with unionism to maintain class solidarity across enterprises. (2) Use another instrument of ownership besides the stock share, like the indivisible and unexchangeable capital accounts developed at Mondragón. (3) Make cooperativization a government-supported project of transcending capitalism within a determinate period of time, supporting workforces in buy-outs of capitalist firms and start-ups of new cooperatives.

Unlike past attempts to build "another world," this one would have no guarantees that history will be on the side of change. That can only be determined by individual decisions on a massive scale.

—*Betsy Bowman*

See also Mondragón Cooperatives; Participatory Economics

Further Readings

Bowman, B., & Stone, B. (2004, August). Cooperativization on the Mondragón model as alternative to globalizing capitalism. *Humanity & Society, 28*(3).

Miller, E. (2004, February). Solidarity economics: Strategies for building new economies from the bottom-up and the inside-out. *Grassroots Economic Organizing: The Newsletter for Democratic Workplaces and Globalization from Below.* Available at http://www.geo.coop/Solidarity EconomicsEthanMiller.htm

Corrie, Rachel (1979–2003)

Rachel Corrie was an American activist who dedicated her life to the pursuit of global peace and justice through nonviolent resistance. She was born on April 10, 1979, to Cindy and Craig Corrie. Rachel attended Evergreen State College in Washington State, where she was active with the Olympia Movement for Justice and Peace.

Rachel traveled to Palestine on January 18, 2003, to join the International Solidarity Movement (ISM) in nonviolent direct action against the Israeli occupation of Palestinian land. She wrote home from Palestine that nothing could have prepared her for the reality of the situation there. After 2 days of ISM training, Rachel participated in a demonstration against the impending war on Iraq and protected local water wells that were under attack by Israeli forces.

Two days before her death, Rachel was interviewed by the Middle East Broadcasting network and said that she felt like she was witnessing the systematic destruction of a people's ability to survive. Corrie was 23 years old when she was killed by the driver of an Israeli Defense Forces (IDF) Caterpillar D9 bulldozer (serial number 949623). On March 16, 2003, Rachel and six other ISM activists tried to prevent the destruction of a Palestinian pharmacist's family home in Rafah, in the Gaza Strip. Rachel was dressed in a bright orange vest with reflective striping as she tried to prevent the home demolition by placing her body in the path of the IDF bulldozer.

Two British citizens were shot in Rafah in the 2 months that followed. Fellow ISM activist, 22-year-old Tom Hurndall, was shot in the head by an Israeli sniper on April 11 as he escorted Palestinian children to safety. He died 9 months later. Award-winning cameraman James Miller was shot in the neck and killed by the IDF on May 2. In this same time period (March–May 2003), 222 Palestinians were killed by Israeli forces.

The families of the three international victims have sought investigations into their deaths. The Israeli government released a report denying responsibility for the death of Rachel Corrie, referring to it as a regrettable accident. On March 25, 2003, Congressman Brian Baird introduced Resolution 111, calling for the U.S. government to investigate Rachel's death. Lawsuits have been filed against the IDF and Israeli Defense Ministry, as well as Caterpillar Inc. Caterpillar's equipment continues to be used to uproot olive trees and illegally demolish Palestinian homes.

Numerous initiatives have been launched to honor Rachel Corrie and continue her work. Such initiatives include rebuilding the home that she was protecting in Rafah, the Olympia-Rafah Sister City Project, and the Rachel Corrie Foundation for Peace and Justice. Rachel's memory is honored in Palestine through the Rachel Corrie Center for Women Empowerment and the Rachel Corrie Children and Youth Cultural Center. Palestinian babies have been named Rachel, and street names carry her name.

Artworks in response to Corrie's death appeared as well, including Suheir Hammad's poem, "*On the Brink of . . .*"; David Rovics's song, "*The Death of Rachel Corrie*"; and the Alan Rickman–directed play, "*My Name Is Rachel Corrie*" in London. The play made its U.S. debut in October 2006 at the Minetta Lane Theatre in New York City. Rachel Corrie left a lasting impression on the work of nonviolence activists worldwide.

—*Muna J. Shami*

See also Nonviolence and Activism; Resistance

Further Readings

Archive for the "Tom Hurndall" category. Retrieved June 1, 2006, from http://www.tomhurndall.co.uk/

Justice for James Miller. Retrieved June 1, 2006, from http://www.justice4jamesmiller.info

Olympia-Rafah Sister City Project. (2004). About ORSCP. Retrieved June 1, 2006, from http://orscp.org/

Palestine Red Crescent Society. (2006). Table of figures: *Total number of deaths and injuries—West Bank & Gaza.* Retrieved June 1, 2006, from http://www.palestinercs .org/crisistables/table_of_figures.htm

Rachel Corrie. Retrieved June 1, 2006, from http://en.wikipedia.org/wiki/Rachel_Corrie

Rachel Corrie Foundation for Peace and Justice. Retrieved June 1, 2006, from http://www.rachelcorriefoundation.org/

U.S. Campaign to End the Israeli Occupation. (2005). *The Caterpillar Campaign: Demanding the end of Caterpillar bulldozer sales to Israel.* Retrieved June 1, 2006, from www.endtheoccupation.org

COTTON, SAMUEL (1947–2003)

Samuel Cotton was a fearless and articulate spokesman within the United States for the eradication of contemporary slavery in Mauritania and Sudan. Cotton graduated with a B.A. degree in sociology from Lehman College, the City University of New York, in 1993. He obtained his M.A. and Ph.D. degrees from Columbia University's School of Social Work and began teaching there in 1998.

Cotton first learned of the existence of slavery in Mauritania and the Sudan from the American Anti-Slavery Group in the early 1990s. His conscience was profoundly disturbed, and his life took a new turn. By 1995, he was sufficiently informed to write several articles on slavery for *The City Sun,* an African American weekly newspaper published in Brooklyn.

With his exposition of the situation in the two North African countries, where Black Africans were routinely being bought and sold, and with his description of the mental and emotional suffering the slaves underwent, Cotton caused a deep stir.

In March 1995, he called Black Africans from all over the United States to a consultative meeting at Columbia University. They agreed to work together to draw the attention of the American public to this 20th century human bondage. Cotton then founded and became executive director of the Coalition Against Slavery in Mauritania and Sudan, made up of abolitionists and human rights groups from Mauritania, Southern Sudan, and North America.

In December 1995, Cotton traveled to Senegal, from where he was taken undercover to Mauritania. He gathered testimonies from slaves and ex-slaves; these testimonies formed the basis of a book and a documentary. *Silent Terror: A Journey Into Contemporary African Slavery* (1998) was recognized as a powerful, truthful, and passionate indictment of slavery in Mauritania, and it soon became a college set text.

Cotton's next initiative was to create a Freedmen's Bureau to educate, feed, clothe, and house runaway slaves in Mauritania. In March 1996, he testified before the U.S. Congress about his findings regarding slavery. He continued writing articles, holding meetings at universities and churches, and speaking at public forums throughout the United States. He appeared in a series of radio and television programs, including debates with members of the Nation of Islam who had made anti-Islam allegations against him.

Cotton's premature death of a brain tumor in December 2003 put an end to these activities. While still alive, he was honored with a Human Rights Fellowship by the Petra Foundation. The American Anti-Slavery Group has established the Dr. Samuel Cotton Memorial Fund to continue the work of this modern-day abolitionist.

—Emilia Ilieva and
Lennox Odiemo-Munara

See also Abolitionist Movements; Activism, Social and Political; Advocacy; Coalition Building; Nation of Islam

Further Readings

Bok, F. (2003). *Escape from slavery.* New York: St. Martin's Press.

Cotton, S. (1995, February 1–7). Arab masters—Black slaves. *The City Sun.*

Cotton, S. (1995, March 22). Sorrow and shame: Brutal North African slave trade. *The City Sun.*

Cotton, S. (1998). *Silent terror: A journey into slavery.* New York: Harlem River Press.

COUNCIL TO AID THE JEWS

See HOLOCAUST, RESISTANCE

COUNTER-RECRUITMENT

A political tactic associated with efforts against war and militarism, counter-recruitment took on particular significance in the U.S. peace movement after 1973. With the suspension of the formal draft which came about at the time of U.S. withdrawal from Southeast Asia at the end of the Vietnam War, the U.S. Armed Forces began a concerted effort to fill its ranks through direct, community-based employment opportunities. Between 1971 and 1974, the U.S. Armed Forces doubled the funding, personnel, and offices dedicated to military recruitment. A steady increase since that time, with special emphasis on high schools and colleges located in low-income neighborhoods, has led to a widespread, decentralized network of counter-recruitment activists.

Counter-recruitment campaigns began largely in place of the draft resistance and conscientious objection projects of traditional peace groups such as the American Friends Service Committee, the Central Committee for Conscientious Objectors, the National Interreligious Service Board for Conscientious Objectors (later renamed the Center on Conscience & War), and the War Resisters League. Strategic differences exist among these groups, including disputes over the efficacy of illegal refusal (to register for the draft or comply with unjust laws), as opposed to work within legal and military structures to extend the rights of conscientious objection to as broad a range of people as possible. Most of these organizations, nevertheless, have lent support to the wide range of local counter-recruitment efforts of the past quarter century.

Throughout the 1980s, as military recruiters became a more consistent and aggressive presence at high school career and college fairs (invited to school-sponsored auditorium, classroom, and guidance counselor presentations), counter-recruiters increased their school-based leafleting and outreach to students and teachers alike. Several key court decisions during this period established basic guidelines for the peace practitioners. In *Vogt v. School Board of Palm Beach County*, a Florida group was granted the right to have draft counseling materials placed in guidance counselors' offices but was denied equal access to school-sponsored career days attended by the military. This decision was based on the premise that counter-recruitment groups were not offering students prospective jobs. In *Clergy and Laity Concerned v. Chicago Board of Education*, a local religious group offering counter-recruitment alternatives to the military was granted the same degree of access as military recruiters. In *San Diego Committee Against Registration and the Draft v. Grossmont Union High School District*, local activists were granted the right to place ads in school newspapers; the court reasoning was that recruitment is a controversial political topic, and as such, it deserved multiple viewpoints even in students' papers not fully protected by the First Amendment. This local precedent is especially important in relation to the 1988 Supreme Court decision (*Hazelwood v. Kuhlmeier*) limiting the rights of freedom of speech in school newspapers that are overseen by a faculty member, using the school name or resources. In *Searcey v. Harris*, an Atlanta-based counter-recruitment campaign won full access to the schools, the court ruling that school districts could not deny access based on their disapproval of an organization's views.

Much of the information presented by counter-recruitment activists centers around the inaccuracies told to potential enlistees during the recruitment process. The fact that, by the U.S. Department of

Defense's own estimates, roughly half of those who join the armed forces find themselves in financial difficulty after one year in service is a highly challenging piece of information, given that a clear majority of those who sign up do so for economic reasons. That military recruiters regularly lie about the type of jobs or job training available to enlistees is often cited. With so many youth joining the military for college tuition assistance, it is also noteworthy that, by the late 1990s, the top recruitment drives were taking place at GED (General Education Development) test centers, where students may have great academic motivation but few resources. The 1990s also saw an increase in recruitment through the Reserves Officer Training Corps (ROTC), a course offered to high schools and junior high schools as a curriculum enhancement.

The 2001 No Child Left Behind Act made funding for high schools contingent upon their supplying student contact information to the military. Combined with the Solomon Amendments, which require universities to allow recruiters on their campus or forfeit federal funding, these national initiatives have sparked waves of protest. The Campus Antiwar Network, formed in 2003, gained notoriety when it staged a disruption of military exercises at Seattle Central Community College at the same time as George W. Bush was being inaugurated. Since then, the Campus Antiwar Network has sponsored hundreds of counter-recruitment protests, forcing the military off of dozens of colleges across the country. They also coordinated a National Day of Counter Recruitment on December 5, 2005, as the Supreme Court was hearing preliminary arguments in the case of *Rumsfield v. Forum for Academic and Institutional Rights*, on the issue of the constitutionality of the Solomon requirements.

A growing diversity of techniques has been the cornerstone of the modern counter-recruitment movement. In San Francisco, organizers took a legislative approach, passing Proposition I, the College Not Combat Act of 2005, which declared the city's opposition to military recruitment in public schools, calling on the government to use the more than $5 billion spent annually on recruitment to go toward educational scholarships. In 2006 in New York City, the War Resisters League published the glossy, student-authored Demilitarized Zone (DMZ), a guide to taking schools back from the military. Popular hip-hop group the Coup devoted their summer 2006 tour to the Not Your Soldier campaign, giving out thousands of counter-recruitment flyers at each of their shows. Speaking tours of Iraq Veterans Against War, a group of young, former enlisted personnel with their own stories of recruitment fraud and the horrors of war, have intensified as the Iraq war went into its third year. More and more peace groups throughout the United States have at least partially accepted the view of longtime San Diego activist Rick Jahnkow: that counter-recruitment organizing is the most practical way to tangibly affect U.S. foreign policy.

—Matt Meyer

See also Campus Antiwar Network; War Resisters' International

Further Readings

American Friends Service Committee. (2006). *Counter-recruitment basics*. Philadelphia: Author.

Jahnkow, R. (2006, January–March). In need of a proactive peace movement. *Draft NOtices* [Newsletter of the Committee Opposed to Militarism and the Draft]. Available at http://comdsd.org

Schenwar, M. (2005, December 5). *Counter-recruitment day sweeps U.S. colleges*. Available at http://www.commondreams.org/views05/1205-32.htm

Theberge, S., Palladino, L., & Heron, S. (2006). *DMZ: A guide to taking your school back from the military*. New York: War Resisters League.

COUNTS, GEORGE (1889–1974)

George Counts, raised in a Populist household in Kansas, was (perhaps second to John Dewey) arguably the most renowned American progressive educator of the 20th century. Counts became famous in pedagogical circles during the 1930s as the leader of a group of radicalized educators who called themselves "frontier thinkers" or "social reconstructionists." They wanted to construct American society along socialist lines via education.

Counts gained fame for a speech at the 1932 annual meeting of the Progressive Education Association titled, "Dare Progressive Education Be Progressive?" Counts implored that education emancipate itself from the influence of the elite. Counts had long focused on class discrimination. In an earlier work, Counts argued that the nation's boards of education were anti-democratic in composition, because they were drawn from the favored economic and social classes. But in his famous lecture before the Progressive Education Association, Counts redirected his analytical lens to educators themselves, exposing them for a tepid commitment to reform.

The amplified radicalism of Counts was partially forged during trips he took to the Soviet Union in the late 1920s, including one in 1929 when he drove the width of the country in a Ford he had shipped there. Counts was favorably impressed by his observations during his trip, after which he called the Soviet project the greatest social experiment of history. Counts placed the fate of the Russian Revolution in education. Counts hoped that progressive educators could reconstruct American society in similar fashion to the Soviets.

However, by the late 1930s, Counts joined numerous other American leftists in their disillusionment with the Soviet Union and Communism. Soon after learning that his Soviet counterparts had been purged and possibly executed by Stalin, the attention he paid to the Soviet schools was to offer a withering critique. This in turn altered his approach to how he wrote about the United States in its relations with the Soviet Union, Communists, and the Popular Front. He believed the American Communist Party had been completely repudiated. Such a strong belief was what compelled Counts to lead an anti-communist faction of the American Federation of Teachers union to power in the late 1930s. He was elected president of the union in 1939 and 1940.

In 1939, Counts and Dewey helped found the Committee for Cultural Freedom, an organizational attempt to separate pragmatic radicalism from communism. By making such a separation, Counts and the Committee for Cultural Freedom argued that communism was barely better than fascism, anticipating the Cold War conflation of the two, what became known as "red fascism." But despite his virulent anticommunism, Counts is probably best remembered for the work he did in the early 1930s when he exposed the class biases of those who controlled the American school system.

—*Andrew Hartman*

See also Communist Party USA; Dewey, John; Populism; Progressive Movement, Education

Further Readings

Callahan, R. (1962). *Education and the cult of efficiency.* Chicago: University of Chicago Press.

Counts, G. (1932). *Dare the schools build a new social order?* New York: Arno.

Cremin, L. (1961). *The transformation of the American school: Progressivism in American education, 1876–1957.* New York: Vintage.

Ravitch, D. (2000). *Left back: A century of battles over school reform.* New York: Simon & Schuster.

COXEY, JACOB S. (1854–1951)

Jacob S. Coxey, a wealthy stone quarry owner from Massillon, Ohio, led the first organized protest of the unemployed. The protest culminated in a march of about 500 unemployed workers, known as Coxey's Army, through the streets of Washington, D.C., in May 1894. In the 1890s, the United States experienced one of the most devastating economic depressions in its history. By 1894, many Americans had reached rock bottom with millions unemployed. A number of workers, notably laid-off railroad construction workers, talked of marching on Washington, D.C., but few made it to the capital. One group that did was the Army of the Commonweal of Christ, led by Coxey.

A Populist with a son that he named Legal Tender in honor of monetary reform, Coxey had a long-standing interest in reform. By the early 1890s, his interest in providing good roads merged with his concerns over unemployment. In 1892, he proposed that Congress hire the unemployed to build better roads, and he created the Good Roads Association to promote this legislation. In 1894, Coxey again sought to address the unemployment problem by combining his good roads program with a financing proposal that would fund the building of a variety of public buildings. With support from several people, Coxey initiated a protest march from Massillon to Washington, D.C., in March 1894. Coxey and his followers took 6 weeks to march 400 miles to the capital, where others sympathetic to the cause joined them. The national press followed the march, and other Coxey's Army groups formed across the nation.

Coxey's Army collapsed quickly when Washington police arrested and jailed Coxey for walking on the grass in violation of the Capitol Grounds Act. He received a 20-day jail sentence and returned to Massillon upon release. However, Coxey's Army and the growing political strength of Populism struck fear into the hearts of many Americans. Critics portrayed Populists like Coxey as socialists whose election would endanger property rights.

For a generation, Coxey's march remained vivid in the public memory. In countless homes, boys and girls grimy from play were warned to clean up or they would look like something from Coxey's Army. Children also reenacted a version of cops and robbers in which youthful Coxeyites stole wagons and were pursued by federal marshals. These parents and children were perpetrating a widespread but incorrect notion that Coxey's Army was merely a collection of dirty thieves.

In reality, Coxey continued as a well-respected political leader. Although the march did not lead to passage of the proposed public works legislation, the fame of the event allowed Coxey to continue in the public limelight for years. In 1896, he unsuccessfully ran for Congress on the Populist ticket. He continued to be involved in politics and finally was elected mayor of Massillon in 1931. He had more success at business and died a wealthy man. In time, the march of Coxey's Army faded from public memory, although its call for public works jobs anticipated a crucial element of the New Deal programs of the 1930s.

—*Caryn E. Neumann*

See also New Deal; Populism

Further Readings

Howson, E. B. (1982). *Jacob Sechler Coxey: A biography of a monetary reformer.* New York: Arno.

McMurry, D. L. (1968). *Coxey's Army: A study of the industrial army movement of 1894.* Seattle: University of Washington Press.

Schwantes, C. A. (1985). *Coxey's Army: An American odyssey.* Lincoln: University of Nebraska Press.

CRAFTIVISM

Craftivism is the practice of engaged creativity, especially regarding political or social causes. By using their creative energy to help make the world a better place, craftivists help bring about positive change via personalized activism. Craftivism allows practitioners to customize their particular skills to address particular causes.

Craftivism is an idea whose time has come. Given the states of materialism and mass production, the rise of feminism, and the time spanned from the Industrial Revolution, the beginning of the 21st century was the right time for the evolution of such an idea. Instead of being a number in a march or mass protest, craftivists apply their creativity toward making a difference one person at a time.

Through activities such as teaching knitting lessons, crocheting hats for the less fortunate, and sewing blankets for abandoned animals, craftivism allows for creativity to expand previous boundaries and enter the arena of activism. In the pre–Industrial Revolution era, craft skills were needed to clothe the family and maintain a working household. As mass production increased, there became no need to knit sweaters for winter warmth or weave baskets to hold vegetables. Crafts were bypassed by modernity.

The do-it-yourself spirit was stifled in the area of wardrobe creativity, and post-9/11, a rising sense of hopelessness to change anything in the world was unleashed. Feminism was still heavily rooted in theory and strength, but enough time had spanned between the economic and social disparities between women and men in the 1970s that women began to look again at domesticity as something to be valued

instead of ignored. Wanting to conquer both a drill and a knitting needle, there was a return to home economics tinged with a hint of irony as well as a fond embracement.

The term *craftivism* surfaced in the first few years of the 21st century and gained an online presence with the website Craftivism.com in 2003 to promote the symbiotic relationship between craft and activism. After craft skills such as knitting regained popularity, the idea emerged that instead of using solely one's voice to advocate political viewpoints, one could use their creativity.

By advocating the use of creativity for the improvement of the world, craftivists worldwide taught knitting lessons, sewed scarves for battered women's shelters, and knitted hats for chemotherapy patients. In a world that was growing increasingly large and unfamiliar, craftivism fought to bring back the personal into our daily lives to replace some of the mass produced. In promoting the idea that people can use their own creativity to improve the world, craftivism allows those who wish to voice their opinions and support their causes the chance to do just that . . . but without chanting or banner waving and at their own pace.

—*Betsy Greer*

See also Feminism; Play, Creativity, and Social Movements

Further Readings

Beal, S., Nguyen, T., O'Rourke, R., & Pitters, C. (2005). *Super crafty.* Seattle, WA: Sasquatch.

Railla, J. (2004). *Hip home ec: Get crafty.* New York: Broadway Books.

Spencer, A. (2005). *DIY: The rise of lo-fi culture.* London: Marion Boyars.

CRAZY HORSE (1841–1877)

The Lakota warrior Tashunka Witco, or Crazy Horse, is one of the most revered American Indian leaders in recorded history. A lifetime protector of his people's way of life, he is best known for having defeated the

U.S. Army in one of the most decisive Indian victories of the 19th century.

Crazy Horse, who was likely born in the winter of 1841–1842, was the son of an Oglala Lakota medicine man and nephew of the Brule chief Spotted Tail. Crazy Horse, too, was gifted mystically. As a young man, he had a dream in which a man marked by blue hailstones and lightning rode a horse safely through a hail of bullets and arrows, only to be pulled down by his own people. The lightning and hail were both strongly associated with the Thunders, powerful beings that called anyone dreaming of them to be a sacred clown, to do the opposite of what was expected. The rider also wore a smooth stone behind his ear and a feather of a red hawk in his unbraided hair, talismans that Crazy Horse adopted throughout his life.

Crazy Horse's opinion of the white people was formed at an early age, when he witnessed the Grattan Incident, in which the U.S. Army, over a stolen cow, opened fire on Conquering Bear's camp. The following year, Crazy Horse happened upon the mutilated bodies of Little Thunder's camp following an army attack. These experiences led him to believe that the whites were a dishonorable race that could not live among the Lakota.

Crazy Horse was a fearsome warrior and leader on the battlefield, and although he participated in all the major battles fought by the Lakota to protect the sacred Black Hills from white intrusion, he was never wounded in battle. He fought in Red Cloud's War and the Fetterman Massacre and led many successful raids against surveying parties for the railroad with the Lakota ally, the Cheyenne. When Red Cloud retired to the reservation, Crazy Horse became war chief of the Oglalas.

In 1876, in response to a campaign to force the rebellious Indians onto the reservation, the Lakota and Cheyenne came together under the leadership of Sitting Bull to mount a resistance. Crazy Horse acted as the military leader. On June 17, he led his warriors to defeat General George Crook at the Battle of the Rosebud and, on June 25, to annihilate General George Custer at the Battle of the Little Bighorn, the most famous battle of the Indian Wars.

When the tribes divided after the battle, Crazy Horse was relentlessly pursued by troops under General Nelson Miles. After a long, hard winter, Crazy Horse and 1,000 Indians surrendered on May 6, 1877, during a battle in which they were out-gunned. Bored by life on the reservation, he became a scout, but enmity among his own people, of which he had once dreamed, forced him to flee. Although he later submitted to the army peaceably, he was taken to a stockade where he tried to break away. In the melee that followed, he was stabbed by a bayonet and died on September 7, 1877.

—*Mara D. Rutten*

See also Sitting Bull; Wounded Knee

Further Readings

Marshall, J. M. (2004). *The journey of Crazy Horse.* New York: Penguin.
Sandoz, M. (1942). *Crazy Horse: The strange man of the Oglalas.* New York: Knopf.

CRITICAL LITERACY

From a critical perspective, literacy is constituted as a set of cultural practices rather than a discrete set of skills. Conceived as a set of practices, literacy is imbued with the hierarchical social meanings, intentions, and values that are a part of the human social and political fabric. In practice, critical literacy is a set of approaches used to analyze and interrogate the ideological constitution of texts. Critical literacy instruction has been implemented with a range of ages, from preschool students to adult literacy learners. Both a process and an outcome, critical literacy puts action and activism at the center of literacy instruction and unveils and disrupts naturalized discourses in order to expose oppression and inequity and seek alternatives.

The History of Critical Literacy

Critical literacy has its foundation in both progressive education reforms and the critical theories of the Frankfurt School. Progressive education reformers consider education for citizenship in democratic society. Historically structured in tiers, formal educational systems have reproduced unequal power relations. Progressive educators have questioned the possibility that a democracy can exist without equal access to education for informed decision making and citizenship. Critical literacy is also part of a larger set of critical educational approaches that emerged as pedagogical proponents of dialectical-materialist philosophy. Critical theory from the Frankfurt School developed a link between theory and society that would connect individual practice with society's aims.

Critical approaches to literacy instruction often deal specifically with the relationship between language and power, how language shapes context, and how context shapes language. Critical perspectives also intersect with feminist and poststructural theories in that they recognize not only the construction of local knowledges but also the inherently indeterminate and unfinished nature of any perspective. Any one perspective is always a specific valuation; it may be critiqued from another point of view. Thus, it is never a final truth, but one truth among many.

Critical literacy is often associated with Paulo Freire's work with adult literacy learners in Brazil. Language and literacy were fundamental to social change for Freire. Freire used generative themes to teach reading and writing, which came from culture circles that learners formed to discuss their grievances with the political and economic structure. The themes were then used as contexts to help participants learn to read and write. Freire's method included an emphasis on praxis: in which action arises from critical dialogues and theory building. Fundamentally, Freire believed that through a literacy based on the systematic study of people's own oppressive life conditions as they relate to their sociohistorical context, people would be able to emancipate themselves.

In some Australian states, critical literacy is part of official school curricula and standards. In contrast, critical literacy occupies a more unofficial status in the United States, dependent on the efforts of teachers both in and outside of the classroom. Teachers have increasingly drawn on critical literacy pedagogy to address issues of race, gender, sexuality, and class. In

a world in which the media are becoming increasingly centralized, critical literacy is more useful than ever in understanding how power is reproduced or contested through texts and literacy practices.

One critique of critical pedagogies, including critical literacy, is that a historical focus on how class operates in society may not take into account the condition of women, people of color, or how racism functions above the individual level, that is, as a part of economic, political, and social structures. Another critique of critical literacy is that it is focused on deconstructive practices and does little to proactively reshape deep institutional and social relationships that hold power. However, one important aspect of critical literacy is the movement from critique to action.

Critical Literacy in Action

In schools, critical perspectives support a movement toward multicultural instruction that begins with students' lives and extends to ways of communicating that have symbolic currency in institutions of power. Within societies that are racially, ethnically, and linguistically diverse, critical literacy questions the naturalized positions of the status quo and reveals a wide range of available positions on societal issues. For example, in the United States, the curriculum's focus has been on a small number of people of color who have actively worked for civil rights and justice for people of color rather than the masses of unknown people who participated in the struggle.

Critical literacy begins with the recognition that texts display messages, viewpoints, and perspectives that can be interrogated by individuals and social groups. Because people create texts according to their values and beliefs about the world, texts imply values. One type of action in critical literacy is the movement from a passive acceptance of hegemonic points of view as natural and inevitable to recognition of how certain discourses are constructed and naturalized in texts.

Critical literacy demands that readers deconstruct texts in order to uncover issues of unequal power relationships, diversity and pluralism, multiple points of view, and personal and communal identities. In action, critical literacy demands that readers ask questions about the purposes and goals of a text, the ways that texts are structured and how language is used, the construction of characters in texts, and whose voices have been left out of texts. Through the questioning that occurs around texts, critical literacy adherents acknowledge and celebrate the diversity of human experiences but also explicitly problematize why some experiences are privileged over others.

Critical literacy is not put into action until texts have been deconstructed using critical questioning and subsequently reconstructed. Reconstruction occurs when people envision how things might be different. Importantly, critical literacy does not seek a final meaning or truth. It works to make texts transformative for people, to compel them to political action. Those involved in critical literacy also produce a wide range of texts that refute hegemonic or dominant discourses that work within exclusionary practices and privilege local voices and knowledge aimed at inclusion, equity, and access.

Teachers and researchers have documented examples of critical literacy in action in a variety of venues. In the United States, for example, one educator involved high school students and their families in the political sphere of school reform. Small groups compiled information, engaged in critical dialogues, and asked representatives to answer challenging questions about the purposes and goals of the reforms. In other settings, young children have educated their families and communities about social and environmental injustice through performances and letter writing. Action within a critical literacy curriculum is the place where the learning of students and their families shapes the conditions of the social, political, and economic environment.

New Directions in Critical Literacy

In the tradition of New Literacy Studies, literacy is increasingly defined in terms of multiliteracies, which involve attention to meanings in modalities other than language, such as the images of advertisements. Critical perspectives ask what voices and perspectives are represented and what perspectives are absent from traditional texts such as novels, history books, and anthologies. More recently, their focus has included multiple literacies in electronic and digital forms of media such as television, websites, and movies.

To further explore the possibilities of action through text construction, educators have begun to consider how theories of multiple literacies intersect with critical literacy. As users become more adept at creating multimodal texts, critical literacy pedagogues conceptualize the user as designer. When people are involved in design, they move beyond the boundaries of written and verbal text and consider how image, movement, and layout create a message. The production of a multimodal text, such as a webpage, film, or painting, affords the user a new set of semiotic resources. For example, the layering of text and image can put two ideas or perspectives into dialogue with each other. Further, because of the increasingly user-friendly technology of personal computers and the World Wide Web, designers find that their texts often have wider and unrevealed audiences. A new direction for critical literacy pedagogy is to consider the ways a variety of semiotic resources can be used in the design of new literacies and new futures.

—Melissa Mosley and Eli Tucker-Raymond

See also Critical Pedagogy; Frankfurt School of Critical Theory; Freire, Paulo; Multicultural Education; Progressive Movement, Education

Further Readings

Comber, B., & Simpson, A. (2001). *Negotiating critical literacies in classrooms.* Mahwah, NJ: Lawrence Erlbaum.

Freire, P. (1970). *Pedagogy of the oppressed.* New York: Herder & Herder.

Freire, P., & Macedo, D. (1987). *Literacy: Reading the word and the world.* Westport, CT: Bergin & Garvey.

Muspratt, S., Luke, A., & Freebody, P. (1997). *Constructing critical literacies: Teaching and learning textual practice.* Cresskill, NJ: Hampton Press.

Shor, I. (1999). *Critical literacy in action: Writing words, changing worlds—A tribute to the life and work of Paulo Freire (1921–1997).* Portsmouth, NH: Boynton-Cook/Heinemann.

Vasquez, V. M. (2003). *Creating a space for critical literacy in K-6 classrooms.* Newark, NJ: International Reading Association.

CRITICAL MASS BICYCLE MOVEMENT

Critical Mass, a nonhierarchical bicycle movement, began in San Francisco in 1992 and spread to several hundred cities worldwide in the decade that followed. By hosting group bike rides on the last Friday of every month, Critical Mass has become part of the urban fabric in a number of American cities, including San Francisco, New York, Portland (Oregon), and Chicago. While group bike rides are not unique phenomena of urban life, Critical Mass is a departure from traditional group rides led by recreational bicycle clubs and formal bike advocacy organizations. Sharing many characteristics of new social movements, Critical Mass rides are intentionally nonhierarchical and pluralistic with no formal ride or movement leaders, no formal organizational sponsor, and no formal political agenda or specific demands for policy changes. Although the meanings associated with Critical Mass rides vary depending on the place and the experience of participants, they are foremost celebratory demonstrations of nonpolluting transportation—a simple yet powerful display of an alternative urban form. In this respect, Critical Mass resembles its urban street party cousin, the Reclaim the Streets movement.

Billed as a celebration of the bicycle rather than a protest or demonstration ride, Critical Mass is an example of a contemporary movement attempting to create new forms of politics outside the traditional government realm. The initial ride, dubbed the Commute Clot, took place in San Francisco in September 1992 as a communal ride home from work and drew about 40 cyclists with roots in the bike messenger community. Subsequently renamed Critical Mass (for a scene in the 1991 documentary *Return of the Scorcher* by San Francisco native and bicyclist Ted White in which bicyclists in China push through intersections once a critical mass is reached), it grew steadily in San Francisco, attracting hundreds of cyclists by the spring of 1993 and growing to over 5,000 in July of 1997. The San Francisco police cracked down on the July 1997 ride, arresting over 100 participants; a subsequent lawsuit was later decided in favor of the cyclists. As the ride grew in size in San Francisco, news of Critical Mass spread over the Internet and via the press with rides appearing throughout the United States and globally, including in Sydney, Chicago, Los Angeles, Paris, Philadelphia, London, Barcelona, Boston, Johannesburg, Zurich, Tokyo, and Taipei. At one time, Critical Mass was estimated to occur in over 300 cities worldwide, but today the number of cities with regular monthly rides is likely below that level.

In spite of Critical Mass's waning global reach, individual rides have nonetheless attracted significant law enforcement attention during periods of increased participation, including lawsuits aimed at shutting down the rides. New York City's ride, in particular the Manhattan Critical Mass (Brooklyn's Critical Mass ride continues to fly under the radar for the most part), has garnered significant attention from police and the city since the Republican National Convention came to New York in late August 2004, coinciding with the monthly ride. In fact, the August 2004 Critical Mass ride turned out to be the opening clash between police and the public at the convention. With an estimated 3,000 to 7,000 cyclists congregated at Union Square Park and local and federal law enforcement on high alert, 264 bicyclists were arrested that August evening; most were held for over 24 hours and had their bikes confiscated and held as evidence for over 3 weeks.

Police attention continued to be focused on the Manhattan ride in the months following the Republican National Convention, with another 300 bicyclists arrested through the end of 2005, for violations such as parading without a permit, failure to disperse, or disorderly conduct. Similar charges have been brought against Critical Mass participants in other American cities. In addition to these individual arrests, the city also filed a lawsuit in state court against Time's Up!, an environmental nonprofit organization based in Lower Manhattan, as well as against four individuals who volunteer for the organization. This suit seeks to require permits for cyclists to both congregate and ride in the streets en masse; however, unlike legal strategies used against other Critical Mass rides, the lawsuit seeks to prevent Time's Up! and the four named individuals from publicizing, and even talking about, Critical Mass. These charges have cast Critical Mass in a new light for many participants;

once viewed in terms of sustainability and safety in numbers for bicyclists, the movement has broadened in significance to encompass the right to assemble in public spaces and freedom of speech.

As the various lawsuits work their way through the courts, the crackdown on Manhattan's Critical Mass has affected the ride in another way: It has reduced the number of bicyclists participating in the monthly Manhattan ride, as many people simply do not want to risk arrest, loss of their bikes, or both. For other participants, though, the crackdown and subsequent broadening of the meaning of the ride to include civil rights appears to have energized their commitment to Critical Mass and justified its importance. Additionally, news of New York City's crackdown on Critical Mass and lessons from the lawsuits continue to motivate participants in other cities, facilitated by the well-established bicyclist networks reaching from San Francisco to Chicago to New York to London. These global bicyclist networks, forged and reinforced by Critical Mass, have helped to raise money for legal expenses associated with the New York lawsuits. Furthermore, news of very large Critical Mass rides, such as one in September 2005 in Budapest that drew 24,000 to 30,000 cyclists, continues to energize the movement. Although the number of cities with regular monthly rides may have peaked toward the end of the 1990s and participation in individual rides fluctuates, the Critical Mass movement remains strong.

—*Susan G. Blickstein*

See also Environmental Movement; Urban Space, Politics of

Further Readings

Blickstein, S., & Hanson, S. (2001). Critical mass: Forging a politics of sustainable mobility in the information age. *Transportation, 28,* 347–362.

Carlsson, C. (Ed.). (2002). *Critical mass: Bicycling's defiant celebration*. Oakland, CA: AK Press.

CRITICAL PEDAGOGY

Critical pedagogy emerged from a wide array of radical theory that wanted to make schooling more democratic and emancipatory by transforming oppressive social processes and structures in schools through praxis and empowering teachers, students, and the community with a critical view of how society perpetuates oppression. It problematizes dominant modes of thinking and pushes teachers to become activists in their approach to addressing social inequalities. Critical pedagogy seeks to address the problems that arise from a society that is inherently unequal, especially in regard to race, class, and gender. Ultimately, critical pedagogy seeks to emancipate oppressed groups and unite people in a culture of critique, struggle, and hope in the quest to end different forms of oppression that exist today. Arising from the Frankfurt School of critical theory founded in 1923, Samuel Bowles and Herbert Gintis's *Schooling in Capitalist America* (1977), the early progressive movement and John Dewey, Miles Horton's work during the civil rights movement, and the efforts in Brazil by activists like Paulo Freire and his seminal book *Pedagogy of the Oppressed* (1970), critical pedagogy greatly influenced many critical scholars in education with their examination of social and cultural issues utilizing a Marxist framework.

One of the first concerns of critical pedagogy is the role that politics plays in people's everyday lives. For example, critical pedagogy seeks to expose the implicit and explicit functions of schooling in a capitalist society. Schools are ideological arenas of struggle and contestation where students are exposed to the dominant culture's beliefs, values, and attitudes. Freire saw the inherent problems when schooling was used to oppress certain groups while empowering others. Freire argued that the function of education should be to put forth a new world and to change existing social structures to become more liberating and empowering. Teaching and learning should not resemble a bank where teachers deposit information into passive students. Instead, teachers and students should be co-creators of knowledge within the classroom, and dominant ideologies should be exposed for critique and discussion. According to Freire, education has reinforced and created myths (about capitalism, heroes, social class, etc.), stressed rugged individualism, separated knowledge from reality, and omitted any discussion of social problems. Teachers and students must understand schooling from this perspective to understand the link between knowledge and power and to become active and critical citizens. This means that schooling is never neutral but instead is always political in nature. Because schooling is political, this means that schooling practices that at one time appeared to be natural are actually supporting the status quo. Thus, classroom learning and instruction cannot be separated from the larger political and social context.

Another concern is the role that culture plays in society. Specifically, schooling legitimates and prepares students for a particular form of cultural and social life. This cultural experience tends to arise from the dominant class and favors forms of knowledge; specific visions of the past, present, and future; and the naturalization of an unequal and tiered society that specifically benefits them. Without access to the cultural capital that society values, students outside of privileged groups do not receive the same educational experiences or socialization, further exacerbating poverty, apathy, and hopelessness. Competition, individualism, and victory are the types of cultural capital that are valued and will be stressed and rewarded in schools. This also means that racism, classism, heterosexism, ableism, and sexism are reproduced in schools. The Frankfurt School is credited as one of the founding centers on critical theory that sought to examine culture and its structural forms from a traditionally Marxist perspective. Herbert Marcuse, Theodore Adorno, and Jürgen Habermas were all influential in the development of critical pedagogy. Their focus on the role that popular culture has in the reproduction of the dominant culture, the importance of economics and its role in human suffering, and the effects of the proliferation of technology in society has guided present-day critical scholars in their examination of how schools reproduce oppression.

Critical pedagogy also takes into account the importance that economics plays in a capitalist society. For example, critical scholars in education are interested in the role of capitalism in how schooling is conducted. This means that schooling does not always provide educational and cultural enrichment and does not give access for upward economic and social mobility. Instead, schools act as a sorting mechanism, giving only some students access to knowledge and experiences that are valued by the dominant culture. These knowledge forms and experiences will give some students the cultural capital necessary to survive and prosper in the current economic and political system. Specifically, critical pedagogy wants to expose the role that school curricula, knowledge, and policies have in this reproduction of inequality. School curricula are aiding in this reproduction by dominant values being reflected in what teachers choose to teach, whose knowledge is valued and passed on, and activities that are chosen for students to participate in. School policies also have economic implications as well. For example, social class is maintained through school practices such as tracking, and poor students do not have access to resources that more wealthy students do. Tracking has also led to a disparity, in that higher numbers of students of color fill the lowest academic courses in public schools. This form of social reproduction leads to a system that allows for different educational experiences, which, in turn, help maintain social positions for specific groups of people (i.e., the dominant class).

Another common thread in critical pedagogy is the focus on power. Taking cues from Michel Foucault's theories on power, critical pedagogy tries to expose the inherently unequal power relationships that exist in all facets of how schools operate: from the curriculum to interpersonal relationships to specific school policies. Foucault argued, however, that power does not just occur in individual relationships ("power over") but emerges from all facets of social life, meaning that power is fluid. This means that power is embedded in all practices and is sometimes reproduced by those who are marginalized and oppressed. Issues of power also emerge when schools choose to validate and endorse specific knowledge forms and processes. It is by no accident that Western European accomplishments are glorified over others. The specific omission of knowledge that sits outside a Eurocentric framework specifically helps reproduce social inequality and keeps valued knowledge forms firmly entrenched in the dominant culture. This also aligns with the critical notion that knowledge and education only reinforce conformity and specific knowledge forms instead of exposing how knowledge that is deemed "objective" is only reinforcing the status quo. Because schooling does not occur in a political vacuum, issues of power and agency will always be present.

Another important concept in critical pedagogy is the importance of ideology. Ideology is a framework of how people view the world; it gives meaning to people's political, social, and economic lives. Ideology is enveloped in every social practice contained in schools and helps to perpetuate unfair and oppressive schooling practices. Using ideology as a tool, critical pedagogy seeks to expose its hidden nature and look at how it is manifested in society and social institutions. This means looking at the ideas, beliefs, and values that are embedded in schooling practices and school curricula. This means exposing students to how ideology manifests itself while also empowering teachers to critically examine the ideological content of what they teach.

Hegemony is another central concept in critical pedagogy. Hegemony refers to the social process of how social institutions, practices, beliefs, values, attitudes, and outlooks are legitimized and naturalized through a dominant group over subordinated groups of people in a specific historical era. Antonio Gramsci, the Italian Marxist who was imprisoned for his political beliefs by Mussolini, argued that the ruling class, or what he called the historical bloc, exercises social control and authority over the subordinate classes through social institutions, such as schools and the government. This social control is often through indirect force, such as the case of schooling, where cultural understandings, values, and ways of looking at the world are transmitted nonviolently. Gramsci also found that the newspapers, television, and other mass forms of media carry the majority opinion and reflect the needs and interests of the dominant class. Although these examples are nonviolent, Gramsci also argued that outright force could be used when the majority of a society agrees to that use of force. Force and consent work reciprocally with each other to secure domination for the social and political elites.

Critical pedagogy does not just exist at the theoretical level. In fact, many critical educators have tried to devise ways in which these theories can be applied in the classroom. Specifically, the concept of counterhegemony arose out of the literature on critical pedagogy. *Counterhegemony* refers to the possibility for oppressed groups to challenge and reconstruct power relationships that will give them a voice that has been silenced. Critical pedagogy argues that education should be used to teach and model this resistance toward social policies that are unfair and oppressive. The main assumption here is that all people have the ability to create and sustain resistance against a dominant group, and this resistance should be nurtured in the classroom by teaching students about social practices, norms, and values that are responsible for reproducing inequality. This also means that students are active participants in the learning process by choosing what they study, addressing problems in their communities, or questioning knowledge put forth in school textbooks. Whatever the form this arises in, resistance is modeled and nurtured through classroom teaching.

Along with this, critical pedagogy supports the notion of praxis. Praxis is the convergence of theory and practice that tries to demonstrate that these can never be separated from each other and that specific actions can produce social change. Praxis is self-generated (by students and teachers), reflective, and dialogic. Thus, any "Truth" claim made (in the classroom or the outside world) is subject to critique and analysis. This critique can only be mediated in a space that is as democratic as possible, thus allowing historically marginalized groups to become active participants in a system that has not traditionally given them a voice. Critical pedagogy forces people to rethink the traditional view that the role of education is merely a technical application of learning theories; instead, the role of education should be toward empowering historically marginalized groups.

Critical pedagogy also places importance on the notion of dialogue. Freire saw dialogue as a critical component to any democratic classroom (and critical pedagogy) because it signifies that students should have an opportunity to question dominant discourses, and it empowers students to challenge oppressive social conditions. Dialogue is a process in which teachers and students are allowed an opportunity to engage with the material they are learning and actively critique the knowledge that they are receiving. Freire argued that through dialogue, a form of consciousness could emerge (what he called *conscientization*) that is an acute awareness of how social conditions are created and maintained. Conscientization also allows students to understand that they have the power to change society to one that is more committed to freedom and social justice.

Critical pedagogy has not come without critique from other critical scholars. Feminists have levied against critical pedagogy being a "boys-only" club and being mired in masculine conceptions of theory, praxis, and knowledge. Other critiques by scholars have found critical pedagogy to be seeking an ultimate "Truth," and prescribing *the* solution for revolutionary emancipation while still silencing those they seek to empower through esoteric language and complex theories traditionally available to privileged groups (i.e., white males). Other critics have argued that teaching is not only political in nature, as critical pedagogy contends, but also moral, which should also guide teaching in public schools.

—Abraham P. DeLeon

See also Anti-Racist Teaching; Foucault, Michel; Frankfurt School of Critical Theory; Freire, Paulo; Gramsci, Antonio; Habermas, Jürgen; Marcuse, Herbert; Marxist Theory; Praxis

Further Readings

Freire, P. (1970). *Pedagogy of the oppressed.* New York: Herder & Herder.

Giroux, H. (1981). *Ideology, culture, and the process of schooling.* Philadelphia: Temple University Press.

Giroux, H. (1983). *Theory and resistance in education: A pedagogy for the opposition.* Amherst, MA: Bergin & Garvey.

Kanpol, B. (1999). Critical pedagogy: An introduction (2nd ed.). Westport, CT: Bergin & Garvey.

Kincheloe, J. (2004). *Critical pedagogy primer.* New York: Peter Lang.

McLaren, P. (1994). *Life in schools: An introduction to critical pedagogy in the foundations of education* (2nd ed.). New York: Longman.

Shor, I. (1992). *Empowering education: Critical teaching for social change.* Chicago: University of Chicago Press.

CRITICAL RACE THEORY

Critical race theory appeared in the mid-1970s and stemmed from an earlier legal movement called critical legal studies (CLS). CLS is a leftist legal movement that challenges legal scholarship and promotes the idea that the civil rights struggle is a long process. Critical legal scholars analyze legal ideology and decipher legal doctrine to expose both its internal and external inconsistencies, revealing how legal ideology has created and sustained class structure. CLS has been critiqued by critical race theorists for failing to address the role of racism. Frustrated with CLS scholars' approach, CRT scholars instead called for centralizing racism in analyzing legal ideology and major policy reform. Leading the CRT movement, Derrick Bell and Alan Freeman challenged CLS scholars' belief in incremental change in civil rights and instead argued that traditional approaches of filing amicus briefs and conducting protests produced smaller gains than before. Soon thereafter, other legal scholars joined in the critique of traditional civil rights strategies.

CRT begins with the premise that racism is a normal part of society and is a permanent part of American life. Critical race theorists expose different forms of racism and critique legal, educational, and other social institutions that perpetuate inequality. It seeks to de-cloak the seemingly race-neutral and color-blind ways in which the law and policy are conceptualized and constructed, with respect to their impact on poor people and persons of color. CRT deconstructs oppressive structures and theorizes how to reconstruct human agency and resistance, with the goal of achieving equity and social justice. Moreover, CRT scholars have critiqued and reinterpreted civil rights law and dominant legal claims of equality, color blindness, and meritocracy.

CRT critiques liberalism for its flawed understanding of the current legal paradigms to be the impetus for social change. The argument is that liberal legal practices support the slow process of arguing legal precedence to gain citizen rights for people of color. Additionally, CRT scholars argue that whites have been the primary beneficiaries of civil rights legislation. An example of this is affirmative action policies. While the intention of this policy was to benefit people of color, white women have been the primary beneficiaries. Even after years of a policy that was intended to benefit people of color, few have benefited. Social scientists have documented the low numbers of students of color in doctoral degrees awarded, as well as faculty positions. Critical race theorists cite this empirical evidence to support the argument that civil rights legislation continues to serve the interests of whites.

Critical race theorists also use social construction theory to reexamine the concept of race as a fluid term, with various social meanings that are socially constructed by the social, political, and historical structures of our society. Social construction theory identifies the process by which people creatively shape reality through social interaction. The social construction of race suggests that human actions have been, and continue to be, subject to historical forces and thus to change. The social construction of reality is the process by which definitions of reality are socially created, objectified, internalized, and then taken for granted. Critical race theorists deconstruct and reconstruct race, informed by the lived experience and the continuous struggle for social justice.

Borrowing from ethnic studies, feminist theory, and Marxist approaches, CRT looks for ways to deconstruct racism in government, law, policy, and schools. As a methodology, CRT is also used to turn margins into places of transformative resistance. Moreover, CRT scholars seek to expose the intricacies of multiple forms of racism by incorporating the intersectionality of race, class, and gender.

Critical race scholars also examine the more covert or subtle forms of racism. These subtle forms of racism, referred to as micro-aggressions, may include subtle nuances and code words, body language, averted gazes, looks, and expressions such as "you people," "articulate black," "highly qualified black," and "reverse discrimination," conveying racially charged meanings. One of the purposes of this body of work is to challenge the status quo and achieve social justice, as well as document the experiences of people of color. Another purpose is to understand how forms of oppression have both material and ideological dimensions. According to

Mari Matsuda, the effects of racism are real, in that racism has an effect on the social and material conditions of people of color. Racism is also ideological. Subordination exists in the ideological, which includes language, the language of law, rights, neutrality, and objectivity. In a racialized society, subordination can serve to make domination seem natural and inevitable, reinforcing whiteness as normative. CRT challenges the objectivity of law and legal doctrine as well as critiques color-blind ideology and the maintenance of white supremacy in education, policy, and law.

Historically, social scientists have represented people of color through traditional social science paradigms, often misrepresenting or ignoring them altogether. More specifically, in the educational literature, paradigms have often relied on racial characterizations and stereotypes. Moreover, literature on instructional approaches for African Americans and Latino/a students often involve some type of remediation, often leading to blaming "at-risk" students as deficient. Much of this literature has been based on cultural deprivation theories connecting race and academic performance, often blaming students of color. Despite its problems, elements of the cultural deprivation paradigm continue to appear in the educational research literature involving racial/ethnic minorities. Cast in a language of failure, critical race theorists are making new efforts to critique these deficit model approaches. Critical race theorists have also engaged in debates regarding assessment. More specifically, they critique the intelligence testing movement, which has been legitimized as scientifically sound. These scientific theories have been used to legitimately oppress students of color, based on racial stereotypes. These tests fail to show what students know; instead, they only indicate what material on the test students do not know.

More recently, CRT has expanded further to include other branches of critical theory, including LatCrit, FemCrit, AsianCrit, and WhiteCrit scholarship. Latino/a critical race theorists (LatCrits) and Asian critical race theorists deconstruct the black-white binary. For example, in the legal arena, LatCrits move beyond the black-white paradigm by analyzing the cultural, political, and economic dimensions of white supremacy, particularly as it affects Latinos/as as individuals as well as collective struggles for social justice. A LatCrit theory is a framework that is used to examine how race and racism affect educational structures and processes that impact Latinos/as. The goal of LatCrit theory in education is to achieve social justice and to link social theory, practice, and scholarship with teaching and the academy with community. More specifically, LatCrit scholars examine communities of various skin tones, accents, cultures, and immigration status.

Feminist critical race theorists problematize race issues and inquire about race and gender. Scholars such as Kimberlé Crenshaw have combined both feminist legal theory with CRT to expose the links between gender and race in the legal arena. Crenshaw et al.'s work brings issues that affect women, such as child care and domestic violence, to the forefront. Crenshaw also addresses the subordination of African American women in society in general, and specifically in law. Patricia Williams, also a feminist critical race theorist, has written a memoir that links feminist jurisprudence with the experiences of black women. Bringing the private into the public, she exposes the reality of both racism and sexism.

Black feminist thought has recently served as a means of unmasking and gaining a deep understanding of the experiences of black women. At the core of black feminist thought are the experiences of black women. Black feminist thought is a critical social theory that has been created in opposition to "women's" experiences. Black feminist thought engages with bodies of knowledge and critiques institutional practices and questions that face U.S. black women as a collective group. Black feminist thought begins with the assumption that African American women have created oppositional, yet reclaim black women's subjugated, knowledge. This involves discovering, reinterpreting, and analyzing the ideas of subgroups within the larger collectivity of black women who have continuously been silenced. Black feminism, a self-conscious struggle on behalf of black women, critiques institutional practices that U.S. black women face collectively. As a collective group, one of the main goals is to name one's own reality. African American women's voices are specialized bodies of knowledge

that have been excluded from the social science literature. The second goal is self-determination, or aiming to have the power to define one's own destiny.

Similarly, critical race theorists, more specifically LatCrit theorists, have relocated Latinas and Chicanas to the center in various research areas, developing a Chicana feminist epistemology by researching the lives and experiences of Chicanas. Chicana feminist epistemology documents the experiences of Chicana students in school, from multiple dimensions, including skin color, gender, class, bilingualism, immigration, migration, and English proficiency. Because the voices of Chicanas and Latinas have largely gone unnoticed and undocumented, the need to document and analyze these experiences remains a challenge. By analyzing Chicanas' relationships and experiences, researchers can gain insight into the relation between Chicanas and structures that shape their lives.

CRT scholars employ alternative methodologies such as storytelling, parables, chronicles, counter-stories, poetry, fiction, revisionist histories, unconventional and creative ways to draw on the lived experiences of people of color and seek to transform social injustices. More specifically, storytelling provides the context for understanding, feeling, and interpreting. It not only provides a means to expose whites to racism through personal narrative, but it can also provide a venue for the marginalized to voice their knowledge and experiences. The telling of stories can serve many purposes for people of color.

For the marginalized, storytelling can serve as a powerful means of survival and liberation. Richard Delgado argues that counter-storytelling, a particular type of storytelling, serves as a tool for unmasking and challenging majoritarian stories that uphold racial privilege. Stories can also serve as a means to destroy complacency and challenge the status quo. Counter-stories about oppression can guide the marginalized through understanding that oppression and can serve as a means of healing. Oppressed groups can use stories as a means of psychic self-preservation as well as lessening their own subordination. Narrative writing essentially legitimizes the personal experiences and perspectives of those who have been excluded from the dominant discourse. Storytelling seeks to expose and subvert the dominant discourse and serves several theoretical and methodological purposes. First, counter-stories can build a sense of community among those at the margins of society by providing a space to share their sense of reality and experiences. Stories build consensus, a common culture of shared understandings. Second, counter-stories can challenge the dominant culture's perspective. Counter-storytelling challenges the accepted ideology, the dominant ideology. And lastly, they can teach people about how one can construct both story and reality. Narrative that focuses on the marginalized can therefore empower the storyteller as well as those who listen.

CRT legal scholars have now begun to grapple with criteria for quality in interpretive research and issues of subjectivity, as they use qualitative research methods. For example, many scholars have discussed issues of positionality and subjectivity in qualitative research. Critical race theorists that utilize qualitative research methods are now dealing with these issues, and trying to understand, for example, how the racialized subject must be understood in the context of social and historical forces. If qualitative researchers take into account their subjects' racialized positions, what does this mean when it comes to the interview process and the interpretation of interview materials?

Other scholars also argue for the need for reflexivity on the part of researchers. Critical race theorists challenge the standardization of conducting qualitative research. They question the traditional notion of the distant researcher and the need to understand subjects, especially racialized subjects. Too often, researchers ignore their own subjective experiences and neglect to address how their own social locations affect their interpretation of research. Some ethnographers, however, have recently begun to write about their positions as researchers while out in the field. Through the perspectives of people of color, and increasingly more often scholars of color, we can learn about how researchers conceptualize notions of subjectivity not only of their subjects but also of themselves. Whether it is by conducting interviews, carrying out observations, or writing up research, critical race theorists utilizing qualitative research are moving beyond traditional qualitative research methods to

investing time in better understanding marginalized populations.

CRT provides a language and a space for people of color to voice their experiences, ultimately legitimizing their experiences which are often invisible to the academic discourse. CRT has been used in analyzing the role of schools for those who have been marginalized, silenced, and disempowered. Critical race theory shows how traditional ways of researching serve to limit the educational opportunities of people of color. However, there is more to critical race theory than providing a means to legitimize the voices of people of color. Critical race theory can also be used as an analytical and conceptual tool that can help scholars create a space for new ways of understanding and theorizing. Re-imagining new ways of knowing and understanding and critiquing Eurocentric, patriarchal, and classist frameworks are necessary for the liberation of all people of color that underlie a "legitimate" way of knowing.

—*Dalia Rodriguez*

See also Anti-Racist Teaching; Anzaldúa, Gloria; Bell, Derrick; *Brown v. Board of Education;* Civil Rights Movement; Feminist Research

Further Readings

Anzaldúa, G. (2003). Speaking in tongues: A letter to third world women writers. In C. Moraga & G. Anzaldúa (Eds.), *This bridge called my back.* Berkeley, CA: Third Woman Press.

Bell, D. (1987). *And we will not be saved: The elusive quest for racial justice.* New York: Basic Books.

Bell, D. (1992). *Faces at the bottom of the well: The permanence of racism.* New York: Basic Books.

Crenshaw, K. (1988). Race, reform and retrenchment: Transformation and legitimation in antidiscrimination law. *Harvard Law Review, 101,* 1331–1387.

Crenshaw, K., Gotanda, N., Peller, G., & Thomas, K. (Eds.). (1995). *Critical race theory: The key writings that formed the movement.* New York: New Press.

Delgado, R. (1989). Storytelling for oppositionists and others: A plea for narrative. *Michigan Law Review, 87*(8), 2411–2441.

Delgado, R., & Stefancic, J. (1992). Critical race theory: Images of the outsider in American law and culture: Can free expression remedy systemic social ills? *Cornell Law Review, 77,* 1248–1297.

Matsuda, M. (1996). *Where is your body? And other essays on race and gender in the law*. Boston: Beacon Press.

Rodriguez, D. (2006, December). Un/masking identity: Healing our wounded souls. *Qualitative Inquiry, 12,* 1067–1090.

Williams, P. J. (1991). *The alchemy of race and rights.* Cambridge, MA: Harvard University Press.

CRITICAL THEORY

See FRANKFURT SCHOOL OF CRITICAL THEORY

CUBAN LITERACY CAMPAIGN

The Cuban literacy campaign was Fidel Castro's 1961 bold educational initiative to eradicate illiteracy in Cuba in one year by bridging the gap between the largely urban educated elite and the island's predominantly illiterate rural workers. The program linked basic literacy to the political education of the people under Castro's newly established revolutionary government. The Cuban literacy campaign not only reduced illiteracy significantly but also united the people around a common cause.

The Cuban literacy campaign officially began on New Year's Eve in 1960 in the capital city, Havana, with Castro's promise before a crowd of 10,000 educators and dignitaries to organize an Army of Education. Prior to this announcement, in September 1960, Castro had declared before the General Assembly of the United Nations his plan to launch a national program with the goal of teaching every illiterate Cuban to read and write. By April 1961, literary foot soldiers were immersed in an intensive training program in Varadero. Then, armed with teacher manuals titled *Alfabeticemos* (Let's Alphabetize) and student textbooks bearing the campaign's slogan *Venceremos* (We will win), they spread out across the country in the single-minded pursuit of teaching basic literacy to every person on the island. Posters dotted the nation proclaiming, "Young men and women, join the Army of the Young Literacy Teachers. . . . A home of a family of peasants who cannot either read or write is waiting for you

now . . . DON'T LET THEM DOWN!" Literate men, women, and even children volunteered to teach. Radio and television played a role by airing advertisements supporting the campaign. Coca-Cola ads encouraged literate people to take refreshing breaks with illiterate people with Cokes and paper and pencils in hand. Slogans, such as "Each one teach one" and "Every home a school," propelled the program.

Ironically, during the year of the campaign, schools were closed for 8 months, so that the people could learn how to read and to write. Brigades of people, known as *brigadistas*, worked as teachers. Teachers from the urban areas moved into the homes of farmers in the country. When houses were too small to accommodate these itinerant teachers, hammocks were provided by the government and teachers slept outside the homes of their pupils. China produced over 100,000 Coleman lantern remakes that were also given by the government to the literary workers to teach reading at night. The lanterns, along with red flags, became symbols for the campaign. The lanterns were hung outside of houses once every member of the family was literate; the flags were hoisted in town squares once an entire village had become literate. The program was national in scope and sought to raise not only the literacy rate but also the political consciousness of the people. Civic education underpinned the entire skill-based part of the program. In sum, approximately 271,000 literate Cubans took to the streets and to the countryside and taught roughly 979,207 illiterate residents of the island basic literacy. And in the process, the political philosophy of Castro was widely disseminated.

The Cuban literacy campaign was interrupted briefly during the Bay of Pigs in April, when for 72 hours, many teachers became soldiers. In total, 42 teachers died during the entire program, including Manuel Ascunce Domenesch and Conrado Benítez, who were murdered by anti-Castro forces. The campaign claimed them as martyrs, further galvanizing the island around the project's aims.

Yet, the counterrevolutionaries were not the only critics of the initiative; there were other critics of the campaign as well. Some claimed the program only taught basic low-level reading. Indeed, the campaign only required reading proficiency at the first-grade level. Others were quick to point out the overtly polit-ical content of the reading materials that emphasized land distribution as well as other communistic prac-tices. Still others questioned how coerced the itinerant teachers' participation in the program was.

The Cuban literacy campaign ended in November 1961 with a drop in illiteracy from 20% to 4%. More than 707,000 people learned to read. Follow-up instruction helped raise the level of literacy to junior high school reading rates. Proponents of the program also noted that the 4% was an inflated number, as it included many new illiterate immigrants.

Both Castro and the country of Cuba declared its literacy campaign a great success. In December 1961, a celebration was held in Revolution Square, complete with scores of people waving giant pencils in the air. In addition, letters from the newly literate reflecting the progress made were sent to Castro. In return, senders received textbooks to continue their studies.

Today, the Literacy Museum that opened in 1964 in Havana houses scores of letters to Castro that offer their readers powerful firsthand accounts of the pro-found impact that the campaign had on the people who learned to read and write under its initiative. Filled with heartfelt thanks to their president and to the literary foot soldiers, they illustrate how the people not only took up his challenge but also achieved its aim. The campaign's slogan, Venceremos ("We will win" or "We shall overcome"), was replaced with Vencimos ("We won"). Lasting friend-ships were forged between people in the country and the city as the nation worked hard together to achieve a shared goal. 1961 became known as the year of edu-cation in Cuba. Not only did the Cuban literacy cam-paign leave a lasting mark on the Cuban people, but it also spread its tenets across the region, as other Latin American countries (e.g., Venezuela) emulated it.

—*Theresa Catherine Lynch*

See also Castro, Fidel; Critical Literacy; Critical Pedagogy

Further Readings

Fagan, R. (1964). *Cuba: The political content of adult education.* Palo Alto, CA: Stanford University Press.

Keeble, A. (Ed.). (2001). *In the spirit of wandering teachers: Cuban literacy campaign, 1961.* Melbourne, Australia: Ocean Press.

Kozol, J. (1978). *Children of the revolution: A Yankee teacher in the Cuban schools.* New York: Delacorte Press.

MacDonald, T. (1985). *Making a new people: Education in revolutionary Cuba.* Vancouver, BC: New Star Books.

CUBAN REVOLUTION

See CASTRO, FIDEL

CULTURE JAMMERS

Coined by the sound collage band Negativland on their album *Jamcon '84,* the term *culture jamming* derives from the Citizens' Band (CB) radio slang for illegally interrupting radio broadcasts with noises and elec-tronic disturbances. Culture jammers similarly intro-duce or unveil such "noise" in capitalist culture itself. Culture jammers could be individual artists, activists, loosely-knit organizations, and even registered corporations unified in their utilization of consumer culture's discourse to illustrate its concomitant ideo-logical failures and distortions. With works ranging from the mildly parodic to the overtly revolutionary, culture jammers appropriate existing hegemonic prac-tices, languages, and aesthetics in order to interrupt the flow of mass media culture and introduce an assess-ment from within the very discourse that is being cri-tiqued. Umberto Eco famously defines culture jammers as activists engaged in semiological guerrilla warfare, which is engendered through the multifarious techniques of adbusting or subvertising, hacktivism, e-mail forwards, audio mixes, billboard liberations, per-formance art, media hoaxes, parody religions, activist "monkeywrenching," and even urban gardening.

These media activists can trace their roots back to the American Great Depression and the New York–based magazine *The Ballyhoo,* which analyzed the language of advertisements and actively encouraged its readers to "Become a Toucher Upper" and join in critiquing advertisements' false promises by artistically intervening in the ads themselves. However, it was the antics of the Situationist International movement of the late 1950s and 1960s and Guy Debord's *The Society of the Spectacle* that gave a theoretical impetus to the practice of culture jamming in the notion of *détournement*. Imagined as a way in which to intervene in the spectacle of consumer culture and the mass media, détournement is a "turnabout" or diversion of the language and practices of the original media into a critique of itself. Kalle Lasn, the founder of Adbusters Media Foundation, the self-proclaimed home of culture jamming, argues that détournement allows for a "jolt" or perceptual shift that can eventually lead to a revolutionary change in cultural perspective and a more active citizenry that is no longer defined by a passive reception of media.

Adbusters Media Foundation's magazine, *Adbusters,* is one of the most visible and often criticized examples of culture jammers at work. It is infamous for its subvertisements, such as the emaciated and dying "Joe Chemo" détourn of Camel cigarettes' mascot Joe Camel, and the promotion of Buy Nothing Day and TV-Turnoff Week. However, culture jamming is not limited to adbusting. A few of the sundry approaches to this form of media activism are exhibited by the following culture jammers: The San Francisco–based Billboard Liberation Front works to reconfigure billboards in order to ultimately reach the goal of a personal billboard for every citizen; ®™ark, a registered corporation, and The Yes Men perpetrate a variety of media hoaxes in order to force an awareness of corporate responsibility for environmental and human costs; and Jonah Peretti, a former MIT student, instigated an e-mail phenomenon recording his attempt to have Nike shoes personalized with the word *sweatshop*. Others include the Guerrilla Girls, anonymous women who appear in various actions and printed pieces while in gorilla masks and under the names of deceased female artists in order to critique misogyny in the art world and in culture at large; Reverend Billy and the Church of Stop Shopping, a New York–based non-profit organization that seeks to take back public "commons" through "gospel choir" performances of anti-shopping songs and revivals at big-box stores; the "organic culture jammers" of guerrilla gardening, who use plants as a political statement in the face of urban clutter; and Billionaires for Bush, a street theater group who don tuxedos and evening gowns as a commentary on who they believe to be George W. Bush's true constituency.

—*Katherine Casey-Sawicki*

See also Adbusters; Billionaires for Bush; Buy Nothing Day; Guerrilla Girls; Media Activism; Situationist International

Further Readings

Baldwin, C. (Director/Producer). (1995). *Sonic outlaws* [Documentary film]. United States: Other Cinema.

Bordwell, M. (2002). Jamming culture: *Adbusters'* hip media campaign against consumerism. In T. Princen, M. Maniates, & K. Conca (Eds.), *Confronting consumption* (pp. 237–253). Cambridge: MIT Press.

Branwyn, G. (1997). *Jamming the media: A citizen's guide to reclaiming the tools of communication.* San Francisco: Chronicle Books.

Debord, G. (1994). *The society of the spectacle* (D. Nicholson-Smith, Trans.). New York: Zone Books.

Jordan, T. (2002). Culture jamming and semiotic terrorism. In *Activism! Direct action, hacktivism and the future of society* (pp. 101–117). London: Reaktion Books.

Klein, N. (1999). *No logo.* New York: Picador.

Lasn, K. (1999). *Culture jam: The uncooling of America.* New York: Eagle Brook.

Sharpe, J. (2001). *Culture jam* [Documentary film]. United States: A Right to Jam Production.

Strangelove, M. (2000). Culture jamming and the transformation of cultural heresies. In *The empire of the mind: Digital piracy and the anti-capitalist movement* (pp. 99–133). Toronto, ON: University of Toronto Press.

Wettergren, Å. (2003). Like moths to a flame—Culture jamming and the global spectacle. In A. Opel & D. Pompper (Eds.), *Representing resistance: Media, civil disobedience, and the global justice movement.* Westport, CT: Praeger.

CYBER RIGHTS

The cyber rights movement believes that one of the most important civil liberty issues is enabling citizens of all races, classes, and creeds to connect to the

Internet. The movement asserts that the Internet should be considered a tool that links everyone together quickly and easily. However, the fact that the Internet links people in different countries with different laws and regulations covering cyberspace makes regulation difficult not only for lawmakers but also for Internet users.

The basic rights promoted by the cyber rights movement are as follows:

- *The right to assemble in online communities.* The movement asserts that as a society in cyberspace, people have to learn how to live inside an environment that is the equivalent of working anarchy. People in cyber communities need to have an awareness of their responsibilities within this anarchy. For this to work, both policymakers and those in the Internet communities need to learn to work together. Policymakers need to understand that Internet communities are capable of governing themselves; thus, politicians should take steps to avoid setting up barriers to this self-governance. At the same time, cyber communities need to find a way to communicate their needs to policymakers in a mature and helpful manner.

- *The right to speak freely.* The movement stresses that in the United States, the federal government needs to affirm that the First Amendment rights enjoyed by print media should extend to the Internet. Additionally, they point out that the concept of copyright does not work well in cyberspace if it is rigidly enforced, as it is outside of the Internet.

- *The right to privacy online.* The movement feels that encryption needs to become commonplace so that the individual citizen no longer feels threatened by those who are already using encryption technology. This will minimize or even eliminate the collection of personal information by making it possible for people to do business online without revealing their personal identity.

- *The right to access regardless of income, location, or disability.* The movement stresses that everyone must be provided with bandwidth—no matter where they are, how much money they make, or what they look like. This means not only making Internet connections accessible to people in public places like libraries and schools but making entire countries wireless so that any citizen can access the Internet at any time.

The cyber rights movement feels that the aforementioned issues are realistic concerns for the future of democracy and equity. Moreover, they believe that the fight for free speech and privacy rights will result in a superficial victory if cyberspace remains segmented, both in control and use, to a majority of the well-educated white elite.

—Malila N. Robinson

See also American Civil Liberties Union (ACLU); Bill of Rights; Community Radio and Television; Electronic Democracy; Free Speech Activism; Media Activism; Media Reform Movement

Further Readings

Godwin, M. (1998). *Cyber rights: Defending free speech in the digital age*. New York: Times Books.

D

DALAI LAMA

According to Tibetan tradition, the Dalai Lama is the incarnation of Avalokitesvara, the Buddha of Compassion, who chose to be reincarnated so that he could serve the people. To date there have been 14 Dalai Lamas.

The First Dalai Lama was called Gedun Drupa. Born in 1391 in the Tsang region of Tibet to a nomadic family, he was ordained in 1411, became a renowned scholar of Buddhist teachings, and founded the Tashi Lhunpo monastery in Shigatse. He died in 1474.

The Second Dalai Lama, Gedun Gyatso, was born to a farming family near Shigatse in 1475. When he was 11 years old, he was recognized as the reincarnation of the First Dalai Lama. He died in 1542.

The Third Dalai Lama was called Sonam Gyatso and was born in 1543 near Lhasa to a wealthy family. In 1546, he was recognized as the reincarnation of Gedun Gyatso. He was fully ordained when he was 22 years old. He established the Namgyal monastery in 1574, which still serves as the Dalai Lama's personal monastery. The Mongolian King Altan Khan conferred on him the title of Dalai Lama, which means "Ocean of Wisdom." Sonam Gyatso died in 1588.

Yonten Gyatso was the Fourth Dalai Lama. Born in 1589 in Mongolia to the Chokar tribal chieftain, he was educated in Mongolia by Tibetan Lamas. He traveled to Tibet in 1601 and was ordained in 1614. He died at the age of 27.

The Fifth Dalai Lama, Ngawang Lobsang Gyatso, was born in the Tsang region in 1617. Although he was identified as the reincarnation of the Dalai Lama, his discovery was kept secret until 1642, once the political turmoil had settled down. He was a great scholar and wielded international political influence. He began the construction of the Potala Palace, which was not completed before his death in 1682. His death was kept secret for 15 years by telling people that the Dalai Lama was engaged in a retreat. Occasionally, someone masqueraded as the Dali Lama so it would appear he was still alive.

Tsangyang Gyatso, the Sixth Dalai Lama was born in 1682 in the Mon Tawang region of India. In 1697 the Emperor and the people were finally informed of the death of the Fifth Dalai Lama and discovery of the Sixth. In 1701 his advisor was killed and the young Dalai Lama, greatly disturbed by this event, rejected the monastic life and never became fully ordained.

In 1708, two years after the disappearance and assumed death of the Sixth Dalai Lama, the Seventh, Kelsang Gyatso, was born in Lithang. The uncertain political situation prevented the young Dalai Lama from traveling to Lhasa to be trained, so he received his training at Kumbum monastery. He was ordained in 1726. Under his reign, the Dalai Lama became the spiritual and political leader of Tibet. He died in 1757.

The Eighth Dalai Lama, Jamphel Gyatso, was born in 1758 in the Tsang region. His parents traced their ancestry to one of Tibet's legendary heroes. He was taken to the monastery in Shigatse at two and a half years old. He was ordained in 1777 and died in 1804.

The Ninth Dalai Lama, Lungtok Gyatso, was born in 1805. He died in 1815 when he was 9 years old.

Tsultrim Gyatso, the 10th Dalai Lama, was born in 1816. He was fully ordained when he was 19 years old. He was always unhealthy and died in 1837.

The 11th Dalai Lama, Khedrup Gyatso, was born in 1838. He was recognized as the new Dalai Lama in 1841 and at a young age took over the political and spiritual responsibilities of the office. In 1856, he died unexpectedly.

Trinley Gyatso, the 12th Dalai Lama, was born in 1856 near Lhasa and was recognized in 1858. In 1873, he took over the political and spiritual responsibilities of Tibet. He died at the age of 20 in 1875.

The 13th Dalai Lama, Thupten Gyatso, was born in 1876 to a peasant couple and was recognized in 1878. He assumed political power in 1895. He and some of his officials fled to India in 1909 after a Chinese invasion. In 1911, he returned to Tibet, where he exercised strong political power, attempting to modernize Tibet and to eliminate some of the more oppressive features of the Tibetan monastic system. He was responsible for establishing the Tibetan postal system, strengthening the Tibetan military, and establishing the Tibetan Medical Institute. He died in 1933.

The 14th Dalai Lama is Tenzin Gyatso. He was born in 1935 in a small village in northeastern Tibet to a peasant family and was recognized at the age of two. In 1949, China invaded Tibet, forcing the Dalai Lama to take over political control of Tibet in 1950. In 1954 he attended peace talks in Beijing with Mao Tse-tung and other Chinese leaders. However in 1959, he fled to India to escape China's brutal suppression of the Tibetan uprising in Lhasa. Dharamsala in northern India is the seat of the Tibetan government-in-exile. The Dalai Lama's appeals to the United Nations resulted in the General Assembly adopting resolutions on Tibet in 1959, 1961, and 1965.

Today, more than 120,000 Tibetans live in exile. The Dalai Lama saw one of the roles of the Tibetan government-in-exile as preserving Tibetan culture. Tibetan refugees and their children have educational and cultural opportunities that maintain their language, history, religion, and culture. The Dali Lama has also worked for a democratic government for Tibet. He has declared that when Tibet is free, he will surrender all political power and resume his life as an ordinary citizen. Although he is the political and spiritual leader of Tibet, he sees himself as a Buddhist monk.

The Dalai Lama is widely known as a man of peace and as a promoter of inter-religious understanding. He consistently advocates nonviolent policies and received the 1989 Nobel Peace Prize for his nonviolent struggle for the liberation of Tibet. In 1987, the Dali Lama proposed a Five-Point Peace Plan for Tibet to make Tibet a free and safe zone for everyone. He has traveled throughout the world and has met with many heads of state, religious leaders, and even famous scientists. He has written numerous books, and has received numerous prizes and awards acknowledging his commitment to peace and unity.

—Lynn W. Zimmerman

Further Readings

Dalai Lama. (1983). My land my people, memoirs of the Dalai Lama of Tibet. New York: Potala.

Dalai Lama. (1990). A policy of kindness. Ithaca, NY: Snow Lion.

Dalai Lama. (1991). Freedom in exile: The autobiography of the Dalai Lama. San Francisco: HarperSanFrancisco.

Dalai Lama. (1992). Worlds in harmony: Dialogues on compassionate action. Berkeley, CA: Parallax Press.

Dalai Lama. (1996). The good heart: A Buddhist perspective on the teachings of Jesus. Somerville, MA: Wisdom.

The Nobel Foundation. (1989). The 14th Dalai Lama. Retrieved May 1, 2006, from http://nobelprize.org/peace/laureates/1989/lama-bio.html

The Office of His Holiness the Dalai Lama. (n.d.) His Holiness the 14th Dalai Lama of Tibet. Retrieved May 1, 2006, from http://www.dalailama.com

The Office of Tibet. (1999). The government of Tibet in exile. His holiness the Dalai Lama. Retrieved May 1, 2006, from http://www.tibet.com/DL/index.html

DALTON, ROQUE (1935–1975)

Roque Dalton was a writer and revolutionary born in El Salvador on May 14, 1935, and murdered on May

10, 1975. He studied law and anthropology at the universities of El Salvador, Chile, and Mexico; worked in journalism; and dedicated himself to literature. He received several national and international awards. Because of his activities and militant politics, he was imprisoned several times and lived in exile in countries such as Guatemala, Mexico, Cuba, Czechoslovakia, Korea, and North Vietnam.

During his life he wrote, struggled, suffered, loved, and died at the hands of his own companions, and that is why Dalton is a considered such a nuisance for those who still deny that another world is possible.

Dalton's literary works were published worldwide and have been gathered in dozens of anthologies (some of them bilingual) in the United States, Europe, and Latin America. Some of them are *Mine, Together With the Birds* (1958), *The Window in the Face* (poetry, Mexico, 1961, introduced by Mauricio de la Selva), *Testimonies* (poetry, La Habana, UNEAC, 1963), *Cesar Vallejo* (essay, LA Habana, 1963), *The Other World* (1963), *Poems* (1967), *Intellectuals and Society* (conversations with writers, Mexico D.F., 1969, translated to Italian), *The Tavern and Other Poems* (1969, Casa de las Americas Award), *Little Hells* (poetry, Barcelona, 1970, introduced by Jose Goytisolo), *Is Revolution the Revolution?* (1970), and *The Forbidden Stories of Tom Thumb* (prose and poems, Mexico, 1974). In 1997, Dalton was named "Meritorious Poet of the Republic" in El Salvador.

—*Adrian Oscar Scribano*

See also FMLN

Further Readings

Dalton, R. (1996). *Small hours of the night*. Willimantic, CT: Curbstone Press.

García Verzi, H. (1986). *Recopilación de textos sobre Roque Dalton*. La Habana: Casa de las Américas, serie Valoración Múltiple.

DANCE AND ACTIVISM

Dance contributes to social change, civic engagement, and activism in multiple ways. Dance can be the antithesis of the values of modern-day capitalism, providing a vehicle for building community and understanding across social boundaries, resisting oppression by contributing to the cultural continuity of oppressed peoples, asking questions and reflecting on sociopolitical discourse through choreography, and embodying social change, simultaneously creating and reflecting social movements toward equality.

The history of dance is somewhat difficult to document, given the ephemeral nature of the form. Dance leaves traces only in pictures, in written and oral descriptions, and by being passed on from dancer to dancer through generations. It can be hypothesized that dance has existed in every culture throughout history, and has served social, religious/spiritual, and artistic functions. In many ways, dance maintains the status quo. In social dances, gender roles and rules of acceptable social behavior are defined. In court dances of all cultures, the aristocracy or monarchy is heralded and praised. Religious/spiritual dances pass on traditional modes of worship. The presentation of dance on proscenium stage, and the development of dance as an entertainment, divided spectator and performer and developed a particular elitism in the art form, connected to the development of physical virtuosity and highly selective skills that segregate dancers from the general public.

However, dance is used in many ways to challenge and change the status quo. Dancing is rooted in physical activity of the body and therefore produces physical awareness. This body consciousness is a counterpoint to the body/mind separation of Western culture. The body/mind separation subordinates kinesthetic knowledge in a hierarchy of knowledge that privileges logical reasoning and concrete evidence instead of the knowledge that is located in the body: emotions, intuition, and physical skill. Dancing subverts this hierarchy by affirming the body's knowledge and its importance, with the potential to develop a morality that is based on emotional responsiveness. Furthermore, dancing inherently resists the lexicon of capitalism. There is no product to buy or sell. Once a dance is over, it is gone. It cannot be effectively captured or purchased. The act of producing dance defies capitalism's emphasis on efficiency, using time and resources for an end result that is transitory and impermanent. Dancing creates community and cross-cultural understanding, unifying participants and offering a transformation that is viscerally experienced. From head-banging to ballroom dancing, movement produces a physical release that counteracts the weight of oppression and cultivates joy. Through dancing, people connect with each other. Additionally, learning the steps of another culture's dance contributes to cross-cultural understanding. Although movement is not a universal language—different cultures have different symbolic systems—the body is a universal instrument that every human can relate to. In this way, physicality is a uniting force, a common ground for creating community. When harnessed to form solidarity and inclusiveness, dance can be a powerful tool for ending social isolation and segregation.

Dancing contributes to cultural continuity, playing an important role in resisting colonialism, imperialism, and cultural obliteration. Only one of many examples, African slaves used dance to maintain their cultural traditions and identity, during (and after) slavery in the Americas. This continuity can be seen in contemporary settings in hip-hop and reggae dances, which carry the same emphasis on polyrhythms and body part isolations. People of the African diaspora also use dance to continue their religious traditions, which use dance and music as a means of worship. The continuation of African-based religious practices in the Western Hemisphere demonstrates the power of dance as a means of resistance to cultural obliteration.

In addition to the inherent ways dance contributes to activism, in the 20th and 21st century, choreographers have used dance as a vehicle for making political statements and asking questions about the world. There is a long tradition of anti-war choreography, beginning with Kurt Jooss's ballet *The Green Table, War Lyrics* by Jose Limon, *Docudance: Nine Short Dances About the Defense Budget and Other Military Matters* by Liz Lerman, *Oh Beautiful* by Deborah Hay, and *one: an anti-war dance* by Juliette Mapp. Choreographers have created work about a wide breadth of sociopolitical issues: race and racism, the HIV/AIDS epidemic, poverty, gay/lesbian/bisexual/transgender identities, and feminism and the experience of women. Because dance begins with the body,

dance often relies on an element of personal history, a unique lens on sociopolitical issues. Of many choreographers, Ralph Lemon and Maura Nguyen Donahue use personal history as a portal to reflecting on larger sociopolitical issues of race and identity, incorporating performance traditions from around the world.

Choreographers also address sociopolitical issues through working in communities. Jawole Willa Jo Zollar and her company, Urban Bush Women, are committed to using dance theater as a catalyst for social change through telling the stories of disenfranchised people, focused especially on the traditions of women in the African diaspora. To that end, Urban Bush Women also engages in community work, through programs like their Summer Institute, which connects professionals and community artists to further the use of dance for social change. Zollar also includes community members in the creation and refinement of her choreography. For *Hair Stories* of 2001, Zollar held "hair parties," gatherings at various community and homes through which Zollar invited participants to discuss hair, view sections of the performance, and build relationships between themselves and the company.

The Liz Lerman Dance Exchange is renowned for its community-based work, pursuing the expansion of the definition of dance and dance with an intergenerational group of dancers, and working on projects to involve communities in the process of making dance. Liz Lerman began working with performers of diverse backgrounds in 1975 in her piece *Woman of the Clear Vision*, which included professional dancers and adults from a senior center. Since then, Liz Lerman has been celebrated for developing innovative ways to make community-based art.

In addition to community-based work, choreographers have developed ways to involve the audience in their performances, challenging the passive role of the spectator. Based on the recognition of the audience as integral in creating meaning through their individual interpretations of choreography, interactive dance performance emphasizes the agency and power of the audience member. In *Pulling the Wool: An American Landscape of Truth and Deception* from 2004, Jill Sigman transformed a two-story gymnasium into a multimedia performance carnival for audience members to navigate, making choices about how they interacted and reacted to the performance. Sigman views this ability to shape their experience as an expression of civic agency. Instead of expressing a single political statement, the performance revealed ambiguity and was open for multiple interpretations. In this way, questioning is activism as it cultivates an engagement with the world.

Similarly, site-specific choreography offers the potential to involve the audience by offering the passerby an unexpected experience. If placed in a prominent and public space, the performance disrupts the flow of everyday life and shifts the viewer's consciousness, developing an interface between performer and the public. In *Salvage/Salvation* from 2001, Clarinda Mac Low created environments on a site, using only the discarded materials found there. The piece always generated conversation with pedestrians who asked about what they are doing. Through dialogue and shifted awareness, choreography has the potential to transform the individual.

Developments in dance—such as the birth of modern dance, contact improvisation, and dance accessibility—embody, create, and reflect social change. The beginning of modern dance in the early 20th century demonstrated (and somewhat preceded) changing social values. Discarding the formality of ballet and the perceived superficiality of vaudeville, modern dance reveled in more natural, organic movement that cherished individual expression, dance for dance's sake, and the human condition. In the 1960s the growth of contact improvisation reflected changing roles between genders, eradicating the status quo in dance where only men lift and support women, and creating instead fluid partnerships between all genders, where everyone could play a physically supporting role. Contact improvisation was part of dance investigations happening at Judson Church in Greenwich Village, where many choreographers were questioning what dance is, stripping dance down to movement essentials and rejecting ideals of virtuosity and special technique. These developments can be seen as a demonstration of the social changes happening in America during the civil rights and anti-war movements, where many social norms were questioned and equality demanded. Similarly, the dance accessibility movement in England reflects the growth of the disability rights movement. Several professional dance companies in England are dedicated to the inclusion of differently abled dancers and challenge ideas of who can be a dancer.

When used intentionally, dance is a powerful tool for asking questions about the world, connecting people, reflecting and discussing political viewpoints, and awakening personal change. Dance is literally the movement of social movements, the embodiment of change and transformation.

—*Jesse Phillips-Fein*

See also Guerrilla Girls; Hip-Hop; Performativity; Play, Creativity, and Social Movements; Postmodernism; Radical Cheerleaders

Further Readings

Albright, A. (1997). *Choreographing difference: The body and identity in contemporary dance.* Middletown, CT: Wesleyan University Press.

Albright, A. (2001). *Moving history/dancing cultures: A dance history reader.* Middletown, CT: Wesleyan University Press.

Auslander, P. (1992). *Presence and resistance.* Ann Arbor: University of Michigan Press.

Banes, S. (1983). *Democracy's body: Judson dance theater, 1962–1964.* Ann Arbor: University of Michigan Press.

Daly, A. (2002). *Critical gestures: Writings on dance & culture.* Middletown, CT: Wesleyan University Press.

Daniel, Y. (2005). *Dancing wisdom: Embodied knowledge in Haitian vodou, Cuban yoruba, and Bahian condemlé.* Chicago: University of Illinois.

Foster, S. (1995). *Corporealities: Dancing, knowledge, and power.* Oxford, UK: Routledge.

Graff, E. (1997). *Stepping left: Dance and politics in New York City, 1928–1942.* Durham, NC: Duke University Press.

Martin, R. (1998). *Critical moves.* Durham, NC: Duke University Press.

Darrow, Clarence (1857–1938)

Clarence Darrow has been called the Attorney for the Damned. In his long legal career as a courtroom lawyer, he defended African Americans, murderers, communists, anarchists, labor radicals, socialists, and iconoclastic classroom teachers. Darrow was a long-time opponent of the death penalty, and his celebrated cross-examination of William Jennings Bryan in the infamous Tennessee "monkey trial" of biology teacher John T. Scopes set back the anti-evolution forces for many decades in the public schools.

Darrow was born in Kinsman, Ohio, the fifth child of Amirus and Emily Eddy Darrow. His father had been prepared in theology, but somewhere in his education he lost his faith and never preached. Growing up, Darrow recognized that his father was considered the village infidel, a sobriquet he accepted rather proudly.

Darrow never liked school and even through law school he devalued formal education, believing it produced narrow minds and not true learning. He was particularly critical of the morality embedded in the school books of the day. The young Darrow deeply resented the forced attendance at Sunday school, which later became the source of a lifelong irreverence for organized religion.

Although Clarence briefly attended Allegheny College, he did not graduate. He became a school teacher in a nearby town. As a teacher he abolished corporal punishment in the school and expanded the lunch break. He also had time to study law. Later he attended the University of Michigan's law school but again did not graduate. He apprenticed to an attorney and passed the Ohio bar at age 21. A short time later he began the practice of law, first in Andover and later in Ashtabula. He learned that he could not be a dispassionate advocate. He had to believe in his client and in the cause. He moved to Chicago in 1887. Almost immediately he became involved with John P. Altgeld, the leading Democratic radical of his time, who later became governor of Illinois. During this period, Altgeld gave Darrow many lessons on power politics.

From his Chicago law office, Clarence Darrow was at the heart of many celebrated cases in the turbulence of the early 19th century. He became the attorney for the United Mine Workers. In 1906 he went to Idaho to defend Big Bill Haywood, secretary-treasurer of the Western Federation of Miners, who was accused of murdering ex-Governor Frank Steunenberg. Darrow gave a long and impassioned plea to the jury. Bill Haywood was acquitted.

Darrow went to Los Angeles, where he defended three union men accused of being involved in the bombing of the *Los Angeles Times*. What Darrow faced in California was bleak. One of the men arrested with the bombers had turned state's evidence and confessed to the plot. It was soon revealed that his clients were actually guilty. Darrow did not want a trial and he did not want certain documents made public implicating the union. He tried for a negotiated sentence. The bombers changed their plea to guilty. The unions backing them were aghast, and Darrow's days as a union attorney ended. A short while later, he had to defend himself against charges that he had tried to bribe prospective jurors. While Darrow pled innocence and spent 8 months defending himself, a careful review of his case by Geoffrey Cowan, a public interest lawyer and a faculty member at UCLA, concluded that he indeed had tried to bribe two jurors in this case. However, after a long and tearful plea by Darrow at his trial, he obtained a not guilty verdict. Darrow then restarted his legal career with a public pledge to continue to help the poor. With few exceptions he stuck to his word.

Darrow today is known as the lawyer who defended John T. Scopes in the famous Tennessee evolution trial encapsulated in the Broadway play and film *Inherit the Wind*. His defense of Loeb and Leopold, who tried to commit the perfect murder, the plot of the novel and film *Compulsion*, was another legal epoch. His defense of an African American family who defended themselves against a white mob in Detroit with an all-white jury in 1926 resulted in a verdict of not guilty.

Clarence Darrow was neither the perfect man nor the perfect lawyer. But few in his profession have left a record of serving the cause of social justice for the poor or the oppressed as well as he did, then or now.

—*Fenwick W. English*

See also Activism, Social and Political; Anarchism; Communism; Debs, Eugene V.; Dissent; Gompers, Samuel; Marshall, Thurgood; Southern Poverty Law Center; Violence, Theories of

Further Readings

Cowan, G. (1993). *The people v. Clarence Darrow.* New York: Random House.

Tierney, K. (1979). *Darrow: A biography.* New York: Thomas Y. Crowell.

Weinberg, A. (Ed.). (1989). *Attorney for the damned: Clarence Darrow in the courtroom.* Chicago: University of Chicago Press. (Original work published 1957)

Darwin, Charles (1809–1882)

Charles Darwin was the British naturalist who first formulated the theory of biological evolution by natural selection, widely regarded as the most significant scientific achievement of the 19th century. Darwin's paternal grandfather was the 18th-century physician and freethinker Erasmus Darwin, who wrote a speculative work on biological evolution, titled *Zoönomia,* in the 1790s. His maternal grandfather was Josiah Wedgwood, founder of the famous pottery. Darwin grew up in Shropshire and later attended Edinburgh University to study medicine, but soon discovered he did not have the stomach for it. Transferring to Christ's College, Cambridge, he came under the influence of John Stevens Henslow, professor of botany. In 1831, Henslow arranged for Darwin to join a surveying voyage on HMS Beagle as personal companion to the ship's captain, Robert FitzRoy. The voyage lasted nearly 5 years and was the turning point in Darwin's life. The Beagle took him to South America, the Galapagos Islands, Tahiti, New Zealand, Australia, and southern Africa, before returning to England in 1836.

During his long trip, Darwin made detailed geological, botanical, and zoological observations and accumulated a large collection of specimens. Back in England, he gained respect for his work as a geologist, including a novel theory of the origin of coral reefs, but by this time Darwin had also privately rejected orthodox accounts of the origin of biological species, which viewed them as having been created in pretty much their present forms. His observations of the similarities between living and fossil mammals, and between the distinct species of plants and animals on the Galapagos Islands and their counterparts on the South American mainland, persuaded him that biological evolution had taken place, even though he was not yet sure how. Within a few years, Darwin had elaborated his entire theory of evolution, the crucial idea being that evolution is the result of natural selection, whereby organisms that are better adapted to their environments are more likely to survive and reproduce, thus passing on their advantageous traits to the next generation.

Although Darwin formulated his theory as early as 1837, it was to be more than 20 years before he finally made it public. The main reason for this delay was his nervousness about challenging the dogmas of orthodox religion, regarded by the upper classes as a bulwark of the status quo during a period of social unrest in early Victorian Britain. In 1839, the independently wealthy Darwin married his cousin, Emma Wedgwood, who unlike him was devoutly religious, adding a personal dimension to this conflict. Darwin and his wife moved to Down House in Kent, and from this period onwards, Darwin was in poor health, which some have speculated was exacerbated by his intellectual anxieties.

Darwin did not go public until 1858, after learning that the young Welsh naturalist Alfred Russel Wallace had reached similar conclusions. The following year, Darwin published his masterpiece, *The Origin of Species,* which makes a methodical case for evolution. Darwin argues that natural selection is a real process, analogous to the way in which plant and animal breeders can dramatically alter the characteristics of a group of organisms over a series of generations by permitting only individuals with desired traits to reproduce. In the natural world, a population of organisms can become better and better adapted to its environment over time, and the characteristics of its members at the end of the process may be very different from those of their ancestors. Darwin goes on to argue that natural selection is capable of giving rise not simply to new varieties but to new species, and that it can in principle account for all the characteristics of existing organisms, even organs of extreme perfection like the human eye.

Finally, Darwin presents an enormous quantity of evidence that natural selection is not only a possible explanation of the origin of species, but that it is the only reasonable one. The data range from the pattern of development revealed in the fossil record, to facts about the geographical distribution of organisms, to structural and developmental similarities between otherwise very different living things. Darwin demonstrates that his view can provide satisfying explanations of such matters, while from the point of view of those who believe in divine creation, they remain conundrums.

Even though Darwin avoided the issue of human evolution in the *Origin* (a subject he was later to discuss at length in *The Descent of Man* of 1871), its publication inevitably sparked intense controversy. Darwin's theory banishes preordained purposes from nature and implies that mental phenomena emerge when matter is arranged in complex ways. One early reviewer condemned Darwin's views for their unflinching materialism, and figures such as Samuel Wilberforce, the Bishop of Oxford, attacked evolution from a religious perspective. But Darwin, who did not engage in the public debate, was ably defended by his scientific supporters, including Joseph Hooker and Thomas Huxley. Within less than a decade, the bulk of the scientific establishment had been won over to evolution, although it took longer for natural selection to be accepted as the central mechanism.

Although Darwin's ideas were initially viewed as a challenge to the existing social order, attempts were soon made to use them in its support. The political theorist Herbert Spencer formulated the doctrine of Social Darwinism, defending laissez-faire economics on the grounds that it represented the principle of the "survival of the fittest" applied to human society. Darwin's cousin, Francis Galton, founded the eugenics movement, which viewed social inequalities as having a biological basis and advocated intervention to "improve" the human stock. Eugenics went out of fashion following its use by the Nazis in the 1930s and 1940s, but new attempts to use Darwinian ideas to explain social inequality have emerged in recent decades, including sociobiology and evolutionary psychology. In turn, these developments have been criticized as ideological misapplications of Darwinism by biologists such as Stephen Jay Gould.

—*Philip Gasper*

See also Eugenics Movement

Further Readings

Desmond, A., & Moore, J. (1994). *Darwin: The life of a tormented evolutionist.* New York: W. W. Norton.

Hodge, J., & Radick, G. (Eds.). (2003). *The Cambridge companion to Darwin.* New York: Cambridge University Press.

Ridley, M. (Ed.). (1996). *The Darwin reader* (2nd ed.). New York: W. W. Norton.

DAVIS, ANGELA (1944–)

Angela Yvonne Davis represents both the typical and the paradoxical in the most-celebrated black American experience. Typical is the convergence in her of the brilliant intellectual—she is a philosopher, a theoretician of black liberation, a feminist theorist, and a writer—and the indefatigable activist. Paradoxical is her having once been among FBI's 10 most wanted criminals, and having later been recognized by the establishment as a historical force with whom to be reckoned.

Davis was born on January 26, 1944, in Birmingham, Alabama. She was inspired from an early age by the alert consciousness of members of her family. Her mother, Sallye Davis, as a college student, participated in the campaign for the freedom of the Scottsboro Boys and was an activist of the National Association for the Advancement of Colored People (NAACP), despite the ban on that organization in Birmingham.

Davis went to Carrie A. Tuggle Elementary School in her hometown, which had the distinction of offering classes in African American culture. She later attended Elisabeth Irwin High School in New York, where she was enrolled in a program for promising southern black students, sponsored by the American

Friends Service Committee. It was there that she came across the *Communist Manifesto,* which, in her own words, had a most powerful impact on her. The origin of her commitment to concrete, practical contribution to the struggle for social change can also be traced to this time. Her earliest activities revolved around Advance, a youth organization associated with the Communist Party.

Immediately upon completion of her high school studies, Davis was offered a scholarship by Brandeis University. She was one of only three black first-year students. Two of her greatest experiences at Brandeis were hearing James Baldwin and Malcolm X on campus. A number of other events accounted for the growth of her international vision. She was a delegate to the Eighth World Festival for Youth and Students in Helsinki, Finland. She was also sent for her junior academic year to the Sorbonne, in France, which was in the grips of youthful revolutionary fervor.

In 1962 Davis met the renowned philosopher Herbert Marcuse, who became her tutor. After graduating from Brandeis, Davis proceeded for graduate work in philosophy to the University of Frankfurt, in Germany. Another famous philosopher, Theodor Adorno, agreed to supervise her Ph.D. dissertation, which was to be in the area of critical theory.

At Frankfurt, Davis was receiving news of the escalation of the black liberation movement. She was shocked by the Birmingham bombing of 1963. Then, in 1965, Malcolm X was assassinated, and unprecedented riots broke out in Selma, Alabama, and in Watts, Los Angeles. Davis realized that she could not continue with her academic work unless she was also politically involved.

She returned to the United States to continue her postgraduate research under the supervision of Marcuse at the University of California at San Diego (UCSD). There, she successfully campaigned for the introduction of programs in ethnic studies, and black studies in particular. Her argument was that the philosophical viewpoint contained in the literature of black experience was superior to that propounded by privileged white philosophers, and it had a transformative power.

While at UCSD, she also ran a so-called liberation academy for a poor black community at Los Angeles.

Angela Yvonne Davis (1944–)

Source: Photo by Nick Wiebe.

Together with Huey Newton, Bobby Seale, and others, in 1966 she set up the Oakland-based Black Panther Party, and was involved in the national Student Nonviolent Coordinating Committee. Most significantly, she became a member of the Communist Party of America, a decision that was to have grave consequences for her life.

Having passed her preliminary doctoral examinations, and without adequate financial means to continue with her dissertation, Davis applied for and was granted a teaching position at the University of California at Los Angeles (UCLA). She was assigned a course in Recurring Philosophical Themes in Black Literature. Her two initial lectures on the life and times of Frederick Douglass offer an analysis of freedom and the role of education in reaching a level of consciousness that requires that the recognition of one's freedom by others be seen as an absolute condition for life. Illustrious examples of scholarship, they were published in 1971 under the title *Lectures of Liberation.*

Davis's first term at UCLA had just started, when the governor of California, Ronald Reagan, and the University of California Board of Regents decided to fire her because of her membership in the Communist Party. Several years of legal battle followed. Eventually, the court fight against the state law prohibiting state universities from hiring communists ended successfully for her, and her contract at UCLA was renewed.

In 1970, Davis was charged in court with conspiracy, kidnapping, and murder, and if convicted, she was to face the death penalty under California law. This was in connection with an attempt by a young black man to rescue three black convicts, who were falsely accused of killing a Soledad Prison guard. Evidence of Davis's proclaimed complicity in the operation was sought due to the fact that one of the guns the youth carried was registered in her name, and also because of her active involvement in the campaign for the release of the three victims, who had become commonly known as the Soledad Brothers. She had persistently argued that they were political prisoners and not criminals, as viewed by the state. (Years later the murder charges against them were dropped.) Her long-standing commitment to prisoners' rights has its origin in that experience.

Frightened by the horrendous frame-up, Davis went underground, earning her a place on the FBI's ten most wanted list, and she was hunted nationwide. She was soon apprehended and incarcerated. Almost immediately after her arrest, a worldwide "Free Angela Davis" movement sprang to life. In July 1972, after 21 months in jail, denied bail, maltreated, Davis was acquitted by a jury of all three charges. By this time she had become an international symbol of the black liberation movement.

In prison, Davis devoted much of her time to the education of incarcerated women and the development of a spirit of solidarity among them. Today she remains a staunch advocate of prison abolition; she has also offered a sustained criticism of racism in the criminal justice system.

She was still in custody when the collection of essays, *If They Come in the Morning: Voices of Resistance* of 1971, which she edited, was published. Soon after, she embarked on her second book, *Angela Davis: An Autobiography* (1974). Besides being what she calls a political account of the people, events, and forces that formed her involvement in the struggle of black Americans, the book is also a philosophical discussion of such issues as race, class, gender, revolution, social transformation, commitment, organizational work, and political prisoners.

Since 1972, Davis has always had a large national, as well as international, platform to address through public speaking, articles in magazines and journals, and books. She has lectured throughout the United States, as well as in Africa, Europe, and the Caribbean. She has continued to actively participate in many political struggles for freedom and justice.

Central to her career has been her work in education. She has taught at various departments at a number of California universities, her lengthiest association having been with San Francisco State University (1978–1991) and the San Francisco Art Institute (1977–1989). In 1990 and 1991 she was an instructor in the Education Program of the San Francisco County Jail. In 1994, she was granted the prestigious appointment to the University of California Presidential Chair in African American and Feminist Studies. Since 1995, she has been a professor in the History of Consciousness Department at the University of California at Santa Cruz, teaching critical theory. Through her writing, especially her books, *Women, Race, and Class* (1981); *Women, Culture, and Politics* (1989); and her most recent works, Davis has played a significant role in the reformation of Marxism and the development of critical theory, black liberation theory, and feminist theory.

—Emilia Ilieva

See also Activism, Social and Political; Advocacy; Anti-Prison Movement; Anti-Racist Teaching; Baldwin, James; Black Panther Party; Black Power; Civil Rights Movement; Communism; *Communist Manifesto;* Communist Party USA; Douglass, Frederick; Feminism; Literature and Activism; Malcolm X; Marcuse, Herbert; Marxist Theory; Student Nonviolent Coordinating Committee (SNCC); Youth Organizing and Activism

Further Readings

Davis, A. (1971). *Lectures on liberation.* New York: New York Committee.

Davis, A. (1974). *Angela Davis: An autobiography.* New York: Random House.

Davis, A. (1981). *Women, race, and class.* New York: Random House.

Davis, A. (1989). *Women, culture, and politics.* New York: Random House.

Davis, A. (1996, Summer). Black women and the academy. *Callaloo, 17*(2), 422–431.

Davis, A. (1998). *Blues legacies and black feminism: Gertrude 'Ma' Rainey, Bessie Smith, and Billie Holiday.* New York: Vintage Books.

Davis, A. (2003). *Are prisons obsolete?* New York: Seven Stories Press.

Davis, A., & Aptheker, B. (Eds.). (1971). *If they came in the morning: Voices of resistance.* New York: Third Press.

Perkins, M. (2000). *Autobiography as activism: Three black women of the sixties.* Jackson: University Press of Mississippi.

Davis, Ossie (1917–2005)

Ossie Davis was one of the most renowned African American personalities in modern American culture, as well as a passionate advocate for social justice. As an actor, playwright, producer, and director, he not only enriched American life through the excellence of his theatrical and cinematic achievements, but also helped transform it along the lines of multicultural humanism.

Davis studied playwriting at Howard University in Washington and then moved to New York to pursue acting under Lloyd Richards. He forged friendships with Father Divine, W. E. B. Du Bois, A. Philip Randolph, Langston Hughes, and Richard Wright. Davis joined the Rose McClendon Players and first appeared in *Joy Exceeding Glory* in Harlem in 1941.

Back from military service after World War II, he made his debut on Broadway in *Jeb,* where he played the title role of a returning soldier who faces racist attacks. He became distinguished for roles dealing with racial injustice and imbued with dignity.

In 1959, he starred on Broadway in *A Raisin in the Sun* by Lorraine Hansberry. It was named best American play of that year by the New York Drama Critics Circle. In such other notable stage performances as *No Time for Sergeants, The Wisteria Trees, Green Pastures, Jamaica, Ballad for Bimshire, The Zulu and the Zayda,* and *I'm Not Rappaport,* he brilliantly articulated the pride, the hope, and the suffering of being black in America.

Davis's first movie role was in *No Way Out* in 1950, Joseph L. Mankiewicz's lauded story of racial hatred, starring Sidney Poitier. His television debut was in 1955 in *The Emperor Jones.* He wrote and directed *Cotton Comes to Harlem* in 1970, one of the first "blaxploitation" films (a genre that refashioned black characterization), and many other films. His breakthrough as a playwright came in 1961 with *Purlie Victorious,* a satire on racial stereotypes. *For Us the Living: The Story of Medgar Evers* is among his best-known television films.

Davis was married to fellow actress Ruby Dee. They became a revered couple of the American stage, two of the most prolific and courageous artists in American culture, and two of the most prominent black role models in Hollywood. Throughout their careers, Davis and Dee worked toward overcoming racial exclusion in the entertainment world and helped open new opportunities for African American actors.

In the 1950s, the couple was nearly blacklisted for protesting the communist witch-hunting of McCarthyism. They raised legal fees for black victims of racial injustices and spoke out on such issues as voting rights and police brutality. The two were among the key organizers of the 1963 March on Washington. Two years later, Davis delivered a memorable eulogy for his assassinated friend, Malcolm X. Davis supported progressive causes until his death.

—Emilia Ilieva and Lennox Odiemo-Munara

See also Activism, Social and Political; Advocacy; Civil Rights Movement; Du Bois, W. E. B.; Evers, Medgar; Film; Hansberry, Lorraine; Hollywood Blacklists; Hughes, Langston; Malcolm X; Multiculturalism

Further Readings

Cutler, J. K. (1999). *Struggles for representation: African American documentary film and video.* Bloomington: Indiana University Press.

Davis, O., & Dee, R. (1998). *With Ossie and Ruby: In this life together.* New York: Morrow.

Donalson, M. (2003). *Black directors in Hollywood.* Austin: University of Texas Press.

Hill, E. G., & Hatch, J. V. (2003). *A history of African American theatre.* Cambridge, UK: Cambridge University Press.

Rhines, J. A. (1996). *Black film/white money.* New Brunswick, NJ: Rutgers University Press.

DAY, DOROTHY (1897–1980)

Dorothy Day is best known as the cofounder of the Catholic Worker movement. In 1932, Day and Peter Maurin established a radical, pacifist organization rooted in the Catholic tradition that provides direct services to the poor and promotes social justice through nonviolent protest and activism. By her own recognition, her life was divided in two parts. Her early years were marked by her devotion to radical causes, as well as a bohemian lifestyle that included love affairs, an abortion, a common-law marriage, and the birth of a child out of wedlock. This phase ended with her conversion in 1927 to Roman Catholicism, an act that was the culmination of nearly a decade of spiritual searching, shortly after the birth of her daughter. Her extraordinary gifts began to reach their full fruition 5 years later when with Maurin she married her deep commitment to Catholicism and her radical beliefs by establishing the Catholic Worker movement. A journalist throughout her life, she is well regarded for her substantial body of writing (much of it first printed in her daily column in the movement's newspaper, the *Catholic Worker*). At the time of her death in 1980, she was widely heralded both for her activism in service of the poor and for her singular contribution to American Catholicism in the 20th century.

Dorothy Day was born in Brooklyn, New York, on November 8, 1897, the third of five children. Early in Day's life, her family moved briefly to San Francisco, but after the earthquake in 1906 they settled permanently in the Chicago area. Although she was baptized as an Episcopalian, Day later actively rejected religion. She attended the University of Illinois for 2 years, but dropped out prior to graduation in order to move to New York City in 1916 to become a writer for a variety of socialist publications. She joined the Industrial Workers of the World (IWW), participated in numerous protests, and was jailed while demonstrating in favor of women's suffrage. Her friends and companions included activists, artists, writers, and journalists who supported radical and socialist causes, including Jack Reed, Malcolm Cowrey, and Eugene

O'Neill. Even during this period of agnosticism, however, she would often follow a night of drinking in a Greenwich Village saloon with friends like O'Neill with silent participation in mass at St. Joseph's Parish across the street, as she reports in her autobiography *The Long Loneliness.*

In 1918, she worked briefly as a nurse's aide in Kings County Hospital. While there, she met an orderly with whom she had a brief affair, resulting in a pregnancy, which she terminated. She drifted after this, traveling and working as a journalist. In Chicago, Day worked on a communist newspaper, and while staying in an IWW flophouse she was mistakenly arrested as a prostitute in a raid. She documented this experience, as well as other prison stays, in her writing, which to this day remains a vivid account of the indignities experienced daily by the poor in the criminal justice system.

Although she did not mention her union in her own accounts of her life, recent biographies of Day establish that this period was followed by a very brief failed marriage when she returned to New York. It hardly lasted as long as her honeymoon trip to Europe. The great love of Day's life was Forster Battenham, an anarchist and biologist whom she would later call her common-law husband. In 1924 she published a novel, *The Eleventh Virgin,* which was largely based on her own life, including her abortion. With the proceeds of this unremarkable book she was able to buy a small cottage on Staten Island near the ocean, in a colony known as the Spanish Camp. Here she lived a bohemian existence with Battenham, Cowley, Caroline Gordon, and others.

The seeds of Day's conversion to Catholicism took root in her domestic life with Battenham when she discovered that she was once again pregnant. Deeply happy, she determined to have her child baptized a Catholic. She named their daughter Tamar Teresa, the former name a Hebrew word meaning "tree," the latter in honor of a great saint and doctor of the Roman Catholic Church. Her own baptism followed shortly after, an act that Day knew would result in the dissolution of her relationship with Battenham, who as an anarchist and an atheist would neither marry her nor accept her new devotion. Day herself gives the best reports of this spiritual journey in two books. The first,

From Union Square to Rome, was an account of her conversion (from the perspective of a former communist, as Paul Elie has noted) published in 1938. The second is a more candid and spiritual account, her autobiography *The Long Loneliness,* published in 1952.

After her split with Tamar's father, Day and her daughter survived on a variety of freelance writing jobs that took her to Hollywood, Mexico, and other places, finally returning to New York. In her autobiography, Day describes how in 1932 she found herself in Washington observing a communist march in support of the poor. Day credits her disenchantment with the anti-religious stance of communism, her subsequent visit to the National Shrine of the Immaculate Conception in prayerful search for new, Catholic-inspired work for the poor, and the near miraculous appearance of Peter Maurin when she returned to New York with the formation of her life's work, the *Catholic Worker.* From that point on Maurin was a seminal influence on her thinking.

Maurin was a French Catholic peasant who believed that Catholic thought needed to be married to the radical commitment to the poor embodied by some social movements of the time. An itinerant preacher and philosopher, he proclaimed his truths on soapboxes in Union Square and by all accounts was a compelling if eccentric figure. He and Day conceived a movement that eventually would be founded on three pillars: publication of a daily newspaper, the *Catholic Worker,* sold on street corners for a penny; the creation of houses of hospitality to provide respite and food for the poor and indigent; and the creation of communal, self-sufficient farms to support this work.

From these beginnings, the Catholic Worker movement evolved under their tutelage to encompass steadfast advocacy of radical social justice. For Day, this meant undertaking a voluntary life of poverty with the movement as the center of her life. The movement stood for pacifism, even in the midst of World War II, for equality for all races, and most importantly as a voice for the poor and dispossessed of society. As she had indicated earlier in her life, Day looked to the saints not merely to help slaves, but also to end slavery.

To comprehend fully the essence of Dorothy Day, one must take account of her Catholic faith and her lifelong commitment to what Paul Elie has termed the *traditional piety* of devotions such as the rosary, the office, and the daily celebration of mass. Prior to her conversion, Day wrote in her autobiography that she did not know what she believed, though she had tried to serve a cause. With her baptism she embraced the simple and radical Christianity she found expressed in the work of another great convert, St. Augustine, in his *Imitation of Christ.* The connection of the Catholic Worker movement to her Catholic faith did not belie her dissatisfaction with the imperfections she saw in the institutional Church. But she maintained committed to the sacraments of the Church until her death, despite her permanent dissatisfaction. Only through the Church could one receive the sacraments.

Throughout most of the 20th century, Day's work realized in a particular way the aspirations and dilemmas of Catholics in an American Church seeking to remain faithful to the teachings of the Beatitudes. In her later life, Day welcomed and explored the *aggiornamento* in the Church brought forth by the Second Vatican Council at the urging of Pope John XXIII. In the 1960s and 1970s, the Catholic Worker welcomed many who worked within the Church to promote radical change and to protest the Vietnam War, most notably the Catholic priests Philip and Daniel Berrigan. As her fame grew and she became the symbol for generations of young people who came to participate in the Catholic Worker in search of social justice, she was known to admonish admirers by saying that she did not want to be called a saint, because she did not want to be dismissed that easily. Despite her protests, others took up her cause for sainthood upon her death and a case for canonization is proceeding. One miracle attributed to her intercession (according to a *Washington Post* report) has been described by author and psychiatrist Robert Coles, an early devotee whose wife's cancer was cured after an encounter with Day.

Another contribution of Day's that continues to grow in significance is her role as a writer on spiritual as well as secular matters. The author of seven books, including two autobiographies and an account of the Catholic Worker movement, *Loaves and Fishes,* she was a frequent contributor to a variety of Catholic publications, including *Commonweal,* and a faithful correspondent to other writers and public figures of her day.

Although *The Long Loneliness* never received the wide popular acclaim of *The Seven Storey Mountain*, her friend Thomas Merton's account of conversion, it remains an influential story of a 20th-century unbeliever's encounter with the deep spiritual truths of contemporary Catholicism. Day and Merton were frequent correspondents, and she remained friends with him until his untimely death in 1968.

Perhaps Day's most significant journalistic contribution is her column "On Pilgrimage," printed daily in the *Catholic Worker* for more than 30 years. In collected short pieces from this source and others published after her death, she emerges as an eloquent as well as passionate advocate for social justice, as an acute observer of her times, and as a transcendent voice for the spiritual life enacted day to day. Like her favorite authors Dickens and Dostoevsky, her writing made the daily plight of the poor a vivid reality for her readers. Contemporary assessments of her writing by critics take her contribution to American Catholic writing of the 20th century quite seriously, and Paul Elie has suggested that together with authors Flannery O'Connor, Walker Percy, and Thomas Merton she is part of a literary School of the Holy Ghost.

Dorothy Day died on November 29, 1980. Her funeral was attended by poor people served in Catholic Worker houses, as well as by the cardinal archbishop of New York. Buried in a simple wooden coffin in Staten Island, she is survived by her daughter Tamar Hennessey, several grandchildren, and the continuing legacy of the Catholic Worker.

—Mary Erina Driscoll

See also Berrigan Brothers; Catholic Worker Movement; Merton, Thomas; Religious Activism

Further Readings

Day, D. (1963). *Loaves and fishes.* San Francisco: HarperSanFrancisco.

Day, D. (1978). *From Union Square to Rome.* New York: Arno Press. (Original work published 1938)

Day, D. (1997). *The long loneliness.* San Francisco: HarperSanFrancisco. (Original work published 1952)

Elie, P. (2003). *The life you save may be your own: An American pilgrimage.* New York: Farrar, Straus & Giroux.

Ellsberg, R. (Ed.). (1992). *Dorothy Day: Selected writings.* Maryknoll, NY: Orbis Books.

Ellsberg, R. (2000). *All saints: Daily reflections on saints, prophets, and witnesses for our time.* New York: Crossroads Press.

Martin, J. (2006). Living in her world: Dorothy Day. *My life with the saints* (pp. 209–228). Chicago: Loyola Press.

Rosin, H. (2000, March 17). Vatican to weigh sainthood for reformer Dorothy Day. *Washington Post,* p. A03.

DEATH PENALTY

See ANTI–DEATH PENALTY MOVEMENT

DE BEAUVOIR, SIMONE (1908–1986)

Simone de Beauvoir was a French existential philosopher, novelist, feminist, and internationally recognized public intellectual. Her ideas on human freedom, ethics, politics, society, and gender relations influenced European and American women's movements of the 1970s and prefigured contemporary disciplines of cultural studies, discourse studies, and women's studies. De Beauvoir wrote incessantly, narrating her life through personal correspondence with family, friends, and lovers, especially with Jean-Paul Sartre, her lifelong partner. Their relationship, self-defined as essential rather than contingent, helped, but did not determine, de Beauvoir's notoriety. She self-consciously and unapologetically wrote into existence the conditions for fame and posterity, compiling more than 40 years of fiction, philosophy, commentary, travel logs, and memoir. Intellectually and politically active to the very end, de Beauvoir renounced the existence of God, never married, loved and slept with numerous men and women, flaunted her high intelligence, and lived a life that often reflected her existentialism: Human beings are communal, responsible for their own actions, and free to conform or challenge social limits.

Born in Paris, de Beauvoir was raised by her mother, a devout bourgeoisie Catholic, and her father, a politically conservative atheist. Her parents' encouragement in her childhood to read and write waned later on as they judged her life actions. De Beauvoir had two early companions, her younger sister, Helene, nicknamed Poupette, and her friend, Elizabeth Mabille, nicknamed Zaza. Poupette often acted as de Beauvoir's first student, and Zaza's early death in 1929 influenced de Beauvoir's existentialism. Her formal education began at an all-girls private Catholic school. She earned a baccalaureate in mathematics and philosophy, and later studied mathematics at the *Institut Catholique* and literature and languages at the *Institut Sainte-Marie.* Her studies continued at Sorbonne, where she prepared for her *agrégation* in philosophy. During this time de Beauvoir met a group of students from the elite school, *École Normale Supérieure.* Jean-Paul Sartre was one of those students. At age 21, de Beauvoir was the youngest student ever to pass her *agrégation.* Her exam scores ranked second only to Sartre, and it was his second attempt. She went on to teach at different secondary schools until a scandal broke out in 1943—she had taken up romantic relations with one of her female students. After an investigation, the school dismissed her and, by choice, she never taught again. De Beauvoir's first novel, *She Came to Stay,* was published also in 1943, beginning her lifelong authorial career. She went on to write numerous novels, often using autobiographical material, especially romantic liaisons, as a source for fiction.

During the early 1940s Nazi occupation of France, de Beauvoir took up politics. She, Sartre, and others founded the left-wing politically independent journal, *Les Temps Modernes* in 1945. Her novel, *The Blood of Others,* published the same year, investigates personal and social responsibilities, and *All Men Are Mortal* (1946) explores the search for immortality as a denial of the present. Her most famous novel, *The Mandarins* (1954), explores the political responsibilities of the intellectual and won the prestigious French literary award, the *Prix Goncourt.* In 1947, de Beauvoir was invited onto the American college lecture circuit. *America Day by Day* from 1948 chronicles her reflections on America. She would write another travel book, *The Long March* in 1957, about communist China. De Beauvoir's appreciation for America did not blind her to American imperialism, and while she often and perhaps naively defended Russian-style communism, she never joined a communist affiliation. De Beauvoir denounced the U.S. bombing of North Vietnam, supported the May 1968 student rebellions, presided over the League of Woman's Rights, and symbolized Second Wave Feminism.

The Second Sex (1949), her most famous work, explores Western society's construction of womanhood. The text calls into question the long-standing assumption that the male counterpart—man—is the measure of all things. This social construction, promulgated by science, literature, psychoanalysis, philosophy, and others, becomes an unquestioned myth, relegating women to second-class humans. De Beauvoir argues that institutions, ideas, and everyday people, especially men, have created asymmetrical gender relations. However, women too have created, and to a degree desire, this situation. Rather than blaming the victim, de Beauvoir points to the inauthentic desire to be taken over by another. While de Beauvoir calls for serious institutional change, she also calls for women to assume an authentic attitude by embracing their freedom to choose and act on their own accord. These ideas, which many people considered heresy, encountered both controversy and acclaim.

De Beauvoir's lifelong intellectual reflections concerned human freedom and our ethical responsibilities to ourselves, each other, and oppressed people. *Pyrrhus et Cineas* (1944) and *Ethics of Ambiguity* (1947) argue that human beings inherently influence and are influenced by others, forever implicating us in the great sociohuman drama. Ignoring and/or denying this influential process prevents our actions from circulating beyond themselves. Such inauthenticity is overcome by consciously choosing life-projects that seek to expand our personal experience and have an impact on the wider world. In her later years, de Beauvoir investigated her obsession with aging. *The Coming of Age* in 1970 critiques social perceptions of the elderly and argues that old age must continue to be a time of productive and committed work. This book followed *The Woman Destroyed* (1968), three novellas that explore the older, no longer sexually desirable woman. Her writings reflected not only her wants and curiosities but also her fears.

Much of what we know about de Beauvoir comes from her own admissions. *Memories of a Dutiful Daughter* (1958), *The Prime of Life* (1960), *Force of Circumstance* (1963), and *All Said and Done* (1972) comprise a four-volume autobiography. *Adieux: A Farewell to Sartre* (1981) chronicles the final years of her relationship with Sartre. And her personal correspondence, published posthumously, enumerates her life as an independent, free woman. Simone de Beauvoir died on April 14, 1986, of pulmonary edema.

—*Jason Del Gandio*

See also Camus, Albert; Nietzsche, Friedrich; Sartre, Jean-Paul

Further Readings

Bair, D. (1990). *Simone de Beauvoir: A biography.* New York: Summit Books.

Card, C. (Ed.). (2003). *The Cambridge companion to Simone de Beauvoir.* Cambridge, UK: Cambridge University Press.

Fallaize, E. (Ed.). (1998). *Simone de Beauvoir: A critical reader.* London: Routledge.

Simons, M. (Ed.). (1995). *Feminist interpretations of Simone de Beauvoir.* University Park: Pennsylvania State University Press.

Debs, Eugene V. (1855–1926)

The premier representative of native-born American socialism in the late 19th and the early 20th centuries was Eugene V. Debs. Debs was originally a labor union leader who made his reputation as an organizer of unskilled railway workers in the 1890s and as a champion of industrial unionism and workers' control.

Eugene Debs (1855–1926) is considered to be the public face of the political socialist movement in America in its early decades.

Source: Courtesy of the Library of Congress.

As the head and three times presidential candidate of the Socialist Party of America, and an exceptionally effective and inspiring public speaker, he became the public face of the political socialist movement in America in its early decades of heady success and advance. Through his example, a uniquely American amalgam of Marxian, populist, and ethically based social activism came to characterize a significant section of the U.S. left.

Born as the son of a prosperous grocery shop owner in Terre Haute, Indiana, Debs worked as a railroad fireman before his father arranged a clerkship for him at a local department store. In the years immediately following, Debs was involved in local politics and, through his secretary-treasurership of the Brotherhood of Locomotive Firemen, in labor union activities. He fully embraced the conservative politics of the Firemen's Brotherhood, claiming that all Americans were equal worker-producers capable of rising to affluence through thrift and hard work. A Democrat by party affiliation, Debs tried to practice what he preached through the various local and state offices that he held, including his brief stint as an Indiana state assemblyman in 1884.

His creation of the American Railway Union (ARU) in 1893 started Debs's gradual transformation into a socialist. The ARU was an industrial union; that is, it accepted as members all, whether skilled or unskilled, who worked on the railroads, and it sought not just higher wages and better working conditions, but also a number of broader social and political goals. These included an end to the court injunctions with which employers tried to prevent strikes, unionization, and collective bargaining, and the building of a nationwide organized labor movement so unified in its class solidarity that it could not be divided by employers' attempts at buying off sections of it. In both regards, Debs's union differed dramatically from the American Federation of Labor (AFL) affiliated craft unions that catered only to the "labor aristocracy" of the skilled.

Debs's message proved appealing, and within a year of its founding, the ALU had some 150,000 members. In a series of aggressive sympathy strikes in the 1890s, Debs proceeded to put the union's mass power to the test, and he proved both an effective mobilizer of his constituency and an astute strategist in industrial conflict. Victories in the Pacific Union and Great Northern strikes were, however, followed by defeat in the legendary Pullman Strike (each in 1894), in which Debs fought to improve the conditions of the manufacturers of Pullman train cars. After some of the strikers tampered with federal mail trains, the railroad employers' organization procured a federal injunction and had federal troops suppress the strike and the ALU. For his role, Debs was imprisoned for 6 months.

While in jail, Debs began to convert to socialism. The extent, exact timing, and agency of his conversion remain open to question, but the end result was Debs's final abandonment of old-style producerism and his embrace of selected aspects of the Marxian social analysis. By no means did Debs become a fully fledged Marxist, for he never entirely accepted Marxian theories about labor value, immiseration, and coming collapse of capitalism, nor the then-popular supposition that corporate concentration was a key agency of socialization. Rather, Debsian socialism revolved around an iconoclastic combination of class-based and semi-evangelical exhortations to social transformation by a unified working class. To him, the corporate capitalist system failed on ethical grounds, and the supposedly cooperationist instincts of the (broadly defined) working class were the only possible alternative, one that should gradually supplant capitalist values, institutions, and modes of operation. The way forward that Debs sketched consisted, on the one hand, of continual self-education of the working class into ever-deeper realization of its ethical superiority and, on the other hand, of workers' control in workplaces that acted as laboratories of the coming socialist order.

For some time, Debs continued to witness for this vision as a supporter of the Populist Party, but in 1897 he joined a number of Western labor activists in founding the Social Democracy of America. A year later, Debs switched to the more doctrinaire Marxist group, the Social Democratic Party, which called for an eventual socialist revolution and issued a number of so-called immediate demands, including demands for workers' unemployment and accident insurance; reduction of hours of work; public works projects; the initiative, referendum, and recall; and the abolition of war. These demands were largely carried over into the Socialist Party of America, which emerged in 1900 after Debs's group merged with another, more Marxian group from the East.

In the Socialist Party, Debs represented the left wing. He continued to champion the industrial unionism model and became an early enthusiast for the Industrial Workers of the World (IWW), a syndicalist group originally composed of Western miners that tried to take industries under workers' control. When this group embraced sabotage and revolutionary violence, Debs disassociated himself from it, but he continued to fight against the craft unionist AFL and against the moderate reformist wing of his party. Throughout the 1910s and the early 1920s, he subjected to severe criticism all those who de-emphasized class war and he hoped to make the Socialist Party into a regular parliamentary group seeking support from the progressively minded in all classes. The passion of his argument alienated reformist Socialists like John Spargo, Victor Berger, and Charles Edward Russell, but endeared Debs to all those whose investment was in the confrontational, ethically charged style of class politics.

Socialist Party presidential candidate for the first time in 1900, Debs did not become a major national figure until 1912. In the elections of that year, he received an unprecedented 900,000 votes. This did not translate into further party growth, however, for in the years following the election, President Woodrow Wilson co-opted many of the Socialists' reform proposals and drained the party both of popular support and many of its leading intellectuals. The anti-war position that Debs championed and his party embraced during World War I made things even worse, although for a brief while in 1917 and 1918 anti-war radicals inflated the party's share of the votes. When he was imprisoned for treasonous speech, Debs himself became a martyred symbol of all those whose anti-war and socialist politics were suppressed under wartime subversion and sedition laws. He was in federal prison from April 1919 to December 1921, and from there he fought his last election campaign.

Pardoned by President Warren G. Harding, Debs returned to public life, but he never fully regained the place in the public's esteem that he had held before the war. For those to whom he was the living, almost mythical embodiment of the American social conscience, his wartime ordeals only added to his luster, but others were all too conscious of how his siding with anti-war radicals and syndicalist revolutionaries had hurt the Socialist Party image and cause. The critics had one further cause to count against him when in the early 1920s Debs became an apologist for the Russian communist dictatorship. Posthumously, however, these grievances tended to be forgotten as Debs's memory was eagerly appropriated by all sections of the American socialist movement. The remembered Debs became the symbol that held together most left-of-center groups and his ethical, populist call for comprehensive change the chief legacy of Debsian socialism.

—Markku Ruotsila

See also Anarcho-Syndicalism; Democratic Socialism; Gompers, Samuel; Industrial Workers of the World (IWW); Marxist Theory; Social Democracy; Social Gospel Movement; Socialism

Further Readings

Brommel. B. J. (1978). *Eugene V. Debs: Spokesman for labor and socialism.* Chicago: Charles H. Kerr.

Fitrakis, R. J. (1993). *The idea of democratic socialism in America and the decline of the socialist party.* New York: Garland.

Ginger, R. (1949). *The bending cross: A biography of Eugene Victor Debs.* New Brunswick, NJ: Rutgers University Press.

Karsner, D. F. (1919). *Debs: His authorized life and letters.* New York: Boni & Liveright.

Salvatori, N. (1982). *Eugene V. Debs: Citizen and socialist.* Urbana: University of Illinois Press.

Tussey, J. Y. (Ed.). (1970). *Eugene Debs speaks.* New York: Pathfinder Press.

DEBT RELIEF MOVEMENT

During the last decade of the 20th century, a network of organizations from several countries formed to address the issue of Third World debt. The escalating level of debt owed by the governments of developing nations was so crippling that basic services in many of those countries began to collapse. Countries owed money to the governments of developed countries, as well as to international economic organizations such as the World Bank and the International Monetary Fund (IMF). The G7, the seven most powerful and wealthy nations, financially backed these organizations.

The debt forgiveness movement demanded an immediate and complete abolishment of all debt owed by the poorest countries. The movement expanded globally in 1996, with the formation of Jubilee 2000. Originally the idea of retired political scientist Martin Dent, Jubilee 2000 was based in the biblical concept of *jubilee,* or the forgiveness of debts and liberation of slaves every 50 years. The Jubilee campaign grew in both the North (developed world) and the South (Third World). Much of the international leadership, however, was based in Great Britain. The Debt Crisis Network (DCN) formed in the United Kingdom as a coalition of debt campaigning agencies. The campaign set the millennium as the deadline. In April 1996, Ann Pettifor, from DCN, became the organization's lead coordinator, and in 1997, Jubilee 2000 and DCN merged to become the Jubilee 2000 Coalition.

It was a high-profile campaign, holding huge public protests and attracting a large celebrity support base. The movement drew a lot of celebrity support. Desmond Tutu became Jubilee 2000 president of the campaign. Pope John Paul supported the movement, as did American evangelical Pat Robertson. Irish rock star Bono became an international spokesperson. The retired boxer Muhammad Ali also became a public supporter of debt forgiveness.

Jubilee 2000 truly represented a grassroots movement. It was both global and citizen-initiated. The organization framed the debt situation in easy-to-understand terms. A central tool of the campaign was a global petition. The Jubilee 2000 coalition's petition went to 166 nations and held a total of 24.2 million signatures. Under Jubilee 2000's criteria, 52 nations qualified for debt forgiveness. This equaled an estimated $350 billion in debt.

Jubilee 2000 ended on December 31, 2000. It succeeded in establishing a popular international social movement and was partially successful in completing its vision. Following the Cologne Summit in 1999, the G8 committed US$100 billion toward relief of multilateral debt and another US$10 billion for bilateral debt. Despite these commitments, by the end of 2000, only two countries had received debt relief. The debt campaigns continue in many countries, but without the international leadership and focus provided by Jubilee 2000 during the late 1990s.

—*Kristen E. Gwinn*

See also Ali, Muhammad; Bono; Tutu, Desmond

Further Readings

Addison, T., Hansen, H., & Tarp, F. (Eds.). (2004). *Debt relief for poor countries.* New York: Palgrave Macmillan.
Buxton, B. (2004). Debt cancellation and civil society: A case study of Jubilee 2000. In P. Gready (Ed.), *Fighting for human rights* (pp. 54–77). London: Routledge.

DE CERTEAU, MICHEL (1925–1986)

A historian of religion, Michel de Certeau became one of the most inventive, interdisciplinary, and collaborative contributors to what we now call cultural studies. De Certeau was born in Chambéry, southeastern France. He was a youth when France capitulated to Germany in 1940. Vichy collaboration disillusioned and enraged him; the extent of the Church's compliance was particularly disillusioning. De Certeau's genius owed much to his ability to feel these passions without capitulating to cynicism.

In the wake of the war, in 1950, he joined the Society of Jesus, and he was ordained in 1956. His scholarly work was focused on the origins of the Jesuits, and on mysticism in early modern Europe, but domestic and world events stimulated a critical and dramatic enlargement of his scholarly concerns.

When in May 1968 French students and laborers took to the streets, de Certeau was editor and contributor to several Catholic journals and magazines. The "Events of May," he said, exposed a breach between what *needed* to be said (by workers, by youth) and what *could* be said (as prescribed or authorized by the reigning conventions). Because what needed to be said could not be said, the protesters were capturing speech, by practicing the social conventions, but in ways that disrupted their authority.

The May protests faltered. However, the fruitfulness of de Certeau's approach would be elaborated in reference to a vast range of themes, including the "discovery" of the Americas, urban experience, language and politics, psychoanalysis and history, and religious belief.

In all this work, de Certeau displayed a keen interest in the microdynamics of social change. His best-known work in English translation, *The Practice of Everyday Life,* discusses the ways of making do that ordinary people fashion out of the dictates of their social position. Always, he attended keenly to these ruses—witting and unwitting—by which those who are situated as objects of knowledge and of power manage to use, and slip by, the structures intended to confine them.

Perhaps most important is the general thrust in de Certeau's body of work to interrogate the advance toward knowledge (the story of history, in an unusually general sense of the word). De Certeau conceived of the writing of history as a recovery of other voices.

Of necessity, history appropriates the voices on which it relies in ways that reflect historians' techniques and institutional expectations.

De Certeau demonstrated how these techniques and expectations were often repressed from the record, thereby constituting—along with the voices appropriated—a veritable hubbub of activity quite unlike the concentrated self-possession of so many historical narratives. In his own histories, he always strived to enable his voice to be altered by its relations to these various others. In this way, de Certeau provided a model of openness to otherness that could not be fixed by his own or any system's tendency to present others as objects of knowledge and as tokens of power.

—Andrew B. Irvine

See also Postmodernism

Further Readings

Ahearne, J. (1995). *Michel de Certeau: Interpretation and its other.* Palo Alto, CA: Stanford University Press.

de Certeau, M. (1984). *The practice of everyday life* (S. Rendell, Trans.). Berkeley: University of California Press.

de Certeau, M. (1988). *The writing of history* (T. Conley, Trans.). New York: Columbia University Press.

de Certeau, M. (2000). *The Certeau reader* (G. Ward, Ed.). Oxford, UK: Blackwell.

DECONSTRUCTION

Deconstruction, the demonstration of multiple, competing, and often contradictory meanings within seemingly stable univocal positions, came to prominence in the mid-1960s and continues to exert a powerful influence across a broad range of disciplines. Although Jacques Derrida coined the term *deconstruction* in his early works, a history of deconstructive analysis can be traced to Friedrich W. Nietzsche and beyond, connecting with Martin Heidegger and Edmund Husserl along the way. Deconstructive analysis, as practiced by Derrida, demonstrates that the substance and coherence of a text—broadly conceived from the traditional notion of a written text to social practice—is as much related to

assumptions and derivative ideas that are excluded, as it is to those that that are included. In other words, meaning is inextricably linked to the constitutive other—silences and exclusions—of the text. Deconstruction aims to render the constitutive other explicit. The exposure of silences and exclusions, together with the contradictions that may ensue, draws sites for activism into clear relief.

The term *deconstruction*, however, has been pejoratively equated with *destruction*. Environmentalists Gary Lease and Michael Soulé exemplify this view, claiming that deconstruction is as destructive to the environment as chainsaws and bulldozers. More generally, however, the charge of destruction is abstract; critics claim that deconstruction shatters unities and leaves it to others to pick up the pieces. As a result, many critics of deconstruction and proponents who are influenced by them emphasize the importance of *reconstruction*. Derrida has repudiated the claim of destruction in numerous interviews and rejected the binary opposition of deconstruction to reconstruction. His rejection of the binary opposition is twofold: first, the opposition invites the misreading that deconstruction is destructive; and second, while supporting the importance of generative analysis, he argues that reconstruction is inadequate. Derrida argues that reconstruction maintains the status quo by simply making something again in the same image. In terms of activism and social justice, the reconstruction of human rights, for example, would replicate existing states of affairs. Derrida insists, however, that deconstruction aims to go further, to displace, change, and improve the current state of affairs. Deconstruction, then, is a deeply political enterprise that has an overt ethical agenda.

Derrida's deconstructive works can be read as posing questions to, eliciting complex responses from, and going beyond the initial formulations of key Western thinkers, including Marx, Saussure, Freud, and Heidegger, and Derrida openly acknowledges that deconstruction is indebted to each. The term *deconstruction* owes its name to Derrida's critical appropriation and translation of Heidegger's terms *Destruktion* and *Abbau,* and questioning, responding to, and going beyond Marx, Saussure, and Freud illuminated leading and interrelated motifs in deconstructive analysis.

The first of these motifs, the critique of the "metaphysics of presence," problematizes the notion of a direct relationship, or immediacy, between speech and writing, thought and consciousness, or the word and the world. The critique of the metaphysics of presence disrupts the purported stability and unity of a text. This argument is, perhaps, best understood through Derrida's deconstruction of Ferdinand de Saussure's structural linguistics. Saussure identified language as a system of signs, which consist of two indissociable elements: spoken words or their written equivalents (signifiers) and concepts (signifieds). For Saussure, signs are arbitrary; they derive their meaning from their opposition to each other rather than through a relationship with a referent, thus, severing the link between the word and the world. Language, then, is a floating system of differences. Consequently, signifieds do not possess meaning in and of themselves. Meaning is continuously differed and deferred, which challenges notions of unity, stability, and truth. Derrida, however, demonstrates that Saussure's argument unavoidably admits the possibility of signifieds without signifiers. In other words, Saussure's argument admits that meaning is not necessarily transacted relationally through a system of differences, but that pockets of pure meaning can exist. This surreptitiously reinstates the metaphysics of presence. Thus, Derrida replaces Saussure's signifier-signified complex with the signifier-signifier, which ensures the endless play of difference that cannot be resolved into a positivity. Derrida introduces the term *différance* to refer to this irrepressible difference.

The second and interrelated motif that emerges in Derrida's engagements with Marx, Saussure, Freud, and Lévi-Strauss is *decentering* the text. This repudiates the belief that words, writings, ideas, and systems of thought are validated by a "center" whose truth they convey. The concept of center is clearly developed at the beginning of Derrida's deconstruction of Claude Lévi-Strauss. Then, performing an immanent critique, adhering strictly to the "rules" that configure the thesis, Derrida demonstrates that Lévi-Strauss implicitly depends on that which he explicitly rejects, thus dismantling the center of the thesis. Demonstrating such contradictoriness, in policy or law for example, can be of great strategic value to social activists. However, decentering necessarily installs an alternative center. Thus, decentering results in cascading centers; decentering cannot rest and the reassuring certitude that centers engender cannot be reclaimed. This will not necessarily motivate social activists to commit to endless deconstruction as Derrida advocates, but it may serve as a salutary and cautionary reminder their successes repose, in turn, upon systems of privileges, silences and exclusions rather than a natural order.

Derrida's famous remark that there is nothing beyond the text has been widely misread as a denial of embodied existence in the material world. If this were the case, Derrida's ideas and social activism would be incommensurable. However, Derrida insists that the statement that there is nothing beyond the text does not deny the existence of the world. This may appear to be an irreconcilable contradiction, but oppositions between the world (sensibility) and text (intelligibility), and between interiority and exteriority, are required for the contradiction to exist. In relation to the former, Derrida's broad conception of text problematizes the opposition of the world and text, and in relation to the latter, his work on the limit problematizes any simple opposition of inside and outside. The apparent contradiction resolves in the view that there is no recourse to an acontextual world.

The statement that there is nothing beyond the text is germane to social activists beyond the acknowledgment that there is no recourse to an acontextual world. Cherished ideals such as social justice, human rights, and freedom do not lie beyond reach of deconstruction. Derrida would exhort activists to interrogate such ideals in order to "expose" their constitutive blindnesses. As a matter of logical consistency, the term *deconstruction* also needs to be deconstructed. Deconstruction cannot, and does not try to, escape this double movement. Every deconstructive gesture is indebted to its constitutive other, which makes the term notoriously elusive.

—Joy Hardy

See also Derrida, Jacques; Nietzsche, Friedrich; Other, the; Postmodernism; Semiotic Warfare

Further Readings

Caputo, J. D. (2000). For love of the things: Derrida's hyper-realism. *Journal for Cultural and Religious Theory, 1*(3), 4–18.

Derrida. J. (1976). *Of grammatology* (G. Hopkins, Trans.). Baltimore: Johns Hopkins University Press. (Original work published 1967)

Derrida, J. (1978). *Writing and difference* (A. Bass, Trans.). Chicago: Chicago University Press. (Original work published 1967)

Derrida, J. (1981). *Positions* (A. Bass, Trans.). London: Althone Press. (Original work published 1972)

Derrida, J. (1982). *Margins of philosophy* (A. Bass, Trans.). Brighton, UK: Harvester Press. (Original work published 1972)

Soulé, M. E., & Lease, G. (1995). *Reinventing nature? Responses to postmodern deconstruction.* Washington, DC: Island Press.

DEEP ECOLOGY MOVEMENT

The first usage of the term *deep ecology* was in a 1973 article written by the Norwegian eco-philosopher Arne Naess, who was greatly inspired by Rachel Carson's seminal work *Silent Spring.* Deep ecology describes a divergent, long-term approach to the mounting ecological crisis that faces industrialized nations, which is distinct from shallow (or reform) ecology. While shallow ecology is often focused on finding short-term solutions for mitigating pollution or fighting resource depletion, deep ecology seeks to combat the approaching ecocatastrophe by establishing an entirely new ontological understanding of the human relationship to nature and the world.

One of the forces working against deep ecology is the prevailing rational/economic ideological paradigm, which commodifies the natural world (hence terms like natural *resources*) and asserts a detached, teleological model of our relationship to nature. Philosophy is particularly well suited to tackle this misconception, because the human-centered understanding of the natural world is deeply rooted in Cartesian Dualism. The bifurcation of our being into the two independent modalities of mind and body, an understanding that we owe to Descartes's *cogito ergo sum* ("I think therefore I am"), considers human consciousness as a transcendent entity that is beyond, and separate from, the natural world.

Thus, deep ecology becomes a philosophical project of cultivating ecological consciousness, by positing humans as inseparable from their environs, and championing intuition instead of logical arguments or deductive reasoning. It promotes a perspective of *biospherical egalitarianism,* which involves a respect and veneration for all forms of life, and *voluntary simplicity,* which entails a personal self-realization about our patterns of consumption and environmental impact.

The rapid adoption of new (typically consumer) technologies is another element of contemporary culture that worries proponents of the deep ecology movement. Borrowing Heideggerian notions of caution in the face of technological innovation, they question the uncritical passivity with which it is often met, and criticize the notion that the adoption of a new technology is invariably progressive and/or inevitable.

Despite the theory-laden underpinnings, deep ecology is not simply a movement of unembodied or inert ideas. Direct action is central to the deep ecology platform, because, as Naess argues, wisdom without underlying action is useless. For example, in 1970 Naess tied himself to the Mardalsfossen waterfall in Norway to protest the building of a dam. He refused to leave until the plans were dropped and was eventually successful in stopping it from being built.

Arne Naess and George Sessions highlight eight points of the deep ecology platform.

1. The flourishing of human and nonhuman life on earth has intrinsic value, independent of the usefulness they may have for narrow human purposes.

2. Richness and diversity of life forms are values in themselves and contribute to the flourishing of human and nonhuman life on earth.

3. Humans have no right to reduce this richness and diversity except to satisfy vital needs.

4. Present human interference with the nonhuman world is excessive, and the situation is rapidly worsening.

5. The flourishing of human life and cultures is compatible with a substantial decrease of the human population. The flourishing of nonhuman life requires it.

6. Significant change of life conditions for the better requires change in policies. These affect basic economic, technological, and ideological structures.

7. The ideological change is mainly that of appreciating the life quality, rather than adhering to a high quality of living. There will be a profound awareness of the difference between big and great.

8. Those who subscribe to the foregoing points have an obligation directly or indirectly to participate in the attempt to implement the necessary changes.

In 1990, inspired by George Session's book *Deep Ecology: Living As If Nature Mattered,* Doug Tompkins and Jerry Mander established the Foundation for Deep Ecology (FDE) in San Francisco, California. They promote the deep ecology platform through book publishing, radio programs, holding events and conferences, and grant-making. Their mission is to support education, advocacy, and environmental initiatives that advance the causes of sustainability, conservation, and the collective reevaluation of our relationship to nature.

—Thomas Kristian Peri

See also Alternative Movements; Carson, Rachel; Climate Change and Global Justice; Direct Action; Environmental Movement; Green Party; Rainforest Action Network; Sierra Club; Voluntary Simplicity

Further Readings

Abram, D. (1996). *The spell of the sensuous.* New York: Vintage Books.

Naess, A. (1989). *Ecology, community, and lifestyle.* Cambridge, UK: Cambridge University Press.

Sessions, G. (1985). *Deep ecology: Living as if nature mattered.* Layton, UT: Peregrine-Smith Books.

DEES, MORRIS (1936–)

Born December 16, 1936, Morris Dees is one of the most significant legal figures to advance civil rights and social justice for historically underserved groups. Despite his upbringing in segregationist Alabama, his parents imparted strong Christian values to Dees that compelled him to redress criminal and civic wrongs through the justice system. Warm interactions with black families, coupled with troubling class-based experiences among whites during his youth, further nurtured his dedication to eradicating the detrimental impact that race and social class exert on individuals' lives. Although Dees was a successful entrepreneur, the reading of Clarence Darrow's *The Story of My Life* provoked him to sell his mail order business and open a law practice devoted to civil rights legislation. The resultant partnership law firm, Levin & Dees, evolved into the Southern Poverty Law Center (SPLC) in 1971.

Dees' legal career is marked by a number of landmark cases and decisions. Examples include integrating the Montgomery, Alabama, Young Men's Christian Association (YMCA) and the Alabama State Troopers, as well as holding white supremacist organizations financially and criminally responsible for unlawful actions against communities of color and immigrants. Substantial monetary awards against groups such as the United Klans of America and Aryan Nations, in fact, have forced some organizations to disband. Despite the critical advances against hate groups, Dees' decision to emphasize Klan activity as a SPLC priority prompted some of its personnel to leave the organization over ideological differences regarding the new legal focus. Additionally, critics outside of the SPLC have accused Dees of drawing few distinctions between white supremacists and other organizations that support limiting immigration, controlling population growth, or upholding the right to bear arms. Detractors primarily question Dees' use of legal approaches that suggest guilt by association rather than evidence of direct involvement.

Beyond the legal arena, Dees gained national prominence as a successful fund-raiser for presidential hopeful George McGovern, former President Jimmy Carter, and Senator Ted Kennedy's 1980 bid for the Democratic presidential nomination. Professionally, Dees received his undergraduate and law degrees from the University of Alabama. He has authored two books, *Hate on Trial: The Case Against America's Most Dangerous Neo-Nazi* and *Gathering Storm: America's Militia Threat.* His autobiography *A Season for Justice,* later rereleased as *A Lawyer's Journey: The Morris Dees Story,* was published in 1991. He is the recipient of numerous awards, including the Martin Luther King, Jr., Memorial and Friend of Education Awards from the National Education Association, Young Lawyers Distinguished Service Award from the American Bar Association, and the Roger Baldwin Award from the American Civil Liberties Union, among other distinctions.

—Carla R. Monroe

See also Southern Poverty Law Center

Further Readings

Chalmers, D. M. (2003). *Backfire: How the Ku Klux Klan helped the civil rights movement.* Lanham, MD: Rowman & Littlefield.
Klebanow, D. (2003). *People's lawyers: Crusaders for justice in American history.* Armonk, NY: M. E. Sharpe.

DE LA CRUZ, SOR JUANA INÉS (1648–1695)

Juana Inés Ramirez de Asbaje was born in San Miguel Nepantla, Mexico, in 1648 (although some biographers say 1651). She was a writer, a scholar, and a servant of God in the Baroque period. Sor Juana was also an advocate for women's rights in education because she believed future generations of women needed to have educators of their own gender. According to Sor Juana, a society can benefit when women are educated, and withholding women from pursuing knowledge went against the tradition of the Catholic Church. Her outspoken stance on controversial subjects, of course, did not please the Church. In 1690, the bishop of Puebla, Manuel Fernandez de Santa Cruz, published a letter Sor Juana had written to him. He introduced it with a letter of his own as "Sor Filotea." In *Carta Atenagorica,* he advises Sor Juana to leave her secular studies and writing and focus on theology. Sor Juana responded with a letter of her own, *Respuesta a Sor Filotea* (1691), in which she defends women's right to higher education. Eventually, she was forced to give up her books and her studies and she spent the last months of her life helping her sisters, until an epidemic took her life in 1695.

In her autobiography, Sor Juana claims she learned how to read and write Latin before the age of 10. From an early age, she had a passion for knowledge and she was known for her beauty, intelligence, and charisma. In 1664, Sor Juana became a lady-in-waiting to the viceroy's wife, marquise of Mancera, in Mexico City. However, court life was not fulfilling. Sor Juana decided that the only way to pursue her passion for knowledge was to become a nun. Because she came from a poor family and was an illegitimate child, she knew her options were limited. As a single woman living in 17th-century Latin America, she did not have the power to continue her studies.

In 1667, Sor Juana entered the convent of the Discalced Carmelites of St. Joseph, but she only stayed 3 months because the monastic life was too harsh on her health. She did not give up. In 1669, she entered the Hieronimite order at the convent of St. Jerome, and she never left its confines until her death. Her most creative period began in 1680. It was during this period that the new vicereine's wife, marquise de la Laguna, countess of Paredes, helped publish three volumes of Sor Juana's work. Sor Juana spent her time at the convent writing poetry, comedies, religious dramas, and liturgies; her apartment-like cell became a salon, a gathering place to exchange ideas. Some scholars and biographers argue that Sor Juana set an example for modern feminism.

—Maria Delis

See also Feminism; Religious Activism

Further Readings

Kirk, P. (1998). *Sor Juana Inez de la Cruz: Religion, art, and feminism.* New York: Continuum.
Paz, O. (1988). *Sor Juana or, The traps of faith* (M. S. Peden, Trans.). Cambridge, MA: Belknap.

DELLINGER, DAVID (1915–2004)

Active nonviolence and social protest were central to the life of David Dellinger, a student in the 1930s and son of an economically and socially prominent family who became involved in politics as he was studying economics at Yale University. He was arrested at a protest where he was supporting the trade union movement. Dellinger left Yale for a time during the Great Depression. He decided to ride the freight trains, sleep at missions, and eat at the soup lines. He then spent a year working in a factory in Maine, in 1936, after finally graduating from Yale.

Dellinger received a fellowship to Oxford University, and became a supporter of the Popular Front government in Spain. When he returned to the United States, he enrolled at the Union Theological Seminary in New York. In 1940, Dellinger refused to register for the military draft. He was arrested and sentenced to a year in prison, and, while in prison, he organized protests against the segregated seating arrangements. His activism led to solitary confinement in the prison. After being released, he was arrested again for refusing to join the armed forces when the United States entered World War II. He was sentenced to another 2 years in prison.

After the war, Dellinger helped create the *Direct Action* magazine in 1945, and criticized the use of atomic bombs on Hiroshima and Nagasaki. A short time later he became the editor of *Liberation,* a position he maintained for more than 20 years.

Dellinger also was a prominent activist in opposition to the Vietnam War. He helped organize the 1967 protest march on the Pentagon. In 1968, he was one of the activists charged with conspiring to incite riots at the Democratic Party Convention. His codefendants included Tom Hayden (Students for a Democratic Society), Bobby Seale (Black Panther Party), Rennie Davis (National Mobilization Committee), and Abbie Hoffman and Jerry Rubin (Youth International Party). These activists, part of the famous Chicago Seven, were eventually acquitted. Dellinger was painted as a stern, evangelical Christian Socialist, and as the chief architect of the conspiracy because of his position as the chairperson of the National Mobilization Committee to End the War in Vietnam.

Dellinger wrote a number of books, including *Beyond Survival: New Directions for the Disarmament Movement* (1985), *Vietnam Revisited: From Covert Action to Invasion to Reconstruction* (1986), and *From*

Yale to Jail: The Life Story of a Moral Dissenter (1993).

He continued to be active in politics, and even into his eighties he continued to take part in protest marches. He was a primary figure in the demonstration against the North American Free Trade Agreement in Quebec City in 2001. He also held regular fasts in an effort to change the name of Columbus Day to Native American Day.

The life of Dellinger suggests to activists that we have more power than we know. Traveling across every state, speaking at gatherings large and small, he was fond of pointing out that efforts for peace and justice were larger and more substantive than at the height of the 1970s. He noted that in the past 30 years that efforts were simply more locally based, and covered a wider range of issues.

—*Pat Lauderdale*

See also Chicago Seven; Direct Action; Draft Resistance; Hayden, Tom; Hoffman, Abbie; Nonviolence and Activism; Seale, Bobby

Further Readings

Gara, L., & Gara, L. M. (Eds.). (1999). *A few small candles: War resisters of World War II tell their stories.* Kent, OH: Kent State Press.

Hunt, A. (2006). *David Dellinger: The life and times of a nonviolent revolutionary.* New York: New York University Press.

DELLUMS, RONALD (1935–)

Ronald Vernie Dellums was born into a working-class ethnic community in west Oakland, California, and it has been the base from which he has carved out his reputation as an outspoken critic of oppression both at home and abroad through almost 40 years of public life. On leaving high school in 1954, Dellums joined the Marines. Turned down for officer training on account of his race, he left after the 2 years he needed to qualify for college financial assistance through the GI Bill. He took degrees at Oakland City College and

San Francisco State University, and a master's degree in social work at UC Berkeley in 1962. While employed as a psychiatric social worker, Dellums got his second education, this time in political activism. He served on Berkeley city council from 1967 to 1970, and in 1971, having run on an anti-Vietnam War platform, Ron Dellums became the representative for California's ninth congressional district.

In early 1971 he called for a full-scale inquiry into U.S. war crimes in Vietnam and, when none was forthcoming, chaired ad-hoc hearings on the issue himself. Dellums also established positions for himself on a range of other important issues throughout his congressional career, from apartheid in South Africa to a national health service, and from support for Israeli-PLO negotiations to the issue of defense spending.

Between 1971 and 1988, Dellums pushed a succession of bills aimed at imposing sanctions on the South African government to end apartheid. While his bills met with conservative opposition in the Senate and the White House, Dellums was at the forefront of positioning the United States within the international sanctions movement. His efforts in support of a national health service met with no such success, as deal-making from the left in pursuit of less radical, seemingly more workable proposals gradually emasculated the legislative efforts of Dellums and like-minded colleagues throughout the 1970s.

In 1973, with the assistance of the Congressional Black Caucus—of which he had been a founding member—Dellums became a member of the House Armed Services Committee (HASC), providing a voice of considered opposition to large defense spending increases throughout his tenure. He was the first member of Congress to call for the termination of funding for the MX missile in 1977 and the Pershing II in 1979; he also opposed the construction of the B-1 bomber and President Reagan's SDI or *Star Wars* program. In 1991 Dellums opposed U.S. military action in Iraq, and in 1993, as chairman of HASC, he sought to persuade President Clinton to honor his campaign commitment to lift the ban on gay men and lesbians in the military.

In 1998 Dellums retired from Congress and took on the presidency of Healthcare International Management Company, a for-profit organization that focused on the provision of coordinated health care in southern Africa. He has also acted as a lobbyist for a range of interests on Capitol Hill. While this seemed to mark the end of his political career, it proved to be only a hiatus. By late 2005 his career had come full circle as he returned to Oakland politics with his candidacy for mayor.

—Dean Williams

See also Anti-Apartheid Movement; GI Bill; Lobbying; Palestine Liberation Organization (PLO)

Further Readings

Dellums, R. V., & Halterman, H. L. (2000). *Lying down with lions: A public life from the streets of Oakland to the halls of power.* Boston: Beacon Press.

Dellums R. V., Miller, R. H., & Halterman, H. L. (1983). *Defense sense: The search for a rational military policy.* Cambridge, MA: Ballinger.

DELORIA, VINE, JR. (1933–2005)

Vine Deloria, Jr., an American Indian from the Standing Rock Sioux tribe, was both an advocate for American Indian rights and a scholar of American Indian culture, history, and law. During the mid to late 1960s, he acted as Executive Director of the National Congress of American Indians (NCAI), a pan-tribal organization that worked on behalf of tribes and lobbied the U.S. Congress in order to secure Indian rights. Under his leadership, the NCAI became increasingly financially sound and became one of the most well-respected American Indian advocacy groups. In 1969 he published *Custer Died for Your Sins: An Indian Manifesto*, a set of essays that critiqued Native Americans' treatment by non-Indians and lauded many of the native cultural traditions that European Americans attempted to eliminate from the American landscape. His work was widely read by Indians and non-Indians alike, many of whom saw it as a refreshing attempt to deromanticize commonly held views of Indian people. This book launched his career as one of the most adamant, articulate, and witty social critics of the era. He went on to a career in law, writing dozens of books on the topic of federal Indian law and policy.

He was born in 1933 to Barbara Sloat and Vine Deloria, Sr., and grew up near both the Pine Ridge and Standing Rock Indian Reservations. His father, a Sioux and an Episcopal missionary, was a well-known figure among many of the reservation communities. He encouraged his son to pursue higher education, and the younger Deloria received his undergraduate degree in the sciences from Iowa State University, and a degree in theology from Lutheran School of Theology in Illinois. His law degree, which he earned from the University of Colorado, Boulder, in 1970, provided the basis for much of his legal scholarship and activism.

Witnessing the grave poverty on the reservations and the surrounding communities, the Deloria became a critic of U.S. Indian policy and agencies—particularly the Bureau of Indian Affairs (BIA)—which he saw as being destructive to the people they pretended to help. He became a spokesperson for Indian sovereignty and self-determination. For him, sovereignty meant allowing American Indian people to develop their own governments, institutions, and policies for improving their lives and lessening the federal government's intrusion. He also promoted a return to the treaty-making process, which the federal government abolished in the 1870s. If the federal government went back to making government-to-government agreements with Indian nations, then this would raise Indian nations to the level of sovereign states and grant a new level of respect to Indian tribal governments.

Outside of advocating a revision of U.S.-Indian relations, Deloria was a great critic of Western science, particularly the social science of anthropology, which he derided as an attempt to fragment the world into its constituent pieces in order to understand them. This method of study, he argued, denigrated the interconnectedness of people, animals, and the planet. Instead, he supported a study of the world and human beings that examined the relatedness of all material and spiritual things. In pursuing this relatedness, he

believed that the broader U.S. population could learn a great deal from Native American culture and thought, which had a long history of examining and learning from connections, rather than encouraging disintegration of the bonds between the spiritual and biological entities in the world.

—*Thomas J. Lappas*

See also American Indian Movement; Deconstructionism; Ecopaganism; Judicial Activism; Law and Social Movements

Further Readings

Cowger, T. (1999). *The National Congress of American Indians: The founding years.* Lincoln: University of Nebraska Press.

Deloria, V., Jr. (1969). *Custer died for your sins: An American Indian manifesto.* New York: Macmillan.

Deloria, V., Jr. (1999). *Spirit and reason: The Vine Deloria, Jr., reader.* Golden, CO: Fulcrum.

Johnson, K. (2005, November 14). Vine Deloria, Jr., champion of Indian rights, dies at 72. *New York Times,* p. A25.

DEMOCRACY

The term *democracy* originates from ancient Greek and means rule by the people (*demos*). Traditionally, political theorists begin their considerations about democracy with aristocratic philosophers like Plato and Aristotle and deduce from there that ancient Greek philosophers opposed the concept of democracy. This is true in one way or another as far as these philosophers concerned, but many other philosophers were critical of Athenian democracy from a humanist perspective—just because it rested upon slavery and excluded women and foreigners from decision making. Epicurus' anti-political position, for example, might be read as a search for a much more comprehensive concept of democracy to include all subordinate classes and sections of society in decision making.

The development of the concept of democracy was not solely due to the ancient Greeks. Democracy as an institution to run general affairs of society is an innovation of a much earlier period. What we read in Plato's and Aristotle's writings is in fact why in Athens the implementation of an earlier form of democracy became problematic. It has to do with the division of society into social classes with contradictory material interests, which throws also some light on the modern problems of democracy. A society with social classes like ancient Greek societies could no longer assimilate the earlier form of democracy that allowed all male and female adults to participate in decision making.

In modern political thought, traditionally the theories of democracy are categorized on how they conceptualize the people, citizenship, majority, and minority. This approach touches one of the most crucial problems of the theory of democracy only on the surface because it takes the division of society into the majority and minority for granted or it leads to a distorted presentation of the problems involved if it accounts merely for elections and issues in governments. Political manipulation and distorted presentations may result in misperceptions of the issues in question; this manipulation may result in elections that may reverse what is the majority and the minority in reality. In Aristotle's political thought, the majority referred to the poor—that is, expropriated sections of society—and the minority is described as propertied nobility. John Stuart Mill's consideration about the tyranny of the majority has to do with the question of what might be the result if subordinate classes, the vast majority of population, are franchised. Provided they are conscious of their real interests, they could easily vote aside propertied classes and expropriate the expropriator. This worry motivates Aristotle in antiquity, as well as Mill in modernity, in the construction of what might be the best form of government. It is this worry that also gave rise to the elitist theory of democracy; for example, the work of Joseph Schumpeter. With Mill's proposal to weight votes in favor of richer and the better educated, the bourgeois democratic thought gives up one of the most essential concepts of democracy: the concept of equality, which is a contribution of Protestant Reformation to modern theory of democracy. This may also explain what Norberto Bobbio observed; namely, that liberal democracies tend to restrict the rights of the people if

they express their will to participate in decision making rather than leaving it to the elites in governments.

Unlike the 19th-century bourgeois democratic thought, however, the 18th-century bourgeois democratic thought has a comprehensive view of democracy, both contractual (Hobbes, Locke, Kant, Rousseau) and historical (Machiavelli, Montesquieu, Hume, A. Smith, J. Millar). It takes into account the problems arising from the structural problems of civil society, as well as those of the state. In the 19th century, however, it comes more and more to be confined to the governmental realm. This is valid as well as for Ronald Dworkin's theory of procedural democracy and Jürgen Habermas's theory of deliberative democracy. Permanently changing structural power relations in civil society in favor of monopolies and monopoly bourgeoisie is no longer problematic. Among contemporary political philosophers, David Held and Peter Singer are perhaps the only ones to refer to the growing power of monopolies in civil society and to the dangers arsing from it.

The concepts of both representative and direct democracy are creations of 18th-century bourgeois democratic thought. In the 19th century it assumed representative democracy. Even contemporary bourgeois thought, despite the fact that modern communications and computers removed many obstacles to direct democracy, accepts Schumpeter's hardly justifiable argument that direct democracy is not compatible with responsible government. But at least since Condorcet's establishment of Jury Theorem, it is almost a common sense that a decision of a large number of only moderately competent people may be more reliable than few hundred experts in governments.

Classical Marxist theory of democracy draws primarily on the study of the broad history of humanity, more particularly on the analysis of the structures in civil society, as well as institutional development of the capitalist state and government. But it inherits also all bourgeois and utopian socialist progressive democratic thought and profits from the Paris Commune experiments. The Marxist theory of democracy is not about establishment and strengthening of the state against society as opposed to bourgeois democratic thought. On the contrary, it is above all concerned about finding ways to abolish the state and bring back the management of general social affairs into society. It wants to democratize all aspects of social life. It is, in other words, foremost concerned about establishing a direct democracy. The socialist state, which is thought to be necessary in the transitory society from capitalism to fully developed communism, is thought to be no longer a state in its classical sense; namely, to be an instrument to suppress the majority by a handful minority of property owners. It is rather envisaged to be a state of the majority to suppress the minority of property owners if (and only if) they act against the establishment of socialism and eventually communism. This aim leads Marxist democratic thought to the historical investigation of the origins of the state. Like many 18th-century bourgeois social and political philosophies, it explains the origins of the state by referring to the establishment of private property and contradictions in civil society. But unlike these philosophies, Marxism does not want to justify private property but substitute it for a common ownership; therefore, it focuses on the question of how private property may be turned into common ownership.

In the light of the experience of the Soviet Union, many contemporary Marxists philosophers suggest that some aspects of Marx's democratic thought needs to be reconsidered, because in the Soviet Union the abolition of private property in the means of production did not lead to the weakening of the state. They suggest to develop further Marxist democratic thought based on the socialist experiences in the 20th century and on the democratic thought of Lenin, Gramsci, and Luxemburg.

The most interesting and new aspect of contemporary debates of democracy is about cosmopolitan or world democracy and ecological democracy. David Held's theory of cosmopolitan democracy draws on a revision of the Kantian notion of perpetual peace. But it could perhaps be more appropriately and comprehensively developed on the basis of what Marx worked out about Paris Commune. The theory of ecological democracy is relatively new and still needs to be worked out in many respects in detail.

—*Doğan Göçmen*

See also Civil Society; Communism; Gramsci, Antonio; Lenin, V. I.; Marxist Theory; Mill, John Stuart; Plato

Further Readings

Bobbio, N. (2005). *Liberalism and democracy.* New York: Verso.

Held, D. (1996). *Democracy and the global order: From the modern state to cosmopolitan governance.* Palo Alto, CA: Stanford University Press.

Held, D. (1997). *Models of democracy.* Palo Alto, CA: Stanford University Press.

Honderich, T. (1991). *Conservatism.* London: Penguin.

Lenin, V. I. (1992). *The state and revolution.* London: Penguin.

Wood, E. M. (1995). *Democracy against capitalism: Renewing historical materialism.* Cambridge, UK: Cambridge University Press.

DEMOCRATIC SOCIALISM

The relationship between democracy and socialism is a curious one. Both traditions are rooted philosophically in the concept of equality, but different aspects of equality are emphasized. Democracy appeals to political equality, the right of all individuals to participate in setting the rules to which all will be subject. Socialism emphasizes material equality—not strict equality, but an end to the vast disparities of income and wealth traceable to the inequalities of ownership of means of production.

Of course there can be material equality without democracy, as well as democracy without material equality. Plato advocated a material equality for the "guardians" of his ideal state. (Those entrusted with ruling would live modestly, take their meals in common, and, to forestall the temptation to enrich themselves, keep their storehouses open for inspection and never handle gold or silver.) Many religious orders have practiced a material egalitarianism while emphasizing strict obedience to one's superiors. Conversely, in most contemporary democratic societies, material inequalities are vast and growing. (The upper 1% of U.S. households now own nearly 40% of all the privately held wealth of the nation.)

From the beginning it has been recognized that political equality is likely to produce demands for material equality. If people are truly *equal*, why should a few be so rich and so many so poor? If the majority can make the laws, what is to prevent them from redistributing the wealth? Political theorists from Plato through the Founding Fathers of the United States, from John Stuart Mill to the present, have warned of this tendency.

Plato saw democracy as inevitably degenerating into tyranny, for the *demos* would try to redistribute wealth, the wealthy would rebel, and the people would call on a strongman to aid their cause, but he would not relinquish power once installed. Alexander Hamilton urged that first-class people, the rich and well born, be given a permanent share of the government, so as to check the imprudence of democracy. Mill worried that the majority would compel the wealthy to bear the burden of taxation, so he proposed that the more intelligent and knowledgeable be allowed multiple votes and that mode of employment serve as a marker for intelligence. He took it to be self-evident that the employer of labor is on average more intelligent than a laborer.

More recently, the Trilateral Commission, a gathering of elites from the United States, Western Europe, and Japan (the brainchild of David Rockefeller and forerunner of the World Economic Forum) issued a widely read report warning that the democratic distemper of the 1960s and early 1970s threatened to render capitalist countries ungovernable.

Unlike the pre-eminent political theorists from antiquity, until quite recently, virtually all the early self-described *socialists* (a term that seems to have been first used as a self-ascription by Robert Owen in 1827) were ardent democrats. Marx and Engels in their *Communist Manifesto* proclaimed that the first step in replacing capitalism with a new and better economic system is to raise the proletariat to the position of ruling class. Marx and Engels and virtually all of their socialist contemporaries saw the political empowerment of society's disenfranchised as a necessary step in the transformation of capitalism into a more humane social order.

Few socialists prior to the 1920s would have imagined a "contradiction" between socialism and democracy. Prior to the Russian Revolution, there were no socialist countries anywhere, nor any fully democratic

ones. (In no country did women have the right to vote. Racial minorities were often excluded from the political process. Dominant capitalist countries presided most undemocratically over their colonial empires.) It seemed obvious to socialists everywhere that democracy was a stepping stone to socialism.

The Russian Revolution changed the equation dramatically. Many socialists began to question the link between socialism and democracy. On the one hand, existing democracies showed themselves to be deeply hostile to socialism. On the other hand, existing socialism turned out to be anything but democratic.

The United States, for example, having gone to war to "make the world safe for democracy," reacted swiftly to the events in Russia (well before the Bolshevik Revolution had become Stalinist), imprisoning the nation's leading socialist, Eugene Debs, along with dozens of other socialist leaders. (Debs had garnered 6% of the vote in the 1912 presidential election, and hundreds of socialists were elected to public office.) Socialist legislators were expelled from office, and the socialist press was banned from the mails.

Moreover, there was virtually no resistance on the part of democratic capitalist countries to the spread of fascism throughout Europe. Indeed, the United States, France, and Britain remained resolutely neutral while the forces of General Franco, aided by fascist Italy and Nazi Germany, waged a successful civil war against the democratically elected government of Spain. So long as anti-democratic forces were anti-socialist or anti-communist, they could count on the support of the democratic governments of the West. Meanwhile, the one country in the world calling itself socialist turned out not to be *democratic* in any recognizable sense of the term.

Some socialists tried to reconcile these deeply disappointing developments by distinguishing between "bourgeois democracy" and "proletarian democracy," the former viewed as fraudulent. Some went on to argue that, given the implacable hostility of powerful capitalist countries to socialism, a dictatorial phase was necessary in order to make the transition to authentic (proletarian) democracy.

Others felt that Stalin had betrayed the revolution. The Soviet Union was declared to be neither democratic nor socialist. Still others, nonsocialists as well as socialists, argued that democracy was a political category, whereas socialism designated an economic system. Hence any of four categories is possible: democratic capitalism, nondemocratic capitalism, democratic socialism, and nondemocratic socialism. There is no necessary connection between democracy and either form of economic organization.

Following World War II, the discourse took another turn. The Soviet Union was no longer the sole representative of actually existing socialism. The Red Army had defeated Hitler's army on the Eastern Front and driven it out of Eastern Europe. As it retreated, pro-Soviet regimes were installed in its wake, none of them democratic. Moreover, a socialist revolution occurred in China, and many were brewing elsewhere in the Third World. In almost all instances these movements, inspired by the successes of Russia and China, had little sympathy for bourgeois democracy.

As the cleavage between socialism and democracy appeared to widen, the connection between capitalism and democracy seemed to grow stronger. Having lost the war, Japan and Germany lost their colonies. So too, soon enough, did most of the other European nations (reluctantly and often only after fierce struggle). The United States, for its part, granted (quasi-) independence to the Philippines. With capitalist fascism and overt colonialism mostly gone (Portugal would retain its African colonies into the 1970s), a new pair of equations gained prominence: capitalism = democracy, socialism = totalitarianism.

Of course the first equation could not be defended intellectually, however much it was embedded in popular consciousness. (In the United States, the Cold War was typically seen to be a battle between democracy and communism.) After all, there had been and still were nondemocratic capitalist countries. Moreover, capitalist democracies continued to support nondemocratic regimes abroad, however brutal, so long as they were anti-communist. On occasion, capitalist democracies would even instigate the replacement of democratically elected governments with viciously authoritarian ones.

The second equation, however, had its intellectual supporters. Milton Friedman (later to be awarded a Nobel Prize in Economics) argued that capitalism was a necessary, although admittedly not sufficient, condition for democracy. He argued that socialism involves replacing decentralized market mechanisms with conscious central planning, and that such central planning is not only inherently inefficient, but it necessarily concentrates power in the hands of the small class of planners. With economic power so concentrated, the concentration of political power is inevitable. Moreover, this concentration virtually rules out dissent, because all media, indeed all jobs of any sort, are controlled by these planners. The inevitable outcome is totalitarianism.

Friedrich von Hayek (also awarded a Nobel Prize in Economics) went still further, arguing that even social democratic reforms intended not to overthrow capitalism, but only to curb the excesses of the market, would have the same result, being nothing less than the road to serfdom.

Hayek's argument was in part a response to a new division that had emerged among socialists, the division between *social democrats* and *democratic socialists*. The former had made peace with capitalism and concentrated on humanizing the system. Social democrats supported and tried to strengthen the basic institutions of the welfare state—pensions for all, public health care, public education, unemployment insurance. They supported and tried to strengthen the labor movement. The latter, as socialists, argued that capitalism could *never* be sufficiently humanized and that trying to suppress the economic contradictions in one area would only see them emerge in a different guise elsewhere (e.g., if you push unemployment too low, you'll get inflation; if job security is too strong, labor discipline breaks down.)

This division has become ever more pronounced since the demise of the Soviet Union. Today the major "socialist" parties of Europe, as well as the Labour Party of Great Britain and many former communist parties, have explicitly distanced themselves from socialism as traditionally understood and are now social democratic parties. There remain smaller parties in almost all countries, often split-offs from the major parties, that retain their allegiance to socialism. In the United States those small parties still bearing the name *socialist* (e.g., Socialist Party USA, Socialist Workers Party) are still committed to socialism, as is the largest socialist organization, the Democratic Socialists of America, an organization that does not consider itself a political party.

Today there are few socialist organizations or self-identified socialist thinkers or activists who do not consider themselves *democratic* socialists. Indeed, the argument is now often made, more forcefully than ever before, that a true democrat, a *radical democrat*, must be a socialist. This argument—a mirror-image of the Friedman argument—purports to show that it is capitalism, not socialism, that is incompatible with genuine democracy.

It is argued that capitalism inevitably gives rise to vast disparities of wealth, and that this economic power inevitably translates into political power. In support of the first clause of the argument, one points to the ever-increasing concentration of wealth in capitalist countries following the collapse of capitalism's ideological rival, the existence of which had checked somewhat capitalism's rapacious tendencies. In support of the second, one points to the enormous role that money plays in contemporary elections, and the fact that virtually all the major media are owned by corporations, which are, in turn, controlled by the wealthy. To these considerations is added a theoretical argument. If an elected government should make a serious attempt to rein in the power of capital, an "investment strike" would ensue, bringing on a severe economic downturn that will have a negative impact on everybody. The offending government will be quickly voted out of office. So long as a small class has such power, real democracy is impossible.

This argument raises a deep question about the meaning of the term *democracy*. Are capitalist democracies truly democratic? The term *socialist* is also much contested. Virtually all socialists have distanced themselves from the economic model long synonymous with *socialism* (i.e., the Soviet model of a nonmarket, centrally planned economy). The validity of the Friedmanite critique of this specific form of socialism has been (at least implicitly) acknowledged. Some have endorsed the concept of *market socialism*,

a postcapitalist economy that retains market competition but socializes the means of production and, in some versions, extends democracy to the workplace. Some hold out for a nonmarket, participatory economy. All democratic socialists agree on the need for a democratic alternative to capitalism. There is no consensus as yet as to what that alternative should look like.

—David Schweickart

See also *Communist Manifesto;* Debs, Eugene V.; Democracy; Engels, Friedrich; Fascism; Harrington, Michael; Marx, Karl; Mill, John Stuart; Owen, Robert; Participatory Economics; Social Democracy; Socialism

Further Readings

Bobbio, N. (1987). *Which socialism? Marxism, socialism, and democracy.* Cambridge, UK: Polity Press.

Busky, D. (2000). *Democratic socialism: A global survey.* New York: Praeger.

Callinicos, A. (1993). Socialism and democracy. In D. Held (Ed.), *Prospects for democracy* (pp. 200–212). Palo Alto, CA: Stanford University Press.

Cunningham, F. (1987). *Democratic theory and socialism.* Cambridge, UK: Cambridge University Press.

Cunningham, F. (1994). *The real world of democracy revisited and other essays on democracy and socialism.* Atlantic Highlands, NJ: Humanities Press.

Dahl, R. A. (1985). *A preface to economic democracy.* Berkeley: University of California Press.

Dahl, R. A. (1989). *Democracy and its critics.* New Haven, CT: Yale University Press.

Gould, C. (1987). *Rethinking democracy: Freedom and social cooperation in politics, economy, and society.* Cambridge, UK: Cambridge University Press.

Harrington, M. (1972). *Socialism.* New York: Bantam.

Howard, M. (Ed.). (2001). *Socialism.* Amherst, NY: Humanities Press.

Schumpeter, J. (1942). *Capitalism, socialism, and democracy.* New York: Harper & Row.

Schweickart, D. (2002). *After capitalism.* Lanham, MD: Rowman & Littlefield.

DEMONSTRATIONS

See STRATEGIES AND TACTICS IN SOCIAL MOVEMENTS

Derrida, Jacques (1930–2004)

Jacques Derrida is one of the most important intellectual figures associated with poststructural and postmodern theory—although he never used the latter term—and is credited with creating the notion of deconstruction. His reassessments of classical metaphysics have posed a substantial challenge to philosophy, his readings of structuralist anthropology have forced serious reconsiderations of thinking in that area, and his discussions of language and literature have had a great impact on these and related fields. In his later life, Derrida increasingly turned his investigations to issues of ethics, justice, and the law, analyzing the legacy of Marxist thought in the wake of the Cold War.

His voluminous writings and broad consideration of questions of *being* in a secular world make him one of the most important thinkers of the 20th century, one whose influence is still in the process of being assessed and whose work is difficult to summarize accurately. He has proven controversial for those engaging in questions of activism and social justice, as his assertion that there are no absolute or transcendental cultural values has challenged people attempting to assert the value of universal human rights. At the same time, his goal of creating an inclusive society to come, one that remains open to change in the future, presents his readers with ways of conceptualizing a world beyond the dichotomies of inside and outside, or inclusion and exclusion.

In 1930 Jacques Derrida was born to a family of Jewish descent in the French colony of Algeria. He grew up in El-Biar and was expelled from his *lycée* by a government eager to please the Vichy regime's anti-Semitic policies in France. His family later moved to France in order to help him pursue his education. Derrida succeeded in the French system, becoming a student and then lecturer at the elite École Normale Supérieure in 1952, where he studied under Michel Foucault and Louis Althusser. He met his future wife Marguerite, a psychoanalyst, in 1953, and in 1957 they married in the United States and eventually had two sons. During the Algerian War of Independence,

Derrida avoided military service by teaching soldiers' children French and English. After this period, Derrida became associated with the leftist avant-garde literary group *Tel Quel* while teaching at the Sorbonne and the École Normale Supérieure. He later dissociated himself from this group, maintaining a complicated position with their political leanings, as he did with most political movements. He finished his *d'état* (roughly equivalent to a doctoral thesis) in 1980, and became the director of studies at the École des Hautes Études en Sciences Sociales. He was a founder of the International College of Philosophy and held a number of visiting and permanent positions at universities in the United States, though he made his home in Paris. He received a number of honorary doctoral degrees and traveled widely prior to his death from pancreatic cancer in 2004.

Derrida emerged into the intellectual spotlight in the late 1960s with his publications "Structure, Sign, and Play in the Discourse of the Human Sciences" and *Of Grammatology.* "Structure, Sign, and Play" was first delivered as a lecture at Johns Hopkins University and then published in the volume *Writing and Difference.* The paper's initial purpose was to critique the vogue of structuralist theory, which was then dominant in much intellectual thought, and which sought the underlying structures that govern all social relations. In it, Derrida proposes a radical rupture against this thinking, asserting that no such underlying structures exist. These early works suggest the project of deconstruction, a notion derived from Martin Heidegger's use of the term *destruction.* Derrida uses the concept of deconstruction to dismantle the assumptions that are present in any text or discourse. He works from the premise that any center or metaphysically grounding notion—such as God, truth, or transcendence—can be demonstrated to be a false or incomplete explanation of how meaning functions. Deconstruction proposes to unsettle sedimented thought patterns. As such, it has the potential to liberate thought from its static or fixed forms and to allow new thinking to occur. Deconstruction is motivated by attempts to disrupt the hierarchical and dualistic modes of thought on which much of Western philosophy, as derived from Plato, is based. The supposed differences or oppositions between, for example, culture and nature can be shown to be artificial through this process, and the valuing of one over the other becomes an arbitrary judgment rather than a transcendent truth. *Of Grammatology* pursues such an investigation by deconstructing the opposition between writing and speech. Once a text relying on such an opposition is destabilized, its meaning opens up and become fluid, enabling alternative interpretations. As a result, deconstruction proposes a challenge to the notions of limits developed in analytic philosophy.

A euphoric explosion of poststructural thought followed Derrida's early works, even as skeptics queried the ethics of this decentered system. Alongside the development of deconstruction and poststructuralism, Jean-François Lyotard and others began to articulate the mind-set of postmodernism, which became inextricably linked to Derrida. Lyotard's statement that the postmodern is evidenced by what he calls an incredulity toward metanarratives—or underlying patterns of thought, such as the ideology of progress—parallels Derrida's disavowal of metaphysics. Critics from Jonathan Culler to Fredric Jameson and Terry Eagleton seized on Derridean and postmodern thinking in their assessments of culture, making postmodernity a dominant mind-set in the last quarter of the 20th century. Processes of deconstruction allowed thinkers like Judith Butler to demonstrate that the dominant sex and gender systems of Western society are social constructs based in what she calls *performativity*, rather than natural modes of being, just as Derrida's thought has enabled the writings of the critic Gayatri Spivak, who has sought to empower subaltern women in the Third World.

Derrida's thinking has proven to be highly controversial. He is sometimes dismissed as too obscure or esoteric in his writing, and many segments of the field of philosophy in particular, have been hostile to Derrida's propositions. In 1992, a group of professors at Cambridge University came to prominence over their objections about plans to award Derrida an honorary degree, while a *New York Times* obituary decried Derrida as obscure, leading to a protest petition from supporters. Critics have charged that Derrida is not only difficult to read, but that his notion of the deconstruction of values leads society into a cultural relativism in which it may no longer be possible to assert that any one thing is better than any other.

Partly in response to his critics and the questions surrounding Martin Heidegger's debated affinities with Nazism, Derrida increasingly turned toward direct investigations of ethics and politics, while insisting that his initial project of deconstruction was founded on these very considerations. His later works sought to demonstrate how deconstruction might free us to construct new, open-ended societies that can become welcoming of difference and remain flexible into the future. His later analyses delved into Marxism, death, the law, and the politics of friendship. He engaged in political advocacy, although he had kept himself distant from conventional politics since his disappointments after the May 1968 student uprisings in France. He contested the American war in Vietnam, was active in cultural activities linked to the anti-apartheid movement against the South African government, and was arrested in 1981 in Czechoslovakia after attending a conference. He met with Palestinian authorities in 1988, protested against the death penalty, supported the release of Mumia Abu-Jamal, and supported Lionel Jospin's socialist candidacy for president of France in 1995. At the time of his death, he was actively opposing the American-led invasion of Iraq in the aftermath of the attacks of September 11, 2001.

Throughout his later writings, Jacques Derrida sought to contrast, for example, justice and the law, discussing the gap between the two and creating a vision of a future justice to come. This vision is in part derived from a Marxist leaning, but one that is based on recognition of the impossibility of making any political or social decision. Once the arbitrariness of the choice is recognized, argues Derrida, its alternatives become visible and might be enacted. The exclusions of the world and its dichotomies can be undone, leading to a deconstructed world of unassimilated differences.

—Kit Dobson

See also Abu-Jamal, Mumia; Anti-Apartheid Movement; Anti–Death Penalty Movement; Deconstruction; Identity

Politics; Intifada (1987–1992, 2000–2003); Marxist Theory; May Revolution, France; Performativity; Plato; Postcolonial Theory; Postmodernism; Rousseau, Jean-Jacques; Spivak, Gayatri

Further Readings

Beardsworth, R. (1996). *Derrida & the political.* London: Routledge.

Derrida, J. (1976). *Of grammatology* (G. Spivak, Trans.). Baltimore: Johns Hopkins University Press. (Original work published 1967)

Derrida, J. (1978). *Writing and difference.* (A. Bass, Trans.). London: Routledge. (Original work published 1967)

Derrida, J. (1994). *Specters of Marx: The state of the debt, the work of mourning, and the new international* (P. Kamuf, Trans.). New York: Routledge.

Lyotard, J. (1984). *The postmodern condition: A report on knowledge* (G. Bennington & B. Massumi, Trans.). Minneapolis: University of Minnesota Press. (Original work published 1979)

DEWEY, JOHN (1859–1952)

John Dewey was an educator, pragmatic and reconstructive philosopher, psychologist, and founder of the progressive education movement. His educational theories and practices in particular were groundbreaking, including support of teacher-student interaction, reflection and experience, and integration with community and democracy.

After obtaining a teacher of philosophy degree at the University of Vermont, Dewey began his educational career by working as a school teacher for several years and then enrolled in the graduate program in philosophy at Johns Hopkins University. There, Dewey studied with George Sylvester Morris, a Hegelian philosopher who became his mentor. He also worked with Stanley Hall, an important experimental psychologist who stressed application of scientific methodology to the human sciences.

After graduation, Dewey was hired into the University of Michigan department of philosophy. There he became increasingly interested in social, political, and economic issues, diverging from idealist philosophy and moving toward pragmatism, struggling with religious issues, and philosophizing about the social nature of the mind and self. In 1886, Dewey married Alice Chipman and gradually began a shift of interests toward public affairs, social justice, and education, focusing on unity of theory and practice.

Dewey moved to the University of Chicago in 1894, as head of the department of philosophy, psychology, and pedagogy, becoming ever more involved in the philosophy of education. He defined the most significant problem of education as the harmonizing of individual traits with the social and moral, underscoring the need for improved theory of schooling and practice to address this problem. Emphasis on the connection of subject matter to the needs, interests, and cognitive development level of students was one of the most novel and enduring of Dewey's ideas. Dewey emphasized attention to both the cognitive and the moral and was strongly opposed to rote learning of facts. Dewey was one of the first educators to actively integrate experience with education.

Dewey founded the experimental University Laboratory School, known as the Dewey School, with the purpose of conducting educational experiments to develop and test educational theories; a platform for reform of pedagogical methods. The Laboratory School was all theory based and flexible in organization, structure, and opportunities. Students were grouped by interests and abilities and exposed to broad and varied curricula and methods. As one example, children learned science by investigating scientific processes as they took place during normal, participatory daily activities that they performed in their classes as experiments, true examples of learning by doing. Unfortunately, administrative difficulties resulted in the closure of the school after 7 years, well before Dewey was able to complete his experimentation.

Educational experimentalism was an underlying theme for much of Dewey's work from this time on. He viewed education as an endless and never fully generalizable experiment. Dewey preferred an educational approach that broadened intellect and developed problem-solving and critical-thinking skills, in direct contradiction to the traditional, back-to-the-basics, memorization-oriented educational programs.

In Chicago, Dewey also had the opportunity to work with many of the top American philosophers of the time and became involved with the political and social issues of the day, including immigration, urbanization, the labor movement, and technology.

Later, Dewey moved from Chicago to the Teacher's College at Columbia, continuing to work on educational issues, publishing, and becoming known worldwide for his work. He was a true public figure, considered by many to be the most public academic philosopher of the 20th century. The public knew him for his involvement in social causes, such as women's suffrage and unionization of teachers, and for his many articles on current social issues in popular magazines. Dewey toured and spoke internationally, visited schools, and continued educational research and the critical study of other educational movements of his day. He was politically active, involved in the American socialist party during the 1930s, committed to fully participatory democracy, and very much opposed to communism. Democracy is a recurring theme in his works, as he believed that only through a democratic society could education for all be improved and a better quality of life provided.

In general, Dewey focused his philosophical interests on theories of knowledge, considering education to be the process of forming fundamental dispositions, intellectual and emotional, necessarily engaged with experience, thinking, and reflection. Dewey believed that a general theory of education is theory of what is valuable enough to be taught to the next generation in order to promote effective adaptation of individuals to their physical and moral environment and prepare the young for future responsibility and success in life. He opposed imposition of education from above and supported educational experiences that utilized opportunities of present life. He felt that educational procedures should not start with facts and truths from outside the ordinary life experiences of the students and that educational experience should be organized and structured to fit the developmental stages of students. In this view Dewey was strongly influenced by Darwinian philosophy, from the standpoint of fit with environment and community, a philosophical perspective that Dewey referred to as *instrumentalism*.

Dewey was a proponent of diversity in education, recognizing that the potential of any given individual is unique, and believing that the goal of the educational system should be to help each individual achieve his or her full individual potential.

In many of his works during this period, Dewey stressed the social dimensions of inquiry. This was a philosophically productive time, during which Dewey and his colleagues were eventually responsible for developing biologically based functional philosophy. Emphasizing action, need, desire, and interest, it was a philosophy dependent on an understanding of the functional unity of individual and environment. Within this framework, Dewey now saw education as a social function, with pluralistic democracy being the best society to foster and sustain freedom, creativity, and growth. He believed democracy was necessary to support education in favor of an improved, shared common life. He argued that education on democratic habits should begin very early in a child's education, and that schools should encourage students to be active members of a community.

The educational ideas that Dewey publicized were very popular, and there is no doubt that he influenced the development of many new educational procedures, although his ideas were never integrated into American public school curricula to the extent he had hoped for. His ideas are viewed as inspirational by many educators (especially informal educators), but the implementation of progressive educational programs has been historically problematic. Dewey's writings are deep, complex, and often misinterpreted. The expansion of progressive education to include many other, often contradictory theories and practices has further complicated popular interpretation of much of Dewey's work. Progressive education was less dominant during the Cold War era, as analytic and phenomenological educational philosophies spread, but resurged in later years. Dewey's ideas are still an important educational philosophy, with ties to many modern curriculum reform efforts. There is great disagreement among adherents of progressive education with respect to Dewey's philosophical principles and school practices, making it very difficult to trace the extent of his influence on public school systems.

Dewey's ideas have often been severely criticized and are still open topics of debate. Critics point to a tendency for application of progressive methods that result in chaotic curriculum and excessive individualism, sometimes even blaming Dewey for what they perceived as the downfall of the American public education system. Dewey countered these critics by pointing out the tendency of some educators to respond to the need for improved education by seizing anything new and different without attention to the underlying theories. He stressed that progressive education is a departure from the old ways, which creates a new set of problems, requiring careful, planned implementation as a philosophy, not just a system. Everything depends on the quality of the educational experiences, with progressive organization of subject matter leading to an understanding of both content and meaning.

Dewey was both a very influential and prolific philosopher and author. Several of his most popular works for educators have been *How We Think, Logic: The Theory of Inquiry,* and *Democracy and Education.* In addition to writing on education, philosophy, psychology, logic, and democracy, Dewey also wrote on the subjects of human behavior, politics, aesthetics, ethics, the nature of a satisfied life, and religion. Today, Dewey's philosophies continue to be studied, continued, and expanded on worldwide, with the Center for Dewey Studies at Southern Illinois a key international focal point for research on Dewey's life and works.

—*Susan L. Rothwell*

See also Critical Pedagogy; Democracy; Hull-House; Progressive Movement, Education

Further Readings

Baker, M. (1966). *Foundations of John Dewey's educational theory.* New York: Atherton.

Boydston, J. (Ed.). (1967–1991). *The collected works of John Dewey* (Vols. 1–37). Carbondale: Southern Illinois University Press.

Bullert, G. (1983). *The politics of John Dewey.* Buffalo, NY: Prometheus Books.

Dykhuizen, G. (1973). *The life and mind of John Dewey.* Carbondale: Southern Illinois University Press.

Hickman, L. (1990). *John Dewey's pragmatic technology.* Bloomington: Indiana University Press.

Hook, S. (1939). *John Dewey: An intellectual portrait.* Westport, CT: Greenwood Press.

Mayhew, K., & Edwards, A. (1966). *The Dewey school.* New York: Atherton.

DICKENS, CHARLES (1812–1870)

Charles Dickens was a 19th-century British novelist, journalist, and social critic. Dickens was born in 1812 in Portsmouth, England, the son of a clerk in the navy pay office. When his father was imprisoned for debt, the young Charles, at the age of 12, was forced to work in a blacking warehouse in order to support the rest of the family. This youthful experience of poverty deeply affected Dickens. Its impact can be felt most poignantly in his novels, in his stories of poor boys like Oliver Twist, David Copperfield, and Pip in *Great Expectations,* who struggle to rise out of the impoverished circumstances of their childhoods to achieve success and respectability. Dickens's own struggles against poverty produced the central contradiction of his adult life and career. His experiences imbued his writing with an ever-present social conscience while at the same time they fostered his own material ambitions. Dickens the grown-up would always suffer from a profound fear of financial insecurity despite his ever-increasing wealth and celebrity.

After working as an office boy, Dickens became a Parliamentary reporter for the London *Morning Chronicle* and embarked on a career in journalism that would set the stage for his future success as a popular novelist and influential editor. The role of journalism in Dickens's career is frequently underestimated. Throughout his life, Dickens was a leading figure in the Victorian periodical press. All the novels that we know so well today saw their first publication in serial form in magazines or newspapers. From 1833 to 1835, Dickens published a series of articles on London street life, which were collected and published together under the title *Sketches by Boz* in 1836. These short pieces chronicled the lives of both the poor and the wealthy in Victorian London, the first industrialized city in the world's history. For example, in a description of a typical London pawn shop, Dickens portrays the representatives of various social classes, each with their individual motives and life stories, gathered together at the pawn brokers to engage in the daily commerce enacted there. The huge success of *Sketches by Boz* led to Dickens's securing of a contract for his first novel, *The Pickwick Papers* of 1837, and launched his literary career. With the publication of the *Sketches* and of *Pickwick,* Dickens found himself a celebrity at the age of 25.

In 1837, Dickens published *Oliver Twist,* the story of an orphan who escapes through equal measures of luck and virtue first from life in a workhouse and then from his apprenticeship to an undertaker and makes his way to the metropolis of London, only to fall in with a gang of thieves, pickpockets, and prostitutes. While chronicling the misfortunes of young Oliver, Dickens simultaneously presented Victorian readers with a compelling portrait of the life of the poor and criminal classes, the left-behinds of British progress and prosperity in the early half of the 19th century. The publication of *Oliver Twist* and other successive novels secured Dickens's status as the most widely read author of his time. In 1842, Dickens visited America for the first time for a series of public appearances that underscored his popularity on both sides of the Atlantic. Dickens expressed his disillusionment with the United States in *American Notes* (1842), a series of travel sketches and dispatches, and in the novel *Martin Chuzzlewit.* His stereotyped portrayal of American life deeply offended his American audience. At the same time, Dickens became an impassioned advocate for the abolition of slavery in the United States.

Alongside his success as a novelist, Dickens also founded and edited a series of widely circulated and highly influential magazines and journals. These publications aimed to satisfy the Victorians' almost insatiable desire for the printed word. Among these were the radical paper *Daily News,* founded in 1846, which Dickens briefly edited; *Household Words,* established in 1850; and its successor, *All the Year Round,* which

Dickens edited from 1859 until his death. Beginning with the semiautobiographical novel *David Copperfield* in 1850, Dickens's various journals and magazines provided an outlet for the serialization of some of his best-known novels, including *Hard Times* (1854), a tale of life in one of the new factory towns of Victorian England; *A Tale of Two Cities* (1859), a treatment of the Reign of Terror in Revolutionary France; and *Great Expectations* (1861), the story of Pip, another poor orphan boy who realizes his dreams of wealth and social status, only to find that all his success is the result of an early, nearly forgotten encounter with an escaped criminal. In addition to his novelistic output, Dickens also involved himself in a number of theatrical productions, including adaptations for the stage of his own novels. He also gave a series of public readings, including a second tour of America in 1868 and 1869. These appearances proved immensely popular and profitable, and Dickens often played to stadium-sized crowds. They were also exhausting, both physically and emotionally, and the pace of Dickens's work and tours contributed to his sudden death in 1870. Dickens left his last novel, *The Mystery of Edwin Drood,* unfinished at the time of his death.

Although he has often been criticized for his inability to portray women realistically and for his constant craving after success and status, Charles Dickens throughout his novels and other writings remained a steady and constant voice for social reform in the midst of Victorian England's reckless embrace of industrial capitalism and technological progress.

—Tony Rafalowski

See also Abolitionist Movements; Literature and Activism

Further Readings

Ackroyd, P. (1991). *Introduction to Dickens.* New York: Ballantine.

Dickens, C. (1997). *Selected journalism, 1850–1870* (D. Pascoe, Ed.). London: Penguin.

Drew, J. M. L. (2003). *Dickens the journalist.* London: Palgrave.

Smiley, J. (2002). *Charles Dickens.* New York: Viking.

DIFFERENCE

The concept of *difference* has long existed in philosophy and social sciences, but it is only in recent decades, with the increased interest in multicultural and gender studies, that it has become a central part of debates in academic, social, and political circles. It is possible to identify two distinct definitions of difference: The first was developed in the modern era, beginning in the Enlightenment, and the second arose in the 20th century, from the 1960s onwards.

During the modern era, democracy appeared with the intention of establishing a universal concept of the human being. This required the elimination of special characteristics and differences and the promotion of equality and equal rights for all. This concept of equality attempted to remove the right to difference that aristocratic and religious elites had established for their own benefit in the form of privileges. However, in reality the new universal project concealed what was in fact the identification the subject's right with those of a white, Western, heterosexual male.

From this point of view, being different meant not being considered part of the human race and, consequently, exclusion from universal rights. Being different was always associated with being the "other," the "exotic," or the "inferior." As a result, much of the oppressed groups' struggle for emancipation was based on assimilation, on showing that those labelled as "different" were not in fact inferior and could carry out generic human tasks if they were given an adequate education and enjoyed equal opportunities. In this sense, cultural difference acted as an ideology that legitimated social inequality.

The positive affirmation of difference began in the social movements of the 1960s with what has been called the *struggle for recognition* of stigmatized and devalued identities. New groups and theories appeared within the feminist movement and began criticizing equalitarian feminism because it was believed that this approach victimized women. Instead, the affirmation of female difference was advocated. At the same time, other groups adopted similar policies, taking the negative concepts of difference previously applied to them and redefining them in terms of pride and empowerment. This was expressed in slogans such as *Black Is Beautiful* and *Gay Pride.*

At the present time, the understanding that difference and diversity are intrinsically good seems to have triumphed, and current debates center on how difference and social equality can fit together satisfactorily. Proof of the acceptance of diversity can be seen in the policies of organizations such as the United Nations. However, the debate about the intrinsic worth of all cultural difference is not over because one important question needs to be addressed. This question is whether racist, sexist, and homophobic elements present in cultural diversity should be respected. Many nations accept that respect for human rights is a necessary requirement for respect of all cultural difference. However, some argue that human rights are in fact a cultural creation of particular societies.

—Ana de Miguel

See also Citizenship; Identity Politics; Postmodernism

Further Readings

Taylor, C. (1992). *Multiculturalism and "the politics of recognition."* Princeton, NJ: Princeton University Press.

Touraine, A. (2000). *Pourrons-nous vivre ensemble? Égaux et différents* [Will we be able to live together? Equal and different]. Paris: Fayard.

Young, I. M. (1990). *Justice and the politics of difference.* Princeton, NJ: Princeton University Press.

DIGITAL ACTIVISM

Digital activism is a form of activism that uses digital media, mainly the Internet, as a key platform for mass mobilization and political action. From the early experiments of the 1980s to the current *smart mobs* and *blogs*, activists and computer specialists have approached digital networks as a channel for militant action. Initially, online activists used the Internet as a *medium* for information distribution, given its capacity to reach massive audiences across borders instantaneously. A more developed undertaking of digital activism or *cyberactivism* approaches the World Wide Web as a *site* of protest, turning virtual space into a ground that mirrors and amplifies street (or offline) demonstrations.

This use of the Web as a valid terrain for social antagonism comes from an understanding of the nomadic nature of the current configuration of hegemonic power. In this scenario, transnational labor and capital flow are indicators of how power is not tied to particular physical spaces but circulates smoothly through the information highway. Digital activists claim that, in order to disrupt the capitalist structures that are favored by the process of globalization, an effective activist action must confront power in its nomadic being by, among other tactics, blocking its free circulation across nation-state borders.

One of the fundamental goals of online activism is to make the body digitally active and not just the passive receptor of power's ubiquitous interpellation that confines individuals to different kinds of data banks. E-mail campaigning is one of the simplest ways in which activists use the Internet as a complement to street action. On the other extreme, *hacktivism* (a form of digital activism that comes out of the hacker culture of the 1980s) aims at breaking in and disrupting websites by altering the patterns of code arrangement. Hacktivists, such as the group Cult of the Dead Cow (cDc), operate based on the philosophy of freedom of information and the rights of people to have unrestricted access to digital resources.

Different digital tactics entail diverse uses of the electronic networks. Text-based practices include e-mail campaigns, text messaging, Web postings, and online petitions to advocate for a determined cause and to generate massive support. *Web defacing* or *cybergraffiti*, a more complex text-based online practice, is an action in which a specialized group of cyberactivists or hacktivists alters the home page of an organization by posting information that holds it accountable for its role in a given conflict. Another way of generating text to create awareness of a political matter is known as *HTML conceptualism*. It

consists of an action in which a group's request of nonexistent pages within an organization's website makes the server return error pages with a message reading, for example, "human rights not found on this server." More performative actions, like "virtual sit-ins" and "e-mail bombs," push the possibilities of online activism a little further, provoking a concrete disruption of the servers' functionality through the concerted action of participants around the world.

Although online political participation always brings up the issue of the digital divide, that is, of the unequal access that different social actors have to technological devices, in many cases online activists narrow the distance between both ends of this division by collaborating with disenfranchised groups in a networked manner. Ricardo Dominguez and his group the Electronic Disturbance Theatre (EDT) take traditional civil disobedience tactics to the Net in support of social movements like the Zapatistas in Chiapas, Mexico; the immigrants subjected to border patrol brutality on the border between Mexico and the United States; or the families of the murdered young women of Ciudad Juárez. In 1998, EDT automated the virtual sit-in, a form of online demonstration in which a networked community gathers on one or several sites to carry out an act of digital dissent. The action is undertaken through a Web-based program, FloodNet, that sends repetitive requests to the targeted Web pages. The protestors' automated "clickings," simultaneously enacted from multiple computers around the world, provoke such an excess of traffic that the targeted site's server is unable to handle it. By clogging the bandwidth, the action affects the site's technological efficiency, slowing down its capacity to retrieve information and eventually provoking its shutting down. In this way, the action combines the activists' appearance in virtual space with their intervention in time, because, as a result of this massive presence, the action disrupts the server's pace. In contrast with hacktivism, which achieves technological efficiency by operating at a *syntactical* level; that is, at the level of code programming, Dominguez locates the efficiency reached by EDT's virtual actions on a *semantic* level. In EDT's actions, myriad symbolic gestures—tied more to the politics of the question and utopia than to a revolutionary overthrowing of power—create disturbance through a poetic reformulation of the link between the real and the virtual. EDT's activism takes much of its symbolic force from the Zapatistas, the Mexican indigenous insurrectionary movement who, through the *communiqués* delivered by their leader, the Subcomandante Marcos, unfolded a creative use of language and technology as powerful weapons against hegemonic power. EDT's actions fall into the category of *electronic civil disobedience,* and, to dissociate them from acts of cyberterrorism or regular hacking, activists ask that these online political gestures comply to certain rules: The actions should always represent a communal interest and not an individual agenda, their motifs and agents should be publicly exposed, they should also include a "live" element linking them to some sort of street action, and they should be easily appropriated and replicated by groups with little or no technological knowledge.

Concepts like *virtual sit-in* or *electronic civil disobedience* show the way in which cyberactivists refer to the rhetoric of the street and to traditional activism in order to make their actions intelligible and meaningful beyond techno-jargon. Similarly, online activism renames street actions as "offline" or "no-fi"; that is, involving no technology, to show the continuity between both online and "live" practices and their value as tactics that can be juxtaposed or alternated depending on the context.

One of the main debates in the field of online activism revolves around the issue of digital correctness bringing hacktivists like Cult of the Dead Cow against other digital activists such as the Electronic Disturbance Theater or The Electrohippies Collective, who carry out virtual sit-ins. The cDc claims that, by blocking access to certain web pages, virtual sit-ins provoke what is called a *denial of service* (DoS), an act that they deem unethical and illegal because it violates the rights secured by the First Amendment of the U.S. Constitution. Similarly, Dominguez from EDT regards cDc's actions as elitist and paramilitary in that they are highly technological and their efficacy does not rely on collective convergence, like EDT's populist campaigns do, but on the level of expertise of a single individual.

As a relatively new field of political action, digital activism invites the question of the concrete efficacy of these gestures that are played out in the virtual realm, a space to which people have different degrees of proximity and engagement. The importance of this kind of activism should not be evaluated in terms of the number of servers that crash as a consequence of these actions. Born in the era of global capital, online activism strives for the generation of a "swarm effect" across borders, a gathering of bodies that is not predicated on corporeal physical presence but on body-machine associations and networked behavior. Digital activist actions always play in tandem with mass-media coverage; that is, a big part of their success depends on generating media attention, another way for the issues at stake to trespass borders.

Online actions can prove of importance in countries where public spaces are highly regulated or militarized. In these cases, online actions signify a better option than "live" actions, putting the electronic body on the front-line when the biological one is at risk. Online protest also plays a vital role when there is a need to assert collective agency against the transnational institutions whose decisions affect the future of local economies and natural resources.

Despite the efforts of online activists to link their actions to traditional protest culture, old-school activists are skeptical about digital activism's real capacity to effect social change. However, scholars in the field point out the importance of cyberactivism in that it generates a radical shift in the use of the Internet and digital technology as an instrument of hegemonic power to the digital as a valid infrastructure for grassroots political mobilization. Digital activism provides new ways for the body to inhabit this realm in an ideally transformative fashion, turning from consumer to agent. This is the principle that contemporary activists and artists follow to account for the power of bodily presence in both its online and offline manifestations. The establishment of governmental secret agencies and laws in an attempt to regulate not only cyberspace but also digital actions has already proved the efficacy of the online body as the radical administrator of its own code.

—*Marcela A. Fuentes*

See also Blogging; Civil Disobedience; Digital Equity; Electronic Democracy; Virtual Sit-Ins

Further Readings

Critical Art Ensemble. (1994). *The electronic disturbance.* New York: Autonomedia.

Critical Art Ensemble. (1996). *Electronic civil disobedience.* New York: Autonomedia.

Critical Art Ensemble. (2001). *Digital resistance: Explorations in tactical media.* New York: Autonomedia.

Fusco, C. (2003). On-line simulations/real-life politics: A discussion with Ricardo Domínguez on staging virtual theatre. *The Drama Review, 47*(2), 151–162.

McCaughey, M., & Ayers, M. D. (Eds.). (2003). *Cyberactivism: Online activism in theory and practice.* New York: Routledge.

Rheingold, H. (2002). *Smart mobs: The next social revolution.* Cambridge, MA: Perseus.

DIGITAL EQUITY

The term *digital divide* was coined in the 1980s to describe gaps in access to computers and the Internet among individuals and groups based on race, gender, socioeconomic status, first language, disability, and other social or cultural identities. Early conceptualizations of the digital divide tended to conceive access only in terms of *physical* access to or ownership of these technologies. In other words, if somebody lived in a household in which the Internet or a computer was available, or if she or he attended a school with a computer lab, that individual was perceived as having Internet or computer access.

But in the 1990s, as critical cultural theorists, social justice educators, and other scholar-activists began to situate and analyze the digital divide within larger analyses of racism, sexism, classism, linguicism, and imperialism, they found these early conceptualizations of the digital divide to be lacking complexity as well as sociohistical and sociopolitical context. For example, by 2000 U.S. women had surpassed U.S. men to become a majority of the U.S. online population. This led many information technology scholars to hail the end of the gender digital divide. But girls and women continued to trail boys and men in educational and career pursuits related to computers and technology, due largely to a lack of encouragement, or blatant discouragement, from educators, peers, the media, and the wider society. And women remained virtually locked out of the increasingly techno-driven global economy while men were more likely to recognize computers and the Internet as tools for economic and professional gain. The equalizing of Internet access rates between girls and boys and between women and men was a significant step toward the elimination of the gender digital divide—a step toward equality. But when more critical scholars with a deeper understanding of equity and social justice looked through a different lens, one painted with the full historical scope of sexism at local, national, and global levels, a much more complex conceptualization for "access" began to emerge. If we are to understand authentically the cross-group gaps in computer and Internet access, these scholars insisted, we first must understand these gaps as symptoms of existing systemic inequities. They began reshaping the digital divide dialogue, broadening its scope, and asking deeper questions about the role of cybertechnologies in education and the larger society.

Emerging from these efforts was the digital equity movement. This movement was, and continues to be, dedicated to (a) challenging the notion that computers and the Internet are inherently the "great equalizers" of society and the world, (b) uncovering ways in which an uncritical endorsement of technological "progress" in the form of educational computer technology is actually contributing to the cycle of inequities, and (c) expanding the digital divide concept of "access" beyond mere physical access to include social, cultural, and political access to these technologies and the social and economic benefits of that access. The base concern of the digital equity movement is that most conceptions of the digital divide, and as a result, most programs designed to close it, are too simplistic and thus replicate the very privilege and oppression continuum they ostensibly aim to dismantle. The base goal of the digital equity movement is to contribute to the larger social justice movement by eliminating digital inequities—racism, sexism, heterosexism, classism, linguicism, ableism, imperialism, and other forms of oppression—as replicated through these electronic media.

The leaders of the digital equity movement include a wide variety of individuals and organizations spanning the world. As in any movement, those involved bring diverse lenses and priorities, some focusing on one dimension of equity (such as sexism), some specializing in a particular form of activism (such as organizing and lobbying government officials), some working in a particular sphere (such as education), and some leading grassroots efforts in a particular region or community. One of the central organizations that bridges these roles is the Digital Divide Network, providing information and points of connection for educators, activists, and policymakers committed to the digital equity movement. The Society for Information Technology and Teacher Education, a branch of the Association for the Advancement of Computers in Education, has also played a leading role in educating and organizing people to battle the digital divide. Digital Sisters, Inc., a nonprofit organization providing technology education for women and children who are traditionally underserved, has emerged as a model for anti-digital-sexism activism. The Center for Democracy & Technology provides several outlets for activism, promoting democratic values in a digital age. Meanwhile, many other organizations including some, like the American Association of University Women and the National Association for Multicultural Education, that are not focused centrally on technology, have become important advocates for the digital equity movement.

Among the many individual pioneers of the digital equity movement, several have made particularly unique and guiding contributions. Andy Carvin, coordinator of the Digital Divide Network, was an early leader of the movement and one of the first scholars to challenge narrowly defined conceptions of computer and Internet access. Cynthia D. Waddell led the fight to apply the Americans with Disabilities Act to the Internet, particularly advocating for accessible Internet content for people with disabilities and the elderly. Susan Herring, professor of Information Sciences at Indiana University, has pushed a broader vision for the gender digital divide since the early 1990s, especially with her studies of the genderization of electronic discourse. Bonnie Bracey, a George Lucas Education Foundation fellow, works as an educator, activist, and lobbyist for digital equity.

In order to highlight and address the complexities of digital inequity and to challenge prevailing shallow understandings of the digital divide, these and other scholars and activists have identified several guiding principles that drive the digital equity movement. One such principle is that we must broaden the meaning of access beyond that of physical access to, or usage rates of, computers and the Internet to include access to equitable support and encouragement to pursue and value technology-related fields, educationally and professionally. So, for example, while the digital equity movement supports the idea of having computers in every school classroom, it also insists that gender role stereotypes that discourage many girls from pursuing possible interests in technology must be eliminated in order to achieve digital equity.

Another principle of the digital equity movement is that all people must have equitably convenient access to computer technology resources (including hardware, software, wired infrastructure, and assistive technology when necessary). This principle pushes against the notion that wealthy people inherently deserve quicker and more convenient access to new technologies such as high-speed Internet access simply because they can afford them. It also challenges the idea that public computer and Internet access, such as that available in libraries and other public spaces, is comparable to computer and Internet access in the comfort of one's own home.

A third digital equity principle is grounded in research that shows that sexist, racist, heterosexist, and other oppressive dynamics observable offline are equally observable online. These dynamics, as manifested online, include the proliferation of Internet-based pornography, the abundance of white supremacist and other hate-based websites, the replication of male-dominated discussion patterns in online forums, and the prevalence of software, including computer games and educational programs, that draw on gender and racial stereotypes. According to this principle, digital equity can be realized only when all people have equitable access to inclusive, nonhostile software and Internet content.

The digital equity movement also is dedicated to the principle that all children must be exposed to new technologies in progressive, pedagogically sound ways. Like the third principle, this one is grounded in research showing that educational uses of computers and the Internet mirror the inequitable practices prevalent when these technologies are not in play. It is not enough, this principle states, to have computers and the Internet in every classroom when some teachers (predominantly those at mostly white and mostly wealthy schools) use them to encourage critical and creative thinking while others (predominantly at schools with large percentages of students of color and students in poverty) use them to replicate the skills-and-drills and lower-level-thinking activities. This means that all teachers, regardless of the schools in which they teach, must have equitable access to continuous professional development on incorporating advanced technologies into their teaching in progressive, pedagogically sound ways.

A fifth principle stipulates that all people must have access to culturally relevant, meaningful, and consumable computer and Internet content. Digital equity scholars whose work digs most deeply into this principle argue, in essence, that simply providing access to software and Internet content is inadequate when little or no relevant content exists for a given group or individual. Research has shown, for example, that online content most relevant to poor or working-class families all over the world—information about jobs, affordable shelter, and assistance programs—is largely nonexistent. Moreover, despite the fact that most Internet users are not first language English speakers, less than one third of all websites are available in languages other than English. According to the global digital equity movement, conceptions of the digital divide concerned only with whether or not individuals or groups have physical access to computers and the Internet fail to capture these crucial intricacies.

Finally, a sixth principle asserts that the inequities that exist among these and other dimensions of access, and the fact that these inequities most negatively affect people already disempowered by racism, sexism, classism, imperialism, and other forms of oppression, necessitate a collective reconsideration of the growing global importance assigned to computers and the Internet. The digital equity movement in this sense calls for a deep and complex reconsideration of the larger sociopolitical and socioeconomic ramifications of the corporation-led push for globalization and these technologies' roles in the globalization process. This principle is based on a central question: How does the growing merger of cyberculture with wider U.S. culture privilege those who already enjoy social, political, and economic access in the broadest sense?

Underlying all of these principles is an insistence that the digital divide be understood as a symptom of larger structures of inequity and injustice. By extension, any plan or program for eliminating the digital divide and achieving digital equity must be connected to and contextualized within larger movements for equity and social justice.

As the digital age spans into the 2000s and toward the 2010s, the digital equity movement continues to apply these principles, critiquing insufficient efforts to close the digital divide and constructing new initiatives to dismantle digital inequities. Meanwhile, the movement grows larger and more global each year as UNESCO and other international organizations begin to highlight, educate about, and fight digital inequities.

—Paul C. Gorski

See also Anti-Racist Teaching; Critical Literacy; Critical Pedagogy; Cyber Rights; Gender Equity Movement in Schools

Further Readings

American Association of University Women (AAUW). (2000). *Tech-savvy: Educating girls in the new computer age.* Washington, DC: AAUW Educational Foundation Research.

Blair, K., & Takayoshi, P. (Eds.). (1999). *Feminist cyberscapes: Mapping gendered academic spaces.* Stamford, CT: Ablex.

Children's Partnership. (2003). *Online content for low-income and underserved Americans.* Washington, DC: Author.

Lenhart, A. (2003). *The ever-shifting internet population: A new look at internet access and the digital divide.* Washington, DC: Pew Internet & American Life Project.

Norris, P. (2001). *Digital divide: Civic engagement, information poverty, and the internet worldwide.* Cambridge, UK: Cambridge University Press.

Solomon, G., Allen, N. J., & Resta, P. (Eds.). (2003). *Toward digital equity: Bridging the divide in education.* Boston: Allyn & Bacon.

Warschauer, M. (2004). *Technology and social inclusion: Rethinking the digital divide.* Cambridge: MIT Press.

DIRECT ACTION

A political method in which persons, without the use of power holders, representatives, professionals, or indirect institutional means, engage practically in social life and realize stated goals. With direct action you realize the intention of the action directly without asking for permission. Direct action might be secret or public, nonviolent or violent, legal or illegal, as well as against or for something. In its most unique variation it transforms the goal into its means. For example, if you want free speech in a dictatorship, you practice free speech and ignore the rules, mind-set, and culture of censorship by publicly making your opposition known—as Charta 77 and other freedom groups did under dictatorship in Eastern Europe before 1989. Or a movement, such as the Plowshares, which wishes for disarmament of nuclear weapons but live in the United States, the most nuclear armed country in the world, put into practice their own disarmament actions at military factories and bases. With hammers, bolt cutters, and other household tools they disarm (or "destroy") weapons equipment and thus enact the biblical prophecy of beating their swords into plowshares.

Thus, direct action attempts to achieve the aspired change through autonomous means, bypassing power holders. It is a kind of do-it-yourself (DIY) culture of politics in which you make wished-for changes yourself. Direct action is the direct intervention into something in society according to activists' own values, ideas, or needs, where perceived problems are directly redeemed or possibilities realized. A popular slogan among direct actionists is "If not now, when? If not you, who?"

Its opposite is *indirect action*; that is, conventional representative politics. It would be indirect to ask leaders, authorities, parents, experts, corporations, or civil servants to solve a problem for you. Direct action varies and might be practical work to create fair trade, ecological villages, direct democracy, cooperatives, or to make your own clothes. It might also be a matter of dramatic actions that confront power structures and state laws.

This tradition was developed in labor struggles and by anarchism since the 19th century (e.g., in Russia and Spain), 20th-century nonviolent movements (e.g., in India), and the anti-authoritarian movements of 1960s (e.g., the situationists in France). The concept is popular today within various radical movements (e.g., militant environmentalists in the United States, Australia, and Norway).

Both academic and activist literature often mistakenly equates the concept with civil disobedience, protest, or demonstration. Some even understand it as necessarily violent and secret. Such confusion increases by the frequent reference to, for example, anarchist assassinations of ruling elites in 19th-century Russia as a propaganda of the deed. Still, the U.S. civil rights leader Martin Luther King, Jr., used the concept regularly but preferred to add the word *nonviolent*. *Nonviolent direct action* is a common term today within various movements in the United States and United Kingdom, often simply as NVDA. An illegal and secret (and sometimes violence-prepared) direct action tradition is cultivated in diverse groups but similar DIY cultures, like the Animal Liberation Front in England, the Autonomen in Germany, and the Black Bloc in the United States.

At times direct action is treated as the opposite of symbolic action. In fact, all human actions that have meaning and are communicated are symbolic. And political actions are clearly meaningful; that is, they have a message beyond what is practically achieved. Instead, it makes more sense to speak about a stronger or weaker symbolism of certain direct actions. Then an action that really achieves its goal, here and now, becomes symbolically strong. If nothing real happens at all, political symbols become quite empty. Then they are only gestures or signs, like political badges or traffic signs. Yet, a new generation of mass-media users, such as the Ruckus Society, one of the organizers of the Battle of Seattle in 1999, transcends this old and assumed dichotomy and use, direct action to increase the political strength of their symbols.

A relevant distinction is that between protest and direct action. The protest is an appeal to authorities to change their mind, policy, or decision, similar to the complaint subjects could present at the mercy of the sovereign in old times. A protest is not a direct change of matters, decisively benefiting those concerned. To shut off the light to save electricity is a legal direct action against nuclear power, while a blockade of a construction site for a power plant would be an illegal one. On the other hand we would have an illegal protest action when a vigil is done on the construction site without directly affecting the work, while a legal demonstration against nuclear power marching to the capital, would be the typical kind of protest.

Gandhi maintained that nonviolence is a form of direct action. In his view, nonviolence is both an effective tool and a value in itself. One's actions should not be guided by short-sighted results but by the strategy of making the means of struggle as much in accordance with the goals as possible. Thus, means are not separated from goals but are *goals in-the-making,* small seeds of the tree we hope for. Goals need to be expressed through the means if they are ever to materialize. So, to Gandhi, the more our way of struggling is formed by democracy, human rights, and solidarity, the more certain it is that we will reach that goal.

If you are against a motorway, then you can close it—like Reclaim the Streets in the United Kingdom—by organizing a street-party in the middle of the road. Then you have, instantly and without any intermediary authorities, defined the road as a party site. On Saturday the 13th of July, 1996, the motorway M41 in London was turned into a gigantic electronic dance-street. Among 10,000 wild dancing participants and under huge carnival figures walking on stilts with massive skirts, some activists with jack hammers broke up the concrete and planted trees in the middle of the motorway, trees saved from the construction of the M11. The goal was realized, autonomously, there and then. Because of direct action, an environmental problem and commercial culture were turned into a free and public space of desire and became a prefiguration of a new society.

Direct action does not necessarily create sustained social change. Its immediate effects or activity might be ignored, reversed, or manipulated, if the activists are too few and vague.

Groups sometimes compensate their small numbers with higher commitment or physical techniques. The "tree hut" people in the United Kingdom climb up in log-threatened trees, build small huts in the branches and connect them to a village with rope-bridges—and stay for months. Other activists might delay construction of a road by chaining themselves to machines or by blocking the road with "tri-pods," (i.e., high platforms on which they sit, making it more difficult to remove them).

Still, the uniqueness of direct action is when the action is a goal in itself—directly *goal-revealing*—or rather when the action embodies, materializes, and realizes directly a value that is valuable in and by itself (what Max Weber described as value rationality). The action is oriented toward values that are intrinsically valuable, not distant goals in a classic understanding of means only valuable to reach an end (goal rationality). A house occupation has a value in itself for homeless—despite other potential consequences, positive as well as negative—which doesn't need external involvement to be fulfilled. Direct action is, therefore, primarily a matter of the self-realization of actors' internally legitimated values. However, the action might be used before, after, or parallel to dialogue, and as a tool to bring an issue to the political agenda and to create increased communication and understanding between parties. For example, when fair-trade activists create projects of actual fair trade, they also make their political demands more visible and attractive for others. This is more difficult for a direct action that stops something in society, is illegal, secret and encompasses a value that is not widely shared by others.

In a direct action you basically act as if you have the right to solve a common problem by yourself, as if legitimate decision makers or equal opponents did not exist. Direct action can thus be anti-democratic if activists avoid communication with others, such as by the use of secrecy and violence. The democratic problem with activists' secret identities is not that they avoid identification by the police (that is a legal problem) but that they undermine democracy by blocking open and critical dialogue. Still, direct action groups are seldom that strong but have to, in the end, also rely on the indirect tool of deliberative democracy.

—*Stellan Vinthagen*

See also Anarchism; Earth First; Libertarians; Performativity; Praxis; Strategies and Tactics in Social Movements; Virtual Sit-Ins

Further Readings

Epstein, B. (2002). The politics of prefigurative community: The non-violent direct action movement. In S. Duncombe (Ed.), *Cultural resistance reader* (pp. 333–346). New York: W. W. Norton.

Knabb, K. (Ed.) (1995). *Situationist international: Anthology.* Berkeley, CA: Bureau of Public Secrets.

Wall, D. (1999). *Earth first! and the anti-roads movement— Radical environmentalism and comparative social movements.* London: Routledge.

DISABILITY RIGHTS MOVEMENT

For many people, the disability movement began in the 1990s, due mostly to the Americans with Disabilities Act (ADA). They are wrong. For others, mostly those who are disabled, the disability movement began in the 1970s. They, too, are wrong. The disability movement began around the middle of the 19th century, gaining impetus after the American Civil War, from which many people returned with disabilities. The effects of rampant industrialization, though, first brought the disabled into the public arena. Since then, society has tried to keep the disabled out of the limelight and in their place. What is their place?

Definitions

There are many different definitions depending on what one is looking at. Over the years, especially since the 1960s, organizations have made adjustments to what they would consider disability. But these definitions have little to do with why there has been activism by people with disabilities. The disabled

have, throughout history, fought against exclusion and prejudice.

Most every nondisabled person will eventually become disabled, probably due to illness or disease, though accident cannot be ignored. At this writing, it is estimated that, at around 54 million, the disabled make up the largest single minority in America. But this number—approximately 20% of the population—is misleading; 54 million is only the number of disabled who are capable of working but are disallowed. Many people with disabilities are working. There are some who don't work and others who can't, mostly children. Many are retired; others have a disability but don't consider themselves disabled. So the number of disabled is somewhat greater than this figure. Yet, in the end, what is normal raises a big question.

Social Stigma

The definition of disability within society goes far deeper than numbers or looks, behavior or physical ability. The definition of disability includes social perceptions—bias and prejudice. These ideas stem from ignorance and fear, according to the literature. Within the public sector, a disabled person is someone who can't function like—and looks different from— the norm. The majority considers itself normal. Because people with disabilities can't do what normal people can in the same way, they are considered inferior or deficient.

People with disabilities are beggars and indigents. The disabled are objects of shame, pity, and ridicule. As such, they should be kept out of sight. Incarcerated, institutionalized, euthanized, prevented from being born, forbidden to marry, sterilized; some of these historical solutions are still practiced. Some children with disabilities are still forbidden schooling. The general population sees disability as a deficit in the individual that is in need of fixing; that is, these people need to be normalized. Many of these images hold even when society has caused the disability, such as due to war or workplace accident. Many of these images are medieval.

More than the physical barriers that keep people with disabilities from living a normal, full life, it is these social attitudinal barriers that are the greatest hurdle to enjoying a good life and that need to be overcome, while the nondisabled enjoy a better or more productive life because of accommodations for the disabled: automatic doors, telephones, typewriters, American football's huddle, the umpires' hand signals in baseball.

History: 19th Century

In 1817 the first permanent school for children with disabilities in the West was cofounded by Thomas Hopkins Gallaudet: the American School for the Deaf. Despite the American Civil War, not much more was accomplished in the way of help for the disabled or their integration into society at large. Yet, the period from 1880 to 1930 was a time of major redefinition via policies and laws and medicine; however, isolating institutions remained the accepted way of dealing with disabilities. While offering more support and training than before, these institutions still took people with disabilities out of the public eye.

Early 20th Century

In 1920 the American Foundation for the Blind was organized and was subsequently supported by Helen Keller. Then, it was a clearinghouse for information and advocacy; now it is a publishing house. In the years leading up to 1920, Keller protested against labor practices and, as a result of her work and the work of others, child labor laws were enacted. It was hoped that, in doing so, disabilities could be prevented. Other laws sought to hold companies responsible for accidents that disabled workers.

The first vocational rehabilitation acts were passed in the 1920s to provide services for the many World War I veterans who were disabled. But the passage of these laws was the result of years of protesting and fighting for both recognition and rights within society. The League of the Physically Handicapped was formed during the Depression in response to the government's anti-disability policies. In 1940 the single most politically powerful organization for the disabled was founded: The National Federation of the

Blind. It was staffed by blind people. In the 1950s, concerned parents began to organize around developmental disability, leading to the founding of the National Association for Retarded Children (now, ARC, Association for Retarded Children) and the United Cerebral Palsy Association.

Late 20th Century

Although the spinal cord injured, those with polio, and psychiatrically disabled began to assert their rights in the 1960s, it was not until the 1970s that the disabled burst their bubble of marginalization and appeared ready for action on the public stage—and would not go away. Perhaps the most important people were Ed Roberts, who founded the first independent living organization in Berkeley, California, in 1972, a movement that has spread over the United States with more than 400 such centers today; and Judy Neumann, who organized Disabled in Action in New York City. Both began with protests over education, Judy winning the first disability-based employment discrimination case in New York City. Both went on to found the World Institute on Disability in 1983. By this time, Justin Dart had entered the fray, eventually becoming known as the "Father of the ADA."

This more recent and far-reaching disability movement took its inspiration from the civil rights movement of the 1960s. Perhaps the most aggressive and effective organization for social change is the American Disabled for Attendant Programs Today (ADAPT), originally organized as the American Disabled for Accessible Public Transit in Denver. Its first action was a demonstration against the Denver transit system in 1978, disabling the running of buses for 24 hours. This action led to further such demonstrations that resulted in national legislation making buses accessible to those people with mobility impairments, including wheelchair users. ADAPT remains an aggressive civil disobedience organization, often relying on the bad press associated with police overzealousness and arrests of people who cannot walk or use their upper extremities.

The Rehabilitation Act of 1973—especially Section 504 that prohibits discrimination in federal programs and services, as well as entities that receive federal funding, mandating removal of architectural barriers—was an important advancement for the movement. Coupled with the 1975 Education of All Handicapped Children Act (now IDEA: Individuals with Disabilities Education Act) and ADAPT's success, these were the most significant legal strides made in the 1970s for inclusion.

In 1985, the Mental Illness Bill of Rights Act, which required protection and advocacy for people with mental illness, was passed after a nearly decade-long battle by parents and families to override and control the abuse that passed for treatment. The Fair Housing Amendments of 1988 forbade discrimination by landlords against the disabled population and their service or companion animals. This was significant in the fight for deinstitutionalization and integration.

All of these piecemeal victories, gained after considerable grassroots activism, led to the signing of the ADA in 1990. Although this act provided broad legal protection everywhere in society, in public or private places, businesses and states have sometimes fought to limit and undermine the various entitlements for a variety of reasons, especially as relates to any kind or compensation for discrimination in employment (as mandated in Title I of the ADA). It is paradoxical that these entities admit the discrimination but claim there is no legal basis for compensation. For the most part, to date they have won the day. Grassroots activism may be effective, especially within the community, but government regulations are not. It is solely by grassroots activism that the government has seen to pass laws. But government regulations—laws—are fought tooth-and-nail as an imposition on the status quo.

Throughout this movement to inclusion, there had been many others who, both in and out of government, have worked assiduously for change, though sometimes not gaining public notice. These people include Frederick A. Fay, who pioneered use of assistance technology and convinced Hertz to provide hand controls in its cars—the first car company to do so. Tim Nugent was the founder of the first disabled student organization in 1947 and the National Wheelchair Basketball Association, while developing self-care techniques for the spinal cord injured and the first

hydraulic lift for buses. Mary Elizabeth Switzer exerted more influence on the upgrading of life for the disabled than anyone else between 1950 and 1969, as head of the Office of Vocational Rehabilitation (now Office of Vocational Rehabilitation). In 1967, she moved to the administration of Social and Rehabilitation Services at Health Education and Welfare.

Thus, despite advancements, the disability movement is still fighting for recognition and civil citizenship status for millions of stigmatized people with disabilities. Legal barriers have been overcome in many instances; attitudinal barriers—prejudice—are not so easily abridged.

—James L. Secor

See also Civil Rights Acts; Civil Rights Movement; Disability Studies; Keller, Helen

Further Readings

Charlton, J. I. (1998). *Nothing about us without us: Disability oppression and empowerment.* Berkeley: University of California Press.

Johnson, M. (2000). *Make them go away: Clint Eastwood, Christopher Reeve and the case against disability rights.* Louisville, KY: Avocado Press.

Longmore, P., & Umansky, L. (Eds.). (2001). *The new disability history: American perspectives.* New York: New York University Press.

Pelka, F. (1997). *ABC-CLIO companion to the disability rights movement.* Santa Barbara, CA: ABC-CLIO.

Shapiro, J. P. (1994). *No pity: People with disabilities forging a new civil rights movement.* New York: Three Rivers Press.

DISABILITY STUDIES

Disability studies is an interdisciplinary area of study, based in the humanities and social sciences, that views disability in cultural, social, and political terms, rather than through the lens of biology or psychology. In these latter disciplines, the primary way of conceptualizing "disability" is typically connected to some form of deficit or measuring distance from the "norm" for purposes of intervention, remediation, and bringing one closer to the established norm. Disability studies challenges this singular view of the construct of disability and aims to present a variety of perspectives on disability, both in contemporary society as well as those from a range of cultures and histories. One goal of disability studies is to challenge the idea of the normal/abnormal binary and to suggest and show that a range of human variation is "normal."

Like African American studies, women's studies, and Latino/a studies in the universities, which were outgrowths of the civil rights and women's movements, disability studies has roots in the disability rights movement (DRM). In the United States, the DRM helped pass legislation relating to the civil rights of individuals with regard to employment (Rehabilitation Act of 1973; Americans with Disabilities Act, 1990), education (Education for All Handicapped Children Act, PL 94–142, 1975), and accessible transportation. The Society for Disability Studies (SDS) was started in 1982 by a group of academics led by Irving Zola. The original name was Section for the Study of Chronic Illness, Impairment, and Disability (SSCIID), part of the Western Social Science Association.

In the United Kingdom, the Union of the Physically Impaired Against Segregation (UPIAS), formed in 1972, was instrumental in politicizing disability. Mike Oliver, a disabled sociologist, wrote the *Politics of Disablement* in 1990, in which he analyzed how a social issue such as disability gets cast as an individual medicalized phenomenon.

While the political movements led social scientists to explorations of disability, the arts and humanities have also taken up the study of disability. The interdisciplinarity that characterizes disability studies allows for a variety of methodologies and approaches to be applied to the study of disability. Some of these include narratives of disability; analysis of representations of disability (in literature, the arts, the law, media); challenging the absence of disabled researchers in the academy; writing or rewriting histories of disability; creating visual art, performance, and poetry that highlights the experiences of disabled people in a world built for the nondisabled; analysis of the social organization of space that excludes people with disabilities; philosophies of justice that speak directly to the interests of the disabled; and narratives and analyses of the experience of living with a disability and how this intersects with race, class, and gender status markers.

More recently, in 2000, Disability Studies in Education has been organized as a Special Interest Group (SIG) of The American Educational Research Association (AERA) as a critique of the segregation, low expectations, poor outcomes, disproportionate classification of students of color, and positivist epistemology that characterizes special education in the United States. The goal of disability studies in any arena is to broaden the understanding of disability, to better understand the experience of disability in society, and to contribute to social change for people with disabilities.

—*Nancy E. Rice*

See also Disability Rights Movement

Further Readings

Albrecht, G., Seelman, K., & Bury, M. (Eds.). (2001). *Handbook of disability studies.* Thousand Oaks, CA: Sage.

Davis, L. (Ed.). (1997). *Disability studies reader.* New York: Routledge.

Gabel, S. (Ed.). (2005). *Disability studies in education: Readings in theory and method.* New York: Peter Lang.

Oliver, M. (1990). *The politics of disablement: A sociological approach.* Basingstoke, UK: Macmillan.

DISSENT

Dissent came into English in the late 16th century as both a general term meaning disagreement in outlook or sentiment and as a specific term meaning difference of opinion in regard to religious doctrine or worship. With both meanings, dissent signified the opposite of consent or assent. Important correlatives threading through the centuries astride dissent include protest, nonconformity, and collectivity.

Dissent is contentious, adversarial, nonconformist political thought and activity that contests, opposes, or transgresses entrenched, commonly expressed ideas, rules, topics, and norms of public interaction and deliberation. Dissent by definition is conflictual. Amid the throes of conflict, dissident citizens and groups often present significant challenges to the social order. Yet for dissident citizens, conflict is not an end; rather, it is a means toward public learning and possibly even the creation of newfound consensus.

Dissident citizens and groups meet the following three criteria: (1) They publicly contest prevailing structures of power and/or the underlying logic of public policy, (2) they engage in some extra-institutional, oppositional tactics, though they may be flexible actors that employ forms of action both inside and outside the institutional pathways of political power, and (3) on at least some issues, they have marginal stances that are not consistently entering the dominant political discourse.

While in its most general sense, the term *dissent* indicates the rejection of commonly held views or disagreement with the ideas, opinions, and views of the majority (e.g., a dissenting opinion in the judicial context: when at least one judge disagrees with the majority decision), dissent goes beyond disagreement or withholding assent. Dissent is a calibration more active than disagreement. Dissident citizens therefore not only disagree with predominant—or even hegemonic—political ideas of their time, but also take action to change their sociopolitical environment. In other words, dissent is the collective mechanism for initiating social change.

As such, dissent involves both a dedication to autonomous thinking as well as a willingness to act on behalf of nonconformist principles, ideas, and ideals. Dissident citizens disregard the resilient, pervasive social pressures to conform not only their thinking, but also their behavior. They often work for causes bigger than themselves, actively pushing to meet the goals and aims of these causes. Practitioners of dissent disagree with and actively oppose official, dominant, or hegemonic doctrines and explicitly express political difference with received ideas in an attempt to widen the path of freedom and improve the vibrancy of civil society.

Dissenting citizens remain outside of much democratic theory that focuses on deliberative democracy and discourse. Dissidents move beyond the activity of deliberative citizens who participate in contained politics within the institutional structures of democracy. Dissident citizens—who see the deliberative role, regardless of how critical it may be, as merely a starting point, rather than an end in itself—engage in transgressive contention using innovative political action that is either unprecedented or prohibited. They take direct action against what they see as problematic political policies, practices, and procedures. They move vigorously against taken-for-granted hegemonic ideas, ideals, and institutions.

Rather than rely on voting, petitioning, and letter writing, dissident citizens create a variety of unconventional public spaces and events—such as protest marches, picket lines, worker strikes, consumer boycotts, and street theater—on the margins and in the fractures of the polity. Dissident citizens can come from anywhere on the political spectrum, but they share a propensity to engage in alternative forms of political engagement that are democratic, innovative, and oppositional.

Dissident citizens do not move beyond the realm of the deliberative, sanctioned public sphere merely for fun. In fact, they view the public sphere as problematic in that the seemingly benign call for cool-headed deliberation can actually be used as an instrument to dictate the terms of discourse that tend to dismiss subordinate, dissident groups. In stratified societies where social inequality exists, it can be very difficult to carve out distinct discursive spaces that allow dissidents to extricate themselves from the repercussions of these social inequalities, because deliberative procedures and processes in the public sphere tend to transpire to the advantage of dominant groups and to the disadvantage of subordinate or subaltern groups. Dissent places checks on the exclusionary nature of consensus-building procedures that are central in deliberative democracy in the public sphere.

In reality, the public sphere is animated by a bedrock contradiction. In order to forge policies that can enhance the freedom, liberty, and autonomy of all citizens, the general public relies on deliberative procedures and practices that exclude many individuals and groups as well as their ideas, interests, and grievances. This chasm between democratic principle and on-the-ground democratic practice leads dissident citizens to forge alternative modes of participation. Rather than relenting to the illusory consensus-based conception of a monolithic, unitary "we," members of historically subordinated groups—like women, racial minorities, gays and lesbians, and workers—form alternative spaces of dissent where they are able to process, adapt, and reformulate their ideas, strategies, and tactics. These zones of dissent provide safe intellectual arenas from which alternative discourses can be catapulted into the mainstream public sphere, thereby widening democracy.

While there are renegade dissident citizens who practice dissent alone (the Unabomber, for example), most work within social movements: concerted, sustained collectivities with common goals and purposes that are buoyed by solidarity and camaraderie as they engage in fractious relations with adversaries, elites, and people in positions of authority.

When faced with vigorous, organized dissident social movements, the state has four options for its response: (1) suppression, (2) mollification, (3) co-optation, or (4) ignoring these movements for change. The state's efforts to suppress dissent, which are meant to discourage such organized contention and prevent it from widening, are a common reaction. Going back centuries, the state's suppression of dissent has occurred in countries across the globe. In fact, the state's propensity to resort to the suppression of dissent has been established both qualitatively and quantitatively by social scientists across time and place. During this time, a variety of dissident citizens and movements from numerous countries have experienced significant and sustained suppression, from Soviet dissidents like writer Andrey Sinyavsky to Chinese dissidents in Tiananmen Square, from African dissidents such as Congolese political leader Patrice Lumumba to U.S. dissidents such as Fred Hampton of the Black Panther Party.

Despite the state's consistent—and sometimes vicious—efforts to suppress the endeavors of dissident citizens, political dissent functions as society's safety valve, a pressure release. If dissidents are not allowed to publicly register their ideas and opinions, they are more likely to resort to violent forms of expression. In fact, by effectively plugging this safety valve, thereby preventing the release of pent-up political pressure, the state may well encourage violent dissent. Such an equation harkens U.S. President John F. Kennedy's admonition that those who stultify peaceful change make violent revolution more of a possibility. In extant democracy, countries are more likely to thrive socially and economically if they embrace dissent and support transparency. By definition, dissident citizens widen the social dialogue, and well-functioning societies benefit from thickened discourse writhing with variegated ideas and opinions.

Dissenting citizens not only speak to perceived dangers and problems in society, but they also speak to the opportunities and possibilities of vigorous political life. Dissidents challenge the axiomatic, taken-for-granted "realities" of prevailing societal discourse(s), as they question the silences, omissions, and limitations of these dominant social constructions. In historical hindsight, dissident citizens are often held up as national heroes. Certainly this is the case in the United States, from Sam Adams and his revolutionary comrades to Frederick Douglass and the slavery abolitionists, from Susan B. Anthony to Martin Luther King, Jr. It is difficult to deny the importance of these dissidents in U.S. history; they are held up as model U.S. Americans precisely because their dissident philosophies strongly challenged the prevailing social discourse of the time, as well as because of their persistent commitment in the face of risk, fear, and sometimes even danger.

As previously mentioned, the term *dissent* has religious roots. Dissent with a capital D designates those who actively opposed the hegemony of the Church of England in the 17th century. These Dissenters were members of Protestant denominations—primarily the Baptists, Presbyterians, Quakers, and the Independents (who later were dubbed Congregationalists)—who eventually combined to overthrow King Charles I before setting up the English Commonwealth.

With the rise of U.S. President George W. Bush, one of the most explicitly religious presidents in U.S. history (he has claimed he believes God wants him to be president), who has enjoyed the fervent support of the Christian Right, this more specific definition of dissent—disagreement with the form of religious worship that prevails or is authoritatively established—may be in line for a comeback. Bush's prayer for the vim and vigor to do the Lord's will in Iraq may engender a new wave of politico-religious dissent to match the fervor of the English Dissidents of previous times.

More commonly acknowledged practitioners of dissent from the contemporary era include Vandana Shiva, Edward Said, Njoki Njoroge Njehu, Oscar Olivera, Leslie Cagan, Nelson Mandela, Cornel West, Noam Chomsky, Robin Hahnel, Amy Goodman, José Bové, Aung San Suu Kyi, Arundhati Roy, Angela Y. Davis, Juan Gonzalez, and Wangari Maathai.

—Jules Boykoff

See also Activism, Social and Political; Battle of Seattle; Bové, José; Campus Antiwar Network; Chicano Movement; Christian Right; Civil Rights Movement; Davis, Angela; Direct Action; Earth First!; Environmental Movement; Government Suppression of Social Activism; Living Wage Movement; Maathai, Wangari; Mandela, Nelson; Nonviolence and Activism; Poor People's Campaign; Resistance; Roy, Arundhati; Said, Edward; Social Movements, Sociology of; Soviet Dissidents; Strategies and Tactics in Social Movements; Suu Kyi, Aung San; Tiananmen Square; Union Movements; Voices in the Wilderness; Welfare Rights Movement; West, Cornel; Women's International League for Peace and Freedom; Women's Suffrage Movement; Youth Organizing and Activism

Further Readings

Benhabib, S. (Ed.). (1996). *Democracy and difference: Contesting the boundaries of the political.* Princeton, NJ: Princeton University Press.

Boykoff, J. (2006). *The suppression of dissent: How the state and mass media squelch USAmerican social movements.* New York: Routledge.

Elster, J. (Ed.). (1998). *Deliberative democracy.* New York: Cambridge University Press.

Fraser, N. (1992). Rethinking the public sphere: A contribution to the critique of actually existing democracy. In C. Calhoun (Ed.), *Habermas and the public sphere* (pp. 109–142). Cambridge: MIT Press.

Sparks, H. (1997). Dissident citizenship: Democratic theory, political courage, and activist women. *Hypatia, 12,* 74–110.

Sunstein, C. (2003). *Why societies need dissent.* Cambridge, MA: Harvard University Press.

Tarrow, S. (1998). *Power in movement: Social movements and contentious politics* (2nd ed.). New York: Cambridge University Press.

DISSENT MAGAZINE

Perhaps the most important voice of social democratic thought in the United States, *Dissent* was the brainchild of Irving Howe, Stanley Plastrik, and Manny Geltman. First published in 1954, *Dissent* sought to provide an option between conventional liberal journals and the more doctrinaire, and outdated, organs of the old intellectual Left. Throughout the 1950s and 1960s, *Dissent* combined a steadfast anti-communist foreign policy with a commitment to domestic social and economic justice. *Dissent* was a passionate voice of opposition to the increased conservatism in American government in the latter 20th century, especially during the years of the Ronald Reagan presidency.

Howe was the primary force behind *Dissent* from its birth until his death in 1993. Howe wanted *Dissent* to provide a voice for genuine third-path democratic socialism. Virtually alone among the organs of ex-independent leftists, like *The Partisan Review, Encounter,* and *Commentary, Dissent* continued to concentrate on issues of labor and work. Throughout the late 1950s and 1960s, *Dissent* published articles on work and unions by such writers as Paul Jacobs, Frank Marquart, Harvey Swados, and Brendan Sexton. In the 1980s and 1990s *Dissent* continued to cover organized labor's declining fortunes. *Dissent* responded to and supported the mainstream civil rights movement from its beginnings.

Dissent was generally supportive of the student activism of the 1960s, but the attempts of Howe and others in the *Dissent* circle to engage many New Leftists often proved disastrous. Howe was leery of what he thought was a tolerance for authoritarianism among groups like the Students for a Democratic Society and his, at times, biting criticism hurt efforts to fuse a positive working relationship with the increasingly radical New Left as the decade wore on.

Howe and *Dissent* were criticized at times for not advocating unilateral withdrawal from Vietnam during the 1960s, but *Dissent* was still fiercely critical of American policy in Southeast Asia during the 1960s and early 1970s. *Dissent* remained sharply critical of American foreign policy in general throughout the 1970s and 1980s. The journal eventually moved from a more pointed democratic socialist perspective to a position of representing the left-liberal wing of the Democratic Party. *Dissent* was modestly optimistic following the election of Bill Clinton to the presidency in 1992. Academics and former New Leftists like Michael Kazin and Todd Gitlin became contributors.

Key to Howe's vision of *Dissent* was the preservation of intellectual and political freedom. *Dissent* has remained to the left of the Democratic Party, but has never strayed from its anti-communist and anti-totalitarian roots.

—*Gregory Geddes*

See also Democratic Socialism; Harrington, Michael; Rustin, Bayard; Trotskyism

Further Readings

Howe, I. (Ed.). (1967). *The radical imagination: An anthology from* Dissent *magazine.* New York: New American Library.

Howe, I. (1982). *A margin of hope.* New York: Harcourt Brace Jovanovich.

Sorin, G. (2002). *Irving Howe: A life of passionate dissent.* New York: New York University Press.

Wald, A. (1987). *The New York intellectuals: The rise and decline of the anti-Stalinist left from the 1930s to the 1980s.* Chapel Hill: University of North Carolina Press.

Walzer, M., & Mills, N. (2004). *50 years of dissent.* New Haven, CT: Yale University Press.

DIVESTMENT

See BOYCOTTS AND DIVESTMENT

DJILAS, MILOVAN (1911–1995)

Milovan Djilas was a Yugoslav politician, activist, and dissident writer. He became known for his daring critique of Tito's communism and for his innovative analysis of the communist bureaucracy. Djilas was born in Podbišće (Montenegro) to a peasant family. He studied law and literature in Belgrade, though he never completed his studies due to his engagement in the communist movement and his imprisonment for anti-royalist activities. Acquainted with Josip Broz Tito, who from 1937 headed the Yugoslavian Communist Party, Djilas joined the Central Committee in 1937 and the Politburo in 1940. He was actively involved in the resistance movement against the Nazi occupation and in the War of National Liberation. He headed the diplomatic mission to the Soviet Union and personally met Stalin, which he later detailed in his book *Conversations with Stalin.* In 1945 he became the Minister for Montenegro in the Yugoslav Government of National Unity; in 1948 he became the head of the Propaganda Department (Agitprop), and in 1953, he became vice president of the Yugoslav Republic. In 1950, together with Edvard Kardelj and Boris Kidrić, he formulated the doctrine of "worker's self-management" and advocated policies of economic decentralization.

Djilas expressed his views about Yugoslav communism in the newspapers *Borba, Nova Jugoslavija,* and *Nova Misao.* His democratic-socialist criticism of the undemocratic and centralizing reforms, as well as the authoritarian leadership style of the party, brought him in direct conflict with Tito. As a result, Djilas was denigrated at the Third Party Plenum in 1954 and removed from the government. Djilas subsequently resigned his party membership.

After an interview with the *New York Times* in 1955, Djilas was tried for spreading anti-state propaganda. He was imprisoned in 1956 for his support of the Hungarian Uprising and remained in prison for the next decade because of the publications abroad of the *New Class: An Analysis of the Communist System* of 1957 and *Conversations with Stalin* of 1962. In the *New Class,* Djilas argued that Soviet-style communism failed to realize the egalitarian claim of Marxism and instead facilitated the emergence of a privileged social stratum of party bureaucrats. As a result, the communist societies were devoid of the bonds of solidarity and comradeship. Commentators on the *New Class* have also emphasized that while it was written from the perspective of revisionist Marxism, it also signified Djilas's initial doubts regarding the accuracy of Marx's dogma of historical materialism.

During his imprisonment Djilas continued his literary activities; writing novels, political essays, a memoir titled *Land Without Justice* (1958), and a translation of Milton's *Paradise Lost* into Serbo-Croatian. When he was released from prison, Djilas continued his dissident writings while being subject to state persecution in the form of a travel and publication ban. In 1980, Djilas wrote Tito's biography, *Tito: The Story from Inside,* which was published abroad.

Djilas was officially rehabilitated in 1989. In postcommunist Yugoslavia, he opposed the Serbian nationalist politics of Milošević's era. He died in Belgrade on April 20, 1995.

—Magdalena Zolkos

See also Communism; Democratic Socialism; Dissent; Lenin, V. I.; Literature and Activism; Marxist Theory; Socialism

Further Readings

Clissold, S. (1983). *Djilas: The progress of a revolutionary.* Middlesex, UK: Maurice Temple Smith.
Reinhartz, D. (1981). *Milovan Djilas.* Boulder, CO: East European Monographs.

DOCTORS WITHOUT BORDERS

Doctors Without Borders (Médecins Sans Frontières) is an international medical and non-governmental organization that provides emergency assistance to individuals in more than 70 countries. Founded in France in 1971 by a group of doctors and journalists to address the famine in Biafra, Nigeria, this humanitarian organization continues to deliver emergency aid to areas of the world torn apart by armed violence, epidemic illness, inadequate health care systems, and disasters (natural and human-made). The health care workers in this organization include physicians, nurses, strategic planners, experts in water and sanitation, administrators, and other nonmedical staff. When intervening after an emergency, the Doctors Without Borders teams work closely with staff that they hire locally to provide the medical relief that is most effective and necessary.

This organization has provided relief in numerous armed conflicts, including the civil wars in Sri Lanka, Liberia, Somalia, Burundi, the Republic of Congo, and Sierra Leone. Doctors Without Borders has also intervened in war situations in Cambodia, Lebanon, the Soviet invasion of Afghanistan, Central America, the Kurdish refugees in northern Iraq, Bosnia, the genocide in Rwanda, the Srebenica massacre, the second war in Chechnya, the U.S.-led coalition invasion of Afghanistan, the U.S. invasion of Iraq, and fighting in the Liberian capital. Their work addressing famine relief includes countries such as Ethiopia, Somalia, North Korea, Southern Sudan, and Angola. In addition, the organization addresses widespread illness in countries, treating infectious diseases such as the epidemics of HIV/AIDS, tuberculosis, meningitis, and malaria in Africa. Regardless of the sociopolitical context of the crisis in a country, the organization methodically assesses the needs of the people in the country that requires assistance. Doctors Without Borders clearly communicates that their mission does not involve partisan politics. Rather, the decision they make about whether to

Throughout Sierra Leone, amputee communities exist and are in urgent need of help since the government does not provide assistance. Amputee communities depend on relief efforts from numerous international organizations. Doctors Without Borders works closely with NGOs such as Global Action Foundation to provide medical services.

Source: Photo by John Daniel Kelly/Global Action Foundation, http://www.go-act.org.

intervene in a country is based on their assessment of the specific needs of the individuals in that country.

Doctors Without Borders is internationally recognized for its rapid response to emergency situations around the globe. The medical teams arrive in countries requiring medical aid fully provisioned with the medical protocols and supplies needed to immediately begin saving lives. Supporting their efforts is their strategic organization of needed medical supplies. For instance, Doctors Without Borders have medical equipment and kits that are specially prepared and prepackaged to treat cholera. Therefore, when a cholera outbreak occurs, they can immediately provide the necessary medical assistance. Due to their effectiveness, the tools and organizing skills that the organization uses as a model of intervention have been replicated by numerous other international relief organizations.

The Doctors Without Borders teams typically work 6 to 12 months when responding to a crisis situation. The expenses that are incurred during assignments are covered by the organization, and sometimes a small stipend is provided as well. Recently, the organization has taken on an advocacy role based on the knowledge garnered from their interventions. For instance, Doctors Without Borders is highlighting the cost-prohibitive challenges of drug prices, the need for research of alternative treatments of illness, and the trade barriers that exist in accessing effective and necessary medical treatment.

—Anneliese Singh

See also Genocide Watch; Human Rights Watch; Non-Governmental Organizations (NGOs)

Further Readings

Leyton, E., & Locke, G. (1998). *Touched by fire: Doctors without borders in a third world crisis.* Toronto: McClelland & Stewart.

Suen, A. (2002). *Doctors without borders.* New York: Rosen.

DORFMAN, ARIEL
(1942–)

Ariel Dorfman is a playwright, essayist, fiction writer, and human rights activist. Born to a Jewish family in Argentina, his family moved from the United States to Chile in 1954, where he would eventually both attend and teach at the University of Chile in Santiago. From 1970 to 1973, Dorfman was a member of the administration of President Salvador Allende, a socialist physician whom the American government had actively opposed. On September 11, 1973, Allende's democratically elected government was violently overthrown in a military coup that put the infamous dictator General Augusto Pinochet in power. Dorfman was forced into exile, living and writing in the United States until the restoration of Chilean democracy began in 1990. Since 1985, he has taught at Duke University in Durham, North Carolina, where he is currently Walter Hines Page Research Professor of Literature and Professor of Latin American Studies.

His play *Death and the Maiden,* perhaps his best-known work, was completed in Chile in the early 1990s as he observed his country's painful transition from authoritarianism to democracy. The politically charged play follows Paulina Salas, a former political prisoner in an unnamed Latin American country, whose husband unknowingly brings home the man she believes to have tortured and raped her more than 20 years before. It is a drama rooted in Chile's particular human rights crisis, yet the lyrical power of Dorfman's writing has made the play a touchstone for exploring similar issues around the world. It has been staged in more than 30 countries; Germany alone had 50 productions running simultaneously in 1993. In 1994 the play was adapted for film, starring Sigourney Weaver and Ben Kingsley, directed by Roman Polanski; one part of Dorfman's "Resistance Trilogy" with *Reader* and the novel *Widows.* Author of the novels *Blake's Remedy, The Nanny and the Iceberg,* and *Konfidenz,* Dorfman can be counted as part of the vibrant politically engaged Latin American literary tradition of Pablo Neruda and Gabriel García Márquez.

Dorfman has been a dedicated public intellectual and prolific commentator on issues related to Latin American politics, American cultural hegemony, war, and human rights, for the *Los Angeles Times, Washington Post, El País, Granta,* and *Le Monde.* He has also worked with organizations such as Amnesty International, Index on Censorship, and Human

Rights Watch. He used his firsthand experience of pre-Pinochet Chile, a functioning democracy with an independent press and judiciary and a military under civilian control, and its sudden end, as a platform for impassioned response to the attacks of September 11, 2001, in essays such as "Americans Must Now Feel What the Rest of Us Have Known" and "Chile: The Other September 11." Dorfman now divides his time between the United States and Santiago.

—Brook Willensky-Lanford

See also Allende, Salvador; CIA Repression of Social Movements; Human Rights Watch; Literature and Activism; Neruda, Pablo; Socialism

Further Readings

Dorfman, A. (1998). *Heading south, looking north: A bilingual journey.* New York: Farrar, Straus & Giroux.

Dorfman, A. (2002). *Exorcising terror: The incredible on-going trial of General Augusto Pinochet.* New York: Seven Stories Press.

DOUGLAS, MARJORY STONEMAN (1890–1998)

Marjory Stoneman Douglas dedicated decades of her 108-year life to various social and environmental causes. She is most often remembered as the Protector of the Everglades. As a columnist, a short story writer, a novelist, and a social and environmentalist activist, Douglas was a force to be reckoned with in Florida because of her ability to garner attention and support from the public and the media.

Douglas was born in Minneapolis on April 7, 1890. She graduated from Wellesley College in 1912 and moved to Miami in 1915 to join her father, Frank Bryant Stoneman, a founder of the *Miami Herald.* Douglas soon became a member of the Florida Equal Suffrage Association and joined a group of women who failed to convince Florida's legislature to ratify the Nineteenth Amendment. Desiring an altruistic way to assist the war effort in Europe during World War I, Douglas volunteered with the Red Cross. She was assigned to the civilian relief department in Paris.

Douglas stayed on after the Armistice in order to help coordinate and publicize refugee relief efforts in the Balkans and other war-torn regions.

Following her return from Europe, Douglas began writing a column for the *Miami Herald.* She promoted women's rights and criticized Miami's housing boom. Two of her greatest achievements as a columnist included establishing the first charity not run by a church in Miami, which was a baby milk fund for the city's impoverished, and generating enough public outcry about the death of a young prisoner that the state legislature abolished the leasing and corporal punishment of convicts. Foreshadowing her work as an environmentalist, some of her columns included artful poems about the Everglades' subtle beauty in response to the descriptions of rapacious developers who characterized it as useless muck.

Douglas's championing of the Everglades continued when she became a professional short story writer. Between 1920 and 1943 she published more than 75 stories, mostly for the *Saturday Evening Post.* Douglas craftily used her enjoyable stories to explore progressive issues such as the New Woman, and to discuss the exploitation of nature by developers, as well as the role of duplicitous real estate agents in Florida's land boom. The unmistakable strength and independence of her often single female protagonists were as strong a model for female readers as any of Willa Cather's pioneering women.

Douglas was instrumental in the establishment of the Everglades National Park. A few weeks before the park's establishment in 1947, Douglas published *Everglades: River of Grass,* which was the first aesthetically pleasing text to describe how the Everglades are a complex and fragile ecosystem. The bestselling book catapulted her to fame, particularly in Florida, where she became the go-to person for queries about the Everglades. Following this success, Douglas used her fame for such issues as persuading Miami's water company to extend services to impoverished, mostly black neighborhoods and founding the first American Civil Liberties Union chapter south of the Mason-Dixon line, in 1955.

Decades later, as Douglas approached her 80s; she became the bonafide leader of the area's environmental movement when she founded the Friends of the

Everglades in 1969. Even as a centegenerian, Douglas's public persona as the tiny but wily and energetic woman who wore the wide-brim hat, positioned her as a Davidesque figure who often triumphed over Goliath-like Big Sugar and other polluting industries in Florida. Douglas was awarded the Presidential Medal of Freedom in 1993. She died on May 14, 1998.

—*Horacio Sierra*

See also Ecofeminism; Environmental Movement; Women's Suffrage Movement

Further Readings

Davis, J. (Ed.). (2002). *The wide brim: Early poems and ponderings of Marjory Stoneman Douglas.* Gainesville: University Press of Florida.

Douglas, M. (1947). *The everglades: A river of grass.* St. Simons Island, GA: Mockingbird Books.

Douglas, M. (with Rothchild, J.). (1987). *Voice of the river.* Sarasota, FL: Pineapple Press.

McCarthy, K. (Ed.). (1990). *Nine Florida stories by Marjory Stoneman Douglas.* Gainesville: University Press of Florida.

McCarthy, K. (Ed.). (1998). *A river in flood and other Florida stories by Marjory Stoneman Douglas.* Gainesville: University Press of Florida.

DOUGLASS, FREDERICK (1818–1895)

African American writer, autobiographer, abolitionist, and diplomat, Frederick Douglass, born Frederick Bailey, is truly one of the most inspiring individuals in American history. Born into slavery in 1818 on Maryland's eastern shore, Douglass grew up without knowing the identities of either his mother or father. In his autobiography, *The Narrative of the Life of Frederick Douglass, an American Slave,* he recounts how he heard rumors that his father was actually the master of the plantation. His mother, as he asserts, was deliberately separated from him when he was an infant to prevent familial bonds from forming between slaves; however, she sometimes visited him

surreptitiously at night, after curfew hours, risking punishment to spend some time with young Frederick. Despite her efforts, when she died, Douglass did not feel any connection to her. He laments this as a typical situation, in which slavery destroyed the natural bonds that should develop between parents and their children.

As a child, he did not experience physical violence, though he witnessed other slaves, including an aunt, being savagely beaten for minor offenses. In 1826, when he was a small child, Douglass was transferred to the household of Hugh Auld in Baltimore, Maryland. The brother-in-law of Douglass' master, Auld had requested a slave to employ as a household servant. Life in Baltimore differed tremendously from that on the plantation on the eastern shore, because many blacks in Baltimore were free—there were more free blacks, in fact, than slaves. Furthermore, while he had been either ignored or mistreated on the plantation, in the Auld household, Douglass received kinder treatment from his new mistress, Sophia Auld.

A woman who had previously earned her own living before marrying, Sophia Auld initially treated young Douglass with the same gentleness she showed her own son, Tommy. When Douglass asked her to teach him how to read, she embarked on the task with enthusiasm. Douglass rapidly made progress and could soon read simple words and string together short sentences. However, when Hugh Auld soon discovered that his wife was teaching a slave child how to read, he immediately stopped the lessons. Douglass recounts the experience as one of the most profound in his life.

The experience disappointed Douglass, who had been making rapid progress, but it also taught him something important—that slavery and oppression were maintained by deliberately denying slaves education and an opportunity for self-improvement; that is, by keeping them ignorant. When he discovered this secret of how whites continued to enslave Africans, Douglass became determined to continue his education, though he would have to rely on his wits.

One of the greatest scenes in American literature is undoubtedly that, recounted in his autobiography, in which Douglass bribes poor white children in his

Baltimore neighborhood with stolen loaves of bread to teach him unfamiliar words and pronunciations. In this steady, wily manner, Douglass cobbled together an education. He read as many books as he could obtain, teaching himself history and other subjects.

After 7 years in Baltimore, Douglass was transferred back to the plantation on which he was raised. He was hired out as a field hand under the supervision of Edward Covey, reputedly a vicious overseer. Having endured several violent beatings, a demoralized Douglass became determined to escape. After an unsuccessful attempt in 1836, he finally succeeded in September of 1838 with the help of abolitionists. Disguised as a sailor, he went to the North, where he began a new life. He married Anna Murray, an African American abolitionist who had helped finance his escape.

The couple lived in Massachusetts and in New York, where Anna turned their home into a station on the Underground Railroad to help other runaway slaves. Douglass became a close associate of William Lloyd Garrison, the era's leading abolitionist and publisher of the abolitionist newspaper, the *Liberator.* With the help of Garrison and his colleagues, Douglass was commissioned by the American Anti-Slavery Society to embark on a lecture circuit, addressing audiences in the Northeast on the evils of slavery, recounting his experiences in bondage.

In 1845, he published his autobiography, *The Narrative of the Life of Frederick Douglass, an American Slave,* in which he revealed his identity. This put him in danger of being discovered, meaning that his former masters could legally reclaim him and recapture him. He spent nearly 2 years in Europe until the danger of his exposure had largely passed.

On his return in 1847, Douglass immersed himself even more deeply in the abolitionist cause, as well as women's rights issues. He founded a newspaper, *The North Star,* in 1847. In July of 1848, he attended the Seneca Falls Women's Rights Convention. Around this time, he began having ideological differences with William Lloyd Garrison; essentially, they differed in their opinions over the U.S. Constitution. Garrison believed it supported and upheld slavery, while Douglass believed it could be used to overturn

and nullify the practice of slavery. They never could reconcile their ideological differences over the issue.

In 1853, Douglass published a short work of fiction, *The Heroic Slave,* which depicted a slave uprising based on a real historic event. His second autobiography, *My Bondage and My Freedom,* appeared in print in 1855.

During the Civil War, Douglass met privately with President Abraham Lincoln three times. He tried to persuade the president that African American soldiers should be allowed to fight in the Union army against the Confederate forces. After the war's end, Douglass eventually moved to Washington, D.C., where he began editing a weekly publication, *New National Era,* advocating civil rights. He also became more politically active and was recruited by government officials for public service, such as serving as the U.S. Marshall for Washington, D.C., and later as the ambassador to Haiti.

In 1882, his wife Anna Murray died, the same year that Douglass published *The Life and Times of Frederick Douglass,* another volume of his autobiography. Two years later he married Helen Pitts, a young white woman who was employed as his secretary. The daughter of fellow abolitionist, Gideon Pitts, Jr., Helen Pitts was almost 20 years younger than Douglass. Their interracial marriage caused a public uproar. In 1886, they took a honeymoon in Europe and the Middle East, touring the region for a year.

On February 20, 1895, Douglass died at his home in Washington, D.C. His legacy stands unparalleled in terms of his influence on later African American activities. He died a man respected by presidents, world leaders, and fellow activists and colleagues. Prominent people, including women's rights leader Elizabeth Cady Stanton, Booker T. Washington, and W. E. B. Du Bois, eulogized him. Douglass had made his mark not just as an abolitionist and black rights leader, but as an advocate for the rights of all oppressed people.

Historians note that his legacy was, undoubtedly, shaped by Frederick Douglass himself. While his life story is a remarkable one, Douglass carefully crafted its presentation through the various volumes of his autobiography and his many speaking engagements and political appointments, always painting himself as a self-made man. Nonetheless, his success helped improve the situation and create opportunities for countless African Americans before and after the Civil War.

—*Susan Muaddi Darraj*

See also Abolitionist Movements; Du Bois, W. E. B.; Lincoln, Abraham

Further Readings

Andrews, W. (Ed.). (1996). *The Oxford Frederick Douglass reader.* New York: Oxford University Press.

Douglass, F. (1845). *Narrative of the life of Frederick Douglass, an American slave.* Boston: Anti-Slavery Office.

Gates, H. L. (Ed.). (1996). *Frederick Douglass: Critical perspectives past and present.* New York: Amistad Press.

McFeely, W. (1991). *Frederick Douglass.* New York: W. W. Norton.

Dow, Unity (1959–)

Unity Dow, Botswana lawyer and human rights activist, was appointed as the first woman judge on the High Court in 1998. She established a women's rights center in her home village, was a cofounder of the Botswana women's rights organization Emang Basadi! (Stand Up, Women!) and of the Women and Law in Southern African research project (WLSA). She is a member of International Women's Rights Watch, and became well-known in Botswana for the Citizenship Case in 1991.

Dow grew up in Mochudi, a large village north of the capital, Gaborone. She received law degrees from the University of Botswana and from the University of Edinburgh. She worked in the Botswana Attorney General's office before going into private practice with a woman partner. In 1986 she joined with other women lawyers, academics, journalists, and political activists, including Athaliah Molokomme, to found Emang Basadi! as an advocacy group for women's

rights, and with women lawyers and researchers from the region to form WLSA. She founded the Methaetsile Women's Information Center to provide legal information and counseling for women who could not afford to pay for legal services.

Emang Basadi! launched a campaign to educate women about their rights and to advocate for reform of laws regarding child support, rape, and married women's property and citizenship rights. From the nation's independence in 1966, citizenship in Botswana's multiparty democracy had been based on birth in the territory. The new law passed in 1984 based citizenship on descent in terms that discriminated against women. Men who married noncitizens could pass on their citizenship to their children, but women who married noncitizens could not. Citizenship carries many educational and economic entitlements in Botswana as well as legal rights. In frontline Botswana in the 1980s, children of women who married exiles from apartheid South Africa would be left stateless.

Advocacy to change the law failed and women's rights groups shifted to a judicial strategy. They supported Dow in filing suit against the law in 1990, based on her marriage to a U.S. citizen and the denial of a passport to their younger daughter, born after passage of the new law. The suit argued that the citizenship law violated the Botswana constitution. The case was decided in her favor in 1991, a victory that was a catalyst for the women's rights movement and led to extensive further reforms of discriminatory laws and to greater inclusion of women in political activism and in public office.

In 1998 Dow was appointed as the first woman judge on the High Court. In addition to her legal work, Dow has written four novels strongly expressing the struggles of girls and women in Botswana for equality and justice, *Far and Beyon', The Screaming of the Innocent, Juggling Truths,* and *The Heavens May Fall.*

—*Judith Imel Van Allen*

See also African Women and Social Justice; Anti-Apartheid Movement; Anti-Colonial Movements, Sub-Saharan Africa; Feminism; Non-Governmental Organizations (NGOs); Socialist Feminism

Further Readings

Holm, J., & Molutsi, P. (Eds.). (1989). *Democracy in Botswana.* Athens: Ohio University Press.

Van Allen, J. (2000). "Bad future things" and liberatory moments: Capitalism, gender and the state in Botswana. *Radical History Review, 76,* 136–168.

DRAFT RESISTANCE

Since America's inception, the debate over the federal government's right to compel Americans into military service (i.e., the right to draft) has evoked passion and dissidence. Some resisters questioned whether the federal government had the authority to compel military service while others disagreed with the premise of the war they were being drafted to fight in. Still a great many others resisted purely on the grounds that they wanted no part of military life, especially if they might have to make the ultimate sacrifice and die for their country. Nonetheless, the debate over the draft predates the Constitution. Americans have been resisting the federal authority to draft American citizens since before Congress was established.

During the constitutional conventions, the founders debated the conditions and authority that could precipitate a draft. Federalists believed a federal draft violated core American values of liberty and republicanism. They compared the prospects of federal authority to compel military service to the recent memory of tyrannical British occupying forces. On the issue of the federal authority to draft, anti-federalists effectively concurred. Their opposition stemmed from a fear of the consequences of juxtaposing the power of the purse and sword. No member or organ of government ought to have the power to fund and raise an army. This consensus on the draft manifested in the resultant language of the Constitution; there was no explicit mention of the power to draft—it is neither condoned nor forbidden. The founders left the question to future generations of politicians. Given the federalists' concern about inalienable rights and the anti-federalists' concern about aggrandized federal power, the final language of the Constitution only mentions militias: state-based organizations with the understood purpose of national (local) defense.

Despite this understanding of the draft and the seemingly universal opposition thereto, 3 years into the War of 1812 and having just witnessed the burning of the White House, President James Madison called for a draft. However, Congress rejected his request citing the founders' concern that they did not have the right to conscript an army. Representative Daniel Webster led the congressional resistance, arguing a draft would infringe on civil and personal liberties and embrace despotism of the worst form.

Thirty-nine years later, President Abraham Lincoln also faced a war and a manpower deficit; however, his draft request met with greater success. On March 3, 1863, the first federal draft in American history took effect. As with every draft since, some potential inductees resisted service by legal means while others employed illegal tactics. Legally a man could avoid service by providing a substitute or paying a $300 commutation fee. For all the resistance efforts to the Civil War draft, none were more infamous than the July 1863 New York City draft riots.

Many New Yorkers resented "Lincoln's War," lamenting that the Civil War had become a rich man's war but a poor man's fight. These tensions culminated on July 13, 1863, when the first draft calls commenced. A fire brigade actually started the riots, setting a draft office ablaze when one of their own was denied exemption as a public servant. Five days of mayhem ensued, engulfing lower Manhattan in a rioting flurry of draft resistance. Though some scholars argue that the riots were more a manifestation of race and class tension than draft protest, the catalyst for the riots is indisputable. The riots began as a direct result of the implementation of the Draft Act and the execution of the first draft calls in New York City.

After the Civil War and in light of the New York City riots, a moratorium on drafts ensued, lasting more than 50 years until World War I when the need for troops trumped fears of a repeat of July 1863. Passed hastily in 1917 as America entered the fight, the Selective Service Act elicited opposition and resistance from numerous Americans. Commutations and substitutions were outlawed; however, a system of deferments replaced them, providing new means to legally avoid service. Though there was no repeat of the New York City riots, there were some prominent episodes of draft resistance. Among them, the two most publicized incidents played out not in the streets or in Congress, but in the U.S. Supreme Court.

The court ruled in 1918 on the constitutionality of the draft itself in *Arver v. United States*, the litmus case for a series of decisions collectively known as the Selective Draft Law Cases. Chief Justice Edward White, writing for the court, ruled for the government, endorsing the constitutional legitimacy of the Selective Service Act and dismissing Arver's argument that a draft violated the Thirteenth Amendment. White ruled a draft was a duty to serve one's country—not a condition of servitude. Scholars debate the accuracy of the historical precedents White cited in his decision; nonetheless, the decision represented a major legal blow to draft resistance. The highest court in America concluded that the framers of the Constitution endorsed compulsory military service.

The second major Supreme Court decision regarding draft resistance during World War I regarded the wartime limits of protected speech. In 1919 in the case of *Schenck v. United States*, the court defined the constitutional limits of speech acts, delineating between protected speech and condemnable actions against the state. Charles T. Schenck distributed pamphlets that encouraged people to talk to their members of Congress in opposition to the Selective Service Act. Writing for the majority, Associate Justice Oliver Wendell Holmes contended speech was not protected when it creates a clear and present danger to an evil Congress is combating. Thus, the court ruled that Schenck was guilty as charged. His encouragement of draft resistance was deemed illegal and unconstitutional.

Though the strain on the draft during World War II and the Korean War was relatively minor (in fact the draft was briefly abandoned in 1947 and 1948), there was a large debate in Congress in 1940 as to whether the United States should return to a policy of drafted manpower, especially in light of the riots during the Civil War and the fallout from the World War I draft. To preserve American readiness, a draft was passed (the Burke-Wadsworth Act) and a selective service system was implemented before American troops entered World War II and before America declared war on any country. Thus, the 1940 draft represented the first peacetime draft in American history, setting a precedent for the next 33 years.

Ultimately, every draft in the 20th century before the Vietnam War met predominant support and compliance. The preponderance of resistance changed, however, during the Vietnam War. Arguably the most pronounced period of draft resistance in American history, it certainly was and remains the most popularized. Nevertheless, many of the means and methods that are now the subject of countless books and movies were tactics already perfected by pockets of resistance during previous wars. Opposition stemmed from the politics behind the war as well as the semantics of the selective service's prosecution of the draft. Some resisters did not support the motivations behind American participation in the war while others were guided simply by self-preservation and a desire not to join the growing death toll. Still others were enraged at the racial and class disparity in the selection process.

Much like during the Civil War, loopholes allowed some men to legally avoid service. The selective service system for draft classification provided various categories for individuals who were not fit or available to serve. The most controversial loophole corresponded to category IV-F, reserved for those physically, morally, or psychiatrically unfit to serve. These conditions ranged from flat feet to homosexuality. While many Americas were legitimately unfit to serve, many more cheated their way into this status. Many men found or paid a friendly doctor to vouch that they had a condition that precluded them from service. Others successfully feigned such conditions when called for induction.

Regardless of one's status, once classified the government issued each young man a draft card. This piece of government identification was to be carried on person at all times and could not be marred or defaced in any way. Thus, when many draft resisters chose to burn their draft cards, they were not only making a political statement, they were overtly defying the law and the selective service system.

Resistance also frequently manifested in terms of evasion. If men could not be found, they could not serve. This logic led between 60,000 and 100,000 men to flee into exile in Canada. Having not implemented a draft in Canada since World War I, and given Canadian political opposition to American participation in the Vietnam War, draft evaders found a haven north of the border. Even after the war ended and President Jimmy Carter pardoned draft evaders in 1977, many exiles chose to remain in Canada.

Draft reforms in the late 1960s remedied some of the larger inequities in the selective service system. Some of the more disparate exemptions were removed, and a lottery system based on birthdays established a colorblind and class-blind determinant of service. Nonetheless, draft resistance continued through 1973 when American ground troop participation in the war ceased and the all-volunteer force replaced the draft. Even then, without a draft to resist, the movement continued to fight for reconciliation and amnesty for draft evaders. Their efforts were rewarded when Jimmy Carter issued his aforementioned pardon in 1977. However, despite early placation of draft resisters, in 1980 Carter reinstituted draft registration. This did not resume active calls to duty but did reinstitute the selective service registry, minimizing the start-up time for the draft machinery should Congress ever decide to resume draft calls. However, since 1973 American military personnel needs have been satisfied without resorting to compulsory service.

This is technically the current status of the draft. Yet, in light of recent political events and military engagements in Afghanistan and Iraq, a new debate over the draft has emerged. As the American military presence abroad increases, the personnel burden has become increasingly strained. This has resulted in what pundits have dubbed a backdoor draft. Stop-loss programs and extensive call-ups of reserve troops have offset increased personnel needs without officially returning to a drafted army. However, this strategy has not duped opponents who ardently oppose any policy and action that constitutes the spirit, even if not the letter, of a draft. While some activists object to this strategy, Congress preferred the status quo to reinstituting a draft. Proof of this political reality was most recently provided on January 7, 2003, when Representative Charles Rangel proposed the Universal National Service Act of 2003. Whether it was a serious suggestion or a political stunt is still debated by scholars; however, despite the efforts of Rangel and his cosponsors, the bill failed in the House by an overwhelming vote of 2 to 402, proving there does not appear to be another draft on the horizon. It also proved that congressional resistance to the draft remains strong.

Ultimately, no draft has ever been enacted without significant debate and subsequent resistance. The quantity and fervor of each have varied in American history based on the popularity of the war and the feelings of the public at the time. Some resisted on philosophic grounds, purporting the government had no right to make the decision to serve for them. Others had more political objections, refusing to support—and in fact fight—for a cause they did not believe in. Still, the largest group remains those who were simply not inclined to risk their life in the army. The debate over the draft in America has always existed and will always exist so long as America has military commitments abroad.

—*Jason Friedman*

See also Carter, James Earl; Counter-Recruitment; Lincoln, Abraham; Roosevelt, Franklin D.

Further Readings

Bernstein, I. (1990). *The New York City draft riots: Their significance for American society and politics in the age of the Civil War.* New York: Oxford University Press.

Fallows, J. (1975). What did you do in the class war, daddy? *Washington Monthly, 7*(8), 5–20.

Freedman, L. (1969). Conscription and the constitution: The original understanding. *Michigan Law Review, 67*, 1493–1552.

Kusch, F. (2001). *All American boys: Draft dodgers in Canada from the Vietnam War.* Westport, CT: Praeger.

Levine, P. (1981). Draft evasion in the north during the Civil War, 1863–1865. *Journal of American History, 67*(4), 816–834.

Lofgren, C. (1976). Compulsory military service under the constitution: The original understanding. *William and Mary Quarterly, 33*(1), 61–88.

Surrey, D. (1982). *Choice of conscience: Vietnam era military and draft resisters in Canada.* New York: Praeger.

DRUG LAWS, RESISTANCE TO

The origins of U.S. drug prohibition lie in the early 20th century. Prior to 1906, there was no drug regulation in the United States and crimes such as drug dealing and drug possession did not exist. The first regulation came with the 1906 Pure Food and Drug Act, which required labeling of ingredients. Passed in the wake of public disgust over Upton Sinclair's slaughterhouse exposé *The Jungle,* the law also required patent medicine and similar nostrums to disclose their ingredients, which often included a healthy dose of morphine or cocaine. The Harrison Act in 1914 banned the distribution of opiates and cocaine and began the prohibition of drugs as a national policy. Although the act had a clause allowing doctors' use in their practices, in 1917 this was interpreted to not allow heroin maintenance to patients.

The Marijuana Tax Act of 1937 was passed with little fanfare. Many legislators were unsure exactly what marijuana was, and there was minimal debate leading up to the floor vote. Sociologist Howard Becker attributed this law to the moral entrepreneurship of Harry Anslinger, the long-standing head of the Federal Bureau of Narcotics, who promoted marijuana as a threat to public safety and luridly linked the drug with Mexican immigration into the Southwest. (The Federal Bureau of Narcotics was the precursor to the Drug Enforcement Administration.)

Early drug laws did not have a major impact on the criminal justice system because of the limited use of some drugs (marijuana) and the medical acceptability of others (cocaine, morphine). The significance of early drug laws lies in the vast expansion of incarceration and the criminal justice system during the 1990s, driven in part by the addition of mandatory minimum sentencing for drug offenses. Resistance to drug laws now focuses mainly on the criminal justice system and the cost and scope of the war on drugs.

During the 1960s and 1970s, marijuana use diffused through the population, greatly increasing the number of people who had tried the drug. As well-educated, middle-class people used marijuana, sentiments toward decriminalization became increasingly favorable.

Jerome Himmelstein's analysis of news reports found that descriptions of the *physical effects* of marijuana changed as the reference group of users changed— marijuana was no longer associated with violence and addiction, but passivity and dependence instead. As drug law affected more middle-class young people, support for drug law reform grew among civil society and politicians concerned about a seemingly unrealistic legal regime of prohibition. The American Bar Association and the American Nurses Association passed resolutions in favor of decriminalization. The New York State Congress of Parents and Teachers Associations passed a similar resolution in 1976.

The possibility of reform seemed to be at its peak in 1977 when President Jimmy Carter spoke to Congress with the message that penalties against drug use should not be more damaging to an individual than the use of the drug itself; he tied this explicitly to the laws against the possession of marijuana in private for personal use. Carter's statement had precedent in earlier reports and official statements. President Nixon commissioned a study of marijuana law and policy in the United States, headed by Raymond Shafer, Republican ex-governor of Pennsylvania. Published in 1972 with the title *Marihuana: Signal of Misunderstanding,* the Shafer commission concluded the criminalization of possession of marijuana for personal use was socially self-defeating and, in the overall scheme of things, did not rank high in ranking of social concerns in the United States. The study recommended de-emphasizing marijuana as a problem.

This conclusion greatly displeased Nixon but suggested the depth of opposition to the nascent drug war. In 1975, the Ford administration released the *White Paper on Drug Abuse,* which also de-emphasized marijuana in relation to other drug problems. It concluded that in light of its widespread recreational use—and the relatively low social cost associated with this type of use—the federal government has been de-emphasizing simple possession and use of marijuana in its law enforcement effort for several years. The Senate also held a number of hearings on relaxation of drug law during the 1970s, with titles such as "Considerations For and Against the Reduction of Federal Penalties for Possession of Small Amounts of Marihuana for Personal Use."

Public opinion measures from the General Social Survey (GSS) saw increasing support for decriminalization in the 1970s, with a peak of more than 30% in 1977. After a long decline in support during the late 1970s and 1980s, the GSS and the data from the Bureau of Justice Statistics find that support for marijuana decriminalization is as high now as it was 30 years ago, with slightly less than a third of the population supporting decriminalization. Among college freshmen, support rises to around 50%, though it is important to note there has always been a gender gap with men more likely to support decriminalization.

The National Organization to Reform Marijuana Laws (NORML) was founded in 1970 and has been the pre-eminent organization advocating against marijuana prohibition. During much of the 1970s, NORML was successful in advancing the agenda of decriminalization of marijuana, with 11 states adopting laws by 1976. However, the emergence of the parental antidrug movement that framed drug use a threat to youth, combined with an increasing governmental focus on the potential health effects of marijuana, stopped federal-level decriminalization from ever being instituted.

NORML has long attracted celebrity support, especially from musicians, filmmakers, and writers. Hunter S. Thompson, Willie Nelson, and Robert Altman have all been members of the board of directors. NORML funds extensive public relations campaigns and recently presented billboards in New York City with Mayor Michael Bloomberg quoted as enjoying his youthful marijuana use.

In 1994, financier George Soros helped found the Lindesmith Institute as part of the Open Society Institute. Public policy professor Ethan Nadelmann left his job at Princeton to become director of the Lindesmith Center in 1994. In 2000, the Lindesmith Center merged with the Drug Policy Foundation to form the Drug Policy Alliance. Like NORML, the Drug Policy Alliance has found common ground with limited-government conservatives; Ethan Nadelmann, founder and executive director of the Drug Policy Alliance, wrote a 2004 cover story for *National Review* opposing marijuana prohibition.

Opposition to the American drug war has taken new forms in recent years. First, Law Enforcement Against

Prohibition, founded in 2002 by mostly retired police and police chiefs, has become increasingly active and vocal in criticizing current drug policy. Because of the credibility of these officials, their opposition to drug law is often well documented in the news media.

Also, student organizations have organized against the war on drugs, especially its educational provisions. Students for a Sensible Drug Policy (SSDP) was founded in 1998 as a response to a federal education spending bill, the Higher Education Act, that denies grants and student loans to anyone convicted of a drug crime. At the time of this writing, SSDP had more than 100 chapters in the United States.

Finally, there is limited development of an international drug users' movement. Activists in Vancouver have had some success with the Vancouver Area Network of Drug Users, which is involved in shaping the city drug policy and negotiating the construction of a safe injection site in downtown Vancouver. Similar networks exist in England, Australia, Belgium, and Thailand, often centered on sexually transmitted disease mitigation. Activist organizations have also been involved in harm-reduction techniques surrounding drug use at public venues. Most notable is DanceSafe, an organization that tests ecstasy pills at raves and publishes the results online.

Many countries also have marijuana-centered political parties. Canada, New Zealand, the United Kingdom, Spain, and Israel all have parties participating in parliamentary elections. The U.S. Marijuana party has chapters in 29 states.

The increasing medicalization of drug use has altered the landscape in reform. The movement for medical marijuana in the 1990s produced several victories, the most far-reaching of which was the passage of California's Proposition 215. Also known as the Compassionate Use Act, the California Proposition passed with 55.6% of the vote and allowed doctors to recommend marijuana to patients. As of this writing, Rhode Island had most recently instituted a medical marijuana law, bringing the number of states with medical marijuana laws to 11. Many municipalities, especially large university towns, also have decriminalization ordinances.

The medical marijuana bills created a conflict between federal prohibitionist drug policy and the ability of states to experiment in a federalist system. The test case was *Gonzales v. Raich* (originally *Ashcroft v. Raich* before John Ashcroft's resignation as attorney general). Angel Raich was a California cancer patient who consumed marijuana under the Compassionate Use Act; along with Diane Monson, a patient whose home was raided by the Drug Enforcement Administration, she brought suit against the government. Their lawsuit questioned the constitutionality of the Controlled Substances Act, which classifies marijuana as having no currently accepted medical use. The root constitutional question was the range of the Commerce Clause, which allows the federal government to regulate both interstate commerce and intrastate commerce that may affect national markets. Raich and Monson argued that because there was no commercial element (all of the marijuana was produced at home or given as gifts) and because the operation was wholly contained to California, the federal government lacked the jurisdiction to regulate this behavior.

In 2005, the Supreme Court ruled 6 to 3 against Raich, concluding that the Commerce Clause was applicable and that the federal government had the right to pre-empt state law. This overturned the 2003 Ninth Circuit Court of Appeals ruling that found in favor of the plaintiffs.

Public opinion polls indicate majority support for medical marijuana nationwide, with little difference by age or gender. Although medical marijuana has been a successful referendum issue at the local and sometimes the state level, the model has for the most part not been extended to other drugs. One exception is the case of Baltimore, with the largest intravenous drug problem in the United States. Mayor Kurt Schmoke created a furor in the 1980s by calling for decriminalization of heroin. However, this reform was never implemented as policy and Schmoke has since retired from office.

Mandatory minimum sentences, which remove judicial discretion in sentencing, have increasingly been applied to drug crimes and have contributed to the growth in incarceration in the United States. Several organizations oppose mandatory minimum sentencing, often with a particular focus on drug offenses. A 1986 Omnibus Crime Bill introduced mandatory minimum for many drug crimes, based on the weight of drugs involved. Although mandatory minimums have been used since the colonial era as a deterrent tool, these laws increased the number of offenses subject to mandatory minimums and made many drug crimes felonies that required a 5- to 10-year prison sentence.

The Sentencing Project was incorporated in 1986 and has become the major source of research and advocacy opposing mandatory minimum sentencing. A related organization, Families Against Mandatory Minimums, was founded in 1991 to advocate for flexibility in sentencing and is active in 24 states and the District of Columbia. The Sentencing Project has released several reports highlighting the racial disparities in criminal justice that stem from mandatory minimum sentencing. Other research by sociologists found that for certain age groups of black men, prison was a more likely life experience than completion of higher education, in part because of mandatory minimum sentencing. Some critical scholars have argued that the greatly expanded criminal justice system and the war on drugs funnel minorities directly from ghettoes to prisons.

Activists have developed several sites dedicated to disseminating information in the drug law reform effort. In addition to the organizations mentioned above such as NORML and Drug Policy Alliance, other notable organizations include the Drug Reform Coordination Network (DRCNet), and DrugSense. The Media Awareness Project, the largest project of DrugSense, focuses on media coverage of drugs and drug law. "Newshawking" volunteers compile drug-related editorials and stories from local, national, and international news sources for dissemination via websites and listserves. DRCNet runs a large newsletter and hosts the Schaffer library of drug policy, with archives of major studies of drug policy and drug law in the United States and abroad. Resistance to drug laws has taken many organizational forms, largely focusing on changing criminal law surrounding drugs and highlighting and combating the inequities of the war on drugs.

—Adam Jacobs

See also Judicial Activism; Law and Social Movements; Moral Panic; Prison-Industrial Complex

Further Readings

Baum, D. (1996). *Smoke and mirrors: The war on drugs and the politics of failure.* Boston: Little, Brown.

Becker, H. (1963). *Outsiders: Studies in the sociology of deviance.* New York: Free Press.

Bonnie, R., & Whitebread, C. (1999). *The marijuana conviction: A history of marijuana prohibition in the United States.* New York: Lindesmith Center.

Himmelstein, J. (1983). *The strange career of marihuana: Politics and ideology of drug control in America.* Westport, CT: Greenwood Press.

Massing, M. (1998). *The fix.* New York: Simon & Schuster.

Musto, D. (1999). *The American disease: Origins of narcotics law.* New York: Oxford University Press.

Simon, D., & Burns, E. (1998). *The corner: A year in the life of an inner-city neighborhood.* New York: Broadway Books.

DUBČEK, ALEXANDER (1921–1992)

Alexander Dubček was the leader of Prague Spring from 1991 to 1992, an effort by reformists within the Czechoslovakia Communist Party to open the political system and introduce economic changes, personified in his slogan "Socialism with a human face." Born in the small Slovak village of Uhrovec, Dubček spent much of childhood in the Soviet Union and later participated in the Slovak Uprising against Nazi occupation during World War II.

Dubček was recruited to become a party administrator in 1949, rising rapidly to become a provincial secretary in 1953, national party secretary for industry in 1960, and Slovak first secretary in 1963. In the early 1960s, Dubček was a member of the Kolder Commission, a party investigation of the Stalinist purges of a decade earlier. His participation on this commission, along with his oversight of industry, solidified his belief in structural reform. Reaching the top ranks of the party in the early 1960s, Dubček cautiously worked to create the necessary conditions to implement his reforms, gathering together like-minded reformists. A cautious approach was necessary because entrenched Stalinists opposed all but the most tepid reforms, and the Stalinist party head and

president, Antonin Novotny, repeatedly tried to oust or demote Dubček, at one point launching a police investigation of Dubček that failed. The attacks on Dubček, led by Novotny, centered on false accusations of "bourgeois nationalism"—for which some senior party officials were jailed during the 1950s—were manufactured over Dubček's continuing advocation of more industrial investment in the Slovak Republic, which lagged behind the Czech lands.

Economic stagnation, rising tensions between Czechs and Slovaks, and pressure for reforms from below created the conditions for changes in the party leadership by late 1967, and in January 1968 the party leadership elected Dubček first secretary, the highest office. Although his reformist credentials and wider anti-Novotny sentiment were important factors in his elevation, another factor was that Dubček was a Slovak; all previous party heads were Czechs and most high party positions had been held by Czechs. A key goal for Dubček was the party renewing its popular support, which was to be done in part by ending the party's pervasive close management of all aspects of government. Through 1968, a majority in the party leadership solidified behind Dubček, but he continued to have to maneuver around internal oppositionists and repeated demonstrations of disapproval from the Soviet Union. In August 1968, Czechoslovakia was invaded by the Soviet Union and four other Warsaw Pact nations, and Dubček was kidnapped from his office by Soviet intelligence agents. Dubček refused to denounce his program but was allowed to remain as first secretary when the Soviets failed to install the coup leaders in power. Although his followers were removed from their offices, he remained in his office in an attempt to stave off reversals of his reforms.

Dubček was forced from office in 1969, stripped of his party membership, and harassed by the secret police for the next 20 years. He worked as a mechanic before retiring, but when the communist regime collapsed in late 1989, Dubček became the head of the national parliament. He energetically opposed the split of Czechoslovakia into two nations. But although a lifelong, unwavering believer in socialism, Dubček was deeply saddened by the betrayal of his ideals and became the leader of the Social Democrats. His return to public life ended prematurely when he was severely injured in an automobile crash in September 1992; he died 9 weeks later.

—*Pete Dolack*

See also Communism; Prague Spring

Further Readings

Williams, K. (1997). *The Prague spring and its aftermath: Czechoslovak politics, 1968–1970.* London: Cambridge University Press.

Du Bois, W. E. B. (1868–1963)

William Edward Burghardt Du Bois was a central figure in the initiation of the Negro protest movement in America, a founder of the National Association for the Advancement of Colored People (NAACP), an advocate for equal rights, a persistent critic of colonialism, the architect of Pan-Africanism, and a preeminent scholar of the black race. Du Bois was born on February 23, 1868, in Great Barrington, Massachusetts. He studied at Fisk and Harvard Universities in the United States and the University of Berlin in Germany. In 1895, he became the first African American to obtain a Ph.D. from Harvard. His "The Suppression of the African Slave Trade" of 1869 opened the authoritative *Harvard Historical Studies* series. In 1894 to 1896, he served as professor of Greek and Latin at Wilberforce University, and in 1896 and 1897, he taught at the University of Pennsylvania.

His academic career was primarily associated with Atlanta University. Du Bois was first there between 1897 and 1910 as professor of history and economics. Alongside teaching, he completed *The Philadelphia Negro* in 1899—an exemplary empirical research in urban sociology with anthropological and demographic dimensions. It is considered the first attempt by an American social scientist to develop a methodology for the discipline of sociology.

In Atlanta, Du Bois organized a series of conferences on urban black people and authored a number of works that defined the situation of blacks in America in striking and insightful ways. Central among them was the much acclaimed *The Souls of Black Folk* of 1903, which has now gone through some 30 editions.

With these works, Du Bois had already asserted himself as a distinguished scholar. But he strongly felt that his academic pursuits would only be meaningful if they were practically linked to the historic demands of the epoch. For him, the greatest challenge of the 20th century was, in his memorable words, the "problem of the color line." To deal with it meant to transform America into a racially integrated society and to achieve the unity and liberation of the whole of Africa. This new turn toward action was stimulated by the deterioration of the racial situation in America, especially in Atlanta, where Du Bois himself was subjected to all manner of restrictions and humiliation off-campus, and where he witnessed lynching every week.

Du Bois created a platform for his work that openly challenged the program and policies of Booker T. Washington. Instead of Washington's insistence on accommodation and submission by black people, Du Bois proposed a demand for equality through all possible means. In opposition to the philosophy of individual education, Du Bois outlined the prospect of the Talented Tenth, an intellectual elite that would lead the black masses to freedom and progress.

As a first step, in 1905, Du Bois founded the Niagara Movement, which sought full citizenship rights for African Americans. He was its general secretary until 1909. In the same year, he was among the founders of NAACP, and from 1910 up to his resignation in 1934, he worked as its director of publicity and research. He was also the editor of its influential organ, *The Crisis.* Through this magazine, Du Bois effectively shaped the character of the organization, set the agenda for black protest, and made Africa an important theme and concern for black Americans.

A pragmatic leader, he had early on emphasized the need for what he called economic democracy. This concern acquired added urgency with the coming of the Great Depression. Du Bois reexamined the whole program of NAACP and proclaimed that it required fundamental revision. In the new situation of further economic marginalization of black people, it was futile to stick to the old liberalism and appeal merely for broad justice and legal reforms. What was essential was to provide opportunities for these people to earn a living, protect and raise their income, and expand their employment. He, therefore, proposed such concrete steps as the establishment of a cooperative commonwealth in the black ghetto, the formation of producer and consumer cooperatives, and the socialization of such crucial black professional services as those of medical doctors and lawyers. But far from being solely a pragmatist, Du Bois also insisted on what he saw as the black people's special mission in the world and envisioned the creation of, in his words, a new and great Negro ethos.

World War I, which Du Bois saw not only as long, cruel, bloody, and unnecessary, but also as unashamedly racist, became that watershed in his life, which made him regard the cause of black Americans as part of the larger cause of colored people everywhere. He concluded that the freedom of Africa is a condition for the emancipation of the descendants of Africa the world over.

In 1919, the Second Pan-African Congress took place in Paris and Du Bois rose as the world leader of that movement. These congresses called for—at the level of internationally formalized opinion—the liberation of the African colonies. They served to highlight the predicament of Africans throughout the world and to create awareness about the indignity of racial discrimination, the wrong of the very existence of the colonial system, and the urgent need of emancipating Africa. Inspired by Du Bois's Pan-Africanism, as a political theory and practical strategy, upon returning to their respective countries, African leaders engaged in the creation of movements for their liberation. The most famous was the Fifth Pan-African Congress, which Du Bois chaired in Manchester in 1945. Among those who attended was Jomo Kenyatta of Kenya and Ghana's Kwame Nkrumah. It is said that this was the event that fired their imagination and led to the decolonization of Africa.

Despite his intense activist involvement, Du Bois continued with his scholarly work. *The Gift of Black Folk* came out in 1924. The year 1933 marked his return to Atlanta University as professor and chair of sociology. He founded and became the editor of *Phylon, the Atlanta University Review of Race and Culture* and initiated the project *Encyclopedia of the Negro.* Another major book of the second Atlanta stint was *Black Folk: Then and Now* from 1939.

Immediately on retirement from Atlanta in 1944, Du Bois returned to the NAACP as director of special research. Later he served, successively, as consultant of the United Nations Organization at San Francisco, chairman of the Council of African Affairs, and chairman of the Peace Information Center. It was for his activities in this latter capacity that he was jailed during the Cold War years of 1950 and 1951. In 1957, he was denied a passport to travel and attend the independence celebrations of Ghana. Du Bois joined the Communist Party of America in 1961.

His most important works of that period are *Color and Democracy* of 1945 and *The World and Africa: An Inquiry into the Part Which Africa Has Played in World History* of 1947. His writings on Africa, in their entirety, constitute a response to his own pioneer call for the honest interpretation of the history of that continent and its people.

Du Bois was also a columnist for the Pittsburgh *Courier* (1936–1938), *Amsterdam News* (New York, 1939–1944), Chicago *Defender* (1945–1948), and *People's Voice* (1947–1948). He wrote for *Current History, Journal of Negro Education, Foreign Affairs,* and *American Scholar.*

On the invitation of President Krumah, in 1961, Du Bois and his wife, Shirley Graham Du Bois—who was also his close associate, the first editor of *Freedomways,* a leading writer, and a composer—moved to reside in Ghana. Soon after, the family chose to become Ghanaian citizens. Du Bois's attention at that stage was focused on his grand project, *Encyclopedia Africana,* whose aim was to trace the developments in the social, political, cultural, historical, and technical spheres in Africa throughout the centuries of its existence.

Du Bois died on August 27, 1963, in Accra. He was accorded a state funeral.

Du Bois was a man of peace. In his 30-year sponsorship of the Pan-African congresses, he insisted on the formulation of programs and tactics of nonviolent and positive action. But he postulated that peace was inseparable from freedom and warned that if force continued to be used by the West as a method of governance in the world, then Africans may, as a last resort, also apply it, to their own detriment and that of humankind. In the same way, he cautioned against compromising the concept of democracy. He was convinced that the prevalence of the problems of poverty, ignorance, disease, and crime made a mockery of the democratic ideal. In 1952, he was awarded the International Peace Prize.

Du Bois was also one of the talented early writers in American literature. He is the author of the drama *The Star of Ethiopia* of 1915 and the novels *The Quest of the Silver Fleece* of 1911 and *Dark Princess: A Romance* of 1928. *The Black Flame* (1957–1961) is a trilogy of historical novels. *Selected Poems* and *The Autobiography of W. E. B. Du Bois* were published posthumously.

Du Bois greatly impressed the minds of his contemporaries. For Paul Robeson he was a leader in the truest sense of that word, and not only of America and the black race, but of the world. Martin Luther King, Jr., emphasized the significance of his pride in the black man, pride that Du Bois derived not from some vague greatness related to color but from the real achievements of black people in struggle, which, he believed, had advanced humanity. His life and work continue to inspire many today. Professor K. Onuwuka Dike sees him as the 20th century's greatest prophet, particularly insofar as the issue of race and the value of human equality are concerned.

—*Emilia Ilieva*

See also Activism, Social and Political; Advocacy; Anti-Colonial Movements, Sub-Saharan Africa; Anti-Imperialism; Anti-Racist Teaching; Civil Rights Movement; Communism; Communist Party USA; Democracy; King, Martin Luther, Jr.; Liberalism; Literature and Activism; National Association for the Advancement of Colored People (NAACP); Nonviolence and Activism; Pan-Africanism; Robeson, Paul; Socialism

Further Readings

Dike, K. O. (1978). Message from Professor K. Onwuka Dike. In J. H. Clarke (Ed.), *Pan-Africanism and the liberation of South Africa: A tribute to W. E. B. Du Bois* (p. 70). New York: African Heritage Studies Association Publications Centre.

DeMarco, J. (1983). *The social thought of W. E. B. Du Bois.* Lanham, MD: University Press of America.

Du Bois, W. E. B. (1903). *The souls of black folk: Essays and sketches.* Chicago: A. C. McClurg.

Du Bois, W. E. B. (1924). *The gift of black folk: Negroes in the making of America.* Boston: Stratford.

Du Bois, W. E. B. (1945). *Color and democracy: Colonies and peace.* New York: Harcourt Brace.

Du Bois, W. E. B. (1947). *The world of Africa: An inquiry into the part which Africa has played in world history.* New York: Viking.

Du Bois, W. E. B. (1968). *The autobiography of W. E. B. Du Bois: A soliloquy on viewing my life from the last decade of its first century.* New York: International Publishers.

Lester, J. (Ed.). (1971). *The seventh son: The thought and writings of W. E. B. Du Bois.* New York: Random House.

Rudwick, E. M. (1960). *W. E. B. Du Bois.* Philadelphia: University of Pennsylvania Press.

DUNAYEVSKAYA, RAYA (1910–1987)

The life of Raya Dunayevskaya fused intense philosophical investigation with active engagement in liberatory social struggles. Dunayevskaya advanced a unique theory of state-capitalism, originated the philosophy of Marxist-Humanism, and founded News and Letters Committees.

Dunayevskaya, born in the Ukraine, settled in Chicago in 1922. As a teenager, she was active in the Young Workers League, a communist youth organization, and the American Negro Labor Congress. Dunayevskaya worked as Leon Trotsky's Russian-language secretary from 1937 to 1938 in Mexico. Following the Hitler-Stalin pact, Dunayevskaya broke with Trotsky, rejecting his defense of Russia as a workers' state.

This break led to her collaboration with C. L. R. James, a Trinidadian Marxist. In 1941, they formed the state-capitalist, or Johnson-Forest Tendency, in the

American Trotskyist movement. In the early 1940s, Dunayevskaya undertook a seminal study of Russia's first Five-Year Plans and concluded that Russia was developing in a state-capitalist, not a socialist, direction.

Dunayevskaya's analysis is unique in that it treats state-capitalism as a new phase in the development of global capitalism. She posited, in opposition to this new phase, both new revolutionary subjects—rank and file workers, African Americans, women, and youth—and new philosophical ground, by way of an original engagement with Marx's *Economic and Philosophic Manuscripts of 1844* and V. I. Lenin's 1914 *Philosophic Notebooks.*

In 1953, Dunayevskaya composed two letters on the "absolutes" of G. W. F. Hegel. In this controversial reading of Hegel, Dunayevskaya locates a dual movement: a movement, in her words, from practice that is itself a form of theory and a movement from theory reaching to philosophy. The letters posit the self-development of revolutionary subjects, through engagement with a philosophy of revolution, as an alternative to both the vanguard party and the view that spontaneous activity alone will give rise to a new society. Dunayevskaya would later identify these letters as the philosophic breakthrough from which her Marxist-Humanism developed.

Dunayevskaya, in 1955, founded a Marxist-Humanist organization, News and Letters Committees. In 1958, she published *Marxism and Freedom,* which explores such diverse ground as the influence of the Paris Commune on Marx's *Capital,* Lenin's plunge into the Hegelian dialectic with the outbreak of World War I, and the struggle of American workers against automation. In her 1973 *Philosophy and Revolution,* Dunayevskaya focuses on the integrality of philosophy and revolution, tracing the relation historically, and emphasizing the Hegelian concept of absolute negativity.

Dunayevskaya's 1982 *Rosa Luxemburg, Women's Liberation, and Marx's Philosophy of Revolution* discusses Luxemburg's feminism and anti-colonialism, explores Marx's *Ethnological Notebooks,* and introduces the pejorative category of "post-Marx Marxism," beginning with the work of Frederick Engels. As her life was drawing to a close, Dunayevskaya prepared extensive notes for a book on philosophy and organization titled *Dialectics of Organization and Philosophy: The "Party" and Forms of Organization Born Out of Spontaneity.*

—Seth G. Weiss

See also Luxemburg, Rosa; Marxist Theory; Trotskyism

Further Readings

Dunayevskaya, R. (2002). *The power of negativity: Selected writings on the dialectic in Hegel and Marx.* Lanham, MD: Lexington Books.

DUSSEL, ENRIQUE (1934–)

Enrique Dussel is widely recognized as one of the most important thinkers of Latin America and the father of a philosophy of liberation. A philosopher by academic training, he has also worked on the history of Latin America, the relation between history and theology of liberation, and the construction of the Americas by the European colonial empires. He has also constructed an elaborate model of social ethics and economics and has lectured widely on economics, philosophy, and social theory. He is one of the most prolific writers of 20th-century Latin America, and his works have been translated in most Western European languages.

The young Dussel started his studies of philosophy at the Universidad Nacional del Cuyo in Mendoza in 1957 and later completed a doctorate of philosophy in Madrid in 1959, a licentiate in religion in Paris in 1965, and a doctorate in history at La Sorbonne in 1967. On his return to his native Argentina, he taught ethics at the Universidad Nacional de la Resistencia (Chaco, 1966–1968), at the Instituto Pastoral del CELAM (Quito, Ecuador, 1967–1973), and at the Universidad Nacional de Cuyo (Mendoza, 1968–1975). However, after Juan Domingo Perón's death in 1974, Argentine underwent a political polarization with escalating violence. Within that violence, right-wing paramilitary groups targeted Dussel, and after a bomb exploded in his home he left for Mexico in 1975 together with his family. In 1975 Dussel became a professor of church history and religious studies at ITES (Mexico, D.F.) and a professor of ethics and philosophy at the Universidad Autónoma Metropolitana/Iztapalapa. Mexico became his adopted country, and years later Dussel took Mexican nationality. Meanwhile, in his native Argentina, communities suffered political repression by the military and long years of democratic instability.

Dussel stresses the importance of oral delivery and the following interaction with an audience as a methodological tool of spoken discourse and recognizes that written texts can never convey the whole depth of spoken lectures. Dussel uses history in order to set the context for a liberating project that includes the liberation from economic structures *ad intra*, as well as the liberation from a Christian situation of empire symbolized in the development of Christianity as a persecuted religion to a colonizing system of Christendom. Within contemporary discussions on economics, philosophy, and ethics, Dussel has made the important distinction between social morality and ethics by suggesting that social moral orders as agreed systems of morality are not always necessarily ethical and can be challenged by Christians as social activists who strive for a just society here and now.

—*Mario I. Aguilar*

See also Abuelas de Plaza de Mayo; Postcolonial Theory

Further Readings

Dussel, E. (1981). *History of the church in Latin America: Colonialism to liberation 1492–1979.* Grand Rapids, MI: Eerdmans.

Dussel, E. (1985). *Philosophy of liberation.* Maryknoll, NY: Orbis.

Dussel, E. (1988). *Ethics and community.* Maryknoll, NY: Orbis.

Dussel, E. (1995). *The invention of the Americas: Eclipse of the other and the myth of modernity.* New York: Continuum.

Dussel, E. (2001). *Towards an unknown Marx: Commentary of the manuscripts of 1861–1863.* London: Routledge.

DWORKIN, ANDREA (1946–2005)

As a radical speaker and writer, Andrea Dworkin was known for her work against pornography, which she argued led to violence against women. Her theories can be found in books, including *Woman Hating, Intercourse,* and *Life and Death.*

Andrea Dworkin was born September 26, 1946, in Camden, New Jersey, to Harry Dworkin and Sylvia Spiegel. Her father was a teacher and devoted socialist who contributed to her social consciousness. Her mother was frequently sick, suffering from heart failure and a stroke before Andrea was of adolescent age. Her mother passed away at the age of 26.

Dworkin attended Bennington College, where she studied literature and actively opposed the war in Vietnam. She was arrested at an anti-war protest at the U.S. Mission to the United Nations and given a forceful physical examination, resulting in lingering pain. She went public about the mistreatment, making domestic and international news. A few years later, the prison in which she was held closed down. Dworkin moved to Greece, where she spent time on her writing before moving back to Bennington for a couple years, resuming her literature studies and campus activism.

Dworkin moved to Amsterdam to interview anarchists associated with the Provo countercultural movement, a Dutch group who incited violent reactions from authorities through nonviolent taunts. She married one of the anarchists, who later abused her. After fleeing the relationship, Dworkin was stuck in the Netherlands for a year enduring hard times, which included working as a prostitute to survive. Her former husband found and beat her. In 1972, Dworkin agreed to smuggle drugs in exchange for a plane ticket to America. The drug deal fell through, but she still was able to return home.

John Stoltenberg, a gay male feminist writer entered Dworkin's life in 1974 and married her in 1998, even though both claimed to be gay. Dworkin died April 9, 2005, in her Washington, D.C., home at 58 years of age. She had been suffering from osteoarthritis in her knees and had been treated for blood clots in her legs, potentially results of hardships and abuse she faced on the streets.

—Maha Shami

See also Anti-Pornography Activism; Feminism

Further Readings

Dworkin, A. (1988). *Letters from a warzone: Writings, 1976–1989*. New York: Dutton.

Dworkin, A. (1989). *Pornography: Men possessing women.* New York: Dutton.

Dworkin, A. (1997). *Intercourse.* New York: Free Press.

Dworkin, A. (1997). *Life and death.* New York: Free Press.

DYLAN, BOB (1941–)

American singer and songwriter, musician, and poet, Bob Dylan is best known for his political protest songs from the 1960s. An icon of the American social unrest that characterized the decade, he incorporated politics, social commentary, philosophy, and literature in his lyrics and produced songs that still enjoy considerable popularity today. Although his more recent work has often received critical acclaim, his subsequent achievements have not attained the wide popularity of his work in the 1960s and 1970s, a time in the United States characterized by social upheaval and turmoil.

Born Robert Allen Zimmerman in Hibbing, Minnesota, to a middle-class Jewish family, Dylan had a fairly uneventful childhood. He exhibited an early interest in music and was particularly intrigued by the emerging genre of rock 'n' roll. Dylan came of age at a time when authority, including parental authority, was being questioned and conventional values were considered suspect. A new era was beginning, and Dylan was there to not only help usher it in but also to shape its direction.

After high school graduation, Dylan enrolled at the University of Minnesota in Minneapolis, where he rarely attended class but often performed folk songs written by others at coffeehouses. It was during this period that he began introducing himself as Bob Dylan or Dillon. He has never explained exactly the source for the pseudonym, sometimes alluding to an uncle and sometimes acknowledging a reference to the Welsh poet Dylan Thomas.

Dylan dropped out of college at the end of his freshman year. In 1961 at the age of 19, he traveled to New York City, finding refuge in Greenwich Village and again playing in coffeehouses. At the time, Greenwich Village was a community known for its support of personal and artistic freedom, and coffeehouses were the venues for aspiring young singers, musicians, poets, and actors.

Dylan was an ardent admirer of Woody Guthrie, the famous country-folk singer who wrote "This Land Is Your Land." Guthrie, hailed by the political left as a true folk poet, had an undeniable influence on Dylan's early music and persona. Indeed, the young Dylan styled himself in appearance, mannerisms, and music after the famed folk singer and owes much of his earlier musical style to Guthrie. Part of the early Dylan mystique arose from people's knowledge that, having learned that Guthrie was dying in a New Jersey hospital, Dylan visited the incapacitated singer and reportedly sang for him.

After playing the coffeehouse circuit in Greenwich Village, Dylan gained some public recognition after a review in the *New York Times* by critic Robert Shelton. John Hammond, a legendary music business figure, signed him to Columbia Records. Dylan's first album debuted in 1961. It contained only two original songs and was destined to mediocre sales and publicity. Despite the undistinguished start, the company approved a second album, *The Freewheelin' Bob Dylan*. Consisting almost entirely of original compositions, this album included two of the most memorable songs of the 1960s, "Blowing in the Wind" and "A Hard Rain's A-Gonna Fall." Dylan attracted growing attention from the folk community with the release of this album.

To understand the immense popularity Dylan gained during the 1960s, one must recognize the importance of the folk movement. The folk music revival existed in juxtaposition to the emerging rock 'n' roll movement. Many folk singers were political radicals who merged politics and culture to offer social commentary, and rock 'n' roll was viewed by them as somewhat hackneyed and banal. Characterized as liberal left-leaning pacifists, the folk community was also in stark contrast with middle-class, right-wing conservatives. Folk musicians used topical song writing to deliver their criticism of middle-class America. For Dylan, folk music reflected the complexities of life.

With the release of *The Freewheeling' Bob Dylan,* influential members of the folk community believed they had found a champion to convey their rage about commercialism, inequities in power, and prejudice. The themes of civil rights and imminent apocalypse were woven into his songs. Through his music, Dylan pointed the finger of guilt at the war makers and the war profiteers. "A Hard Rain's a-Gonna Fall," a song with metaphorical imagery making veiled references to nuclear apocalypse, struck a chord as the Cuban Missile crisis developed only a few weeks after Dylan began performing it. At a time when segregation was the norm, "Blowing in the Wind" challenged the social and political status quo of the period and heralded the shift of mainstream white American opinion behind the civil rights movement. With these songs, there was an apparent new direction in modern songwriting. Dylan developed a unique blending of stream of consciousness poetry with social consciousness, often set to the stylings of traditional folk music.

During this period, numerous Dylan songs point to the systemic nature of the problems that agitated many young people through the lens of specific individuals in specific settings. In "Who Killed Davey Moore?" Dylan points his finger at the ethical complicity of a whole society in the death of a boxer killed in the ring. Similarly, in "North Country Blues," a song about a woman in an iron mining town in Minnesota, Dylan decries the results of market forces, perhaps one of the initial musical protests against globalization.

Rather than continue to perform primarily for his white liberal fans (and following in the footsteps of Guthrie), Dylan expanded his audience. In 1963 he sang at a voter registration concert in a cotton field to a mainly black audience. The song "Only a Pawn in Their Game" suggested that the white assassin of Medgar Evers, an official from the National Association for the Advancement of Colored People (NAACP), was in fact part of a system that was racist at its core and that focusing solely on the assassin would not bring the guilty to justice. That same year Dylan took part in the March on Washington and performed this song and another before Martin Luther King, Jr., delivered his "I Have a Dream" speech that came to epitomize the movement. Joining other folksingers, including Odetta, Joan Baez, and Peter, Paul, and Mary, Dylan helped usher in a new movement that placed the demand for equality at the center of American consciousness.

The Times They Are A-Changing was released in early 1964, and indeed the political, social, and cultural climate was shifting. *Another Side of Bob Dylan,* released in the summer of 1964, reveals that personal changes were taking place for the young singer, suggesting that his former identity as protest singer for the folk community was dissipating. Gone were the "finger-pointing" songs that had made him famous and in their place came more personal ballads and love songs.

Defying all efforts to categorize him, Dylan was clearly uncomfortable with the label of "protest singer" but even more so of "voice of his generation." Even as he was being hailed as Woody Guthrie's heir, master of the topical folk song, Dylan was refocusing his attention. The folk community became increasingly skeptical when he started writing surreal narratives instead of the topical songs expected of folk musicians. When Dylan replaced his acoustic guitar for an electric one, the folk purists viewed this as the final betrayal.

Recorded in 1965, *Bringin' It All Back Home* included both acoustic and electric songs but definitely sent the message that Dylan had turned away from his folk music roots. Rather than the sole singer on stage strumming his acoustic guitar and blowing his harmonica, Dylan now made his musical statements with an electric guitar and a back-up band. He made his breakthrough to the pop world in the summer of 1965 with the release of "Like a Rolling Stone" from the album *Highway 61 Revisited,* his first full-fledged rock 'n' roll album.

Dylan's first electric performance at the Newport Folk Festival in 1965 earned him boos from about half the crowd, a scene that would be duplicated on his European tour, where he was called "Judas" for apparently forsaking the acoustical folk music that had made him an icon. Without doubt, his decision to expand into electrical music was influenced by the British bands that were appearing on the pop charts. However, his refusal to be pigeonholed by any musical label was a strong motivator (and continues to motivate him today), and Dylan ultimately outgrew the movement that had helped gain him recognition.

Seen with the hindsight of 3 decades, the drama of Dylan's break with the folk movement seems more of an evolutionary change than a revolutionary one. Undoubtedly, the "defection" of Dylan had an impact on the folk music movement, but perhaps most notably on the careers of folk musicians. They watched the spotlight of popular culture dim around them while the melding of poetry, music, and protest, heralded by Dylan moved to the rock scene. Despite the allegations that he had "sold out" by "plugging in," Dylan brought to electric music the same complexity and social insight he had used to transform acoustical music, delivering many unforgettable songs in a way that brought the worlds of music and literature together. While songs about specific instances of social injustice were rarer, Dylan's migration made it acceptable for other rock musicians, including, for example, John Lennon, to use their music to express their social views, something unheard of before.

In 1966 Dylan sustained injuries in a motorcycle accident. After the accident, he became a recluse. By his own admission, the accident provided him the opportunity to get away from the overwhelming spotlight that had followed him for the past few years. The mystique and intensity that was Dylan transformed fan adulation into stalking and deification, to the point that Dylan felt persecuted. During this period, he preferred to focus on his growing family obligations but still produced albums and wrote the soundtrack for a film, *Pat Garrett and Billy the Kid,* which included the classic, "Knockin' on Heaven's Door."

In 1971 Dylan was cajoled into playing for the Concert for Bangladesh at Madison Square Garden. He appeared in 1974 with other singer-songwriters of the 1960s at a Friends of Chile benefit aimed at helping prisoners of the Pinochet regime. In 1976, he released "Hurricane," a narrative meant to raise awareness about Rubin Carter, a boxer convicted of murder on suspect evidence and eventually released

from prison in 1985. In late 1978 he announced he was a born-again Christian and released a series of Christian albums. He returned to secular recording with the 1983 release of *Infidels.*

In the 1980s, Dylan made a case for not playing Sun City in South Africa and promoted American farmers at Live Aid, which in turn gave rise to the Farm Aid project. But the purpose and drive of the 1960s was not readily apparent when he performed in 1985 at the first Farm Aid with Tom Petty & the Heartbreakers and later toured intermittently with them and other big-name groups. He enjoyed some fame as a member of the musical group, the Traveling Wilburys. In 1988 he began the Never Ending Tour. To this day, Dylan tours year-round, playing both large venues and small, sharing the stage with numerous icons of American music.

Dylan's accolades are numerous. He received a Lifetime Achievement award in 1991 at the Grammy Awards and played at President Bill Clinton's inauguration. His first album of original material in 7 years was released in 1997, *Time Out of Mind,* which earned him the Best Album award at the 1998 Grammys. He authored a first installment of his memoirs in 2004 titled *Chronicles: Volume 1. No Direction Home: Bob Dylan,* a Martin Scorsese documentary, followed in 2005. This documentary included rare interviews with the normally reticent Dylan as he recalled his rise to fame in the 1960s. He recently released, through a large coffee chain, the *Live at the Gaslight 1962* album and also contracted to host a radio show for XM satellite radio.

Dylan's successes are many. He has stood as a symbol of societal protest, made innovative music, wrote remarkable lyrics, and executed lucrative business deals, all the while maintaining the position of cynical observer and outsider. He has written and performed songs in nearly every American musical genre, including not only folk and rock, but also country, blues, gospel, and Latin American as well. Yet, he refers to himself simply as a song and dance man. His career is marked with various highs and lows, but his impact has been enormous . . . and he is not done yet.

—Susan R. Wynn and Harris Cooper

See also Benefit Concerts; Guthrie, Woody; Protest Music; Rock 'n' Roll

Further Readings

Dylan, B. (2004). *Chronicles* (Vol. 1). New York: Simon & Schuster.

Edmonds, B. (2005). Revolution in his head. In M. Blake (Ed.), *Dylan: Visions, portraits & back pages.* New York: DK.

Kane, P. (2005). Boy wonder. In M. Blake (Ed.), *Dylan: Visions, portraits & back pages.* New York: DK.

Marqusee, M. (2003). *Chimes of freedom: The politics of Bob Dylan's art.* New York: New Press.

Scorsese, M. (Director). (2005). *No direction home: Bob Dylan* [Motion picture]. United States: Paramount Pictures.

Shelton, R. (1986). *No direction home: The life and music of Bob Dylan.* New York: Beech Tree Books.

Stuart, B. (2005). Protest and survive. In M. Blake (Ed.), *Dylan: Visions, portraits & back pages.* New York: DK.